Encyclopedia of

# LITERARY CRITICS

## AND CRITICISM

Volume 2

Encyclopedia of

# LITERARY CRITICS

## AND CRITICISM

Volume 2
L–Z

*Consultant*
John Sutherland

*Edited by*

CHRIS MURRAY

FD

FITZROY DEARBORN PUBLISHERS
LONDON • CHICAGO

FITZROY DEARBORN PUBLISHERS
919 North Michigan Avenue – Suite 760
Chicago, IL. 60611
USA

*or*

310 Regent Street
London W1R 5AJ
England

Editors: Edith Summerhayes and Radojka Miljevic
Proofreaders: Edith Summerhayes and Nicola Bennett
Researchers: Michael Brett and Rowland Hughes
Indexer: Drusilla Calvert

**British Library Cataloguing in Publication Data**
Encyclopedia of literary critics and criticism
    1. Criticism – Encyclopedias    2. Critics – Encyclopedias
    I. Murray, Chris
    801.9′5′03

ISBN 1–57958–144–7

**Library of Congress Cataloging in Publication Data is available.**

First published in the USA and UK 1999

Typeset by Florence Production Limited, Stoodleigh, Devon
Printed and b███████████████████ Bath Press, Bath

# CONTENTS

# ALPHABETICAL
# LIST OF ENTRIES

# ENTRIES BY CATEGORY

## INDIVIDUALS

'Abd al-Qāhir al-Jurjānī
M. H. Abrams
Joseph Addison
Theodor Adorno
Alan of Lille
Dámaso Alonso
Louis Althusser
Anandavardhana
Luciano Anceschi
Aristotle
Matthew Arnold
Antonin Artaud
W. H. Auden
Erich Auerbach
Saint Augustine
Irving Babbitt
Francis Bacon
Mikhail Bakhtin
Giuseppe Baretti
Owen Barfield
Roland Barthes
Matsuo Bashō
Georges Bataille
F. W. Bateson
Charles Baudelaire
Jean Baudrillard
Vissarion Belinskii
Andrei Belyi
Pietro Bembo
Walter Benjamin
Eric Bentley
Henri Bergson
Bharata
Bhartrhari
R. P. Blackmur
Harold Bloom
Giovanni Boccaccio
Johann Jakob Bodmer
Nicolas Boileau-Despréaux
Wayne C. Booth
Jorge Luis Borges
Paul Bourget
Fredson Bowers
Malcolm Bradbury

A. C. Bradley
Bertolt Brecht
André Breton
Cleanth Brooks
Van Wyck Brooks
Ferdinand Brunetière
Edmund Burke
Kenneth Burke
Michel Butor
Lord Byron
Callimachus
Italo Calvino
Lodovico Castelvetro
Geoffrey Chaucer
Nikolai Chernyshevskii
Cicero
Hélène Cixous
Samuel Taylor Coleridge
Pierre Corneille
Malcolm Cowley
R. S. Crane
Benedetto Croce
Jonathan Culler
Ernst Robert Curtius
Dante
Donald Davie
Paul de Man
Francesco De Sanctis
Gilles Deleuze
Jacques Derrida
Denis Diderot
Dionysius of Halicarnassus
Nikolai Dobroluibov
Fedor Dostoevskii
John Dryden
Joachim du Bellay
Terry Eagleton
Umberto Eco
Leon Edel
Joseph von Eichendorff
Boris Eikhenbaum
T. S. Eliot
Richard Ellmann
Ralph Waldo Emerson

Georgii Plekhanov
Plotinus
Edgar Allan Poe
Alexander Pope
Georges Poulet
Ezra Pound
Mario Praz
Vladimir Propp
Marcel Proust
Aleksandr Pushkin
George Puttenham
Qudāma Ibn Ja'far
Quintilian
Jean Racine
John Crowe Ransom
Sir Herbert Read
I. A. Richards
Christopher Ricks
Paul Ricœur
Alain Robbe-Grillet
Jean-Jacques Rousseau
John Ruskin
Thomas Rymer
Edward Said
Charles-Augustin Sainte-Beuve
George Saintsbury
Jean-Paul Sartre
Ferdinand de Saussure
Julius Caesar Scaliger
Friedrich Wilhelm Joseph Schelling
Friedrich Schiller
August Wilhelm Schlegel
Friedrich Schlegel
Arthur Schopenhauer
Third Earl of Shaftesbury
George Bernard Shaw
Percy Bysshe Shelley
Viktor Shklovskii
Sir Philip Sidney
Andrei Siniavskii
Karl Wilhelm Ferdinand Solger
Susan Sontag

Wole Soyinka
Gayatri Chakravorty Spivak
Madame de Staël
George Steiner
Stendhal
Algernon Charles Swinburne
John Addington Symonds
Arthur Symons
Hippolyte-Adolphe Taine
Allen Tate
Tzvetan Todorov
J. R. R. Tolkien
Lev Tolstoi
Jane P. Tompkins
Lionel Trilling
Giangiorgio Trissino
Ts'ao P'i
Ki no Tsurayuki
Iurii Tynianov
Miguel de Unamuno y Jugo
Paul Valéry
Giovanni Verga
Aleksandr Veselovskii
Giambattista Vico
Voltaire
Robert Penn Warren
Joseph Warton and Thomas Warton
Ian Watt
René Wellek
Oscar Wilde
Raymond Williams
Edmund Wilson
William K. Wimsatt, Jr.
Johann Joachim Winckelmann
Yvor Winters
Virginia Woolf
William Wordsworth
William Butler Yeats
Nijō Yoshimoto
Edward Young
Vasilii Zhukovskii
Émile Zola

# CHRONOLOGICAL SURVEYS

American Literary Theory to 1900
American Literary Theory: Twentieth
    Century
Arabic Literary Theory
British Literary Theory: Twentieth Century
French Literary Theory: Twentieth Century
Chinese Literary Theory
Classical Greek and Roman Literary
    Theory

Continental Theory
Indian Literary Theory
Japanese Literary Theory
Literary Theory in the Age of Victoria
Medieval Literary Theory
Modern Literary Theory
Neoclassical Literary Theory
Renaissance and Restoration Literary
    Theory

# THEORIES AND APPROACHES

Archetypal Criticism
Biblical Criticism: Allegory and Typology
Black Literary Theory and Criticism
Criticism
Cultural Criticism
Deconstruction
Dialogic Criticism
Feminist Criticism
Film Criticism
Frankfurt School, The
Gay Theory and Criticism
Geneva school, The
Hermeneutics
Linguistics and Literary Studies

Marxist Theory and Criticism
Modernism
Narratology
New Criticism
New Historicism
Phenomenological Criticism
Postmodernism
Psychoanalytic Criticism
Reader-Response Criticism
Reception Theory
Romanticism
Russian Formalism
Semiotics
Structuralism

# CONCEPTS

Absurd, The
Aestheticism
Author, The
Canon
Classic, The
Comedy
Discourse
Drama: Theory and Criticism
Epic
Erotic, The
Existentialism
Gothic
Grotesque
Humanism, Renaissance
Ideology
Intertextuality
Lyric
Metaphor
Metonymy
Mimesis

New Pragmatism
Novel: Theory and Criticism
Parody
Pastoral
Plot
Popular Literature: Approaches to Genre
Popular literature: Critical Reception
Postcolonial Literature and Theory
Prague School, The
Realism
Rhetoric
Sensibility
Sincerity
Style
Sublime
Surrealism
Symbolism
Translation
Yale School, The

# CHRONOLOGICAL LIST

# OF INDIVIDUALS

| | | |
|---|---|---|
| c. 427 B.C.–347 B.C. | Plato | Greek philosopher |
| 384 B.C.–322 B.C. | Aristotle | Greek philosopher |
| c. 305 B.C.–240 B.C. | Callimachus | Greek scholar and poet |
| 106 B.C.–43 B.C. | Cicero | Roman writer and rhetorician |
| 78/54 B.C.–7 B.C. | Dionysius of Halicarnassus | Greek teacher and rhetorician |
| 65 B.C.–8 B.C. | Horace (Quintus Horatius Flaccus) | Roman poet and writer |
| 1st century A.D. | Longinus | Greek theorist |
| c. 35 A.D.–c. 96 A.D. | Quintilian (Marcus Fabius Quintilianus) | Roman rhetorician and teacher |
| c. 120 A.D.–after 180 A.D. | Lucian | Greek writer and critic |
| 187 A.D.–226 A.D. | Ts'ao P'i | Chinese poet |
| 3rd century A.D. | Bharata | Indian dramatic theorist |
| 205 A.D.–270 A.D. | Plotinus | Greco-Roman philosopher |
| 261 A.D.–303 A.D. | Lu Chi | Chinese Poet |
| 354 A.D.–430 A.D. | Saint Augustine (Aurelius Augustinus) | Christian scholar, philosopher, and writer |
| c. 375 A.D.–c. 422 A.D. | Macrobius | Latin philosopher and writer |
| c. 465 A.D.–c. 522 A.D. | Liu Hsieh | Chinese philosopher and theorist |
| c. 500–600 | Fulgentius | Christian Latin writer |
| c. 560–636 | Saint Isidore of Seville | Spanish theologian and scholar |
| 7th century | Bhartrhari | Indian grammarian and philosopher |
| 9th century | Anandavardhana | Indian theorist |
| c. 884–c. 945 | Ki no Tsurayuki | Japanese critic and editor |
| ?–c. 948 | Qudāma Ibn Ja'far | Arabic theorist and philologist |
| ?–1087 | 'Abd al-Qāhir al-Jurjānī | Arabic theorist and grammarian |
| 1110(/1130)–1203 | Alan of Lille (Alanus de Insulis) | French philosopher and poet |
| c. 1200–? | Geoffrey of Vinsauf | English scholar |
| 1211–1285 | Hāzim al-Qartājannī | Arabic theorist, grammarian, and poet |
| 1265–1321 | Dante (Durantè Alighieri) | Italian poet |
| 1304–1374 | Petrarch (Francesco Petrarca) | Italian poet and writer |
| 1313–1375 | Giovanni Boccaccio | Italian writer |
| 1320–1388 | Nijō Yoshimoto | Japanese poet |
| c. 1343–1400 | Geoffrey Chaucer | English poet |
| 1466?–1536 | Desiderius Erasmus | Dutch theologian, scholar, and critic |
| 1470–1547 | Pietro Bembo | Italian scholar and poet |
| 1478–1550 | Giangiorgio Trissino | Italian poet and scholar |
| 1484–1558 | Julius Caesar Scaliger | Italian-French scholar and writer |
| 1500–c. 1574 | Antonio Minturno (Antonio Sebastiani) | Italian critic and scholar |
| 1504–1573 | Giambattista Giraldi Cinthio | Italian playwright and theorist |
| 1505–1571 | Lodovico Castelvetro | Italian critic and playwright |
| 1522–1560 | Joachim du Bellay | French critic, poet, and translator |
| c. 1525–1577 | George Gascoigne | English writer and critic |
| c. 1530–1590 | George Puttenham | English critic |
| 1533–1592 | Michel Eyquem de Montaigne | French essayist and writer |

| 1554–1586 | Sir Philip Sidney | English poet and critic |
| 1554 (baptized)–1624 | Stephen Gosson | English critic and writer |
| 1555–1628 | François de Malherbe | French poet, writer, and translator |
| 1561–1626 | Francis Bacon | English statesman, philosopher, and essayist |
| 1573–1637 | Ben Jonson | English poet, playwright, and critic |
| 1606–1684 | Pierre Corneille | French dramatist and critic |
| 1621–1695 | Jean de La Fontaine | French writer |
| 1631–1700 | John Dryden | English poet, critic, and translator |
| 1636–1711 | Nicolas Boileau-Despréaux | French critic and poet |
| 1639 (baptized)–1699 | Jean Racine | French playwright and writer |
| c. 1643–1713 | Thomas Rymer | English critic, translator, and editor |
| 1644–1694 | Matsuo Bashō | Japanese poet, traveler, and teacher of poetry |
| 1645–1696 | Jean de La Bruyère | French writer, critic, and translator |
| 1651–1715 | François de Salignac de La Mothe-Fénelon | French theologian and writer |
| 1668–1744 | Giambattista Vico | Italian philosopher |
| 1671–1713 | Third Earl of Shaftesbury (Anthony Ashley Cooper) | English writer and critic |
| 1672–1719 | Joseph Addison | English essayist and critic |
| 1676–1764 | Benito Jerónimo Feijóo y Montenegro | Spanish writer and critic |
| 1683–1765 | Edward Young | English poet and critic |
| 1688–1744 | Alexander Pope | English poet, translator, and critic |
| 1694–1778 | Voltaire (François-Marie Arouet) | French writer and critic |
| 1696?–1782 | Lord Kames (Henry Home, Lord Kames) | Scottish jurist, legal historian, philosopher, and critic |
| 1697–1769 | Kamo No Mabuchi | Japanese writer and philologist |
| 1698–1783 | Johann Jakob Bodmer | Swiss critic, historian, and translator |
| 1700–1766 | Johann Christoph Gottsched | German critic and philosopher |
| 1702–1754 | Ignacio de Luzán y Claramunt | Spanish writer and critic |
| 1709–1784 | Samuel Johnson | English writer, editor, and lexicographer |
| 1711–1776 | David Hume | Scottish philosopher |
| 1712–1778 | Jean-Jacques Rousseau | Swiss-born French writer, critic, and social theorist |
| 1713–1784 | Denis Diderot | French editor, writer, and theorist |
| 1717–1768 | Johann Joachim Winckelmann | German art historian and critic |
| 1719–1789 | Giuseppe Baretti | Italian-English critic and lexicographer |
| 1722 (baptized)–1800 | Joseph Warton | English critic and poet |
| 1724–1804 | Immanuel Kant | German philosopher |
| 1727–1790 | Thomas Warton | English critic and poet |
| 1729–1781 | Gotthold Ephraim Lessing | German critic and playwright |
| 1729–1797 | Edmund Burke | Irish-born writer and politician |
| 1730–1801 | Motoori Norinaga (Ozu Norinaga) | Japanese writer and philologist |
| 1739–1803 | Jean-François de la Harpe | French writer and critic |
| 1744–1803 | Johann Gottfried Herder | German writer |
| 1749–1832 | Johann Wolfgang von Goethe | German poet, novelist, playwright, and critic |
| 1759–1805 | Friedrich Schiller | German poet, playwright, and theorist |
| 1766–1817 | Madame de Staël (Anne Louise Germaine, Baroness of Staël-Holstein) | French critic and writer |
| 1767–1845 | August Wilhelm Schlegel | German translator and critic |
| 1770–1831 | Georg Wilhelm Friedrich Hegel | German philosopher |
| 1770–1850 | William Wordsworth | English poet |
| 1772–1829 | Friedrich Schlegel | German critic and writer |
| 1772–1834 | Samuel Taylor Coleridge | English poet and critic |
| 1775–1854 | Friedrich Wilhelm Joseph Schelling | German philosopher, writer, and critic |
| 1777–1811 | Heinrich von Kleist | German writer and playwright |
| 1778–1830 | William Hazlitt | English critic and essayist |
| 1780–1819 | Karl Wilhelm Ferdinand Solger | German philosopher and critic |
| 1783–1842 | Stendhal (Marie-Henri Beyle) | French novelist |
| 1783–1852 | Vasilii Zhukovskii | Russian poet, translator, and critic |
| 1788–1824 | Lord Byron (George Gordon, sixth Baron Byron) | English poet and critic |
| 1788–1857 | Joseph von Eichendorff | German poet, writer, and critic |
| 1788–1860 | Arthur Schopenhauer | German philosopher |

| 1791–1872 | Franz Grillparzer | Austrian dramatist and critic |
| 1792–1822 | Percy Bysshe Shelley | English poet |
| 1795–1821 | John Keats | English poet |
| 1797–1856 | Heinrich Heine | German poet and writer |
| 1799–1837 | Aleksandr Pushkin | Russian poet and writer |
| 1802–1885 | Victor Hugo | French novelist, poet, and playwright |
| 1803–1882 | Ralph Waldo Emerson | American essayist and critic |
| 1804–1869 | Charles-Augustin Sainte-Beuve | French critic and writer |
| 1805–1872 | Giuseppe Mazzini | Italian critic and essayist |
| 1806–1873 | John Stuart Mill | English writer, critic, and polemicist |
| 1809–1849 | Edgar Allan Poe | American writer and poet |
| 1810–1850 | Margaret Fuller | American critic and social reformer |
| 1811–1848 | Vissarion Belinskii | Russian critic |
| 1811–1872 | Théophile Gautier | French writer and critic |
| 1817–1883 | Francesco De Sanctis | Italian critic, translator, and essayist |
| 1819–1900 | John Ruskin | English social and cultural critic |
| 1821–1867 | Charles Baudelaire | French poet and critic |
| 1821–1881 | Fedor Dostoevskii | Russian novelist |
| 1822–1888 | Matthew Arnold | English poet and critic |
| 1828–1889 | Nikolai Chernyshevskii | Russian critic and writer |
| 1828–1893 | Hippolyte-Adolphe Taine | French critic and writer |
| 1828–1910 | Lev Tolstoi | Russian novelist and writer |
| 1836–1861 | Nikolai Dobroliubov | Russian critic and poet |
| 1837–1909 | Algernon Charles Swinburne | English poet and critic |
| 1838–1906 | Aleksandr Veselovskii | Russian critic and translator |
| 1839–1894 | Walter Pater | English critic and writer |
| 1840–1868 | Dmitrii Pisarev | Russian critic |
| 1840–1893 | John Addington Symonds | English critic |
| 1840–1902 | Émile Zola | French novelist, writer, and critic |
| 1840–1922 | Giovanni Verga | Italian writer and critic |
| 1842–1898 | Stéphane Mallarmé | French poet and critic |
| 1843–1916 | Henry James | American novelist and critic |
| 1844–1889 | Gerard Manley Hopkins | English poet and Jesuit priest |
| 1844–1900 | Friedrich Nietzsche | German philosopher |
| 1845–1933 | George Saintsbury | English critic, historian, and biographer |
| 1849–1906 | Ferdinand Brunetière | French critic |
| 1851–1935 | A. C. Bradley | English critic |
| 1852–1935 | Paul Bourget | French writer and critic |
| 1854–1900 | Oscar Wilde | Irish writer, dramatist, and essayist |
| 1856–1912 | Marcelino Menéndez y Pelayo | Spanish writer and critic |
| 1856–1918 | Georgii Plekhanov | Russian writer and theorist |
| 1856–1950 | George Bernard Shaw | Irish dramatist and critic |
| 1857–1913 | Ferdinand de Saussure | Swiss linguist |
| 1858–1915 | Rémy de Gourmont | French writer and critic |
| 1859–1941 | Henri Bergson | French philosopher and writer |
| 1863–1929 | Arno Holz | German critic and poet |
| 1864–1936 | Miguel de Unamuno y Jugo | Spanish philosopher, writer, and critic |
| 1865–1933 | Irving Babbitt | American critic, translator, and editor |
| 1865–1939 | William Butler Yeats | Irish poet, dramatist, and critic |
| 1865–1945 | Arthur Symons | English writer and critic |
| 1866–1952 | Benedetto Croce | Italian philosopher and critic |
| 1867–1936 | Luigi Pirandello | Italian playwright and writer |
| 1868–1933 | Stefan George | German poet, critic, and theorist |
| 1871–1922 | Marcel Proust | French novelist and critic |
| 1871–1945 | Paul Valéry | French writer and poet |
| 1874–1929 | Hugo von Hofmannsthal | Austrian poet, dramatist, and critic |
| 1875–1933 | Anatolii Lunacharskii | Russian writer and critic |
| 1875–1955 | Thomas Mann | German novelist and writer |
| 1876–1944 | Filippo Tommaso Marinetti | Italian writer and critic |
| 1879–1965 | Percy Lubbock | English critic and writer |

| 1879–1970 | E. M. Forster | English novelist and critic |
| 1880–1931 | Friedrich Gundolf (Friedrich Gundelfinger) | German writer and critic |
| 1880–1934 | Andrei Belyi (Boris Nikolaevich Bugaev) | Russian writer and critic |
| 1882–1941 | Virginia Woolf | English novelist and critic |
| 1882–1973 | Jacques Maritain | French religious philosopher and critic |
| 1883–1917 | T. E. Hulme | English poet and theorist |
| 1885–1930 | D. H. Lawrence | English novelist, poet, and critic |
| 1885–1971 | Georg Lukács | Hungarian theorist and critic |
| 1885–1972 | Ezra Pound | American poet and critic |
| 1886–1956 | Ernst Robert Curtius | German scholar and critic |
| 1886–1959 | Boris Eikhenbaum | Russian theorist |
| 1886–1963 | Van Wyck Brooks | American critic and writer |
| 1886–1967 | R. S. Crane | American critic |
| 1888–1965 | T. S. Eliot | American-born English poet, dramatist, and critic |
| 1888–1974 | John Crowe Ransom | American critic and poet |
| 1889–1976 | Martin Heidegger | German philosopher |
| 1891–1937 | Antonio Gramsci | Italian writer and political theorist |
| 1891–1962 | Hu Shih | Chinese critic |
| 1892–1940 | Walter Benjamin | German writer, critic, and theorist |
| 1892–1957 | Erich Auerbach | German-born American scholar |
| 1892–1973 | J. R. R. Tolkien | South African-born English novelist and scholar |
| 1893–1968 | Sir Herbert Read | English writer, poet, and critic |
| 1893–1970 | Roman Ingarden | Polish philosopher |
| 1893–1979 | I. A. Richards | English critic, writer, and linguist |
| 1893–1984 | Viktor Shklovskii | Russian critic |
| 1894–1943 | Iurii Tynianov | Russian theorist |
| 1895–1970 | Vladimir Propp | Russian folklorist and critical theorist |
| 1895–1972 | Edmund Wilson | American writer and critic |
| 1895–1975 | Mikhail Bakhtin | Russian theorist and critic |
| 1895–1978 | F. R. Leavis | English critic |
| 1895–1985 | Robert Graves | English poet, writer, and critic |
| 1896–1948 | Antonin Artaud | French writer, actor, and playwright |
| 1896–1966 | André Breton | French poet and theorist |
| 1896–1982 | Roman Jakobson | Russian-born American linguist and theorist |
| 1896–1982 | Mario Praz | Italian writer on literature and art |
| 1897–1962 | Georges Bataille | French writer and editor |
| 1897–1993 | Kenneth Burke | American writer and critic |
| 1898–1956 | Bertolt Brecht | German playwright and critic |
| 1898–1963 | C. S. Lewis | English writer, critic, and scholar |
| 1898–1989 | Malcolm Cowley | American editor and critic |
| 1898–1990 | Dámaso Alonso | Spanish poet and critic |
| 1898–1998 | Owen Barfield | English critic, writer, and teacher |
| 1899–1979 | Allen Tate | American writer and critic |
| 1899–1986 | Jorge Luis Borges | Argentine writer, poet, and critic |
| 1900– | Hans-Georg Gadamer | German philosopher and critic |
| 1900–1968 | Yvor Winters | American critic and poet |
| 1901–1978 | F. W. Bateson | English literary critic and editor |
| 1901–1981 | Jacques Lacan | French psychoanalyst and theorist |
| 1902– | Georges Poulet | Belgian critic and theorist |
| 1902–1950 | F. O. Matthiessen | American critic and editor |
| 1903–1969 | Theodor Adorno (Theodor Wiesengrund) | German critic and philosopher |
| 1903–1995 | René Wellek | Austrian-born American theorist |
| 1904–1965 | R. P. Blackmur | American critic and poet |
| 1904–1969 | Witold Gombrowicz | Polish critic and writer |
| 1905–1975 | Lionel Trilling | American critic and writer |
| 1905–1980 | Jean-Paul Sartre | French philosopher and writer |
| 1905–1989 | Robert Penn Warren | American teacher, critic, poet, and novelist |
| 1905–1991 | Fredson Bowers | American bibliographer, editor, and critic |
| 1906–1984 | William Empson | English critic and poet |
| 1906–1994 | Cleanth Brooks | American critic and editor |

| 1906–1997 | L. C. Knights | English critic and scholar |
| 1907–1973 | W. H. Auden | English-born American poet and essayist |
| 1907–1975 | William K. Wimsatt, Jr. | American critic and editor |
| 1907–1997 | Leon Edel | American biographer, critic, and editor |
| 1908– | Claude Lévi-Strauss | Belgian-born French anthropologist and theorist |
| 1910–1970 | Charles Olson | American critic and poet |
| 1911– | Luciano Anceschi | Italian philosopher and critic |
| 1911–1980 | Marshall McLuhan | Canadian critic and writer |
| 1912– | M. H. Abrams | American critic and editor |
| 1912– | Walter J. Ong | American essayist and critic |
| 1912–1991 | Northrop Frye | Canadian critic and theorist |
| 1913– | Paul Ricœur | French critic |
| 1914–1965 | Randall Jarrell | American poet, critic, and teacher |
| 1915–1980 | Roland Barthes | French writer and cultural critic |
| 1916– | Eric Bentley | English-born American critic, writer, and translator |
| 1917– | Leslie Fiedler | American critic and writer |
| 1917– | Ian Watt | English critic |
| 1917–1992 | A. J. Greimas | Lithuanian-born French semiotician |
| 1918– | Martin Esslin | Hungarian-born English drama critic |
| 1918–1987 | Richard Ellmann | American biographer and critic |
| 1918–1990 | Louis Althusser | French political philosopher |
| 1919– | Frank Kermode | English critic and writer |
| 1919– | Es'kia (Ezekiel) Mphahlele | South African writer and critic |
| 1919–1983 | Paul de Man | Belgian-born American critic |
| 1921– | Wayne C. Booth | American critic and teacher |
| 1921–1988 | Raymond Williams | Welsh critic and writer |
| 1921–1997 | Hans Robert Jauss | German literary theorist |
| 1922– | Alain Robbe-Grillet | French novelist, writer, and theorist |
| 1922–1993 | Iurii Lotman | Russian critic and theorist |
| 1922–1995 | Donald Davie | English poet and critic |
| 1923– | René Girard | French cultural critic |
| 1923– | Hugh Kenner | Canadian critic |
| 1923– | Murray Krieger | American critic |
| 1923–1985 | Italo Calvino | Italian novelist, editor, and critic |
| 1925–1995 | Gilles Deleuze | French philosopher |
| 1925–1997 | Andrei Siniavskii ("Abram Tertz") | Russian writer and critic |
| 1926– | Michel Butor | French writer and critic |
| 1926– | Clifford Geertz | American cultural anthropologist and critic |
| 1926– | Wolfgang Iser | German theorist |
| 1926–1984 | Michel Foucault | French philosopher and writer |
| 1927– | Norman N. Holland | American critic |
| 1928– | J. Hillis Miller | American critic and editor |
| 1929– | Jean Baudrillard | French cultural critic |
| 1929– | Geoffrey H. Hartman | German-born American critic and editor |
| 1929– | George Steiner | French-born American critic and writer |
| 1930– | Harold Bloom | American theorist and critic |
| 1930– | Jacques Derrida | French philosopher and critic |
| 1930– | Gérard Genette | French critic and editor |
| 1930– | Luce Irigaray | Belgian-born French psychoanalyst, writer, and critic |
| 1931– | Marjorie Perloff | American critic |
| 1932– | Malcolm Bradbury | English novelist and critic |
| 1932– | Umberto Eco | Italian writer, semiotician, and critic |
| 1933– | Christopher Ricks | English teacher, critic, and editor |
| 1933– | Susan Sontag | American essayist, critic, and novelist |
| 1933–1982 | John Gardner | American novelist, translator, and critic |
| 1934– | Fredric Jameson | American critic and theorist |
| 1934– | Wole Soyinka | Nigerian playwright, poet, and novelist |
| 1935 | David Lodge | English novelist and critic |

| 1935– | Edward Said | Palestinian-American cultural critic |
| 1936– | Sandra M. Gilbert | American critic |
| 1937– | Hélène Cixous | French writer, theorist, and critic |
| 1937– | Jerome J. McGann | American critic, editor, and theorist |
| 1938– | Stanley Fish | American critic |
| 1938– | Ngugi wa Thiong'o | Kenyan writer |
| 1939– | Tzvetan Todorov | Bulgarian-born French theorist |
| 1940– | Jane P. Tompkins | American critic and educator |
| 1941 | Annette Kolodny | American critic |
| 1941– | Julia Kristeva | Bulgarian-born French critic and theorist |
| 1942– | Gayatri Chakravorty Spivak | Indian cultural critic |
| 1943– | Terry Eagleton | English critic, writer, and editor |
| 1944– | Jonathan Culler | American critic |
| 1944– | Susan Gubar | American critic |
| 1946– | Stephen Heath | English critic, editor, and translator |
| 1950– | Henry Louis Gates, Jr. | American critic and editor |
| 1953– | Toril Moi | Norwegian theorist and critic |

# L

## Jean de La Bruyère

French writer, critic, and translator

**Born:** Paris, France; August 17, 1645
**Died:** Versailles, France; May 11, 1696

### Biography

Jean de La Bruyère was born on August 17, 1645, into a middle-class Parisian family, the eldest of seven children born to Élisabeth and Louis de La Bruyère. Apparently, he spent most of his childhood years in the French countryside and studied in a school run by the Oratorians. In 1665 he completed his law studies at the University of Poitiers. Soon after his graduation, he was admitted to the bar in Paris. Little is known about the next two decades of his life.

In 1684, upon the recommendation of the celebrated French preacher and moralist Jacques-Bénigne Bossuet, La Bruyère was appointed tutor to the Duke of Bourbon, scion of the influential Condé family, who were close cousins to Louis XIV. This relatively well-paying position also gave La Bruyère access to the court at Versailles. After the marriage of his pupil in 1685, he became secretary and librarian, remaining in the service of the Condés until his death in 1696.

In 1688 he published the first edition of his masterpiece, *The Characters*, which, during the last eight years of his life, he revised and expanded eight times. In 1693 he was elected to the French Academy. On May 10, 1696, he participated in one of its public sessions and that evening suffered a fatal stroke, dying early in the morning on May 11, 1696, at Versailles. La Bruyère never married.

### Influence

Since the late seventeenth century, La Bruyère has been admired as a master of French prose who skillfully and subtly analyzed artificiality and injustice in society as well as the moral motivation for human behavior. Scholars, however, have generally misunderstood or overlooked La Bruyère's importance in the history of French literary criticism. La Bruyère's *The Characters* and Charles Perrault's *Parallèle des anciens et des modernes* (1688–1692; four volumes) were both first published in 1688. In his comparative study, Perrault argued that the literary masterpieces of seventeenth-century France rivaled and even surpassed those produced in ancient Greece and Rome. During the last years of the seventeenth century, there was a lively exchange of critical ideas in France which is now referred to as the "Quarrel of the Ancients and the Moderns." La Bruyère and several other French writers questioned Perrault's assertion and affirmed that modern French writers could attain true originality only through the systematic and creative imitation of admired literary works from the classical period. La Bruyère believed that the brilliant reworking of classical themes and subjects in Jean Racine's tragedies should serve as a model for his compatriots.

The literary theory and aesthetic judgments developed in the first chapter of *The Characters* illustrate the central role of the classical tradition in seventeenth-century French literature. Although many readers may disagree with La Bruyère's evaluation of specific authors or poets, he did develop a consistent system for distinguishing between superficial and profound works of literature. His assessments of seventeenth-century French writers were generally quite accurate and revealed profound insights into the true originality of such writers as Racine, Pierre Corneille, and François de Malherbe.

### Analysis

Two chapters in La Bruyère's *The Characters* deal extensively with literary theory and composition. He argues persuasively that gifted writers and preachers, through their mastery of style and keen insight into the human condition, convey to their audience a sense of the sublime. The role of the literary critic, according to La Bruyère, is to analyze the artistry by which a true writer attains the sublime.

What, however, constitutes the sublime in a work of literature? La Bruyère established a close connection between nature and the sublime. Like many other literary critics of his century, he encouraged young poets to imitate "nature" and to write "naturally." The key question is to define what La Bruyère meant by imitating nature.

He clearly believed that the systematic study of classical letters was absolutely essential both for writers and for literary critics. A young poet wishing to describe the beauty of nature should first read Virgil's *Eclogues* (43–37 B.C.; also known as *Bucolics*) and *Georgics* (c. 37–29 B.C.) in order to understand the stylistic techniques and rhetorical devices which the master used to convey the aesthetic pleasure which natural beauty brings.

Great poets describe the quintessence of human feelings in a style which is appropriate both for the subject matter chosen and for the audience. La Bruyère believed that there existed in literature "a point of perfection" which only true geniuses, such as Virgil, Horace, and Racine, could achieve in their masterpieces. Stylistic brilliance by itself, however, does not suffice to explain literary excellence: beauty and truth must be expressed simultaneously. La Bruyère defined the complex nature of literary composition when he wrote, "One must express truth in order to write naturally, powerfully, and delicately." It is essential that the expression of truth be perceived as significant and "natural" not merely for one generation or society, but in many different societies and for several successive generations. Aesthetic interpretations from extremely diverse groups of attentive critics and readers will determine whether a well-written work is truly sublime.

La Bruyère was keenly aware of the relationship between the search for values and the development of a personal style and greatly admired creativity and originality within established stylistic and literary conventions. He praised, for example, the elegant tension in Malherbe's formal poetry, considering that the poet "knew nature." La Bruyère clarified this comment by affirming that Malherbe's style captured "at the same time the noblest and the most beautiful" creations of nature.

La Bruyère believed that each creative poet or writer develops a unique "rich and uniform style" which no one else should ever attempt to imitate. A poet's personality and the specific literary genre which he or she perfects will determine the level of stylistic formality appropriate for a work. He admired consistency in writers and regretted that Molière had written light farces in addition to his elegant five-act verse comedies such as *Le Misanthrope* (1666; *The Misanthrope*, 1709) and *Tartuffe: Ou, L'Imposteur* (1664, 1667; *Tartuffe*, 1732). Similarly, La Bruyère held in the highest esteem the stage tragedies written by Corneille between *Le Cid* (1637; *The Cid*, 1637) and *Polyeucte* (1642; English translation, 1655) but expressed disdain for the dramatist's early comedies and the late tragedies written between *Œdipe* (1659) and *Suréna* (1674; English translation, 1960). His disparaging remarks on these works had the unfortunate result of convincing generations of French readers that very few of Corneille's thirty-two plays were truly worthwhile. It has only been since the end of the 1940s that critics have come to appreciate the rich diversity of Corneille's talents as a playwright. The same thing happened to other writers: those seventeenth-century works judged harshly by La Bruyère fell into a critical disfavor which lasted for generations. In recent decades, however, critics have learned to appreciate what one scholar has called the "plural unity" in seventeenth-century French theater.

Although La Bruyère clearly believed that certain forms of artistic creativity were more significant than others, he realized that it would be foolish to use a single critical standard to evaluate works from widely different genres, recognizing the need for flexibility in literary criticism. He understood that a listener's reactions to a tragedy and a sermon differ profoundly. Aesthetic criteria which enable one to judge Racine's originality as a playwright properly may well be inappropriate for a scholar who wishes to describe the stylistic and rhetorical effectiveness of the sermons of Louis Bourdaloue and Bossuet. He reflected at length on the complexity of the emotional and aesthetic reactions to various literary genres popular in his day. In *The Characters*, he describes specifically reactions to operas, stage tragedies, and sermons, noting perceptively that opera composers and librettists, tragic playwrights, and preachers seek to convey different truths to their listeners, whose expectations and reactions vary for each art form.

La Bruyère's negative perception of opera may well surprise modern admirers of psychologically powerful works by such composers as Wolfgang Amadeus Mozart, Richard Wagner, Giuseppe Verdi, and Richard Strauss. The critic had good reason for his opinion: when La Bruyère first published his treatise in 1688, opera had been performed in France for only fifteen years. In addition, the only operas known to Frenchmen at that time were those by Jean-Baptiste Lully, whose most frequent collaborator was librettist Philippe Quinault. The thirteen Quinault-Lully operas were essentially stage tragedies set to music. As a result, La Bruyère believed that the genre made fewer demands on audiences than did tragedies. In his opinion, an opera was a visual spectacle which "enchanted our eyes and our ears" but did not express a sense of dramatic and psychological tension. For this reason, he preferred Racine's and Corneille's tragedies to Lully's works.

Although not believing that Lully's elegant operas were totally satisfying, La Bruyère nevertheless affirmed that they "gave us an idea" of what opera could become. His insight is readily apparent: Lully's example would directly influence French composers until the middle of the eighteenth century, and Jean-Philippe Rameau's numerous operas would owe much to Lully's pioneering work.

Although La Bruyère expressed only mitigated praise for opera, he greatly admired the tragedies of Racine and Corneille. Unlike most critics, however, La Bruyère did not attempt to explain what their tragedies meant, realizing that it would be foolish and haughty for a critic to assert that a tragedy by Racine necessarily had a specific meaning. Thus he did not commit what later scholars would call the "intentional fallacy." No critic can possibly know Racine's intentions; a critic can, however, describe quite properly the emotional effect of a tragedy on spectators and readers.

La Bruyère agreed with Aristotle that a skillful performance of a powerful tragedy can produce a cathartic effect on spectators and thus purge or purify them emotionally. Tragic masterpieces produce lasting catharsis in their audience. La Bruyère described how gifted playwrights control psychological reactions to their tragedies:

> The tragic poem grabs your heart from the very beginning, scarcely leaves you throughout the play time to breathe or to relax, or if it does give you some respite, it is to plunge you again into new abysses and new alarms.

This analysis describes very accurately an audience's emotional reactions to Racine's first important tragedy, *Andromaque* (1667; *Andromache*, 1674). At the beginning of act 1, Andromache, the widow of the Trojan hero Hector and the mother of their very young son Astyanax, is the prisoner of a Greek king, Pyrrhus. The Greeks, inspired by a sense of vengeance, demand that Pyrrhus execute Astyanax. In each of the first four acts, Pyrrhus threatens to kill Astyanax unless Andromache marries him. The proud Andromache wishes to reconcile her fidelity to Hector with the need to save the boy's life, and though realizing that Pyrrhus is violent and untrustworthy, she has no choice. When she finally agrees to marry the king, she has some hope of success. The audience suffers with Andromache throughout this tragedy. Although Pyrrhus is assassinated between the fourth and fifth acts of the play, according to Greek mythology, Astyanax did in fact die at a very young age. Thus there is no hope for him and his mother. La Bruyère's critical approach to tragedy describes well the many profound emotional reactions experienced during a performance of any significant tragedy.

Racine and Corneille frequently modified their literary sources in order to make their tragedies seem believable and truthful to their contemporary audiences. They felt justified in modifying historical events or ancient mythology so that their plays would produce a more powerful effect on their spectators. For example, Racine justified allowing Astyanax to live longer than he did in the legends so that the audience could experience for the entire tragedy the terror felt by Andromache. If Astyanax were already dead, *Andromache* would be less meaningful.

Preachers, however, cannot take such liberties in order to make their sermons more effective. La Bruyère and numerous other seventeenth-century French critics greatly admired sermons by such famous preachers as Bourdaloue and Bossuet. La Bruyère appreciated not only their eloquence but also their thoughtful analyses of the complex motivation for human behavior. Indeed, even today, the sermons of these masters of French prose can be read with pleasure.

La Bruyère argues persuasively that sacred oratory is essentially different from all other forms of literary discourse. An essayist, a poet, or a playwright can always invent new arguments. A preacher, however, must discuss sublime and universal topics without modifying the biblical narratives on which all sermons must be based. An effective preacher impresses his audience first with his high moral character and only then persuades it with his "noble simplicity." An eloquent sermon develops a "unique but capital truth" which appeals to passions and moral beliefs in order to produce "persuasion in our minds and fear in our hearts." La Bruyère reminds his reader that a sermon, unlike an essay, is more than an abstract discourse: a sermon is intended to inspire a love of virtue so that actions can be made in conformity to God's will.

The demands placed on preachers are so great that few can write truly original and personal sermons. It may be possible to imitate a lyric poet, but no one can successfully imitate a sacred orator. La Bruyère compared Bourdaloue with Cicero and argued that no one could ever reproduce the brilliance and eloquence of either orator. This comparison may seem excessive to modern readers unacquainted with Bourdaloue's well-written sermons. La Bruyère's contemporaries, however, would have judged his comparison a very perceptive critical assessment.

La Bruyère's literary criticism constituted a significant contribution to the Quarrel of the Ancients and the Moderns. This lively exchange of aesthetic ideas, which took place during the last years of the seventeenth century, dealt with the complex relationship between the classical and modern traditions. Bernard de Fontenelle and Perrault, the main apologists for the moderns, believed that writers and critics should feel free to explore themes not treated extensively during the classical era. Nicolas Boileau-Despréaux and La Bruyère, the main defenders of the ancients, were afraid, however, that such a position would result in superficial and ephemeral works of literature and criticism.

La Bruyère and Boileau believed that their contemporaries could attain true originality only through the systematic and creative imitation of respected poets, orators, literary theorists, and playwrights from classical Greece and Rome. They believed that the most significant literary criticism should always refer to such pioneering and insightful works as Aristotle's *De poetica* (c. 334–323 B.C.; *Poetics*) and Horace's *Ars poetica* (c. 17 B.C.; *The Art of Poetry*). In these classical masterpieces, La Bruyère discovered that literary critics should analyze the emotional and aesthetic effect of literary texts on readers and spectators. In the 1980s such a theoretical approach would have been called reader-response criticism. La Bruyère's insightful analyses of reactions to tragedies, poems, and sermons inspired similarly creative literary criticism by such important eighteenth-century French literary theorists as Voltaire and Denis Diderot.

## Principal criticism

*Les Caractères: Ou, Les Mœurs de ce siècle*, 1688, 1689–1694
    (*The Characters: Or, The Manners of the Age*, 1699)

## Other major works and literary forms

Jean de La Bruyère owes his literary fame solely to
*The Characters*, a book of moral philosophy and social
criticism. His other works are of much less importance.
The editions of *The Characters* published during his lifetime also included his translation of the fourth-century B.C.
*Charaktēres* of Theophrastus, a Greek moralist. French
scholars, however, proved generations ago that La Bruyère
had translated into French not the original Greek text but
rather a 1592 Latin translation by Isaac Casaubon.

In 1699, three years after his death, *Dialogues posthumes
du sieur de La Bruyère sur le quiétisme* (posthumous
dialogues on quietism) was published. A Parisian publisher
and bookseller attributed this work to La Bruyère, although
this attribution is suspect. Quietism is an unorthodox belief
which encourages such a total submission to God's will that
no actions are undertaken alone. The practitioner of this
belief ideally retreats into extreme and abnormal passivity.
Since La Bruyère was a practicing Catholic and both the
Vatican and the French bishops had expressed strong disapproval of this philosophy, readers and critics since 1699
have wondered why he would write an entire work criticizing such an odd religious position.

NONFICTION
*Discours de réception à l'Académie française*, 1693 (*M.
    Bruyère's Speech upon His Admission into the French
    Academy*, 1713)
*Dialogues posthumes du sieur de La Bruyère sur le quiétisme*,
    1699

TRANSLATION
*Les Caractères de Théophraste*, 1688, 1689–1694 (of
    Theophrastus' essays; *The Moral Characters of Théophrastus*,
    1713)

MISCELLANEOUS
*The Works*, 1713 (2 volumes)
*Œuvres*, 1865–1878

## Further reading

Jasinski, René. *Deux Accès à La Bruyère*, 1971.
Kirsch, Doris. *La Bruyère: Ou, Le Style cruel*, 1977.
Knox, Edward C. *Jean de La Bruyère*, 1973.
Landry, Jean-Pierre. *La Bruyère*, 1996.
Richard, Pierre. *La Bruyère et ses "Caractères,"* 1965.
Roukhomosky, Bernard. *L'Esthétique de la Bruyère*, 1997.
Van Delft, Louis. *La Bruyère moraliste*, 1971.
——. *La Bruyère ou du spectateur*, 1996.
Yarrow, P. J. "La Bruyère," in *A Literary History of France*.
    Vol. 2, *The Seventeenth Century*, 1967. Edited by
    P. E. Charvet.

EDMUND J. CAMPION

*See also* Boileau-Despréaux; Corneille; Malherbe;
Neoclassical Literary Theory; Racine

# Jean de La Fontaine

French writer

**Born:** Château-Thierry, France; July 8, 1621
**Died:** Paris, France; April 13, 1695

## Biography

Jean de La Fontaine was born on July 8, 1621, in Château-
Thierry, a village on the Marne in the Champagne region
of France. An indifferent student at school – with an
apparent distaste for pedagogues and pedagogy – La
Fontaine became an inspector of forests and waterways in
1652. Not altogether happy with this post (although
he continued to serve in it for many years) or with the
marriage he had made in 1647 to Marie Héricart, he left
Château-Thierry for Paris in 1658, after his wife insisted
on a separation by contract. He had, however, by 1658,
already spent much time in Paris and had made important
connections there.

Living in an age of patronage, La Fontaine was especially lucky to secure a series of generous patrons, beginning with Nicolas Fouquet, a minister of finance for Louis
XIV, and ending with Madame de La Sablière, in whose
home La Fontaine lived the last twenty years of his life,
and who once claimed that she would never go anywhere
without her dog, her cat, and La Fontaine. His first literary
piece was a play in imitation of Terence, *L'Eunuque* (1654;
*The Eunuch*). It was followed ten years later by *Contes et
nouvelles en vers* (*Tales and Short Stories in Verse*, 1735)
a series of for the most part licentious tales adapted from
Giovanni Boccaccio, Ludovico Ariosto, and numerous other
writers. La Fontaine continued to publish various series of
these tales until shortly before his death, when, under some
pressure from the Church, he delivered a halfhearted renunciation of them. His fables, published in three parts, have
made his reputation. In 1683 he was elected to the French
Academy. He died in Paris on April 13, 1695.

## Influence

Because La Fontaine was only implicitly a literary critic, his
influence is perforce an implicit matter. Henry David
Thoreau is said to have lived out some of Ralph Waldo
Emerson's literary pronouncements, and perhaps it can be
argued that La Fontaine in some measure "lived out" in
his various writings some of the critical precepts of Nicolas
Boileau-Despréaux, whose *L'Art poétique* (1674; *The Art
of Poetry*, 1683) became in the last quarter of the seventeenth century a bible of sorts for literary theorists. Unlike
many of those theorists, however, La Fontaine did not
become a rule-bound fool, a slave to Boileau's or anyone
else's tastes. He is generally thought to have sided with the
cause of the ancients in what Jonathan Swift later called
"the battle of the books," a controversy concerning the
question of the respective merits of ancient and modern

writers; in fact, however, he was a voracious and tolerant reader who drew on influences both classical and modern and whose numerous innovations as a versifier paved the way for later experiments in French prosody. The Romantic writers Jean-Jacques Rousseau and Alphonse de Lamartine abhorred La Fontaine: Rousseau believed the morality implicit in the fables unfit for children; Lamartine found La Fontaine generally poisonous. Modern French writers such as Paul Valéry and Jean Giraudoux, however, have admired La Fontaine's versatility and moral complexity and have written for the most part favorably of him.

## Analysis

In *The Art of Poetry* Boileau wrote, "If you wish to deserve the regard of the public, constantly vary your style when writing. Too even a style, one that is always uniform, is brilliant in vain: the brightness will put us to sleep." La Fontaine's career as a writer and implicit theorist of writing can be seen as a long attempt to live up to this advice. He was fond of saying, "*Diversité, c'est ma devise*" (diversity, that is my motto), and so it was: diversity of theme, style, genre. So wide were La Fontaine's tastes in reading that it is difficult, if not impossible, to say what writer he favored over all others, but certainly his enthusiasm for Horace was great, because Horace was for him a poet of every tone and thus eminently worthy of close attention and emulation.

In *The Esthetics of Negligence: La Fontaine's "Contes"* (1971), John C. Lapp has suggested a valuable way of looking at and subdividing the *négligence* of La Fontaine, that studied carelessness that is a hallmark of his works, diverse though they may be. Lapp claims that *négligence* comprises two elements. The first, irresponsibility, is the denial that one's work has a special purpose. In La Fontaine's preface to the 1665 edition of the *Contes*, he suggests such an absence of special purpose, and later, in his commentary on the fables, he argues that not all fables ought to have explicit morals, that the reader ought sometimes to be left with "something to think about." It was just such a notion that caused Rousseau to inveigh against the "immoralism" of La Fontaine and to suggest that the fables had no place on the reading lists of children. The second subdivision is spontaneity, the apparent ease with which writing is done, its "cavalier" nature. Aristotle had urged gentlemen who played musical instruments to take pains not to learn to play them too well, and, at least in theory, neoclassical critics were prepared to assent to this advice. La Fontaine reported that he wished to give in his work the impression of a conversation rather than an academic conference. In the process of creating such an impression, he doomed himself to the eventual scorn of Romantic writers, for whom enthusiasm was a great virtue and who preferred a more emotional variety of spontaneity. Writing, according to one version of Romantic doctrine, is supposed to come out of suffering and to bear the marks of that

suffering. If, as William Wordsworth supposed, the emotion that is the basis of writing is to be recollected in tranquillity, the emotion is nevertheless to be placed in the foreground, the tranquillity in the background. It is clear that La Fontaine labored to make his art; the labor, however, is not apparent enough for the Romantic temperament.

In *Clymène* (1671), a small fantasia in dramatic form, La Fontaine announced certain critical principles, among them his sincere devotion to art, which is strong, despite the disclaimer of irresponsibility; his sense – here expressed by Apollo – that the current age of poetry is an Iron Age and that the good old days are to be much longed for; and the neoclassical doctrine of imitation, with which La Fontaine clearly agreed, with certain reservations. A great synthesizer of old and new, La Fontaine was able to be neoclassical in essence and yet not to fall victim to the absurdities of those critics and writers who followed the letter, rather than the spirit, of classical maxims. Even one hundred years after La Fontaine flourished, the grip of such thoughtless adherence was still strong in Europe, as can be seen by the out-cry that occurred in England when Benjamin West dressed the soldiers of his painting *The Death of Wolfe* in coats, breeches, and cocked hats rather than the classically acceptable togas.

One imagines La Fontaine smiling at such excesses as this, despite an occasional and apparently reflexive deference on his part to the unconditional wisdom of the ancients. In one of his prefaces, he says, after having cited Quintilian on the nature of narrative, "Need I substantiate the statement? That it is Quintilian's is enough."

Nevertheless, one here senses the same sort of obligatory allegiance to a classical sage that a Frenchman was bound to express when writing something intended for the approval of Louis XIV. Ultimately, any adherence on La Fontaine's part to the wisdom of either ancients or moderns was of the thoughtful variety. One must imitate, one must borrow, to be sure, but one must also be ready to apply new twists in the process, to supplant the Alexandrine with *vers libre* (free verse), to turn Aesop's industrious ant into a dour and mean-spirited figure. In his *Épître à Huet* (1687; a verse epistle addressed to Huet, the Bishop of Soissons), La Fontaine defends his right to take liberties with his sources, thus announcing a theory of judicious adornment. In *Clymène*, Apollo says that no topic is ever exhausted, and La Fontaine stood ready, with his tireless skills as an innovator in verse, narrative, and moral perspective, to prove the truth of Apollo's pronouncement.

In *Relation d'un voyage en Limousin* (1663; an account of a trip to Limousin), La Fontaine demonstrates what might seem, given the epoch in which he lived, an unusual aversion to regularity. Noting that the cathedral there is made up of three different architectural styles, he writes, "*Toutes ces trois pièces ne font, Dieu merci, nulle symétrie*" (all three styles have, thank God, no symmetry). This comment appears to celebrate the freedom to appropriate whatever has been thought, felt, and made, and to do with it as one pleases, to adorn stories, or cathedrals, in manners as surprising, as asymmetrical, as one wishes.

In his fables, La Fontaine does not bring to bear the scruples of the entomologist or the naturalist, and certainly he bridles at the pedestrian insistences of rule-bound neoclassical critics who fell prey time and again to mindless acceptance of the least dictate of arbiters of taste from Aristotle to Boileau. Nevertheless, with freedom comes responsibility: if one is not obliged to get the entomology of insects right, one is obliged to be faithful to the truth of human nature. If the Alexandrine is dispensed with, one must study the "carelessness" of free verse so as to keep it from turning into prose.

When Olivier Patru, a lawyer and friend of Boileau and La Fontaine, questioned La Fontaine's versifying of Aesop's prose, wondering whether such adornment would not destroy the conciseness which is the essence of fable, La Fontaine responded in his preface with a most graceful statement in defense of diversity and catholicity: "I would merely ask that he . . . concede that spartan graces and the French muses are not too incompatible to be persuaded at times to walk hand in hand." Later in the same preface, La Fontaine defends his occasional omitting of a moral:

> I have sometimes done so, but only when I could not include it appropriately, or where the reader could supply it himself. In France we consider only what pleases: the one requisite and, so to speak, the only one. It has never seemed to me a crime to ignore the ancient conventions if one could not adhere to them gracefully.

If one considers for a moment how many critics at the time did believe it a crime to ignore ancient conventions, one begins to see how striking and even revolutionary such a remark was. In two late fables, "The Candle" and "The Scythian Philosopher," La Fontaine slyly but strikingly explodes the neoclassical myths of uniformity and conformity, at the same time defending the principle of judicious diversity. "The Candle" deals with a foolish taper which, having noted that clay, when baked in fire, hardens to durable brick, decides to attempt a similar hardening, with predictable consequences. La Fontaine then parallels this behavior with that of the taper's spiritual ancestor Empedocles, who committed what La Fontaine thought a supreme folly when he threw himself into a volcano in order to prove that he was a god. The fabulist pronounces a hard judgment on both taper and philosopher:

> Could logic's fool led astray
> Have proved better its lack of philosophy.
> Each differs from the rest: don't think that the folk you see

Who make up the world have been nursed as you were nursed!
In the pot, our wax Empedocles vanished instantly
But was not more a fool than the first.

The foolishness consists of not knowing what one is, what one's limitations are. Like Horace, La Fontaine recognized that he was no Homer, no singer of epic songs. The wisdom of any writers, ancient or modern, consists in remaining true to their specific talents and recognizing their limitations; La Fontaine repeatedly justifies his emendations of old tales and fables on these grounds. In "The Scythian Philosopher," a denizen of Scythia journeys to Greece and meets a sage who is busy pruning his garden. At first the Scythian does not understand what the sage is doing. The sage attempts to instruct him: "Remove sere boughs and when they are gone,/ One has benefited what remain." The Scythian, sounding for all the world like a critic fresh returned from a reading of Aristotle or Boileau, returns to his native country and acts upon his garbled understanding of the sage's counsel:

> The Scythian returned to his bleak shore,
> Seized his own pruning hook, was at work hour on hour,
> Enjoining upon any in the vicinity
>     That they work – the whole community.
> He sheared off whatever was beautiful,
> Indiscriminately trimmed and cut down,
>     Persevering in reduction
>     Beneath new moons and full
> Till none of his trees could bear.

It is in such brilliant jibes as these that La Fontaine makes his great impression as a theorist.

In another part of the same preface in which La Fontaine made his fine defense of catholicity, he discusses his determination to write fables and his awareness that, even if he did not succeed in them, his efforts would bring to him the credit of having opened a way for others. Thus it may be said that La Fontaine's great legacy as critic and literary theorist lies in his having provided a model. He went about what he was doing with great acuity, he chose his own examples from an immensely wide stock, he made the most judicious use of those choices, and he exercised classical restraint in the matter of his limits. His own description of his fables is in itself a sterling example of perceptive, economic criticism: *Une ample comédie à cent actes divers,/ Et dont la scène est l'univers* (an ample comedy of a hundred diverse acts, of which the scene is the universe). Small wonder that a poet and critic of similarly wide learning and curiosity such as Paul Valéry should have sung the praises of La Fontaine in the twentieth century.

## Principal criticism
*Discours à Mme de La Sablière*, 1679
*Épître à Huet*, 1687

## Other major works and literary forms
Much of Jean de La Fontaine's critical writing can be found only in the fables, novels, tales, discourses, and prefaces for which he is most famous. These works include *Contes et nouvelles en vers* (1664, 1665; *Tales and Short Stories in Verse*, 1735), *Fables choisies, mises en vers* (1668, 1678, 1694; *Fables Written in Verse*, 1735), and *Les Amours de Psyché et de Cupidon* (1669; *The Loves of Cupid and Psyche*, 1744). There exists no English edition of his complete works. The most recent French edition is *Œuvres complètes* (1991; two volumes). A selection of miscellaneous works, excluding his fables and tales, is contained in *Œuvres diverses* (1942).

NOVEL
*Les Amours de Psyché et de Cupidon*, 1669 (*The Loves of Cupid and Psyche*, 1744)

PLAYS
*L'Eunuque*, 1654
*Clymène*, 1671
*Daphné*, 1682 (libretto)
*Galatée*, 1682 (libretto)
*L'Astrée*, 1692 (libretto)

POETRY
*Adonis*, 1658
*Le Songe de Vaux*, 1659
*Contes et nouvelles en vers*, 1664, 1665 (*Tales and Short Stories in Verse*, 1735)
*Deuxième partie des contes et nouvelles en vers*, 1666 (*Part Two of Tales and Short Stories in Verse*, 1735)
*Fables choisies, mises en vers*, 1668, 1678, 1694 (*Fables Written in Verse*, 1735)
*Troisième partie des contes et nouvelles en vers*, 1671 (*Part Three of Tales and Short Stories in Verse*, 1735)
*Nouveaux Contes*, 1674 (*New Tales*, 1735)
*Poèmes et poésies diverses*, 1697

NONFICTION
*Relation d'un voyage en Limousin*, 1663

MISCELLANEOUS
*Æuvres complètes*, 1933 (2 volumes)
*Æuvres diverses*, 1942

## Further reading
Bared, Robert. *La Fontaine*, 1995.
Birberick, Anne L., ed. *Refiguring La Fontaine: Tercentenary Essays*, 1996.
Danner, Richard. *Patterns of Irony in the Fables of La Fontaine*, 1985.
De Ley, Herbert. *Fixing Up Reality: La Fontaine and Lévi-Strauss*, 1996.
Guiton, Margaret O. *La Fontaine: Poet and Counterpoet*, 1961.
Hamel, Frank. *Jean de La Fontaine*, 1911.
King, Ethel. *Jean de La Fontaine*, 1970.
Lapp, John C. *The Esthetics of Negligence: La Fontaine's "Contes,"* 1971.
Mackay, Agnes. *La Fontaine and His Friends*, 1973.
Rubin, David Lee. *A Pact with Silence: Art and Thought in the Fables of Jean de La Fontaine*, 1991.
Sutherland, Monica. *La Fontaine*, 1953.
Vincent, Michael. *Figures of the Text: Reading and Writing (in) La Fontaine*, 1992.
Wadsworth, Philip A. *Young La Fontaine: A Study of His Artistic Growth in His Early Poetry and First Fables*, 1952.

JOHNNY WINK

See also  Boileau-Despréaux; La Bruyère; Neoclassical Literary Theory

# Jean-François de la Harpe
French writer and critic

**Born:** Paris, France; November 20, 1739
**Died:** Paris, France; February 11, 1803

## Biography
Jean-François de La Harpe was born on November 20, 1739, the son of Jean-François de La Harpe, a former artillery captain, and Marie-Louise Devienne. On his father's death in May, 1749, the family found itself completely destitute. That same year a parish priest introduced the young La Harpe to the headmaster of the Collège d'Harcourt, who gave him a scholarship and a solid education, based primarily on the study of classical languages and authors. A bright pupil, La Harpe received numerous awards, and thanks to his acquaintance with some students from good families, he entered society in 1758 and became a protégé of the Marquess de Ximenes. In November, 1763, his first play was successfully performed, consolidating his place in society. More important, however, it secured for him Voltaire's lasting support and friendship. La Harpe espoused his master's literary views and took his part in literary and political quarrels. This prominent vantage on the literary scene did not always translate into financial security, however, and La Harpe gladly accepted the post of editor of the *Mercure de France* as well as that of Parisian literary correspondent for Prince Paul, the heir to the throne of Russia, who granted him a pension of one thousand pounds that was to last from 1775 to 1779. Money earned from prizes given to laureates of competitions organized by different academies and the stipend for his professorship at the Lycée contributed to ensure his livelihood.

Unfortunately, the political torment that was to engulf France did not spare him; despite his ardently proclaimed Republican views, he fell victim to the Reign of Terror. Jailed in March, 1794, La Harpe was freed in July of that year by Maximilien François Marie Isidore de Robespierre's fall. As a result of his imprisonment, La Harpe became a very different man, having undergone during his internment a conversion which made him loudly denounce his former convictions and friendships. His last years were marked by constant illness and financial worries caused by his inability to work. He died in Paris on February 11, 1803, and on December 29, 1838, his remains were transferred to the Père Lachaise Cemetery.

## Influence

There is no doubt that La Harpe's *Lycée*, his best-known and most systematic work, was quite influential in the early nineteenth century, since it was reedited at least twenty times from 1800 to 1833. Later, however, his dogmatic approach and narrow admiration for the seventeenth-century French masters were denounced by Victor Hugo, Alfred de Vigny, and Gustave Flaubert, and led to near oblivion in the twentieth century. This negative judgment was not shared by all: Ferdinand Brunetière, among others, was lavish in his praises of La Harpe in his *L'Évolution des genres dans l'histoire de la littérature* (1890). While acknowledging his weaknesses, Brunetière remarked that the *Lycée* contained useful judgments and precious information on the seventeenth and eighteenth centuries and confirmed the originality of La Harpe's immense enterprise. The 1960s and 1970s saw a revival of interest in La Harpe's critical work as attested by the studies of Andrew Hunwick and Christopher Todd.

## Analysis

La Harpe did not compose a formal treatise on literary criticism, but principles governing his views on the matter can be gleaned from his newspaper articles, his *Correspondance littéraire*, some discourses, and especially his *Lycée*.

Like most eighteenth-century critics, La Harpe adopted the neoclassical theory of literature based on the traditional distinction of the different genres, the imitation of nature, and the obedience to certain rules. He strongly believed, following the thinking of the seventeenth century, that there are certain principles of literature valid for all times and nations. He greatly admired the French masters of the preceding century and thought that at times the moderns had even surpassed the ancients they were imitating, especially in the realm of the theater. He shared with them the conviction that the desire to please and not morality, as Denis Diderot and other of his contemporaries believed, was the artist's first responsibility to the public.

Good writers were to imitate nature, but La Harpe did not advocate a slavish imitation of nature which could lead to unsavory realism. All artists had to choose and embellish according to the theory of decorum, lest they offend their readers. Thus, they needed to possess "good taste," a prerogative of polite society and a quality derived from the study of literary models and the knowledge of the rules pertaining to art. La Harpe found it as difficult to define good taste as he found it difficult to define its opposite, to which he alluded even more often. Because of their nonconformity to his ideals, he condemned French literature of the Middle Ages and Renaissance, as well as the works of Dante, William Shakespeare, John Milton and others, although he did recognize that these "monsters" contained some beautiful parts which were composed according to "the rules of art." Another abstract notion, as slippery as taste, was that of genius; because of the vagueness of the term, many critics were led to attribute it to writers who had none. La Harpe believed that he would not fall victim to such error, convinced as he was that the presence of genius could be demonstrated. In the case of a tragic poet, the critic should examine whether the topics are properly chosen, the structure is well conceived, the situations are interesting and probable, the characters conform to nature, and the style is the correct expression of feelings and passions. Having conducted this thorough examination, critics, without erring, can then formulate their conclusions.

This self-assurance never left La Harpe, who believed that he was supremely qualified to perform his task as critic. Some, however, objected to the critic's role – which is to analyze the pleasure derived from literature and to judge the literary production of the past and the present – as being useless, since nothing new could be said and beauty, nature, and reason belong to all times. To those, La Harpe answered that critics could add to the unchangeable principles a host of new and useful observations. Thanks to their judgment and sensibility, they could analyze writers' strengths as well as their weaknesses. The critique of even a famous author could yield some riches, true genius being inexhaustible. The critic's role was thus that of guiding authors and enlightening readers through a careful analysis of works – a task which La Harpe took seriously during his long career as arbiter of good taste in literature.

In poetry, he advocated a blend of correct language, moderate use of figures, and skillful versification and favored direct, simple, elegant verses, although they are, by their very nature, more ornate than prose. Classical rules about rhythm or hiatus should be observed. Run-on lines, antitheses, mixing of verses of different patterns were to be kept to a minimum. Nevertheless, La Harpe, himself a poet, realized that well-crafted lines do not make poets out of versifiers, for poetry remains the most difficult and beautiful of the arts. In the appreciation of poetry, the reader's ears and heart are involved, and to a lesser degree his or her mind, since poetry's primary aim remains pleasure resulting from the harmony between ideas and form and not from the ideas alone. Despite this statement, La Harpe nevertheless continued writing satires in verse in which he mercilessly depicted his enemies, expounded his literary creed, and defended true genius against envious writers.

Although La Harpe never finished an epic, he was quite interested in the genre as practiced by the ancient poets and by Voltaire as well. A very difficult genre, and a truly noble one, the epic, which, unlike tragedy, could not rely on the artifice of the stage, was to present a unified action through its different episodes. Finding a suitable theme which would at once be heroic, moving, and moral, however, proved to be difficult, since the mythology which served the ancients so well could not be replaced by Christianity, the latter's marvels being mysteries and not merely fables. Nevertheless, this difficulty did not prevent La Harpe, after his conversion, from starting a Christian epic, entitled *Le Triomphe de la religion*. Death interrupted this work, whose main interest lay in its style, which echoed those of Virgil, Boileau, and Jean Racine and confirmed his adherence to classical rules of versification. Yet poets could turn to other fields for inspiration, to history for example, as did Voltaire in his *La Pucelle d'Orléans* (1755, 1762; *The Maid of Orleans*, 1758, also as *La Pucelle: Or, The Maid of Orleans*) and *La Henriade* (1728; *Henriade*, 1732), which La Harpe called tasteless.

If La Harpe was critical of his friend's epics, the same cannot be said of his analysis of Voltaire's tragedies. According to him, Voltaire and Racine had fulfilled all the conditions that genius required. Tragedy was highly regarded by the eighteenth century, which still admired the productions of the preceding century. Dramatic theory was still basically that of Aristotle. Thus, La Harpe recommended that the action be a serious one: he did not allow any distraction from it and consequently deprecated Shakespeare's plays as being thoroughly marred by their blend of buffoonery and tragedy. He also objected to plays whose mundane subjects and characters could not move the spectators as tragedy did, but he did so not as vigorously, since it represented a lesser genre.

It should be said that La Harpe did not cling unwaveringly to the rules of unity concerning action, time, and place. In his opinion, only the first was necessary to retain the public's attention, but he still thought that the exposition had to contain all the essential parts of the play. Furthermore, the plot had to unfold in a continuous manner, and gratuitous events and extra characters had to be firmly proscribed in order not to detract from the protagonists and their fates.

As to comedy, judged less difficult and less important than tragedy, it nevertheless remained a serious genre whose principal object was to give moral lessons while entertaining the spectators. It should imitate nature, depicting humanity in its unchanging aspects. Thus, La Harpe objected to such improbabilities as the transformation, within a mere twenty-four hours, of a miser into a generous man. True comedy, as practiced by the great Molière, was to show not the particular (a result of specific and changing mores and situations) but the eternal in human nature. True comedy, like true tragedy, could thus withstand the supreme test, that of posterity.

Since literary critics of the day retained the hierarchy of the genres, the novel was much maligned. La Harpe's attitude toward this category was no different from that of his contemporaries. He judged it to be inferior and governed by no rules. Still, and to his credit, he expressed his admiration for some works of fiction, such as Mme de La Fayette's *La Princesse de Clèves* (1678; *The Princess of Clèves*, 1679), Alain-René Lesage's *Histoire de Gil Blas de Santillane* (1715–1735; *The History of Gil Blas de Santillane*, 1716, better known as *Gil Blas*), Voltaire's tales, Abbé Prévost's *Histoire du chevalier des Grieux et de Manon Lescaut* (1731; *Manon Lescaut*, 1734), and Henry Fielding's *The History of Tom Jones, a Foundling*, 1749.

La Harpe, a true believer in the classical tenets of literature, was not as dogmatic as his enemies portrayed him, although his admiration for authors of the past made him unable to appreciate any new trend in literature and his reliance on French good taste forbade him to see the originality and genius of non-French writers. His willingness to endorse Voltaire's causes as well as his irascible character caused him to become involved in many lengthy battles, as exemplified by his thirty-year duel with critic Pierre Clément, his contemporary. He certainly can also be faulted for having burnt what he once had adored since, after his conversion of 1794, he turned from ardent supporter of the philosophes to bitter adversary, finding no epithet strong enough to denounce Diderot and his atheism, stooping even to criticism of his former mentor, Voltaire. Nevertheless, his importance as a critic should not be overlooked. For years he had the power, because of his numerous articles, to make or break a literary reputation. Yet his influence went beyond the eighteenth century itself with the publication of the *Lycée*, which despite gaps, represented a new and ambitious enterprise in the field of literary history. Louis de Fontanes, the founder of *Mercure de France*, an influential paper of the period, went so far as to write in 1801 that the work was nothing less than an invaluable supplement to the national education of French youth. Again in 1803 in the obituary he composed after La Harpe's death, he stated that France was mourning the loss of an excellent critic, an opinion shared by Charles-Augustin Sainte-Beuve, François Auguste René Chateaubriand, and, later, by Brunetière. To modern minds, however, he remains the last representative of a literary tradition that was soon to be swept away by Madame de Staël's theories and the Romantic revolution.

## Principal criticism

*Conseils à un jeune poète*, 1775
*Lycée: Ou, Cours de littérature ancienne et moderne*, 1799–1805 (16 volumes)
*Correspondance littéraire*, 1801–1807 (6 volumes)
*Mélanges inédits de littérature de J. F. de La Harpe*, 1810
*Commentaire sur le théâtre de Voltaire*, 1814
*Discours sur la poésie sacrée*, 1822

## Other major works and literary forms

In addition to critical works, Jean-François de La Harpe wrote several tragedies, the first and best one being *Comte de Warwick* (1763), which brought him early recognition as it was successfully performed on the stage of the famous Comédie-Française. La Harpe was also a poet: some of his poems are literary treatises, in Nicolas Boileau-Despréaux's fashion (*Le Poète*, 1766; *Conseils à un jeune poète*, 1775), while others treat literary quarrels in a satiric vein (*L'Ombre de Duclos*, 1773, *Les Prétensions*, 1770). He seems to have excelled at light verse written for social occasions, although he did try his hand at the epic genre as in the *Héroïdes nouvelles* (1759) and *Le Triomphe de la religion: Ou, Le Roi martyr* (1814), which was interrupted after the sixth canto by his death. He also published many discourses, *Des malheurs de la guerre* (1767), *Éloge de Henri IV, roi de France* (1769), and *Éloge de Racine* (1772).

PLAYS
*Comte de Warwick*, 1763
*Timoléon*, 1764
*Pharamond*, 1765
*Gustave Wasa*, 1766
*Mélanie: Ou, La Religieuse*, 1770
*Barnevel*, 1778
*Les Barricades*, 1778
*Les Brames*, 1781
*Jeanne de Naples*, 1781
*Philoctète*, 1783
*Coriolan*, 1784
*Virginie*, 1786

POETRY
*Héroïdes nouvelles*, 1759
*Le Poète*, 1766
*Les Prétensions*, 1770
*L'Ombre de Duclos*, 1773
*Conseils à un jeune poète*, 1775
*Le Triomphe de la religion: Ou, Le Roi martyr*, 1814

NONFICTION
*Des malheurs de la guerre*, 1767
*Éloge de Henry IV, roi de France*, 1769
*Éloge de Racine*, 1772

### Further reading
Hunwick, Andrew. *La Critique littéraire de Jean-François de La Harpe, 1739–1803*, 1977.
Todd, Christopher. *Voltaire's Disciple: Jean-François de La Harpe*, 1972.
Wellek, René. *A History of Modern Criticism: 1750–1950*. Vol. 1, *The Later Eighteenth Century*, 1955.

CAMILLE GARNIER

*See also* Brunetière; Neoclassical Literary Theory; Sainte-Beuve

# Jacques Lacan
French psychoanalyst and theorist

**Born:** Paris, France; April 13, 1901
**Died:** Paris, France; September 9, 1981

## Biography

Jacques Marie Émile Lacan was born, grew up, worked, and died in Paris, the intellectual capital of France and of postwar Europe, the center of the structuralist and post-structuralist movements which he helped found. Son of businessman Alfred Lacan and of Émilie Baudry, Lacan studied medicine and psychology in Paris, receiving his doctorate in psychiatry in 1932. During his student days he associated with Surrealist poets and painters, among them Salvador Dalí, who credits Lacan with helping him develop the "paranoid style" in art. Lacan had undergone psychoanalysis with Rudolph Loewenstein, who broke off the sessions in order to emigrate to the United States and develop ego psychology with Heinz Hartmann. It has been conjectured that this improper ending to Lacan's own analysis had much to do with his later vituperations against ego psychology and American psychiatry. In 1934 Lacan married Marie-Louise Blondin and in the same year joined the Faculté de Médecine de Paris, teaching and practicing at the Hôpital Sainte-Anne. The insistence by Lacan and some of his colleagues that psychiatry not be considered a branch of medicine – Lacan is not out to "cure" his patients, but to reveal a truth to them – led to their secession from the Paris Psychoanalytic Society in 1953 and to their subsequent founding of the French Psychoanalytic School. This was to be the first of many schisms and controversies surrounding Lacan. The French Psychoanalytic School turned on him eleven years later, expelling its cofounder in order to remain a part of the International Psychiatric Association (run by Americans with little sympathy for Lacan's ideas). Allegedly at issue were Lacan's famed "short sessions," that is, analyses in which the analyst decides when to end each session rather than follow the standard scheme of fifty-minute blocks.

Suddenly deprived of a place to teach, Lacan was rescued by his friends Claude Lévi-Strauss and Marxist philosopher Louis Althusser, who used their influence to provide him with a title and a lecture hall at the École Normale Supérieure. It was at this point that Lacan's lectures, collectively called *Le Séminaire* and previously given mainly to students of psychiatry, began to attract a wide audience and to become a modern salon for Parisian intellectuals. The publication in 1966 of Lacan's magnum opus, *Écrits*, confirmed his position at the forefront of structuralism. So influential did Lacan become that the École Normale Supérieure felt compelled to eject him in 1968 on the suspicion that his lectures had helped fuel the student riots which were gripping Paris. Sherry Turkle, whose *Psychoanalytic*

*Politics* (1992) describes the role played by psychoanalytic theory in France's social upheaval, confirms that suspicion with a listing of Lacan's credentials as a radical:

> There is the Lacan who criticized the "discourse of the University" before such talk had become popular. There is the Lacan who signed manifestos in support of the striking students in May 1968, and the Lacan who sided with jailed student leaders. There is the Lacan who warned the students not to be seduced by the government's attempts to cool them out with promises of dialogue and participation .... And of course, there is the story ... of Lacan putting student leader Daniel Cohn-Bendit in the back of his own Jaguar and successfully smuggling him across the border into Germany.

Lacan's Freudian School of Paris relocated to the University of Paris branch at Vincennes, until suddenly a gravely ill Lacan declared it dissolved in order to end the war of succession. Jacques-Alain Miller had become heir apparent to Lacan by marrying his daughter Judith (from his second marriage to Sylvia Makles), upsetting a number of people who had worked longer with Lacan and believed themselves more appropriate successors. Lacan's move seemed to have the opposite effect from what he intended, touching off legal battles and endless recriminations. The final dissolution of the Freudian School of Paris was done by vote, a process carried out somewhat like the condemnation of Socrates, in a large lecture hall under the eyes of the dying Lacan in 1981. Eyewitness Catherine Clément describes the scene:

> One by one the Lacanians climbed the platform to cast a vote for or against the dissolution of their School .... That cardboard urn contained not only the ballots cast by the members of the dead School but also the ashes of "Lacan." He knew it. I don't think he gave a damn.

A few months after this extraordinary event, Jacques Lacan died in Paris at the age of eighty.

## Influence
Lacan was one of the most influential theorists of the 1970s and 1980s. His work formed a nodal point (or "knot," to use one of Lacan's favorite topological metaphors) among several movements: it derived many of its basic ideas from structuralism, particularly from the linguistics of Ferdinand de Saussure and Roman Jakobson and from the anthropology of Lévi-Strauss. On the other hand, Lacan's application of structuralist theories of the sign and of exchange to the realm of psychoanalysis gave enormous impetus to the poststructuralist movement. In this process Lacan almost single-handedly brought the discipline of

psychoanalysis back to its founder Sigmund Freud's insistence upon language as the key to understanding the unconscious – a shift in emphasis which has given new life to psychoanalytic literary interpretation. Finally, French feminist theory, psychoanalytic and linguistic in outlook, can be seen as a collective response to Lacan's insistence on the (non)position of woman outside Western discourse.

## Analysis
Besides Edgar Allan Poe's story "The Purloined Letter" (1844), Jacques Lacan also took as his model for psychoanalysis and the problems of interpretation the famous joke in which one Jew shouts at the other: "Why are you lying to me? Yes, why do you lie to me saying you're going to Cracow so I should believe you're going to Lemberg, when in reality you *are* going to Cracow?" Many years earlier, Freud had interpreted this joke as a profound questioning of the nature of truth: "Is it the truth if we describe things as they are without troubling to consider how our hearer will understand what we say?"

Lacan called this discrepancy between person and expression the realm of the Symbolic. One cannot mean anything personally but must always express oneself through language, which Lacan called the Other because it always implicates the hearer in a dialogue. The Symbolic in Lacan is opposed to the Imaginary, a realm of personal wholeness and unity. One of Lacan's earliest discoveries is of the "mirror stage" ("stade du miroir"), in which the child conceives of itself as a whole through self-contemplation in a mirror. This image (hence "Imaginary") provides a kind of illusory exoskeleton for the subject. Trying to define what one "is" in the conflict between these two realms is as impossible as trying to determine the real destination of the addressee in the joke.

So central did Lacan consider this joke that he used it in two of his most important works, "Seminar on 'The Purloined Letter,'" and "The Insistence of the Letter in the Unconscious," both collected in his *Écrits*. The joke appears each time with different city names. The change of names and the anonymity of the characters reinforce the fact that this joke signifies through its dialectical structure. All that matters to the joke, then, besides there being two people trying to communicate, is that there be two cities, which represent two different destinations. In other words, the meaning of the joke lies not in a single destination but in the opposition created between the two choices. (In "The Insistence of the Letter in the Unconscious," Lacan provides the additional example of two identical bathroom doors, one bearing the signifier "Ladies," the other "Gentleman." Any difference between the two bathrooms is entirely contained in their respective namings.) Lacan brought this notion of meaning as opposition, a central concept of structuralism impressed upon Lacan by his friends Jakobson and Lévi-Strauss, to bear upon the Oedipal situation at the heart of Freud's theory. Freud had theorized that the Oedipal conflict involved the child's renouncing his desire for the mother because he fears castration by the father. Lacan notes that everything begins with the idea of a lack: the father has the phallus, the mother is supposed to but does not. Thus the phallus, which Lacan calls the primal signifier, signifies through its absence. The Oedipal conflict is thus redefined as the conflict between the imaginary positing of something present, whole, and single, and the deferral of that object as the beginning of desire and of language.

Thus the beginning of language is the beginning of a series of deferrals of meaning, of a chain of "metonymies" in Lacan's terminology, which can also be seen operating in this joke. One character alone could be said to possess the knowledge of where he was going. The problem begins when he attempts to communicate that knowledge to another through linguistic symbols. Veracity immediately becomes a weapon of deception, and personal expression is inundated by signifying convention. It only becomes possible to express one's true intentions through a circuitous route, which may never succeed – there is after all no guarantee that saying "I'm going to Lemberg" will be read as meaning "I'm going to Cracow." There is also no guarantee that the complainant is correct in his perception of mendacity in the other. In general, the joke shows that interpretation is not something that is done to language but is a part of signification in general.

In any communicative situation, Lacan would say, there is the possibility of dialectical reversal, of truth being changed into untruth through the workings of the Symbolic. He notes in one of his central works, *The Language of the Self*:

> Even if it communicates nothing, the discourse [of the joke, of psychoanalysis, of literature] represents the existence of communication; even if it denies the obvious, it affirms that the Word constitutes the Truth; even if it is destined to deceive, here the discourse speculates on faith in testimony.

The two characters in the joke can be substituted by such concepts as the id and the ego, the analyst and the analysand, or the text and the reader. The joke's indeterminacy is indicative of repression, that is, of the subject's inability to perceive the workings of his own unconscious, whose meanings disappear at the moment he attempts to specify them. As Malcolm Bowie phrases it, "whenever we arrive at the cave of the unconscious, it is always closing time; the only way that we have of gaining access is to be inside already. The structure of the unconscious is knowable only by those who are prepared to admit and espouse its inexhaustible capacity for displacement." It is primarily the psychoanalyst who has taken charge of this attempt to render the unconscious into speech, and the relation between analyst and patient is, as the following quotation from Clément shows, analogous to and as problematic as the relationship between the speakers in the joke:

Lacan says that the subject, in analysis, is a question in search of an answer by way of speech. Lacan's thought has consistently remained open to the infinite perspectives of mythology, whose secret powers have helped to shape his ideas. The question must not link up with its answer, just as the son must not link up with its mother, just as the client must not link up with the analyst. The essential thing is to find the right therapeutic distance between the two, neither too close nor too far.

Finally, the relationship between the two speakers in the joke is also analogous to the reader's own relation to the mysteries of literature or to the often impenetrable pronouncements of Lacan himself. True to his belief in the impossibility of direct communication, Lacan couched his theory in a prose of extreme density full of allusions, puns, and poetry. One may be tempted to disregard Lacan's message because one doubts his sincerity, because one doubts that there is a "meaning" behind his words, because one doubts that he is "going to Cracow" as he (does not) say he is. Lacan would respond that the reading process which includes doubt and incomprehension is the only useful one.

Lacan as critic is literally a dreamer; his ideal of literature is *Finnegans Wake* (1939), James Joyce's oneiric masterpiece. Scraps and fragments of literature or songs appear and are used by the dream not for their content, but as pure signifiers pointing to something else. Literature gives to the dreamer not its own meaning, but rather a plethora of signifiers with which the dreamer will attempt to construct a rebus for his own meaning, to paint a disguised and scrambled portrait of his unconscious desires. The texts which appear in Lacan's essays (texts of Blaise Pascal, Molière, Jean Racine, Edgar Allan Poe, Stendhal, G. W. F. Hegel, the Upanishads) do so not in their own right but as scraps for bricolage, patches to be woven into the always unfinished quilt of Lacanian theory.

Even a text treated exhaustively, such as Poe's "The Purloined Letter," is read as an allegory of psychoanalysis, as a demonstration of the workings of the signifying chain, without any hope or desire for revealing Poe's "intentions." It is the letter, the text, which "in-tends," which exists on the inside, while both the human subject of writing and its final meaning are always elsewhere. The essay, playing on the double meaning of "letter" as missive and as typographical unit, elaborates how the purloined letter functions as a pure signifier. The letter's content or signified – never revealed in the story – is irrelevant to its ability to bring the characters into repeated triangular confrontations reminiscent of the Oedipal triangle, of the relation between the three Freudian components of human personality (id, ego, superego), and of the relation between the two speakers and the reader of the joke with which this essay began.

According to Lacan, literature always represents a particularly clear path to the excess of signification occurring in the unconscious. "Literature is the place in which form is itself 'put on the couch,' analysed rather than simply followed," writes one Lacanian critic. The form which is analyzed is that of language, of rhetoric as the process of linguistic signification regardless of its content. Thus the other work in the *Écrits* in which literature features prominently is aptly titled "The Insistence of the Letter in the Unconscious." The essay attempts to provide a psychoanalytic basis for rhetoric. By equating metonymy with the Freudian term "displacement," and metaphor with "condensation," Lacan in this essay customizes the theory of the metaphoric and metonymic poles outlined by Roman Jakobson and Morris Halle in *Fundamentals of Language* (1956) to psychoanalytic theory. In a similar refinement on the theory of the sign as union of signifier and signified (S/s), originally outlined by Saussure in his *Cours de linguistique générale* (1916; *Course in General Linguistics*, 1959), Lacan defines their relationship as the "incessant sliding of the signified under the signifier." By this Lacan means that the signified, identified by Saussure as a concept which the signifier points to, is in fact merely another signifier. This elusiveness of the signified leads back to the joke which began this essay; "what this structure of the signifying chain discloses is the possibility I have, precisely in so far as I have this language in common with other subjects, . . . to use it in order to signify *something quite other* than what it says." This is a psychoanalytic view of language, formed from working with patients whose problem is precisely an inability to formulate unconscious desires in language. Hysterical symptoms, dreams, and procrastination are all signifiers produced by this incessant sliding. The signified, the basic trauma or Oedipus complex which produces these symptoms, remains hidden.

Lacan characterizes poetry as a form of writing which exposes the signifying chain by drawing one's attention precisely to the multitude of signifiers to which each single signifier points: "One has only to listen to poetry . . . for a polyphony to be heard, for it to become clear that all discourse is aligned along the several staves of a score. There is in effect no signifying chain that does not have, as if attached to the punctuation of each of its units, a whole articulation of relevant contexts suspended 'vertically,' as it were, from that point." Reading poetry is the closest one can come to reading the unconscious.

Lacan's achievement as a literary theorist is analogous to that of the German philosopher Martin Heidegger, whom he often quotes. Heidegger claimed that poetic and philosophical discourse were of the same order, and his readings of the poems of Friedrich Hölderlin and Rainer Maria Rilke revealed the philosophical systems "contained" within them. Similarly, Lacan's analyses of Poe and of Marguerite Duras reveal that psychoanalysis and literature undertake a similar investigation of language and of the human mind.

In his study of the latter writer, Lacan has stated most baldly the principle, implicit in all of his writings as it is in those of Freud, that in his subject matter the artist "always precedes [the psychoanalyst], who does not need to play the psychologist where the artist has blazed the trail for him . . . . The praxis of the letter [or of language or of literature] converges with the usage of the unconscious." The generality of this equation of literature and psychoanalysis rescues the latter from its repetitive and demeaning analyses of literature as a product of mental abnormality.

Virtually the whole of contemporary French theory has been touched in one way or another by Lacan's many ideas. Roland Barthes, for example, uses Lacanian ideas of castration and of the signifying chain in his own highly original fashion in *S/Z* (1970; English translation, 1974). In their *Capitalisme et schizophrénie: L'Anti-Oedipe* (1973; *Anti-Oedipus: Capitalism and Schizophrenia*, 1977), Gilles Deleuze and Félix Guattari draw on Lacan's notions of the decentered subject imprisoned within the symbolic to project a revolutionary antipsychiatry which valorizes schizophrenia. Julia Kristeva's *Séméiotiké* (1969), which sees a similar freedom in what she calls the "semiotic" realm, uses a number of Lacanian ideas. The philosopher Paul Ricœur, in frequent attendance at the seminar, was inspired by Lacan to consider the relation between psychoanalysis and philosophy in *De l'interpretation: Essai sur Freud* (1965; *Freud and Philosophy: An Essay on Interpretation*, 1970). Luce Irigaray, a psychoanalyst expelled from Lacan's school for heresy, intends the title of her book of feminist theory *Ce sexe qui n'en est pas un* (1977; *This Sex Which Is Not One*, 1985) as a response to Lacan's famous pronouncement "La Femme n'est pas" (woman does not exist). Even Jacques Derrida's vehement objections to Lacan's interpretation of Poe in "Le Facteur de la vérité" (1975; English translation – The Postman of truth, 1987) cannot conceal a fundamental indebtedness to him for bringing Freud into a philosophical context. Whether in opposition or in direct dependence, all these theorists – and many others – owe an immense debt to Lacan. Undoubtedly more students of literature, especially those unable to read him in the original, will come into contact with Lacan through these (slightly) more readable disciples and opponents than through direct contact with Lacan's own words.

In summarizing the importance and difficulty of Lacan's thought, it is useful to recall M. H. Abrams' title *The Mirror and the Lamp: Romantic Theory and the Critical Tradition* (1953) and his statement that "in any period, the theory of mind and the theory of art tend to be integrally related and to turn upon similar analogues, explicit or submerged." Lacan is thus to postmodernism what John Locke was to neoclassicism and Freud was to modernism. Abrams' title *The Mirror and the Lamp* is a reminder that the two master concepts available for the functioning of the human mind, that of passive reflector and that of creative light, are always metaphorical and cannot be grounded unambiguously in scientific data. In his insistence on the ego as a mirage and on human beings as spoken by language Lacan is definitely an adherent of the mirror metaphor – which in fact he explicitly uses to describe the ego as a fantasy. Lacan's deflation of the terms Imaginary and Symbolic, two terms which are central to the Romantics' definition of creative and linguistic power, into psychological concepts working against the possibility of creativity or individuality, shows this basic opposition. So also Lacan's transformation of Poe's letter from the method of intersubjective communication into typographical mark without meaning constitutes a rejection of the signified and of any notion of content, intention, or final meaning.

It is therefore at its most basic level, at the level of its root metaphor, that Lacan's system is most vulnerable. This vulnerability is all the more striking given the fact that Lacan, unlike Freud, does not provide his readers with extended case histories, clinical data, or objective references to other psychological findings. His case is built essentially upon analogies with Jakobsonian linguistics and with the structural anthropology of Lévi-Strauss. It presupposes an acceptance of the shifting of meaning away from individuals into the structures in which they are imbricated.

## Principal criticism

"Le Problème du style et la conception psychiatrique des formes paranoïaques de l'expérience," 1933
"Fonction et champ de la parole et du langage en psychanalyse," 1956 (*The Language of the Self: The Function of Language in Psychoanalysis*, 1968)
"Le Séminaire sur 'La Lettre volée,'" 1956 ("Seminar on 'The Purloined Letter,'" 1973)
"L'Instance de la lettre dans l'inconscient ou la raison depuis Freud," 1957 ("The Insistence of the Letter in the Unconscious," 1966)
"Le Désir et son interprétation," 1959–1960 ("Desire and the Interpretation of Desire in *Hamlet*," 1977)
"Hommage fait à Marguerite Duras du *Ravissement de Lol V. Stein*," 1965
*Écrits*, 1966 (*Écrits: A Selection*, 1977)
"Of Structure as an Inmixing of an Otherness Prerequisite to Any Subject Whatever," 1970
"Joyce le symptôme," 1982
*Joyce avec Lacan*, 1987

## Other major works and literary forms

As a practicing psychoanalyst, Jacques Lacan has published technical articles and reviews of interest mainly to specialists. Early in his career, however, Lacan also published, in the noted Surrealist journal *Minotaure*, articles on the style of paranoiacs (listed above) and on the sensational crime of the Papin sisters. These articles are related to Lacan's doctoral thesis on paranoia, *De la psychose paranoïaque dans ses rapports avec la personnalité* (1932; psychotic paranoia and its bearing on personality). He also contributed an article on familial psychopathology to the *Encyclopédie française*.

Lacan is perhaps best known for his cultivation of the academic lecture. His seminars, *de rigueur* for the Parisian intelligentsia and often attended by one thousand or more auditors, were recorded by a stenographer and over the course of several decades were transcribed and published – without scholarly apparatus or correction of errors – by Jacques-Alain Miller. Carefully prepared but delivered extemporaneously, the seminars are unique verbal constructs playing on the differences between oral and written language; naturally, their transcription lacks the special intonation, phrasing, and physical presence with which Lacan bewitched his audience. Of the volumes of *Le Séminaire* which have made their way into print (twenty-four are projected), two have special importance: *Livre XI, les quatre concepts fondamentaux de la psychanalyse* (1973; *The Four Fundamental Concepts of Psychoanalysis*, 1977) contains, as its title indicates, a basic exposition of Lacan's ideas; *Livre XX, encore* (1975; *The Seminar of Jacques Lacan*, 1988), containing Lacan's theory of female sexuality, of importance to one branch of feminist theory, has found partial translation in *Feminine Sexuality* (1982). The journals *Ornicar?* and *Scilicet*, founded by Lacan, also contain parts of the seminars. *Ornicar?* also contains Lacan's apologies for the three times he created schisms in the French psychoanalytic profession: "La Scission de 1953" (1976), "L'Excommunication" (1977), and "Après la dissolution" (1980). As his influence grew, Lacan extended his seminar to the airwaves in *Télévision* (1974; *Television*, 1987).

NONFICTION
*De la psychose paranoïaque dans ses rapports avec la personnalité*, 1932
*Le Séminaire: Livre XI, les quatre concepts fondamentaux de la psychanalyse*, 1973 (*The Four Fundamental Concepts of Psychoanalysis*, 1977)
*Télévision*, 1974 (*Television: A Challenge to the Psychoanalytic Establishment*, 1990)
*Le Séminaire: Livre I, les écrits techniques de Freud*, 1975 (*Freud's Writing on Technique*, 1987)
*Le Séminaire: Livre XX, encore*, 1975 (*The Seminar of Jacques Lacan*, 1988)
*Le Séminaire: Livre XXII, RSI*, 1975
*Le Séminaire: Livre XXIII, le sinthome*, 1976–77
*Le Séminaire: Livre XXIV, l'insu que sait de l'une bévue s'aile à mourir (l'insuccès de l'unbewusste)*, 1977–79
*Proposition du 9 octobre 1967*, 1978
*Le Séminaire: Livre II, le moi dans la théorie de Freud et dans la technique de la psychanalytique*, 1978 (*The Theory of the Ego in Psychoanalytic Theory and Practice*, 1987)
*Le Séminaire: Livre III, les psychoses*, 1981 (*The Psychoses*, 1993)
*Les Complexes familiaux*, 1984 (*The Family Complexes*, 1988)
*Le Séminaire: Livre VII, l'éthique de la psychanalyse*, 1986 (*The Ethics of Psychoanalysis*, 1992)
*The Works of Jacques Lacan*, 1986
*Le Séminaire: Livre VIII, le transfert dans sa disparité subjective, sa prétendue situation, ses excursions techniques*, 1991
*Le Séminaire: Livre XVII, l'envers de la psychanalyse*, 1991
*Le Séminaire: Livre V, les formations de l'inconscient*, 1993
*Le Séminaire: Livre IV, la relation d'objet*, 1994

## Further reading

Bowie, Malcolm. *Freud, Proust, and Lacan*, 1987.

Clark, Michael. *Jacques Lacan: An Annotated Bibliography*, 1984.

Clément, Catherine. *The Lives and Legends of Jacques Lacan*, 1983.

Davis, Robert Con, ed. *Lacan and Narration: The Psychoanalytic Difference in Narrative Theory*, 1984.

Felman, Shoshana. *Jacques Lacan and the Adventure of Insight: Psychoanalysis in Contemporary Culture*, 1987.

Gallop, Jane. *The Daughter's Seduction*, 1982.

Lacoue-Labarthe, Phillipe. *The Title of the Letter: A Reading of Lacan*, 1992.

Leupin, Alexandre, ed. *Lacan and the Human Sciences*, 1991.

MacCabe, Colin. *The Talking Cure: Essays in Psychoanalysis and Language*, 1981.

MacCannell, Juliet Flower. *Figuring Lacan: Criticism and the Cultural Unconscious*, 1986.

Macey, David. *Lacan in Contexts*, 1988.

Muller, John P., and William J. Richardson, eds. *The Purloined Poe: Lacan, Derrida, and Psychoanalytic Reading*, 1987.

Ragland-Sullivan, Ellie. *Jacques Lacan and the Philosophy of Psychoanalysis*, 1986.

Roudinesco, Elisabeth. *Jacques Lacan: Outline of a Life, History of a System of Thought*, 1997.

Schneiderman, Stuart. *Jacques Lacan: the Death of an Intellectual Hero*, 1983.

Smith, Joseph H., and William Kerrigan, eds. *Interpreting Lacan*, 1983.

Turkle, Sherry. *Psychoanalytic Politics*, 1992.

Zizek, Slavoj. *Looking Awry: An Introduction to Jacques Lacan through Popular Culture*, 1991.

THOMAS O. BEEBEE

*See also* French Literary Theory: Twentieth Century; Kristeva; Psychoanalytic Criticism; Structuralism

# D. H. Lawrence

English novelist, poet, and critic

**Born:** Eastwood, Nottinghamshire, England; September 11, 1885

**Died:** Vence, France; March 2, 1930

## Biography

David Herbert Lawrence was born on September 11, 1885, in Eastwood, in the Midlands district of England, the second youngest of five children born to Lydia Beardsall, formerly a schoolteacher, and Arthur John Lawrence, a coal miner at nearby Brinsley. Lawrence attended the Beauvale Board School in Eastwood until 1898, when he won a scholarship to Nottingham High School. From 1902 until 1905 he served as an uncertified teacher at Eastwood British School; in 1906 he entered Nottingham University College for a two-year teacher training course. Yet by 1910, when he completed his first novel, *The White Peacock* (published the next year), he had abandoned teaching and was determined to become a writer. In 1912 he left Croydon, where he had been a teacher at the Davidson Road School, to elope with Frieda Weekley, traveling to Germany. With the publication of *Sons and Lovers* during 1913, he came into his own as a literary figure. By 1914 he had married Frieda, established important friendships with J. M. Murray and Katherine Mansfield, and published his first collection of short fiction, *The Prussian Officer and Other Stories* (1914). Yet Lawrence's difficulties with censors (*The Rainbow* was suppressed within weeks of publication), and with the military (in 1917 Frieda and he were expelled from Cornwall as suspected spies) intensified his anguish as a pacifist throughout the wartime years. By 1919 Frieda and he left England forever – except for three brief return visits. During their travels to Italy, Germany, Ceylon, Australia, Mexico, and New Mexico, Lawrence wrote and published prolifically, despite declining health. In 1930 he died of tuberculosis at a sanatorium in Vence, France.

## Influence

A moral critic with a strong bias toward psychological interpretation, Lawrence has exerted a wide influence on Western critics. Among notables who have asserted the important values of Lawrence's criticism are Edmund Wilson in the United States and F. R. Leavis in Great Britain. Wilson included the whole of *Studies in Classic American Literature* (1923) in his edited work *The Shock of Recognition: The Development of Literature in the United States Recorded by the Men Who Made It* (1943, 1955). According to Wilson, Lawrence's work is "one of the few first rate books ever to have been written on the subject." Leavis, editor of *Scrutiny* and author of *The Great Tradition: George Eliot, Henry James, Joseph Conrad* (1948), judged Lawrence "the finest literary critic of our time – a great critic if ever there was one."

## Analysis

In his essay on Walt Whitman, included in *Studies in Classic American Literature*, Lawrence declares his literary creed: "The essential function of art is moral. Not aesthetic, not decorative, not pastime and recreation. But moral." With this judgment, Lawrence joins the great liberal moral critics of the nineteenth century: John Ruskin, John Stuart Mill, Matthew Arnold. Yet, unlike his Victorian predecessors, Lawrence as a critic is rarely moralistic; he abjures a conventional moral doctrine – whether socialist ethic, Unitarianism, or Christian culture – as a touchstone to compare his artistic values. Instead, he favors "a passionate implicit morality, not didactic. A morality which changes the blood, rather than the mind." To Lawrence, "blood consciousness" is a biological, psychological reality. In the blood, the essential nature of the ego, an individual – just as a whole people or a nation – identifies itself. Lawrence believes that, once the blood is changed, "the mind follows later, in the wake."

What, precisely, is blood consciousness? For Lawrence's readers, the phrase has complex meanings. The writer believes that consciousness defines the whole artist – not what the person imagines himself to be, not a mask or image that he assumes in his writings, but his true essence. This essence, Lawrence insists, is often disguised by the "subterfuge" of artistic form. Nevertheless, it manifests itself, consciously or below the level of conscious intention, through the fable of the artist. In "The Spirit of Place," Lawrence writes, "Art-speech is the only truth. An artist is usually a damned liar, but his art, if it be art, will tell you the truth of his day." Such "truth" is rooted in biological or psychological reality, in the "blood." Even when the artist attempts to write a mere tale, an escapist fantasy, the tale tricks him into telling the truth, exposing the reality of life. Lawrence recognizes two "blankly opposing morals, the artist's and the tale's." He urges his readers: "Never trust the artist. Trust the tale. The proper function of a critic is to save the tale from the artist who created it."

How does criticism accomplish this objective? Lawrence examines the psychological and sociological framework of a literary work in order to understand its underlying myth. In his tart, witty essay on Benjamin Franklin, he ridicules the American philosopher's rigid moral code, antiquated and unrealistic, because it is founded on the myth of "the perfectibility of man." To explode Franklin's framework of narrow morality, Lawrence first attempts to establish the intellectual context of the writer's materialistic prudence. At the heart of Franklin's prudence, his common-sense application of principles that lead to "success," Lawrence discovers a cowardice: the American is fearful of the art of living. Such cowardice produces a complacent, not a true, morality, for it excludes the dangerous element of the human id (instinct, urge, the impulse toward sexuality) and subdues the ego (self-awareness) into a timorous "moral machine," intended to protect the individual.

Perhaps Lawrence's most original contribution to twentieth-century criticism is his examination of anthropological and sociological mythic patterns. In his two brilliant essays on James Fenimore Cooper, he exposes the myth of the good "red man," the Native American, who must bow to the interests of the less-noble white European. To prove his contention, Lawrence breaks down the writing "formula" employed by Cooper (and by Cooper's contemporaries) according to stereotypical roles in caste and social class. Lawrence is interested less in the ways in which Cooper's characters function in the novel to advance the plot than in the ways they represent social types. As a consequence, Lawrence's criticism is rarely tied to the form or structure of a work, to an examination of the aesthetic means by which the artist achieves his or her effects. Instead, Lawrence examines the mythic structure of that work in order to judge the artist's success or failure in depicting real people (those whose blood consciousness is psychologically revealed) in real-life situations. On that basis, he judges the moral content as well as the artistic power of the work as life-enhancing or, its opposite, life-inhibiting.

In his reviews and occasional essays, his introductions to different volumes, and his early, ambitious *Study of Thomas Hardy* (1936), Lawrence applied to various writers and works the same standard of moral judgment that he develops in *Studies in Classic American Literature*. For example, in his controversial essay on William Shakespeare's *Hamlet, Prince of Denmark* (c. 1600–1601), Lawrence places the play in the sociological context of Elizabethan England and observes in the Prince of Denmark a man caught between "the reaction from the great aristocratic to the great democratic principle." To Lawrence, Hamlet decides that "Father and King" must die, because the "great religious, philosophic tide, which had been swelling all through the Middle Ages, had brought him there." In a similar manner, Lawrence explores the psychosociological basis of Thomas Mann's craft. Mann, he argues, treats the theme of sickness and decay from more than an aesthetic basis; the roots of Mann's consciousness are in nineteenth-century neurosis. Lawrence sees in Mann the "unwholesome" neuroticism of Gustave Flaubert, the myth of psychological corruption expressed as physical or moral sickness.

Just as writers reveal their authentic blood consciousness through their art, so do peoples and nations. Lawrence argues that a whole national ego, or "IT," develops from mythic patterns. In "The Spirit of Place," he declares that "the true liberty will only begin when Americans discover IT, and proceed possibly to fulfil IT. IT being the deepest *whole* self of man, the self in its wholeness, not idealistic halfness." As a critic, Lawrence wishes to identify and expose "true liberty" for his readers so that they will understand themselves and learn better how to live. To him, the great value of art is to reveal, through the subterfuge of "art-speech" (including myth), the realities of wholesome, psychologically vital, ego-fulfilling life.

Because Lawrence discovers very few literary works that, in their totality, treat vital aspects of life, his criticism – especially to the casual reader – may appear abusive, or as critic Richard Foster puts it, "criticism as rage." Generally speaking, Lawrence's rage is real. As early as *Study of Thomas Hardy* (written from 1914 to 1915), Lawrence rages against antiquated moral laws. Addressing Angel Clare's crass rejection of Tess in *Tess of the D'Urbervilles* (1891), Lawrence writes:

> It is not Angel Clare's fault that he cannot come to Tess when he finds that she has, in his words, been defiled. It is the result of generations of ultra-Christian training, which had left in him an inherent aversion to the female, and to all in himself which pertained to the female.

To Lawrence, the dead hand of the past is almost always present, almost always extinguishing the vital spark.

For readers familiar with the more nearly genteel conventions of most literary critics from Lawrence's generation, the writer's tone as well as his rhetoric may seem elusive. Is Lawrence facetious, sarcastic, or merely argumentative? Some of his criticism, written in staccato bursts, has the effect of machine-gun volleys, spattering a wide target without precision. Such essays (among his most original) as "Surgery for the Novel – or a Bomb," "Art as Morality," "Morality and the Novel," "Women Are So Cocksure," and "Why the Novel Matters" contain passages of rage and vituperation as well as reasoned discourse, personal idiosyncrasy as well as sound literary scholarship. Yet the reader should be forewarned: Lawrence's wit is nearly always deadly serious; his seeming facetiousness almost always glosses an earnest argument.

As a critic, Lawrence attempts to rouse readers from their torpor, not to comfort them with conventional wisdom. In particular, his objective is to restore the "life-quality" to literature, no matter if he must raise the hackles of his readers to stimulate vitality. For Lawrence, literature matters very deeply. Art re-creates the world, from sterility to vitality, from passivity to blood consciousness. Among other critics of the twentieth century, Lawrence stands foremost as a prophet in the Romantic tradition, one who proclaims a new age of authentic morality, authentic vitality.

## Principal criticism
*Study of Thomas Hardy*, written 1914–1915, published 1936
*Studies in Classic American Literature*, 1923
*À Propos of Lady Chatterley's Lover*, 1930 (expansion of *My Skirmish with Jolly Roger*, 1929)

## Other major works and literary forms
In addition to the works listed above, D. H. Lawrence published numerous critical articles, reviews, and introductions to various volumes. Most of the articles, reviews, and introductions are included in *Phoenix: The Posthumous Papers of D. H. Lawrence* (1936); others are included in *Phoenix II: Uncollected, Unpublished, and Other Prose Works* (1968). Psychological studies that touch on aesthetic or literary matters, often indirectly, are *Psychoanalysis and the Unconscious* (1921) and *Fantasia of the Unconscious* (1922). *Reflections on the Death of a Porcupine and Other Essays* (1925) further treats a range of literary and psychological themes.

Lawrence's major fiction includes *Sons and Lovers* (1913), *The Rainbow* (1915), *Women in Love* (1920), *The Plumed Serpent* (1926), and *Lady Chatterley's Lover* (1928). He published many other novels (one which was issued posthumously), several volumes of short stories and short novels, and some travel literature. In addition, several volumes of his selected and collected letters have appeared since 1932.

NOVELS
*The White Peacock*, 1911
*The Trespasser*, 1912
*Sons and Lovers*, 1913
*The Rainbow*, 1915
*Women in Love*, 1920
*The Lost Girl*, 1920
*Aaron's Rod*, 1922
*Kangaroo*, 1923
*The Boy in the Bush*, 1924 (with M. L. Skinner)
*The Plumed Serpent*, 1926
*Lady Chatterley's Lover*, 1928
*The Virgin and the Gipsy*, 1930

SHORT FICTION
*The Prussian Officer and Other Stories*, 1914
*England, My England*, 1922
*The Ladybird*, 1923
*St. Mawr: Together with the Princess*, 1925
*The Woman Who Rode Away and Other Stories*, 1928
*Love Among the Haystacks and Other Stories*, 1930
*The Man Who Died*, 1931 (also known as *The Escaped Cock*, 1929)
*The Lovely Lady and Other Stories*, 1933
*A Modern Lover*, 1934
*The Complete Short Stories of D. H. Lawrence*, 1955, 1961

PLAYS
*The Widowing of Mrs. Holyroyd*, 1914
*Touch and Go*, 1920
*David*, 1926
*A Collier's Friday Night*, 1934
*The Complete Plays of D. H. Lawrence*, 1965

POETRY
*Love Poems and Others*, 1913
*Amores*, 1916
*Look! We Have Come Through*, 1917
*New Poems*, 1918
*Bay*, 1919
*Tortoises*, 1921
*Birds, Beasts, and Flowers*, 1923
*Collected Poems*, 1928
*Pansies*, 1929
*Nettles*, 1930
*The Triumph of the Machine*, 1931
*Last Poems*, 1932
*Fire and Other Poems*, 1940
*Phoenix Edition of Complete Poems*, 1957
*The Complete Poems of D. H. Lawrence*, 1964

NONFICTION
*Twilight in Italy*, 1916
*Movements in European History*, 1921
*Psychoanalysis and the Unconscious*, 1921
*Sea and Sardinia*, 1921
*Fantasia of the Unconscious*, 1922
*Reflections on the Death of a Porcupine and Other Essays*, 1925
*Mornings in Mexico*, 1927
*Pornography and Obscenity*, 1929
*Assorted Articles*, 1930
*Apocalypse*, 1931
*Etruscan Places*, 1932
*The Letters of D. H. Lawrence*, 1932 (Aldous Huxley, editor)
*Phoenix: The Posthumous Papers of D. H. Lawrence*, 1936

*The Collected Letters of D. H. Lawrence*, 1962 (2 volumes)
*Phoenix II: Uncollected, Unpublished, and Other Prose Works*, 1968

## Further reading

Becket, Fiona. *D. H. Lawrence: The Thinker as Poet*, 1997.
Cura-Sazdanic, Ileana. *D. H. Lawrence as Critic*, 1969.
Fernihough, Anne. *D. H. Lawrence: Aesthetics and Ideology*, 1992.
Foster, Richard. "Criticism as Rage: D. H. Lawrence," in *A D. H. Lawrence Miscellany*, 1961.
Gordon, David J. *D. H. Lawrence as a Literary Critic*, 1966.
Leavis, F. R. *D. H. Lawrence: Novelist*, 1956.
——. *Thought, Words and Creativity: Art and Thought in D. H. Lawrence*, 1976.
Morrison, Claudia C. *Freud and the Critic: The Early Use of Depth Psychology in Literary Criticism*, 1968.
Scherr, Barry J. *D. H. Lawrence's Response to Plato: A Bloomian Interpretation*, 1996.
Singh, Tajindar. *The Literary Criticism of D. H. Lawrence*, 1984.
Wilson, Edmund. *The Shock of Recognition: The Development of Literature in the United States Recorded by the Men Who Made It*, 1943, 1955.

LESLIE B. MITTLEMAN

*See also* British Literary Theory: Twentieth Century; Leavis

# F. R. Leavis

English critic

**Born:** Cambridge, England; July 14, 1895
**Died:** Cambridge, England; April 14, 1978

## Biography

Frank Raymond Leavis was born on July 14, 1895, in Cambridge, England, and was educated at the Perse School and Cambridge University. He spent virtually his entire life in that university town. He had great admiration for and was deeply attached to his father, a sensitive, cultivated, deeply musical man, who owned a musical instrument shop in Cambridge. After serving in the Ambulance Corps during World War I, Leavis won a scholarship to Emmanuel College.

As an undergraduate, he began specializing first in history but changed to English. The works that influenced his thoughts about literature, culture, and society were those by George Santayana, Matthew Arnold, T. S. Eliot, and Ford Madox Ford. As a schoolboy in 1912 he had subscribed to Ford's *The English Review*. He was attracted to Ford's belief that in the contemporary industrial world, the higher cultural values should be preserved by a small minority, which, however, should resist removing itself from life.

As a student in Cambridge's new English School, he was stimulated by such teachers as Mansfield Forbes and particularly I. A. Richards, the advocate of practical criticism. He was impressed by the Edgell Rickword's periodical *The Calendar of Modern Letters*, which insisted on maintaining high critical standards in a period of cultural decline. In 1924 Leavis wrote his doctoral thesis on the periodical literature of the eighteenth century, "The Relationship of Journalism to Literature: Studies in the Rise and Earlier Development of the Press in England." In it, he notes how periodical literature can influence the reading public.

He started tutoring English literature at Emmanuel College, and many recall him as a dynamic teacher who challenged the establishment with his theories on literature and the university. He annoyed the English faculty in the 1930s when he began lecturing to his class on contemporary writings, such as James Joyce's *Ulysses* (1922).

In 1929 Leavis married Queenie Roth, with whom he collaborated on numerous critical studies. Not popular with the English faculty, he was denied a permanent post as lecturer until 1936, at Downing College. He was appointed a reader in English twenty-four years later and continued in that post until 1962. In 1966 he undertook a lecture tour of the United States. He later held visiting professorships at the Universities of York, Wales, and Bristol. Several universities, including Aberdeen, Belfast, Delhi, Leeds, and York, awarded him honorary doctorates. He was made a Companion of Honour in 1978, just prior to his death on April 14.

## Influence

Many consider Leavis to be the most influential British critic of the twentieth century. Though he abjured making comprehensive and systematic theoretical statements, such as René Wellek and Austin Warren's *Theory of Literature* (1942) or Northrop Frye's *Anatomy of Criticism* (1957), through his teaching at Cambridge University from 1937 to 1962 and his numerous critical studies of writers whom he considered to have a place in the "great tradition" of English literature, he drastically changed the approach to literary studies that was current in universities when he began to teach. He directed attention to the text, away from literary history and biography, insisting that the reader must come to grips with the words on the page, not with extrinsic matters. Others, such as Richards and the New Critics, were moving in the same direction, but it was Leavis who was most influential in establishing this new approach to literary studies. Up to the 1970s Leavis' approach was a dominant one in many universities. He has had his share of detractors, as would be expected of any major critic; and there were in several English departments intensely committed polarized camps of Leavisites and anti-Leavisites.

## Analysis

It is important to understand that for Leavis, literary criticism does not operate in a social vacuum; it must be concerned with maintaining high cultural standards. A serious interest in literature, he states, "cannot be merely literary"; it derives from "a perception of – which must be a preoccupation with – the problems of social equity and order and of cultural health." Like many of the figures who influenced him, such as Richards and Eliot, Leavis believes that contemporary society is in a state of cultural decline. This decline can be arrested by adhering to the finer values of English literature, the mainstay of the English cultural tradition. Those professing the function of criticism – who, by necessity, always will be in a minority – must strive to uphold a high standard of criticism and use the educational system, particularly the English schools and departments of universities, to raise cultural standards. Leavis stresses that they should not indulge in debilitating and fatuous aestheticism and remove themselves from life, an injunction which explains why Matthew Arnold is one of the older critics who most appealed to him. Leavis shares Arnold's credo that literature should be seen as a "criticism of life" and not as "art for art's sake," and he admires Arnold's insistence on critical intelligence and critical standards, defending Arnold's advocacy of touchstones by which literary works are judged. Despite Leavis' interest in the cultural health of society, he insists on a distinction between the literary and the social or cultural critic. The literary critic's field is literature. Though it "is pleasant to hope that, when he writes or talks about political or 'social' matters, insight and understanding acquired in literary studies will be engaged," the concern "of the literary critic as such is with literary criticism."

In articulating his ideas of literary criticism, Leavis makes clear that he perceives criticism as a distinct discipline at the center of the intellectual and cultural life of civilized society. For him, evaluation of the text is the principal function of criticism. He rejects the concentration on literary biography and history that was still prevalent in the universities at the beginning of the twentieth century. Critical evaluation, however, does not require or depend on formulation of a rigid poetics or theory of literature. Leavis shows little interest in philosophical theories or in a systematic postulation of his principles. His approach is an empirical one, as is illustrated by his famous recantation of his early evaluation of Charles Dickens as simply an entertainer. The critic is concerned with critical principles. In a healthy critical climate, a "centre of real consensus" soon establishes itself by constant concrete agreement and disagreement among critics rather than by abstract discussion of values, norms, and criteria. Leavis, then, believes in a collaborative process, a creative interplay of judgment, a "common pursuit." This approach informs the editing of *Scrutiny*; the editors see readers and contributors as belonging to a reciprocal group that helped to shape the journal. Leavis rejects absolutism and "fixed and definite criteria." He stresses the need for firm, decisive assessments, but requires always room for disagreement: "Collaboration may take the form of disagreement, and one is grateful to the critic whom one has found worth disagreeing with."

In providing decisive and insightful literary evaluation, the critic helps to educate the public and to shape contemporary cultural and intellectual life: "Criticism, when it performs its function, not merely expresses and defines the 'contemporary sensibility'; it helps to form it ... to persuade an effective 'contemporary sensibility' into being." By sensibility, Leavis refers not simply to feelings and emotions, but to feelings and emotions informed by intelligence and morality. By morality, Leavis does not suggest narrow moral or religious criticism, which he rejects as no substitute for literary criticism. Moral values do enter into evaluation of a literary work, but they are invoked only when relevant by the critic whose judgment must reflect intelligence and sensibility.

Evaluation and judgment arise from close analysis of the text. This is the central aspect of Leavis' literary criticism: the focus must always be the "words on the page." The critic must respond "fully, delicately and with discriminating accuracy to the subtle and precise use of words." Leavis believed that one could develop such proficiency in few languages other than one's own, which may in part explain why his own literary criticism is primarily on works in English. He approaches analysis as a constructive and creative process. It is not "a dissection of something that is already and passively there." It is a "process of creation in response to the poet's words," in which, "by a considering attentiveness, we ensure a more than ordinary faithfulness and completeness."

The difference between Leavis' analysis and that of Richards, who pioneered the idea of practical criticism, is that Richards advocates that criticism could become more systematic and codified. Though Leavis sees criticism as a discipline, he rejects this "scientific" approach: "Criticism can never be a science: it is, in the first place, much too personal, and in the second, it is concerned with values that science ignores." Leavis also argues that critical analysis of the language of the text is not undertaken merely for the sake of analysis; the purpose of such scrutiny is to reveal the text's statement on human experiences. A serious interest in literature cannot confine itself "to the scrutiny of the 'words on the page' in their minute relations, their effects of imagery and so on; a real literary interest is an interest in man, society and civilization."

Leavis' emphasis on the text leads him to reject the need for contextual reading of a literary work. He dismisses scholarship and literary history that put the literary work in the context of its time and place: "There is no more futile study than that which ends with mere knowledge *about* literature." Leavis assumes that the critic would have an understanding of the civilization that produced the work, but he rejected contextual aid as indispensable to analysis.

In rejecting the "historical" and "scholarly" approaches, Leavis does not shun tradition. In fact, a central concern for him is the preservation of cultural tradition, which he conceives primarily in terms of literature. It is important to recognize and give currency to the great works of English literature: "Largely conveyed in language, there is our spiritual, moral and emotional tradition, which preserves the 'picked experience of ages' regarding the finer issues of life." The English schools or universities are the best guardians of tradition, for "universities are recognized symbols of cultural tradition – of cultural tradition still conceived as a directing force, representing a wisdom older than modern civilization."

Leavis insists that the writer should adhere to the spoken language, not to a literary rendition of it that is widely removed from the current idiom. The diction of speech has what he calls "body" and "substance." In poetry, William Shakespeare, John Donne, Gerard Manley Hopkins, Eliot, and the later William Butler Yeats are among the writers who employ the spoken diction; Edmund Spenser, John Milton, and Alfred, Lord Tennyson, are among those who use a literary language, divorced from actual experience that cannot achieve "concrete realization." This is a recurring phrase in Leavis' criticism, by which he means that language must create and enact, not merely say. He criticizes John Dryden because in his poetry "emotion doesn't emerge from a given situation realized in its concrete particularity; it is stated, not presented or enacted." Leavis judges Joyce, moreover, to be interested primarily in words for their own sake, not in what they say.

In his criticism of the novel, Leavis points out that the great novels show an affirmation of "the possibilities of life," which is, for him, a fundamental criterion. The major novelists that he allows into the great tradition all have this affirmation: Jane Austen, George Eliot, Nathaniel Hawthorne, Dickens, Mark Twain (whose *Huckleberry Finn* of 1884 he ranks as "one of the great books of the world"), Henry James, Joseph Conrad, and D. H. Lawrence. Much of Leavis' praise of Lawrence, with whose work he is preoccupied throughout his career as a critic and whom he considers the greatest novelist of the century, has to do with the positive affirmative values that Leavis discovers in Lawrence's work. Speaking of the intensity of *St. Mawr* (1925), he says that it is not an intensity "of repulsion and rejection"; it is "essentially creative, a marvellous and triumphant expression of the creative force of life, in its very nature an affirmation."

Though Leavis' approach to literary studies was officially disapproved of by the English faculty at Cambridge, he has had considerable influence on contemporary literary criticism and is perceived by many as the most influential British critic of this century. He disseminates his ideas through the center for English studies that he established at Downing College, Cambridge; through *Scrutiny*; through his numerous essays and books; and through his students and disciples, many of whom themselves achieved reputations as critics: L. C. Knights, D. A. Traversi, and Martin Turnell

in Britain, Marius Bewley in the United States, and Henri Fluchère in France. Leavis' advocacy of close analytical and aesthetic reading of the text, combined with a firm awareness of the value and importance of what it has to say about life, established the dominant pattern of modern British criticism until the 1970s.

Leavis' criticism is similar to the New Criticism, which flourished between 1940 and 1960, in that both schools believed in looking closely at the text (though the New Critics tended to stress the technical, the paradoxical, and the ambiguous) and both were influenced by Eliot's ideas about literature and criticism. The difference is that Leavis' criticism emphasizes the moral and social conviction and relevance of the text, while the New Critics are concerned with the spiritual values inherent in the text. Leavis' criticism is one of the progenitors of structuralism, with which it shares the common emphasis on close analysis of the language of the text, but it stands distinctly apart from structuralism's rejection of what Leavis insistently advocated: that art cannot be insulated from life and judged by different standards.

## Principal criticism

*Mass Civilization and Minority Culture*, 1930
*D. H. Lawrence*, 1930
*New Bearings in English Poetry: A Study of the Contemporary Situation*, 1932
*How to Teach Reading: A Primer for Ezra Pound*, 1932
*For Continuity*, 1933
*Culture and Environment: The Training of Critical Awareness*, 1933 (with Denys Thompson)
*Revaluation: Tradition and Development in English Poetry*, 1936
*Education and the University: A Sketch for an "English School*," 1943
*The Great Tradition: George Eliot, Henry James, Joseph Conrad*, 1948
*The Common Pursuit*, 1952
*D. H. Lawrence: Novelist*, 1955
*Two Cultures? The Significance of C. P. Snow*, 1962
*Anna Karenina and Other Essays*, 1967
*Lectures in America*, 1969 (with Q. D. Leavis)
*English Literature in Our Time and the University*, 1969
*Dickens the Novelist*, 1970 (with Q. D. Leavis)
*Nor Shall My Sword: Discourses on Pluralism, Compassion, and Social Hope*, 1972
*Letters in Criticism*, 1974
*The Living Principle: "English" as a Discipline of Thought*, 1975.
*Thoughts, Words, and Creativity: Art and Thought in Lawrence*, 1976

## Other major works and literary forms

F. R. Leavis was closely associated with the launching in 1932 of *Scrutiny: A Quarterly Review*, which became one of the most influential literary journals of the twentieth century. He was actively involved as editor and contributor with the seventy-six issues, contributing the valedictory issue in October, 1953. He wrote more than one hundred reviews of creative and critical volumes mainly in *Scrutiny* and *The Cambridge Review*, reviewing such works as William Empson's *Seven Types of Ambiguity* (1930), Katherine Mansfield's *Novels and Novelists* (1930), William Butler Yeats' *The Winding Stair and Other Poems* (1933), and Edmund Wilson's *The Wound and the Bow* (1941). Leavis published numerous essays on culture and education, but his ideas on these aspects of society can best be considered in relation to his literary theories and criticism with which they are closely integrated. During the 1960s he was involved in a controversy with C. P. Snow, the scientist-novelist, over the relationship in contemporary society of the scientific and literary cultures. Leavis' position appears in *Two Cultures? The Significance of C. P. Snow*, the most famous of his social essays, in which he attacks unsparingly Snow's idea of a separate scientific culture distinct from the traditional humanistic culture.

NONFICTION
*Scrutiny: A Quarterly Review*, 1932–1953 (editor, with others)
*Towards Standards of Criticism: Selections from "The Calendar of Modern Letters,"* 1933 (editor)
*Determinations: Critical Essays*, 1934 (editor)
*A Selection from Scrutiny*, 1968 (editor)
*Mill on Bentham and Coleridge*, 1950 (editor)
*The Critic as anti-Philosopher: Essays and Papers*, 1982 (G. Singh, editor)
*"Valuation in Criticism" and Other Essays*, 1986 (G. Singh, editor)

## Further reading
Bell, M. *F. R. Leavis*, 1988.
Bilan, R. P. *The Literary Criticism of F. R. Leavis*, 1979.
Boyers, R. *F. R. Leavis: Judgement and the Discipline of Thought*, 1978.
Buckley, Vincent. *Poetry and Morality: Studies in the Criticism of Matthew Arnold, T. S. Eliot, F. R. Leavis*, 1959.
Greenwood, Edward. *F. R. Leavis*, 1978.
Hayman, Ronald. *Leavis*, 1976.
Kinch, M. B., W. Baker, and J. Kimber. *F. R. Leavis and Q. D. Leavis: An Annotated Bibliography*, 1989.
McCallum, Pamela. *Literature and Method: Towards a Critique of I. A. Richards, T. S. Eliot and F. R. Leavis*, 1983.
McKenzie, D. F., and M-P. Allum. *F. R. Leavis: A Check-List 1924–1964*, 1966.
Robertson, P. J. M. *The Leavises on Fiction*, 1981.
Samson, Anne. *F. R. Leavis*, 1992.
Thompson, D., ed. *The Leavises: Recollections and Impressions*, 1984.
Walsh, William. *F. R. Leavis*, 1980.
Watson, George. *The Literary Critics*, 1962.
———. *The Leavises, the "Social" and the Left*, 1977.
Wellek, René. "F. R. Leavis and the *Scrutiny* Group," in *A History of Modern Criticism: 1750–1950*. Vol. 5, *English Criticism, 1900–1950*, 1986.

VICTOR J. RAMRAJ

*See also* British Literary Theory: Twentieth Century; Eagleton; Williams

# Gotthold Ephraim Lessing

German critic and playwright

**Born:** Kamenz, Saxony; January 22, 1729
**Died:** Brunswick, Saxony; February 15, 1781

## Biography

Gotthold Ephraim Lessing was born on January 22, 1729, in Kamenz, Saxony, the oldest of thirteen children. His father, a pastor, came from a family steeped in the traditions of theology and law. Under his father's guidance, the young Lessing acquired his interest in books and learning. In June, 1741, he entered St. Afra, a famous monastic school for princes, in Meissen. He left the school after only five years because, in his own words, he had nothing more to learn there. He then entered the University of Leipzig as a student of theology. After a few changes of faculty and a move to Wittenberg University, Lessing gave up his studies to join his cousin Christoph Mylius in Berlin, where Mylius, an early follower of Johann Christoph Gottsched, lived as a writer. In 1751 Lessing returned to Wittenberg University and received a master of arts degree in 1752. He then returned to Berlin to resume his freelance writing career.

In 1760, plagued by monetary problems, Lessing accepted a position as private secretary to General von Tauentzien, Governor of Silesia. The five years he spent in the general's service were productive ones. His most influential critical work, *Laokoon: Oder, Über die Grenzen der Mahlerei und Poesie* (1766; *Laocoön: An Essay on the Limits of Painting and Poetry*, 1836), and *Minna von Barnhelm: Oder, Das Soldatenglück* (1767; *Minna von Barnhelm: Or, The Soldier's Fortune*, 1786) were written during this time. In 1767 Lessing left Berlin for Hamburg, where he became a critic of the German National Theater, which was the first large-scale theater independent of the courts in Germany. His critical commentary on the productions were collected in the *Hamburgische Dramaturgie* (1767–1769; *Hamburg Dramaturgy*, 1889).

When the National Theater failed, Lessing was forced once again to seek employment. He found it in Wolfenbüttel, as a librarian. It was in this small, secluded town that he produced the bulk of his theological writings. After a long and complicated courtship Lessing married the widowed former actress and businesswoman Eva König in 1776. Only a year after their marriage, she died in childbirth along with their newborn son. Lessing died on February 15, 1781.

## Influence

Lessing's knowledge of ancient Greek and Roman comedy informed his awareness of the dramatic form, which went beyond the critical and aesthetic awareness of his contemporaries in depth and complexity. He introduced elements of the English sentimental drama and novel to the German audience. His greatest accomplishment, however, was the constant search to draw distinctions and to challenge entrenched positions. He transcended the "easy" optimism of Enlightenment thought with its mechanistic interpretations. At the root of his productions as a literary critic, as a dramatist, and as a religious and philosophical thinker lies the interest in its relevance for human life. Lessing challenged the contemporary philosophy of Christian von Wolff, who popularized the thinking of Gottfried Wilhelm von Leibniz. Both believed in the automatic perfectibility of history. Lessing, however, placed the burden to perfect the human condition on the individual and one's responsibility to make informed and critical ethical choices in an ever-changing world. Lessing's sensitivity to the situational flux of what constitutes an ethical choice and its representation in literary works is what distinguishes him as one of the first "modern" thinkers.

## Analysis

*Briefe, die neueste Litteratur betreffend* (1759–1760; letters on current literature), one of Lessing's early forums for literary criticism, represents a group effort by Lessing, Friedrich Nicolai, and Moses Mendelssohn. The periodical was presumably initiated by Lessing. These articles were influenced by the tradition of the *moralische Wochenschriften*, periodicals intended to disseminate popularized information and ideas from philosophy, literature, and the sciences.

The goal of *Briefe, die neueste Litteratur betreffend* was to provide an assessment of the contemporary literary situation in Germany. By choosing to represent the aesthetic ideas as fictitious letters to an officer, the authors disassociate themselves from the accepted modes of literary criticism, that is, to produce a systematic treatise in the tradition of the philosophy and aesthetics of the ancients. Dynamic, provocative conclusions take the place of descriptive, detailed analysis.

In one of the most important issues, the seventeenth, Lessing attacked Gottsched, the most prominent literary theorist of the day, who had tried to refine the quality of the German theater. Lessing's criticism was mainly directed against Gottsched's introduction of the theory and practice of French classicist theater. Lessing claimed that the French tastes, as they are represented by the plays of Pierre Corneille and Jean Racine, do not correspond with the German national character. Instead, he proposed to look to England, and especially to William Shakespeare, for models. According to Lessing, the genius of Shakespeare was his ability to achieve a well-rounded play without the superficial formal considerations proposed by Gottsched.

*Laocoön*, Lessing's most famous critical work, discusses the distinctiveness and limitations of poetry and painting as artistic spheres. In this widely received treatise, Lessing challenged the convention of regarding the visual arts as superior to poetry and the conviction that the latter is modeled after the former. He based his opinion on careful observation of the antique Laocoön statue and on a painstaking interpretation of Virgil's description of Laocoön's struggle to the death in the *Aeneid* (c. 29–19 B.C.). Laocoön, priest of Apollo, protested against the admittance of the wooden horse of Ulysses within the walls of Troy. The horse was, nevertheless, allowed to enter, and Laocoön was punished by the gods for his attempt to cross their purposes: two huge serpents came out of the sea and attacked his two sons. As Laocoön hastened to their aid, he himself became entwined in the deadly coils.

Lessing's investigations of the difference between painting and poetry revolve around the specific characteristics of their respective materials and the distinct nature of signification. They are informed by an extensive study of the ancients, in particular of Aristotle, Plato, and Horace. Characterizing his mode of presentation as that of an open-eyed stroller, he gave his deliberately structured essay the air of chance observations. This form constitutes a purposeful departure from the rationalistic method of deduction practiced by his predecessors, specifically Gottsched.

The contemporary acceptance of the basic similarity of the arts served as a point of departure. In *Laocoön* Lessing goes on to outline the trend in present-day plastic art toward allegory (telling a story with a visual art object). It is literature, however, which is defined by a tendency toward description. Thus the contemporary view of the visual arts, with an affinity to allegory, confuses the distinct features of these two significantly different forms of art. By clearly differentiating the plastic arts, which consist of "figures and colors in space," from poetry, which is composed of "sounds in time," Lessing liberates poetry from its subservient position.

In his elaborations on the Laocoön statue, Lessing also demonstrates how vital it is for the visual artist to choose the most advantageous, the most pregnant moment, which in the imagination of the onlooker incorporates the previous and subsequent stages of the event as well. In contrast to this fixed spatial image, poetry provides the listener or reader with a linear series of fleeting images, which form a whole only in the mind of the beholder. Homer serves as an ideal model of the true poet, who circumvents the need for description in his art. Instead of describing the visual image of the famous shield, he evokes it by describing its production. Consequently, the poet is able to depict a more complex phenomenon than the sculptor, who can treat only relatively simple ideas that can be represented through the depiction of bodies. Lessing maintains that the poet has more liberty in portraying more intense passions while the ancient ideal of beauty forces moderation on the sculptor. He goes on to explain that had Laocoön been portrayed at the height of agony it would be a contortion; the body would have "lost the beautiful contours of its natural state." "The ancient artists either refrained from depicting such emotions or reduced them to a degree where it is possible to show them with a certain measure of beauty." It is noteworthy that Lessing, with respect to the ancients, assigned the aesthetic ideal of beauty a higher importance than the truth of the emotion: "The scream had to be softened to a sigh, not because screaming betrays an ignoble soul, but because it distorts the features in a disgusting manner." Thus he insists that the ancients did not portray negative or transient emotions such as anger, fury, or even laughter, because the permanence would reduce such a state to ugliness.

Unlike the more general *Laocoön* treatise, *Hamburg Dramaturgy* was written with a very specific purpose: it was meant to provide a critical evaluation of the newly founded National Theater in Hamburg, which was the first attempt to free the stage from the patronage, and thus the influence, of the courts. As such it was an important step in the intellectual emancipation of the bourgeoisie. Lessing's *Hamburg Dramaturgy* focuses on the plays, on formal considerations of the various dramatic forms, and on the performances themselves, the acting and the actors.

In order to liberate the German stage from the dominance of French classicist theater, Lessing returned to the source, the poetics of the ancients – especially to the poetic writing of Aristotle – and demonstrated that the French, especially Corneille, had misunderstood Aristotle. With the rejection of the dogmatic influence of France, Lessing wished to clear the path for the budding German theater and at the same time provide it with a solid aesthetic base. Lessing's reinterpretation of Aristotle provided the backdrop for his own theory of genuine tragedy, as opposed to the shallow and artificial tragedy of the French stage. In particular, Lessing differentiated between the essential rules, such as the unity of action as the first dramatic law of the ancients, and the merely consequential rules of the unity of place and time. He goes on to explain that the latter unities were merely informed by the necessities of the Greek stage and the presence of a chorus. These rules served as a means to simplify the action by reducing it to its bare essentials. Through simplicity it became the ideal action. He criticized the French for following Aristotle only in letter, not in spirit. Failing to understand the inner value of the rules, they placed more importance on the outer unities of action.

Another major issue raised by the *Hamburg Dramaturgy* was the question of the ultimate goal of tragedy. Lessing charged the translators with having misrepresented what Aristotle considered the aims of tragedy, pity and fear, by interpreting them as pity and terror. This error in translation, he contended, obscured the true nature of fear as it was conceived by the Greek philosopher. Pity and fear, Lessing continues, are emotions that the audience and not the characters are experiencing: the plight of the tragic hero arouses sympathy in the audience but also fear, for the spectators should feel that the character's fate might be their own. Connected to this line of argument is the Aristotelian

demand for mixed characters because a perfect person should not suffer without any fault on his or her part. For Lessing's own concept of tragedy, these Aristotelian notions became essential.

In *Wie die Alten den Tod gebildet* (1769; *How the Ancients Represented Death*, 1879), Lessing takes issue with the unquestioning acceptance of traditional beliefs and the tendency to superimpose contemporary values and interpretations on artifacts of earlier historical epochs. Lessing demonstrates his objections with the example of the representation of death. Eighteenth-century art historians assumed that the representation of death as a skeleton, traditional in Nordic countries, symbolized the same in antiquity. This belief seemed to stem from the fact that depictions of skeletons can be found in murals and other art objects. Lessing considers this opinion erroneous, since it fails to establish whether the object truly represents death or whether it stands for another notion. Based on his own evaluation, he maintains that the ancients represented death as a small, winged boy, the twin brother of sleep, leaning on a reversed torch, holding a wreath with a butterfly. Lessing interprets the wreath as the mortuary garland and the butterfly as the emblem of the departed soul. Representing death in such a manner would entail a completely different interpretation of its meaning. Lessing admits that there are illustrations of skeletons in antique art, but he maintains that they depict not death as such but a glimpse into the future – what humans will resemble after they have died – to remind humanity to live life to the fullest. The essay is an important example of Lessing's method of analysis, which, in true Enlightenment fashion, reevaluates any traditional view.

Lessing redirected attention from the French stage toward the English stage, paving the way for the *Sturm und Drang* movement, which further liberated German playwrights from the rigid rules of classicist drama. Lessing's close analysis of the nature of unity in drama as an inner form was consequently taken up by the younger generation. By reexamining the logic of drama, Lessing was instrumental in directing the attention of the German audience toward Shakespeare, who had, since Gottsched, been a negative model for irregular and irrational theater. The next generation would make Shakespeare its ideal, because he was able to portray "true" nature, not simply idealized nature.

Lessing's investigation of the sign character of art, which he briefly touched on in *Laocoön* and which he intended to expand in a third part, is yet another contribution to literary theory. In a letter to Nicolai in 1767 Lessing elaborated on this concept and distinguished natural signs (mainly found in the visual arts) and arbitrary signs (found in literature). In a dialectical synthesis he arrived at the conclusion that only theater could overcome this division and turn arbitrary signs into natural signs. The nature of linguistic signs was addressed again in the twentieth century by semioticians.

## Principal criticism

*Theatralische Bibliothek*, 1754–1758
*Briefe, die neueste Litteratur betreffend*, 1759–1760 (editor)
*Laokoon: Oder, Über die Grenzen der Mahlerei und Poesie*,
    1766 (*Laocoön: An Essay on the Limits of Painting and
    Poetry*, 1836)
*Hamburgische Dramaturgie*, 1767–1769 (*Hamburg Dramaturgy*,
    1889)
*Wie die Alten den Tod gebildet*, 1769 (*How the Ancients
    Represented Death*, 1879)

## Other major works and literary forms

While Gotthold Ephraim Lessing is justly referred to as the
first literary critic who offered a thorough aesthetic treatment of literary forms of representation, he is also the most
prominent preclassical dramatist in Germany. Many of his
plays, especially the early comedies, modeled closely after
ancient comedies, seem to have served as an exercise in
dramatic form per se. (The relationship between Lessing's
theoretical works and his plays is an interesting one: the
playwright never completely follows the rules set forth by
the critic but modifies them in the light of a perceived
aesthetic need.)

His first success came with his bourgeois tragedy *Miss
Sara Sampson* (1755; English translation, 1789). Lessing
must be credited for introducing this new genre, which had
its roots in England, to Germany. His comedy *Minna von
Barnhelm: Oder, Das Soldatenglück* (1767; *Minna von
Barnhelm: Or, The Soldier's Fortune*, 1786) has become a
classic and is still performed on the German stage. His next
bourgeois tragedy, *Emilia Galotti* (1772; English translation, 1786), is often interpreted in the light of his theory
of drama as exemplified in his *Hamburgische Dramaturgie*
(1767–1769; *Hamburg Dramaturgy*, 1889). *Nathan der
Weise* (1779; *Nathan the Wise*, 1781), written in verse, was
his last play.

In addition to his role as the leading critic and dramatist in the preclassical age, Lessing produced theological and
philosophical writings emphasizing the nondogmatic,
humanitarian aspects of religion. His most important theological works include *Von der Duldung der Deisten* (1774;
translated in *Theological Writings*, 1956), *Ernst und Falk:
Gespräche für Freimaurer* (1778; *Masonic Dialogues*, 1927)
and *Die Erziehung des Menschengeschlechts* (1780; *The
Education of the Human Race*, 1858).

SHORT FICTION
*Fabeln nebst Abhandlungen*, 1759 (*Fables*, 1773)

PLAYS
*Damon: Oder, Die wahre Freundschaft*, 1747
*Der junge Gelehrte*, 1748
*Die alte Jungfer*, 1749
*Die Freigeist*, written 1749, published 1755 (*The Freethinker*,
    1838)
*Samuel Henzi*, written 1749, published 1753 (verse)
*Die Juden*, written 1749, published 1754 (*The Jews*, 1801)
*Der Misogyn*, 1755

*Miss Sara Sampson*, 1755 (*Lucy Sampson: Or, The Unhappy
    Heiress*, 1789; better known as *Miss Sara Sampson*, 1895)
*Philotas*, 1759
*Minna von Barnhelm: Oder, Das Soldatenglück*, 1767 (*Minna
    von Barnhelm: Or, The Soldier's Fortune*, 1786)
*Emilia Galotti*, 1772 (English translation, 1786)
*Nathan der Weise*, 1779 (verse; *Nathan the Wise*, 1781)
*The Dramatic Works of G. E. Lessing*, 1879

NONFICTION
*Kritische Briefe*, 1753
*Abhandlungen vom weinerlichen oder rührenden Lustspiel*, 1754
*Vade mecum für den Hrn. Sam. Gotth. Lange*, 1754
*Pope ein Mataphysiker!*, 1755
*Abhandlungen über die Fabel*, 1759 (*Treatises on the Fable*, 1773)
*Briefe antiquarischen Inhalts*, 1768
*Zerstreute Anmerkungen über das Epigramm*, 1771
*Zur Geschichte und Literatur*, 1773
*Von der Duldung der Deisten*, 1774 (English translation in
    *Theological Writings*, 1956)
*Das Testament Johannis*, 1777
*Eine Duplick*, 1778
"*Eine Parable*," 1778
"*Axiomata*," 1778
*Anti-Goeze*, 1778
*Ernst und Falk: Gespräche für Freimaurer*, 1778 (*Masonic
    Dialogues*, 1927)
*Die Erziehung des Menschengeschlects*, 1780 (*The Education of
    the Human Race*, 1858)

TRANSLATION
*Das Theater des Herrn Diderot*, 1760 (2 volumes)

MISCELLANEOUS
*Selected Prose Works*, 1879
*Sämtliche Schriften*, 1886–1924 (23 volumes)

## Further reading

Allison, Henry E. *Lessing and the Enlightenment: His
    Philosophy of Religion and Its Relation to Eighteenth-
    Century Thought*, 1966.
Batley, Edward Malcolm. *Catalyst of Enlightenment, Gotthold
    Ephraim Lessing: Productive Criticism of Eighteenth-century
    Germany*, 1990.
Berghahn, Klaus. "From Classicist to Classical Literary Theory
    1730–1806," in *A History of German Literary Criticism*,
    1988. Edited by P. U. Hohendahl.
Bieber, Margarete. *Laocoön: The Influence of the Group Since
    Its Rediscovery*, 1942.
Brown, F. Andrew. *Gotthold Ephraim Lessing*, 1971.
Eckardt, Jo-Jacqueline. *Lessing's* Nathan the Wise *and the
    Critics, 1779–1991*, 1993.
Howard, William Guild, ed. *Laokoon: Lessing, Herder, Goethe*,
    1910.
Rudowski, Victor A. *Lessing's Aesthetica in Nuce: An Analysis
    of the May 26, 1769, Letter to Nicolai*, 1971.
Schlaffer, Heinz. *Bürger als Held: Sozialgeschichtliche
    Auflösungen literarischer Widersprüche 1973, 1981. The
    Bourgeois as Hero 1989.* Translated by James Lynn.
Wellbery, David. *Lessing's "Laokoon": Semiotics and Aesthetics
    in the Age of Reason*, 1984.

KARIN WURST

*See also* Goethe; Gottsched; Herder; Kant; Schiller

# Claude Lévi-Strauss

Belgian-born French anthropologist and
theorist

**Born:** Brussels, Belgium; November 28, 1908

## Biography

It may help to understand the aesthetic qualities of Claude Lévi-Strauss' writing to learn that he was the son not of an academic, scientist, or clerk, but of an artist. His father, Raymond Lévi-Strauss, was a painter, and his mother, Emmy (née Lévy), was related to painters. Born in Brussels, Lévi-Strauss was sent to his grandfather in Paris upon the invasion of Belgium at the outbreak of World War I. He thus grew up in France, receiving his education at Versailles and later at the University of Paris, where he studied law and philosophy. He taught for two years without enthusiasm at lycées in Mont-de-Marsan and in Laon, and then, as he himself puts it, "my career was decided one day in the autumn of 1934, at nine o'clock in the morning, by a telephone call from Célestin Bouglé, who was then head of the École Normale Supérieure." Out of the blue, Bouglé suggested that Lévi-Strauss, who up to that point had shown no penchant for anthropology, apply for a post as professor of sociology at the University of São Paulo, Brazil. While occupying this post from 1934 to 1937, and in the following year while under French sponsorship, Lévi-Strauss and his wife, Dina Dreyfus, made several expeditions into the Brazilian backlands, visiting tribes such as the Nambikwara, Caduveo, and Bororo. No sooner had he returned to Europe than war broke out, and he was pressed into military service. When France fell in 1941 the Jewish Lévi-Strauss was lucky to catch a boat for the United States. Lévi-Strauss opens his best-selling autobiography *A World on the Wane* (better known as *Tristes Tropiques*) with an account of his nervous stay on Martinique awaiting entry into the United States.

As a Fellow of the New School for Social Research in New York during the war, he met and collaborated with linguist and literary critic Roman Jakobson, absorbing many of Jakobson's views on structural linguistics into his anthropological methodology. It was with Jakobson's collaboration that Lévi-Strauss was to write his only detailed analysis of Western literature, the controversial "Charles Baudelaire's 'Les Chats.'" Immediately after the war Lévi-Strauss, now married to his second wife, Rose-Marie Ullmo, became a cultural attaché to the French Embassy in Washington, D.C., where he undoubtedly was allowed to indulge his avocational passions for literature, music, and art. In 1950 he became director of studies at the École Pratique des Hautes Études in Paris, his chair bearing the interesting title "Comparative Religion of Nonliterate Peoples." During the 1950s he left France on occasion for fieldwork in Pakistan and the South Pacific.

His later chair at the Collège de France, held from 1959 to 1982, bears the more mundane title of "social anthropology." Finally, Lévi-Strauss' connection to literature appears again in his election to the Académie Française in 1973: his chair had been previously held by the noted dramatist Henry de Montherlant. Lévi-Strauss was married to his third wife, Monique Roman, in 1954, and she bore him a son, Laurent, who joined Matthieu, Lévi-Strauss' son from the marriage to Ullmo. Lévi-Strauss has made Paris his permanent home.

## Influence

Lévi-Strauss is an anthropologist whose interest in myth overlaps with that of literary theory and whose general influence extends far beyond the boundaries of his own field. George Steiner wrote in 1966 that "Monsieur Lévi-Strauss's influence on the life of ideas in France . . . is, perhaps, second only to that of [Jean-Paul] Sartre. But the exact nature of that influence is not easy to define." Soon it was to surpass Sartre's, as Lévi-Strauss (along with Jakobson, Roland Barthes, and others) made structuralism the dominant mode of literary analysis in France and elsewhere. Indeed poststructuralism, as the name implies, would be unthinkable without structuralism and hence also owes a great debt to Lévi-Strauss.

Aside from his work on myth, Lévi-Strauss has had little to say directly about literature or literary theory. Nevertheless, sentences from even his most technical anthropological works have shown up in works of literary criticism, testifying to his unique ability to throw light on human signifying processes in general.

## Analysis

Following Lévi-Strauss' own predilection for binary thinking, it is convenient to note two ways in which his thought has influenced Western literary theory and criticism. There is first of all the question of "content," of Lévi-Strauss' central ideas concerning the nature of man. Then there is the question of "method" and of Lévi-Strauss' central role in the development of structuralism.

A single example will serve to illustrate how Lévi-Strauss' ideas about humanity have influenced literary criticism. In a study entitled "The Courtship of the Family" (1981), critic John Allen Stevenson borrows the idea, developed by Lévi-Strauss in *The Elementary Structures of Kinship*, that the origin of the incest prohibition lies in its ensuring an exchange of women, which in turn is the foundation of social relations. Stevenson finds that in Samuel Richardson's *Clarissa: Or, The History of a Young Lady* (1747–1748) "these patterns [of exchange] – dominant in modern as well as primitive cultures – are systematically inverted or attacked." Clarissa's family does not wish to exchange her, and this asocial attitude brings about the novel's tragic sequence of events. One may go on to note that for Lévi-Strauss, the exchange of women constitutes a language –

language, like marriage exchange, is constitutive of society – and that in the epistolary novel *Clarissa*, the exchange (in this case the nonexchange) of women finds both its parallel and its deferral in the exchange of letters. Other critics – Jacques Ehrmann in "Structures of Exchange in *Cinna*" (1966), for example – have looked for "structures of exchange" in literary works in a more general sense.

Stevenson's equation of modern and primitive cultures, necessary in order to justify the use of anthropology to analyze Western literature, rests upon an even more fundamental idea in Lévi-Strauss' work, namely that the undeniable differences between "primitive" and "modern" societies disguise their deeper similarities. This idea informs one of Lévi-Strauss' most famous books, *The Savage Mind*, the title of which Dan Sperber insists could more accurately have been translated as "Untamed Thinking." The published translation makes it sound as though Lévi-Strauss supported the view that primitive peoples think differently from the way moderns do. Yet in fact, he is affirming the opposite, that all peoples engage in an "untamed thinking" anterior to rationality, that in fact the "same logical processes are put to use in myth as in science, and that man has always been thinking equally well." Thus he invented the punning title *Mythologiques*, that is, "mytho-logics," for his monumental study of mythical thinking. Lévi-Strauss has been able to draw striking examples to support his universalist position. He is able to see totemism in the way the French name their pets or relate to race horses, and he claims that Sigmund Freud's use of the Oedipus myth "should be included among the recorded versions of the Oedipus myth on a par with earlier or seemingly more 'authentic' versions." Such a pronouncement seeks to diminish radically the historical and cultural distance between ancient Greece and modern Europe by declaring that the use of myth as a problem-solving tool remains the same in both cultures.

Structuralism is the methodology which enables Lévi-Strauss to bridge the gap of appearances, which enables him to write of primitive peoples both as alien and as familiar; it is also as one of the founders of this methodology that Lévi-Strauss has influenced literary theory most profoundly. In a 1945 article entitled "L'Analyse structurale en linguistique et en anthropologie" ("Structural Analysis in Linguistics and in Anthropology), Lévi-Strauss has acknowledged four basic ideas which he has borrowed from linguistics (a discipline he declares to be the only social science worthy of the name): signifying as an unconscious process, relations rather than individual terms as basic units of meaning, the importance of system, and the search for general rules. To put it another way, linguistics has taught that meaning is always achieved by (mostly unconscious) acts of selection and combination within a system which is ultimately reducible to a limited number of oppositions.

These simple principles inform Lévi-Strauss' "The Structural Study of Myth," a landmark essay which

has literally changed the direction of reading. Whereas previously the Oedipus myth had been read horizontally, as a sequence of events occurring to its heroes through time, Lévi-Strauss proposed that the meaning of the myth can be derived only through a vertical, nonchronological reading of its component parts. That Oedipus sleeps with his mother first and then blinds himself because he has discovered the awful truth of his incest is no longer important. Rather, the two events are significant only as representatives of two paradigmatic categories, "overvaluing of blood relations" and "crippledness." With the help of two additional categories composed of other events and names in the myth, Lévi-Strauss arrives at its underlying meaning, that the "overrating of blood relations is to the underrating of blood relations as the attempt to escape autochthony is to the impossibility to succeed in it." The myth is thus seen as a logical puzzle attempting to resolve the fundamental contradiction between practical human perception of biological origins ("born of two") and a cosmology positing plantlike autochthonic origins ("born of one"). In numerous other articles and books, Lévi-Strauss goes on to analyze other myths as resolutions of similar oppositions. A central oppositional pair (life/death, above/below, raw/cooked) is always posited as being resolved or at least confronted by the workings of the myth.

Lévi-Strauss' relentless search for oppositions and the two-dimensional reading process which enables him to find them have had the greatest impact on literary theory. True to the metaphor of structure, Lévi-Strauss even proposes to make the reading process three-dimensional: a myth should be read in all of its variants, since the differences between variants will also prove to be systematic and meaningful. The utter break which Lévi-Strauss makes with more traditional methods of interpretation is most clearly seen in a suggestion, made at the end of his article, that at the point when analysis turns to three dimensions, a computer will be needed – undoubtedly the first suggestion that the meaning of a literary text can best be fathomed by a machine. At this point, a whole change in vocabulary is necessary: "meaning" must be replaced by "structure," "interpretation" by the more appropriate term "perception of structure."

Indeed, in his only detailed analysis of a work of Western literature – done in conjunction with the linguist Jakobson, to whom he owes so much of his method – Lévi-Strauss desires that his preliminary pages of completely objective phonological and grammatical observations on the sonnet "Les Chats" (1847) by Charles Baudelaire "blend together, complete each other or merge, and endow the poem with the value of an absolute object." Because of its seemingly scientific objectivity, bolstered by the use of terminology from linguistics, the essay on Baudelaire has become the single most famous – though hardly the most successful – structural analysis of a work of literature. The detailed grammatical and phonological observations are used to demonstrate that the poem has several different "axes," that there are several different ways in which the poem can be divided. Just as a myth consists of all of its variants, so the poem's structure consists of the tensions between all of its possible divisions. These divisions mark movements at the level of meaning from the extrinsic to the intrinsic, from the empirical to the mythological, and from the real to the surreal. The cats as subjects of the poem unify these oppositions; thus, the poem is seen as carrying out the same function of mediation between cosmological contradictions as Lévi-Strauss had posited for myth in primitive cultures.

As Michael Riffaterre has pointed out in "Describing Poetic Structures: Two Approaches to Baudelaire's *Les Chats*" (1966), such an analysis of the poem as an "absolute object" conflicts with common notions of what a poetic text does: namely, to call forth responses from the reader. Thus Riffaterre dismisses half the divisions in the poem made by Lévi-Strauss and Jakobson because they "make use of constituents that cannot possibly be perceived by the reader; these constituents must therefore remain alien to the poetic structure, which is supposed to emphasize the form of the message, to make it more 'visible,' more compelling." Two questions are at work here. The first is whether the methodology of structural linguistics or of structural mythography can be applied to the study of poetry. In *Structuralism in Literature* (1974), Robert Scholes concludes that it cannot, at least not in the purely linguistic form which Jakobson and Lévi-Strauss have attempted:

> The structuralists are quite right in suggesting that critics should borrow descriptive terminology from linguistics, simply because it is the best we have. But linguistic description will not solve the problem of literary response .... If poetry offered us only messages framed in special poetic structures, the problem would be easy, and attention to the specifics of grammar and syntax in the poetic message would lead to a true understanding of poetic achievement.

The more crucial question asked by Riffaterre is how structure, in myth or in poetry, can be meaningful unless it is perceived. Lévi-Strauss would no doubt respond by saying, as he does throughout his work, that structure is always perceived, but at the level of the unconscious. Besides language itself, trained musician Lévi-Strauss can also call upon music as an example of communication through a structure which escapes the consciousness of most of its listeners. One perceives order or disorder in music without understanding what makes it so. Nevertheless, by definition the theory of unconscious interpretation escapes proof or disproof.

If Riffaterre rejects Lévi-Strauss' two-directional reading and play of oppositions in order to return to a more traditional method in which words mean in and of themselves and reading proceeds from beginning to end, deconstruction

wishes to retain the essence of Lévi-Strauss' method while jettisoning its search for a basic opposition structuring texts. Thus, in an article devoted primarily to the thought of Lévi-Strauss, philosopher Jacques Derrida characterizes the difference between structuralism and deconstruction as follows:

> There are thus two interpretations of interpretation, of structure, of sign, of play. The one [structuralism] seeks to decipher, dreams of deciphering a truth or an origin which escapes play and the order of the sign, and which lives the necessity of interpretation as an exile. The other [deconstruction], which is no longer turned toward the origin, affirms play and tries to pass beyond man and humanism .... The second interpretation of interpretation, to which Nietzsche pointed the way, does not seek in ethnography, as Lévi-Strauss does, the "inspiration of a new humanism."

The significance of the thought of Lévi-Strauss can be usefully compared with that of another thinker, Sigmund Freud, the founder of psychoanalysis, a discipline Lévi-Strauss has named as one of his three sources of youthful inspiration (the other two are Marxism and geology). Both men believe that there are universals of human thought which work at the unconscious level. For Lévi-Strauss this universal would seem to be the machine of binary opposition, working ruthlessly with the aid of natural phenomena and narrative units to identify and then mediate logical antinomies. Both men are, to use a term Lévi-Strauss applies to mytho-logic, *bricoleurs* (improvisational handymen), drawing their ideas from whatever comes to hand, be it science or literature, and writing texts which are, aside from their disputed truth value, brilliant works of verbal art. Conversely, both men have had a profound influence on virtually all humanistic and social disciplines. Both men prefer the indirect to the direct method of interpretation; for both, meaning always lies somewhere other than on the surface of the dream, myth, or work of art under examination. That is the sticking point for both thinkers: the very ingenuity – others might say "casuistry" – with which they arrange data in order to prove their theories is fascinating, yet in the end unconvincing, at least to those clinging to the tradition of Western logic. For both men have revealed another, unconscious logic more fundamental than that of rationality. It is no wonder that literary exegetes, who owe their living to the fact that literary expression is often indirect, would embrace the innovations of these thinkers with perhaps more enthusiasm than they have been received by the scientists within their own disciplines. Those scientists have reproved both thinkers with constructing theories that are ultimately unprovable. In the end, however, unprovability does not matter, for both men have wished less to prove something than to found the new "languages" of psychoanalysis and of structuralism. It helps little to characterize a language or a metaphor as "right" or "wrong," "logical," or "illogical." As George Steiner remarks, "it is not, primarily, as anthropology or ethnography that [Lévi-Strauss'] fascinating body of work may come to be judged and valued, but as extended poetic metaphor."

## Principal criticism

"The Structural Study of Myth," 1955
"'Les Chats' de Charles Baudelaire," 1962 (with Roman Jakobson; "Charles Baudelaire's 'Les Chats,'" 1971)
*Mythologiques*, 1964–1971 (*Introduction to a Science of Mythology*, 1969–1981), includes *Le Cru et le cuit* (*The Raw and the Cooked*), *Du miel aux cendres* (*From Honey to Ashes*), *L'Origine des manières de table* (*The Origin of Table Manners*), and *L'Homme nu* (*The Naked Man*)
*Regarder, Ecouter, lire*, 1993 (*Look, Listen, Read*, 1997)

## Other major works and literary forms

Besides his myth studies, the most important of which have been listed under Principal criticism above, Claude Lévi-Strauss has made major contributions to two other areas of anthropology: to the theory of kinship relations in his first major book, *Les Structures élémentaires de la parenté* (1949; *The Elementary Structures of Kinship*, 1969), and to the study of totemism both in *La Pensée sauvage* (1962; *The Savage Mind*, 1966) and in *Le Totémisme aujourd'hui* (1962; *Totemism*, 1963). The brilliant writing in his autobiographical ethnography *Tristes tropiques* (1955; *A World on the Wane*, 1961, better known as *Tristes Tropiques*, 1964) first brought Lévi-Strauss widespread fame. He has written on various other topics and has outlined his views of anthropology and of structuralism in *Anthropologie structurale* (1958; *Structural Anthropology*, 1963) and *Anthropologie structurale II* (1973; *Structural Anthropology, Volume Two*, 1976) as well as in numerous other books, articles, reviews, lectures, and research reports, the latter collected in *Paroles données* (1984; *Anthropology and Myth*, 1987). He also has given an extraordinary number of interviews. George Charbonnier's collection *Entretiens avec Claude Lévi-Strauss* (1961; *Conversations with Claude Lévi-Strauss*, 1969) is of particular interest, art being one of the main topics of their discussion.

NONFICTION
*La Vie familiale et sociale des Indiens Nambikwara*, 1948
*Les Structures élémentaires de la parenté*, 1949 (*The Elementary Structures of Kinship*, 1969)
*Introduction à l'œuvre de Marcel Mauss*, 1950 (*Introduction to the Work of Marcel Mauss*, 1987)
*Race et Histoire*, 1952 (*Race and History*, 1958)
*Tristes tropiques*, 1955 (*A World on the Wane*, 1961, better known as *Tristes Tropiques*, 1964)
*Anthropologie structurale*, 1958 (*Structural Anthropology*, 1963)
*Leçon inaugurale*, 1960 (*The Scope of Anthropology*, 1967)
*Entretiens avec Claude Lévi-Strauss*, 1961 (George Charbonnier, editor; *Conversations with Claude Lévi-Strauss*, 1969)
*La Pensée sauvage*, 1962 (*The Savage Mind*, 1966)
*Le Totémisme aujourd'hui*, 1962 (*Totemism*, 1963)

*The Bear and the Barber*, 1963
*The Culinary Triangle*, 1966
*La Racisme devant les sciences*, 1973
*Anthropologie structurale II*, 1973 (*Structural Anthropology, Volume Two*, 1976)
*La Voie des masques*, 1975 (2 volumes; *The Way of the Masks*, 1982)
*Myth and Meaning*, 1979
*Le Regard éloigné*, 1983 (*The View from Afar*, 1985)
*Paroles données*, 1984 (*Anthropology and Myth*, 1987)
*La Potière jalouse*, 1985 (*The Jealous Potter*, 1988)
*Hommage à André Roussin décédé le 3 novembre 1987*, 1987
*De près et de loin*, 1988
*Des symboles et leur doubles*, 1989
*Histoire de Lynx*, 1993 (*The Story of Lynx*, 1995)

## Further reading

Boon, James A. *From Symbolism to Structuralism: Lévi-Strauss in a Literary Tradition*, 1971.
Champagne, Roland A. *Claude Lévi-Strauss*, 1987.
Derrida, Jacques. "Structure, Sign, and Play in the Discourse of the Human Sciences," in *Writing and Difference*, 1978.
Jenkins, Alan. *The Social Theory of Claude Lévi-Strauss*, 1979.
Lapointe, François H., and Claire C. Lapointe. *Claude Lévi-Strauss and His Critics: An International Bibliography of Criticism, 1950–1976*, 1977.
Leach, Edmund. *Claude Lévi-Strauss*, 1970.
Mehlmann, Jeffrey. "Punctuation in *Tristes tropiques*," in *A Structural Study of Autobiography: Proust, Leiris, Sartre, Lévi-Strauss*, 1974.
Paz, Octavio. *Claude Lévi-Strauss: An Introduction*, 1970.
Sperber, Dan. "Claude Lévi-Strauss," in *Structuralism and Since*, 1979. Edited by John Sturrock.
Steiner, George. "Orpheus with His Myths: Claude Lévi-Strauss," in *Language and Silence*, 1974.

THOMAS O. BEEBEE

*See also* French Literary Theory: Twentieth Century; Jakobson; Structuralism

# C. S. Lewis

Irish-born English writer, critic, and scholar

**Born:** Belfast, Ireland; November 29, 1898
**Died:** Oxford, England; November 22, 1963

## Biography

Clive Staples Lewis was born on November 29, 1898, in Belfast, Ireland, to Albert James Lewis and the former Flora Augusta Hamilton. His father was a successful lawyer, his mother a writer and mathematician, so Lewis and his brother, Warren, grew up in comfortable, bookish surroundings. Mrs. Lewis died in 1908, and the sons were sent to boarding school in England, a British institution which Lewis came to loathe. He won a scholarship to University College, Oxford, but World War I duty intervened. He served as a second lieutenant and was wounded in action.

Lewis entered Oxford in 1919. He remained there for thirty-five years, first as a student and lecturer at University College, then as a Fellow and tutor at Magdalen College. During these years Lewis wrote most of his books and gradually reasoned himself into a Christian convert; he also became a close friend of J. R. R. Tolkien while at Oxford. In 1954 he was appointed to the chair of Medieval and Renaissance Literature at Cambridge University, where he taught until his death. He married Joy Davidman, an American reader who had initiated a long correspondence with him, in 1956. She died of bone cancer in 1960. Lewis' death from a heart attack occurred on November 22, 1963, the same day on which the novelist Aldous Huxley and the American president John F. Kennedy died.

## Influence

Lewis was a valuable, even necessary, restraining influence upon the excesses of the New Criticism. When the New Critics insisted upon a close reading of the text as the sole analytical tool required for evaluating literature, Lewis reminded them that every literary work is written by some person at some time in some place – within some cultural context. In *The Discarded Image*, he attempts to show what fruits medieval and Renaissance literature will yield to the reader who does not impose a modern sensibility and modern conceptions upon it. Elsewhere, he engages in the spirited defense of writers such as Percy Bysshe Shelley and Rudyard Kipling, against whom he believes twentieth-century critics have overreacted in their rejection of nineteenth-century conventions.

## Analysis

Lewis was a truly phenomenal writer. His fields were medieval and Renaissance literature. Such was his scholarly standing that, for the prestigious *Oxford History of English Literature*, he was commissioned to write volume 3, *English Literature in the Sixteenth Century, Excluding Drama*. In an age of specialization, however, he did not confine himself to his specialty; his literary criticism addresses every period. His knowledge was encyclopedic and, like an earlier generalist and Christian apologist, G. K. Chesterton, he wrote on any and every subject. His literary criticism was overshadowed by his fiction and religious writings, which developed a wide following. Yet his reasoned and eloquent defense of the Christian life, within a literary milieu in which that was a decidedly minority view, would alone be enough to secure his reputation.

Lewis' criticism, like his fiction and theology, emphasizes the interplay between reason and imagination. He did not, as did the Romantic critics, see these two faculties as being necessarily in opposition. For Lewis, myth was the means by which humanity, from prehistory to modern times, had communicated its most deeply felt truths to later generations. Lewis' critical, creative, and metaphysical views were of a piece and, for him, the power of Christianity lay in its combining of imagination with reason. Its central mystery, the Incarnation, was at the same time its most rational aspect. When God became human, myth became fact. Lewis had lost his faith during his unhappy days at public school, and his wartime experiences had not restored it. By 1929, however, his intellect rather than enthusiasm had brought him (very much against his will, he makes clear in his autobiography) to Christian conversion.

It is not possible to pigeonhole Lewis' criticism. He was not a formalist or New Critic; nevertheless, he shared with the New Critics the conviction that each text warrants a sensitive reading and a thorough examination of its iconography. Lewis' first literary ambition was to be a great poet and, although that ambition was not realized, he possessed the poet's awareness that every word in every line can be crucial to a proper assessment of the work. Lewis was at odds with the trend of poetry in the 1920s and 1930s; he wrote and warmly defended the long narrative poem, which had fallen into disfavor elsewhere.

Lewis was not a linguistic critic, but he was fascinated with language, especially figurative language. In "Bluspels and Flalansferes: A Semantic Nightmare" in *Rehabilitations and Other Essays*, he responds to those who wish writings about language to be scientific rather than rhetorical; he specifically mentions I. A. Richards, a leading light among the New Critics. Lewis' thesis is that language is innately metaphorical, and the user is seldom free of the rhetorical implications of even the so-called dead metaphor. He argues that the best writers have been those who have intuited this truth. In the essay, Lewis characterizes himself as a rationalist, but he relates rationality to imagination. Reason, he states, finds the truth, but meaning antecedes both truth and falsehood, and imagination finds the meaning. It is also interesting to note that in Lewis' celebrated space trilogy (*Out of the Silent Planet*, 1938; *Perelandra*, 1943; *That Hideous Strength: A Modern Fairy Tale for Grown-ups*, 1945) he makes his protagonist, Dr. Elwin Ransom, a noted philologist.

Lewis was not an Aristotelian (genre) critic, enamored of the theory of inherent forms. In "High and Low Brows," another of the essays from *Rehabilitations and Other Essays*, he tackles the issue of good books and bad, and of what makes a work "literature." He presses for abolition of the distinction between high- and low-brow writing. The former term, he argues, protects too many bad books, while the latter robs others of deserved praise. In *An Experiment in Criticism*, he elaborates a suggestion that literature be judged by the way people read it. Lewis does not, on the other hand, suggest that taste is purely relative – quite the reverse. He observes elsewhere that to believe a person can get the same kind and degree of pleasure from commonplace art as from great art is to believe that one can get as drunk from water as from spirits.

Lewis was not an impressionistic critic, whose only criterion was his personal emotional response to the work. In fact, he believed that a school of criticism could be just as arbitrary as an individual in formulating and applying its principles. In "Shelley, Dryden, and Mr. Eliot," the first and longest of the essays in *Rehabilitations and Other Essays*, Lewis responds to "John Dryden," an essay which the brilliant poet and New Critic T. S. Eliot published in 1932. Lewis believes that the assessment in that essay of Dryden as a greater poet than Shelley is motivated by Eliot's hidden poetic agenda. Lewis' defense of Shelley, while not glossing over his weaknesses, is spirited and detailed. It concludes with the observation that some anti-Romantics (here Lewis excludes Eliot) have repudiated Shelley as a result of their willful misunderstanding of his best work. Another apologia, "Kipling's World," in *Selected Literary Essays*, begins with a disclaimer. Lewis admits that he has never taken Kipling to his heart, but he also notes that he never reads Kipling without experiencing renewed admiration for his work and wonders how any reader of taste can doubt that he is a very great artist. Lewis goes on to explore, with many specific references to the author's works, the roots of the considerable critical antipathy for Kipling. He concludes by advising critics of Kipling's gods, discipline and work, to add the necessary correctives to them, not deny their literary authenticity.

If historical criticism is defined as that school of critics who see their duty as the analysis of the literary work in the light of the past, then here is where the reader addicted to taxonomy might feel most comfortable in placing Lewis. Clearly though, Lewis did not confuse history with biography; he asserts in *The Personal Heresy* that a book should never become the mere vehicle for steeping oneself in the personality of its author. "Our English Syllabus" in *Rehabilitations and Other Essays*, although specifically addressing the teaching of English literature at Oxford, makes an implicit critical statement. Lewis insists that the teacher (which can be read as critic) need not and should not offer assistance to the student (which can be read as reader) in the consideration of current literature. The teacher (critic) should offer assistance only where assistance is truly needed. Lewis likens the student (reader) who requires assistance in understanding the work of his contemporaries to a grown man who requires a nurse's assistance in blowing his own nose. In Lewis' best-known critical works, he has offered the truly needed assistance.

*The Allegory of Love* examines the medieval idea of love as reflected in the poetry of the period. So integral to the medieval mentality and so foreign to the modern sensibility is the notion of courtly love, that medieval love poetry is scarcely comprehensible without some knowledge of it. Lewis argues in this book that cultural, and literary, history is not simply like the string of stations along a railway line through which, in chronological order, the train will pass. The past brings with it accretions for the present and these accretions must be constantly reexamined. *The Discarded Image* sketches for the modern reader the roots – classical, theological, cosmological, and conventional – of medieval and Renaissance literature. *English Literature in the Sixteenth Century, Excluding Drama*, seven hundred pages in length, is an extremely valuable and readable work of literary history.

Lewis' criticism can be separated from his religious writings, but there is usually a close correspondence between the two. The clarity of his argument is the chief virtue of each. His influence has probably been greater in the religious sphere. He was one of those brilliant converts, like Saint Paul and Saint Augustine, who lent a measure of intellectual respectability to their faith. After his conversion, he surely felt a closer kinship to Geoffrey Chaucer, John Milton, John Donne, and the other great Christian poets of England. He has been characterized as a writer who has made a difference, someone who has altered the way his readers think about literary and Christian ideas.

It should not be surprising that Lewis' literary criticism so often borders upon the metaphysical. Walter Hooper, the editor of Lewis' *Selected Literary Essays*, reminds the reader that Lewis originally read "Greats" at Oxford and sought a fellowship in philosophy before finally turning to English literature. Lewis states his literary position clearly in the concluding sentences of "Bluspels and Flalansferes": "And so, admittedly, the view I have taken has metaphysical implications. But so has every view."

## Principal criticism

*The Allegory of Love: A Study in Medieval Tradition*, 1936
*The Personal Heresy: A Controversy*, 1939 (with E. M. W. Tillyard)
*Rehabilitations and Other Essays*, 1939
*A Preface to "Paradise Lost": Being the Ballard Matthews Lectures, Delivered at University College, North Wales*, 1941, 1942
*Hamlet: The Prince or the Poem?*, 1942
*The Abolition of Man: Or, Reflections on Education with Special Reference to the Teaching of English to the Upper Forms of Schools*, 1943
*The Literary Impact of the Authorized Version*, 1950
*English Literature in the Sixteenth Century, Excluding Drama: The Completion of the Clark Lectures*, 1944, 1954
*Studies in Words*, 1960, enlarged 1967
*An Experiment in Criticism*, 1961
*The Discarded Image: An Introduction to Medieval and Renaissance Literature*, 1964
*Spenser's Images of Life*, 1967
*Selected Literary Essays*, 1969 (Walter Hooper, editor)

## Other major works and literary forms

C. S. Lewis was a man of letters in the truest sense which that appellation can convey. He was a renowned scholar of English literature, especially of the medieval and Renaissance periods. He was a former atheist turned Christian apologist. His spiritual autobiography, *Surprised by Joy: The Shape of My Early Life* (1955), is in the tradition of Saint Augustine's *Confessions* (c. 400) and John Henry Newman's *Apologia pro Vita Sua* (1864). Lewis also wrote novels (in some of which he deftly combines science fiction and Christian theory), children's books, poetry, sermons, philosophy, linguistic treatises, and devotional books. He published some of his poetry under the pseudonym Clive Hamilton and some of his nonfiction as N. W. Clerk.

NOVELS
*Out of the Silent Planet*, 1938
*Perelandra*, 1943
*That Hideous Strength: A Modern Fairy Tale for Grown-ups*, 1945
*The Great Divorce: A Dream, 1945*
*Till We Have Faces: A Myth Retold*, 1956

SHORT FICTION
*The Dark Tower and Other Stories*, 1977

POETRY
*Spirits in Bondage: A Cycle of Lyrics*, 1919 (as Clive Hamilton)
*Dymer*, 1926 (as Hamilton)
*Poems*, 1964
*Narrative Poems*, 1969

NONFICTION
*The Pilgrim's Regress: An Allegorical Apology for Christianity, Reason, and Romanticism*, 1933
*The Problem of Pain*, 1940
*Broadcast Talks*, 1942 (also as *The Case for Christianity*, 1943)
*Christian Behaviour: A Further Series of Broadcast Talks*, 1943
*Beyond Personality: The Christian Idea of God*, 1944
*Miracles: A Preliminary Study*, 1947
*The Weight of Glory, and Other Addresses*, 1949
*Mere Christianity*, 1952
*Surprised by Joy: The Shape of My Early Life*, 1955
*Reflections on the Psalms*, 1958
*Shall We Lose God in Outer Space?* 1959
*The Four Loves*, 1960
*The World's Last Night and Other Essays*, 1960
*The Screwtape Letters and Screwtape Proposes a Toast*, 1961
*A Grief Observed*, 1961 (as N. W. Clerk)
*Beyond the Bright Blue*, 1963
*Letters to Malcolm: Chiefly on Prayer*, 1964
*Christian Reflections*, 1967
*Letters to an American Lady*, 1969
*God in the Dock: Essays on Theology and Ethics*, 1970
*Undeceptions: Essays on Theology and Ethics*, 1971
*The Joyful Christian: 127 Readings from C. S. Lewis*, 1977

CHILDREN'S LITERATURE
*The Lion, the Witch, and the Wardrobe: A Story for Children*, 1950
*Prince Caspian: The Return to Narnia*, 1951
*The Voyage of the Dawn Treader*, 1952
*The Silver Chair*, 1953
*The Horse and His Boy*, 1954
*The Magician's Nephew*, 1955
*The Last Battle: A Story for Children*, 1956

ANTHOLOGY
*George Macdonald: An Anthology*, 1945 (editor)

MISCELLANEOUS
*Of Other Worlds: Essays and Stories*, 1966

## Further reading

Barratt, David. *C. S. Lewis and His World*, 1987.
Como, James. "The Critical Principles of C. S. Lewis," in *Bulletin of the New York C. S. Lewis Society*. II (March, 1971), pp. 5–10.
Goldberg, S. L. "C. S. Lewis and the Study of English," in *Melbourne Critical Review*. V (1962), pp. 119–127.
Green, Roger Lancelyn, and Walter Hooper. *C. S. Lewis: A Biography*, 1974.
Nassar, Eugene Paul. "Metacriticism," in *The Rape of Cinderella: Essays in Literary Continuity*, 1970.
Sayer, George. *Jack: C. S. Lewis and His Times*, 1988.
Sundaram, P. S. "C. S. Lewis: Literary Critic," in *Quest*. LX (January–March, 1969), pp. 58–66.
Walsh, Chad. *The Literary Legacy of C. S. Lewis*, 1979.
Watson, George. *The Literary Critics: A Study of English Descriptive Criticism*, 1964.
Wilson, A. N. *C. S. Lewis: A Biography*, 1990.

PATRICK ADCOCK

*See also* British Literary Theory: Twentieth Century; Tolkien

# Linguistics and Literary Studies

Linguistics, as the scientific study of language, was often drawn upon by literary critics in the twentieth century. This focus on scientific rigor became particularly important in the 1960s, since the study of literature within universities was being subjected to demands for more systematic and replicable analysis. Rather than simply reading literary works in order to evaluate their quality in relation to other literary works, it was thought necessary to be able to provide general descriptions of the structural qualities of literature. Turning to the study of language enabled critics to develop more systematic forms of analysis, and this focus on language has remained with literary criticism, since the demise of structuralism, especially within poststructuralism and deconstruction. This demand for greater professionalism within the university study of literature resulted in the development of two forms of more scientific study which have at times worked in tandem: structuralist criticism, and linguistic criticism or stylistics.

Structuralism is heavily indebted to the linguistic system developed by the Swiss linguist Ferdinand de Saussure; it involved a focus on the structural and formal qualities of literary and other texts, at the expense of meaning and interpretation. This meant that structuralist critics made the assumption that the linguistic analysis of the sentence, consisting of various functional entities, could be extended to the level of the text as a whole; thus a narrative could be described in terms of its "grammar" and the components of that grammar could be described. Narrative analysis, or narratology, has proved to be an immensely productive form of analysis, focusing on the components of the plot and story of a text and analyzing the different roles and functions of action and description. Structuralist critics, like linguists, were more interested in the general rather than specific features of texts, and thus developed a form of analysis, termed "poetics," which tried to formulate general rules that could be applied to all literary texts. This was in stark contrast to more traditional literary analysis, where the specific text and its author were generally the focus of analysis, and the goal of criticism was to provide the most comprehensive and coherent interpretation of a work.

Linguistic criticism or stylistics (treated separately by Ronald Carter but conflated for the purposes of this discussion) took a slightly different trajectory to structuralism although it too was indebted to linguistics. Whilst structuralism drew on the general features of linguistics, and from time to time incorporated some of the technical vocabulary of linguistics, it did not attempt to perform linguistic analyses of texts as such. Its concerns were more with identifying general features of texts than with explaining certain effects within literature through the use of linguistics as a descriptive or explanatory framework. Stylistics has always been torn between two aims and its proponents are often not clear as to which aim they have: the first is to use linguistics in order to describe features within literary texts (literature here being seen as qualitatively different to other texts); the second is to analyze literature using linguistics in order to test out linguistic rules and systems, thus discovering something at the theoretical level about linguistics. It must be said that most stylistics and linguistics critics have the first aim.

One of the first linguistic tasks which stylisticians engaged in was the description of individual literary styles. The writings of Ernest Hemingway, William Faulkner, and William Shakespeare were described in terms of the ways in which they differed from "ordinary" language, or from the writings of other authors. It was considered that these writers in particular had very idiosyncratic styles and it was therefore hoped that it would prove possible to describe a writer's "grammar." This had a number of problematic assumptions. Firstly, that writers have utterly distinct styles grammatically; secondly, that they are consistent; and finally, that there is something against which these styles could be contrasted and measured for their supposed deviance. One of the major problems of this type of linguistic criticism, however, is that it seems to have no real point in terms of interpretation. Being able to describe something in terms of its component parts is interesting, and being able to describe the difference between, say, Shakespeare's style and Christopher Marlowe's style, is, at an academic level, important. But this type of description seems to serve no function as such in terms of interpretation or analysis; it tells us nothing about the texts themselves, nor about the effect that this type of style, in contrast to any other, has on readers.

Another concern of early stylisticians was to describe so-called "literary" language. This focus stemmed from early Russian Formalist work on the specialness of literary language, which stylisticians felt it would be possible to describe formally using linguistic terminology. This task proved to be more complicated than was at first envisaged since it became clear on analysis that literary language was not quite as uniform as had been anticipated, and also it was very difficult to know what norm literary language should be contrasted with. Because literary language was considered to be a "rule-breaking" language, the examples which were analyzed were generally poems by, for example, e. e. cummings or Dylan Thomas, where the poets had developed very clear guidelines or grammars for the language of a particular poem. However, it became clear when analyzing novels or less "deviant" poetry, that not all literary language could be described in terms of its linguistic deviation from a norm.

Another potentially very useful aspect of linguistics is discourse analysis – a system of analyzing conversation by categorizing the functions of larger stretches of interaction than individual sentences. Thus, within discourse analysis, the aim is to try to analyze stretches of conversation into whether they are functioning to, for example, end the interaction or to change the topic of conversation. This analysis of units above the level of the sentence, that is, of discourse, has been particularly successful in the analysis of drama. Those using discourse analysis have largely analyzed the functions of stretches of speech by particular characters and the way that conversational contracts are established between participants as to what sort of language is permitted, what is considered as polite, and so on. This type of analysis can be particularly rewarding when it focuses on the way that power relations inform the type of linguistic choices which are made in a text.

Linguistics has also been drawn upon by literary critics to try to describe in a more rigorous fashion the effects and responses to literature (a useful source of articles on this subject is the journal *Language and Literature*). What many linguistic critics have used linguistics for is to analyze the way in which language plays a key role in terms of the way that the reader is manipulated by the author/narrator. By the systematic analysis of narrative, and particularly point of view and focalization (the position from which the narrative is told and the focus of the narrative), the linguistic critic is able to see the way that readers are led to believe certain pieces of information or to feel certain emotions in relation to situations and characters. This concern with manipulation has been at the heart of many linguistic analyses of literature, particularly in relation to discussions of ideology. Ideology is considered by many critics to be the world-view and belief systems of those in positions of power which is imparted to others and believed by them or contested by them. Critical linguists are those critics who wish to expose the mechanisms whereby ideological messages are relayed to readers and "owned" by them, as if they were their own opinions. (Most critical linguists are in fact concerned to analyze nonliterary texts such as newspapers and advertisements; however, their work has clear implications for literary texts as well.)

Michael Halliday, on whose linguistic system much of this critical linguistic work has been based, used "systemic" linguistics in order to describe the world-views which were presented to the reader, particularly in the work of William Golding. For example, he described the actions of the central characters of the novel *The Inheritors* (1955) in order to demonstrate that choice of verbs and the type of verbs chosen systematically add up cumulatively to a particular set of beliefs about the way that the world functions. His work was drawn upon by Deirdre Burton, who used this analysis of verbal processes in Sylvia Plath's novel *The Bell Jar* (1963) in order to describe the way that female characters can be seen in certain works of literature to be "acted upon" rather than responsible for their own actions. This type of analysis of transitivity (who does what to whom) has been central to feminist linguistic work on literature.

Perhaps linguistic criticism is at its most useful and productive when it is used in the analysis of manipulation and the emotional and ideational effects that are achieved in the reader. When linguistic criticism is taken to its logical extreme, for example, in a "pure" grammatical description of the language of literature, it can seem rather pointless. For example, John Sinclair pushed linguistic criticism as far as it is possible for it to go in terms of the description of a poem when he simply gave a grammatical description of a poem and suggested that that was as much as linguistics should do. However, even in the process of simply describing the grammatical structures of a poem, it is clear that Sinclair is focusing on certain aspects of the poem rather than others, and his focus on these features is led, perhaps at an unconscious level, by what he takes the meaning of the poem to be. Thus although interpretation is something which Sinclair is working to dispel from his analysis, interpretation precedes the analysis and informs it.

Linguistic criticism is thus that form of literary criticism which tries to make literary study more rigorous and systematic, moving it away from simple emotional and evaluative responses to literature, to a more scientific concern with the way that certain effects are achieved. Describing these effects necessarily brings into play questions of gender, race, and class, both in terms of analysis of the narrator, narrative structure chosen, and the characters represented in the text, but also in terms of the intended or ideal reader which the text constructs. Although this type of linguistic analysis is at an early stage, it is clear that linguistic categories can help to describe the way that the reader is positioned by the text, and can construct for himself or herself an alternative position of intelligibility. This type of linguistic criticism is concerned to move away from notions

which bedeviled early stylistic analysis, where there was an assumption that there was one meaning of a text, and that the role of the critic was to make that interpretation explicit. In more recent work it has become clear that although the text positions readers in certain ways, they, because of their social position and political consciousness, can react in line with the text's positioning or can resist that address. Thus, this type of criticism is trying to develop a form of linguistic analysis which can deal with a multiplicity of interpretations and reader positions, whilst still providing a framework of analysis. Although variables such as gender, race, and class are ones which theoretical linguistics tries to hold at bay, within the analysis of literature it is essential that they be considered, and that they be seen as informing linguistic choices, rather than being considered as extralinguistic features.

### Further reading

Barthes, Roland. "Structural Analysis of Narrative," in *Image/Music/Text*, 1977.

Burton, Deirdre. *Dialogue and Discourse: A Sociolinguistic Approach to Modern Drama Dialogue and Naturally Occurring Conversation*, 1980.

——. "Through Dark Glasses: Through Glass Darkly," in *Language and Literature: An Introductory Reader in Stylistics*, 1982. Edited by Ronald Carter.

Carter, Ronald, ed. *Language and Literature: An Introductory Reader in Stylistics*, 1982.

——, and Paul Simpson, eds. *Language, Discourse and Literature: An Introductory Reader in Discourse Stylistics*, 1989.

Fowler, Roger. *Linguistic Criticism*, 1986.

Halliday, Michael. "Linguistic Function and Style: An Inquiry into the Language of William Golding's *The Inheritors*," in *Literary Style: A Symposium*, 1977. Edited by S. Chatman.

Lee, David. *Competing Discourses: Perspective and Ideology in Language*, 1992.

Mills, Sara. *Feminist Stylistics*, 1995.

Sinclair, John. "Taking a Poem to Pieces," in *Essays on Style and Language*, 1966. Edited by Roger Fowler.

Toolan, Michael. *Narrative: A Critical Linguistic Introduction*, 1988.

Weber, Jean Jacques, ed. *The Stylistics Reader*, 1996.

SARA MILLS

*See also* Deconstruction; Metaphor; Metonymy; Russian Formalism; Saussure; Structuralism

# Literary Theory in the Age of Victoria

The rich and seemingly infinite variety of the Victorian Age is reflected in the literary theories and criticism of the era. After a violent reaction to all things Victorian in the early part of the twentieth century, chiefly precipitated by Lytton Strachey, Paul Elmer More, and T. S. Eliot, the latter half of the century witnessed a major critical reappraisal of the era, including a positive revaluation of its criticism and fresh understandings of its importance for later thought. Thus, while the twentieth century has been rightly characterized as the age of criticism, the lineage of most of its critical perspectives is traceable to the work of the Victorians.

During the sixty-four years of Victoria's reign (1837–1901), English criticism took surprising new turns as it reflected the fundamental intellectual and spiritual concerns, paradoxes and dualities, and hopes and despairs of the time. Fueled by the emergence, growth, and multiplication of periodicals and newspapers, greatly aided by an ever-growing readership educated at London's new University College (founded in 1828), in the workingmen's institutes, and in the Society for the Diffusion of Useful Knowledge (founded in 1826), and buttressed by the National Education Act (1870), modern literary criticism was born and nurtured in this era. It was inspired, in part, by the "lower" (linguistic/textual) and "higher" (historical/ interpretive) biblical criticism practiced in Germany. It was assisted both by the rediscovery, editing, and textual analysis of Anglo-Saxon and Middle English works and by notions imported from Europe. Highly influenced also by the new historicism at work in France and England and the new art criticism of John Ruskin (1819–1900), the criticism of literature grew and flourished in an unprecedented profusion. The historical, cultural, ethical, and humanistic criticism produced by a growing number of critics was largely responsible for the adoption of the study of English language and literature in the ancient universities at Oxford and Cambridge and the beginnings of formulating a canon of English literature – a canon to which the works of the Victorians themselves were added in the twentieth century.

It is useful to bear in mind that the Victorians, endowed with a new sense of history, thought of themselves as living in an age of transition between a yesterday clearly identified with the pastoral Middle Ages and an uncertain tomorrow predicated upon a confused present replete with conflicting claims. No better capsule of the age exists than the opening paragraph of diametrically opposed superlatives ("the best of times"/"the worst of times") in Charles Dickens' *A Tale of Two Cities* (1859). The transitional nature of the period is the reason for the fundamental difficulty its students invariably face: for every assertion about it, a counter-assertion is possible; every generalization can be proved and disproved. So well and thoroughly documented is this complex age that even the wary are susceptible to "selective Victorianism." Moreover, the daunting bulk of Victorian critical prose must be viewed in the light of an even more daunting body of philosophical, religious, and scientific prose (particularly Charles Darwin's), together with voluminous cultural and social commentary and the apparently endless stream of works in the popular press.

To appreciate the varied strands of criticism in this fecund Victorian period, it is necessary to appreciate the principal intellectual currents of the time and to recognize that four ways of life were contending with one another for dominance and that each way had within it some obvious and some subtle variations. Put simply, the four major strains of thought were Romanticism, utilitarianism (sometimes called Benthamism), Christian humanism, and secular humanism, each of which informed the criticism of literature, since endemic to any theory of criticism is a theory of culture. It is also the case that as some critics evolved their philosophies of criticism changed, that some critics eschewed any philosophical system, that each brand of humanism sometimes proceeds from and sometimes shades off into Romanticism, and that somewhat shifting perspectives characterize the entire era, especially its last thirty years.

Thus, the distinctions often made among the literary theorist or critic, the historian of culture, taste, and aesthetics, the moralist, and the social critic blur when one seeks to account for the great thinkers and critics of the era, particularly among the earlier Victorians, who tried to "see life whole" and sought to integrate their theories of literature and criticism with their views of society and its values. Surely this is the case with Thomas Babington Macaulay (1800–1859), Thomas Carlyle (1795–1881), and John Ruskin, the three eminent earlier Victorians whose works both reflected and defined orthodox Victorianism.

Macaulay began his literary career in the 1820s as a contributor to *Knight's Quarterly Magazine* and soon became a renowned writer for the *Edinburgh Quarterly*, achieving lasting recognition for his essay on John Milton. Macaulay's work displays the era's convictions about progress and politics and focuses on the life and times of the authors whose work he examined, often to the neglect of their actual work. His clear adherence to the bourgeois values of his time and promulgation of those values in his historical and critical writings both assured his popularity and placed him among the chief prophets of progress and shapers of Victorian culture, thought, and art through the mid-century. This master of the utilitarian spirit amply illustrates in his work the axiom that criticism both springs from and buttresses a vision of culture.

Facing Macaulay across an unbridgeable gulf is the essentially Romantic Carlyle. His work is far more traditionalist and backward-looking, reflecting his reaction to the pervasive notions of materialism and material progress central to the social theory of Jeremy Bentham (1748–1832) and his followers. Thus, for example, in his reaction against materialism and the subjection of the one to the many, Carlyle asserts the primacy of the individual and the spiritual nature of the universe, drawing his inspiration from German transcendental philosophy. Like Macaulay, Carlyle was already established as a literary and social critic by the time of Queen Victoria's accession to the throne; he remained a force in Victorian letters for nearly fifty more years. Although his literary criticism is slight in volume as compared with his social and political works, it is nevertheless important for its introduction of German literature and thought to England and for its establishment of nonfictional prose as a medium well suited for carrying ideas to a mass audience. Suffused with moral sentiment and favoring an earnest sincerity as the hallmark of true literature, Carlyle's criticism sprang from the conviction, amply illustrated by his passionate advocacy of writers who evinced the quality, that literature, and poetry above all, was necessarily didactic. Carlyle, then, strove to establish the notions that literature was more than an amusement and that, read rightly, it could exert a great moral force.

While he was not a specifically literary critic, Ruskin deserves mention here, since he led the age in art criticism and helped form Victorian attitudes toward art and toward culture generally. His many volumes constitute the triumph of Victorian realism and prudery in the criticism of art. One literary dimension of his criticism is his curious application of the Romantic theory of poetry to the art of painting in his defense of J. M. W. Turner, a practice Charles Baudelaire also used in his defense of Eugène Delacroix. Again at the intersection of painting and poetry, Ruskin examined the work of the Pre-Raphaelite Brotherhood (formed in 1848). Praising Dante Gabriel Rossetti (1828–1882) and the other members of the brotherhood, Ruskin gave respectability to what might otherwise have been a marginal movement. The Pre-Raphaelites are notable for their advocacy and conscious imitation of Raphael and his medieval predecessors and represent, with William Morris (1834–1896), a remarkable aspect of Victorian critical and creative work, a medievalism popularized early in the century by Sir Walter Scott. This highly romanticized medievalism represents yet another paradox of the age: it was an era consecrated to Benthamite progress yet at odds with progress as it sought refuge in an earlier, presumably more innocent time. Like members of the Oxford Movement of the 1830s and 1840s in the Anglican church, who advocated a return to ritual and decoration absent since the Reformation, the Pre-Raphaelite Brotherhood elevated nostalgia. A major difference between the two movements, however, was the Oxford Movement's assertion of religious authority as opposed to the Pre-Raphaelites' declaration of freedom from received artistic authority. A later advocate and biographer of Rossetti whom Ruskin influenced both positively and negatively came to be as great an advocate of the art, architecture, poetry, and music of the Renaissance as Ruskin was their puritanical detractor: Walter Pater (1839–1894), founder of the aesthetic school of criticism. A great difference between Ruskin's and Pater's aesthetic theories has become clearer to succeeding generations in that Ruskin's insistence that art must be seen in a total context fell victim to Pater's much more selective focus on artistic elements and the

pleasurable sensations they produce. As a Calvinist, Ruskin had emphasized the social values of aesthetics and ethics; Pater, on the other hand, dismissed philosophical or moral claims upon art as external to it. Early in his career, Pater subscribed to the notion already popularized in France by Charles Baudelaire and Théophile Gautier: art for art's sake.

Before a full consideration of Pater, who achieved popularity and eminence in the 1870s, it is appropriate to examine two formidable and very different mid-Victorians who influenced him. Matthew Arnold (1822–1888) achieved distinction as a poet whose work has much in common with that of the Romantics and as an essayist who argued forcefully for Christian humanism. His critical achievement remains difficult to assess, and his principal critical tenets are open to varied interpretation and revaluation. Indeed, his prose writings are filled with self-contradictory and ambiguous elements. Like many of his contemporaries, he was attempting the difficult task of constructing an alternative world-view in the light of Darwin's new and startling theories of natural selection and evolution put forth in *On the Origin of Species* (1859) and *The Descent of Man and Selection in Relation to Sex* (1871).

Darwin's was not the first nineteenth-century voice to dissent from the praise of the Great Chain of Being, but it was the most eloquent. Earlier work in geology and paleontology had put into question the traditional interpretations of the Creation story in Genesis. The findings of German biblical scholarship, set forth in such works as David Friedrich Strauss' *Das Leben Jesu, kritisch bearbeitet* (1835–1836; *The Life of Christ: Or, A Critical Examination of His History*, 1843), unsettled traditional notions about Christianity. In France, Auguste Comte's philosophical positivism began forming the basis of a religion of humanity intended to supplant a worn-out Christianity. In England, Samuel Taylor Coleridge's attacks on common philosophical assumptions and his call for renewal early in the century were still being heeded by Arnold and his contemporaries. In this highly charged world of the 1860s and 1870s, with conservative rationalist thought jostled by doubt, science, skepticism, and no little cynicism, Arnold tried to reconstruct a theory of culture and to apply it to religion, social organization, and literature. In this as in every aspect of his life, Arnold was a seeker after truth and an able expositor of his findings.

As he strove to define culture, the relation of poetry to culture, and the function of criticism, Arnold bent his efforts to exhibit in his work a certain temper of mind, to present himself as the chief apostle and high priest of a new religion of culture. Using the guiding premises that literature is fundamentally a criticism of life and that literary criticism has for its function the discovery, analysis, and transmission of the best that is known and thought in the world, Arnold consistently attempted to establish a basis for a literary canon, spanning the centuries from Homer to his own time, that would include only the best and that would serve to shore up culture in the face of anarchy. In his famous *Essays in Criticism* (1865, 1888), Arnold followed Carlyle in adopting the roles of sage and prophet. Examining these roles gives the student of Arnold's prose an entry to the moral imperative in his work, a moral sense that poetry and criticism serve an ennobling and sacred purpose in the rites of culture. The suggestion that Arnold tried to create a religion of art, or to substitute art for religion, overlooks the subtle complexities of some of his thought but is still suggestive of one fruitful reading of his criticism and the secular-theological bent his work takes. Implicit in this view is a principle of authority at work in organizing the best in literature and culture to fashion it into a religion of humanity with at least the trappings of Christianity.

Poised against Arnold and clearly derisive of Carlyle is their contemporary Algernon Charles Swinburne (1837–1909), whose libertine and fleshly poetic concerns matched his critical concern for spreading the gospel of Charles Baudelaire and Victor Hugo in England. Swinburne's criticism, especially his rehabilitation of William Blake, sounded a new note in Victorian England: the battle cry of "art for art's sake." Like the earlier French Romantics, he set out to shock the middle class (the very philistines whom Arnold wanted to educate for the spread of culture) and to challenge the values of respectability and propriety by taking for his poetic themes a frank if decadent sensuality and overtly sexual behavior. So, too, in his criticism of the 1860s and early 1870s, Swinburne defended and celebrated French writers of the Romantic decadence who had proclaimed the artistic necessity of alienating themselves from society and its conventional restraints.

Swinburne's example is crucial to an understanding of most subsequent criticism that does not have cultural unity as its goal. Consequent upon alienation from society and dissociation from the middle class (for whom the Pre-Raphaelites, for example, painted and wrote) was the rapid retreat of artistic literature (especially poetry) from mass popularity and appeal, the segregation of artists into their various bohemias, and the retreat of criticism to academia. Artists and critics in the modern dispensation, then, use private voices to speak in public and seek expression more than communication.

Swinburne, it must be stressed, was far from representative of Victorian literary taste and criticism, though he did represent one reaction to the post-Darwinian world. John Morley, for example, a critic, biographer, historian, editor of the *Fortnightly Review*, and charter member of the Victorian radical intelligentsia, expressed his serious displeasure with Swinburne's *Poems and Ballads* (1866). Robert Buchanan, in a famous 1871 essay that could be a parody of itself, also decried "the fleshly school of poetry" and vehemently reasserted the values and morals of the middle class against the license he found in Rossetti and

Swinburne. Rossetti's "The Stealthy School of Criticism" (1872) was a measured rebuttal that set forth his aesthetic principles in a more moderate vein than did Swinburne's reply. It is also the case that Swinburne's pose of art for art's sake is only one element, possibly reflecting a temporary vogue, in his criticism, which is otherwise founded upon the critical principles of his French master, Hugo.

With Arnold and Swinburne providing very different views of culture and the public and private functions of literature, the stage was set for Walter Pater to become the most influential critical voice of the remainder of the Victorian Age. Pater's contribution to the criticism of the age was the formulating of an aesthetic criticism at odds with both Ruskin's art criticism (especially in its treatment of the Renaissance) and Arnold's attempted objectivity and establishment of a literary canon. Dismissing utilitarianism and moral aims, negating the "facile orthodoxy of Comte, or of Hegel," Pater's aesthetic criticism challenged Victorian solutions (Benthamism, positivism, Christian humanism) with a Romanticism that was self-conscious in its artistic vision and critical perspective and so went beyond Romanticism to share in the new tradition of secular humanism. In Pater's scheme, the key critical act involves knowing one's own impressions of a work as they really are, as opposed to the Arnoldian effort to see the object as in itself it really is – an effort which, as Pater showed, is doomed to futility. Success in life, then, consists in gathering multiple impressions of pleasure, of living as a "hard gem-like flame." With the publication of *Studies in the History of the Renaissance* (1873), Pater gained unwelcome notoriety as one in league with Swinburne (as indeed he was) in proclaiming art for art's sake. Like the medievalism of Rossetti and Morris, which Pater admired, the postulation of art for art's sake was in part a reassertion of the values of the Romantic rebellion against a highly industrialized society dominated by a middle class of stolidly conventional thought and morality.

In Pater's hands, art was no longer the didactic instrument Macaulay, Ruskin, Carlyle, and Arnold had made of it; instead, it became a refuge of pleasure in a world of "sick hurry and divided aims." Although his subsequent work did not have the same impact as *Studies in the History of the Renaissance* (which was, for Oscar Wilde, Pater's "Golden Book"), his examination of and comments on writers such as Gustave Flaubert, Stendhal, Baudelaire, Émile Zola, and Prosper Mérimée inspired a widespread interest in French literature that had surprisingly profound repercussions for the remainder of the Victorian Age and the twentieth century. Clearly, Pater is a central figure in a confused age, a writer whose critical perspective ratified the dichotomy between the artist and ordinary people, the critic and the public, despite the paradoxical fact that Pater opened the possibility of aesthetic criticism to all who would try it. This tension between the democratization of criticism and the elitism of the critic has been played out since Pater's formulation of aestheticism. Although a long-standing dissociation continues to exist between poetry and criticism on the one hand and the accessible world of popular culture on the other, it remains unclear whether the "aesthetic man" whom Ruskin opposed but Pater exalted will be replaced by the artist at home in the public sphere.

With a few notable exceptions, subsequent critics of the Victorian Age followed the example set by Pater. His willingness to write about controversial figures such as Baudelaire ("Romanticism," 1876), once Arnold had recanted his earlier enthusiasm for George Sand and Swinburne was no longer an active force in criticism, made Pater a leading influence. He clearly prepared the way for George Saintsbury (1845–1933) to begin his extraordinarily long and productive career with an 1877 essay on Baudelaire, followed by his series of histories and collections of French and English literature. Saintsbury's monumental three-volume work, *A History of Criticism and Literary Taste in Europe from the Earliest Texts to the Present Day* (1900–1904), began publication just before the end of Victoria's reign and established his reputation as the new century's leading academic critic. Saintsbury followed Pater in divorcing literature from didacticism but superseded Pater's aestheticism with an undisguised hedonism. He also meticulously avoided formulating a metaphysics of literature or principles of criticism. In denying literature a moral dimension or a pedagogical aim, Saintsbury further isolated literature from other modes of cultural expression; he consistently emphasized the formal and stylistic aspects of literature while passing over its content.

A more open disciple of Pater, Edmund Gosse (1849–1928), labored on behalf of French and Scandinavian literature in England and had as his purpose in criticism not instruction but appreciation – sharing the pleasures literature afforded him. His sharing, unlike that of his more flamboyant contemporaries, was cautious and reserved, marked by a concern for propriety that would exasperate Virginia Woolf and many others in the twentieth-century reaction against Victorianism. Like Saintsbury, Gosse was a professional critic; he wrote somewhat flawed histories of English literature and was among those responsible for the rediscovery and appreciation of the seventeenth-century Metaphysical poets, chiefly in calling attention to the extraordinary poetry and prose of John Donne.

Both Saintsbury and Gosse operated on principles that were embraced by many as the aesthetic movement grew. To later students of the period, however, these two are less noteworthy than other critics who achieved great notoriety in the last decades of Victoria's rule. George Moore (1852–1933), a key figure in the Celtic renaissance that had its origins in the nineteenth century, brought to his criticism the principles Pater had enunciated along with Parnassian notions that he had gathered in Paris. Moore's critical originality in a vein authorized by Pater (and

approved by him in a review of Moore's art criticism) is to be found in an impressionistic series of critical insights that tumble forth upon the page in an often-elliptical manner that does not admit discursive analysis. Although the resultant lack of consistency in his judgments at times diminishes the value of his work, his criticism is highly original in blending many of the currents of thought he had encountered in France, currents that transformed English literature and criticism in the 1890s.

Arthur Symons (1865–1945), an important contributor to *The Yellow Book* (1894–1897) and editor of *The Savoy* (1896), followed Pater's lead by writing aesthetic criticism that explored French literary and critical theory. More than any of his colleagues in the Rhymers' Club, William Butler Yeats (1865–1939) among them, Symons was thoroughly imbued with French Decadence and the spirit of the *fin de siècle*, reveling in the literature of an intense self-consciousness, an over-subtilizing, and a spiritual and moral perversity that he characterized as a new and beautiful and interesting disease. His highly important essay "The Decadent Movement in Literature" (1893) chronicles the state of literature in his age from an appreciative critical perspective. Since its original periodical publication, the essay has often appeared, in condensed form, as a prelude to his most important volume, and one of the most important of the Yellow Decade, *The Symbolist Movement in Literature* (1899). Yet a comparison of the works yields a very different authorial perspective: in the later work, Symons moves beyond aestheticism into mysticism, reflecting the unprecedented attention given to the occult in literary and critical thought during the first half of the period known formally as the Transitional Age (1880–1920).

Far more elusive is the critical thought and writing of Oscar Wilde (1854–1900). Patently aesthetic, frequently coy, elliptical, and paradoxical, Wilde's criticism derives from some of Pater's notions and (what is usually overlooked) some of Arnold's tenets, while still remaining highly original. For many, the brilliantly witty style Wilde employed has obscured the serious theories of aesthetics he set forth in his criticism and illustrated in his plays and fiction. Notably, he explored the complex relationships of art and life from a wholly different angle of vision from Arnold's. Indeed, Wilde's mimetic theory, not that art imitates life but that life imitates art, is far more psychologically complex than the theories of many of his contemporaries. Wilde's criticism, however, has fallen victim to the frivolous posturing in which he engaged and thus has not been fully explored. Still, his anti-Romanticism (placing man over nature and artifice above all), his antididacticism (emphasizing the symbolic), and his acute perception that the imagination is an independent faculty conspire to place him in the modernist line that has roots in Arnold's thought and, even more, in Pater's. Indeed, modernism cannot be said to have been born in the twentieth century, for its childhood and adolescence can be seen in the reign of Victoria. Modernism is incipient in Arnold and in Pater, in Thomas Hardy and in Joseph Conrad; it is also at the core of Symons' thought and surely present in all Wilde's work.

With this brief look at the aesthetic movement's impulses and products – many of them later flowerings of Romanticism and manifestations of a secular humanism emphasizing private vision – it is well to recall the comment made by Yeats during his period of fascination with aesthetic/Decadent theory: he believed that people would increasingly reject the opinion that poetry is a "criticism of life" in favor of the notion that it is a revelation of a hidden life. Thus, at the end of Victoria's era, the case for literature as a revelation of a hidden life had superseded the Arnoldian premise, just as new explanations for all human behavior were being explored in Vienna by Sigmund Freud – whose *Die Traumdeutung* (*The Interpretation of Dreams*, 1913) appeared in 1900 – and in England by Henry Havelock Ellis (1859–1939) and others.

Although many other literary critics who wrote during the Victorian Age have a just claim on the student's attention, examination of one important group is essential in any survey of the criticism of the period: the radical critics sometimes classified as the unbelievers, among them Frederic Harrison (1831–1923), T. H. Huxley (1825–1895), John Morley (1838–1923), and Sir Leslie Stephen (1832–1904). Some brief mention of the latter phase of William Morris and the early years of George Bernard Shaw (1856–1950) will shed further light on the vision of radical criticism in the late nineteenth century.

John Stuart Mill (1806–1873) is justly regarded as the most representative thinker of the Victorian era, and many elements of his thought are reflected in the work of several important critics of the time. His advocacy of Benthamism was tempered by an appreciation of the traditions and order celebrated by Coleridge. Though Mill's literary theories were set forth only in review articles, never synthesized in a longer work, he was highly influential in his dissemination of the ideas of Romantic poets and German and French philosophers. Three stages in Mill's evolving response to literature involve an early Benthamite concern for the political and moral content of art (to 1828), a second phase, during which he attempted, like Carlyle, to synthesize literary truth into a larger world-view (1828–1837), and a third stage (from 1837), during which he focused on the pragmatic utility of literature rather than on empirical truth. His agnosticism (a term coined by Huxley, "Darwin's Bulldog") influenced and attracted many to his circle. Thus, while Arnold, Swinburne, Pater, and subsequent mainstream and aesthetic critics pursued their critical inquiries, Mill and the radical rationalists and positivists pursued theirs.

As noted above, Darwin's findings challenged accepted views of the individual and society; earlier skeptics had already managed to cast doubt on traditional Christian beliefs. By the 1860s, unbelief had become respectable amid the ferment of lost and found bases of belief. It is remarkable, nevertheless, that thinkers of widely disparate views could still come together regularly to discuss and debate controversial issues. The members of the Metaphysical Society did exactly that between 1869 and 1880; they counted in their number the Roman Catholic Henry Cardinal Manning, Huxley, the poet laureate Alfred, Lord Tennyson, Ruskin, and Prime Minister William Ewart Gladstone. The rationalism, positivism, agnosticism, and socialism of Victorian England found their expression in the literary theory and criticism of these and other writers. It is a stream of criticism that has long been neglected in surveys of Victorian criticism.

Morley deserves to be remembered as much more than the man who took exception to Swinburne's erotic verse and, a few years later, less exception to Pater's new Cyrenaicism. Sympathetic to the avant-garde in politics and literature, Morley was chosen to succeed G. H. Lewes as the editor (1867–1882) of *The Fortnightly Review*. Under his leadership, the journal continued its war on the Victorian establishment and published pieces by Swinburne, Pater, Arnold, Stephen, Huxley, and Harrison. Bringing his rationalism to bear upon literature, Morley produced a wealth of essays and some volumes highly sympathetic to contemporary French and English literature. A critic in the mode of Arnold but without the investment in Christianity, Morley consistently looked to literature for an expression of the intellectual currents and tendencies of the time and, like many of his peers, for a synthesis of the age. A devout humanist, he prized "art for man's sake," a perspective that characterized his editorship of *The Fortnightly Review*, *The Pall Mall Gazette*, and the English Men of Letters series.

Huxley, the controversial prophet of science militant who elaborated and popularized Darwin's thought, was not a critic of literature but must be recognized for his influence on those in his circle of agnostic writers and, negatively, those at the opposite pole of faith. Huxley's defense of Darwin forced members of his generation to confront the implications of evolutionary thought for their understanding of the human race and morality, yet with a reasonableness that made the acceptance of new ideas less traumatic than it might have been. Harrison, like Huxley an unbeliever but unlike him a positivist, was attacked by Huxley; Arnold, too, characterized him as a leading proponent of anarchy. His criticism of contemporary literature, collected in *Studies in Early Victorian Literature* (1895) and *Tennyson, Ruskin, Mill, and Other Literary Estimates* (1899), evidences his apostleship of positivism and humanism and reveals him to have been an extraordinarily perceptive observer of his own era.

Stephen rounds out the number of distinguished unbelievers whose criticism of life and of literature constituted a major force in Victorian consciousness. With Harrison and Morley, Stephen helped to build a theory of historical development that represented a clear alternative to the theories of theologians, idealists, and pre-Darwinian rationalists. Through his studies of Samuel Johnson, Alexander Pope, Jonathan Swift, George Eliot, and Robert Louis Stevenson, as well as through the works he wrote for his grand creation, the *Dictionary of National Biography* (1882–1970), Stephen served as a disseminator but not necessarily an originator of ideas. Thus, to read Stephen is to learn much about his age from a basically positivist perspective, marked by the intentional fallacy and an appreciation of the moral element in literature. Stephen also has the distinction of having adapted Comte's thought into the most notable quasi-Marxist theory of intellectual history in Victorian England.

The Marxist or socialist question occupied many of the late Victorians. William Morris, for example, disenchanted with his own Pre-Raphaelitism, never quite abandoned his medievalism but became a militant socialist in his cultural criticism. The young George Bernard Shaw too was imbued with a spirit of socialism that colored such literary criticism as *The Quintessence of Ibsenism* (1891) and the view of the place of art and literature expressed in *Fabian Essays in Socialism* (1889), which he edited. The Fabian socialist perspective, eschewing Marxism and utopianism alike, was and remains an active force in the criticism of society and, by extension, of literature.

Criticism in the Age of Victoria, then, is richly varied, more than ample in bulk, diffuse in its aims and accomplishments, and unquestionably relevant to the many schools and strains of critical inquiry in the twentieth century. To summarize this diverse body of criticism and to assert for it its rightful place in the development of subsequent literary criticism, one may turn again to Dickens and replicate the claim "that some of its noisiest authorities insisted on its being received, for good or evil, in the superlative degree of comparison only."

## Further reading

Altick, Richard D. *Victorian People and Ideas: A Companion for the Modern Reader of Victorian Literature*, 1973.
Buckley, J. H. *The Victorian Temper: A Study in Literary Culture*, 1951.
Cevasco, G. A. *The 1890s: An Encyclopedia of British Literature, Art, and Culture*, 1993.
Dale, Peter A. *The Victorian Critic and the Idea of History*, 1977.
De Laura, David, ed. *Victorian Prose: A Guide to Research*, 1973.
Gibbons, Tom. *Rooms in the Darwin Hotel: Studies in English Literary Criticism and Ideas 1880–1920*, 1973.
Houghton, Walter E. *The Victorian Frame of Mind, 1830–1870*, 1957.
Levene, George, and William Madden, eds. *The Art of Victorian Prose*, 1968.
McGann, Jerome, ed. *Victorian Connections*, 1989.
Meisel, Perry. *The Myth of the Modern*, 1987.
Miller, J. Hillis. *The Disappearance of God: Five Nineteenth-Century Writers*, 1963.
Mitchell, Sally, ed. *Victorian Britain: An Encyclopedia*, 1988.
Roston, Murray. *Victorian Contexts: Literature and the Visual Arts*, 1996.

JOHN J. CONLON

*See also* Aestheticism; Arnold; Hopkins; Mill; Pater; Ruskin; Symbolism; Swinburne; Symonds; Symons; Wilde

# Liu Hsieh

Chinese philosopher and theorist

**Born:** Chü, Guan Province, China; c. A.D. 465
**Died:** c. A.D. 522, China

## Biography

Although Liu Hsieh's exact date of birth is not recorded, various sources indicate that he may have been born in 465 in the district of Chü in Guan (Shantung) Province, China. Early in Liu Hsieh's childhood, his father, a middle-ranking military officer, died and left his family impoverished. Liu was forced to leave his family and seek shelter in a Buddhist temple. He stayed under the care of a renowned and learned Buddhist monk, Seng You, for more than ten years. During this period Liu studied Buddhist philosophy extensively, which later helped him to formulate the comprehensive framework for his critical theories.

After the completion of his masterpiece, *The Literary Mind and the Carving of Dragons*, he began to enjoy a literary reputation, which paved the way for a political career during the Liang Dynasty (502–557). Serving first in low-ranking positions, Liu, in approximately 507, became the chief magistrate in the district of T'ai Mo (located in Chechiang Province) and earned a reputation as a just administrator. Several years later he began to work as a secretary for the crown prince, Hsiao Tung, a patron of literature. Liu was ordered by Emperor Hsiao Yen to edit the Buddhist sutras in Ding Lin Temple. Once the task was completed, Liu asked for the emperor's permission to become a Buddhist monk. Less than a year after becoming a monk, Liu died, in approximately 522. Because of his poverty, as well as his religious beliefs, he never married.

## Influence

Because of his comprehensive theory, Liu Hsieh has been a source of inspiration for both writers and critics in the Chinese literary tradition. His study not only greatly enhanced the critic's understanding of classical Chinese literature but also offered the writer principles exemplary for literary composition. As a result of his work, a systematic and objective literary criticism became possible in China. His metaphysical concept of literature also led to the appearance of the Zen school of criticism. Furthermore, he helped to correct the overly embellished writings of his era, which were seen as spurious, lacking genuine senti-ment. Through his efforts to change this style of literature, Liu set the course for an eventual countermovement in the T'ang and Sung dynasties (618–1279), when writers attempted to emulate the style of the classics.

## Analysis

In the history of classical Chinese literature, Liu Hsieh is regarded as the greatest of literary critics. His only existing critical work is *The Literary Mind and the Carving of Dragons*. Written in verse, *The Literary Mind and the Carving of Dragons* is not only a masterpiece in criticism but also a literary work of great aesthetic quality. Liu Hsieh's critical work appeared at a time of great political turmoil in Chinese history; literature, however, thrived. The pursuit of literary fame had long been in vogue by Liu's time, as a result of the promotion of literature by Emperor Wei Wen (187–226), known as Ts'ao P'i. Liu himself made it clear in his postface to *The Literary Mind and the Carving of Dragons* that he wrote the book with the intention of obtaining literary fame. Because of the excessive develop-ment of literature, many of Liu's contemporaries experi-enced difficulty in finding new subject matter for their literary creations and, instead, made diction their primary concern. They endeavored to distinguish themselves through the creation of an ornate, idiosyncratic style without proper regard for the content of their work. To correct this narrow view of literary creation, Liu made it his task to construct a literary theory that would address this issue of creativity. In addition, his dissatisfaction with the critical work of the past motivated him to contribute significantly to the field of literary criticism.

As a result of Buddhist influence, which was introduced into China in the first century, Liu Hsieh began his literary theory with the metaphysical exploration of the nature of *wên*, which means, depending on the context, "literature," "culture," or "the configuration of natural phenomenon." As an inevitable manifestation of the natural process, *wên* (literature), he states, coexists metaphysically with the universe. The mind creates language and literature; nature, however, fosters human beings and, by doing so, causes them to be the mind of nature. Consequently, literature is viewed as the mind of nature and has its transcendental basis with the formation of the universe. In the light of this metaphysical relationship between nature and humans, a sage is a writer who is able to perceive the essence of this world and render it into literature. Through the sage-writer, truth is most effectively expressed; through literature, the sage-writer, in turn, comprehends truth. This metaphysical approach to literature is quite different from the traditional pragmatic approach, which Liu originally inherited as part of his cultural upbringing. Moving beyond the boundary of this conventional Confucianist approach, Liu ventured to raise his theory to a cosmic level and traced the origin of literature to the creation of the world.

Based on the creative process of nature, literary compo-sition, according to Liu, should be refined expressions of natural feelings, an appropriate blending of form and content. He illustrates this idea with the example of a tree with blossoms: a tree would have to be sturdy and healthy in order to bloom fully. Therefore emotions – the content – should precede language – the form – in literary creation. Because ancient writers composed in order to express their feelings, while many later writers simulated their emotions in order to write, Liu thus held ancient classics as the model for genuine literary writing. Liu's esteem for the classics is not blind worship of antiquity, an idea commonly accepted in Chinese tradition. He used the unadorned style of the classics to remedy the extremely ornate and idiosyncratic writings of his era.

His concept of literary composition is further illustrated in his study of genres. Classifying Chinese writings into twenty genres, some of which overlap, Liu specified the particular norms required by each. His thorough study of each genre – its definition, historical development, and representative writers – helped to formulate a practical guide for writers.

In discussing the formation and development of litera-ture, Liu exhibits an excellent knowledge of history. While previous critics, such as Ts'ao P'i and Lu Chi (261–303), emphasized the importance of individual talent, Liu stressed the politico-historical influence upon a writer. Although Liu also recognized the significance of individual genius, he employed many other approaches that would account for the formation of literature. His study of the historical devel-opment of Chinese literature led him to conclude that an emperor's policy is normally one of the dominant factors influencing the way in which literature is created. In Liu's own illustration, the influence of emperors on writers is like wind blowing over water – wherever the wind blows, the waves follow.

Inheriting a traditional Confucianist view, Liu also incor-porated a social approach into his critical theory. As a social being, a writer is inevitably influenced by society and should create literature that will in turn influence society. In his analysis of the historical development of Chinese literature, he indicates that literature of the recent past has degener-ated as a result of its lack of concern for society and the preoccupation with the private world of the self. Regardless of its concern for society, literature is not equivalent to social propaganda. Therefore, Liu advises the writer to use metaphorical expressions rather than explicit statements to voice his or her social concerns.

Liu also employed a geographical approach. The creative process, as Liu sees it, originates in the correspondence between a poet's mind and the natural environment. This relationship between the poet and nature is a reciprocal one: the poet views nature with feelings; nature inspires the poet with emotions. As a result, the natural environment finds expression in literature. Basing his analysis on the theory of geographical influence, Liu observed the two contrasting styles in Chinese literature: the unadorned style of the north represented by the poetry collection *Shih Ching* (c. 1066–541 B.C.; the *Book of Songs*) and the florid style of the south represented by the collection *Li Shao* (c. 298 B.C.; encountering sorrow). Critics before Liu had certainly noted these two different styles of ancient poetry. It was Liu, however, who attributed the difference to a geographical influence, a new approach that found favor among many later critics.

The greatest contribution Liu made to Chinese literary theory was his establishment of a methodology in literary criticism. Since its appearance in the third century, Chinese literary criticism had been based more on personal impressions than on objective standards. Critics in general judged a literary work in accordance with subjective feelings rather than on an established methodology. Revolting against this tradition of subjective criticism, Liu advocated an objective approach. The problem with literary criticism, according to Liu, does not lie so much in the difficulty of a literary text as in a critic's knowledge of and approach to the text. The process of critique is the opposite of literary creation. Whereas a poet feels before creating a literary work, a critic studies the work before being able to feel with the poet. As long as there exists the literary text, Liu argues that, through the study of the text, a critic can always detect the author's original ideas and emotions, thereby making criticism possible. The study of a text thus becomes the focus of Liu's theory of criticism. Before studying a work, critics, he suggests, should rid themselves of every kind of bias. For example, they should not exalt ancient literature above contemporary writings, nor should they approve or disapprove of works simply because they may or may not have the same style or approach as their own. In Liu's view, a critic needs to consider the various aspects of a work, such as content, organization, diction, meter, imagination, and originality. Liu's emphasis on the intrinsic merits of a literary work and his demand for invariable standards marked the beginning of a new era of criticism based on an objective and systematic study of literature.

Although Liu's theory has commanded great respect throughout Chinese literary history, *The Literary Mind and the Carving of Dragons* surprisingly failed to attract the attention of his contemporaries when it first appeared. Liu, however, was able to solicit the respected opinion of one of the leading literary and political figures of his day, Shen Yue (441–512). Shen praised the work and, from that day on, Liu was famous. His book, which is a synthesis of Confucianist and Buddhist thought, has since his time been widely read and admired, exerting an enormous influence on Chinese literature. Both writers and critics found inspiration in his theory of literature and criticism. His advocacy of an ideal blending of content and form, feeling and language, helped to end the practice of an ornate style of writing and to stem the development of erotic literature, which was referred to as "poetry of the palace." Eventually, his theory paved the way for the countermovement in the T'ang and Sung dynasties, when writers returned to the unadorned style of the classics.

Apart from rectifying the literary trend of his time, Liu greatly influenced the future development of Chinese literary criticism. His investigation of the metaphysical nature of literature later developed into the school of Zen criticism, which was primarily concerned with the relationship between literature and the universe. Because of his studies and interpretations, the significance and development of ancient literature became easily comprehensible. Furthermore, his approaches have been widely applied to this day. His establishment of a methodology in criticism undoubtedly made Chinese critics aware of the importance of using objective principles. As a result of his efforts, Chinese criticism became a systematic study of literature rather than an expression of personal sentiment.

## Principal criticism

*Wên-hsin tiao-lung*, c. sixth century (*The Literary Mind and the Carving of Dragons: A Study of Thought and Pattern in Chinese Literature*, 1959)

## Other major work and literary forms

Liu Hsieh is known primarily as a literary theorist. His only other work is a long philosophical essay entitled "Mieh Huo Lun" (c. 507; on extinguishing all doubts). This work is a debate in which Liu defends Buddhism against conventional Chinese thought.

NONFICTION
"Mieh Huo Lun," c. 507

## Further reading

Ch'en, Shou-yi. *Chinese Literature*, 1961.
Chi, Ch'iu-lang. "Liu Hsieh as a Classicist and His Concepts of Tradition and Change," in *Tamkang Review*. IV (April, 1973), pp. 89–108.
Liu, James J. Y. *Chinese Theories of Literature*, 1975.
Rickett, Adele Austin. *Chinese Approaches to Literature from Confucius to Liang Ch'i-ch'ao*, 1978.
Shao, Paul Young Shing. "Liu Hsieh as Literary Theorist, Critic and Rhetorician," in *Dissertation Abstracts International*. 42, no. 8 (February, 1982), p. 3605A
Shih, Vincent Yu-chung. Introduction to *The Literary Mind and the Carving of Dragons: A Study of Thought and Pattern in Chinese Literature*, 1959.
Wong, W. L. "The Carved Dragon and the Well Wrought Urn: Notes on the Concept of Structure in Liu Hsieh and the New Critics," in *Tamkang Review: A Quarterly of Comparative Studies between Chinese and Foreign Literatures*. 14, nos. 1–4 (Autumn–Summer, 1983–1984), pp. 555–568.

VINCENT YANG

*See also* Chinese Literary Theory; Lu Chi

# David Lodge

English novelist and critic

**Born:** London, England; January 28, 1935

## Biography

David Lodge was born and raised in the largely working-class Dulwich area of south London. His Catholic upbringing and education, his experiences during and immediately after World War II, and his period of national service are among the biographical facts that Lodge turned to narrative advantage in his early novels: *The Picturegoers* (1960), *Ginger, You're Barmy* (1962), and *Out of the Shelter* (1970). However, it is as a writer of comic campus novels that Lodge is best known as an imaginative writer. *The British Museum is Falling Down* (1965), his first comic novel, draws on his experiences as a married Catholic graduate student at University College, London (Lodge married in 1959), and was written under the influence of his friend and fellow novelist/critic Malcolm Bradbury. *Changing Places* (1975) draws on Lodge's tenure at the University of Birmingham from 1961 to 1987 and the year he spent as a visiting professor at the University of California, Berkeley, during the 1960s. *Small World* (1984) revisits these settings while greatly expanding the campus novel genre in and for the age of the "global campus" with which Lodge became familiar as his international reputation grew. Lodge retired early (1987) from his teaching post at Birmingham to devote himself full-time to writing: not only criticism, reviews, and novels (*Paradise News*, 1991, and *Therapy*, 1995), but a play entitled *The Writing Game* (1991) and television adaptations of his own work and that of others, most notably Charles Dickens' *Martin Chuzzlewit*.

## Influence

Lodge's chief claim to fame as a critic and literary theorist is not as an original thinker but instead as a versatile and highly influential adapter, interpreter, disseminator, and evaluator of many of the most important critical and theoretical trends of the postwar period. As a self-described formalist "conditioned by the Arnoldian tradition," Lodge has taken a keen interest not only in how novels work but in why it should matter that they work the way they do. As he has pointed out, formalist criticism tells us everything about a novel except why narrative matters, why people need it. At a time when literary theory has grown increasingly rarefied, self-involved, and detached from its ostensible subject and increasingly inaccessible to nonspecialists, Lodge has remained interested in theory's practical uses and applications and in the consequences of specific theories and of the theoretical turn in general. Equally important, he has sought, in a variety of ways, to bridge the growing distance between academic and general audiences, between literary criticism and literary journalism,

with his novels often serving as a vital link between the two. *Nice Work* (1988), for example, comically updates the "condition of England" novel for an era of high-flown theories on the one hand and economic austerity in academia as well as in industry on the other. Although by no means overtly or ideologically polemic in his thinking or his writing, Lodge, both as critic and as comic, gently satiric novelist, does have a preferred position which he unobtrusively propounds. His interest in and practice of "critical pluralism" and the comic novel imply an essentially liberal humanist position, with a decided Catholic twist. This subtext manifests itself most in the way Lodge's practice as popular campus/Catholic novelist and respected critic builds on "the thesis of Frank Kermode's brilliant and stimulating study, *The Sense of an Ending*, where he argues that the history of fiction is the history of a continuous dialogue or dialectic between credulity – our wish to believe – and scepticism – our wish to be told the truth."

## Analysis

In his first major work of literary criticism, *The Language of Fiction* (1966), Lodge takes issue with the tendency on the part of New Critics to prize poetry over prose and with critics of the novel who either have adopted the tools of the New Criticism in an unnecessarily narrow way (for the study of imagery and symbolism only) or have turned away from the language of fiction altogether to pursue other approaches (the mythic and the psychological in particular). Contending that the poetry–prose dichotomy is false, Lodge proposes a continuum having the poetic at one end, the prosaic at the other, with most writing falling somewhere in-between. In a rather bold move for the time, Lodge resists the overvaluing of poetic prose stylists such as Gustave Flaubert and Marcel Proust to the detriment of the significant but less self-apparent artistry of realist writers whose prose is generally believed to be merely serviceable (and therefore easily translatable). Much of *The Language of Fiction* is therefore devoted to making the case for realism as art using the same New Critical tools previously applied to poetry and poetic prose. However, Lodge warns, linguistic analysis should not replace literary analysis. The problem with the kind of purely "scientific stylistics" practiced by Michael Riffaterre and others is that it fails to deal not just satisfactorily but at all with questions of value that are central to the novel as Lodge defines it.

In asserting this point, Lodge makes clear his liberal humanist position and bias. "In literary discourse, the writer discovers what he has to say in the process of saying it, and the reader discovers what is said in responding to the way it is said." Although the individual literary work has an objective existence which must be acknowledged and can be objectively/linguistically described, the value of a given work derives from its being part of not a specific historical context, as his friend Bradbury claims, but "a process of human communication which is not amenable to objective description." In this way, Lodge combines the axiological concerns of an F. R. Leavis with the close scrutiny of Riffaterre's "scientific stylistics" to arrive at the following position: that values are embedded in and inseparable from the novelist's specific use of language. "For ultimately language is the only tangible evidence we have for those vast, vague, unreliable qualities which we bandy about in literary criticism: 'truth to life,' 'moral seriousness,' 'psychological insight,' 'social awareness.'" Part of a larger resurgence of interest in the novel after two decades of neglect inspired by the fashion for New Criticism and the usefulness of New Critical methods in the greatly expanded systems of higher education in the United States and Britain, *The Language of Fiction* quickly became the touchstone for other critics of the novel. Having made his case, Lodge, however, moved on to other, more recent literary tools and theories by which he could strengthen and update the case for the art of realism in a postrealist age. His subsequent interest in structuralist, semiotic, narratological, and dialogical theories would also lead him to question the wisdom of his influential first book and its "overly stylistic approach."

Having settled his quarrel with, and made his appropriation of, the New Criticism in *The Language of Fiction*, Lodge moved on to a new challenge in *The Novelist at the Crossroads* (1971). Impressed by Frank Kermode's *The Sense of an Ending*, Lodge set out to challenge the argument made by Robert Scholes in another recent, equally influential critical study, *The Fabulators*. Rather than reject realism out of hand as a viable option for the contemporary novelist, as Scholes does in making his case for the more or less fantastic, irrealist, metafictional novels of John Barth, John Fowles, Kurt Vonnegut, and others, Lodge posits a "period of unprecedented cultural pluralism" in which the contemporary novelist faces two equally appealing but mutually exclusive possibilities: fabulation, which is impatient with reality, and "empirical narrative," which is impatient with fiction. Loyal to both but lacking confidence in either alone (as well as in the ability to reconcile them), the novelist finds him- or herself at a crossroads (especially the English novelist aware of his or her own provincialism and inadequacy in the face of American expansiveness). There the novelist hesitates – indeed he or she builds his or her hesitation into the novel (as Lodge does in *Changing Places*). The result is a form that Lodge calls "the problematic novel," with its "modest affirmation in the future of realistic fiction" as opposed to the dead ends of those two "radical forms," Scholes' fabulation and Truman Capote's and Norman Mailer's nonfiction novel. The problematic novel implies a restored realism as well as a Kermode-like "balance between credulity and scepticism." It is precisely this latter point, the playing back and forth between faith and doubt, that provides a measure of coherence to what is otherwise a rather disparate group of essays that make up most of the pages of *The Novelist*

*at the Crossroads and Other Essays on Fiction and Criticism*. These include essays on one of Lodge's favorite subjects, Catholic novelists, as well as essays about the doubtful value of the Neo-Aristotelian approach to contemporary criticism (such as Bradbury's). The reader also finds a certain faith on Lodge's part in the value of innovative fiction. This is a faith tempered by a degree of skepticism about innovative fiction's most enthusiastic and perhaps least discriminating supporters. ("Have we come to handle the avant-garde too gently?" Lodge asks in an essay on William Burroughs.) Lodge expresses a similar ambivalence and concern about the future of criticism as a collaborative enterprise, a conversation as it were, able to maintain its contact with an audience of general readers.

Lodge's own desire to maintain contact with an audience of nonspecialists, for whom he wishes to serve as guide and interpreter rather than distant god in an academic ivory tower of specialization and specialized vocabulary, comes up against his equally powerful desire to put the kind of realistic fiction that he and the general audience prefer on a firm theoretical foundation at a time when innovative fiction and theories of the writerly text seem about to declare realism as dead, or at least as retrograde, as old-fashioned ideas about "the author." Thus the problematic brilliance of *The Modes of Modern Writing* (1977). Drawing on the distinction between metaphor and metonymy made by the structural linguist Roman Jakobson, Lodge attempts to devise "a comprehensive typology of literary discourses . . . capable of describing and discriminating between all types of text without prejudging them." The problem of labeling and prejudging is one Lodge finds particularly troubling. Writing that is not considered modern is considered realistic and therefore retrograde, and dismissed as if no further analysis were necessary. In place of the poetry–prose continuum posited in *The Language of Fiction*, Lodge now offers the opposition between metaphor and metonymy along with a brief history of modern English literature in terms of oscillation (between the two poles) rather than evolution. According to this formulation, realism is not less literary and less advanced than modernism, merely more inclined to exploit metonymy rather than (as modernist texts do) metaphor. In an inspired if not entirely convincing move, Lodge uses Roland Barthes' *S/Z* to support his position, contending that what Barthes demonstrates is not in fact the poverty of the readerly realistic text but its richness in so far as in realism "nothing is ever merely referential." Equally impressive but more persuasive is Lodge's typological analysis of postmodern fiction which leads him to conclude that although individual postmodern writers clearly prefer one pole or another, metaphor or metonymy, postmodern fiction overall employs both equally but in "radically new ways." The result, Lodge goes on to note, is liberating but because postmodernism is "essentially a rule-breaking kind of art," it only makes sense if others are keeping the rules, which is to say the rules of realism, either conventional or restored.

Lodge's engagement with the latest critical theories and the challenges they pose continues in *Working with Structuralism* (1981). Once again the challenge is twofold: to the kind of realistic fiction and to the kind of criticism, comprehensible to the lay reader, that Lodge prefers but sees is under continued threat. The question then, for Lodge, is not as Robert Frost puts it in one of his poems, "what to make of a diminished thing" (or two things in Lodge's case), but "how to work with structuralism . . . without being dominated by it." Drawing on the work of the Russian Formalist critics and more recent narratologists (especially Gérard Genette and Seymour Chatman), Lodge reformulates the oscillation between metaphor and metonymy from *The Modes of Modern Writing* as one between *fabula* and *sjuzet*, narrative and narration, or more simply between what a novel says and how it says it. What one generation of writers foregrounds, the *what* for example, the next puts in the background so as to better foreground the other, the *how*, and so on. Put in semiotic terms, where the generation of late-nineteenth-century realists foregrounded the signified (crudely understood, the sign's or signifier's referent or meaning), the generation of early-twentieth-century modernists that followed them foregrounded the signifier (and with it the process of signification and signs as arbitrary, altogether human constructs). In making this claim, Lodge is in effect returning to the point made in his previous book: that we can only understand and appreciate what one generation of writers does by comparing and contrasting their works with those who come before and after them and, further, that each is equally literary, albeit each in its own way.

If Lodge's next book, *After Bakhtin* (1990), is a more satisfying explanation of recent literary theory than *Working with Structuralism*, the reason may well be that in Mikhail Bakhtin's theory of the dialogical novel Lodge found a concept more in tune with his own thinking and a theorist who cared just as deeply as Lodge does about not only the language and structure of fiction but about the necessary linkage between language and value as well and about criticism as "a contribution to human knowledge." Although *After Bakhtin* mainly comprises essays published before Lodge retired from his position at the University of Birmingham, the collection itself was published shortly after and reflects its author's deep dissatisfaction with the inaccessibility and self-involvement of much recent criticism, the failure of its practitioners to be sufficiently interested in criticism as a mode of exploration and explanation. In much the same way that Bakhtin rescues the author from the death sentence that poststructuralism imposed, Lodge wishes to resuscitate criticism as a way of understanding and a means of communication. Lodge's position here is, of course, deeply conservative, though his conservatism should not be construed as

aesthetically or politically reactionary. His varied forays into many of the new critical theories of the postwar period led him to believe that his early faith in the language of fiction had been not so much wrong as incomplete and that narrative and narration form a language of their own, whose deep structure structuralism and poststructuralism could help make visible. That task done, Lodge resumed the role he felt too many literary critics had abjured, making literature accessible and understandable to interested readers who were not literary specialists. Thus *The Art of Fiction* (1992), which borrows its title from Henry James' famous essay and which comprises fifty short essays on literary topics from "Beginning" to "Ending" that were originally written for the *Independent on Sunday* at the request of that newspaper's literary editor, Blake Morrison, and *The Practice of Writing* (1996), "a collection of occasional prose pieces" mainly written after his retirement (just as those in the earlier collection *Write On*, 1986, had been written before). Many of these essays deal with Lodge's own practice as a writer as well as with his belief that the purpose of criticism should be "to demystify and shed light on the creative power." Both directly and indirectly, the two books evidence the ever charitable Lodge's faith in writing in general and realism in particular and his hope for its future in the face of theory's challenge. Noting realism's resilience and sturdiness, he wonders, perhaps a bit too optimistically, whether "the practice of writing" evident in the proliferation of university writing programs "may supersede the fashion for theory which began in the nineteen-sixties, and now seems to have exhausted the energy and interest of even its devotees."

## Principal criticism
*Language of Fiction*, 1966
*Evelyn Waugh*, 1971
*The Novelist at the Crossroads and Other Essays on Fiction and Criticism*, 1971
*The Modes of Modern Writing: Metaphor, Metonymy, and the Typology of Modern Literature*, 1977
*Working with Structuralism: Essays and Reviews on Nineteenth- and Twentieth-Century Literature*, 1981
*Write On: Occasional Essays '65–'85*, 1986
*After Bakhtin: Essays on Fiction and Criticism*, 1990
*The Art of Fiction: Illustrated from Classic and Modern Texts*, 1992
*The Practice of Writing*, 1996

## Other major works and literary forms
In addition to his literary criticism, David Lodge has written a large number of reviews for a variety of publications ranging from the Catholic newspaper *The Tablet* to the *Times Literary Supplement* and the *New York Review of Books*. He has also written revues, a play, a handful of short stories and television adaptations, and edited a number of works, most notably *Twentieth Century Literary Criticism: A Reader* (1972) and *Modern Criticism and Theory* (1988). His formidable reputation as a literary critic

is surpassed by his work as a novelist: *The Picturegoers* (1960), *Ginger, You're Barmy* (1962), *The British Museum is Falling Down* (1965), *Out of the Shelter* (1970), *Changing Places* (1975), *How Far Can You Go?* (1980), *Small World* (1984), *Nice Work* (1988), *Paradise News* (1991), and *Therapy* (1995).

## Further reading

Bradbury, Malcolm. "The Language Novelists Use," in *Kenyon Review*. 29 (1966), pp. 122–136.
Brooke-Rose, Christine. *A Rhetoric of the Unreal*, 1981.
D'Haen, Theo. "Fowles, Lodge, and the 'Problematic Novel,'" in *Dutch Quarterly Review of Anglo-American Letters*. 9 (1979), pp. 162–175.
Eagleton, Terry. "The Silences of David Lodge," in *New Left Review*. 172 (1988), pp. 93–102.
Haffenden, John. *Novelists in Interview*, 1985.
Morace, Robert A. *The Dialogic Novels of Malcolm Bradbury and David Lodge*, 1989.
Moseley, Merritt. *David Lodge*, 1991.
Smallwood, Philip. *Modern Critics in Practice*, 1990.
Widdowson, Peter. "The Anti-History Men: Malcolm Bradbury and David Lodge," in *Critical Quarterly*. 26 (1984), pp. 5–32.

ROBERT A. MORACE

*See also* Bradbury; British Literary Theory: Twentieth Century; Ricks

# Longinus

## Greek theorist

**Born:** Place unknown; early to mid-first century A.D.
**Died:** Place unknown; mid- to late first century A.D.

## Biography

Longinus wrote in Greek, had a broad knowledge of literature, nursed an antipathy to conventional rhetoric-oriented modes of criticism, and addressed his essay to a Roman citizen named Postumius Terentianus. His essay challenged and used as a point of departure an identically titled essay by one Caecilius of Calacte, a Sicilian rhetorician of the first century B.C. Apart from wisps of biographical information to be inferred from the text itself, such as his having written two treatises on synthesis (which are not extant), there is not much more, if anything, that one can say with certainty about Longinus.

Longinus' real identity is difficult to establish. The earliest manuscript includes in the title of the work the name "Dionysius Longinus" and, in a list of contents, the cryptic addition "Dionysius or Longinus." The author commonly known as Longinus could be Dionysius of Halicarnassus, a prolific rhetorician who lived in Rome after 30 B.C., or Cassius Longinus, an Athenian rhetorician of philosophical inclination who was a friend, or at least an acquaintance, of the philosopher Plotinus (c. A.D. 204–270). Cassius Longinus went on to teach at Palmyra and Zenobia and was executed in A.D. 273 as an enemy of Rome. That the author was probably neither of these individuals but a rhetorician of the first century A.D. is the argument of scholars who assume that the work's style is different from that of Dionysius of Halicarnassus and is alien to the style of the third century A.D. These scholars maintain that the work itself reflects temporal proximity to Caecilius of Calacte. The argument is far from convincing, but, until the identity of the author is indisputably established, the name Longinus will be used.

## Influence

Longinus is the contributor of the concept of "the sublime" to literary criticism. His exposition of the term has prevailed since its inception in late classical antiquity. *On the Sublime* provided eighteenth- and early-nineteenth-century authors with their focus on the inexplicable factor that elevates literature to what Alexander Pope called "a grace beyond the reach of art," or, as William Wordsworth put it, the "light that never was, on sea or land,/ The consecration, and the Poet's dream." The Longinian aesthetics of the sublime as the transcendent element that transmutes a literary work into more than the sum of its parts persisted in literary criticism and can be found even in the higher criticism of the later twentieth century. Any student of the sublime in art must acknowledge Longinus as not the inventor of the term but the critic who formulated and stabilized the concept.

## Analysis

Longinus describes the sublime (*hypsous*) as "a certain high excellence of expression by virtue of which the greatest writers of prose and poetry have achieved preeminence and timeless recognition." He lists three impediments to sublimity and five sources of it. The impediments are affectation, cold pedantry, and sentimentality. The sources are great intellectual conception, forceful and spirited emotion, figures of thought and figures of speech, dignified phrasing, and *synthesis*.

The first two sources of excellence constitute the major conflicting elements that great art reconciles. Specifically, these are intellection and emotion, or, to use the words of the author, *noesis* and *pathos*. These initially give form to the character of the artist, who in turn gives them form as literary expression. The remaining three sources embellish and intensify that expression.

Figures of thought are to be differentiated from figures of speech as *noesis* is differentiated from *pathos*. Longinus does not provide examples of figures of thought, noting only that they appeal to the intellect. He does, however, provide many examples of figures of speech and the ways in which they appeal to the emotions. He claims, for example, that rhetorical questions by their very configuration yoke and intensify intellectual practicality and stirring emotion. He asserts his claim, moreover, in the form of two rhetorical questions. He goes on to tell his addressee that figures are most effective when they are concealed or unobtrusive, and in the telling he unobtrusively introduces similes. His compendium of figures of speech, all exemplified from literature and oratory and many further exemplified by his manner of presenting them, include apostrophe, oath, rhetorical question, asyndeton, anaphora, polysyndeton, historical present, direct address to the second person, abrupt change from third- to first-person speech, and periphrasis. The missing segments of the essay doubtless included many others.

Dignified phrasing is "the selection of appropriate and splendid words" and "well-chosen words are," as such, "the light of the mind." Dignified phrasing extends to the use of metaphors, similes, and hyperbole. These are akin to figures of thought in that they make one think, and they are most effective when used in contexts of *pathos*. Figures which entail comparison lead the mind to apprehend not only the similarity of the apparently dissimilar elements but also the unity of them. When this mental apprehension is achieved through an emotional passage there is a union of *noesis* and *pathos*, of thought and emotion, which is evidence of sublimity.

*Synthesis*, the fifth source of sublimity, was explicated by Longinus in two earlier works and is addressed only briefly in *On the Sublime*. Nevertheless, an important instrument of *synthesis* is discussed: harmony, the means by which those attendant upon an artwork are given the experience of *pathos* without being subjectively affected by it. According to Longinus, "Harmony, which is inherent in human beings, is an impressive instrument, not only of persuasion and pleasure but also of emotions with freedom." Some scholars reject the phrase "emotions with freedom" (*met eleutherias kai pathous*) and substitute "grandeur and emotions" (*megalègorias kai pathous*). To do so is to change the reading of the authoritative manuscript and to eliminate a significant feature of Longinian theory.

"Emotions with freedom" are emotions that one feels but by which one is not controlled. In any real situation, such as death or failure or triumph or love, a person feels emotions and is at their command. Artistic harmony makes it possible for a person to feel real emotions without being their thrall. If one is not subject to the emotions one feels, one can think objectively about them, study them as they are being felt. This simultaneous experience of emotions and rational consideration of those same emotions is the harmony of *pathos* and *noesis*. Sublime art reflects the harmony of the creative artist and produces a contextual harmony to which those who appreciate the work of art are inherently receptive.

An earlier theory of "emotions with freedom" is Aristotle's doctrine of *catharsis*. Tragic drama, according to Aristotle, elicits emotions to effect a purging of them. Purging is to be understood not so much in the sense of elimination as in the sense of refinement. The audience is not purged of emotions exactly; the emotions elicited from the audience are themselves purified, or purged of what can make them harmful to their human progenitors. Tragic drama gave audiences the ability to feel emotions without being enslaved by them and within a freedom that further enabled the audiences to think about what it was that they were feeling.

Longinus, concerned with all verbal art and not exclusively with tragic drama, links literature to music and expatiates on word arrangements, word rhythms, and verbal euphony as contributing to a music of words by means of which *noesis* and *pathos* are amalgamated.

> Are we not to consider, then, that *synthesis*, being a certain harmony of verbal contexts which are natural to human beings and which strike not only the ears but also the mind, giving rise to various ideas of words, intellections, actions, beauty, and melody, all of which are inherent to us and nurtured within us, and at the same time, by the variety and combination of its sounds, introducing the *pathos* that is present in the speaker and his listeners in a common experience, fashioning greatness by a construction of contexts – are we not to consider, then, that synthesis, by all these means in simultaneity, charms us, confers dignity, worth, and sublimity upon us as well as upon its contexts, and in every respect gives directions to our thoughts?

This lengthy and complex rhetorical question articulates the idea that *synthesis* both conduces to *noesis* with *pathos* and conjoins them with the result that their union is sublimity. Equally significant is the idea that the artist and the recipient of art are merged in a common experience.

Longinian theory holds that an artist's *noesis* enables the artist to give sublime expression to either *noesis* or *pathos*. Sublimity may exist without *pathos* but not without *noesis*. Both *noesis* and *pathos* must be present, however, where *synthesis* is the source of sublimity: both are part of the artist's character, both are ingrained in the artist's work, and both are finally experienced by the audience in a veritable *synthesis* of artist and audience or reader.

In his critique of a poem by Sappho, which is among the most famous parts of this essay, Longinus shows the *synthesis* of *noesis* and *pathos* in the artist herself and argues that the poem appeals to the reader's intellect in a rendition of erotic emotion. Sappho, according to Longinus, presents the sublime idea of an emotion, a *noesis* of *pathos*. She identifies erotic fever with fire, for example, and fire is also a symbol of illumination or enlightenment. The symbol accordingly unifies the *pathos* of love and the *noesis* of that *pathos*: the mind is enlightened about a strong emotion which is depicted through the physical symptoms of that emotion (including the union of such different concepts as heat and cold, sight and sound, semblance and actuality, the irrational and the rational, and pleasure and pain).

The image of light informs another area of Longinian theory and may indeed exhibit something of a link with Plotinus' use of the image in *Enneads* (first transcribed c. A.D. 256):

> When the soul suddenly apprehends light, one sees; this light both derives from and is intellectual apprehension. We must consider it to be present to us when, like a god coming into a room in answer to a prayer, it illuminates us; if there is no coming there is no illumination. Likewise the unilluminated soul is unseen of itself; but, being illuminated, it has what it seeks.

Longinus insists that, if visionary literature is taken literally instead of allegorically, it is unseen (*athea*, which most scholars translate as "godless"). "Our soul," he writes, "is inherently stirred by the genuinely sublime, and . . . is imbued with delight and exultation, as though it had created what it has apprehended." It can be seen by these quotations that both Longinus and Plotinus conceive of the soul, the core of human subjectivity, as having within itself the light that it seeks and finding that light by means of that light itself.

Light, vision, and recognition are considered to be constituents of that sublimity which is the soul of the artist, of art itself, and of the apprehension of art. The author quotes from Homer's *Iliad* (c. 800 B.C.) passages about gods and humans seeing, about marine monsters seeing and recognizing Poseidon, about blind Ajax praying for light, and about fire in the mountains. He invokes the sublimity of the passage in Genesis in which God says "Let there be light." He uses the simile of lesser lights disappearing in the greater light of the sun. In all of this the soul is taken to be the sublimity of the body and, as already noted, well-chosen words are taken to be "the light of the mind."

Sublimity as the soul that enlightens itself by appropriate expression would be tantamount to a solipsism if it were not for the individual sources of sublimity that exist independently until they are synthesized. In Longinian theory the two major sources of sublimity, intellection and emotion, are as distinct as mind and body, until the experience of art synthesizes them.

The impact of Longinus on his contemporaries cannot become a subject of speculation until it is determined who Longinus was and in what century he lived. The absence of ancient commentary upon his work may be indicative of a lack of attention to it in his own time or of his having had the last word on the subject; in any event, the survival of his essay attests its wide readership.

Longinus was little known and received scant attention during the Middle Ages. The earliest extant manuscript of *On the Sublime* was produced in the tenth century. It is now identified as "Parisinus 2036" (or simply "P"). Seventeen pages (about 1,050 lines) of this folio manuscript

were lost after its production and ten subsequent manuscripts, obviously based on P, have the same lacunae except for their retention of the work's first and last pages, both among the seventeen missing from P.

The first printed version of *On the Sublime* appeared in 1554 in Basel; it was edited by Francesco Robortelli. Between 1555 and 1694 there were seven more printed editions, five of them Latin translations and one French translation by Nicolas Boileau-Despréaux, published in 1674. In the eighteenth century, as editions of the work proliferated, the great wave of Longinianism came into being, succeeded by waves of scholarly interest during the nineteenth and twentieth centuries. Textual scholarship concerning *On the Sublime* tended to supplant Longinian formation of literary and critical theory.

So it is that one must turn to the eighteenth century to estimate properly the import of Longinus. Adumbrating this import was the first English translation in 1652 by John Hall. Eight years earlier John Milton, in *Of Education*, had listed Longinus, along with Plato, Aristotle, Phalereus, Cicero, and Hermogenes, as an exemplary student of poetics. Boileau's French translation initiated a Longinian continuity in critical theory that was not to wane until the early nineteenth century.

John Dryden, in the late seventeenth century, and John Dennis, in the early eighteenth, propagated the work. Joseph Addison referred to it in a number of *The Spectator* essays during 1711 and 1712. Alexander Pope, author, with John Arbuthnot and John Gay, of a comedy entitled *Three Hours After Marriage* (1717), presented Dennis as "Sir Tremendous Longinus." Earlier, Pope had included an accolade to Longinus in his *Essay on Criticism* (1711):

> Thee, bold Longinus, all the Nine inspire,
> And bless their critic with a poet's fire.
> An ardent judge, who, zealous in his trust,
> With warmth gives sentence, yet is always just;
> Whose own example strengthens all his laws,
> And is himself the great Sublime he draws.

Later, in 1727, Pope published a prose parody entitled *Bathous: Or, The Art of Sinking in Poetry*. Casual overtures to Longinus by Jonathan Swift, in *On Poetry: A Rhapsody* (1733), for example, and Laurence Sterne, in *Tristram Shandy* (1759–1767), indicate the extent to which Longinus had become familiar to the literate and commonplace as an arbiter of taste.

The chief contributions of *On the Sublime* to standards of excellence in the eighteenth century were the work's concentration on the relationship of the artist's character to his or her art (and to the recipients of that art) and the concept of reconciled antitheses, or the union of dissimilar elements. Oddly, both notions are consistent with Romanticism, which nevertheless came to reject *On the Sublime* as a set of classical rules.

Serious but limited consideration was given to Longinus by T. R. Henn and Samuel H. Monk in the 1930s, and by Elder Olson and Allen Tate in the 1940s, but later critics and critical theorists largely ignored the "sublimist." He did, however, regain a modicum of favor with a few modernist critics, particularly among the deconstructionists, who strove to obliterate the distinction between criticism of literature and criticism of criticism, and ultimately between literature and criticism. Like the last lines of the accolade from Pope quoted above, the observation by Geoffrey H. Hartman that "Longinus is studied as seriously as the sublime texts he comments on" conveys well the lofty status of the theorist.

## Principal criticism
*Peri hypsous* (*On the Sublime*)

## Other major works and literary forms
*On the Sublime* is the only work attributed to Longinus.

## Further reading
Ashfield, Andrew, and Peter de Bolla. *The Sublime: A Reader in Eighteenth-century Aesthetic Theory*, 1996.
Ferguson, F. *Solitude and the Sublime*, 1992.
Grube, G. M. A. "Longinus, On Great Writing," in *The Greek and Roman Critics*, 1965.
Henn, T. R. *Longinus and English Criticism*, 1934.
Librett, Jeffrey S., ed. *Of the Sublime: Presence in Question*, 1993.
Lyotard, Jean-François. *Lessons on the Analytic of the Sublime*, 1994. Translated by Elizabeth Rottenberg.
Monk, Samuel H. *The Sublime: A Study of Critical Theories in Eighteenth-Century England*, 1935.
Olson, Elder. "The Argument of Longinus' *On the Sublime*," in *On Value Judgments in the Arts and Other Essays*, 1976.
Russell, D. A. Introduction to *Longinus On Sublimity*, 1965.
St. Marin, Demetrio. *Bibliography of the "Essay on the Sublime,"* 1967.
Saintsbury, George. *A History of Criticism and Literary Taste in Europe from the Earliest Texts to the Present Day*. Vol. 1, *Classical and Mediaeval Criticism*, 1900.
Tate, Allen. "Longinus and the 'New Criticism,'" in *The Man of Letters in the Modern World*, 1955.

ROY ARTHUR SWANSON

*See also* Classical Greek and Roman Literary Theory; Horace; Plotinus; Sublime

# Iurii Lotman

## Russian critic and theorist

**Born:** Petrograd, U.S.S.R.; February 28, 1922
**Died:** Tartu, Estonia; 1993

## Biography
Iurii Lotman, the son of Mikhail and Aleksandra Lotman, was a graduate of Leningrad University. He married Zara G. Mints in 1950; they had three sons. His wife was also his collaborator at Tartu University in Soviet Estonia, where Lotman was professor of Russian literature. Lotman founded the Tartu School of semiotics in 1964, and went on to organize internationally renowned seminars in Kiaariku, near Tartu. These activities brought together large numbers of outstanding scholars from the Soviet Union and from around the world in a common endeavor: to deepen and extend the understanding of culture as one of the most important factors in human interaction.

Although, under Communism, Lotman and other Soviet semioticians were conversant with developments in the West, and although their works became increasingly well known (despite the scarcity of translations and the small number of copies printed), free interaction and the exchange of ideas were still discouraged. One explanation for this situation was that the work of the Tartu School had been rather controversial in the Soviet Union. Lotman had been criticized for being too subjective and schematic and for adopting the structuralist position, which is by nature suspect, since it tends to isolate aesthetic and theoretical considerations from more practical concerns.

By training and inclination, Lotman was a literary historian. He was nurtured in the great Russian philological tradition that conjoined the study of literature with intellectual trends and social history. His biography of the Decembrist Ivan Dmitriev and his studies of Nikolai Karamzin, Aleksandr Pushkin, and other eighteenth- and nineteenth-century Russian writers are examples of the best of this tradition. With the rise of semiotics in the early 1960s, however, Lotman was armed with new tools which enabled him to tackle traditional problems. He then began to search for general principles and laws governing the structure of a text, the language in which it is composed, its function in a culture, and its relationship to society.

## Influence
Lotman's particular contribution to literary studies has been to conceptualize literature as a socially functioning and historically continuing semiotic phenomenon that both creates and prescribes communication of information. His original thoughts on this subject have not only made him the leading Soviet semiotician/structuralist of his time but also an outstanding figure in the international semiotics movement. The influence of Lotman and the Moscow-Tartu School has been deeply felt in both Europe and the Americas.

## Analysis
Since Lotman's theory of literature is most immediately influenced by the closely related concepts of semiotics and structuralism – he acknowledges as his predecessors Ferdinand de Saussure, Roman Jakobson, and the Russian mathematician Andrei Kolmogorov – it is useful to discuss these two terms briefly in their Western and Eastern

European context before giving an overview of Lotman's work. In his book *Literary Theory: An Introduction* (1983), Terry Eagleton differentiates the terms in the following general way:

> The word "structuralism" itself indicates a *method* of enquiry, which can be applied to a whole range of objects from football matches to economic modes of production; "semiotics" denotes rather a particular *field* of study, that of systems which would in an ordinary sense be regarded as signs: poems, bird calls, traffic lights, medical symptoms and so on. But the two words overlap, since structuralism treats something which may not usually be thought of as a system of signs as though it were – the kinship relations of tribal societies, for example – while semiotics commonly uses structuralist methods.

Literary structuralism developed in the 1960s as an attempt to apply to literature the methods of Saussure, the Swiss founder of modern structural linguistics. Language, for Saussure, is a system of signs to be studied "synchronically" (as a complete system at a given point in time) rather than "diachronically" (in historical development). A sign in literature is an element of the text, or the notable absence of an element, perceived against the background of the text, or it is the text taken as a whole, perceived against the norms of a particular period. Saussure argued that signs consist of two aspects: the "signifier" (the aspect of pronunciation or writing) and the "signified" (the aspect of meaning). The relation between the signifier and signified is arbitrary; the relation between the sign and what it refers to (the "referent") is also arbitrary. No individual sign in the system has meaning in itself; it acquires meaning only by its difference from other signs. The signs of one system (for example, the words of natural or ordinary language) can be the signifier of another system (for example, poetic language) which is superimposed on them. In his linguistic studies, Saussure was not interested in investigating actual speech (*parole*) but in the objective structure of signs which makes speech possible (*langue*). Lotman views Saussure's distinctions between *langue* and *parole* as examples of the theoretical apparatus of any sign system – *langue* – and of the realization or employment of individual signs in specific contexts – *parole*.

In the 1920s Saussure's linguistics had a tremendous impact on a group of literary theorists who became known as the Russian Formalists. Prominent members of the group included Jakobson, Viktor Shklovskii, Boris Eikhenbaum, and Boris Tomashevskii. While Formalism approaches literature "structurally," analyzing the sign itself rather than its referent, it is not overtly concerned with meaning as a function of difference. When Jakobson, leader of the Moscow Linguistic Circle, a Formalist group founded in 1915, emigrated to Prague in 1920, he became not only one of the major theoreticians of Czech structuralism (in the newly founded Prague Linguistic Circle) but also an important link between Russian Formalism and modern structuralism. Lotman's literary theory is indebted to the poetics of Jakobson and develops from it a "structure" which seeks a systematic approach to a literary text.

Jakobson and the Prague School maintained that the "poetic" essentially places language in a kind of self-conscious relation to itself. For them, Saussure's stress on the arbitrary relation between sign and referent, word and object, helped to detach the text from its context and make it an autonomous object. The Czech structuralists, even more than the Formalists, insisted on the structural unity of the work. Its elements were to be understood as functions of a dynamic whole, with one particular level of the text (the *dominanta*) acting as a determining influence which subsumed all other textual levels. For Lotman, the "energy" of poetry results from the constant battle among competing levels or systems.

Any object of structural investigation, according to Lotman, must be viewed as an interrelated and interdependent system consisting of a number of basic units and the rules of their possible combinations. Although self-regulating by an internal feedback mechanism, the system may be a part of other systems. To study "structure," then, is to study the constructive elements of the poetic work in relation to the artistic whole.

Since its formulation in 1867 by the American logician Charles S. Peirce, semiotics has expanded beyond logic and linguistics to address communication studies (Lotman employs the language of information theory in his literary studies), anthropology, psychology, sociology, history, and art criticism. Although it uses structural methods, as a science of signs and sign systems, semiotics studies the basic characteristics of all signs and their combinations, for example, the words of natural and artificial languages, the tropes of poetic language, or mathematical symbols. It also treats systems of signs, such as the languages of various poetic schools, codes (for Lotman, a "code" is any verbal or nonverbal communication system created consciously or unconsciously; Lotman often uses the words "code" and "system" interchangeably), and animal communication systems. From the semantic perspective, poetics, or a view of the literary text as a complex sign, isolates the devices (such as plot, rhythm, meter) existing between the signified, which is the subject matter, and the signifier, its verbal embodiment.

As a semiotician, Lotman views the poetic text as a multilevel system in which meaning exists only contextually, governed by sets of similarities and differences. In poetry, it is the nature of the signifier – the patterns of sound and rhythm constructed by the marks on the page – that determines what is signified. A poetic text is "semantically saturated," that is, it condenses more "information" than any other type of discourse. For modern communication theory, in general, an increase in "information" leads to a decrease in "communication"; for Lotman, however, this is not the case in poetry because of its unique kind of internal organization. Poetry produces a more complex set of messages than any other form of language. Poems are "bad" when they do not carry significant information, since in Lotman's estimation "information is beauty."

Every literary text is composed of many systems (for example, lexical, graphic, metrical) and achieves its effects by constant clashes and tensions between these systems, according to Lotman's theory. Each of the systems becomes a norm from which the others deviate, erecting a code of expectations which is ultimately violated. In this way, each system in the text, to use Shklovskii's term, "defamiliarizes" the others, disturbs their regularity, and casts them into relief. As one of the poem's systems threatens to become too predictable, another disrupts and transforms it. Consequently, the literary work continually enriches the denotation of words, generating new meanings by the clash and juxtaposition of its various levels almost ad infinitum. Each word in the text is linked by a set of formal structures to several other words, and its meaning is always "overdetermined": the result of several different determinants acting together.

For Lotman, the poetic text is the most complex form of discourse imaginable, condensing together several systems, each of which contains its own tensions, parallelisms, repetitions, and oppositions, and each of which is continually modifying all the others. A poem, according to Lotman, can only be reread, not read, since some of its structures can be perceived only retrospectively. Whatever the reader perceives in the text is only perceived by contrast and difference, since an element which had no differential relation to any other would remain invisible. Yet even the absence of certain devices – what the Formalists and Lotman would call a "minus device" – may produce textual meaning. If the codes which the work has generated lead the reader to expect, for example, a certain rhyme which does not occur, this absence may be as effective a device of generating meaning as any other. The literary work, then, is a continual generating and violating of expectations, a complex interplay of the regular and the random, patterns and deviations.

Despite its unique verbal plenitude, Lotman does not consider that poetry, or literature in general, can be defined by its inherent linguistic properties. He insists that literary texts are entities of great complexity which are created through the use of various invented "subcodes." Literary texts then activate these subcodes in the mind of the reader. The meaning of the text is not only an internal matter; it is also a matter of the text's relation to larger systems of meaning, to other texts, codes, and norms in literature and society as a whole. Its meaning is also relative to the reader's "horizon of expectations." It is the reader, then, who by certain "receptive codes" at his or her disposal identifies an element

in the work as a "device"; the device is not simply an internal feature but one perceived through a particular code and against a definite textual background. Lotman's view of poetry, then, stresses the need for the reader to engage actively in creating meaning. He also maintains, however, that the poet and the poem must continually work against habitual modes of perception, thought, and speech, what he calls the "automism of language":

> The aim of poetry, of course, is not "devices" but a knowledge of the world and the relationship among people, self-knowledge, and the development of the human personality in the process of learning and social communication . . . the goal of poetry coincides with the goal of culture as a whole. But poetry realizes this goal specifically, and an understanding of its specific character is impossible if one ignores its mechanism, its internal structure. This mechanism actually is more readily revealed when it enters into conflict with the automism of language.

As opposed to French structuralists and semioticians, who have been establishing parameters of individual systems and the relation of these systems to their component parts, and who deny or who do not even consider the possibility of any correspondence between semiotic studies and reality (literature, in their view, is a closed system whose elements have meaning only as parts of other systems), Lotman and the Moscow-Tartu School have asserted that semiotic systems model reality. They do not proceed further, however, to investigate the nature of this modeling, since they assume that the theory of meaning cannot be formulated before the technical details of the code are known. At least since the 1970s Lotman has studied the mutual influence of culture and an individual text in order to elaborate a theory of information and has investigated whether semiotics can succeed in reaching inside the modeling system to its intrinsic relational meanings and outside the modeling system to its place in the historical environment of a period.

In Lotman's view, all communication systems model the world in some way. A primary modeling system – language is the only known one – is one which is constructed independently of other modeling systems. Secondary modeling systems, however, are constructed in conjunction with the primary system, as is the case, for example, with religion, art, and myth; since language is the primary system, it is assumed that all other systems have a linguistic basis. Lotman argues that external similarity between words, as used in primary and secondary communication, makes confusion of the two modes common.

The ultimate implication of Lotman's, and the Moscow-Tartu School's, work is that human beings not only communicate with signs but are largely controlled by them as well. A sign system has the capacity to mold or model the world in its own unique image. Shaping the minds of society's members to fit its structure, a sign system not only passively mirrors reality but also actively transforms it. The world, then, appears to be a hierarchy of codes or "languages" that can be read or embodied in texts. Semiotic mechanisms govern the way individuals perceive the world and convey ideas to others.

In summary, Lotman's theory of literature is a theory of poetic language, of meaning formation, of poetic generation, of literature in history, and of literature in a culture functioning as a semiotic system. Considering literature to be the central and most typical manifestation of culture, he constructed a method of analysis that accounts for ideological and cultural values, and that is applicable to structures of thought as well as structures of language.

## Principal criticism
*Lekskii po strukturalnoi poetike: Vvedenie, teoriia stikha*, 1964 (*Lectures on Structural Poetics: Introduction, the Theory of Poetry*, 1968)
*Struktura khudozhestvennogo teksta*, 1970 (*The Structure of the Artistic Text*, 1977)
*Analiz poeticheskogo teksta: Struktura stikh*, 1972 (*Analysis of the Poetic Text*, 1976)
*Universe of the Mind: A Semiotic Theory of Culture*, 1991 (Ann Shukman, translator)

## Other major works and literary forms
Iurii Lotman's bibliography consists of about five hundred items. Aside from his theoretical work on structural poetics and semiotics, he expanded his studies to include culture, specifically theater, film, and the visual arts. His works on the typology of culture are considered by some critics to be his most interesting and significant contributions to semiotic studies. He also edited several journals and series of papers produced by the Moscow-Tartu School.

NONFICTION
*Khudozhestvennaia struktura "Evgeniia Onegina,"* 1966
*Stati po tipologii kultury*, 1970
*Semiotike kino i voprosy kiinoestetiki*, 1973 (*Semiotics of Cinema*, 1976)
*A. S. Pushkin: Biografiia pisatelia*, 1981
*Semiotics of Russian Culture*, 1984 (with Boris A. Uspenskii)

## Further reading
Baran, Henryk, ed. *Semiotics and Structuralism: Readings from the Soviet Union*, 1976.
Champagne, Roland A. "A Grammar of the Languages of Culture: Literary Theory and Yury M. Lotman's Semiotics," in *New Literary History*. IX (1978), pp. 205–210.
Johnson, D. Barton. Introduction to *Analysis of the Poetic Text*, 1976.
Kristeva, Julia. "On Yury Lotman," in *PMLA*. 109, no. 3 (1994), pp. 375–384.
Shukman, Ann. "The Canonization of the Real: J. L. Lotman's Theory of Literature and the Analysis of Poetry," in *PTL: A Journal for Descriptive Poetics and Theory of Literature*. I (1976), pp. 317–338.
——. *Literature and Semiotics: A Study of the Writings of Y. M. Lotman*, 1977.
Thompson, Ewa M. "Yurij Lotman's Literary Theory and Its Context," in *Slavic and East European Journal*. II (1977), pp. 225–238.

GENEVIEVE SLOMSKI

*See also* Jakobson; Prague School; Semiotics

# Lu Chi
## Chinese poet

**Born:** Hua T'ing, Yangtze Delta, China; 261
**Died:** Loyang, China; 303

### Biography
Lu Chi (whose *tzŭ*, or courtesy name, was Shih-hêng) was born in 261 at Hua T'ing, the family's country estate, in the Yangtze Delta region of the southern kingdom of Wu (the modern Kiangsu Province), China. He was the fourth of six sons of Lu K'ang, a marquess (*hou*) and the commander in chief of the Wu armies. His grandfather was Lu Hsün, a duke (*kung*) and army general whose martial talent had helped to found the Wu kingdom.

Lu Chi and his younger brother, Lu Yün, were given scholarly training, and they both began writing poetry at a young age. Their education, however, was interrupted by the death of their father in 275. Lu Chi entered the army with the rank of captain to oversee his father's personal troops. His two elder brothers received higher ranks in the army on the northern frontier. Lu Chi served in the army until 280, when the Wu emperor surrendered to the Tsin forces. Lu Chi's elder brothers were killed, but he and Lu Yün escaped and returned to Hua T'ing. There, in the words of E. R. Hughes, they "barred their door and devoted themselves to study" for the next decade.

As Hughes suggests, it must have been during this period that Lu Chi and Lu Yün "served their apprenticeship" as writers. Judging by Lu Chi's later work, he must have continued his study of the Confucian classics, read the Confucian expositor Hsün-tzŭ, and explored the thought of the Taoists Lao-tzŭ, Lieh-tzŭ, and Chuang-tzŭ. Also, apparently, during this period Lu Chi married and had two sons.

In 290 the two brothers journeyed northward to Loyang, the capital of the Tsin Dynasty, to seek their fortunes at the court. Lu Chi obtained a series of official posts, serving several princes, and at one time being an adviser to the emperor Hui Ti. Since the emperor was weak, the various princes continually vied with one another in an effort to seize power. In 302 Lu Chi was in service to Prince Yin, who decided to attack his brother (or half brother) Prince I, the latter having overcome the emperor in the capital.

The prince appointed Lu Chi commander of one flank division and Mêng Chao commander of the other. They were to advance jointly and engage the enemy. Although Lu Chi advanced as ordered, Mêng Chao did not, wishing to revenge himself on Lu Chi for having reported him to the prince earlier for allowing his troops to pillage. Lu Chi's forces engaged the enemy without proper support and were ignominiously defeated. Influenced by Lu Chi's enemies, Prince Yin ordered Lu Chi arrested and executed together with his two sons. His last words prior to his beheading were, in Hughes' translation: "The crying of the cranes of Hua T'ing, never shall I hear them again!" His fame today, as Hughes says, "rests primarily on his *fu* poems, on his *Wên Fu* in particular."

## Influence

Professor Ch'ên Shou-yi, of Pomona College, has termed Lu Chi "the first important writer in the kingdom of Wu [one of the Three Kingdoms]" and "the first important representative of the southward extension of Chinese civilization." He states that Lu Chi's poetic essay was so highly regarded that it became "scriptural" in its authority. This statement is supported by the tributes paid Lu Chi by later critics and their discussions of his views. His poetic essay was also included in later judiciously selected anthologies and in larger collections whose editors sought to preserve and make available to readers the best literature of the past.

## Analysis

The Three Kingdoms – Wei, Shu, and Wu – emerged following the disintegration of the Han Empire in 220. Although the Han Empire eventually succumbed to forces it could not control, it contributed mightily to the future of Chinese civilization: Confucianism was adopted as the official philosophy, and an imperial academy was established to train civil servants, using the Confucian classics as textbooks. Buddhism was introduced into China from India and competed with a native Taoism, which on the philosophical level taught a spiritual way of life. Important developments also took place in literature, especially the invention of the new poetic form called the *fu*. The *fu* was to dominate Chinese literary expression for the next five centuries.

The Han *fu* originated as a coalescence of the new form of the *sao* which came into being during the Warring States period (404–221 B.C.) and the rhetoric of Hsün-tzǔ. The Han *fu*, although flexible, was long, ornate, and full of pomp. During the epoch of the Three Kingdoms (220–265), two poets, Tso Su, who flourished from 265 to 305, and Lu Chi, sought to modify the Han *fu*. Although an imitator of Pan Ku (32–92), Tso Su insisted on a factual, topographical *fu*. On the other hand, Lu Chi went in the direction of the lyrical, imaginative *fu*, as seen in his *Wên fu* (c. 302; *Essay on Literature*, 1951) and other *fu* poems, such as his *Huai-t'u fu* (thinking of earthly things) and *Ta-mu fu* (splendid evening).

Lu Chi was a master of the *fu*, which some Western critics call "rhymeprose." The original title of *Essay on Literature* literally means "a *fu* on literature." It is, generally speaking, on the order of such Western poems as Horace's *Ars poetica* (c. 17 B.C.; *The Art of Poetry*), Nicolas Boileau-Despréaux's *L'Art poétique* (1674), and Alexander Pope's *An Essay on Criticism* (1711), except that they are in verse. The *Essay on Literature* consists mostly of parallel lines or antithetical couplets of six or four characters – what the Chinese term *ssǔ-liu wên*, that is, "four-and-six prose" – with rhyme schemes.

Anyone who attempts a rational reconstruction of Lu Chi's *Essay on Literature* must take into account that it is a poem, although in prose. Imaginative, figurative, and lyrical, its language is often indefinite in meaning. Yet in terms of the *fu*'s generic rules – employing as it does sentence and clausal parallelism, called *p'ien-wên* style, with a rhyme scheme – it is limited to "double-harness" thinking and word selection dependent on sound pattern.

Lu Chi's theory of literature is multiperspectival and involves metaphysical, psychological, aesthetic, technical, and instrumental views. He obviously believed that all these factors enter into the creation of an original literary work and that none is more important than another, although some may be more basic than others.

It was customary for the *fu* writer to provide a foreword. In his foreword, Lu Chi expresses several basic ideas which may be regarded as the premises of his theory. First, a text reflects the mind of its author, and hence the poet's mind is to a degree knowable. Second, since "beauty and excellence" are governed by an author's diction and expression, and these factors are "infinitely variable," the text needs to be evaluated and criticized. Third, because the connections between signifiers and the signified are purely arbitrary, an author is obliged to struggle with the text in an effort to choose words which conform as nearly as possible to whatever he or she has experienced. Fourth, the great literary works of the past, sanctioned by memorability, survival, and admiration by generations of astute readers, represent "glorious accomplishments" and are models that can nourish and inspire living authors, even though circumstances have changed and living authors are obliged to create something "new." Finally, although an axe handle (literature) is made "by cutting wood [nature] with an axe [literature]," – art imitates art – the workings of creation are so intricate and mysterious that words generally prove inadequate to explain them.

Although a confirmed Confucian, Lu Chi's metaphysics was Taoist. Poets must take account of their relation to the universe. Its center (*chung-chü*) is within the poet; from this position one observes the vast extent of the universe and contemplates its mystery (*hsüan*). In the Taoism of the Three Kingdoms, "The Learning of Mystery" was identified with the *Tao*, or the Way, which is Non-Being (*wu*). The earlier Lao-tzǔ states: "The Way brings forth all things" and "All things in the world are brought forth in Being (*Yu*), and Being is brought forth in Non-Being (*Wu*)." As the One (*i*),

Being produced the Two (*yin and yang*), which produce the myriad things (*wan-wu*). Lu Chi sees the poet struggling with the Great Void (*hsü-wu*), or Non-Being, forcing it to yield up Being, which is the source of all the shapes and features of nature (*hsing*).

Yet in this instance the poet as writer is not interested in the real or physical world but in words, the symbols used to represent the poet's percepts and concepts of that world. Lu Chi writes:

And 'tis sound rung out of Profound Silence [*chi-k'uan*].
In a sheet of paper is contained the Infinite,
And, evolved from an inch-sized heart [*ts'un hsin*], an endless panorama.
The words, as they expand, become all-evocative. . . .

To Lu Chi, writing provides visible traces of Heaven and Earth. It shows the writer's relation to nature as well as to the *Tao*, or the Way, which is beyond nature.

Lu Chi's theory of the creative process embraces the idea of inspiration stemming from meditation, awareness and sensitivity, feelings and emotions, intuition and reason, and linguistic expression. The two chief stimuli of inspiration are the great literary works of the past and the cyclical processes and multitudinous forms and appearances of nature. As a result of a deep awareness and sensitivity, the poet's feelings and emotions are aroused by such stimuli. Having previously identified intuitively with the cosmic *Tao*, the poet reacts directly to whatever has been perceived and seeks to give linguistic expression to these emotions, to trace them symbolically. To Lu Chi, such inspiration is an involuntary act of free, joyous play, intuitive and irrational. It does not matter whether laughter or tears are evoked. At such a moment, Lu Chi writes,

You cannot hinder its coming or stop its going.
It vanishes like a shadow, and it comes like echoes.
When the Heavenly Arrow [*t'ien-chi*] is at its fleetest and sharpest, what confusion is there that cannot be brought to order?
The wind of thought bursts from the heart; the stream of words rushes through the lips and teeth.
Luxuriance and magnificence wait the command of the brush and the paper.

Once the words are written, however, reason and literary discipline come into play as the text is evaluated, corrected, and revised, in a rational, decision-making process.

Since Lu Chi viewed the composing of a poem as similar to an act of the *Tao*, he held that meditation (*ch'an*) is the proper way to enter into the creative process. By suspending sense perceptions and concentrating the intuition, the poet is able to apprehend eternity and infinity and introduce them into the writing. In Lu Chi's words:

In the beginning,
All external vision and sound are suspended,
Perpetual thought itself gropes in time and space;
Then, the spirit at full gallop reaches the eight limits of the cosmos,
And the mind, self-buoyant, will ever soar to new insurmountable heights.

Feeling is then sparked in the poet to illuminate all the images which flow into the mind. This process is called "intuitive thinking" (*shên szŭ*).

Lu Chi does not neglect the aesthetics of poetry. He remarks that "we may speak of beauty [*yen*] and ugliness [*chih*], of good [*hao*] and bad [*o*] [in each literary work]." He continually speaks of "order," "orderly arrangement," and "reason" [*li*]. He also repeatedly refers to "colorfulness" [*wu-sê*], "harmony" [*ho*], and the importance of reciprocity between "form" [*hsing*] and "meaning" [*ch'ü*]. He habitually thinks in terms of "consummate artistry" and "luxurious elegance" [*shêng tsao*]. Of the poet, he says: "Now he selects ideas and fixes them in their order; he examines words and puts them in their places./ He taps at the door of all that is colorful; he chooses from among everything that rings . . . . He traps heaven and earth in the cage of form." He continues: "Ideas should be cleverly brought together; language should be beautifully commissioned./ And the mutation of sounds and tones should be like the five colors of embroidery sustaining each other."

Technically, Lu Chi draws many important distinctions between good and bad writing. Perhaps the most important one is his stand that good writing is "new" and "original." Fully aware that texts are made from other texts, he stresses the danger of slavish imitation, recalling the aphorism "One man sings, and three men do the refrain." He mentions the common state of nerves called "artist's guilt" – the fear that one's writing is perhaps too derivative.

In terms of instrumentalism, Lu Chi's *Essay on Literature* illustrates well the way authorial intention can be contrary to the writing performance. His "coda," as it were, is a conscious effort to placate those Confucians who believe that the sole purpose of literature is the maintenance of virtue. The aim and the thrust of the argument of the poem, however, is clearly to present, to pay tribute to, and to glory in the workings of the mysterious *Tao*.

By the sixth century, the impact of Lu Chi's *Essay on Literature* was felt throughout the literary world in China. When Liu Hsieh composed the first book-length study of the main problems of literature, *Wên-hsin tiao-lung* (c. sixth century; *The Literary Mind and the Carving of Dragons: A Study of Thought and Pattern in Chinese Literature*, 1959), he paid tribute to Lu Chi. Radical critic Chung Jung discussed Lu Chi's literary theory in his *Shih p'in* (c. 513–517; levels of poetry). Hsiao T'ung included the *Essay on Literature* in his anthology *Wên hsüan* (c. 501–531; *Wen Xuan: Or, Selections of Refined Literature*,

Vol. 1, *Rhapsodies on Metropolises and Capitals*, 1982), together with more than fifty of Lu's other pieces. In or near 628 the T'ang statesman, scholar, and critic Li Shan favorably appraised the *Essay on Literature* in his commentary on Hsiao T'ung's anthology.

Perhaps the highest tribute paid to Lu Chi was the inclusion of his works by the great Ch'ing emperor Ch'ien Lung (who ruled from 1736 to 1796) in his monumental Imperial Library collection, which was so voluminous that it was never printed. Lu's works, however, were printed in the twentieth century in the smaller version of the Imperial collection, called the *Ssŭ-k'u ch'üan-shu* (1772–1794; *Complete Works* [of the Imperial Library] *in Four Divisions*, 1919–1936).

Three English translations of the *Essay on Literature* have appeared and there are also French and Russian translations. Studies of Lu's essay, written in the East and West, continue to appear.

## Principal criticism
*Wên fu* (c. 302; *Essay on Literature*, 1951)

## Other major works and literary forms
Lu Chi was renowned in his day as a poet and prose writer. In addition to writing official documents and civil service examination questions, he wrote analytical essays and poems. Two lengthy essays of his are *Po lun* (the dialectic of destruction) and *Wu-chiao-wei lun* (discussion of the five grades of nobility). He also left seventy or more poems of various types: four-syllable poems, five-syllable poems (*ku-shih*), lyrics (*yüeh-fu* and *shih*), odes (*sung*), and prose poems (*fu*). A selection of Lu Chi's lyric poems was included by Hsü Ling in his anthology *Yü-t'ai hsin-yung* (545; *New Songs from a Jade Terrace*, 1982).

## Further reading
Chen, Shih-hsiang. Introduction to *Essay on Literature Written by the Third Century Chinese Poet Lu Chi*, 1952 (revised edition).
Chou, Ju-chang. "An Introduction to Lu Chi's *Wên fu*," in *Studia Serica*. IX (1948), pp. 42–65.
Fang, Achilles. "Rhymeprose on Literature: The *Wên Fu* of Lu Chi (A.D. 261–303)," in *Harvard Journal of Asiatic Studies*. XIV (1951), pp. 527–566.
Frodsham, J. D. *An Anthology of Chinese Verse*, 1967.
Fung, Yu-lan. *A Short History of Chinese Philosophy*, 1948. Edited and translated by Derk Bodde.
Hamill, Sam. "Lu Chi: *Wên Fu* ('The Art of Writing'), Translation with Introduction," in *The American Poetry Review*. XV (May/June, 1986), pp. 23–27.
Holzman, Donald. "Literary Criticism in China in the Early Third Century A.D.," in *Asiatische Studien*. XXVIII (1974), pp. 111–149.
Hughes, E. R. *The Art of Letters: Lu Chi's "Wên Fu,"* A.D. 302, 1951.
Knoerle, Mary Gregory. "The Poetic Theories of Lu Chi, with a Brief Comparison with Horace's *Ars Poetica*," in *Journal of Aesthetics and Art Criticism*. XXV (1966), pp. 137–143.
Liu, James Y. *Chinese Theories of Literature*, 1975.

RICHARD P. BENTON

# Percy Lubbock
## English critic and writer

**Born:** London, England; June 4, 1879
**Died:** Lerici, Italy; August 1, 1965

## Biography
Percy Lubbock was born on June 4, 1879, in London, the fourth of the six sons of Frederick Lubbock and the former Catherine Gurney. The Lubbock family had long been prominent in banking, education, and Liberal politics, while the Gurneys were well-known Quakers and philanthropists. Lubbock was educated at Eton College, where his tutor, Arthur Benson, the brother of novelist E. F. Benson, introduced him to such literary friends as Henry James and Edmund Gosse, and at King's College, Cambridge, where his fellow students included E. M. Forster and Lytton Strachey, though he was not close to either.

After Cambridge, he worked for the Board of Education in London for two years. From 1906 to 1908 he was librarian of Bibliotheca Pepysiana at Magdalene College, Cambridge, a post obtained for him by his friend Benson, then master of Magdalene. He next moved to London to work as an essayist and reviewer until World War I, which he spent with the British Red Cross, becoming head of the department for locating missing persons. He married Lady Sybil Cuffe in 1926 and lived in Italy at Fiesole and later Lerici until the beginning of World War II, when he and his wife went to Montreux, Switzerland, where she died in 1943. Lubbock returned to Lerici after the war; he died there in 1965.

## Influence
Lubbock's single work of criticism has been called the first study to treat the novel seriously as an art form. Ensuing works – from Forster's *Aspects of the Novel* (1927) to Wayne C. Booth's *The Rhetoric of Fiction* (1961) and even to the theories of the deconstructionists – owe something to Lubbock's analysis of the form of the novel and the methods the novelist employs to create this form. Novelists themselves have acknowledged the influence of *The Craft of Fiction*; Graham Greene, for example, said that early in his career he paid more attention to unity and point of view "after studying Percy Lubbock's admirable primer."

## Analysis
The significance of *The Craft of Fiction* was not seen by most of its reviewers, but Forster, in *Aspects of the Novel*, praised Lubbock's contribution: "Those who follow him will lay a sure foundation for the aesthetics of fiction." The book remained in disfavor for a time because it was judged too academic, but by 1944 Allen Tate was comparing it with Aristotle's *Poetics*, saying that Lubbock "had incomparably

the more difficult job to do." This job involved virtually inventing a means for describing the aesthetics of the novel. As Lubbock wrote of the critics of his time:

> we discuss the writer, we discuss the people in his book, we discuss the kind of life he renders and his success in the rendering. But meanwhile the book, the thing he made, lies imprisoned in the volume, and our glimpse of it was too fleeting . . . to leave us with a lasting knowledge of its form.

Lubbock's purpose is to reveal this form.

René Wellek and Austin Warren have called *The Craft of Fiction* "a Poetics of the novel based on the practice and the theory of Henry James." Lubbock considered his friend James "the only real *scholar* in the art." He acknowledges his debt to the theoretical commentary in James' prefaces and letters:

> the novel in its wayward exuberance had hardly been held to any serious account of its practice till it was called to confront the most magisterial of its makers. Henry James took the whole of its conduct in hand with a large assurance that cleared the air of certain old and obstinate misunderstandings, if only by loftily ignoring them.

Lubbock borrows much of his critical terminology – picture, scene, panorama, drama, subject – from James, yet he adds much more. His achievement, according to John W. Aldridge, "consists in his having elevated the products of both James' critical and his creative sensibility to the status of a closely reasoned esthetic of literary form."

Lubbock's goal is to make the readers of novels aware that the novel is an art form and that much can be gained by determining what methods the novelist is emphasizing, defining these methods, noticing how the writer changes or manipulates them, and deciding why the novelist has made certain choices and whether they are the most appropriate ones. Lubbock's aesthetics are hardly prescriptive, demanding only that the novelist "be consistent on *some* plan . . . . A critic, then, looks for the principle on which a novelist's methods are mingled and varied – looks for it, as usual, in the novelist's subject, and marks its application as the subject is developed."

Much of Lubbock's argument centers on the proper balance between what he calls the scenic, or pictorial, and the dramatic elements of a novel. The visual terminology he adapts from James is appropriate given his belief that "the art of fiction does not begin until the novelist thinks of his story as a matter to be *shown*, to be so exhibited that it will tell itself . . . . The book is not a row of facts, it is a single image." The novelist's ability to use art to control what the reader "sees" helps to distinguish the novel from the play, where no such control is possible.

At the same time, however, the pictorial qualities of a novel must still be dramatized. (Like James, Lubbock prefers internal drama to external action.) What happens in a novel, according to Lubbock, is that the various aesthetic tools are

> alternated, united, imposed one on another, this point of view blended with that, dramatic action treated pictorially, pictorial description rendered dramatically . . . . In well-fashioned work it is always interesting to discover how method tends to be laid upon method, so that we get, as it were, layers and stratifications in the treatment of a story.

Lubbock's work is revolutionary in recognizing this complex structure in the novel.

The novel's artistry depends upon how well the pictorial and dramatic elements are blended. Lubbock argues that the less dramatic the subject of a novel is, "the more it is needful to heighten its flat, pictorial, descriptive surface by the arts of drama." Failure to recognize the need to employ a dramatic technique thus weakens a novel, as when William Makepeace Thackeray imposes authorial intrusions. Lubbock believes in the possibility of an ideal shape through which the novel creates the illusion of reality and believes that it can be achieved through dramatic rather than narrative form – through enactment, not description. He acknowledges, however, that the dramatic form is not necessarily the best form for all circumstances in a novel; method is dictated by the subject.

Most of the commentary on Lubbock's contribution to an aesthetics of fiction stresses his observations about point of view. In discussing the pictorial aspects of Gustave Flaubert's *Madame Bovary* (1857; English translation, 1886), Lubbock explains how the novel's scenes are depicted from several points of view. As a result, Flaubert presents Emma Bovary both objectively and subjectively, making the reader conscious of his presence as well as hers. According to Lubbock, "The whole intricate question of method . . . I take to be governed by the question of the point of view – the question of the relation in which the narrator stands to the story." For Lubbock, manipulation of point of view should be the novelist's primary concern.

Although Lubbock understands that there are times when first-person narration has certain limitations, he prefers it to omniscient narration: "When the point of view is definitely included in the book, when it can be recognized and verified there, then every side of the book is equally wrought and fashioned." Lubbock believes that "it is much more satisfactory to know who the story-teller is, and to see him as a part of the story, than to be deflected away from the book by the author, an arbitrary, unmeasurable, unappraisable factor." The first-person narrator allows the novelist to disguise his or her voice, to be more artistic. Lubbock's enthusiasm for the apparent absence of the novelist and for James causes him to overstate his case when he claims that *The Ambassadors* (1903) is seen entirely from the point of view of Lambert Strether, ignoring that someone refers to the protagonist as "poor Strether."

Occasional contradictions and oversimplifications in *The Craft of Fiction* result, in the words of Timothy P. Martin, from Lubbock's attitude that the novel is "an artifact rather than a product of the artist's imagination and experience." Lubbock, in a sense, anticipates structuralist criticism in his concern with the reader as much as the writer, a reader who must re-create or reconstruct the form of the novel: "So far from losing ourselves in the world of the novel, we must hold it away from us, see it all in detachment, and use the whole of it to make the image we seek, the book itself." Lubbock thinks that the reader should prefer the pleasure of creation to that of losing personal identity in a world of illusions.

This detachment Lubbock calls for in the reader is perhaps the major difference between his theory of the novel and that of James, who aims at heightening the illusion of reality. James is also concerned with the moral side of art, but Lubbock almost ignores it, using "moral" only three times in *The Craft of Fiction*. One final connection between Lubbock and James is the groundbreaking analysis of James' later novels. According to Tony Tanner, sophisticated analysis of James begins with Lubbock, "the first to examine the actual operational details" of James' technique.

*The Craft of Fiction* has been criticized for numerous prejudices and deficiencies. Forster, for all his admiration of Lubbock, maintains that the book merely tells one how to write Jamesian novels. Many critics have complained that Lubbock ignores unique contributors to the form of the novel, Marcel Proust in particular. Timothy Martin, who has written perhaps the best analysis of Lubbock's book, points out that although Lubbock claims that form must serve the subject of a novel, most of *The Craft of Fiction* shows how subject should be the servant of form. The most common complaint is with Lubbock's style, called mandarin by Cyril Connolly, mannered and overly complicated by Robert Liddell.

Most of the commentary, however, affirms Lubbock's lofty position as a theorist of the novel. His book, writes Ashley Brown, "remains a starting point for the criticism of fiction," and Liddell says that "other aesthetic critics of the novel are only gleaning after Lubbock." Finally, Mark Schorer's rhetorical question suggests Lubbock's contribution: "Without Lubbock's respect for the artist in the novelist, the loose form of the novel would have floundered on for how many more years without the prestige that, as a form of art, it had always deserved?"

## Principal criticism
*The Craft of Fiction*, 1921

## Other major works and literary forms
Although best known as the author of *The Craft of Fiction*, Percy Lubbock also wrote novels, biographies, childhood reminiscences, essays, and reviews. His novel *The Region Cloud* (1925) is considered a weak imitation of Henry James, while his novel *Roman Pictures* (1923) is notable for its manipulation of a naive protagonist/narrator. Of his five biographies, the study of his friend Edith Wharton has received the most attention. His most significant work beyond his criticism is his editing of the final volumes in the New York edition of the collected works of Henry James and the first collection of James' letters.

NOVELS
*Roman Pictures*, 1923
*The Region Cloud*, 1925

NONFICTION
*Elizabeth Barrett Browning in Her Letters*, 1906
*Samuel Pepys*, 1909
*George Calderon: A Sketch from Memory*, 1921
*Earlham*, 1922
*Mary Cholmondeley: A Sketch from Memory*, 1928
*Shades of Eton*, 1929
*Portrait of Edith Wharton*, 1947

EDITED TEXTS
*A Book of English Prose*, 1913
*The Ivory Tower*, by Henry James, 1917
*The Middle Years*, by James, 1917
*The Sense of the Past*, by James, 1917
*The Letters of Henry James*, 1920
*The Novels and Stories of Henry James*, 1921–1923
*The Diary of Arthur Christopher Benson*, 1926

MISCELLANEOUS
Harkness, Marjory Gore, ed. *Percy Lubbock Reader*, 1957

## Further reading
Auchincloss, Louis. "My Dear Blest Percy," in *The New Criterion*. III (May, 1985), pp. 83–85.
Brown, Ashley. "Homage to Percy Lubbock," in *The Southern Review*. XV (January, 1979), pp. 22–33.
Goodman, Susan. *Edith Wharton's Inner Circle*, 1994.
Liddell, Robert. "Percy Lubbock," in *The Kenyon Review*. XXIX (September, 1967), pp. 493–511.
Martin, Timothy P. "Henry James and Percy Lubbock: From Mimesis to Formalism," in *Novel*. XIV (Fall, 1980), pp. 20–29.

MICHAEL ADAMS

*See also* James

# Lucian

Greek writer and critic

**Born:** Samosata, Syria; c. 120
**Died:** Athens, Greece; after 180

## Biography

What Lucian writes of himself is all that is known of him. He was born in Samosata, the capital of Commagene, in Syria (modern Turkey). As a youth, he was apprenticed to a sculptor. He became a student of rhetoric, under whose auspices is not known. Eventually he became an advocate and wandered, plying his trade, through Ionia, briefly settled at Antioch, and wandered again through Greece, Italy, and Gaul. By the age of forty he was an experienced rhetorician and speech writer, and he returned to his homeland to write the bulk of the material upon which his reputation rests.

He did not completely abandon travel, however, and even engaged in some adventuring. As a rather elderly man he obtained a position as procurator (a judicial post) of part of Egypt. There is some inference from his own work that he suffered from gout; he may have died of it. There is no evidence for the exact date of his death.

## Influence

Lucian is above all a satirist, and his status often suffers from the view that his efforts at literary criticism are critical rather than creative – that he only dismantles the works or opinions of others and offers nothing constructive in return. While this may be true of many of his dialogues, there are positive aspects to his critical works, and he was not above granting wholehearted approval to writings he considered truly worthy.

As a satirist, his influence stretches from Desiderius Erasmus to Sir Thomas More, from François Rabelais and Jonathan Swift to Percy Bysshe Shelley's circle. As a literary theorist, he was an Atticist, a supporter of the ancient Greek styles, as opposed to those popular in the Roman Empire of the second century. His writings play no major role in accounting for the history of critical theory itself, but his critical efforts are worthwhile, as they demonstrate the range and power of his unique mind.

## Analysis

Lucian's world has been described by John Jay Chapman as "the Romanized, pacified, citified, luxurious, lettered, Hellenized, dissolute Mediterranean world." Such times breed satirists. In this case, a man with knowledge of Greek traditions and lore, but without formal training in the ancient philosophies, took aim at any topic, genre, or theory which attracted his attention. His place in the history of criticism is determined as much by what he was as by what he wrote. Satire is older than Lucian, but Lucian may be the oldest satirist.

Lucian the satirist pervades Lucian the literary critic. In the society in which he lived he was the "character," the outsider, always on the attack and frequently attacked in return. His satire was often cruel, but he was not afraid to turn it on himself if the situation warranted: truth was truth, common sense was common sense, the attack must be pressed no matter who the victim. Ultimately, he probably suffered the chronic disease of the satirist: supreme dissatisfaction with all things, combined with a never-ending search for a literary form that did not smack of extremism or artificiality.

Lucian's ability to look at all subjects from the outside could have been a product of his training. He writes that he was largely self-supporting. He learned rhetoric in his early years from experience, travel, and practice – not from formal schooling. An example of the attitude he developed is evident in *A Professor of Public Speaking*, in which a potential student of the subject is facetiously invited to decide between learning rhetoric the real, difficult way, or to acquire it via modern shortcuts. The dialogue is a merciless embarrassment of the lazy modern. The school of experience is obviously preferable to a method which promises success without labor. These may be the bitter, raving opinions of a man who had given up rhetoric, as Lucian had, but they are primarily the attack of one who has earned his position, his money, and his talent, and who believes that there is no substitute for hard work. He is outside the new way, looking in at the mainstream. Society has sacrificed quality for expedience and separated the real thinkers from the masses who would make everything instantly comprehensible. Does the critic then move only in a small circle of erudite sophisticates (a solution that creates as many problems as it solves) or does he quit the genre entirely? Lucian chooses the path of the outsider.

Similarly, Lucian's critiques of pompous style, rhetorical trickery, exaggerated academic pursuits, and poor historiography all support the theory that the critic must be brutally honest and have no emotional attachment to his subject. Detachment and honesty are exhibited best when Lucian attacks his own concerns as a rhetorician, an Atticist, or a philosopher. An Atticist – some critics say a very superficial one, some say simply a moderate one – he mercilessly attacks the more dedicated Atticists for their absurd pursuits. He rakes solecists over the coals for seeking the arcane while ignoring the obvious. When caught in a mistake himself, as he is in *The Mistaken Critic*, the gloves come off, the attack is brutal, and the impression is of a critic who can never be satisfied: all literary effort is either insufficiently elevated or artificially formed.

Lucian's lifelong search for satisfaction is best reflected in the wide range of his efforts and the often self-contradictory behavior he exhibited. He tried his hand at almost every available genre and is credited with inventing – or perfecting – one of them, the dialogue. At each new effort, he deprecated the previous ones and the purposes to which they were put.

Detractors point out that it was easy for Lucian to satirize. He did not succeed at any real literary effort, and his knowledge of ancient poetry, rhetoric, and philosophy was just deep enough to allow him to destroy the current manifestations of these endeavors, but only by setting them up as straw men. In particular, Lucian's few forays into the criticism of classical poetry come under heavy attack, because he did not have, or at least did not express, any theoretical knowledge of the genre, only a thematic one. These are stringent views of Lucian, and they provide his own best defense. He reports, in one of his apologies, that indeed he is not a wise man, but that he never claimed wisdom; few satirists have. If Lucian is a thematic critic, it is because theme is the product – the application of literature – and the product, as any real rhetorician knows, is the most important aspect of literature. The practical, the useful, towers over Lucian's work. If we dismiss him as too theoretically irrelevant, we dismiss our conscience.

The measure of Lucian the critic is Lucian the satirist. The influence of his writings, his place in history, is most obvious when the times are like his. Other outsiders, other dissatisfied satirists whose criticism knows no bounds, owe him their positions; the ability of societies and cultures to tolerate them probably began with Lucian. That beginning led to tradition. Specific works of Lucian that influenced specific writers of later ages are not as important as the general stature of the man.

Lucian criticized fanatical Christians in a way that almost doomed his reputation to that of a heretic. As he was discovered during the Renaissance, it took the special perceptions of Sir Thomas More and Desiderius Erasmus to make Lucian the man emerge from Lucian the critic. That one may criticize without completely condemning was a Humanist thought and not in the truly critical spirit of Lucian. Yet his example cannot be ignored, even if it came in through the back door. Erasmus' fifty-six *Colloquies* (1522–1533, nine volumes) owe much to the Lucianic dialogue. More's *Utopia* (1516) is a product of *A True History*. François Rabelais was much like Lucian: versatile, well-traveled, well-read, well-spoken, witty, obscene, and energetic. Lucian was his favorite Greek writer. It is no surprise that Rabelais' satires, notably *Gargantua* (1534) and *Pantagruel* (1532), reflect a desire for moderation and a distaste for tyrannical methods.

Lucian often satirized people by removing them from their normal surroundings, for purpose of comparison. The age in which satire and reason coexisted, the eighteenth century, bred the same method. Lucian's "outsider" persona was evident in Jonathan Swift, and *A True History* is clearly evident in *Gulliver's Travels* (1726).

The influence of Lucian is present in the Romantic period as well. Walter Savage Landor's *Imaginary Conversations of Greeks and Romans* (1853) echoes Lucian's dialogues,

as does *The Pentameron* (1837) in which Giovanni Boccaccio and Petrarch discuss Dante's poetry. Thomas Love Peacock's satirical efforts, especially those aimed at "fashionable" literature, contain the essence of Lucian: rough handling with little or no constructive effort to replace what is satirized.

Lucian is, in many respects, the most accessible of the classic writers. His skepticism, his tendency to drop a concept at the first sign of corruption, and his inclination to drop out rather than correct, are all very modern. Lucian wanted a world that contained universal respect for the past, common agreement on values and precepts, and practical literature, unsullied by poor thought, blatant superstition, or political motive. He never got it, but his position as the leading critic of an age much like this age makes him more than relevant. Chapman points out: "He was Romanized, and we are Romanized." If this is so, then modern readers should heed his method and his truth.

## Principal criticism

*Dikē phōnēentōn* (The Consonants at Law)
*Lexiphanes*
*Pōs dei historian sungraphein* (History as It Should Be Written)
*Rhētorōn didaskalos* (A Professor of Public Speaking)
*Pseudologistēs ē peri tēs apophrados* (The Mistaken Critic)
*Dēmosthenous enkōmion* (In Praise of Demosthenes)
*Pseudosophistēs ē soloikistēs* (The Sham Sophist)

## Other major works and literary forms

Lucian survives in more than eighty works. The range of his efforts is impressive, but the quality is inconsistent. Rhetorical works, criticism, biography, romances, dialogues, and poetry all received his attention. His satirical works are in many respects prototypical. It is common to trace the romance, and perhaps even the novel, to his *Alēthōn diēgēmatōn* (A True History), a fantastic story of a journey to the moon. His minor pieces are precursors of the essay.

Lucian's fame rests on the Lucian Dialogues, which combine the Platonic Dialogue with the comedy of Aristophanes, with wide variance in style and worth. They are sometimes brutal attacks on everything from ancient poets to philosophy, and from religion to manners. His "biographies" are mostly anecdotal, his rhetorical works derivative, and his mock-tragic poems unimportant.

NOVEL
*Alēthōn diēgēmatōn* (A True History)

NONFICTION
*Nekrikoi dialogoi* (Dialogues of the Dead)
*Enalioi dialogoi* (Dialogues of the Sea Gods)
*Theōn dialogoi* (Dialogues of the Gods)
*Hetairikoi dialogoi* (Dialogues of the Courtesans)

MISCELLANEOUS
*Certaine Select Dialogues of Lucian, Together with His True Historie*, 1634
*Lucian's Works*, 1684

## Further reading

Baldwin, Barry. *Studies in Lucian*, 1973.
Branham, R. Bracht. *Unruly Eloquence: Lucian and the Comedy of Traditions*, 1989.
Chapman, John Jay. *Lucian, Plato, and Greek Morals*, 1931.
Craig, Hardin. "The Vitality of an Old Classic: Lucian and Lucianism," in *The Written Word and Other Essays*, 1953.
Frye, Northrop. *Anatomy of Criticism*, 1957.
Hadas, Moses. *A History of Greek Literature*, 1950.
Harmon, A. M. Introduction to *The Works of Lucian*, 1913–1959.
Jones, C. P. *Culture and Society in Lucian*, 1986.
Lesky, Albin. *A History of Greek Literature*, 1963. Translated by James Willis and Cornelis Heer.
Murray, Gilbert. *A History of Ancient Greek Literature*, 1897.
Robinson, Christopher. *Lucian and His Influence in Europe*, 1979.

DAVID P. SMITH

*See also* Classical Greek and Roman Literary Theory; Horace; Longinus; Quintilian

# Georg Lukács

## Hungarian theorist and critic

**Born:** Budapest, Hungary; April 13, 1885
**Died:** Budapest, Hungary; June 4, 1971

## Biography

Georg Lukács was born on April 13, 1885, in Budapest, Hungary. He came from a wealthy Jewish family; his father was a banker in Budapest. Lukács studied at the universities of Budapest and Berlin. The philosopher Georg Simmel and the sociologist Max Weber were his teachers. After travels in Italy, Lukács lived in Heidelberg, where he belonged to Max Weber's circle. The publication of a collection of his essays, *Die Seele und die Formen* (1911; *Soul and Form*, 1974), established Lukács as a critic of international reputation in Central Europe.

In 1917 Lukács returned to Budapest, joined the Communist Party of Hungary, and became People's Commissar for public education in the short-lived government of the Hungarian Communist republic of 1919. After its overthrow by the counterrevolutionary forces under Admiral Horthy de Nagybánya, Lukács was forced to flee to Austria, where he settled in Vienna.

When, in 1923, Lukács published *Geschichte und Klassenbewusstsein: Studien über Marxistische Dialektik* (*History and Class Consciousness*, 1971), the Communist International charged him with "revisionism," a charge that was to haunt him for the rest of his life. When a similar charge was brought against him in 1929, he withdrew from politics. From 1929 to 1931 he lived in Moscow and from 1931 to 1933 in Berlin, where he was involved in the organization of the League of Proletarian Revolutionary

Writers. After Adolf Hitler's seizure of power, he emigrated to the Soviet Union, where he worked at the Philosophical Institute of the Academy of Sciences, laying the foundation for his major works.

In 1945, at the end of World War II, Lukács returned to Budapest after twenty-five years of exile. In the period in which Hungary aligned itself with the Soviet Bloc, renewed accusations of revisionism caused Lukács again to withdraw from political life. When a popular anti-Communist revolt broke out in October, 1956, a new coalition government under Imre Nagy declared Hungary neutral and withdrew from the Warsaw Pact. It was in this brief coalition government that Lukács served as Minister of Culture. Soon, however, Soviet troops suppressed the revolt, and Lukács was deported to Romania.

In 1957 he was allowed to return to Budapest, and with his brief political career over, he devoted himself until his death in 1971 to his studies in aesthetics, ontology, and ethics. Although he was essentially ignored by the Communist establishment in Eastern Europe for the rest of his life, he was buried in Budapest with all due Party honors. All major newspapers in the West published obituaries, acknowledging his contributions to literary criticism and intellectual history.

## Influence

Lukács, perhaps the most influential Marxist literary critic in the twentieth century, reinterpreted the canon of European literature from the eighteenth to the twentieth century to establish a model for Marxist literary criticism and Marxist history of literature. Lukács offered a more sophisticated theory of literature than the official doctrine of Socialist Realism. He developed into an opponent of Stalinism in literature and had no tolerance for the inferior products of Socialist Realism. He rehabilitated some of the proscribed writers of the past, such as Fedor Dostoevskii, and supported writers in conflict with Socialist Realism, such as Aleksandr Solzhenitsyn. Lukács showed how the "great realism" of early-nineteenth-century writers such as Johann Wolfgang von Goethe, Lev Tolstoi, and Honoré de Balzac could serve as a model for twentieth-century literature. Thus, Lukács praised the works of Thomas Mann, while denouncing James Joyce, Franz Kafka, and Bertolt Brecht.

## Analysis

As a literary scholar and critic, Lukács was primarily concerned with the historical, political, and social dynamics of literature. Literature to Lukács was not simply a political tool or social documentation. In fact, he stressed the originality and freedom of the writer's imagination. He pointed out how artistic imagination reflects the reality of the historical process, elevating events and circumstances that may appear devoid of meaning to the level of symbolic significance. The outstanding feature of Lukács' theory of literature is that literature as a form of art has the function of "a seeing, hearing, and feeling organon of humanity – of humanity in every human being." Literature, therefore, plays a most important role in the development of our consciousness of humanity; it forms an integral part of the process of freeing us from our state of alienation.

Lukács' approach to literature was philosophical, his vision of history was Marxist, and his aesthetics was Hegelian. G. W. F. Hegel was most influential in the sense that Lukács adopted his view of the historical development of form in art. From Hegel and Karl Marx, Lukács evolved his own philosophy of history, which was formulated in *History and Class Consciousness*. A major work in Marxist philosophy, this book integrated Marx's interpretation of history – a chronicle of human emancipation from the class struggle – with Hegel's concept of totality. Its particular significance for the theory of literature lies in the fact that, in it, Lukács had articulated the basic framework from which his literary criticism could be developed.

In *Die Theorie des Romans: Ein geschichtsphilosophischer versuch über die Formen der grossen Epik* (completed in 1916, published as a book in 1920; *The Theory of the Novel: A Historico-Philosophical Essay on the Forms of Great Epic Literature*, 1971), which marked Lukács' transition from the Neo-Platonism and Neo-Kantianism of his early essays in *Soul and Form* to Hegelianism, Lukács relates the genres of epic and novel to Western intellectual history. Epic poetry, he maintains, expresses a sense of the "extensive totality of life," as experienced in Greece at the dawn of history. The novel is regarded as "an expression of the transcendental homelessness" of modern humanity, its development being paralleled by the decline of religious myth and the rise of scientific ideology. *The Theory of the Novel* was Lukács' first step in formulating his theory that artistic forms can be perceived in terms of historical development.

It was after Lukács' emigration to the Soviet Union that the doctrine of Socialist Realism was officially proclaimed. Under the ideological umbrella of this doctrine, Lukács began to develop his own theory of the "great realism." Basing his theory on Lenin's epistemology in *Materializm i empiriokrititsizm* (1908; *Materialism and Empiriocriticism*, 1927), which posits a "real world" that is independent of the mind, Lukács considered art a special form of reflecting "reality that exists independently of our consciousness." The work of art, however, does not mirror reality directly, only indirectly. Works of art that reflect reality directly were condemned by Lukács as "naturalistic," while those that are too far removed from reality were denounced as "formalistic." This aesthetic theory became the basis of Lukács' literary criticism for the years to come. His "great realism" differed from Socialist Realism in paying more attention to the classical heritage and in deemphasizing the importance of adhering to the Party line in literary works. Lukács' literary taste gravitated to the writers of the

eighteenth and nineteenth centuries, however conservative they may have been, and he was always opposed to mere propaganda literature. He repeatedly refused to endorse the Socialist Realist writers of the Stalinist era, an attitude for which he was to be attacked by the Communist Party in the late 1950s.

During the 1930s Lukács participated in the discussion on the origins and goals of German expressionism that was published in the German exile journal *Das Wort* in Moscow during the period 1937 to 1938, and that was to become one of the most important debates in the history of Marxist aesthetics. The two major antagonists, Brecht and Lukács, were both vehemently opposed to German Fascism. Brecht maintained that Communist writers must break radically with traditional forms and that they must utilize modern techniques. Lukács sought to employ the liberal and humanist traditions of bourgeois art as allies against Fascism, condemning at the same time modern art as decadent or formalist. Thus, Lukács denounced James Joyce, John Dos Passos, and Alfred Döblin, while praising Maxim Gorky, Romain Rolland, and Thomas and Heinrich Mann for their realism.

In *Der historische Roman* (1935; *The Historical Novel*, 1962) Lukács cited the historical novel, as represented by Sir Walter Scott, Balzac, and Tolstoi, as the prime example of realist literature, since this type of narrative demonstrates not only the effect of historical reality upon literature but also the interrelationship of economic and social developments with literature and art. The integrity of the genre, threatened by the romanticists and the conservatively bourgeois writers after the revolution of 1848, is reestablished by Anatole France, Stefan Zweig, Lion Feuchtwanger, Romain Rolland, and Heinrich Mann.

Lukács' studies in European realism are characterized by questions such as "Balzac or Flaubert?" and "Tolstoi or Dostoevskii?" Making the representation of reality the criterion for his judgment, Lukács decided in favor of Balzac and Tolstoi. Balzac exemplified Friedrich Engels' idea of "triumph of realism," that is, a great writer cannot but portray reality, even if such reality conflicts with his or her ideology. In the case of Gustave Flaubert, Lukács is critical of the writer's preoccupation with literature as "revelation of the inner life," which does not constitute reality in Lukács' opinion.

Thomas Mann, for Lukács, is one of the great realists, "the last great bourgeois writer" and representative of German humanism. In his *Thomas Mann* (1949; *Essays on Thomas Mann*, 1964) Lukács traces Mann's brand of realism back to Goethe. In his studies *Skizze einer Geschichte der neueren deutschen Literatur* (1953; an outline of the history of modern German literature) and *Die Zerstörung der Vernunft* (1954; *The Destruction of Reason*, 1981) Lukács demonstrates the interrelationship between political and intellectual history in German literature and philosophy; he points out a progressive and a regressive trend within German culture, rationalism, and humanism as represented by Gotthold Ephraim Lessing, Goethe, Hegel, Heinrich Heine, Marx, and Thomas Mann on the one hand and irrationalism and barbarism as represented by the "romanticists" Richard Wagner and Friedrich Nietzsche on the other hand. In these studies, Lukács attempts to analyze the German catastrophe of the Nazi era while also formulating designs for a better future.

Lukács had a somewhat troubled relationship to modern literature and displayed a conservative animosity toward all forms of modernism. He saw the increasing obsession with psychopathology as central to all modernist literature – a theme which he developed at some length in his work *Wider den missverstandenen Realismus* (1958; *Realism in Our Time: Literature and the Class Struggle*, 1964). The great exception was Thomas Mann, ideal model of the modern writer for Lukács. Brecht, on the other hand, was labeled a Formalist, and Franz Kafka stood condemned as a representative of decadence. Brecht's concept of "alienation" (*Entfremdung*) and his idea of an "epic" or "dialectic theater" did not fit into Lukács' concept of great realism. Even though Lukács finally did justice to the most important playwright of his time, he did so by according him a place within the cathartic drama in the tradition of Aristotle and Lessing, which amounts to a basic misunderstanding of Brecht's contribution to modern drama.

In *Realism in Our Time*, Lukács perceived the opposition of realism versus antirealism (avant-gardism and decadence) in terms of the conflict of peace versus war. The problem of international politics became crystallized for Lukács in the literary question "Thomas Mann or Franz Kafka?" Lukács saw the experience of modernism expressed in the feeling of angst, or universal anxiety, as portrayed in Kafka's short stories and novels. Kafka's portrait of people submitting fatalistically to a seemingly senseless fate discouraged people from taking charge of their lives and coming to grips with history for the sake of progressing humanity. While never denying that Kafka was a serious, important writer, Lukács did not consider him a model for a literature of the future.

The last phase of Lukács' literary criticism is characterized by his opposition to manifestations of Stalinism in literature, such as the mandatory expression of Socialist Realism and political control of the artist in general. He energetically fought the "expedient character" of Stalinist theories of art, working for what he called the "liquidation of Stalinism in literature." In this context, Lukács hailed Aleksandr Solzhenitsyn as a major force in re-directing Socialist Realism toward the revolutionary origins of socialist literature during the 1920s. He compared the Russian author to Joseph Conrad and Ernest Hemingway and extolled the virtues of Solzhenitsyn's criticism of the Stalinist period in his novels. According to Lukács, these novels marked Solzhenitsyn as heir to the best tendencies in modern realism and to the tradition of Tolstoi and Dostoevskii in Russian literature. Lukács was not able to predict Solzhenitsyn's exile to the United States, but he noticed a basic pessimism in his work that is alien to a typically socialist writer.

During these last years, Lukács also adopted the Aristotelian concept of mimesis (imitation of reality) and catharsis in place of Lenin's theory of reflection. *Die Eigenart des Ästhetischen* (1963; the specific nature of the aesthetic), which forms part of a projected magnum opus of his later years, introduces Aristotle's definition of art as mimesis, stressing the anthropomorphic, evocative, and especially the cathartic function of art.

Although *Zur Ontologie des gesellschaftlichen Seins* (1971–1973; "On the Ontology of Social Existence," volume 1 of *Marx's Basic Ontological Principles*, 1978), the first Marxist ontology written since Marx, was completed before his death, a planned work of ethics had only been begun at his death. Lukács' projected autobiography is preserved in outline in *Gelebtes Leben: Eine Autobiographie im Dialog* (1981).

World literature in the Goethean sense was always the primary goal of Lukács' literary criticism. As one of the most important and stimulating Marxist theoreticians of literature and aesthetics, Lukács influenced decisively the theory and practice of literary criticism not only in Eastern Europe but also in Western Europe and in the United States. Any formalist, structuralist, or poststructuralist school of literary criticism cannot fail to benefit from the historical perspective that Lukács brought to the understanding of literature.

## Principal criticism

*Die Seele und die Formen*, 1911 (*Soul and Form*, 1974)
*Die Theorie des Romans: Ein geschichtsphilosophischer Versuch über die Formen der grossen Epik*, 1920 (*The Theory of the Novel: A Historico-Philosophical Essay on the Forms of Great Epic Literature*, 1971)
*Der historische Roman*, 1935 (*The Historical Novel*, 1962)
*Goethe und seine Zeit*, 1947 (*Goethe and His Age*, 1968)
*Essays über Realismus* 1948
*Der russische Realismus in der Weltliteratur*, 1949 (partial translation in *Studies in European Realism*, 1964)
*Thomas Mann*, 1949 (*Essays on Thomas Mann*, 1964)
*Deutsche Realisten des 19. Jahrhunderts*, 1951
*Balzac und der französische Realismus*, 1952 (partial translation in *Studies in European Realism*, 1964)
*Skizze einer Geschichte der neueren deutschen Literatur*, 1953
*Beiträge zur Geschichte der Ästhetik*, 1954
*Probleme des Realismus*, 1955
*Wider den missverstandenen Realismus*, 1958 (*Realism in Our Time: Literature and the Class Struggle*, 1964)
*Schriften zur Literatursoziologie*, 1961
*Ästhetik, Teil 1: Die Eigenart des Ästhetischen*, 1963 (2 volumes)
*Über die Besonderheit als Kategorie der Ästhetik*, 1967
*Solschenizyn*, 1969 (*Solzhenitsyn*, 1970)
*Heidelberger Philosophie der Kunst: 1912–1914*, 1974
*Heidelberger Ästhetik: 1916–1918*, 1975
*Entwicklungsgeschichte des modernen Dramas*, 1981

*Moskauer Schriften: Zur Literaturtheorie und Literaturpolitik, 1934-1940,* 1981

## Other major works and literary forms

In addition to the books listed above, Georg Lukács published a number of books on German and neo-Marxist philosophy, on Communist Party ideology and politics, and several hundred articles, essays, and reviews. While many of these deal with topics of world literature, others consider the interrelationships among history, culture, and revolution on a more general level. Above all, Lukács was one of the most prominent figures in neo-Marxist philosophy, and many of his book titles reflect his productivity and stature in this field.

NONFICTION

*Geschichte und Klassenbewusstsein: Studien über Marxistische Dialektik,* 1923 (*History and Class Consciousness,* 1971)
*Lenin: Studie über den Zusammenhang seiner Gedanken,* 1924 (*Lenin: A Study on the Unity of His Thought,* 1971)
*Moses Hess und die Problem der idealistischen Dialektik,* 1926
*Der junge Hegel,* 1948 (*The Young Hegel,* 1976)
*Karl Marx und Friedrich Engels als Literaturhistoriker,* 1948
*Schicksalswende: Beiträge zu einer neuen deutschen Ideologie,* 1948
*Existentialismus oder Marxismus?,* 1951
*Die Zerstörung der Vernunft,* 1954 (*The Destruction of Reason,* 1981)
*Niezsche és a fasizmus,* 1964
*Von Nietzsche bis Hitler: Oder, Der Irrationalismus und der deutschen Politik,* 1966
*Gespräche mit Georg Lukács: Hans Heinz Holz, Leo Kofler, Wolfgang Abendroth,* 1967 (*Conversations with Lukács,* 1975)
*Writer and Critic, and Other Essays,* 1970
*Zur Ontologie des gesellschaftlichen Seins,* 1971-1973 (3 volumes partial translation in *Marx's Basic Ontological Principles,* 1978)
*Political Writings: 1919-1929,* 1972
*Marxism and Human Liberation: Essays on History, Culture, and Revolution,* 1973
*Politische Aufsätze,* 1975-1977 (2 volumes)
*Gelebtes Leben: Eine Autobiographie im Dialog,* 1981
*Georg Lukács: Briefwechsel 1902-1917,* 1982 (partial translation in *Georg Lukács: Selected Correspondence, 1902-1920: Dialogues with Weber, Simmel, Buber, Manheim, and Others,* 1986)
*Reviews and Articles from "Die rote Fahne,"* 1983

## Further reading

Arato, Andrew, and Paul Breines. *The Young Lukács and the Origins of Western Marxism,* 1979.
Bahr, Ehrhard, and Ruth G. Kunzer. *Georg Lukács,* 1972.
Bernstein, J. M. *The Philosophy of the Novel: Lukács, Marxism and the Dialectics of Form,* 1984.
Congdon, Lee. *The Young Lukács,* 1983.
Demetz, Peter. *Marx, Engels, and the Poets: Origins of Marxist Literary Criticism,* 1967 (revised edition).
Gluck, Mary. *Georg Lukács and His Generation, 1900-1918,* 1985.
Heller, Agnes, ed. *Lukács Reassessed,* 1986.
Jameson, Frederic. *Marxism and Form: Twentieth Century Dialectical Theories of Literature,* 1971.
Kardarkay, Arpad. *Georg Lukács: Life, Thought and Politics,* 1991.
Királyfalvi, Béla. *The Aesthetics of György Lukács,* 1975.
Lichtheim, George. *George Lukács,* 1970.
Löwy, Michael. *Georg Lukács: From Romanticism to Bolshevism,* 1980.
Mészáros, István. *Lukács' Concept of Dialectic, with Biography, Bibliography, and Documents,* 1972.
Parkinson, George H. R., ed. *Georg Lukács: The Man, His Work, and His Ideas,* 1970.
Pike, David. *Lukács and Brecht,* 1985.
Rockmore, Tom. *Lukács Today: Essays in Marxist Philosophy,* 1988.

EHRHARD BAHR

*See also* Adorno: Benjamin; Brecht; Eagleton; Gramsci; Marxist Theory and Criticism; Realism

# Anatolii Lunacharskii

Russian writer and critic

**Born:** Poltava, Ukraine, Russian Empire; November 23, 1875
**Died:** Menton, France; December 26, 1933

## Biography

Anatolii Lunacharskii was born in Poltava, a city southeast of Kiev in the Ukraine, on November 23, 1875. He was the son of Aleksandr Antonov, a state councillor, and Aleksandra Lunacharskaia (who retained the surname of her former husband). It is possible that Antonov's radical political leanings may have contributed to Lunacharskii's early interest in socialist thought. He grew up alongside three older stepbrothers and a younger brother; when the family moved to Kiev, he was educated in a local Gymnasium. With other students, he became involved in revolutionary agitation among local workers and artisans. Though he read widely and in many subjects, he was denied academic advancement, probably because of his political activities. When it became clear that he could not expect admission to any Russian university, Lunacharskii left for Europe; in 1895 he commenced a period of study at the University of Zürich. He began to associate with Russians living abroad, however, and again became involved with leftist groups.

Shortly after returning to Russia, he was arrested, and in 1902 he was sentenced to two years of internal exile under police surveillance. During a 1904 visit to France, he met Lenin for the first time. During the Russian revolution of 1905, he returned again to his native country, where he took an active part in radical political work; in 1907 he emigrated once more. Although for a time Lunacharskii and Lenin differed over theoretical questions, once they were reconciled Lunacharskii's assistance became invaluable to the Bolshevik leader. Lunacharskii returned to Russia in May, 1917, two months after the monarchy had been swept away by revolution. In November, when the first Soviet government was formed, he became the commissar of education. In spite of some qualms – he threatened to resign his position if harm came to Russia's cultural monuments – he proved effective in generating support for the new regime. Some observers contended that he was second only to Leon Trotskii as an effective and persuasive spokesman for the Bolshevik Party. By promoting the development of educational institutions, he also did much to assist in the spread of literacy.

Lunacharskii was married twice: to Anna Malinovskaia in 1902, and to Natal'ia Aleksandrovna Sats in 1922. During his later years he became involved with diplomatic work abroad. Beginning in 1927 he served with the delegation that prepared Soviet disarmament proposals for presentation to the League of Nations. In 1929 he left the commissariat of education after some of its functions were transferred to other bodies. Failing health, as well as misgivings about the political regimentation that increasingly affected Soviet life, troubled him during his later years. His last appointment was as ambassador to Spain, but before he could take up his post he died from arteriosclerosis in Menton, France, on December 26, 1933.

## Influence

During his work in the Soviet commissariat of education, Lunacharskii exercised great influence, and it seems likely that the innovative and wide-ranging spirit of Soviet culture during the 1920s owed much to his broad and tolerant vision of socialist aesthetics. Although Lunacharskii's own preferences were definite and clear-cut, he did not insist upon political conformism. Not only did he favor certain experimental approaches to literature and art, but in many ways Lunacharskii also encouraged interest in foreign writers who were thought to be sympathetic to Soviet ideals. This effervescent period came to an abrupt end when Lunacharskii left the commissariat of education; in 1934, shortly after his death, Socialist Realism officially became the guiding doctrine of Soviet writers. Enforced adherence to specified standards thereafter led to monotonous and stereotyped forms in most Soviet literature. Years later, however, when cultural restrictions were relaxed, many Soviet writers began to look to Lunacharskii's writings for guidelines in the development of a Marxist framework that would permit diversity in literary styles and techniques.

## Analysis

Lunacharskii's literary theories were formulated against a background of ideological controversy and political tension that was inevitably reflected in his works. His erudition and breadth of vision, however, gave many of his writings a wider scope. He had an impressive command of foreign languages – including English, French, German, Italian, and Latin – which allowed great latitude for his comparative studies. His critical studies examine not only Russian literature but also that of other countries. As with various other Marxist writers, his efforts to apply dialectical materialism sometimes led to some rather abrupt and arbitrary efforts at classification. Moreover, many of his studies were written in some haste, in response to literary issues as they arose; other works were composed specifically in connection with anniversaries, literary gatherings, or other major events. Nevertheless, many of his articles convey a view of literature that transcends partisanship; he was generally unwilling to condemn other authors on purely ideological grounds. Furthermore, he was fascinated with the possibilities opened by innovations that had appeared during his own time; his interest in the theater, for example, led him into a corresponding interest in film. He ventured the opinion that motion pictures could serve as the most effective medium for the dissemination of ideas. At the same time, his respect for the literary heritage of Russia and Europe led him to support the widespread publication of more traditional works. There was thus an eclecticism to Lunacharskii's approach to literary questions, an eclecticism which, though narrowed at times by his Marxist outlook, allowed judgments that were particularly diverse and provocative by official Soviet standards.

Lunacharskii's philosophical views were not entirely consistent, nor were they always in accord with the ideas of other Marxist thinkers. While he was a student in Switzerland, at about the age of twenty, he came under the influence of Richard Avenarius, who espoused a doctrine of empiriocriticism that was derived from the teachings of the philosopher and physicist Ernst Mach. Although ideas of this sort were not meant specifically to support or to rebut Marxist conceptions, they did suggest that distinctions between Idealism and materialism would not need to be recognized. Lunacharskii, seizing upon such notions, began to regard Marxism as having a mission analogous to that of traditional faiths; furthermore, he contended that, once it was maintained that religion derived its support from the credence accorded it by its followers, Marxism could be considered to have a similar function: it could supply purpose and value to the lives of political activists. The idea that traditional religion could be superseded by dedication to Marxist ideals was most clearly apparent in Lunacharskii's early writings on socialist thought. For a time, Maksim Gor'kii's philosophical outlook began to converge with that of Lunacharskii where the enterprise of *bogostroitelstvo* (god-building) was concerned, and in places Gor'kii's novels reflect this concern for deeper truths. In time, however, interest in this idea dwindled; for his part, Lunacharskii deferred to Lenin's argument that empiriocriticism could not be reconciled with the tenets of dialectical materialism. Nevertheless, some traces of this notion can be seen in later works such as Lunacharskii's writings on education; at times he suggested that commitment to the ideals of enlightenment could serve as an independent basis for the inspiration and edification of the masses. In other ways he seemed to regard literature as having a special calling and purpose in affecting the views of its readers.

On other counts, the ideological issues raised in Lunacharskii's works did not seem to impose specific limitations as to particular schools of criticism. Frequently, he noted progressive traits in great authors from the past and ascribed their shortcomings to problems of the social context in which they worked. Class consciousness and political leanings became more important criteria in Lunacharskii's considerations of modern writers, yet he was able to appreciate a diversity of literary techniques and styles. Thus, for example, he praised the work of Symbolist writers whose views could be reconciled with socialist ideals; those who evaded social commitments he tended to censure. He vigorously disapproved of Formalism as a literary movement, but he found positive traits in those who espoused Futurism from a leftist standpoint. Others of that inclination, notably those who supported rightist movements in European politics, he denounced. In commenting on leading trends in Soviet literature, Lunacharskii frequently spoke approvingly of realism; still, he did not insist upon precise delineations in his discussion of the theoretical bases of various works. Indeed, he suggested that form was not a decisive element in determining the value of literary works. Toward the end of his life, Lunacharskii did write a series of articles in support of Socialist Realism. Although in those works he defended the conceptions officially set forth by the Soviet government, he did not attach restrictive connotations to his formulation of this theory.

While Lunacharskii's views were widely respected within Russian revolutionary circles, some differences of judgment arose when the ideas of other leading theorists came into play. He acknowledged the contributions of Georgii Plekhanov, the first major Russian thinker to embrace Marxism; there was some discord, however, over political issues, notably in view of Plekhanov's leading position in the Menshevik Party. Lunacharskii also took Plekhanov to task for his views on modern literature, which Lunacharskii believed to be overly doctrinaire. Lunacharskii sometimes was bemused by the attitude toward literature of Lenin, who took little interest in experimental approaches to modern poetry, even where a professedly proletarian outlook was expressed; Lenin also manifested some impatience when Lunacharskii pursued his avocation as a playwright even during troubled and decisive periods for the Soviet state. Nevertheless, Lenin accorded him his full confidence in the administration of educational and cultural affairs. There was genuine respect between them, and Lunacharskii became fond of citing statements Lenin had made indicating his awareness of literary concerns. Some differences became apparent, however, where the ideas of other Bolshevik theoreticians were concerned. To a greater extent than Trotskii, who also wrote on this

subject, Lunacharskii maintained that some forms of continuity might remain where past and present ideas were conjoined in new proletarian forms of literature. There is some evidence that during his later years Lunacharskii was disquieted by the mechanistic interpretations advanced by followers of Soviet premier Joseph Stalin, though he did not outwardly take issue with official Soviet doctrines.

Lunacharskii's writings on classical Russian literature reveal a keen appreciation for the achievements of great authors which coexisted – at times uneasily – with a critical eye toward the political implications of their works. In some cases, he was inclined to speculate on the position major writers would have taken in the context of later struggles, when radical and revolutionary leaders came out in open opposition to the czarist regime. He showed particular approval for the views of Aleksandr Radishchev, who toward the end of the eighteenth century had produced a fictional account of a journey between St. Petersburg and Moscow; Lunacharskii held that in his exposition of the evils of serfdom Radishchev had manifested an outlook that was not merely liberal but indeed revolutionary. Among writers of the early nineteenth century, Lunacharskii had high regard for the dramatist Aleksandr Griboedov, whose comedies were a vehicle for trenchant social commentary.

In examining the works of Aleksandr Pushkin, Lunacharskii encountered some odd dilemmas for his form of Marxist criticism. Although he regarded Pushkin as the first major author to convey Russia's cultural ethos, he expressed some reservations about the great poet's aristocratic ancestry and his association with others of his class. On aesthetic grounds, Lunacharskii found Pushkin's works original and superbly crafted; in many instances, their literary quality was beyond reproach. Lunacharskii found it significant that Pushkin had come under suspicion on the part of the autocracy and had spent part of his later career under government surveillance. Moreover, the broad and varied appeal of Pushkin's creative works among the literary public proved that his themes transcended the narrow concerns of an elite. Lunacharskii also recognized the attainments of Mikhail Lermontov and Nikolai Gogol', in whose works he discerned an implicit critique of their society.

Lunacharskii traced the development of literary criticism, discussing the works of Greek, Roman, and early modern theorists; some of his more important historical writings deal with the progress of critical thought in Russia. He particularly sought to determine the extent to which earlier literary critics and theorists had anticipated Marxist lines of analysis or had shown some concern for the well-being of the masses. He had warm praise for the efforts of Vissarion Belinskii, who had produced influential works during the fourth and fifth decades of the nineteenth century; to Belinskii belonged the honor of having established social consciousness as a central criterion by which literary efforts could be assessed. Lunacharskii maintained that in some respects Belinskii had foreseen the emergence of the proletariat as a political and social force; indeed, had he lived later, Belinskii almost certainly would have supported the Bolsheviks. Lunacharskii also wrote at some length on the literary studies of Nikolai Chernyshevskii, who was regarded as important by some Marxist critics but who had also been reproached for his utopian and seemingly unsystematic point of view. While acknowledging that Chernyshevskii's ideas did not in all respects accord with Marxist perspectives, Lunacharskii considered that his socialist leanings had been a vital stepping-stone in the progress toward Soviet Marxist literary theory.

Rather definite political standards were applied in Lunacharskii's judgments of creative writers from the later nineteenth and early twentieth centuries. By that time, liberalism, populism, and socialism had won adherents among the intelligentsia, and it was possible to identify various writers with specific current ideological positions. Lunacharskii's use of such criteria, however, did not so much signal disapproval as an effort to point the way toward positive and constructive approaches to literature. Thus, he lavishly praised the work of Ivan Turgenev for its style, construction, and psychological insights; still, he found fault with Turgenev's characterization, largely on the grounds that his depictions of political groups bordered on mere caricature. Lunacharskii regarded the work of Fedor Dostoevskii as profound and powerful, and he maintained that Dostoevskii was adept at penetrating the seemingly contradictory aspects of human thought and aspirations. Still, Lunacharskii found reactionary traits in some of the novelist's later works, and he maintained that Dostoevskii was overly preoccupied with physical and moral illness. Lunacharskii wrote more extensively about Lev Tolstoi than on any other classical figure, perhaps because he found perplexing certain apparently conflicting elements in the great writer's work. Lunacharskii expressed wonderment at the remarkable vitality and panoramic scale of Tolstoi's novels. His depictions of rural life and his sympathies for the peasantry were also deemed worthy of praise. On the other hand, Tolstoi's point of view, though anticapitalist, implied an actual retreat from the political confrontations that repeatedly arose in later imperial Russia. In considering Tolstoi's interpretations of Christian duty, Lunacharskii echoed Lenin's judgment that such ideas were original but dangerous. Lunacharskii also found ideological problems in the work of Anton Chekhov; though he possessed significant artistic talents, he resembled Tolstoi and Dostoevskii in his inability to settle upon any positive standpoint where social questions were concerned.

In studies of writers who were contemporary with him, Lunacharskii showed some flexibility and restraint. In discussing the work of those who had remained in Russia after the Soviets had come to power, he was inclined to deal at least as much with aesthetic questions as with the political positions implied in their writings. He maintained that Maksim Gor'kii was a world-class writer, one who understood the dialectical significance of the struggle in literature between the old world and the new. Gor'kii's experiences of working-class life supplied authenticity to works that centered upon proletarian concerns. Lunacharskii had a particularly high regard for Gor'kii's narrative fiction, which he regarded as deeply realistic; his handling of scenery also was cited as moving and impressive. Lunacharskii did maintain that some aspects of his work were overly fantastic.

Lunacharskii contended that under a socialist state new forms of artistic expression would flourish. In his studies of Soviet literature, he discussed the various directions that new writing had taken. He depicted the verse compositions of Vladimir Maiakovskii as exemplifying a gigantic process of creation which had clear implications for the poetry of the future. He noted the extent to which Maiakovskii seemingly had overturned established patterns of style, usage, and rhythm; in some ways, his posture as a writer bordered on the oratorical. On such matters Lunacharskii was willing to suspend judgment; indeed, he seemed uncertain as to what standards of judgment should be applied to experimental works.

Lunacharskii praised Sergei Esenin, whose poetry was meant to express peasant attitudes and mores. It is worth noting that numerous writers who subsequently fell into official disfavor received some sympathetic understanding from Lunacharskii; in particular, he supported the creative efforts of the great poet Osip Mandel'shtam. He also noted some promising features in the writings of Boris Pasternak. Authors who were later known for their conventional political views – such as the novelist Mikhail Sholokhov – also received favorable treatment in some of Lunacharskii's articles. Lunacharskii maintained that Konstantin Stanislavskii's conception of the drama combined classical and revolutionary features in a manner that encouraged hope for the future of Soviet theater.

Lunacharskii's writings on foreign literature, though numerous and often enough well-informed, have not received great attention outside the Soviet Union. Although he attempted to deal with the many ages and traditions of Western culture, he was particularly attracted to themes that arose in his other works. For example, he was concerned with tracing the development of the Faust legend as it had appeared in various literary forms; indeed, this conception was featured in his own dramatic writing. Other studies evaluated the work of notable authors from a standpoint of historical materialism and attempted to place modern writers within the context of ongoing literary and ideological controversies. Thus, many of Lunacharskii's later articles dealt with authors whom he regarded as politically sympathetic, such as Bertolt Brecht and Henri Barbusse; other essays considered problems in the ideological views of Romain Rolland. This conjunction of political and aesthetic criticism also affected his writings on other major figures; he had some positive comments, for example, on the efforts of Anatole France. He also evinced his appreciation for innovative qualities found in the works of leading British writers. Thus, by later criteria, Lunacharskii's standpoint was distinguished by its relative tolerance; moreover, his view of literary endeavors was cosmopolitan to an extent that became unusual among later guardians of Soviet cultural standards.

## Principal criticism

*Etiudi kriticheskie i polemicheskie*, 1905
*Otkliki zhizni*, 1906
*Etiudi: Sbornik statei*, 1922
*Idealizm i materializm: Kultura burzhuaznaia i proletarskaia*, 1923
*Literaturnye siluety*, 1923
*Meshchanstvo i individualizm*, 1923
*Osnoviy pozitivnoi estetiki*, 1923
*Istoriia zapadnoevropeiskoi literatury v ee vazhneishikh momentakh*, 1924 (2 volumes)
*Protiv idealizma: Etiudi polemicheskie*, 1924
*Teatr i revoliutsiia*, 1924
*Tolstoi i Marks*, 1924
*Etiudi kriticheskie: Zapadnoevropeiskaia literatura*, 1925
*Kriticheskie etiudi (Russkaia literatura)*, 1925
*Ot Spinozy do Marksa*, 1925
*O teatre: Sbornik statei 1926*
*Ocherki marksistskoi teorii iskusstv*, 1926
*Na Zapade*, 1927
*Teatr segodnia: Otsenka sovremennogo repertuara i stseny*, 1927
*N. G. Chernyshevskii: Stati*, 1928
*O Tolstom: Sbornik statei*, 1928
*Iskusstvo i molodezh'*, 1929
*Lenin i literaturovedenie*, 1934
*Iubilei: Sbornik iubileinykh rechei i statei (1931–1933)*, 1934
*Klassiki russkoi literatury: Izbrannye stati*, 1937
*Kritika i kritiki: Sbornik statei*, 1938
*Stat'i o Gorkom*, 1938
*Stat'i o teatre i dramaturgii*, 1938
*Russkaia literatura: Izbrannye stati*, 1947
*Stat'i o literature*, 1957
*O teatre i dramaturgii*, 1958 (2 volumes)
*Stat'i o Chernyshevskom*, 1958
*Stat'i o sovetskoi literature*, 1958
*On Literature and Art*, 1965
*Siluety*, 1965
*Izbrannye stat'i po estetike*, 1975
*Ocherki po istorii russkoi literatury*, 1976

## Other major works and literary forms

At intervals during his career, Anatolii Lunacharskii wrote short stories, poetry, and dramatic works; during the later portion of his career, he also tried his hand at film scenarios. His interest in certain themes and ideas was also reflected in translations of works by European writers. His *Faust i gorod* (1918; *Faust and the City*, 1923) represents an attempt at a socialist interpretation of the well-known legend. *Oliver Kromvel* (1920) and *Foma Kampanella* (1920–1922) deal with historical protagonists who represent earlier revolutionary traditions. *Osvobozhdennyi Don Kikhot* (1922) adapts themes from Miguel de Cervantes' novel, with some political commentary added to reflect Lunacharskii's social concerns.

During a certain period, Lunacharskii promoted a form of Marxist thought which was meant to supersede traditional religious teachings; such ideas were explored in *Religiia i sotsializm* (1908–1911). Various writings on atheism and problems of religious belief were later compiled in *Pochemu nel'zia verit' v boga? Izbrannye ateisticheskie proizvedeniia* (1965) and *Ob ateizme i religii* (1972). Lunacharskii's writings on the philosophy of education were collected in *A. V. Lunacharskii o narodnom obrazovanii* (1958) and *O vospitanii i obrazovanii* (1976). *Evropa v pliaske smerti* (1967) deals with the period of World War I, and *Velikii perevorot (Oktiabrskaia revoliutsiia)* (1919) and *Revoliutsionnye siluety* (1924; *Revolutionary Silhouettes*, 1967) concern major figures and issues from the Russian Revolution.

SHORT FICTION
*Idei v maskakh*, 1912

PLAYS
*Korolevskiy bradobrey*, 1906
*Piat' farsov dlia liubiteli*, 1907
*Faust i gorod*, 1918 (*Faust and the City*, 1923)
*Komedii*, 1918
*Magi*, 1919 (*The Magi*, 1923)
*Foma Kampanella*, 1920–1922
*Ivan v raiu*, 1920
*Oliver Kromvel*, 1920
*Vasilisa Premudraia*, 1920 (*Vasilisa the Wise*, 1923)
*Kantsler i slesar'*, 1921
*Iskushenie*, 1922
*Osvobozhdennyi Don Kikhot*, 1922
*Bomba*, 1923
*Dramaticheskie proizvedeniia*, 1923 (2 volumes)
*Three Plays*, 1923 (includes *Faust and the City*, *Vasilisa the Wise*, and *The Magi*)
*Medvezh'ia svad'ba*, 1924 (*The Bear's Wedding*, 1926)
*Podzhigateli*, 1924
*Iad*, 1926
*Barkhat i lokhmotia (Svadba Adriana Van-Brouera)*, 1927 (with Eduard Stucken)
*Bankirskii dom*, 1929
*Baronskaia prichuda*, 1929
*Kometa*, 1929
*Izbrannye dramy*, 1935
*P'esy*, 1963

POETRY
*Kontsert*, 1926

NONFICTION
*Religiia i sotsializm*, 1908–1911 (2 volumes)
*Italiia i voyna*, 1917
*Velikii perevorot (Oktiabrskaia revoliutsiia)*, 1919
*Problemy narodnogo obrazovaniia (Sbornik statei)*, 1923
*Vvedenie v istoriiu religii (v 6 populiarnikh lektsiiakh)*, 1923
*Revoliutsionnye siluety*, 1924 (*Revolutionary Silhouettes*, 1967)
*Partiia i revoliutsiia: Sbornik statei i rechei*, 1924
*Iskusstvo i revoliutsiia: Sbornik statei*, 1924
*Tretii front: Sbornik statei*, 1925
*Prosveshchenie i revoliutsiia: Sbornik statei*, 1926
*Desiat' let kul'turnogo stroitelstva v strane rabochikh i krestian*, 1927

*Voprosy sotsiologii muzyki: Sbornik statei*, 1927
*Narodnoe obrazovanie v SSSR v sviazi s rekonstruktsiei narodnogo khoziaistva*, 1929 (with Nikolai Skrypnik)
*Stat'i ob iskusstve*, 1941
*V mire muzyki: Stat'i i rechi*, 1958
*A. V. Lunacharskii o narodnom obrazovanii*, 1958
*Stat'i i rechi po voprosam mezhdunarodnoi politiki*, 1959
*Lenin i narodnoe obrazovanie*, 1960
*Pochemu nel'zia verit v boga? Izbrannye ateisticheskie proizvedeniia*, 1965
*Lunacharskii o kino: Stat'i vyskazyvaniia, stsenarii, dokumenty*, 1965
*Ob izobrazitelnom iskusstve*, 1967 (2 volumes)
*Evropa v pliaske smerti*, 1967
*Vospominaniia i vpechatleniia*, 1968
*Ob ateizme i religii*, 1972
*Chelovek novogo mira*, 1967
*O vospitanii i obrazovanii*, 1976
*Lenin Through the Eyes of Lunacharskii*, 1980
*O massovykh prazdnestvakh, estrade, tsirke*, 1981
*On Education: Selected Articles and Speeches*, 1981
*Ob iskusstve*, 1982 (2 volumes)

TRANSLATIONS
"Pered litsom roka: K filosofii tragedii," 1903 (of Johann Wolfgang von Goethe's play *Faust*)
*Faust*, 1904 (of Nicolaus Lenau's play *Faust: Ein Gedicht*)
"Stikhotvoreniia," 1905 (of poems from Ludwig Scharf's *Tschandala-Lieder*)
"Pravda o shekspirsovskom teatre," 1916 (of Romain Rolland's critical essay "La Vérité dans le théâtre de Shakespeare")
"Krasnoie solntse: Krasnaia melnitsa," 1918 (of poems from Charles-Maurice Couyba's *Chansons rouges*)
*Lirika*, 1920 (of Conrad Ferdinand Meyer's poetry collection *Gedichte*)

EDITED TEXTS
*Sovetskaia kul'tura*, 1924; (with Iurii Steklov)
*Ocherki po istorii russkoi kritiki*, 1929–1931 (2 volumes; with Pavel Lebedev-Polianskii)
*Zvenia: Sborniki materialov i dokumentov po istorii literatury, iskusstva i obshchestvennoi mysli XIX v.*, 1932–1933 (4 volumes; with Vladimir Bonch-Bruevich)

MISCELLANEOUS
*Sobranie sochinenii*, 1963–1967 (8 volumes)
*A. V. Lunacharskii: Neizdannye materialy*, 1970
*V. I. Lenin i A. V. Lunacharskii: Perepiska, doklady, dokumenty*, 1971

## Further reading

Bullitt, Margaret M. "A Socialist Faust?" in *Comparative Literature*. XXXII, no. 2 (1980), pp. 184–195.
Fitzpatrick, Sheila M. *The Commissariat of Enlightenment: Soviet Organization of Education and the Arts Under Lunacharskii, October 1917–1921*, 1970.
Holter, Howard R. "The Legacy of Lunacharskii and Artistic Freedom in the USSR," in *Slavic Review*. XXIX, no. 2 (1970), pp. 262–282.
O'Connor, Timothy Edward. "Did Lunacharskii Contribute to Stalin's Cult of Personality?," in *European Studies Journal*. XII, no. 1 (1995), pp. 17–38.
——. *The Politics of Soviet Culture: Anatolii Lunacharskii*, 1983.
Price, M. Philips. "Anatole Lunacharskii: A Personal Note," in *Slavonic and East European Review*. XII (1934), pp. 728–730.
Stacy, Robert H. *Russian Literary Criticism: A Short History*, 1974.
Tait, A. L. *Lunacharskii: Poet of the Revolution (1875–1907)*, 1984.
Yassour, Avraham. "Philosophy-Religion-Politics: Borochov, Bogdanov, and Lunacharskii," in *Studies in Soviet Thought*. XXXI, no. 3 (1986), pp. 199–230.

J. R. BROADUS

*See also* Belyi; Plekhanov

# Ignacio de Luzán y Claramunt

Spanish writer and critic

**Born:** Zaragoza, Spain; March 28, 1702
**Died:** Madrid, Spain; May 19, 1754

## Biography

Ignacio de Luzán y Claramunt was born on March 28, 1702, in Zaragoza, Spain, second son of Antonio de Luzán y Guaso, Governor of Aragon, and his wife, Leonor Pérez Claramunt. Orphaned at an early age, Luzán was brought up by a paternal uncle, a priest, who took the youngster to Italy. Luzán would remain there, residing in several cities, for eighteen years. In Sicily he completed his doctoral studies in civil and canon law and added to his already impressive command of foreign languages – Latin, Catalan, Italian, and French – by becoming proficient in German and Greek. Of delicate health, Luzán was an avid reader, showing a clear preference for literature and history and committing to memory the best poetry of Italian, Greek, and Latin writers.

Upon the death of his uncle in 1729 Luzán moved to Naples to live with his older brother, then governor of the Castle of San Telmo. He returned to Spain in 1733, where he married María Francisca Mincholet three years later. They had three sons and a daughter.

Luzán found it difficult to make a living in spite of a distinguished birth, numerous connections, and a superior education. He was unable to secure the patronage of the court and failed to elicit financial support from his friends. Though his writings were much admired by a small circle of intellectuals – he was elected to the Royal Spanish Language Academy and the Royal Academy of History in Madrid – they never produced financial rewards for their author. Luzán enjoyed his first steady income following his appointment as secretary of the Spanish embassy in Paris in 1747; after 1750 he was again in Madrid, occupying a series of poorly paid yet honorable posts, such as the superintendency of the Royal Mint and the treasury of the Royal Library. He died on May 19, 1754, in Madrid, entrusting his children and his small estate to his illiterate wife.

## Influence

Luzán is considered to have anticipated the rationalist and neoclassical aesthetic principles that became the norm in Western European letters during the second half of the eighteenth century. To say that he was the father of Spanish neoclassicism, however, would be an exaggeration. Many of his contemporaries greatly admired his erudition, his concern for the promotion of classical aesthetic principles, and his insistence on the preeminence of order and the need for laws in the art of writing. At the same time, Luzán's criticism of the works of revered national figures – the Golden Age playwright Lope de Vega y Carpio in particular – served to invalidate many of his literary theories within Spain. Several of his contemporaries, as well as future generations of critics, would remember him as a highly cultured author whose aesthetic code, though useful for appreciating classical literature, failed when applied to works that best exemplified the genius of his own people. This allegedly anti-Spanish tone of Luzán's *La poética* – at times attributed to the extensive education that he acquired abroad – would serve to account for the overall limited appeal of his ideas.

## Analysis

Luzán's major work of literary criticism, *La poética*, was an attempt to present in a careful and well-argued form the author's major aesthetic concerns. Luzán's extensive travels, broad education, and command of foreign languages and literatures contributed to his formulation of an artistic theory that tended to emphasize the preeminence of the universal and objective as the foundation of any serious poetic pursuit. Luzán's views reflect, foremost, a deliberate reaction against certain tendencies displayed by Spanish authors of the second half of the seventeenth and the early part of the eighteenth centuries. A period of relatively little innovation and literary productivity, it was characterized by an adherence to obsolete Baroque forms and by a total lack of originality. Luzán wanted to encourage a literary revival and a stylistic renewal and believed that what was required was the acceptance by his contemporaries of classical artistic tenets. Aristotle and Horace were his principal sources and his role models. Luzán's *La poética*, then, was a highly erudite and well-argued effort to persuade Spanish writers to accept those literary principles that Luzán believed had stood the test of time.

*La poética* is divided into four books. Book 1 is devoted to a philosophical examination of the origins and development of poetry in general, book 2 examines the lyric, book 3 is centered on drama, and book 4 on the nature and definition of the epic. Books 1 and 3 are generally regarded as the more important because they contain the author's most serious expression of his philosophy of literary composition.

At the foundation of Luzán's aesthetic lay his belief that literature must be written following certain principles and rules. Spaniards, he asserted, were especially reluctant to accept the notion that natural talent alone is insufficient to achieve literary perfection. Unaided inspiration is similarly imperfect. Rules are a necessary element of literary production; they are derived from reason, which is universal, and confirmed by tradition. Luzán believed in the timeless applicability and nonarbitrariness of sound aesthetic principles; he frequently cited Aristotle's *Poetics* (c. 334–323 B.C.), which in both form and substance served to confirm Luzán's own arguments. Respect for and adherence to tradition do not necessarily imply, the author assured the reader, that there is no room for new ideas. "It would be commendable," Luzán wrote sarcastically, "to reject gold from the Indies just because it comes from the New World." Nevertheless, the Spanish writers Luzán criticized most repeatedly were berated for their neglect of the teachings of the masters that preceded them and for their disregard of the established laws of artistic expression. His most frequent targets were two of the most distinguished figures of Spanish letters: the playwright Lope de Vega, charged with pandering to popular tastes, and the poet Luis de Góngora y Argote for his penchant for ornate language and obscure metaphors.

Luzán wished to restore to Spanish literature, and to Spanish poetry in particular, certain principles he believed had been forgotten: order, reason, verisimilitude, nobility, and good taste. Numerous poets of his own country had once succeeded in achieving the required level of perfection. The main exponents of poetic virtue to Luzán were three Spanish writers of the sixteenth century: Garcilaso de la Vega, Juan Boscán de Almogáver, and Fray Luis de León. To Luzán, good poetry had to meet a set of standards. It should be the imitation of the universal or of the particular in nature, in verse form, for utility, pleasure, or both. Poetry should seek to instruct and to enlighten but also to delight; it should be written for the reader, not the writer, and it should reflect either some objective reality or a strong fictitious possibility. Good poetry is not devoid of invention; this invention, however, should never be extravagant. The poet should refrain from obscure metaphors and avoid all that is complicated, illogical, pedantic, disorderly, and chaotic. Verse should be well-proportioned, clear, and judicious.

Luzán is at his most eloquent when discussing the qualities of theater or dramatic poetry. In this regard, the standards he proposed for the genre are a direct counterpart to his critique of foibles and abuses of Golden Age (and Baroque) dramaturgy. He criticized seventeenth-century playwrights on such issues as the lack of verisimilitude of characters and plot lines, the excessive number of coincidences and chance encounters, and the frequent use of onstage tricks such as duels and sword fights. The aesthetic principles he advanced would serve to eliminate much of the artifice, frivolity, and manipulation of the spectator that he associates with the Spanish stage from the Golden Age to his own day.

For Luzán, good theater, both tragedy and comedy, should be an uplifting experience. In the case of tragedy, it should also be enlightening and instructive and thus serve a higher moral purpose. Good tragedy for him is "a dramatic representation of a great change of fortune suffered by kings, princes, and personages of high quality whose . . . adversities and dangers may so promote terror and compassion in the soul of the spectator that he is cured and purged of these and other passions." As with classical drama, the principles of which he so admired and emulated, Luzán believed that history – Spanish history in particular – should be the source of inspiration for dramatic plots.

Luzán proposed a rather narrow and strict adherence to the three dramatic unities of time, place, and action as essential for good drama. A single work should not represent more than the actual time the audience would spend watching the play. Only under special circumstances should the time of the action exceed actual or real time, and even then it is recommended that it be only for an hour or two. Moreover, the place of the action should remain the same throughout the play; he rejected what he perceived as the chaos created by constant scene changes – even within a single act – common in productions of his day. He judged the different locations of scenes as contrary to experience, and any possible pleasant distraction that such a change may produce for the audience was not deemed of sufficient merit to justify its practice. The action itself should focus on a single line, avoiding as much as possible, again, the distraction and confusion of subplots and other story-line complications. The spectators should focus their undivided attention on the issues and developments of the main characters without concern for peripheral matters, which may add color and spectacle, but inevitably detract from the impact of the overall work by dividing attention and misleading the audience. In his effort to simplify and even to eliminate theatrics and gimmicks onstage, Luzán longed for a theater that was less popular, less eager to entertain the masses, favoring productions that would provide stimulation for audiences not simply at the sensory level but on a higher intellectual and moral plane as well. Luzán's theater would have favored the elimination of all dramatic elements that fail to coincide with reality, as well as those that provide unnecessary complication, overstimulate audiences, and demand too emotional a response. Instead, he championed works that uplift and instruct.

In spite of the fact that many of the aesthetic judgments that Luzán articulated in La poética became the literary credo of the neoclassical movement in both Spain and Western Europe, later generations of writers and critics found it difficult to acknowledge a debt to him. They judged his insistence on law and order as essential standards for literary creation too narrow and stifling. Some of his detractors point to the poor quality of Spanish neoclassical theater in general, which followed many of Luzán's principles, as the best proof of the narrowness of his critical insights.

Furthermore, Luzán's approach to literary criticism differs sharply from the techniques that most modern readers are accustomed to expect. As is the case with the classical tradition that he emulated, Luzán tended to cite a passage of a work – or even a complete work – as an illustration of a general statement made about the genre as a whole. Individual passages were never analyzed in their own right; their meaning, verbal structure, philosophical content, and author's voice were not relevant considerations in this approach. The reader of Luzán never learns why, specifically, a poem is good. As a consequence, Luzán's La poética is best remembered as an example of eighteenth-century erudition and a serious statement of neoclassical aesthetics, rather than as an indispensable tool of literary analysis.

## Principal criticism

*La poética: Ó, Reglas de la poesía en general y de sus principales especies*, 1737, revised 1789
*Discurso apologético de don Íñigo de Lanuza, donde procura satisfacer los reparos de los señores Diaristas sobre la "Poética" de Luzán*, 1741
*Carta latina de Ignacio Philalethes a los padres de Trévoux sobre lo que se dice en las "Memorias" del mes de marzo del año pasado de 1742 acerca de las cosas literarias de España*, 1743
*Memorias literarias de París*, 1751

## Other major works and literary forms

In spite of the fact that Ignacio de Luzán y Claramunt had an active career as a writer, poet, and translator, most of his creative work has not survived. Several of his writings were never published, and many were lost after his death. That they existed is undoubted because they are mentioned in a biographical account of Luzán written by his son and namesake to accompany the second edition of *La poética: Ó, Reglas de la poesía en general y de sus principales especies* (the poetics: or, rules of poetry in general and of its principal types). The inventory of Luzán's writings prepared by his son includes a variety of original poetic compositions of various lengths, numerous comedies, several translations into Spanish of French theater pieces, and a few short prose works.

POETRY
*Poesías*, 1952

## Further reading

Alvarez, Roman, and Theodore Braun. "An Example of Luzán's Influence on Eighteenth-Century Dramatic Practice: A Question of Prologues," in *Eighteenth-Century Life*. 8, no. 3 (1983) pp. 88–91.
Beltrán, José Checa. "Los clásicos en la preceptiva dramática del siglo XVIII," in *Cuadernos de Teatro Clásico*. 5 (1990), pp. 13–31.
Cano, Juan. *"La Poetica" de Luzan*, 1928.
Cerreta, F. V. "An Italian Source of Luzán's Theory of Tragedy," in *Modern Language Notes*. LXXII (1957), pp. 518–523.
Cook, John A. *Neo-Classic Drama in Spain*, 1959.

McClelland, Ivy L. *Ignacio de Luzán,* 1973.

Makowiecka, Gabriela. *Luzán y su "Poética,"* 1973.

Pellisier, Robert E. "The Reintroduction of Aristotelian Rules of Criticism in Spain through Luzán's 'Poetica,'" in *The Neo-Classic Movement in Spain During the XVIII Century,* 1918.

Robertson, J. G. "Italian Influence in Spain: Ignacio de Luzán," in *Studies in the Genesis of Romantic Theory in the Eighteenth Century,* 1923.

Rudat, Eva Kahiluoto. "From Preceptive Poetics to Aesthetic Sensibility in the Critical Appreciation of Eighteenth-Century Poetry: Ignacio de Luzán and Esteban de Arteaga," in *Dieciocho: Hispanic Enlightenment.* 11, no. 1(1988), pp. 37–74.

Sebold, Russell P. "A Statistical Analysis of the Origins and Nature of Luzán's Ideas on Poetry," in *Hispanic Review.* XXXV (1967), pp. 227–251.

——. Introduction to *La poética,* 1977.

CLARA ESTOW

*See also* Feijóo y Montenegro

# Lyric

Literature is traditionally divided into three genres: lyric, epic, and dramatic. While this division is often attributed to the ancient Greeks, typically to Plato and Aristotle, neither author ever specifically addressed the topic of lyric poetry. While they would have, of course, been aware of the lyric genre, long practiced by such renowned poets as Sappho and Pindar, both writers restricted their analyses to the mimetic, or representational, narrative poetry exemplified by the drama and epic, intentionally excluding consideration of verse that does not consist in the imitation of an action. The earliest efforts to explicitly group all nonnarrative, expressive poetry under the label of the lyric, as a genre forming part of a system with the narrative genres of drama and epic, appear to be Renaissance models only loosely indebted to their putative classical ancestry. The Spanish humanist Francisco Cascales (1567–1642) offers perhaps the most carefully constructed of these early models in his *Tablas Poéticas* (1617). Cascales still bases his approach on the concept of imitation as developed by Aristotle and Horace, but his comprehensive fivefold division – major epic, minor epic, tragedy, comedy, and lyric – is readily reducible to the familiar tripartite model. Even in Cascales, however, such forms as eclogues and elegies, which would now be considered lyric, are classified as minor epics on the grounds that they do not involve singing and dancing, and similar questions as to the boundaries and dimensions of the lyric genre persist.

A number of dominant lines of analysis may be singled out from the ongoing effort since the Renaissance to define the lyric. One influential approach extends the classical definition of poetry as imitation by postulating that, while epics and dramas present imitations of actions, lyrics present imitations of the act of expressing emotions and thoughts. Another approach differentiates the genres by the status of the speaker: in lyric, the poet speaks directly in his or her own voice; in drama, only the characters speak; and in the mixed form of epic, sometimes the poet speaks (as narrator) and sometimes the characters speak (in quoted dialogue). Conversely, the lyric mode has been defined on the basis of audience: the turning away from actual listeners to address absent or imagined interlocutors is identified as the characteristic trope of lyric. A series of attempts have been made to classify the genres according to their degrees of affinity with past, present, and future tenses: E. S. Dallas, for example, identified the lyric as the genre of the future tense, while Emil Staiger classified it as a past-tense form, and John Erskine (among others) associated it with the present tense.

Each of these definitional schemes derives from genuine insights into the genre, but each also has its weaknesses and loopholes, and all have proven more valuable as general concepts than as tools for actually classifying real works of literature. Even broader complications have resulted from efforts to fold newer or neglected genres into this system (the autobiography is sometimes classified as a modern lyric form, for example, as part of the vexed question of what to do with literary nonfiction in these arrangements), as well as from attempts to reconcile the master scheme of three primary genres with the multitude of subtypes within each genre (the sonnet, ode, eclogue, ballad, and so on, all arguably types of the lyric, are also, confusingly, themselves usually called genres, and the term "lyric" is itself frequently used to mean something like "any short poem," making the "lyric" as a poem a subtype of the lyric as a genre).

Despite the lack of general consensus about the conclusions reached by such theories, the valuable insights underlying them have been periodically revived, as modern theorists attempt to separate the wheat from the chaff, replacing idiosyncratic responses with more durable foundations. Roman Jakobson has argued that the lyric form has genuine linguistic connections to the first person and to the present tense. The elaborate models of Northrup Frye and Franz Stanzel (who includes a spectrum of genres including such hybrids as the lyric drama, lyric novel, and lyric dialogue), while not reducible to such categories as temporal mode or grammatical person, do include them among the key generic attributes. Jonathan Culler has contributed a series of important essays that reevaluate conventional ideas about the lyric persona, the absent audience, and the structure and interpretation of lyrics within the frameworks provided by contemporary literary theory.

One of the more striking modern approaches to the definition of the lyric, adopted by critics such as Käte Hamburger, Henri Bonnet, and Gilbert Durand, cuts the Gordian knot by dividing the genres along the axis of subjectivity and objectivity, reducing the triad to lyric (including autobiography and first-person novels) and fiction (which contains epic and drama, and some "lyric" forms such as the ballad). Gérard Genette has raised the alternative possibility that it might make equal sense to consider a fusion of the lyric and epic, leaving the drama apart as the only rigorously objective, nonnarrated, genre. Obviously the weight of centuries remains a powerful obstacle to such sweeping revisions, and perhaps the most generally recognized model of the system of genres retains the traditional triad, albeit much modified from its earliest versions: the drama (now more often in prose than in the classical verse forms); the epic, extended to cover all fiction (literary nonfiction, as usual, remains confused territory); and the lyric, which has become the inclusive category for virtually everything that modern readers now think of as poetry. While even so conservative a reformulation of the genres owes precious little to their supposed classical origin – the definition of poetry now becomes, ironically, precisely those works that Plato and Aristotle exempted from their own definitions – it has gained widespread general acceptance by offering an intuitive simplicity and fitting modern common-sense notions about the lyric as preeminently constituting the genre of poetry.

## Further reading

Culler, Jonathan. "Poetics of the Lyric," in *Structuralist Poetics*, 1975, pp. 161–188.
de Man, Paul. "Anthropomorphism and Trope in the Lyric," in *The Rhetoric of Romanticism*, 1984, pp. 239–262.
Frye, Northrup. *Anatomy of Criticism: Four Essays*, 1957.
Genette, Gérard. *The Architext: An Introduction*, 1992.
Hosek, Chaviva, and Patricia Parker, eds. *Lyric Poetry: Beyond New Criticism*, 1985.

WILLIAM NELLES

# M

## Macrobius

Latin philosopher and writer

**Born:** Possibly North Africa; c. A.D. 375
**Died:** Place unknown; c. A.D. 422

### Biography

Macrobius Ambrosius Theodosius was probably born in the third quarter of the fourth century, outside Italy. In *The Saturnalia*, he writes that he was "born under an alien sky," and he makes many references to Egypt. Consequently, his birthplace is often conjectured to have been in Egypt.

Little is known for certain of his life save that he had a son, Eustachius, to whom he dedicated *The Saturnalia* and the *Commentary on the "Dream of Scipio."* Based on internal evidence, the *Commentary on the "Dream of Scipio"* was probably written before *The Saturnalia*. In many manuscripts, Macrobius' name is followed by the words *vir clarissimus et illustris*, an official title indicating that he held high government positions. As a result, he is often identified with a contemporary Macrobius named in the *Codex Theodosianus* (Theodosian code), who was Vicar of Spain in 399, Proconsul of Africa in 410, and Grand Chamberlain in 422. Macrobius would have been required to have been a Christian in order to hold the last office, yet he makes no references to Christianity in any of his extant works. This is no reason to doubt the *Codex Theodosianus* references, however, since several later Roman writers who were professed Christians did not mention Christianity in their works.

### Influence

Macrobius was a Roman philosopher, grammarian, and encyclopedist of the fourth and fifth centuries whose work became the most influential statement of Neo-Platonism of the Middle Ages. He was a sustaining force of classical learning for nearly a millennium. Highly regarded by such authors as Dante and Geoffrey Chaucer, Macrobius' *Commentary on the "Dream of Scipio"* presents a compendium of information and an exposition of the basic philosophical doctrines of Neo-Platonism, both moral and natural.

While very popular, readable, and accessible, Macrobius' interpretation of the classical liberal arts cannot be considered either an accurate or an adequate statement of classical knowledge. Unfortunately, Macrobius, like so many other compilers and commentators, used intermediate sources, often as many as ten sources removed from the original works of Plato and Aristotle. Therefore, even though the *Commentary on the "Dream of Scipio"* preserves within it "Somnium Scipionis," the lost sixth book from Marcus Tullius Cicero's *De republica* (c. 51 B.C.; *The Republic*), it is of much greater interest to the medievalist than to the classicist, since its influence is far greater than its originality.

In the longer but less significant compendium, *The Saturnalia*, Macrobius again includes discussions of literary, antiquarian, and philological themes, but he also preserves fragments of the earlier writers Quintus Ennius and Gaius Lucilius. Most important, he presents a lengthy criticism of Virgil representative of the practical nature of Roman literary criticism, which focused almost exclusively on rhetorical style and depth of knowledge rather than poetic meaning.

### Analysis

The works of Macrobius are typical of that literary style and genre begun in Rome in the first century after Christ. This type of writing was overwhelmingly governed by the use of rhetoric and stock themes, and it discouraged original work. As Edward Gibbon commented, it created "a cloud of critics, of compilers, of commentators," which "darkened the face of learning." Indeed, Macrobius himself denies literary merit in *The Saturnalia*, claiming its purpose is the presentation to Eustachius, his son, of a variety of subjects arranged to form "a body coming together like the parts of a coherent whole." Although Macrobius wrote that he intended the *Commentary on the "Dream of Scipio"* as an elucidation of Cicero, the work functions as a compendium also.

Typical of the writers of this period, Macrobius depended heavily on outside sources. Often he took lengthy sections directly from the works of other writers. In *The Saturnalia*, originally an extensive seven-book imaginary dialogue but incomplete in its extant version, Macrobius presents the conversation of twelve characters on the eve of the Saturnalia. Half of them represent Roman nobility, and each of the other six is interested in a separate branch of learning. All were probably real people who never actually met and are presented as having clear personality traits, yet their words are taken from the writings of others.

This is especially true in their lengthy discussion of Virgil. The ideas, and often the words, belong to the critics of Virgil, both hostile and friendly, who were numerous in the time before Macrobius. Suetonius Tranquillus, in his *Vita Vergili*, probably written in the first century, notes that, like Homer, Virgil had detractors, such as Carvilius, Marcus Vipsanius Agrippa, and Herennius. Also in the first century, Asconius Pedianus wrote a reply to the detractors of Virgil, *Contra obtrectatores Vergilli*, and although names of other laudatory critics are unknown, praise of Virgil was common since the poet's works were used time and again to illustrate correct grammar and rhetoric to students.

Still, problems were created from the heavy dependence on sources: inaccuracies, superficial discussions, and incorrect attributions. For example, in his *Commentary on the "Dream of Scipio,"* Macrobius borrows Cicero's character P. Cornelius Scipio Aemilianus Africanus Minor, the hero of the Third Punic War. Scipio has a dream about his adoptive grandfather, Scipio Africanus Major, while visiting Masinissa, King of Numidia, in Africa in 150 B.C. Macrobius carefully preserves and correctly attributes the "Dream of Scipio" to Cicero within his lengthy two-book commentary; still, the work is also a compilation of general information attributed to Plato. Ironically, the major source used by Macrobius is not Plato at all but primarily Porphyry and, to a far less extent, the lofty and metaphysical Plotinus. It was common practice for Roman compilers to depend upon recent summaries of the Greeks, while trying to appear as if they were drawing directly from the classical sources. Thus, although the work serves as a compendium of Neo-Platonic thought, it lacks a clear chronology and confuses events from classical and later Roman times.

Macrobius intended his writings to be useful and organized, and their diversity and antiquarian subject matter make them fascinating even today. His philosophical and moral treatises were highly respected by patristic writers. In the *Commentary on the "Dream of Scipio"* Macrobius constructs lengthy arguments proving the Platonic and Ciceronian belief in the origin and descent of souls and life after death. He also condemns suicide and praises the contemplative life. Although not Christian, he expounds upon the Neo-Platonic trinity of *deus, mens,* and *animus* (God, Mind, and Soul) and supports the immortality of the latter using the statements of twenty-one philosophers.

Macrobius' scientific hypotheses were perhaps even more widely respected. He describes the geocentric universe, the positions of the seven planets, and the motion and harmony of the spheres. His writings on world geography kept alive the belief in a spherical earth, divided into four quarters by oceans, and also preserved Eratosthenes' figure of 252,000 stadia as the circumference of the earth. His chapters on number theory include the conventional statements about the virtues of numbers within the sacred Pythagorean decade and an excellent explanation of Pythagorean doctrine that numbers underlie all physical objects. These concepts dominated scientific thinking in the Middle Ages.

Macrobius' literary criticism of Virgil sheds light on Roman literary standards. Following the Roman belief that a thorough education included a complete understanding of the works of Virgil, the central topic in *The Saturnalia* is an appreciation of Virgil. Praise of his works forms the subject matter of books 4, 5, and 6 and parts of books 1 and 3. According to standards of the time, Macrobius praises Virgil for his style, his erudition, and his authority in every discipline: philosophy, astronomy, augural law, pontifical law, rhetoric, and, most of all, Greek and Latin authors – namely, Homer. Book 4 of *The Saturnalia* illustrates Virgil's best use of rhetoric while book 5 concentrates on his use of Greek models, particularly Homer's *Iliad* and the *Odyssey*. Macrobius cites examples when Virgil supersedes, equals, or fails to match the quality of Homer in the wealth and realism of detail, and he notes the use of repetition, metrics, narrative, catalogs, and proverbs. He considers such extensive knowledge and skill remarkable since Virgil was a Venetian of peasant stock.

Macrobius belongs to a select group of late Roman writers of the fourth, fifth, and sixth centuries whose stated purpose was to make an orderly presentation of the classical liberal arts and sciences; while he may be sketchy and incorrect, he must be credited as one of the very few writers who kept alive classical learning and philosophy as a source for medieval science and scholasticism during the Middle Ages for nearly a millennium. Neo-Platonism may be more accurately presented by Plotinus, Porphyry, Iamblichus, and Proclus, but it is Macrobius who was widely read and understood because of his lucidity and succinctness. Considered pagan rather than patristic, Macrobius' writings were preserved in monasteries where monks apparently believed that both Christian and pagan writings were a part of their cultural inheritance. His works were particularly important after 1100 and are said to have been rediscovered at the beginning of the Italian Renaissance, primarily by lay writers.

Earlier medieval writers seem to have been more influenced by *The Saturnalia*. Isidore of Seville cites many of Macrobius' "scientific" explanations in his *Etymologies* (c. 633), such as the discussion of the ring finger, types of drinking vessels, and the fresh water of the Black Sea. In a similar manner, Saint Bede, the Venerable, refers to the Roman day and month in *De temporum ratione* (725) as they are described in an abridgement of *The Saturnalia*, no longer extant. Finally, John of Salisbury directly quotes many sections of *The Saturnalia* in the *Policraticus* (1159) and, interestingly, seems to be using a more complete text than is extant today.

Macrobius' *Commentary on the "Dream of Scipio"* was far more influential in the later medieval period. Its influence was wide-ranging. Serving as an encyclopedia of natural and moral philosophy, this work was unusually popular, perhaps because of its comparably small size combined with its breadth of topics and doctrines of great concern in the Middle Ages. Considered equal to Cicero, Macrobius was respected as a goodly writer of antique times who had written the only pagan statement on human affection accepted by the patristic writers of the twelfth century. Giovanni Boccaccio read Macrobius avidly and may have been influenced by the commentary in his description of the transmigration of Arcita in his *Teseida* (c. 1341). Dante considered him equal in stature to Boethius, and critics suggest that the form and first idea of Dante's *Inferno* (c. 1320) were suggested by the apologue to the *Commentary on the "Dream of Scipio."* Boethius himself named Macrobius a *vir doctissimus* (knowledgeable man) in his *Commenta in Isagogen Porphyrii* (c. 500), and Peter Abelard called him "a remarkable philosopher and interpreter of the great Cicero" and considered him first among Platonists.

Most famous of the English writers influenced by Macrobius is Chaucer. Along with Dante, Boethius, and Cicero, Chaucer thought of Macrobius as one of the *vetere*. As a writer who often used the dream framework, Chaucer clearly respected the dream form which Macrobius enshrined and explored in his commentary. In Chaucer's time, Cicero's "Dream of Scipio" was identified more closely with Macrobius as a part of the whole of the commentary. Macrobius, however, is not responsible for this, as he clearly assigns the "Dream of Scipio" to Cicero in line 31 of the commentary. Still, in four of the five references to Macrobius by Chaucer, Macrobius seems to be identified as both author and commentator of the "Dream of Scipio." In *The Romance of the Rose* (c. 1370), Chaucer begins by describing:

An authour, that hight Macrobe,
That halt not dremes false ne lees,
But undoth us the avisioun
That whylom mette king Cipioun.

In *The Book of the Duchess* (c. 1370), Chaucer describes Macrobius as "He that wrot al th' avysyoun / That he mette, kyng Scipioun." In *The House of Fame* (1372–1380), Chaucer merely confuses Scipio as being the king, but again he attributes the "Dream of Scipio" to Macrobius in "The Nun's Priest's Tale" in *The Canterbury Tales* (1387–1400).

It is only in the *Parliament of Fowls* (1380) that Chaucer makes clear that Cicero wrote the "Dream of Scipio" and Macrobius "roughte nat a lyte." Yet Chaucer devotes seven stanzas of the "Proem" of the *Parliament of Fowls* to a summary of the "Dream of Scipio" and finds the entire work a great inspiration.

After the Middle Ages, Macrobius continued as a highly regarded writer, particularly because of the growing interest in cosmology among scholars. Thirty-five editions of Macrobius' commentary are known to have been printed between 1472 and 1628. John Skelton refers to Macrobius as the authority who treated Scipio's dream with wisdom, Ben Jonson cites Macrobius in his notes to the *Hymenaei* (1606) in the seventeenth century, and as late as the eighteenth century, in *The Life of Samuel Johnson* (1791), James Boswell recalls Johnson quoting Macrobius, thereby showing the extent of the reading in which he indulged.

Clearly, Macrobius played a significant role in the history of Western culture as an encylopedist who, because of his ability to make readable diverse topics in classical culture, was an important influence on the writers of the next thousand years.

### Principal criticism
*Commentarii in somnium Scipionis*, c. 400 (*Commentary on the "Dream of Scipio,"* 1952)
*Saturnalia*, c. 400 (*The Saturnalia*, 1969)

### Other major works and literary forms
Only one other work of Macrobius is known, a treatise entitled *De differentiis Graeci Latinique verbi* (on the differences of the Greek and Latin verb), written at an unknown date. The work has been lost and is only known in a medieval abridgement, doubtfully attributed to John Duns Scotus.

NONFICTION
*De differentiis Graeci Latinique verbi*, date unknown

### Further reading
Davies, Percival Vaughan. Introduction to *The Saturnalia*, 1969.
Stahl, W. H. Introduction to *Commentary on the "Dream of Scipio,"* 1952.
Whittaker, T. *Macrobius: Or, Philosophy, Science, and Letters in the Year 400*, 1923.
Willis, J. *Macrobius*. Vol. 1, 1963.

VICKI K. ROBINSON

*See also* Classical Greek and Roman Literary Theory; Fulgentius; Medieval Literary Theory

# François de Malherbe

French poet, writer, and translator

**Born:** Caen, France; 1555
**Died:** Paris, France; October 16, 1628

## Biography
François de Malherbe was born in the French city of Caen in 1555 and completed his primary and secondary studies in Caen and Paris. He studied classical literature first at the

University of Basel and then at the University of Heidelberg. In 1581 he married Madeleine de Carriolis. Their first two children died in early infancy, and their one daughter, Jourdaine, died in 1599 at the age of eight. In 1601 their youngest son, Marc-Antoine, was born; he would cause his parents grave concern. In 1622 he was arrested in Aix-en-Provence for reasons that are still unclear, and two years later he killed a man in a duel. Both times his father had to use his political influence to protect him from legal penalties. Finally, in July 1627 Marc-Antoine was killed. Letters written after his son's violent death reveal that Malherbe had become profoundly unhappy, and he died in Paris on October 16, 1628.

During his lengthy career Malherbe served several influential French noblemen in Provence and in Paris, and on several occasions, Henri IV and Louis XIII recognized the quality of his verse by honoring him with monetary awards. In order to remain in royal favor, Malherbe frequently wrote poems praising members of the royal family, since monetary awards or "pensions" were renewed annually. Although such conventional poems of praise were in fact written on command, their formal elegance should not be underestimated. By his poetry, correspondence, and literary criticism, Malherbe contributed significantly to French intellectual life in the first three decades of the seventeenth century.

## Influence

Malherbe codified the conventions of French versification and taught generations of French poets how to compose technically correct verse. Both as a lyric poet and as a literary theorist, he was suspicious of subjectivity and sentimentality and he affirmed that one could describe objectively the art of poetry and appropriate techniques for evaluating poetry. In his influential 1674 *L'Art poétique* (*The Art of Poetry*, 1683), Nicolas Boileau-Despréaux declared that Malherbe's critical method "still served as a model" for both poets and literary theorists.

Although Malherbe's stylistic approach to lyric poetry helped many generations of French critics to present their analyses of poetry logically and to avoid eclecticism, it did adversely affect the reception of Renaissance poetry by French critics of the seventeenth and eighteenth centuries. Malherbe assumed that his aesthetic standards could be applied to all lyric poetry written in French, and his literary criticism was rather inflexible. Because of his belief that such important sixteenth-century poets as Pierre de Ronsard, Joachim du Bellay, and Philippe Desportes had expressed themselves in artificial styles, their refined poetry fell into critical disfavor; it would not recover until the nineteenth century.

## Analysis

Malherbe's commentary on the writings of Desportes, the last important French Renaissance poet, constitutes his major contribution to literary theory. Like such eminent French lyric poets as Ronsard and du Bellay, Desportes firmly believed that a truly creative poet had to develop an original style and that style and lyricism should reflect his changing personality. As literary interest evolved, so did style. In the 1570s and 1580s Desportes composed elegant and often tongue-in-cheek adaptations of Roman love poetry; as he aged, he began to write formal verse on religious themes; finally, in 1603 he published a verse translation of the Book of Psalms which his contemporaries greatly admired. Desportes was a Catholic priest. His verse translation of the Psalms was viewed as a Catholic response to the well-known verse translation of the Psalms by the French Protestant poet Clément Marot. Desportes was a learned poet whose works and style reveal his evolving interests.

According to Malherbe, the extraordinary diversity of Desportes' poetry represented unacceptable eclecticism. Unlike Desportes, Malherbe admired above all thematic and stylistic consistency in poets, believing that poets should express their ideas logically, clearly, and precisely and should systematically avoid personal and thus subjective interpretations of reality. Clarity was much more important than originality.

A critic who reads both Desportes' poetry and Malherbe's commentary on Desportes realizes that their writings illustrate radically different methods for interpreting poetry. Desportes believed that the inherent individuality of each poet should encourage critics to recognize and appreciate each unique poetic voice. Tolerance was extremely important to Desportes, who willingly shared with younger poets, including Malherbe, his personal library and his own vast knowledge of classical letters so that they could develop their own poetic style. Unlike Desportes, Malherbe distrusted individuality and believed that all French poets should conform to detailed conventions. Although Desportes was certainly not indifferent to the rules of French versification, he did not believe that the strict observance of conventions constituted a significant poetic accomplishment. Unlike Malherbe, Desportes was convinced that objective criteria can never properly describe emotional and aesthetic reactions to poetry, and his lyric poetry expresses not the logical development of arguments but rather the process by which ideas occurred to him. On an emotional and aesthetic level, the reader responds positively to Desportes' refined and very personal poetry.

In evaluating Desportes' theory, Malherbe was extraordinarily dogmatic and judgmental both in his written commentary and in his conversations with Desportes. According to Honorat de Beuil, the seigneur de Racan, a French poet who agreed with Malherbe's poetics, one evening, while he was dining in Desportes' house, Desportes offered Malherbe a copy of his recently published verse translation of the Psalms. Malherbe rejected this kind gesture, telling Desportes, "Your soup is worth more than your Psalms." Such a rude and thoughtless remark has prejudiced numerous readers against Malherbe. Although his remarks on Desportes are often of questionable value, they do define quite clearly two key problems in the interpretation of poetry, namely the relationship between tradition and originality in poetry and the proper role of subjectivity in literary criticism. Although polemic in nature, Malherbe's theoretical writings caused generations of French critics to reflect quite seriously on the difficulties involved in evaluating poetry. Malherbe strove to attain total objectivity in literary criticism, and his extreme position may well have constituted a healthy reaction against the impressionistic assessments of poetry so prevalent in late-sixteenth-century France. Although his disparagement of Desportes is not at all persuasive, his very method causes the reader to reflect both on the nature of poetic creativity and on the criteria used to interpret poetry.

Malherbe believed that a poem should be immediately understandable to all readers, and modern readers admire the logical and effective presentation of ideas and emotions in his poetry. In his view, a poem was a self-contained artifice which did not require from its readers a knowledge of previous literary treatments of similar themes or motifs. The very title of Malherbe's most famous poem, *Consolation à Monsieur Du Périer sur la mort de sa fille* (consolation to Mr. Du Périer on the death of his daughter), creates specific expectations in readers and may well remind them of similar poems in which poets tried to console themselves or friends following the death of a child. Malherbe's poem, however, makes no reference to these other poems; his eloquent verse seems to exist in a literary vacuum. In his *Commentaire sur Desportes*, Malherbe argued repeatedly that it was inappropriate if not pedantic for poets to display too much erudition, believing that poetic creativity required the eloquent expression of new ideas and not the artistic reworking and transformation of respected literary sources from the classical era.

Malherbe's attitude toward poetic originality constituted a significant break with Renaissance poetics. Such important Renaissance critics as Desiderius Erasmus and du Bellay frequently repeated their conviction that literary works of lasting value can be produced only through the creative imitation of specific literary texts which readers recognize and admire. Love poetry, for example, was extremely popular during the French Renaissance. It would be wrong, however, to seek in such poetry the authentic representation of personal insights into the force of passion. Critics should rather strive to appreciate the true creativity in the imaginative reworking of conventional Roman love poems by such refined poets as Marot, Ronsard, and Desportes. It is essential that the classical literary sources for such French love poems be recognized lest the relationship between convention and originality in the works of Marot, Ronsard, and Desportes be badly misinterpreted. Although Malherbe himself knew Latin literature extremely well, he

argued in *Commentaire sur Desportes* that such learned poetry interfered with the reader's emotional and aesthetic reactions to lyric poetry. Thus Malherbe's commentary and Desportes' love poetry illustrate radically different approaches to the composition and interpretation of poetry.

It is most helpful that modern editions of Desportes' poems also include Malherbe's commentary, since although Malherbe disliked Desportes' poetic practice, he correctly identified the classical sources for Desportes' poems. Desportes clearly wrote for learned readers who shared his enthusiasm for Latin poetry and who would recognize his elegant reworking of the conventions of Latin love poetry. Originality for Desportes meant not the expression of new ideas but rather the artistic amplification of admired poems from the classical period. Desportes' 1600 elegy "Que serviroit nier chose si reconnuë?" (What would be the purpose of denying such a well-known thing?) and Malherbe's analysis of this elegy illustrate very clearly their opposing attitudes toward poetic originality.

Malherbe correctly identified Albins Tibullus' *Elegia II* (c. 27 B.C.) as the direct literary source for Desportes' poem. Malherbe, however, dismissed Desportes' elegy as nothing more than an elegant translation of Tibullus' poem, stating that Desportes was incapable of attaining true poetic creativity and suggesting that even the creative imitation of a literary source was unworthy of a true artist. Desportes clearly thought otherwise; he understood that the love elegies of Tibullus were formal speeches in which an unsympathetic lover tried unsuccessfully to persuade his indifferent mistress to sleep with him, and it is abundantly clear that neither Tibullus nor Desportes expected readers to respond positively to such ineffective speeches. Indeed, it is the very artificiality of the lover's speeches to his beloved which is appreciated. In his imitation, Desportes translated into French only forty lines from Tibullus' poem. Desportes' elegy, however, contains one hundred and twenty-six lines; eighty-six of them express an ironic commentary on Tibullus' poem. Desportes' true originality in this elegy was his ability to parody the conventions of Latin love poetry and to make Tibullus' poem more amusing for his contemporary audience.

In his book-length study on Malherbe's commentary, Ferdinand Brunot concluded perceptively that Malherbe simply had not understood Desportes' poetry. Creativity has radically different meanings for these two poets. Malherbe believed that poetic originality required the development of new themes or ideas. This idea represented a very modern approach to literary composition. Like most classical poets, Desportes was convinced that a truly imaginative poet did not create new themes or situations but rather developed a unique poetic voice. Francesco Della Corte has argued persuasively that the elegies of Tibullus are important because they combine "pure eloquence" with "natural and singular spontaneity." This paradoxical combination of eloquence and artistic spontaneity constitutes an impressive stylistic accomplishment. In his direct imitation of Tibullus' elegies, Desportes also produced this refined mixture of eloquence and spontaneity, re-creating in French the Roman's stylistic brilliance with much wit and subtlety. Malherbe, however, did not recognize the creativity in Desportes' style largely because he discovered no new themes or situations in his poetry. His own literary theory prevented Malherbe from appreciating Desportes' refined artistry.

Throughout the seventeenth century Malherbe's literary theory provoked strong reactions, both positive and negative. Critics such as Boileau and Jean Chapelain admired Malherbe because his literary theory enabled them to avoid subjectivity in evaluating the originality and technical merits of French poems. Other seventeenth-century French writers, however, admired Malherbe's lyric poetry but questioned the significance of his theoretical writings; Théophile de Viau, for example, believed that the critical method developed by Malherbe might well prevent many readers from appreciating the stylistic brilliance in poems which imitate specific literary sources. Perhaps Malherbe's greatest contribution was that his literary theory inspired lively critical discussions in seventeenth-century France concerning the complex relationship between imitation and creativity in poetry.

## Principal criticism
*Commentaire sur Desportes*, 1605–1606

## Other major works and literary forms
Although François de Malherbe's literary career lasted more than forty years, only one hundred and thirty-seven poems can definitely be attributed to him. Malherbe was a perfectionist: he rewrote several times his most important poems, until he became convinced that he could not possibly express his ideas more accurately and eloquently. Malherbe demanded of himself the same high critical standards he applied to others' poetry. His most admired poems are his *Les Larmes de Saint Pierre* (1587; the tears of Saint Peter) and his *Consolation à Monsieur Du Périer sur la mort de sa fille* (c. 1600; consolation to Mr. Du Périer on the death of his daughter). The latter poem describes powerfully and effectively the universal feelings of grief which any parent experiences upon the death of a child and seems to be a very personal poem. Raymond Lebègue, a modern scholar, in fact, discovered that Malherbe had originally written this poem after the death of his own eight-year-old daughter, Jourdaine, in 1599. Malherbe then modified his poem and offered it to his friend François Du Périer. Malherbe's well-crafted poems are still held in the highest esteem.

Malherbe is also famous for his extensive correspondence with Nicolas Fabride Peiresc, a nobleman from Provence. From 1606 until 1628 the poet wrote frequently to Peiresc on a wide variety of personal and aesthetic topics. After Malherbe's death in 1628, Peiresc published all of his friend's letters. Like many other writers of the sixteenth and seventeenth centuries, Malherbe believed that there was an art to letter-writing, and readers can still admire the artistic spontaneity and profound portrayal of human feelings to be found in his correspondence. Malherbe was also a learned Latinist who translated works by Livy and Seneca.

POETRY
*Les Larmes de Saint Pierre*, 1587
*Consolation à Monsieur Du Périer sur la mort de sa fille*, c. 1600
*À la reine, sur sa bienvenue en France*, 1600
*Prière pour le roi Henri le Grand*, 1605
*Prière pour le roi allant en Limousin*, 1607
*Poésies*, 1626

NONFICTION
*Lettres à Peiresc*, 1628
*Les Lettres de Monsieur de Malherbe*, 1630

TRANSLATIONS
*Le XXXIIIᵉ livre de Tite Live*, 1616 (of Livy's history *Ab urbi condita libri*)
*Traité des bienfaits de Seneque*, 1630 (of Seneca's treatise, *De beneficiis*)

MISCELLANEOUS
*Œuvres complètes*, 1862–1869 (5 volumes)

## Further reading
Abraham, Claude. *Enfin Malherbe: The Influence of Malherbe on French Lyric Prosody*, 1971.
Brunot, Ferdinand. *La Doctrine de Malherbe d'après son "Commentaire sur Desportes,"* 1891.
Floeck, Willfried. *Esthétique de la diversité: Pour une histoire du baroque littéraire en France*, 1989. Translated by Gilles Floret.
Fromilhague, René. *Malherbe: Technique et création poétique*, 1954.
Hammond, Nicholas, *Creative Tensions: An Introduction to Seventeenth-Century French Literature*, 1997.
Ponge, Francis. *Pour un Malherbe*, 1965.
Rubin, David Lee, and Mary B. McKinley, eds. *Convergences: Rhetoric and Poetic in Seventeenth-Century France*, 1989.
Winegarten, R. *French Poetry in the Age of Malherbe*, 1954.

EDMUND J. CAMPION

*See also* Boileau-Despréaux; La Bruyère; Neoclassical Literary Theory

# Stéphane Mallarmé
French poet and critic

**Born:** Paris, France; March 18, 1842
**Died:** Valvins, France; September 9, 1898

## Biography
Stéphane Mallarmé was born in Paris on March 18, 1842. His father, Numa Florence Joseph Mallarmé, a government

official, and his mother, Élisabeth Félicie Desmolins, both came from middle-class backgrounds, and the family's circumstances were quite comfortable. His early years, however, were scarred by tragedy: when his mother died in 1847, he and his younger sister, Maria, were sent to live with their maternal grandparents, after which their father remarried and moved away. At the age of ten, Mallarmé was sent away to boarding school, and five years later his sister died, which was another severe shock to Mallarmé's turbulent and largely unhappy childhood.

Mallarmé left school at the age of eighteen, having already decided to become a writer, and finally settled upon teaching as a means of supporting himself. He spent nine months in London studying English, returning to France in 1863 and accepting the first of a series of teaching posts that would take him to Tournon, Besançon, and Avignon before he permanently settled in Paris in 1871. He married Marie Gerhard in 1863 and became the father of Geneviève in 1864 and Anatole in 1871, the latter dying in 1879 after a long illness that came close to shattering Mallarmé's sanity.

During the 1870s Mallarmé's name often appeared in the leading literary periodicals, but the financial strains of supporting a family on his modest salary forced him to spend much of his free time on hackwork, such as editing fashion magazines and writing school textbooks. In 1880 he began to host the famous *mardis* (Tuesdays) at which such luminaries as Paul Verlaine, Joris-Karl Huysmans, and Édouard Manet were regular guests, and he gradually became recognized as the leading poet of the day. This recognition enabled him to retire from teaching in 1893; during the remainder of his life he was able to devote more time to writing and reading. He died on September 9, 1898, in the quiet village of Valvins, where he had spent most of the years of his retirement.

## Influence

Mallarmé was one of the major figures involved in the creation of the Symbolist movement in France. In his difficult, allusive, but often fruitfully suggestive poetry and prose, literature was weaned away from direct statement and reoriented toward the possibilities of implication and association. His influence upon the practice of other poets was immense: William Butler Yeats, Rainer Maria Rilke, Wallace Stevens, and Paul Valéry are among the many who acknowledged his importance as a stimulus to their conceptions of poetry as well as to the writing of poetry itself.

Mallarmé's specific contributions to literary theory are not easily differentiated from his contributions to literature. His writings on Symbolism had a significant impact upon the thinking of such Russian Formalist critics as Andrei Belyi, Valérii Briusov, and Viktor Shklovskii, particularly with regard to their emphasis upon style and technique rather than content; as mediated through Arthur Symons' seminal *The Symbolist Movement in Literature* (1899;

revised and enlarged, 1908 and 1919), Symbolism became a standard term in the critical vocabulary of figures as diverse as Kenneth Burke, T. S. Eliot, and Northrop Frye. Mallarmé is probably best viewed, however, as a rich source of stimulating ideas about literature rather than as the originator of a coherent body of literary theory.

## Analysis

As a theorist concerned with both defining and creating poetry, Mallarmé appears in the somewhat paradoxical guise of a rigorous craftsman dedicated to the making of essentially mysterious objects. As he remarked in an 1891 letter, he had no use for poets who thought that they need only affix words to their perceptions in order to describe them satisfactorily:

> They deprive the mind of the delicious joy of believing that it is creating. To name an object is to do away with three-quarters of the enjoyment of the poem which is derived from the satisfaction of guessing little by little; to suggest it, that is the illusion. It is the perfect handling of the mystery that constitutes the symbol: to evoke an object little by little in order to show a state of mind or inversely to choose an object and to disengage from it a state of mind, by a series of unriddlings.

It was the "perfect handling of the mystery" which obsessed Mallarmé throughout his career; from it followed a consuming interest in the basic unit of literary craftsmanship, the word.

Words, for Mallarmé, have two fundamental properties: they have meaning and they have sound. Their meanings are not, except in inferior and uninteresting kinds of writing which are content "to name an object," finite, however, nor are they exactly equivalent to anything to which one can point in the material world. When combined with one another, the interactions among their collective nuances are capable of creating further subtleties of meaning which may even come as a surprise to their author. It follows that poetry – which for Mallarmé was always the highest form of literature – is not, as Samuel Taylor Coleridge has it, "the best words in their best order," but something more akin to "those evocative groupings of words which, at each stage of our constant experimentation with them, produce previously unknown and unpredictable effects."

Mallarmé believed that sound was the other primary consideration for those who wanted to create fine poetry. Although he was a great lover of music, he did not think, as is sometimes maintained, that poetry should attempt to emulate it: he saw the two arts as alternative faces of that unknowable mystery, that "Idea" as he sometimes referred to it in his later and more esoteric writings, which favored each with intimations and suggestions as to what might lie behind glimpses of its worldly manifestations. It was in the resonances between two words or a small group of words that he sought to catch the ear of his readers, as he experimented with the possibilities presented by such basic sonic properties of language as consonant-vowel opposition and the modification of initial by terminal consonants.

The end result of the poet's manipulation of words, of the sometimes trial-and-error and sometimes purely intuitive methods that must be used, is still not to be identified with any external object. In his essay "Crisis in Poetry," Mallarmé combined poetic theory and poetic language in articulating this position:

> Done away, the claim, aesthetically an error, although it governed masterpieces, to enclose in the subtle paper of the volume anything but for example the horror of the forest, or the dumb thunder strewn in the foliage; not the intrinsic dense wood of the trees.

The question then becomes exactly what is being captured in the poet's ventures into a milieu where impressions are not transformed into significations; it is here that Mallarmé's literary theories become essentially – and to a degree opaquely – metaphysical in character.

Philosophical Idealism, in his case, is the consequence of profound dissatisfaction with material reality. As a young man, he expressed this discontent in the form of yearning for a release from the mundane and for contact with the ideal; he soon realized, however, that this connection would not in itself answer his needs. Hypothesizing that the ideal could be known through the exercise of rational faculties, he attempted to illuminate it with the cold light of reason; after at first despairing when this light seemed to reveal only a vast emptiness, he then became convinced that concealed within this emptiness there lay a realm of ideal forms accessible to the nonrational powers of the human mind. This conclusion was very much influenced by Mallarmé's reading of G. W. F. Hegel, whose theory of "objective Idealism" argued that finite human minds were dependent fragments of an infinite absolute mind.

These abstract philosophical ideas had a very real effect upon Mallarmé's poetic practice. Previously, it had been generally agreed that poets had to immerse themselves in reality as a means of preparing to write about it; for Mallarmé, reality became something to be rigorously avoided, as the poet tried to create a void within the self which would be filled by the ideal forms hidden in the infinite world. He distilled this concept into the phrase "the pure work implies the disappearance of the poet," and in one of his sonnets he used the image of an uninhabited room littered with the ashes of burned manuscripts to symbolize the kind of mental vacuum which might then be filled by knowledge of the infinite.

This theory may seem to contradict Mallarmé's concern with words as the units of literary craftsmanship, but in fact, he was able to reconcile the latter with his theory of the ideal. The poet still had to express, to communicate, the nature of what had flowed into the voided mind, and it was here that matters of word choice and juxtaposition resumed their importance as fundamentals of poetic art. Words could not exactly correspond to ideal forms any more than they could exactly correspond to real objects; nevertheless, they were capable of evoking the spiritual essence of what the poet had seen and of acting as a bridge between the worlds of the finite and the infinite.

In the process of working out this very complex notion of how true poetry could be written, Mallarmé made a number of experiments with poetic form that reflected his radical rethinking of what a poem is. Since it was the poet's task to suggest, to hint, and even coyly to play games with readers as part of the effort to involve them in the creation of the poem, the abolition of traditional forms was a necessary prelude to encouraging a state of mind alert to allusions, as opposed to one satisfied with identifying correspondences between words and objects. Mallarmé's interest in the prose poem was an early manifestation of his desire to transcend literary conventions, an interest still bound to events in the real world although he hoped "to write as it struck my poet's eye" before such occurrences have been buried under the banalities of "reporters jockeying to assign to each thing its common character."

Mallarmé's prose poems were a criticism of standard literary practices; in his later poems, however, he actively sought to destroy them. He began by dispensing with almost all punctuation, since these visible grammatical signs had no place in verse that deliberately avoided the obvious, ignored normative grammar, and refused to engage in signification. He rewrote many of his earlier poems in an attempt to make them more syntactically ambiguous, and therefore more open to varying interpretations.

In his final years Mallarmé produced the formidably difficult *Dice Thrown Never Will Annul Chance*, which breaks up its originating sentence into widely separated fragments and then intersperses them with subordinate clauses in typography that swoops across pages and scatters italics and capitals in every direction. *Dice Thrown Never Will Annul Chance* is a work that envisages the abolition of linear writing, a consummate demonstration of how the arrangement and interaction of words become determinants of alternate meanings, and an achievement that foreshadows much twentieth-century literary experimentation.

It would be difficult to overestimate the impact of Mallarmé's ideas about writing upon subsequent generations. In France, Valéry adopted the poet's philosophical Idealism as a guiding principle in exploring the world of ideas, and Marcel Proust admired his evocative use of words as symbols: the famous passage at the beginning of *Du côté de chez Swann* (1913; *Swann's Way*, 1922), in which the narrator's childhood memories are evoked by the taste of a small cake, is a textbook example of Symbolism's literary potential. In the realm of the theater, playwrights such as Villiers de L'Isle-Adam, Maurice Maeterlinck, and Paul Claudel found his work a stimulus to the creation of stage atmospheres pregnant with mystery and hallucination.

Among English-language writers, Yeats and Eliot were both deeply influenced by the Symbolist ethos which Mallarmé was so instrumental in developing, Yeats through his reading of de L'Isle-Adam and Symons' *The Symbolist Movement in Literature*, Eliot directly, as indicated by the phrase in *Four Quartets* (1943), "To purify the dialect of the tribe," which is an almost literal rendering of "*Donner un sens plus pur aux mots de la tribu*" from Mallarmé's poem "Le Tombeau d'Edgar Poe" (the tomb of Edgar Poe). James Joyce, Gertrude Stein, and Stevens are among the other major English and American writers who explicitly acknowledged Mallarmé's influence.

In Germany, Rilke and Stefan George were deeply affected by Symbolist practice, as were the Russian poets and critics Belyi and Briusov. Among the most eloquent tributes to Mallarmé's example is that paid by the Mexican writer Octavio Paz:

> Mallarmé's work represented more than the birth of a style or a movement: it was the appearance of an open form, the purpose of which was to escape linear writing. A form that destroys itself and starts all over: it is reborn only to fall to pieces again and reconstruct itself again. . . . Any work that really counts as our century goes on, whether in literature, music, or painting, is governed by a similar principle.

As for literary criticism per se, Mallarmé's influence can be discerned in the work of Frye, Burke, and Eliot, although, by and large, Symbolism seems to have been too diffuse a set of ideas to have had much direct impact upon the course of literary theory. Frye's emphasis upon the nonreferential status of the literary text, Burke's inquiries into the symbolic functions of language and Eliot's search for the exact words to express rarefied states of the soul are all participants in the historical development of Symbolist ideas. Yet it is in literature, rather than in theories about literature, that Mallarmé's work became an abundant source of stimulating ideas and arresting examples, and it is among the major creative writers of the twentieth century that his influence is of incontestable importance.

## Principal criticism
"Variations sur un sujet," 1895
"Crises de vers," 1897 ("Crisis in Poetry," 1982)
*Divagations*, 1897

## Other major works and literary forms
During his lifetime Stéphane Mallarmé's poetry appeared in *Les Poésies de Stéphane Mallarmé* (1887), *Album de vers et de prose* (1887), *Vers et prose* (1893), and *Un Coup de dés jamais n'abolira le hasard* (1897; *Dice Thrown Never Will Annul Chance*, 1965), followed soon after his death by a second and enlarged edition of his *Les Poésies de Stéphane Mallarmé* in 1899. *Poésies* (1970; *The Poems*, 1977) is the standard and most complete edition of his verse, although it omits *Igitur* (1925; English translation, 1974), an early unfinished work. His prose poetry appeared in two of the volumes listed above, *Album de vers et de prose* and *Vers et prose*, as well as in *Pages* (1891) and the posthumously published *Pour un "Tombeau d'Anatole"* (1961; *A Tomb for Anatole*, 1983). His complete works have been published in France in *Œuvres complètes de Stéphane Mallarmé* (1945), his letters in the volumes of *Correspondance* published between 1959 and 1984, and a massive compilation of biographical material in *Documents Mallarmé* (1968–1971, three volumes). Three collections offer a selection of his work for the English-language reader: *Selected Prose Poems, Essays, and Letters* (1956), *Mallarmé* (1965), and *Selected Poetry and Prose* (1982).

POETRY
*L'Après-midi d'un faune*, 1876 (*The Afternoon of a Faun*, 1956)
*Les Poésies de Stéphane Mallarmé*, 1887, 1899
*Les Poésies d'Edgar Poe*, 1888 (translation)
*Un Coup de dés jamais n'abolira le hasard*, 1897 (*Dice Thrown Never Will Annul Chance*, 1965)
*Igitur*, 1925 (English translation, 1974)
*Poems by Mallarmé*, 1936 (Roger Fry, translator)
*Herodias*, 1940 (Clark Mills, translator)
*Selected Poems*, 1957
*Les Noces d'Hérodiade*, 1959
*Pour un "Tombeau d'Anatole,"* 1961 (*A Tomb for Anatole*, 1983)
*Poésies*, 1970 (*The Poems*, 1977)

NONFICTION
*Petite Philologie à l'usage des classes et du monde: Les Mots anglais*, 1878
*Les Dieux antiques*, 1880
*Correspondance*, 1959–1984 (10 volumes)
*Documents Mallarmé*, 1968–1971 (3 volumes)

MISCELLANEOUS
*Album de vers et de prose*, 1887
*Pages*, 1891
*Vers et prose*, 1893
*Œuvres complètes de Stéphane Mallarmé*, 1945
*Selected Prose Poems, Essays, and Letters*, 1956
*Mallarmé*, 1965
*Selected Poetry and Prose*, 1982

## Further reading
Bowie, Malcolm. *Mallarmé and the Art of Being Difficult*, 1978.
Cassedy, Steven M. *The Flight from Eden: The Origins of Modern Literary Criticism and Theory*, 1990.
Cohn, Robert Greer. *Toward the Poems of Mallarmé*, 1965.
Fowlie, Wallace. *Mallarmé*, 1962 (revised edition).
Houston, John Porter. *Patterns of Thought in Rimbaud and Mallarmé*, 1986.
Kearns, James. *Symbolist Landscapes: The Place of Painting in the Poetry and Criticism of Mallarmé and His Circle*, 1989.

Millan, Gordon. *Mallarmé: A Throw of the Dice*, 1994.
Peason, Roger. *Unfolding Mallarmé: The Development of a Poetic Art*, 1996.
St. Aubyn, Frederic Chase. *Stéphane Mallarmé*, 1969.
Wooley, Grange. *Stéphane Mallarmé, 1842–1898*, 1981.

PAUL STUEWE

*See also* Baudelaire; Continental Theory; Gourmont; Symbolism; Valéry

# Thomas Mann

German novelist and writer

**Born:** Lübeck, Germany; June 6, 1875
**Died:** Zurich, Switzerland; August 12, 1955

## Biography

The second of five children, Thomas Mann was born in Lübeck, Germany, on June 6, 1875. His father was a prominent local official from a family of grain merchants; his mother, who was partly of Portuguese descent, added a distinctive element to his background. Thomas Mann later asserted that his artistic temperament in part was derived from her. Although his academic progress was slow and fitful – it took him five years to complete a three-year Gymnasium course – from his adolescence Thomas Mann regarded creative writing as his particular calling. His father died in 1891, and later Thomas moved to Munich; he also traveled in Italy. In various ways he followed the example of his older brother, Heinrich Mann, who had taken up literary pursuits and subsequently achieved some distinction. After Thomas Mann had published some of his stories, the success of his first novel, in 1901, projected him into the ranks of leading German writers. In 1905 he married Katia Pringsheim, who was from a prominent family of Jewish bankers and scholars. Among the three sons and three daughters who were born to them, several became known for their literary efforts in their own right much later.

Mann's major novels and short stories earned for him lasting renown in his own country, and translations increased the reception of his works elsewhere. In addition to other honors, in 1929 he was awarded the Nobel Prize for Literature. Thereafter, however, he was caught up in political travails; after the Nazi seizure of power in 1933, he came under increasingly direct attack in his native land. He lived in Switzerland for a while, and for a time he carried a Czechoslovakian passport. In 1938 he emigrated to the United States, where he lived in Princeton, New Jersey, and Pacific Palisades, California. In 1944 he became a United States citizen. As the outstanding spokesperson for German culture and letters in exile, his pronouncements on

Germany's fate and its literary heritage were widely followed while his later novels were received as major new works. When he later returned to Europe, he made his home in Switzerland; he also visited various German cities to make commemorative statements in connection with important cultural events. In spite of the infirmities of advancing age, he continued with his efforts on novels and other writings which showed further dimensions of his literary vision. While his mind remained active until the end, he succumbed ultimately to arteriosclerosis and died in Zurich on August 12, 1955.

## Influence

During his long and varied literary career, Mann dealt personally with many important writers and thinkers; many of his letters were addressed to leading thinkers of his time. While for the most part contacts of this sort had to do with the reception of his fictional works, often enough issues involving his critical ideas also arose. He was personally acquainted with authors whose literary renown had preceded his own, such as Gerhart Hauptmann; other creative writers, including Arthur Schnitzler and Hugo von Hofmannsthal, also directly manifested their interest in Mann's work. Among those of his own generation, Mann frequently exchanged ideas and impressions with Hermann Hesse and André Gide. In time certain affinities emerged among their literary conceptions. The philosopher and historian Benedetto Croce acknowledged the inspiration he received from Mann's works, and indeed he dedicated one of his major studies to the German writer. Although it would seem unlikely that his essentially literary ideas affected the development of psychoanalytic thought, it is worth noting that friendly personal relations developed between Mann and Sigmund Freud. The distinguished critic Georg Lukács warmly praised Mann's creations; even from his Marxist standpoint, which Mann did not share, Lukács considered his novels as approaching an ideal type which would set the standard for other works.

Many of Mann's critical works were composed during the difficult period beginning with the collapse of democratic institutions in Germany and ending in the aftermath of World War II. During that time, he upheld classical cultural ideals which seemed threatened by Nazi demands upon German thinkers and writers. He also maintained that the timeless achievements of German literature and philosophy could furnish inspiration even under the most demanding political circumstances. After World War II, the importance of Mann's literary creations and the vitality of his critical insights were accepted in East and West Germany. Although in some respects modern German literature has moved in other directions, the significance of his views has been reflected in the works of later writers such as Siegfried Lenz, Günter Grass, and Heinrich Böll. His accomplishments have been recognized by authors and scholars in many other countries as well.

## Analysis

The sources of inspiration that were important in Mann's fiction figured prominently in his critical writings. His literary studies, which for the most part were composed after his reputation had been established through his novels and stories, recorded his debt to major thinkers and writers; in various instances he suggested as well that characteristic views of important figures had produced distinct approaches to intellectual pursuits that had a specific appeal of their own. While at times in his critical writings he referred to important literary figures from his own day, in many places he was particularly concerned to elucidate the specific features of great works from the past that exercised continuing fascination over readers of later generations. Often, as well, he would consider the biographical factors affecting literary efforts that had contributed in full measure to the development of Western culture. Contrasts and seeming anomalies were important to him; morbid and introspective thinkers interested him to the same degree as those with a positive and cosmopolitan outlook. At times he mused upon the differences that seemed to affect German and more broadly European conceptions of aesthetic values; that similar divergences may have affected those of other national cultures was suggested in places as well. In the essays and speeches that are included among Mann's critical offerings, there is a delicate balance between the formal and the offhand, where style and tone were adapted to the occasions for which such works were prepared; in some respects the shifting emphases and syntactic versatility that are notable in his narrative fiction appear as well in his studies of other writers and their literary ideas.

One of Mann's most celebrated early essays, "Goethe und Tolstoi: Fragmente zum Problem der Humanität" (1922; "Goethe and Tolstoi," 1929), dealt with the specific qualities and virtues of two great figures whose works exemplified respectively the distinctive ethos of the literary awakening in Germany and the cultural efflorescence of nineteenth-century Russia. Although previously among scholars it had not been common to seek similarities between Johann Wolfgang von Goethe and Lev Tolstoi, Mann suggested that such resemblances illustrated those features that supported the universal appeal of their great works. Both of them had pursued autobiographical themes in their writings; both had become well known for the efforts through their own lives to realize the ideals embodied in their artistic conceptions. For neither man was a contemplative existence tolerable. Although in their viewpoints they differed markedly – Goethe's cultural idealism stood at some distance from traditional religion, while Tolstoi espoused his own notions of Christian socialism – the vital forces of living experience were prominently evident in the forms of creative expression each of them adopted. Although paradoxically both men in their quest for literary truth were seemingly impelled by fascination with the forces of negation, as well as more positive urges, oppositions of this sort

appeared to heighten the attachment of each of them to the higher values they had sought. Mann drew a sharply etched contrast with two other great writers; he maintained that on the other side Friedrich Schiller and Fedor Dostoevskii seemed to epitomize the ascendancy of thought and spirit; their world of ideas was of a different sort from that directly felt and described by Goethe and Tolstoi. In their detachment from nature and the world, there was a certain quality that was decidedly gloomy and murky. While Mann's grasp of Russian literary history owed much to translations of secondary works, particularly those of Dmitrii Merezhkovskii, the importance of Russian themes in his critical writings was evident at a number of intervals. In one of his most famous literary pronouncements, from 1928, Mann designated Tolstoi's *Anna Karénina* (1875–1877; English translation, 1886) as the greatest social novel that had ever been written. In other places he discussed his great interest in Dostoevskii for having raised profound and disturbing questions about the human soul.

In various writings, Mann renewed his efforts to uncover the secrets of Goethe's creativity. A theme that imbued Mann's first novel, and was raised in statements about the cultural outlook in the city of his birth, concerned bourgeois values and habits of mind. A rather favorable consideration of such attitudes was expressed in "Goethe als Repräsentant des bürgerlichen Zeitalters" (1932; "Goethe," 1932). Mann maintained that much of Goethe's work expressed the quest for freedom that had begun to prevail during the early nineteenth century. Further antinomies had agitated German intellectual life and had left their traces in Goethe's writings; cosmopolitanism vied with more narrowly national creeds, while in a longer historical perspective the spirit of the Protestant Reformation contrasted with the classical humanism that Goethe had inherited from the eighteenth century. From Goethe, Mann derived some of the conceptions he developed in his own novels. In addition to *Lotte in Weimar* (1939; *The Beloved Returns*, 1940), which presents an imaginative account of the aging poet's return encounter with love in a youthful guise, *Doktor Faustus: Das Leben des deutschen Tonsetzers Adrian Leverkühn, erzählt von einem Freunde* (1947; *Doctor Faustus: The Life of the German Composer Adrian Leverkühn as Told by a Friend*, 1948) was inspired in part by Goethe's play, *Faust*. In "Goethe und die Demokratie" (1949; "Goethe and Democracy," 1950), Mann maintained that the importance of the great writer's thought for the modern age lay in his affirmation of enduring values and ideals in the face of the Romantic age's preoccupation with images of death. In this sense, though during his own time Goethe did not favor broad public participation in political life, his views still presaged the eventual advance of democracy rather than the rise and fall of totalitarian systems.

Elsewhere, Mann paid tribute to other great writers from past ages. His address "Rede über Lessing" (1929;

"Lessing," 1933) emphasized the importance of critical conceptions in the development of aesthetic theory. He maintained that Gotthold Ephraim Lessing's view of intellectual activity implied a humane outlook that was at once both national and natural. In another essay, Mann considered instances where in his drama Heinrich von Kleist combined mythological motifs with skillfully devised comic sequences. Much later, in the introduction to an American edition of Kleist's prose fiction, he recommended such works for the artful use of narrative tension, which is one of their distinguishing characteristics. One of the authors most frequently mentioned in Mann's critical writings was Friedrich Schiller; indeed, situations involving differences between his typical work habits and those of Goethe were depicted in some of Mann's fiction. In other writings, Mann took particular note of Schiller's works on aesthetic theory as well as his poetry and drama. A well-rounded statement on his place in German literature was delivered in *Versuch über Schiller* (1955), one of the last written works of Mann's career. He described Schiller as animated by an unswerving spirit of adventure, which was expressed tirelessly through his literary efforts; yet this impulse was tempered by a sense of realism that frequently was not recognized. Mann took note of Schiller's extraordinary sensitivity and maintained that the great struggles of his creative life were conducted ultimately within himself. Suggesting once more the typology that he had developed in his earlier work, Mann found it significant that Schiller's writings had enjoyed widespread popularity in Russia; indeed, Dostoevskii had received his ideas with enthusiasm. On the other hand, though Schiller's troubled and turbulent existence produced works that in many respects varied from those that Goethe's more refined and tranquil nature had created, it was significant that in later life admiration and respect prompted Goethe to accord the other man a high place among literary figures of that time. In this sense, the possibility was raised that seemingly antithetical types conceivably might be reconciled to the extent that they possessed complementary qualities.

Among writers of the nineteenth century, Mann discussed at times those whose works had left particularly memorable impressions upon him. He had high praise for the verse of Theodor Storm, who he maintained had composed some of the most haunting and poignant love poetry in the German language. Mann found it remarkable that Theodor Fontane had displayed youthful vigor of a heightened sort in verse that was written at a time of life when others would have yielded to the more sedate sentiments of advanced age. Other writings indicated the esteem in which Mann held authors he had come to know in the course of his own career. In his memorial statement on Hugo von Hofmannsthal, in 1929, he declared that it was tragic for the other writer's efforts to have suffered so severely as a consequence of the upheaval in values and ideals that had come in the wake of World War I. In

*Der Zauberberg* (1924; *The Magic Mountain*, 1927), Mann had rendered a thinly veiled caricature of Gerhart Hauptmann, and also of Georg Lukács; afterward he expressed some regrets, and several years later he delivered a formal public statement setting forth Hauptmann's literary achievements. Toward the end of his life, Mann contended that there were positive qualities in fictional portraits of the sort that he had devised while he called to mind as well the remarkably inventive and evocative aspects of Hauptmann's work.

In Mann's works there was often some congruence between literary conceptions and musical or philosophical motifs. After his first major fictional efforts had appeared, he declared at one point that the guiding lights of his creative work were the ideas of Richard Wagner, Arthur Schopenhauer, and Friedrich Nietzsche. Indeed, in some of his narrative fiction Mann had alluded to opera as suggesting the awakening of aesthetic consciousness. Mann explained his long-standing devotion to Wagner's compositions in essays such as "Leiden und Grösse Richard Wagners" (1933; "Sufferings and Greatness of Richard Wagner," 1933), in which he presented some rather striking interpretations of the musical writer's place in intellectual history. Mann contended that in many respects Wagner was able to capitalize upon theatrical and sensual elements in productions that made virtues of those very qualities. Wagner may have begun his efforts as a dilettante, but he elevated that characteristic into art by the very force of his genius. On other fronts, Mann tended to defend Wagner from his detractors by maintaining that the great composer was neither as nationalistic nor as hostile to Christianity as had sometimes been asserted. Moreover, Mann contended that Wagner possessed poetic gifts that should not be disregarded. Essays on leading philosophers also revealed some of the individual lines along which Mann's thoughts were drawn. In a study of Schopenhauer, he depicted the well-known thinker as having shown a musical temperament; though he was a pessimist by nature, his outlook also evinced a humanism tempered by objectivity which belied more facile interpretations of his work. Mann also regarded Schopenhauer's ideas on will and the self as marking a vital and pathbreaking stage in the development of psychological thought. Early in his career, Mann had valued the teachings of Nietzsche, particularly as they had explored problems of individual and social consciousness that had been important underlying concerns in his own works. During his later years, Mann drew back from this reading of Nietzsche, though throughout he regarded his ideas as having significant applications in literature. In "Nietzsches Philosophie im Lichte unserer Erfahrung" (1947; "Nietzsche's Philosophy in the Light of Recent History," 1958), Mann contended that even by overreaching himself the celebrated thinker had come upon towering insights. Mann had a particularly high regard for the philosophical speculation in Nietzsche's work, which he maintained had revealed new dimensions of human drives and aspirations. On the other hand, his preoccupation with the conflict between intellect and instinct had, in Mann's view, led Nietzsche to overstate the hazards of dedication to the life of the mind; he had also misjudged the influence of moral standards in modern society.

In his depiction of fictional characters, Mann had shown the workings of the unconscious mind, and at times he discussed his interest in leading psychological theories. His judgments of such ideas displayed an essentially literary conception which made use of such doctrines in ways that accorded with his own reading and insights. His essay "Freud und die Zukunft" (1936; "Freud and the Future," 1937) paid homage to the founder of modern psychoanalysis. Indeed, Mann maintained that, without any systematic study of modern philosophy, Sigmund Freud had reached conclusions that were foreshadowed in the works of Schopenhauer and Nietzsche, and in fact had proceeded well beyond them. Freud's determination that the underlying sources of human conduct enveloped the conscious ego and created imperatives of their own represented a major stage in the understanding of the mind; primitive urges thus could be recognized where thought and behavior seemed affected by conflicting drives. Mann was of the opinion that the future of humanity could benefit from advances in this area, and he called for greater daring in utilizing discoveries that had been made.

Many of Mann's other pronouncements were delivered by way of reviews, commemorative statements, and brief recollections. Often writers and issues that had intrigued him during his early career were discussed in his subsequent critical offerings. Interest and attention were aroused partly by Mann's position as one of the outstanding prose writers of his time, and partly by the original and somewhat individual evaluations he delivered of major works. In certain respects, the body of his critical writing has been regarded in this light by subsequent scholars. Mann was not a partisan of any school of criticism; many of his statements represented, rather, his personal views on major authors and their efforts. Nevertheless, to the extent that the origins of his own creative works could be traced to specific cultural traditions, his views could be considered important; often enough they were supported by a serious and painstaking reading of literary sources. Moreover, that his judgments should be cited in connection with many literary issues is indicative of the degree to which they remain provocative yet grounded in enough erudition and good sense to warrant renewed attention and consideration.

## Principal criticism

*Rede und Antwort*, 1922
*Bemühungen*, 1925
*Die Forderung des Tages*, 1930
*Three Essays*, 1932
*Past Masters and Other Papers*, 1933
*Leiden und Grösse der Meister*, 1935
*Freud, Goethe, Wagner*, 1937
*Order of the Day: Political Essays and Speeches of Two Decades*, 1942
*Adel des Geistes: Sechzehn Versuche zum Problem der Humanität*, 1945 (*Essays of Three Decades*, 1947)
*Neue Studien*, 1948
*Altes und Neues: Kleine Prosa aus fünf Jahrzehnten*, 1953
*Versuch über Schiller*, 1955
*Nachlese: Prosa 1951–1955*, 1956
*Last Essays*, 1958
*Addresses Delivered at the Library of Congress*, 1963
*Wagner und unsere Zeit*, 1963 (*Pro and Contra Wagner*, 1985)
*Reden und Aufsätze*, 1965 (2 volumes)
*Essays*, 1977–1978 (3 volumes)
*Goethes Laufbahn als Schriftsteller: Zwölf Essays und Reden zu Goethe*, 1982

## Other major works and literary forms

Thomas Mann's literary stature has rested in almost equal measure upon his achievements with the novel and in short fiction. His first full-length work, *Buddenbrooks: Verfall einer Familie* (1901; *Buddenbrooks*, 1924), is a family saga redolent with themes of decadence and fatalism. Among his major novels, *Der Zauberberg* (1924; *The Magic Mountain*, 1927) is possibly the most renowned; it considers the actual and the metaphorical aspects of illness against a background of European values in upheaval during the period leading to World War I. Mann's most ambitious effort, *Joseph und seine Brüder* (1933–1943; *Joseph and His Brothers*, 1934–1944), poses questions of morality and betrayal in an archetypal setting drawn from the Old Testament. *Lotte in Weimar* (1939; *The Beloved Returns*, 1940) presents a fictional recounting of events from the life of Johann Wolfgang von Goethe. Brooding thoughts upon Germany's destiny were set forth in Mann's modern version of the legend surrounding Faustus in *Doktor Faustus: Das Leben des deutschen Tonsetzers Adrian Leverkühn, erzählt von einem Freunde* (1947; *Doctor Faustus: The Life of the German Composer Adrian Leverkühn as Told by a Friend*, 1948). *Bekenntnisse des Hochstaplers Felix Krull: Der Memoiren erster Teil* (1954; *Confessions of Felix Krull, Confidence Man: The Early Years*, 1955), though left unfinished, is a witty and engaging work which is based on some deft pieces of characterization.

Among Mann's most important shorter works, *Der kleine Herr Friedemann* (1898; *Little Herr Friedemann*, 1928) is one of the earliest of note; *Tonio Kröger* (1903; English translation, 1914) depicts the travails of a youth caught between his artistic temperament and the demands of actual life. *Der Tod in Venedig* (1912; *Death in Venice*, 1925), probably the most celebrated of Mann's stories, takes up concerns with a writer's sense of identity, his conception of creativity, and inexorable mortality in an evocative and subtly crafted narrative. Other works, such as *Herr und Hund* (1919; *Bashan and I*, 1923, also known as *A Man and His Dog*, 1930), *Unordnung und frühes Leid* (1926; *Disorder and Early Sorrow*, 1928), and *Mario und der Zauberer* (1930; *Mario and the Magician*, 1930), are fine examples of Mann's delicate precise style and studied restraint in the achievement of architectonic thematic ends. He also wrote one play and some short verse offerings. The outlook of Mann's political writings varied widely. During World War I he upheld German cultural ideals in *Betrachtungen eines Unpolitischen* (1918; *Reflections of a Nonpolitical Man*, 1983); under the Weimar Republic he defended liberal democratic institutions. In later works he resolutely declared his opposition to National Socialism and its ambitions. In 1930 he produced a brief autobiographical sketch. The most extensive compilation of his correspondence is his *Briefe* (1961–1965; partial translation, *Letters of Thomas Mann, 1889-1955*, 1970). His *Tagebücher* (1977–1986), in six volumes, present impressions of his life recorded between 1918 and 1946; an abridged translation of the first four volumes appeared as *Diaries 1918–1939* (1982).

## NOVELS

*Buddenbrooks: Verfall einer Familie*, 1901 (*Buddenbrooks*, 1924)
*Tonio Kröger*, 1903 (novella; English translation, 1914)
*Tristan*, 1903 (novella; English translation, 1925)
*Königliche Hoheit*, 1909 (*Royal Highness*, 1916)
*Der Tod in Venedig*, 1912 (novella; *Death in Venice*, 1925)
*Herr und Hund*, 1919 (novella: *Bashan and I*, 1923, also known as *A Man and His Dog*, 1930)
*Der Zauberberg*, 1924 (*The Magic Mountain*, 1927)
*Unordnung und frühes Leid*, 1926 (novella; *Disorder and Early Sorrow*, 1928)
*Mario und der Zauberer*, 1930 (novella; *Mario and the Magician*, 1930)
*Joseph und seine Brüder*, 1933–1943 (*Joseph and His Brothers*, 1934–1944), includes *Die Geschichten Jaakobs* (*Joseph and His Brothers*, also as *The Tales of Jacob*), *Der junge Joseph* (*The Young Joseph*), *Joseph in Ägypten* (*Joseph in Egypt*), and *Joseph, der Ernährer* (*Joseph the Provider*)
*Lotte in Weimar*, 1939 (*The Beloved Returns*, 1940)
*Die vertauschten Köpfe: Eine indische Legende*, 1940 (*The Transposed Heads: A Legend of India*, 1941)
*Das Gesetz*, 1944 (*The Tables of the Law*, 1945)
*Doktor Faustus: Das Leben des deutschen Tonsetzers Adrian Leverkühn, erzählt von einem Freunde*, 1947 (*Doctor Faustus: The Life of the German Composer Adrian Leverkühn as Told by a Friend*, 1948)
*Der Erwählte*, 1951 (*The Holy Sinner*, 1951)
*Die Betrogene*, 1953 (*The Black Swan*, 1954)
*Bekenntnisse des Hochstaplers Felix Krull: Der Memoiren erster Teil*, 1954 (*Confessions of Felix Krull, Confidence Man: The Early Years*, 1955)

## SHORT FICTION

*Der kleine Herr Friedemann*, 1898 (*Little Herr Friedemann*, 1928)
*Erzählungen*, 1922
*Children and Fools*, 1928
*Stories of Three Decades*, 1936
*Ausgewählte Erzählungen*, 1945
*Stories of a Lifetime*, 1961

## PLAY

*Fiorenza*, 1906

## POETRY

"Gesang vom Kindchen," 1919

## NONFICTION

"Friedrich und die grosse Koalition," 1915 ("Frederick and the Great Coalition," 1929)
*Betrachtungen eines Unpolitischen*, 1918 (*Reflections of a Nonpolitical Man*, 1983)
*Lebensabriss*, 1930 (*A Sketch of My Life*, 1960)
*Achtung, Europa!*, 1938
*Dieser Friede*, 1938 (*This Peace*, 1938)
*Vom künftigen Sieg der Demokratie*, 1938 (*The Coming of Victory of Democracy*, 1938)
*Deutsche Hörer!*, 1942 (*Listen, Germany!*, 1943)
*Die Entstehung des "Doktor Faustus": Roman eines Romans*, 1949 (*The Story of a Novel: The Genesis of "Doctor Faustus,"* 1961)
*Briefe*, 1961–1965 (3 volumes; partial translation, *Letters of Thomas Mann, 1889-1955*, 1970)
*Tagebücher*, 1977–1986 (6 volumes; partial translation, *Diaries 1918–1939*, 1982)

## MISCELLANEOUS

*Gesammelte Werke*, 1956 (12 volumes; includes critical writings in volumes 10–11)
*Gesammelte Werke*, 1960–1974 (13 volumes; includes critical writings in volumes 9–11)
*Werkausgabe*, 1980–1986 (20 volumes; includes 3 volumes of critical writings)
*Frage und Antwort: Interviews mit Thomas Mann 1909-1955*, 1983
*Thomas Mann's "Goethe and Tolstoi": Notes and Sources*, 1984

# Further reading

Bloom, Harold, ed. *Thomas Mann*, 1986.
Ezergailis, Inta Miske. *Male and Female: An Approach to Thomas Mann's Dialectic*, 1975.
Hayman, Ronald. *Thomas Mann: A Biography*, 1996.
Heller, Erich. *The Ironic German: A Study of Thomas Mann*, 1958.
Heller, Peter. "Goethe und Tolstoi: Notes on Thomas Mann's Typology of the Artist," in *Germano-Slavica*. II, no. 6 (1978), pp. 439–451.
Jahn, Gary R. "A Note on the Concept of the Artist in Thomas Mann and Dmitry Merezhkovsky," in *Germano-Slavica*. II, no. 6 (1978), pp. 451–454.
Kaufmann, Fritz. *Thomas Mann: The World as Will and Representation*, 1957.
Lukács, Georg. *Essays on Thomas Mann*, 1964. Translated by Stanley Mitchell.
Marcus, Judith. *Georg Lukács and Thomas Mann: A Study in the Sociology of Literature*, 1987.
Neider, Charles, ed. *The Stature of Thomas Mann*, 1947.
Prater, Donald. *Thomas Mann: A Life*, 1995.
Reed, Terence James. *Thomas Mann: The Uses of Tradition*, 1974.
Ridley, Hugh. *The Problematic Bourgeois: 20th Century Criticism and Thomas Mann's Buddenbrooks and The Magic Mountain*, 1994.
Swales, Martin. *Thomas Mann: A Study*, 1980.
Travers, Martin. *Thomas Mann*, 1982.
Vaget, Hans Rudolf. "Georg Lukács, Thomas Mann, and the Modern Novel," in *Thomas Mann in Context: Papers of the Clark University Centennial Colloquium*, 1978. Edited by Kenneth Hughes.

J. R. BROADUS

# Filippo Tommaso Marinetti

Italian writer and critic

**Born:** Alexandria, Egypt; December 22, 1876
**Died:** Bellagio, Italy; December 2, 1944

## Biography

Filippo Tommaso Marinetti was born on December 22, 1876, in Alexandria, Egypt. He was the second son of an Italian family living abroad; his father, Enrico, was an attorney who in time amassed a sizable fortune from international commercial transactions, and his mother, Amalia Grolli Marinetti, was originally from Milan. During his youth Marinetti lived in several countries. Although he was expelled from a French Jesuit school in Egypt, evidently for having distributed copies of Émile Zola's novels among his fellow students, in 1893 he commenced university studies in Paris. He subsequently pursued a legal education in Italy, at the universities in Pavia and Genoa. In 1898, however, he won first prize for a free-verse composition he had submitted to a contest sponsored by a French theater organization. Although the following year he defended a thesis on problems of the monarchy under a parliamentary government, he never practiced law; instead, he embarked on various literary ventures. He published several volumes of poetry and drama, and in 1905 he became one of the founders of the international journal *Poesia*, which carried experimental verse from many contributors. In 1909 he published his first manifesto on Futurism and announced that radically innovative forces could transform literature and art. The approaches he advocated were displayed in some of his subsequent fictional efforts; he began to associate himself with other journals as well.

Themes of war as a creative and purifying force were derived in part from Marinetti's own experiences. In 1911 he was on hand as a correspondent during Italy's invasion of Libya; during the next year he also reported on the first of the Balkan Wars, which supplied images he incorporated in his poetry. In 1915 Marinetti was arrested following a demonstration in favor of Italian belligerence during World War I; when Italy did enter the conflict, Marinetti fought with some distinction on the Alpine front. He was wounded, and toward the end of the war he was decorated for valor in action. Shortly thereafter he married Benedetta Cappa, a painter and writer; in time three daughters were born to them.

Marinetti was a fervent supporter of Fascism; he had come to know Benito Mussolini and welcomed his political ascendancy. Indeed, in some of his publications Marinetti argued that Fascist principles resembled Futurist thinking as it could be applied to problems of government and public life. He received various honors in his own country; in 1929 he became a member of the Accademia d'Italia. Nationalism and militarism remained important elements of his thought. In spite of his relatively advanced age he participated in the Ethiopian War of 1935–1936. Later, when such questions were raised by Italian journalists, he denounced anti-Semitism, however, as incompatible with genuine Italian patriotism. During World War II he joined Italian troops in Russia, where in 1942 and 1943 he was involved in some rather hazardous engagements. Upon his return, he remained loyal to the Fascist regime; after the short-lived Republic of Salò was founded in northern Italy, he settled briefly in Bellagio. He died there from a heart attack on December 2, 1944.

## Influence

For a certain period, in one form or another, Marinetti's Futurist conceptions of literature and art were received by writers and thinkers from many countries. Although in some cases the effects were short-lived, in other instances the exuberant vitality and energy of his aesthetic vision left clear traces. Early in their careers, Wyndham Lewis and D. H. Lawrence were notably affected by his ideas, as was Hart Crane; partly in answer to Marinetti's example, Ezra Pound became a leading advocate of new variations in approaches to poetry. Although as a partisan for the Bolsheviks Vladimir Maiakovskii espoused a political position that was nearly a negative mirror image of Marinetti's rightist standpoint, the Russian writer was heavily indebted to Futurist methods. Marinetti's influence probably reached its zenith during the second decade of the twentieth century; later, particularly as a result of his personal alignment with Fascist ambitions and doctrines, his ideas fell into desuetude. For a number of years after World War II little was written or said about Marinetti and his literary conceptions, but eventually many of his works were published in new editions. Not only have Italian writers and literary historians been moved to reconsider Marinetti's place in critical theory, but also translations and other studies of his life and work have awakened interest in his contributions to the literature of the modern age.

## Analysis

Marinetti is the specific individual most closely associated with the conception of Futurism: a movement which rejected the past and all of its relics and posited that civilization was at the threshold of a new historical epoch. Essentially all the movement's proponents attested his role in formulating and expounding such ideas as part of a broadly-based creative vision. For that matter, Marinetti's notions of modernity asserted that similar underlying approaches could unite various forms of literary expression, such as poetry, drama, and prose fiction; the means he employed in each genre seemed to converge with those he utilized in others. He also promoted uses of the graphic arts by which variations in typefaces could convey unusual effects; experiments of this sort with his verse compositions led to some interesting forays into visual art which resembled the later efforts of Dadaist painters. Another production of this sort was a self-portrait which cast aside any pretenses at exact representation. Marinetti contended that the theater should be dominated by noise and spectacle; at times he maintained that the purpose of the cinema was to render printed books outmoded. He asserted as well that clothing and cuisine were susceptible to his theories; he appeared at times in what he described as a Futurist vest, and he helped devise an organization of dinner plates which suggested words and phrases taken from Futurist pronouncements. Many of Marinetti's writings had political and social overtones; at times he suggested that his ideas could provide foundations for bold new forms of government which would reject the vacillation and compromise of past regimes. Although he believed that his views on political life were distinctive in their own right, his teachings were eventually assimilated by larger doctrines, while his support for Italian intervention in World War I, and for Fascism thereafter, was used by political groups for their own ends.

Early in his career Marinetti declared that he and his followers had certain specific aims which consisted in the exaltation of traits that he held were necessary attributes of Futurist artists and writers. He maintained that courage and struggle were necessary in any creative work. Insomnia and ceaseless activity, as well as devotion to the cult of speed, were characteristics of those who should pursue literary callings. In his "Premier manifeste du futurisme" ("The Founding and Manifesto of Futurism," 1919), he asserted certain principles which subsequently were invariably associated with his views. His claim that an automobile in full racing trim was more beautiful than the *Victory of Samothrace* was widely quoted; he went on to contend that his movement derived its fervor from the glorification of war, which he regarded as having a hygienic function. Patriotism and militarism in his view were positive virtues, which were complemented by scorn for women. Museums, libraries, and other cultural repositories he considered useless relics which could as well be destroyed; they were no more uplifting than graveyards. For that matter, he was willing to concede that when his generation had become old they might well be consigned to the oblivion of decay, while younger and yet more vigorous Futurist artists would come to the fore. Other manifestos from this period, such as "Tuons le clair de lune" ("Let's Murder the Moonshine"), promoted the destruction of old values as part of a program which he asserted would open the way for new and qualitatively different cultural achievements. Salient themes in his writings included a forceful positive emphasis on the creations of modern technology, particularly motor vehicles and power engines. Electricity he regarded as vital as exemplifying new relations between matter and energy; accordingly, he insisted that frenetic movement was necessary for any Futurist efforts. Indeed, he contended that a new aesthetic of speed could overthrow all past bounds of time and space, liberating men and machines for unremitting endeavors of every sort.

The applications of an outlook of this sort to literature were set forth in his "Manifeste technique de la littérature futuriste" ("Technical Manifesto of Futurist Literature"), in which Marinetti maintained that syntax must be destroyed and punctuation replaced by mathematical symbols; adjectives and adverbs should be expelled from the Futurist vocabulary. There remained nouns and images; Marinetti proposed various semantic inventions while declaring that metaphors suggesting the metal and motion of propellors and machine guns were appropriate for capturing the spirit of a new age. Critical commentators depicted Marinetti's ideas as a congeries of disjointed arguments, feelings, and assertions, and indeed others from that period found his notions easy targets for their parodies. On the other hand, because of the outspoken novelty of his conceptions and the zeal with which he promoted them, Marinetti for a time had numerous followers.

Apart from a certain number of contemporaries whom he identified as kindred spirits, there were few creative thinkers for whom Marinetti expressed any sort of respect or approval. He was, however, willing to acknowledge that some positive qualities could still be found in authors from the past, even when he regarded their conceptions as essentially outdated. Thus, for example, he believed that the works of Dante might well remain part of his nation's cultural legacy but should not be accorded abject veneration. Other dislikes and preferences were set forth in collections of essays such as *Le Futurisme*. Although he was inclined to discount the significance of many previous writers, he counted some authors from the nineteenth century among his predecessors. In particular, Marinetti mentioned Symbolist poets; in this category he included Edgar Allan Poe and Charles Baudelaire, as well as Stéphane Mallarmé and Paul Verlaine. Evidently, he believed that their innovations regarding form were vital, as otherwise Marinetti reproached them for yielding excessively to nostalgic and sentimental yearnings. His own tastes were varied but rather selective; another small group of writers whom he described as direct precursors of Futurism included Walt Whitman, Émile Zola, and Émile Verhaeren. In various connections Marinetti also suggested that he had derived some inspiration from the works of Friedrich Nietzsche; in addition to support for the conviction that old values no longer could be sustained during the modern age, Marinetti may have found Nietzsche's use of declamatory devices instructive as a matter of form. Nevertheless, Marinetti showed some disdain for what he regarded as the overly serious and self-concerned element of Nietzsche's outlook; indeed, Marinetti considered Nietzsche a representative of a Germanic cultural tradition which was incompatible with the national ideals of militant Futurism. Marinetti also had some caustic remarks about the standpoint conveyed in the works of Richard Wagner. In "À bas le tango et Parsifal" ("Down with the Tango and Parsifal"), Marinetti denounced compositions which presented drawn-out sequences of romance, parting, and grief; he contended, rather, that more direct themes of virility and possession should dominate the musical stage.

The lengthiest and the most telling of Marinetti's critical judgments were delivered in his *D'Annunzio intime* and *Les Dieux s'en vont, D'Annunzio reste*. In these works he denounced the literary standing of Italy's premier poet, whom he had seen personally, while he recorded some observations which were not far from outright caricature. Marinetti objected specifically to what he regarded as weak and sickly traits in the works of Gabriele D'Annunzio. He maintained that memory and nostalgia were emphasized to excess; D'Annunzio had, he argued, given way to idealizations of female beauty and romantic sentimentality that, in Marinetti's view, were utterly to be abjured. He also reproached D'Annunzio for a preoccupation with the past, which had led to a fascination with historical antiquity that was unseemly in any creative writer. On the other hand, Marinetti regarded certain French writers whom he had known as important representatives of ideas which resembled his own. In particular, he cited the efforts of Alfred Jarry, whose evocations of decadence and disregard for prevailing mores had foreshadowed similar themes in Futurist efforts. Indeed, at various times, Marinetti arranged for Jarry's contributions to appear in the poetry journal he had helped to establish. Guillaume Apollinaire also showed some interest in Marinetti's ideas, and short articles of his were featured in publications such as *I manifesti del futurismo* (1914). Nevertheless, while the Italian writer was anxious to claim Apollinaire as a leading figure in his movement, there is evidence that Apollinaire was somewhat diffident in his reception of Futurist ideas and considered them only part of a larger concern with modernism in various forms of literary expression.

As it was conceived by Marinetti and his associates, Futurism connoted both attitudes and approaches to form that were openly at odds with past practices; on both fronts, their stance was insistently iconoclastic. Marinetti, whose first literary efforts were poetry, increasingly dispensed with more conventional terms in favor of usages he had devised himself; his efforts in this genre moved toward a kind of free verse which he frequently characterized as *parole in libertà*, or words at liberty. Odd and seemingly random semantic associations were juxtaposed with onomatopoeic inventions in works where repetitive passages alternated with abrupt transitions which recorded seemingly disjointed thoughts. The results, which were presented in works such as *Zang tumb tuuum*, produced impressions of a strident declamatory posture, heighted by Marinetti's frequent use of bold capitals. Similar techniques in *8 anime in una bomba* were used to create effects of prose narrative merging with poetry, with more typographical special effects added for emphasis or variety. Marinetti maintained that a purpose lay behind his studied disregard for conventional literary restraints; indeed, to overthrow them was the first task of Futurism. In the preface to *The Untamables*, he depicted his aims as encompassing those of symbolic poetry, the fantastic or adventure novel, and social-philosophical commentary. Elsewhere in his fictional works, curious poses were struck in order to demonstrate the seemingly divergent paths by which Futurist doctrines yielded efforts which, he contended, would supersede previous forms of poetry and narrative prose. On the other hand, once a certain number of variations had been explored, many of Marinetti's compositions seemed largely to elaborate on themes and methods that he had developed in his earlier works.

During the later phases of his career, Marinetti edited various anthologies which were meant to display the Futurist conceptions of other writers; he also composed brief studies of authors whom he regarded as important within the movement. He showed some adeptness as a translator from Romance languages; his renditions of various works, including those of Mallarmé and Cornelius Tacitus, were considered important. Although he continued to expound his theories, however, and to produce further poems and novels, his efforts aroused less interest than they had earlier, during that vibrant period of the early twentieth century when his ideas received widespread attention and publicity. It would seem likely that when Marinetti became an honored figure in Fascist Italy, his influence elsewhere diminished proportionately. In some respects it could also be argued that, for all its insistence on the unending quest for innovation, Futurism drew from a limited stock of ideas; once those had begun to run low, Marinetti and others like him fell back on essentially redundant means of expression or were driven to proclaim their conceptions in forms that were more bizarre than original. Nevertheless, though Marinetti's influence fell into abeyance for quite some time, and after his death there was little discussion of his doctrines, in due course renewed attention to his writings and his critical views served to reaffirm his importance among modern creative thinkers.

## Principal criticism

*D'Annunzio intime*, 1903
*Les Dieux s'en vont, D'Annunzio reste*, 1908
*Le Futurisme*, 1911
*Guerra sola igiene del mondo*, 1915
*Come si seducono le donne*, 1916
*Democrazia futurista*, 1919
*Les Mots en liberté futuristes*, 1919
*Futurismo e fascismo*, 1924
*Arte fascista*, 1927
*Marinetti e il futurismo*, 1929
*Il paesaggio e l'estetica futurista della macchina*, 1931
*Teoria e invenzione futurista*, 1968
*Selected Writings*, 1972
*Collaudi futuristi*, 1977
*Let's Murder the Moonshine: Selected Writings*, 1991 (R. W. Flint, editor; R. W. Flint and Arthur A. Coppotelli, translators)

## Other major works and literary forms

Filippo Tommaso Marinetti often announced his literary ideas in creative works which were meant to demonstrate the applications of his views. He was fluent in French as well as his native Italian, and for a time he wrote poetry and prose as well as criticism in both languages. Among his early verse collections, *La Conquête des étoiles* (1902) and *Destruction* (1904) herald themes which also appear in his later efforts. Marinetti's experiments with form, for which he became well known, are carried forward in works such as *La Bataille de Tripoli (26 octobre 1911)* (1912) and *Zang tumb tuuum: Adrianopoli, ottobre 1912* (1914). Some efforts attempt to produce the effects of several genres; *Le Monoplan du Pape* (1912), for example, represents his notions of a novel in verse.

Marinetti's dramatic writing challenges conventional sensibilities. (For example, *Le Roi bombance*, published in 1905, addresses amorality.) Some plays were intended to illustrate the principles upon which he asserted theatrical productions should be based. Odd traits from his other works were introduced, and, in advance of Luigi Pirandello, with whom Marinetti otherwise had little to do, some efforts for the stage seem to issue an invitation for the audience to participate.

There is a marked unevenness in Marinetti's narrative writing. His novel *Mafarka le futuriste* (1909) is a prolonged and chaotic work; for *8 anime in una bomba* (1919) Marinetti drew upon dramatic and verse techniques in an attempt to demonstrate his versatility. His short novel *Gli indomabili* (1922; *The Untamables*, 1972) was composed along somewhat similar lines but conveys a curiously pessimistic outlook. Autobiographical themes come to the fore in some of Marinetti's other prose works.

NOVELS
*Mafarka le futuriste*, 1909
*L'isola dei baci*, 1918 (with Bruno Corra)
*8 anime in una bomba*, 1919
*Un ventre di donna*, 1919 (with Enif Robert)
*L'alcòva d'acciaio*, 1921
*Gli indomabili*, 1922 (*The Untamables*, 1972)
*Il club dei simpatici*, 1931

SHORT FICTION
*Gli amori futuristi*, 1922
*Scatole d'amore in conserva*, 1927
*Novelle colle labbra tinte*, 1930

PLAYS
*La Momie sanglante*, 1904
*Le Roi bombance*, 1905
*Poupées électriques*, 1909
*Elettricità sessuale*, 1920
*Il tamburo di fuoco*, 1922
*Prigionieri*, 1927
*Vulcano*, 1927
*L'oceano del cuore*, 1928
*Il suggeritore nudo*, 1930
*Patriottismo insetticida*, 1939

*Teatro*, 1960
*Il teatro della sorpresa*, 1968

POETRY
*La Conquête des étoiles*, 1902
*Destruction*, 1904
*La Ville charnelle*, 1908
*La Bataille de Tripoli (26 octobre 1911)*, 1912
*Le Monoplan du Pape*, 1912
*Zang tumb tuuum: Adrianopoli, ottobre 1912*, 1914
*Scelta di poesie e parole in libertà*, 1918
*Spagna veloce e toro futurista*, 1931
*Poemi simultanei futuristi*, 1933
*L'aeropoema del Golfo della Spezia*, 1935
*Il poema africano della divisione "XXVIII ottobre,"* 1937
*Il poema non umano dei tecnicismi*, 1940
*Canto eroi e macchine della guerra Mussoliniana*, 1942
*Quarto d'ora di poesia della X Mas*, 1945
*Poesie a Beny*, 1971
*Stung by Salt and War*, 1987

NONFICTION
*A di là del comunismo*, 1920
*Primo dizionario aereo italiano*, 1929 (with Fedele Azari)
*La Cucina Futurista*, 1932 (*The Futurist Cookbook*, 1989)
*Il fascino dell'Egitto*, 1933
*La grande Milano tradizionale e futurista: Una sensibilità italiana nata in Egitto*, 1969 (partial translation, "Great Traditional and Futurist Milan: An Italian Sensibility Born in Egypt," 1972)
*Lettere ruggenti a F. Balilla-Pratella*, 1969
*Carteggio*, 1978 (with Aldo Palazzeschi)
*Scritti francesi*, 1983

TRANSLATIONS
*Versi e prose*, 1916 (of Stéphane Mallarmé's *Vers et prose*)
*Le Syphon d'or*, 1924 (of Francesco Cangiullo's *Il sifone d'oro: Versi*, 1913)
*La Germania*, 1928 (of Tacitus' *Germania: De origine situ Germanorum*)

EDITED TEXTS
*Enquête internationale sur le vers libre et manifeste du futurisme*, 1909
*I poeti futuristi*, 1912
*I manifesti del futurismo*, 1914
*Teatro futurista sintetico*, 1915–1916
*Noi futuristi*, 1917
*I nuovi poeti futuristi*, 1925
*Carlinga di aeropoeti futuristi di guerra*, 1941

MISCELLANEOUS
*Opere*, 1968–1969

## Further reading

Bronner, Stephen Eric. "F. T. Marinetti: The Theory and Practice of Futurism," in *Boston University Journal*. XXV, no. 2 (1977), pp. 48–56.

Clough, Rosa Trillo. *Futurism: The Story of a Modern Art Movement, a New Appraisal*, 1961.

Festa-McCormick, Diana. "Marinetti's Murder of the Moonlight and the Kinetics of Time," in *Centerpoint*. II, no. 3 (1977), pp. 50–54.

Joll, James. "F. T. Marinetti: Futurism and Fascism," in *Intellectuals in Politics*, 1960.

Perloff, Marjorie. *The Futurist Movement: Avant-garde, Avant Guerre, and the Language of Rupture,* 1986.

Rainey, Lawrence. "The Creation of the Avant-Garde: F. T. Marinetti and Ezra Pound," in *Modernism Modernity.* 1, no. 3 (September, 1994), pp. 195–219.

Rawson, Judy. "Italian Futurism," in *Modernism, 1890–1930,* 1976. Edited by Malcolm Bradbury and James McFarlane.

Schnapp, Jeffrey. "Politics and Poetics in Marinetti's *Zang tumb tuuum,*" in *Stanford Italian Review.* V, no. 1 (1985), pp. 75–92.

Vinall, Shirley W. "Marinetti and the English Contributors to *Poesia,*" in *The Modern Language Review.* LXXV, no. 3 (1980), pp. 547–560.

Wagstaff, Christopher. "Dead Man Erect: F. T. Marinetti, *L'alcòva d'acciaio,*" in *The First World War in Fiction,* 1976. Edited by Holger Klein.

Webster, Michael. *Reading Visual Poetry after Futurism: Marinetti, Apollinaire, Schwitters, Cummings,* 1995.

Zurbrugg, Nicholas. "Marinetti, Boccioni, and Electroacoustic Poetry: Futurism and After," in *Comparative Criticism.* IV (1982), pp. 193–211.

J. R. BROADUS

*See also* Hulme; Pound


# Jacques Maritain

## French religious philosopher and critic

**Born:** Paris, France; November 18, 1882
**Died:** Toulouse, France; April 28, 1973

## Biography

Jacques Maritain was born on November 18, 1882, in Paris, was baptized in the French Reformed church, and received religious instruction as a liberal Protestant. Educated at the Sorbonne from 1901 to 1906, he rebelled against the dominant rationalistic philosophies of the day and joined a circle of friends which included the renowned poet Charles-Pierre Péguy and Maritain's future wife and lifelong collaborator, Raïssa Oumansoff. After their marriage in 1904 they were converted to Roman Catholicism by Léon Bloy. They were also liberated from what they believed to be sterile positivism by the lectures and writings of Henri Bergson at the Collège de France, but his teachings merely paved the way for their own discovery of Saint Thomas Aquinas.

Maritain served as professor of philosophy at the Institut Catholique de Paris from 1914 to 1933, during which time he built his reputation as the premier apologist for Christianity in France. Unaffected by World War I and its aftermath, he remained a typical conservative scholar who opposed modern democracy, along with twentieth-century changes in society, until 1926, when Pope Pius XI condemned the Action Française as a political organization which had illegitimately merged right-wing, clerical-monarchist politics with the Church. Maritain obeyed the Pope and rose to international stature as he encountered increased hostility at home from the die-hard conservative defenders of the Action Française. As a result of this pressure, he left France to serve at the Institute of Medieval Studies in Toronto from 1933 to 1945. After World War II he remained in the United States and served at several universities before he retired in the late 1950s. When his beloved Raïssa died in 1960 he returned to France to spend the rest of his days in a monastery. He lived in Toulouse with the Little Brothers of Jesus, a Dominican monastic order, which he joined in 1969; he died among its members on April 28, 1973.

## Influence

Maritain offered a vision of unity and order based upon the Thomistic formulations of the Christian religion. At first, this resuscitated Thomism represented a counterattack against the fragmentation of knowledge which was being brought about by the spread of science and the specialization of knowledge. Against the materialistic philosophies of positivism (also called scientism) and economic determinism (capitalism and socialism, or liberalism and Marxism), Maritain argued that there is an existential, spiritual reality which lies beneath surface appearances and events. Against the aestheticism of art for art's sake, Maritain insisted that human art is doomed to sterility and failure if it cuts itself off from the world of nature and humanity.

In later years Maritain pitted this Thomistic Christianity against the equally comprehensive claims of existentialism, which flourished in the peculiarly French setting provided by such intellectuals as Jean-Paul Sartre and Albert Camus. Against their secular atheism, which in the name of freedom denied transcendental meaning, Maritain affirmed that there is a personal God in charge of the universe, that there is a Christian art (not church art) which bears within it the characteristics of Christianity, and that there are human beings who create Christian art as an act of labor which continues the labor of divine creation.

## Analysis

In *Art and Scholasticism,* Jacques Maritain laid out the Thomistic aesthetic system, which he elaborated but from which he did not deviate, setting forth his fundamental notion that art is an expression of God's creation. Creating their works not *ex nihilo* (from nothing) as did God in the beginning, human artists do not copy but instead continue His creation. Drawing from preexisting materials, the human artist must base himself in nature to discern and draw forth the spiritual reality which is immanent there. Since this spiritual reality is also transcendent, that is in and from God, the human artist who probes for and re-creates this spiritual reality in material form is performing not only an aesthetic act but a moral one as well. The quest for beauty is also the quest for truth and is itself a manifestation of goodness.

Maritain perceived an overarching unity with everything in its place as in a hierarchy. Contrary to the rationalists, both philosophical and scientific, who would separate the aesthetic impulse from reason, Maritain insisted that beauty was true. Although he acknowledged that unconceptualizable knowledge was rooted in the emotions and received in the preconscious life of the intellect, he argued that the artist's creations were intentional and intuitive and therefore a manifestation of rationality. There was primordial chaos and there was primitive emotional expression, but there was also coherence and order in the same hierarchy of spiritual expression.

Similarly, contrary to the moralists, both religious and secular, who would separate the aesthetic impulse from morality, Maritain insisted that beauty was good. Although acknowledging that art could promote illusion and seduce the unwary, he maintained that the artist's creations were a continuation of divine creativity and a manifestation of morality. Choosing Aristotle's notion of intuition penetrating to the Platonic form as opposed to Plato's rejection of art as an image of an image, Maritain placed the aesthetic act with the rational act as supremely moral.

In believing that the unity and coherence of art was rational and that the unity and purity of art was moral, as he propounded throughout his life, Maritain insisted that art was ultimately religious. By "religious," he meant Roman Catholic Christian as defined by the theology of Aquinas. By "art," he did not mean, however, what he called "church art" (that is the depiction of crucifixes, cathedrals, madonnas, martyrologies, and biblical stories); rather, he meant art which was infused with "the character of Christianity."

Maritain ascribed three defining attributes to "Christian art," which could be called popular, theological, and religious. By "popular," Maritain meant that the art must be "legible" and "finished." Because art is intended to instruct the people, it must be clear, that is, legible to those it is to serve, and completely in the mode peculiar to its style, that is, finished. An example of illegible art would be a house without a staircase; an example of unfinished art, a church without an altar. By "theological," Maritain meant that the art must be dependent upon the theological wisdom of the Christian religion. This dependence is not a matter of genre or technique but of what he called "intellectual signification." He illustrated his argument with a 1670 decree from the Holy Office forbidding artists from making crucifixes so grotesque that they provoked disgust rather than pious attention. By "religious," Maritain meant that art must tap religious emotion, but he emphasized that in this realm there are no inflexible rules to be followed. Instead, he stated that the artist must participate in the life of the Church as both a worshipper and a creator: the inner spirit and the outer substance must be in harmony.

In summary, Maritain denied that the artist's desire to please the senses is inherently seductive. He acknowledged the risk, noting that humanity is fallen and corrupted; nevertheless, he contended that the artist's urge to create is a continuation of the divine. As long as it is rooted in the emotions of the people, this art will please the higher senses and encourage the human spirit to reach toward God. Similarly, despite the temptations of rationalism, Maritain defended the artist's desire to please the mind: as long as it is guided by Christian faith, which unites the emotions of the people and the coherence of the divine order, art will illuminate God's creation.

As Maritain grew older, he became more lyrical in his writing. His attempt to encompass all reality in art was expressed in *Creative Intuition in Art and Poetry*:

This transient motion of a beloved hand – it exists an instant, and will disappear forever, and only in the memory of angels will it be preserved, above time. Poetic intuition catches it in passing, in a faint attempt to immortalize it in time. But poetic intuition does not stop at this given existent; it goes beyond, and infinitely beyond. Precisely because it has no conceptualized object, it tends and extends to the infinite, it tends toward all the reality, the infinite reality which is engaged in any singular existing thing.

From a "transient motion of a beloved hand" to "infinite reality," Maritain encompasses the motion, the observation, the poetic intuition, and the divine order.

## Principal criticism

*La Philosophie bergsonienne*, 1914 (*Bergsonian Philosophy and Thomism*, 1955)
*Art et scolastique*, 1920 (*The Philosophy of Art*, 1923; better known as *Art and Scholasticism*, 1962)
*Distinguer pour unir: Ou, Les Degrés du savoir*, 1932 (*The Degrees of Knowledge*, 1937)
*Frontières de la poésie et autres essais*, 1935 (*The Frontiers of Poetry*, 1962)
*La Philosophie de la nature: Essai critique sur ses frontières et son objet*, 1935 (*Philosophy of Nature*, 1951)
*Situation de la poésie*, 1938 (*The Situation of Poetry*, 1955)
*Creative Intuition in Art and Poetry*, 1953
*The Responsibility of the Artist*, 1960

## Other major works and literary forms

In addition to the books listed above, Jacques Maritain published works on philosophy, theology, and politics. In attempting to resurrect and vindicate Thomism, the medieval Catholic philosophy of Saint Thomas Aquinas which had been declared "the official philosophy" of the Roman Catholic church by Pope Leo XIII in 1879, Maritain wrote several hundred articles, essays, and book reviews on metaphysics, epistemology, ethics, morals, and social and political philosophy. Lectures from his extensive teaching and special appearances at academic conferences were also published in book form.

NONFICTION
*Humanisme intégral*, 1936 (*True Humanism*, 1938)
*Education at the Crossroads*, 1943
*La Personne et le bien commun*, 1947 (*The Person and the Common Good*, 1947)
*Man and the State*, 1951
*The Range of Reason*, 1952
*Approches de Dieu*, 1953 (*Approaches to God*, 1954)
*On the Philosophy of History*, 1957
*Reflections on America*, 1958

## Further reading

Doering, Bernard E. *Jacques Maritain and the French Intellectuals*, 1983.
Dunaway, John M., ed. *Exiles and Fugitives: The Letters of Jacques and Raissa Maritain, Allen Tate, and Caroline Gordon*, 1992.
Evans, Joseph W. *The Social and Political Philosophy of Jacques Maritain*, 1955.
——. *Jacques Maritain: The Man and the Achievement*, 1965.
Gallagher, Donald, and Idella Gallagher. *The Achievement of Jacques and Raïssa Maritain: A Bibliography, 1906–1961*, 1962.
Phelan, Gerald B. *Jacques Maritain*, 1937.
Redpath, Peter A., ed. *From Twilight to Dawn: The Cultural Vision of Jacques Maritain*, 1990.
Rover, Thomas D. *The Poetics of Maritain: A Titanistic Critique*, 1965.
Tamosaitis, Anicetus. *Church and State in Maritain's Thought*, 1959.

DAVID R. STEVENSON

*See also* French Literary Theory: Twentieth Century

# Marxist Theory and Criticism

Marxism is a social, economic, and political theory derived from the writings of Karl Marx and various followers, notably Friedrich Engels and Vladimir Ilyich Lenin. It claims both to be a scientific theory and to be committed to revolutionary social change. Marxist literary criticism assumes that literature must be understood in terms of that theory and, by implication at least, one of the main purposes of Marxist criticism is to further social change. The fundamental Marxist assumption is that the economic *base* of society determines the nature and structure of the ideology, institutions, and social practices that form the *superstructure* of that society, exemplified in the educational system, law, religion, and politics. Literature is seen as part of that superstructure. The most influential form of early Marxist criticism assumed that there was a direct relation between the socioeconomic infrastructure of society and such practices as literature: literature was seen as a product of ideology, the role of ideology in Marxist terms being to provide legitimation for the power of the ruling class. This type of criticism is sometimes called reflective or "vulgar" Marxism since it sees literary texts as directly reflecting socioeconomic forces.

One of its practitioners was the British Marxist Christopher Caudwell. In a discussion of nineteenth-century English poets in his book *Illusion and Reality* (1937), entitled "English Poets: The Decline of Capitalism," he writes that "Arnold, Swinburne, Tennyson and Browning, each in his own way, illustrate the movement of the bourgeois illusion in this 'tragic' stage of history." He goes on to say of Tennyson's poem *In Memoriam*: "Like Darwin, and even more Darwin's followers, he projects the conditions of capitalist production into Nature (individual struggle for existence) and then reflects this struggle, intensified by its instinctive and therefore unalterable blindness, back into society, so that God – symbol of the internal forces of society – seems captive to Nature – symbol of the external environment of society."

Such a reflective approach was not, however, the only form of Marxist criticism in the earlier half of the twentieth century. In the Soviet Union there were a number of critics who attempted to combine Marxist theory with Russian Formalist criticism. These critics were associated with Mikhail Bakhtin, who, though not apparently a committed Marxist himself, cooperated with these critics to produce some important studies, notably *The Formal Method in Literary Scholarship* (1928) with P. N. Medvedev and *Marxism and the Philosophy of Language* (1929) with Valentin Voloshinov. Though these studies are critical of a purely formalist approach to literature (one which focuses on style, technique, and literary devices rather than meaning or content), they believe that it is possible to combine Marxism and formalism dialectically in what Bakhtin and Medvedev call a "sociological poetics." With the emergence of the Stalinist era in the Soviet Union, this literary critical approach was suppressed.

Another critic of the first half of the century who had strong connections with Marxism but who rejected the reflective approach was the German critic and treatise writer Walter Benjamin. He was sympathetic to modernism (in contrast to most Marxists, who identified it with a decadent bourgeois ideology), and in one of his most influential essays, "The Artist as Producer," he argues that the most revolutionary art cannot merely replicate traditional forms if it is going to further social change. This will merely lead to art being consumed by a bourgeois audience, even if such art is apparently committed to Marxist ideas. Benjamin was a major advocate of the work of the German dramatist Bertolt Brecht, a committed Marxist, but one who rejected the dominant Marxist aesthetic of socialist realism, an approach to art that required it to conform to Marxist doctrine and promote socialist aims.

During the Stalinist era, the major Marxist critic was the Hungarian Georg Lukács, a supporter of socialist realism and a fierce opponent of modernism in the arts. Lukács was a Marxist in the Hegelian tradition, but though he was committed to the view that literature reflected the social reality that produced it, he did not accept that the relationship between social reality and the literary text was a simple deterministic one. For Lukács there was a "form" to history that literature should incorporate in its structures. He objected to modernism on the grounds that modernist writers rejected such a conception of form in favor of mere subjectivism or a concentration on aspects of life that were of little significance. The literary genre he favored most was the nineteenth-century realist novel, and he argued that the greatest of such novels did not merely reflect the dominant bourgeois ideology but embodied in their form an implicit critique of that ideology that allowed them to expose its contradictions. He called the type of realism in such works "critical realism." For Lukács, what was important in the novel was "typicality." In his book *The Meaning of Contemporary Realism* (1958) he wrote: "The *typical* is not to be confused with the *average* . . . nor with the *eccentric* . . . . A character is typical, in this technical sense, when his innermost being is determined by objective forces at work in society . . . . The typical hero reacts with his entire personality to the life of his age." Lukács defines socialist realism as a politically self-conscious form of critical realism since it is "based on a concrete socialist perspective" and uses such a perspective "to describe the forces working towards socialism *from the inside*." However, he accepts that during the Stalinist period, socialist realism was compromised, and instead "thought up a poetical substitute for naturalism, 'revolutionary romanticism,' instead of attempting an ideologically correct aesthetic solution."

Marxist criticism in the later half of the twentieth century saw a shift away from the reflective model. The major intellectual influence on this change was the French Marxist philosopher Louis Althusser, in works such as *Lenin and Philosophy and Other Essays* (1971), a collection of essays written between 1964 and 1969. He was opposed to Hegelian or humanistic readings of Marx, which tended to concentrate on his earlier writings, and focused instead on the later writings in which Marx attempted to establish a system that was scientifically based. Althusser also drew on structuralist ideas and this alignment between Marxism and structuralism made Marxist criticism more appealing to critics who were not committed Marxists but were in broad sympathy with it or who accepted its analysis in part. Two aspects of Althusser's revision of Marxism were especially influential because they allowed Marxist criticism to break away from the reflective model – the first was the concept of social formation, the second that of ideological state apparatuses. The notion of "totality" – the entirety of social reality, in which all parts of the whole were seen as expressing its essence – had dominated in Hegel-influenced Marxist thinking. Althusser substituted for "totality" the concept of "social formation": a structure of various levels without a center rather than a totality in which the economic level determined the structure of all the other levels. The various levels, he argued, possessed "relative autonomy" and were "overdetermined," that is, determined

by a complex network of forces, with the economic base being the ultimate determinant, but at very far remove. Althusser defined the various elements of the social formation, such as legal, religious, educational, and artistic institutions, as "ideological state apparatuses," and redefined ideology as "a representation of the imaginary relationship of individuals to their real conditions of existence" rather than as "false consciousness," which had been how it had been understood by earlier Marxists. Each particular state apparatus creates its own form of ideological discourse and, through a process Althusser defines as "interpellation," calls upon individuals to take up a "subject position," one which serves the interests of the dominant class.

Althusser's theory created the intellectual conditions for forms of Marxist criticism that drew on ideas from a variety of sources, such as structuralism, psychoanalysis, and discourse theory. The first major literary study in which Marxism and structuralist thinking were aligned was Pierre Macherey's *A Theory of Literary Production*, first published in French in 1966 and in English in 1978. Macherey, a French philosopher who had collaborated with Althusser, sees meaning in literary texts as "decentered" and not reflective. For Macherey, the ideology governing a work cannot be separated from the question of form since the literary text is "rooted in historical reality" not in a direct way "but only through a complex series of mediations." Thus history is not directly accessible in literature and so can be apprehended only indirectly. In literature, history is discovered by focusing on divisions which constitute the work's "unconscious": "the unconscious which is history, the play of history beyond its edges, encroaching on those edges." Macherey argues that literary representation is under the control of ideology and the role of criticism is to reveal history not as a presence in the text but as an absence: that which ideology excludes but which can be discerned in the fissures or gaps in the text which expose the incoherence of its ideology. The critic therefore does not look for order, coherence, and harmony, for what fits together, but rather for what does not fit; the text enables "ideology to speak of its *own absences*" and thus "to escape from the false consciousness of self, of history, and of time."

Macherey compares the critic's interest in the relationship between text and history with Freudian focus on the relationship between the conscious and the unconscious, for the unconscious is never directly accessible but can only be understood through interpreting such phenomena as dreams and slips of the tongue. The apparent order of a literary work is only "an imagined order" based on "the fictive resolution of ideological conflicts," and the critic's role is to expose the incoherences, gaps, and absences that are part of that resolution since ideology is always incoherent and contradictory. Though Macherey uses the word "defect" to describe such gaps or absences in the text, no adverse criticism of the literary work is implied since this is where the "truth" of the work is to be found.

Althusser and Macherey changed the direction of Marxist criticism, and all later Marxist critics have had to confront their work. The leading British Marxist critic Terry Eagleton has clearly felt their effect in his major theoretical study *Criticism and Ideology* (1976). Eagleton goes part of the way with Macherey in agreeing that ideology being put to work within a text exposes the gaps and silences in that ideology which can then be made to speak. However, he is unhappy with Macherey's concept of "absence," which he sees as "an essentially negative conception of the text's relation to history." In other words, he is reluctant to discard the reflection model as completely as Althusser and Macherey do. He believes it is still possible to preserve a direct relation between text and history by means of a complex series of mediations that govern the relation between text and history. He recognizes that history can be present in the text only as ideology, so that reality in the text is therefore "pseudo-reality," but he believes there can be a "science of ideological formations" and that one can study "the laws of the production of ideological discourses as literature." Thus, in looking at a writer such as George Eliot, he sees her work as an attempt "to resolve a structural conflict between two forms of mid-Victorian ideology" – a belief in individualism and the need for social laws to prevent individualism taking irresponsible forms – so that "the historical contradictions at the heart of Eliot's fiction [are recast] into ideologically resolvable terms." Eagleton's critical perspective has continued to evolve and his later criticism combines Marxism with poststructuralism, as can be seen in his book *William Shakespeare* (1986) in which he writes of *Antony and Cleopatra*: "What deconstructs political order in the play is desire, and the figure for this is Cleopatra .... She is, as it were, pure heterogeneity, an 'infinite variety' which eludes any stable position."

Possibly the most ambitious Marxist critical study of the past thirty years or so is Fredric Jameson's *The Political Unconscious* (1981). Jameson has strong sympathies with the Hegelian Marxist tradition as exemplified in the work of Lukács but he attempts an ambitious reconciliation of Lukács with Althusserian Marxism in a totalizing criticism that can also embrace non-Marxist critical perspectives, such as formalism, archetypal criticism, structuralism, and poststructuralism. He sees Marxism as a "master code" which underlies all other forms of criticism. Even the most detailed formalist or textual analysis, he argues, is governed by a philosophy of history even if critics are unaware of it. Like Eagleton, Jameson does not want to give up the idea that all levels of the superstructure are essentially similar in structure to the economic base and directly determined by it. He argues that such a concept still functions in Althusser's theory. Working with an implicitly psychoanalytical model, Jameson sees history as an "absent cause" since it does not exist separately from its products, and as history cannot be separated from politics it functions as a "political unconscious." Jameson, like Althusser and Macherey, does not regard ideologies as forms of false consciousness, but as "strategies of containment" which repress knowledge of the contradictions which are the product of history, history for him being driven by the "collective struggle to wrest a realm of Freedom from a realm of Necessity." Works of art are the most complex products of ideologies as strategies of containment and the Marxist critic's role is to restore "to the surface of the text the repressed and buried reality of this fundamental history." Works of art for Jameson have developed complex strategies to deny the exploitation and oppression which is the reality of history since Jameson accepts Walter Benjamin's dictum that "[t]here has never been a document of culture which was not at one and the same time a document of barbarism." The Marxist critic looks for clues and symptoms which reveal the way literary texts evade the realities of history or refuse to acknowledge contradictions. Since history is an absent cause and so not directly accessible except in textual form, "our approach to it and to the Real itself necessarily passes through its prior textualization, its narrativization in the political unconscious."

What has been striking about modern developments in Marxist criticism is how recent Marxist critics have not been willing to accept Marxism as a fixed system but have moved it forward through dialectical confrontations with other forms of thought, such as psychoanalysis, structuralism, and poststructuralism, with the result that even at a time when Marxist politics is in crisis as a result of the break-up of the Soviet Union, Marxist criticism still remains a force in modern critical theory and practice.

## Further reading

Baxandall, Lee, and Stefan Morawski, eds. *Marx and Engels on Literature and Art*, 1973.
Benjamin, Walter. *Illuminations*, 1970.
——. *Understanding Brecht*, 1973.
Bennett, Tony. *Formalism and Marxism*, 1979.
Caudwell, Christopher. *Studies in a Dying Culture*, 1938.
Craig, David, ed. *Marxists on Literature*, 1975.
Demetz, Peter. *Marx, Engels and the Poets: Origins of Marxist Criticism*, 1967.
Eagleton, Terry. *Myths of Power: A Marxist Study of the Brontës*, 1975.
——. *Marxism and Literary Criticism*, 1976.
Frow, John. *Marxism and Literary Criticism*, 1986.
Jameson, Frederic. *Marxism and Form: Twentieth-Century Dialectical Theories of Literature*, 1971.
Lukács, Georg. *The Historical Novel*, 1937.
Mulhern, Francis, ed. *Contemporary Marxist Literary Criticism*, 1992.
Trotsky, Leon. *Literature and Revolution*, 1923.
Williams, Raymond. *Marxism and Literature*, 1977.
——. *Problems in Materialism and Culture*, 1980.

K. M. Newton

*See also* Althusser; Benjamin; Eagleton; Frankfurt School; Gramsci; Ideology; Jameson; Lukács; Williams

# F. O. Matthiessen

American critic and editor

**Born:** Pasadena, California; February 19, 1902
**Died:** Boston, Massachusetts; April 1, 1950

## Biography

Francis Otto Matthiessen, the youngest of four children, was born in California in 1902. His parents were separated when he was five years old and were formally divorced when he was thirteen. Matthiessen's intellectual life began when he entered Yale University in 1919. His teachers and friends there introduced him to the life of the mind, and he developed a love for that university which lasted all of his life. At Yale he also became convinced of the necessity for social and political action, a concern which would later surface in his literary criticism.

After an outstanding career at Yale, from which he graduated in 1923, Matthiessen won a Rhodes scholarship to Oxford University and received a bachelor of letters degree in 1925. While traveling by ship to England in 1924 he met the painter Russell Cheney, a man twenty years his senior, and the two men immediately fell in love. They developed a remarkably stable relationship that lasted until Cheney's death in 1945. The two men bought a house in Kittery, Maine, where they spent summers and as many weekends as possible. Matthiessen's experiences as a homosexual helped him to understand and sympathize with the plight of economic and social outsiders, a sympathy which compelled him to become a socialist at a time when such a political orientation was perilous for an academic. Matthiessen's studies in England were supplemented by travel in Europe, to which he frequently returned; his European experience enabled him to judge American literature not only in terms of its own development but in terms of its place in world civilization as well.

Upon his return to the United States, Matthiessen began graduate study at Harvard University and received a master of arts degree in 1926 and his doctorate in 1927. He returned to Yale to teach for two years, but administrators at Harvard had recognized his brilliance and had made him attractive offers, so he returned to that school in 1929 and spent the rest of his academic life there. Although he was known among the student body for his lectures, he preferred the private method of instruction with a few self-motivated students, and Harvard rewarded this propensity by appointing him head tutor at Eliot House and finally chairman of the Board of Tutors in history and literature. Throughout his tenure as a tutor, he produced criticism of the highest quality, crowned by his masterpiece, *American Renaissance*, in 1941. With others, he helped to develop the American civilization program, one of the first interdisciplinary programs at any American university.

Matthiessen's belief that the contemplative and politically active lives should be united is shown by the leading role he played in the establishment at Harvard of a chapter of the American Federation of Teachers, a labor union affiliated with the American Federation of Labor, and by his active participation in the affairs of the Massachusetts Civil Liberties Union. After World War II he took part in an American studies seminar in Salzburg and expressed his deep concern for the reconstruction and progress of Eastern Europe in *From the Heart of Europe*. In 1948 Matthiessen seconded the nomination of Henry Wallace at the Progressive Party convention and subsequently campaigned for him.

Matthiessen continued his scholarly work with major books on Henry James, the James family, and Theodore Dreiser, but the depression which had caused him to seek admission to a hospital in 1938, during the pressure-filled time when he was writing *American Renaissance*, began to haunt him again. In 1950, disillusioned by the failure of socialist democracy in Czechoslovakia, a country he had come to love during his last European visit, disheartened by the increasing trend toward political conservatism in the United States, discouraged by Harvard's turn toward vocational training at the expense of liberal educational values, and most of all, shattered by the loss of Russell Cheney five years earlier, Matthiessen took his own life by leaping from the twelfth-floor window of a Boston hotel.

## Influence

It is impossible to read, study, or teach the classic works of nineteenth-century American literature without encountering the ideas of F. O. Matthiessen. Using in *American Renaissance* a critical approach which he first developed in his book on T. S. Eliot – a close examination of the form of a work not only as a further revelation of content but also as an expression of the society and cultural milieu in which the author worked – Matthiessen demonstrated the continuity of American political and social thought with its art. In the early twentieth century, not only English but also American critics joked that there was no American literature, because there was no American culture. (While Matthiessen was an undergraduate at Yale University, Herman Melville's *Moby Dick* was shelved in the library under cetology.) That such an opinion now seems absurd is a testament to the light that Matthiessen shed on the great works of American literature. That his critical method seems only ordinary common sense is further evidence of his pervasive influence.

## Analysis

Matthiessen's theory of literature was that a work of art could not be analyzed by breaking it into separate categories of form and content, but that the critic understood the content and cultural background of a work of art by closely examining its form. He began his professional training at a time when Romantic and biographical critics such as Van Wyck Brooks (later a frequent target of Matthiessen's critical barbs) and Chauncey Brewster Tinker, whom Matthiessen knew at Yale, dominated the academic scene. Tinker's course on the Romantic poets was exactly that, a survey of the lives of the men behind the poetry of the early nineteenth century, rarely dealing with their poetry. Other dominant critics such as Vernon L. Parrington, Irving Babbitt (Matthiessen's colleague at Harvard), and Paul Elmer More stressed literature as the vessel through which cultural tradition was carried from one generation to another. These critics stressed intellectual history and moral force at the expense of technical analysis and minimized the effect of art and the aims of the artist.

By the 1930s Matthiessen's critical career had begun, and the formalist school of the New Criticism, led by John Crowe Ransom, Cleanth Brooks, and others, had also begun to react strongly against the critical approach of the older critics, but its method of close textual analysis worked best for lyric poetry. To resolve the critical controversy which stressed one element of criticism at the expense of the other, Matthiessen set himself in *American Renaissance* the enormous task of defining the impact of the five great writers of the mid-nineteenth century – Ralph Waldo Emerson, Henry David Thoreau, Nathaniel Hawthorne, Herman Melville, and Walt Whitman – not by extracting the content of their writing from its form or by narrowly examining technique at the expense of cultural significance, but by demonstrating how the ideas of the time and the personal approach of each of these writers revealed content and background through perfectly realized form.

The shortest section of Matthiessen's huge book deals with Emerson, whom Matthiessen recognized as the least of the five as an artist. Matthiessen showed the efficacy of his own critical theory by demonstrating that the form of Emerson's writing slid off into the inexpressible, vague realm of the transcendental just as Emerson simultaneously lost his grasp of his ideas. Although as an artist and a thinker Emerson could not be judged first-rate, as an inspirer of others, he was first among all American writers. In the accounts of the works of the other four writers, Matthiessen frequently refers to Emerson's thought and example for the impact they had on the life and writing of the other authors and the light they shed on their work.

Perhaps Matthiessen's most important achievement in *American Renaissance* is his refutation of the charge that Thoreau was a mere cheerleader or a preacher to the converted. Through his careful analysis of Thoreau's prose, Matthiessen shows that Thoreau found through clear statement and profound metaphor a form for the Emersonian ideas of freedom, independence, and democracy that had more force than the writings of Emerson himself.

Earlier, in *The Achievement of T. S. Eliot*, Matthiessen had performed a similar service for Eliot's reputation, saving him from the charge of obscurity and modern pessimism. Matthiessen showed that Eliot had revived the skepticism of the seventeenth-century Metaphysical poets and applied it to modern verse forms, thus creating a voice which assimilated the past yet spoke to the twentieth century. Matthiessen's task in that volume was made easier because the two men had become friends during Eliot's stay at Harvard in the early 1930s and because Eliot had already defended himself in his own essays, particularly "Tradition and the Individual Talent." Matthiessen's later work on James was facilitated in like manner, since James also believed that content went unheeded without the proper form to express it and gave the critic a lead in his prefaces to his works.

Both Hawthorne and Melville performed an important service by examining the darker side of humanity's nature which Emerson overlooked. Hawthorne understood sin and Melville evil, and Matthiessen noted that Hawthorne's allegorical technique was based not only on his examination of the American Puritanical character but also on his use of his spiritual forebears, John Bunyan and Edmund Spenser. Similarly, Melville's expansiveness had roots not only in his review of the commercial America in which he lived but also in his affinity for the world-view of William Shakespeare and his familiarity with the stern morality of the Old Testament. Of the five writers he examines, however, Matthiessen is least successful in fitting the explosive Melville to his theory that proper artistic expression must be fitted to an apt form.

Finally, Whitman gave expression to the Emersonian American ideal in a new literary form that was truly American, since Whitman was a protestant and a democrat, in the philosophical sense of those terms, in a way that the bookish Emerson, the withdrawn Thoreau, and the stern Hawthorne and Melville could never have been. Again, Matthiessen had some problems fitting Whitman to his theory, as he checked off the list of Whitman's familiar excesses. The poet's marked fondness for foreign terms, for example, cannot be made to fit the democratic standard for content or the American standard for form.

Although Matthiessen never defines the term "renaissance," its meaning in his book on American literature can be inferred from his book on Elizabethan translation, which was based on his doctoral dissertation. He demonstrated that a few English prose translators sought through their vigorous prose not merely to copy the great works of other cultures such as ancient Rome and Renaissance Italy and France, but instead to present those works in a manner which would speak to their contemporaries. Thus they helped to create the Elizabethan Renaissance with an entirely new synthesis that redefined tradition in a specifically English sense. Similarly, the American writers of the mid-nineteenth century translated the political ideas that had given birth to America into an artistic form that created a new American character.

The most telling criticism that can be raised against Matthiessen is that, because of his strong emphasis on tradition and the role of the artist in reshaping that tradition to fit his own ends, he tends to explain the nineteenth century with reference only to what preceded it, not what followed. There is in Matthiessen's writing hardly a reference to Sigmund Freud, for example, or to any other twentieth-century thinker. In his last book, on Theodore Dreiser, Matthiessen sees that novelist more as a presenter and synthesizer of ideas formed in the Gilded Age than as a twentieth-century writer. The two world wars were personally devastating to Matthiessen's political and social ideas, yet they are hardly mentioned in his critical writings. Still, his work is fundamental to an understanding of the giants of American literature.

## Principal criticism
*Sarah Orne Jewett,* 1929
*Translation: An Elizabethan Art,* 1931
*The Achievement of T. S. Eliot: An Essay on the Nature of Poetry,* 1935
*American Renaissance: Art and Expression in the Age of Emerson and Whitman,* 1941
*Henry James: The Major Phase,* 1944
*The James Family: Including Selections from the Writings of Henry James, Senior, William, Henry, and Alice James,* 1947
*Theodore Dreiser,* 1951
*The Responsibilities of the Critic: Essays and Reviews by F. O. Matthiessen,* 1952

## Other major works and literary forms
F. O. Matthiessen edited *Stories of Writers and Artists by Henry James* (1944), *The American Novels and Stories of Henry James* (1947; with Kenneth B. Murdock), and *The Oxford Book of American Verse* (1950). In addition, he wrote more than one hundred articles and reviews, including the chapters "Edgar Allan Poe" and "Poetry" in *The Literary History of the United States* (1948). The most significant of these pieces have been collected in *The Responsibilities of the Critic.* He also wrote two nonfiction works: *Russell Cheney, 1881–1945: A Record of His Work* (1947) and *From the Heart of Europe* (1948), the former an assessment of the life and art of his longtime friend and companion and the latter his reflections on his travels through Eastern Europe in 1947.

NONFICTION
*Russell Cheney, 1881–1945: A Record of His Work,* 1947
*From the Heart of Europe,* 1948

EDITED TEXT
*The American Novels and Stories of Henry James,* 1947 (with Kenneth B. Murdock)

ANTHOLOGIES
*Stories of Writers and Artists by Henry James,* 1944
*Herman Melville: Selected Poems,* 1944
*The Oxford Book of American Verse,* 1950

## Further reading
Bergman, David. "F. O. Matthiessen: The Critic as Homosexual," in *Raritan.* 9 (Spring, 1990), pp. 62–82.
Cain, William E. *F. O. Matthiessen and the Politics of Criticism,* 1988.
Cheyfitz, Eric. "Matthiessen's American Renaissance: Circumscribing the Revolution," in *American Quarterly.* 41 (June, 1989), pp. 341–361.
Gunn, Giles B. *F. O. Matthiessen: The Critical Achievement,* 1975.
Hyde, Louis, ed. *Rat and the Devil: Journal Letters of F. O. Matthiessen and Russell Cheney,* 1978.
Sarton, May. *Faithful Are the Wounds,* 1955.
Stern, Frederick C. *F. O. Matthiessen: Christian Socialist as Critic,* 1981.
Sweezy, Paul M., and Leo Huberman, eds. *F. O. Matthiessen, 1902–1950,* 1959.

JAMES BAIRD

*See also* Babbitt; Brooks, Van W.; American Literary Theory: Twentieth Century

# Giuseppe Mazzini
Italian critic and essayist

**Born:** Genoa, Italy; June 22, 1805
**Died:** Pisa, Italy; March 10, 1872

## Biography
Giuseppe Mazzini was born on June 22, 1805, in Genoa. His father was a doctor and sent his son to the University of Genoa, where Mazzini received a law degree in 1827. In that same year Giuseppe Mazzini joined the Carbonari, a secret society that demanded a unified Italian state which would be governed through a liberal constitution and be free of foreign domination and influence. Mazzini's activities led to his arrest in 1830 and exile in 1831. While in Marseilles, he founded *Giovine Italia* (Young Italy), a society dedicated to a liberated and unified Italian republic; in 1833 Mazzini established the Young Switzerland and Young Europe organizations. He envisioned a Europe consisting of free, national states bonded together through a general support of liberal political principles. In 1837 Mazzini moved to London, where he continued to write political tracts and literary essays. He remained in England until the revolutions of 1848 began, when he returned to Italy and became involved in the short-lived Roman Republic, only to return to England as a political failure.

Mazzini resumed his writings, which were designed to attract the support of the liberals and liberal regimes throughout Western Europe to the cause of a unified Italy; he founded the Friends of Italy in 1851. Mazzini was not seriously involved in any of the subsequent developments which affected the unification of Italy – the Franco-Piedmontese War against Austria (1859), the Prussian-Austrian War (1866), nor the Franco-Prussian War

(1870–1871). Identified with the failure of 1848, Mazzini and other early advocates of Italian nationalism were discredited; their positions of leadership were assumed by such individuals as the Piedmontese prime minister, Count Camillo Benso di Cavour, and his king, Victor Emmanuel II. The emergence of the Italian state, for which Mazzini had labored for decades, developed as a result of traditional practices and concepts rather than as a consequence of the ideology espoused by Mazzini.

While in England, Mazzini produced critical essays on Dante, Johann Wolfgang von Goethe, Lord Byron, Thomas Carlyle, and others, as well as essays on his thoughts on the philosophy of music and art. He became a friend of Algernon Charles Swinburne and George Meredith. Mazzini spent most of his last years in Lugano, Italy. He died of pleurisy in Pisa on March 10, 1872.

## Influence

Mazzini is known primarily as the advocate of national self-determination throughout Europe and the view that the modern individual would realize happiness only through his or her role as a citizen of a nation-state. Mazzini's role as a significant literary theoretician and critic was recognized by his contemporaries and has been studied more fully during the late twentieth century. In his studies of Dante, Carlyle, Goethe, Byron, and others, Mazzini developed analyses which included an evaluation of the writer's approach to individuality, national identity, God, and the dichotomy between objective and subjective argumentation. Mazzini's voluminous literary essays and reviews constitute a consistent apology for a literature in which humankind reaches a sense of fulfillment and an identification with the good through contributing to the progress of the nation-state. Mazzini's literary criticism complemented his political tracts and served to advance the cause of the Italian national movement known as the Risorgimento.

## Analysis

Mazzini was educated and lived through his formative period during the Romantic era. The impact of the philosophy of the era and the accompanying literary movement on Mazzini can be detected in his writings throughout his life. While it would be rash to label Mazzini an ideologue, one must observe that throughout his life his writings – political, philosophical, and literary – exhibited a consistency in ideology and intent which is anomalous. Mazzini was an intellectual who possessed few distinct ideas but who excelled at applying those ideas through hundreds of writings during a professional career which lasted for almost fifty years. (His collected works, *Scritti editi ed inediti di Giuseppe Mazzini*, published between 1906 and 1943, fill one hundred and six volumes.) He was an Italian nationalist and liberal republican who maintained that individualism, materialism, and secularism had diverted humankind from the good which would be attained only

through leading a life of action predicated upon a reverence for and commitment to traditional values – God, family, and country.

In his discussion of Italian literature in the essay "Of an European Literature," Mazzini advanced the basic tenets of his literary theory when he wrote:

> The character of every literature is determined by the institutions of the country, and the existing diversity is but the natural result of those civil and political conditions which excite or depress, promote or restrain intelligence.

Writing during the turbulent decades of the early and mid-nineteenth century, Mazzini, the advocate of an Italian state and republic, argued that Italy no longer possessed a national literature. He urged his fellow Italians to study other national literatures so that they would become acquainted with the various manifestations of the relationships of the individual as a citizen of a nation-state; this study of foreign literatures should not result in Italian writers providing literary imitations in lieu of a seminal Italian literature. To Mazzini, the citizens of the new Italy would engage in social and political action; they would be individuals who live and act in harmony, not subservience, in their relationship to God, the family, and the state. Among such citizens, the genuine European writer would be a poet-philosopher.

Writing in his "Preface to Literary Works," more than thirty years later, Mazzini lamented the failure of Italians to develop a national literature. This failure was brought about by the propensity of Italian writers to surrender their art and identity as Italians in return for personal comfort and position. Through a sometimes exquisite sense of accommodation, Italian writers advanced local or regional interests at the expense of the nation. Other factors which contributed to this failure to develop a unique national literature were a lack of respect for Italian history and the great figures of Italy's past, and an insidious envy of contemporary writers who attempted to break out of the mold of mediocrity. Mazzini suggested that the underlying cause for this situation was the separation of literature from the Italian tradition, and the subordination of the natural values inherent in Italian life to the artificial values imposed by foreign literary movements. Mazzini also argued that materialism and the accompanying cult of individualism had played a part in the decline of Italian literature. Materialism and individualism corrupted the Italian view of women, the concept of love, and an identity with a higher national purpose and future. Mazzini informed Italian writers that it was their duty to create a national literature which would repudiate materialism and individualism and reestablish traditional values based on faith and universal principles.

Mazzini's view of literature as the instrument and expression of nationalism was developed in other writings.

In 1844 Mazzini published "On the Minor Works of Dante"; this study was the result of his readings of Dante's works rather than an examination of the existing literature on Dante. In this passionate essay, Dante is portrayed as the preeminent writer of all time and the foremost expression of the high standards of a once-proud Italian literature. Dante's writings reflect his sufferings and his hopes for himself and for Italy. To comprehend Dante, Mazzini contended, one must study his minor works before venturing into *The Divine Comedy*. In these works, the simplicity of the true is revealed through an examination of Dante's concept of love, which encompasses opposing universals – the natural and supernatural, the objective and the subjective – and provides a purified unity which serves as the optimum world-view. Mazzini asserted that the aim of Dante's concept of love was synonymous with the "National Aim" which was the unification of Italy. This aim would be realized through the development of national unity which is part of God's design for Italians. A new imperium would be established which would maintain the peace. Mazzini considered Dante to be the prophet of the Italian nation.

In his study of Byron and Goethe, Mazzini concluded that they were leaders of two different schools of individuality. Byron, with his egocentric emphasis on every aspect of living, advanced a subjective approach to individuality; solitary man is a failure for not having lived life fully among his contemporaries and for not confronting the moral dilemmas of life, for not distinguishing good from evil, and for not acting decisively when action is required. Mazzini's Goethe valued the objective approach to individuality; while Byron was caught up in the turmoil and chaos of the period, Goethe exhibited a rather indifferent, almost detached and sterile, attitude. Goethe compartmentalized the world and, through his developing skepticism, emphasized the external aspects of life. Byron, in contrast, emphasized inner experience. Both writers, Mazzini believed, failed to portray the whole person and human needs. Both advanced the cause of equality, but both lacked the power and the imagination to break from their self-imposed literary and philosophical limitations. Mazzini concluded that Goethe and Byron, to many the literary titans of the age, exemplified the manifest problems associated with an emphasis on individuality.

In "On the Genius and Tendency of the Writing of Thomas Carlyle," Mazzini presented a devastating attack on the English historian and man of letters. He argued that Carlyle's thought was flawed by his failure to recognize collective intelligence as the dynamic force of history. Carlyle confined himself to the individual and emphasized the achievements of great men; Mazzini countered by stating that the collective whole, Humanity, is the expression of the conscious greatness of a people. Carlyle was not able to understand or appreciate the nature of government and a person's relationship to it. Mazzini noted that

Carlyle's failure to understand the meaning of government and political reform movements severely restricted the value of his work. He concurred with Carlyle's primacy of the spiritual and the invisible over the natural and the visible. Mazzini differed, however, with the author of *The French Revolution* (1837) when he wrote:

> We must come to the conviction that there exist no rights but those which result from the fulfilment of duty; that our concernment here below is not to be happy, but to become better; that there is no other object in human life than to discover, by collective effort, and to execute, every one for himself, the law of God, without regarding individual results.

These sentiments reflect aspects of the dominant philosophic movement of the period, German Romantic Idealism, which emphasized the significance of the group at the expense of the individual. Immanuel Kant, Johann Gottlieb Fichte, and G. W. F. Hegel were the primary advocates of this school of philosophy. Mazzini concluded that Carlyle was dominated by a sense of fatalism, of hopelessness, because he restricted his vision to God and the individual. He argued that the progress of the good, that is, the nation, in the light of spiritual values, is the only useful end. Carlyle's emphasis on the individual eliminated the concept or the need of the nation; Mazzini found such a position unacceptable. Where Carlyle advanced the role of the hero in history, Mazzini maintained that history was motivated by religious values and conducted through the political and social actions of societies. Through stressing the individual and his relationship to God, Carlyle represented a more medieval and antiprogressive intellectual stance than the philosophy of hope and progress advanced by Mazzini.

On several occasions during his long literary career, Mazzini discussed the genre of poetry. In "On the Historical Drama," he stated that poetry reflects the creativity of a national culture and literature; it refreshes and renews the nation in its commitment to spiritual values. Through poetry, the writer can reach the heart of the nation and, once contact is made, the people can be informed of ultimate considerations. Mazzini warned that poetry can be rendered sterile by the failure of the poet to stress the issues of humanity and the future. Poets are not to be preoccupied with the past except insofar as such study would result in the further development of the nation. Mazzini was more optimistic about poetry in his article "Thoughts Addressed to the Poets of the Nineteenth Century." In this work Mazzini emphasized the transcendent nature of poetry. Poetry is enthusiastic and enduring, and the people of Europe await the arrival of a new generation of creative and progressive poets. In "Of an European Literature," Mazzini advanced the notion that the great poet was the servant of humanity, a writer who experienced and wrote of the joys and sufferings of his fellow countrymen and who contributed to the development of the concept of collective humanity. In a letter to Mrs. Emilie Hawkes (1855), Mazzini denounced the poet Giacomo Leopardi, who was considered to be the most respected Italian poet of the early nineteenth century. Leopardi, after an early success as a poet, became absorbed in the study of literary criticism, and developed into a classicist and a skeptic. Leopardi continued to write poetry, and it was this despondent and formal poetry which Mazzini denounced as not constituting a contribution to art or to the nation.

In many ways Mazzini's literary theory and criticism was emblematic of his period. There was a general recognition that the attempt to reestablish the old order at the Congress of Vienna would be a short-lived victory for the forces of reaction and that new dynamic forces were at work. Mazzini's emphasis on collective humanity developed through his literary criticism along with his continuing commitment to the collaboration of literature and nationalism. Literature was more than just a means to an end – the nation state; once the state was realized, literature would sustain it through spiritual renewal. During his lifetime Mazzini, who spent many decades in exile, commanded the attention of an international audience which extended well beyond the limits of the Italian peninsula. His influence on the development of national literatures is obvious. While he argued that Dante was the prophet of the Italian nation, Giuseppe Mazzini emerged as the herald of a unified Italy and modern Italian literature.

## Principal criticism

"Dell'amor patrio di Dante," 1826 ("Dante's Love of Country," 1870)
"D'una letteratura europea," 1829 ("Of an European Literature," 1894)
"Della fatalita considerata come elemento drammatico," 1830 ("On Fatality Considered as an Element of the Dramatic Art," 1865)
"Del dramma storio," 1830 ("On the Historical Drama," 1865)
"Ai Poeti Del Secolo XIX," 1830 ("Thoughts Addressed to the Poets of the Nineteenth Century," 1894)
"Della Byron e Goethe," 1839 ("Byron and Goethe," 1870)
"Genio e tendenze di Tommasco Carlyle," 1843 ("On the Genius and Tendency of the Writings of Thomas Carlyle," 1867)
"Opere minori di Dante," 1844 ("On the Minor Works of Dante," 1867)
"On Leopardi," 1855
"Prefazione," 1862 ("Preface to Literary Works," 1865)

## Other major works and literary forms

In addition to the works cited above, Giuseppe Mazzini wrote hundreds of significant essays and reviews which were received well and studied throughout Western and Central Europe during the mid-nineteenth century and which influenced the development of liberalism and nationalism throughout Europe.

While most of Mazzini's essays were directly associated with political themes, many addressed literary and artistic themes. Throughout Mazzini's essays, the theme of human progress through national identity and commitment prevails. Mazzini denounced the cults of materialism and individualism which emerged during the nineteenth century; he opposed Marxism as a disruptive and nonprogressive historical force which was devoid of value. Among Mazzini's more noteworthy essays are "Filosofia della musica" (1833; "The Philosophy of Music," 1867), "Faith and the Future" (1835), "Storia della Rivoluzione Francese di T. Carlyle" (1840; "On Carlyle's History of the French Revolution," 1843), "I doveri dell'uomo" (1844; "The Duties of Man," 1862), "Pensieri sulla Democrazia in Europa" (1847; "Thoughts upon Democracy in Europe," 1875), "La Santa Alleanza dei populi" (1849; "The Holy Alliance of the Peoples," 1875), "Condiziono e avvenire dell'Europa" (1852; "Europe: Its Condition and Prospects," 1870), and "Roma del Popolo" (1871; "To the Italians," 1894). Mazzini also founded and edited three journals, *Giovine Italia* (Young Italy), *Le Jeune Suisse* (Young Switzerland), and *Pensiero ed azione* (Thought and Action), and he established a newspaper, *Apostolato popolare* (Apostleship of the People).

NONFICTION
*Life and Writings of Joseph Mazzini*, 1864–1870 (6 volumes)
*Essays by Joseph Mazzini*, 1894
*Scritti editi ed inediti di Giuseppe Mazzini*, 1906–1943 (106 volumes)
*Mazzini's Letters to an English Family*, 1920–1922 (3 volumes)
*Giuseppe Mazzini, Selected Writings*, 1945

## Further reading

Hales, E. E. Y. *Mazzini and the Secret Societies: The Making of a Myth*, 1956.
Roberts, William. *Prophet in Exile: Joseph Mazzini in England*, 1989.
Rudman, Harry William. *Italian Nationalism and English Letters: Figures of the Risorgimento and Victorian Men of Letters*, 1966.
Sarti, Roland. *Mazzini: A Life for the Religion of Politics*, 1997.
Smith, Denis Mack. *Mazzini*, 1996.

WILLIAM T. WALKER

*See also* Croce; De Sanctis

# Jerome J. McGann

American critic, editor, and theorist

**Born:** New York, New York; July 22, 1937

## Biography

Jerome John McGann obtained his bachelor's degree at LeMoyne College in 1959, followed by an M.A. from Syracuse University in 1962. He completed his doctorate at Yale University in 1966 as a Fulbright Fellow. From 1966 to 1969 he held the post of assistant professor at the University of Chicago, becoming an associate professor in 1969 and a full professor in 1972. In 1975 he moved to the Johns Hopkins University, and in 1980 he became the Dreyfuss Professor of Humanities at the California Institute of Technology. While at CalTech, McGann also worked as adjunct professor of English at the University of Southern California. In 1986 he was appointed Commonwealth Professor at the University of Virginia, and became the John Stewart Bryan Professor in 1993. He has received numerous awards and honors throughout his career, including two Guggenheim fellowships and the Melville Cane Award from the American Poetry Society in 1973 for his study of Algernon Charles Swinburne, which was named "The Year's Best Critical Book about Poetry." He has been named to the American Academy of Arts and Sciences, and in 1996 he received an Honorary Doctorate of Humane Letters from the University of Chicago. McGann has an international reputation as a prolific essayist and lecturer, and has served on numerous editorial boards. In 1960 he married Anne Lanni, and they have three children.

## Influence

McGann's central achievement is to have brought the ideological concerns of poststructuralism into the realm of critical textual editing. His extensive work on the theory of critical editing was instigated by his own experience editing Lord Byron's poetry. His most influential critical writing has been a development of the arguments first outlined in *A Critique of Modern Textual Criticism* (1983), and it is this single study which has had the greatest impact upon recent critical thought and methodology. Although his own scholarship has tended to focus on the Romantic and modernist periods, and on poetry as a literary form, McGann's endeavor is demonstrate that editorial practice and literary criticism are inseparable. His criticism has consistently developed a "materialist hermeneutics": a critical approach to the interpretation of a literary work which acknowledges the work as a physical location that includes a linguistic text, but is not merely a linguistic text. McGann's method incorporates into textual criticism an awareness of all the material signifiers of a historical literary work – its typeface, its layout, and all practical editorial interventions, as well as the design of the volume as an object in itself. McGann refers to these features of the text as the "bibliographical codes" that have commonly been overlooked by critical editors in favor of the linguistic text alone. This highly socialized and historicized approach has ramifications for critical analysis and the editing of literary works from all periods. McGann regards the literary text as a social product which is always tending toward a collaborative state; his refusal to accept that the author's intentions should be necessarily the dominant factor when determining the copy-text for a critical edition is a scholarly enactment of the poststructuralist decentering of the author. It is this aspect of McGann's work that has impinged upon recent critical methods, and has challenged empirical assumptions of the critical edition as an ahistorical foundation for literary studies.

## Analysis

McGann's early critical volumes on Byron and Swinburne – *Fiery Dust: Byron's Poetic Development* (1969), *Swinburne: An Experiment in Criticism* (1972), and *Don Juan in Context* (1976) – demonstrate Romantic scholarship which is ideologically conscious and textually astute. It was not until after he had commenced the editing of Byron's complete poetical works in 1971 that McGann first delved into the theory of critical editing as set out by critics such as W. W. Greg and Fredson Bowers. He began to question the reasoning behind their selection of the author's manuscript as the copy-text for a critical edition of a literary work, and challenged the more widespread – even Romantically inspired – assumption of the primacy of a literary author's "final intentions."

*The Romantic Ideology: A Critical Investigation* and *A Critique of Modern Textual Criticism* (both 1983) serve as companion texts in the commencement of a rigorous, materialist approach in McGann's criticism. They address themselves to McGann's area of study – Romanticism – and the textual mediation and critical dissemination of this body of literature, but despite McGann's specificity of interest his findings have inferences for critical approaches to all literary periods. *The Romantic Ideology* is self-consciously directed to the analysis of ideological constructs within the literary text and its resultant criticism, and McGann locates his own discussion in relation to the work of Louis Althusser and Terry Eagleton. While the study focuses on poetry and criticism of the Romantic period, it does so within the context of their transmission in post-Romantic culture. McGann may be seen shifting from the specifics of his area of expertise to a more wide-reaching analysis of the state of contemporary textual criticism and critical editing.

*A Critique of Modern Textual Criticism* is McGann's most influential text and establishes the foundation for a proposed materialist hermeneutics: a concentration on all the "bibliographical codes" of a literary work. This is an approach that he continues to develop in later studies such as *The Textual Condition* (1991) and *Black Riders: The Visible Language of Modernism* (1993). The *Critique* is a response to the editorial approach to the literary text established by Fredson Bowers, W. W. Greg, and G. Thomas Tanselle. Bowers' methods were developed largely from Greg's "The Rationale of Copy-Text" (1950), and Tanselle, despite some reticence, can also be grouped as an inheritor of Greg's approach. These critics had, with slight modifications, brought to literary studies the "Lachmann Method" from classical scholarship. Named after Karl Lachmann, a nineteenth-century classicist, the Lachmann

Method aimed to construct an ideal authorial text (the original being nonexistent) by deducing its content from later versions of variable reliability. Reacting against this critical standpoint, McGann's *Critique* demonstrates a general advocacy of materialist texts; he states a preference for historical *versions* of literary texts rather than "critical editions" or "constructed" eclectic editions founded on this copy-text theory. McGann takes issue with the basic tenet of the Greg-Bowers editing method that assumes the primacy of the author's final intentions as demonstrated at the manuscript stage of composition. McGann places his textual debate in a contemporary ideological context, and alternatively places the methods of Greg, Bowers, and their followers within the history of classical philology.

The *Critique* seeks to challenge the empiricism of the Greg-Bowers editorial approach, but not, McGann has since insisted, to undermine any conception of the author as the source of authority and meaning in literary texts; rather, it attempts to historicize the author, and to overthrow the still prevalent Romantic notion of the author as the *sole* originator of a literary text. In 1983 such ideas of ideological decentering were not new to critical discourse by any means, but McGann's *Critique* constitutes an early appearance of such poststructuralist concerns within the discipline of scholarly editing. His argument against the "intentionalists" is that their endeavor to "cleanse" the text of the various "corruptions" which it acquires as it moves into the social (printed) forum, is to deny the practicalities of textual production in the modern period. McGann is opposed to any idealistic conception of the "text itself" (which is an outmoded "modernist essentialism" according to D. C. Greetham in his 1992 introduction to the *Critique*). He asserts that literary scholars are wrong to simply take up the editing processes of classical scholarship – the Lachmann Method – which McGann finds unsatisfactory and flawed in its idealistic empiricism:

Lacking the author's original documents, possessing only a more or less extensive set of later manuscripts, the classical editor developed procedures for tracing the internal history of these late manuscripts. The aim was to work out textual errors by revealing the history of their emergence. Ultimately, the method sought to "clear the text" of its corruptions and, thereby, to produce (or approximate) – by subtraction, as it were – the lost original document, the "authoritative text."

McGann is not dismissive of the method, but he regards it as an outmoded approach from another historical paradigm, and not suited to the reproduction of modern literary texts. The existence of two versions of William Shakespeare's *King Lear* serves as McGann's most succinct example of the inadequacy of an eclectic, or conflated, critical edition. The approach to editing of Shakespeare's work was thrown into crisis by new discoveries concerning the two printed texts of the play; rather than being two "relatively corrupted" texts of a lost and pure original, they were now considered to be two "relatively reliable" texts of two distinct versions of the same play. Thus any critical approach which directs itself solely toward a single, idealized canonical conflation of textual material is necessarily inadequate when confronted by the actuality of modern textual production, which continually creates distinct, equally canonical, historical versions of single "works." McGann finds himself closer to Philip Gaskell's preference for an early printed edition as copy-text, than to Fredson Bowers' preference for the manuscript. For McGann the socialized text is always superior, and multiple historical versions are more accurate than any intentionalist construction of an ideal text.

McGann argues against Bowers' view that the editorial intervention of the publisher, in producing substantial changes in the text and its format, is necessarily a corruption of the "authoritative text"; Bowers maintains this view regardless of whether or not the author allowed the publisher (reluctantly or otherwise) to make such changes. Essentially, McGann departs from Greg's copy-text rule, in which the first published edition is a "later" text in the ancestry, and where supreme authority is given to the author's manuscript. Tanselle, although critical of Greg, had stopped just short of "allowing" the first printed edition. McGann suggests that Tanselle had failed to see the historical dimension of both literary production and subsequent critical texts themselves. McGann calls on James Thorpe's claim that, in the modern, printed era, "The work of art is . . . always tending toward a collaborative status, and the task of the textual critic is always to recover and preserve its integrity at that point where the authorial intentions seem to have been fulfilled." McGann regards the social transmission of the printed text within its historical context as being wholly integrated with the author's intention, asserting that literary works "are fundamentally social rather than personal or psychological products"; they "do not even acquire an artistic form of being until their engagement with an audience has been determined." McGann's point is that even prior to the manuscript stage a literary work is a collaborative endeavor, albeit originating from the author:

As soon as it begins its passage to publication it undergoes a series of interventions which some textual critics see as a process of contamination, but which may equally be seen as a process of training the poem for its appearances in the world.

Additionally, at the printing stage, the literary work is a mutable entity; it is reliant on the originating author but, due to the practicalities of the physical creation of books, it is also a socialized production its own right:

"Final authority" for literary works rests neither with the author nor with his affiliated institution; it resides in the actual structure of the agreements which these two cooperating authorities reach in specific cases.

The conclusion of the *Critique* is that any decision as to what will constitute the copy-text of a critical edition must continue to take into account what is known of the "author's intentions," but it must also acknowledge the history of the text's production, and the history of the text's transmission and reproduction. The "author's intentions" cannot be assumed to constitute the determining factor in all instances. Rather than shifting the authority in a Barthesian sense from the author to the work and hence to the "text," McGann instead argues for a shifting and variance of competing authorities. He proposes a tentative terminology for this discussion in his essay "Theory of Texts" (1988): "social text," which is McGann's constant subject, operates at three social, collaborative levels designated as "the work," "the version," and "the text," all of which involve a textual interaction between the author and various readers.

*Towards a Literature of Knowledge* (1989) is based on the Clark Lectures which McGann delivered at Trinity College, Cambridge, in 1988. Its subject initially might not seem to sit comfortably with McGann's insistence upon the limitations of the author's authority – which is that the literary imagination constantly seeks to "make statements" and to "communicate." Nevertheless, McGann's position is that all texts are "social texts," and hence are social communications foremost. His study examines the poetry of William Blake, Lord Byron, Dante Gabriel Rossetti, and Ezra Pound, emphasizing that poems are not merely reflections on "truth" and representations of sociohistoric circumstance, but are factive documents which enact that circumstance, making (often incommensurable) assertions and transmissions within their temporal context. An interpretation of a poem is not itself a revelation of meaning, but a part of the history of a poem's interpretation. McGann's position ultimately remains characteristically poststructuralist when he asserts that while poetry "aspires towards the condition of knowledge," it does so in vain.

*The Textual Condition* takes up its discussion where the *Critique* ended. McGann notes that Tanselle, in his essay "The Editing of Historical Documents" (1978), had recognized a serious lack of consideration of the "physical form" of textual documents in historical scholarship, and McGann resolves to pursue this materialist notion firmly with regard to the study of literary works. Paying particular attention to the highly textualized poetry of Ezra Pound's *Cantos*, he proposes a rigorous, materialist hermeneutics in the study of literature; literature defined precisely as ink arranged into patterns on pages within a volume: "The object of poetry is to display the textual condition." Pound's poetry is notoriously alert to the microscopic significance of the various bibliographical codes that constitute the text. For McGann, the *Cantos* serve as an extreme example of textual signification: although literature is written language, it is never "merely" linguistic but functions as a result of the practical phenomenology of reading. That is to say, the images evoked by the poetry are not simply a function of "words and strings of words" but also a result of "abstract constructions of the page as a visual field." Similarly, Pound's allusiveness encourages a "radial" process of reading which deflects attention from the text itself; the reader is constantly "decoding one or more of the contexts that interpenetrate the scripted and physical text." At a further extension, the "bibliographical codes" which determine the meaning of the physical text also include its reception and critical presentation – the pre- and post-publication structures such as announcements and reviews. McGann offers T. S. Eliot's *The Waste Land* as a text that epitomizes this radial nature, and one which is particularly pertinent in a discussion of twentieth-century critical methods. Eliot's poem was never merely linguistic but radial from its first appearance; it emerged within a context of pre-publication discussion and analysis which necessarily structured the text, even for its earliest readers. McGann suggests a paradox within the ideals of the New Criticism, with its championing of close reading and anti-intentionalism, despite the characteristics of poems such as Eliot's which thrived in an era of New Criticism yet were framed within extensive radial structures of textual meaning and authority.

In *The Textual Condition*, McGann reiterates his sense of an ideological crisis in modern textual practice which he reduces to an amusing dictum that represents contemporary American textual scholarship as he sees it: "Thou shalt not mix literary criticism and editorial practice." McGann's holistic, materialist approach necessarily confronts this tendency, wherein the multifarious bibliographical codes of a literary work combine to constitute the text; hence any editorial practice must have an absolute effect upon the criticism of the text and any determination of its meaning or signification. For McGann, literary criticism and editorial practice are inextricably and definitively linked.

McGann carefully distinguishes his assertion of the continual instability of the text from the same assertion in poststructural critical theory by placing it in materialist terms. In fact, McGann's position is even more radical, and he explicitly charges critics as diverse as Paul de Man and G. Thomas Tanselle with "textual idealism." While much critical theory explores the instability of the linguistic text, it simultaneously assumes (or fails to question) "the stability of the material text – the interpretive location, or material object." McGann constantly asserts the variance of the interpretive location – the historical version, or the altered layout or typeface, or the re-editing of a literary work: "Interpretive differentials (or the freedom of the reader) are not the origin or cause of the variation, they are only its most manifest set of symptoms." As he makes clear near the start of this study, "The textual condition's only immutable law is the law of change."

*Black Riders* takes its title from Stephen Crane's volume of poetry – *The Black Riders and Other Lines* – which was published in 1895. McGann sees in Crane's original volume a deliberate emulation of the bibliographical innovations of the Pre-Raphaelites some years earlier. An additional connotation of the title, which Crane was likely to have been aware of, is that "riders" is the name given to the series of rollers which assist the distribution of ink on the paper in a printing press. McGann regards Crane's unusual typescript (which presents the poetry in the center of the page in entirely capitalized text) as being symptomatic of a general characteristic of modernist poetics: an emphasis on the "material features" of poetry, which is itself "a system of material signifiers." McGann finds in this early modernist text a physical manifestation of contemporary theoretical concepts. It is symptomatic of McGann's general argument that the poetry from this original volume has been widely reproduced with an almost total disregard for its idiosyncratic typographics. McGann describes Crane's poems, in their original published form, as "Barthesian writings, already fully conscious that the poetic field is self-signifying." *Black Riders* concentrates on the bibliographical codings of the work of poets such as William Morris, and the general typographics of modernist and postmodernist poetry. McGann's assertion is that twentieth-century English poetry arises directly from, and expresses, the revolution in printing technology which had begun late in the previous century. McGann is insistent upon the importance of poetry as a medium in which socialized philosophical and aesthetic concepts are enacted within historical periods: he devotes a chapter to the notion of expressible "truth" in poetry. McGann's faith in poetry as a vessel for linguistic and textual "truth" goes hand in hand with his examination of the limitations of the text and the continual instability of the material location of the text. He employs the dialogue form to dramatize the limitations of a single, directed exposition as a form of argument. His justification for this compelling technique is that when a fully developed argument approaches the "horizon of its own truths," it inevitably exposes itself to "disconfirmation and critique." Here McGann exhibits his poststructuralist tendencies once again, complicating his discourse by textually acknowledging its amenability to linguistic deconstruction.

McGann's most recent publication, *The Poetics of Sensibility: A Revolution in Literary Style* (1996), pursues his belief in the communicative aspiration of literary works by attempting to critically recover – through close reading, ironically – those "poetries of sensibility and sentiment" of the eighteenth century that were ignored or discounted by the trends of New Criticism. This critical movement had explicitly dissociated the interpretable content of a poem from the (subjective) sensibility that engendered the work. Famous New Critical protocols like the Intentional and the Affective Fallacies in effect forbade the critical deployment of the stylistic conventions of sensibility and sentimentality.

McGann's campaign against the "modernist essentialism" which assumes a determined, stable material text informs *The Poetics of Sensibility*, but the emphasis of textual authority is paradoxically on the side of the contextualized, socialized literary author rather than the ahistorical critic (for McGann, all literary critics are historicized – admittedly or otherwise). He suggests that this study is a part of the same ongoing critique of the "academic legacy of modernism" which has informed his approach to critical editing and his delineation of the hermeneutics of the material text. McGann continues to provide an opposition to the empirical critical editing practices still prevalent in contemporary literary scholarship.

## Principal criticism

*Fiery Dust: Byron's Poetic Development*, 1969
*Swinburne: An Experiment in Criticism*, 1972
*Don Juan in Context*, 1976
*The Romantic Ideology: A Critical Investigation*, 1983
*A Critique of Modern Textual Criticism*, 1983
*The Beauty of Inflections: Literary Investigations in Historical Method and Theory*, 1985
*Social Values and Poetic Acts*, 1988
"Theory of Texts," in the *London Review of Books*, February 18, 1988
*Towards a Literature of Knowledge*, 1989
*The Textual Condition*, 1991
*Black Riders: The Visible Language of Modernism*, 1993
*The Poetics of Sensibility. A Revolution in Literary Style*, 1996

## Other major works and literary forms

Jerome J. McGann is a prolific writer and contributes regularly to a host of literary journals. His recent work on electronic texts and hypertext theory is a natural evolution of his analysis of the material hermeneutics of the text. McGann is particularly interested in the manner in which the electronic medium will affect critical processes and the teaching of literature, and this has led to a number of essays which are available electronically, including "The Rationale of Hypertext" (1994) and "Radiant Textuality" (1995). He is currently compiling *The Complete Writings and Pictures of Dante Gabriel Rossetti: A HyperMedia Research Archive*. An accompanying book on Rossetti's work, and a study of Lord Byron and William Wordsworth, are forthcoming. McGann has written four volumes of poetry, the most recent being *Four Last Poems* (1996).

POETRY
*Air Heart Sermons*, 1976
*Writing Home*, 1978 (with Janet Kauffman)
*Nerves in Patterns*, 1979 (with James Kahn)
*Four Last Poems*, 1996

EDITED TEXTS

*Edward Bulwer-Lytton's Pelham, or The Adventures of a Gentleman*, 1972
*Byron: The Complete Poetical Works*, 1980 (7 volumes)
*Historical Studies and Literary Criticism*, 1985
*Textual Criticism and Literary Interpretation*, 1985
*The Manuscripts of the Younger Romantics: Byron*, 1985–1989 (with Alice Levine; 4 volumes)
*Oxford Authors: Byron*, 1986
*Victorian Connections*, 1989
*Postmodern Poetries*, 1990 (special verse issue)
*The New Oxford Book of Romantic Period Verse*, 1993
*Laetitia Elizabeth Landon: Selected Writings*, 1998 (with Daniel Riess)

## Further reading

Fischer, Michael. "The New Criticism in the New Historicism: The Recent Work of Jerome J. McGann," in *The New Criticism and Contemporary Literary Theory: Connections and Continuities*, 1995. Edited by William J. Spurlin and Michael Fischer.

Gorman, David. "Pictures of Great Detail: Jerome McGann's Social Values and Poetic Acts," in *Works and Days: Essays in the Socio-Historical Dimensions of Literature and the Arts*. 8, no. 1 (15) (Spring, 1990), pp. 89–97.

Shaw, Philip, and Steven Earnshaw. "Interview with Jerome McGann," in *The Cambridge Quarterly*. 22, no. 4 (1993), pp. 355–369.

MICHAEL BRETT

*See also* Bateson; Bowers

# Marshall McLuhan

## Canadian critic and writer

**Born:** Edmonton, Canada; July 21, 1911
**Died:** Toronto, Canada; December 31, 1980

## Biography

Herbert Marshall McLuhan was the son of Herbert Ernest and Elsie Naomi (née Hall) McLuhan. His father sold insurance, while his mother was well known throughout Canada as an elocutionist. The McLuhans lived in western Canada – first Alberta, then Winnipeg, Manitoba. McLuhan first planned to become an engineer, but he shifted to literature after entering the university.

He attended the University of Manitoba, earning a B.A. in 1933 and an M.A. in 1934. He developed a lasting admiration for the modernist writers, especially Ezra Pound, T. S. Eliot, and, above all others, James Joyce. McLuhan's works are studded with references to the Irish author's writings and filled with quotations from his books, especially *Finnegans Wake* (1939).

McLuhan next studied at Trinity Hall, Cambridge University. He completed his B.A. in 1936, his M.A. in 1940, and his Ph.D. in 1942. The topic of his dissertation, titled "The Place of Thomas Nashe in the Learning of His Time," is significant, for Nashe was the Elizabethan writer whose mixture of styles, genres, and rhetoric most closely corresponds to McLuhan's own fascination with the impact of media.

During the 1930s, while doing research at the Huntington Library in California, McLuhan met Corinne Keller Lewis; they were married on August 4, 1939. The couple had six children.

McLuhan converted to Roman Catholicism during the 1930s. Most of his academic career was spent at Catholic schools: St. Louis University in Missouri, Assumption University in Windsor, Canada, and St. Michael's College, the Roman Catholic unit of the University of Toronto, where he taught from 1946 until his retirement.

In 1963 McLuhan became director of the University of Toronto Centre for Culture and Technology, and in 1966 he was appointed to the Albert Schweitzer Chair in Humanities at Fordham University; thereafter he shared his time between Fordham and Toronto.

McLuhan retired from the University of Toronto in 1979. On New Year's Eve, 1980, he died in his sleep.

## Influence

One of the most original and stimulating of twentieth-century critics and theorists, McLuhan brought both scholarly and popular attention to the role of media in shaping human lives and culture. His frequently repeated dictum that "the medium is the message" encapsulated a truth which has become a key element in modern thought: that the manner in which a communication is presented can be just as important – and will sometimes have more lasting impact – than the content of the message itself. McLuhan was particularly concerned with demonstrating the effect of the modern electronic media – radio, television, computer systems – which he claimed were creating one vast "global village," reversing the impact of centuries of linear print, which he termed "the Gutenberg galaxy."

McLuhan's theories found favor with many, outraged many others. During the mid-1960s and early 1970s he was extremely influential in both academic and nonacademic circles, particularly advertising and mass communications. After his initial fame (some would say notoriety) subsided, the key elements of McLuhan's theories and observations remained, and in the works of such authors as Walter Ong they have been shown to be essential tools for the study of modern literature and culture.

## Analysis

In his 1967 work, *The Medium Is the Massage*, McLuhan provides a brief summary of his basic thesis:

> Societies have always been shaped more by the nature of the media by which men communicate than by the content of the communication. . . . The alphabet and print technology fostered and encouraged a

fragmenting process, a process of specialism and of detachment. Electric technology fosters and encourages unification and involvement. It is impossible to understand social and cultural changes without a knowledge of the workings of media.

This approach, which places emphasis on medium rather than content, has a classical example in Plato's *Phaedrus* (c. 370 B.C.), where Socrates deplores writing, since the use of this artificial aid to memory will destroy true learning and wisdom and must lead to their replacement by a superficial appearance of knowledge. Aristotle also addresses the topic, for in his discussion of catharsis, the stirring and purging of the emotions brought about by works of art, he maintains that this beneficial effect is possible only if the work has a proper form, presentation, or appearance. In other words, the medium as well as the message affects the spectator or reader.

Among modern philosophers, Ludwig Wittgenstein is among the best known for his view that language is a picture of reality, thus his famous dictum that "the limits of language mean the limits of my world." It is difficult to conceive of a stronger statement about the power inherent in the medium of communication.

Such thoughts, however, were limited primarily to abstract philosophical discussions. The relationship between the means of communication and its impact on society was posed in a more practical fashion in the twentieth century by Harold Innis, a fellow Canadian who had a profound influence on McLuhan. In *Empire and Communications* (1950) and *The Bias of Communication* (1951), Innis advanced the thesis that societies develop in unique ways directly determined by their technologies of communication. Communication for Innis meant more than the conscious exchange of information; it embraced an entire galaxy of human activities. The fur trade, for example, was of decisive importance in the establishment of white settlers in Canada, and the communications involved in that trade – from dealing with the native Indians, to tracking the animals, to marketing the pelts – formed a communications network that influenced all Canadian life.

Innis regarded communication systems as patterns which determine a society's character. The Roman Empire was made possible by an interlocking network of order and regularity. Its famous roads laced all parts of the empire together, and on those roads – without parallel in ancient times – the legions marched, and each legion had the same organization, the same weapons, the same uniforms. This regularity pervaded Roman life and would not have been possible without Rome's communications network.

Following Innis' lead, McLuhan offered his own interpretation of the relationships between communications media and society. The exposition of his thought is not linear; rather, it is accomplished through thought-provoking, often-startling collages of thought and comment that may appear random at first but upon closer inspection reveal new and definite patterns. The straightforward presentation here can only hint at the richness found in McLuhan's own works.

McLuhan defines media as all things that are extensions of some human faculty. Clothing, for example, is a medium, since it is an extension of the skin; the wheel, an extension of the foot. Most students of McLuhan have little difficulty with definitions such as this; when, however, he explains the book as an extension of the eye, or the electronic media as an extension of the human central nervous system, then some criticism begins.

McLuhan supports his definitions with a three-pronged argument. First, media carry information, regardless of whether the recipients recognize it. That information may be overt and intentional, such as the content of a book; it may be covert and unintended, such as the impact that printing has on a reader or the message conveyed by a certain style of dress or fashion of hair.

Second, the strongest effect comes from the nature of media, rather than their content. According to McLuhan, media alter human environments by changing the ratio of human senses – that is, the sense to which the media appeal the most. As he writes, "When these ratios change, men change."

Third, McLuhan argues that the change in humans and their perceptions results in changes in their overall attitudes. As he puts it, punning on his own remark that the medium is the message:

> All media work us over completely. They are so pervasive in their personal, political, economic, aesthetic, psychological, moral, ethical, and social consequences that they leave no part of us untouched, unaffected, unaltered. The medium is the massage. Any understanding of social and cultural change is impossible without a knowledge of the way media work as environments.

In other words, the media surround humankind, causing profound changes, but as environments they are invisible. McLuhan makes media, and their effects, visible by providing literally hundreds of examples. Two of the more far-ranging and well-known must stand for them here.

McLuhan devotes much attention to the effects of writing and printing. He posits that preliterate societies have hearing as their primary sense; in his terms, the ratio of sense perception is tilted toward the ear. Unable to write, people in such societies must communicate through speech. A characteristic of sound is that it comes from all directions, and persons who live in such "acoustic space" perceive reality as a series of simultaneous relationships.

This oral-aural culture was first weakened by the invention of the phonetic alphabet, which began shifting the ratio of the senses away from sound toward sight. In McLuhan's words, it gave man "an eye for an ear." In contrast to hearing, sight is more definite, more structured, more controllable by human beings. The visual sense forces man to break reality down into bits and pieces, which are then reassembled in an order characterized by repeatability, regularity, and continuity.

Speech, memorized or rote, changes from utterance to utterance; writing remains the same. When people could inscribe their words and later retrieve them or pass them on to others without direct physical contact, their sense of the world around them subtly but powerfully shifted. The uniformity and repetition of writing caused people to become more independent and at the same time more isolated.

This process was dramatically accelerated by the invention of printing, which established the pattern for the next five hundred years of our culture. While writing tends toward uniformity, printing absolutely ensures it; endless copies of a book spill from the press, and each book carries the same letters in the same order. The eye completely dominates the other senses.

From the invention of the printing press, McLuhan sees such disparate developments as perspective in painting (developed in the Renaissance after artists began to see reality from an objective point of view), the Industrial Revolution (the book was the first mass-produced artifact), and mechanization, which breaks the organic whole of the universe – or human society – into artificial components to be handled as discrete units.

Having established the wide-ranging impact of linear print on human beings and their culture, McLuhan next examines the effect of the electronic media. McLuhan notes that a change can be discerned in the popular media, especially the press, following the spread of the telegraph, one of the first examples of the new electric systems of communications. The format of newspapers began to involve more of the reader's senses than only the visual. The mix of unrelated stories on the same page, and later the appearance of photographs amid the print, produced a shift in the ratio of the senses, making the reader more like a listener in the preliterate cultures, where there is no single, definite point of view.

According to McLuhan, the very nature of the electronic media – irrespective of content – has this effect on human beings, and its impact was increased during the twentieth century as those media became more sophisticated and more pervasive. A common characteristic of electronic media is that they require participation and involvement by the audience; they utilize all senses simultaneously, rather than favoring sight as print does. In McLuhan's terminology, such media are "cool," whereas media that provide information exclusively to a single sense – print, for the eye – are "hot." This distinction between "hot" and "cool" media became a key point in McLuhan's theories.

For McLuhan, the "cool" medium par excellence is television, which demands close participation from its viewers because they must fill in the gaps and spaces that actually make up most of the screen. When so much of a person's sensorium is engaged in receiving and interpreting experience, McLuhan argues, the actual content presented by the television becomes almost inconsequential, because the total effect is so overwhelming.

In a perceptive article in *McLuhan: Hot and Cool* (1967), Tom Wolfe posed the essential question about McLuhan: "What if he is right?" If McLuhan's theories about the media and their effects are wrong, then he can be dismissed as an intriguing eccentric; if McLuhan is right, then profound changes will have to be made in the approach to media, starting with a broader understanding of the term itself.

During his career McLuhan's theories elicited both admiration and scorn; such reactions were particularly acute during the 1960s and 1970s, when he became most widely known. Indeed, so passionately did the debate rage that objective consideration of his ideas was rare, and the question posed by Wolfe was answered, on both sides, more by faith than by facts.

McLuhan's central concept is sound: the impact of a medium is largely dependent upon its form. His elaboration of specific examples of this truth is persuasive and provocative. It seems clear, from his studies and those of other scholars, that the phonetic alphabet, literacy, and printing made fundamental changes in Western culture, changes that were caused as much by the medium as by its messages. McLuhan further observed a second shift: from the orientation fostered by linear print ("the Gutenberg galaxy," as he termed it) to that of the new electronic age. He traced the development of the electric network, pointed out the changes it had already accomplished, and speculated on greater changes yet to come. While some of his ideas might seem far-fetched and his presentation innovative to the point of irritation, he was a remarkably perceptive and creative observer.

The impact of media on human beings and their societies, the concept that "the medium is the message," and a new and deeper understanding of how people are altered by their technologies – for these insights, McLuhan's work is destined to have lasting value for students of literature, the arts, and culture in general.

## Principal criticism

*The Mechanical Bride: Folklore of Industrial Man*, 1951
*Explorations in Communication*, 1960 (with E. S. Carpenter)
*The Gutenberg Galaxy: The Making of Typographic Man*, 1962
*Understanding Media: The Extensions of Man*, 1964
*The Medium Is the Massage: An Inventory of Effects*, 1967 (with Quentin Fiore)
*Through the Vanishing Point: Space in Poetry and Painting*, 1968 (with Harley Parker)

*War and Peace in the Global Village*, 1968 (with Fiore)
*The Interior Landscape: The Literary Criticism of Marshall McLuhan, 1943–1962*, 1969
*Counterblast*, 1969 (with Parker)
*From Cliché to Archetype*, 1970 (with Wilfred Watson)
*Culture Is Our Business*, 1970
*Take Today: The Executive as Dropout*, 1972 (with Barrington Nevitt)

## Other major works and literary forms

Several of Marshall McLuhan's books, including his first, *The Mechanical Bride*, and later ones such as *The Medium Is the Massage* and *Culture Is Our Business*, employ a mixture of illustrations, bold page design, and innovative typography to present the author's views. This technique allows McLuhan to reinforce his thesis that the manner in which a message is presented is as important as the content – perhaps more important. The technique is one that McLuhan used during an earlier and extremely formative period in his career.

These unique presentations have their foundation in the Journal *Explorations in Communication*, which McLuhan coedited with Edmund Carpenter from 1953 through 1957. *Explorations in Communication* was published by the Centre for Culture and Technology at the University of Toronto, and its nine issues presented their subjects – primarily media and their effects – through striking, highly unusual page formats, daring graphic design, and mixtures of typographical forms, reminiscent of the Dada school of modern art. Given the fresh displays of information, the epigrammatic, thought-provoking statements, and the subject matter involved, this publication expresses the essence of McLuhan's subsequent work. It could be said that McLuhan's later work is the continuation of *Explorations in Communication* by other means.

NONFICTION
*Letters of Marshall McLuhan*, 1987 (Molinaro, Matie, Corinne McLuhan and William Toye, editors)

ANTHOLOGIES
*Selected Poetry by Alfred, Lord Tennyson*, 1956
*Voices of Literature*, 1964–1965 (2 volumes; editor, with Richard J. Schoeck)

## Further reading

Duffy, Dennis. *Marshall McLuhan*, 1969.
Gordon, W. Terrence. *Marshall McLuhan: Escape Into Understanding*, 1997.
Miller, Jonathan. *Marshall McLuhan*, 1971.
Rosenthal, Raymond, ed. *McLuhan: Pro and Con*, 1967.
Stearn, Gerald, ed. *McLuhan: Hot and Cool*, 1967.
Theall, Donald. *The Medium Is the Rear View Mirror: Understanding McLuhan*, 1971.

MICHAEL WITKOSKI

*See also* Baudrillard; Ong

# Medieval Literary Theory

Medieval literary theory comprises a wide range of texts from different disciplines written over a long but only vaguely defined period of time. The field resists clear demarcation because of the nature of the study of the liberal arts during the Middle Ages, when literary theory was not recognized as a separate discipline, and because of the continuing influence of classical models throughout the period, an influence that tends to blur the boundary between classical and medieval ideas.

The great concerns of medieval scholars were with preserving the achievements of the fallen Roman Empire and with adapting that body of learning to the changed conditions of a new Christian empire. As a result, the influence of classical traditions on medieval literary theory is so pervasive that no definite or even closely approximate date can be set as a dividing line between the two periods. Writers such as Saint Augustine (354–430) or Boethius (c. 480–524) are considered by some authorities to be late classical writers, by others to be early medieval writers. Both were conscious of themselves as followers, coming after a body of classical tradition, yet they were read throughout the Middle Ages more as authorities within that tradition than as representatives of a break with it.

This difficulty in locating a watershed has led some current writers to argue that the dividing point between classical and medieval grammar, to take one example of an academic discipline crucial to the history and development of literary theory, is as late as the twelfth century. For this reason, it will be more productive to consider a few representative works clearly pertaining to one period or the other than to attempt a strictly chronological survey.

Medieval scholars, following classical models, divided most of the arts and sciences into two major categories: the trivium, which dealt with the study of words, was composed of grammar, rhetoric, and dialectic (or logic); the quadrivium, which dealt with the study of mathematical concepts, was composed of arithmetic, geometry, music, and astronomy. The different kinds of knowledge were placed into one or another of these seven categories. Literary theory – or poetics, as it was more likely to be called – could be assigned by different writers to different categories, and this assignment would naturally have an effect on the approach to the subject.

Within this framework, poetics was viewed most commonly as part of either grammar or rhetoric. It was also possible, however, to classify it as a part of logic. The Arab philosopher Averroës (1126–1198), in his commentary on Aristotle's *De poetica* (c. 334–323 B.C.; *Poetics*), argued that the work belonged to logic, of which poetry was one branch, an idea followed at least in part by writers as late as the sixteenth century. Other classifications moved literary theory outside the trivium and quadrivium proper and aligned it with ethics or moral philosophy. A further complication for medieval literary theory was a result of the distinction often made between religious writings, especially the Bible, and secular writings, especially those by pagan authors. Whether the same methods of reading and interpretation applied to both types of text was frequently disputed throughout the Middle Ages. By the end of the medieval period – or, alternatively, at the beginning of the Renaissance, since similar problems in finding boundaries exist at the other end of the period – some writers had concluded that these two genres might be in many important respects similar.

These problems were all closely related, and no simple division of them can be entirely satisfactory. For expository purposes, however, three main aspects of the development of medieval literary theory may be broadly outlined: the adaptation of models derived from classical grammar and rhetoric to the literary analysis of secular writing, the further adaptation of these models of literary analysis for use in scriptural exegesis, and, finally, a generalized model within which even secular texts could be analyzed in terms of their ethical and moral principles, almost as if they were themselves scriptures.

Given that many classical treatises on literary theory were widely known throughout the medieval period, it is in some respects surprising that medieval critics were more likely to turn to classical grammar or rhetoric rather than poetics for their sources. While the most important of these sources, Aristotle's *Poetics*, was little known outside the Arabic-speaking world during this period, others were readily available. The reason behind this relative neglect would seem to be that the medieval writers' concerns were different from those of their predecessors. In fact, before becoming useful even to the Arab theorists who had access to it, Aristotle's work had to undergo significant distortions, particularly through the introduction of the ideas that poetry is a branch of logic and that poetry can be defined as the art of praising and blaming, notions quite foreign to Aristotle but useful for the analysis of Arabic poetry.

The works most commonly available to scholars working in Latin, as opposed to Arabic, would have been the works of writers such as Donatus (fourth century), and these were built around discussions of the drama, as was the *Poetics*. The difficulty with using these models was that classical drama disappeared nearly completely during the Middle Ages. In the absence of a context within which to apply theories about drama, approaches through grammar or rhetoric, which applied more generally to linguistic productions, seemed more fruitful to medieval theorists.

The Roman rhetorician Quintilian (c. 35–96) had defined grammar as the science of correct speaking and the reading of the poets. The first half of his formulation would seem to have affinities with rhetoric, the second with literary interpretation – and this inclusive view of grammar survived throughout the medieval period. The English ecclesiastic John of Salisbury (c. 1115–1180) followed this approach

in affirming that "poetry belongs to grammar, which is the mother and source of its study."

This orientation toward literary analysis produced extensive commentaries, or glosses, on major classical authors such as Virgil and Horace. These commentaries began with a brief biography of the author, followed by an outline of the form and genre of the work being discussed and then a long set of notes analyzing individual lines and even words of the text. Such notes would explain difficult vocabulary or expressions, identify poetic meters and figures, and offer moral interpretations of passages.

The late classical commentary on Virgil by Servius, to take an example widely followed during the Middle Ages, was basically a series of footnotes giving definitions of unfamiliar words or brief explanations of references to myths. These notes did not aim to achieve some comprehensive interpretation of Virgil's work; they were meant only to clarify specific passages. Such commentaries were not undertaken, however, with the exclusive or even primary aim of literary interpretation of the text, but to teach the methods underlying good writing, to develop eloquence in the student by providing models for imitation. More important, the study of these secular texts was seen as preparation for interpreting the Bible, a point which will be discussed more fully below. John of Salisbury explained how these educational functions were served by the grammatical curriculum developed by Bernard of Chartres, who flourished during the early twelfth century:

Bernard of Chartres, the richest fountain of literary learning in modern times, taught the authors in this way: he pointed out what was simple and what conformed to rule; he called attention to grammatical figures, rhetorical colors, and sophistic fallacies; he showed where a given text was related to other disciplines. . . . He expounded the poets and orators to those of his students who were assigned as preliminary exercises the imitation of works in prose or verse. Pointing out skillful connections between words and elegant closing rhythms, he would urge his students to follow in the steps of the authors. . . . He bade them reproduce the very image of the author, and succeeded in making a student who imitated the great writers himself worthy of posterity's imitation.

The study of rhetoric built upon the study of grammar and overlapped it in many ways. The grammatically oriented commentary on Virgil by Servius cited above may be paralleled to the rhetorically oriented commentary by Donatus on the same subject. In the introductory letter to his son which prefaces the work, Donatus argues the inadequacy of the grammatical approach and proposes to study Virgil's *Aeneid* (c. 29–19 B.C.) rhetorically, as one might study an oration. He accordingly classifies the epic as a specific rhetorical type, as an example of epideictic, or demonstrative, rhetoric, concerned with blame or, as in the case of the *Aeneid*, praise of an individual. He then gives an analysis, heavily influenced by Ciceronian principles, of Virgil's rhetorical techniques.

Classical rhetorical treatises such as those by Cicero (106–43 B.C.), especially his youthful book *De inventione* (86 B.C.), were copied throughout the medieval period and became themselves the subjects of extensive commentaries. The classical tradition had divided the study of rhetoric into five parts: invention, the methods for discovering what to say about a given topic, for generating ideas about it; disposition, the ordering and arrangement of these ideas; style, the formulation of specific words and figures of speech to express the material; delivery (or elocution), the rules of effective speaking; and memory, the techniques for recalling these ideas in their proper order and expression. Medieval writers concerned themselves primarily, though not exclusively, with the component of style, as the citation from Bernard of Chartres suggests. While Cicero, along with most other classical rhetoricians, was concerned with public speaking, whether in political, judicial, or ceremonial contexts, medieval authors adapted these rhetorical principles to a variety of new ends. The three most important of these applications were to the writing of letters, sermons, and poetry.

The classical authorities had left no separate works dealing with techniques of letter writing, probably because the subject would have been adequately treated during the general course of a liberal education. After the collapse of the Roman Empire, however, there was a long period of disruption which caused educational systems to lose continuity, though in places such as Gaul and Germany the Roman schools did persist for some time after the fall of Rome itself in the year 410. With increasing need for communication between rulers – especially within the increasingly large and complex hierarchy of the administration of the medieval Church – the need for standardized forms and techniques for letter-writing grew.

The Benedictine monk Alberic, of the monastery of Monte Cassino in Italy, is credited with the first systematic application of the principles of Ciceronian rhetoric to the *ars dictaminis*, or the art of letter-writing, in the year 1087. Such treatises were written throughout the medieval period and well into the Renaissance. Especially important to these writers was the treatment of the salutation, the specific terms in which to address readers of different social and ecclesiastical levels. Such a concern reflects not only the rhetorical roots of their approach but also the complexity of the increasingly stratified society within which such treatises were needed.

Another distinctively medieval adaptation of classical rhetoric was the development of manuals of the art of preaching, or *ars praedicandi*. Preaching was the primary form of oral discourse in the medieval world, just as oratory of various types had been the most important form of public

discourse in the classical world. Again, it was the rhetoric of Cicero, especially his ideas about the principles for first dividing the theme into components and then separately elaborating upon each component in turn, which provided the foundation for most of these manuals for writing the thematic sermon. By 1322, the probable date of Robert of Basevorn's *Forma praedicandi* (the form of preaching), these techniques had become so thoroughly refined and standardized that he was able to compare and contrast the distinct approaches of the Oxford and Paris schools virtually point by point on the twenty-two ways of ornamenting a sermon. The rhetorical basis of these handbooks is further suggested by the typical concluding section dealing with delivery or elocution, which discussed such matters as modulation of voice and the appropriate uses of gesture and humor.

The third major reformulation of classical rhetoric for the purposes of literary description and analysis was in the proliferation of rhetorical models of poetry, what might be called rhetorical poetics. Perhaps the most widely followed work in this tradition was the *Poetria nova* (The New Poetics, 1967; best known as *Poetria nova*) of Geoffrey of Vinsauf, probably written between 1208 and 1213. Its author was an Englishman who had studied in Paris and traveled in Italy, and the work brings together many ideas that must have been current throughout medieval Europe. The popularity of the work during the Middle Ages is suggested by the fact that it survives in some fifty manuscripts. That twenty of these manuscripts are translations into English suggests that it was a popular textbook. The work is written in Latin verse and was intended for aspiring poets. The outline of the book gives clear indications of its debt to classical rhetoric, especially that of Cicero:

1. Dedication to Pope Innocent III (lines 1–42)
2. Idea versus subject matter in poetry (43–86)
3. Arrangement (87–201)
4. Amplification and abbreviation (202–736)
5. Difficult ornaments of style (737–1093)
6. Easy ornaments of style (1094–1587)
7. Theory of conversions (1588–1761)
8. Theory of determinations (1762–1841)
9. Miscellaneous prescriptions (1842–1968)
10. Memory (1969–2031)
11. Delivery (2032–2066)
12. Epilogue (2067–2117)

Certain aspects of this scheme, particularly the emphasis on the theories of conversions and determinations, would seem to be derived from grammatical models rather than rhetoric. The debt to Horace's *Ars poetica* (c. 17 B.C.; *The Art of Poetry*), known in the Middle Ages as the *Poetria*, is suggested by the title, which implies that the work follows or supersedes Horace's work, which was also associated with the grammatical tradition. Yet the grounding of the work as a whole on the five-part structure of classical rhetoric, with its fairly clear divisions into sections on invention (ideas), arrangement, ornamentation, memory, and delivery, is evident. The opening of the treatise proper after the conventional dedication is often cited as one of the quintessential formulations of medieval notions about the methods of poetic composition:

> If a man has a house to build, his hand does not rush, hasty, into the very doing: the work is first measured out with his heart's inward plumb line, and the inner man marks out a series of steps beforehand, according to a definite plan; his heart's hand shapes the whole before his body's hand does so, and his building is a plan before it is an actuality. . . .
>
> When a plan has sorted out the subject in the secret places of your mind, then let Poetry come to clothe your material with words.

This discussion makes explicit what is implicit in the outline of the book, which allots about forty lines to the discussion of invention and more than seventeen hundred to ornamentation: poetic composition was seen primarily as a matter of style. One could make any subject into poetry by adorning it sufficiently with the ornaments of style. The suggestion that content is separable from form to this extent, however dubious a proposition in terms of modern theory, may have provided a justification for the application of these models of analysis, derived from secular sources, to scriptural texts.

As suggested above, medieval theologians, while maintaining clear distinctions between the relative authority of secular and scriptural texts, believed that training in the analysis of literature could be valuable preparation for the more important task of interpreting the Bible. Theologians would draw upon the principles of literary criticism developed for the study of secular texts to the extent that these techniques were applicable to the language of the Scriptures. As a result, one can find examples of the relatively straightforward application of rhetorical criticism to the Bible.

Augustine, for example, illustrated the notion of the three levels of style, the grand, middle, and plain, a notion derived from the *Rhetorica ad herrenium* (c. 86–82 B.C.) ascribed to Cicero, by reference to examples drawn from religious writings. Peter Abelard (1079–1142) argued that "all sacred Scripture, in the manner of rhetorical speech, intends either to teach or to move," a precept which implies a wide range of connections to be made between scriptural exegesis and the kinds of literary theory that had been derived from the classical rhetorical tradition. Literary form could also be seen as a useful method for classifying the parts of the Scriptures. Petrus Aureolus, writing about 1319, applied a scheme developed for secular poetry to sacred poetry:

> It should be known that poetic song is divided into three kinds. Into *Carmina*, which are songs of joy . . ., Elegies, which are songs of sorrow . . ., and Dramatic poems, which are songs of love. And this should be known: the decantative part of divine Scripture with regard to the mode of sacred poetry is divided into the Book of Psalms, which contains poems of joy and sweet pleasure, and the Book of Lamentations, which contains elegies of misery and sadness, and the Song of Songs, which contains dramas of beauty and love.

For the analysis of other aspects of sacred writings, however, new techniques had to be developed which extended literary theory beyond the kinds of analysis called for by secular literary forms. The best-known of these interpretive principles is the method of fourfold exegesis, summarized by Guibert of Nogent in a preface to his commentary on Genesis (1084):

> There are four ways of interpreting Scripture. . . . The first is history, which speaks of actual events as they occurred; the second is allegory, in which one thing stands for something else; the third is tropology, or moral instruction, which treats of the ordering and arranging of one's life; and the last is ascetics, or spiritual enlightenment, through which we who are about to treat of lofty and heavenly topics are led to a higher way of life. For example, the word Jerusalem: historically, it represents a specific city; in allegory it represents holy Church; tropologically or morally, it is the soul of every faithful man who longs for the vision of eternal peace; and anagogically it refers to the life of the heavenly citizens, who already see the God of Gods, revealed in all His glory in Sion.

Such an approach was particularly valuable in interpreting biblical texts whose apparent literal meaning was difficult to reconcile with the supposed principles of the faith. The Song of Songs provides a convenient example. On the literal level, it appears to describe erotic encounters recorded by the lascivious Solomon, to whom the work was ascribed. In his commentary on the work (c. 1130), William of Saint-Thierry explains the historical, or literal, meaning of the song but also defines its spiritual sense; rather than describing mere human love, the song could be read to be a celebration of the mystical marriage between Jesus Christ and Holy Church.

While the intended effect of this application of literary theory to the Bible was to operate primarily in one direction – the focusing of attention on the ways in which the literal reading of the sacred text was to be augmented and extended by the addition of figurative readings – an effect in the other direction also occurred. Such analysis provided a precedent for arguing that secular poetry, even that written by pagans and having no obvious moral value, could also be read and interpreted as having valuable allegorical and moral significance.

An influential late classical (or early medieval) model for this type of analysis was *Virgiliana continentia* (*The Exposition of the Content of Virgil According to Moral Philosophy*, 1971) by Fabius Planciades Fulgentius (c. 500–600). Just as Servius had written a commentary on Virgil from a grammatical point of view and Donatus had discussed his work from a rhetorical orientation, Fulgentius' exposition, as the title suggests, turns from the trivium to the category of ethics for the emphasis of his commentary. His method for extracting moral philosophy from pagan poetry was influential throughout the Middle Ages, establishing a precedent for similar commentaries on other classical poets. Pierre Bersuire, for example, provided an analysis of Ovid's *Metamorphoses* (c. A.D. 8) in his *Reductorium morale* (1350–1362), which virtually ignores the superficial prurient interest of many of the stories and concentrates on drawing out the morality hidden in the profane text. Treatments of this nature helped to establish a common ground for secular and sacred writings which was exploited by later Humanist writers, particularly by Dante (1265–1321) and Giovanni Boccaccio (1313–1375).

Dante's major contributions to late medieval (or early Renaissance) literary theory are his analysis of the distinction between theological and poetic levels of meaning and his defense of the use of the vernacular rather than Latin for poetry. Dante argued that secular poetry had four levels of meaning which were parallel to the four levels described in scriptural exegesis: a poem could be analyzed at the literal, allegorical, moral, and spiritual (or anagogic) levels. The difference for analysis would be most significant, somewhat surprisingly, at the literal level. While theology is true in all four senses, secular poetry is false at the literal level.

This idea that poets are disseminators of falsehood had long formed the basis of disparaging critiques of such poetry. Dante's approach rehabilitated the status of secular poetry by emphasizing that it could be not only true but also spiritually edifying at the higher levels of meaning. He also argued that understanding of the literal level was essential to correct interpretation of these higher levels, a position that implies the unity of the literal and figurative meanings of a work and denies the clear division between form and content that was frequently maintained in textual analysis. According to Dante, one must always work from the literal level first:

> Therefore, for this reason, I will regularly analyze the literal sense of each *canzone* first, and after that I will analyze the allegory, that is, what is the hidden truth, and from time to time I will touch on the other senses in passing, as time and place permit.

An even stronger defense of secular poetry was presented by Boccaccio in his *Genealogia deorum gentilium* (genealogy of the gentile gods), a defense which he apparently worked on for a period extending from about 1343 to sometime after 1370. He uses the methods of allegorical interpretation to demonstrate that even pagan myths contain moral truths and that the reading of and reference to these myths is entirely appropriate for Christians. In subsequent chapters, he responds to general charges which were frequently made against secular poetry in the Middle Ages: that it was trivial, false, and even sinful.

Boccaccio took the Humanist position that poetry embodies a broad range of truths and serves a social function in communicating them in a pleasurable way. He extended his defense by arguing that poetry is the result of inspiration originating in the bosom of God and that the first poetry was written by early priests in praise of God. This line of reasoning led him to make the allegation "that the pagan poets are theologians," a claim that he softened somewhat by making a distinction between "physical" and "sacred" theology, but which nevertheless represents a valuation of secular poetry which seems to be a sign of the transition from medieval to Renaissance ideas regarding the nature and value of literature.

## Further reading

Auerbach, Erich. *Literary Language and Its Public in Late Latin Antiquity and in the Middle Ages*, 1958.
Baldwin, Charles S. *Medieval Rhetoric and Poetic*, 1928.
Curtius, Ernst Robert. *European Literature and the Latin Middle Ages*, 1948.
Minnis, A. J. *Medieval Theory of Authorship: Scholastic Literary Attitudes in the Later Middle Ages*, 1982.
Murphy, James J. *Rhetoric in the Middle Ages: A History of Rhetorical Theory from Saint Augustine to the Renaissance*, 1974.
———. *Medieval Eloquence: Studies in the Theory and Practice of Medieval Rhetoric*, 1978.
———. *Medieval Rhetoric: A Select Bibliography*, 1989.
Preminger, Alex, O. B. Hardison, Jr., and Kevin Kerrane, eds. *Classical and Medieval Literary Criticism: Translations and Interpretations*, 1974.
Spearing, A. C. *Criticism and Medieval Poetry*, 1972.
Stock, Brian. *The Implications of Literacy: Written Language and Models of Interpretation in the Eleventh and Twelfth Centuries*, 1983.
Trimpi, Wesley. *Muses of One Mind: The Literary Analysis of Experience and Its Continuity*, 1983.
Zumthor, Paul. *Toward a Medieval Poetics*, 1972.

WILLIAM NELLES

*See also* Alan of Lille; Saint Augustine; Boccaccio; Chaucer; Dante; Fulgentius; Geoffrey of Vinsauf; Saint Isidore of Seville; Petrarch

# Marcelino Menéndez y Pelayo

Spanish writer and critic

**Born:** Santander, Spain; November 3, 1856
**Died:** Santander, Spain; May 19, 1912

## Biography

Marcelino Menéndez y Pelayo was born in Santander, Spain, on November 3, 1856. His father was Marcelino Menéndez Pintado, a teacher of mathematics. His mother was Jesusa Pelayo, daughter and sister of physicians. Though respectable, the family was of modest means. At an early age Menéndez displayed an extraordinary intelligence and a prodigious memory. After completing secondary school in his native Santander in 1871, he attended the Universidad de Barcelona, transferring to the Universidad de Madrid after two years. Four years later in 1875 when not yet twenty, he completed his doctoral studies in literature there, writing his dissertation on the topic of the novel among Latin writers of the classical period. He impressed his classmates and teachers with his superior erudition, energy, and intelligence. In 1878, in a case without precedent, he won the prestigious chair of Critical History of Spanish Literature at the Universidad de Madrid at the tender age of twenty-one.

During the next several years he published incessantly, earning election to such prestigious bodies as the Royal Spanish Language Academy (1881) and the Royal Spanish Academy of History (1883). His intellectual interests were impressive and wide-ranging. In addition to his many books on literature, philosophy, and aesthetic theory, he wrote a multivolume work on the history of Spanish science and an equally detailed analysis of religious heterodoxy in Spain. Increasingly, because of his firm religious beliefs and his eloquent defense of religious orthodoxy, he became a spokesman for Catholic ideals and institutions at a time when many liberal intellectuals were attacking the Church. After 1884, continuing his academic and scholarly work, he entered the political arena and was elected to represent first Majorca and then Zaragoza in congressional elections. Menéndez y Pelayo became director of the National Library in 1898 and director of the Royal Spanish Academy of History in 1909. He died three years later, in 1912. He never married and left no direct descendants.

## Influence

Menéndez is credited with having been the founder of the modern school of literary criticism in Spain. Dámaso Alonso, himself an eminent critic, asserts that, before Menéndez, literary criticism in Spain not only was chaotic but also was practiced primarily by non-Spaniards. Menéndez's work changed all that by giving the entire enterprise the required discipline and erudition. Menéndez's techniques of literary analysis, which entailed an examination of all internal and external aspects of a work, required the use of extensive historical and documentary materials as essential elements in the understanding of any artistic creation. This emphasis accounts for his reputation as the most eloquent exponent of the method of analysis that became widely accepted as the foundation of modern scholarship in the field of the history of literature. He is believed to have anticipated Benedetto Croce and, in his insistence on the indispensability of examining literature in the light of external and objective historical facts, to have influenced future generations of Spanish historians such as Ramón Menéndez Pidal and Américo Castro.

## Analysis

For some time, Menéndez was much admired for the breadth of his knowledge, his prolific writing, and his role in encouraging serious literary scholarship among his contemporaries in Spain and abroad. Literary scholars began to argue, however, that his writings, copious as they were, did not contain a well-developed and coherent body of ideas that could be regarded as a systematic aesthetic code and the basis on which to build a theory of literary criticism. The skepticism inherent in this position was occasioned by the fact that Menéndez had planned to synthesize his ideas, scattered throughout his many works, into a comprehensive statement, and that he intended for this statement to constitute the closing section of his magisterial *Historia de las ideas estéticas en España* (history of Aesthetic Ideas in Spain). Instead, the multivolume work closed with a discussion of French Romanticism, and readers are left without an explicit treatment of the author's personal aesthetic philosophy.

A reappraisal of Menéndez's ideas has taken place since the 1950 publication by Manuel Olguín of an article arguing that in spite of the lack of a clear and direct statement by Menéndez, his aesthetic ideas permeate his entire work. Olguín proceeds to extract what he believes to be Menéndez's artistic creed. Olguín's insights have been accepted by scholars ever since.

The foundation of Menéndez's aesthetics is the belief that each artistic creation or "aesthetic fact" results from the synthesis of matter and form. Form is both the creative function – the spiritual, free, and universal ideal – and its impact on matter itself. Matter is numerous different things, all reflecting the world of phenomena. It is the materials from the physical world such as words, sounds, and colors that the artist uses for creation. It is also the conceptions and theories from the outside world that are incorporated into a work of art. Last, but not least, matter is the emotional content of that work. An aesthetic fact incorporates the act of creation and the finished product; its form and substance, its spiritual and material elements which, while clearly distinct, cannot be separated.

Equally inseparable are freedom or the agent of creativity (the inspiration that impels an artist to create) and the established precepts and principles of style that give shape to this creativity. Menéndez believes that freedom is essential in the artistic act and that aesthetic creation should be independent, for its own sake, not constrained to serve any other purpose than itself. It should also not reflect the interests of a particular nation, time, class, ideology, or cause. At the same time, he also holds that the artistic fact is not synonymous with absolute freedom, especially with regard to its external elements; even geniuses must work within the established and accepted technical limits of their genre. A finished work of art must reflect the merger of artistic ideology and fact, of ideas and form, striving for a quality that Menéndez terms "ideality." It is achieved, states Olguín,

> only when the artist is capable of becoming immersed in the material reality of life and nature, because it is in that reality alone that the legitimate ideality or universality of art is hidden. Moreover, to be able to discover ideality or universality in the concrete and transitory world of individuality is what constitutes the very core of the artist's activity.

In Menéndez's thought, there is no opposition between realism and idealism in art; the two categories are mutually inclusive. His concept of ideality as the true aim of art accounts for the expression of the universal and ideal with the tools of the concrete.

Menéndez's ideas concerning literary criticism are a direct result of his theory of aesthetics. The appreciation of art is not simply an intellectual act, nor is it a purely emotional one; feeling and judgment should coalesce and interact in exactly the right proportion. Literary critics should be equipped with all the material tools necessary for their task, but they should also possess a set of aesthetic principles that would serve to guide their taste. Olguín summarizes Menéndez's definition of literary criticism as

> the analysis, description, classification, and evaluation of literary works; hence . . . the qualifications of the critic: erudition, artistic sensibility, and an intimate knowledge of the general principles of aesthetics.

Critics, moreover, should not be peripheral characters, nor should their work be merely ancillary. Their work, like the artist's, is in principle creative. They place themselves between the artist and the public. In this role, equipped as they must be with facts and objective knowledge of the circumstances surrounding the creation of a particular work, they must also have some first-hand knowledge of the creative process itself, of the intricacies of the workings of the genre from having practiced it and understood the forces and motives that lead to creative expression. Although critics are not expected to achieve, or to have

achieved, a high level of proficiency in the practice of a particular genre, they are required to have directly experienced the dynamics of the creative process from within. In this light, critics are also artists; their work is not only an erudite and intellectualized reaction to a work of literature or an abstract exercise, but also a creative act in its own right. Literary criticism, like the artistic fact, is an inseparable alliance of matter and form. Menéndez states:

> The first thing that is required to write about art is to have lived intimately with art; to have loved it for its own sake, for the spiritual enjoyment it provides, much more than for its social importance or the polemics it might create; to allow the light of beauty to penetrate the soul, simply and calmly; to exercise personally the artistic fantasy, in which the true critic always participates to some degree; . . . to become proficient in the technical aspects of at least one of the arts, not so much to produce art, as to learn how it is produced, . . . how to tame and defeat the resistance of material elements [in the act of creation].

Menéndez classifies criticism into four categories. Historical criticism examines literary sources and the external factors that accompanied the production of a particular work. Philosophical or high criticism seeks to establish universal principles. External criticism analyzes bibliographic, linguistic, and paleographic elements. Internal criticism, in turn, concentrates on a work's aesthetic merits. Menéndez advocates a system of critical standards wherein all four methods would be integrated. Such a system would avoid the pitfalls and shortcomings associated with each: the excessive focus on social causation of the historical school, which tends to underestimate the role of the individual creator, the tendency among critics to use external techniques of criticism to turn literary history into lists and catalogs, the vagueness of the philosophical school, and the subjectivity of the internalists. Using the best that each has to offer would result in a system in which each would serve to check the excesses of the other and to complement its deficiencies. Literary criticism, then, would be the emotional response of a critic to a piece of work, guided by intimate knowledge of all aspects of that work and tempered by a general philosophy of art.

No discussion of Menéndez's aesthetics would be complete without a brief reference to his attitude toward religion and redemption. While it is clear that he argued against the use of art for any ideological, moral, or political purpose, Menéndez also believed, as Pedro Laín Entralgo has pointed out, that the ideality essential to the artistic fact is perfectly and completely fulfilled in the teachings of Christianity. Christ is the ultimate representation of the aesthetic fact, uniting in His person both the metaphysical and the historical, the ideal and the material.

## Principal criticism

*Estudios críticos sobre escritores montañeses*, 1876
*Horacio en España*, 1877
*Calderón y su teatro*, 1881
*Historia de las ideas estéticas en España*, 1883–1910 (9 volumes)
*Estudios de crítica literaria*, 1884–1908 (5 volumes)
*Orígenes de la novela*, 1905–1915 (4 volumes)
*Estudios sobre el teatro de Lope de Vega*, 1919–1927 (6 volumes)
*Estudios y discursos de crítica histórica y literaria*, 1941–1942
   (7 volumes)

## Other major works and literary forms

Marcelino Menéndez y Pelayo was one of Spain's most prolific authors, producing more than two hundred different titles. When his complete works were published – *Edición nacional de las obras completas de Menéndez Pelayo* (1940–1974) – in an effort supported by the Spanish government, the collection consisted of sixty-seven volumes. Displaying remarkable erudition, he wrote on a variety of subjects, showing a marked preference for literary history, history in general, and the histories of science, philosophy, and religion. He also edited a number of anthologies and produced numerous essays on wide-ranging topics. In the area of creative writing, his output was relatively small; he wrote some poetry but achieved distinction as an academician and learned critic rather than as a creative writer.

NONFICTION
*Historia de los heterodoxos españoles*, 1880–1882 (3 volumes)
*La ciencia española*, 1887–1888 (3 volumes)
*Bibliografía hispanolatina clásica*, 1902 (10 volumes)
*Historia de la poesía castellana en la edad media*, 1911–1961
   (3 volumes)
*Introducción y programa de literatura española*, 1934
*Edición nacional de las obras completas de Menéndez Pelayo*,
   1940–1974 (67 volumes)
*La filosofía española*, 1955

ANTHOLOGY
*Antología de poetas líricos castellanos*, 1890–1906 (10 volumes)

## Further reading

Alonso, Dámaso. *Menéndez Pelayo, crítico literario*, 1956.
Campomar, Marta M. "Menéndez Pelayo and Neo-Catholic Aesthetics in the Nineteenth Century," in *Essays on Hispanic Themes for Gareth Alban Davies*, 1987, pp. 171–192. Edited by C. A. Longhurst.
Laín Entralgo, Pedro. *Menéndez Pelayo*, 1945.
Olguín, Manuel. "Marcelino Menéndez Pelayo's Theory of Art, Aesthetics, and Criticism," in *University of California Publications in Modern Philology*. XXVII (1950), pp. 333–358.
Sainz Rodríguez, Pedro. *Estudios sobre Menéndez Pelayo*, 1984.
Sánchez Reyes, Enrique. *Biografía crítica y documental de Marcelino Menéndez Pelayo*, 1974.
Zulueta, Emilia de. *Historia de la crítica española contemporánea*, 1966.
———. *Menéndez y Pelayo*, 1968.

CLARA ESTOW

*See also* Unamuno y Jugo

# Metaphor

Metaphor is an important and often debated term in several disciplines, namely philosophy and anthropology (the nature of consciousness, the construction of perceived "reality," and the origins of language), psycholinguistics (language and cognition), and literary theory (rhetorical/ poetic trope or figure of speech). In the most general terms, it designates a verbal/symbolic relationship (usually based upon similarity) between two concepts or images which mutually describe or enhance each other; we are able to recognize conceptually (and intuitively) a similarity within dissimilarity or an identity within difference. For example, the sentence "My love [*a*] is a rose [*b*]" suggests that *a* and *b* are related because of perceived similarities (red lips, soft skin, fragrant smell, and so on). It has been customary (since the critical work of I. A. Richards) to speak of *a*, "love," as being the "tenor" of the metaphor and *b*, "rose," as being the "vehicle" of the comparison. Metaphor proper is to be distinguished from a simile (a comparison using the words "like" or "as") and from metaphoric metonymy/ synecdoche (a comparison based not upon similarity but rather on the contiguity or physical proximity of the two objects/one concept being a part of a larger whole, as in the expression "all hands on deck"). Extremely elaborate and extended metaphoric comparisons (as in the poetry of John Donne) have been termed "metaphysical conceits." Since all words or signs (or rather the signifiers of signs) have the potential to be used as metaphors, we speak of the meaning (or what is signified in a sign) as being either literal, that is, the object/concept itself, or figurative, that is, metaphoric.

Metaphor as a philosophical problem of language came to the fore in the nineteenth and twentieth centuries. Many thinkers (Friedrich Nietzsche and Suzanne K. Langer, for example) have argued that metaphor is fundamental to human perception of reality (and not only literary reality); it is, of course, true that metaphoric expressions are commonly found in everyday/nonpoetic discourse (we speak of the metaphoric "leg" of a table or ask metonymically "Give me a hand," for example). Nietzsche even argued that much of everyday speech consists of "frozen" or reified metaphoric expressions which we no longer consciously perceive as being metaphors and which influence our perception of what constitutes the "real." The contemporary deconstructionist philosopher Jacques Derrida has taken Nietzsche a step further by asserting that much of the terminology of Western metaphysics – key words such as "idea" or "essence" – consists of faded or "dead" metaphoric vocabulary. Structuralist poetics also contributed greatly to the discussion of metaphor in the twentieth century. Prague structuralist Roman Jakobson's study of the linguistic behavior of individuals suffering from aphasia (a brain disfunction affecting language behavior) showed two types of language disruption, one in which relations of similarity/contrast or metaphor predominated (similarity disorder) and one in which relations of contiguity/proximity or metonymy were most prevalent (contiguity disorder). Jakobson sought to relate these polarities to central notions of Ferdinand Saussure's structuralist linguistics, namely to the latter's notion that all language/linguistic signs and utterances are generated through processes of selection and combination. From this Jakobson formulated a definition of poetic discourse as the projection of symbolic equivalences based upon selection/combination. The metaphoric mode can be found in Romantic/Symbolist poetry and the metonymic mode in realist/naturalist texts. The French structuralist psychoanalyst Jacques Lacan elaborated these ideas in terms of the structure of the psyche, namely that symptoms of mental disfunction are essentially metaphoric in nature (based on similarity to the cause of the neurosis/psychosis) and that psychic desire is metonymic (based on a continuous psychic displacement of desire itself onto other objects).

Roland Barthes, one of the most provocative of the French structuralist thinkers, examined modern cultural "mythologies" as "poetic" structures with ideological/political implications in his book on bourgeois culture and style *Le Degré zéro de l'écriture* (1953; *Writing Degree Zero*, 1967) and his collection of essays on popular French culture *Mythologies* (1957; *Mythologies*, 1972). All words/signs (sign = signifier + signifed or the word/sign "apple" is made up of the letters "a-p-p-l-e" and the fruit designated or signified by these letters) can take on a metaphoric meaning which can then become a second order signifier itself, that is, it can generate a second order of symbolic or connotative meaning with an independent life of its own. For example, the word "apple" can become a metaphor for the warmth and coziness associated with mother and childhood as in the well-known phrase "Mom's apple pie." This metaphoric sign of "apple (as mother's care)" can then become itself a sign/signifier for the signified concept of the "American democratic way of life," that is, of a particular political and social ideology, or what Barthes calls a modern "myth." Barthes suggested that this second order of symbolic or metaphoric meaning remains essentially invisible to most people and is often confused with the "natural" order of the world. We confuse what is a product of history (language and political/social ideology) with nature (the world as it is in and of itself) and this confusion of history and nature is often used (consciously and unconsciously) to justify the political and social status quo by those in power. Barthes' insight into the ideological nature of metaphor and the perception (or misperception) of "reality" is akin to Nietzsche's view of metaphor "hidden" in everyday language. Barthes' provocative view of metaphor, myth, and literary style takes the topic of metaphor beyond the more traditional area of the study of rhetorical tropes into the broader field of semiotics or the study of signs and the signification process.

## Further reading

Cooper, David E. *Metaphor*, 1986.

Frye, Northrup. *Northrup Frye, Myth and Metaphor: Selected Essays 1974–1988*, 1992.

Highwater, Jamake. *The Language of Vision: Meditations on Myth and Metaphor*, 1995.

Hintikka, Jaako, ed. *Aspects of Metaphor*, 1994.

Lakoff, George, and Mark Johnson. *Metaphors We Live By*, 1983.

——, and Mark Turner. *More than Cool Reason: A Field Guide to Poetic Metaphor*, 1989.

Ortony, Andrew. *Metaphor and Thought*, 1993.

Parker, Gillian S. *An Aesthetic Theory for Metaphor*, 1999.

Sacks, Sheldon, ed. *On Metaphor*, 1979.

Steen, Gerard. *Understanding Metaphor in Literature: An Empirical Approach*, 1994.

Turner, Victor Vitter. *Dramas, Fields, and Metaphors: Symbolic Action in Human Society*, 1975.

THOMAS F. BARRY

*See also* Linguistics and Literary Studies; Metonymy

# Metonymy

A rhetorical device or figure of speech, metonymy is an example of figurative or metaphorical language in general. Figurative language occurs when words signify more than just their literal or "dictionary" meaning. Like all metaphorical language, metonymy presents an association or comparison between two objects. Unlike the simile and the metaphor proper, which involve a comparison of two things based upon the principle of similarity or resemblance, metonymy exploits associations based on the use of cause in place of effect, on contiguity (the physical proximity of the two), or on the use of a part to represent a whole. Synecdoche is a term sometimes used for the latter particular type of metonymy in which the part represents the whole, as in the common expression "Please give me a hand" or speaking of the "crown" or the "throne" when referring to a king or queen. Many philosophers of rhetorical language and literature have expressed dissatisfaction with the terms metaphor, metonymy, and synecdoche because the distinctions among the three concepts are so general and vague that they often become blurred and imprecise. At times what is regarded as a metonymy based on correspondence or contiguity appears to merge with what might be considered a metaphor based upon resemblance in so far as all metonymy is ultimately a device of figurative or metaphoric language in general.

In traditional discussions of literary theory, metonymy was often considered something of a minor (or at least lesser used) figure of speech in comparison with the rather more common device of metaphor proper. This changed somewhat in the twentieth century with the advent of structuralism, especially in the work of the Russian Formalist scholar Roman Jakobson. Jakobson was researching a topic in psycholinguistics (the study of how the mind processes language), namely the speech disorder of aphasia which is usually the result of some kind of brain damage. Patients showed two types of speech problems: one in which "metaphoric" displacements occurred based upon similarity and the other dominated by "metonymic" errors based upon contiguity. For example, when a patient meant to speak of his girlfriend whose lips were a beautiful red he would say "rose," a metaphoric error. Another might say "hat" when he meant to speak of his mother because she was wearing a colorful hat, a metonymic mistake. Jakobson concluded that these aphasic errors pointed to the two fundamental psycholinguistic operations governing all language, namely the act of selection or picking one word from a number of similar possibilities (what the Swiss structuralist Ferdinand de Saussure called the "paradigmatic" axis of language) and the act of combination or putting these words into a spatial order (what Saussure called the "syntagmatic" axis). Jakobson saw these functions as being related to the literary-rhetorical devices of metaphor and metonymy respectively and to entire discourse structures based upon the two, indeed even to the entire structural processes of the mind. He thereby put – correctly or incorrectly – the lesser used notion of metonymy on an equal level with metaphor in terms of the literary criticism of texts. Jakobson and others concluded that whole literary discourse structures – the literature of Romanticism for example – might be characterized as being largely "metaphoric" whereas others – realist literature being one – were predominantly "metonymic." Gustave Flaubert's famous realist novel *Madame Bovary* (1857), for example, does contain an extended and very detailed description of the young Charles Bovary's schoolboy hat that would seem to be a clear instance of metonymy but which, as the narrator Flaubert points out, is, in all its ugly gaudiness and bad taste, a symbol or metaphor of Charles' pedestrian personality. Metonymy is clearly present here but blurs, if not into an example of metaphor proper, then most certainly into figurative or metaphoric language.

Metonymy has now come to be associated – largely due to Jakobson's work – with modernist and postmodernist theory and writing, especially in the works of the British novelist and critic David Lodge and those of the French novelist and critic Alain Robbe-Grillet, the structuralist critic Roland Barthes, and the (post-)structuralist psychoanalyst Jacques Lacan. Modernist and postmodernist literature embraces, as both the legacy and extension of nineteenth-century realist tendencies and the twentieth-century existential movement, a rejection of all illusion – and the symbolizing constructions of all metaphoric language – and hence also a distrust of all notions of "truth" and "meaning." Literary description seems to focus on objects and random details. Robbe-Grillet rejects all metaphoric language because it links human consciousness and the physical world in a "tragic complicity" or a forced sympathy that

suggests a humanization of nature where none actually exists. The natural world in truth *is* independent of human beings and mute to any demands for sympathy. His novels depict a world of "surfaces" in which mute objects exist and which denies any human efforts to insert subjective meaning. Barthes also calls for a literary description – which he called a "zero degree" style – which is "self-reflexive," that is, which points to the fact that literature is above all an attempt to give, indeed to impose, meaning and human subjectivity onto reality. All metaphoric language – metaphor and metonymy – represents for these writers an act of artificiality and also one of the domination of nature. The early works of the Austrian writer Peter Handke are influenced by Barthes and Robbe-Grillet. The short novel *Die Angst des Tormanns beim Elfmeter* (1970; *The Goalie's Anxiety at the Penalty Kick*, 1972), for example, shows a psychotic character whose consciousness and vision is decidedly metonymic: he compulsively gives "meaning" to the random details and objects he encounters, reading the world, as it were, as if it were a "text."

The post-Freudian psychoanalytic theories of Lacan – who argues that the human mind is structured along the lines of language or a linguistic-sign system – take Jakobson's important metaphor/metonymy opposition into the realm of the unconscious. Lacan suggests that the symptomology of psychic disturbance (Sigmund Freud's patients with hysteria, for example) resembles the process of metaphor as one of substitution of one word (or signifier) for another and thus illustrates Freud's idea of displacement. Metonymy points to the origin of desire – the pivotal "want" (or lack of being) within the subjective self – in the unconscious in that its substitution of a part (or signifier) for the whole (the signified) demonstrates the signification process of the fragmented or incomplete self pointing to a whole that is absent or missing, that is "desired" in order to achieve a completeness that is ultimately unattainable. Metonymy in Lacan assumes a privileged position with respect to metaphor in that all symptoms are ultimately grounded in desire.

## Further reading

Cooper, David E. *Metaphor*, 1986.
Culler, Jonathan. *Structuralist Poetics. Structuralism, Linguistics, and the Study of Literature*, 1975.
——. *The Pursuit of Signs. Semiotics, Literature, Deconstruction*, 1981.
Devenyi, Jutka. *Metonymy and Drama. Essays on Language and Dramatic Theory*, 1996.
Hawkes, Terence. *Structuralism and Semiotics*, 1977.
Jameson, Frederic. *The Prisonhouse of Language*, 1972.
Lodge, David. *The Modes of Modern Writing. Metaphor, Metonymy, and the Typology of Modern Literature*, 1977.
Ullmann, Stephan. *Language and Style*, 1964.

THOMAS F. BARRY

*See also* Jakobson; Linguistics and Literary Studies; Lodge; Metaphor

# John Stuart Mill

English writer, critic, and polemicist

**Born:** London, England; May 20, 1806
**Died:** Avignon, France; May 7, 1873

## Biography

John Stuart Mill was born on May 20, 1806, in Pentonville, a district of London, the eldest son of James Mill and Harriet Burrow Mill of Yorkshire. James Mill was a prominent British intellectual and social critic and an associate of Jeremy Bentham, the founder of English utilitarianism. John Stuart Mill's *Autobiography* (1873) describes the education that his father designed for him; by the time Mill was an adolescent, he was multilingual and had acquired an extensive knowledge of ancient, medieval, and modern philosophy, higher mathematics, literature, and history. In 1823, at the age of seventeen, Mill was employed by the British East India Company as an assistant examiner; he remained with India House, eventually attaining the position of chief of the examiner's office (1856), until the dissolution of the British East India Company in 1858.

During his long tenure at India House, Mill produced several book-length studies and hundreds of essays on philosophy, politics, economics, religion, and literature. He emerged as the standard-bearer of English utilitarianism during the period from 1840 to 1870. After his retirement he produced several significant works, including *On Liberty* (1859), *Considerations on Representative Government* (1861), and *Utilitarianism* (1863). Mill was a staunch advocate of political reform; he advanced the cause of female suffrage, called for land reform in Ireland, and expressed his support for Northern abolitionists during the American Civil War. Mill was elected a Member of Parliament from Westminster in 1866. He died on May 8, 1873, at his retirement home in Avignon.

## Influence

Mill extended the philosophical principles and values of utilitarianism to literary subjects. His writings on contemporary and classical literature in the *London and Westminster Review* constituted an influential and provocative contribution to English letters. Throughout his theoretical and critical writings, Mill advanced the cause of freedom and equality.

## Analysis

In one of his earliest (1824) published essays, "Periodical Literature," John Stuart Mill argued that English literature was in need of wide-ranging improvements. While Mill faulted French writers for their preoccupation with sentimentality and declamation, he contended that they were still outdoing their English counterparts. During the next several decades Mill addressed issues on literary theory and criticism in numerous essays; he eventually altered his opinions on the value of French literature. Not surprisingly, the liberal advocate of English utilitarianism was sharply critical of prevailing tastes and embraced a philosophical approach to literature. Mill was concerned with the place of literature in culture; though at all times he measured his world against his criteria for the new utilitarian future, he possessed a fluid intellect and was not averse to changing his mind.

While Mill was in many ways a philosophical futurist, he maintained that the Greek contributions in literature and philosophy were exemplary. In "Early Grecian History and Legend" (1846) and "Grote's *History of Greece*" (1853), he observed that the Greeks laid the foundations of Western civilization and created the basis for high literary culture. It was Mill's hope that the same intellectual and moral forces which transformed the Greeks from barbarians into civilized beings would reemerge to bring European society into a new utilitarian age of liberty and happiness. Literature, especially poetry, was to have an important role in this political and economic revolution.

Mill's writings on poetic theory were quite extensive; most of them were published during the 1830s and 1840s. Drawing on the poetry and criticism of Samuel Taylor Coleridge and William Wordsworth, Mill defined poetry as the expression of emotion which is natural and spontaneous. Poets are those whose spiritual and sensuous ideas are bonded together. Emotion is essential to the poet of nature, who views the world in poetical form and describes it accordingly; "secondary poets" see reality as prose and try to describe it through poetry. Mill noted that the great poet is shaped by both nature and culture. He wrote: "Every great poet, every poet who has extensively or permanently influenced mankind, has been a great thinker . . . has had his mind full of thoughts, derived not merely from passive sensibility, but from trains of reflection, from observation, analysis, and generalization." In this statement, one can detect the philosopher's methodology and, to a degree, the element of detachment that characterized Mill's study of literature. His literary criticism was marked by a certain restrained formality which rendered his literary insights inconclusive. It was political and economic values that were primary for Mill; his literary and aesthetic views were derivative and supportive.

In "Poems and Romances of Alfred de Vigny" (1838), Mill discussed the distinction between a conservative or royalist poet and a liberal or radical poet; the frame of reference is essentially political. The conservative poet is preoccupied with a passion for the past and ascribes value to things and situations which are established, settled, and regulated; his heroes exemplify endurance and self-control, and beauty and virtue are to be found through natural growth arising from fixed habits. The liberal or radical poet has developed a conviction that mankind's future must be shaped by reform and innovation; the liberal poet values the exercise of free will and finds his heroes among those who struggle against the status quo. For the liberal poet, beauty and virtue are active qualities which spring from efforts to effect change – that is, progress in society.

In "Thoughts on Poetry and Its Varieties" (1833), Mill delineated a distinction between poetry and eloquence and argued that nations as well as individuals can be measured by whether they are concerned with poetry or with eloquence. The most significant element in distinguishing eloquence from poetry is the matter of an audience. While eloquence by definition requires an audience, poetry is not concerned with an audience; it flows naturally from the poet's unconscious mind. Mill stated that nations which produce excellent poetry are those which are least dependent upon world approval; nations which excel in eloquence are therefore the least poetical and independent and tend to suffer from insecurity and self-doubt.

Mill offered evaluations of the works of some of the prominent poets of his age. For example, he was critical of Alfred de Vigny's *Eloa: Ou, La Sœur des anges* (1826), which was written in heroic verse. Denouncing the work as excessive – in emotion and in the use of language – and as corrupting the French language's natural rhythm and harmony, Mill concluded that Vigny was not of the first rank of French poets. In his study of Coleridge, Mill recognized that Coleridge was a great poet who had done much to reawaken the dormant intellect and emotions of the English by challenging the establishment and its values at the turn of the nineteenth century. Actually, however, Mill's essays dwelled more on the role of Coleridge as a political and economic philosopher than on his poetic achievement. In that context, Coleridge was judged to have fallen short of the standards of Bentham, whom Mill praised for his disciplined intellect. In a consideration of the early works of Alfred, Lord Tennyson, Mill concluded that, while poetic talent was evident, it was a talent that was in need of nurturing and development.

In 1838 and 1840 Mill published essays on the poetry of Richard Monckton Milnes, a Member of the House of Commons and a participant in the Coleridgian reaction of this period. In his initial essay, Mill appears to have been overwhelmed by the depth and scope of Milnes' poems. Milnes, who was involved in efforts to reform the Anglican church and the rebuilding of the aristocracy, appeared to Mill to transcend contemporary politics and to identify with issues which commanded the attention, if not the allegiance, of all. In his poetry, Milnes stressed the need to view morality as a comprehensive and dynamic force for good; while adhering to the restrictions of the moral code, Milnes laid emphasis on positive obligations for commitment and action. A happy person was one who had developed clarity of vision, arrived at basic tenets of belief, and acted accordingly. To the liberal Mill, Milnes was defining the ideal citizen – the new citizen for the age of utilitarianism. Two years later, in "Milnes's Poetry for the People," however,

Mill denounced Milnes for his poem "Specimens of Poetry for the People." Arguing that the poem had been written in haste and that it was underdeveloped, Mill questioned whether the poem should have been written at all. He was critical of Milnes' style and structure, as well as the philosophical substance of the work; Milnes' poetical arguments in favor of the poor were as disorganized as his style was unpolished.

Mill contended that the essence of fiction was the same as it was for poetry: the truth. While poetry is concerned with the soul, fiction provides an accurate portrayal of life: "Other knowledge of mankind, such as comes to men of the world by outward experience, is not indispensable to . . . poets: but to the novelist such knowledge is all in all; he has to describe outward things, not the inward man; actions and events, not feelings." The union of poetry and fiction, when effected properly, can result in the fullest possible expression of each through drama. The greatness of William Shakespeare's works, according to Mill, resulted from the artistic combination of poetry and fiction.

In addition to poetry and fiction, Mill was concerned with analyzing historical literature and the philosophy of history. Bentham's utilitarianism was predicated on a philosophy of history which was progressive, revolutionary, and antiestablishment; Mill applied this concept of history in his analysis of several contemporary works. Mill studied the arguments on the concept of history advanced by Comte de Saint-Simon, Robert Owen, and Auguste Comte and developed criticisms of the works of Thomas Carlyle, Sir Walter Scott, and George Grote. Mill judged Scott's works to be of little value because they lacked structure and a philosophical base and were designed for popular consumption by an uncritical public. In contrast, Mill praised Grote's multivolume *History of Greece* (1846–1856), despite its stylistic deficiencies and contradictions, because it was structured as a philosophical history.

Throughout his literary and historical studies, Mill was a defender of utilitarian principles and interests. For him, poetry, fiction, drama, and history reached their fullest capacity for good when they promoted human equality and liberty.

## Principal criticism

"Periodical Literature," 1824
"Scott's Life of Napoleon," 1828
"Alison's History of the French Revolution," 1833
"Two Kinds of Poetry," 1833
"What Is Poetry?," 1833
"Thoughts on Poetry and Its Varieties," 1833
"Browning's *Pauline*," 1833
"Writings of Junius Redivivus I," 1833
"Writings of Junius Redivivus II," 1833
"Tennyson's Poems," 1835
"Armand Carrel," 1837
"Poems and Romances of Alfred de Vigny," 1838
"Ware's Letters from Palmyra," 1838
"Milnes's Poems," 1838

"M. de Tocqueville on Democracy in America," 1840
"Coleridge," 1840
"Milnes's Poetry for the People," 1840
"Macaulay's *Lays of Ancient Rome*," 1843
"Michelet's *History of France*," 1844
"Guizot's Essays and Lectures on History," 1845
"Early Grecian History and Legend," 1846
"Grote's *History of Greece*," 1853
"'De l'Intelligence' par H. Taine," 1870

## Other major works and literary forms

In addition to the literary pieces listed above, John Stuart Mill wrote extensively in philosophy, religion, politics, and economics. In his *Utilitarianism* (1863), he attempted to refine Jeremy Bentham's principle of "the greatest happiness of the greatest number." Mill concerned himself with the intellectual issues of his time and advanced in his writings provocative positions on liberty, representative government, and the political rights of women. His *Autobiography* was published posthumously in 1873.

NONFICTION
*A System of Logic*, 1843
*Essays on Some Unsettled Questions in Political Economy*, 1844
*Principles of Political Economy*, 1848
*Dissertations and Discourses*, 1859
*On Liberty*, 1859
*Considerations on Representative Government*, 1861
*Utilitarianism*, 1863
*Examination of Sir William Hamilton's Philosophy*, 1865
*Auguste Comte and Positivism*, 1865
*The Subjection of Women*, 1869
*Autobiography*, 1873
*Three Essays on Religion*, 1874

## Further reading

Abrams, M. H. *The Mirror and the Lamp*, 1958.
Britton, K. W. *John Stuart Mill: Life and Philosophy*, 1969 (second edition).
Glassman, Peter. *J. S. Mill: Evolution of a Genius*, 1985.
Halevy, Elie. *The Growth of Philosophical Radicalism*, 1952 (revised edition).
Hayek, F. A. *John Stuart Mill and Harriet Taylor: Their Friendship and Subsequent Marriage*, 1951.
Packe, Michael St. John. *The Life of John Stuart Mill*, 1954.
Plamenatz, J. *The English Utilitarians*, 1949.
Robson, J. M. "J. S. Mill's Theory of Poetry," in *Mill: A Collection of Critical Essays*, 1969. Edited by J. B. Schneewind.
Skorupski, John, ed. *The Cambridge Companion to Mill*, 1997.
Stafford, William. *John Stuart Mill*, 1999.
Wood, John Cunningham, ed. *John Stuart Mill: Critical Assessments*, 1998.

WILLIAM T. WALKER

*See also* Arnold; Literary Theory in the Age of Victoria; Ruskin

# J. Hillis Miller

## American critic and editor

**Born:** Newport News, Virginia; March 5, 1928

## Biography

Joseph Hillis Miller, Jr., was born on March 5, 1928, in Newport News, Virginia, to Joseph Hillis Miller and the former Nell Critzer. He grew up in upstate New York, where his father was president of Keuka College and then a high official within the state university system. The Protestant upbringing provided by his parents would remain influential. In 1949 he married Dorothy Marian Jones, with whom he had three children.

Miller earned his B.A. at Oberlin College in 1948, before attending graduate school at Harvard University. He was awarded an M.A. in 1949 and a Ph.D. in 1952. From Harvard, Miller went to Williams College as an instructor in English, before moving to The Johns Hopkins University, where he taught from 1953 to 1972. During these years Miller's critical writing reflected the influence of a colleague, phenomenologist Georges Poulet.

When the works of Jacques Derrida and Paul de Man convinced Miller of the ultimate impossibility of language to achieve the goal of communion between consciousnesses, Miller became a deconstructionist. He turned his talents at close textual reading to finding those places in the text itself which undercut or otherwise hindered the development of univocal meaning. In 1972 he transferred to Yale University. There he became famous, along with Geoffrey H. Hartman, de Man, and Harold Bloom, as one of the Yale deconstructionist critics. By 1979 he had become Frederick W. Hilles Professor of English and professor of comparative literature. In the fall of 1986 Miller joined the department of English and comparative literature of the University of California at Irvine.

## Influence

Miller's impact on American literary theory and practice derives largely from his ability to fuse European theory with Anglo-American literary practice. In his preface to the paperback edition of *The Disappearance of God* (1965), after commenting on his use of European phenomenology, Miller says,

> The happiest result would be the creation of another indigenous criticism, one assimilating the advances of European criticism in the past twenty years, but reshaping these to our peculiarly American experience of literature and its powers.

As phenomenologist or as deconstructivist, Miller demonstrates the application of literary theory to the analysis of literary texts based upon close reading of particular texts.

While determining the identifying characteristic of an author's consciousness or denoting the hindrances to meaning within a text, he validates the American assumption of the uniqueness of each author and of each of the author's works.

During the 1960s he was influential in expanding the interests of American criticism beyond the self-imposed limits of New Criticism by analyzing the entire corpus of an author's work rather than a single poem or novel. As the preeminent spokesman for deconstruction during the 1970s, Miller was instrumental in familiarizing the American academy with its assertions and methods. Again, he shows how application of the theory to individual works contributes to an understanding of the complexity of the meaning of the work.

## Analysis

"It seemed to me when I began the study of literature, as it still seems to me now, that one of the most obvious characteristics of works of literature is their manifest strangeness as integuments of words." So Miller declares in his sixth major book of literary criticism, *Fiction and Repetition*. From an early training in science, he retains the attitude of seeing things as problems to be solved. Thus his career has been a process of trying out different literary theories – New Criticism, phenomenology, deconstruction – to find one that best accounts for the strangeness of literature itself or for the uniqueness of any particular novel or poem. In the movement from each theory to the next, he carries whatever remains of value from the earlier to the later approach. Among the assumptions of New Criticism that Miller retains are commitments to "account for the totality of a given work" and to close reading of the text as the first step toward this accounting.

Unsatisfied with the New Critical or formalist devotion to the text as a product to be explicated without reference to its external context, Miller found in the phenomenology of the Geneva School of critics of consciousness a theoretical basis for extending the realm of interpretation. In the preface to *The Disappearance of God*, Miller asserts that

> the comprehension of literature takes place through a constant narrowing and expansion of the focus of attention, from the single work of an author, to the whole body of his works, to the spirit of the age, and back again in a contraction and dilation which is the living motion of interpretation.

This shifting back and forth among the words of the text, to other texts of the author, to the literary, social, historical, or philosophical context of the writer serves as the general method of Miller's first five books, all written from the perspective of phenomenology. In these books, Miller attempts to identify the particular set of characteristics of vision that defines the consciousness of the author under study.

A basic assumption is that each major author is unique and that this individuality is a function of the relationships among the particular images and ideas that form his or her consciousness. Since consciousness is revealed through words, close reading of the text remains as important to Miller as it is to any New Critic. A novel then becomes "the embodiment in words of a certain very special way of experiencing the world." The task of the critic becomes one of assimilating the consciousness of the author by interpreting the words of the text. "Through the analysis of all the passages, as they reveal the persistence of certain obsessions, problems, and attitudes, the critic can hope to glimpse the original unity of a creative mind."

Whereas the traditional formalist approaches the text as a finished work of art, Miller approaches it as a process. He sees the text "not as a product of a preexistent psychological condition, but as the very means by which a writer apprehends and, in some measure, creates himself." These attempts at self-definition continue as long as the author continues to write. Consequently, the critic must not stop with the analysis of one particular work but must, as in Miller's books on Charles Dickens and Thomas Hardy, analyze the entire corpus of the author in order to achieve the goal of comprehending as thoroughly as possible the consciousness of the author.

Nor is the novel or poem a mere product of its age, but rather a factor in the defining of the spirit of the age. Miller consistently explores the relationships between the words of the text and their various contexts in the belief that meaning is a function of these relationships. *The Disappearance of God, Poets of Reality*, and *The Form of Victorian Fiction* all focus on the relationship between the consciousness of particular authors and the spirit of the age. In these books, Miller identifies the "cogito," the center or origin of the unity of the author's consciousness, with his or her sense of the absence or death of God. The Romantic writers Thomas De Quincey, Robert Browning, Emily Brontë, Matthew Arnold, and Gerard Manley Hopkins strive to reestablish a symbolic connection between transcendent being and their natural environment. The novelists of realism replace transcendence with intersubjectivity, a vision of society as a pattern of consciousnesses. This intersubjectivity culminates in a generalized Victorian consciousness for which the narrator becomes the spokesman. *Poets of Reality* extends the investigation into the twentieth century through the consciousnesses of Joseph Conrad, William Butler Yeats, T. S. Eliot, Dylan Thomas, Wallace Stevens, and William Carlos Williams as they encounter the concept of nihilism and work their ways through it to a sense of presence, or unity, with the natural world.

> The unity of twentieth century poetry is suggested by the fact that these authors are in the end poets not of absence but of proximity. In their work reality

comes to be present to the senses, present to the mind which possesses it through the senses, and present in the words of the poems which ratify this possession.

During his phenomenological stage then, for Miller, words were translucent; interpreting the words of a text would lead to an understanding of an author's concept of reality. In *The Form of Victorian Fiction*, however, Miller noted that the novelists came to change their notion of society as "a system in which each element has a center and foundation outside itself to a view of it as a system which founds itself, as a sentence generates its own meaning." The change of assumptions from phenomenology to deconstruction is a change of assumption about the nature of language. The phenomenological Miller thought that language was essentially referential, a mirror, if not of reality, at least of the consciousness of the author. The deconstructive Miller sees language as reflexive and therefore ultimately indeterminate. Miller was able to go over to deconstruction so readily because Derrida and de Man were able to present the nonreferentiality of language so that, for him, phenomenology was no longer tenable.

As a deconstructionist, Miller sees that meaning in the novel or poem is generated by the relationship among the words that compose the work rather than by reference to an external reality. The effects and their causes are linguistic and therefore located within the text rather than in the consciousness of the mind of the author or critic. The subject of literature becomes language itself. In "Arachne's Broken Woof," Shakespeare's plays become profound explorations of "the possibilities inherent in the English language as it inherits the concepts, figures, and stories of Occidental culture." Made up of words, literary texts exemplify the indeterminacy of language. Indeterminacy means "the alternation between specific possible meanings between which the text doesn't allow a decision." Miller's preferred term for this is "heterogeneity." There is no right reading of the text, but there are deeper or more complex readings. The best readings would seem to be those that take into account the most ambiguities, or assertions and denials, just as the greatest works of literature are those that embody these complexities.

The best readings will be the ones which best account for the heterogeneity of the text, its presentation of a definite group of possible meanings which are systematically interconnected, determined by the text, but logically incompatible.

Miller applies his close reading techniques to the tracing of figures of speech and other rhetorical patterns in search of instances of aporia, or breakdown in meaning, to show the ultimate heterogeneity of the text. A deconstructive reading is not applied to the text from an external source but is intrinsic to the text itself. "Deconstruction is not a dismantling of the structure of a text but a demonstration that it has already dismantled itself." The text dismantles itself because it contains elements that cannot be reconciled with one another. In *The Linguistic Moment*, Miller finds patterns of "irreconcilable self-contradiction" in the poetry of major poets writing in English, from William Wordsworth to Williams and Stevens. For each poet the contradiction may be different, but it is expressed at that point in the poem which Miller identifies as the "linguistic moment": "the moment when language becomes problematic and assumes a momentum of its own" and therefore undercuts the mimetic or hermeneutic grounds of meaning. In *Fiction and Repetition*, he advances a theory of narrative based on two opposing types of repetition, one mimetic, or based on similarity, the other based on difference, both active within any story. The presence of these logically incompatible patterns of repetition is the source of the heterogeneity of the novels he discusses. Similarly, the combination of the technique of close reading with the study of tropes reveals the absence of any determining ground for absolute meaning. The text is always open to both closed and open readings because figures of speech work both ways, to support a single meaning and to deny one at the same time; they assert similarity and difference simultaneously. Miller systematically extends his project to reconfigure the traditional critical approaches to the novel in particular and narrative in general through four books: *Ariadne's Thread*, *Illustration*, *Topographies*, and *Reading Narrative*. Through the application of such tropes as catachresis, personification, anastomosis, and anacoluthon to a wide variety of texts, he deconstructs the practices of interpretation through the tracing of patterns of imagery or action, character, interpersonal relations, setting, ideology, and plot. The task of the critic is, then, not to discover one all-explaining meaning but to explore as many of the movements toward meaning as is feasible. Daniel R. Schwarz has said that "the great value of Miller's work is to teach us that the centre may be elusive or inexplicable or both."

In *The Ethics of Reading* and *Versions of Pygmalion*, Miller explores how the radical indeterminacy of works of literature demands personal responsibility of both writer and reader for the interpretation of the text. His belief in the heterogeneity of texts puts him at odds with critics who approach literature from the point of view of political, theological, psychological, or other ideologies. This is the argument behind *The Ethics of Reading*.

Without the rhetorical study of literature, focused on language, its laws, what it is, and what it can do, particularly on the role of figurative language in interfering with the straightforward working of grammar and logic, we can have no hope of understanding just what the role of literature might be in society, in history, and in individual human life.

The "strangeness" of literary language in Miller's terms saves literature from being reduced to ideology.

## Principal criticism
*Charles Dickens: The World of His Novels*, 1958
*The Disappearance of God: Five Nineteenth Century Writers*, 1963
*Poets of Reality: Six Twentieth Century Writers*, 1965
*The Form of Victorian Fiction: Thackeray, Dickens, Trollope, George Eliot, Meredith, and Hardy*, 1968
*Thomas Hardy: Distance and Desire*, 1970
*Fiction and Repetition: Seven English Novels*, 1982
*The Linguistic Moment: From Wordsworth to Stevens*, 1985
*The Ethics of Reading: Kant, de Man, Eliot, Trollope, James, and Benjamin*, 1986
*Versions of Pygmalion*, 1990
*Ariadne's Thread: Story Lines*, 1992
*Illustration*, 1992
*Topographies*, 1995
*Reading Narrative*, 1998
*Black Holes*, 1999

## Other major works and literary forms
J. Hillis Miller has written many articles, essays, and reviews in addition to the books listed above. He clarifies his version of deconstruction in reviews. It was his review of M. H. Abrams' *Natural Supernaturalism: Tradition and Revolution in Romantic Literature* (1971) that dramatized the conflict between deconstructive and traditional literary theory and sparked the sharp critical debate in literary journals during the 1970s. Miller served as the principal proponent of deconstruction throughout this debate. Miller's renowned reply to Abrams' response took its final form as "The Critic as Host," Miller's contribution to *Deconstruction and Criticism* (1979; edited by Harold Bloom and others). The exigencies of debate spurred Miller to publish as articles in literary journals what would become chapters in his books. Among the most significant for literary theory are "Stevens' Rock and Criticism as Cure," which appeared in *The Georgia Review*, and "Ariadne's Thread: Repetition and the Narrative Line," in *Critical Inquiry*.

EDITED TEXTS
*Dickens Criticism: Past, Present, and Future Direction*, 1962 (with others)
*The Act of the Mind: Essays on the Poetry of Wallace Stevens*, 1965 (with Roy Harvey Pearce)
*William Carlos Williams: A Collection of Critical Essays*, 1966
*Aspects of Narrative: Selected Papers from the English Institute*, 1971
*The Well-Beloved*, by Thomas Hardy, 1976

## Further reading
Atkins, G. Douglas. "J. Hillis Miller, Deconstruction, and the Recovery of Transcendence," in *Reading Deconstruction – Deconstructive Reading*, 1983.
Cain, William E. "Deconstruction in America: The Literary Criticism of J. Hillis Miller," in *The Crisis in Criticism: Theory, Literature, and Reform in English Studies*, 1984.

Lawall, Sarah N. *Critics of Consciousness: The Existential Structures of Literature*, 1968.
Leitch, Vincent B. "The Lateral Dance," in *Deconstructive Criticism: An Advanced Introduction and Survey*, 1982.
Moynihan, Robert. *A Recent Imagining: Interviews with Harold Bloom, Geoffrey Hartman, Paul de Man, J. Hillis Miller*, 1986.
Pease, Donald. "J. Hillis Miller: The Other Victorian at Yale," in *The Yale Critics: Deconstruction in America*, 1983. Edited by Johnathan Arac, et al.
Salusinszky, Imre. "J. Hillis Miller," in *Criticism in Society*, 1987.
Schwarz, Daniel R. "The Fictional Theories of J. Hillis Miller: Humanism, Phenomenology, and Deconstruction in *The Form of Victorian Fiction* and *Fiction and Repetition*," in *The Humanistic Heritage: Critical Theories of the English Novel from James to Hillis Miller*, 1986.

WILLIAM McDONALD

*See also* Deconstruction; deMan; Phenomenological Criticism

# Mimesis

In general terms, mimesis (from the Greek for "imitation" or "representation") refers to the relationship between a work of literature and the world – more specifically, to the degree to which a text can be seen as reflecting "reality."

The analysis of mimesis begins with Plato. In the tenth book of his *Republic* (388–368 B.C.), Plato explains that the purpose of a painting or a literary work is not to imitate reality but rather to represent the artist's or writer's perception of reality in an aesthetically pleasing manner. It would be arrogant for a writer to claim that he or she has presented reality as it actually is for all human beings. Plato illustrates the meaning of "mimesis" by indicating that a skilled painter could produce a portrait of a carpenter which would convey to viewers an "idea" of what a carpenter might well look like. In this same passage from the *Republic* (596b), Plato adds that a painter does not need to have any knowledge about carpentry in order to produce an effective portrait of a carpenter. We do not even need to know the model's identity. The person who poses for this portrait need not even be a carpenter because it is the "idea" of what a carpenter should look like which is more important than what this artist's model actually looks like. By its very nature, the meaning of "truth" will vary from one person to another, from one generation to another, and from one society to another. Artistic and literary works which convey different levels of meaning and different types of pleasure to a wide variety of readers and viewers enrich our lives by helping us to understand more deeply what our daily experiences and our personal perceptions of reality mean to us individually. Plato argues that it is not relevant to criticize artistic or literary works because they are not accurate representations of what actually happened at a certain historical moment. It would be foolish, for example, to criticize *The Iliad* by arguing that this epic was untruthful because it depicted historical events which never occurred and mythological characters who never existed. The Trojan War may, in fact, have never taken place and the characters in this epic never existed, but such comments would be irrelevant for a reader of Homer's masterpiece. Homer presented very effectively profound psychological truths by his profound analysis of how very diverse characters react to the horrors of a lengthy and unnecessary war.

The concept of mimesis was further developed by Aristotle, for whom "imitation" was a central feature of all the arts. Typical of his extensive use of the concept is his definition of tragedy as the "imitation of an action," in this case the fall of a noble man or woman. In his *Poetics* (c. 334–323 B.C.), Aristotle also states that different literary genres require different forms of "mimesis," in other words should reflect different aspects of life – hence comedies should represent characters from the lower classes, whereas tragedy should represent characters from the higher social orders. Aristotle's concept of mimesis was to have a profound effect on the development of literary theory and criticism.

The concept of "mimesis" later became a central tenet of literary criticism in such important theoretical works as Horace's *Art of Poetry* (c. 17 B.C.) and Erasmus' *The Ciceronian* (1528). Horace, Erasmus, and Latin literary critics referred to "mimesis" as "imitatio." The use such writers make of "imitatio" also reflects a profound change in the concept, now referring not only to the "imitation" of the world, but also to the imitation of classical models. This shift in meaning, which brought a new significance and subtlety to the concept, became a central feature of classically inspired theories of literature. The change in meaning can be clearly seen in *The Ciceronian*, where Erasmus distinguishes between servile and creative "imitatio." In this witty dialogue, he ridicules a pedant named Nosoponus, who admires Cicero so much that he uses in his own Latin sentences only those words found in Cicero's extant works. Erasmus argues that a true "imitatio" of Cicero's works would require us to adapt his style and arguments to treat contemporary concerns.

Although the term "mimesis" and its Latin equivalent "imitatio" remained in common usage in literary criticism for centuries, the word "mimesis" (with its emphasis on the relationship between a work and the world it reflects) acquired a new prominence with the publication of Erich Auerbach's book *Mimesis: The Representation of Reality in Western Literature*, first in the original German in 1946 and then in an English translation by Willard Trask in 1953. The twenty chapters in this extraordinary book explore the subtle artistry by which such diverse writers as Homer, Michel Eyquem de Montaigne, William Shakespeare, Miguel de Cervantes, and Virginia Woolf express in their own voices their understanding of the diversity of the human condition. Each chapter begins with a lengthy quotation of a specific text by a famous writer. Auerbach then presents a detailed stylistic analysis of each text and shows how each text reveals profound insights into both the originality of each writer's contribution to the representation of the evolving nature of his or her society and the importance of that specific writer in the literary movement or historical moment in which the work was created. Auerbach shows that a detailed analysis of the skill by which a writer expresses the effect of significant social changes on fictional characters can lead readers to appreciate more thoroughly both the literary talents of that writer and the evolving nature of many different societies and cultures. Stylistic analysis, as developed so creatively by Auerbach, is inseparable from reflections on social changes. Objective historical studies may well enable us to see the big picture and appreciate how traumatic events such as civil war and revolution can disrupt an entire country, but Auerbach suggests that the artistic "imitation" or "representation" of such major social transformations in works of fiction, plays, or poems can truly enable us to appreciate at a very personal level how such changes transformed the lives of ordinary people. Readers may feel detached from historical treatises about distant events which may not seem relevant to their daily lives, but a skillfully created work of fiction can enable them to see beyond dated social conventions in order to understand the portrayal of universal human experiences with which we can still identify.

## Further reading

Aristotle. *Poetics.*
Auerbach, Erich. *Mimesis: The Representation of Reality in Western Literature*, 1946 (English translation, 1953).
Golden, Leon. *Aristotle on Tragic and Comic Mimesis*, 1992.
Janaway, Christopher. *Images of Excellence: Plato's Critique of the Arts*, 1995.
Levine, George, ed. *Realism and Representation: Essays on the Problem of Realism in Relation to Science, Literature, and Culture*, 1993.
Lyons, John, and Stephen G. Nichols, Jr., eds. *Mimesis: From Method to Mirror, Augustine to Descartes*, 1982.
Mitchell, W. J. T. "Representation," in *Critical Terms for Literary Study*, 1990. Edited by Frank Lentricchia and Thomas McLaughlin.
Plato. The tenth book of his *Republic.*
Verdenius, W. J. *Mimesis: Plato's Doctrine of Artistic Imitation and its Meaning to Us*, 1962.

EDMUND J. CAMPION

*See also* Aristotle; Auerbach; Realism

# Antonio Minturno

(Antonio Sebastiani)

Italian critic and scholar

**Born:** Traetto, Italy; 1500
**Died:** Crotone, Italy; c. 1574

## Biography

Born Antonio Sebastiani in 1500, Minturno followed the usage of the Humanists by assuming the Roman name of his native town of Traetto. Before becoming Bishop of Ugenta in 1559, he had lived and studied in various Italian cities, chiefly Naples, sometimes as the disciple of the Aristotelian scholar Agostino Nifo and sometimes in the service of various noblemen. He was elected to the Academio Pontaniono in 1526, called to the University of Rome by Julius III in 1551, and sent on a mission to the Council of Trent in 1553. It has been argued that the atmosphere of the Counter-Reformation can be seen in the moralistic tone of Minturno's criticism and in his distaste for the "barbarous" style of the romance. Transferred to the see of Crotone in 1565, he is believed to have died in 1574.

## Influence

In judging Minturno's influence, one should keep in mind that he lived during a time of crucial change in the history of European criticism; one could say that this period saw the beginnings of modern European criticism. Well into the sixteenth century little was known of Aristotle's *De poetica* (c. 334–323 B.C.; *Poetics*), and what was known came by way of a confused and incomplete version of Averroës' commentary. Two crucial events helped bring the *Poetics* to the attention of scholars: the first printing of Aristotle's Greek text (1508) and the appearance of translations into Latin (1498) and Italian (1549). Of the numerous commentaries and expansions that followed, Minturno's *Arte poetica* (art of poetry) was one of the first. Minturno's influence is difficult to separate from the influence of other Italian Renaissance critics, especially Lodovico Castelvetro and J. C. Scaliger, but the ultimate effect of the commentaries was to establish Aristotle (along with Horace) as the supreme authority on criticism until the end of the eighteenth century. The specific influence of Minturno can be seen in the work of Sir Philip Sidney in England and Jean Vauquelin de La Fresnaye in France.

## Analysis

When adapting the system of Aristotle's *Poetics* for the criticism of modern literature, Minturno was faced with two problems. First, the *Poetics* says little or nothing about any genres other than the narrative and dramatic forms, and second, there already existed in modern literature recognized masterpieces which did not fit the system (or at least

did not fit the mechanical rules which most of the Renaissance and neoclassical critics seemed to think were the essence of Aristotle). The first problem could be met by the expansion and interpretation of Aristotle. The second could have led, but seldom did, to the rejection of Aristotle; it could have led to the rejection of the moderns or of those aspects of their art which did not follow classical precedent; or it could have led to various compromises and rationalizations in which the modern ways were somehow proved compatible with Aristotle after all. This last solution was generally the way of English critics such as John Dryden – and the Italian Torquato Tasso, too, when, in *Gerusalemme liberato* (1581; *Jerusalem Delivered*, 1600), he elected to use the romance materials popularized by Ludovico Ariosto but with a form based on Aristotle and Homer.

Minturno wrote two massive treatises in dialogue form: *De poeta libri sex*, written in Latin and amounting to more than five hundred pages, and *Arte poetica*, written in Italian and amounting to more than four hundred pages (Minturno sometimes called it "*Della toscano poesia*," of Tuscan poetry). The material from the *Poetics* is expanded, first by the use of Horace (who is accepted as an authority equal to Aristotle), then by Plato, and finally by the rhetorical writers Quintilian and Cicero (though here poetic is no longer subordinated to rhetoric as it had been by some earlier writers). On one point Minturno may be thought to deviate from Aristotle, who was anything but didactic in his theory of criticism. Minturno follows Horace's idea that poetry should please and instruct (*delectare* and *prodesse*), though often he uses a formulation taken from Cicero's rhetoric: "*docere, delectere, movere*" (touch, please, and move – or transport). It was the Horatian formula which was generally accepted by later critics, but the occasional use of "move" perhaps encouraged an emotional concept of poetry. Another key term used by Minturno and some English critics was *admiratio* (admiration), which might be used to justify the incredible. As might be expected given Minturno's clerical character, the moral element was emphasized: poetry can provide consolation in misfortune and drive out noxious passions.

On the key Aristotelian element of imitation, Minturno offers an interpretation which greatly expands the subject matter of poetry from Aristotle's "imitation of action" to include "life and manners," "the semblances of all things public and private," and "all kinds of doctrine, all the arts, all varieties of writings." Equally flexible is his manner of classifying the genres. Poems are of three kinds: epic, scenic (dramatic), and melic (lyric). More important, each type can be divided according to whether the persons depicted are humble, great and serious, or in between, so that pastoral poetry, with its humble characters, becomes a species of epic, while Virgil's *Georgics* (c. 37–29 B.C.) and similar "instructions about things" become epics of the intermediate class. There would even be a place here for the novel, except that Minturno, following Aristotle in making fiction rather than verse the defining character of poetry, in the end rejects the use of prose as contrary to the practice of the ancients. (Neither he nor any other critic of the time had any such concept as "literature.")

Minturno may seem to have offered a very flexible interpretation of Aristotle, but he was rigid in two respects. First, he accepted literally the "rules" Aristotle (and Horace) gave for constructing the plots of the major genres. Second, where rules were not laid down by Aristotle, Minturno insisted on following the practice of the ancient poets. Even Ovid, with his "wonderful power of arrangement," "does not merit the name of poet," since he does not follow Aristotle's rules for the epic plot.

Considering Italian tastes at this time, one sees why Minturno would dismiss Ariosto's *Orlando furioso* (1516–1532; English translation, 1591), for in his sequel to Matteo Maria Boiardo's *Orlando innamorato* (1483, 1495; Roland in love), Ariosto had used the materials of medieval romance, the product of "crude and barbarous writers." (Here, some historians have seen evidence of Minturno's Counter-Reformation prejudices.) Minturno does not believe, however, that the material is absolutely unacceptable, for he gives suggestions as to how Ariosto might have arranged his episodes better. What barbarians cannot do, apparently, is create a new kind of art to replace Aristotle and Horace; they may have had "the light of nature," but natural endowment without art does not make a perfect work.

Like the neoclassical critics, Minturno holds that nature and art are always and everywhere the same, however they may differ in "accidental qualities." According to Minturno, the universal practice in his time was to follow the ancients in all the arts (which included medicine and military affairs), for "truth is one, and that which is once true must of necessity be always true." Minturno cannot deny that Ariosto was a most excellent poet and was using materials worthy of epic poetry in a language capable of any subject, but his poetry was not of the kind that Aristotle and Horace taught. In effect, Ariosto had made not only knights but also poetry itself "errant." What Ariosto had done was to have not one hero but many, not one action but many. Minturno does allow for a number of episodes, provided that all are subordinated to one central action, as episodes in Homer's *Iliad* (c. 800 B.C.) are subordinated to the central episode of the wrath of Achilles.

Tragedy and comedy provided less controversy than the epic, since Italian drama had produced no Shakespeare to challenge the rules of Aristotle, but there is something of interest in Minturno's "ethico-medical" theory of catharsis. The spectacle of great men thrown into unhappiness teaches one not to put trust in worldy things and to endure misfortune with a patient spirit. Minturno interprets Aristotle to mean that pity and fear in art drive out more than pity and fear: they drive out all unrestrained passions. Thus, the poet

is like a physician who uses poisonous medicine to cure an illness. As for comedy, following both the precept of Aristotle and the practice of the ancients, Minturno argues that the comic dramatists, who invent names as the characters and the subject require, are the most universal and hence the most philosophical of poets.

Whatever his precise influence, Minturno gave an early version of what was later known as neoclassicism, which originated in Italy and was adopted by the French and later by the English critics. Minturno, like the neoclassicists, deserted Aristotle to accept Horace's moralistic definition of the function of poetry. He followed Aristotle in viewing poetry as imitation and in seeing imitation – though here he is somewhat ambiguous – as dealing less with truth than with things like the truth. He followed Aristotle in putting much emphasis on genres, and although he in effect multiplied Aristotle's genres by subdivision and by admitting the imitation of things other than actions, he limited his conception of genre by insisting on the rules and the purity of genres. By accepting Ariosto's material and rejecting his form, Minturno fostered a conception of the epic which was followed by Tasso and John Milton. He accepted the general conception of poetry as resulting from genius and art, while perhaps playing down the element of genius. The system was still alive, although under siege, two hundred years after his death.

## Principal criticism
*De poeta libri sex*, 1559
*Arte poetica*, 1563

## Other major works and literary forms
While Antonio Minturno is chiefly remembered for his critical works, he was also a voluminous writer in prose and verse. His Petrarchan lyrics and Virgilian eclogues were less valued than his biblical poetry and his epigrams. More interesting were his pastoral novel *L'Amore innamorato* (1559; love in love) and his correspondence, collected in the volume *Lettere* (1549; letters). The variety of his creative works is significant, as he greatly expanded Aristotle's list of genres.

NOVEL
*L'Amore innamorato*, 1559

POETRY
*Rime e prose*, 1559

NONFICTION
*Lettere*, 1549

## Further reading
Gilbert, Alan H., ed. *Literary Criticism: Plato to Dryden*, 1940.
Hathaway, Baxter. *The Age of Criticism: The Late Renaissance in Italy*, 1962.
Krailsheimer, A. J. ed. *The Continental Renaissance, 1500–1600*, 1971.

Saintsbury, George. *A History of Criticism and Literary Taste in Europe*, 1902.
Weinberg, Bernard. *A History of Literary Criticism in the Italian Renaissance*, 1961.

JOHN C. SHERWOOD

*See also* Castelvetro; Giraldi Cinthio; Renaissance and Restoration Literary Theory; Trissino

# Modern Literary Theory

## From the New Criticism to the New Pragmatism

Modern literary theory began with an effort by English and American critics to understand and to justify literature as a type of discourse essentially different from other types of discourse, such as those used by the physical and social sciences. Although it may appear obvious that a poem or a story differs from a psychological case history or a scientific report, the distinction is not so clear-cut; both kinds of discourse can use the same words and sometimes even the same sentence patterns, and both kinds of discourse make statements about some phenomenon – sometimes the same phenomenon. For example, a book on the history of whaling in New England may make some of the same kinds of statements that *Moby Dick* makes.

Most readers, however, agree that the purpose to which language is put in poetry is different than the purpose to which it is put in a psychological report. Moreover, most readers believe that the statements a novel makes refer to something different from the statements a history book makes; whereas the first refers to a "made-up" world, the second refers to a "real" world. Finally, most readers think that the effects of statements in a scientific or historical discourse are different from the effects of statements in poetry.

Such issues are not as simple as they were once thought to be. Indeed, before the beginning of modern literary theory, literature was often believed to be secondary to other verbal forms; literary works were studied as historical documents or for their social content or philosophical themes. Modern literary theory, beginning primarily with the great modernist British poet and critic T. S. Eliot, changed all that forever.

To be sure, not everyone before Eliot believed that literature, particularly poetry, used language the way other verbal forms did. For example, the nineteenth-century British poet and critic Samuel Taylor Coleridge noted that poetry differed in an essential way from other kinds of language use, for its purpose is a unique kind of pleasure which results from the reader's perception of the intrinsic unity of all of its parts. In the United States, Edgar Allan Poe argued strongly that both poems and short tales depended on a highly unified structure to communicate their singular effect. This point of view became even more pronounced at the end of the nineteenth century with the advent, especially in England and Europe, of the so-called aesthetic school of poetry, which insisted that a poem was important for its own sake, not because it contained important ideas.

## Modernism

Actually, what Eliot contributed to this development of a particularly "modern" notion of literature was a group of critical pronouncements about literature's uniqueness which crystallized the views of other poets and thinkers. For example, Eliot suggested that art is more concerned with emotional expression than with the logical ideas on which other verbal forms focused; furthermore, Eliot argued, the only way of expressing emotion in literature is by means of a verbal "objective correlative," a set of objects, a situation, or a chain of events which, even though it seemed to be made up of mere concrete, sensory details, served as a verbal equivalent of the emotion. This idea that poetry communicated meaning by means of concrete detail rather than by means of abstractions was an important step in the critical effort to establish that poetry used language in a distinct way.

Eliot's perception that the language of poetry was unique was soon followed by the arguments of British critic I. A. Richards that the kinds of "statements" poetry used were different than those in other forms of discourse. In *Science and Poetry* (1926, 1935), Richards noted that although poetry does make statements, they are not statements that have to be verified as they do in scientific forms; they are instead "pseudostatements," which are justified not because they correspond to facts but rather because they serve the attitudes of the speaker or organize the attitudes of the reader. The "truth" of poetry is relative to the perspective of the speaker; it does not depend on a correspondence to that which it seems to refer.

## The new criticism

These and other ideas of Eliot and Richards found their way into American criticism primarily as a result of the enthusiasm and efforts of a small group of teachers and students at Vanderbilt University in Tennessee. Led by John Crowe Ransom, a young faculty member at Vanderbilt, the group included Donald Davidson, Allen Tate, Robert Penn Warren, and Cleanth Brooks. Although Ransom was the first to use the term "New Criticism" in a book of that name in 1941, the circulation of the central ideas of what has also been called "formalist," "contextual," or "objective" criticism was mainly a result of the publication of two highly influential literature textbooks by Brooks and Warren: *Understanding Poetry: An Anthology for College Students* (1938) and *Understanding Fiction* (1943). In addition to these texts, other books important to the development of the New Critical approach were Ransom's *The World's Body* (1938), Tate's *Reason in Madness:*

*Critical Essays* (1941), Brooks's *The Well Wrought Urn: Studies in the Structure of Poetry* (1947), and William K. Wimsatt, Jr.'s *The Verbal Icon: Studies in the Meaning of Poetry* (1954).

The most basic and pervasive assumption of the New Criticism was that the meaning of a work is not equivalent to what the artist "intended" when he wrote it, for poetic language is so highly connotative that the ultimate meaning of a work of art exceeds any original intention. To get at a work's meaning, the reader had to engage in a close analytical reading of the work itself. In fact, as Ransom said, a poem should be "nearly anonymous," for even though it has the poet's name attached to it, it should represent him not as he is in real life but rather as a sort of idealized fictitious personality. This notion gave rise to the widespread tactic of New Critical readers to determine the "persona," or dramatized speaker, of the poem before attempting to understand its meaning.

The New Critics not only insisted that the poem was independent of the poet but also maintained that the poem was independent of the reader. The reader had to be careful not to impose his or her values on the work but to allow the poem to establish its own rules for being read. The poem was seen as a highly unified object which communicated something significant about human experience by the very choice, arrangement, and balance of its individual parts; the reader could discover this meaning by reference to nothing more than the poem itself.

Yet, although the New Critics argued strongly against both the "intentional fallacy" and the "affective fallacy," these should not be confused with the "art for art's sake" belief commonly associated with poets and critics of the late nineteenth century in Britain and Europe. New Critics were also interested in the content, or theme, of the work. They simply believed that the poem's theme is too complex to be some discursive idea purposely placed within the poem by the author and plucked out by the reader like a raisin from a cake. The Anglo-American formalists thought that poetry reveals truth in a way substantially different from other discursive forms. Whereas science focuses on truth in terms of abstractions or generalities, poetry deals with truth in terms of concreteness. Because experience is more complex than the abstractions of scientific language will allow, poetry is more "true" and more "complex" in its use of language than science is.

According to Wimsatt, the complexity of a work's form is an indication of the sophistication of its content, and in an essay entitled "The Language of Paradox," Brooks argued that whereas the scientist wants to freeze language into widely accepted denotations, poetry breaks these agreements in perpetually new ways. The primary device used for breaking these agreements is metaphor, and metaphor, argued the New Critics, is by its very nature always ironic and paradoxical. Thus, the values that the New Critics sought were those of complexity, irony, tension, and paradox.

The New Criticism's method of getting at the meaning of literary works was so powerful between the 1930s and the 1950s that it dominated college English classes across the United States. Indeed, for all of its theoretical statements, the New Criticism was less a theory of literature than a method of interpreting individual literary works. It had little to say about what characterized literature in general or what relationships existed among literary works either past or present; it only spoke to the explication of an individual poem or story. Ironically, this shortcoming was made clear by the publication of a book in 1949 that is perhaps the high point of Anglo-American formalism, René Wellek and Austin Warren's *Theory of Literature*.

Although Wellek and Warren were more committed to formalist criticism than to any other mode of critical thought outlined in their survey of critical approaches, they were also aware that the New Criticism had failed to understand literature as a whole. In what should have been a foreshadowing of the critical invasion of structuralist and phenomenological approaches twenty years later, Wellek and Warren summarized and cited many European efforts to develop a unified theory of literature. Yet, because many of these efforts were still untranslated into English and because of the firmness with which New Criticism had held the English-speaking intellectual establishment, these new ideas about a poetics of literature would not gain much recognition until the late 1960s.

## Neo-Aristotelian criticism

In the meantime, the first challenge to the New Criticism came from within the Anglo-American establishment itself. Although such scholars as R. S. Crane, Elder Olson, and Richard McKeon (who were members of what came to be known as the Chicago School, or the Neo-Aristotelians) were challenging the ideas of Eliot and Richards throughout the 1940s, their work did not attract much attention until 1952, with the publication of a collection of essays by various members of the group entitled *Critics and Criticism: Ancient and Modern*, edited by Crane.

Claiming a return to Aristotle, the Neo-Aristotelians shared with the New Critics an emphasis on what was specifically "literary" about literature rather than on such extraliterary concerns as history, philosophy, and psychology. They took issue with the New Critical focus on the "language of poetry," however, and its essential qualities of irony and paradox. They insisted on the importance of the larger units of structure of the work, particularly the plot, as, according to Aristotle, an "imitation of an action." Moreover, returning to Aristotle's concern with genre, which was largely missing from the New Critical approach, they also developed ways to differentiate various poetic forms based on this notion of plot as imitation.

One of the most pernicious effects of the New Criticism, argued the Neo-Aristotelians, was that its emphasis on tight, logical linguistic structure largely dependent on paradoxical metaphors gave obvious precedence to the Metaphysical poetry of the seventeenth century and the modernist poetry which emulated it. The real damage to hopes for a poetics, or a general theory of literature – according to the chief theoretician of the group, Elder Olson – was that such a false demand that all literary works embody tension and paradox demolished the theory of genres, the crucial mediator between the individual work and the whole of literature.

More specifically, argued the Chicago School, by favoring metaphysical or symbolist poetry, the New Critics ignored the large forms such as the drama or the novel, especially the eighteenth and nineteenth century pre-symbolist novel which focused more on character and plot than on language. Indeed, the analysis of such novels became the privileged ground of the Neo-Aristotelians, just as lyric poetry had been the favored ground of the New Critics. Yet in spite of encouraging such important studies as Wayne C. Booth's *The Rhetoric of Fiction* (1961) and Sheldon Sack's *Fiction and the Shape of Belief* (1964), the Chicago School of criticism never achieved its goal of stimulating a broader study of genre. This important underlying idea necessary for a unified poetics did not get its impetus until 1957, when the publication of Northrop Frye's *Anatomy of Criticism: Four Essays* marked the second attack on New Criticism's focus on the interpretation of the individual literary work.

## Myth criticism

Although Frye is the best-known spokesman for what is now called archetypal or myth criticism, this theoretical approach actually started with a group of classical scholars at the University of Cambridge in the early twentieth century. Myth criticism, however, did not become widespread as an alternative to the New Criticism until the 1950s; its challenge began, as did that of the Neo-Aristotelians, as an attack on New Criticism's atomism or focus on the individual work. Such critics as Frye, Francis Fergusson, and Richard Chase accepted the Cambridge School's comparative focus on the generic relationship between literary works rather than works standing alone.

An even more important precursor of the modern mythic method than the Cambridge critics was philosopher and social anthropologist Ernst Cassirer. A follower of the philosopher Immanuel Kant, who also influenced the Anglo-American formalists, Cassirer argued that reason alone cannot lead to truth; in addition to reasoned theoretical thinking, which seeks knowledge by abstracting from concrete experience, there is a mode of thinking which Cassirer calls "mythical thinking" which focuses on immediate experience. Art, which shares some similarities with mythical thinking, is not the reproduction of some pre-existent, ready-made knowledge but rather a means to the creation or discovery of a hitherto nonexistent knowledge. Mythical thinking does not discover reality the way science does, says Cassirer, by searching for a central feature of an object; instead, it gives human beings an intuition of the forms of things.

The critic Philip Wheelwright makes Cassirer's views more explicitly applicable to literature in his books *The Burning Fountain* (1954) and *Metaphor and Reality* (1962). He agrees with Cassirer that to try to deal with all matters through logico-scientific language is futile; being exact, which is the aim of logical language, is not always desirable. Sometimes, especially when dealing with human relations, writes Wheelwright, one desires the openness, suggestiveness, relativity, and, what Wheelwright calls "perspectival individuality," which only the language of literature provides.

Northrop Frye contributes most to the so-called mythic method, especially as a means of developing a unified poetics. In the "Polemical Introduction" to his influential *Anatomy of Criticism*, Frye made several controversial critical statements which challenged the atomistic approach of the New Critics. First, Frye argued strongly for a unified field of study called "criticism," the first principle of which is the assumption of total coherence of literature as a whole. Literature is not a series of works spread out in historical time, insisted Frye, but an order of words spread out in conceptual space from some kind of theoretical center which it is the job of criticism to find and describe.

Although Frye's ambitious attempt to describe this conceptual framework in his *Anatomy of Criticism* in terms of elaborate theories of modes, symbols, and genres stimulated much debate in the critical establishment, his central contribution to modern literary theory can be summarized briefly. When Frye referred to archetypes, he did not mean individual mythic images embodied in literary works; rather, he meant associative clusters of symbols which connect one poem with another. The study of genres must be based on the study of the conventional nature of these symbols or artistic devices. In this crucial way, Frye laid the foundation for structuralism, which swept through England and the United States in the 1960s and 1970s.

Furthermore, Frye's argument that individual works were projections of more general themes, as well as his structural approach to highly formalized individual works, also made the rediscovery of 1920s Russian Formalism more acceptable to Anglo-American critics. According to Frye, when a critic examines the theme of a work seen as its total design, he isolates that aspect of it which is conventional and held in common with other works of the same type. It is the critic's task to describe literary shape, and literary shape, argues Frye, comes not from life but from literature and thus ultimately from myth itself. Of the various contexts possible for studying literature, the archetypal context, because it comes from literature, is the context with which critics should be most concerned.

## Russian Formalism

It is an interesting coincidence of modern literary theory that while T. S. Eliot and Richards were laying down the basis for the brand of Anglo-American formalism that was to dominate criticism through the 1950s, a group of critics in Russia were working independently to develop a comparable approach to literature – one which, however, was not widely known in the West until the 1960s and 1970s, when it became highly influential. The major work of the Russian Formalists grew out of two groups of critics: the St. Petersburg Opoyaz group and the Moscow Linguistic Circle.

When Formalist approaches to literature were politically discouraged in the Soviet Union in the late 1920s, Roman Jakobson, an important member of the Moscow group, left the Soviet Union to become a founding member of what was to be known as the Prague Linguistic Circle. As a result, Jakobson is the crucial connecting link between Formalism of the 1920s and structuralism of the 1960s. Another important member of the Prague group, René Wellek, has already been mentioned as being partially responsible for introducing some Russian Formalist ideas to American critics in 1949 through his *Theory of Literature*.

Like the Anglo-American New Critics, the Russian Formalists were primarily concerned with determining the principles by which literature could be distinguished from "nonliterature." The central principle, as expressed in an essay by Viktor Shklovskii entitled "Art as Technique," was that of "defamiliarization," or the process of "making strange." According to Shklovskii, as human perception becomes habitual it becomes automatic and thought processes become abbreviated and algebraic until the world of objects is treated only as a world of abstract shapes. Art, however, exists so that the "sensation" of life, which has been lost to habit and abstraction, can be recovered. Artists use literary conventions, or devices, to make objects "unfamiliar" and thus to increase the difficulty and length of perception, for perception is an aesthetic end in itself. The purpose of art, insisted Shklovskii in what is perhaps the key assertion of the Russian Formalists, is to experience the "artfulness" of the object; the object itself (the work's referential content) is not important.

The theories of the Russian Formalists have had important implications for the study of literary history, the study of the structure of fiction, and the study of genre. For example, the notion of literary devices or conventions made it possible for critics to talk about literary history as the evolution of genres. Poetic forms, argues Jakobson, evolve as a result of shifts in the relationships between the components that make up a generic system. Historical shifts take place when elements that were once considered primary become secondary in this hierarchial system or when elements that were once taken seriously are parodied by "foregrounding" or "laying bare" the devices that communicated them.

The Russian Formalist focus on purely literary devices is what distinguishes it from Anglo-American formalism. Whereas the New Critics were primarily interested in how technique revealed the thematic aspect of individual literary works, the Russian Formalists were interested in technique for its own sake. For example, one of the most famous Russian Formalist essays on an individual work, Boris Eikhenbaum's essay "How Gogol''s "Overcoat" was Made" clearly illustrates the difference between the two schools. Whereas the American formalists would be interested in how the technique of the story reflects the ironic theme of Nikolai Gogol''s story, Eikhenbaum argued that Gogol' did not wish to present a certain type of theme or content; rather, he simply used the theme of the little man at the mercy of incomprehensible social forces as an excuse to create a literary style based on a particular kind of Russian folktale.

In short, for the American formalists, the technique of a literary work existed for the sake of discovering its theme. For the Russian Formalists, however, the theme of the work existed simply to make possible the author's "play" with technique. For this reason, the Russian Formalists were drawn to works in which the technique was particularly obvious, works which bared their devices and thus referred to their own process of being written. Thus, for the Russian Formalists, the eighteenth-century novel *Tristram Shandy* (1759–1767), which frequently calls the reader's attention to the fact that he or she is reading a novel instead of observing a mirror of reality, is the most typical and most novelistic of all novels, for it takes as its subject matter the process of storytelling itself.

The Russian Formalist approach that most influenced the structuralist movement of the 1960s and 1970s was the study of fiction as a structure of individual motifs. According to the Formalists Eikhenbaum and Boris Tomashevskii, when approaching fiction one must make an initial distinction between the series of events which a writer takes as his or her subject matter and the specific structure that results when the writer presents the completed piece of fiction to the reader. Although one may be tempted to think of both these series of events as the same, the former is merely the raw material, whereas the latter is the transformation of the raw material by means of purely literary conventions. The former has been often translated as *fabula*, or story, whereas the latter is referred to as *sjuzet*, plot or discourse.

A second Russian Formalist notion that later proved highly influential is the idea of a "motif" as being the smallest particle of thematic material in a story. Such motifs, the irreducible building blocks of a story, are contained within individual sentences: for example, "the boy left home," "he met an old man," "they entered a cave," and so on. Whereas the *fabula* is merely the aggregate of these motifs in a causal, chronological order, the *sjuzet* is the organization of the motifs in strategically justifiable ways which the Russian Formalists call "motivation."

This approach means that a group of works hypothetically of the same type or genre can be broken down into their various motifs, or smallest meaningful particles. These particles can then be rearranged in terms of their similarity of function or purpose so that more general similarities of the structure of the genre as a whole can be determined. Basically, that is what the Russian critic Vladimir Propp did in his influential study *Morfologiia skazki* (*Morphology of the Folktale*), which, although first published in 1928, was not translated into English until 1958. Working with a limited number of folk tales or fairy tales, Propp broke the tales down into units based on their shared motifs. He argued that different motifs describe different actions, or "functions," that recur in the tales even though the characters and their attributes may differ. Although there may be numerous motifs in Russian fairy tales, Propp argued there were only thirty-one different functions in such tales. Such an approach to the study of the generic elements of fiction became one of the foundations of 1960s and 1970s structuralism.

## Structuralism

Taking its initial cue from Russian Formalism, structuralism began as a reflection of the need to understand literary criticism as a unified scientific field of study rather than the practice of the explication of individual works of art. Concerned not with meaning but more generally with what makes meaning itself possible, structuralism gets its most powerful and immediate impetus from the methods of modern linguistics as developed primarily by Swiss linguist Ferdinand de Saussure. The seminal document of modern structuralism is *Cours de linguistique générale* (1916; *Course in General Linguistics*, 1959), a collection of Saussure's lecture notes edited by some of his students.

The central ideas of Saussure which have proved most useful to literary theory by the structuralists are fairly easy to summarize, although their implications have proved highly complex and controversial. Saussure's basic assertion was that "language" should not be thought of simply as a horde of those words used for communication. Instead, language is made up of both individual utterances (which Saussure called *parole*) and the general system of language which makes such individual utterances possible (which Saussure called *langue*). Although individual utterances make up the governing system of language, they do so not as an aggregate of utterances but rather as an elaborate system of generative principles.

Furthermore, the individual "sign," such as that designated by a single word in a language, is also made up of two parts. First, there is the sound that is made when one utters the word "house"; then, there is the concept present in the mind when one utters such a word. The sound image Saussure calls the "signifier," whereas he calls the mental concept the "signified." What is important to remember about these two notions is that there is no intrinsic or "necessary" relationship between the two. There is no essential quality of "houseness" inherent in the sound of the word "house." The relationship between the two is purely arbitrary and conventional; it results from the tacit agreement of those who belong to a certain speech community that such a sound image will signify such a concept.

The final important distinction Saussure made is the distinction between studying a phenomenon, such as language or literature, as it develops over time (which Saussure calls a "diachronic" study) and studying it as it exists at any one given moment in time (which Saussure calls a "synchronic" study). These two approaches for studying a cultural phenomenon are related to the realization that all utterances and other examples of sign systems communicate simultaneously in two different ways. First, they function along the linear, time-bound axis, as the sentence, "the dog bites the boy" communicates by the syntactic relationship between the signifiers "dog," "bites," and "boy." Second, they function along a vertical, spatially fixed axis that exists tacitly for each of the signifiers in the string on the basis of similarity of function. For example, the signifier "dog" could be replaced by "cat," "snake," or "lion" – in short anything that might plausibly perform the same function as the signifier "dog." The linear relationship between the signifiers in the string is called the "syntagmatic" relationship, whereas the spatial relationship is called the "paradigmatic" relationship. The first is governed by the principle of contiguity or combination of signifiers, whereas the second is governed by the principle of similarity, or substitution.

In *Fundamentals of Language* (1956, with Morris Halle), Roman Jakobson suggests that the distinction between the syntagmatic and the paradigmatic corresponds not only to the two basic ways that simple linguistic chains signify but also to the two basic means by which larger units of linguistic chains such as literary works signify. All discourse, says Jakobson, communicates along two lines of meaning: One topic may lead to another through the process of combination based on contiguity, or a topic may lead to another through the process of substitution based on similarity. The first corresponds to the trope known as "metonymy," whereby something is suggested by something else contiguous to it; for example, a doghouse may "stand for" a dog because a dog lives there. The second corresponds to the device known as "metaphor," whereby something is suggested by something else that can be substituted for it; for example, a dog can be referred to as an animal, a pet, man's best friend, a pest, and so on.

The first significant attempt to use the linguistic approach to apply to a signifying phenomenon other than language itself was the effort by French anthropologist Claude Lévi-Strauss to understand myth. In his most familiar discussion, "The Structural Study of Myth," a chapter from his 1958 book *Anthropologie structurale* (*Structural Anthropology*, 1963), Lévi-Strauss laid out an approach to myth which has since been used for the study of literary fictions.

Myth is story, says Lévi-Strauss, made up of basic constituent units or distinctive features which share similar functional traits. Yet these units are larger than the units of phonemes or morphemes which make up language; thus, Lévi-Strauss calls them "gross constituent units" and terms them "mythemes." After breaking down the myth into mythemes, or units based on similarity of function, Lévi-Strauss then determines how these units are related to one another in what he calls "bundles of relations." He then reads the myth not in terms of one event after another in a causal-chronological relationship but rather in terms of the logical relationships between the various sets, or "bundles."

In this way, Lévi-Strauss breaks down the syntagmatic flow of the myth based on contiguity, groups the resulting motifs together into paradigmatic sets based on similarity, and then reads the paradigmatic sets in terms of their logical relationships. The result is, as Jakobson stated in his famous essay "Closing Statement: Linguistics and Poetics," similarity is imposed onto contiguity, and thus equivalence is made the constitutive device of the sequence. In other words, the syntagmatic, which is "just one thing after another" and therefore meaningless, is transformed into paradigmatic sets made up of units based on similarity which communicate by logical relationships. Lévi-Strauss' method has served as the model for further studies of literary narratives, as if they were structured the same way language is.

Structuralist critics have been primarily concerned with various ways to extrapolate from the study of language a method for the study of literature. The most basic way they attempted to do this in the 1960s was to treat literature as a second-level language system above language itself. Although a poem or a story is made up of language and thus can be broken down into such units as phonemes and morphemes, structuralists made use of Saussure's ideas of the distinction between *langue* and *parole* to refer to a distinction within literature itself between the individual work of art (*parole*) and the system of genre (*langue*) to which it belonged or between the genre (*parole*) and the larger system of literature as a whole (*langue*). Carrying this approach even further, they suggested that literature was not only made up of language, it was "like" a language in many other ways as well. The field of study that has made the most extensive use of such linguistic approaches is the field that structuralism may be said to have invented: narratology.

Drawing their inspiration initially from Propp's *Morphology of the Folktale*, such narratologists as A. J. Greimas, Claude Bremond, and Tzvetan Todorov were concerned with identifying the fundamental elements of narrative and their laws of combination. Perhaps the most familiar to Anglo-American readers is Todorov, whose collection *Poétique de la prose* (1971; *The Poetics of Prose*, 1977) made his approach easily accessible. Basically, Todorov reduces the action in individual stories to a basic syntactic summary and then analyzes that summary by focusing on active verb forms in the stories such as "to change," "to transgress," "to punish," and so on. It has often been pointed out that whereas such an approach works most effectively with highly formalized works such as stories and tales, it works least effectively with more "realistic" works such as the novel. The structuralist approach to narrative, claim many of its critics, drains the human content out of literary works and then deals only with their mathematically pure, linguistic-like structure.

## Reader-response theory

Because of this refusal to deal with the human origin of the work, its human content, or its human effect on the reader, the structuralist approach was challenged almost as soon as it began by critics concerned with the "subjectivity" of literature, particularly with the subjective involvement or response of the reader. There are two distinct sources for literary criticism which focuses on the reader: the phenomenological theory derived from Edmund Husserl and the psychoanalytic theory derived from Sigmund Freud. The first has often been called "reception aesthetics," whereas the second has been termed "transactive criticism."

Phenomenologists criticize such linguistically based approaches as structuralism because they try to fix invariant patterns in literary works and thus abstract the human being out of the work's concrete experience. The most subtle spokesman of phenomenology's interest in understanding the subjectivity of literature is philosopher Paul Ricœur. Yet Ricœur's discussions of how meaning is created – in *La Métaphore vive* (1975; *The Rule of Metaphor*, 1977) – and how history is like narrative – in *Temps et récit* (1983; *Time and Narrative*, 1984, 1986, 1988) – have had less effect on literary criticism than European reception theory, introduced in German in the late 1960s by Hans Robert Jauss.

Making use of Husserl's basic notion that one perceives reality through an abstract structure of expectation (termed "horizons"), Jauss argues that to study literary history, the focus should be on the reader's literary horizons, that is, the structure of generic norms the reader has internalized as a result of all previous texts he or she has read. Following this same approach, Wolfgang Iser, the best-known spokesman for reception theory in the United States, focuses on reading as a dynamic process during which the reader continually fills in what Iser calls "gaps of indeterminacy" in the text – gaps which are there because the artwork never completely corresponds to real objects. Iser's reader is not one who brings his or her unique experience to the reading experience; instead, Iser's reader is an "implicit reader," one who alters the self to fit the kind of reader that the work requires. Thus, the reading experience is a dynamic interchange with the text, not a passive experience; the person you are for the time you are reading *Huckleberry Finn*, for example, is not quite the same person you are when you read *The Scarlet Letter*.

Another well-known advocate of reader-based criticism is American critic Stanley Fish, who has called his approach to literary texts "affective stylistics." Like Iser, Fish's notion of a reader is not one who brings to the text all the individualities that define him or her in everyday life but what some have called a "superreader," one who interacts with the text in a highly sophisticated, rhetorical way. Fish says that the so-called objectivity of a text is a dangerous illusion; reading, and thus the text itself, constitutes a temporal, not a spatial, experience, contrary to what formalists, myth critics, and structuralists contend. A sentence, for example, argues Fish, is not an object but an event, something that happens to the reader with his or her participation. Fish monitors the temporal flow of the experience as it is structured by what the reader brings with him or her; thus, he can chart reader response as it develops over time.

In contrast to phenomenologically based reader-response theory, which focuses primarily on the reader's general and rhetorical expectations as he or she reads the work, psychoanalytically based reader-response theory focuses on the reader's specific response based on his or her unique personality or identity. The best-known advocate of this brand of criticism, transactive criticism, or Buffalo criticism, because it originated from State University of New York, Buffalo, is Norman Holland.

Holland's first major theoretical book, *The Dynamics of Literary Response* (1968), came at a time when New Criticism's explication of individual poems was beginning to pall on critics and students and when much psychoanalytic criticism up to that point, influenced both by formalism and myth criticism, had degenerated into the simple interpretative task of searching for dream or myth symbols in literary works. Holland argued that Freud's theories, particularly in his study of wit and jokes, offered the basis for a general theory about the dynamic transaction between reader and text in which basic interests or themes in the reader's personality "constructed" themes in the text.

Thus, like Fish, Holland urges that texts should not be studied as objects but rather as dynamic transactions between readers and texts. Holland argues that by means of literary form (which works like defense mechanisms in human beings) and by means of literary meaning (which works like sublimation in human beings), literature can transform unconscious desires in the reader into a higher aesthetic, intellectual, and moral unity. This unity, which not only exists in the text but also is created by the needs of the reader, should be the focus of the critic.

Another influential critic within this psychoanalytically based reader-response tradition is David Bleich, whose first book, *Reading and Feelings: An Introduction to Subjective Criticism* (1975), had a major impact on the way literature is taught in the classroom, particularly the high school classroom, in the United States. His more substantial theoretical book, *Subjective Criticism* (1978), criticizes Holland for dwelling on the objectivity of the text, as the New Critics did, and instead offers a radical new "subjective" paradigm of thought which is based on epistemological issues of how one "knows"; consequently, Bleich connects psychoanalytically based reader-response theory with some of the issues that have dominated phenomenologically based theories about the reader.

## Deconstruction

It is an interesting irony of modern criticism that even as structuralism was being introduced to American critics in 1966 at a conference at The Johns Hopkins University entitled "The Languages of Criticism and the Sciences of Man," a relatively unknown philosopher named Jacques Derrida delivered a paper entitled "Structure, Sign and Play in the Discourse of the Human Sciences" which was already seriously challenging structuralism. In this milestone essay, Derrida challenged the basic assumptions of structuralism as illustrated by Claude Lévi-Strauss; then, in 1967, with a series of important but often dense and unreadable books – including *La Voix et le phénomène: Introduction au problème du signe dans la phénoménologie de Husserl* ("*Speech and Phenomena," and Other Essays on Husserl's Theory of Signs*, 1973), *De la grammatologie* (*Of Grammatology*, 1976), and *L'Écriture et la différence* (*Writing and Difference*, 1978) – he further undercut structuralism's philosophical foundations as established by Ferdinand de Saussure. His approach, which has come to be called "deconstruction," is to analyze such thinkers as Lévi-Strauss, Saussure, and Edmund Husserl in such a way as to show that their own arguments create a basic contradiction which itself is the key to understanding.

As a result of Derrida's critique of structuralism, the movement never really got started in the United States. Moreover, by the time it was introduced to English-speaking critics, its most influential advocate in Europe, Roland Barthes, had already begun to offer his own challenging critique, primarily in his work *S/Z* (1970; English translation, 1974). Whereas in his earlier critical statements Barthes, like other structuralists, had appealed to a general structure, something equivalent to Saussure's notion of *langue*, from which one could derive an analysis of an individual text, or *parole*, in *S/Z* Barthes analyzed a short novel by Honoré de Balzac as being a work which instead of having a single *parole*-like system governed by its dependence on a large *langue*-like system, is a system in and of itself. Barthes argued that there is no transcendent or primary model equivalent to *langue* but rather that each text is traversed by numerous codes which constitute its meaning. The implication of this shift is that if the text does not have a meaning determined by a transcendent code, it may have numerous meanings which are created by the reader as he or she applies the various procedures demanded by the multiple codes that traverse it.

Still, Derrida's challenge to structuralism's assumptions of a transcendent code has had the most powerful impact on contemporary literary theory. In his 1966 presentation at the Johns Hopkins conference on structuralism, Derrida challenged the methodology of Lévi-Strauss on the basis of what he called Lévi-Strauss' tacit nostalgia for a central and transcendent "presence," or "fixed origin." Derrida exposed the Kantian basis of structuralism and dismisses as a fiction, although a functional fiction, the a priori mythic consciousness on which all forms of formalist criticism, from the Russian Formalists to the structuralists, had depended.

In referring to Saussure's influential distinction between signifier and signified, Derrida argued that there was no transcendent signified to which a signifier referred but that a signifier referred only to other signifiers in an endless play of signifiers. Derrida insisted that the structuralist endeavor was based on what he called a "metaphysics of presence," that is, some hypothetical mythic moment when signifier and signified were intrinsically related and indivisible. Derrida has claimed that this illusion is damaging, for it allows one to avoid dealing with fragmentary reality on the assumption that there is some unified, pure meaning, or reality, that can be grasped. According to Derrida, everything is a mediated "text"; there is nothing outside the text, and the only things to which texts can refer are other texts.

Derrida also dismissed the assumption of linguistics that writing is secondary to and derivative of speech, for this, he said, is merely another version of the "metaphysics of presence." To believe that writing is secondary to speech is to believe that although writing is a highly mediated sign system that one must interpret, its source is in speech, which, by comparison is unmediated, and thus its truth is immediately knowable. Derrida argued, however, that it is an illusion to think that truth is apparent at the moment of speech. In fact, once it is shown that speech is susceptible to the same distance and difference from meaning as writing itself is and thus not a primary source of truth, then writing can be studied as the model of what Derrida called a "metaphysics of absence," which allows for the "free play of signifiers." According to Derrida, there has never been an original source; there has never been anything but a string of substitutional signifiers in a chain of differences moving toward infinity. The most basic implication of Derrida's approach to literary criticism is that if a work can have no ultimate meaning, then it can have limitless meanings.

It is this basic implication that American followers of Derrida, primarily the so-called Yale School – which includes Geoffrey H. Hartman, J. Hillis Miller, the late Paul de Man, and Harold Bloom – have most taken to heart. Although these critics differ in many particulars in terms of their engagement with the ideas of Derrida, they all proceed on the assumption that the notion of referentiality is an illusion. A sign, says Miller, marks not the presence of, but the absence of, an object. All the world is a text in which there are not facts, only interpretations. De Man argued that what reading reveals is the confrontation with a language that always vacillates between the promise of some referential meaning and the rhetorical subversion of that meaning. Only Bloom differs in his approach by focusing on the problem of literary history from a psychoanalytic point of view. Although he agrees that every text is an "intertext," he argues that literary history is the history of the clash of the strong personalities of young poets in conflict with powerful previous poets or precursors. Literature develops by means of purposeful "misreadings" by present poets of previous ones.

Structuralist and deconstructionist theories about the nature of literature have also been integrated into two of the most pervasive and powerful models for the analysis of human experience in Western culture – Marxism and psychoanalysis. Although both of these models were subject to charges of reductionism when first used by literary critics in the early part of the twentieth century, more recent approaches to Marxism, derived primarily from the so-called Frankfurt School of social theorists, and more recent explorations in psychoanalysis, derived from the work of French analyst Jacques Lacan, have attempted to make use of the linguistic revolution to understand better Marx's critique of society and Freud's concept of the unconscious.

The best-known Marxist theorists of the Frankfurt School are Theodor Adorno, its chief aesthetician, who argues that the greatness of the artwork is that it allows those things to be heard which ideology conceals, and Louis Althusser, who urges that critics lay bare the author's "problematic," that is, the unconscious infrastructure, or base, of his "potential thoughts," which make up the existing "ideological field" within which he works. Pierre Macherey makes the connection between Marxism and structuralist and poststructuralist theories even more obvious in *Pour une théorie de la production littéraire* (*A Theory of Literary Production*), originally published in Paris in 1966 and translated into English in 1978.

For Macherey, criticism is not explication, nor is literature mimetic. Criticism is a form of knowledge; its object is not the literary work but rather a product of literary criticism itself. Whatever phenomenal reality is revealed by the literary work has no prior existence; it is simply the product of the laws of the work's production, and the task of criticism is to reveal these laws. In an effort to connect the concept of "ideology" with linguistic theories about structure, Macherey argues that ideology cannot be reduced to a set of concepts; ideology is, in fact, the tacit internalized realm of structures itself. It is this realm of the unsaid and the unsayable which makes the said possible. For Macherey, the task of criticism is not to try to articulate the unsaid, the so-called latent meaning, but rather to lay bare the laws of the production of the said.

The maverick French psychoanalyst · Jacques Lacan, strongly influenced in his reading of Freud by Saussure and Lévi-Strauss, argues that the unconscious is structured like a language and therefore needs to be understood linguistically. Yet he begins to sound more deconstructionist than structuralist in his approach when he argues that the signifier is privileged over the signified and that the child's early ego development is based on an illusion of wholeness and totality which obscures the reality of one's fragmentary self. Rivaling Derrida in the complexity and density of his ideas and his prose style, Lacan's theories, which have been termed "French Freud," have had a profound influence on psychoanalytic approaches to criticism in the United States. The journal *Yale French Studies* has been most instrumental in disseminating the views of Lacan, primarily in the writings of such critics as Shoshana Felman, Peter Brooks, and Barbara Johnson, who have offered Lacanian approaches to Henry James, Charles Dickens, and Edgar Allan Poe.

Throughout the 1970s, critics such as Hartman, de Man, and Miller carried on a vigorous defense of deconstruction against more traditional critics, primarily in the most important journals of modern literary theory, such as *Critical Inquiry, New Literary History*, and *Diacritics*. As might be expected, traditional critics have accused deconstructionists of being subjective, relative, unreadable, and perversely contradictory. Indeed, if one follows Derrida's line of thought and rejects any ultimately absolute meaning, then literary analysis becomes justified not on the basis of its truth value but on the basis of whether it is interesting. Deconstructionists do not strive for some final reading of a work; they attempt to present an engagement with the work that rivals the work itself for its fictionality and imaginative structure.

It is this ultimate divorce, not only from historical and social referentiality but also from any responsibility either to the world or to the text, that has led to a reaction against deconstruction in the 1980s that may mark a return, although a return with a crucial difference, to the view of literary works as cultural documents of political and historical significance that gave rise to the formalist or New Critical revolution in the first place.

## Feminist criticism

The most vocal and visible of these calls for a return to the social and historical context of literature comes from feminist criticism. Generated out of the so-called women's liberation movement of the late 1960s and early 1970s, feminist criticism began with the 1970 publication of Kate Millett's *Sexual Politics*, which exposed the sexism inherent in the writing of several important male authors. As the consciousness of more women became raised to sexism in all aspects of American life, the movement exerted enough influence on higher education to make women's studies programs a pervasive phenomenon on university campuses;

a related phenomenon was the development of feminist academic approaches to history, sociology, philosophy, and literature.

Feminist literary criticism as an academic field of study began with several primary projects. First, feminist critics focused on the sexist biases male writers were often guilty of embedding in their works – biases which have become unquestioned paradigms of belief. Feminist critics made the literary establishment take them seriously by arguing that there are undeniable connections between the exploitation of women in society and the depiction of women as sexual objects in male erotica and pornography. The result of this project has been not only a revision of critical attitudes about the literature of the past but also a new sensitivity to what feminists regard as literary misogyny in the present.

Second, feminist critics argued that the established canon of so-called great literary works in Western culture was developed and maintained by males and therefore needed to be expanded to include valuable but previously ignored works by female writers. A corollary of this demand for the expansion of the existing canon was the call for the reevaluation of literary works by females which had been previously "misinterpreted" by the prevailing male critical establishment. Some American writers newly discovered as a result of this insistence are Kate Chopin, Rebecca Harding Davis, and Charlotte Perkins Gilman. Writers reclaimed from critical scorn include Harriet Beecher Stowe, Rebecca West, and Susan Glaspell.

Another important project for feminist criticism has been the establishment of female writers as a countertradition of literature characterized by a radically different consciousness and value system from those embodied in the so-called great tradition of male writers. Such critics as Patricia Meyer Spacks in *The Female Imagination* (1975) and Elaine Showalter in *A Literature of Their Own: British Women Novelists from Brontë to Lessing* (1977) argued that women writers have often been concerned with matters considered peripheral by men and that they have thus expressed the value of a subculture within the framework of society at large. Perhaps the best-known and most influential study to focus on what has come to be known as a female literary tradition is *The Madwoman in the Attic: The Woman Writer and the Nineteenth-Century Literary Imagination* (1979) by Sandra M. Gilbert and Susan Gubar, who argue that the very idea of authorship and thus literary authority has always been unyieldingly paternalistic.

Feminist criticism has frequently been challenged for its lack of a rigorous theoretical framework. Although it has made liberal use of critical approaches from structuralist and poststructuralist theories of the literary text, because it has focused more on the social content of literature than on its specifically literary form, many feminist critics seem to agree that it is most closely aligned with Marxist sociology and aesthetics in its political and polemical focus on a dominant ideology's power to repress a significant social group.

Moreover, although feminist critics seemed at first to be a close-knit group, considering themselves a "sisterhood" devoted to the same liberating task, once the necessary negative critiques of male-dominated literary theory and criticism had been published, many feminist critics disagreed about what should constitute a positive poetics. Some have argued that feminist criticism should remain pluralistic and thus avoid the traps of reductionism which have beset other theoretical frameworks. Others have declared that women should focus on the social content of literary works, ignoring their aesthetic form as being irrelevant to feminist concerns. Still others have insisted that a feminist poetics should be developed out of how the feminine consciousness gives rise to linguistic styles and literary structures unique to women. Although no coherent approach has emerged from this debate, there is little doubt that feminist criticism has been the most influential new movement in American literary criticism in the late 1980s.

## The New Pragmatism

Whereas feminist criticism marks a divergence from modern theory's predominantly formalist approach to literature simply because it has been more interested in the social content of the literary work than its form, a group of critics loosely termed the "New Pragmatists" have mounted a direct assault on the formalist tradition and have urged a return to approaches which focus on the authorial "intention" of the work, its socially human referent, and its sociohistorical context. Although Marxist critics such as Fredric Jameson – who announced that the "moral" of his book *The Political Unconscious: Narrative as a Socially Symbolic Act* (1981) was "Always historicize!" – have been associated with this new movement, the group that is usually designated by the term "New Pragmatism" comprises primarily faculty members at the University of California at Berkeley.

The New Pragmatism's basic attack against modern literary theory has been outlined by Berkeley professors Steven Knapp and Walter Benn Michaels in two articles published in 1982 and 1987 in the journal *Critical Inquiry*, entitled "Against Theory" and "Against Theory II: Hermeneutics and Deconstruction." The philosophical basis of Knapp and Michaels' arguments and assumptions is primarily derived from German thinker Hans-Georg Gadamer, who argues that criticism cannot find a basis for an absolute meaning in a literary work unprejudiced by history, and from his best-known follower, Hans Robert Jauss, who argues that the literary work must be studied in terms of the various historical moments of its reception.

Knapp and Michaels insist that a text means what its author intends it to mean and that any effort to establish a method of interpretation based on a general theory of language is doomed. Aligning themselves with Gadamer, Knapp and Michaels claim that the interpretive history of a literary text is part of the meaning of the text itself. They not only attack the formalist notion that linguistic and literary conventions determine the meaning of a text but also complain that hermeneutics and deconstruction only partially reject such conventionalism. Although these latter two theories no longer argue for an absolute and unchanging meaning, they still allow a text to "acquire" a meaning independent of the author's intention.

According to Knapp and Michaels, the theoretical impulse which has dominated literary criticism in the twentieth century tries to separate concepts that should not be separated; primarily, theory tries to separate meaning from intention and language from speech acts. Because theory is nothing else than the attempt to escape practice, Knapp and Michaels call for the end of the theoretical enterprise. By rejecting studies which are based on the assumption that literary works are autonomous verbal constructs, textual opportunities for reader dynamics, or intertextual grids of floating signifiers, the New Pragmatism has come full circle, returning to a focus on the artwork as both radically referential and intentional.

## Conclusion

Modern literary theory in the late 1990s reached a point ripe for rebellion and reactionism. The basic problem is a crippling schism between assumptions about the nature of literature as it is taught in schools and undergraduate classrooms and the nature of literature as it is written about in the scholarly and critical journals and taught in the major graduate research institutions. Whereas the New Criticism was straightforward enough in its philosophical assumptions and its pedagogical approach to be accessible to anyone able to read the language, structuralist and poststructuralist approaches seem so complicated and dense that they are accessible only to a relative few who sometimes seem determined to keep it that way. The result is that the approaches which literature professors must master in order to publish contributions to criticism in books and journals are based on so many diverse and sophisticated philosophical assumptions that they can only be successfully taught in the most advanced graduate classes. It has become increasingly difficult to maintain these two critical "houses" without one or the other falling into disrepair and disrepute.

Despite this confusion, the revolution in literary theory which has taken place between the 1960s and the 1990s has found its way into the classroom and affected the way that college graduates think about the study of literature. Teachers and students have more respect for literary criticism as a rigorous, even scientific, study. Furthermore, the increase in literary theories has suggested that the study of literature is by its very nature an interdisciplinary study which yields knowledge which is just as valuable as other disciplines in both the "hard" and the "soft" sciences.

If there is one central theme which has dominated literary criticism in the twentieth century, it is the idea that human reality is not a simple aggregate of data that can be determined by simple empirical investigation. Consequently, modern literary theory has argued that instead of being a mirror held up to an ostensible reality "out there," literature is reflective of the dynamic process whereby the human mind constructs reality. Thus, the old referential relationship between the world and the work – that literature "reflects" reality – has been turned upside down to suggest that literature "constitutes" reality. Instead of taking the reader further from the direct experience of literature, as some traditionalists have claimed, modern literary theory has deepened appreciation and understanding of the literary work as a significant model of the means by which we know what we know.

## Further reading

Barry, Peter. *Beginning Theory: An Introduction to Literary and Cultural Theory*, 1995.

Barthes, Roland. *Critical Essays*, 1972.

Bloom, Harold, et al. *Deconstruction and Criticism*, 1979.

Culler, Jonathan D. *Structuralist Poetics: Structuralism, Linguistics, and the Study of Literature*, 1975.

Derrida, Jacques. *Of Grammatology*, 1976.

Eagleton, Terry. *Literary Theory: An Introduction*, 1983.

Eco, Umberto. *A Theory of Semiotics*, 1976.

Erlich, Victor. *Russian Formalism: History, Doctrine*, 1981.

Frye, Northrop. *Anatomy of Criticism: Four Essays*, 1957.

Gilbert, Sandra M., and Susan Gubar. *The Madwoman in the Attic: The Woman Writer and the Nineteenth-Century Literary Imagination*, 1979.

Hawkes, Terrence. *Structuralism and Semiotics*, 1977.

Iser, Wolfgang. *The Act of Reading: A Theory of Aesthetic Response*, 1978.

Jameson, Fredric. *The Prison-House of Language: A Critical Account of Structuralism and Russian Formalism*, 1972.

Leitch, Vincent. *Deconstructive Criticism: An Advanced Introduction and Survey*, 1982.

Newton, K. M. *Twentieth Century Literary Theory: A Reader*, 1988.

Scholes, Robert. *Structuralism in Literature: An Introduction*, 1974.

Selden, Radman and Peter Widdowsom. *A Reader's Guide to Contemporary Literary Theory*, 1993.

Showalter, Elaine, ed. *The New Feminist Criticism: Essays on Women, Literature, and Theory*, 1985.

Tompkins, Jane, ed. *Reader-Response Criticism*, 1980.

Wellek, René, and Austin Warren. *Theory of Literature*, 1949 (revised edition, 1956).

CHARLES E. MAY

# Modernism

Modernism is a catch-all term for the numerous artistic and cultural movements of the late nineteenth and early twentieth centuries (to be distinguished from the "modern age," which began with the end of the medieval period and the beginning of the Renaissance). In the broadest terms, it is the time period from 1880 to 1945 with the years 1900 to 1925 usually recognized as being those of the most intense modernist activity. Concentrated for the most part in the urban centers of turn-of-the-century Paris and Vienna but encompassing cities from Berlin and London to New York and Chicago, it signifies a widespread revolution in the arts of music, painting, architecture, philosophy, and literature associated with a wide variety of creative individuals ranging from Arnold Schoenberg, Pablo Picasso, Ludwig Wittgenstein, James Joyce, T. S. Eliot, Virginia Woolf, William Faulkner, and Franz Kafka. The intellectual roots of the modernist phenomenon extend back to the late eighteenth and nineteenth centuries with figures as disparate as Immanuel Kant, Arthur Schopenhauer, Gustave Flaubert, and Friedrich Nietzsche. Modernism is characterized by the rejection of tradition, aestheticism/aesthetic self-consciousness, abstraction/nonrepresentationalism, discontinuity, and a heightened sense of the irrational/subjective and the absurd. The term is applied to such a wide variety of artistic trends and individuals that some critics prefer to speak of various modernisms (for example liberal, conservative, experimental modernism, and so on).

It may be argued that the intellectual roots of modernism lie to a large extent in the transcendental Idealism of the German philosopher Immanuel Kant. Traditionally aesthetics has been guided by the Aristotelian notion that art is mimesis or the imitation of nature, by the idea that art should be didactic or instructive of moral/ethical teachings, and by the belief that art is the result of divine inspiration or revelation. Mimetic, didactic, or inspired art is grounded in the belief in a universe (that is, both nature and God) which is ultimately knowable through human perception. Kantian epistemology and metaphysics, as explicated in his *Kritik der reinen Vernunft* (1781; *Critique of Pure Reason*, 1854), suggests that what we know as "reality" – the world as a "phenomenon" – is in fact the product or the construction of the categories of our cognition (time, space, causality, relation, and so on). Absolute reality (as it really is and not as it is constructed by our minds) or indeed the divine Godhead – both of which Kant called the noumenon or the "Thing-in-Itself" – cannot be known through human perception. With this insight, the basis for art as mimesis and didactic becomes extremely problematic at best. The modern artist is summarily freed from the responsibility of reproducing nature and the divine will.

Kant discusses the implications of this viewpoint for art and aesthetics in the *Kritik der Urteilskraft* (1790; *Critique of Judgment*, 1892). The artist/genius chooses the form and purpose of the work of art alone; the work of art forms a "universe" of its own and the artist is its sole "creator." The realm of the artwork is the only place in which the human being is totally free from the external yoke of physical necessity and the internal dictates of moral law. Traditional art had been subservient to nature and the divine; now art was to be an end in itself. Art and the imagination became the domain of absolute freedom and transcendence. The position of the artist was virtually elevated to that of a religious figure or seer. The artist is now spoken of as being a kind of uniquely free "genius" who lives and creates from his or her own set of laws. From this modernist viewpoint came the turn-of-the-century trend called aestheticism or "art for art's sake": the religion of art. The modernist aesthetes – Stefan George or Oscar Wilde, for example – were often associated with a decadent and elitist lifestyle by the bourgeois classes.

In his explication of aesthetic judgment, Kant distinguished clearly between logical ideas or discourse – scientific concepts, for example – which are appropriate to the rational human faculty, and aesthetic ideas or discourse – emotive metaphors, for example – which are a function of the human imagination or intuition. Logical concepts are appropriate to statements about external facts but they are inadequate when they attempt to depict inner, emotional experience which can, however, be intimated in aesthetic ideas. Logical discourse is essentially denotative, that is, it conveys by necessity only simple, literal meaning (the "logical attribute" of scientific discourse); aesthetic discourse deals with the evocative, connotative nuances of language. The primary vehicle for these nuances of meaning conveyed in aesthetic discourse is metaphor, a poetic device through which associations are invoked (Kant termed it an "aesthetic attribute" of poetic language). This distinction – between the language of art and that of science – is fundamental to the discussion of modernism. This separation between aesthetic ideas and rational discourse (as well as the empirical or everyday experience from which logical concepts are customarily drawn) gives modernist art its often apparently discontinuous, abstract, and sometimes irrational or "surreal" quality.

This move within turn-of-the-century modernism toward the expression of subjective realities was given further impetus through the so-called "depth psychology" or psychoanalysis of Sigmund Freud, most especially with the publication of his *Die Traumdeutung* (1899; *The Interpretation of Dreams*, 1900). Freud's "discovery" of the unconscious opened up a virtual Pandora's box of aesthetic possibilities in the depiction of what lies hidden from the domain of the conscious mind and what is expressed often through the unusual metaphoric symbolism of the individual's dream world. The subtly disquieting, "uncanny" dreamlike fiction of Kafka and the highly unreal work of the Surrealists in both writing and painting, for example, owe their debt to the spirit of early Freudian research into the nature and forms of subjective realities.

The Freudian, as well as the Kantian, notion of the individual being divorced from an invisible or undisclosed world (be it the unconscious or the noumenon) suggests that modernism also contains an important movement toward what might be called a crisis of the subject, that is,

the individual consciousness is indeed liberated from the constraints of objective reality but also remains irrevocably "alienated" from it. The issue of the alienation of the self – the turning inward of consciousness – (and the twentieth-century existential philosophy to which it is related) becomes a major theme in many modernist works of art. The nineteenth-century roots of existentialism are closely associated with the philosophy of Nietzsche and his overall influence on the spirit of modernism is enormous. Not only his radical condemnations of the Christian religion, middle-class value systems, and European culture and civilization in general, which contributed to the modernist rejection of all prior tradition, but also his far-reaching and more fundamental critiques of meaning and truth (and the important role of language in creating meaning) contributed to the modernist sensibility of radical doubt and to a newly defined and yet disorienting sense of radical nihilism. Not a few modernists (Hugo von Hofmannsthal, for example) were struck by a crisis of language in which words were regarded as being incapable of expressing any vision of an authentic or existential reality. Nietzsche's extreme pessimism stood as a counterpoint to the cultural optimism – a boundless faith in the promise of science and technology – that was to be found in some modernist movements.

Another important aspect of twentieth-century modernism is again to be found in the nineteenth-century German Idealism of Kant as well as in the literary writings of Friedrich Klopstock, Johann Gottfried Herder, Johann Wolfgang von Goethe, and Johann Schiller: the work of art as organism and the primacy of form over content (the aesthetics of inward form). Since Kant argued that the work of art constituted a unique domain of absolute freedom in which the artist/genius reigns supremely, then its form or structure would be dictated solely by its own inner workings – as a plant develops organically from a seed – and not by any external considerations of normative rules of composition, content, or function. Style (the way something is said) becomes more significant than content (what is said): the medium is the message. The French novelist Gustave Flaubert, another important precursor of modernism and consummate stylist, also maintained the primacy of style in writing; indeed, style or form itself becomes the real content of the work of art. Form which becomes content delineates in many respects the modernist artistic program of expressionists such as Vasilii Kandinskii (and the later American abstract expressionists such as Jackson Pollock). The combination of a nonmimetic, absolute art, and style as an end in itself lends itself to the rise of the formal abstractionism found in modernist expressionism and the cubism movement as exemplified by the later Picasso. The movement toward abstraction also suggests a shift to essentialism in both the form and function of art, depicting only what is fundamental in shape and form and viewing art solely in its aesthetic/nonutilitarian function. The latter trend leads again to the association of aestheticism with modernism. Art, the creation of form, becomes the only path to the creation of meaning.

A further important predecessor to modernism and its abstract expression can be found in yet another nineteenth-century German philosopher, namely Arthur Schopenhauer, who valued music – its abstract formal/mathematical relationships – as the highest art form because of its nonrepresentational nature. His aesthetics of musicalization influenced Richard Wagner, Charles Baudelaire, Stéphane Mallarmé (and French Symbolism), as well as the aestheticism and expressionism movements in many countries. Indeed, it has been argued that the adoption of the aesthetics of musical composition by all modes of artistic creation is the single most important feature of modernist art. Schopenhauer's nihilism (as well as that of Nietzsche) also influenced the sense of cultural despair/relativism – the millennial sense of doom at the ending of 1900 – and the rejection of all tradition found in much modernist writing.

A word should be said about the current critical debates concerning the terms modernism and postmodernism. The latter emerges in the postwar period first of all as an expression of the growing awareness that the artistic and cultural movements of modernism have come to a conclusion and that we have embarked upon a new cultural and artistic era. As with modernism, however, there are numerous theories concerning what postmodernism is, and some indeed contradict each other. In any case, we might summarize these postmodernisms and suggest they involve an awareness of the following themes: the pervasive role of mass/popular culture and the dominance of international capitalism in postindustrial nations; the insights of the poststructuralist thought of Jacques Derrida, Michel Foucault, Jacques Lacan, and others; the new feminist analyses of "male"/phallocentric ideologies and the promotion of an alternative "female" position; and an aesthetics of openness, indeterminacy, multiplicity, pluralism, and an intertextuality which favors the calculated (and sometimes ironic) "citing" or quoting of the past. The more definitive description of postmodernism and its relation to modernism remains to be seen.

## Further reading

Bradbury, Malcolm, and James McFarlane, eds. *Modernism 1890–1930*, 1976.
Ciari, Joseph. *The Aesthetics of Modernism*, 1970.
Cronin, Anthony. *A Question of Modernity*, 1966.
Eysteinsson, Astradur. *The Concept of Modernism*, 1990.
Faulkner, Peter. *Modernism*, 1977.
Garvin, Harry R., ed. *Romanticism, Modernism, Postmodernism*, 1980.
Huyssen, Andreas. *After the Great Divide: Modernism, Mass Culture, Postmodernism*, 1986.
Kampf, Louis. *On Modernism: The Prospects for Literature and Freedom*, 1967.
Kiely, Robert, ed. *Modernism Reconsidered*, 1983.
Kubal, David. *The Consoling Intelligence: Responses to Literary Modernism*, 1982.
Quinones, Ricardo. *Mapping Literary Modernism: Time and Development*, 1983.
Reiss, Timothy J. *The Discourse of Modernism*, 1982.
Stevenson, Randall. *Modernist Fiction. An Introduction*, 1992.
Wilson, Edmund. *Axel's Castle: A Study in the Imaginative Literature of 1870–1930*, 1984.

THOMAS F. BARRY

# Toril Moi

## Norwegian theorist and critic

**Born:** Farsund, Norway; November 28, 1953

## Biography

Born and educated (in French Studies) in Norway, Toril Moi has served as the director of the Center for Feminist Research at the University of Bergen, Norway, as a distinguished lecturer in French at Oxford University (Lady Margaret Hall), and (as of writing, 1999), as professor of literature and Romance studies at Duke University in the United States. Her interests are in the area of theoretical studies and include feminist theory, psychoanalytic theory (Sigmund Freud), French phenomenology (Jean-Paul Sartre, Simone de Beauvoir, Maurice Merleau-Ponty), and ordinary language philosophy (Ludwig Wittgenstein, John Austin, Stanley Cavell). Her research and teaching has focused on three major areas, namely questions concerning sexuality, sex, gender, and the body; melodrama, skepticism, and the "ordinary" in theater and film (Henrik Ibsen and August Strindberg); and the history of "free love" and other critiques of traditional bourgeois marriage since the late eighteenth century.

## Influence

Moi has been a major figure in contemporary academic discussions of feminism, especially feminist literary theory, since the publication of her first book, *Sexual/Textual Politics* in 1985. Her lucid and perceptive explications of issues in feminist literary theory and of the intellectual positions of leading feminist thinkers such as Simone de Beauvoir and Julia Kristeva, as well as her significant editorial work on important compilations of essays, have made her writings a staple of undergraduate and graduate course reading lists on modern feminism throughout the world. Moi is extremely evenhanded in both her praise and criticism of other feminist writers and critics and this fact has earned her the professional respect of her peers.

## Analysis

Before we can examine the specific publications of Toril Moi, a brief discussion of modern feminism in general would seem appropriate. At the onset let a central fact be stated: the majority of societies (both Occidental, Oriental,

and African) around the world have been historically patriarchal, that is, the inheritance of land (and the economic,
political, social, and psychological power that this implies)
has been to the (usually oldest) male child; women were
considered to be expendable and indeed, in some societies,
even a property to be traded. It must always be kept in
mind that the operative and crucial word here is *power* in
all its varied manifestations. This imbalance in the assig-
nation of power is still the case today in many areas of the
world. In most Western countries, however, women did
gain a measure (more or less) of political emancipation in
the universal suffrage movements of the first half of the
twentieth century. World War II gave many women an
experience of economic emancipation as they labored in
wartime industries and lived without their soldiering
husbands, a freedom which many were loath to relinquish
when their male partners returned home. In the United
States many did, however, return to the status quo during
the 1950s and they sought to emulate an imagined ideal of
wife, mother, and homemaker widely promulgated in
cinema and the new medium of television. The civil-rights
movement of African-Americans (and the general spirit of
protest and rebellion) of the 1960s encouraged the emergence of a new (and more assertive) feminist movement
which sought to emancipate all women and to explore the
nature of women's experience in all its dimensions,
including the literary. Feminists are also accustomed to
make the following lexical distinctions: "female" means
biologically-based gender differences, "feminine" refers to
a mode of thinking/behavior that is largely socially
transmitted, and "feminist" designates the attempt by both
women and men to uncover patriarchal, gender-based
ideologies and their consequences.

To illustrate the importance of the feminist perspective
for literary studies, we can briefly examine the issue of the
"canon" of great literature. The canon refers to the authoritative and elite list of literary texts which are considered
to have perennial cultural-humanistic value and which are
routinely taught to students (usually in the form of anthologies of great literature published for secondary school and
university class reading lists) with the claim that these books
convey a universally valid and authentic vision of life.
William Shakespeare is clearly part of the list for English
language literature as is Johann Wolfgang von Goethe for
German literature or Molière for French. To be included in
the canon conveys great status and privilege and one way
of viewing this inclusion is to see it in terms of power, be
it social, economic, political, or cultural power. Perhaps the
most important meaning of power in this context is the
very power to judge: *who* is listed in the canon and
*who* is not. The literary canon, it can be argued, represents
power as cultural value and what is deemed valuable is
always designated by those "in power." Such decisions have
been traditionally made by the professorial elite of academe,
that is, the selection of texts has been institutionalized

(which is, as it were, a way to cement power) within a
select community that has been, for the most part until
fairly recently, made up exclusively, in the majority of
Western societies, of white middle-class males whose
choices may well reflect their own parochial/patriarchal
values. By its very definition, the canon represses texts
which are *other* (or noncanonical) and here this generally
means literary works by women, nonwhites, the poor, and
any other group excluded from the power elite. The question faced by Moi and other feminist literary theoreticians
is whether or not a separate canon of women's writing
should be established or whether or not all canons should
be abolished because they are essentially repressive and
exclusive. Such issues of the canon in literary theory are
symptomatic of larger philosophical problems facing postmodern societies such as multiculturalism or cultural
pluralism (admitting the universal validity of all cultures)
versus the maintenance of individual (but perhaps biased
or parochial) cultural values and norms of behavior.

Moi's *Sexual/Textual Politics* examines through
insightful critical discussions the history of modern feminist literary theory and as such it makes an excellent introductory text. The particular critical acumen which Moi
brings to her discussions involves a clear emphasis on the
socioeconomic as well as the psychoanalytic dimensions of
literature and, perhaps more importantly, a constant awareness of the hermeneutic dimensions of literary criticism and
theory. Both emphases involve the assumption that the
meaning of the text/author are never absolute in and of
themselves but rather are always a product of the context
in which they are viewed. Sociological and psychoanalytic
approaches emphasize that textual meanings are embedded
within a complex matrix of social-cultural-psychological
factors and in Moi's case these dimensions must include
gender-specific issues in any attempt to understand a literary
text. Hermeneutics – the science and study of how we
interpret texts, of how meaning is generated – examines
the sometimes hidden or unspoken assumptions (what the
German philosopher Hans-Georg Gadamer called the
"horizon of expectations") about the nature of meaning
which the critic/reader brings to any given text. In other
words, if we have certain presumptions about what is meaningful in a text, then we only "see" those dimensions which
involve our conscious and unconscious assumptions; other
aspects of the work are simply not "seen." Thomas Kuhns,
the well-known historian of science, called this set of
presumptions a "paradigm," a matrix of factors which
constitute the "reality" we perceive. Feminism asks us to
perform a "paradigm shift," a radical change in our perception of gender relationships.

As an example of what Moi's critical approach intends,
let us examine the introductory chapter of her book in
which she critiques hermeneutic assumptions in Elaine
Showalter's discussion of the 1929 Virginia Woolf text,
*A Room of One's Own*, from Showalter's 1977 critical

work on British women writers, *A Literature of Their Own*. Showalter criticizes Woolf's work for lacking a unified and committed feminist point of view – suggesting rather a politically detached, passive, and highly subjective female aestheticism/modernism which seeks to "transcend" gender politics – and adopting instead continuously shifting, multiple perspectives that leave the reader with no definitive existential-feminist position to identify with; Woolf (for Showalter) abdicates her feminist "duty" to depict the lives of real women. Moi argues that specific theoretical assumptions concerning literature and politics – and the criteria which define the canon of *good* writing – underlie Showalter's position, literary-critical assumptions which have their roots in well-established (that is, institutionalized) patriarchal ideologies. Showalter's criteria owe a debt to the proletarian realism of Marxist critic Georg Lukács who proscribes that the novel depict three-dimensional, fully rounded human characters and relationships – realistic human "types" – with which the reader can identify and thereby gain insight into the dynamics of personality, history, and society. Moi (and other feminist theoreticians) suggests that this traditional and bourgeois humanism is in fact gender-based, a male ideology which posits – in analogy to the male member – a monolithic, rigid, and unified vision of the self (the Freudian fully "integrated personality") always in control/domination of the situation, that is, of itself and others. The feminine position – again in analogy to female anatomy – presents a much needed contraposition to this masculine view: a self that is indeed multiplicitous, always in flux, shifting, and allowing itself and others the freedom and openness to generate alternative realities rather than proscribing a unitary, canonical, and unyielding view of the "real" self. Although the genital analogies to modes of thinking may seem somewhat spurious to some, the biological basis of different gender sensibilities is indeed significant (when "nature" is not overly stressed over "nurture") and the feminist intellectual position is well taken; it clearly affords the reader a more balanced view of the true nature of literary production. In short, Moi's principal criticism is that Showalter has not sufficiently examined the ideological-theoretical assumptions with which she examines a literary text. The first part of Moi's book deals with authors and trends within Anglo-American feminist criticism and she continues her examinations of hidden ideological-critical assumptions in well-known feminist texts such as Kate Millet's *Sexual Politics* (1970), Ellen Moer's *Literary Women* (1977), and Sandra Gilbert and Susan Gubar's *The Madwoman in the Attic* (1979) as well as the work of prominent representative theoreticians such as Showalter, Annette Kolodny, and Myra Jehlen. Issues under discussion among these critics are whether the practice of "literary theory" itself is a masculine/patriarchal activity, whether there are "feminine" and "masculine" modes of writing and reading texts, questions concerning (patriarchal) humanism and the creation of a less oppressive "female" canon, and difficulties in even formulating a conceptual ground upon which to generate a feminine aesthetic when the very issues are defined within male/patriarchal "humanist" categories. Moi argues that the answer lies in the area of sexual politics, that is, in the dynamics of gender-based assignations of political and material power.

The second part of *Sexual/Textual Politics* examines the thought of prominent French feminists, most notably Simone de Beauvoir, Hélène Cixous, Luce Irigaray, and Julia Kristeva. Since Beauvoir is the subject of Moi's second book publication, we will look briefly at her appraisals of the other French thinkers. While Anglo-American feminists tend to be pragmatically text- and author-centered as well as skeptical of Freudian psychology and all theory, French feminists are given to elaborate and radical philosophical theorizing which often presupposes knowledge of thinkers from Friedrich Nietzsche and Martin Heidegger to Jacques Derrida and Jacques Lacan and is therefore rather difficult to access for the average reader. The flamboyant Cixous is a good example of such involved and radical feminist literary theorizing and Moi's evaluation of her work is again very evenhanded, both critical and cognizant of Cixous' achievement. Cixous considers herself more poet than philosopher and as such her pronouncements are seemingly contradictory. In brief, she seeks (in the manner of Derrida) to deconstruct textuality (and the hierarchy of all patriarchal language) and to construct a completely liberated vision of female writing which is utopian and harks back to the Lacanian Imaginary – a womblike state – when the self is not yet distinguished from the all-giving and all powerful Mother. Moi (understandably, given her realistic estimations of the importance of the materiality of power, politics, and ideology in gender relations) criticizes Cixous' apolitical and nonmaterialist stance. Moi's criticism is essentially the same for the feminist thought of Luce Irigaray, a practicing psychoanalyst. Irigaray is caught in the same dilemma of theory that plagues her French colleagues, that is, she seeks to deny the logocentric/phallocentric essentialism – Derrida's idea that Western philosophy is guided by the incorrect notion that essential reality is centered in the word/*logos* – of patriarchal discourse yet she attempts nonetheless to define the metaphysical essence of what is female/feminine and thereby traps herself in a contradiction. Irigaray's works practice a sophisticated analysis of male texts – sometimes involving an exaggerated mimicry of their discourse as a way to expose their phallocentrism – which reveals a "masculine" dependence on seeing/viewing as the criterion of what is reality whereas the "feminine" modality privileges touching. Moi rejects such ahistorical metaphysical idealism in favor of materialist analyses which transcend facile concepts of what men and women are.

Moi explicitly aligns herself with the thought of the Bulgarian-born thinker Julia Kristeva. Kristeva rejects the structuralist view of language as being a static system and prefers a notion of language as dynamic process: all meaning is produced through and in context (Moi calls this semiotics or textual theory) which is essentially infinite since we can always conceive of another context (including the context of other texts themselves, which Moi and Kristeva term intertextuality). Interestingly, Kristeva's view privileges poetic discourse – the productivity of language – as a central arbiter of meaning since it is a product of the imagination and thus establishes not merely contexts that are real but also the horizon of contexts that are possible or even conceivable. On the other hand, this view also indicates that the act of naming is very much an act of power as the attempt to organize and to regulate/control the perception of reality (and as such is subject to ideological abuse). Thus Kristeva believes that definitions of "female/feminine" are constructs of patriarchal discourse and have no real meaning outside of that context; real women (as individuals or a group) are essentially marginalized within this ideologically biased discourse structure. Ever mindful of political/materialist concerns, Moi mentions that Kristeva's critical analyses, as those of all intellectuals, (unfortunately) constitute themselves a more or less marginal activity within postindustrial capitalism.

Moi's 1994 study *Simone de Beauvoir: The Making of an Intellectual Woman* examines the life of one of the most important twentieth-century feminists and intellectuals. Moi considers Beauvoir's 1949 work *Le Deuxième Sexe* (*The Second Sex*, 1984) to be of monumental importance to the concerns of modern women – the "greatest feminist essay of this century" – and a text which is still highly relevant to feminists today. The "Simone de Beauvoir" whose life Moi considers is the person represented in and through her writings (and the writings about her); in other words, Moi takes her subject Beauvoir's "life" as a "text" to be deciphered. Moi writes about the varied social, psychological, educational, and material forces and the discourse structures within a patriarchally organized world (as well as about the literary and philosophical texts Beauvoir herself produced) which made or "constructed" Beauvoir the person into the intellectual/textual "Beauvoir" that she became in the eyes of others. Moi calls her approach the writing of a "personal genealogy" and it is to be distinguished from the traditional linear/historical mode of biography. She divides her book into three "textual moments" which she discerns in Beauvoir's life/texts.

First, Moi looks at a conversation held in 1929 between Beauvoir (aged 21) and Jean-Paul Sartre (aged 24), as they prepare for the orals in the prestigious *agrégation* examination in philosophy, in which Beauvoir seeks to explain her philosophical ideas to the older (and more distinguished) Sartre and he – in what Moi calls "logical violence" – demolishes her arguments, leaving her feeling intellectually inferior and emotionally devastated. Moi discusses the educational background of the two

intellectuals, with Sartre clearly being the more privileged of the pair. The interesting fact here, however, is that Beauvoir – who was in love with Sartre – convinces herself that his superiority/her inferiority is somehow "natural," a function of male-female differences. Moi looks at the complex psychosexual needs and the patriarchal social structures at work in Beauvoir's lifelong adoption of a subordinate intellectual "speaking position" (Moi's term) to Sartre who was, despite his great intellect, somewhat of a male chauvinist cad. At work here is what another feminist theoretician, Michèle Le Doueff, calls an "erotico-theoretical" relationship, that is, when the woman idealizes the man's intellect as equivalent to his phallic power. In such a situation, an intellectual woman who shows herself to be more "intelligent" than the man she desires would jeopardize the sexual relationship with that man. Simply put, Beauvoir was forced to deny – at great personal expense – a significant part of her psychological identity. It is, in part at least, this almost masochistic dependence on Sartre that has caused many (especially French) intellectuals to denigrate Beauvoir's achievement.

Second, Moi examines another conversation, held in 1946, between the two thinkers in which Beauvoir realized (again) that the social status of men and women is indeed very different; this meeting eventually led to the writing of *The Second Sex*. Moi seeks to explore Beauvoir's conceptions of what it meant to be a woman in detailed discussions of the (overly melodramatic) novel *L'Invitée* (1943) as well as *The Second Sex*. Moi holds Beauvoir's novel to be "melodramatic" because of its existential import and this is because the text is in many ways a response to Sartre's monumental (and in its way equally melodramatic) opus on existential philosophy, *L'Être et le néant* (1943; *Being and Nothingness*, 1966). Both Sartre and Beauvoir tend to sexualize (unconsciously) the terms of their philosophical discussions and Moi considers at length the psychological implications (in terms of gender/power relationships) of such a practice. In *The Second Sex*, Beauvoir analyzes with great sympathy and understanding the experience of being born female within a world dictated by the demands of patriarchal authority in its varied manifestations from fathers and sons to lovers and husbands. Yet along with its polemics and analyses, Moi finds Beauvoir's work to be a "powerful narrative of liberation" which offers a vision of hope to all women of a world in which feminism would no longer be a necessity. Moi also regards it as the "founding text" for the materialist feminism which she herself seeks to practice.

Third, Moi investigates the older Beauvoir's autobiographical writings in which the latter discusses her profound feelings of depression and personal emptiness. Moi analyzes the latter's personal psychology and the meaning writing assumed in her life. In what Nietzsche would call a "human, all too human" attempt to defend herself against overwhelming existential feelings of loneliness and separation (especially in the case of male love and approval and most notably in the case of Sartre), Beauvoir ironically sacrificed the very self she sought to protect by refusing to assert her own identity when it would put her in conflict with patriarchal demands. Her fate is in no way unique and remains one that is faced by all women living under patriarchal strictures: an oscillation between dependence and independence, love and loneliness, happiness and despair. The result of this conflict for Beauvoir was a lifelong existential self-alienation, an estrangement from her own identity as a thinking and feeling female human being, which produced intermittent but debilitating states of depression and obsessive thoughts of old age and death. As an intellectual woman, Beauvoir was conscious (to varying degrees at least) of the gender issues at stake and verbalized them in/through her letters and diaries as well as the literary and philosophical texts and, as with most writers who directly confront difficult existential themes, she sought a personal transcendence in/through the act of writing.

Moi has identified herself on several occasions with "materialist feminism" and a final word might be said concerning the meaning of this term. One thinks immediately of the dialectical materialism usually associated with Marxist socialism, but this is only one aspect of its significance for Moi and other feminist theoreticians (as is suggested in the 1994 collection of essays which Moi coedited). A materialist feminism is not only about the social, political, and economic transformation of society (although this is indeed a crucial aspect) but about the transformation of the patriarchal psychological and social (behavioral) structures – what we might, borrowing from Thomas Kuhns' often cited concept, call the "patriarchal paradigm" – which dictate the lives of individual women and men. Whereas Marx argued that material/economic production was the basis of all social superstructures (art, law, education, and family for example), a feminist materialism suggests that perceived (patriarchal) gender relationships dictate/regulate much of these other social activities including the economic.

## Principal criticism
*Sexual/Textual Politics: Feminist Literary Theory*, 1985
*Feminist Theory and Simone de Beauvoir*, 1990
*Simone de Beauvoir: The Making of an Intellectual Woman*, 1994
*What is a Woman? And Other Essays*, 1999

## Other major works and literary forms

EDITED TEXTS
*The Kristeva Reader*, 1986
*French Feminist Thought*, 1987
*Materialist Feminism*, 1994 (with Janice Radway)

THOMAS F. BARRY

See also Cixous; Feminist Criticism; Gilbert and Gubar; Irigaray; Kristeva

# Michel Eyquem de Montaigne
French essayist and writer

**Born:** Château de Montaigne (near Bordeaux), France; February 28, 1533
**Died:** Château de Montaigne, France; September 13, 1592

## Biography
Michel Eyquem de Montaigne's great-grandfather, Ramon Eyquem, purchased the château of Montaigne in 1477, and Pierre Eyquem, the essayist's father, enlarged it. Pierre, a prosperous businessman, married Antoinette de Louppes, the daughter of a Spanish-Jewish family; at the château on February 28, 1533, Montaigne was born. In an age of religious and political contention, the family was remarkably tolerant, a trait which the essayist also exhibited strikingly in his life and writing. He was tutored early and exclusively in Latin, with the result that long before he continued his education at the Collège de Guyenne at Bordeaux he was an accomplished and enthusiastic Latinist. Later he studied law and spent his early working years as counselor in a court of law at Bordeaux. He disliked the law but established a close friendship with Étienne de La Boétie, whose early death affected Montaigne profoundly. In 1565 he married Françoise de La Chassaigne; of their six children, only one survived infancy.

At his father's death in 1568 the title and estate of Montaigne passed to him. Three years later he retired from public life, until 1581, when he began four years of service as the mayor of Bordeaux. Three different French kings proffered him court appointments; most of the time from 1572 until his death, however, he spent reading and composing *The Essays*. Troubled by ill health in his later years, he died on September 13, 1592.

## Influence
As the inventor of the personal essay, Montaigne initiated the portrayal of the self in discursive prose. Mainly by his practice but also by his observations on his craft, he established the principles of a form related to, but distinctly different from, autobiography. He portrayed himself candidly in the act of reflection on his subject material rather than as a master or expert. The provisional quality of his writing made *The Essays* unique, and their flexibility prompted countless imitations, especially by journalists after the rise of the periodical in the eighteenth century.

## Analysis
Although Montaigne's essays are not so random and unstructured as they initially seem, he felt no obligation to confine himself to his nominal subject; consequently, his criticism is scattered throughout his one hundred and seven essays. Much of what he says about poetry typifies Renaissance theory without breaking new ground. For

example, he agrees with Plato – the Plato of the *Ion* (c. fourth century B.C.) – that poetry is a divine gift and that the poet operates in a divine "frenzy," but his critical remarks taken collectively do not suggest too literal an adherence to this long-popular theory which acknowledges the mystery of creativity by denying responsibility or rational control to the poet. Because "divine poetry is above the rules and reason," however, it lifts its audience out of the realm of everyday life. Indeed, Montaigne testifies to the power poetry has exerted over him from earliest childhood. Addressed to the emotions, it "ravishes and overwhelms" reason to stir its listener or reader at a deeper level. Montaigne does not urge the appropriation of this emotional dynamite to promote moral education, as do contemporaries such as Edmund Spenser and Sir Philip Sidney; instead, he savors its effect personally. Poetic form contributes: "It seems to me that a thought, when compressed into the numbered feet of poetry, springs forth much more violently and strikes me a much stiffer jolt." This observation, itself a compression of several ideas, including the paradox that the restraints of measure can somehow enhance "violence," demonstrates Montaigne's knack for absorbing commonplaces and expressing them personally.

His ranking of the great poets also shows him to be conventional, though not slavishly so. He rates Virgil, Lucretius, Catullus, and Horace above all others, but in preferring Virgil's *Georgics* (c. 37–29 B.C.) to his *Aeneid* (c. 29–19 B.C.) he departs from the more usual Renaissance opinion that the former was an intermediate step between pastoral and epic, a honing of the poet's skills before venturing upon his masterpiece. Montaigne applauds the relative polish of the *Georgics*, which, unlike the *Aeneid*, Virgil had time to finish. It is easy to see why a man who wrote that "the most beautiful lives . . . are those that conform to the common human pattern, with order, but without miracle and without eccentricity" would enjoy poems celebrating the life and work of the simple farmer. Montaigne also displays a maverick taste in favoring the fifth book of the *Aeneid*, the account of the funeral games in memory of Aeneas' father, over the more generally popular preceding book on Aeneas' encounter with Dido or the following one describing his visit to the underworld.

Montaigne has little to say of contemporary writers. His essay "Twenty-nine Sonnets of Étienne de La Boétie" is only a brief introduction to works of a dear friend. He acknowledges other contemporaries thus:

It seems to me that poetry too has flourished in our century. We have a wealth of good craftsmen in that trade: Daurat, Beza, Buchanan, L'Hôpital, Montdoré, Turnebus. As for those writing in French, I think they have raised its poetry to the highest point it will ever reach; and in the respects in which Ronsard and Du Bellay excel, I do not consider them far removed from the perfection of the ancients.

He makes two other passing references each to Pierre de Ronsard and Joachim du Bellay and makes no others to any of the famed Pléiade. By comparison, he quotes Horace, Lucretius, and Virgil more than one hundred times each in *The Essays* and classical prose writers Cicero, Seneca the Younger, and Plutarch even more often.

Renaissance writers were inveterate classicists, but there is a particular reason for Montaigne's almost exclusive attention to Roman writers. (The main exception, the Greek Plutarch, he read in a French translation.) Latin, not French, was Montaigne's first language from the time his father employed a non-French-speaking tutor and instructed him to let the boy, then a mere infant, hear nothing but Latin. Thus Montaigne's sensitivity to Latin literature was not mere book learning, and his grasp of Latin style exceeded that of most, if not all, of his contemporaries. Because he read for pleasure as he matured and wrote as an enthusiast rather than as an objective critic, the temptation is to dismiss his opinions as mere partialities, but his early saturation in the classics and the abiding love of them that grew out of his education give his judgments the stamp of the expert – at least with respect to his favorite writers.

In two parts of his long essay "On Some Verses of Vergil," his critical acuteness comes into focus. He quotes a passage from the eighth book of the *Aeneid* in which Virgil describes the lovemaking of Venus and Vulcan and then goes on to discuss the differences between marital and extramarital love, but twenty pages later, after citing a somewhat similar passage from Lucretius on a coupling of Venus and Mars, Montaigne examines the diction of the two quotations. What he admires most are the colorful active verbs and the adjectives, which he proceeds to list, curiously intermingling words from both poets. His remarks at this point constitute his most trenchant utterance on the art of poetry:

These good people needed no sharp and subtle play on words; their language is all full and copious with a natural and constant vigor. They are all epigram, not only the tail but the head, stomach, and feet. There is nothing forced, nothing dragging; the whole thing moves at the same pace. . . . This is not a soft and merely inoffensive eloquence; it is sinewy and solid, and does not so much please as fill and ravish; and it ravishes the strongest minds most. When I see these brave forms of expression, so alive, so profound, I do not say "This is well said," I say "This is well thought."

Good description is not merely manipulation of language; it is perception, a matter of seeing "more clearly and deeply into the thing." The solidity of such language is a function of mental fiber. The great poet has an "able mind" which can use the language more resourcefully and innovatively and thus enrich it through his efforts.

In this essay and elsewhere Montaigne attacks Petrarchan conceits and "vain subtleties." He is not directing his scorn primarily at Petrarch, however, but at the excesses of his imitators. His remarks on this subject call to mind the later critical assaults on decadent metaphysical conceits. Montaigne was no enemy of metaphor as such, for most of his Virgilian-Lucretian word list was metaphors and his own prose is highly and effectively metaphorical. For Montaigne, nevertheless a first-rate mind had no need of any but direct, vigorous language.

Although an admirer of poetry, Montaigne wrote about prose as a practitioner, and his critical views on prose, though no more systematic, are more suggestive and influential. The major critical controversy of his time with respect to prose pitted the eloquence and majesty of Cicero against Seneca's plain style. Montaigne saw in Cicero's great orations the contrivances of a wily lawyer and politician. Suspecting a lack of sincerity and truth in the language of public persuasion, he proclaimed himself persuadable rather by what comes from the heart.

A more serious objection to studied eloquence is that it turns attention away from its subject: "Fie on the eloquence that leaves us craving itself, not things!" Montaigne's conviction that style can distract the reader from subject matter – a view shortly thereafter elaborated by the first English essayist, Francis Bacon – leads him frequently to quote Seneca on the virtues of plain and simple prose. Yet Montaigne admires Cicero's letters to his friend Atticus most ungrudgingly, for they reveal not only history but Cicero's personality, his "soul," as well. Montaigne's interest in the inner person anticipates the later neoclassical and Victorian fondness for letters, memoirs, and biography – including autobiography. It is no accident that Montaigne cites Plutarch so often; if Cicero was the great ancient revealer of self, Plutarch yielded to no one in the art of revealing other selves. Long before James Boswell revered Plutarch as the "prince of ancient biographers," Renaissance geniuses such as Montaigne and William Shakespeare were in various ways taking advantage of Plutarch's gift for disclosing "what comes from within."

Although Cicero, Seneca, and Plutarch wrote works that today are classified as essays, Montaigne, in using for the first time the word *essai* to designate a literary form, was inventing a new and personal form of prose composition and in the process defining it. The word was already well established grammatically as both substantive and predicative in French and English. Geoffrey Chaucer had used it in its earlier English form, "assay," two centuries earlier, to mean "test" or "attempt" or "trial," and its French equivalent shared the same cluster of meanings. No one before Montaigne, however, had thought of using the word to name a specifically literary test or attempt or trial.

To appreciate the significance of this new application for an old word, it is useful to consider the words "author" and "authority." An authority writes from mastery and as

such delivers knowledge – a finished product, as it were – to the reader. The authors of classical antiquity were authorities. In Chaucer's time there was no significant difference between an author and an authority, both words coming into England from the Latin *auctor* by way of Old French. The author of *The Essays* disavows authority. He is not presenting the conclusions of an expert but is inviting the reader to look on as he tries, tests, conducts experiments. By "trying on" the essayist's observations, the reader cooperates in a continuing test of their applicability.

The subject of these trials and try-outs is very personal: "I am myself the matter of my book." Montaigne thereby becomes the father of all personal essayists. It should be noted that Bacon, while owing more than his title to Montaigne, is making an "attempt" not particularly on himself but on moral ideas. Since Bacon's essays were not received as the tentative exercises they purported to be, he in effect continued the tradition, established in antiquity, of what is now referred to as the formal essay. In short, he became another authority, while Montaigne's personal essays served as models for a distinctly different type of literary endeavor. One has only to think of its great practitioners in one era – William Hazlitt, Thomas De Quincey, and Charles Lamb in the early nineteenth century – to realize how influential Montaigne's invention became.

Not only in practice but also in scattered but fruitful critical observations Montaigne provided a theoretical basis for the familiar essay. He objected to the divisions of traditional prose compositions such as the oration, stating that they were inimical to the simple effect for which he strove. Since essays were by definition tentative, he had to feel free from the restrictions of a preestablished form, which he compared to tight clothing and uncomfortable furniture. Oddly enough, he believed not in correction but in addition as his mode of alteration, his explanation being that once he released his work, it no longer belonged to him. If he found it necessary to change his work substantively, he preferred to "speak better elsewhere." Accretions in the form of ornaments or further development he considered true to the original version. This concept of form, adumbrating Samuel Taylor Coleridge's "organicism," permits the work to grow, although it is "always one."

Although few essayists have rivaled him in open-endedness (some of his essays run only a page or two, the longest well over a hundred pages), generations of essayists have profited from his emphasis on flexibility and allowed themselves to "go roaming" like their master. He recommended the essay as a vehicle for independence, for increasing one's capacity by mental exercise rather than by the acquisition of knowledge. Because essays are not chapters in a book, they can be taken up or put down easily by writer or reader as either sees fit. Montaigne's invention would prosper when periodicals came into fashion in the eighteenth century and created both a need and a large audience for individual essays.

The habit of independent reflection, divorced from causes or creeds and encouraging the discovery of self, is a Renaissance legacy; self-investigation, however, became a legitimate literary endeavor only in the autobiographies of Benvenuto Cellini and Geronimo Cardano in Montaigne's lifetime. Lacking chronological ordering or any other systematic development of his life, Montaigne's essays hardly constitute an autobiography but instead present "some features of my habits and temperament," as he says in his preface. Such apparent self-indulgence must have mystified his contemporaries, who were inclined to the opposite vice of self-immolation in religious and political controversies whose rationales they took no part in developing.

*The Essays* embody and occasionally assert as yet unrealized literary implications of Renaissance Humanism. If life is worth living for its own sake, and human personality is worth developing, then a book which essays the revelation of any individual personality is similarly justifiable. What Walt Whitman wrote nearly three centuries later – "I celebrate myself and sing myself" – applies equally well to Montaigne, and though his vision was not Whitman's democratic one, the self of Montaigne's essays, like Whitman's, became by extension the selves of those readers who have over the generations tested their experiences against the author's. Thus both writers avoid egotism by looking not only inward at themselves but outward at mankind as well. That such writing is taken for granted today is the most obvious measure of Montaigne's continuing influence.

## Principal criticism

*Essais*, 1580, 1588, 1595 (*The Essays*, 1603, John Florio translation)

## Other major works and literary forms

Aside from *The Essays*, which Michel Eyquem de Montaigne continued to augment over a period of a dozen years, he is chiefly noted for his *Journal du voyage* (1774; *Travel Journal*, 1842), based on a manuscript no longer extant. It is a diary, written partly in French, partly in Latin, of a journey to Switzerland, Germany, and Italy undertaken in 1580 and is important as a source of observations later used in *The Essays*. Montaigne also left letters and a 1569 translation of Raymond de Sebond's *Theologia Naturalis*, a fifteenth-century Latin work purporting to demonstrate philosophically the existence and nature of God.

NONFICTION
*Journal du voyage*, 1774 (*Travel Journal*, 1842)

TRANSLATION
*La Théologie naturelle*, 1569 (of Raymond de Sebond's *Theologia Naturalis*)

## Further reading

Auerbach, Erich. "L'Humaine Condition," in *Mimesis*, 1953.
Bowman, Frank. *Montaigne*, 1965.
Burke, Peter. *Montaigne*, 1981.
Croll, Morris W. "The Anti-Ciceronian Movement: 'Attic' and Baroque Prose Style," in *Style, Rhetoric, and Rhythm*, 1966. Edited by J. Max Patrick et al.
Emerson, Ralph Waldo. "Montaigne: Or, The Skeptic," in *Representative Men*, 1903.
Frame, Donald M. *Montaigne's Discovery of Man: The Humanization of a Humanist*, 1955.
———. *Montaigne's Essais: A Study*, 1969.
Friedrich, Hugo. *Montaigne*, 1991.
Sayce, Richard A. *The Essays of Montaigne: A Critical Exploration*, 1972.
Screech, Peter M. A. *Montaigne and Melancholy: The Wisdom of the Essays*, 1983.
Starobinski, J. "Montaigne on Illusion: The Denunciation of Untruth," in *Daedalus*. 108 (1979), pp. 85–101.
Tetel, Marcel. *Montaigne*, 1974.

ROBERT P. ELLIS

*See also* Bacon; Humanism; Renaissance; Renaissance and Restoration Literary Theory

# Motoori Norinaga

(Ozu Norinaga)

Japanese writer and philologist

**Born:** Matsusaka, Japan; June 21, 1730
**Died:** Matsusaka, Japan; November 4, 1801

## Biography

Motoori Norinaga was born Ozu Norinaga in the town of Matsusaka in Japan's province of Ise in 1730. He came from a family of relatively prosperous cotton wholesalers who owned several shops in Edo, the political center of Japan. As a result of his father's death in 1740 and the poor financial management by his elder stepbrother, the shops were sold, and he and his mother lived off the invested proceeds of the sale.

Clearly, no expense was spared on the young thinker's education, and in 1752 his mother sent him to the ancient capital of Kyoto in order to study medicine. During his five years there he changed his name to Motoori, the name by which his samurai ancestors were known, studied Confucianism under Hori Keizan, as well as classical and contemporary poetics, and became familiar with the philological studies of Keichū.

In 1757 Motoori returned to Matsusaka to practice medicine, and it was also about this time that he read his first essay by Kamo no Mabuchi, who was to become the major influence on his work. In 1763 Motoori had his only meeting with Mabuchi, when the latter spent the night in Matsusaka after touring the nearby Ise Shrines. The two maintained a lively and occasionally bitter correspondence during Mabuchi's remaining years.

Motoori lived the rest of his life in Matsusaka, where his private nativist academy, the Suzunoya, flourished. He frequently traveled to Nagoya, Kyoto, and other cities, communicating his theories on classical literature and verse, as well as his views on the Japanese polity to dominial officials and members of the traditional court aristocracy.

## Influence

Motoori is regarded as the preeminent formulator of critical perspectives on Japan's classic work of fiction, *Genji monogatari* (*The Tale of Genji*, 1925–1976), written by Murasaki Shikibu about 1004. Motoori also formulated a major theory of Japanese poetics and wrote commentaries on the three prime anthologies of Japanese verse: *Manyōshū* (c. 759; *The Manyōshū*, 1929–1969), *Kokinshū* (c. 905; *Kokinshū: A Collection of Poems Ancient and Modern*, 1984), and *Shin kokinshū* (c. 1205) – the last two partially translated in *Japanese Court Poetry* (1961). He had more than five hundred students registered in the private school which he operated out of his home, though his main "disciples," Hirata Atsutane and Ban Nobutomo, knew Motoori only through his writings.

## Analysis

It was in 1757 that Motoori became influenced by Mabuchi's work and wrote his own first essay discussing his views on poetics, titled "Ashiwake obune" (small boat among the reeds). The essay addressed the much-debated issue of whether versification was of benefit to either the individual or the polity. Adopting a position largely consistent with the views of his future teacher Mabuchi, Motoori drew a distinction between the essence (*hontai*) of poetry and its potential (*mochiyuru tokoro*). Motoori argued that this essence was of no use whatever in either assisting the governing of the country or regulating the individual, but that by virtue of its capacity to express one's heartfelt emotions, verse made it possible for people to understand one another better and thereby contributed indirectly to the maintenance of social order. Though Motoori significantly amplified and refined his poetics in later years, he never repudiated this assumption concerning the potential of verse to contribute to political stability.

In 1763, shortly after his only face-to-face meeting with Mabuchi, Motoori wrote two essays which expressed his fundamental views on literary criticism and poetics. The first, *Shibun yōryō*, applied the concept of *mono no aware* to an analysis of *The Tale of Genji*, and the second, *Isonokami sasamegoto* (personal views on poetry), applied the concept to verse. Both works were written in 1763, and they represent exceptionally mature articulations of views which Motoori retained during the remaining thirty-eight years of his life.

The term *mono no aware* defies translation. In its most literal sense, it refers to the sadness, or pity (*aware*) of things (*mono*), that is, the emotive qualities of objects,

forces of nature, and even persons. As Motoori used the term, however, it suggests a heightened sensitivity to the emotional and affective dimensions of human experience. *Mono no aware* accordingly is something people possess whenever they exhibit such instinctive and acute sympathy with the actions of others that the passing of moral judgment upon those actions becomes extraneous. This *mono no aware* is expressed, according to Motoori, whenever persons write of what they feel in their hearts.

In *Shibun yōryō*, Motoori wrote that what distinguished *The Tale of Genji* as a work of literature was the fact that its author, Murasaki Shikibu, was able to express *mono no aware* through the realistic depictions of the emotions of the major characters. In this way she succeeded in drawing the reader into a sympathetic relationship with the characters; didactic or moralistic interpretations of the work become meaningless. Motoori argued that because of Murasaki's descriptive and narrative skills, her readers are never tempted to ask whether a character's actions are morally right or wrong; instead, her readers are impelled to reflect on whether they have participated in such actions or shared those emotions. Motoori's conclusion is that the only legitimate criterion for evaluating a work of fiction is not its morally edifying properties but its capacity to evoke this quality of emotional engagement on the part of the reader. In this respect Motoori was directly challenging the didactic traditions of literary criticism that *The Tale of Genji* had inspired for most of the preceding seven and a half centuries in Japan. His perspective on *The Tale of Genji* continues to influence contemporary Japanese literary criticism.

Though there is no evidence that Mabuchi ever read *Shibun yōryō*, it is unlikely that he would have disagreed with the thrust of Motoori's remarks. Mabuchi regarded *The Tale of Genji* as a "feminine" work representative of a "feminine age," and in this respect he favored earlier works which he believed evoked a more "masculine" spirit, a spirit which he regarded as more purely Japanese. In other respects, Motoori's emotionalism was essentially consistent with Mabuchi's perspectives on literature. It was Motoori's poetics, however, which directly challenged the views of Mabuchi: while Mabuchi extolled the poetics of Japan's earliest extant anthology of poetry, *The Manyōshū*, Motoori admired the poetics of the *Shin kokinshū* anthology; while Mabuchi disdained poetic sophistication in favor of linguistic purity, Motoori evaluated poetry in terms of its elegance and refinement; while Mabuchi regarded ancient verse as the most effective medium for the communication of an allegedly ancient masculine spirit, Motoori prized the feminine and insisted that all verse be evaluated solely in terms of its artistic integrity independent of the time or circumstances of its composition.

Motoori's differences with Mabuchi stemmed largely from the fact that while Mabuchi regarded the composition of verse as an essentially spontaneous event which occurs when one's emotions can no longer be contained, Motoori regarded versification as a far more calculated affair. Motoori described it as a deliberate act (*waza*), which occurred in response to the sadness of a situation; what distinguished an exceptional verse from a mediocre one, he argued, was the degree of sophistication (*aya*) represented in its words. It was on these grounds that Motoori esteemed verses from later anthologies such as the *Kokinshū* and *Shin kokinshū* over those from the *Manyōshū*. In this respect Motoori's perspectives on literature and verse were actually more consistent with the avant-garde "art for art's sake" perspectives of the Confucian teachings of Ogyū Sorai than with the prevailing sentiments among the followers of nativism (*kokugaku*).

During his lifetime Motoori earned a reputation not only as a major literary critic but also as Japan's preeminent philologist, and this combination of gifts has caused him to be regarded as the most important of Japan's nativist writers. Despite the encouragement from Mabuchi that he concentrate on *The Manyōshū*, Motoori chose instead to comment on the *Kojiki* (712; *Records of Ancient Matters*, 1882, 1968), which was written in a comparably opaque form of Sino-Japanese. Like *The Manyōshū*, the *Records of Ancient Matters* was written entirely in Chinese characters, using them both phonetically and for their semantic value, but without strict rules of consistency. This style made the *Records of Ancient Matters* an unintelligible work in later centuries and encouraged those with an interest in early Japan to use the *Nihon shoki* (720; *Chronicles of Japan*, 1896), a practice of which Motoori disapproved because the work was written in classical Chinese, and he insisted that Japanese "truths" were not communicable in a foreign language. After more than three decades of work on the project, he completed the commentary on *Records of Ancient Matters*.

Unlike Mabuchi, whose nostalgic, patriotic, and literary ideals converged in his study of *The Manyōshū*, Motoori's postulations concerning a native ancient Way remained largely separate from his literary criticism. While Motoori prized classical works written largely between the early eleventh and the early thirteenth centuries, he otherwise chose to extol the merits of far more ancient times in Japan, times which he perceived to have been unsullied by the contagion of Chinese Confucianism. Like Mabuchi, Motoori believed that the same "true hearts" which had inspired life in ancient Japan might be reanimated in the present, but he tended to present these views more in the vocabulary and structure of a contemporary religion.

The majority of Motoori's students were attracted more by his lectures on works drawn from the native classical literature than by his views on the ancient Way. His private academy, the Suzunoya, was at the time the most successful such venture in Japan, a fact made all the more remarkable by virtue of its location in Matsusaka, outside Japan's major cities. After his death in 1801 the administration of the school was continued by his adopted son, Motoori Ōhira, who enjoyed a measure of success as a philologist and literary critic. Motoori's most famous disciples, Hirata Atsutane and Ban Nobutomo, actually never met him but were nevertheless sufficiently inspired by his writings to develop their own theories concerning the ancient past and its Way.

Motoori's celebrity continues in modern times: there are more studies of him in Japanese than of any other nativist thinker or critic, and he remains the only nativist thinker to have been the subject of a book-length monograph in English. Many of his ideas concerning the ancient polity in Japan were incorporated into the ultranationalist ideology during the decades preceding World War II. Interest in Motoori continued after the war, as the celebrated Japanese literary critic Kobayashi Hideo made him the subject of a special study which was serialized in the popular magazine *Shinchō* over a period of twelve years before finally being published in book form in 1977. The city of Matsusaka constructed a Motoori Norinaga museum to house his manuscripts and other memorabilia, and the museum has become one of the city's major tourist attractions, attesting the ongoing interest in Japan's most famous nativist literary critic.

## Principal criticism

Motoori Norinaga's work was published for the first time in twentieth-century collections, long after it became influential. Thus, written dates are used throughout.

*Shibun yōryō*, 1763
*Isonokami sasamegoto*, 1763
*Man'yōshū tama no ogoto*, 1779
*Shin kokinshū Mino no iezuto*, 1791
*Kokinshū tōkagami*, 1794
*Genji monogatari tama no ogushi*, 1796
*Tamakatsuma*, 1801

## Other major works and literary forms

Motoori Norinaga produced many nonfiction texts about his native Japan – all of which are most often associated with their written dates, for the reason noted above. In 1798 he wrote an autobiography, *Ie no mukashi monogatari*. He also kept a diary, known as *Zaikyō nikki*, written from 1752 to 1757 in Kyoto. Motoori composed several collections of verse and wrote dozens of essays on other subjects. Most of these essays concerned his views on ancient Shinto, which he believed to be Japan's native ancient Way (*kodō*), and related topics such as the ancient calendar or the location of the sun goddess, Amaterasu.

Motoori also wrote a primer for his students titled *Uiyamabumi* (1798), as well as two essays for dominial authorities concerning his views on political economy, *Tamakushige* (1786), and *Hihon tamakushige* (1787), which remained a confidential, uncirculated document until after Motoori's death. His magnum opus, however, was his *Kojiki den* (1798), a philological study of and commentary on Japan's most ancient extant history, the *Kojiki* (compiled by Ō no Yasumaro in 712; *Records of Ancient Matters*, 1882, 1968), on which Motoori worked for more than three decades.

NONFICTION
*Zaikyō nikki*, 1752–1757
*Tamakushige*, 1786
*Hihon tamakushige*, 1787
*Ie no mukashi monogatari*, 1798
*Kojiki den*, 1798
*Uiyamabumi*, 1798
*Motoori Norinaga-ō shokan shū*, 1933 (letters)

MISCELLANEOUS
*Motoori Norinaga kōhon zenshū*, 1923 (2 volumes)
*Motoori Norinaga zenshū*, 1926–1927 (10 volumes)
*Motoori Norinaga zenshū*, 1968–1977 (22 volumes)

## Further reading

Matsumoto, Shigeru. *Motoori Norinaga: 1730–1801*, 1970.
Nishimura, Sey. "First Steps into the Mountains: Motoori Norinaga's *Uiyamabumi*," in *Monumenta Nipponica*. XLII (Winter, 1988), pp. 449–493.
Nosco, Peter. *Remembering Paradise: Nativism and Nostalgia in 18th-Century Japan*, 1990.
Ueda, Makoto. *Literary and Art Theories in Japan*, 1967.
Yoshikawa, Kōjirō. *Motoori Norinaga*, 1977.
——. *Jinsai, Sorai, Norinaga*, 1985.

PETER NOSCO

*See also* Japanese Literary Theory; Kamo No Mabuchi

# Es'kia (Ezekiel) Mphahlele

## South African writer and critic

**Born:** Marabastad township, Pretoria, South Africa; December 17, 1919

## Biography

Es'kia (Ezekiel) Mphahlele was born on December 17, 1919, in Marabastad township, Pretoria, South Africa. After an impoverished childhood, which saw him spend eight unhappy years away from his parents in the northern Transvaal with his paternal grandfather, he made his way to Adams College, Natal, earning a teacher's diploma, which secured for him a position as Afrikaans and English teacher at Orlando High School, Johannesburg. Though he was exposed to the African languages of his parents and to Afrikaans, he acquired a proficiency in English, which was the language of the schools he attended.

As an external student, he earned a B.A. (with honors in English) and an M.A., with distinction, from the University of South Africa. His master's thesis was entitled "The Non-European Character in South African English Fiction"; it was later published in a revised form as *The African Image*. Banned from teaching in South African government schools because of his protesting the apartheid education policy, he eventually became, in 1957, a reporter and literary editor of *Drum*, the journal in English for Africans. That year he left South Africa, complaining that, not allowed to teach and to write by the ever more stringent racial policies, he felt stifled.

He began two decades of wandering in exile, holding various university and cultural positions in Nigeria, Paris, Kenya, Zambia, and the United States. In 1968 he earned his Ph.D. in creative writing for his novel *The Wanderers* at the University of Denver, joining the faculty of that university in 1970. Four years later he moved to the University of Pennsylvania, and in 1978 he returned to South Africa. (He has since changed his name to Es'kia Mphahlele.) The government vetoed his first appointment as Professor of English at Turfloop, the university of the north, but allowed him an inspectorship of schools in the northern Transvaal. Later he became a senior research fellow at the African Studies Institute at the University of Witwatersrand, where he teaches African and comparative literature and does his own research on African languages and literatures. Like many other South African exiles, he has stated that he could not stay away from his country forever, for it is deeply rooted in his life. While his children remained in the United States, his wife, née Rebecca Mochadibane, whom he married in 1945, returned with him to South Africa.

## Influence

As short-story writer, autobiographer, novelist, and poet, Mphahlele has contributed as much as any other writer to the establishment of African literature in English. His importance has been equally considerable in his role as literary and cultural essayist. He is among the most controversial and influential of modern African critics. His *The African Image* is the first extensive work of literary criticism and theory by an English-speaking African writer. In the classrooms of various universities, at numerous conferences and congresses, in essays and books, he has made seminal and pioneering observations on the major literary and cultural issues, such as the nature of black aesthetics, negritude, and protest literature. He has led the opposition to Léopold Senghor's elitist and romantic conception of negritude. His denunciation of negritude is shared by many prominent black African writers, including Wole Soyinka of Nigeria, Sembène Ousmane of Senegal, and Lewis Nkosi of South Africa. In examining these literary and cultural issues, he has provided insightful critical commentary on many African, Caribbean, and Afro-American writers.

## Analysis

Two aspects of Mphahlele's critical writings should be noted from the start. First, he offers his theories of literature not in a systematic, sustained form, as Northrop Frye does in

*Anatomy of Criticism* (1957); his ideas emerge from his musings on writers, predominantly from Africa, and on African culture, society, and politics, which, for him, are integrally linked to African literature. Second, he concerns himself primarily with literary theories that are relevant to African literature; he is familiar with European and American critical theories, but he acknowledges them only to the extent that they have bearing on, or have been assimilated into, African literature.

At the core of Mphahlele's critical theory is his concern with defining black consciousness and examining how this consciousness affects black – particularly black African – literature and society. He begins by rejecting the conception of African consciousness put forward by the advocates of negritude, the term used by Aimé Césaire, the black poet from Martinique, to describe the cultural movement that urges the black man consciously to assert his blackness and to take pride in the history, culture, and thought that existed in Africa before the intrusion of the white man. The term became a rallying cry for many, such as Léopold Senghor of Senegal, who sought a pan-African oneness and a distinct "African Personality," the term used in 1958 by Kwame Nkrumah, then Prime Minister of Gold Coast (now Ghana).

Mphahlele rejects negritude, first, because it is too preoccupied with the past to the exclusion of the realities of contemporary life. He recognizes the value of traditional African culture but not the obsessive, mystical cultivation of it. It is sheer escapism to seek refuge in memories and to deny that the present African experience necessitates the exposure to other cultures and values. He issues "a warning to those Africans who think of culture as an anthropological thing that belongs in the past." The current confrontation with "other ways of life," he insists, "must give as valid a definition to our culture as its historical past." Like Frantz Fanon, he perceives the consequence of negritude to be a mawkish romanticism, quaint exoticism, and tedious slogans.

Mphahlele dissociates himself from the negritudist's categorical rejection of non-African, particularly European, culture. Such insularity suppresses possible enrichment from sources that have already made their mark on African culture. African writers should not be apologetic about Western elements in their own writing. Would the advocates of an exclusively black aesthetics, he asks, reject such elements that are embedded in African literature as the Western novel's form and structure, the "objective correlative," classical or Christian allusions and symbols, ambiguity of meanings, or the abjuring of mere exhortation or propaganda in poetry? He points out that African societies have traditional tales and epics, but not the novel form of today, "which is the product of an individual mind not of group activity." He rejects as simplistic the notion that the Western writer, unlike the African, emphasizes form more than content and that African culture, unlike that of Europe, is based on emotion and passion: the Africans are

not "the only section of the human race who are full of passionate intensity."

Negritude, Mphahlele contends, approaches the African experience as homogeneous, ignoring fundamental differences in politics, history, and racial composition. There are "broad elements of the 'African Personality' that we can be sure are common to most of our societies on this continent": the importance in the social structure of the extended family, of communal responsibility, of gravitating toward other people rather than to places and things, of ancestral spirits, and of audience participation in performances. There are also many common myths and legends. The writer who ignores the distinct individuality of the various communities is falsifying and simplifying the African experience. A vast difference exists between those regions of Africa with a large number of European settlers and others with a European minority, and between exclusively black regions, such as West Africa, and the multiracial ones, such as South Africa. Mphahlele reprimands the enthusiasts of negritude, in particular Senghor, for not being aware of "cultural crosscurrents that characterize artistic expression in multi-racial societies." Senghor and other Francophone African writers are narrowly concerned with their own problems of identity. As Mphahlele says, negritude "answered their own needs as people so assimilated into French culture that they felt cut off from their African roots." Living in a multiracial and multicultural society, the South African black has to learn to synthesize the traditional and the Western cultures, both of which are a part of his psyche. Mphahlele is not blind to the faults of Western culture and the horrors of the apartheid regime – as is made abundantly clear in the revised version of *The African Image*, which has a much-diminished liberal tone; still, he has seen "too much that is good in Western culture . . . to want to repudiate it." The black South African is both captive and admirer of Western culture. An ambivalent creature, he constantly experiences the "need to make choices" and the "dialogue between the two selves" that never ends. "The pendulum swings between revulsion and attraction, between the dreams and the reality of a living past and the aspirations, the imperatives of modern living." The question for the South African black is not whether he "can go back to ancestral worship" but how the ancestral past can help him "snap out of the trance" induced by Western education.

The South African experience also differs from that of black communities such as Nigeria and Ghana, where black Africans are in the ruling and middle classes. To them, negritude is a game for aesthetes, encouraging complacent narcissism and sterile nostalgia. In South Africa, because of the problem of segregation, black people remain members of the proletariat, and what is created by black artists is a proletarian art, not an elitist, debilitating aestheticism removed from social actualities. Mphahlele believes that every writer is "committed to something beyond his art, to a statement of value not purely aesthetic, to a 'criticism of life.'" In proletarian writing, this is even more in evidence, for the writer wants to show the people where to go, to educate them "for an immediate end."

Such commitment and intention, however, should not take the form of propaganda; there must be "literary worth" to the work and the writer must take a stand without resorting to blatant propaganda. Mphahlele quotes Leon Trotskii's remark in *Literature and Revolution* (1923) that the "proletariat has to have in art the expression of the new spiritual point of view which is just beginning to be formulated within him, and to which art must help him give form." Yet Mphahlele immediately rejects Trotskii's prescription that the art form of the proletariat should be "incompatible with pessimism." Commitment should not blind the writer to the shortcomings of his society; in fact, Mphahlele says, it should help him to perceive his community's weaknesses. He commends the writers who achieve a balance of commitment and artistic integrity, such as Kofi Awoonor and Gabriel Okara, but condemns those who indulge in attitudinizing and sloganizing, such as W. E. B. Du Bois in some of his poems.

Mphahlele praises "protest poetry" once it adheres to an aesthetics he considers basic to all poetry: poetry communicates a communal voice through an individual experience or a particular private emotion. He finds this integration of the communal and the personal in the poetry of such poets as the South African Dennis Brutus and the American Gwendolyn Brooks, but not in Claude McKay, the Caribbean-American, who overemphasizes the universal at the expense of the particular and communal.

South African poetry, Mphahlele believes, follows Afro-American protest literature. In fact, he argues that South African blacks have much more in common with Afro-Americans than with Francophone and Anglophone West Africans. The American and the South African both live in societies dominated by whites; they experience a similar cultural predicament, caught between rejection and acceptance of the dominant culture and between sharing in the life of their respective countries as a whole and asserting their own cultural importance; and they both realize that they cannot escape to an ancestral past, despite its romantic appeal, but must try to reconcile themselves to a way of life for which their urban upbringing and Western education have prepared them.

Though Mphahlele rejects Senghor's concept of negritude as romantic and elitist, he accepts Césaire's, whom he considers "the sanest and most competent poet of the movement"; his poetry "is always at grips with political realities and could seldom be charged with romantic lyricism." Many African writers have shared Mphahlele's view of negritude, including his fellow South Africans Nkosi, Ousmane, and the Nigerian Soyinka, who has dismissed negritude with the epigrammatic observation that the tiger does not have to proclaim its tigritude. Many militant figures, however, have attacked Mphahlele for rejecting the first neo-African literary movement that sought to instill pride and assertiveness in black Africans, and for not repudiating Western culture altogether. Mphahlele does not reject the concept of a black aesthetics, though he raises serious questions about negritude. As he has stated, Fanon, Soyinka, and himself share "a certain negritude," if negritude is defined as any black consciousness, whether it is merely a sense of importance of being black, or black independence, or a drive for black power, or the forced acceptance "of blackness in fenced-in conditions such as in South Africa where you can't possibly do otherwise," or "the mere lyrical expression of black identity."

## Principal criticism
*The African Image*, 1962, revised 1973
*A Guide to Creative Writing*, 1966
*Voices in the Whirlwind and Other Essays*, 1972
*Let's Write a Novel*, 1981

## Other major works and literary forms
When Es'kia Mphahlele published his first book of literary criticism, *The African Image*, in 1962, he was already an established short-story writer, in which role he is perhaps better known. His first collection of stories, *Man Must Live and Other Stories* (1947), describes life in the urban black ghettos of South Africa, drawing extensively from his own experience, as he does in almost all of his fiction. He describes this early collection as "escapist stuff." *The Living and Dead and Other Stories* (1961) contains some of his best pieces of fiction, such as the title story and "The Master of Doornvlei." *In Corner B* (1967) includes four reprints from the earlier volumes and two stories set uncharacteristically outside South Africa, in Nigeria. A selection from these volumes was republished in *The Unbroken Song: Selected Writings of Es'kia Mphahlele* (1981).

Mphahlele off and on has written poems, ten of which are included in *The Unbroken Song*. He has published an acclaimed autobiography, *Down Second Avenue* (1959), which portrays his life up to his departure from South Africa in 1957. His first novel, *The Wanderers* (1971), is a thinly veiled autobiography which has a protagonist whose life closely parallels Mphahlele's during his last years in South Africa and his subsequent exile in Africa and Europe. *Chirundu* (1979), his second novel, is set not in South Africa but in a fictional version of Zambia in the 1960s; it examines a political figure's fall from power and his trial for polygamy. In addition to these creative pieces, Mphahlele has written many literary reviews and cultural articles and has coedited, with Ellis Ayitey Komey, *Modern African Stories* (1964) and edited Penguin's *African Writing Today* (1967).

NOVELS
*The Wanderers*, 1971
*Chirundu*, 1979

SHORT FICTION
*Man Must Live and Other Stories*, 1947
*The Living and Dead and Other Stories*, 1961
*In Corner B*, 1967
*Father Comes Home*, 1984 (children's fiction)
*Renewal Time*, 1988

NONFICTION
*The Unbroken Song: Selected Writings of Es'kia Mphahlele*,
    1981
*Poetry and Humanism: Oral Beginnings*, 1986
*Echoes of African Art*, 1987

EDITED TEXTS
*Modern African Stories*, 1964 (coedited with Ellis Ayitey
    Komey)
*African Writing Today*, 1967 (editor)

AUTOBIOGRAPHY
*Down Second Avenue*, 1959
*Afrika My Music: An Autobiography 1957–1983*, 1984

MISCELLANEOUS
*Bury Me at the Marketplace: Selected Letters of Es'kia
    Mphahlele 1943–1980*, 1984

## Further reading

Akosu, Tyohdzuah. *The Writings of Es'kia (Ezekiel) Mphahlele:
    South African Writer*, 1995.
Barnett, Ursula A. *Ezekiel Mphahlele*, 1976.
Gayle, Addison, Jr. "Under Western Eyes," in *Black World*.
    XXII (July, 1973), pp. 40–48.
Lindfors, Bernth, et al. "Interview with Ezekiel Mphahlele," in
    *Palaver*. 1972, pp. 39–44.
Manganyi, N. C. *Exiles and Homecomings: A Biography of
    Es'kia Mphahlele*, 1983.
Moore, Gerald. "Ezekiel Mphahlele: The Urban Outcast,"
    in *Twelve African Writers*, 1980.
Nkosi, Lewis. "Conversations with Ezekiel Mphahlele," in
    *Africa Report*. July, 1964, pp. 8–9.
Obee, Obee. *Es'kia Mphahlele: Themes of Alienation and
    African Humanism*, 1998.
Thuynsma, Peter N., ed. *Footprints Along the Way: A Tribute
    to Es'kia Mphahlele*, 1989.
Woeber, Catherine, and John Read. *Es'kia Mphahlele:
    A Bibliography*, 1989.

VICTOR J. RAMRAJ

*See also* Black Literary Theory and Criticism; Ngugi wa
Thiong'o; Postcolonial Literature and Theory; Soyinka

# N

## Narratology

Narratology is, quite simply, the study of narratives. But what are narratives? Stories, tales, legends, myths, jokes, and, according to Roland Barthes (1977), "epic, history, drama, comedy, mime, painting, stained glass windows, cinema, comics, news items, conversation. . . ." If this seems somewhat all-embracing, let us ask what all these items have in common: the answer, simply, is a *sequence* of events connected by causality and probability. As E. M. Forster observes in *Aspects of the Novel* (1927), "the king died and then the queen died" is a story, while "the king died and then the queen died of grief" is a plot, the crucial addition here being "of grief." "The train left the station" is not a narrative, nor is it a story or a plot – it is simply a statement of an event. In order to have a narrative, events must be located in space and time. So the primary task of the narratologist will be the study of how events are linked, the degree of motivation among them, and the effect they have on the characters of the story. Thus annals, diaries, journals, timetables, weather forecasts, do not constitute narratives unless the teller has organized them into a logically coherent, meaningful sequence.

The narratologist will probably commence with the Russian Formalist distinction, as adumbrated by Viktor Shklovskii, between *fabula* and *sjuzet*, a distinction that focuses on time in narrative. *Fabula*, or story, is the basic range of events in chronological order; *sjuzet* is the way in which these are actually presented. Tales can begin *in medias res*, the action can stop for description, commentary, or what in drama used to be called comic relief. A story can skip several years or linger for ten pages on something that happens in a second (as in the opening pages of Alain Robbe-Grillet's 1955 novel *Le Voyeur*). We can have flashbacks (analepses) – particularly common in cinema – or anticipations (prolepses) – "Jill, who was to die so tragically three years later . . . ." Detective stories almost inevitably have to be told in retrospect: the murder has already happened, so the task is to reconstruct the events leading up to it. Indeed, time in narrative is an extremely complex issue. The French narratologist Gérard Genette systematizes this in three modes: *order*, *duration*, and *frequency*. The first simply refers to how the events "really" occurred as opposed to the order in which they are presented in the text. *Duration* relates to the amount of time that things would actually have taken up as opposed to how long the text takes to describe them. *Frequency* is simply how often any one event is narrated in the text. Seymour Chatman, in *Story and Discourse* (1978), points out that there are five different degrees of time in narrative fiction. We can have *summary*, in which the discourse time is shorter than the story time; we can also have *ellipsis* in which the discourse time is zero – for example in William Shakespeare's *The Winter's Tale*, sixteen years pass between the end of Act 2 and the beginning of Act 3, but even the most tolerant theater-goer would hardly have the stamina to sit that out in real time. In *scene* the discourse time and the story time are equal; this hardly ever happens, except in passages of dialogue. Chatman also points out that when the discourse time is longer than the actual story time we have what he terms a *stretch* – the cinema is particularly good at this, and a classic example would be the scene on the Odessa steps in Sergei Eisenstein's film *The Battleship Potemkin*. And, finally, a *pause* simply represents a hiatus in the narrative, despite the fact that the story is going on. This is usually encountered in the space between chapters or where the author, as frequently in the novels of Émile Zola, takes time out to describe or demonstrate objects such as a train, a house, or a garden.

Of course a tale implies a teller, and here we have three types of narrator: autodiegetic, homodiegetic, and heterodiegetic. The first refers to someone who is telling his or her own story (for example Pip in Charles Dickens' *Great Expectations*). The second is more concerned with an onlooker who is present in person but not talking about him- or herself but the events he or she witnessed (for example Mr. Lockwood in Charlotte Brontë's *Wuthering Heights*, recalling the narration of Mrs. Dean who herself is recalling the events she witnessed and participated in. Heterodiegetic narration is third-person, omniscient storytelling.

The narratologist will also be interested in the distinction between what Roland Barthes called "catalytic" and "indexical" material and what Chatman refers to as "kernels" and "satellites." In both terminologies the first refers to an event that moves on the action of the story, while the second supplies atmosphere or description (for example the color of the wallpaper where the murder took place). Some novelists – for example Henry James – spend a lot of time on indexical material while not much happens in the story; others (notably Ernest Hemingway) prefer to concentrate on action.

It is worthwhile here to spend a little more time on Barthes' seminal article "The Structural Analysis of Narrative." He points out that the inductive method of studying each individual narrative is "Utopian" and instead proposes a deductive method, that is a "hypothetical model of description" to provide a structuralist paradigm for the analysis of "millions of narratives." Linguistics, we know, cannot analyze beyond the sentence, but structuralism can borrow its procedures to regard a narrative as one long sentence constructed out of interrelated functional units: everything in the story has its relevance. Take the sentence "Bond picked up one of the four phones"; one might suppose that "four" is irrelevant, but in the context it connotes "a highly developed bureaucratic technology." Barthes goes on to elaborate the distinction we have already referred to between *catalysts* and *indices*, pointing out that each can be subdivided: *nuclear* or *cardinal* functional units produce a change of state in the narrative ("Tom shot the policeman and escaped") while a *catalytic* function is still an action but is more likely to establish habit than affect the direction of the narrative ("That Thursday Tom went to the pub"). *Indices* establish fixed features ("Every Thursday Tom goes to the pub"), while the subdivision of *indexical* functions provides general information, usually to establish a sense of realism ("At that time Tom was aged thirty-one") [author's examples]. Barthes then proceeds to discuss the relationship between the narrator and his or her characters, criticizing the traditional concept of the omniscient narrator who, like God, knows everything that goes on inside his or her fictive creations. Barthes concludes by dismissing the concept of realism, claiming that true mimesis (imitation of life) is possible only in directly reported dialogue. Barthes' work has been profoundly influential, but many have found this essay too theoretical to be applied to analysis of actual texts, a deficiency Barthes was subsequently to remedy in *S/Z*, a minute analysis of "Sarrasine," a short story by Honoré de Balzac.

Other narratologists draw on different traditions, notably Shlomith Rimmon-Kenan in *Narrative Fiction* (1983). Basing her approach on the Russian Formalist Boris Tomashevskii's definition of narrative as a *succession* of events, she develops the Formalist distinction between *fabula* and *sjuzet* via Genette's threefold *histoire*, *récit*, and *narration*, which she translates as "story," "text," and "narration." This is clearly a useful schema wherein "story" relates to the actual events in chronological order, "text" is the actual presentation of these events, and "narration"

is the way they are told. To take a familiar example, the actual events in the *fabula* of Shakespeare's *Hamlet* occur as follows: (1) the mutual attraction of Claudius and Gertrude; (2) the murder of the old Hamlet; (3) the assumption of the throne and the recall of Hamlet from Wittenburg; (4) the hasty marriage; (5) the first appearance of the ghost; (6) the return of Hamlet to Denmark; (7) the plan with his friends to see "if this thing appears again"; and (8) Act 1, scene 1, line 1.

Another crucial aspect of narratology is the distinction between focalization (the consciousness through which the story is told) and point of view (the attitude adopted by the focalizer). Take the sentence in Dickens' *Great Expectations*: "As I passed the church, I felt . . . a sublime compassion for the poor creatures . . . I promised myself that I would do something for them and formed a plan in outline for bestowing a dinner of roast beef and plum pudding, a pint of ale and a gallon of condescension upon everybody." The story is focalized through the eyes of the young Pip, but the point of view is obviously that of the older Pip as he narrates the story thirty years later. No child would talk about "a gallon of condescension." This points again to the importance of time in narration, and Rimmon-Kenon devotes an entire chapter to this aspect, building upon the categories of Genette that we have already noted.

As for characters, the structuralist approach to narrative tends to regard these as "actants" – agents of action – rather than imitations of "real" people. Rimmon-Kenan tries to redress this imbalance, building on Chatman's paradigm of character "traits" and devoting an entire chapter to the way character can be defined directly by the author or by name, speech, external appearance, and environment.

Another major contribution made by Rimmon-Kenan is her clear exposition of F.I.D. (free indirect discourse), that is to say, a statement in a text without any reportorial verbs. Her example sums it up clearly: *direct discourse* (She asked, "Do you love me?"); *indirect discourse* (She asked if he loved her); F.I.D. (Did he love her?). Rimmon-Kenan covers various aspects of narratology too complex to be examined here, but all in all provides a clear, detailed introduction to this somewhat amorphous Leviathan of textual analysis.

One final element in narratology should be mentioned: this is the role of the so-called "implied author" and "implied reader." Clearly there is a real author, but this is of no interest except to the biographer or where certain elements of the author's life are transported into the fiction, as in James Joyce's early novel *Stephen Hero* (first published in 1944); there is also a real reader, but this could be anybody. The implieds, however, are extrapolations from the text, the implied author being that presence whose voice we feel controlling the choice of characters, narrative modes, setting, and so on, very often distinct from the narrator – hence we have adjectives like "Dickensian." We also feel that a text is being directed at a particular kind of reader, though this may be more difficult to define and may depend on genre; for example, the love romance, the thriller, the family saga, and the soap opera seem to have inbuilt expectations of the kind of general readerly competence (rather than the idiosyncratic response of the individual reader) that will fully actualize them.

Narratology aspires to being a *science* of narrative, to discovering those general structural features that form the basis of all narratives (literary and nonliterary alike). Its approach is abstract and formalist. As a consequence, it necessarily ignores many of those features that are generally seen as forming integral elements in the literary analysis of a specific text. Similarly, it may seem unhelpful in exploring the relationship between text and author, and between text and social context. Nevertheless, its increasingly subtle models of narrative have provided power tools of analysis, and not merely in literature but also in such disciplines as history and philosophy (for example Arthur C. Danto's 1985 *Narration and Knowledge: Including the Integral Text of Analytical Philosophy of History*).

### Further reading

Bal, Mieke. *Narratology*, 1985.
Barthes, Roland. "Introduction à l'analyse structurale des récits," in *Communications*, 8, 1966 ("The Structural Analysis of Language," in *Image, Music, Text*, 1977).
Bonheim, Helmut. *The Narrative Modes*, 1982.
Chatman, Seymour. *Story and Discourse*, 1978.
Cohen, Steven, and Linda M. Shires. *Telling Stories*, 1988.
Genette, Gérard. *Narrative Discourse*, 1980.
Martin, Wallace. *Recent Theories of Narrative*, 1986.
Onega, Susana, and José Angel García. *Narratology*, 1996.
Prince, Gerald. *A Dictionary of Narratology*, 1987.
Rimmon-Kenan, Shlomith. *Narrative Fiction*, 1983.
Scholes, Robert, and Robert Kellogg. *The Nature of Narrative*, 1966.
Stanzel, F. K. *A Theory of Narrative*, 1984.
Toolan, Michael J. *Narrative: A Critical Linguistic Introduction*, 1988.

A. W. LYLE

*See also* Eco; Genette; Greimas; Propp; Russian Formalism; Semiotics; Todorov

# Neoclassical Literary Theory

For almost a century and a half, from the mid-1600s through the early 1800s, European literary practice and theory were dominated by aesthetic assumptions and attitudes now called "neoclassical." Neoclassicism was not, however, a simple set of concepts and criteria. It was instead a tapestry of ideas and principles that seem well-defined from a distance but which blur upon close inspection.

Even the chronological boundaries of the neoclassical period are hazy. By 1650 France had a well-established neoclassical movement, but no other European country did. By 1800 neoclassicism was spent in France, England, and Spain, but it was still strong in Italy and Russia. Moreover, neoclassicism is not easily distinguished from its predecessor, the Renaissance, or from its progeny, Romanticism. Students of history are always tempted to draw strong contrasts between cultural periods; in reality, one era slides imperceptibly into another.

The central tenets of neoclassicism are as difficult to define as are its time boundaries. Several factors complicate the matter. First, neoclassical criticism found expression in many key works of poetry, drama, and fiction as well as in works of analysis and scholarship. Second, neoclassical criticism flourished at different times in different countries to different degrees. What is a central tenet in one such flourishing is a tangent in another. Third, neoclassical attitudes crossed from one nation to another but seldom in linear fashion.

Influence was rather recursive and reciprocal, so that the original giver became the receiver. For example, between 1660 and 1690 English critics drew heavily on French critics in extolling wit as a literary virtue; forty years later French critics learned from their English counterparts the power of sentiment. Fourth, beneath the apparent stability of neoclassical concepts lurked problems and paradoxes which caused those concepts to change rather than to remain fixed.

This essay examines the tapestry of neoclassical criticism to discern those patterns that seem most sharply defined, brings to light less apparent gaps or rough edges, and surveys the course of neoclassical criticism in several major European literatures.

## Central ideas of neoclassical criticism

Neoclassicism was based on admiration for the cultures of ancient Greece and the Roman Empire. These cultures were credited with the highest achievements in art, philosophy, politics, and literature. According to neoclassical theory, Greco-Roman writers established and perfected the principal literary genres for all time. The few Greco-Roman critical works that survive – especially Aristotle's *De poetica* (c. 334–324 B.C.; *Poetics*), Horace's *Ars poetica* (c. 17 B.C.; *The Art of Poetry*), and Longinus' *Peri hypsous* (first century A.D.; *On the Sublime*) – are models of insight into ancient literature and of methods for analyzing any literature. Neoclassicism worked from the assumption that the literary artist's task is to instruct readers in religious, moral, and ethical truths by casting them into dramatic or poetic form. The critic's task is to judge the dramatist's or poet's work, to award it immortality or to consign it to oblivion. Armed with sure criteria for evaluating literary qualities (as exemplified by the practices of ancient writers or as defined by ancient critics), the critic examines works by his contemporaries to see how close each comes to, or falls short of, classical achievement.

First, the neoclassical critic looked to see how well the writer imitated nature. "Nature" here does not refer to the physical parts of the world – earth, sky, sea – but to the order built into the universe by the Creator. The universe's order is visible in the way the planets, stars, sun, and moon dance in regular rotation; order is also visible in the way that the cycle of seasons brings forth life, takes it away, and returns it. Nature – order – is also evident in the Creator's greatest achievement, humanity, whose soul, mind, and body were designed to function harmoniously. In the neoclassical model, then, writers imitate nature by showing patterns of universal and human order in their works.

For the neoclassicist, literature, too, existed in an ordered pattern, a hierarchy of genres. Genres such as epic and tragedy ranked high because they depict the interventions of Providence in nature (such as when the gods spared Aeneas at Troy so that he could found Rome) and human nature at its noblest (for example, Oedipus accepting his terrible destiny). Genres such as satire and comedy ranked low because they treat nature in situations of daily life, when Providence does not intervene, and capitalize on the follies and faults of human behavior. Ancient writers established the genres and modeled the distinctive characteristics of each. Early neoclassical critics tended to assume that the hierarchy of genres was as immutable as the laws of nature.

The neoclassicists' tidy theory was that if a work clearly exhibits the characteristics appropriate to the genre, it possesses literary quality; if it omits characteristics or intermixes characteristics from two different genres, it lacks literary quality. In order to judge fairly and consistently, neoclassical critics strove to articulate precise rules for each genre. They sought to delineate and apply rules for plot, character, setting, and language. Where ancient critical sources failed to address a particular topic, neoclassical critics deduced rules from the practice of ancient poets. There were rules governing the depiction of divine intervention in the epic (through "machinery"), the setting of the action in tragedy (limited to one place), and the proper manner of speech of shepherds in pastoral verse.

The critic was to pay special attention to one rule that applied to all genres: decorum. In neoclassical practice, decorum dictates both the relationship between writer and reader and the relationships between fictional characters. Decorum demands that the writer set an emotional tone that is appropriate for the genre. The type of passionate outburst that is natural in lyric poetry is inexcusable in the epic, where the poet is to preserve Olympian detachment; the serious tone of tragedy must not be broken by comic interruptions.

Decorum dictates how the plot unfolds. In tragedy, death must not occur onstage but off; a messenger reports the event to the audience. In lyric poetry, erotic love is depicted through symbols, not realistic description. Decorum dictates

that characters conform to the stereotypes of their social class: a servant must be more cowardly than a lord, a lady must be more virtuous than her maid. Characters must speak according to social rank: a king is articulate, even poetic; a horse dealer speaks rough prose at best.

Finally, a critic was to judge how well an author's work mixed instruction with pleasure. It was important that some important truth be clearly and accurately conveyed. The critic was to study the pleasant fictions of plot and characterization and assess the varied devices of figurative language. The dramatist or poet who enhanced instruction with his fictions received high praise; writers who diverted readers from instruction by exaggerated inventions or fantasies were condemned.

Neoclassical critics' proper focus was literature written for an educated society, following the distinction made by Aulus Gellius, a second-century Roman commentator, between writing for educated persons and writing for common persons. Only the first is *classicus*; only the first has literary qualities. These qualities reflect the interests and attitudes of an aristocratic audience: elegance, order, and tastefulness. *Classicus* literature embodies the hopes, fear, ambitions, duties, and perquisites of a society's leadership class. It enables the older generation to pass on its values to the younger generation. Neoclassical critics thus stressed the social role of literature and grouped themselves into social units – salons, literary clubs, academies – when they discussed it. These organizations were a forum for the public articulation of general cultural standards and specific judgments about individual writers. The establishment of the Académie Française is the archetypal example. The academy was founded in 1635 to debate and decide cultural and literary questions: was a certain word purely French in its etymology? Who among contemporary poets ranked with the Immortals? Members of the academy considered the evidence and rendered an authoritative judgment. A literary work that violated social propriety or harmony in some way was likely to be censured. Public, communal assessments tended to stress correctness as a literary virtue.

In sum, neoclassical criticism viewed literature as a social construct to accomplish social purposes by displaying social virtues.

## Problems and paradoxes

In the abstract, then, neoclassical theory looks like a coherent tapestry. In fact, however, the tapestry's weavers left many gaps and rough edges. Yet the flaws proved felicitous; because the theory was not logically rigid or perfectly consistent, it left room for its practitioners to follow their own course, to challenge one another and to rethink their understanding of literature. The better neoclassical critics perceived and outgrew the theory they inherited.

One weakness of neoclassical theory is its professional vocabulary. Its proponents seldom assigned specific definitions to terms such as "nature," "decorum," "instruction," or "pleasure" until someone challenged them; articulating a term better often changed its connotations. Those who were content with the general meaning of the terms tended to apply them poorly in particular cases. Remove the titles from the plays reviewed by John Dennis (an early-eighteenth-century English critic), and his commentaries seem identical. Early neoclassical critics tended to make abstract judgments that sounded learned but committed the critic to no specific point of view. This general, ill-defined literary vocabulary allowed anyone who could speak the jargon to pose as an arbiter of merit. In England, would-be critics who used terms they could not define became figures of ridicule to knowledgeable neoclassical critics such as John Dryden and Samuel Johnson.

A second weakness of neoclassical criticism is its surprisingly casual attitude toward the ancient texts upon which it relied. Many neoclassical critics resembled the modern Fundamentalist interpreters of the Bible who trust the sacred text – even a translated sacred text – to be self-explanatory. Only a few early neoclassical critics believed that readers might understand Greco-Roman writers better by drawing on information from allied disciplines. (It is true that linguistics and archaeology were only in their infancy at this time, but what research was available received little attention from literary scholars.) Only lip service was given to the notion that a critic had to know each ancient writer's time and place as well as his works; in practice, biographical and philological research was usually perceived as pedantry. By the mid-eighteenth century, however, neoclassical critics were better prepared to ground their observations in wide-ranging learning. Denis Diderot practiced literary criticism as part of the *encyclopédiste* effort to coordinate knowledge in the arts and sciences. Johnson turned to criticism after writing an English dictionary and collating numerous editions of William Shakespeare's plays. The burgeoning academies also influenced the trend: to keep up with the learned circle, critics had to incorporate new knowledge into their judgments.

A third weakness lay in the perceived relationship between literary values and social norms. In the seventeenth and eighteenth centuries, European societies experienced numerous intellectual, political, and religious upheavals. During contentious times, literature became a battleground where opposing ideas clashed. Plays and poems often took partisan positions, and critics sometimes made favorable pronouncements on literary works whose principal merit was actually that their authors held opinions about culture, the church, or the state that accorded well with those of the critic. This polemical streak in neoclassical literature and criticism makes for lively reading even when the issues themselves no longer matter.

That the neoclassical pursuit of stable, universal norms sometimes led to squabbling over transient social issues is only one irony. Also ironic – even paradoxical – is that neoclassicism sometimes prompted a reaction against ancient culture by valuing it so highly. This controversy is termed the "Quarrel of the Ancients and the Moderns"; it developed within all European neoclassical movements but burst forth most dramatically in France and in England.

Such conflicts arose when admiration for Greco-Roman culture clashed with national pride. Neoclassicists urged their contemporaries to bring their own culture up to the level of ancient achievement; critics ceaselessly judged modern works by a classical yardstick. Some Grecophile critics never found a modern work that they could acknowledge as the equal of ancient poems or plays. Other, less fanatic critics recognized that at some points modern accomplishments had matched or surpassed the ancients' work. For example, Europe had explored and colonized two continents, North and South America, that had been *terra incognita* to the ancients. European inventions such as the printing press and the compass had revolutionized education and commerce. Furthermore, Europeans believed that Christianity afforded them a divine revelation of truths that the ancient pagans with their myths had never known, or had perceived only dimly. Many Europeans readily concluded that they would surpass Greco-Roman literary achievements eventually, if not immediately. If classical poets could win eternal fame with pagan fictions, imagine what Christian poets could achieve with divine revelation. The more critics spurred writers to emulate the past, the harder it became to deny the worth of modern authors' achievements. Though neoclassicists began by calling ancients "giants" and moderns "dwarfs," partisans of modernity quickly pointed out that even dwarfs stood higher and saw farther than the giants on whose shoulders they perched.

The first explicit showdown between the party of the ancients and the party of the moderns occurred in France. In a speech delivered at the Académie Française in its first year, the dramatist François de Boisrobert asserted that Greek drama lacked the elegance and good taste of contemporary French drama. If audiences failed to appreciate plays by modern writers such as himself, the fault could be laid at the door of audiences' false expectations based upon ancient theatrical practice. Boisrobert apparently spoke for many writers. A decade later, Jean Desmarets de Saint-Sorlin trusted to the inherent superiority of his epic poems about Christian conversion; two decades afterward, Bernard le Bovier, sieur de Fontenelle, pointed out the virtues of his own contemporary pastoral poems in smooth couplets in comparison to Theocritus' and Virgil's country poems in "rough" meters.

Charles Perrault summed up a generation's complaints when, at a January, 1687, meeting of the Académie Française, he named a dozen French poets whose works, in his estimation, surpassed Homer's and Virgil's. Perrault expanded his attack in *Parallèle des anciens et des modernes* (1688–1697; parallels of the ancients and the moderns), an entertaining but ill-informed series of dialogues ridiculing pedantic neoclassicists. Perrault's continuing assault inspired several replies. One was a satiric pamphlet by François de Callieres, *Histoire poétique de la guerre nouvellement déclarée entre les anciens et les modernes* (1688; a poetic history of the war lately declared between the ancients and the moderns), that attempted to puncture egos on both sides. Nicolas Boileau-Despréaux penned a more scholarly response, *Réflexions sur Longin* (1694; reflections on Longinus), which accurately (though somewhat peevishly) exposed Perrault's weak knowledge of ancient culture. Many writers and critics joined the fray with hasty verse and ill-tempered prose. Other scholars stepped in to reconcile Perrault and Boileau before the battle went beyond the printed page. To make peace, Boileau retracted some of what he had written. No compromise, however, could change the conviction of a growing number of writers that admiration of the classics was an implied rebuke to their own writing. The dispute was something of a tempest in a teapot, but it is significant for the manner in which it was conducted: as a debate, conducted in print, of a critical tenet, to be adjudicated by an audience of learned peers. The Quarrel of the Ancients and the Moderns was a foreshadowing of critical controversies that before 1800 would challenge every major neoclassical premise. Each dispute ended with a retraction similar to Boileau's that recognized a critic's own national literature as the primary object of literary study.

A second paradox in neoclassicism emerged as the period progressed. It grew from the assumptions that literature's purpose is to teach and criticism's purpose is to evaluate the teachers. Both assumptions presume that there is an audience to be addressed. Early neoclassicists identified that audience as the class of educated aristocrats who provided a country's economic, social, and political leadership. The late seventeenth and early eighteenth centuries was a time, however, when in several European countries a new mercantile class arose to challenge the aristocracy's position of leadership. If this new class were to provide leaders, those individuals would have to be educated as the aristocracy was educated. Therefore, writers and critics turned to the task of reshaping the classical heritage for a new audience. This process, which led to the redefinition and expansion of neoclassical literary ideas, can be most readily seen in eighteenth-century British culture. Reaching out to educate a new audience, neoclassicists changed the very heritage they aspired to communicate.

The criticism of Joseph Addison early in the century and of Johnson at mid-century show how rapidly and extensively the change occurred. Addison was educated in the classics at Magdalen College, University of Oxford; he wrote criticism and verse in Latin. He attempted a career in politics, allying himself with the Whig Party in its electoral contests with the Tories. In this context, Addison's classical knowledge was extremely useful: he could dignify Whig panegyrics with classical allusions and find precedent for Whig policies in classical history. He joined forces with Sir Richard Steele to produce two periodical papers, *The Tatler* (1709–1711) and *The Spectator* (1711–1712, 1714), whose purpose was to educate polite society – composed of both hereditary aristocrats and self-made entrepreneurs – regarding art, theater, literature, and ideas. Designed to bring "Philosophy out of the closets and libraries . . . into Clubs and Assemblies," these essays in *The Tatler* and *The Spectator* disseminated high culture in small daily doses. Each issue (one sheet printed on two sides) began with a Latin epigraph which set the tone or theme; for the average reader's sake, it was translated. Each issue treated a different topic, some serious (immortality, the virtues of a gentleman, qualities of an epic) and some light (fashion trends, social fads, eccentric personality types). Addison and Steele offered learning made easy, instruction in pleasing small packages. About a quarter of the essays address literary topics such as tragic conventions, the role of wit, ballad themes. These efforts to educate a new audience about the value of reading imaginative works led Addison to reassess the traditional notion of how literature pleases. In a landmark piece of criticism, "The Pleasures of the Imagination," he examined why and how readers enjoy literature or other art forms. These essays provoked a debate and continuing investigation among eighteenth-century critics, who supported, rebutted, or expanded Addison's concepts. By the nineteenth century "imagination" – not an important neoclassical concept – had become the central concept of Romanticism as a result of this continuing critical discussion.

Johnson began his career in literary criticism by following in Addison and Steele's footsteps. Johnson produced two periodical papers, *The Rambler* (1750–1752) and *The Idler* (1758–1760). Like his predecessors, Johnson was fascinated by reader psychology. Observing that readers enthusiastically perused biographies, novels, and works of travel, Johnson decided to apply critical methods to the study of these new genres. Cataloging their purposes and conventions, Johnson unashamedly added them to the list of classical genres. For Johnson, the hierarchy of genres was not fixed but mutable, open to newcomers. Johnson also stretched neoclassical thinking in another way: he recognized that one critic cannot be the sole arbiter of literary immortality. The critic must recognize the force of judgments by the community of readers. A classic is defined not by the critic's application of a universal standard but by evidence that generations of readers continue to be pleased and instructed: "What mankind have long possessed they have often examined and compared," Johnson wrote of the works of William Shakespeare, "and if they persist to value the possession, it is because frequent comparisons have confirmed opinion in its favour."

As critics became more willing to expand the definition of literature, writers felt less constrained to cite classical precedent. Henry Fielding made a valiant, half-serious, half-comic effort to explain his novel *The History of the Adventures of Joseph Andrews, and of His Friend Mr. Abraham Adams* (1742; best known as *Joseph Andrews*) as a descendant of a classical genre, the "comic epic." The novel flourished thereafter, and subsequent novelists did not share Fielding's urge to justify a work's pedigree. In the second half of the neoclassical period, there was little literary achievement in the classical genres, but there was a flood of fascinating works in popular genres. The willingness of neoclassical critics to dispense with Aulus Gellius' distinction between writing for the learned and writing for the less educated seems to have freed writers to explore new realms of literature.

To conclude, while neoclassical theory about literature contained a core of axioms and assumptions, it also contained gaps and paradoxes that encouraged further thinking. Though neoclassicism's century-and-a-half dominance in European literature has sometimes been seen as a sign of inertia or unthinking rigidity, it may be viewed instead as a sign of fundamental soundness. Neoclassical theorists were asking the right questions about literature and were sensible enough to entertain changing answers. The pattern is evident in the course of neoclassical movements in Europe.

## France

The neoclassical era in France from 1600 to about 1715 is considered to fall into three distinguishable periods. During the formative period, lasting until 1660, writers reacted against the literary and grammatical excesses inspired by the Renaissance rediscovery of the classics. Copying Italian and Spanish literati, Renaissance French writers had enthusiastically embraced Greco-Roman mythology and coined or incorporated Latin words. The critics of the formative period reacted against these trends, preferring a reasoned, less exuberant embrace of classical culture. Critics aimed to purify and standardize the language, articulate rules (especially the unities of time, place, and action) for the drama, and develop a prose style with literary qualities. The movement toward coherent formulation of literature's philosophical and technical aspects was aided by the increasing availability of ancient works in translation. Contemporary social, political, and religious circumstances – especially the resolution of the Protestant-Catholic struggle for ascendancy – encouraged a desire for stability at all levels. Order and rule in the arts, as well as in society, seemed desirable and achievable. The agent for order was the aforementioned Académie Française, composed of critics, philologists, theorists, and scholars. Their common inspiration was Aristotle's *Poetics*, from which they derived literary principles that soon solidified into dogma. The most influential members were Jean Chapelain (1595–1674) and Jean-Louis Guez de Balzac (1594–1654).

Neoclassicism peaked in France between 1660 and 1690, an era called *l'Age de raison* (the Age of Reason). During this period neoclassical principles were frequently articulated by writers in prefaces to their plays, poems, and prose. Landmark works of the time include Pierre Corneille's *Discours* and *Examens* (both 1660), Molière's *Tartuffe: Ou, L'Imposteur* (1664, 1667; English translation, 1732) and *Le Misanthrope* (1666; *The Misanthrope*, 1709), Jean Racine's *Andromaque* (1667; *Andromache*, 1674), and Boileau's *Les Satires* (1666–1711; English translation, 1711–1713).

To imitate nature successfully, the French neoclassicists believed, the writer must depend upon reason rather than genius, imagination, or inspiration. They defined reason as intelligence, judgment, and a concern for truth. A writer must possess reason, a quality whose outward sign would be his good character. A skilled writer had to be a man of common sense, one who checked spontaneity and repressed strictly personal emotion. The neoclassical writer who valued reason attended to questions of probability; he was pleased by that which is generally rather than exceptionally true. The writer therefore had to know his subject thoroughly before he attempted to convey it to his readers. For the French neoclassicist, then, intellect was the real shaping force of literature.

From these principles, the French neoclassicists deduced that the way to artistic perfection was through the rules regulating decorum and genre. By observing the rules, writers displayed the quality of *goût* (taste), an instinctive discernment or artistry that allowed them to draw from classical texts the ideas or spirit that matched the mood of the contemporary audience.

The third period of French neoclassicists was a time of decline; its terminal point was, fittingly, the death of Louis XIV in 1715. It was in this time that the mean-spirited Quarrel of the Ancients and the Moderns arose. Gradually, the important writers of the previous age died, leaving no successors. In later criticism, the attempt to promulgate rules for the creation of new works – rather than simply describing and analyzing existing works – became hopelessly mired in unverifiable speculation and outbursts of petty jealousy.

The second half of the eighteenth century in France was not formally a neoclassical period but was influenced by the classics in a different way. A loose grouping of intellectuals called the philosophes turned to Greek and Roman civilization in search of secular values. Convinced that Christianity was a stumbling block to political and social reform in Europe, the philosophes sought in classical culture the formula for a harmonious, moral society which had no need for divine revelation. The philosophes ransacked ancient literature to find examples of ethical behavior. Voltaire (1694–1778) advocated a return to ancient models of drama because they display characters who take civic duties to heroic length. Diderot argued in *Discours sur la poésie dramatique* (1758) that drama's purpose is to instruct the audience that human nature is basically good, thereby prompting feelings of good humor and benevolence. Both Voltaire and Diderot wrote literary criticism as one aspect of a wide-ranging exploration of disciplines such as history, politics, philosophy, and religion. The philosophes were also *encyclopédistes*, engaged in compiling a reasoned, systematic understanding of human society. Like the early neoclassicists, they honored reason; unlike the early neoclassicists, they did not perceive reason to be built into the universe, the society, or the individual. Rather, an age of reason became a goal toward which every society must work.

## Britain

Though early-seventeenth-century writers such as Ben Jonson and John Milton expressed appreciation for the classical heritage, the English neoclassical period had its real beginnings in 1660, when Charles II was restored to the throne. Having spent the fifteen years of Commonwealth government in exile, Charles had developed a taste for things French. During the next thirty years, English writers and critics looked to French literature for models, though they did not always look with unqualified enthusiasm. John Dryden illustrates the ambivalent English attitude: while acknowledging the classics and their French imitators as models, Dryden suggested that English apprentices would soon outstrip their teachers. His *Of Dramatic Poesy, an Essay* (1667) gives ancient writers their due but expresses preference for the moderns, then gives a polite nod to French drama but asserts that English writers have more liveliness, despite their lack of Gallic orderliness.

Early English neoclassicism differed markedly from the French because it lacked the theoretical center that the Académie Française provided. Individual critics such as Thomas Rymer (in *A Short View of Tragedy*, 1693) and John Dennis (in *The Advancement and Reformation of Poetry*, 1701) repeatedly judged modern poets by the standard of ancient poets but displayed a willingness to explore new concepts. Dennis, for example, discusses the Roman critic Longinus, whose idea of sublimity has to do more with passion than with reason. English writers were generally less adulatory of the past than were the French. Many English literati were taken with Sir Francis Bacon's idea of the "New Philosophy" (that is, the scientific method), which promised rapid progress in natural science and technology far beyond anything Greco-Roman culture had known. In addition, many authors and critics recognized that Great Britain already possessed a great poet and dramatist, William Shakespeare – despite his "little Latin and less Greek." Unstinted praise of the ancients suggested an ignorance of Shakespeare's genius. English neoclassicists saw the classics less as a high achievement far unequaled by native poets than as a standard by which to separate first-rate poets from those who were second-rate.

A second stage of neoclassicism spanned the first forty years of the eighteenth century. Its primary exponents were Alexander Pope, Jonathan Swift, and the previously mentioned Addison. Pope, both poet and critic, is the quintessential neoclassical writer. Determined from youth to become England's greatest poet, Pope wrote his way up the hierarchy of genres. From imitations of earlier English poets, he proceeded to pastoral, mock-epic, satire, epistle, and ode. Pope's classical locus was Horace, the Roman poet whose verse embodies the social virtues of urbanity, fellowship, and intelligent leisure.

Pope's Horatian approach to literary criticism is most evident in *An Essay of Criticism* (1711), a verse treatise on the art of judging literature. Though Pope was only twenty-three when he wrote it, the poet's voice is wise in the ways of writers and critics. He schools fellow critics in the ways of judging with moderation: avoid hasty evaluation, recognize virtues as well as faults, remember the rules but allow genius to override them. Pope casts his advice in reasoned, balanced couplets that demonstrate his mastery of critical principles:

> Those rules of old discovered, not devised,
> Are Nature still, but Nature methodized.

> A little learning is a dangerous thing;
> Drink deep, or taste not the Pierian spring.

> A perfect judge will read each work of wit
> With the same spirit that its author writ.

> True wit is Nature to advantage dressed;
> What oft was thought, but ne'er so well expressed.

Wit was for Pope's generation of authors what *goût* was for French neoclassical writers: the ultimate demonstration that a poet fully understood an idea and could express it to contemporaries in a way that simultaneously instructed and delighted.

The harmonious world of literary criticism depicted in *An Essay of Criticism* is poetic rather than actual. Pope and his contemporaries became embroiled in controversy in regard to several issues, chief among which was the question of what constituted true knowledge of ancient literature. This issue came to the fore during the British version of the Quarrel of the Ancients and the Moderns. Sir William Temple had published in 1692 an essay immoderately praising the past, "Of Ancient and Modern Learning," wherein he held up as literary models the letters of the sixth-century B.C. Sicilian king Phalaris. Two University of Cambridge scholars, William Wotton and Richard Bentley, deflated Temple's balloon by proving that the letters had actually been composed centuries after Phalaris' time. Temple's protégé Swift then rose to his patron's defense, ridiculing Wotton and Bentley as nitpicking scholars who in their attention to textual questions had become oblivious to the spirit of literary works. Swift's *A Tale of a Tub* and *The Battle of the Books* (both 1704) attack modern meanness, contrasting it with ancient magnanimity. Though Swift rarely emulated Greco-Roman literary models in his own writings, he fiercely defended the classical spirit. Pope and Swift joined forces with John Arbuthnot to create a fictional embodiment of modern scholarship, the pedantic Martinus Scriblerus, who prefers questions of textual accuracy to questions of ethics or morality. Philological study was, in fact, providing more accurate texts of classical literature and challenging critical clichés, but the strongest neoclassical voices shortsightedly claimed that no one need drink from the "Pierian spring" of grammar, linguistics, or archaeology. Thus, Swift and Pope brilliantly parodied as pedantry a new scholarship that would soon transform literary criticism.

At the same time, however, Addison's "pleasures of the imagination" approach was becoming increasingly prevalent. The aesthetics of literature occupied the third Earl of Shaftesbury (Anthony Ashley Cooper), Edward Young, Mark Akenside, and other poets and critics who sought to define the pleasure experienced by readers of poetry and fiction. Samuel Johnson used the standard of reader response to defend Shakespeare's plays against charges that the Bard's failure to observe the classical unities of time, place, and action constituted a literary fault. Johnson's criticism differed markedly from that of Pope and Swift because of the value Johnson placed on scholarship. Johnson's lexicography (he published *A Dictionary of the English Language* in 1755) and textual editing (he published an edition of Shakespeare's plays in 1765) undergirded his criticism. The scholarship that Pope and Swift called pedantry Johnson practiced as art. After Johnson, literary criticism stood firmly on its own feet, no longer merely a second-rate discipline of glossing imaginative works. Moreover, criticism was no longer ahistorical. The works of Richard Hurd, the Wartons (Joseph and Thomas), and Hugh Blair began to trace consciously the evolution of literary ideas and critical standards.

The traditional bifurcated neoclassical view – there were the ancients, now there are the moderns – had given way to a linear world-view of evolution and development. The change had been initiated by the growing realization that "genre," "instruction," and "pleasure" were dynamic rather than static concepts.

## Italy

The Italian neoclassical era began later than the French and English; it started in the mid-eighteenth century and lasted until the early nineteenth. It was also distinctive in lacking the nationalistic and social implications which generated controversy elsewhere. Italians, on whose soil the Roman Empire had risen and fallen and the Renaissance had begun, did not see the classical heritage as an external intrusion.

Italian neoclassicism, then, became rooted in the visual and plastic arts, not in visions of society. Literary criticism was explored more in imaginative than in scholarly works.

The year 1690 marked the beginning of a movement that served as an important prelude to Italian neoclassicism. Fourteen scholars founded the Accademia dell' Arcadia (commonly called simply the Arcadia), modeled on the Académie Française. They were interested in eliminating the Baroque taste for excessively flowery, highly ornamented language; they wished to promote a more disciplined, standardized poetic vocabulary. Instead of championing reason (like the French) or wit (like the English), the Arcadians championed sublimity and passion. Of primary interest to them was literary historiography. One of the academy's first achievements was Giovan Mario Crescimbeni's *Istoria della volgar poesia* (1698, 1714; history of vernacular poetry). Arcadian "colonies" began to spring up throughout Italy.

As the eighteenth century unfolded, the Arcadia's efforts to guide literary practice and theory toward discipline and simplicity coincided with the flourishing of neoclassicism in France and England. Racine, Corneille, Boileau, Pope, Addison, and other neoclassical writers were widely read in translation and frequently imitated. The burgeoning neoclassical spirit was given particular impetus by the aesthetic theories of Johann Joachim Winckelman. German by birth, Winckelman worked in Rome as an archaeologist and an art historian. He came to espouse a theory that the ancients, with their preference for straight lines, defined shapes, and static scenes, had discovered the secret of ideal beauty. By mid-century neoclassical theories and principles had become dominant throughout Italy.

Italian poets turned increasingly toward classical subjects: finding Greco-Roman parallels for contemporary persons or events, expressing intellectual rather than emotional reactions, reinterpreting ancient myths. As happened during the Age of Reason in France, poets adopted the custom of prefacing their imaginative works with treatises that explained or defended the writer's approach. Important works of the period include Giuseppe Parini's *Il giorno* (1763–1804; *The Day*, 1927), with its companion *Sui principi di belle lettere* (1770–1773; principles of belles lettres), Agostini Paradisi's *Versi sciolti* (1762; unrhymed hendecasyllables) and *Saggio metafisico sopra l'entusiasmo nelle belle arti* (1769; a metaphysical essay on enthusiasm in fine arts), and Luigi Lamberti's poems describing the sculptures at the Villa Borghese. Italian literary neoclassicists focused principally on poetry, considering it the verbal embodiment of visual or plastic aesthetics. Little critical attention was given to drama or to the question of genre.

Italian neoclassicism lasted into the nineteenth century as a coherent movement because it was comparatively unthreatened by Romantic sensibility. It had already incorporated elements of this sensibility by establishing the primacy of poetry and championing the individual pursuit of ideal beauty.

## Spain

*Neoclasicismo* was the prevailing tendency in eighteenth-century Spanish literature. Its origin was more political than cultural. In 1700 Philip V, a relative of Louis XIV of France, ascended the Spanish throne. Just as the Restoration of Charles II in 1660 had "Frenchified" aristocratic culture in England for three decades, in Spain the accession of Philip inspired a passion among the educated classes for French manners and cultures. These *afrancesados* led the neoclassical movement as well as its later companion movement, the Enlightenment.

The primary architect of Spanish neoclassical theory was Ignacio de Luzán y Claramunt. After being educated in Italy, Luzán served as a diplomat in France. Inspired by his membership in several foreign academies, Luzán attempted a consolidation of neoclassical theories in *La poética: O, Reglas de la poesía en general y de sus principales especies* (1737, 1789; poetry: or, the rules of poetry in general and of particular kinds). His treatise repeats the central tenets of most neoclassical movements: the writer is a craftsman concerned with formal matters and a teacher concerned with moral instruction; the work is an imitation of nature and helps people learn how to order the state and themselves. Luzán focused on epic and tragedy, the highest genres of poetry.

Luzán's text articulated ideas which encouraged the formation of numerous Spanish academies on the French and Italian model. An academy might be formal (for example, the Real Academia Española de la Lengua) or informal (such as the Fonda de San Sebastián, a *tertulia* or gathering at the San Sebastián Inn in Madrid). Madrid was the capital of neoclassical culture because it contained the nation's most important theater. Here flourished the Spanish version of the Quarrel of the Ancients and the Moderns. The argument concerned the virtues of Baroque drama (the plays of Lope de Vega y Carpio and Pedro Calderón de la Barca had been an important part of the Golden Age of Spanish art and literature) compared to a contemporary drama inspired by French neoclassicism. Plays by Agustín de Montiano y Luyando (such as *Virginia*, 1750) and by Leandro Fernández de Moratín had plots and characters drawn from antiquity, held to the unities, and were marked by declamation more than action. Their authors attempted to restore a psychological realism that the Baroque predilection for ostentatious scenery and rhetorical excesses had obscured.

Academies fostered discussion about literary and other topics by sponsoring journals, whose content was modeled either on the informal essays of Addison and Steele or on the formal treatises of the Académie Française. In the academies, discussions sprang up about the same political and philosophical problems that intrigued the philosophes and *encyclopédistes* in France. Like the French Enlightenment, the Spanish *Ilustración* turned to the classical heritage in a quest for a secular alternative to Christianity. The growing debate concerning which philosophical and moral truths were universally true made increasingly irrelevant the didactic strain in neoclassical literature and criticism.

Opposition to neoclassicism eventually arose from some, such as the satirist Juan Pablo Forner y Sagarra (1756–1797), who wondered how far Spanish writers would go in imitating the French. He and others feared that native Castilian words would soon disappear as French ideas imposed Gallicized diction.

## Russia

Russia's neoclassicism, like Spain's and England's, originated with a monarch. Peter the Great modernized and Westernized Russia in the late seventeenth and early eighteenth centuries. Russian writers contributed to the transition by studying and reformulating European literary ideas for Russia's educated society. As French was the Russian aristocracy's language, it was French neoclassicism that heavily influenced Russian ideas and interpretations.

Russian neoclassicism was the most eclectic of the European movements, for reasons that are clear: the country's great distance from Western Europe (and thus from the easy interchange of ideas), its lack of contact with the Renaissance, and its more rigid social order. Neoclassicists' first priority was to familiarize Russians with Greco-Roman history, writers, and literary ideas. Early popularizers such as Feofan Prokopovich (1681–1736) and Aleksandr Sumarokov (1718?–1777) relied heavily on Boileau, the clearest and most forceful of French theoreticians. They accepted his central tenets that linked instruction and giving pleasure, upheld the ancients as models for emulation, and advocated a clear but elegant style.

The question of literary style was crucial for Russians. The original literary language was Church Slavonic, whose limited vocabulary of theological, moral, and liturgical terms made it unsuitable for most European topics. (One writer, charged with translating a French gardening book, tried to commit suicide after wrestling with diction and vocabulary problems.) Moreover, spoken Russian did not fit easily with versification rules that emphasized accentuation as the determining factor in regular metrical patterns. Up to 1750 two questions occupied Russian critics: how to match style to genre and how to establish metrical rules.

Realizing that neoclassical genres such as epic and tragedy could shape national identity, Russian poets and dramatists attempted imitations of classical epics and French drama. There were some successes – such as Mikhail Khersakov's *Rossiada* (1779), and Yakov Knyazhnin's *Vadim Novgorodskii* (1789) – but in general the significance of such works was political. Imitation of literary conventions was not accompanied by critical reflection.

The most congenial poetic genre to Russian poets was the ode, which was less rigid in form and theme than were the "higher" genres. Gavrila Derzhavin was the most prominent practitioner of the ode as a form of civic expression in the Roman tradition. Russian rulers from Peter the Great to Catherine the Great enjoyed well-crafted odes that celebrated military or diplomatic triumphs – and they gave handsome rewards to those who wrote them.

Russian neoclassicists became most theoretical when discussing whom the poet ought to instruct and upon which topics he ought to instruct them. One obvious, though potentially dangerous, audience was the monarch. Another obvious audience was the educated aristocracy and the less educated emerging commercial class. This concern for instruction prompted Russian interest in the periodical essay (in imitation of *The Tatler* and *The Spectator*) and the novel. Catherine the Great supported the foundation of the journal *Vsyakaya vsyachina* (1769–1774; all kinds of things) aimed at teaching her court about manners and culture. Its editor, Nikolai Novikov, saw no reason not to lecture the empress herself, but Catherine tired within a few years of his lessons in statecraft. *Vsyakaya vsyachina*'s attempts at refining Russian sensibilities and reforming their behavior according to European standards was a noble goal but politically dangerous. A later journalist, Nikolai Karamzin, promoted novels as the best literature to educate the heart as well as the head of the common reader. In critical commentary rare for a Russian neoclassicist, Karamzin speculated about the psychological and aesthetic effects of different kinds of plots or characters.

In summary, Russian criticism in the eighteenth century passively accepted French and English neoclassical ideas, except where features of the Russian language demanded changes in metrical theory or principles of diction. Neoclassicism's greater impact was to enshrine the idea that poets and critics were to serve the state. This idea survived in Russia even as it withered in other European literatures. In the twentieth century this notion became the basis for the official literary aesthetic of the Soviet Union, Socialist Realism, whose central principles resemble those of early neoclassicism.

## Conclusion

In a sense, neoclassicism has never disappeared. The literature of classical Greece and Rome continued to influence and inspire writers after 1800. Neoclassical criticism never disappeared either, although it has gone through many permutations. The original neoclassical premise – that a timeless, universal standard for literary judgment exists – has come to seem simplistic. Yet the effort to articulate that standard necessitated research, the assembling of evidence, the articulation of coherent ideas, and the careful definition of terms. These tasks, in turn, have generated a process of thinking that is important, not for the conclusions it reaches, but for the discoveries it yields. The critical

tapestry, which its neoclassical designers planned to hem and finish, is still being woven.

## Further reading

Adams, Robert M. *The Roman Stamp: Frame and Façade in Some Forms of Neo-Classicism*, 1974.
Atkins, J. W. H. *English Literary Criticism: Seventeenth and Eighteenth Centuries*, 1951.
Barry, Peter. *Beginning Theory: An Introduction to Literary and Cultural Theory*, 1995.
Guerard, Albert. *France in the Classical Age*, 1956.
Highet, Gilbert. *The Classical Tradition*, 1949.
Johnson, James William. *The Formation of English Neoclassical Thought*, 1967.
Jones, Richard Foster. *Ancients and Moderns: A Study of the Background of the Battle of the Books*, 1936.
Lodge, David, ed. *Modern Criticism and Theory*, 1988.
Pocock, Gordon. *Boileau and the Nature of Neo-classicism*, 1980.
Selden, Raman. *A Reader's Guide to Contemporary Literary Theory*, 1985.
Wellek, René. *The Rise of English Literary History*, 1941.
——. *A History of Modern Criticism: 1750–1950*. Vol. 1, *The Later Eighteenth Century*, 1955.

ROBERT M. OTTEN

**Britain** *See also* Addison; Burke, E.; Dryden; Hume; Johnson; Jonson; Lord Kames; Pope; Shaftesbury; Warton and Warton; Young

**France** *See also* Boileau-Despréaux; Corneille; Diderot; Fénelon; La Bruyère; La Fontaine; La Harpe; Racine; Voltaire

**Germany** *See also* Gottsched; Winckelmann

**Spain** *See also* Luzán y Claramunt

# New Criticism

New Criticism emerged in the 1930s and played a dominant role in American literary criticism until the end of the 1960s. Though it is primarily an American phenomenon, the major influences on it were either British by birth or adoption. The criticism of T. S. Eliot was crucial. Eliot had great status as one of the leading modernist writers and his criticism was therefore perceived to be of special value. Modernist literature presented traditional forms of literary criticism with a problem, for the work of such writers as James Joyce, Ezra Pound, and T. S. Eliot seemed resistant to conventional criticism. A new kind of criticism was clearly needed to engage with modernist texts. Eliot's redefinition of tradition in his essay "Tradition and the Individual Talent," his formulation of critical concepts such as the "objective correlative," and his rethinking of the literary canon in his elevation of Jacobean drama and

Metaphysical poetry, together with his questioning of the status of poets such as John Milton and Percy Bysshe Shelley, had a major influence on New Criticism.

Though Eliot's criticism had theoretical implications, he was not a literary theorist in any orthodox sense. Literary theory, however, emerged in the 1920s in the work of I. A. Richards. His studies *The Principles of Literary Criticism* (1924) and *Practical Criticism* (1929) were crucial to the development of New Criticism. Another significant influence was the work of Richards' pupil William Empson, who applied ideas derived from Richards' theory of literature to the close analysis of poetry in his book *Seven Types of Ambiguity* (1930).

For both Richards and Empson literary criticism needed to engage in detail with literary texts. In *Practical Criticism*, Richards had shown how inadequate even Cambridge University students were at analyzing poetry when presented with poems as pure texts without any indicators such as the author's name to offer guidance as to how they should be read or interpreted. Richards' experiment and its main critical implication – that texts which deserved to be categorized as literary should be capable of being interpreted coherently so that every element of form and meaning could be seen as an essential part of the text's structure – had a fundamental effect on the emerging New Criticism.

The term "New Criticism" was derived from John Crowe Ransom's book *The New Criticism* (1941). In addition to Ransom, the other major figures associated with it were R. P. Blackmur, Cleanth Brooks, Allen Tate, Robert Penn Warren, and W. K. Wimsatt. Where the New Critics differed from Richards was in their emphasis on the words of the text rather than on psychology. For Richards, a poem is a coherent ordering of impulses, and when properly read this coherence is transferred from the poem to the mind of the reader, enabling the reader to achieve a sense of wholeness of being. The New Critics, however, shifted the focus from psychology to the poem as a structure of words which had an independent existence. In the greatest poetry, meaning, structure, and form interact in such a way that one cannot be separated from the others. The New Critics have been called formalists but their formalism was different from that of the Russian Formalists. The latter had little interest in meaning as such: they tended to redefine content as having a formal function and the purpose of form was to defamiliarize the reader's habitual perspectives. Though the New Critics, like the Russian Formalists, denied that form and content were separable in literature, they were interested in meaning. In his essay of 1951, "The Formalist Critic," Cleanth Brooks asserted that "form is meaning."

The centrality of "meaning" in New Critical theory led to a critical emphasis on interpretation during the period in which the New Criticism was dominant. However, the New Critics denied that the meaning of a literary text was paraphrasable: literary meaning could not be discussed independently of the form of a work. Their notion of form was unlike traditional concepts which highlighted such elements as rhythm and meter, structural patterning, and genre. Rather, the New Critics conceived of form as an organic relation between all the elements of a work which interacted in such a way as to manifest a text's meaning, and the role of criticism was to demonstrate this. That was as much as criticism could do since the meaning of a text was beyond paraphrase and could only be embodied concretely in the work itself.

The New Critics' concept of form was almost certainly affected by T. S. Eliot's claim in an essay on the Metaphysical poets that a "dissociation of sensibility" had taken place in the seventeenth century, a cultural change which had created a radical division in consciousness through separating feeling and intellect. For Eliot, writers whom he admired in the early seventeenth century, such as Jacobean dramatists and Metaphysical poets, could think in terms of feeling through "a direct sensuous apprehension of thought." The early New Critics accepted Eliot's version of literary history and admired most those writers unaffected by the "dissociation of sensibility" and modernists such as Eliot himself who endeavored to overcome it. One of the tasks of criticism was to demonstrate the presence of this unity of sensibility, or the lack of it, in literature.

I. A. Richards had also been affected by Eliot's concept but he had expressed it in psychological terms. In his *Principles of Literary Criticism* he had distinguished between poems "built out of sets of impulses which run parallel" and poems in which there is an extraordinary "heterogeneity of distinguishable impulses. But they are more than heterogeneous, they are opposed." The New Critics, however, projected such heterogeneity and opposition of impulses onto the poem itself. It is the structure of the poem which fuses heterogeneous and opposed elements into unity, and it is particularly characteristic of writing which is unaffected by or which has gone beyond the "dissociation of sensibility" that it unifies opposed and heterogeneous elements. Cleanth Brooks, in his essay "The Heresy of Paraphrase" (1947), describes poetic structure as follows:

> The structure meant is certainly not 'form' in the conventional sense in which we think of form as a kind of envelope which 'contains' the 'content.' . . . The structure meant is a structure of meanings, evaluations, and interpretations; and the principle of unity which informs it seems to be one of balancing and harmonizing connotations, attitudes, and meanings . . . . It unites the like with the unlike.

It is this concept of structure in which unity and diversity are combined that leads to the habitual use in early

New Critical discourse of such terms as "ambiguity," "paradox," "complex of attitudes," and, most prominently, "irony." In critical practice the New Critic sets out to display the form and structure of a work so as to show how heterogeneous or opposed elements are unified through ambiguity or irony or paradox, which are not mere devices but integral to poetic form.

It is possible that there were cultural reasons why the New Critics were so committed to a formalism that unified heterogeneity and oppositions. Most of the American New Critics were conservative in political outlook and viewed with alarm the apparent anarchy of contemporary history, most powerfully expressed in literary terms in a work like Eliot's *The Waste Land*. In a world in which "the centre cannot hold," as William Butler Yeats put it in his poem "The Second Coming," the value of literary works which could confront the contradictory and disparate yet incorporate them without simplification in a structure in which the center *did* hold was clear. In poetry the human imagination could triumph over the contradictory or the chaotic without the need to accept religious belief or political ideology or philosophical system. At the end of "The Heresy of Paraphrase" Brooks wrote: "If the poet, then, must perforce dramatize the oneness of the experience, even though paying tribute to its diversity, then his use of paradox and ambiguity is seen as necessary," and this provides us with "an insight which preserves the unity of experience and which ... triumphs over the apparently contradictory and conflicting elements of experience by unifying them into a new pattern." An implication of this is that literary criticism itself is a reenactment of the unifying process embodied in the literary text itself, so that criticism, like literature, also creates order and coherence out of the contradictions and conflicts of the world.

The New Critics attached particular value to Metaphysical poetry, particularly the lyrics of John Donne. For Samuel Johnson, writing in the eighteenth century, Metaphysical poetry discovered "occult resemblances in things apparently unlike" so that the "most heterogeneous ideas are yoked by violence together," but for the New Critics this made Metaphysical poetry embody their ideal of form. The early New Criticism had tended to concentrate on lyric poetry and doubts had been expressed as to whether it could be appropriately applied to longer forms such as plays and novels. Critics such as Brooks attempted to overcome such objections by applying New Critical method to longer works. In his study *The Well Wrought Urn* (1947), a title significantly derived from a Donne poem, he writes on *Macbeth* in an essay entitled "The Naked Babe and the Cloak of Manliness." For Brooks the play has a poetic rather than a dramatic structure. Imagery is elevated above plot in importance, with the emphasis being given to recurrent images that appear to be contradictory. He focuses on the image "a naked new-born-babe,/ Striding the blast," an image which contains a contradiction since

the weakest of creatures has strength to outface the turmoil of nature. After an intricate analysis Brooks argues that the play overcomes such an apparent contradiction since a "naked new-born babe" can create pity as a force of nature that can eventually defeat a murderer. He concludes his analysis by arguing that what for him are the two dominant images in *Macbeth* – the naked babe and daggers clothed in blood – "are facets of two of the great symbols which run throughout the play." The play, he argues, creates unity out of such diametrical oppositions.

New Criticism generated comparatively little theory. Though critics such as Brooks wrote occasionally on theoretical topics, their main interest was in critical analysis. W. K. Wimsatt was the most theoretically minded of the New Critics and is best remembered for two essays, written together with Monroe C. Beardsley, that attempt to theorize central New Critical assumptions: "The Intentional Fallacy" and "The Affective Fallacy," first published in 1946 and 1949 respectively. The purpose of these two essays is to justify the New Critical emphasis on the text itself rather than on the role of the author or the audience's response. The position they take is rather more subtle than most discussions of these essays would tend to suggest. It is a crude reading of the essays which would claim that they assert that authorial intention is irrelevant to the meaning of a text and that audience response is of no literary interest. They recognize that language is a historical phenomenon and therefore one needs to take into account what words meant when a author committed them to paper and also how an audience contemporary with the text would have responded to them. But one should not ask what the author meant, as meaning is embodied in the text, and the critic should also not be concerned with the diversity of individual response: "The critic is not a contributor to statistically countable reports about a poem, but a teacher or explicator of meanings."

New Criticism eventually came to dominate American academic criticism. In an essay written in 1937, "Criticism, Inc.," John Crowe Ransom attacked professors of literature for not really being critics, and claimed that "the students of the future must be permitted to study literature, and not merely about literature." By emphasizing close reading rather than historical knowledge, New Criticism made it possible for students to feel they had a more active role to play in literary studies and could enter into critical dialogue with their teachers. The New Critics also produced textbooks which had great influence on the teaching of literature, notably Brooks and Warren's *Understanding Poetry*, the first edition of which appeared in 1938, and this gave New Criticism a pedagogical advantage over more traditional teaching methods.

As New Criticism became increasingly established in American universities, it gradually changed its nature. If one looks at New Criticism in the 1950s and 1960s, there is much less emphasis on paradox, ambiguity, or irony as being intrinsic to literary form. There was a greater emphasis on incorporating as much of the text as possible within its thematic structure. For example, John M. Ellis in his *Theory of Literary Criticism* (1974), a work which defends some central New Critical concepts, writes: "The most general statement of structure . . . is equally a statement of thematic structure and therefore of the meaning of the text. The test of statements of this kind is simply comprehensiveness – they must synthesize and thus make sense of as much of the text as possible." The redirection of New Criticism toward thematic unity and comprehensiveness made it possible for it to be applied easily to fiction and drama, whereas the earlier New Critics had been most at home with lyric poetry. The later New Criticism also was more compromising in its attitude toward authorial intention and historical context: it became legitimate to make use of them if this helped to understand the structure of the work.

One significant result of these modifications to New Criticism was an explosion of interpretations of literary texts. Despite comprehensiveness as a criterion in judging whether one interpretation was superior to another, in practice it was difficult to decide among interpretations on this principle. This led to a certain disillusionment with later New Criticism, as one can see in an essay like Susan Sontag's "Against Interpretation" (1964). Allied to the professionalization of literary criticism, New Criticism seemed to be producing merely an accumulation of interpretations. In this context, the climate was right for the emergence of alternative critical perspectives such as structuralism, deconstruction, and New Historicism, though New Criticism, in the English-speaking world at least, continues to interact with all of these and remains a force in the teaching of literature.

## Further reading

Brooks, Cleanth. *Modern Poetry and the Tradition*, 1939.
——. *The Well Wrought Urn: Studies in the Structure of Poetry*, 1947.
——. "In Search of the New Criticism," in *American Scholar*. 53 (1983–1984).
de Man, Paul. "Form and Intent in the American New Criticism," in *Blindness and Insight*, 1971.
Empson, William. *Seven Types of Ambiguity*, 1930.
Krieger, Murray. *The New Apologists for Poetry*, 1956.
Lentricchia, Frank. *After the New Criticism*, 1980.
Ransom, John Crowe. *The New Criticism*, 1941.
Richards, I. A. *The Principles of Literary Criticism*, 1924.
——. *Practical Criticism: A Study of Literary Judgement*, 1929.
Tate, Allen. *Essays of Four Decades*, 1968.
Wellek, René. *A History of Modern Criticism, 1750–1950*. Vol. 6, *American Criticism, 1900–1950*, 1986.
Wimsatt, W. K., Jr. *The Verbal Icon: Studies in the Meaning of Poetry*, 1954.

K. M. NEWTON

*See also* American Literary Theory: Twentieth Century; Blackmur; Brooks, C.; Ransom; Richards; Tate; Warren; Wimsatt

# New Historicism

New Historicism is a critical movement which flourished in the late 1970s and during the 1980s. New Historicists operate by fusing two key issues in criticism since the 1960s: the "linguistic turn" of poststructuralist and deconstructive criticism, and a return to historical readings. These two impulses are aptly summarized in Louis Montrose's often repeated catchphrase: "the historicity of texts and the textuality of history." Texts, he insists (as do all New Historicist critics) are embedded in particular histories. Those histories, in turn, are embedded in language, since we only access those histories through the texts which represent them. Since all these texts use language which is seen as elusive and unfixed, "textual" history effectively calls for the kinds of close reading strategies which, as Stephen Greenblatt remarks in a recent essay, literary critics have as part of their "disciplinary tool kit." In their choice of text events to analyze, and in their manner of analyzing those events, New Historicists develop many of their ideas by fusing the ethnography of the anthropologist Clifford Geertz with the philosophic history of Michel Foucault. New Historicist essays began appearing in the late 1970s, but the groundbreaking text was the 1980 publication of Stephen Greenblatt's *Renaissance Self-Fashioning: From More to Shakespeare*. This book was followed in 1983 by the founding of the journal *Representations*, initiated by Greenblatt and several of his colleagues at the University of California at Berkeley, where the journal is still published. In its volumes, and in Greenblatt's many subsequent publications, can most clearly be seen the strategies of New Historicism as well as their limitations.

## Clifford Geertz and thick description

Geertz's ethnography became celebrated in the late 1960s, just as the major New Historicists were moving from graduate school into university posts. His writings have been enormously influential on New Historicist practice, especially the essays collected in *The Interpretation of Cultures: Selected Essays* (1973) and *Local Knowledge: Further Essays in Interpretive Anthropology* (1983). From the first, New Historicists were beguiled by the much anthologized "Deep Play: Notes on the Balinese Cock Fight" (1971); and from the second, by "Centers, Kings and Charisma: Reflections on the Symbolics of Power" (1983), especially by the section evoking the pageantry which Queen Elizabeth I of England deployed with great political skill. Here Geertz showed literary critics how they might read Renaissance English culture in new ways. With Geertz as their great exemplar, New Historicists have completely changed criticism of Renaissance texts; those changes can now also be seen in the criticism of texts from many different periods and national cultures.

Geertz practices "thick description," a term he borrows from the Oxford philosopher Gilbert Ryle. Geertz "thickly describes" – in other words, unearths the underlying meaningful structures of – local events and local interactions, and from those interactions generalizes whole societies. For Geertz, the concrete or the actual must always precede the abstract. He insists on what Greenblatt calls "the touch of the real." New Historicists were excited by the advantage Geertz offered them: his ethnography always focused on what had actually happened. He spun these happenings in elegant webs of significance; he turned them into elaborately constructed fictions. But their "touch of the real" meant that, in a crucial sense, they were more "real" than the literary fictions which New Historicists had been trained to describe: plays, poems, novels. They yearned to link those fictions with the world Geertz and his subjects seemed to inhabit. Geertz might describe a cockfight, a Moroccan bazaar, an Islamic ritual: his eye would light on an apparently small object or event and through thick description evoke its meanings.

Here there is a key crossover. Geertz's first degree was in English and philosophy; thus, in a sense he still closely reads events as if they themselves were art objects, lyric poems, or Renaissance portraits. He thus showed New Historicists how they could read; the advantage he offered them was an enormous expansion in the range of materials they might then read. If all events were accessed through texts, critics need not confine themselves to traditional literary and canonical texts.

A standard New Historicist essay would begin by reading an explorer's journal, an account of an exorcist, or perhaps some gossip from the court of Henry VIII or Elizabeth I. This would be read as thoroughly as, say, New Criticism might read a Shakespearean sonnet. This would then be linked with other excerpts from quite different texts. Finally the New Historicist, in a standard move, would turn to a literary example, usually a small passage or a scene from a play. There would be no attempts at a complete, or "closed," reading of the text. Rather, the strategy would be to link together, somewhat loosely, a whole series of apparently unrelated items. From these readings the New Historicist would, like Geertz, then attempt to generalize the workings of a society.

All literary methods have ideal forms, modes of writing which respond most readily to the proposed method. For New Historicism, the "anecdote" as Joel Fineman points out, is really the preferred form. Since Herodotus, anecdotes have offered layered and complex descriptions of events and persons; in their rich looseness, anecdotes are perfectly structured for the kinds of stories New Historicists wished to tell.

## Geertz as storyteller

If New Historicists allowed Geertz to lead them away from the unreal world of canonical fiction, then he also always reminded them that the descriptions of this "real" world were also fictions, texts wrought and crafted. Highly elaborate stories, such as Geertz's accounts of cockfighting, could only be told by highly self-conscious storytellers. In Geertz's work the ethnographer is always present, collecting data and shaping the ethnographic fiction. Geertz for the most part reports on his own fieldwork. He can describe "being there" because, as his field notes show, he really was there. New Historicists setting out to describe English Renaissance culture (or any other historical period) could not achieve the same access, despite Greenblatt's confessed desire to "speak with the dead" as an ethnographer speaks with the living. As they make the dead speak, however, New Historicists have been keen to remind readers of their own voices. The critic is always present, arranging, commenting, ironizing. Like Geertz, the major New Historicists have been self-conscious stylists. Many of them also, like Geertz, have been autobiographical, Greenblatt most obsessively so, revealing progressively his intellectual and personal history. As they disclose the symbolics of power in the Renaissance, these reflections worry over the relationship between New Historicism and the workings of power in the modern world. As Stanley Fish acerbically remarked: "they are nervous their careers are going well."

## Michel Foucault and power relations

With Geertz as their model, New Historicists attempted a "poetics of culture," turning Renaissance culture into a series of art objects. But they also aspired to a poetics of power. For this they turned to Michel Foucault, whose studies of madness, reason, discipline, and punishment exercised huge influence through the 1970s and into the 1980s. In the early 1980s Foucault visited Berkeley annually; this helped energize in person the ideas sparked by reading his works. New Historicists shared with him many political experiences. Foucault had witnessed the 1968 uprisings in Paris, and had seen the force of protest crushed by the power of the republic. Similarly, New Historicists were young, liberal teachers who witnessed the campus protests in the United States, and the crushing of those protests by federal and state forces. Greenblatt and Montrose began writing while Ronald Reagan was governor of California and Richard Nixon president of the United States. Their fascination with the symbolics of power, the invisible forces manifested in a street parade or a court masque, as well as with the brute force of power, reflect this combination of personal and intellectual experiences. Greenblatt and Montrose clearly projected their own anxieties into the European past. With Foucault to assist them, they saw not a golden age, as previous critics had done, but rather a dark mirror for their own troubled times.

The events of 1968 showed how forcefully states would seek, when threatened, to enforce their own power. What preoccupied Foucault and his New Historicist followers was not so much the defeat of "freedom fighters" but rather the capacity of the state to withstand such urgent challenges. Why had the populace not risen to support the students and workers in Paris? The answer was provided partly by Foucault and partly by the French political philosopher Louis Althusser. The state's control of its citizenry was internal rather than external. The state subjected its peoples by creating them as subjects, devising fixed categories under which people could be described and thus controlled. This was the conjunction Foucault evoked as "power/knowledge." The categories sane/insane, homosexual/heterosexual, male/female, slave/freed could thus be used to proscribe activity. This would happen not with regulation but with more invisible forms of ideological pressure, through institutions, literature, entertainments. The populace would have the illusion of being free to choose their status and activities; in fact they would be in thrall to an omnipresent state. For many, Foucault thus made sense of the complexity of capitalist societies, saturated with media events and spectacles of pleasure. In turn he offered New Historicists insight into the complex workings of Renaissance monarchies. Renaissance England, it seemed to them, was as beset by chaos, by enemies within and without, as the contemporary world. How could you effectively rule such turmoil? Their explanations projected Elizabeth I as a cunning constructor of images of herself and her kingdom, purveying fictions of splendor as well as propaganda to her people. Underneath the theatrical charisma, her regime was harsh and oppressive. Rebellion might be attempted but effectively would be impossible. Renaissance writers were thus trapped in subtle webs of power politics, just as New Historicists felt themselves trapped by what Althusser calls "Ideological State Apparatuses."

## Renaissance

New Historicists thus reject previous models of Elizabethan England, spurning in particular images of social wholeness and cosmic harmony. Here E. M. W. Tillyard's useful primer of Elizabethan beliefs, *The Elizabethan World Picture* (1963), became an object of derision. Tillyard's depiction of Renaissance beliefs in the need for harmony and order in the world were taken as an insistence that the Elizabethan world was always harmonious and cosmically ordered. For New Historicists, rather, the Renaissance was dark, fragmented, painful. It responded well to reading by anecdote because larger frameworks would not in fact make sense. England of the 1590s, then, came to seem like the first postmodern epoch in Western culture. This investment in the Renaissance was not accidental. Deconstructive and poststructuralist approaches had been successfully applied to texts from later periods, proving especially fruitful in rereading Romantic texts by William Wordsworth, Percy Bysshe Shelley, and John Keats. Yet, into the 1980s, the canon of Renaissance texts had seemed immune to new readings, imprisoned in the patterns of an older historicism. Readings were historical, but they tended to absorb Renaissance ideas or events into canonical texts, and not the other way round. The canon was still sealed off, a separate, precious category, from the era which produced it. New Historicists looked for a more dynamic relationship between texts and their societies. If a society could be shown to form a text, then you could also show that texts in turn reshaped the society from which they came. For New Historicists understood Marshall McLuhan's sound bite – the medium is the message – as a fundamental truism. If they wished to write about the forms of power, they sought also to show the power of literary forms to reshape the world. This has proved easier to assert than to prove, a beguiling possibility rather than a demonstrable fact, for lyric poems which can be shown by themselves to have changed the world turned out to be hard to find.

## Influence

In the late 1980s there seemed to be almost as many commentators on New Historicism as avowed practitioners. New Historicists had quickly, it seemed, achieved positions of intellectual eminence. They were then forced to defend that eminence against hostile fire. They were frequently denounced for not being intellectually coherent, for not having, in fact, a proper method at all. Rather, New Historicists were seen to be arch *bricoleurs*, making up their method as they went along, concocting a paradigm stew of anthropology, Marxism, history, and psychology. Responses to these charges were serendipitous. Greenblatt in particular was happy to admit his eclectic mix of approaches. Like Geertz, he clearly preferred to keep doing what he had always done, touching and poeticizing the real, leaving grand theories to different intellects.

Though obsessed with the processes of power, New Historicism was also thought to be apolitical. Its readings, on the whole, suggested the monolithic and inventive nature of the state, capable of the subtlest forms of exclusion and suppression. New Historicists, moreover, had practiced their own forms of exclusion. Though they had tried to renovate the canon, they had largely focused on highly canonical figures. They were evangelists, in other words, for the much spurned "dead white males" of the literary canon. They ignored writings by women and other minorities, preferring instead another reading of *King Lear*. For some critics, New Historicists were not nearly political enough.

Yet New Historicism, by the late 1990s, had inspired new approaches which themselves might turn out to be politically more effective. The strategy of thick description and the local reading of power relations could be seen in subaltern studies and postcolonial approaches more generally. New Historicism could also be seen as fertilizing feminist scholarship as well as gender studies and its offshoots in queer theory. Scholars in all these areas were as keen as Greenblatt or Geertz to put themselves in the picture they were evoking. At its stammering worst, this led to tedious self-aggrandizement. The confession blocked the view of the text or period the confessor tried to describe. At its best, though, New Historicism continued to inspire productive and influential work. The return to the "real" Greenblatt hoped for was clearly in place. Locating texts inside the material circumstances of their creation and reception had become accepted literary practice. The flagship journal *Representations* continued to publish influential material from an eclectic range of disciplines; New Historicist studies continued to emerge. Denunciations of New Historicism remained part of the Anglo-American literary scene. The citation indexes, however, suggested that, if the frequency of citings was anything to go by, New Historicism still had something to say.

## Further reading

Brannigan, John. *New Historicism and Cultural Materialism*, 1998.
Fineman, Joel. *The Subjectivity Effect in Western Literary Tradition*, 1991.
Geertz, Clifford. *The Interpretation of Cultures: Selected Essays*, 1973.
——. *Local Knowledge: Further Essays in Interpretive Anthropology*, 1983.
Greenblatt, Stephen. *Renaissance Self-Fashioning: From More to Shakespeare*, 1980.
——, ed. *Representing the English Renaissance*, 1988.
——. *Learning to Curse: Essays in Early Modern Culture*, 1990.
Montrose, Louis. *The Purpose of Playing: Shakespeare and the Cultural Politics of the Elizabethan Theatre*, 1996.
Tillyard, E. M. W. *The Elizabethan World Picture*, 1963.
Veeser, H. Aram, ed. *The New Historicism*, 1989.
——, ed. *The New Historicism Reader*, 1994.

MARK HOULAHAN

*See also* Geertz

# New Pragmatism

The term "New Pragmatism" first emerged as the result of the publication of an article entitled "Against Theory" by Steven Knapp and Walter Benn Michaels in the journal *Critical Inquiry* in 1982. This article provoked a flurry of rejoinders and also further articles replying to their critics by Knapp and Michaels. "Against Theory" was clearly influenced by the work of the philosopher Richard Rorty and the critic and theorist Stanley Fish, though Knapp and Michaels take the view that Rorty and Fish do not go far enough.

In "Against Theory" Knapp and Michaels define theory as "a special project in literary criticism: the attempt to govern interpretations of particular texts by appealing to an account of interpretation in general." They see contemporary theory as having two forms: first, the attempt "to ground the reading of literary texts in methods designed to guarantee the objectivity and validity of interpretations";

and second, following the failure of interpreters to agree about objectivity and validity, "an alternative mode of theory that denies the possibility of correct interpretation." Knapp and Michaels claim both these approaches rest on a mistake.

As an instance of the incoherence of the theoretical project, they point to the debate about the validity or invalidity of authorial intention in relation to literary interpretation. They claim that there cannot in fact be intentionless meanings, and so the debate between anti-intentionalists such as the New Critics and intentionalists such as E. D. Hirsch and P. D. Juhl is simply pointless. One cannot choose either to pay attention to or to disregard intention, for there can be no meaning without intention; intention cannot either be added to or subtracted from language. They conjure up a situation in which lines of a poem are produced by some natural process like the effect of waves on sand. Such lines would not be language, they claim, but only "accidental likenesses of language. They are not . . . an example of intentionless meaning; as soon as they become intentionless they become meaningless as well." In terms of literary theory, therefore, the New Critics and other textualists are wrong to believe that language exists independently of human intention; but equally intentionalists like Hirsch are wrong to concede that there can be intentionless meanings, and that intentionalism can therefore be defended only on moral grounds. Interpretation is inevitably and unavoidably an attempt to recover intention, though Knapp and Michaels do not discuss the argument that intention cannot be seen merely as an individual phenomenon but is shaped by such supra-individual forces as culture or history or the unconscious.

Knapp and Michaels accept Stanley Fish's position that theory can have no practical consequences since one can never maintain a theoretical position that stands outside practice. Nor can theory be separated from belief: "In our view . . . the only relevant truth about belief is that you can't go outside it." They conclude that theory "is the name for all the ways people have tried to stand outside practice in order to govern practice from without. Our thesis has been that no one can reach a position outside practice, that theorists should stop trying, and that the theoretical enterprise should therefore come to an end."

Stanley Fish responded to Knapp and Michaels in an essay entitled "Consequences," published in *Critical Inquiry* in 1985, in which he thoroughly aligned himself with a New Pragmatist position. He argues that he, like Knapp and Michaels, is committed to an antifoundationalist theory, one associated with the "anti-essentialism" of Richard Rorty, though he adds that this is only a theory in the ironic sense that it is "an argument against the possibility of theory." Foundationalism claims that there are beliefs that are foundational in that all other beliefs rest upon them, and furthermore that these foundational beliefs cannot be questioned without threatening all beliefs. Fish argues that the dire consequences that foundationalists assert will result from antifoundationalism can never happen. The reason, he argues, is that one does not need to control or guide practice from a position outside it because all practices have rules built into them. If they did not, they would not be able to function as practices. He rejects the view that theory can lead to the "foregrounding of beliefs and assumptions" and so guide practice since this assumes that one can somehow achieve a position that does not depend on beliefs or assumptions, which Fish argues is impossible. He believes that there is no need to seek out rules or constraints or shared standards as all individuals are unavoidably enmeshed in cultural practices that are inevitably rule governed: the subject is always socially constrained and "will always be guided by the rules or rules of thumb that are the content of any settled practice." New Pragmatism is therefore not so much a theoretical position as a theoretically informed critique of theory itself.

### Further reading

Fish, Stanley. *Doing What Comes Naturally: Change, Rhetoric, and the Practice of Theory in Literary and Legal Studies*, 1989.
Mitchell, W. J. T., ed. *Against Theory: Literary Studies and the New Pragmatism*, 1985.
Rorty, Richard. *Consequences of Pragmatism (Essays: 1972–80)*, 1982.

K. M. NEWTON

*See also* Fish

# Ngugi wa Thiong'o

## Kenyan writer

**Born:** Kamiriithu village, near Limuru, Kenya; January 5, 1938

## Biography

Ngugi wa Thiong'o (known until his name change in 1970 as James Ngugi) was born in 1938 in Kamiriithu village near Limuru in the Kiambu District of the Central Province of Kenya. He came from a large family: his father had four wives and twenty-eight children. His elementary education – first in a mission school and then in a Gikuyu nationalist school – was interrupted by the Mau Mau War of 1952. This bitter Gikuyu uprising against the British is the basis for Ngugi's first novels.

Ngugi attended Alliance High School, known as the Eton of East Africa. His higher education was at Makarere University in Uganda and Leeds University in England. His teaching career began at University College, Nairobi, where he later became head of the department of literature. Ngugi was imprisoned without trial for the whole of the year 1978. He has lived in self-imposed exile in England since 1982 because of the oppressive political conditions in Kenya.

Ngugi married Nyambura in 1961 and has five children. He has traveled widely, having visited the United States several times, Europe, the Soviet Union, Australia, and New Zealand.

## Influence

Ngugi is undoubtedly the most articulate and influential of the artist-critics of Africa who have taken a radical Marxist position. A true Marxist, he believes that literature should not merely reflect life but change it by exposing the real sources of corruption and exploitation and by inspiring the wretched of the earth to rise in rebellion and claim their birthright: Ngugi's criticism – literary, social, political, and cultural – is prophetic in spirit: it is a judgment as well as a call to action.

## Analysis

In an interview with Hansel Nolumbe Eyoh on March 30, 1985, Ngugi gave the following definition of literature:

> Literature is like thinking in images about the world we live in. I therefore see literature as a very important weapon, if you like, in the ideological struggle, in the battle for how we perceive ourselves – in the struggle for communal and individual self-definition.

This quotation gives a fairly accurate idea of Ngugi's concerns as a writer and critic. The aim of the ideological struggle is, however, not only to alter the way in which people perceive themselves – it is also to change the world, to banish from it the corruption and exploitation which make it impossible for people to realize their full potential as human beings. It took Ngugi some time to arrive at this position, and it is possible to trace three distinct stages in his evolution and growth as a critic. The first stage extends from his early life to 1964, when he completed his studies at Makarere University and left for higher studies at Leeds. The second stage extends from 1964 to his involvement in the Kamiriithu festival in 1976, and the third from that time onward.

Ngugi began expressing himself on social, political, literary, and cultural affairs quite early in life. He wrote his first two novels, a play, and several short stories while he was still a student at Makarere. Along with these, he was writing a fortnightly column for the Nairobi paper *The Sunday Nation*. His critical opinions at the time were those of a liberal humanist nurtured in the Romantic tradition. "A creative writer," Ngugi asserted, "is concerned with the expression of the music and strife in his own soul." Though he did not dismiss the idea of commitment, acknowledging that an artist cannot be wholly detached from social problems, he believed that the artist's main duty is to retain his or her own individuality and to resist giving people what they want. In an article entitled "African Writers Need a New Outlook," he said: "Protest writing and Negritude

... are poses and attitudes. They have left a large area of permanent human experience unexplored."

There was a drastic change in Ngugi's views following his arrival in Leeds in 1964. There, he was introduced to radical socialist thought – the writings of Karl Marx, Friedrich Engels, Vladimir Ilich Lenin, and Frantz Fanon. The atmosphere at the university was revolutionary: his supervisor, Arnold Kettle, was a Marxist; the student group led by Alan Hunt was Marxist, as well. One of his fellow students was Grant Kamenju, who has come to be known as one of the founders of Black Aesthetics. Fanon's *Les Damnes de la terre* (1961; *The Wretched of the Earth*, 1965) came as a revelation to Ngugi. Having learned from his Algerian experience, Fanon justified the use of violence by the oppressed to regain not only their freedom but also, and even more, their self-respect. The greatest damage that colonialism had done to the colonized was to inculcate in them a sense of inferiority by denigrating their culture. African countries were still not free: flag independence was only an illusion of freedom, for the national bourgeoisie which had come to power in the newly independent countries was a comprador class, managing the economies of these countries in the interests of its neocolonial masters. The peasantry alone was the truly revolutionary class. From Engels, Ngugi learned the meaning and significance of dialectic; from Marx, the materialist interpretation of history, the theory of social class, faith in the proletariat, and the proletariat's ability to build a new future. From the early Marx, who defined Communism as "transcendence of human alienation" and "positive humanism," Ngugi derived the concept of alienation, or more correctly, self-alienation. Lenin's writings on capitalism provided him with an understanding of the main source of imperialism.

The Marxist influence is clearly discernible in the critical essays which were collected in *Homecoming* in 1972. His scholarly work on the literature of the West Indies between 1965 and 1967 and his year's stay in the United States between 1970 and 1971 had convinced him of the similarity of the problems facing black people everywhere. Hundreds of years of ill-treatment by the white slavers and imperialists and denigration of their culture by missionaries and European intellectuals, from G. W. F. Hegel to Hugh Trevor-Roper, and by racist writers, such as Rider Haggard, Isak Dinesen, Elspeth Huxley, and Robert Ruark, had affected the way blacks perceived themselves. It is the business of the writer to end this alienation and to restore to the black people their lost self-respect – what Ngugi calls building a communal home for all Africans.

Ngugi recognized that he was not the first among African or black writers to diagnose this problem. Caribbean writers such as George Lamming, Edward Brathwaite, and Orlando Patterson and Americans such as Richard Wright have graphically portrayed the black condition. African writers such as Chinua Achebe, Wole Soyinka, and Okot p'Bitek have enabled blacks to resume the broken dialogue with their own gods. With rare exceptions, however, such as Richard Wright or George Lamming, the belief has persisted among most African intellectuals and artists – the leading spirits of the negritude movement being an outstanding example – that cultural liberation is an essential condition for political liberation. In *Homecoming*, however, Ngugi argued that it is wrong to think of culture as prior to politics:

Political and economic liberation are the essential condition for cultural liberation, for the true release of a people's creative spirit and imagination. It is when people are involved in the active work of destroying an inhibitive social structure and building a new one that they begin to see themselves. They are born again.

Since literature is primarily concerned with what any political and economic arrangement does to the spirit and values governing human relationships, it is the duty of the writer to make the people aware of the harm that capitalism and its natural extension, colonialism, do to the heart and soul of the individual and society. If Africans are to achieve true national cultures which will restore a "meaningful self-image" to the individual and prove the opportunity to realize one's full potential as a human being, they must fully Africanize and socialize their political and economic life. Persons who believe that they can maintain colonial, economic, and other social institutions and graft an African culture onto them are sadly mistaken; colonial institutions can only produce a colonial mentality.

Thus, in *Homecoming* Ngugi is critical of writers such as Achebe and Soyinka. In a review of Achebe's powerful novel *A Man of the People* (1966), Ngugi doubts that characters such as Obi Okonkwo, Nanga, Odili, and Max – or political parties, such as the Common People's Convention – can behave in a radical way while operating within, and in fact espousing, the given economic and social setup. In the same way, though Soyinka is very effective in exposing corruption and injustice, when it comes to suggesting solutions he "does not know where to turn." The characters shown in a positive light are, with the exception of the artists, cynics or tribal reactionaries. "Soyinka's good man is the uncorrupted individual: his liberal humanism leads him to admire an individual's lone act of courage, and thus often he ignores the creative struggle of the masses." He fails to see the social dialectic, "the present in the historical perspective of conflict and struggle." This is a serious failure, for it is not enough for the African artist, standing aloof, to view society and highlight its weaknesses. The writer is not outside the battle. By diving deep into the collective unconscious of the people, the writer can seek the root, the trend of the revolutionary struggle. Having once assessed this trend, the writer must be committed to the majority, the struggling masses, and give a moral direction and vision to the struggle which, in spite of temporary setbacks, ultimately is bound to succeed.

The 1970s saw Ngugi's increasing identification of art with the people. The decisive event was his involvement in the activities of his native village through the Kamiriithu Community Educational and Cultural Centre. Ngugi and a colleague were asked to produce a working script of a play, and their response was *Ngaahika Ndeenda* (1977; *I Will Marry When I Want*, 1982). During rehearsals, the peasants changed the play completely. The process of metamorphosis, involving discussion of the play's content, its language, even its form, was a decisive experience for Ngugi – "the true beginning of my education." He claimed he was learning his language anew and rediscovering the nature and power of creative work. The critical theory Ngugi began to espouse is startlingly new as well as revolutionary. Good plays are not so much the work of individual playwrights as the results of communal effort. The theater is a kind of literary and ideological workshop and school where the writer learns to write and also receives the correct ideological orientation by sitting at the feet of the people. The people are qualified to be the teachers because of their fine sense of language, which is much more discriminating than that of the playwright alienated by a bourgeois colonial education. Their richer possession of indigenous culture has made them intimate with the forms and techniques of dramatic production – ritual, song, dance, and mime. They have a true knowledge of the actual conditions in which the masses live, and they know history.

A knowledge of this history would show the playwright, as it had shown Ngugi, that there are two diametrically opposed traditions of Kenyan history, culture, and aesthetics. The first tradition is the people's revolutionary culture of outspoken courage and patriotism; the second is the bourgeoisie's colonial culture of silence and fear, developed primarily as a reaction to the first, in order to humiliate the African people into accepting the oppressor's view of history. The first tradition carried the aesthetic line that struggle to change an oppressive status quo was a good thing. The foreign missionary churches, on the contrary, and the colonial religions and cultures promulgated by them carried the aesthetic line of the beauty of reveling in slavery.

A natural corollary of identifying art with the people is adoption of their language. Language was the means by which imperialism brought about the spiritual subjugation of the people of Asia and Africa, the most important vehicle through which its power fascinated and held their souls prisoner. Therefore, if the people of Asia and Africa want to win their spiritual freedom, they will have to stop writing in European languages and learn to express themselves in their own languages, by establishing close contact with the people. Finally, the real language of African theater, as of other literary forms, is to be found in the struggles of the oppressed, for it is out of those struggles that a new Africa is being born.

The contribution of Ngugi to the theory of criticism is distinct and impressive, and his influence on African and Third World critics is deep as well as extensive. Some idea of this influence can be obtained from the essays included in the collection *Marxism and African Literature* (1985), edited by Georg M. Gugelberger. Ngugi is contrasted with Soyinka and held up as the model of a progressive and Third World writer and critic, who accepts his identity with the wretched of the earth and is determined to end all exploitation and oppression. This estimate is just, for Ngugi is a committed critic who firmly believes that literature cannot escape the class power structures that shape everyday life. As he asserts in *Writers in Politics* (1981), every writer is a writer in politics; the only question is what and whose politics, whether of the people or of those social forces and classes which try to keep the people down. With his fearless, forceful, and clear articulation of issues, Ngugi has lifted African/black critical debate from notions of race to those of class. By vehemently rejecting efforts to make a religion of skin color, as seen in the formulation of concepts such as African Socialism, Ngugi has expanded the parameters of critical discourse and made it possible to talk in terms of Third World literature. His critical vision is broad enough to embrace progressive writers from around the world, such as William Blake, Maksim Gor'kii, Mikhail Sholokhov, Bertolt Brecht, and Kim Chi Ha.

## Principal criticism

*Homecoming: Essays on African and Caribbean Literature, Culture, and Politics*, 1972
*Writers in Politics*, 1981
*Detained: A Writer's Prison Diary*, 1981
*Barrel of a Pen: Resistance to Repression in Neo-Colonial Kenya*, 1983
*Decolonising the Mind: The Politics of Language in African Literature*, 1986
*Writing Against Neocolonialism*, 1986
*Moving the Centre: The Struggle for Cultural Freedoms*, 1993
*Writers in Politics: A Re-engagement With Issues of Literature and Society*, 1997
*Penpoints, Gunpoints, and Dreams: the Performance of Literature and Power in Post-Colonial Africa*, 1998

## Other major works and literary forms

Ngugi wa Thiong'o is one of the leading writers of modern Africa. He has published novels, plays, short stories, children's books, and collections of essays. He is a distinguished novelist, whose *A Grain of Wheat* (1967) and *Petals of Blood* (1977) are among the finest novels to come out of East Africa. As his main concern is the freedom and resurgence of Africa, his interests are wide and comprehensive. He has written and spoken on subjects which are social, political, economic, educational, and cultural. As a more effective instrument for the propagation of his ideas, Ngugi has turned increasingly to the theater and film. Regarding language as one of the most powerful instruments used by imperialism to enslave the African mind, he gave up writing in English and began writing in his mother tongue, Gikuyu, in 1977. He has translated his novels, plays, and children's books written in Gikuyu into English. Ngugi had continued to write essays and lectures in English, but in 1986 he announced that the book *Decolonising the Mind* was his farewell to English as a vehicle for any of his writings. Since then he has maintained a political refusal to employ "alien languages" in his work, instead embracing Gikuyu and Kiswahili, although he continues to lecture in English.

NOVELS
*Weep Not, Child,* 1964
*The River Between,* 1965
*A Grain of Wheat,* 1967
*Petals of Blood,* 1977
*Caitaani Mutharaba-Ini,* 1982 (*Devil on the Cross,* 1982)

SHORT FICTION
*Secret Lives and Other Stories,* 1975

PLAYS
*The Black Hermit,* 1962
*This Time Tomorrow: Three Plays,* 1966 (includes *The Rebels, The Wound in My Heart,* and *This Time Tomorrow*)
*The Trial of Dedan Kimathi,* 1974 (with Micere Githae-Mugo)
*Ngaahika Ndeenda,* 1977 (with Ngugi wa Mirii; *I Will Marry When I Want,* 1982)
*Maitu Njugira,* 1982 (with Ngugi wa Mirii; *Mother, Sing for Me,* 1986)
*Matigari ma Njiruungi,* 1986

CHILDREN'S LITERATURE
*Njamba Nene na Cibu King'angi,* 1982 (*Njamba Nene and the Flying Bus,* 1986)
*Njamba Nene na Mbaathi i Mathagu,* 1984 (*Njamba Nene's Pistol,* 1986)

## Further reading

Amuzu, Koku. *Beyond Ideology: Literary Technique in Ngugi's "Petals of Blood" and "Devil on the Cross,"* 1997.
Cook, David, and Michael Okenimkpe. *Ngugi wa Thiong'o: An Exploration of His Writings,* 1983.
Gugelberger, Georg M., ed. *Marxism and African Literature,* 1985.
Killam, Gordon Douglas. *An Introduction to the Writings of Ngugi,* 1980.
——, ed. *Critical Perspectives on Ngugi wa Thiong'o,* 1984.
Moore, Gerald. *Twelve African Writers,* 1980.
Robson, Clifford B. *Ngugi wa Thiong'o,* 1979.
Sicherman, Carol. *Ngugi Wa Thiong'o: A Bibliography of Primary and Secondary Sources, 1957–1987,* 1989.
Tsabedze, Clara. *African Independence from Francophone and Anglophone Voices: A Comparative Study of the Post-Independence Novels by Ngugi and Sembene,* 1994.

GOVIND NARAIN SHARMA

*See also* Black Literary Theory and Criticism; Mphahlele; Postcolonial Literature and Theory; Soyinka

# Friedrich Nietzsche

German philosopher

**Born:** Röcken, Saxony, Prussia; October 15, 1844
**Died:** Weimar, Germany; August 25, 1900

## Biography

Friedrich Nietzsche was born on October 15, 1844, in Röcken, Prussia. His father died at an early age and he was reared by his mother and his sister Elizabeth. Nietzsche was a bright and studious boy, although physically rather weak and sickly. He attended the universities at Bonn and Leipzig, where he studied theology and classical philology. In 1865 he discovered the thought of the dour and pessimistic Arthur Schopenhauer, whose work made a profound impression on the young man. In 1868, Nietzsche met Richard Wagner, whose magnetic personality and dynamic music also impressed him. During his student days at Leipzig, Nietzsche's work in Greek and Roman philology was of such sophistication and maturity that his professor recommended that he be appointed professor at the University of Basel even before he had completed his dissertation.

Nietzsche began teaching in 1869, and during his early years there he also made frequent visits to his friend Wagner. By 1876 his chronic health problems forced him to resign from the university and his relationship to Wagner had begun to deteriorate. Nietzsche spent the following years living alone in boardinghouses in various European cities and working intensely on his books. He began to exhibit the signs of extreme mental derangement, possibly the results of a long-term syphilitic infection. In January 1889, while in Turin, Italy, Nietzsche collapsed in the street and never regained his former clarity of mind. He was cared for by his mother and sister, the latter setting up a Nietzsche archive and issuing an affordable edition of his writings. Nietzsche died on August 25, 1900.

## Influence

Nietzsche's ideas have been a seminal force in modern literature, philosophy, and literary theory. Within the domain of German literature and thought, his work influenced the writings of Sigmund Freud, Alfred Adler, Arthur Schnitzler, Ludwig Wittgenstein, Rainer Maria Rilke, Thomas Mann, Franz Kafka, Hermann Hesse, Martin Heidegger, and expressionist authors such as Gottfried Benn, Carl Sternheim, and Georg Kaiser. Non-German authors influenced by Nietzsche include some of the greatest names of the twentieth century: George Bernard Shaw, D. H. Lawrence, William Butler Yeats, Eugene O'Neill, Jean-Paul Sartre, Albert Camus, and André Malraux. In modern literary theory, his ideas have shaped the thought of Michel Foucault, Jean Lyotard, and Jacques Derrida.

## Analysis

Nietzsche was never a builder of comprehensive philosophical systems in the manner of more traditional philosophers such as Immanuel Kant and G. W. F. Hegel. His writings tend toward the aphoristic and consist primarily of pointed observations and reflections on various themes and topics. His ideas subsequently changed and evolved throughout his life. Nietzsche's remarks on aesthetics and criticism are scattered throughout his works.

Before there can be a discussion of Nietzsche's reflections on aesthetic issues, the overall context of his thought should be established briefly. In 1865 he first read and was profoundly influenced by *Die Welt als Wille und Vorstellung* (1819; *The World as Will and Idea*, 1883–1886), the major work of Arthur Schopenhauer. The latter's ideas suggest that the absolute reality of the universe is the Will, a mindless and irrational life force that is indifferent to the hopes and fears of humanity, itself only a manifestation of this universal cosmic energy and its ceaseless striving or desire for creation and destruction. All "reality" as it appears to the human perspective is only illusion or image. The basic condition of individual existence is suffering, and humanity's only escape is either asceticism, a cessation of desire, as is suggested by Christianity, Buddhism, and most other religions, or the momentary transcendence offered to the individual by art and the aesthetic experience.

In contemplating art, the individual is able to remove himself from the unceasing activity of the Will and may reflect upon it with a degree of objectivity. For Schopenhauer, music is the highest art form, because, unlike other genres (such as painting, literature, or sculpture), it is nonmimetic – that is, music does not seek to reproduce a "reality" (which for Schopenhauer is actually mere appearance) but depicts directly the essence of the cosmos, the Will. Schopenhauer's thought, with its high estimation of music, consequently also appealed to Nietzsche's older friend, the composer Richard Wagner.

Schopenhauer's ideas deeply affected the young Nietzsche, forming the starting point for the latter's first major and best-known work, *The Birth of Tragedy Out of the Spirit of Music*. Nietzsche sought to correct the sentimentalized image of the ancient Greeks, an idealized portrait of a childlike, happy people in tune with nature, which had shaped the ideas of writers such as Johann Joachim Winckelmann, Johann Wolfgang von Goethe, and Friedrich Schiller during the preceding era of German neoclassicism. He asserted that the triumphs of Greek culture – its art and religion – sprang not from a feeling of naive harmony and well-being in life but rather from a profound sense of the suffering inherent in human existence. The Greeks had created their pantheon of immortal gods and their art out of a deep need for the salvation of illusion. Existence, as Nietzsche goes on to assert in one of the more famous pronouncements from *The Birth of Tragedy Out of the Spirit of Music*, is justified only as an aesthetic phenomenon. Without the salutary illusion of art, human beings could not bear the weight of life.

As the title suggests, Nietzsche's first work was devoted to a study of the origins of tragedy in Greek culture. He sees tragic art as the product of two fundamental psychological/aesthetic/cultural impulses, which he labels with the names of two prominent god figures: Dionysus, the nature deity of wine, intoxication, and fertility, and Apollo, the deity of poetry, the imagination, and dreams. Both relate to modes through which man can escape the suffering of existence: drunkenness (Dionysian) and fantasy (Apollonian). The Dionysian element is that of music and dance, wine and sexuality, the ecstatic intoxication in which the individual loses himself or herself and merges with the totality of the universe (Schopenhauer's Will). The Apollonian represents the integrity or wholeness of the individual (as in painting and sculpture), the beautiful illusion of images found in dreams and in lyric poetry.

The synthesis of these two artistic impulses produced "tragedy" (its Greek etymology suggests "goat-song," referring to the animal sacred to Dionysus), in which the rhythmic and lyric hymns (dithyrambs, or songs in honor of Dionysus) of the chorus comment upon as well as celebrate the rise and fall of the exemplary individual, the hero whose pride and arrogance produce only suffering for himself and others. Tragedy combined music and dance in the form of the chorus (Dionysian) with the spoken dialogue of the individual actors (Apollonian). Tragic art, asserts Nietzsche, grew out of a ritual celebration of each human being's suffering and his or her eventual return to the totality of the Will. Nietzsche sees tragedy as an affirmation of the life process not from the point of view of the individual, however – for whom it is only pain and suffering – but from the standpoint of the Will itself. Through the cathartic identification of the audience with the events depicted onstage, the individual gains a momentary experience of transcendence. Authentic tragedy is an affirmation of life, including suffering. For Nietzsche, Greek tragic art achieved its zenith in the works of Aeschylus and Sophocles.

With the plays of the younger tragedian, Euripides, comes the decline of truly tragic art, according to Nietzsche. Euripides' works evidence the influence of the Sophists – above all, that of Socrates. In Euripides' plays, human suffering is often ascribed to social injustice (as in *Medea*), which can be alleviated by rational measures, rather than to the inherent nature of human existence. Logical argument between the characters seems to replace the lyric discourse of his older colleagues' works. For Nietzsche, Socratism represents the optimism of science and the faith in progress and happiness brought about by the exercise of reason. Thus, the earlier tragic art of the god Dionysus stands in conflict with the rational optimism of Socrates. The latter's position has dominated Western culture, claims Nietzsche, and has led humankind astray.

Science, like art, is itself merely another creator of myths, an illusion that has come to regard itself as absolute truth. This is an important point, because it ties in with Nietzsche's overall vision of "truth" and its relationship to language. All seemingly absolute truths and values could actually be termed aesthetic illusions, the product of language; they are only rhetorical tropes, metaphors which, in the course of time, have come to be regarded as (or confused with) "facts" or "reality," linguistic constructions that have become reified and which constitute a veritable cemetery of old and institutionalized perceptions. This is Nietzsche's post-Kantian perspectivism, the idea that truth is a function of one's point of view codified in linguistic forms. Thus the creative use of language, as in the literary text, presents its audience with new and fresh perspectives, new and vital "truths," and is to this degree superior to the "dead" truths perpetuated within human society in institutions such as religion, law, and education. This insight into aesthetic language and the perception of truth is Nietzsche's most significant contribution to modern philosophy. *The Birth of Tragedy Out of the Spirit of Music* ends with Nietzsche's praise of the music of his then-close friend, Wagner. The latter's operas (such as *Tristan und Isolde*), Nietzsche maintained, had brought about the rebirth of a truly tragic Dionysian art and had served to counterbalance the false optimism of a Socratic culture.

In *Human, All Too Human*, composed after his break with Wagner, Nietzsche writes negatively about artists whose nebulous creations bring only temporary relief from suffering. This position is more a result of a rejection of everything Wagner represented than a denial of his previous position that art as illusion serves an important function for humankind. In Nietzsche's later works, the Dionysian comes to be associated with the positive, life affirming side of man and is opposed to Christianity and Buddhism, which he regards as negative, life-denying forces, since they advocate a rejection of and withdrawal from this world.

In *The Will to Power*, a compilation of notes and ideas on which Nietzsche was working when he went insane, art, or the will to creation, is associated with the will to power. The latter concept represents an almost biological notion of the force to create, to generate and promote the life, growth, and vitality of the organism. By its nature, art constitutes a life-affirming expression, and a culture's ability to produce and view tragedy is to be regarded as a sign of its vital strength, not its weakening pessimism. The will to produce art is linked in certain sections to the drive of sexuality, and here Nietzsche anticipated to a degree the theories of Freud, who himself found a kindred spirit in the former's works, especially in the notion of the relationship between aesthetic creation and erotic sublimation.

The reception of Nietzsche's ideas began at about the time of his death in 1900 and has been pervasive. Freud as well as major German writers such as Mann, Hesse, and Kafka were deeply influenced by his notions of art, society, and cultural development. The concepts of the Apollonian and Dionysian from *The Birth of Tragedy Out of the Spirit of Music*, for example, clearly shape Mann's well-known novella *Der Tod in Venedig* (1912; *Death in Venice*, 1925). The expressionist writers of the period from 1910 to 1925 were also profoundly affected by Nietzsche's critique of bourgeois German society, as well as his ecstatic visions of cultural transformation. Nietzsche is considered to be one of the forerunners of modern existentialism, and his emphasis on the theme of art and transcendence has been important to thinkers such as Heidegger, Sartre, and Camus. Nietzsche's views on language and its relationship to truth have shaped the poststructuralist thought of intellectuals such as Derrida, whose notions of grammatology and the myth of writing and presence owe much to Nietzsche, and Foucault, whose notion of the episteme as a structural principle of an individual's or a culture's worldview also recalls Nietzsche's work. Much of twentieth-century writing and philosophy would be unthinkable without Nietzsche's influence.

## Principal criticism

*Die Geburt der Tragödie aus dem Geiste der Musik*, 1872 (*The Birth of Tragedy Out of the Spirit of Music*, 1909)
*Menschliches, Allzumenschliches: Ein Buch für freie Geister*, 1878 (*Human, All Too Human*, 1910, 1911)
*Die fröhliche Wissenschaft*, 1882, 1887 (*The Joyful Wisdom*, 1910)
*Also sprach Zarathustra: Ein Buch für Alle und Keinen*, 1883–1885 (*Thus Spake Zarathustra*, 1896)
*Der Fall Wagner*, 1888 (*The Case of Wagner*, 1896)
*Der Wille zur Macht*, 1901 (*The Will to Power*, 1910)

## Other major works and literary forms

Friedrich Nietzsche was a philosopher and essayist whose aphoristic writings covered a wide range of topics: religion, music, cultural criticism, and classical philology, as well as the more traditional philosophical fields of epistemology and aesthetics. Nietzsche also wrote some poetry and composed music.

NONFICTION
*Unzeitgemässe Betrachtungen*, 1873–1876 (4 volumes; *Thoughts Out of Season*, 1909, 2 volumes)
*Jenseits von Gut und Böse: Vorspiel einer Philosophie der Zukunft*, 1886 (*Beyond Good and Evil*, 1907)
*Zur Genealogie der Moral*, 1887 (*On the Genealogy of Morals*, 1896)

MISCELLANEOUS
*The Complete Works of Friedrich Nietzsche*, 1994 (Ernst Behler, editor)

## Further reading

Ackermann, Robert John. *Nietzsche: A Frenzied Look*, 1990.
Allison, David B., ed. *The New Nietzsche*, 1977.
Burgard, Peter J., ed. *Nietzsche and the Feminine*, 1994.
Danto, Arthur C. *Nietzsche as Philosopher*, 1965.
Derrida, Jacques. *Spurs: Nietzsche's Styles*, 1979. Translated by Barbara Harlow.

Gane, Laurence. *Introducing Nietzsche*, 1998.
Gillespie, Michael Allen and Strong, Tracy B., eds. *Nietzsche's New Seas. Explorations in Philosophy, Aesthetics, and Politics*, 1988.
Heller, Erich. *The Importance of Nietzsche*, 1989.
Hollingdale, R. J. *Nietzsche*, 1973.
Holub, Robert C. *Friedrich Nietzsche*, 1995.
Kaufmann, Walter. *Nietzsche: Philosopher, Psychologist, Antichrist*, 1950.
——. *Tragedy and Philosophy*, 1968.
Krell, David Farrell. *Nietzsche: A Novel*, 1996
——. *Infectious Nietzsche*, 1996.
Magnus, Bernd and Higgins, Kathleen Marie, ed. *The Cambridge Companion to Nietzsche*, 1996.
Nehamas, Alexander. *Nietzsche: Life as Literature*, 1985.
Oliver, Kelly and Pearsall, Marilyn, eds. *Feminist Interpretations of Nietzsche*, 1998.
Rickels, Laurence A., ed. *Looking After Nietzsche*, 1990.
Sallis, John. *Nietzsche and the Space of Tragedy*, 1991.
Schutte, Ofelia. *Beyond Nihilism: Nietzsche without Masks*, 1984.
Shapiro, Gary. *Alcyone: Nietzsche on Gifts, Noise, and Women*, 1991.
Silk, M. S., and J. P. Stern. *Nietzsche on Tragedy*, 1981.
Stern, J. P. *A Study of Nietzsche*, 1979.
Thomas, R. Hinton. *Nietzsche in German Politics and Society, 1890–1918*, 1983.
Zeitlin, Irving M. *Nietzsche: A Re-Examination*, 1994.

THOMAS F. BARRY

*See also* Deconstruction; Derrida; Existentialism; Foucault; Heidegger; Schopenhauer

# Novel: Theory and Criticism

The novel has been a form capable of assimilating elements of many other genres, and an account of its antecedents would have to include not only epic, romance, picaresque, pamphlets, travelogues, letters, histories, chronicles, memoirs, biographies, autobiographies, and folk tales, but also elements of drama and poetry. The word "fiction" derives from the Latin *fingere*, to fashion (in clay), while "history" comes from the Greek *historia*, finding out, narrating, and "novel" evolves from the Italian *novella storia*, "new story." Fashioning, finding out, narrating the new, evoke not only the ideas and practices involved in the writing *of* fiction, but also the cultural processes involved in writing *about* fiction. The concept of the novel has emerged through a gradual process in which it became distinguished from the romance, the epic, the history, and the satire. If the history of criticism can be seen as an ongoing attempt to understand literature in terms of successive parts of the literary process, then *criticism* of the novel is notable partly for its stress on continuity, thus the various lines of argument militating around social realism, or liberal humanism. In contrast, the *theory* of the novel is the history of a sequence of exclusions, thus the variable exclusion of the author, the reader, or the literary and historical context, depending on the theory.

To begin with criticism of the novel, the idea of art as *mimesis*, as an imitation of life, goes back to Plato and Aristotle. Eighteenth-century definitions of the emergent genre by Henry Fielding and Daniel Defoe tended to stress that it was truer to ordinary life than other literary forms. This line of argument has led to the central paradigm of what a novel should be – a mirror of social reality. Ian Watt's *The Rise of the Novel* (1957) relates the emergence of the novel to the increasing social and cultural power of the commercial middle class and the consequent rise of individualism and empiricism. He argued that the main tradition was the realist line starting with Fielding and Defoe, and continuing via Jane Austen and Charles Dickens. Watt was explicating a view held generally amongst novel practitioners and critics alike for many years, although these assumptions have survived quite radical aesthetic realignments. A good example would be the modernist emphasis on subjectivity, which implies that reality is seen differently by different individuals. Both Virginia Woolf and Henry James retain the idea of mimesis by interiorizing it, so for Woolf it is the reality of internal mental flux that is reflected, whereas for James reality is filtered through the unique artistic sensibility of the writer.

This modernist stress on the "art" of fiction filtered through the twentieth century in various guises, most notably in the work of Northrop Frye, Wayne C. Booth, and J. Hillis Miller. Yet it has proved more durable still in an alternative guise, which concentrates on fiction's bearing on our experience of reality. Such criticism encompasses a huge diversity of scholarly writing, most frequently emanating from Cambridge, England. It includes the rigorous close reading of I. A. Richards' *Principles of Literary Criticism* (1924) and William Empson's *Seven Types of Ambiguity* (1930), the moral canonizing of Q. D. Leavis' *Fiction and the Reading Public* (1932) and F. R. Leavis' *The Great Tradition* (1948), and the theoretical adeptness of Raymond Williams' *Culture and Society* (1958) and Frank Kermode's *The Sense of an Ending* (1967).

Postwar critical theory has transformed literary criticism by posing radical challenges to the idea of realism, principally as a result of the philosophical relativism which has its origins half a century earlier in the thinking of Friedrich Nietzsche, Sigmund Freud, and Henri Bergson. Moreover, structuralist and poststructuralist literary theory has questioned the whole concept of mimesis by arguing that words cannot refer in any direct way to a preexisting reality. Ferdinand de Saussure's *Course in General Linguistics* (1915) finds its critical apogee in Roland Barthes' *S/Z* (1975), although the most controversial criticism in contemporary times has originated from the deconstructive theories of Jacques Derrida. His *Of Grammatology* (1976) and *Writing and Difference* (1978) provide a metatheory engaging with texts purely on semantic terms, and are bent upon showing how fiction cannot possibly succeed in meaning what it manifestly tries to mean: "there is nothing outside the text, or, the text has no outside."

The diversity of theoretical approaches and the possibility of dialogic exchange which all of this produces is crucial to the productivity of criticism of the novel, so that a total synthesis would be neither possible nor desirable. However, if one sought to identify a single area which is of importance in most literary theory since the 1960s, the problem of the subject (that is, the self) would be a likely candidate. The psychoanalytical theory of the unconscious (see Norman Holland, Harold Bloom); the Marxist conception of the subject as interpolated in ideology (see Georg Lukács, Fredric Jameson); the deconstructive subversion of belief in origins or the self-presence of the subject (see later J. Hillis Miller); the postcolonial critique of the alienation of spurious universality to culturally specific images of the self (Edward Said, Gayatri Spivak); the location of all subject utterances as participants in a dialogue based on power and authority (Mikhail Bakhtin); and the feminist analysis of the imposition of socially constructed gender roles (Julia Kristeva, Elaine Showalter): all of these tend to call into question the belief in the autonomy and unity of the free individual in favor of a conception of subjectivity as constructed, traversed, and intersected by discursive social formations.

Indeed, it may still seem obvious to many to read a novel as expressing the vision of one individual (the author), including mimetic representations of fictional individuals (the characters), communicated via the text to another individual (the reader), and interpreted by him or her in terms of the universal features of "human nature." However, literary theory, and its practical analogue, literary criticism, have systematically questioned all the assumptions of individuality, mimesis, self-expression, universality, and referentiality which are implicit in such a model, and will continue to do so for the foreseeable future.

## Further reading

Bakhtin, M. M. *The Dialogic Imagination*, 1981.
Barthes, Roland. *S/Z*, 1975.
Bergonzi, Bernard. *Exploding English*, 1990.
Booth, Wayne C. *The Rhetoric of Fiction*, 1961.
Eco, Umberto. *The Role of the Reader*, 1974
Genette, Gérard. *Narrative Discourse*, 1980.
Hillis Miller, J. *Fiction and Repetition*, 1980.
Hutcheon, Linda. *Narcissistic Narrative*, 1984.
Iser, Wolfgang. *The Implied Reader*, 1972.
Lodge, David. *Language of Fiction*, 1966.
Lubbock, Percy. *The Craft of Fiction*, 1921.
Rimmon-Kenan, S. *Narrative Fiction*, 1983.
Roberts, A. M. *The Novel*, 1993.
Showalter, Elaine. *A Literature of Their Own*, 1978.
Watt, Ian. *The Rise of the Novel*, 1957.

SIMON C. BAKER

*See also* Bakhtin; Barthes; Leavis; Lodge; Lubbock; Mimesis; Narratology; Popular Literature: Approaches to Genre; Watt

# O

## Charles Olson

American critic and poet

**Born:** Worcester, Massachusetts; December 27, 1910
**Died:** New York, New York; January 10, 1970

### Biography

Charles John Olson was born in Worcester, Massachusetts, on December 27, 1910, the only child of an Irish mother and Swedish postman father. He was president and valedictorian of his high school class, and in his senior year he won a trip to Europe in the National Oratorical Contest. Olson graduated Phi Beta Kappa from Wesleyan University in 1932 and received his M.A. in 1933. From 1934 to 1936 he worked as an instructor of English at Clark University. In the fall of 1936 he entered Harvard as one of the first doctoral candidates in the new American studies program. He completed his course work but left when he won a Guggenheim Fellowship and then worked as the publicity director of the American Civil Liberties Union. During this period Olson and Constance Wilcock were married. He joined the Office of War Information (OWI) in 1942, advancing to associate chief of the Foreign Language Division. He resigned in 1944, protesting policies of the OWI director which prevented him from resisting Axis propaganda aimed at creating dissension among Americans of minority ancestry. His political career ended when he turned down an offer to become assistant postmaster general and an appointment to a high Treasury Department post in early 1945.

In 1946 Olson began visits to Ezra Pound at St. Elizabeths Hospital which lasted until 1948 and started to publish his first poems in magazines such as *Harper's Magazine* and *The Atlantic*. His study of Herman Melville, *Call Me Ishmael*, was published in 1947 after ten years of revision. In 1950 the first Maximus poem was written, and his groundbreaking "Projective Verse" essay appeared in *Poetry New York*. His friendship with Robert Creeley began after Creeley turned down several of Olson's poems, submitted by a friend for Creeley's new magazine. Olson's typical response was to start a thousand-letter exchange.

After spending six months in Yucatan studying Mayan civilization, Olson moved to North Carolina, where he became an instructor at the experimental Black Mountain College. In 1951 he became rector of the college, and he and his wife had a daughter, Katharine. That marriage ended, and in 1954 Olson married Elizabeth Kaiser; they had a son, Charles Peter, in 1955. Olson closed the college when funds ran out in 1956 and returned with his family to New England.

In 1960 Olson began a series of readings at colleges which culminated in his appearance at the Poetry Conference in Vancouver, British Columbia, in 1963. He joined the faculty of the State University of New York at Buffalo that fall. His wife died in an automobile accident in 1964. In 1965 he received the Oscar Blumenthal-Charles Leviton Prize from *Poetry* magazine and was the central figure at the Berkeley Poetry Conference.

In 1966 he returned, as he had many times when he was between positions, to Gloucester, Massachusetts, to continue work on the Maximus poems. He spent much of 1967 in Europe, and in 1969 he accepted a post as visiting professor at the University of Connecticut, but was hospitalized with cancer of the liver shortly after Thanksgiving and died in a New York City hospital in January, 1970.

### Influence

Olson's landmark essay, "Projective Verse," which presents a philosophy of poetic composition crucial to an understanding of a line of American poetry running from Walt Whitman through the most contemporary postmodernists, is a necessary counterbalance to the classic British perspective of the New Critics. Drawing on the work of Pound and William Carlos, Olson expressed and explored concerns of rhythm and language central to poetry in the twentieth century, providing vital encouragement to many writers isolated by their originality. "It is as if the whole area lifted," Williams commented when he first read Olson's work.

In addition, his essays on historical process drew other areas of interest into the domain of literary theory, paralleling structuralist concerns with archaeology, geology, physics, and aesthetics, and his theories of cartographic construction contributed to the dissolution of rigid generic classifications and the expansion of typographic possibility. Finally, his poems are a reminder that an artist can maintain a vision of moral integrity while developing his or her aesthetic obsessions, and that an absorption in intellectual exploration does not exclude the use of song in the spirit of the lyric mode.

## Analysis

Although he rightly regarded himself as a premier postmodernist because he had seized and then surpassed the ideas generated by "the revolution of the word," Charles Olson's critical thinking is built on an intensive consideration of ancient, pre-Hellenistic civilizations. Combining the solid academic training he had at Harvard, which produced a firm literary foundation based on William Shakespeare and the Romantic poets, with much imaginative, speculative reading of unconventional thinkers outside the mainstream of academic life (the classicist Eric Havelock, the geographer Carl Sauer, the writer Edward Dahlberg), Olson gradually developed a conception of an ideal culture which he believed existed prior to the fragmentation of consciousness that he located in the declining years of the Greek millennium. As his ideas took shape, he sought to bring them to bear on mid-twentieth-century American society, hoping to restore the poet to the place of a respected seer (such as Homer or Hesiod) in a community which recognized the poet as a storehouse of collective knowledge and as a perceptive commentator on the specific events of the time. To do this, Olson wrote poetry which he hoped would clarify the virtues of the type of society (such as the Greek polis) he valued, as well as extensive essays, correspondence, and lectures. All of these forms mutated and merged throughout his writing – "... a poet, when he's alive, whether he talks or reads you his poems, it's the same thing" – which he designed as a demonstration of the power and effectiveness of poetic consciousness.

As he put it in *Human Universe and Other Essays* (1965), citing "the American push to find an alternative discourse to the inherited one" as his basic thrust, a massive and total rejection of conventional European rationalist thought and language was necessary to create literature "equal, that is, to the real itself." For Olson, "the real" had been concealed by centuries of dualistic thinking which separated mind and body, the rational and the mystical, conscious perception and subconscious intuition, and ultimately, humanity from the natural world. His intellectual formulations led him to such theoretical approaches to the restructuring of artistic expression as the substitution of glyphic or emblematic language for standard alphabets, the replacement of the artificial subject-predicate syntactical arrangement with a more flexible mode he called "parataxis," and the reestablishment of the primitive/abstract model as a better depiction of reality than the classical/representational one. Each of these revisionary tendencies was a method for cutting away the accumulated legacy of subjective bias inscribed in the languages of the West (and thus in patterns of thought). If subjectivity ("the ego-position") were overcome, Olson believed, an artist would be open to the full range of authentic experience necessary to restore to human community its unruly, primal energy.

It was Olson's interest in the essential physicality of energy itself that led him beyond his singularly original but still fundamentally cerebral approach to literary theory. In becoming a "proprioceptive" (the physical soul) critic, Olson was following a logical progression from his distaste for the purely rational. He began by stressing the sensual – all the senses – as a counterweight, recalling the legends of the sailors of Gloucester, the center of the great New England whaling industry, with admiration, noting the primordial aspect of human contact with *okeanos*, the vast realm of mystery and pleasure.

He extended this still-theoretical consideration into the sphere of the directly personal as his intense delight with dance induced him to make connections between language gestures and the gesture of the body in motion. As a teenager in 1929 he had studied with Constance Taylor, who taught exercises in posture, and he had performed a small part with Léonide Massine's Ballet Russe in the 1930s. As Martin Pops points out, for Olson "dance returns man to egoless reciprocity, to the condition of Ishmael in the sea at the end of *Moby Dick*." The idea of dance as a "graphic of drama" enabled Olson to develop a literal model of the poet/cartographer's ordering of space and time; just as dance expressed the latent energy potential of the body, so poetic language and form could express the shape of the poet's mind in action. This perception – stated another way by the dancer Yvonne Ranier as "the mind is a muscle" – underscored the directly body-conscious philosophy of composition Olson developed in the "Projective Verse" essay of 1950.

Written at a time when accepted styles of poetic analysis were dominated by the ideas of the New Critics, Olson's declaration provided a theoretical construct for examining an alternative tradition in American literature running from Whitman through Pound and Williams and on to Olson's contemporaries. These writers were essentially being ignored by established critics who were more comfortable with the British-influenced poetry of Emily Dickinson, Robert Frost, Wallace Stevens, and T. S. Eliot. In a sense, Olson's essay made legitimate an outlaw muse. It is not, however, a guide for analyzing "open verse" or a method of explaining the work of those poets whose attitudes toward their writing approximated Olson's ideas of "composition by field." Rather, it offers some insights into the process of poetic awareness and explores the ways in which language works at a most basic level.

Probably the most significant statement in the essay is Olson's contention that "FORM IS NEVER MORE THAN

AN EXTENSION OF CONTENT," a direct challenge to the view that "perfected" classic forms are models to emulate – "well-wrought urns" so to speak. Put in other terms, Creeley's proposition that "there is a way of saying something inherent in the thing to be said" expresses the same idea, both Creeley and Olson insisting that the shape of the poem grow as an organic entity independent of preconceptions. Thus, "ONE PERCEPTION MUST IMMEDIATELY AND DIRECTLY LEAD TO A FURTHER PERCEPTION," so that the poem transfers energy (or "inspiration," to use a more traditional term) "where the poet got it ... by way of the poem itself to, all the way over to, the reader." Olson saw a poem as a "high-energy construct," recalling Pound's famous definition of "language charged with meaning," but went beyond Pound by postulating that the syllable is, like a subatomic particle, the most fundamental component of the kinetics of language, and that the syllable is most specifically responsive to the motion of the mind. Then, challenging metrical conventions that determine poetic form in "closed" verse, Olson maintained that the rhythms of the poem reflect the rhythms of the life of the poet, that measure replaces meter as a means of organizing poetry, and that the rhythmic measure of the line is determined by the breath pattern of the poet. Overarching the entire poem, or perhaps sequence of poems, Olson posited a threefold matrix, forces he called in his explanatory "Letter to Elaine Feinstein" (1959) "topos," suggesting location or landscape, "typos," indicating the manner and style of the subject, and "tropos," meaning the totality of the experience. In other words, the energy generated by the field of consideration (morphology) is managed or maneuvered through an expression of the self through language (typography) into full experiential awareness (mythology).

Olson's own poems are complements to and demonstrations of his theories. As George Butterick, the premier Olson scholar, summarizes them, his techniques in practice "include processual (in Whiteheadean terms), 'openness,' discovery rather than recovery of form, reward by image, syncopation, incremental associations, [and] paratactic forwarding." On paper, the lines, word clusters, signs, and devices are displayed and arranged over the entire frame of the page. Olson's control of rhythm, pitch, timbre, and his use of emphasis – pauses, word-bursts, varying tempi (obviously more evident in performance) – are all part of an effort to make punctuation "obey the law of the breath" and reflect the condition of the neuromuscular and cardiovascular systems of the poet. One might say that poets teach themselves while their readers listen. In this way, the poetic persona is one of action, contrary to Olson's criticism of Pound's vision of the poet contemplating the world from a position Olson described as "the beak of his ego."

"It is difficult to remember the isolation a writer such as I felt in the fifties," Gilbert Sorrentino recalls in reference to the initial impact of Olson's work. Speaking for many of the poets grouped under the heading "Black Mountain" in Donald Allen's anthology of discovery, The New American Poetry (1960), Robert Duncan stated, "For all the poets who matter to me in my generation Charles Olson has been a Big Fire source."

Olson's extraordinary physical presence (he was about six-foot eight-inches tall) and enthusiasm had something to do with his influence, but his theories have withstood his absence from the scene, particularly as a growing familiarity with his ideas has reduced resistance to them. The establishment critics who felt threatened and confused both by Olson's ideas and by his often aggressive coterie are now in retirement, and Olson's students have now themselves taken positions in the universities, putting Olson's ideas in a more approachable context. Even the anthologies cautiously prepared for undergraduate literature survey courses have begun to include his poetry. The small press journals that published Olson's work have become part of valuable collections in libraries, and although Olson felt like "an old schlump from Gloucester" when reading with Beat poets, such contemporary poets as Allen Ginsberg, Ed Sanders, and even Amiri Baraka (who as LeRoi Jones published Olson in Yugen) have reflected his ideas in their work. Sorrentino's observation that "Everyone else in the world today who cares for poems has learned from Olson" is more an exaggeration of scope than of effect.

On the other hand, conservative countertrends are still very powerful in universities and particularly in secondary schools. For all of their brilliance and originality, Olson's theories have not been espoused by a poet as popular with the American public as, for example, Frost, or even Eliot, was. Many of the poems written by Olson's students and friends seem to be primarily addressed to one another, and, while a supportive community has always been essential for the arts, this kind of hermetic enclosure mocks some of Olson's essential social concerns. What is likely to endure in Olson's work is the genuine change in consciousness of what a poem is; there has been a widening of scope that is irreversible. Olson's introduction of a type of "middle voice" between the authoritarian rhetoric of Pound's public postures and the introspective indulgence of Eliot's private stance may eventually lead to some version of the artist as a valued member of a social community known for his or her work rather than for a certain celebrity.

Contrary to some charges, Olson was not a revolutionary so much as a restorer or conservator who knew that "what does not change/is the will to change," and who knew that the artist's reactions to the procession of experience are vital in the maintenance of human awareness. His resistance to life-strangling systems is the linchpin of his work, and his insistence on the primacy of the flexible Ishmael over the rigid, doomed Ahab is a testament to the artist's need to respond to all that has gone before in order to remain ready for all that is to come.

## Principal criticism

*Call Me Ishmael: A Study of Melville*, 1947
"Projective Verse," 1950
*Mayan Letters*, 1953
*Human Universe and Other Essays*, 1965
*Selected Writings*, 1966
*Causal Mythology*, 1969
*Letters for "Origin," 1950–1956*, 1969
*The Special View of History*, 1970
*Poetry and Truth: The Beloit Lectures and Poems*, 1971
*Additional Prose: A Bibliography on America, Proprioception, and Other Notes and Essays*, 1974
*The Post Office*, 1975
*Muthologos: Collected Lectures and Interviews, 1978–1979* (2 volumes)
*Charles Olson and Robert Creeley: The Complete Correspondence*, 1980– (8 volumes; George F. Butterick, editor)

## Other major works and literary forms

Charles Olson is the author of *The Maximus Poems 1–10*, a long poem or sequence of poems that continues the tradition of the epic of the self begun by Walt Whitman in *Leaves of Grass* (1855–1892) and continued by Ezra Pound in the *Cantos* (1917–1968), Louis Zukofsky in *"A"* (1978), and William Carlos Williams in *Paterson* (1946–1958). Olson also wrote many shorter poems, which have been gathered in *The Collected Poems of Charles Olson* (1987); numerous letters in addition to those which specifically discuss his literary theories; essays on politics and the arts; memoirs; and a dance-play based on Herman Melville's *Moby Dick: Or, The Whale* (1851) called "The Fiery Hunt" (in *The Fiery Hunt and Other Plays*, 1977), which he sent to the Martha Graham dance company.

SHORT FICTION
*Stocking Cap: A Story*, 1966

PLAYS
*The Fiery Hunt and Other Plays*, 1977

POETRY
*Y & X*, 1948
*Letter for Melville 1951*, 1951
*This*, 1952
*In Cold Hell, in Thicket*, 1953
*The Maximus Poems 1–10*, 1953
*The Maximus Poems 11–22*, 1956
*O'Ryan 2 4 6 8 10*, 1958 (expanded edition, *O'Ryan 12345678910*, 1965)
*The Distances*, 1960
*Charles Olson: Reading at Berkeley*, 1966 (transcription)
*The Maximus Poems IV, V, VI*, 1968
*Archaeologist of Morning: The Collected Poems Outside the Maximus Series*, 1970
*The Maximus Poems, Volume 3*, 1974
*The Horses of the Sea*, 1976
*The Maximus Poems*, 1983
*The Collected Poems of Charles Olson*, 1987

NONFICTION
*On Black Mountain*, 1971

## Further reading

*Boundary 2: A Journal of Postmodern Literature*. II (Fall / Winter, 1973 / 1974). Special Olson issue.
Butterick, George F. *A Guide to the Maximus Poems of Charles Olson*, 1978.
Byrd, Don. *Charles Olson's Maximus*, 1980.
Cech, John. *Charles Olson and Edward Dahlberg: A Portrait of a Friendship*, 1982.
Charters, Ann. *Olson / Melville: A Study in Affinity*, 1968.
Christensen, Paul. *Charles Olson: Call Him Ishmael*, 1979.
Clark, Tom. *Charles Olson: The Allegory of a Poet's Life*, 1991.
Clarke, John. *From Feathers to Iron*, 1987.
Maud, Ralph. *Charles Olson's Reading: A Biography*, 1995.
Paul, Sherman. *Olson's Push: "Origin," "Black Mountain," and Recent American Poetry*, 1978.
Ross, Andrew. *The Failure of Modernism: Symptoms of American Poetry*, 1986.
Seelye, Catherine. *Charles Olson and Ezra Pound: An Encounter at St. Elizabeths*, 1975.
Von Hallberg, Robert. *Charles Olson: The Scholar's Art*, 1978.

LEON LEWIS

*See also* American Literary Theory: Twentieth Century; Pound

# Walter J. Ong

## American essayist and critic

**Born:** Kansas City, Missouri; November 30, 1912

## Biography

Walter Jackson Ong was born on November 30, 1912, in Kansas City, Missouri, the son of Walter Jackson Ong and Blanche Eugenia (Mense) Ong. He studied at Rockhurst College, a small Catholic school in Kansas City run by the Jesuit Order. After receiving his B.A. from Rockhurst in 1933, he spent two years in newspaper and other commercial positions. He entered the Missouri Province of the Society of Jesus in 1935 and went through the traditional education of a Jesuit, spending two years in a novitiate, where he studied Latin and Greek and where he underwent rigorous ascetic training, including a thirty-day retreat based on the *Exercitia* (c. 1548; *Spiritual Exercises*) of Saint Ignatius. He studied philosophy at Saint Louis University, a Jesuit institution since 1828 and one with which he would become closely associated for the rest of his career. He received his Ph.L. (licentiate in philosophy) in 1940 and his M.A. in 1941.

During regency, a period of practice teaching for Jesuit scholastics, he was an instructor for two years in English and French at Regis College in Denver. In 1944 he began his theological training at Saint Louis University, and during his first three years of studies he also taught English. He was ordained a priest in 1946, and after another year of theology he received his S.T.L. (licentiate in sacred theology).

In the early 1950s Ong studied at Harvard University, where he came under the influence of Perry Miller and began his important work on Petrus Ramus. He received his doctorate from Harvard in 1955, by which time he had already become an assistant professor at Saint Louis University. He quickly passed through the academic ranks at Saint Louis, becoming a full professor in 1959. While retaining his professorship in English, he was named Professor of Humanities in Psychiatry in the school of medicine in 1970.

Ong was twice a recipient of Guggenheim Fellowships (in 1949 and 1951), and he has long been a member of the Advisory Board of the John Simon Guggenheim Memorial Foundation. He has served as visiting professor at Yale University, McGill University, and several other American and foreign universities, including positions in the Middle East and Central West Africa. He was president of the Modern Language Association in 1978, and his work in the humanities has been honored by various awards both in the United States and Europe.

After his retirement from St. Louis University in 1984, Ong used his time to reassess his work. For example, in *Hopkins, the Self, and God* he returned to the poetry of Gerard Manley Hopkins, the English Jesuit about whom he had written so insightfully early in his career. He now saw an evolutionary view of time in Hopkins' poems, but he also argued that the Jesuit poet's faith, like Ong's own, was deepened rather than threatened by scientific ideas. During Ong's eightieth-birthday celebrations, as he reflected on his life as priest and scholar, he beheld a unity in the great variety of his contributions, since everything in the universe, which is being constantly created by God with profound wisdom, is interrelated.

## Influence

Ong's reputation has derived from his living intellectually along several important divides: the religious and secular worlds, Catholicism and Protestantism, Renaissance and modern cultures, the sciences and humanities. In particular, his career has embodied the interfaces of word and culture, and one of his most influential themes has been the evolution of the word from early orality to present literacy. Some of his discussions about the differences between oral and chirographic (writing) cultures show similarities to those of Marshall McLuhan, but Ong has grounded his insights on much more thorough scholarship than McLuhan, and thus he has had a much more lasting influence among literary intellectuals.

Ong's message was initially directed to Catholic thinkers, and he became well known in Europe and the United States for his literate analysis of American Catholicism, especially for his treatment of the religious-secular dialogue in a pluralist society. In relating theology to culture, Ong has made bold use of evolutionary themes. For him, the Christian dispensation is closely tied to the evolution of the material world, since both the Christian and the evolutionary views involve a linear rather than a cyclic sense of time.

For most scholars, the greatest value of Ong's work lies in his erudite research into such cultural phenomena as the nature of Ramism, the rhetorical tradition in Western culture, and the evolution of communication media. In literature, his approach to the New Criticism, structuralism, and deconstruction from the standpoint of a classicist has proved valuable and provocative, as have his general cultural insights into literary phenomena as varied as Tudor prose style and James Joyce's stream-of-consciousness technique.

## Analysis

Throughout his career, Ong has explored the structuring of the human psyche through the culture nurturing it. For Ong, the human being is, paradoxically, an open closure – open, because knowledge of the entire universe is available to him or her, and closed, because humans make systems, which both limit and enrich their knowledge. The human being is thus an adventure in knowledge, and knowledge's story is humanity's story.

Human knowledge changes with time, and this change is more than cumulative: it is self-accelerating. Before the development of writing, human knowledge evolved slowly, but with the appearance of chirographic culture, knowledge could be stored, leading to knowledge becoming both more exteriorized and more interiorized. The exteriorization of knowledge can be seen in the great developments of science and technology. The interiorization of knowledge is more obvious in literature. For example, James Joyce's *Finnegans Wake* (1939), with its baroque interiority, is more personalized than Henry Fielding's *Tom Jones* (1749), with its emphasis on plot machinations. These works also illustrate the human being's changing relationship to time itself. As knowledge of the past grows, people know more about the present, for they can both connect the present with the past and differentiate it from the past. Thus, the knowledge explosion breeds a deep sensitivity to the present moment, felt as the front of past time, moving inexorably into the future.

Ong's literary theory grew out of his analysis of the evolution of consciousness and out of his studies on the sixteenth-century logician and educational reformer Ramus. In the 1950s Ong's work on Ramus and his milieu made him aware of the shift in sensibility brought about by the development of typography. In his writings, Ramus reduced all argumentation to one art of discourse, which he called indifferently logic or dialectic. He associated logic with spatial models, most notably the model of dichotomized divisions, often arranged in tabular form for the analysis of everything under the sun. Ramus divided a subject into two parts, subdivided each of these parts into two, and so on. The new medium of typography could reproduce these spatial constructs much more easily than manuscript writers could. The Ramist account-book organization of knowledge appealed strongly to the Protestant and bourgeois mind, and Ramism became a movement complexly related to Scholasticism, Humanism, typography, Puritanism, and pedagogical techniques. Ong sees Ramism as an attempt to simplify knowledge through noetic bookkeeping, and it illustrates a shift that brought Western man to react to words less as sounds and more as items in space. Its confident rationalism allies Ramism with the Cartesianism that followed it. In literature, Ramism contributed to the development of a stark scientific literary style.

In *The Barbarian Within, and Other Fugitive Essays and Studies* and *The Presence of the Word*, Ong analyzed more fully the evolution of modes of thought and verbal expressions from oral culture through the typographic patterns that succeeded it. In these works, Ong saw communication as the human being's central activity. Communication has passed through three stages, marked by the media through which the word is transmitted: the oral-aural (voice and ear) stage, when all verbal communication was oral; the chirographic-typographic stage, when communication was through writings; and the electronic stage, when communication is practically instantaneous via radio, television, and computer. When media change, what is communicated changes. For example, typographic culture is linear, and thus it encourages the habit of assimilating material in sequences, one item after the other.

According to Ong, the simultaneity associated with our new electronic culture is having an impact on literature. For example, the experience captured in Ezra Pound's *Cantos* starts in Idaho, dwells sporadically on the troubadours, and even includes Chinese ideograms. The problem for modern individuals therefore is not that the past has evaporated but rather that it is too much with them. The reach of human beings now extends more deeply into time and space, but the result has been that the tips of their fingers are farther from their hearts. This development can be seen in such modern novels as George Orwell's *Nineteen Eighty-Four* (1949) and Aldous Huxley's *Brave New World* (1932), which address the ascendancy of the mechanical and the elimination of the truly human. Ong, too, has expressed his concern for the modern dehumanization of life and has allied himself with such personalist philosophers as Emmanuel Mounier, Gabriel Marcel, and Martin Buber.

In *Rhetoric, Romance, and Technology*, Ong shows how the history of rhetoric has mirrored the evolution of society. Until the modern technological age, Western culture could be meaningfully described as rhetorical in that it made an art of its orality. With the advent of the Industrial Revolution, rhetoric was not eradicated but rather displaced and rearranged. Modern rhetoric has become more visual, not only through the use of pictures for persuasion but also through the presentation of words as objects (display type).

For Ong, Romanticism appeared as a result of man's noetic control over nature, a counterpart of technology. Novels developed in full only with the Romantic movement, because they are products of the interiorization encouraged and implemented by print. The humanities in modern times have developed a close alliance with print, but since print is now interwoven with newer media – radio, television, the cinema – with which it interacts and by which it is transformed, the humanities and the literary works that are often their subjects will, in turn, evolve and reshape themselves with the evolution of culture.

*Interfaces of the Word* develops ideas connected with those in Ong's previous works, but he groups his new studies around two related themes: change and alienation and growth and integration. The technological history of the word has evolved in dialectical patterns. For example, the world of orality was torn to pieces by print, which then created a new kind of culture based on analysis and self-consciousness that has since been fragmented into new constellations of thought.

Alienation, a favorite diagnosis of modern man's plight, has not been commonly thought of in terms of the technological history of the word, but it appears to Ong that the inventions of print and electronic verbalization have helped to bring about a new kind of alienation. These inventions have restructured consciousness by affecting a person's presence to the world and to himself, creating new interior distances within the psyche. To personalities shaped by literacy, oral folk often seem unprogrammed, given simply to soaking up existence. With the appearance of writing and print, the consciousness associated with orality underwent a cleavage, dividing knowers from the external universe and from themselves. This division made possible much of modern science, art, and literature, but it did so at the price of splitting up the original unity of consciousness. People in this new culture are strongly conditioned to bestow more and more reality to the printed word, and dictionaries codify this understanding. Away from print, all is chaos.

An example from literature of the distancing of the word by writing is Ong's analysis of the writer's audience. If communication is viewed mechanistically, with information traveling back and forth between two terminals, then there is no special problem with the audience, but if one puts aside the mechanistic model and looks at communication in its human actuality, then problems with the writer's audience begin to manifest themselves. Unlike oral communication, where the context is provided by the face-to-face situation, communicative writing comes with no such actuality. Thus, the writer has to take into consideration the real social and psychological states of possible readers.

That leads to Ong's concept of fictionalized audiences, because in modern culture writers need to imagine an audience – for example, as entertainment seekers or reflective sharers of their experience. Correspondingly, the audience must fictionalize itself: readers have to play the role in which the author has cast them. Ernest Hemingway, for example, assumes a relationship with the reader that is marked by tight-lipped empathy based on manly experience. The role in which Hemingway casts the reader is different from anything demanded in earlier literature. Indeed, some features of the Hemingway style (his calculated exclusion of most descriptive qualifiers, for example) would have repelled sixteenth-century readers.

Ong's *Fighting for Life* marks yet another stage in his investigation of the history of human consciousness. In several of his earlier essays Ong was driven back to the biological side of human nature, for consciousness always has a biological complement. An essential element in Charles Darwin's view of evolution is the struggle for existence, and Ong probes how competition is embedded in various levels of culture. He argues that the struggle for dominance, crucial among many animal species, is more critical for human males than for females, helping males to manage persistent insecurity and to establish sexual identity. Ong also shows how adversary procedures have influenced social, linguistic, and intellectual history. The human being's internalization of agonistic drives, he concludes, can foster new discoveries within the self. In order to know oneself, one must know that something else is set against one, psychologically as well as physically. Adversativeness has also become a tool of modern literary criticism; for example, binary opposition is the basis of much of structuralism.

*Orality and Literacy* summarizes Ong's lifework. In this book he makes clear that he does not belong to any school of interpretation, because there is no school of orality and literacy, nothing that could be called the equivalent of the New Criticism or structuralism or deconstruction, although awareness of the interrelationship of orality and literacy can influence what is done in these and other schools.

From the time of his studies on Ramus through the three volumes of his essays that have been collected under the title *Faith and Contexts*, Ong's work has evolved into its own history of culture. In treating the transit from oral to typographic cultures, he ingests and adapts much American and European scholarship. Though he accepts the uniqueness and unrepeatable nature of the human person, he also believes that the human person's place in the cosmos has evolved in a structured way over the ages. Furthermore, he is convinced that the orality-literacy interaction enters into man's ultimate concerns and aspirations. All religious traditions have their origins in an oral past and all make use of the written word, an interiorization of the oral tradition in sacred texts. In Christianity, orality-literacy polarities are especially acute, for Jesus Christ is known as the Word of God. In Trinitarian teaching, God the Father speaks His Word, and this belief is at the core of the written Word of God, the Bible. Thus, Ong brings his literary theory back to the source of his own vocation, the relationship of God's Word to particular human beings in history. Ong hopes that his writings lead others to enter into the modern evolution of consciousness toward greater interiorization and greater openness.

## Principal criticism

*Ramus, Method, and the Decay of Dialogue: From the Art of Discourse to the Art of Reason*, 1958
*Ramus and Talon Inventory*, 1958
*The Barbarian Within, and Other Fugitive Essays and Studies*, 1962
*In the Human Grain: Further Explorations of Contemporary Culture*, 1967
*The Presence of the Word: Some Prolegomena for Cultural and Religious History*, 1967
*Rhetoric, Romance, and Technology: Studies in the Interaction of Expression and Culture*, 1971
*Why Talk?*, 1973
*Interfaces of the Word: Studies in the Evolution of Consciousness and Culture*, 1977
*Fighting for Life: Contest, Sexuality, and Consciousness*, 1981
*Orality and Literacy: The Technologizing of the Word*, 1982
*Hopkins, the Self, and God*, 1986
*Faith and Contexts, Vol. 1: Selected Essays and Studies, 1952–1991*, 1992
*Faith and Contexts, Vol. 2: Supplementary Studies, 1946–1989*, 1992
*Faith and Contexts, Vol. 3: Further Essays, 1952–1990*, 1995

## Other major works and literary forms

Most of Walter J. Ong's writing has been in the essay form, and several of the books listed above are collections of essays. Some of his essays are strictly literary – for example, his classic study of Gerard Manley Hopkins' sprung rhythm – but the majority of his work is more eclectic, and within a single essay the reader may encounter references to subjects as seemingly unrelated as technology and literature, sociobiology and theology, neurophysiology and metaphysics. Ong's forte is to reveal illuminating connections among apparently diverse subjects from the viewpoint of a deeply felt Christian personalism.

NONFICTION
*Frontiers in American Catholicism: Essays on Ideology and Culture*, 1957
*American Catholic Crossroads: Religious-Secular Encounters in the Modern World*, 1959

EDITED TEXTS
*Darwin's Vision and Christian Perspectives*, 1960
*Knowledge and the Future of Man: An International Symposium*, 1968
*Petrus Ramus, Audomarus Talaeus: Collectaneae Praefationes epistolae, Orationes*, 1969
*Petrus Ramus, Scholae in Liberales Artes*, 1970
*John Milton, Logic*, 1982

## Further reading

Bailey, L. P. "Reverend Walter Jackson Ong, S. J.: A Selected Bibliography," in *Bulletin of Bibliography*. XXX (January, 1973), pp. 39–41.

Cargas, H. J. "Walter Ong, S. J.," in *Catholic Library World.* XLVII (November, 1975), p. 185.

Farrell, Thomas J. "Developing Literacy: Walter J. Ong and Basic Writing," in *Journal of Basic Writing.* II (Fall/Winter, 1978), pp. 30–51.

Graham, William A. *Beyond the Written World: Oral Aspects of Scripture in the History of Religion,* 1988.

Nielsen, Mark. "A Bridge Builder: Walter J. Ong at Eighty," in *America.* (November 21, 1992), pp. 404–406, 413–414.

Toolan, David. "The Male Agony According to Walter J. Ong," in *Commonweal.* (November 20, 1992), pp. 13–18.

Wimsatt, William K., and Cleanth Brooks. *Literary Criticism: A Short History,* 1957.

ROBERT J. PARADOWSKI

*See also* Dialogic Criticism; McLuhan

# P

## Parody

Parody – from the Greek *paroidia*, a "mock song" or burlesque – is a form of literary imitation in which distinctive characteristic aspects of the original, usually the style, are exaggerated. The purpose of parody is usually humor or satire, though it can also be used to extend a work's range of thematic and stylistic references. Ben Jonson, in his comedy *Every Man in His Humour* (printed 1601), describes parody as a "gift to make [the text] absurder than it was." In other words, parody has customarily been regarded as a critical method of ridiculing "high" texts that have expectations above their station. The earliest example we have of this is the *Batrachomyomachia* (*Battle of the Frogs and Mice*) possibly by Homer, but certainly in existence from about the fifth century B.C., which the classical scholar Gilbert Murray described as a "good parody of the fighting epic": here the larger-than-life heroes of *The Iliad* are reduced to small, squabbling animals.

This points to an important fact, often overlooked, that parody can make fun of content as well as form. A classic case of this would be Henry Fielding's novel *The Adventures of Joseph Andrews and his Friend, Mr. Abraham Adams* (1742), described by the author as "written in imitation of the manner of Cervantes." If he had simply said, "imitation" his text could be honorific, but "manner" gives the game away. An "exact quotation" from an original text put in an entirely different context can produce a comic effect, as also can "surprise anti-climaxes" and even sonic imitation. An example might be the parody of Virgilian hexameters in English: "Here is the eight o'clock news/ For Monday the tenth of September."

Parody, of course, is not confined to literature: there are countless examples in music, ranging from Jacques Offenbach's *La Belle Hélène* (1865), which mercilessly yet affectionately mocks the Helen of Troy legend, to Gilbert and Sullivan's tongue-in-cheek emulations of Italian opera in *Trial by Jury* (1875), or Franz Reizenstein's brilliant set of variations on "The Lambeth Walk" (1938), where he captures the styles of Chopin, Verdi, Mozart, Beethoven, Wagner, and Lizst. This could be described as affectionate parody, purely for the sake of entertainment and intending no satirical mockery, but the listener has to have cognisance of the styles of the original composers. Similarly in painting: Linda Hutcheon dramatically juxtaposes the classically poised *La Grande Odalisque* (1814) of the French artist Ingres with the soft pornographic *Plenti-Grandi-Odalisque* of 1973 by the American artist Mel Ramos.

Hutcheon also significantly notes that parody is distinct not only from imitation, but also from related forms such as burlesque (bringing elevated characters to a low level), travesty, pastiche (a collage of disparate fragments), plagiarism (as in D. M. Thomas' novel *The White Hotel*, 1981), and allusion. Parody is closely related to intertextuality: if you do not know the original text it is unlikely that you will appreciate or recognize the parody (except perhaps in longer works like Stella Gibbons' *Cold Comfort Farm*, 1932, which can be enjoyed as a novel in its own right even if you do not know the novels, such as Mary Webb's *Precious Bane*, 1924, that Gibbons is poking fun at). However, it is important to note that lesser forms of parody such as television comedy or take-offs in satirical magazines like *Private Eye* date rapidly and die once their contemporaneity is lost.

It is important to stress that parody need not be reductive: John Fowles' painter Breasley (in the novella *The Ebony Tower*, 1974) parodies Uccello's painting *Night Hunt* (1468) as a "homage," acknowledging the fact that as an artist he will never aspire to the heights of his Renaissance counterpart. Similarly, Francis Ford Coppola's film *Apocalypse Now* (1979) is a parody of Joseph Conrad's story *Heart of Darkness* (1902) but in no way could it be described as amusing or satirical. Alexander Pope's mock epic *The Rape of the Lock* (1712, 1714) presents us with a more complex form of parody: it imitates epic style and structure but does not make fun of the form itself, rather it exploits it to make satirical fun of contemporary society through stressing, by implication, the gulf between the great heroes of the epic and the trivial protagonists of today.

Crucial to all kinds of parody, as Hutcheon points out, is the degree of difference between the original and the parody: Iris Murdoch's *The Black Prince* (1973) is certainly a parody of William Shakespeare's *Hamlet* (1603), but there are large amounts of extraneous material and its aim is in no way to make fun of the original, rather to utilize it as a hypotext to give greater depth and historical universality to her narrative. Hutcheon goes on to point out that the distance between text and hypotext, unlike that created by, for example, citation or intertextuality, must be ironic, although that irony need not be satirical or destructive. Parody, as we have seen, can be paying a compliment to its predecessor. Of course, it is preferable, in some cases essential, to know the predecessor, but certain major works such as Miguel de Cervantes' *Don Quixote* (1605, 1615), a parody of sixteenth-century chivalric romances, have achieved an autonomy of their own.

Of course there are degrees of parody, ranging from the obvious to the highly elitist, such as Vladimir Nabokov's parody of academic indexes in his novel *Pale Fire* (1962), where one indexical reference simply leads to another ad infinitum; or Malcolm Bradbury's parody of himself (and, by extension, all deconstructive scholarship) in his novel *My Quest for Mensonge* (1987).

## Further reading

Bennett, David. "Parody, Postmodernism, and the Politics of Reading," in *Critical Quarterly*. 27, no. 4 (Winter, 1985).
Crews, F. C. *The Pooh Perplex*, 1979.
Hutcheon, Linda. *A Theory of Parody*, 1985.
Lee, Guy. *Allusion, Parody and Imitation*, 1971.
Parrott, E. O. *Imitations of Immortality*, 1986.
Rose, Margaret. *Parody/Metafiction*, 1979.
——. *Parody: Ancient, Modern, and Post-Modern*, 1993.
Zaranka, W. *Brand-X Fiction: A Parody Anthology*, 1983.

A. W. LYLE

# Pastoral

Samuel Johnson, writing of John Milton's poem *Lycidas*, described its form as "that of the pastoral – easy, vulgar, and therefore disgusting." Nominally a pastoral poem is concerned with sheep and shepherds; in *Lycidas* Milton pays lip service to this convention, but, like many pastoralists before him, he uses the form as a stalking-horse under which he aims at far more serious matters. It is this pretense and seeming insincerity which offended Johnson. However, in a more sober essay in the *Rambler* for July 24, 1750, he accepted a wider definition of pastoral as "a poem in which any action or passion is represented by its effects upon a country life," and gave it as his opinion that the characters need not be actual shepherds and shepherdesses, nor the location a remote Arcadia set in the long-lost Golden Age.

In so doing Johnson distanced himself from the prevailing view of the eighteenth century that the pastoral was indeed concerned with pastoralists, though more usually presented in idealistic than realistic terms. The French critic René Rapin (1621–1687), for example, a firm advocate of classical decorum, laid down rules for the composition of pastoral poems which decreed that the subject-matter should be both innocent and pure and "fitted to the Genius of a Shepherd," the style appropriately simple and ingenuous, the tone "soft and easy," and that the structure should be that of the eclogue, in other words alternating between two speakers. However, his rival, Bernard le Bovier de Fontenelle (1657–1757), dispensing with the absolute necessity for sheep and goats, argued that the essence of pastoral consisted in "the Idea of Quietness" and a sophisticated relaxation that would appeal to readers satiated with ambition and courtly turmoil. The bland and artful verse resulting from such prescriptions (seen at its best in Alexander Pope's youthful pastorals) was condemned by subsequent critics (many of them, including William Wordsworth, poets themselves), for whom George Crabbe spoke when, in *The Village*, he condemned "sleepy bards" who prolong the "flattering dream" of conventionalized pastoral, and proposed instead to "paint the cot,/ As Truth will paint it, and as bards will not."

Nevertheless, the eighteenth century's classicizing version of pastoral was not the genuinely classical norm. What it sought to regularize – on the supposed authority of the classical poets Theocritus, Bion, Moschus, and Virgil – was eclectic; in its own critical pronouncements it had frequently to exclude the elements of realism in Theocritus' *Idylls*, and at best to apologize for the high-toned digressions in Virgil's *Eclogues*. The Renaissance, though less critically self-conscious, had been truer to its classical Greek and Latin predecessors by being prepared to vary widely – from what "E. K." in his "Epistle Dedicatory" to Edmund Spenser's *Shepheardes Calendar* (1579) called a "pastorall rudenesse," to a rhetorically elaborate style which included allegorical treatment of the most serious issues of politics, morality, and religion. Especially in their preoccupation with the idea of the Golden Age, Renaissance writers used the pastoral not merely as a form of escape, but as a standard by which to look at, and judge, the values of the present. In Christopher Marlowe's celebrated poem "The Passionate Shepherd to His Love," the shepherd invites his mistress to live with him and be his love and enjoy all the pleasures "That valleys, groves, hills, and fields/ Woods, or steepy mountains yields"; but the answer put in the mouth of the Nymph by Sir Walter Ralegh emphasizes the fading nature of these joys and the human deceit that produces "A honey tongue, a heart of gall." This is a critical reaction which would have been recognized and endorsed by countless English sixteenth- and seventeenth-century pastoral poets, from Spenser and Michael Drayton to William Shakespeare and Andrew Marvell – and, indeed, by Marlowe himself.

Not surprisingly, modern criticism has focused particularly on the Renaissance. The ground was prepared and the map laid out by W. W. Greg in his *Pastoral Poetry and Pastoral Drama* (1906), which comprehensively covers the whole range of European pastoral. The "pastoral ideal," and its link with the concept of the Golden Age, is central for him; and though, somewhat inconsistently, he writes of its "escape" function, he is generally clear that its recurrent theme is "the recognition of a contrast, implicit or expressed, between pastoral life and some more complex type of civilization." This is the idea taken up and expanded elaborately, and with characteristic ingenuity, by William Empson in *Some Versions of Pastoral* (1935). For Empson pastoral is itself a complex genre, using the apparently naive, simplifying concept of an unsophisticated mode of existence as a means of expressing, and reflecting upon, a more complicated attitude of mind and social reality. The pastoral becomes a "process of putting the complex into the simple." More thoroughly than either Samuel Johnson or Fontenelle, Empson is prepared not only to abandon the traditional requirement that the pastoral should relate to shepherds and shepherdesses, but to move well outside the continuing sense that it is something which should at least be associated with the countryside and rural society. His discussion of particular examples includes not only *The Beggar's Opera* (which John Gay's contemporary Jonathan Swift may have occasioned by his ironic proposal for a "Newgate pastoral"), but the much less obvious, though ingeniously defended, "pastoral" *Alice in Wonderland*. The term is stretched so far that at times it seems to be defined by little more than the peculiarly Empsonian sense of ambiguity and ironic juxtaposition.

Critics such as Frank Kermode and Peter Marinelli also allow themselves considerable latitude, but manage to remain somewhat nearer the traditional definition of pastoral. Kermode's chief interest is in the Renaissance, and his focus is on the interaction of the naive and sophisticated (usually, however, from the point of view of the latter) and the bearing this has on the Renaissance preoccupation with Nature versus Art. (His extension of "pastoral" to *The Tempest* is based on its use of the nature/nurture theme.) This is an opposition which, he suggests, has particular relevance for English writers of the sixteenth and seventeenth centuries since they have their roots in a rural society, but belong to a time of deracination and urbanization.

Marinelli is more interested in Arcadia as what he calls "the landscape of an idea," and in the recurrent theme of escape and return as developed in pastoral narratives and plays. In arguing that the pastoral is also very much alive in the nineteenth and twentieth centuries, he suggests that the Golden Age has now become located in childhood, and that just as the contrast of Art and Nature is seen in a perspective that owes most to Art, so childhood is viewed in what is essentially an adult perspective.

Much of the best in more recent criticism of the pastoral is to be found in studies of individual authors and works that are felt to be touchstones of the peculiar complexity of the form and its associated themes. Among these authors the most important earlier ones are Spenser, Shakespeare, Milton, and Marvell, and the most important single works *The Shepheardes Calendar*, *Lycidas*, and *As You Like It*.

The last, in particular, has come to be viewed as the very acme of Shakespearean comedy and a central reflector and critique of Renaissance pastoral. The continuing vitality of pastoral in the nineteenth and twentieth centuries is strongly associated with the development of regionalism. The critics who deal with it are interested in such novelists as George Eliot, Thomas Hardy, and D. H. Lawrence; and they tend to focus on such works as *Silas Marner*, *Under the Greenwood Tree*, *Far From the Madding Crowd*, *Sons and Lovers*, and *The Rainbow*. In poetry the equivalent figures include William Blake, Wordsworth, Hardy, Robert Frost, Edward Thomas, and Seamus Heaney.

## Further reading

Alcorn, John. *The Nature Novel from Hardy to Lawrence*, 1977.
Chaudhuri, Sakunta. *Renaissance Pastoral and its English Development*, 1989.
Cullen, Patrick. *Spenser, Marvell, and Renaissance Pastoral*, 1970.
Draper, R. P., ed. *Thomas Hardy: Three Pastoral Novels: A Casebook*, 1987.
Empson, William. *Some Versions of Pastoral*, 1935.
Greenlaw, Edwin. *Shakespeare's Pastorals*, 1916.
Greg, W. W. *Pastoral Poetry and Pastoral Drama*, 1906.
Kermode, Frank, ed. *English Pastoral Poetry from the Beginnings to Marvell*, 1952.
——. Introduction to *The Tempest*, 1954.
Levin, Harry. *The Myth of the Golden Age in the Renaissance*, 1969.
Lodge, David. Introduction to *The Woodlanders*, 1974.
Loughrey, Bryan, ed. *The Pastoral Mode: A Casebook*, 1984.
Marinelli, Peter V. *Pastoral*, 1971.
Squires, Michael. *The Pastoral Novel: Studies in George Eliot, Thomas Hardy and D. H. Lawrence*, 1975.
Ward, John Powell. *The English Line: Poetry of the Unpoetic from Wordsworth to Larkin*, 1991.
Whitfield, J. H., ed. *Battista Guarini: Il pastor fido*, 1976.

Studies of pastoral in relation to Shakespeare's *As You Like It* include:
Barber, C. L. *Shakespeare's Festive Comedy*, 1959.
Brissenden, Alan. Introduction to *As You Like It*, 1993.
Draper, R. P. "Shakespeare's Pastoral Comedy," in *Études anglaises*, January–March 1958.
Jenkins, Harold. "As You Like It," in *Shakespeare Survey*. 8, 1955.
Lascelles, Mary. "Shakespeare's Pastoral Comedy," in *More Talking of Shakespeare*, 1959. Edited by J. Garrett.
Young, David. *The Heart's Forest*, 1972.

R. P. DRAPER

# Walter Pater

English critic and writer

**Born:** London, England; August 4, 1839
**Died:** Oxford, England; July 30, 1894

## Biography

Born on August 4, 1839, in London, England, Walter Horatio Pater was the third of four children of Maria (née

Hill) and Richard Glode Pater, a surgeon in practice in London's East End. After his father's early death in 1842, Pater's family moved to Enfield and then in 1852 moved near Canterbury, where Pater attended King's School. Pater studied at Queen's College, Oxford, took a B.A. and an M.A. there, and was elected a Fellow of Brasenose College at Oxford, a post he held until his death. His active life as a critic began with work as a reviewer in the 1860s. He achieved public recognition with the publication of *The Renaissance*, a volume that sparked considerable controversy. Pater led the quiet life of a scholar: tutoring, lecturing, reading, writing, and traveling. A bachelor, he lived with his sisters Hester and Clara in Oxford and, for a time, in London, when not in his rooms at Brasenose. An intensely private person whose writings made him a figure of some controversy, Pater achieved quiet fame in Oxford and London and public recognition at the University of Glasgow, where, shortly before his death, he received an honorary doctoral degree. Pater died on July 30, 1894, and is buried in Holywell Cemetery, Oxford.

## Influence

Pater's influence extended to many self-styled disciples, Oscar Wilde, Arthur Symons, and George Moore among them, and to the literary theory and practice of William Butler Yeats, T. S. Eliot, Ezra Pound, Virginia Woolf, Henry James, and James Joyce. As one of the principal interpreters of French Romanticism in the nineteenth century, Pater changed the course of British literature and criticism in his century through his early apologia for "art for art's sake" and the promulgation of aesthetic criticism. After nearly a half century of being out of fashion, Pater's work became highly influential in the late twentieth century, particularly among British and American critics. The impulses and methodologies of many branches of modern and postmodern criticism are easily traced to Pater's work.

## Analysis

Walter Pater has been variously hailed and denounced as an impressionist critic, as an aesthete whose early championing of art for art's sake became codified by his disciples to bring about a dissociation between art and morality, and as a Decadent under whose influence the artistic excesses and untidy lives of the men of the 1890s were played out. While his work is partially susceptible to these interpretations, they do not adequately capture his theory and practice. His most controversial work, the conclusion to *The Renaissance*, in which he makes his case for art for art's sake, was withdrawn from the volume's second edition and revised for inclusion in the third and fourth editions. Yet he remains notable in the popular imagination for promoting that theory.

*The Renaissance* quite clearly marks a departure from Victorian criticism and the work of its quintessential representatives, John Ruskin and Matthew Arnold. Indeed, Pater

has in mind a corrective to their critical postures from the outset of his epoch-making volume. Having posited the idea that the Beautiful, far from being the Platonic universal Ruskin sought, is relative, and that definitions of beauty must be concrete and expressed in formulas that delineate its special manifestations, Pater proceeds to define his critical aims. Citing Arnold's phrase, Pater writes:

> "To see the object as in itself it really is" has been justly said to be the aim of all true criticism whatever; and in æsthetic criticism the first step towards seeing one object as it really is, is to know one's own impression of it as it really is, to discriminate it, to realise it distinctly.

In elaborating on the practices of the aesthetic critic, Pater introduces not only his volume but also his lifelong critical practice.

In the course of this seminal preface, Pater cites one of his critical mentors, Charles-Augustin Sainte-Beuve. He also introduces such key words as "formula," "virtue," and "temperament" and the relativity of beauty reminiscent of Charles Baudelaire. These and other elements point to the French origins of his newly anglicized brand of aesthetic criticism. In fact, the preface consolidates the patterns of his earlier essays and reviews, sets the tone for all of his subsequent criticism, and continues his work with fresh ideas he imported from France. Chief among those ideas is the critical model he used most, the "literary portrait" fundamental to Sainte-Beuve's criticism. He also appropriated the method and temper of Jules Michelet's historical writing. In addition, deeply attracted to the relativism in Baudelaire's criticism, Pater pursued it to its logical end in "The School of Giorgione" (1877, added to *The Renaissance* in 1888), only to find it leading to an abyss from which he had to retreat in order to continue writing criticism credibly.

Aesthetic criticism, as Pater defined it, has the appearance of scientific order, just as Eliot's criticism would have early in the twentieth century: both use similar chemical metaphors for the critical process. In Pater's usage the critical expression of observation is the disengagement of the virtue by which a work of art or a life produces a distinct impression of beauty or pleasure and the notation of that virtue "as a chemist notes some natural element, for himself and others." Yet since aesthetic criticism depends upon knowing one's own impression and what produced it, the critical process is not objective but essentially subjective. Aesthetic criticism is also eclectic and far from systematic. In his conclusion to *The Renaissance*, Pater makes this very point by asserting not only the need for vigilant personal observation and experience itself (and "not the fruit of experience") but also the necessity of "for ever curiously testing new opinions and courting new impressions, never acquiescing in a facile orthodoxy of Comte, or of Hegel, or of our own." Further, Pater stresses that theories, ideas, systems, and conventions that require the sacrifice of any part of experience are to be eschewed. The aesthetic critic, then, by implication, cannot be systematic or require the faith of others in that criticism. Pater thus entirely democratizes criticism in contrast to Arnold's enshrining it as an activity of those few who would preserve culture.

Pater, as aesthetic critic, adopted a posture of "appreciation" and titled a book of critical essays *Appreciations*. The theory of appreciation focuses positively upon beauty and pleasure: thus Pater is rarely negative in his writings, nor sharply critical of others, but rather passes his time discriminating virtues and not entering into contentious debate. So much does he wish to create a harmonious House Beautiful of art, artists, and the accomplished forms of human life that he avoids controversy and the negative elements of the subjects he appreciates. Thus in *The Renaissance* he celebrates Peter Abelard without mentioning his fate, and in an essay on Romanticism he reconciles the classic and the Romantic by calling upon Stendhal and by applying a definition of the classic written by Johann Wolfgang von Goethe (via Sainte-Beuve) to the poetry of Baudelaire. Thus he reconfigures the definitions so as to reverse their original applications and mold them to his own ends.

The Romanticism Pater favored, primarily French Romanticism, suffuses his fiction and criticism to the extent that he continually draws parallels, sometimes unlikely ones, between French and English culture. Hence, for example, in a discussion of style in which he glorifies Gustave Flaubert as "the martyr of style," he extols Flaubert's workmanship as a model for all writers, including the English. In his lecture/essays on Plato, he not only brings to bear a peculiarly Romantic view of Plato and his philosophy but also compares Spartan culture to English culture and Athenian to French. Moreover, his Romantic disposition influences and colors his treatment of such visual artists as Sandro Botticelli, Michelangelo, and Leonardo da Vinci in the literary portraits he draws of them.

As an aesthetic critic of pronounced Romantic sensibility, Pater spent the majority of his life introducing his readers to topics and figures unknown or underappreciated in late-Victorian England. He is largely responsible for introducing Botticelli to the modern world, wrote positively of Baudelaire (following Algernon Charles Swinburne's lead), and appreciated Stendhal long before any other did in England and most in France. He also popularized Flaubert and Prosper Mérimée, wrote in defense of Émile Zola, and drew attention to lesser-known writers such as Henri-Frédéric Amiel, Jules Lemaître, and Octave Feuillet. Yet out of diffidence and caution he did not write of the French Symbolists or the Decadents of the 1880s and early 1890s.

Pater's influence has had three distinct phases. The first dates from his publication of *The Renaissance* until roughly after World War I and was extraordinarily great. The younger generation at Oxford seized upon his novelty and was profoundly moved by it. As an undergraduate, Wilde was strongly drawn to Pater's criticism, and for him *The Renaissance* became his "Golden Book." Pater's influence on Wilde also extends to Wilde's daring play *Salomé* (1893; English translation, 1894), one source of which is a short story by Flaubert that Pater sent to him in the 1870s. Others, such as George Moore, took Pater's cue and began modeling their work on contemporary French writers. Moore, for example, following Pater's general lead, adopted Zola's brand of naturalism. Symons, another self-proclaimed disciple and an early biographer of Pater, adapted the form of *The Renaissance* to his own purposes of chronicling the Symbolist movement in France. Yeats goes so far in his own autobiography as to assert of the young writers of the 1890s that they were all Paterians. Still other members of the Rhymers' Club, Lionel Johnson and Ernest Dowson among them, took up Pater's interest in France and pursued its latest flowerings in a Decadent artificiality. Although Pater distanced himself from his disciples and their literary output, and indeed wrote a critical review of Wilde's *The Picture of Dorian Gray* (1891), he had begun the aesthetic movement and his later dissociation from it could not stem the tide. Pater's influence also clearly extended to such writers as Marcel Proust, Woolf, and Joyce.

As Pater's influence waxed in his own era, it would severely wane in the period from the 1920s through the mid-1950s. Changes in critical fashion begun by such critics as Paul Elmer More and Eliot put Pater completely out of favor. Yet in Eliot's case, his virulent attack on Pater concealed a critical debt that took decades to come to light. Just as his chemical metaphor for criticism, for example, has its precursor in Pater's *The Renaissance*, so his "objective correlative," the notion of a relative somewhere in the world of thought and its correlative somewhere in the world of language, comes from Pater's *Appreciations*. Eliot's criticism combined with Thomas Wright's flawed biography of Pater and the disastrous ends of several of Pater's disciples effectively removed Pater from popularity until a rebirth in literary criticism in the 1950s and 1960s reversed that trend.

In the 1940s and 1950s, powerful critics such as Graham Hough, Frank Kermode, René Wellek, and Iain Fletcher began a movement toward more active interest in Pater, and a major impetus for this came in response to Fletcher's essay "Why Not Take Pater Seriously?" Pater's work has since become a major force in literary criticism and literary theory. His work has attracted notice from critics whose approach derives from the study of semiotics, from critics whose focus is upon the reader's response to work, from psychological critics, and from those who practice the criticism of deconstruction.

## Principal criticism

*Studies in the History of the Renaissance*, 1873, revised as *The Renaissance: Studies in Art and Poetry*, 1877, 1888, 1893

*Appreciations: With an Essay on Style,* 1889
*Plato and Platonism: A Series of Lectures,* 1893
*Greek Studies: A Series of Essays,* 1895
*Essays from the "Guardian,"* 1896

## Other major works and literary forms

Remembered principally for his influential criticism, Walter Pater also published a novel, *Marius the Epicurean: His Sensations and Ideas* (1885), a fictionalized version of themes central to *Studies in the History of the Renaissance,* generally known as *The Renaissance.* He also wrote short fictional studies, entitled *Imaginary Portraits* (1887), and left unfinished the second novel in his contemplated trilogy, *Gaston de Latour: An Unfinished Romance* (1896).

NOVELS
*Marius the Epicurean: His Sensations and Ideas,* 1885 (2 volumes)
*Gaston de Latour: An Unfinished Romance,* 1896

SHORT FICTION
*Imaginary Potraits,* 1887

## Further reading

Brake, Laurel. *Walter Pater,* 1990.
Conlon, John J. *Walter Pater and the French Tradition,* 1982.
Court, Franklin E., ed. *Walter Pater: An Annotated Bibliography of Writings About Him,* 1979.
Dale, Peter A. *The Victorian Critic and the Idea of History: Carlyle, Arnold, and Pater,* 1977.
De Laura, David. *Hebrew and Hellene in Victorian England: Newman, Arnold, and Pater,* 1969.
Donoghue, Dennis. *Walter Pater: Lover of Strange Souls,* 1995.
Fletcher Iain. *Walter Pater,* 1959.
Inman, Billie Andrew. *Walter Pater's Reading: A Bibliography of His Library Borrowings and Literary References,* 1981.
Keefe, Robert and Janice. *Walter Pater and the Gods of Disorder,* 1988.
Levey, Michael. *The Case of Walter Pater,* 1978.
Loesberg, Jonathan. *Aestheticism and Deconstruction: Pater, Derrida, and DeMan,* 1991.
McGrath, F. C. *The Sensible Spirit: Walter Pater and the Modernist Paradigm,* 1986.
Moliterno, Frank. *The Dialects of Sense and Spirit in Pater and Joyce,* 1997.
Monsman, Gerald C. *Walter Pater,* 1977.
Shuter, William. *Rereading Walter Pater,* 1997.
Sieler, R. M. *Walter Pater: The Critical Heritage,* 1980.
Williams, Carolyn. *Transfigured Worlds: Walter Pater's Aesthetic Historicism,* 1990.
Wright, Samuel. *A Bibliography of the Writings of Walter Pater,* 1975.

JOHN J. CONLON

*See also* Aestheticism; Arnold; Literary Theory in the Age of Victoria; Ruskin; Symonds; Symons

# Marjorie Perloff

American critic

**Born:** Vienna, Austria; September 28, 1931

## Biography

Marjorie Perloff is one of the foremost American critics of contemporary poetry. Her work has been especially concerned with explicating the writing of experimental and avant-garde poets and relating it to the major currents of modernist and, especially, postmodernist activity in the arts, including the visual arts and cultural theory. She took her first degree at Barnard College, New York, followed by an M.A. and Ph.D. (in 1965) at CUA (Catholic University of America) in Washington, D.C. CUA also provided her first teaching post (as assistant and then associate professor) from 1966 to 1971. She moved to the University of Maryland as full professor in 1971, remaining there five years before moving to California in 1976. She has been a professor at Californian universities since 1976, with ten years at the University of Southern California, till 1986, and since then at Stanford University, becoming Sadie Dernham Patek Professor of Humanities in 1990. Her immense energies and enthusiasm as a writer and teacher have been devoted to creating a public for the work of writers whom many others have wanted to dismiss as too difficult, obscure, or marginal. Her own writing is always anything but that; as Frank Kermode has said, Marjorie Perloff is fun to read. She has never been a critic who wraps her insights in a daunting verbal carapace which only the truly intrepid can penetrate. She writes to explain, and always communicates her insights through vivid juxtapositions, formulations, and examples.

## Influence

While the American mainstream of academic poststructuralist theory in recent years has concentrated its efforts chiefly on such areas as Renaissance drama and modern prose fiction, partly in reaction against the New Critical generation's stress on poetry, Perloff has never wavered from her commitment to modern and contemporary poetry, a commitment which constantly seeks to extend her generation's "New Critical" enthusiasm for major modernist poets like William Butler Yeats, Ezra Pound, and T. S. Eliot, taking in the postwar tradition of American poetic innovation which runs through the Black Mountain Poets, the New York Poets, the Beats in the 1950s and 1960s, and through to the Language Poets of the 1980s and 1990s. (Language Poetry, a key interest of Perloff's, is a radical form of poetry which arose in the 1970s in the United States, especially in San Francisco and New York. In its "pure" form it rejects "reference" out to an objective world beyond the page, so that the poem is not "about" anything – it is simply the "actuality of the words." It also rejects the "tyranny" of the lyrical "I" whose experience is narrated or explored through poetry. Instead, it focuses attention on sentence, phrase, linguistic register, and verbal patterning. Prominent practitioners are Charles Bernstein, Lyn Hejinian, and Bob Perelman.) Perloff's strong interest in related "avant-garde" poetry activity in Britain (and, indeed, in Canada and in the rest of Europe) from the 1970s onward marks her out as highly unusual among major American critics. Indeed, it would be true to say that the major academic and commercial success of contemporary avant-garde poetries in the United States is partly due to the succession of lively, lucid, and enlightening critical books and articles which she has produced since the early 1980s. Likewise, the comparative obscurity which remains the fate of the related British "experimental" poetries can be said to be due to the continuing absence from the critical scene of a "British Perloff."

## Analysis

Perloff's three earliest books are her only ones devoted entirely to a single poet, but each marks a step closer to the field which she made her métier. They are *Rhyme and Meaning in the Poetry of Yeats* (1970), *The Poetic Art of Robert Lowell* (1973), and *Frank O'Hara: Poet Among Painters* (1977). This sequence of books also suggests a gradual "Americanization" of her interests, and perhaps also hints at her refusal to be bowled over by deconstruction. Her book on the New York poet Frank O'Hara sees his work as part of a matrix of related cultural and artistic activity, rather than isolating it, in the New Critical fashion, as a uniquely supercharged variety known as "literature." Placing poetry within a cultural continuum in this way quickly becomes the keynote of her approach. Instead of reading the "words on the page" she reads the words (as she has said) off the page and into the immensely active urban and technological cultures from which innovative poetries invariably arise. As she says in the Preface to *Radical Artifice: Writing Poetry in the Age of Media* (1991), "There is today no landscape uncontaminated by sound bytes or computer blips, no mountain peak or lonely valley beyond the reach of the cellular phone and the microcassette player. Increasingly, then, the poet's arena is the electronic world."

In 1981 Perloff produced her first book in what became her settled manner of dealing with a broad range of modern and contemporary culture and treating poetry "within the arts," under the title *The Poetics of Indeterminacy: Rimbaud to Cage*, a book which sees broad lines of continuity between modernist and postmodernist culture. This project of establishing a network of interconnections between modernism and postmodernism is characteristic of Perloff's mature project, in sharp contrast to that of her contemporary, and rival, the critic Helen Vendler, whose consistent line has been to elevate the status of classic modernists like T. S. Eliot and Wallace Stevens while

seeming to denigrate that of the present-day avant-garde. Vendler has, it is true, singled out specific contemporary poets as exemplary (such as John Ashbery) but she has never "endorsed" a whole body of varied work by different figures in the way that Perloff, for the past decade and a half, has engaged with the work known as Language Poetry. Where Vendler searches for the individual heirs to the literary heroes of the recent past, Perloff is fascinated by the intense debates about language, poetry, culture, and the self which cluster about the Language Poets. The *Poetics of Indeterminacy* is also the first of Perloff's books to emphasize the importance of the musician and cultural theorist John Cage, a figure on whose exemplary centrality she becomes increasingly insistent. The other three books in this "middle" phase of her career are *The Dance of the Intellect: Studies in the Poetry of the Pound Tradition* (1985), *The Futurist Moment: Avant-Garde, Avant-Guerre, and the Language of Rupture* (1986), and *Poetic Licence: Studies in Modernist and Postmodernist Lyric* (1990), all, again, establishing deep-level connections and affinities between modernism and postmodernism.

But it should be emphasized that Perloff's notion of the postmodern takes up early definitions of it by critics such as Ihab Hassan in the 1970s. Hassan's *The Literature of Silence* (1967) made a case for a new kind of post-Holocaust, post-Hiroshima writing which rejected traditional Western literary-aesthetic norms, resulting in texts which were either violent or obscene, like those of Henry Miller and Norman Mailer, or else reticent, randomized, and indeterminate, like those of Samuel Beckett and John Cage. This critical approach responded to the well-known pronouncement of Theodor Adorno that "After Auschwitz ... to a write a poem is barbaric." Such notions of silence, randomness, and openness seemed to posit the possibility of a "post-aesthetic" kind of writing which acknowledged the failure of the century's high culture to prevent a return to barbarism. "Postmodernism" in this sense represented a literature which recognized the failure of "high culture," even that of the great modernists like Pound, Eliot, Rainer Maria Rilke, and Thomas Mann, so that the anti-elitism, anti-authoritarianism, and anarchism of this kind of postmodernism had what Perloff calls a "cutting edge" – it was polemical and political, and had not yet been formulated primarily as "play." But 1967 was also the year of the three books which brought Jacques Derrida to fame, and marked the beginning of the rise of poststucturalism in the United States. Derrida's seminal essay "Structure, Sign, and Play" had first appeared in 1966, and very quickly the notion of "semantic instability" became dominant in the humanities, not as the specific quality of the postmodern "open text," but as the necessary linguistic condition of all texts. Thus, in its later phase, postmodernism becomes "play" rather than "anarchy," celebrating what Jameson called "a new depthlessness," and "a waning of affect." Perloff sees the shift in emphasis from "openness" to "depthlessness," in discussions of postmodernism between the 1970s and the 1980s, as symptomatic. The "dissolution of the subject," favored by 1980s postmodernism and poststructuralism, far from being something to celebrate, is actually the state of mind that engendered Stalinist purges, the Holocaust, and Hiroshima. Perloff, of course, offers no neat solution to this contradiction, but she points out that many of the classic modernists had already lost faith in those "meta-narratives" before their demise was proclaimed in the 1980s. Perloff's point is that unless we reappraise modernism, we cannot understand postmodernism, or will at best be left with a deracinated version of the phenomenon in which we are compelled to relive the, after all, quite recent past, without being aware that that is what we are doing. Perloff, then, is far from accepting the dominant notions of postmodernism uncritically. She asks of postmodernism what might be called "developmental" questions, such as "How did we ever get ourselves into this mode of critical thinking?" This is not a rhetorical question, and she means to stimulate us into retracing the process step by step, a proceeding which is conspicuously free of the poststructuralist queasiness about considering questions of origin and development.

One of Perloff's great strengths as a critic and theorist, then, is that while her career reaches its highpoint as deconstruction sweeps the board in America, her work retains its independence and is not swept along with it, whether in the form of extreme partisanship or extreme opposition. Instead of reacting, as so many American critics did, by developing an exaggerated horror for the New Critical "formalism" of the previous generation, she retains many elements of this native American product and refuses to trade it in for the new European model of literary study. Hence, all her essays at some point reproduce a poem, or a substantial proportion of one, and enter into close critical engagement with it. The difference between hers and the typical New Critical essay is that the poem is not isolated as a "verbal icon" detached from every other aspect of life. Rather, she is likely to relate poems to broader (and often interlocking) cultural contexts, such as aspects of business and commercial culture (for example, the way messages are conveyed by iconographic business calling cards, as in *Radical Artifice*), and the close textual explication is placed within a generously panoramic literary context, with a clear and sharp line of argument which maps a large expanse of literary territory in a memorable way. A classic example of this kind of broad contextualizing is her essay "After Free Verse: The New Non-Linear Poetries," which argues that while free-verse was speech-based, image-based, and individually expressive writing which centered on the line as its unit, there is now a new kind of "post-linear" writing, represented by Language Poetry, which centers on "the word as such," or on the "aphoristic fragment," and is designed for the eye (it is "page-specific") more than the ear. A formulation of this kind seems to empower the reader

in a dramatic way with a new and comprehensive way of seeing a major segment of twentieth-century poetry – what more could be asked of a literary critic and theorist? Such mappings and formulations, of course, always prove too rigid once we actually get into the field and begin to encounter the examples in quantity. But the point is that they send us into the field with some confidence, and with a hypothesis to test, and Perloff herself makes the point earlier in the essay about the necessary crudeness of our literary maps by presenting five American poems, without at first naming the poets, and asking us to decide in which of the well-known camps ("Beat," "Black Mountain," "Deep Image," and so on) each poet belongs. The answers, of course, are surprising, but this does not prove the categories to be meaningless: it simply means that the test will often (as it should) modify the hypothesis.

Perloff's best-known and most influential book is *Radical Artifice: Writing Poetry in the Age of Media*, which appeared in 1991 and is very much the best starting point for readers new to her work. The book seeks to situate the flight from "transparency" (that is, language which aims to look and sound "natural," to sound like "real" talk) to "artifice" (that is, poetic language which foregrounds its own artificiality, for instance, by arranging itself in a series of blocks or clusters on the page). This shift is characteristic of the modernist and postmodernist writers she most admires today, who write within "the discourses of art and the mass media," for it is naive to suppose that "a 'poem' could exist in the United States today that has not been shaped by the electronic culture that has produced it." The book maps the transition from "free verse" (where the line was the unit) to "post-linear," "post-subjective" poetry, where the operative unit is "the word as such," and the page itself as a visual and spacial entity. The notion of "procedural play" is also introduced, whereby the artist works within a grid of strictly regulated randomness (for instance, by allowing word occurrence in the text to be decided by an *a priori* mathematical sequence). Such procedures bring us full circle, imposing restrictions on "self-expression" which are as fundamental and pervasive as the old iambic metrics abandoned by the modernists. The final chapter in the book is on the musician and theorist John Cage, whose work supplied explicit theoretical formulations of "procedural play."

Her next book, *Wittgenstein's Ladder: Poetic Language and the Strangeness of the Ordinary* (1996), takes another major cultural figure from the mid-century period who is not himself a poet, but whose work provides ways of understanding and situating poetry, the philosopher Ludwig Wittgenstein. As she writes, "I am less interested in 'influence,' always a nebulous quality, than in analogue. It is fascinating to see that Wittgenstein's stringent and severe interrogation of language has provided an opening for the replacement of the 'autonomous,' self-contained, and self-expressive lyric with a more fluid poetic paradigm – a paradigm based on the recognition that the poet's most secret and profound emotions are expressed in a language that has always already belonged to the poet's culture, society, and nation, the irony being that this 'belonging' need not make the poetry in question – Robert Creeley's and Rosmarie Waldrop's, Ron Silliman's and Lyn Hejinian's, the Fluxus box or the Joseph Kosuth 'investigation' – any less moving." This encapsulates the rationale for her whole approach to poetry: in spite of the long tradition of rhetorical criticism which has emphasized the separateness of poetic language, Perloff emphasizes that poets do not invent language, but share it with the rest of society, including artists, philosophers, political activists, and business people. As she says in the quotation above, this does not make the poetry any less moving, for avant-garde techniques are not just cerebral – which is always, and only, the way they look at first sight – they are also emotive and humanizing, and this fact counters the "depthlessness" and the "waning of affect" which are so prominent in more dominant accounts of postmodernism. Again, then, Perloff is a theorist whose work has maintained its distinctiveness in the face of the rapid homogenization of literary criticism and theory by such all-embracing concepts as poststructuralism and postcolonialism. We need her distinctive voice more than ever as literary theory (which was instigated by Aristotle) enters its third millennium.

## Principal criticism

*Rhyme and Meaning in the Poetry of Yeats*, 1970
*The Poetic Art of Robert Lowell*, 1973
*Frank O'Hara: Poet Among Painters*, 1977
*The Poetics of Indeterminacy: Rimbaud to Cage*, 1981
*The Dance of the Intellect: Studies in the Poetry of the Pound
    Tradition*, 1985
*The Futurist Moment: Avant-Garde, Avant-Guerre, and the
    Language of Rupture*, 1986
*Poetic Licence: Studies in Modernist and Postmodernist Lyric*,
    1990
*Postmodern Genres*, 1990
*Radical Artifice: Writing Poetry in the Age of Media*, 1991
*Wittgenstein's Ladder: Poetic Language and the Strangeness of
    the Ordinary*, 1996
*Poetry On and Off the Page: Essays for Emergent Occasions*,
    1998

## Further reading

Duric, Dubravka. "Interview with Marjorie Perloff," in *Kosava*.
    21 (September, 1994), pp. 54–56.
——. "Radical Artifice in the 90s: An Interview with Professor
    Marjorie Perloff," in *The Rising Generation*. 151, no. 8
    (November 1, 1995), pp. 2–10.

PETER BARRY

*See also* American Literary Theory: Twentieth Century

# Petrarch

(Francesco Petrarca)

Italian poet and writer

**Born:** Arezzo, Italy; July 20, 1304
**Died:** Arquà, Italy; July 18, 1374

## Biography

Francesco Petrarca was born in Arezzo, Italy, on July 20, 1304. The son of a Florentine political exile, he moved early in life to Avignon, France, seat of the papacy. His formal education there was traditional. Despite his great love of literature, at his father's insistence he prepared for a career in law, studying at Montpellier and Bologna. After his father's death Petrarch returned to Avignon and began an ecclesiastical career. Although he never went beyond minor orders, it brought him preferments and patronage that permitted him a career in literature and scholarship.

Petrarch's poetry dates from 1330, three years after he saw Laura (a fictional name, since her real identity is unknown), the lady who became his inspiration. He traveled widely on commissions for ecclesiastical and civil authorities, meeting many of the great figures of his day and fostering his growing reputation as a writer and scholar. In 1341 he was crowned poet laureate in Rome. During the next fifteen years he produced the bulk of his work, which he honed and polished through many years.

Petrarch continued to travel to Italy, France, Germany, and Flanders, frequently returning to the Avignon area to write. His interest in his illegitimate children (a daughter and a son), his wide circle of friends, and his continuing work filled his later years. He never tired of writing and study and continued to work to the day of his death at Arquà, near Padua, on July 18, 1374.

## Influence

Petrarch was the first Italian scholar to criticize medieval theory and form. He wished to return to the canons of classical tradition, which he found superior to those of the centuries that intervened between his own day and the Age of Antiquity. He called for a revival of ancient languages and literature, particularly Latin, although he attempted to work with Greek documents later in his career. Not only did he consider ancient literature important for its own sake, but he also saw it as the guide for contemporary and future literature. He considered medieval writing barbarous. Described by later scholars as the first Humanist of the Renaissance spirit and as "the first modern man," he popularized and widely influenced the Italian Renaissance.

His famous library, assembled during his many trips to various parts of Europe, encouraged pioneering philological studies, while his lyric poetry influenced that genre throughout Europe for centuries.

## Analysis

One would search in vain for a full statement or cohesive essay by Petrarch on literary theory or the role of criticism. Yet embedded in his work and life there are clear patterns and overt explanations that are instructional and important for an understanding of his criticism. The influence of his traditional education and preparations for a legal career faded with his discovery of the ancients. It was the writings of the authors of the Roman world that first developed his awareness of literary form and meaning. His criticism was rooted in his acceptance of classic models.

Petrarch considered the written word far superior to the spoken word, for the former survived to instruct posterity and reached the many rather than the few. To use the written word effectively was his goal, but to reach it, knowledge of classical Latin was essential. He describes in his letters the laborious method he used to learn Ciceronian Latin with its complex periodic sentences. He copied Cicero's works, absorbing the words, the structure, and the thought until they were part of him. Cicero became a friend, a confidant to whom he could address correspondence as to a contemporary.

Great as his love and admiration of classic authors grew, his own work was not mere imitation. He sought truth from these sources to inform his own writing. He believed in the universality of the wisdom of the past but insisted on its relevance for his own age; in one of his letters, Petrarch likens his use of ancient materials to the work of bees that take nectar from many flowers but transform it into new creations of wax and honey. He made a careful distinction between ideas gleaned from classical sources and the style in which he transmitted them. Petrarch declared his style to be his own, remarking on several occasions that even if it were unpolished and uncouth he preferred it to that of someone else. By way of illustration, he explains that he would rather have a cloak cut to his own measure than someone else's cloak, even if the latter were richer or more ornate. He seems to suggest that while any role might fit any actor, any style does not fit any writer: writers must find their own style and keep it their own as they refine, polish, and improve it. It was characteristic of Petrarch to believe that his work was never finished. He reworked and rewrote his material for years before permitting his manuscripts to circulate. Therefore, it is extremely difficult to date his works, and much scholarly debate continues in regard to this problem.

Petrarch's passion for collecting ancient manuscripts led him to scour monasteries and archival deposits across Europe, thus creating an extremely valuable library. Collating and emending these prizes led to the foundation of philological studies of considerable worth, though they were pioneering efforts. In Liège, Petrarch found a lost work of Cicero which contained lengthy discussions of the art of poetry. Although Cicero's work as a poet affords him only a minor place in Roman literary history, he did refine verse form and had an influence on the work of Virgil and Catullus. Petrarch imbibed all that Cicero wrote, particularly discussions of the choice of rhyme scheme at the end of hexameter lines. Undoubtedly this discovery encouraged Petrarch to undertake an epic poem known as *Africa* – a theme which his acquaintance with Virgil's *Aeneid* (c. 29–19 B.C.) had already suggested. The work, more admired by his own age than by subsequent ones, is evidence of his continuing development of a formal, theoretical approach to poetic expression. His most lasting work is *The Sonnets and Stanzas of Petrarch*. Not only is it the fullest example of Petrarch's vernacular poetry, but many statements about his theory of poetry are included in its lines as well. It contains more than three hundred poems and establishes the scheme of what came to be known as the Petrarchan sonnet. The sonnet is composed of an octet, or eight-line stanza, with rhyme scheme *abbabba*, followed by the sestet or six-line stanza, with the pattern *cdecde*. Usually the sestet makes specific a general statement posed in the octet. Other poetic forms that Petrarch devised are equally rich and complex, demonstrating the seriousness with which he strove to apply his artistic theories.

Texture, tone, and emotional context were equally important to him. The poems are divided into two parts, with the idealized Laura as the focal point. The first section deals with the years up to Laura's death; the second covers the years without her earthly presence. Primarily expressions of love, the poems also reflect religious beliefs and an appreciation of the beauty of nature. Petrarch had a sharp eye for the scenic beauty of the various regions where he traveled, and depiction of nature was one of his most impressive accomplishments.

Petrarch's critical approach to ancient writings was not slavish and did not preclude dissatisfaction if those writers fell short of their own stated goals. He was angered by slips in scheme or content, and as his knowledge of vocabulary and syntax improved, he was quick to point out how the ancients might have improved their work.

Although it never became an insurmountable problem for him, Petrarch was sometimes caught between his religious convictions and the call of the pagan past. In some of his work he felt called upon to express his belief in the supremacy of religious truth, yet secular knowledge from the pre-Christian era involved human truths that were not incompatible with the revealed truth of Scripture. In one of his dialogues, a Christian chides a writer of Humanistic studies. The writer protests that his fervent faith protects him from error, but his defense seems weak. During his visits to Rome, Petrarch wrote detailed descriptions of the city. He remarks at the beginning of these essays on the numerous Christian and Roman shrines. In the body of the work, however, there is little said of the Christian sites – indeed, they are entirely neglected in one piece – while the pagan sites are described in lyrical terms.

Petrarch's preoccupation with Rome led to his interest in the history of the Roman world. He believed that the historian's task is to find accurate evidence on which to base an interpretation of singular events and wider historical developments. His interest in history led to his belief that great men have an extraordinary impact upon history. Indeed, he believed, it is the juxtaposition of great lives at certain momentous periods of crisis that creates history. Although prose and poetry have different goals, according to Petrarch, fictional writers benefit from accurate historical information even if they romanticize their subject or add dramatic elements to heighten the impact of their story.

It is important to note that Petrarch viewed the history of Rome not from an aesthetic point of view but from a critical one, easily accepted by modern historians. His discussion of history is reminiscent of the attitude of Edward Gibbon, the eighteenth-century historian. A new conception of history was developing in Petrarch's mind. His division of history into six ages, the latter three being the ancient, the barbarous, and the new (a revival of the ancient), created a new sense of chronology.

Petrarch's constant pleas for a return to the quality of ancient writing constituted a crucial aspect of his scheme of the divisions of European history. He spoke to posterity as well as to his contemporaries in demanding that a new age be created. His interpretation of history, widely accepted among his contemporaries, included the view that the Middle Ages had produced little of literary worth, despite the maintenance of the Christian faith. Though Petrarch did not castigate all medieval writers, he considered the best of them to have been ill-fated, doomed to live in dark and barbarous times. He acknowledged that some were men of genius despite the handicap of living in a dismal age.

Petrarch never doubted the values of Christianity. He was well acquainted with the writings of the Latin Fathers of the Western Church. He had no difficulty with blending Saint Augustine and Cicero. This sense of the compatibility of Christian and Humanist values led to his encouraging the Church to embrace the new approach to learning; he welcomed knowledge from all sources and therefore valued literature as an instructional tool.

Petrarch's concept of the role of literature was founded in the belief that it is the measure by which a civilization's worth can be gauged. He had no doubt that it was the noblest and most useful of studies. All of his criticism reveals his deepest conviction: good literature contains material of ethical value; it leads to the improvement of humanity, both individually and collectively.

The exceptional place of Petrarch in literary criticism is a result of the combination of his life, writing, and ideas, which are inextricably bound together. His correspondence represents a diary of his travels. His travels, interspersed with periods of tranquillity, gave him material and time for reflection, expressed and given shape in the works that he produced.

Petrarch left his mark on Western civilization in both obvious and subtle ways. His impact on form and theory has been noted. His leadership of the Renaissance movement in Italy is also clear. The subtle areas are harder to delineate, but no less real. His deep religious feelings are undeniable, but he also prized human individuality and, above all, human love, which is a reflection of the Divine. If Petrarch believed that human beings were sinful creatures, as he did, he also believed that, created in the image and likeness of God, they were intrinsically good and capable of producing good. Thus, with many other thinkers of his age, he contributed to a new sense of human achievement and human worth.

## Principal criticism

*Rerum familiarium libri*, written 1325–1366 (English translation, 1975–1985)
*Collatio laureationes*, 1341 (*Coronation Oath*, 1955)
*Secretum meum*, 1353–1358 (*My Secret*, 1911)
*Senilium rerum libri*, wr. 1361–1374 (*Letters of Old Age*, 1966)

## Other major works and literary forms

In addition to the works noted above, Petrarch wrote dialogues and treatises on religious topics as well as personal essays on moral theology. His fame as a poet was widespread. His lyric poetry, best exemplified by the *Rerum vulgarium fragmenta* (1470; also known as *Canzionere*; *The Sonnets and Stanzas of Petrarch*, 1879), was written in the vernacular in 1373. Petrarch also wrote epic poetry in Latin. His historical works include biographies of men of ancient and medieval times; *Africa* (1396; English translation, 1977), while demonstrating his poetic talent, is also historically accurate, evidencing serious research on the career of Scipio Africanus. Some of Petrarch's studies defy classification in modern terms, but even his occasional pieces are important for an understanding of his career and contributions.

POETRY
*Epistolae metricae*, 1363 (*Metrical Letters*, 1958)
*Bucolicum carmen*, 1364 (*Eclogues*, 1974)
*Africa*, 1396 (English translation, 1977)
*Trionfi*, 1470 (*Tryumphs*, 1565; also as *Triumphs*, 1962)
*Rerum vulgarium fragmenta*, 1470 (also as *Canzoniere*; *The Sonnets and Stanzas of Petrarch*, 1879)
*Rime disperse*, 1826 (also as *Estravaganti*; *Excluded Rhymes*, 1976)

NONFICTION
*Psalmi penitentiales*, 1342–1347
*Rerum memorandum libri*, 1343–1345
*De vita solitaria*, 1346 (*The Life of Solitude*, 1924)
*De viris illustribus*, 1351–1353 (reorganized as *Quorundam virorum illustrium epithoma*, completed by Lombardo della Seta)
*Invectivarum contra quendam magni status hominen sed nullius scientiae aut virtutis*, 1355
*Itinerarium Syriacum*, 1358 (also as *Itinerarium breve de Ianua*)
*Sine nomine*, 1359–1360 (*Book Without a Name*, 1973)

*De remediis utriusque fortunae*, 1366 (*Physicke Against Fortune*, 1597)
*De sui ipsius et multorum ignorantia*, 1367 (*On His Own Ignorance and That of Many*, 1948)
*Posteritati*, 1370–1372 (*Epistle to Posterity*, 1966)
*Invectiva contra eum qui maledixit Italiae*, 1373
*De otio religioso*, 1376
*Miscellaneous Letters*, 1966

MISCELLANEOUS
*Opera quae extant omnia*, 1554, 1581

## Further reading

Bergin, Thomas. *Petrarch*, 1970.
Bishop, Morris. *Petrarch and His World*, 1963.
Boyle, Marjorie O'Rourke. *Petrarch's Genius: Pentimento and Prophecy*, 1992.
Dubrow, Heather. *Echoes of Desire: English Petrarchism and its Counter-Discourses*, 1995.
Foster, Kenelm. *Petrarch*, 1984.
Kennedy, William John. *Authorizing Petrarch*, 1994.
Mann, Nicholas. *Petrarch*, 1984.
Roche, Thomas P. *Petrarch and the English Sonnet Sequences*, 1989.
Wilkins, Ernest H. *Life of Petrarch*, 1961.

ANNE R. VIZZIER

*See also* Boccaccio; Dante; Renaissance and Restoration Literary Theory

# Phenomenological Criticism

In the wake of the ideological crisis surrounding World War I, a time of relativism and irrationalism, the German philosopher Edmund Husserl initiated a philosophical method to develop a new (subjective) certainty. Husserl thus became the modern founder of phenomenology, a method through which he attempted to explain the structure of experience in terms of consciousness and the relations between the human subject and the world, history, and other persons. Phenomenology also underwrote a literary criticism devoted to investigating the world as reflected through an author's consciousness and represented by the corpus of his or her literary works. A phenomenological approach was taken by the American critic J. Hillis Miller and the Geneva School of criticism of the 1940s and 1950s, which included the Belgian-born Georges Poulet, the Frenchman Jean-Pierre Richard, and the Swiss Jean Starobinski and Jean Rousset. Phenomenology also influenced reader-oriented critics like the German Wolfgang Iser and the American Stanley Fish. They regarded a literary work as what is given to the consciousness of the reader rather than as something objective or independent. As "reader-response" critics they describe how a reader interprets a text in the act of reading, a process of making connections and filling in the gaps of the text in such a way as to participate in the production of its meaning.

A work is constituted by the reader's experience. Also influenced by phenomenology is "reception theory," or "the aesthetics of reception," developed by Hans Robert Jauss. Instead of the reader's individual response, the focus of this approach is the history of a work's critical reception in the course of the changing norms or "horizon of expectations" of different historical periods that cause a work to be interpreted differently. These diverse but interrelated critical approaches have their roots in Husserlian phenomenology.

## Phenomenology

Husserl's purpose as stated in *The Crisis of the European Sciences* (1935) was to make philosophy an "absolutely self-sufficient science of the spirit" and thereby to counteract the irrationality of a world in which the center cannot hold. The modern development of phenomenology includes philosophers such as Martin Heidegger, Hans-Georg Gadamer, Paul Ricœur, and Maurice Merleau-Ponty, and, more recently, John Searle, Thomas Nagel, Francisco Varela, and Robert Forman.

Husserl began by proposing that the philosopher reject the "natural attitude" of the ordinary person with the unprovable presuppositions about the world of objects and metaphysical truths. He questioned the common-sense assumption that things exist in the world independently of our perceptions and that our perceptions are reliable. Although we may not be able to know for certain whether things exist in themselves, we can at least be certain through first-hand experience whether or not the objects of our awareness are illusory. If objects cannot be known as things in themselves, as the German philosopher Immanuel Kant had argued, then we might better regard them as things intended or posited by consciousness. This leads to the definition of consciousness as always positing an object: all consciousness is thus consciousness of something insofar that awareness is never devoid of empirical, phenomenological content. Consciousness is not passive but "intends" its objects of awareness. Anything beyond our range of immediate awareness is ignored or "put in brackets" in the attempt to establish certainty, a primal move in this new science that Husserl called "phenomenological reduction." By excluding anything not "immanent" to consciousness, Husserl gave two things priority: human consciousness and pure phenomena.

By designating pure phenomena as the bracketed object of awareness, Husserl was not concerned with individual objects in time and space but rather with universal essences. The purity of phenomena resides in the unchanging and essential nature of things, not in their temporal forms. If he could establish the pure essence of phenomena, Husserl believed he could take philosophy "Back to the things themselves," away from the excessive abstraction of a purely conceptual knowledge. His aim was to develop a science of human consciousness that would reveal not merely particular knowledge but the timeless foundation of all knowledge. Like Kant before him, he strove to found a "transcendental" philosophy based on a "transcendental" subject. Phenomenological reduction thus concerned itself, for instance, not with the particular horse but with the "universal essence" of horses and the state of awareness necessary to perceive it.

## Phenomenology and literary criticism

Husserlian phenomenology as the basis for literary criticism has been criticized as a form of ideal abstraction detached from the world of concrete experience. It was considered an idealism or an intuitionism that speculated on the abstraction of consciousness rather than an empirical exploration of concrete existence. Terry Eagleton, for example, criticized phenomenology as an authoritarian theory based solely on intuition and the assumption that phenomena can be intended subjectively without having to be interpreted through reasoned argument. Nonetheless, phenomenology is one of the longest-standing philosophies of the twentieth century and has had a significant influence on literary criticism. Even the Russian Formalists and the New Critics of the first third of the twentieth century, like Husserl, "bracketed off" the world in order to focus on the act of knowing the text itself as an autonomous object. Phenomenological criticism and its derivatives strive to give a reading of a text as a manifestation of consciousness, whether the author's, the reader's, or a combination of the two. The Geneva School, for instance, tried to apprehend the unity of an author's consciousness as reflected in the unity of style, symbols, and patterns of imagery inherent in the text. Rather than investigating the author's biography, phenomenological critics would "bracket off" the real author and investigate the "deep structures" of the mind embodied by the work. These structures become the "content" of the work for the phenomenological critic, just as form becomes the "content" of a work for the Russian Formalists.

Historical and cultural critics accused the early phenomenological critics for their allegedly misguided attempt at a disinterested or objective reading of literature and for leading to a mere passive reception. As an essentialist, antihistorical approach, phenomenological criticism neglects the function of language and the power of cultural forces exerted on the critic. Particularly egregious for Marxist and postmodernist critics is that Husserl seemed to conceive of meaning as predating language, as a preordained idea directly knowable through language defined as a transparent window to a referent in the author's consciousness. But for Husserl consciousness consists of a relation between subject and object, or between "intentional acts" and "intentional objects." Consciousness is thus never pure but always culture-dependent, with each intention influencing the objects of perception according to the attitudes and interests embodied by the perceiver as part of a "horizon" of possibilities imposed by any given historical context.

The historical nature of meaning led Martin Heidegger, Husserl's most celebrated student, to elaborate on the interdependence of expectation and understanding in *Being and Time* (1927). Heidegger defines not only understanding but also human existence as a process of projection through which we anticipate future interpretations according to past experience. This anticipatory structure of interpreting the raw data of experience strongly influenced later phenomenological critics, particularly Hans-Georg Gadamer and Paul Ricœur who developed a method of reading and interpretation known as hermeneutic phenomenology.

With his own hermeneutical (interpretive) phenomenology, Heidegger broke with Husserl's transcendental phenomenology. He insisted on the irreducible historical context or "givenness" of human existence, which in *Being and Time* he called *Dasein*, or "being-there." Heidegger thus substituted his mentor's emphasis on consciousness with a form of existentialism, an emphasis on the experience of being-in-the-world. He tried to decenter the human subject, arguing that we are not really transcendent or dominant in relation to the world but rather culturally constructed products. Because of our conditioning or "preunderstanding," we are never self-identical but always projecting ourselves into the future. This notion of difference or the lack of unity also extends to language, which always pre-exists the individual subject, an idea that parallels the later theories of structuralism and poststructuralism as developed by theorists such as Roland Barthes and Jacques Derrida.

In *Phenomenology of Perception* (1945) the existential phenomenologist Maurice Merleau-Ponty rejects Heidegger's later notion of consciousness as transcendental and instead situates it in the body and sensory experience. Because consciousness is incarnate, our perceptions are largely determined by the social and political pressures of our historical context. Roman Ingarden, the Polish founder of phenomenological aesthetics who also disclaimed the notion of a transcendental consciousness, developed a theory of art as intersubjective and stratified. Regarding the opposition of the real and imaginary, Ingarden argues that a literary work does not lead an autonomous existence but depends on the intentional acts of both author and readers, which give the work an intersubjective life with a historical origin. The work both depends on and transcends the consciousnesses of author and readers. On the one hand, a work as an "aesthetic object" needs to be concretized by readers. On the other hand, a work consists of four strata – sounds, meaning, narrative viewpoint, and referent – which extend "horizontally" in time; thus any particular act of reading, which is by definition a temporal process, can only be a partial actualization of a work's strata. The reader assesses a work through a set of pre-understandings, beliefs, and expectations which in turn are modified in the process of reading, which becomes a hermeneutic circle – a move from a whole which is simultaneously part of another whole, or a contexts within contexts, and so on. Reading is thus not a straightforward and cumulative affair but a complex process of shifting inferences, anticipations, and revisions.

Wolfgang Iser, who is classified both as a reader-response critic and a reception theorist of the Constance School, speaks of the techniques and conventions or "codes" of literary works and the "strategies" needed to interpret them, a view he develops in *The Act of Reading* (1978). We need to interpret a work according to its codes, but these codes lend themselves to a variety of interpretations, each of which is valid provided it is internally coherent. For reception theorists like Iser and Gadamer the work consists of textual indeterminacies or gaps that the reader must normalize or fill. The work in turn interrogates the reader and usually "disconfirms" preconceptions in a manner parallel to the defamiliarization of Russian Formalism, thereby leading the reader from the book to a deeper self-awareness. Readers have a greater degree of freedom in actualizing a text in reception theory than they do for Ingarden, who believed that textual indeterminacies were intentional and had to be concretized correctly. But even for Iser the polyphonic potential of a work's pluralistic meaning had to be contained to preserve the reader as a unified subject. Later structuralist and poststructuralist critics like Roland Barthes and Jacques Derrida accept the radical indeterminacy of texts and reject the notion of a unified reading subject.

In Iser's approach, as distinct from Russian Formalism, New Criticism, structuralism, and poststructuralism, the critic's task is not to interpret the text as an object, but rather to explain its effects on the reader: "The phenomenological theory of art lays full stress on the idea that, in considering a literary work, one must take into account not only the actual text but also, and in equal measure, the actions involved in responding to that text." In this way reader-response criticism and reception theory constitute a reaction against formalism. Iser subdivides the term reader into "implied reader" and "actual reader." The implied reader is the reader created by the text as "a network of response-inviting structures" that predispose the actual reader to interpret the text in a particular way. The actual reader's response, however, will also be affected by the sum total of his or her real-life experience. Thus reading involves an ongoing interaction between the implied and actual readers. The expectations of the actual reader are continually adjusted according to the response-inviting structures of the text, a process in which our memory of the characters and events in the story interact with our own extra-textual experience and with the evolving story itself.

The text, moreover, embodies certain values and norms that interact with each other implicitly and that the reader must concretize. These suggested norms or concepts of reality can only be actualized into a work of literature by the reader who explicitly fills in the textual blanks or gaps.

In "Interaction Between Text and Reader," Iser defines communication in literature as

> a process set in motion and regulated, not by a given code, but by a mutually restrictive and magnifying interaction between the explicit and the implicit, between revelation and concealment. What is concealed spurs the reader into action, but this action is also controlled by what is revealed . . . the blank in the fictional text induces and guides the reader's constitutive activity. . . . The reader fills in the blank in the text, thereby bringing about a referential field; the blank arising in turn out of the referential field is filled in by way of the theme-and-background structure; and the vacancy arising from juxtaposed themes and backgrounds is occupied by the reader's standpoint, from which the various reciprocal transformations lead to the emergence of the aesthetic object.

Which then has greater power in the construction of meaning, the text itself or the reader filling in the blanks? Iser sides ultimately with phenomenology, allowing greater sway to the reader's experience of filling in the text's partial indeterminacies. Yet by engaging the reader into concretizing its blanks, the text wields the power to modify the reader's world-view through an expansion of consciousness.

In the late 1960s the German reception theorist Hans Robert Jauss added a historical perspective to reader-oriented criticism. He attempted to find a compromise between theories that ignore history and those that ignore the text by integrating text, history, and reader. Jauss used the notion of "paradigm shifts" developed by Thomas Kuhn in *The Structure of Scientific Revolutions* (1970). When a new paradigm or scientific model challenges an older paradigm whose concepts begin to prove inadequate or contradictory, then a paradigm shift occurs in which new assumptions are established, as in the shift from Newtonian to quantum physics. Similarly Jauss uses the phase "horizon of expectations" to describe how the criteria that readers use to judge a work shift over time. Literature and interpretation exist within a particular horizon. As the critical horizon changes, so does the interpretation of a work. The meaning of a work therefore is not universal or fixed but constantly shifting as the criteria brought to bear on it undergo transformation during the course of history. Readers of different historical periods would interpret a work differently, and the total meaning of a work would have to take into account the accumulation of all reader responses – ultimately an impossible task. The question then arises which meaning of a work would have the greatest authority, that of its original context and first interpretation, that of the present, or a combination of the two?

Jauss finds his answer through the philosophical hermeneutics of Hans-Georg Gadamer, who argued that past literature must be interpreted through a dialogue between past and present, a fusion of horizons. Our understanding of the past will depend on our present world-view, the horizon or paradigm of expectations that constitute our cultural context. Since we cannot know the past directly but only through our present perspective, our knowledge of the past comprises a fusion of past and present. The ordinary gap between subject and object in this way diminishes, for the past work continues to live in the present though the reader's consciousness. The difficulty in a fusion of horizons, however, is that in deriving a hermeneutics (interpretation) of totality the critic is tempted to skew the accumulation of past readings of a work in favor of an emerging totality most relevant to the critic's own perspective.

In *Readings and Feelings: An Introduction to Subjective Criticism* (1977), the American critic David Bleich takes a psychoanalytic approach to the text/reader question. He practices a "subjective criticism" that sees literary interpretation as a formulation of the critic's personal desires and expectations which are projected or "discovered" in a work. By establishing a psychological connection between the quest for self-knowledge and the interpretation of a text, Bleich resolves the text/reader question like Iser on the side of the reader. But if the reader is in control, then the text seems intrinsically undefined and excessively blank. The American critic Norman Holland, also taking a psychoanalytic approach, tries to hold on to the text in resolving the text/reader question by maintaining a connection between the text and the reader's personal associations. In *5 Readers Reading* (1975), he asserts that the reader must be responding to something in the text more than "marks on the page," at least a network of possibilities for the reader to psychologically actualize, but again he resolves the text/reader issue in the reader's favor. But the text has its defenders. In *Validity of Interpretation* (1967), the American hermeneuticist E. D. Hirsch, Jr., following Husserlian phenomenology, argues that the inherent system of expectations in a work may allow a number of different interpretations. But these are valid mainly as the work's "significance" and do not replace the author's "meaning" inherent in the text.

The American reader-oriented critic Stanley Fish tries to avoid the ambiguities of the text/reader question, though with doubtful success. He developed an approach called "affective stylistics" that resembles Iser's criticism in emphasizing the adjustments caused in the reader's expectations by the reading process. But unlike Iser, Fish focuses more on individual sentences and their immediate, local effect on the reader's interpretation. He argues that literary and nonliterary language are the same, as in their use of tropes, and can thus be approached with the same strategies. In analyzing John Milton's *Variorum* (variant texts), for instance, Fish contends that the sentence, "Nor did they not perceive the evil plight," cannot be read as equivalent to "they perceived the evil plight," for the double negative suspends the reader between shades of meaning that require an adjustment of expectation and interpretation. He considered the best reader for his affective stylistics to be an "informed reader" who had the "linguistic competence" necessary to understand a work. He himself epitomized this linguistic competence in his own interpretations, but these became accounts not of reading per se but of his own idiosyncratic readings. In *Is There a Text in This Class?* (1980), Fish expands his approach to include the idea of "interpretive communities" who apply similar strategies of reading. But such communities seem to undermine the possibility of unique interpretations such as Fish's own reading of Milton. Fish has been faulted for not resolving the text/reader question but only deferring it, since his conceptions of "interpretive communities" and "competence" are themselves open to interpretation and thus problematic. Nevertheless, even without a systematic theoretical framework, Fish has been an influential reader-response critic.

Although phenomenological and reader-oriented criticism have been unable to resolve the text/reader question, they have still been remarkably influential and productive. Their major accomplishment has been to argue effectively against formalist approaches to literature by defining interpretation as an active process that engages the reader. Through phenomenological criticism, literature has been redefined in terms of reading, which is no longer seen as a static event whose outcome is solely determined by the text. Instead the phenomenological experience of the creative and interpretative acts can be described in terms of a series of contexts within contexts. For Husserl consciousness is culture-dependent regardless of its mysterious source. The whole of the author's consciousness is simultaneously part of a cultural (or wider interior) whole, which is part of a social (or exterior) whole, in an ever expanding series of wholes that are parts of other wholes – or "holons," to use a term coined by Arthur Koestler. Phenomenological criticism validates the author's primal holon as part of another whole, the artwork itself, which mediates between the consciousness of author and reader. The reader engages in a similar process in the interpretive act, which begins with the reader's consciousness and extends through ever widening contexts toward the author's consciousness, via texts, history, and the horizon of expectations. In exploring the links between these interrelated contexts, reader-oriented criticism has permanently changed the definition of literature. As Jonathan Culler puts it, "the 'literariness' of literature may lie in the tension of the interaction between the linguistic material and readers' conventional expectations of what literature is."

## Further reading
Booth, Wayne C. *The Rhetoric of Fiction*, 1961.
Chatman, Seymour. *Narrative Structure in Fiction and Film*, 1978.

Detweiler, Robert. *Story, Sign, and Self: Phenomenology and Structuralism as Literary Critical Methods*, 1978.

Eagleton, Terry. *Literary Theory: An Introduction*, 1983.

Falk, Eugene H. *The Poetics of Roman Ingarden*, 1981.

Forman, Robert K. C., ed. *The Innate Capacity: Mysticism, Psychology, and Philosophy*, 1998.

Halliburton, David. *Poetic Thinking: An Approach to Heidegger*, 1981.

Ihde, Don. *Hermeneutic Phenomenology: The Philosophy of Paul Ricœur*, 1971.

Landgrebe, Ludwig. *The Phenomenology of Edmund Husserl*, 1981. Edited by Donn Welton.

Lee, Edward N., and Maurice Mandelbaum, eds. *Phenomenology and Existentialism*, 1967.

Madison, Gary Brent Madison. *The Phenomenology of Merleau-Ponty: A Search for the Limits of Consciousness*, 1981.

Magliola, Robert. *Phenomenology and Literature: An Introduction*, 1977.

Nagel, Thomas. *A View from Nowhere*, 1986.

Palmer, Richard E. *Hermeneutics: Interpretation Theory in Schleiermacher, Dilthey, Heidegger, and Gadamer*, 1969.

Ricœur, Paul. *Husserl: An Analysis of His Phenomenology*, 1967.

Searle, John R. *The Mystery of Consciousness*, 1997.

Spiegelberg, Herbert. *The Phenomenological Movement: A Historical Introduction*, 1976 (second edition).

Tompkins, Jane P., ed. *Reader-Response Criticism: From Formalism to Post-Structuralism*, 1980.

Wilber, Ken. *The Eye of Spirit*, 1998.

WILLIAM S. HANEY II

*See also* Geneva School; Heidegger; Miller; Poulet; Ricœur

# Luigi Pirandello

Italian playwright and writer

**Born:** Girgenti, Italy; June 28, 1867
**Died:** Rome, Italy; December 10, 1936

## Biography

Luigi Pirandello was the second of the six children of Stephano Pirandello and Caterina Ricci Gramitto Pirandello. He went to universities in Rome and in Bonn, Germany, where he wrote his thesis on the Sicilian dialect of his native Girgenti (now Agrigento) and earned his doctorate in Romance philology in 1891. In 1894 he married Antonietta Portulano and took up residence in Rome, where their three children were born. The flooding of his father's sulphur mines in 1903 made Pirandello dependent on his teaching job at the Magistero, where he taught from 1897 to 1922. His wife suffered her first major breakdown in 1903 as a result of the financial disaster, and Pirandello insisted on caring for her despite her condition, later diagnosed as paranoid schizophrenia. Not until 1919 was Antonietta committed to an institution, where she died forty years later.

While Pirandello's novel *Il fu Mattia Pascal* (1904; *The Late Mattia Pascal*, 1923) brought him fame, he was in his forties before he gave dramatic embodiment to human illusion which, for him, constituted reality. His fame as playwright was established with Rome and Paris productions of *Sei personaggi in cerca d'autore* (1921; *Six Characters in Search of an Author*, 1922) in 1921 and 1923, and with the Milan production of *Enrico IV* (1922; *Henry IV*, 1923) in the intervening year.

Pirandello's political heritage, his temperament, and his own experience were all factors in his approach to politics. In 1924 he became a supporter of Benito Mussolini, and, sponsored by state subsidies for his Teatro d'Arte di Roma, he and his company toured England, France, Germany, Austria, and South America from 1925 to 1928. He believed in Italian Fascism as some kind of patriotic myth, and he emphatically believed that politics had nothing to do with art.

Pirandello was awarded the Nobel Prize for Literature in 1934. He died in 1936, and his insistence on the simplest of funerals was honored, even though Il Duce was outraged at the lost opportunity for a huge state funeral. There was no ceremony, and Pirandello's body was taken in a pauper's hearse to be cremated. Nevertheless, Pirandello had the last word: he had arranged that his signature be the first on his own funeral register.

## Influence

It is Pirandello's plays for which he is internationally famous. As Pirandellian and theater scholars have argued, Pirandello's influence on twentieth-century drama is manifest in such diverse playwrights as Jean Anouilh, Jean-Paul Sartre, Albert Camus, Samuel Beckett, Eugene O'Neill, Harold Pinter, Edward Albee, and Tom Stoppard. Pirandello's examination of reality, of art and illusion, and his theatrical innovations have affected experimental theater around the world. His principal essay, *L'umorismo* (1908, 1920; *Humor*, 1974) is important for an understanding of his plays, which continue to yield new insight with every examination.

As a theorist, Pirandello is important because his ideas provide insight into his theater, which remains enigmatic and powerful, and because, as Frederick May suggests, his fiction and his plays aesthetically coincide with the relativistic theories of modern science and modern philosophy. Pirandello is not, however, known primarily as a theorist; his fame rests on his achievements as a dramatist.

## Analysis

In all his writings Pirandello is invariably concerned with the problems of human identity, of reality, of art and illusion. He is no solipsist, even though he does not believe in any objective reality. For Pirandello, reality is completely subjective and illusory, and the idea that the subjectivity of any individual necessarily coincides with the subjective realities of other individuals is an illusion. He does not believe that only the self is real when the identity of the self exists in varying forms, or masks, only in relation to others – however unknowable their respective realities may be. The self would exist in a void, without identity or knowledge of itself, if it were not for the identities it assumes in relation to others. Ultimately, the human psyche is unknowable, and all that can be known about the identity of the self is the mask or masks assumed by that self.

Each person wears many masks, and constantly shifts masks as he or she progresses through time. Hence, the mask, or the way the self appears to others, is all that others can know of the self. If appearance is the only knowable reality, that reality is constantly changing. Each person seeks to establish a mask that is both pleasing and accepted by others. The consistency of any mask, however, is undermined by the changes wrought by time; therefore, no living individual can achieve coherent form. Nevertheless, as the self seeks to achieve form and consistency in the flux of living, so the artist seeks to impose form and order on the chaos of human experience.

It is not surprising, then, that Pirandello focuses in his work on character, on the perceptions of his characters. Like human beings, Pirandello's characters think because they feel and feel because they think. Human anguish derives from the conflict between differing perceptions of reality. Since the self cannot escape the pressure of others' perceptions, it dons masks, or roles, which may not be as false as they are fleeting. These masks conceal the self not only from others but from itself: the self lives in constant fear of exposure by others and of inadvertent self-discovery. The multiple roles played by every individual make manifest the multiplicity of human personality. This multiplicity and the fluidity of experience preclude any consistency to the roles or masks that are assumed for others. Hence, identity can never be verified. Because there is no way of verifying the human reality with which Pirandello is concerned, identity is an ongoing paradox.

In *Humor*, Pirandello presents his image of the humorist, who studies this enigma. The humorist perceives humor differently from the comic writer, the ironist, or the satirist – none of whom experiences the feelings of the opposite. For the comic writer, the perception of the opposite (*avvertimento del contrario*) leads only to laughter, and the comic writer, like the ironist and the satirist, is not concerned with the feelings or motivations of either the perceived or the perceiver. Ironists would cease to exist if they identified with their implied opposites. Satirists, in presenting their perception of the opposite, the discrepancy between what is and what should be, are moved probably by indignation and certainly by a sense of distance and superiority, as are the ironists. The Humorists, however, recognize themselves in what initially appears to be opposite, and thus their perception of the opposite is followed by a feeling of the opposite (*sentimento del contrario*). The humorist knows that "the condition of a man who is constantly somewhat off key, who is like a violin and double bass at the same time; of a man in which a thought cannot originate without the opposite or contrary thought originating at the same time, . . . is a condition which, in its very abnormality, can only be bitterly comic."

Aware of the conflicting facets of every situation, the humorist is characterized by a dual perception which results both in laughter followed by empathy and in constant reversals. Given a hero, humorists will render the unheroic; pomp, and they will perceive the irreverent; the trivial, and they will elucidate the significant. Thus, the conception of the humoristic artist is inevitably double and multiform, involving different, seemingly contradictory views.

For Pirandello, art has reality which life cannot provide: a character can achieve an immortality which no living person can ever hope to achieve. Art, however, must deal with life: "art, like all ideal or illusory constructions, also tends to fix life: it fixes it in one moment or in various given moments." Acutely aware that each moment yields to successive moments and that this flow, both of time and of consciousness which is outside time, constitutes human life, Pirandello argues that art must concern itself with the multiplicity of human masks. Each must be presented as it is perceived and as it seeks acceptance of its own self-created significance. The simultaneity of presentation, perception, and acceptance of human illusion can be accomplished only in the theater.

Pirandello's method of characterization is opposed to traditional methods. Where others create character by accumulating details and information until a coherent personality is revealed, Pirandello offers no more coherence of personality in art than he perceives there to be in life. Typically, he offers one image of a character and then proceeds to other images or masks. Whether his plays are located in a villa or on the stage itself, the world presented is not that of everyday reality; it is the world of the humorist conceived and presented in terms of the mask, the mirror, and *construirsi* or the building up of character.

While the humorist insists on the abyss between appearance and reality, the humorist as dramatist can insist that appearance is reality, that each character appear in the guise of a specific mask. The mask must be perceived by the audience as either true or false, acceptable or not acceptable, and only through the drama does the audience discover that each mask conceals other masks or forms. Humorists are the only ones whose dual vision allows them to penetrate the masks and to perceive the nakedness both of the characters, or phantasms, and of human beings, who also cloak themselves in theatrical illusions. Hence we have Pirandello's title for his plays, *maschere nudi*, or "naked masks." Clearly, his view of artists and their art is inseparable from his view of life.

In 1908 Pirandello's essay *Humor* sparked a neverending battle between him and Benedetto Croce, the Italian philosopher whose journal, *La critica*, contains his reviews of Pirandello's work from 1909 to 1935. Croce accused

Pirandello of neither creating art nor formulating philosophy. He argued that Pirandello's dramaturgy consisted of sleight-of-hand sophistries which had no substance. He denied any validity to Pirandello's concept of humor because it was not presented systematically, and he failed to comprehend Pirandello's emphasis on aesthetic technique. The two men never understood each other, and their dispute was continued after their deaths by their supporters. Critics may still reveal their attitude toward Pirandello's ideas and work by their stance on the Pirandello / Croce feud.

Pirandello has been misunderstood by the critics who praise him as well as by those who damn him, in spite of the overwhelming recognition of the importance of his work. His work has been damned as philosophical, as dealing only with ideas and with characters who are either abstractions or spokesmen for their author. While Pirandello emphatically objected to any overly intellectual approach to his plays, he accepted the praise of Adriano Tilgher and endorsed Tilgher's analysis in terms of dichotomies. Tilgher's influence on Pirandello's later plays remains a matter of controversy, but there is no question about the international impact of Pirandello's early and greatest plays, *Six Characters in Search of an Author* and *Henry IV*.

These two plays are the proper subject of books and lengthy essays, but even a brief examination reveals the humorist at work. The paradox of identity is central to both plays. The masks worn by the *dramatis personae* both limit and yet fail to define their identities, for as Eric Bentley stresses, the truth is always concealed in Pirandello's plays. If the struggle is within the protagonist in *Henry IV*, in *Six Characters in Search of an Author* the struggle is between the Characters and their surrogate author, the Stage Manager. The audience is given the Characters who have their own realities, the Actors who portray the realities of others, the Stage Manager, and Madame Pace, who is neither Character nor Actor. Once the audience accepts the forms presented, various questions must be confronted: do the Characters want an author? or does each Character, in particular the Father and the Stepdaughter, want his or her view of reality to be accepted by others to the exclusion of other views? and why did their author abandon the Characters? The question of what is art and what is reality is inescapable: if the Characters are fixed forever in a certain period of their lives, what exactly can one know about them? The Father and the Stepdaughter have quite different perceptions which they want others to accept.

*Henry IV* presents a character who has assumed the identity of the eleventh-century German emperor Henry IV. Fixed in his mind for twelve years at the moment when he fell from his horse while masquerading as Henry IV, "Henry" has been lucid for eight of the twenty years that he has been confined as insane – when he is visited by those from the past who want to know if he has been cured.

"Henry" must choose whether to remain in his known role from the past or to enter a moving world from which he has been absent for twenty years. In his passion as a sane man, "Henry" commits murder and forgoes any future participation in the unknown chaos of living.

Pirandello has repeatedly been accused of pessimism. Robert Brustein, for example, who maintains that twentieth-century theater would be totally different if it were not for Pirandello, describes his philosophy as unrelentingly pessimistic. Certainly, there can be no doubt that Pirandello was alienated from the world around him or that he typifies the alienation of the twentieth century. He is, however, most clearly perceived as an absurdist. As Pirandello hypothesizes toward the end of *Humor*, it is conceivable that Prometheus might finally have realized that the enormous Jupiter whom he has been battling is, in fact, an immense shadow cast by his own light; he might have realized that Jupiter would cease to exist if he extinguished this light, but he will not and he cannot do so without himself ceasing to exist. So it is with humorists who cannot cease focusing on the shadow or phantasm which would not exist if it were not for their light. So it is with each individual who will continue to see darkness only because he or she has light.

In his book on the influence of Pirandello on French theater, Thomas Bishop argues that "besides Pirandello, only Shakespeare and Ibsen have left such a legacy, and it is unlikely that either has affected the theater of a single country of any one era more than the author of *Sei personaggi*." Pirandello's theory of the humorist as manifested in his plays may have struck some of his contemporaries as bizarre, but it revolutionized the theater. His theory of human reality and his presentation of all the shattered realities of the past were crucial to the development of twentieth-century drama.

## Principal criticism
*Arte e scienza*, 1908
*L'umorismo*, 1908, revised 1920 (*Humor*, partial translation 1966, complete translation 1974)

## Other major works and literary forms
Luigi Pirandello was an extraordinarily prolific writer; he began writing poetry as a youth. His complete works, including *novelle* or short stories (many of which are quite long), seven novels, and forty-four plays, amount to some ten thousand pages. He planned to write three hundred and sixty-five stories, one for each day of the year, and the first volume of a fifteen-volume series, *Novelle per un anno*, appeared in 1922. The plays of his late career frequently derive from his earlier fiction.

NOVELS
*L'esclusa*, 1901 (*The Outcast*, 1925)
*Il turno*, 1902 (*The Merry-Go-Round of Love*, 1964)
*Il fu Mattia Pascal*, 1904 (*The Late Mattia Pascal*, 1923)

*Suo marito*, 1911
*I vecchi e i giovani*, 1913 (*The Old and the Young*, 1928)
*Si gira*, 1916 (*Shoot! The Notebooks of Serafino Gubbio, Cinematograph Operator*, 1926)
*Uno, nessuno, centomila*, 1925 (*One, None, and a Hundred Thousand*, 1933)

SHORT FICTION

*Amori senza amore*, 1894
*Beffe della morte e della vita*, 1902
*Quando'ero matàto*, 1902
*Bianche e nere*, 1904
*Erma bifronte*, 1906
*La vita nuda*, 1910
*Terzetti*, 1912
*Le due maschere*, 1914
*Erba del nostro orto*, 1915
*La trappola*, 1915
*E domani, lunedi*, 1917
*Un cavallo nella luna*, 1915
*Berecche e la guerra*, 1919
*Il carnevale dei morti*, 1919
*Novelle per un anno*, 1922–1937 (15 volumes)
*A Horse in the Moon and Twelve Short Stories*, 1932
*"Better Think Twice About It!" and Twelve Other Stories*, 1933
*"The Naked Truth" and Eleven Other Stories*, 1934
*Four Tales*, 1939
*"The Medals" and Other Stories*, 1939
*Short Stories*, 1959
*"The Merry-Go-Round of Love" and Selected Stories*, 1964
*Selected Stories*, 1964
*Short Stories*, 1964
*The Oil Jar and Other Stories*, 1995

PLAYS

*La morsa*, in Sicilian as *L'epilogo*, 1898, in French 1910 (*The Vise*, 1928)
*Scamandro*, 1909
*Lumìe di Sicilia*, 1910 (*Sicilian Limes*, 1921)
*Il dovere del medico*, 1912 (*The Doctor's Duty*, 1928)
*Se non così . . .*, 1915
*All'uscita*, 1916 (*At the Gate*, 1928)
*Liolà*, 1916 (English translation, 1952)
*Pensaci, Giacomino!*, 1916
*Il berretto a sonagli*, 1917 (*Cap and Bells*, 1957)
*Così è (se vi pare)*, 1917 (*Right You Are (If You Think So)*, 1952)
*La giara*, 1917 (*The Jar*, 1928)
*Il piacere dell'onestà*, 1917 (*The Pleasure of Honesty*, 1923)
*Il giuoco delle parti*, 1918 (*The Rules of the Game*, 1959)
*Ma non è una cosa seria*, 1918
*La patente*, 1918 (*The License*, 1964)
*L'innesto*, 1919
*L'uomo, la bestia, e la virtù*, 1919
*Come prima, meglio di prima*, 1920
*La Signora Morli, una e due*, 1920
*Tutto per bene*, 1920 (*All for the Best*, 1960)
*Sei personaggi in cerca d'autore*, 1921 (*Six Characters in Search of an Author*, 1922)
*Enrico IV*, 1922 (*Henry IV*, 1923)
*L'imbecille*, 1922 (*The Imbecile*, 1928)
*Vestire gli ignudi*, 1922 (*Naked*, 1924)
*L'altro figlio*, 1923 (*The House with the Column*, 1928)
*L'uomo dal fiore in bocca*, 1923 (*The Man with the Flower in His Mouth*, 1928)
*La vita che ti diedi*, 1923 (*The Life I Gave You*, 1959)

*Ciascuno a suo modo*, 1924 (*Each in His Own Way*, 1924)
*Sagra del Signore della nave*, 1924 (*Our Lord of the Ship*, 1928)
*Diana e la Tuda*, 1926 (*Diana and Tudo*, 1950)
*L'amica della mogli*, 1927 (*The Wives' Friend*, 1949)
*Bellavita*, 1927 (English translation, 1964)
*La nuova colonia*, 1928 (*The New Colony*, 1958)
*Lazzaro*, 1929 (*Lazarus*, 1952)
*O di uno o di nessuno*, 1929
*Sogno (ma forse no)*, 1929 (*I'm Dreaming, But Am I?*, 1964)
*Come tu mi vuoi*, 1930 (*As You Desire Me*, 1931)
*Questa sera si recita a soggetto*, 1930 (*Tonight We Improvise*, 1932)
*I giganti della montagna*, 1931–1937 (*The Mountain Giants*, 1958)
*Trovarsi*, 1932 (*To Find Oneself*, 1943)
*Quando si è qualcuno*, 1933 (*When Someone Is Somebody*, 1958)
*Maschere nudi*, 1933–1938 (*Naked Masks: Five Plays*, 1952, Eric Bentley, editor)
*La favola del figlio cambiato*, 1934
*Non si sa come*, 1934 (*No One Know How*, 1960)
*Collected Plays*, 1987–1996 (English translation, 4 volumes)

POETRY

*Mal giocondo*, 1889
*Pasqua di Gea*, 1891
*Pier Gudrò*, 1894
*Elegie renane*, 1895
*Elegie romane*, 1896
*Scamandro*, 1909 (dramatic poem)
*Fuori de chiave*, 1912

NONFICTION

*Pirandello's Love Letters to Marta Abba*, 1994

MISCELLANEOUS

*Opere*, 1966

## Further reading

Bishop, Thomas. *Pirandello and the French Theater*, 1960.
Büdel, Oscar. *Pirandello*, 1966.
Cambon, Glauco, ed. *Pirandello: A Collection of Critical Essays*, 1967.
Caputi, Anthony Francis. *Pirandello and the Crisis of Modern Consciousness*, 1988.
Cincotta, Madeleine Strong. *Luigi Pirandello: The Humorous Existentialist*, 1989.
DiGaetani, John Luis, ed. *A Companion to Pirandello Studies*, 1991.
Giudice, Gaspare. *Pirandello: A Biography*, 1975.
Matthaei, Renate. *Luigi Pirandello*, 1973. Translated by Simon and Erika Young.
Oliver, Roger W. *Dreams of Passion: The Theater of Luigi Pirandello*, 1979.
Paolucci, Anne. *Pirandello's Theater: The Recovery of the Modern Stage for Dramatic Art*, 1974.
Ragusa, Olga. *Luigi Pirandello*, 1980.
Starkie, Walter. *Luigi Pirandello, 1867–1936*, 1965.
Vecchio-Musti, Manlio Lo. *Bibliografia di Pirandello*, 1952.
Vittorini, Domenico. *The Drama of Luigi Pirandello*, 1935.

CAROL BISHOP

*See also* Bergson; Croce

# Dmitrii Pisarev

Russian critic

**Born:** Znamenskoe, Russia; October 2, 1840
**Died:** Dubbelna, Russia; July 4, 1868

## Biography

Dmitrii Pisarev was born on October 2, 1840, to a cultured gentry family of modest means. His background thus differed from many of his fellow radicals and the *raznochintsy* (people of various ranks); the two other most prominent radical critics of his generation, Nikolai Chernyshevskii and Nikolai Dobroliubov, were both the sons of priests and received their initial education at seminaries. Pisarev instead was sent by his family to St. Petersburg to attend a Gymnasium, and in 1856 he entered the history and literature department of the university there. By early 1859 he was writing reviews for *Rassvet* (dawn), a journal for educated young women. The opportunity to express his ideas in print inspired Pisarev to select and describe works that would edify his readers.

While still a student, during the latter part of 1859 and early 1860, Pisarev suffered what today would be called a nervous breakdown; it was brought on by a combination of overwork and unrequited love. He was hospitalized for several months but recovered sufficiently to complete his studies. Immediately upon his graduation from the university in 1861, he became a major contributor to *Russkoe slovo* (the Russian word), a onetime moderate journal that under the new leadership of Grigorii Blagosvetlov came to rival *Sovremennik* (the contemporary) as a center for radical thought.

In 1862 he wrote a rejoinder to an anti-Herzen pamphlet written by a czarist police agent, who used the pseudonym Shedo-Ferroti. When Pisarev's work, which openly called for the overthrow of the monarchy, was discovered by the police among the papers of the person who had solicited it, Pisarev was arrested and incarcerated in the Peter and Paul Fortress. Unlike Chernyshevskii, however, he was not exiled, and within a year he managed to resume his literary career from prison. He was pardoned only after four and a half years, and as a result, the most significant essays of his truncated career were written while he was in jail.

During this time a bitter polemic broke out between *Sovremennik* and Pisarev's *Russkoe slovo*, with each journal claiming to be the true heir to Chernyshevskii's legacy. Pisarev took a leading part in the controversy, but by the time of his release, his physical and spiritual health had suffered. Both *Sovremennik* and *Russkoe slovo* had been closed by the authorities. He began to publish in Blagosvetlov's new journal, *Delo* (the deed), but soon broke with his old ally and began an association with another journal that was under the control of Nikolai Nekrasov and other former staff members of *Sovremennik* – his erstwhile rivals. Pisarev's difficult situation was not helped by his close collaboration with Maria Vilinskaia-Markovich (who published under the name Marko Vovchok); once again he appears to have become involved in a one-way romantic relationship. When he drowned on July 4, 1868, at the age of twenty-seven, while swimming by himself at a seaside resort, many of his contemporaries suspected that his death was a suicide.

## Influence

After the untimely death of Dobroliubov in 1861 and the arrest of Chernyshevskii in 1862, Pisarev, although himself jailed for some time, emerged as the leading radical critic of his day. While his significant deviations from the positions of Vissarion Belinskii and Chernyshevskii, along with the extreme opinions that he often expressed on aesthetic questions, were partly responsible for a severe feud among the radicals, his arguments were well received by many of the writers and critics of his day. In particular, his call for a socially and politically relevant literature as well as his concentration on the psychological makeup of the literary figures he analyzed found echoes among his contemporaries. The idiosyncrasy of certain theoretical statements, however, eventually caused the Populist and then the Marxist critics to look toward the other radicals of the 1850s and 1860s for inspiration. During the Soviet era it became fashionable to regard Pisarev as a curiosity – a critic with some good intentions, but whose formulations often represented a step "backward" from the ideas of his older contemporaries. To some extent even within the Soviet Union and to a greater degree since its demise, however, the originality and verve of his approach, to say nothing of his innate literary taste and skill as a stylist, have continued to prove attractive.

## Analysis

It is not easy to fit Pisarev into a critical school. On the one hand, his materialism and positivism, combined with his radical political views, would seem to make him a natural successor to Chernyshevskii and Dobroliubov. On the other, he quarreled violently with many of their closest followers and, even while borrowing much from both men, differed from them on key issues. Pisarev, it must be said at the outset, enjoyed making extreme and even outrageous statements, which in many cases were actually out of keeping with the main position he was taking in his essays. The more quotable passages, however, remained in the popular imagination. More substantially, he was more of an iconoclast than his older contemporaries. Thus many radical critics condemned Ivan Turgenev's *Ottsy i deti* (1862; *Fathers and Sons*, 1867), seeing in Bazarov, the novel's chief figure, a parody of Dobroliubov or Chernyshevskii or both. Pisarev, however, liked the character. He listed the traits that might repel most readers:

Thus Bazarov, everywhere and in everything, does only what he wishes or what seems to him to be advantageous or convenient. He is ruled only by his whims or his personal calculations. Neither over himself, nor outside himself, nor within himself does he recognize a moderator, a moral law or principle.

To Pisarev these qualities simply indicate the extent to which Bazarov stands above his contemporaries; in any case, they are more than offset by Bazarov's sincerity, his intelligence, and the correctness of his beliefs. If most radicals recoiled from the term "nihilist" (the term used by Turgenev to describe Bazarov and his ilk), then Pisarev embraced it. The notion of a person who would accept nothing as given, who was given to pure empiricism and an unquestioned faith in science, had great appeal to him.

Pisarev's fellow radicals were also frequently taken aback by his almost cheerful willingness to hold positions that seemed contradictory. He was, for example, a strong believer in individualism and in the independent development of the self, but at times he also came out as a determinist, one who holds that the needs of society specify the ways in which people should act. At one point he said about Bazarov that "his desire to live for his pleasure was stronger than his desire to be consistent." The same would seem to have been true of Pisarev, who wrote copiously and rapidly (in many cases his first draft was also his last) and who was apparently not greatly bothered by changes in his own beliefs or by statements that contradicted earlier assertions even within the same article.

As with the other radical critics, Pisarev's attitudes toward literature owe much to his readings in philosophy. Unlike the others, however, he had little interest in G. W. F. Hegel, even as a figure against whom to react, and he was not influenced by Ludwig Andreas Feuerbach's materialism. Instead the main inspiration came from such popularizers as Karl Vogt and Ludwig Büchner, who saw humanity's development as crudely determined by its biological or physiological essence – significantly, Bazarov recommends Büchner's *Kraft und Stoff* (1855; *Force and Matter*, 1870) in Turgenev's novel. Pisarev's consequent interest in natural science and positivism was furthered by the historical writings of Henry Buckle and by Charles Darwin's *On the Origin of Species*, which to Pisarev offered a neat biological explanation for humanity's development.

Having associated science with progress, Pisarev came to exalt what he called critical thinking and "realism." The concrete and the empirical were of positive value to him, while he rejected all that was abstract or vague – what he called "aesthetic" in his essay "Realisty" (1864; "The Realists", 1965).

What we like unaccountably, we like only because we have grown accustomed to it. If this unaccountable sympathy is not justified by the judgment of our critical thinking, then evidently it is impeding our intellectual development. . . . If aesthetic feeling prevails we shall take a step backwards, toward the reign of routine, intellectual impotence, harm, and darkness.

As Pisarev's critics have remarked, his use of terms such as "aesthetic" was often imprecise and malleable. Yet the word clearly had a certain set of associations for him. In a related essay, "Razrushenie estetiki" (1865; the destruction of aesthetics), he provided a commentary to Chernyshevskii's *Esteticheskie otnosheniia iskusstva k deistvitel'nosti* (1855; the aesthetic relationship of art to reality). An important part of Chernyshevskii's argument was the claim that beauty in art can never equal the beauty in nature; thus, he defined what might be called a "realistic aesthetics." Pisarev contended that since each individual has a particular concept of the beautiful, no objective criterion for this category exists. Hence he claimed that there can be no basis for a theory of aesthetics at all. The implications for art are clear: if beauty cannot be defined, then works are to be discussed only in terms of their content, not their form or structure. If a work's value rests primarily or entirely on its supposed aesthetic qualities, it has no place in Pisarev's canon. He went on to express a decided utilitarianism: for an artistic work to be good, it must be useful, in the sense of benefiting a broad range of society.

For all of his talk of society's needs, though, Pisarev never lost sight of the individual, and in his practical criticism he was constantly drawn to strong figures, such as Bazarov. Like Chernyshevskii, Pisarev believed that all people are egoists, but he distinguished between good and bad egoists. For him an aesthete's egoism is self-centered and unrestrained; the realist's egoism is rational, calculating, and ultimately for the good of society. Yet Pisarev did not want external restraints. Hence in one of his earliest essays, "Idealizm Platona" (1861; "Plato's Idealism," 1958), he attacked Plato's view of the state as ultimately authoritarian, claiming that his political writings showed "no respect for the individual" and placed the citizen "under humiliating restraints."

Given Pisarev's dislike of the purely aesthetic and his call for a utilitarian art, his rejection of many acknowledged classics is not surprising. He was particularly hard on Russian writers, at one time saying that even the best of Russian writers were only embryonic poets. Typically, within the same essay ("The Realists"), he finally did praise a handful of writers, including Nikolai Gogol', Nekrasov, Aleksei Pisemskii, and Fedor Dostoevskii. Like the other radical critics, Pisarev preferred Gogol', whom he saw as a realistic writer, over Pushkin. Nevertheless, he went far beyond the others in denigrating Pushkin's significance for Russian literature; in "Pushkin i Belinskii" (1865; Pushkin and Belinskii), he singled out Gogol', rather than Pushkin, as the founder of modern Russian literature. Pisarev even attacked Belinskii for exaggerating Pushkin's role in Russian literary history.

The phrase "Boots are more significant than Shakespeare" came to be widely ascribed to Pisarev. As it turns out, however, the words were not his: the saying derives from some parodic comments in Dostoevskii's works. The association is, however, indicative of Pisarev's reputation. Yet for all of his attacks on aesthetics, he greatly admired those whom he recognized as titans (he saw no middle ground): William Shakespeare, Dante, Lord Byron, Johann Wolfgang von Goethe, Heinrich Heine, among others. To some degree, Pisarev's demands for literature (though not necessarily his specific preferences) coincided with those later expressed by Lev Tolstoi. Good form may be necessary, but it is not sufficient or even important by itself; literature must be engaged and must help people progress toward a better life.

Pisarev's influence on his contemporaries appears first of all in his insistence that literature deal accurately and insightfully with matters that are of broad contemporary importance. His criteria for realism and accuracy were sufficiently strict that he often disagreed with his fellow radicals. Thus he took issue with Dobroliubov's praise of Katerina in Aleksandr Ostrovskii's play *Groza* (1859; *The Storm*, 1899). To Pisarev she was hardly the optimistic figure that Dobroliubov portrayed, nor did he see much significance in her tragedy on any but the purely personal level. Similarly, he was unenthusiastic about Saltykov-Shchedrin's satire, in which he detected an absence of ideological direction. Since Pisarev was opposed to the reigning political and social order, he was inclined toward those writers who clearly expressed a negative view of contemporary Russian life. By this criterion he preferred Pisemskii to Turgenev, and Turgenev to Ivan Goncharov.

If Pisarev sometimes disagreed with Dobroliubov on specifics, he nevertheless helped solidify the trend of using literary works as an excuse for writing about social issues. Thus "Pogibshie i pogibaiushchie" (1866; the perished and the perishing) starts off as a review of Dostoevskii's *Zapiski iz mertvogo doma* (1861–1862; *The House of the Dead*, 1881) and goes on to provide a critique of Russia's seminaries, which are compared unfavorably to the prisons Dostoevskii describes. For all of his disinterest in questions of style and structure, Pisarev was capable of analyzing characters' psychological makeup in a manner that was sensitive and frequently penetrating; this interest too was reflected in the essays of other critics. Examples in his own writing include his descriptions of Turgenev's heroes in both "Bazarov" (1966) and "The Realists," as well as his comments on Dostoevskii's *Prestuplenie i nakazanie* (1866; *Crime and Punishment*, 1886) in "Bor'ba za zhizn'" (1867–1868; "A Contemporary View: 1867"). In the latter piece, too much emphasis may be put on the social cause of Raskolnikov's crime, but the character's self-deception and inner turmoil are captured.

Finally, Pisarev, like the other radical critics of his generation, helped make literature both less and more important than it was before. By placing science above literature and insisting on the "real" over the "aesthetic," Pisarev reduced art to the subservient roles of popularizing certain ideas and providing exposés of shortcomings in society. Yet when he talked of writers whom he admired – and he did admire some literature – Pisarev clearly believed that the "titans" possess a particularly profound understanding of life. In portraying that understanding and conveying it to others, the best writers can both inspire and direct human progress.

## Principal criticism
"Zhenskie tipy v romanakh i povestiakh Pisemskogo, Turgeneva i Goncharova," 1861
"Russkii Don-Kikhot," 1862 ("Russian Don Quixote," 1958)
"Tsvety nevinnogo iumora," 1864 ("Flowers of Harmless Humor," 1903)
"Motivy russkoi dramy," 1864
"Realisty," 1864 ("The Realists," 1965)
"Progulka po sadam rossiiskoi slovesnosti," 1865
"Pushkin i Belinskii," 1865
"Razrushenie estetiki," 1865
"Posmotrim!," 1865
"Mysliashchii proletariat," 1865 ("Thinking Proletariat," 1958)
"Pogibshie i pogibaiushchie," 1866
"Genrikh Geine," 1867 ("Heinrich Heine," 1958)
"Bor'ba za zhizn'," 1867–1868 ("A Contemporary View: 1867," 1961)
"Bazarov," 1966 (writtten 1862)

## Other major works and literary forms
While the great bulk of Dmitrii Pisarev's writing is concerned either directly or indirectly with literature, he also devoted essays to philosophical, social, and economic matters. In addition, his unquestioning faith in science's ability to answer all questions and to better the lot of humanity – as well as his belief that no endeavor was more important than the popularization of science – can be seen in his "Progress v mire zhivotnykh i rastenii" (1864; "Progress in the Animal and Vegetable Worlds," 1958), a piece that did much to introduce Charles Darwin's *On the Origin of Species* (1859) to a broad audience in Russia. In "Pchely" (1868; "Bees," 1958), Pisarev reworked an allegorical essay by Karl Vogt to create a sharp satire on Russian political and social institutions of the 1860s. Early in his career, Pisarev published "Nasha universitetskaia nauka" (1863; our academic learning), an attack on the Russian university system that is written in the form of a memoir and provides intriguing glimpses into his personal development and outlook.

NONFICTION
"Idealizm Platona," 1861 ("Plato's Idealism," 1958)
"Skholastika XIX veka," 1861 ("Nineteenth-century Scholasticism," 1958)
"Nasha universitetskaia nauka," 1863
"Progress v mire zhivotnykh i rastenii," 1864 ("Progress in the Animal and Vegetable Worlds," 1958)

"Pchely," 1868 (written 1862; "Bees," 1958)
"O broshiure Shedo-Ferroti," 1920 (written 1962; "Shedo-Ferroti's Pamphlet," 1958)
*Selected Philosophical, Social, and Political Essays,* 1958

## Further reading

Copleston, Frederick C. *Philosophy in Russia: From Herzen to Lenin and Berdyaev,* 1986.
Edie, James M., et al., eds. *Russian Philosophy.* Vol. 2, 1965.
Kuvakin, Valery A., ed. *A History of Russian Philosophy from the Tenth through the Twentieth Centuries* Vol. 1, 1994.
Lampert, Evgenii. *Sons Against Fathers: Studies in Russian Radicalism and Revolution,* 1965.
Masaryk, Thomas G. *The Spirit of Russia.* Vol. 2, 1955 (second edition).
Moser, Charles A. *Esthetics as Nightmare: Russian Literary Theory, 1855–1870,* 1989.
Pereira, N. G. O. "Challenging the Principle of Authority: The Polemic Between *Sovremennik* and *Russkoe Slovo,* 1863–65," in *The Russian Review.* XXXIV (1975), pp. 137–150.
Pereverzev, V. F. "Theoretical Premises of Pisarev's Criticism," in *Soviet Studies in Literature.* 22, nos. 2–3 (1986), pp. 36–53.
Pozefsky, Peter. "*Smoke* as 'Strange and sinister commentary on *Fathers and Sons,*'" in *The Russian Review.* LVII (1995), pp. 571–86.
Proctor, Thelwall. *Dostoevskij and the Belinskij School of Literary Criticism,* 1969.
Terras, Victor. *Belinskij and Russian Literary Criticism: The Heritage of Organic Aesthetics,* 1974.
Walicki, Andrzej. *A History of Russian Thought from the Enlightenment to Marxism,* 1979.

BARRY P. SCHERR

*See also* Belinskii; Chernyshevskii; Dobroliubov; Dostoevskii; Veselovskii

# Plato

## Greek philosopher

**Born:** Athens, Greece; c. 427 B.C.
**Died:** Athens, Greece; 347 B.C.

## Biography

Plato was born in Athens around 427 B.C., the son of aristocrats Ariston and Perictione. Because he came from a wealthy family, Plato received a thorough education; in his youth, he is said to have written verse and even tragedy. He formed a strong attachment to the philosopher Socrates, and his growing dissatisfaction with political participation reached a peak when Athens put Socrates to death in 399 B.C., on charges of corrupting the youth and introducing new gods to the city. Shortly after his mentor's death, Plato left Athens and visited Egypt, Cyrene, southern Italy, and Sicily. It was during these years away from Athens that he wrote his early dialogues, including the *Apologia Socratis* (*Apology*), the *Protagoras,* the *Ion,* and the *Gorgias.* In

Sicily, Plato met the tyrant Dionysius I, then at the height of his power, and also Dionysius' young brother-in-law Dion, with whom he formed a lifelong friendship.

In 387 B.C. Plato returned to Athens and founded his school, the Academy. This middle period saw the production of Plato's most important work, the *Republic,* and also the *Symposium,* the *Cratylus,* and the *Phaedrus.* When Dionysius I of Syracuse was succeeded by his son, Dionysius II, Dion wrote to Plato, and in 366 B.C. Plato returned to Syracuse, probably intending to follow up the theories of the *Republic* with political action and experimentation. The realities of court intrigue intervened, however, and soon Dion was exiled and Plato returned to Athens, where he wrote the *Sophist* and the *Politicus* (*Statesman*). In 361 B.C. Dion sent a trireme to Athens to bring Plato back to Syracuse to intercede for him with Dionysius. Things did not go well, however, and Plato was relieved to be allowed to return to Athens in 360 B.C. In 357 B.C. Dion raised an army, seized Syracuse, and forced Dionysius to flee; he ruled for four years before a conspiracy led by Callipus, one of Plato's students, toppled his regime and killed Dion, causing Plato great sorrow. Plato devoted the last part of his life to teaching in the Academy and to his last dialogues, including the *Laws.* He died in 347 B.C.

## Influence

Because his literary criticism is preceded in Greek literature only by occasional comments from poets and philosophers, literary criticism and theory in the West are rightly said to begin with Plato's discussions of rhetoric and poetry. His student Aristotle responded to Plato's work with two systematic treatises, *De poetica* (c. 334–323 B.C.; *Poetics*) and *Technē rhetorikēs* (c. 334–323 B.C.; *Rhetoric*), showing far less concern than his mentor with the ethical and social aspects of poetry and rhetoric and more interest in the details of composition. Of the major Roman critics who followed, virtually all show the influence of Plato in choice of subject and in content. The Neo-Platonic period of the third through fifth centuries A.D., under the influence of figures such as Plotinus and Porphyry, saw the writing of commentaries on Plato's works and an application of Platonic principles in commentaries on other literary texts. The European High Renaissance of the sixteenth and seventeenth centuries was marked by a resurgence of interest in Platonic thought, especially in the educational function of poetry and in theories of inspiration and imitation. Plato's ideas of inspiration and literary symbolism continued to be influential in the nineteenth and twentieth centuries, not only in literary criticism, but also in the work of such poets as William Blake, Percy Bysshe Shelley, William Butler Yeats, and Wallace Stevens.

## Analysis

Plato's views on literary criticism and theory are presented not in straightforward, systematic treatises but in complex dramatic dialogues which aim to shed light on the issues through dialectical discussion. The dialogues, which center on Plato's teacher, Socrates, pose difficulties for the scholar who seeks to extrapolate from them a consistent notion of Plato's ideas. There is casual movement from one topic to another, and literary topics are considered secondary to wider discussions of ethics, politics, and morality; Plato uses irony, often very subtly, which can mislead the reader, and the dialogues seldom issue in clear statements and conclusions. The reader must examine a series of dialogues, written over a period of time, and grapple with apparent inconsistencies in order to discover Plato's views on a particular topic.

In his dialogues, Plato treats both rhetoric and poetry. The primary discussions of rhetoric are found in the *Cratylus*, the *Protagoras*, the *Gorgias*, and the *Phaedrus*. Plato intimates his own views of rhetoric both by having his characters speak about it in a theoretical way and by having them give speeches exemplifying certain rhetorical styles. The *Cratylus* deals with a relatively minor branch of rhetoric, the study of etymology and the origin of language, which was in Plato's day still in its infancy. The sophist Hermogenes maintains that names in a language are merely conventional and may be changed at will; the philosopher Cratylus believes that names are natural and true. Amid a playful series of absurd etymologies, Socrates gives a view intermediate between those of his fellow interlocutors: that language is a rational act, giving expression to real differences between things.

In the *Protagoras*, the title character, a famous sophist, is asked to explain the purpose of his teaching. His reply, that he plans to educate Hippocrates (the student presently before him) in politics and citizenship, leads to the central question of the dialogue: can virtue be taught? Socrates is doubtful, and Protagoras responds with a fable of the origin of humanity which purports to illustrate the teachability of virtue. Socrates' cross-examination moves toward the concept of the unity of all separate virtues. After a brief digression on Simonides, Socrates returns to the unity of virtues, asserting to a now skeptical Protagoras that virtue, which he identifies with knowledge, must be teachable. Although the speakers have reversed their original positions, the dialogue produces no definitive results, and it is agreed that the inquiry must be taken up again at a later time. An interesting aspect of the dialogue is its presentation of the sophistic style of rhetoric through Protagoras' speeches; there is also the ridicule of Prodicus' etymological studies during the discussion of Simonides. Plato's ear for rhetorical style and his ability to parody thus aid in his presentation of rhetorical theory.

The *Gorgias* continues the debate between Socrates and the sophists, in greater depth and in a more complex dramatic structure. Here the rhetorical inquiry is interlaced with a broader discussion of the moral basis of politics. The dialogue consists of three conversations, the first of

which is between Socrates and the famous orator Gorgias. It begins in a manner reminiscent of the earlier, aporetic dialogues, with a question – what is rhetoric about? – to which various answers are suggested and then shown by Socrates to be inadequate. Socrates eventually determines that rhetoric is a manufacturer of conviction involving belief, but not absolute knowledge, concerning right and wrong. Gorgias attempts to turn this into an advantage: the rhetorician therefore has greater influence than trained experts, and the ability to speak allows the individual to compete with experts from all fields. Yet if the speaker has no real knowledge of matters such as justice, how can he act with moral correctness? Gorgias says that he will teach his student to discern between right and wrong, but this conflicts with his earlier statement that rhetoric is morally neutral, and a teacher cannot be held responsible for the abuse of rhetoric by his students. Somewhat befuddled, Gorgias retires from the discussion, and his place is taken by his student, Polus.

In the conversation with Polus, who had published a treatise on rhetoric, Socrates presents a theory of the arts or skills (*technai*) which tend to the health of the body and the soul: for each of the genuine arts (such as medicine or lawmaking) there is a corresponding counterfeit, a type of flattery or cajolery (such as cooking or rhetoric). Clearly, rhetoric fares poorly in this scheme. Polus' heated assertion, in response, of the great power wielded by the rhetorician leads to a discussion of the opposition of might and right, and on into the wider issues of justice and happiness. Socrates' paradoxical statements, that committing injustice is worse than suffering it and that the unjust person is less unhappy if he or she is punished, lead to an extremely ironic conclusion about the advantages of rhetoric: that it can be employed to serve one's self-interest by bringing about one's own punishment and also by preventing one's enemies from being punished, thus ensuring their unhappiness.

With the entrance of Callicles, Socrates' third opponent, the conflict between rhetoric and philosophy sharpens. Callicles is a typical Athenian democrat, intensely practical, who promotes a "natural justice" whereby one follows one's own instinctive desires, obeying only the law of nature and equating "good" with "pleasurable." In his view, rhetoric is the best road to power and the surest guarantor of personal safety in a democracy. Socrates counters with a dialectical proof that good cannot be equated with pleasure. He returns to his theory of arts, now adding tragedy to the "counterfeit" category occupied by rhetoric and cooking, since this medium aims at the gratification of mass audiences. Thrusting at the heart of Callicles' views, Socrates proves next that true happiness depends upon temperance and self-control rather than the gratification of one's desires. The best self-defense in life, he adds, is against one's own commission of injustice. Trained practitioners, whose own lives are in order, are needed to direct the improvement of their fellow citizens. Socrates argues that Athens has never produced a true statesman, with the sole exception of himself, but he refuses Callicles' urgings that he serve the state in the conventional political manner and avoid unpopularity. This part of the dialogue is ominous, hinting strongly at the future danger to Socrates (the dramatic date of the dialogue is 405 B.C., six years before Socrates' execution). Socrates' moral philosophy prevails here over the false rhetoric of the politician Callicles, but the wider issue of the relationship between the philosopher and the state has not been exhausted, and Plato will return to it in the *Republic*.

Plato's inquiries into the nature and use of rhetoric culminated in the *Phaedrus*, where the discussion of rhetoric plays against an unlikely partner, an examination of Eros (love). Socrates meets Phaedrus, who has just heard a speech by the famous orator Lysias on why it is better for a young boy to yield to a nonlover than to a lover. From a written manuscript Phaedrus reproduces the speech, which is banal, repetitive, and disorganized, a good example of false rhetoric. (Other examples of false rhetoric are offered in the earlier dialogue, the *Symposium*, in the ornamental speech of Pausanias and the extravagant, mannered style of Agathon.) Socrates is then induced to treat the theme himself, and he offers a conventional speech in which the inevitable points are made, but better organization and an initial definition of Eros mark it as an improvement over Lysias' speech. Socrates, however, almost immediately regrets the exercise – he has blasphemed a great god – and prepares to embark on a recantation. In this, his second speech, Socrates praises Eros as a form of divine madness, closely related to the inspired areas of prophecy, poetry, and mysticism. The speech also contains a famous metaphor wherein the soul is compared to a charioteer driving two winged horses: when the impure part of the soul is sufficiently controlled by the better part, the soul flies toward eternity, where it glimpses Reality. Socrates enumerates a hierarchy of souls, arranged according to how much Reality has been glimpsed; seekers of wisdom and lovers top the list, while poets are sixth and sophists ninth, followed only by tyrants.

Socrates' second speech in the *Phaedrus* is followed by a discussion of rhetoric, which begins with Socrates' statement that writing and speaking are not intrinsically shameful, though doing them badly is. The interlocutors turn to establishing criteria for good and bad writing and speaking. Phaedrus puts forth the conventional idea, attributed to Gorgias in the *Gorgias*, that a speaker need not have real knowledge of his subject as long as he seems to his audience to have it. Socrates proves by dialectic that even successful deceit requires true knowledge of how things resemble and differ from one another, and attempts to persuade and influence souls must be predicated on an understanding of different types of souls. He also offers more concrete advice on the composition of speeches: the writer must define his subject, and the speech needs a definite structure with every part in its proper place. Turning back to his own two speeches on Eros, with their opposing conclusions, Socrates explains the method he calls dialectic, with its two components, collection and analysis. A discussion of fifth-century orators, along with a review of the relevant technical terms and devices, demonstrates the inferiority of conventional rhetoric. The true art of rhetoric requires the outlook and method of philosophy; orators, and even poets, if their compositions are based on truth, are worthy to be called philosophers. A final important point is the superiority of the spoken word, when it includes dialectic, to the written. The *Phaedrus* shows that rhetoric and philosophy, which oppose one another in the *Protagoras* and the *Gorgias*, need not be adversaries at all, if rhetoricians will acquire the true knowledge of philosophy.

Plato's dialogues also exhibit apparently conflicting attitudes toward poetry. A recurring theme is the idea that poets are inspired by god and Muse, so that aspects of their work cannot be accounted for rationally. While often filled with beauty, poetry is basically emotional rather than rational, and herein lie its dangers. This idea, which appears briefly in the *Apology*, is considered at greater length in the *Ion*, where Socrates punctures the claims of a self-confident rhapsode that poets and their interpreters are able to teach the arts of life. These claims are misplaced, Socrates demonstrates, because Ion's ability, like that of the poets, is not art (*technē*), but a product of divine inspiration. This inspiration cannot be called knowledge; furthermore, it actively excludes knowledge. In the *Phaedrus*, Plato returns to the subject of inspiration during Socrates' second speech about Eros: here a distinction is made between two types of madness, that which stems from mortal maladies and that which arises from supernatural release from the conventions of life. Poetic inspiration is classed among the latter. Paradoxically, the poet ranks low in the hierarchy of souls that Socrates proposes subsequently. Perhaps Plato's apparently inconsistent attitude toward poetic inspiration results from a consideration of different types of poetry, or a distinction between good and bad poetry.

In the *Republic*, Plato explores the role of poetry in an ideal political system: is exposure to poetry, especially dramatic poetry, desirable in the ideal republic? The question occurs initially in books 2 and 3, in which Socrates discusses the education of the guardians of his proposed state. Censorship guidelines are suggested, especially for the mythological stories told to the young. Stories which are ugly and immoral must be eliminated; writers must show divine nature as always good and responsible only for good; the gods must not be shown changing, using magic or illusions, or telling lies; poets must speak well of the afterlife. Furthermore, heroes should not be shown lamenting, the stories must value truth and self-control, and excessive laughter must be avoided. (Although some of these difficulties with mythological poetry traditionally are addressed by allegorical interpretations, Plato later – at the beginning of the *Phaedrus* – rejects this approach.)

Plato introduces the concept of *mimesis* (imitation), first using it in the sense of an actor or a speaker playing a role. Such role-playing, Socrates warns, can cause psychological harm. Socrates classifies the genres of literature according to the degree of *mimesis* contained by each: comedy and tragedy are wholly dramatic, the dithyramb is strictly narrative, and other genres, especially epic, comprise some dramatic and some narrative elements. It is parenthetically noted that a single poet cannot write both tragedy and comedy – the same notion against which Socrates argues, at least in theory, at the close of the *Symposium*. Returning to the topic of the education of his guardians, Socrates now states that these individuals should only be allowed to play characters who are brave, religious, and self-controlled. Especially troubling are actors capable of playing a wide variety of roles; such players will be excluded from the ideal commonwealth.

The discussion now becomes technical, as it moves into the areas of meter, music, and rhythm. Much of this material is not accessible to the modern reader, but the main point is clear: a song consists of words, musical mode, and rhythm; the words must conform to the standards already established for literature in general, and the musical mode and rhythm must then be appropriate to these words. Musical modes that evoke undesirable emotions – dirges, for example – must be avoided, and the community will retain those musical modes which are congruent with courage, restraint, and temperance.

Socrates moves on to discuss the aim of education in all the arts, as well as in poetry and music. Good rhythm and good poetry go along with good character; excellence and grace of form and content in discourse, musical expression, and rhythm all depend on goodness of nature. Education should lead to insight into the "images" (Platonic forms) of moral and spiritual excellence. Poetry must express the "image" of noble character.

Book 10 presents a less optimistic view of the possible role of poetry in an ideal political system. Here Socrates discusses the long-standing quarrel between poetry and philosophy. One problem is the traditional hold which poetry, especially Homeric poetry, exercises over the Greek mind: many people consult these verses for advice in ethical and practical questions. Poetry is thus a rival of philosophy. There are other reasons that this slavish consulting of the poets is foolish: no one, not even a poet, can be expert in every area, and the fact that a poet can render a word-picture realistically does not imply an exhaustive knowledge of the phenomenon which is pictured. This notion of "realism" leads into a brief discussion of Platonic forms and to an attack on "realistic" art which is, in fact, far removed from reality because it represents semblance rather than truth. A bed is used as an example: there is the Platonic

ideal, or form, of bed; the carpenter's material bed; and finally, a painter's depiction of a material bed. Since only the form, bed, is real, and the carpenter's bed a mere imitation (*mimesis*, used in another sense), the painter's bed is twice removed from reality, an imitation of an imitation. In the same way, the poet produces unsubstantial images, like a person holding up a mirror to nature.

Dramatic poetry now comes under Plato's most serious attack: the idea is put forth that it must be excluded from the ideal commonwealth. Drama is especially deficient because it appeals to emotions rather than reason and is therefore more subject to illusions. Moreover, a truly temperate individual is unlikely to be presented on the tragic stage. Tragedy and comedy, by encouraging emotions to which one is normally ashamed to yield, ultimately undermine character. (Tragedy, according to the later *Philebus*, 360–347 B.C., is an especially emotional medium, since the viewer weeps and experiences enjoyment simultaneously.) Unless poetry can be adequately defended from these charges, it must be restricted in the ideal state to the praise of gods and heroes.

The ethical consideration of the arts is reprised in Plato's late work, the *Laws*. A few guidelines are set down – poetry must imitate the universal, and poetry will be subject to censorship – and the poets are readmitted to the ideal commonwealth. While the importance of arts in the formation of character remains a consideration, a new function is now added, that of cultural recreation to restore lost emotional balance. (Here Plato comes close to Aristotle's later ideas about tragedy's beneficial emotional catharsis.) Pleasure can be a criterion for judging the arts, but whose pleasure should it be? After discussing the preferences of various groups, the main speaker (designated as "an Athenian") concludes that one must consider the pleasure of an educated, virtuous few, rather than that of the mob. The proper judge of drama must be an instructor, not a disciple, of the theater, and people must praise only what they sincerely enjoy. Art is to be judged by these criteria: moral content and effect, pleasure given, and correctness of imitation.

In book 3 of the *Laws*, the speaker discusses the causes of decline in poetry, especially dramatic poetry. He looks back nostalgically at a period when the boundaries separating various genres and forms were clear and impassable. More recently, he notes, the genres have become confused, as the tastes of the masses are taken more into account. The result is a "theatrocracy," a "tyranny of the theater." The speaker wishes to strengthen the boundaries between genres and rule out excessive emotionalism. Specific decisions in the ideal state will be made by an officer in charge of education and a board of men who are more than fifty years old, who will select appropriate kinds of poetry and performance, leaning toward representations of the good life, praise of the gods, and other elevating topics. A later section refers very briefly to comedy, whose chief value is said to lie in articulating what is laughable so that the listener may avoid behaving in a ridiculous manner. Citizens, however, will keep their distance, and the writing and acting of comedies will be relegated to slaves and foreigners.

Plato's attitude toward literature is complex and ambivalent. Both rhetoric and poetry are powerful forces in the community, with great capacity to influence the minds of the young. For this reason Plato felt compelled to examine the proper role of poetry in society. While his attack on poetry in the *Republic* has given him the reputation of being hostile to literature, a careful reading of the *Phaedrus* and the *Laws* shows a deeper understanding and respect for both rhetoric and poetry; nor should the reader overlook the strong dramatic element in Plato's own works, the dramatic dialogues themselves. Plato raised the question of censorship, with which all subsequent societies have had to deal, but he did not come to a clear, unequivocal conclusion on the subject. His last comments on poetry, found in the *Laws*, restore balance to the discussion by returning to the notion of pleasure and reconsidering art as an integral and important part of life, but the moral content and effect of literary works remains a crucial criterion. Plato refused to consider literary criticism and theory separately from issues of ethics, politics, and morality; all are part of a single, seamless philosophical web.

## Principal criticism
Although Plato's individual works cannot be dated with exactness, there is consensus among scholars as to a four-period division (early, middle, later, and last). *Protagoras, Ion*, and *Gorgias* fall into the early period (399–390 B.C.)
*Cratylus, Symposium, Politeia (Republic)*, and *Phaedrus* are from the middle period (388–366 B.C.)
*Nomoi (Laws)* was written during the last period (360–347 B.C.)

## Other major works and literary forms
Including those listed above, the surviving work of Plato consists of about twenty-seven dialogues. (Others that have been attributed to him are now considered spurious.) There are also thirteen epistles, but, with exception of three or four, most of them are of doubtful authenticity.

NONFICTION
*Laches, Charmides, Euthyphro, Lysis, Hippias minor, Hippias maior, Apologia Socratis (Apology)*, all early period (399–390 B.C.)
*Meno, Euthydemus, Menexenus, Phaedo, Parmenides, Theaetetus*, all middle period (388–366 B.C.)
*Sophist, Politicus (Statesman)*, both later period (365–361 B.C.)
*Philebus, Timaeus, Critias*, all last period (360–347 B.C.). There are also thirteen epistles, of which only a few are considered authentic.

## Further reading
Atkins, John William Hey. *Literary Criticism in Antiquity: A Sketch of Its Development.* Vol. 1, 1934.
Else, Gerald F. *Plato and Aristotle on Poetry*, 1986.

Green, W. C. "Plato's View of Poetry," in *Harvard Studies in Classical Philology*. XXIX (1918), pp. 1–75.
Grube, G. M. A. *The Greek and Roman Critics*, 1965.
Hare, R. M. *Plato*, 1982.
Murdoch, Iris. *The Fire and the Sun: Why Plato Banished the Artists*, 1977.
Roberts, W. Rhys. *Greek Rhetoric and Literary Criticism*, 1963.
Ryle, Gilbert. *Plato's Progress*, 1966.
Tigerstedt, E. N. *Plato's Idea of Poetical Inspiration*, 1969.
Vicaire, Paul. *Platon: Critique littéraire*, 1960.

LAURA STONE BARNARD

*See also* Aristotle; Classical Greek and Roman Literary Theory

# Georgii Plekhanov
## Russian writer and theorist

**Born:** Gudalovka, Russia; December 11, 1856
**Died:** Terioki, Finland; May 30, 1918

## Biography
Georgii Plekhanov, the son of a minor nobleman, Valentin Plekhanov, graduated from the Voronezh Military Academy in 1873. After briefly attending the Konstaninovskoe Military School in St. Petersburg, he enrolled in the Mining Institute. The lure of political radicalism was too strong to resist, however, and in his second year Plekhanov left the institute to join the ranks of the revolutionaries. By 1876 he was a member of the Land and Freedom Party and working for a peasant, socialist revolution. He was arrested twice in the next two years. By 1879 he broke with the party, preferring agitation to violence and the urban worker to the peasant. He organized the short-lived Black Partition Party, but, fearing another arrest, he went abroad in 1880 and did not return to Russia until 1917.

While he was in exile, his contributions to political life were exclusively literary. Following three years of studying Marxist theory, he broke completely with revolutionary Populism by organizing the Liberation of Labor Party, which was designed to spread Marxist ideas among Russian workers. His parting with agrarian socialism was expressed in *Sotsializm i politicheskaia borba* (1883; political struggle).

Not until the mid-1890s did Plekhanov's movement attract a significant following. Meanwhile he wrote a major work, *In Defense of Materialism*, which Lenin said reared a whole generation of Russian Marxists. While still in exile in Geneva, Plekhanov urged his allies to link up with the working-class activists in 1898 to form the Russian Social Democratic Labor Party.

While representing Russian Social Democracy in the Second International, he launched a literary war against several heresies, including German revisionism, legal

Marxism, anarchism, and economism. In 1900 he helped to sponsor a party newspaper, *Iskra* (the spark). When differences of opinion emerged at the 1903 Party Congress, he parted with Lenin, joining L. Martov's Mensheviks. The revolutionary events of 1905 discredited Plekhanov's orthodox insistence on the revolutionary potential of the bourgeoisie and the passivity of the peasantry. Yet he clung to his former views, criticizing the Bolsheviks for seeking a premature seizure of power.

From 1906 to 1909 he tried to reunite the two wings of Russian social democracy without success. His goal was partly hampered by continued geographical separation from his colleagues but even more so by an inflexibility and arrogance which became accentuated in his middle age. Plekhanov scandalized his associates by supporting the Allied war efforts against Germany in a series of articles in the Paris-based *Prizyv*.

Surprised by the February Revolution that toppled the czar, he joyfully returned to Russia with his wife on March 31, 1917, after thirty-seven years in exile. He was welcomed by the revolutionary ranks and, unlike Lenin who returned days later, he supported the Provisional Government. He did not participate in government, however, but published articles promoting political unity and compromise. Not only did he aid the government of Aleksandr Kerenskii, he favored continued hostilities against Germany as well. He lost influence, however, among the masses, and Bolshevik guards harassed him as "an enemy of the people."

When his tuberculosis worsened, Plekhanov moved to Finland, where he died in a sanatorium in Terioki on May 30, 1918. His philosophical and historical contributions came to be highly respected in the Soviet Union.

## Influence

Although Plekhanov's primary influence was in radical politics (he founded the first Russian Marxist political party in 1883) and in philosophy (he was the first to use the expression "dialectical materialism"), he is also esteemed as the parent of Marxist literary criticism. Influenced by French historian Hippolyte Taine, Russian critic Vissarion Belinskii, and German philosopher Karl Marx, Plekhanov was the first Russian to interpret literature in terms of modern materialist philosophy. Unlike the Populist writer Nikolai Chernyshevskii and the followers of the Socialist Realist principles of the Stalin era, Plekhanov, despite his materialism, insisted on the autonomy of the artist. From 1917 to 1931 he was esteemed as the founder of Marxist aesthetics; he was denounced in the following year when his aesthetics were contrasted with those of Lenin. Since the cultural thaw of the 1950s his writings on art and literature have slowly become a popular alternative to the official cultural doctrine.

## Analysis

Although literary criticism occupied but a small part of Plekhanov's life, he was nevertheless the first to apply seriously the principles of dialectical materialism to art and literature. Upon his return from Geneva he wrote a series of critical pieces on literature in the 1880s. His subsequent return to political activism lasted until the 1905 revolution in his homeland. Despite his acknowledged intellectual brilliance, he no longer could lead. Perhaps that is why, after 1906, he turned his energies to writing *Art and Social Life*. Genuinely interested in aesthetics, Plekhanov warned that political control of artistic expressions would destroy creativity.

Plekhanov's starting point in literary criticism was the dialectical analysis of Marx. Art, literature, even human consciousness were but part of the superstructure of life, dependent upon the economic base, having no independent existence of their own. Differences in artistic inspiration were traced to the economic aspirations of different classes in society. When a social class became extinct so, too, did the aesthetics that were associated with that class.

Yet if such a view diminished the role of the man of letters, did it also diminish the role of the literary critic? Plekhanov responded that the roles were analogous. If the novelist or poet was constrained in his or her ideas by laws of social development, so, too, was the critic. There could be no thought of changing literary ideas, there was no reason for prescriptions; one could locate the good and the bad art but never urge what should be done.

Leon Trotskii once referred to Plekhanov as a Marxian Belinskii, a reference to the famed literary critic of the early nineteenth century. A relative of Belinskii on his mother's side, Plekhanov relied on Belinskii's insistence that artistic content was absolute truth in order to justify the importance of content as well as form. Such content, or truth, for Plekhanov was inseparable from beauty. Thus, when he found wanting a correct depiction of society in a literary work, he could claim a deficiency on aesthetic grounds.

Plekhanov saw as the principal task of a critic the need to reduce each work of literature to terminology understood by the sociologist – namely, the class basis of the work. Such an objective view could not lead to any condemnation of a school of art or literature, since each reflects the social and economic conditions of its society. To the extent that bourgeois artistic inspiration was directed against an outdated feudal order it could be beautiful; when used to sustain a bourgeois culture, it was false and unartistic.

Plekhanov found additional support not only in a few comments of Karl Marx but also in the writings of Taine, the French historian who maintained that the critic's task was to explain, not to disparage. To illustrate the extent to which aesthetic inclinations depend on economic conditions, Plekhanov refers to Chernyshevskii's often-cited example of the differing perceptions of feminine beauty on the part of noblemen and peasants. The heavy, robust peasant woman with a colorful complexion was bound to appeal to the muzhik who worked hard and admired strength. To this same muzhik, the society woman, on the other hand, was pallid and frail because she did not work hard enough each day to circulate her blood properly, hence her proclivity for headaches.

After identifying the class nature of a literary work, the second task of the critic is to evaluate the form. Here one can see that despite his assent to the ideological basis of literature, Plekhanov is not the father of Socialist Realism. That Soviet formula was composed in the 1930s and, although weakened by internal criticism for more than a generation, was still in force in the late 1980s. Socialist Realism judges artistic works primarily as they promote the practical goals of a developing Communist society. For Plekhanov, however, art must never be merely tendentious; truth and beauty must appeal to the audience apart from utilitarian concerns.

Although he quoted Friedrich Engels in support of his views on the independence of artistic inspiration, and although he was widely regarded until 1917 as the leading Russian theoretician of Marxian thought, Plekhanov's views on literature and art came to be regarded as dangerous and unsound. He confused some of his readers with his attempts to harmonize the Marxian analysis of literature as super-structure with his insistence on the autonomy of beauty and truth.

Plekhanov agreed with his ideological allies that the psychology of art was ultimately related to those productive or nonproductive elements in society that give rise to inspiration. Nevertheless, that inspiration was not crudely expressive of class interests and should even become independent of the economic base, however much it owed its origins to it. Although only a Marxist writer might hope to escape his critique of content, Plekhanov's contempt for state-directed art and his thoughts on the autonomy of beauty would later relegate his views on aesthetics to obscurity.

His frequent condemnation of tendentious literature was at the root of his hatred for state-directed artistic expression. Art, as superstructure, could only reflect – not generate – change, in Plekhanov's view. Not only were efforts to prescribe or propagandize feeble, they were un-Marxian as well. It was precisely his acceptance of Marxian laws of development that caused Plekhanov's split with Lenin on matters of aesthetics as well as of political revolution.

In his analysis of French literature of the seventeenth century, *Unaddressed Letters*, Plekhanov saw the elegance of classicism as the natural expression of absolute monarchy. In Taine he saw a kindred spirit when the Frenchman noted that great literature was simultaneous with great civilizations; it was no accident that Aeschylus, Sophocles, and Euripides wrote during the glories of ancient Athens and that Jean Racine, Molière, and Pierre Corneille emerged at the pinnacle of French power.

According to Plekhanov, Taine was correct when he saw that the literary influence of one society upon another was in direct proportion to the similarity of their social conditions. No influences result under dissimilar social conditions: French dramatists and English writers borrowed inspiration from one another during the seventeenth century, but the English could never fully imitate the French, whose milieu of royal absolutism was foreign to them. Similarly, the different social conditions of Rome ensured that Virgil's *Aeneid* (c. 29–19 B.C.) would be no mere copy of Homer's *Odyssey* (c. 800 B.C.); similarly, Racine's Achilles appeared naturally more like a French marquess than a Greek warrior.

Plekhanov shared with Taine the further thought that an artistic school disappears when that society disintegrates. Changes in human conditions bring changes in human conceptions. Plekhanov asks what causes the change in those conditions, believing that Taine was correct in noting that the state of mind flows from the social environment; it was left to Marx, however, to show why and how that environment first changes.

The reason classical values persist among the French and English in the revolutionary age of the next century is that the bourgeoisie saw opportunities to contrast the values of antiquity with those of the corrupt aristocrats of their own day, much as Tacitus, when praising the Germans, had used the inspiration of an earlier day to condemn the loss of values in Rome. When classicism became outdated after 1789, it quickly gave way to its Romantic successor.

When, in Plekhanov's own day, Romanticism was challenged by the supporters of the laboring classes' new social values, neither artistic inspiration nor social reconstruction was necessarily improved. Plekhanov found the utilitarianism of Chernyshevskii's novel, *Chto delat'?* (1863; *What Is to Be Done?*, c. 1863), bereft of beauty. The radical politics of the Populist writer N. I. Naumov were useful but lacking in artistic expression. Plekhanov saw the same flaw in Maksim Gor'kii's *Mat* (1906; *The Mother*, 1906), a novel more appropriate for the logician than for the writer of images. Plekhanov also criticized the Symbolist poets (Zinaida Gippius, Dmitrii Merezhkovskii, and Nikolai Minskii) for excessive individualism, creating for themselves a narrow society which denied the opportunity to see the world as it was.

Why was literature so barren of content in the late nineteenth century? In his essay on Henrik Ibsen, Plekhanov sympathized with the Norwegian dramatist's critique of petty bourgeois values but found his prescriptions vague and abstract. Indeed, he found this same shortcoming in most writers of his day. Yet he was compelled to admit that Lev Tolstoi's outdated feudal outlook was conveyed with beauty. Nikolai Gogol', Fedor Dostoevskii, and Tolstoi were all creative geniuses but nevertheless were mere children when addressing fundamental issues. Soviet critics detected an inconsistency here, asking whether false ideas can really convey beauty.

To those in the 1920s who wished to promote a progressive Socialist art, followers of Plekhanov responded that scientific criticism of literature revealed that the obligation of the writer was meaningless and irrelevant. For a decade Plekhanov's ideas on art reigned supreme, despite his Menshevik past and the passivity of his Marxian aesthetics. Even after the great industrial experiment began in 1928, when all segments of society were mobilized to win the battle on the economic front, Plekhanov's aesthetics remained popular. Supporters simply ignored the passivity of his approach or argued that critics such as Anatolii Lunacharskii exaggerated his ideas. Nevertheless, times and opinions were changing. By 1929 the voluntarist theories so essential to the success of the First Five-Year Plan challenged the passive, Menshevik-oriented notions in many fields and Plekhanov's ideas came under vigorous scrutiny. It was not until 1931, however, that his supporters were routed and his errors in art and literature enumerated. The triumph of voluntarism and unbridled utilitarianism was complete.

Plekhanov's own inconsistencies may have worked in his favor when the chief ideological arbiter of artistic expression, Andrei Zhdanov, initiated a modest revival of Plekhanov's aesthetic ideas after 1946. Plekhanov's annoyance with tendentious literature was lauded by the new generation of writers after Joseph Stalin's death in 1953, although his Menshevism was still unacceptable.

## Principal criticism
"Gleb I. Uspensky," 1888 (English translation, 1981)
"S. Karonin," 1890 (English translation, 1981)
Chapter 5 of *K voprosu o razvitii monisticheskogo vzgliada na istoriiu*, 1895 (*In Defense of Materialism: The Development of the Monist View of History*, 1947)
"N. I. Naumov," 1897 (English translation, 1981)
*Pisma bez adresa*, 1956 (written 1889–1900; *Unaddressed Letters*, 1957)

## Other major works and literary forms
Georgii Plekhanov is still regarded in the Soviet Union as the "father of Russian Marxism," and most of his writings are explications of that ideology. The twenty-four volumes of his *Sochineniia* (works) published in Moscow from 1923 to 1927 also include theoretical, practical, and polemical works on Marxist politics and economics, Party differences, and Russian history and philosophy. After 1903 he was an editor of the Social Democratic newspaper *Iskra* (the spark).

NONFICTION
*Sotsializm i politicheskaia borba*, 1883
*Ob agitatsii*, 1894
*Ocherki po istorii materializma*, 1896 (*Essays in the History of Materialism*, 1934)
*K voprosu o roli lichnosti v istorii*, 1898 (*Role of the Individual in History*, 1940)
*Vademecum*, 1900
*Osnovnye voprosy marksizma*, 1908 (*Fundamental Problems of Marxism*, 1929)
*Iskusstvo i obshchestvennaia zhizn'*, 1912–1913 (*Art and Social Life*, 1936)
*O voine*, 1915

*Istoriia russkoi obshchestvennoi mysli*, 1918 (*History of Russian Social Thought*, 1938)
*Sochineniia*, 1923–1927 (24 volumes)

## Further reading
Baron, Samuel H. *Plekhanov: The Father of Russian Marxism*, 1963.
——. "Plekhanov, Trotsky, and the Development of Soviet Historiography," in *Soviet Studies*. XXVI (July, 1974), pp. 380–395.
——. "The Resurrection of Plekhanovism in Soviet Historiography," in *Russian Review*. XXXIII (October, 1974), pp. 386–404.
——. *Plekhanov in Russian History and Soviet Historiography*, 1995.
Fomina, V. A. "The Struggle of Plekhanov Against Modernism in Art," in *Questions of Philosophy*. No. 3 (1951), pp. 105–111.
——. Introduction to *Georgy Plekhanov: Selected Philosophical Works*, 1974 (5 volumes).
Haimson, Leopold. *Russian Marxists and the Origins of Bolshevism*, 1954.
Reed, Christopher. *Religion, Revolution, and the Russian Revolution, 1900–1912*, 1980.
Rubin, Burton. "Plekhanov and Soviet Literary Criticism," in *American Slavic and East European Review*. XV (1956), pp. 527–542.
Steila, Daniela. *Genesis and Development of Plekhanov's Theory of Knowledge: A Marxist Between Anthropological Materialism and Physiology*, 1991.
Treadgold, Donald W. *Lenin and His Rivals: The Struggle for Russia's Future, 1898–1906*, 1955.
Wolfe, Bertram D. *Three Who Made a Revolution*, 1984.

JOHN D. WINDHAUSEN

*See also* Belinskii; Chernyshevskii; Lunacharskii

# Plot

"*Plot*" is an Anglo-Saxon word meaning originally a spot of ground. It is another form of "*plat*," closely related to "*plan*," meaning a design or scheme for the spot of ground, drawn on a flat surface. One meaning of the term evolving over time was, specifically, the design or scheme for a literary work.

The earliest formal discussion of plot in a literary sense was undertaken in the fourth century B.C. by Aristotle. In his *Poetics* (c. 334–323 B.C.), Aristotle declares that every tragedy (only the portion of the *Poetics* dealing with tragedy has survived) must have six parts: plot, character, diction, thought, scenery, and song. Aristotle then asserts that plot is the first and most important thing in tragedy. Until the twentieth century, plot – along with character, perhaps – retained this primacy.

Aristotle actually writes of the "fable" of the tragedy, by which he means its story or plot. His most famous observation is that every tragedy must be a whole; that is, the tragedy – its plot – must have a beginning, a middle, and an end. This deceptively simple analysis means the plot must begin with a situation containing the potential for conflict and thus drama, the middle must proceed organically from that beginning, and the resolution of conflict at the end must issue from the seeds found in the incidents of the middle. He is adamant that, as the complications must arise out of the plot itself, so must the unraveling of the plot. The unraveling should not be brought about by supernatural intervention.

In their theater, the ancient Greeks used some kind of car or conveyance to lower an actor portraying a god from the top of the skene (the façade behind the acting area) to the ground. This god often descended for the purpose of resolving the central conflict of the play. Even the very great playwright Euripides resorted to this device on several occasions. The term *deus ex machina* (god from a machine) has come to mean any coincidental or contrived resolution of the complications of the plot. Aristotle also argues that the episodic are the worst of all plots and actions. The reader must wonder, however, if Aristotle would have judged these episodic novels to be inferior works of art: *Don Quixote* (1605, 1616) by Miguel de Cervantes, *Tom Jones* (1749) by Henry Fielding, and *The Adventures of Huckleberry Finn* (1884) by Mark Twain.

Some critics have drawn a distinction between the terms story and plot. The novelist E. M. Forster wrote that a story is "a narrative of events in their time-sequence. A *plot* is also a narrative of events, the emphasis falling on causality."

The form of the traditional plot has six elements, as follows. (1) Point of attack – the most propitious moment to introduce setting, character, and conflict. One possibility is *in medias res*, beginning the action in the middle of things. Since this was the practice of the epic poet Homer, it has been widely imitated. (2) Exposition – a setting forth of who the characters are and what has happened before the beginning of the work. (3) Rising action – usually a series of conflicts facing the protagonist, each more difficult to resolve than the one preceding it. (4) Climax – the point at which the protagonist faces the central conflict, the turning point, the highest point of interest. (5) Falling action – incidents necessary to the narrative but occurring after the turning point. (6) Dénouement – (literally, an "untying") the explanation or outcome of the action.

Until the twentieth century, writers ordinarily arranged the incidents of the plot in chronological order. Occasionally, the forward movement of the narrative would be interrupted by a flashback, the portrayal of some earlier episode. Conversely, an incident would sometimes foreshadow later developments in the narrative. Still, the basic arrangement of the incidents was sequential in time.

By the end of the nineteenth century, however, some fiction writers, for example Joseph Conrad, were experimenting with plots that, rather than proceeding in a straight chronological fashion, moved backward and forward in time. A master of this technique in American literature was

William Faulkner. His 1930 short story "A Rose for Emily" serves as an excellent example. The story begins on the day of Miss Emily Grierson's funeral. Miss Emily, the protagonist, has died at the age of seventy-four. The second scene flashes back to her middle age. The third scene flashes back another thirty years to a time only two years after her father's death. Then the narrative moves backward again to events of the three days following his death. Only at this point does the plot begin to move – fitfully – forward in time, through more of Miss Emily's youth and middle age. Part V of the story returns to the day of the funeral, by which time exposition and foreshadowing have helped to prepare the reader for the shocking conclusion. The author's technique elaborates his theme, that the past is always a part of the present. In his longer works, Faulkner uses chronology even more imaginatively.

Throughout the twentieth century, James Joyce, Virginia Woolf, Ernest Hemingway, and many later writers of "literary" fiction progressively stressed character and style – particularly style – over plot. In fact, there was a decided reaction against the traditionally constructed plot as described above. The fashion for the "stream of consciousness" technique, tracing the mind's random associations and private symbolism, produced narratives that were often fascinating and puzzling in equal measure. Eventually, some writers abandoned plot altogether, arguing that since life does not consist of carefully constructed plots, plotted fiction and drama misrepresent human life rather than point up its truths. A group of French writers led by the novelist and screenwriter Alain Robbe-Grillet feel obliged only to provide the raw material for a novel. The novelist and the reader, they say, create the novel together, each bringing his or her own personality, experiences, and biases to the task. Therefore, every novel is many novels, as various as are its readers. In Robbe-Grillet's novel *Topologie d'une cité fantôme* (1976; *Topology of a Phantom City*, 1977), the central dramatic incident, as well as every character, major or peripheral, is thoroughly ambiguous.

Another twentieth-century movement has been called "magic realism." A work so designated has a firm plot, but the reality of the plot is invaded by the supernatural, dream, myth, or fantasy. Often, key questions are never answered, or key identifications are never made. Some practitioners in the Americas are John Barth, Bernard Malamud, and Thomas Pynchon (United States), Jorge Luis Borges (Argentina), and Gabriel García Márquez (Colombia). In Britain, John Fowles, Martin Amis, and Salman Rushdie employ such plots in their fiction, as do Harold Pinter and Tom Stoppard in their plays and screenplays.

Yet, in the realm of "popular" fiction – adventure, romance, mystery, fantasy, horror – the traditional plot continues to be the central element in the novel, short story, or drama, and shows no sign of relinquishing that dominant role, the role which Aristotle originally ascribed to it.

## Further reading

Aristotle. *Poetics.*

Booth, Wayne C. *The Rhetoric of Fiction,* 1961.

Brooks, Peter. *Reading for the Plot: Design and Intention in Narrative,* 1984.

Chatman, Seymour. *Story and Discourse: Narrative Structure in Fiction and Film,* 1980.

Cooper, Lane. *The Poetics of Aristotle, Its Meaning and Influence,* 1963.

Forster, E. M. *Aspects of the Novel,* 1927.

Goodman, Paul. *The Structure of Literature,* 1962.

Levin, Richard Louis. *The Multiple Plot in English Renaissance Drama,* 1971.

Polti, Georges. *The Thirty-six Dramatic Situations,* 1940.

Young, James Nicholas. *101 Plots Used and Abused,* 1961.

PATRICK ADCOCK

*See also* Aristotle; Narratology

# Plotinus

## Greco-Roman philosopher

**Born:** Lycopolis, Egypt; A.D. 205
**Died:** Campania, Italy; A.D. 270

## Biography

Plotinus was probably born in Lycopolis in Upper Egypt. Some scholars think that he may have been a Hellenized Egyptian, but most see him as thoroughly Greek, both the product and the exponent of Greek thought. Porphyry begins his *Plotini vita* (A.D. 303; *Life of Plotinus,* 1917) with the words "Plotinus seemed ashamed of having a body," and this reveals the reason information about him is so meager. Plotinus, who cared little about his body's biography, could never be cajoled into telling of his ancestry, early life, or education. Scholars have learned that in his twenty-eighth year he became interested in philosophy and went to Alexandria to attend the lectures of some eminent teachers, all of whom he found uninspiring. His enthusiasm was fueled, however, when a friend took him to hear Ammonius Saccas, a former Christian who had somehow reconciled the teachings of Plato and Aristotle. Plotinus found in Ammonius the man for whom he had been looking, and he became Ammonius' student for eleven years.

In 243 Plotinus, hoping to learn something about Oriental philosophies, joined the Persian expedition of the Roman emperor Gordianus III. Before Plotinus could meet any Eastern sages, Gordianus was murdered by mutinous soldiers in Mesopotamia. Plotinus made his way to Antioch and then to Rome, where he settled at the age of forty. He made his living there by teaching, and by the time Porphyry made his acquaintance in 263, Plotinus had achieved some renown. He arbitrated several disputes without alienating either side, and many of his friends, when they were near death, appointed him guardian of their children. As a result, his house was full of young boys and girls, whose education he conscientiously monitored. Among his many admirers was Emperor Gallienus, whom Plotinus failed to persuade to found a Platonic community in an ancient Pythagorean site in Campania.

Plotinus' Roman years were filled with teaching, writing, and controversy. He abhorred the views of the Gnostics, a heretical Christian sect that thought salvation could be attained only by a certain few whose esoteric knowledge allowed them to transcend matter. He wrote a vigorous attack against their beliefs, and, through Porphyry, organized a campaign against them. During his last years, Plotinus suffered from a debilitating illness that some have identified as tuberculosis and others as leprosy. The sickness caused his friends to avoid his company, and he retired to a country estate near Minturnae in Campania. His physician was with him when he died in 270. His last words, "I am striving to give back the Divine in myself to the Divine in the All," were spoken as a snake slithered beneath his bed and crawled into a hole in the wall.

## Influence

Plotinus was the last of the great Greek philosophers, and he developed one of the most important systems of thought, comparable to those of Aristotle and Saint Thomas Aquinas. Later critics considered him the founder of a new philosophical school, Neo-Platonism, although he would have been surprised to be so regarded, since he saw himself as a Platonist pure and simple. Besides Plato, he was influenced by Aristotle and the Stoics, and out of this complex philosophical inheritance he created a set of ideas that shaped the views of Western thinkers from Saint Augustine to Henri Bergson. His immediate influence was on the Christian Middle Ages, and his psychological analysis of the soul became the basic framework of mystical theology.

Plotinus' importance for literary theory derives from his aesthetics, which differed from Plato's doctrine of art as the imitator of nature. For Plotinus, both art and nature impose on matter a structure based on archetypal forms (models of reality flowing from the Divine One). For centuries, his theory on beauty was the work by which he was known, and Plotinian aesthetics influenced Aquinas and Dante, whose conception of the mystical poetic vision as an imaginative intuition of spiritual reality owed much to Plotinus. During the Renaissance, Marsilio Ficino's cosmology made use of Plotinus' system of emanations from the Divine One, and Ficino's aesthetics was based on a Plotinian theme – the beauty that draws the soul to God. One can find Plotinian ideas in the *Monadology* of Gottfried Wilhelm Leibniz, written in 1714, and in the eighteenth and nineteenth centuries Neo-Platonic aesthetics contributed to the flowering of German and English literary criticism. Johann Wolfgang von Goethe, for example, studied Plotinus extensively and made use of his ideas about beauty through order and unity. Samuel Taylor Coleridge's definition of beauty as the intuition of the interrelationships of parts to one another, and of all parts to the whole, came from Plotinus.

One can even find Plotinian themes in twentieth-century literature – most notably in James Joyce's use of the term "epiphany" to denote a sudden spiritual manifestation: an object radiates its essence through the clothing of its appearance and thus becomes the symbol of a spiritual state. For Joyce as for Plotinus, the commonest object can be the source of an epiphany.

## Analysis

Plotinus did not address literary theory specifically in the *Enneads*, but he had much to say about the beautiful as a problem not only of metaphysics but also of art, and these aesthetic ideas had implications for literary analysis. Artists, in his view, do not reproduce images of objects but draw on the ideas from which nature itself is constructed. For the modern Italian thinker Benedetto Croce, Plotinus' ascent into the transcendental realm of "Ideas" placed his theory of art beyond the category of criticism. Aristotelian realism certainly played a diminished role in Plotinus' aesthetic theory, and he was not as concerned as Aristotle with definitions, genres, and other technicalities for discussing the comic, tragic, and satiric in literature. It was not by an astute analysis of imaginative works that Plotinus made his contribution to aesthetics but through his emphasis on the Divine One as the radiating source and constitutive principle of all being.

The Plotinian system developed in the *Enneads* teaches that all being, whether material or spiritual, is constituted by the emanation, expansion, or overflow of an existentially rich but ineffable One. The One is not merely numerical but the ocean of being from which the multiplicity of levels and plurality of beings in the universe flow. Between the One and brute matter are located descending grades of reality. Beneath the One, whose intimate life is incomprehensible, is the World of Ideas, which scholars variously term the Divine Mind, Intelligible Principle, and World Mind. Emanating from the Divine Mind, but existing on a lower plane of reality, is the World Soul (often called the Universal Soul or the Soul of All). The World Soul also contains nature and individual souls, for according to Plotinus this World Soul has created all material beings and has ordered the universe.

The relevance of this Plotinian doctrine for aesthetics and literary theory can be grasped by analyzing the central element in his system: the relation between unity and multiplicity. In the *Enneads*, Plotinus makes a virtue of unity. He argues that, deprived of unity, anything in this world – a person, a painting, a poem – ceases to be what it is. Just as a human being, without his or her unifying soul, falls into fragments, so too a literary work without a unifying form loses its being. Plotinus, therefore, associates beauty with an ideal form. When the ideal form enters a

work of art, it orders chaos into cooperation: it brings the parts into a harmonious whole. Plotinus thus sees beauty as a creative and molding force and enthrones it in this organized unity. The notions of harmony, order, and proportion link the beautiful and the good. Since objects participate in form, they are beautiful, and since they aid humans in a mystical union with the One, they are good.

Plotinus' aesthetic theory poses a problem: how can the perfect One produce something that becomes evil? If the One is good and beautiful, how can the bad and the ugly be explained? Plotinus resolves this problem by saying that evil is really nothing: it is an absence, a void where something ought to be. He uses the image of gradually diminishing light and the notion of increasing multiplicity to explain this idea. The One, morally seen, is good, and the material world is also good, because it is an expression of the Beauty above. The natural world encompasses all the perfection permitted by its lower order and, as such, embodies that from which it descends, its higher origin. Unformed matter, however, is evil, in the sense that it lacks form and unity.

Another illustration of the relationship between the One and matter is Plotinus' comparison of the universe to a series of concentric rainbows. The One is the central circle of pure, white light, radiating through concentric shells of increasingly darker colors to blackness at the outer limit. Matter is therefore the blackest, lowest, last, and least emanation of the creative power of the Divine One – the fringe at which the World Soul's activity comes to a halt.

What are the implications of this Plotinian doctrine for literary theory? The matter of literature is made up of the writer's many experiences – recalcitrant and obstructive stuff, as anyone who begins to write can attest. The task of the writer seeking to make a beautiful work is to master the amorphousness of this matter by some ideal form. If this material is not successfully mastered by a pattern, then he or she makes something ugly. For Plotinus, a literary work is infected with evil if it embraces diverse elements without reconciling their interrelationships and thus leaving these parts to their own mastery. The beautiful literary work, then, is a synthesis of its parts to form a coherent whole.

The notion of participation is another important aspect of Plotinus' analysis of the beautiful. He emphasizes that beauty does not consist in symmetry, proportion, and the relationship of parts to the whole, for if it did, beauty could be identified with these relationships, which are multiple. Instead, beauty is a form that, being one, creates unity. By their participation in the ideal form, things are beautiful.

From this analysis of Plotinus' aesthetics it is clear that he valued physical beauty not for itself but because it served as an approach to the real beauty of intelligence in the divine. When a person encounters beauty in a literary work, he should, according to Plotinus, withdraw into himself, turning away from the material beauty that gave him joy, because he must realize that these beautiful things are copies and vestiges of the divine. Indeed, there are dangers in these beautiful things, because the person who pursues them uncritically is like the man who tried to follow a beautiful shape playing over the water and sank into the depths and drowned. Clearly, Plotinus did not accept art for art's sake. Rather, works of art should provide human beings with a taste for the divine. The poet, having experienced sensuous tones, rhythms, and patterns, must learn that the words that quicken his or her pulse have in them an intelligible harmony, and only the mind's eye can contemplate this harmonious beauty. It is in the intelligible realm that beauty dwells.

Plotinus had a more elevated view of artists and writers than did Plato. In the Platonic view, artists work with copies of copies and are thus at a double remove from reality. In the Plotinian view, artists enjoy a more than usually full participation in the Divine Intelligence and the Ideal World. The artist goes back to the Ideas from which nature derives. Furthermore, much of the artist's work is truly his own: he is a creator of beauty who adds form where nature is lacking. The kind of unity and intelligibility enjoyed by the Plotinian object of art is not that of a species but of an individual so intensely organized as to be microcosmic, that is, rich in implications for the whole universe. For example, allegory plays a double role within the Plotinian framework. Allegory looks upward to a transcendental plane of richer and purer being, but at the same time it retains the basic operation of a language system in which every term has a concrete meaning. In Plotinus' system, the unity of a literary work allows human beings to transcend the heterogeneity of this world and ascend to the Divine One that is so simply unified as to be conceivable only by symbolic, or in this case allegoric, methods.

Symmetry was a criterion of beauty much respected by ancient critics, but symmetry presented a problem for Plotinus. He asserted that symmetry is neither a necessary nor a sufficient condition for beauty. It is not necessary because things lacking any symmetry of parts can be beautiful. Indeed, such things as sunlight, single tones, and monochromatic colors are especially beautiful for Plotinus because of their close relationship to the One. Symmetry is not a sufficient condition for beauty because a symmetrical object can lose its beauty. For example, when a human body becomes lifeless, it loses most of its beauty, though not its symmetry.

For Plotinus, then, the sun is devoid of parts; it is not beautiful by symmetry but by its wholeness and brilliance. Works of art, too, should be brilliant: clear and clean, not murky and muddy. The beauty of brightness is the outcome of unification. It comes from the conquest of darkness inherent in brute matter by the pouring in of light, which, for Plotinus, is the ideal form or rational principle. The idea of brightness as intelligible form is closely connected with another Plotinian idea – that beauty is discerned chiefly through the sense of sight, because sight is most sensitive to pattern and form.

Plotinus' aesthetic theory, and what it says derivatively about literature, did not start as a theory of beauty but as a theory of the world and the One. It was soon clear, however, that the Plotinian emphasis on unity, order, and radiance had implications for art and literature. The physical world and everything in it, including art and literature, emanate from the divine, and the path to mystical union with the divine is both an ascent, a movement upward from below, and a penetration, a movement from the external to the internal. The contemplation of works of art and the experience of literary works can be steps on the ladder of this ascent, but Plotinus makes it clear that these are early steps. In order to reach the final steps, the soul has to prepare itself by purity of heart and ascetical practices, and these acts involve turning away from all material things, including art and literature.

According to Plotinus, the artist must ascend toward a vision of the beautiful, where he or she finds the model of his or her creations, but this vision is not the highest of which his soul is capable. The highest level is reached when his soul devotes itself to contemplation, in which memory, sensibility, and discursive reasoning progressively disappear. Then it reaches a mystical union with the ineffable Presence. This union is beyond thought or expression in words; it is a unity of love in which the lover is no longer conscious of any distinction between himself and the beloved. Once attained, this union makes all else seem worthless, including the great beauties of art and literature.

## Principal criticism
*Enneads*, c. A.D. 300–305

## Other literary forms
Plotinus is known primarily as the author of the *Enneads*. According to his biographer, Porphyry, Plotinus wrote nothing until he was fifty. Then he composed a series of fifty-four philosophical essays that originated from his seminar discussions and were intended for his students. About thirty years after Plotinus' death, Porphyry categorized and published these essays in six groups of nine tractates each (the groups were called "enneads," from the Greek *ennea*, meaning nine). Discussions relevant to Plotinus' theory of art and literature occur mainly in the first ennead, sixth tractate, and the fifth ennead, eighth tractate. All the enneads are highly discursive and allusive, and their subject matter ranges over the entire field of ancient philosophy, including physics, cosmology, psychology, logic, epistemology, and metaphysics.

## Further reading
Armstrong, Arthur Hilary. *The Architecture of the Intelligible Universe in the Philosophy of Plotinus*, 1940.
Bréhier, Émile. *The Philosophy of Plotinus*, 1958.

Deck, John N. *Nature and Contemplation and the One: A Study in the Philosophy of Plotinus*, 1967.

Emilsson, E. K. *Plotinus on Sense-Perception: A Philosophical Study*, 1988.

Gerson, L. P. *Plotinus*, 1996.

Hadot, Pierre. *Plotinus or the Simplicity of Vision*, 1994.

Inge, William R. *The Philosophy of Plotinus*, 1968 (2 volumes).

Katz, J. *Plotinus' Search for the Good*, 1959.

Lloyd, A. C. *The Anatomy of Neoplatonism*, 1990.

Merlan, P. *From Platonism to Neoplatonism*, 1960.

O'Daly, G. J. *Plotinus' Philosophy of the Self*, 1973.

O'Meara, D. J. *Plotinus: An Introduction to the Enneads*, 1993.

Rist, John M. *Plotinus: The Road to Reality*, 1967.

Schroeder, F. M. *Form and Transformation: A Study in the Philosophy of Plotinus*, 1992.

ROBERT J. PARADOWSKI

*See also* Saint Augustine; Classical Greek and Roman Literary Theory; Plato

# Edgar Allan Poe

American writer and poet

**Born:** Boston, Massachusetts; January 19, 1809
**Died:** Baltimore, Maryland; October 7, 1849

## Biography

Edgar Poe was born in Boston on January 19, 1809, to actor parents, Elizabeth Arnold and David Poe. Poe's father deserted the family soon after his son's birth, and Elizabeth moved to Richmond, Virginia. When she died in December, 1811, Edgar Poe was left an orphan. He was taken in by John Allan, a wealthy tobacco exporter, and his wife. They renamed him Edgar Allan Poe, although they never legally adopted him. From 1815 to 1820 Poe was with the Allans in Great Britain. In 1820 they returned to Richmond. In 1826 Poe became a student at the University of Virginia, but unpaid gambling debts precluded his returning.

In the late 1820s Poe's literary career began in earnest. *Tamerlane and Other Poems* appeared in 1827, the same year Poe enlisted in the army under a pseudonym. Securing an honorable discharge in 1829, Poe published another volume of poetry, then entered West Point the following year. Poe soon realized that an army career was inappropriate for him, so he disobeyed regulations in order to secure dismissal (1831). He moved in with an aunt, Maria Clemm, living in Baltimore, and began publishing stories. In 1835 he became assistant editor of the *Southern Literary Messenger*, from which position he helped shape American canons of taste and criticism. In 1837 he left the newspaper to move to New York with his cousin and now wife, Virginia Clemm, and his aunt. He became an editor with *Gentleman's Magazine*, then the editor of *Graham's Magazine*, the *Evening Mirror*, and by 1845 he was sole editor of the *Broadway Journal*. The same year he published his most famous poem, "The Raven," as well as *Tales* and *The Raven and Other Poems*.

After the death of Virginia in 1847 Poe had a number of romantic episodes. He became engaged to his boyhood sweetheart, now the widowed Sarah Royster Shelton. En route to New York from Richmond to escort his aunt, Maria Clemm, to the wedding, Poe stopped in Baltimore, where he was found semiconscious on October 3, 1849, outside a polling booth. He died in a hospital four days later, never having regained full consciousness.

## Influence

Poe's influence in literary criticism has been extensive, for he used his position as writer of literary reviews and as editor to urge a more critical approach to the literature of his time. He was interested in the artifact itself, not in the artist behind the work, nor in the moral or intellectual lessons the artifact might foster. Poe eschewed contemporaneous flaunting of opinion, which tended to be impressionistic and general, in favor of an analytical discussion of such items as plot, diction, tone, rhythm, rhyme, unity, and so on.

In keeping with his analytical interests, Poe argued that the artifact must be evaluated on its own merits. While this notion hardly seems radical now, Poe was writing at a time when nationalism in literature was greatly in vogue. Poe's influence can thus be traced in any critical theory that espouses art for art's sake alone. The so-called New Criticism of the twentieth century endorsed Poe's aesthetic values, applied his principles, and developed a vocabulary to describe what Poe had focused upon a century earlier. For this reason, Poe's influence as a literary critic of the nineteenth century has been more significant and more lasting than that of perhaps any other American critic of his time, although recognition of this fact has been overpowered by Poe's reputation as a writer of short stories and poems. In recent decades, Poe's own criticism has been even further eclipsed as poststructuralist critics have shown a renewed interest in his fiction and its particular amenability to detailed semiotic and psychoanalytic approaches. A notable example is Jacques Lacan's analysis of Poe's story "The Purloined Letter." In the case of Roland Barthes, whose "Textual Analysis of Poe's 'Valdemar'" concentrates on Baudelaire's translation of the story, it is possible to see the continuing influence of Poe's writing on French critical thought which began with the Symbolists in the nineteenth century.

## Analysis

As his bibliography indicates, Poe was an active and prolific reviewer during the years that he edited various magazines. He made a name for himself early in his career, when he wrote for the *Southern Literary Messenger*. Criticism at this time was expected to be a well-written essay by a man who was cultured, educated, and informed. Because he had lived in and attended schools in England, Poe could manage this ambiance very well. On the other hand, however, he was not able to rise above some of the petty bickering and *ad hominem* attacks that surfaced in the popular magazines of his day. He found plagiarism sometimes in the slightest of similarities, and there is no doubt that he wasted his energy and his intellect in vituperations against writers whom history would prove insignificant.

Poe did have the opportunity, however, to write about famous English and American writers, such as William Wordsworth, Samuel Taylor Coleridge, Charles Dickens, Thomas Carlyle, Edward Gibbon, Percy Bysshe Shelley, and Leigh Hunt on the English side, and Henry Wadsworth Longfellow, William Gilmore Simms, Ralph Waldo Emerson, and Nathaniel Hawthorne, among others, on the American side. These are the writers who provided Poe with material of substance and artistry worthy of his talent as critic. With all these writers Poe exercised certain critical principles that he articulated later in his own writings of critical theory.

First of all, Poe attempted to promulgate literary criticism as a science. Because literary criticism has progressed so rapidly today, to the point where most English departments teach courses in the field, Poe's insistence on objectivity may not seem radical. It is worthwhile remembering, however, the highly subjective nature of what passed as criticism during the early to mid-nineteenth century. Literary critics frequently praised work for political and social reasons entirely removed from the issue of literary merit. A critical "review" could become an excuse for an independent essay on a subject central or tangential to the substance of the literary work at hand, it could provide the stepping-off point for a sermon, or it could initiate an autobiographical reflection having no relationship to the work under review. Poe insisted on looking directly at the literary artifact, on analyzing it, on discussing the work as it fulfilled certain expectations regarding effect, tone, diction, rhyme, and so on. In this way Poe helped to shape literary criticism into a distinct and unique literary form.

So intent was Poe on destroying the image of the artist as an inspired genius that he wrote an essay which professed to explain the process by which the famous poem "The Raven" came to be written. In "The Philosophy of Composition," Poe details an almost mechanical regimen. He reports that he made careful calculations and decided upon the length of the poem, its province (beauty), and its tone (sadness, achieved through melancholy). He then determined that a refrain would most successfully attain the desired effect. The appropriate sounds having been determined, Poe decided on the word "nevermore" as a refrain because it had the necessary sounds, then imagined an occasion for repetition of the refrain and a situation that would make that repetition reasonable. After all these calculations and decisions had been made, only then, Poe claims, did he put pen to paper. When he finally began to write, he wrote not the first stanza of the poem, but the stanza that would be the climax. By beginning at the end, Poe insisted, he could more easily write all the stanzas that would lead to the desired effect of the climactic stanza. The process outlined by Poe was dramatically at odds with notions of creativity prevalent at the time and further argued that creativity was an objective science that could be plotted and planned. Ideas of "genius" as the source of creativity were clearly beside the point.

Reviewing at a time when American writers were trying to establish an American literature distinct from English influence, Poe refused to step on the nationalist bandwagon. He objected to the practice of praising American writers simply because they were American and criticizing foreign literature simply because it was foreign. Poe even went so far as to generalize that most English literature was better than that being produced in the United States. In arguing this way, Poe was not being unpatriotic, but demonstrating his fidelity to artistic values beyond social or national interference. As a matter of fact, Poe was so determined that his critical writings address aesthetic interests exclusively that he wanted his contributions to the *Southern Literary Messenger* to be known as "critical notices" rather than by the conventional term, "reviews." Poe ascribed to impartial analysis, even if he was unable always to live up to his own high standards given the volume of material that passed across his desk and the amount of sheer hackwork he was forced to produce.

In some of the early reviews, Poe applied critical principles that he later articulated in theoretical writings. In a review of Longfellow's 1841 *Ballads and Other Poems*, for example, Poe foreshadowed principles and definitions that would later be elaborated in "The Poetic Principle." To begin, Poe insisted that there was no such thing as a long poem. If a work were long, according to Poe, it could not possibly have the characteristics that make something a poem. Yet a poem must have a certain duration. Something too short, something epigrammatic, would also not qualify as poetry because it is incapable of producing an effect. Poe insisted that there is an optimal length for a poem; in "The Philosophy of Composition" he set the number at one hundred lines. He arrived at that number by determining that that is about the length a person can tolerate at a single sitting. If one is forced to interrupt the reading, then unity is lost and totality of effect forsaken. While there was doubtless some need to counter prevailing trends of admiring a work simply because of length alone, Poe's criterion for length backed him into the unfortunate corner of having to disparage all long poetic works, including classic epics and later masterpieces such as John Milton's *Paradise Lost* (1667).

Poe was also greatly concerned with totality of effect. A work of art should aim to produce in its audience a single effect; Poe's view of literature thus can be said to be "affective" since affecting the reader or listener is a main goal.

All components of a literary work were to contribute to producing this single effect. Because of this requirement, unity is an extremely important criterion in Poe's evaluation process.

Poe constantly waged war on what he called in "The Poetic Principle" the "heresy of *The Didactic*," the notion that to be meritorious a poem should inculcate a moral. Poe insisted that a poem's moral or statement of "truth" is in no way a measure of its aesthetic merit. In making this claim, Poe divided the world of the mind into three distinct parts: "Pure Intellect, Taste, and the Moral Sense." In this schema the Intellect concerns itself with Truth; Taste addresses the Beautiful; and the Moral Sense reflects Duty. Poe then eliminates intellect and the moral sense, truth and duty, as being irrelevant to the true concern of poetry, the realm of taste alone. Taste, then, lies intermediate between Truth and the Moral Sense, but is infinitely more important than either. Taste helps the individual appreciate the Beautiful. The Beautiful for which Poe aims is not common and earthly, but "supernal beauty," the beauty above and beyond one, which can be appreciated, if at all, only by quick, brief apprehensions. Poetry thus seeks to facilitate the individual's apprehension of supernal loveliness, and to this end all aspects of a poem must be unified in working. The "Poetic Principle," then, is the individual's universal and eternal aspiration for Beauty. To Poe, this can be achieved only by "an elevating excitement of the Soul." The definition of poetry itself, the poetry of words, follows from Poe's explanation of the "Poetic Principle." Poetry is defined as "The Rhythmical Creation of Beauty." There are media other than language for expressing the poetic sentiment, to be sure, such as music and the visual arts, but all have the same goal and the same ultimate criterion: Taste.

What Poe claims for the poetry of words applies as well to the short story as to verse. In his review of Hawthorne's 1837 *Twice-Told Tales*, Poe mentions many of the same criteria used in judging verse. For example, producing a single effect is as important in the short story as in the poem. The requirement of a single sitting obtains in perusing prose as in poetry. Poe maintains that the reader can be attentive to prose for a longer period of time than to poetry, yet the restrictions of the single sitting limit the length of a prose piece to something that can be read in anywhere between a half hour and two hours. Just as his criterion for length necessarily dismisses certain forms of verse such as the epic, in prose Poe finds that the novel is an unworthy and ineffective genre. Because Hawthorne's tales are superbly unified to bring out a single effect, because every word of Hawthorne's tales contributes to the work's design, Poe praises the tales lavishly, although he later objects to Hawthorne's penchant for allegory. Poe respects Hawthorne's genius and his style; his admiration helped to bring Hawthorne the public acclaim he deserved.

Because Poe's own short stories have been so influential in the development of the modern short story, and because they fulfil so satisfactorily Poe's critical prescriptions, there are those who say that Poe's criticism is merely self-serving, that he arbitrarily composed critical principles to accommodate his own writing. Yet to write creatively what one professes critically should not be considered unusual. It is more likely that Poe wrote his own short stories and poems as he had come to believe they should be written given his extensive reading in the literary production of his day, occasioned by his employment as editor and reviewer. Far more culpable would he be if he had criticized other writers according to one set of principles and used another set of guidelines for his own work.

During his lifetime Poe suffered from a sense of not belonging to the literary establishment, that of Boston primarily. He was always underpaid, and always as an adult lived a hand-to-mouth existence. He was understandably embittered by the better economic situation of men far inferior to him in imagination, intellect, and talent. In addition, the truth is that America did not respect Poe's talent during his lifetime and that he was appreciated in France long before he gained respect in his own country. Charles Baudelaire translated several of Poe's writings, but some American critics have gone so far as to say that the French Symbolists liked Poe only because Baudelaire improved Poe's writings in the process of translation. Poe's reputation suffered as well because he had the misfortune of leaving Rufus W. Griswold as his literary executor. No one has yet been able to determine what possible motives could have inspired Griswold to the heights of calumny and slander in which he engaged against Poe both personally and professionally after Poe's death. Only in time has the truth about Poe begun to emerge, and as it has emerged, Poe's status as critic and creative writer has climbed consistently upward.

Poe's great triumph as a critic was also the biggest obstacle he faced in his lifetime – he was a literary anachronism, out of time, out of step. When twentieth-century criticism moved away from traditional nineteenth-century approaches, from its historical and biographical orientation, the world recognized how progressive Edgar Allan Poe had been. His insistence on demystifying the artistic process, on applying universal criteria of judgment, and on esteeming the value of art for its own sake has placed Edgar Allan Poe among the great literary critics, philosophers, and theoreticians of all time.

## Principal criticism

All articles below appeared in the *Southern Literary Messenger*
Review of William Cullen Bryant's *Poems*, 1835
"Letter to B——," 1836
Review of Bryant's *Poems*, 1837
Review of Thomas Babington Macaulay's *Critical and Miscellaneous Essays*, 1841
Review of Charles Dickens' *Barnaby Rudge*, 1842
Review of Henry Wadsworth Longfellow's *Ballads and Other Poems*, 1842
Review of Nathaniel Hawthorne's *Twice-Told Tales*, 1842

Review of Rufus W. Griswold's *The Poets and Poetry of America*, 1842
Review of Griswold's third edition of *The Poets and Poetry in America*, 1843
Review of James Russell Lowell's *Poems*, 1844
"The Longfellow War" articles, 1845
Review of Bryant's *Complete Poetical Works*, 1846
"The Literati of New York City," 1846
"The Philosophy of Composition," 1846
Review of Hawthorne's *Twice-Told Tales* and *Mosses from an Old Manse*, 1847
Review of Lowell's *Fable for Critics*, 1849
"The Poetic Principle," 1850
*Literary Criticism of Edgar Allan Poe*, 1965
*Essays and Reviews*, 1984

## Other major works and literary forms

Edgar Allan Poe was preeminently the master of the short story. He developed the genres of science fiction, detective and mystery stories, and psychological studies, especially tales of the divided self, and he is best known for his tales of the macabre. Although writing short stories was more financially rewarding, Poe preferred poetry, and he was a poet of considerable talent. He wrote one long prose narrative, *The Narrative of Arthur Gordon Pym* (1838). He also wrote in prose a philosophical explanation of the universe, *Eureka: A Prose Poem* (1848), which he requested be judged as a poem after his death.

NOVEL
*The Narrative of Arthur Gordon Pym*, 1838

SHORT FICTION
*Tales of the Grotesque and Arabesque*, 1840
*The Prose Romances of Edgar A. Poe*, 1843
*Tales*, 1845
*The Other Poe: Comedies and Satires*, 1983

PLAY
*Politian*, 1835-1836

POETRY
*Tamerlane and Other Poems*, 1827
*Al Aaraaf, Tamerlane, and Minor Poems*, 1829
*Poems*, 1831
*The Raven and Other Poems*, 1845
*Eureka: A Prose Poem*, 1848
*Poe: Complete Poems*, 1959

NONFICTION
*The Letters of Edgar Allan Poe*, 1948

MISCELLANEOUS
*The Complete Works of Edgar Allan Poe*, 1902 (17 volumes)
*Collected Works of Edgar Allan Poe*, 1969, 1978 (3 volumes)

## Further reading

Alterton, Margaret. *Origins of Poe's Critical Theory*, 1965.
Barthes, Roland. "Textual Analysis of Poe's 'Valdemar,'" in *Untying the Text: A Post-Structuralist Reader*, 1981.
Bloom, Clive. *Reading Poe, Reading Freud: The Romantic Imagination in Crisis*, 1988.
Buranelli, Vincent. "Critical Attitudes," in *Edgar Allan Poe*, 1977.
Foerster, Norman. "Poe," in *American Criticism: A Study in Literary Theory from Poe to the Present*, 1928.
Foust, R. E. "Aesthetician of Simultaneity: E. A. Poe and Modern Literary Theory," in *South Atlantic Review*. XLVI (May, 1981), pp. 17-25.
Jacobs, Robert D. *Poe, Journalist and Critic*, 1969.
Johnson, Barbara. "The Frame of Reference: Poe, Lacan, Derrida," in *Psychoanalysis and the Question of the Text*, 1978.
Lacan, Jacques. "Seminar on 'The Purloined Letter,'" in *Yale French Studies* 48 (1972).
Marks, Emerson. "Poe as Literary Theorist: A Reappraisal," in *American Literature*. XXXIII (November, 1961), pp. 296-306.
Meyers, Jeffrey. *Edgar Allan Poe: His Life and Legacy*, 1992.
Muller, John P., and William J. Richardson, eds. *The Purloined Poe: Lacan, Derrida and Psychoanalytic Reading*, 1988.
Saintsbury, George. *A History of Criticism and Taste in Europe*, 1904.
Snell, George. "First of the New Critics," in *Quarterly Review of Literature*. II (1946), pp. 333-340.
Wilson, Edmund. "Poe as a Literary Critic," in *The Nation*. CLV (October 31, 1942), pp. 452-453.
Woodberry, George E. *Edgar Allan Poe*, 1885.

PAULA KOPACZ

*See also* American Literary Theory to 1900; Baudelaire; Emerson; James

# Alexander Pope

English poet, translator, and critic

**Born:** London, England; May 21, 1688
**Died:** Twickenham, England; May 30, 1744

## Biography

The son of a well-to-do Roman Catholic merchant, Alexander Pope was born in London but spent his later childhood at Binfield in Windsor Forest. He attended two schools but left school permanently at the age of twelve. At about that time he developed Pott's disease, a bone ailment which caused him frequent serious pain for the rest of his life and left him a humpbacked dwarf. He began writing poetry early and sent a poem to Henry Cromwell in 1709, the result being that Cromwell and a number of established writers urged him to submit his *Pastorals*, written when he was sixteen, for publication. They were published in 1709, and Pope then moved to London, where he had many friends in the literary world, including the writer who became his closest friend, Jonathan Swift. He also became a member of the well-known Scriblerus Club, which included Swift, John Gay, and other writers and noblemen interested in writing. His first important work, *An Essay on Criticism*, established him as a poet, and he continued to write and publish extensively throughout his life.

Pope bought a house on the river Thames at Twickenham in 1719 and lived there for the rest of his life, visited frequently by his friends from London and also visiting London frequently. He never married. He died in 1744, a victim of his bone ailment and kidney disease.

## Influence

The three most important literary critics in the neoclassical age were John Dryden, Pope, and Samuel Johnson. Dryden was an important influence upon Pope, though more in the use of the heroic couplet than in criticism; Pope, in turn, was an important influence on Johnson. All three were also influenced by the great critics of Greece and Rome, especially Aristotle and Horace.

## Analysis

*An Essay on Criticism* is the last of a long series of poems in Italian, French, and English owing a debt to the Roman poet Horace's *Ars poetica* (c. 17 B.C.; *The Art of Poetry*); it is, however, unlike the others in being addressed not to poets but to critics. Long considered (especially in the nineteenth century) to represent the extreme of neoclassical theory and attitude, *An Essay on Criticism* is quite various in its views, and rarely arbitrary. A major point at the beginning, and a sort of explanation of why Pope chose to address critics rather than poets, is that he believed bad criticism to be much more dangerous than bad poetry, bad critics to be much more numerous than bad poets, and bad critics to be bad because education was likely to be misleading or because they had tried to be poets and, having failed at it, turned to criticism. He then makes a major neoclassical point: the critic, like the poet, should know his or her limitations and stay within his or her limits. Otherwise, the result will be, for both poet and critic, dullness, which is, for Pope, the ultimate fault in writing of any kind. Moreover, he believed that the poet should also be the critic: a phenomenon common in English literature up to Pope's day, from Sir Philip Sidney and Ben Jonson, to Dryden. Though Pope could not know it, this tradition would continue with such later poet-critics as Johnson, William Wordsworth, Samuel Taylor Coleridge, Matthew Arnold, and T. S. Eliot.

Pope's first and most important advice to critics, as it would be to poets, is to "follow nature" – that is, to conform to universal truth, nature being "the source, and end, and test of art." A problem here, he goes on to say, is that "wit and judgment often are at strife," wit here apparently meaning – it has various meanings in the poem – what could be called creativity, whereas actually wit and judgment should call on each other for assistance. His next point is that the ancient rules for literature (that is, those of the Greeks and Romans) do conform to nature, and hence should be followed; while this idea is in part neoclassical, Pope does not imply that the much stricter rules of his own and the previous generation ("dull receipts how poems should be made") should be followed. What one should do, whether poet or critic, is read and understand the great writers of the past and learn from them how to follow nature.

He then proceeds to explain, in a passage clearly not the extreme of neoclassical thought, that the critic needs to realize that a successful poem will have beauties that must be accepted without explanation and hence are beyond reference to existing rules; that is, genius can go beyond rule and "snatch a grace beyond the reach of art"; what the genius has done, if it can be verbalized, then becomes a rule. A fault of critics in this context is that they may fail to see a poem, as one might fail to see a picture, from the right perspective, and hence see faults where faults do not exist. He then uses as an example one that would now seem, from a modern perspective, more Romantic than neoclassical: "In prospects, thus, some objects please our eyes/ Which out of nature's common order rise,/ The shapeless rock, or hanging precipice."

Pope then proceeds to offer further explanations for why bad critics are bad critics. The first is pride, pride here meaning that one feels no need to learn from others. The good critic needs constantly to learn from his or her contemporaries and from great writers and critics of the past, and hence to recognize truth when he or she sees it – truth, in a neoclassical sense, not of new ideas (which apparently cannot exist) but of "what oft was thought but ne'er so well expressed."

The second fault of bad critics is that they may be interested only in figures of speech or in style, not in thought, whereas style should be "the dress of thought" and of value not for its own sake but for how it makes thought clear without calling attention to itself. The third fault is judging a poem exclusively by its meter and demanding that the meter be perfectly regular. Pope's own meter is astonishingly various for its day, and his own advice is simply that "the sound must be an echo to the sense" and not call attention to itself in this way either. The fourth fault is going to extremes – admiring or fault-finding too much. The fifth, typical of its day, is to be prejudiced for or against ancient or modern writers: critics should recognize that what is true wit is true wit, no matter when it was written. The sixth fault is to go along with whatever is popular, regardless of whether it deserves to be, or, at the opposite extreme, to be against whatever is popular simply because it is popular. The last fault is to be inconsistent: to keep changing one's mind, perhaps to conform to, or oppose, the current fashion in taste, though, as Pope says later, one should not be afraid to change one's mind if a change is genuinely required.

Pope then turns to what the critic should do: praise "true merit," even if no one else has done so; avoid allowing one's learning to become prejudice; avoid being overcritical: "Good nature and good sense must ever join;/ To err is human, to forgive divine." If anger and scorn cannot be avoided altogether, they should be spent on that which deserves them: obscenity and blasphemy – though even then one should be careful to avoid seeing such things where they do not actually exist. Next, one should be diplomatic when one must point out faults, avoid sounding oversure of oneself. Still, if one sees important faults in generally meritorious authors, one should not hesitate to point them out. One should give praise or blame where it is due, without concern for whether the writer is a friend or an enemy; one should not waste one's time criticizing writers who are third-rate.

In the concluding part of the poem, Pope first makes the point that the present day, unlike the days of ancient Greece and Rome, has very few critics who meet the criteria that he has been establishing; he then proceeds to praise those Greeks and Romans who did meet them: Aristotle, Horace (who, rather like Pope himself, "charms with graceful negligence, / And without method talks us into sense"), Dionysius, Petronius, Quintilian, and, finally, Longinus, for whom his praise is once again far from strictly neoclassical. He examines how such critical excellence disappeared after the Fall of Rome and how it recovered in Italy in the Renaissance. He seems to speak adversely of French criticism: "But critic-learning flourished most in France. / The rules, a nation born to serve, obeys, / And Boileau still in right of Horace sways." This again would not be a strictly neoclassical attitude. He then turns to England – where, he seems to believe, proper criticism did not flourish until the seventeenth century. He concludes with a summary of what a good critic is:

> Careless of censure, nor too fond of fame,
> Still pleased to praise, yet not afraid to blame,
> Averse alike to flatter or offend,
> Not free from faults, nor yet afraid to mend.

Pope's preface to his translation of the *Iliad* centers on a comparison of Homer and Virgil, with a strong preference for Homer. He begins by saying that it is "universally" agreed that Homer had the greatest invention (that is, imagination) of any writer ever; he clearly considers invention to be the most important quality of a great poet. Yet, Pope says, most critics prefer an orderly genius, more closely related to judgment than to invention, because the quality of such a writer is easier to assess. Homer's "amazing invention" produced "unequaled fire and rapture," and hence he does not merely describe but makes the reader see and hear what is happening. This kind of invention is very rare: "exact disposition, just thought, correct elocution, polished numbers may have been found in a thousand, but this poetical fire ... in very few," the few, Pope says, including John Milton and William Shakespeare. While there were certainly contemporaries of Pope who would have agreed with what he says here, it nevertheless sounds, in its emphasis on imagination and emotion, more nearly Romantic than neoclassical.

Pope then proceeds to show how Homer's "vast invention exerts itself," by going through the elements of an epic (or tragedy) in Aristotle's *De poetica* (c. 334–323 B.C., *Poetics*). First is fable (that is, plot), which he says Homer invented: as in the *Iliad*, there should be a single plot, relatively brief in time, with clear-cut cause and effect, the cause in the *Iliad* being the wrath of Achilles. Virgil, in the *Aeneid*, Pope says, uses a much greater length of time and does not have so brief and easily verbalized a cause.

Second is character: Pope finds that in Homer even a single aspect of character, such as courage, varies widely among the courageous, and that Homer's characters have great diversity and complexity, whereas Virgil's are simpler and more uniform. Next, Pope treats language – actually Aristotle's fourth category. Pope finds in the *Iliad* far more conversation, as opposed to narration, than one would expect in an epic; that this is a virtue, in being dramatic; and that the language always fits the speaker remarkably well – whereas, once again, Virgil uses dialogue less and makes it much less individual. As for Aristotle's third category, sentiments or thoughts, Pope says that Homer's thoughts have the "grandeur and excellence" of those in Scripture, though his thoughts may also at times be "low and vulgar," and that Virgil never achieves either the height or the depth of Homer. Finally, Pope turns to what some had found to be defects in Homer, and, while not denying that they exist, says that the "seeming defects" resulted, apparently, from the early and relatively uncultured age in which Homer lived.

Pope then turns to the problem of translation. A literal translation, he says, will not do, apparently not, as one would probably expect, because a literal translation is never adequate, but rather because, in a typical neoclassical and earlier English attitude, Greek is a language superior to English. What is necessary is to "transfuse the spirit of the original" and give the translation a "poetical style."

Pope's preface to his edition of Shakespeare seems unusually favorable for his day, though an occasional attitude is expressed with which modern readers would almost surely disagree. He begins by saying that Shakespeare is that English poet who is "the fairest and fullest subject for criticism" and that he has the most, and most noticeable, "beauties and faults of all sorts." Yet he attempts to show both that some of the faults are not Shakespeare's own and that some supposed faults are not faults at all.

He first deals with Shakespeare's merits. First, he was the most original of all writers, since even Homer got some of his material from Egyptian sources – a rather odd view, since he later points out, correctly, how much Shakespeare derived from ancient, and earlier modern, history and literature. He declares the poetry of Shakespeare to have been inspiration, another attitude that modern readers would call Romantic, and says that he is "not so much an imitator, as an instrument, of nature." He then praises him for his presentation of characters, saying in a famous statement that, if the plays were printed without the names of the characters, their speech is so individual that readers could assign the proper name to every speech. He then praises him for his effect on the emotions, without any evidence of effort, so that one weeps at the right places and also laughs at the right places; certainly Pope is right in the implication that few, if any, writers before Shakespeare had been successful in both comedy and tragedy.

Pope then turns to Shakespeare's defects, saying that he can account for many of them. The salient point is that Shakespeare had to please the common people; thus, as Pope observes in a famous comment, "To judge therefore of Shakespeare by Aristotle's rules, is like trying a man by the laws of one country who acted under those of another." Further, being himself an actor, he had to write in such a way as to draw audiences, and hence he did not so much make mistaken judgments as an author but rather right judgments as an actor. Pope then turns to the issue of whether Shakespeare lacked education, pointing out, correctly but uncommonly in Pope's day, that "there is a vast difference between learning and languages," and that his plays make clear that his knowledge was extensive. Pope then explains his belief that the errors of Shakespeare's early editors and printers account for many of the errors regarded as his.

After explaining how he himself edited the plays, Pope concludes the preface with a favorable comparison highly unusual for his day: Shakespeare, he says, is like Gothic architecture in being "more strong and more solemn," whereas more "regular" (that is, rulebound) writers are more like a neat and elegant modern building. The great majority in Pope's day regarded the Gothic unfavorably, and it became popular again only as the Romantic period was approaching, near the end of the century.

Both of Pope's prefaces are valuable, though his most important work in criticism is, and will remain, *An Essay on Criticism*, one of the broadest, most comprehensive, and permanently important works of criticism in the eighteenth century.

## Principal criticism
*An Essay on Criticism*, 1711
Preface to *The Iliad of Homer*, 1715
Preface to *Works of Shakespear*, 1725
*The Literary Criticism of Alexander Pope*, 1965

## Other major works and literary forms
With the exception of the two prefaces, which were in prose, all Alexander Pope's more important work was written in heroic couplets. Besides *An Essay on Criticism*, Pope's major poems include *The Rape of the Lock* (1712, enlarged 1714), *Windsor Forest* (1713), *The Dunciad* (1728-1743), *An Essay on Man* (1733-1734), *Imitations of Horace* (1733-1737), and *Epistle to Dr. Arbuthnot* (1735). His translation of *The Odyssey*, done with two assistants, was published in 1725 and 1726. *The Works of Mr. Alexander Pope* appeared between 1717 and 1741.

POETRY
*Pastorals*, 1709
*The Rape of the Lock*, 1712, enlarged 1714
*Windsor Forest*, 1713
*Cytherea*, 1723
*The Dunciad*, 1728-1743
*Moral Essays*, 1731-1735
*An Essay on Man*, 1733-1734
*Imitations of Horace*, 1733-1737
*Epistle to Dr. Arbuthnot*, 1735
*One Thousand Seven Hundred and Thirty-eight*, 1738
*Epilogue to the Satires*, 1738
*The Twickenham Edition of the Poems of Alexander Pope*, 1939-1967 (11 volumes; John Butt, editor)

NONFICTION
*Peri Bathos: Or, The Art of Sinking in Poetry*, 1727
*Mr. Pope's Literary Correspondence*, 1735-1737
*The Correspondence of Alexander Pope*, 1956 (5 volumes; George Sherburn, editor)

TRANSLATIONS
*The Iliad of Homer*, 1715-1720
*The Odyssey of Homer*, 1725-1726

EDITED TEXT
*Works of Shakespear*, 1723-1725 (6 volumes)

MISCELLANEOUS
*The Works of Mr. Alexander Pope*, 1717-1741

## Further reading
Barnard, John. *Pope: The Critical Heritage*, 1973.
Bloom, Harold, ed. *Alexander Pope*, 1986.
Deutsch, Helen. *Resemblance and Disgrace: Alexander Pope and the Deformation of Culture*, 1996.
Erskine-Hill, Howard, ed. *Alexander Pope, World and Word*, 1998.
Fairer, David. *The Poetry of Alexander Pope*, 1989.
Foxon, David. *Pope and the Early Eighteenth-Century Book Trade*, 1991.
Keener, Frank M. *An Essay on Pope*, 1974.
Kowalk, Wolfgang. *Alexander Pope: An Annotated Bibliography of Twentieth Century Criticism, 1900-1979*, 1981.
Mack, Maynard. *Alexander Pope: A Life*, 1985.
Rogers, Pat. *Hacks and Dunces: Pope, Swift and Grub Street*, 1980.
Rumbold, Valerie. *Women's Place in Pope's World*, 1989.
Sherburn, George W. *The Early Career of Alexander Pope*, 1934.
Tillotson, Geoffrey. *On the Poetry of Pope*, 1938.
Warren, Austin. *Pope as Critic and Humanist*, 1929.
Williams, Carolyn D. *Pope, Homer, and Manliness: Some Aspects of Eighteenth-Century Classical Learning*, 1992.

JACOB H. ADLER

*See also* Addison; Dryden; Johnson; Neoclassical Literary Theory

# Popular Literature: Approaches to Genre

Much of the most substantial and interesting criticism of popular literature is genre-based. Work relating to individual texts or authors tends to be of article or chapter length and there are relatively few general critical surveys of the field. Popular genres, however, have attracted increasingly sophisticated critical attention and there is now a substantial literature relating to five major genres: romance, science fiction, the Western, horror, and thrillers. Typically, critics have attempted one or more of the following: to plot chronologically the development of the genre; to identify its "essence" – the characteristics which distinguish it from other genres; or to explore its appeal to readers. Genre also provides the principle on which a great deal of popular fiction is published and sold.

The chronological survey was typical of many early approaches to popular genres, notably that of Howard Haycraft. Work of this kind invariably provides useful information but beyond that the principle recommendation is more often the author's enthusiasm than his or her critical insights. The Russian folklorist Vladimir Propp attempted in 1928 to identify the essence of the folk-tale genre. Though its level of sophistication now appears modest, his work is an important landmark in the study of popular genres. Adopting a structuralist perspective, Propp identifies the thirty-one "functions" which comprise the basic units of narrative which advance the plot in all the examples of folk tale he analyzed. Though not all examples include all thirty-one functions, the order of those which do appear does not vary; the folk tale emerges as a genre in which abundance and variety at the level of detail is contained within narrative systems of substantial uniformity.

A later and more sophisticated approach, whose perspective is still primarily that of structuralism, informs Umberto Eco's influential essay on Ian Fleming's James Bond novels. Eco identifies a schematic narrative consisting of nine "moves" which are necessarily present in each and every James Bond novel, though not necessarily in the same order. Eco is more concerned with exploring meanings than with judgments of value. But his references to narrative as "game" and to the author's cynical manipulation of plot and reader do, however, highlight an important set of value-based judgments which have become central to common assumptions about popular genres. On the one hand we have "serious literature," which flows from the spontaneous creativity of authors of genius; on the other hand we have popular genres, which are mechanically, sometimes cynically, formulaic, and whose predictability must necessarily bore all but the least demanding (or most highly manipulated) reader. An important early essay by John Cawelti reserves the term "genre" for canonical literature in contradistinction to "formula literature," which refers to the accumulated and predictable conventions of popular literary categories.

Such value-laden positions point us toward a key critical issue surrounding popular genres. In the face of such monumental predictability, how do we account for the pleasures manifestly and continuously experienced by large numbers of readers? Eco provides some initial pointers toward solutions: "The reader's pleasure consists of finding himself immersed in a game of which he knows the pieces and the rules – and perhaps the outcome – drawing pleasure simply from the minimal variations by which the victor realizes his objective." The issue is dealt with most comprehensively and persuasively, however, by Steve Neale, who explains the reader's pleasure in all genres precisely in a creative tension between the predictable and unexpected components. Neale's conflicting pleasures are "process" and "position" – the former linked with movement, the latter with stasis (and with the predictability flowing from genre conventions). The pleasures of process and position are interdependent, process resisting the boredom of endless stasis (in which nothing happens) and position preventing the profoundly unsettling experience of an excess of process (in which too much happens).

Even the most cursory survey of the critical literature makes it clear that the earlier listing of five principal popular genres is problematic. May we in full confidence subsume Gothic and fantasy as subgenres of horror? Or do we need to expand our list by treating each of these as a genre in its own right? Is it valid to propose a genre "the thriller" which will legitimately embrace the categories classic detective, "hard-boiled dick," and espionage fiction? This is the central inquiry of one of the most extensive explorations of a specific popular genre, Jerry Palmer's work on thrillers, where the case is convincingly argued that the "tough thriller" and the traditional detective story do indeed cohere generically. Palmer concludes: "my contention is that the 'tough thriller' and the traditional detective story are variations on the same theme and that such differences as there are are insignificant in comparison with what they have in common." Neale's monograph usefully reminds us that we cannot plot fixed and impermeable boundaries between genres: "Generic specificity is a question not of particular and exclusive elements . . . but of exclusive and particular combinations and articulations of elements, of the exclusive and particular weight given in any one genre to elements which in fact it shares with other genres."

During the 1980s and 1990s work on popular genre continued to draw on and develop earlier critical perspectives; James Twitchell's study of horror, for example, identifies three central myths and three narrative formulas at the heart of the genre. Increasingly, however, structuralist approaches are complemented by perspectives drawn from poststructuralism, psychoanalysis, and feminism. The result has been the substantial extending of our understanding both of the historical contexts in which genres develop and are reworked, and also of the pleasures of those who read them. Tania Modleski and Janice Radway both discuss romance from a feminist perspective and both are concerned primarily to explore readers' pleasure. Methodologically they diverge: Radway's use of ethnographic research contrasts with Modleski's exclusively theoretical approach in which psychoanalytic debates inform an influential discussion of Gothic and "Harlequin" romances (the US equivalent of the British Mills and Boon novels). Their conclusions, however, are broadly similar. Both argue that reading romances involves active selection and the assertion of specifically "feminine" values. In identifying space in which consuming romance acquires oppositional potential, Modleski and Radway were instrumental in contesting the view that the pleasure women readers find in romance novels is exclusively bound up with the endorsement and passive acceptance of patriarchy. Rosemary Jackson's work combines a psychoanalytic perspective with a very strong sense of the historical context of horror/Gothic/fantasy literature. This perspective is further developed by Carol ·Clover in her study of the horror genre. Clover's approach to horror, however, is largely concerned with film, and is indicative of an increasing closeness and interdependence in recent years of literary and cinematic popular forms, both at the point of production and as the focus of critical discussion.

## Further reading

Berger, Asa. *Popular Culture Genres: Theories and Texts*, 1992.
Cawelti, John. "The Concept of Formula in the Study of Popular Literature," in *Journal of Popular Culture*. 3 (1969).
Clover, Carol. *Men, Women and Chain-saws*, 1992.
Cranny-Francis, Anne. *Feminist Fiction*, 1990.
Eco, Umberto. *The Bond Affair*, 1977.
Haycraft, Howard. *Murder for Pleasure*, 1941.
Jackson, Rosemary. *Fantasy: The Literature of Subversion*, 1981.
Longhurst, Derek. *Gender, Genre and Narrative Pleasure*, 1989.
Modleski, Tania. *Loving with a Vengeance: Mass-Produced Fantasies for Women*, 1984.
Moylan, Tom. *Demand the Impossible: Science Fiction and the Utopian Imagination*, 1986.
Neale, Steve. *Genre*, 1980.
Palmer, Jerry. *Thrillers: Genesis and Structure of a Popular Genre*, 1978.
Propp, Vladimir. *Morphology of the Folktale*, 1928.
Radway, Janice. *Reading the Romance*, 1984.
Twitchell, James. *Dreadful Pleasures: An Anatomy of Modern Horror*, 1985.
Wright, Will. *Sixguns and Society: A Structural Study of the Western*, 1975.

BOB ASHLEY

*See also* Novel: Theory and Criticism

# Popular Literature: Critical Reception

The serious criticism of popular literature began, as an isolated and self-consciously pioneering intellectual enterprise, during the 1930s, and although considerable advances have been made since, its position in the academy remains an uneasy one. It is widely regarded as an attempt to deal seriously with material which is essentially trivial, which is commonly ignored, frequently derided, sometimes suppressed. And yet it is precisely this despised popular literature – and not the highly regarded classics – which constitutes for many readers their principal, perhaps their *only*, reading material. Commentators have demonstrated almost ad nauseam the extent to which the readership of the likes of Stephen King and Agatha Christie is overwhelmingly greater than that of respected canonical authors. Slowly, over the twentieth century, criticism has responded to this high level of cultural visibility with the realization that such material cannot simply be ignored. The clarity of such realization is, however, balanced by the uncertainties it opens up: what kind of critical approaches are appropriate to King and Christie? Do we ask the same value-based questions of both popular and classic texts alike? If we do, the likelihood is that we quickly reach the unhelpful impasse of equating the popular with trash – which is simply to complete the circle by reaffirming the very assumptions the inquiry seeks to challenge. The recognition that appropriate, probably different, questions need to be asked is at the heart of the criticism of popular texts, and this has generated a critical literature never far removed from engaging with problems of method. Critical debate has generated a plethora of competing approaches, drawing on and sometimes influencing many of the wider intellectual projects of the twentieth century, notably structuralism, poststructuralism, Marxism, feminism, postmodernism, and psychoanalysis.

The most influential early readings were those of the British critics Q. D. Leavis and George Orwell. Both constitute an early recognition by literary figures of the significance of popular forms. Neither, however, achieves the fully dispassionate open-minded analysis Leavis explicitly identifies as her goal. Thus for Leavis, the appeal of popular literature is to "herd prejudice" and its effect is "to debase the emotional currency by touching basely on fine issues"; popular texts are identified as both symptom and cause of the wider cultural malaise Leavis is seeking to identify and to resist. In Orwell's essay the analysis of James Hadley Chases' gangster novel *No Orchids for Miss Blandish* is prefaced by the words "Now for a header into the cesspool." Chase was a British writer strongly influenced by American models and for Orwell the novel typifies the vulgarizing and brutalizing impact of American cultural influence widely perceived by British literary intellectuals in the mid-twentieth century as a threat to the integrity of national culture. Neither Leavis nor Orwell is able to overcome the impulsion toward the distancing of self from material which is perceived as potentially harmful trash. In this context fully dispassionate analysis is improbable. It was from the late 1960s on that significant advances toward a dispassionate open-minded critique of popular fiction began to emerge. Much of the work was located in the new academic field of cultural studies and is heavily dependent on the absorption and application by British and American critics of continental European theory. A key influence is structuralism, whose aspirations to scientific objectivity and concern with the meanings as opposed to the value of texts offered ways of bypassing some of the earlier difficulties. John Cawelti offers an important early attempt to explain the workings of individual popular texts in terms of the genre conventions and rules within which individual texts operate. The aspiration is to discover *how* texts work; concerns about value and effects are unimportant.

From the early 1970s the range of critical inquiry broadened from the largely formal concerns of structuralism to a poststructuralist interest in the cultural contexts of popular texts. Simultaneously, there was a growing interest in readers – this involved a shift away both from the idea of a reader as someone who is "subject to" the manipulative efforts of authors, and from the structuralist idea that "texts read their readers," toward the notion of the reader as someone who, alongside texts and authors, is an active participant in the production of meanings within particular historical contexts. Roland Barthes' essay was a seminal text in this shift. It is a polemical work, arguing that the traditional focus of Western criticism on the author is anachronistic and that it is at the point of consumption that meaning is generated. More recent work drawing on feminism, psychoanalysis, and postmodernism has further refined the focus on the reader, and especially the reader's pleasure. For example, insights into ways in which women's romance works to foreground (and arguably to "celebrate") experience which is marginalized in the wider culture, and analyses of the complex pleasures experienced by readers who are simultaneously liberated from and reminded of limitations to their own fulfillment, move us some way on from earlier readings of romance literature which simply sought to demonstrate the ideological pervasiveness of patriarchy.

Any suggestion of a smooth and unproblematic emergence out of darkness into critical enlightenment in the study of popular literature must, of course, be resisted. Awareness of the skepticism of academic colleagues has bred a defensiveness among critics of popular forms which at worst can lead to an almost unreadable obscurity. At this point concern for method crosses over into the obscurantism of texts whose difficulty may seek to endorse the intellectual rigor of the exercise. Despite this – and to a degree because of it – the old prejudices persist and it is

still difficult for student and critic alike to become liberated from negative estimations of the study of popular literature. In Harriet Hawkins' book the classics/trash split is successfully problematized. As the argument proceeds, however, one is aware of a distinctly superior kind of trash as the focus of attention of an author who seems to be distancing herself very successfully from the worst of the "junk." Whilst recording the very real progress in the decades since Leavis wrote her book, it remains entirely appropriate to conclude by recognizing the obstacles to critical engagement with the popular which still remain deeply embedded in the common notions of our literary culture.

## Further reading

Ashley, Bob, ed. *Reading Popular Narrative: A Source Book*, 1997.
Barthes, Roland. "The Death of the Author," 1968, reprinted in *Image, Music, Text*, 1977.
Bennett, Tony, ed. *Popular Fiction: Technology, Ideology, Production, Reading*, 1990.
Cawelti, John. *Adventure, Mystery and Romance*, 1976.
Hawkins, Harriett. *Classics and Trash: Traditions and Taboos in High Literature and Popular Modern Genres*, 1990.
Leavis, Q. D. *Fiction and the Reading Public*, 1932.
McCracken, Scott. *Pulp: Reading Popular Fiction*, 1998.
Orwell, George. "Raffles and Miss Blandish," in *Collected Essays, Journalism and Letters*, Vol. 3, 1968.
Palmer, Jerry. *Potboilers: Methods, Concepts and Case Studies in Popular Fiction*, 1991.

BOB ASHLEY

*See also* Fiedler; Tompkins

# Postcolonial Literature and Theory

Beginning around the time of the Renaissance, at the apex of European mercantilism and outward expansion, colonialism reached its zenith during the nineteenth century with the now notorious "scramble for Africa." In the aftermath of World Wars I and II, the exhausted imperial powers could neither exert the level of control necessary to maintain their overseas territories, nor morally justify their continuation. As a result, colonialism began to unravel, and it was into the "gaps" caused by the European retreat around the 1950s that the colonized asserted themselves. More precisely, this was the time of the Algerian war of independence against France, the Mau Mau uprisings in Kenya, the dethroning of Egypt's King Farouk, and the faint rumblings of dissent in Indo-China and the Levant. While this resistance largely involved armed struggle, intervention also occurred (as Edward Said points out in his *Culture and Imperialism*) on the cultural and aesthetic levels: thus there emerged what has come to be termed *postcolonial literature* – writing by the (post)colonial subject as resistance to colonial subjugation.

Within the colonial paradigm, cultural subjugation meant the transformation or representation of lands and regions as spaces of mystique and exoticism for the European traveler, as in André Gide's novel *The Immoralist*; or as sinister, impenetrable spaces which nonetheless held out the promise of commercial exploitation, as in Joseph Conrad's novella *Heart of Darkness*. Moreover, it involved representations of the colonized as irrational, overemotional, disorderly, and incoherent – familiar examples include Dr. Aziz in E. M. Forster's *A Passage to India*, and the chaotic, swirling crowds of Lahore in Rudyard Kipling's *Kim*. Where existing or traditional cultural forms were recognized by the colonizers, their value was generally undermined by categorizing them as naive, mythic, superstitious, or aesthetically crude – all rationales for situating colonized cultures *outside* the modern Eurocentric sphere. It was to these biased representations that postcolonial literature responded, not only to *reverse* the fictionality of the colonizer's narrative but also to show how colonial representations had had an impact on the totality of life for the colonized, from the formation of colonial public policy and education, to constructions of identity (based upon partial and political viewpoints).

While it is important not to collapse the colonial condition into an undifferentiated set of experiences, there are nonetheless certain thematic parallels which much postcolonial literature, from Africa to New Guinea, shares in common (Ashcroft, et al, *The Empire Writes Back: Theory and Practice in Post-Colonial Literatures*). Writing from different countries and cultures, the Kenyan Ngugi wa Thiong'o in his novel *A Grain of Wheat* and the Indian Raja Roa in his novel *Kanthapura* both express the simultaneous pain and triumph involved in the struggle for independence. Likewise, the sense of displacement and alienation in one's own land and within one's own psyche is addressed in the West Indian novelist George Lamming's *In the Castle of My Skin* as well as in the Nigerian Chinua Achebe's *No Longer at Ease*. Metaphoric themes that wrestle with the crisis of identity in a decolonizing world are also extensively used in diverse postcolonial literatures, for example in the Trinidadian V. S. Naipaul's *A House for Mr. Biswas*, and in *Remember the House* by the Indian novelist Santha Rama Roa. Many postcolonial writers have employed the literary forms and techniques of the colonial power's own language, and so used allegory, disrupted narrative flow, magic realism, irony, and so on to create alternative views of the colonial situation. This appropriation demonstrates the ability of postcolonial writers to use the "tools" of metropolitan language – the language emanating from the colonial center, the metropolis – against itself. The strategic application of this alteration, however, lies not only in the appropriation of these literary techniques themselves, but in the way they are self-consciously used to demonstrate alternative and oppositional *ideological* principles, as well as to expose dubious and biased

ones. The Indian-born novelist Salman Rushdie exemplifies this cleverly crafted appropriation in many of his novels, notably in *Midnight's Children*, *The Satanic Verses*, *The Moor's Last Sigh*, and *Shame*, as does Arundhati Roy in her Booker Prize-winning novel *The God of Small Things*.

While thematic parallels signify the ubiquitous nature of the colonial project, they do not however mean that colonized countries, regions, or people should be conflated into an undifferentiated amalgam or unit called "the colonized." Instead, it is important to recognize the variation of other crucial factors and how they function – economic, political, social, and cultural structures – within different colonized regions as well as within the colonizing power itself. In other words, there is no *essential* colonial reality or sensibility but rather *multiple realities* created by a monolithic Eurocentric endeavor. Consequently, a theoretical framework emerges to address these complex and multifaceted variables as they relate to the colonial condition. Paralleling postcolonial literature therefore is the discipline of *postcolonial theory* or *criticism* whose focus is on the ideological and political but without necessarily excluding the aesthetic. Rather, postcolonial theory is an inclusive and inquisitorial field that probes the relationships between the center and the peripheries, the colonizer and the colonized. It can also be seen as a "corrective" to the hegemonizing impulse of Western-centered discourse.

In the vanguard of postcolonial theory is the Martinique-born poet and playwright Aimé Césaire, whose 1950s essay "Discourse on Colonialism" galvanized subsequent theories and movements, most notably the concept of "negritude," a social and literary movement. In collaboration with Léon Damas and Léopold Senghor, Césaire's negritude movement promoted the rich cultural accomplishments of people of color in order to resist assimilation. Another Martinican founder of postcolonial theory is the psychotherapist Franz Fanon, whose books *The Wretched of the Earth* and *Black Skin, White Masks* are profound philosophical analyses of the psychological as well as the socioeconomic factors inherent in colonialism. In this sense, Fanon sees racism as a consequence of political oppression. In the following decade, the Palestinian-American Edward Said's *Orientalism* would become the foundational text of postcolonial criticism. For Said, postcolonial writing – literary and theoretical – is a form of resistance to highly dubious Western constructions of the "Orient." In *Culture and Imperialism*, Said scrutinizes the colonial formation through the prisms of culture and narrative.

The production of postcolonial theory has grown exponentially over the decades with certain principle terms and key figures coming up frequently. Examples include Gayatri Spivak's "subaltern studies" as well as her Marxist-feminist critiques in *In Other Worlds*; Homi Bhabha's propositions on hybridity, mimicry, and ambivalence embedded in colonial discourse ("Of Mimicry and Man: The Ambivalence of Colonial Discourse"); Barbara Harlow's concentration on writing as resistance (*Resistance Literature*); and Abdul JanMohamed's concept of "manichean duality" (*Manichean Aesthetics: The Politics of Literature in Colonial Africa*), where colonial conflict is posed in terms of a struggle between the forces of light and dark, good and evil, or, more specifically, God and Satan.

More recently, the dimensions of postcolonial theory have expanded to address ever more complex relationships, particularly in the fields of feminism and cultural studies. Postcolonial feminists argue for more inclusive critiques where the position of women within the colonial framework is scrutinized to illuminate the "double-bind" of colonial *and* gender oppression. And scholars in the field of cultural studies such as Masao Miyoshi and Arif Dirlik question the premature appellation of the prefix *post*-colonial when the globalization of culture and capital may be leading humanity toward a *neo*-colonial condition.

## Further reading

Appiah, A. K. "Is the Post- in Postmodernism the Post- in Postcolonial?," in *Critical Inquiry*. 17, no. 2 (Winter 1991), pp. 336–357.

Ashcroft, Bill, et al. *The Empire Writes Back: Theory and Practice in Post-Colonial Literatures*, 1989.

Bhabha, Homi K. "Of Mimicry and Man: The Ambivalence of Colonial Discourse," in *October*. No. 28 (1984).

Eagleton, Terry, et al. *Nationalism, Colonialism and Literature*, 1990.

Fanon, Franz. *The Wretched of the Earth*, 1964.

——. *Black Skin, White Masks*, 1967.

Guha, Ranajit, and Gayatri Spivak. *Selected Subaltern Studies*, 1988.

Harlow, Barbara. *Resistance Literature*, 1987.

JanMohamed, Abdul. *Manichean Aesthetics: The Politics of Literature in Colonial Africa*, 1983.

Mukerjee, Arun P. "Whose Postcolonialism and Whose Postmodernism?," in *World Literature Written in English*. 30, no. 2 (1990), pp. 1–9.

Parry, Benita. "Problems in Current Theories of Colonial Discourse," in *Oxford Literary Review*. 9, no. 7 (1987), pp. 27–58.

Said, Edward. *Orientalism*, 1978.

——. "Representing the Colonized," in *Critical Inquiry*. 15, no. 2 (1989), pp. 205–225.

——. *Culture and Imperialism*, 1993.

Spivak, Gayatri C. *In Other Worlds: Essays in Cultural Politics*, 1987.

——. *The Postcolonial Critic: Interviews, Strategies, Dialogues*, 1990.

LORRAINA PINNELL

*See also* Black Literary Theory and Criticism; Gates; Mphahlele; Ngugi wa Thiong'o; Soyinka; Spivak

# Postmodernism

"Postmodernism" is a term usually applied to the period in literature and literary theory since the 1960s, though some regard postmodernism as the prevailing intellectual mood since World War II ended in 1945. Numerous philosophers, critics, and belletristic writers can be seen as precursors or early representatives of the cultural and aesthetic approach that would come to be called postmodernism, among them Martin Heidegger, Walter Benjamin, Bertolt Brecht, Jorge Luis Borges, and Roland Barthes. Unlike other avant-garde or "progressive" movements before it, postmodernism rejects the metaphysical underpinnings of Western thought and culture at the very deepest level. Postmodernism is characterized by a strikingly radical skepticism toward all aspects of Western culture, the impetus for which many practitioners of postmodern theory themselves trace back to the writings of the nineteenth-century philosopher Friedrich Nietzsche. Nietzsche's spiritual descendants seek, in so many words, a new kind of meaning independent of the prevailing cultural "myth" of objective truth.

## Defining terms

What exactly is meant by the label "modernism" and how does postmodernism differ from it? In the English-speaking world, modernism has a very specific meaning among most literature scholars, referring not to the "modern age" since the Enlightenment, or to "modern" in the sense of contemporary, but to the period after World War I, when T. S. Eliot, James Joyce, William Butler Yeats, Ezra Pound, and Gertrude Stein (among others) were in their heyday. Their collective effort represents an attempt to revive Western literature without advancing the realist tradition or the bourgeois morality of the nineteenth century. The war effectively extinguished the optimism once invested in rationality and technological progress by Western culture, but it was hoped that a new, more critical literature and culture could be established. The period is marked by the search for totality in art, as in James Joyce's "book to end all books," *Ulysses* (1922). Modernism thus still exhibits the desire for order, albeit new forms of order, in its aesthetics, while postmodernism, coming in the wake of yet another world war, abandons the search for totality altogether and sets out to particularize, question, and subvert. Postmodernism offers no suggestion of anything like a comprehensive substitute world-view.

Postmodernism means to make a clean break with the past in the sense that the past and its way of looking at the world become the subject of satirical, often sarcastic "play" with historical figures, texts, and ideologies. Postmodernism represents a final disillusionment with Western cultural preconceptions and indulges in a merciless "rethinking" of history, pedagogy, and aesthetics in literature, the visual arts, and architecture. This disillusionment peaked in the culturally and politically rebellious years of the 1960s, during which time the prestige of the United States, a putative champion of traditional Western values, was called into question by a protracted, brutal, and ultimately unsuccessful interventionist war in Southeast Asia. By the same token, postmodernism in the days after the end of the Cold War (1945–1989) is no closer to offering direction, but asserts only its prerogative to question infinitely and to subvert.

Finally, it is fair to say that the adjective "postmodern" refers to virtually all nontraditional literature written in the years after World War II, as suggested above, but "postmodernist" connotes a programmatic aesthetics, a construct of various critics speaking with different voices, since the 1960s. A postmodernist novel is self-consciously so; a postmodern novel, on the other hand, means it shows some or all of certain common assumptions of postmodernism, but may have been written before the term gained currency.

## Common assumptions

Since some critics resist the label "postmodernist" and still others deny there actually exists a movement or school of postmodernism, it is best to identify the common assumptions usually in play when scholars use the term. First, the postmodernists can be said to see language as the multilayered medium within which we must search for meaning, all the while aware of the impossibility of absolute knowledge. Meaning, as deconstructionists like Jacques Derrida insist, is a matter of contrast within linguistic contexts; it is created by difference, not by the identity of the sign (word) with that which the sign represents.

The boundary between fact and fiction is often dissolved in postmodernism. Neither historiography nor science writing is exempt from skepticism about its fundamental tenets, and like narrative fiction, both are regarded as human constructs and inventive creations. Borrowing from the terminology of Thomas Kuhn's philosophy of science, postmodernists regard the modern, rationalistic, technologically oriented world-view as a "paradigm" that will one day be replaced by the paradigms of a new world-view, just as the heliocentric universe replaced the Ptolemaic system. Relativity underscored the limits of Newtonian physics, and forced the twentieth century to readjust fundamentally the received paradigm for the behavior of the physical world. Science, it is argued, cannot be regarded as decisive, complete.

Indeed, for the postmodernist there is nothing absolute or eternal. All meaning, all value is historically conditioned. On the societal level, the rituals and conventions of culture, to paraphrase Michel Foucault, are tired, in need of abandonment or renewal, and ultimately arbitrary. Any culture, when analyzed "archeologically," is motivated at various levels by the need to dominate and control. Postmodernism aims at freedom from the shackles of the past, especially the intellectual shackles of the past. It is concerned with exposing structures of power, both political and cultural.

Another common assumption in postmodernism is that there is nothing necessarily essential about human beings; the idea of human nature is itself a human construct among many. Thus, the concentration on depicting universal experience in traditional literature is irrelevant and illusionary.

Finally, the postmodern art object is not "self-sufficient" but exists in relation to other texts and consciously refers to other works of art (intertextuality). It borrows and manipulates freely, without any of the traditional deference for the works of high culture (or their creators).

## Literature in the era of postmodernism

In the years after World War II many writers emerged with innovative techniques and narrative content reflecting to one degree or another the intentions of postmodernism. These include John Barth, Italo Calvino, Günter Grass, Kurt Vonnegut, and Jorge Luis Borges, among others.

World War II and its aftermath form the context within which the first generation of postmodern writers set at least some part of their stories. They focus often on the contrast between received "noble ideals" and the willingness of opposing sides to employ utterly barbarous technological means to defeat each other through "total war." This depravity and mayhem on a mass scale renders any distinction between "high" and "low" culture meaningless. While veterans of World War I expressed a similar disillusionment, for the postmoderns the repugnance is complete. The popular American novelist and playwright Kurt Vonnegut uses the example of the fire-bombing of Dresden, Germany (an architectural and cultural jewel with scant military and no industrial significance), as a backdrop for his 1969 novel *Slaughterhouse-Five*. An even darker, more grotesque note is struck by Thomas Pynchon in his unrelentingly scathing *Gravity's Rainbow* (1973). As is typical for postmodern literature, the narrative advances tortuously, in flashbacks and flashforwards, and is frequently interrupted.

In Germany, too, a new style of writing appeared after 1945. Günter Grass constructs in baroque detail a fascinating prewar and wartime tale from the perspective of a young boy (Oskar) who decides to stop growing up when the hostilities begin. The story is accompanied by a metanarrative and framed by the remarks of the adult Oskar, now being cared for in an asylum. *Die Blechtrommel* (*The Tin Drum*) appeared in 1959 and was immediately heralded as an immensely innovative literary triumph. An English translation appeared in 1962. (It should be mentioned that Bertolt Brecht paved the way for a new, postwar aesthetics in Germany with his concept of "audience alienation," known by the German term *Verfremdungseffekt*, and other methodological innovations in drama, poetry, and prose.)

Besides the stupidity of war, another subject of primary importance in postmodern literature is ethnicity. Postmodern writers who depict the experience of racism and segregation in the United States include E. L. Doctorow, Toni Morrison, and Alice Walker, among others. Postmodern literature is also increasingly concerned with the institutionalized exploitation of women and with feminist issues in general. Salman Rushdie's novels challenge and transcend cultural conventions and parochial mentalities, in two different worlds, the Islamic as well as the European.

Clearly, any literature that assails injustice as postmodern(ist) literature so often does is not nihilistic or devoid of values, however much it wishes to be free of conventions and traditional attachments. However, the postmodern approach is one which more often than not exposes rather than explicitly condemns. By the same token, postmodernism accepts and embraces mass culture and goes out of its way not to turn up its nose. Andy Warhol's pop art images are the visual counterpart to the literary use of "cultural icons" and items of mass production, where once literature celebrated and participated in "high culture" apart from and superior to other crafts and trades.

As for specific techniques, the novels of postmodernism are often self-conscious "meta-narratives" – they do not tell a story without commenting on the narrative enterprise and paradoxically questioning their own claims to narrative and epistemological validity. (The British author John Fowles is a master of this sort of postmodernist inversion and ambiguity, though his inversions are final ones, occurring at the end of the narrative, with alternative conclusions, as in *The French Lieutenant's Woman*, 1969.) In the works of many other writers, narrative ambiguity permeates the text, however, bewildering many readers. Conventional perspective is also absent. Postmodernist literature shirks the omniscient third-person narrative voice and often "floats" perspective among several narrators. This kind of literature also often excerpts or "samples" from other documents (of various kinds) and playfully manipulates history and historical figures, as in the works of Umberto Eco, Milan Kundera, Ian Watson, and others. Ironically, the postmodernist self-assertiveness toward "high culture" (not as much a sweeping disdain as a reaction against exaggerated cultural deference) results often in a new type of arcane, even elitist literature; rarely in the history of literature has any movement been as academic and self-referential as postmodernism.

## Postmodernist critical theory

Recent research has increasingly focused on postmodernist critical theory's conceptual borrowings from the fields of elementary particle physics and special relativity theory as they burgeoned in the first half of the twentieth century. This cross-disciplinary influence occurred despite the obscurity, for most people, of the mathematical intricacies of modern physics, largely because Albert Einstein, Werner Heisenberg, and others wrote specifically for the broader public concerning their ideas. For instance, the scientific conclusion that light behaves as both wave and particle – and that these two manifestations of the same phenomenon are not mutually exclusive but can be unified in theory – was encouraging for those already convinced that ambiguity and paradox needed to assume a larger role in

philosophy as well as art. Einstein's challenge to absolute time in his denial of large-scale simultaneity, that is, the existence of absolute time for all observers in the cosmos, was also a liberating notion for those who wished to apply the principle of relativity to Western cultural conventions and metaphysics.

The most important scientific concept for postmodernist thought is however the idea, borrowed from quantum mechanics, of "indeterminacy" at the very basis of material reality. Statistical probabilities can be determined for the position and identity of an electron at any given time, but beyond that our measurements cannot go with any certainty. And by attempting to "lift the veil" we disturb the natural state of the atom; the act of observation alters the phenomenon we observe.

Thus, the principle of the "indeterminacy of the text," discussed by critical theorists since the 1960s, has its roots at least in part in ideas being discussed in physics in the 1920s. Derrida has been the prime voice in that realm of postmodernist discourse, though the American Stanley Fish is also known for his extensive arguments against determinacy. The naive notion that a text exists independently of its perception by a reader or audience is the starting point for its "deconstruction." Multiple readings are possible, desirable, even necessary. The autonomy of the text, sacred in New Criticism, is toppled in postmodernism; we are free to explore multiple possibilities in interpreting any poem, play, or prose narrative. William Shakespeare's plays may be performed not only in modern, anachronistic dress, but simultaneously in eclectic costumes from various periods. Postmodernism toys with conventions, rewrites history, and answers to no authority but its own hermeneutical conscience.

The term "postmodernism" was first used in the 1960s by literary critics such as Ihab Hassan and Leslie Fiedler. They were joined by Susan Sontag in arguing for the postmodernist aesthetic. The postmodernist critical approach soon made its way to Paris and Frankfurt and was taken up by Julia Kristeva and Jean-François Lyotard, and taken on by Jürgen Habermas, who believes that postmodern literature succeeds in the negative purpose of "problematizing" but ultimately delivers no "positive content." Defenders of postmodernism often respond that such criticism misses the point; postmodern writers expose questions of reality – they do not provide explicit answers about reality.

## Further reading
Barthes, Roland. *Critical Essays*, 1972.
Fish, Stanley. *Is There a Text in This Class? The Authority of Interpretive Communities*, 1980.
Foster, Hal, ed. *Recodings: Art, Spectacle, Cultural Politics*, 1985.
Foucault, Michel. *An Archeology of Knowledge*, 1972.
Froula, Christine. "Quantum Physics/Post-Modern Metaphysics: The Nature of Derrida," in *Western Humanities Review*. 39 (1985), pp. 287–313.

Hassan, Ihab. *Liberations: New Essays on the Humanities in Revolution*, 1971.

Hutcheon, Linda. *A Poetics of Postmodernism: History, Theory, Fiction*, 1988.

Huyssen, Andreas. *After the Great Divide: Modernism, Mass Culture, Postmodernism*, 1986.

Jameson, Frederic. *Brecht and Method*, 1998.

Kristeva, Julia. *Desire in Language*, 1980.

Lyotard, Jean-François. *The Postmodernist Condition: A Report on Knowledge*, 1984.

McHale, Brian. *Postmodernist Fiction*, 1987.

Nash, Christopher. *World Postmodern Fiction: A Guide*, 1993.

Simpson, David. *The Academic Postmodern and the Rule of Literature: A Report on Half-Knowledge*, 1995.

Sontag, Susan. *Against Interpretation and Other Essays*, 1967.

Stephens, Julie. *Sixties Radicalism and Postmodernism*, 1998.

White, Hayden. *Metahistory: The Historical Imagination in Nineteenth-Century Europe*, 1973.

MARK R. McCULLOH

*See also* Barthes; Baudrillard; Deconstruction; Derrida; Foucault; Intertextuality; Modernism

# Georges Poulet

Belgian critic and theorist

**Born:** Chênée, Belgium; November 29, 1902

## Biography

Georges Poulet has had a distinguished transatlantic career as a critic of international renown. He has taught French literature at the University of Edinburgh, The Johns Hopkins University, and the universities of Zurich, Switzerland, and Nice. The first volume of his *Études sur le temps humain* (1949; *Studies in Human Time*, 1956) won the Prix Sainte-Beuve in 1950; the second volume, *La Distance intérieure* (1952; *The Interior Distance*, 1959), was awarded both the Grand Prix de la Critique Littéraire in 1952 and the French Academy's Prix Duvchon for a work in philosophy in 1953; in 1959 the University of Geneva bestowed on him an honorary doctorate, as did the University of Nice in 1966 and the University of Edinburgh in 1971. In 1979 he received the Prix International de la Critique.

## Influence

Poulet is the most sophisticated, ambitious, and influential member of a group of critics, variously termed critics of consciousness, phenomenologists, genetic critics, existential philosopher-critics, or simply the Geneva School, since virtually all of them have had formal associations with the University of Geneva and are linked by bonds of reciprocal intellectual impact as well as friendship. This cohort exerted considerable authority in both European and American literary circles from the early 1960s to the mid-1970s, displacing the aestheticist formalism of the New Critics only to be in turn supplanted by poststructuralists, Derridean deconstructionists, and reader-response receptionists.

## Analysis

The New Criticism, dominant in the American critical landscape for a generation from the mid-1930s onward, viewed the literary work as an artifact, an autonomous object with its own structure and mode of being. New Critics such as John Crowe Ransom, Allen Tate, Cleanth Brooks, Robert Penn Warren, and R. P. Blackmur considered criticism a category of objective knowledge, akin to anthropology or chemistry, yielding a definitive conceptualization of its subject matter. They therefore committed themselves to probing studies of the linguistic properties of a particular text, closely considering its imagery, symbolism, paradoxes, tone, texture, irony, ambiguity, and other aspects of its special literary language. They refused to locate the meaning of a work beyond its particular, verbal organization, ignoring or minimizing its intellectual background, social milieu, the author's biography, and its psychological or moral effects on a reader. Their outstanding achievement was the establishment of standards for astute and subtle textual analysis.

To the Genevists, the critical universe looks drastically different. For them the literary work is not an objective, closed structure of meanings evident or latent in the words of a poem, play, or novel; instead, it is part of the writer's consciousness, of his or her state of mind. The writer has brought a certain mode of consciousness into a fusion of mind and words called a literary text, and the critic must seek to ascertain that consciousness and communicate it to others. The subject of the text is not "what it says" via a verbal structure and signals, but the critic's hypothesis of the author's *cogito* – the author's perception and creation of his or her literary identity. J. Hillis Miller, once Georges Poulet's colleague and disciple at Johns Hopkins, has defined this kind of criticism as "primordially consciousness of the consciousness of another, the transposition of the mental universe of an author into . . . the critic's mind."

The Genevists eliminate clear distinctions between critic, writer, and work: they regard the movement of the text as indistinguishable from the movement of thought which is the critique, or from the creative act which produced the work. They view the formal and stylistic uniqueness of a text not as self-referential and contextual, but as the revelation of the writer's own being, the confession of his or her state of consciousness. Their criticism is a personal adventure – the critic's empathic identification with the psyche of the creator. Since the Genevists refuse to grant the text any intrinsic, self-sufficient life, they assemble endless, restless metaphors as they attempt to imprint the text's nature in the mind of the reader. What they aim at is extremely bold and hazardous: to perform a parallel act of composition with the work's creator, so as to capture its imaginative synergy. In sum, the Genevists join the author in a common enterprise of achieving literary meaning; they regard their criticism as itself a form of literature.

Poulet owes only a minor intellectual debt to the founder of phenomenology, the German philosopher Edmund Husserl. Husserl sought to describe human consciousness – he called it the *Lebenswelt* (lived world) – as a universal epiphenomenon common to all human beings. Poulet, to the contrary, seeks to ascertain and share the unique consciousness of a particular writer. His phenomenalism is far closer to that of the French philosopher-critic Gaston Bachelard. In *La Psychanalyse du feu* (1937; *The Psychoanalysis of Fire*, 1964), Bachelard attempted to demonstrate that the four elements, earth, fire, water, and air, are the foundations for myth and imagery and thus for poetic consciousness, with the poet using them for his or her world of sensibility and imagination. In two later works, *La Poétique de l'éspace* (1957; *The Poetics of Space*, 1964) and *La Poétique de la reverie* (1960; *The Poetics of Reverie*, 1969), Bachelard insists that the poetic image has its own being and dynamism, and therefore should become the subject for an ontology of poetics which would seek to account for its existence and essence. In his stress on images and patterns of consciousness, his search for meanings which can be applied to the movement of consciousness which constitutes its author, Bachelard accords with Poulet. He considers any distinction between the author and the work to be artificial and untenable; so does Poulet. He regards the critic as the cocreator of the literary text; so does Poulet. He sees the formal structure of a work as an obstacle to the reader's identification with the poetic will which is the source for creative achievement; so does Poulet.

In an illuminating essay, "Phénoménologie de la conscience critique" (1968; "Phenomenology of Reading," 1969), Poulet recounts his experience in reading a book. As soon as he starts reading, the gap between writer and reader is bridged: "You are inside it; it is inside you; there is no longer either outside or inside. . . . I am aware of a . . . consciousness; the consciousness of another, . . . in this case the consciousness is open to me, welcomes me, lets me look deep inside itself, and even allows me . . . to think what it thinks, and feel what it feels."

Poulet maintains that the experiential world can be divided into exterior objects and interior objects. The former, such as vases, statues, and sewing machines, give the viewer no inside access. This is not true of a book: "It asks nothing better than to exist outside itself, or to let you exist in it." A book "wants" to transcend its material condition and change into a mental, interior universe of language and concepts as it is being read. Where does the object called a book end up? No longer, concludes Poulet, in a spatial dimension: "There is only one place left for this new existence: my innermost self."

Poulet's overriding critical concern is thus with the genesis of the literary work in the human consciousness, with its creative rather than reflective or expressive function. He therefore turns inward toward an explanation of the psyche as the unmediated, irreducible, asocial originator of the work – before the mind achieves duration, and before the work becomes a sociohistoric phenomenon. The critic's aim is to catch the author's consciousness – or *cogito*, as Poulet often calls it – when it is still in a virgin condition, not yet penetrated by what Poulet has termed "the thick bulk of its objective content."

Poulet is here asking the reader to believe that consciousness can be grasped as a pure texture, as the precise tone which persists in a particular author's writing throughout his or her work. Surely this is a drastically simplified psychology, even if the reader is generous enough not to ask awkward questions about the neurophysiological facts of adult interaction. Poulet wants the reader-critics to efface their own habits, beliefs, and desires, to dispossess themselves of all of their experiences and characteristics, in effect to empty themselves of self. Instead, he wants the reader-critic to achieve an empathic state of harmony with an author's *cogito* that amounts to virtually uncanny identification and re-creation. For Poulet the aim of reading is to assume the creative essence of another being. The reader-critic's task is not only to discover but also to enter intuitively and relive the inner life of every writer as if it were his or her own. The writer, text, and reader may begin the aesthetic transaction as three; Poulet's aim is to make them one.

In his preface to *The Interior Distance*, Poulet seeks to establish a basic paradigm for his criticism of communion: two persons – the author and the reader – start at a distance from each other, then create a space in which they unite their minds. His essays constitute attempts to describe this "interior distance" that can be overcome by sensitive interpretation: "My thought is not made up solely of my thoughts; it is made up also, even more perhaps, of all the *interior distance* which separates me from, or draws me closer to, that which I am able to think. . . . The distance is not merely an interval; it is an ambient milieu, a field of union."

Poulet's criticism proves most illuminating when he can apply it to largely introspective writers, such as Maurice de Guérin, Sébastien-Roch Nicolas Chamfort, and Stéphane Mallarmé. It fails in varying degrees, however, with more extroverted authors such as Victor Hugo and Honoré de Balzac; Poulet's assessments cut and press these men's achievements to accommodate the tight, metaphysical frames of the *cogitos* he has conceived for them. Thus Poulet posits a "Balzacian being" whom he defines as "the space in which a world is reflected and also the movement by which this world spreads itself out." Yet nowhere in his fifty-five-page essay on Balzac does Poulet mention money, clothes, furniture, or people encountering other people – despite discussing a writer whose appetite for the material world and its human comedy was the most zestful in the history of fiction.

Poulet's problems with Hugo and Balzac illustrate the rigidity of his critical stance. He applies his *cogito*-tracking unvaryingly to writers differing drastically in thought, temperament, experience, and expression. His results are bound to be uneven, as he underdocuments and over-schematizes, concentrating on the attitudes to temporal and spatial relationships each of his subjects is deemed to express in a continuum controlled by his – the critic's – sensibility.

What chiefly distinguishes Poulet's criticism from that of other Genevists is his insistence that consciousness need not have a referent, whether it be subject or object. He affirms over and over again that consciousness need be aware of nothing but itself, that it is a solitary yet universal condition which is the hidden center of every human mind apart from and independent of the experiential world. His premises are Platonic and Cartesian, professing as the essential element of literature a state of mind prior to and separate from the dense sensuousness of objects or texture of human relationships. His is purely and solely a consciousness of consciousness, entitling him to the central and pivotal place in the Geneva School.

The older members of this school were Marcel Raymond and Albert Béguin. Raymond's best-known book, *De Baudelaire au surréalisme* (1933; *From Baudelaire to Surrealism*, 1947), traces the history of modern French poetry along lines of inner spiritual affinities, disregarding what he considers irrelevantly external features of specific influences and derivations. Like Poulet, whom he deeply influenced, Raymond seeks to feel his way backward from the mass of motifs and objects which fill a writer's consciousness toward the pure moment when consciousness is as yet empty of all but itself. He calls this kind of criticism "creative participation." Albert Béguin began as Raymond's friend and disciple. His most distinguished work, *L'Âme romantique et le rêve* (1937), was hailed by Poulet in a 1954 article as "revealing the very essence of the dream's nature." Béguin's conversion to Catholicism in 1940, however, radically affected his subsequent choice of subjects, steering him away from studies of the poetic imagination to a personal quest for salvation.

In his turn Poulet has had considerable effect on the younger Genevists, including Jean-Pierre Richard, Jean Rousset, Jean Starobinski, and J. Hillis Miller. Richard studied with Poulet at the University of Edinburgh and received high praise from his mentor when he published *Littérature et sensation* (1954); in turn he dedicated to Poulet his *L'Univers imaginaire de Mallarmé* (1961). Like Poulet, Richard seeks to define the writer's consciousness by mapping his mental world, considering any text by the writer merely a single emanation of what he terms the author's "fundamental project." Rousset is a former student

of Raymond who, in texts such as *Forme et signification* (1962), tries to relive the adventure of the work's creation by interpreting it as a clue to the author's mind. Starobinski is the most eclectic of the Genevists. Trained as a physician as well as a professor of literature, he studies human consciousness in its physiological as well as verbal expressions, committed to interpreting literature through such motifs as the mask, the look, or the village festival.

Miller is the only American critic who has associated – or, more precisely, did associate – himself with the criticism of consciousness. He came to know Poulet at Johns Hopkins during the mid-1950s and dedicated his first book, *Charles Dickens: The World of His Novels* (1958), to him. Miller, however, has been consistently more style-conscious and formalistic than other Genevists. In his preface to the Dickens study, he tries to negotiate a compromise between phenomenological and New criticism: "A poem or novel is indeed the world refashioned into conformity with the inner structure of the writer's spirit, but at the same time it is that spirit given, through words, a form and substance taken from the shared solidity of the exterior world." From about 1970 Miller renounced consciousness criticism in favor of Derridean deconstruction, concluding that a literary text is a continuous flow of irreconcilable and contradictory meanings, so that, in the final analysis, all reading must constitute at least a partial misreading.

Recent critical movements have had a short shelf-life, and Poulet's criticism has not been exempted from this fate of all-too-temporary modishness: it has been attacked from a variety of perspectives. Freudian interpreters have questioned the concept that consciousness rather than the unconscious represents the originating point for a literary work. Poststructuralists such as Michel Foucault are skeptical of the possibility of ascertaining any origin of consciousness that would govern an author's creativity. Psycholinguists contend that Poulet's overlapping coincidence of the creator's and critic's zones of consciousness is an impossibility, since another person's mind is ultimately alien and impenetrable to even the most discerning evaluator.

Formalists (New Critics) attack Poulet's work on the central ground that, by ignoring or disdaining the discrete, unique existence of the literary object, he consequently rejects its nature as an organic whole, its coherence of structure and meaning, its verbal craft and contour. They insist that literary judgment must be exercised primarily on the work, not on its author. The poet may, as William Wordsworth declared, be a man speaking to men, but he speaks by means of a poem.

The most formidable rejection of consciousness criticism is that mounted by the deconstructionist movement, headed by Jacques Derrida and Paul de Man. The Derrideans question the basic assumptions of Western philosophy originating with Plato. They regard the desire for a center or origin of all structures – such as Poulet's *cogito* – as the fallacy of "logocentrism," discussed in Derrida's *De la grammatologie* (1967; *Of Grammatology*, 1976), which is grounded on a metaphysics of "presence." Derrida and his followers argue that all reliances on such a tradition of "presence" are illusory and unverifiable. They call instead for a new tradition of *différance* – a word which, in French, fuses the senses of being different and deferring. They insist that reader-critics can never establish a limit to a text, and that everything written can be read in different and contradictory contexts, regardless of the writer's intention. Hence all readings are at best uncertain and provisional, resulting in a deadlock of incompatible interpretations that cannot be broken. De Man, in a subtle essay on Poulet collected in *Blindness and Insight* (1971), tries to claim him as an unintentional deconstructionist by pointing out contradictions in Poulet's several critical essays on Marcel Proust. In an early essay, de Man states, Poulet sees Proust turning toward the past and failing to find it a firm link between himself and the world. In a later analysis, Poulet finds Proust discovering in the past "the creative moment par excellence, the source of Proust's poetic imagination as well as the center of the critical narrative." In a still later study, Poulet reverses perspective again, granting the past no priority over the present or future in Proust's fiction. While de Man regrets Poulet's reluctance to accept the self-consuming nature of literature, he nevertheless concludes his appraisal by calling Poulet's critical performance "one of the major works of our time."

## Principal criticism

*Études sur le temps humain, I*, 1949 (*Studies in Human Time*, 1956)
*Études sur le temps humain, II: La Distance intérieure*, 1952 (*The Interior Distance*, 1959)
*Les Metamorphoses du cercle*, 1961 (*The Metamorphoses of the Circle*, 1967)
*L'Éspace proustien*, 1963 (*Proustian Space*, 1977)
*Études sur le temps humain, III: Le Point de départ*, 1964
"Bachelard et la conscience de soi," 1965
*Trois Essais de mythologie romantique*, 1966
*Benjamin Constant par lui-même*, 1968
"Phénoménologie de la conscience critique," 1968 ("Phenomenology of Reading," 1969)
*Qui était Baudelaire?*, 1969 (*Who Was Baudelaire?*, 1969)
*La Conscience critique*, 1971
*Entre moi et moi: Essais critiques sur la conscience de soi*, 1977
*La Poesie Éclatée: Baudelaire / Rimbaud*, 1980 (*Exploding Poetry: Baudelaire / Rimbaud*, 1980)

## Other major works and literary forms

Georges Poulet is known primarily for his literary theory.

## Further reading

Alexander, Ian W. *French Literature and the Philosophy of Consciousness*, 1984.
De Man, Paul. "The Literary Self as Origin: The Work of Georges Poulet," in *Blindness and Insight*, 1971.
Lawall, Sarah. *Critics of Consciousness: The Existential Structures of Literature*, 1968.

Miller, J. Hillis. "The Literary Criticism of Georges Poulet," in *MLN*. 78, no. 5 (1963), pp. 471–488.
——. "The Geneva School," in *Critical Quarterly*. VIII (Winter, 1966), pp. 305–321.

GERHARD BRAND

*See also* French Literary Theory: Twentieth Century; Geneva School; Phenomenological Criticism

# Ezra Pound

## American poet and critic

**Born:** Hailey, Idaho; October 30, 1885
**Died:** Venice, Italy; November 1, 1972

## Biography

Ezra Loomis Pound was born in Hailey, Idaho, on October 30, 1885. His father, who ran the land office in Hailey, moved the family to Philadelphia, where he worked as the assistant assayer at the United States Mint. Reared in the Philadelphia suburbs, Pound attended local public schools and the Cheltenham Military Academy. He entered the University of Pennsylvania in 1901. He transferred to Hamilton College in 1903, received a Ph.B. in 1905, and returned to the University of Pennsylvania, only to study abroad for a year on a fellowship in London and Madrid. After returning to Philadelphia for another year of graduate work, he completed his M.A. in Romance languages.

In the fall of 1907 Pound taught Romance languages at Wabash College in Crawfordsville, Indiana. After he was fired in early 1908 he took a trip to Europe, a trip which, in effect, began his literary career. He moved to Italy and published his first collection of poems in Venice and then moved to London later the same year and became active in several artistic circles. In London, Pound wrote poetry, music, and literary criticism, lectured on Romance literature, and edited and collaborated on literary journals and anthologies, promoting new writers and the new art movements of Imagism and vorticism. From among his many literary acquaintances, he met Dorothy Shakespear, a watercolorist, and they were married in 1914.

Pound left for Paris in 1921 and extended his circle of influence and friendship to include expatriate writers such as Ernest Hemingway and James Joyce. He met Olga Rudge, a concert violinist, and together they had a daughter, Mary. In 1924 Pound moved to Rapallo, Italy, continuing his writing, editing, and research and maintaining his literary contacts.

During World War II, Pound made a series of radio broadcasts for Rome Radio. Although he saw his actions as an effort to end the fighting between Italy and the United States, he was charged with treason at the end of the war.

Initially imprisoned by the United States government in a detention camp in Pisa, he was brought to the United States to stand trial.

Pound was declared medically unfit for trial and, from 1946 to 1958, was committed to St. Elizabeths Hospital for the criminally insane in Washington, D.C. He continued to write at St. Elizabeths, while friends and young writers visited him. When his indictment for treason was dismissed, he returned to Italy. Except for short trips, he lived the rest of his life with his daughter and son-in-law in Castle Brunnenburg in the Tirol and with Olga Rudge in Venice, where he died in 1972.

## Influence

In his introduction to Pound's *Literary Essays* (1954), the poet and critic T. S. Eliot wrote that Pound brought about a "revolution of taste and practice," adding that Pound's critical writings "form the *least dispensable* body of critical writing in our time." Pound succeeded in shaking up then, as his ideas have since, much of the stagnation and narrow-mindedness found in literary criticism. Pound also influenced the field directly by fighting to get jobs or patrons for unsuccessful but talented writers so they would be free to write.

Twentieth-century critics' strong interest in comparative literature and interdisciplinary studies can be directly attributed to Pound. Comparative studies were virtually nonexistent early in the twentieth century; thus Pound wrote, and many have followed his example, about music, sculpture, and painting. He inspired, annoyed, and baffled scholars when he wrote about and translated Chinese poetry and Japanese drama, while encouraging people to read Arthur Rimbaud, Catullus, and troubadour poets.

Pound influenced the critical theories of objectivism and projectivism and, by breaking the narrow focus of criticism, indirectly influenced the popular acceptance of the many new and experimental critical theories of the twentieth century, some of which he might very well have disdained. Yet, perhaps more than any other critic in the twentieth century, Pound has influenced those actually writing literature. Even those writers who deny his ideas or influence have to contend with Ezra Pound.

## Analysis

Pound's poetry is often indecipherable, his economic theory occasionally perplexing. Yet his attitude toward the usual state of criticism, his views on its ideal function, and his own approach to achieve this ideal were always clear, simple, and consistent:

I really do not give an underdone damn about your terminology so long as you understand it and don't mess up the meaning of your words. And (we might add) so long as you, as reader, try to understand the meaning of the text (whatever text) you read.

Pound's criticism was almost always this blunt and contentious. For the most part, he hated critics. Regardless of whether he discussed medieval poetry or Italian politics, he usually blasted "half-knowing and half-thinking" critics and pointed out the shortcomings of contemporary criticism. In *Jefferson and/or Mussolini* (1935), he refers to academic writers as "lily-livered letterati." In his essay "Cavalcanti" in *Make It New* (1934), he notes that critics were "normally a bore and a nuisance." In the essay "How to Read," Pound points out how critics "talk all around the matter," do not "define their terms," and "don't say frankly that certain authors are . . . bores."

Pound believed that critics should provide a service to humanity. The function of criticism, the responsibility of the critic, was to discriminate – to select the best authors, ideas, and works – and save the public from wasting its time and effort reading mediocre work. Pound's theory restated the critical position of the nineteenth-century British poet and critic Matthew Arnold, in that the best ideas should prevail. "If I am being 'crucified for an idea' – that is, the coherent idea around which my muddles accumulated," Pound related to Donald Hall in *The Paris Review* (1963), "it is probably the idea that European culture ought to survive, that the best qualities of it ought to survive along with whatever other cultures, in whatever universality." Guided by this ideal, the Poundian critic should point out discoveries that may have been overlooked; the rare critic who has a "perception of relations," relates these discoveries to others in literature. The critic "construct[s] cloacae to carry off the waste matter, which stagnates about the real work, and which is continuously being heaped up and caused to stagnate by academic bodies." Finally, "the critic most worth respect is the one who actually causes an improvement in the art he criticizes." In short, the critic's role is close to that of a teacher, as Pound exemplified himself by promising in his titles to offer "A Few Don'ts" as well as an *ABC of Reading* and *Guide to Kulchur*.

Pound promoted a *Weltliteratur* (world literature), establishing, as he wrote to Harriet Monroe in 1913, a "universal standard that pays no attention to time and country." From the best the critic has gathered together, the artist "makes it new." This regenerative process was mythologically illustrated by the Egyptian god Osiris, the symbolic source of renewed life, resurrected by his sister, Isis, who gathered his scattered limbs from all over the world. To regenerate the dead or dying art of literature, Pound addressed the subject of language. According to Pound, "great literature is simply language charged with meaning to the utmost possible degree," and he believed the difference between prose and poetry was merely that "the language of prose is much less highly charged." Since the nineteenth century, poetry has lost its supremacy in communicating human experience. Pound believed that the serious writers, such as the novelist Stendhal, tired of the frills and padding found in verse, chose prose as their medium. So, "for some time the important developments of language as means of expression were the developments of prose." Poetic language needed to be revitalized and streamlined, cleared of useless forms, archaisms, and abstractions: "It is as important for the purpose of thought to keep language efficient as it is in surgery to keep tetanus bacilli out of one's bandages." All writers, poets, and critics needed to use natural speech and to use no word that did not contribute to one's meaning. Pound admired Arthur Rimbaud and the ancient Roman poet Catullus, their poetry being "unencumbered by non-functioning words."

Pound was always interested in energy and how language captures and transfers it. A revitalized language provides the energy to revitalize thought and, by this, art and society. He wrote, "I believe that any precise use of words is bound in the long run to be useful to the state and the world at large." Pound believed it possible to generate a literary renaissance and, beyond this, a cultural and political renaissance. The critic's contribution to this renaissance was distributing a healthy supply of the best ideas and information – not mucking up or enervating the system with vague language: "I suggest that we throw out all critics who use vague general terms."

The goals that Pound set for criticism, then, were ambitious and arrogant, perhaps one could say American – he would not allow himself to be constricted. Given these goals, however, and out of critical necessity, the theorist needs a method to determine what should survive. Even for the active critic, there is simply too much "out there" in time and place to read it all.

Pound proposed a critical shortcut, a "new method of scholarship," in a series of articles entitled "I Gather the Limbs of Osiris," published in *The New Age* from 1911 to 1912. While Pound's terminology changed during his career, the distinctive character of his imagination, this urgency for condensing, simplifying, and distributing information about anything – a poem, a writer, an art or economic theory – was constant.

Pound called the approach the method of "Luminous Detail," stressing, however, that it was not really new but had been adopted by all good scholars "since the beginning of scholarship." Instead of confusing readers with details and vague generalities, the critic must find, select, and distribute luminous details, "certain facts [that] give one a sudden insight into circumjacent condition, into their causes, their effects, into sequence, and law."

Pound distinguishes between the "symptomatic" and the "donative." The symptomatic reflects the character and tendencies of the time, mirroring "what one might have expected in such and such a year and place. They register." The donative also fits into the time, but it is special, absorbing what and who came before, revealing what was always present but not apparent and contributing a new discovery. For Pound, a sestina of Pico della Mirandola was symptomatic, a canzon of Arnaut Daniel donative.

Throughout his criticism, Pound saw the world as divided between the active and the passive, those who fed a system and those who bled it. In "How to Read," for example, he classified writers as either inventors, masters, or diluters of literature. Pound suggested that Benito Mussolini had a fondness for the inventors:

The secret of the Duce is possibly the capacity to pick out the element of immediate and major importance in any tangle; or, in case of a man, to go straight to the center, for the fellow's major interest. "Why do you want to put your ideas in order?"

Pound stressed this sense of immediate importance when he propagated his own critical discoveries. In 1912 in London, along with H. D., Richard Aldington, and T. E. Hulme, he provided the credo for the Imagist "school" of poetry, Imagism. He stressed the "direct treatment of the 'thing' whether subjective or objective" and urged the poet "to use absolutely no word that does not contribute to the presentation." He compacted the definition of the poetic image into the formula of "that which presents an intellectual and emotional complex in an instant of time."

Shortly after proclaiming the fundamentals of Imagism, Pound discovered the Chinese written character. In 1913 Mary Fenollosa, the widow of an American scholar of Chinese and Japanese, Ernest Fenollosa, who died in 1908, brought Pound her husband's notebooks. From these notebooks, Pound edited and published *The Chinese Written Character as a Medium for Poetry* (1920). Fenollosa's work provided Pound with fresh critical support for his ideas about language and poetry.

The Chinese character, or ideogram, simultaneously – in an instant of time – represented the picture, or image, of the "thing" itself, a noun, and the "thing in motion," its verb. "Chinese notation . . . is based upon a vivid shorthand picture of the operations of nature," so the character for sunrise, for example, reveals exactly that: a tree, a horizon, and the sun rising behind and above them. As an ideal model, the Chinese character could revitalize the English language, rid it of its sluggishness and imprecision; the Chinese "ideographic roots carry in them a verbal idea of action."

Pound's theory directly reflected his impatient and combative critical temperament. He was impatient with extraneous and insignificant detail. He was impatient with the medium of his own craft, language, which by its narrative nature depended on time. Yet the Chinese character came closest in language to overcoming this limitation by "concretely and vividly" expressing "the interaction of things" instantly.

Creating images instantly is the "language" of the visual arts. Not long after advertising Imagism, Pound, along with the painter Wyndham Lewis and the sculptor Henri Gaudier-Brzeska, claimed to discover around 1914 what was at the very core of art itself: the vortex. The new art movement was vorticism. Pound coined a new term, but his critical ideas – his call for a concrete image, for swift and easy transmissions of energy – were the same. Pound theorized that all art, be it poetry, painting, or sculpture, centered on and contained a center of intense energy, a vortex: "a radiant node or cluster . . . from which, and through which, and into which, ideas are constantly rushing." Vortices could be detected in different countries at various times, generating political, social, and artistic energy.

Pound put vorticism into action, organizing the interdisciplinary magazine *Blast*. *Blast No. 1* was published in 1914. *Blast No. 2*, the final publication, followed a month after the Vorticist Exhibition, organized by Pound and many of the same artists contributing to *Blast*. The multinational and artistic diversity was certainly Poundian. The two *Blasts* and the exhibition included work by the sculptors Gaudier-Brzeska and Jacob Epstein, the painters Lewis and Edward Wadsworth, and the photographers Malcolm Arbuthnot and Alvin Coburn (who later produced "vortographs"). In addition, the exhibition included vorticist tables, tea trays, linen, rugs, and stained glass windows, supporting Pound's belief that generating a renaissance is possible.

*Blast*, like Pound, brought the arts together in a critical format. While promoting the new art, Pound and the vorticists attacked the outdated ideas and useless forms of established art. The vorticist manifesto in *Blast No. 1*, for example, blasted with some good-humored abuse the British Academy and "BOURGEOIS VICTORIAN VISTAS," "SENTIMENTAL HYGIENICS," Edward Elgar, the "years 1837 to 1900," "DALY'S MUSICAL COMEDY," "FEAR OF RIDICULE," the "LONDON COLISEUM," "VEGETABLE HUMANITY," "ROUSSEAUISMS (wild Nature cranks)," the "BRITANNIC ÆSTHETE CREAM OF THE SNOBBISH EARTH," and "RHETORIC OF EUNUCH and STYLIST."

As he found details to illuminate his theory for language, poetry and the image in Fenollosa, he found a form and order for language in the plastic arts:

> Gaudier had discriminated against beefy statues, he had given us a very definite appreciation of stone as stone; he had taught us to feel that the beauty of sculpture is inseparable from its material and that it inheres in the material.

Pound believed that the sculptor Constantin Brancusi best exemplified the aesthetic that "a work of art has in it no idea which is inseparable from the form."

Since the idea determines the language and the form, it was important to Pound that nothing, or as little as possible, interfered with the transmission, from the ideas in one's mind to the page. When writers used artificial language and archaic forms for their own sake, they obscured, falsified,

or covered up the fact that they simply did not have any ideas. This critical relation between idea and form remains at the center of contemporary aesthetics throughout the century, from Charles Olson's Projective Verse, based on Robert Creeley's "FORM IS NEVER MORE THAN AN EXTENSION OF CONTENT," to the concrete and language-centered poets who believe that form is content.

Pound was constantly discovering useful forms and ideas for his own writing, and his literary criticism, like that by other poet-critics such as William Wordsworth and T. S. Eliot, usually supported his own poetry. "The people I have written about," he told Hall in *The Paris Review*, "were the most important to me." When discussing another artist or genre, he was often talking about himself or his poetry, especially the *Cantos*.

Music as well as sculpture inspired Pound's ideas for language and literature: "Gaudier had developed a sort of form-fugue or form-sonata by a combination of forms." Pound found in the songs of the troubadours of Provence the union of words and music, sound and meaning, the divorce of which is effecting the decline of poetry. The best of the troubadours, Arnaut Daniel, writing between 1180 and 1200, brought "new words into writing" and made "new blendings of words." Provençal language was "growing weary," and Pound claimed that Daniel "tried to make almost a new language . . . and make new things possible."

Other Pound finds were the "medieval clean line," seen in the "precision of statement" in Dante's verse, the linear quality of Giotto's frescoes, and the inner structure of Byzantine architecture (the "ornament flat on the walls, and not bulging and bumping and indulging in bulbous excrescence"). He wished to bring together and capitalize on these energies, these vortices, as did the Quattrocento under state patronage: "the Quattrocento shines out because the social power coincided with the vortices of creative intelligence."

The trick for Pound was how to use all of his ideas and incorporate all of the forms to establish a unified and guiding theory for a work of art. Gaudier-Brzeska, he noted, achieved a combination of forms, but the sculptor Brancusi "has set out on the maddening more difficult exploration toward getting all the forms into one form." Confucius, too, provided Pound with the overriding insistence on order. In Canto 13, his "Confucius Canto," Pound wrote: "If a man have not order within him/ He can not spread order about him."

In seeming to summarize his studies in the visual arts and music and their relation to language, Pound concluded that "language is charged or energized" in three ways; in other words, "there are three 'kinds of poetry'": *melopoeia*, *phanopoeia*, and *logopoeia*. *Melopoeia* is charged with "some musical property, which directs the bearing or trend . . . over and above plain meaning." *Phanopoeia* is charged by "a casting of images upon the visual imagination," resulting in poetry "wherein the feelings of painting and sculpture are predominant." *Logopoeia* is charged by the play of language itself, "the dance of the intellect among words."

Yet to set all of his ideas in order – poetry and art, politics, and society – Pound became obsessed with economics. Energy was being wasted in "aimless and destructive effort." Instead of machines allowing people to work less, freeing workers from the drudgery of monotonous and dehumanizing work, people had to work more or take out loans to purchase necessary goods. Pound thought of artists, spending their creative energies not creating, not purchasing real goods, and not paying off the principal, but trying to pay off interest, a nonexistent value. Bankers kept charging interest after the initial loan and service, increasing their own wealth although they provided nothing in return. Pound centered on the central evil in this system, *usura* (usury), interest-bearing loans, defined in Canto 74 (1948) as "lending/ that which is made out of nothing." The culprits were bankers, an international gang of thugs, as he called them. *Usura* encourages a lack of discrimination between useful and useless products, priced and distributed without regard to their individual and social value. *Usura* is counterproductive, because it ties people to useless work, discouraging meaningful and creative work: "With usury," Pound decries in Canto 51 (1937), "the stone cutter is kept from his stone/ the weaver is kept from his loom by usura." Governments (also victims because they, too, borrow money and waste more energy paying off the interest than the principal) are empowered to create money; they can, therefore, lend money and charge a reasonable, onetime fee, for service and handling. Governments should follow the example of the great medieval and Renaissance patrons of the arts.

Pound's ideals might seem naive to modern readers, but he lived in a time when people believed that they could – and they often did – change the world for the better. New political orders were created. The three-hundred-year-old Russian Romanov dynasty gave way in 1917 to the Soviet Union and a new "social experiment." Soviet artists, as well as American artists (such as the dancer Isadora Duncan and the architect Frank Lloyd Wright), believed that new social and political orders were possible through their art. Indeed, the artists were not always dreaming. After a decade of revolution, and more than three centuries of oppression, the Irish Free State was created in 1922. The visionary poet William Butler Yeats, leader of the Irish Renaissance and a friend of Pound, served in its new senate.

Critics of Pound generally point out a contradiction within his theory. Pound believed vehemently in communicating directly to the common person and fighting the snobbery and pretentiousness of academics. Yet he developed his own elitist system – preserving the best – and refers or alludes to writers or works in Chinese, Greek, and Latin, often without translating. Aware of this himself, Pound countered, "How the deuce is one to avoid it? Several ideas

occurred to humanity before I bought a portable typewriter." Pound's critical school is democratically aristocratic. Unlike the economic system he abhorred, his system is open (as are libraries) to anyone who makes the useful effort.

## Principal criticism

*The Spirit of Romance*, 1910
*Gaudier-Brzeska: A Memoir Including the Published Writings of the Sculptor and a Selection from His Letters*, 1916
*Instigations of Ezra Pound, Together with an Essay on the Chinese Written Character by Ernest Fenollosa*, 1920
*Antheil and the Treatise on Harmony*, 1924
*How to Read*, 1931
*ABC of Reading*, 1934
*Make It New*, 1934
*Polite Essays*, 1937
*Guide to Kulchur*, 1938
*Literary Essays*, 1954
*Impact: Essays on Ignorance and the Decline of American Civilization*, 1960
*Patria Mia and the Treatise on Harmony*, 1962
*Ezra Pound and Music: The Complete Criticism*, 1977
*Ezra Pound and the Visual Arts*, 1980

## Other major works and literary forms

As one of the most prolific writers of the century, Ezra Pound wrote in many different media. Early in his career, he supported himself editing and writing for literary magazines. As a music and art critic for *The New Age* between 1917 and 1921, he wrote nearly four hundred entries, many pseudonymously, and he regularly contributed essays and reviews on sculpture, painting, and drama to *The Egoist*.

Regardless of the literary form, Pound's career was dedicated to poetry. He published his own poetry in magazines and anthologies, and, beginning with *A lume spento* in 1908, he published more than a dozen books of verse. The Imagist "In a Station of the Metro" and his satirical parody *Hugh Selwyn Mauberley* (1920) are two famous early poems, and – because of Pound's famous extensive editing of T. S. Eliot's *The Waste Land* (1922) – some argue that the poem is as much Pound's as it is Eliot's. Pound's lifelong poetic effort, however, was the epic *Cantos*. The *Cantos*, containing more than one hundred poems, or cantos, were published in parts over a span of some fifty years. In 1949 Pound received the Bollingen Award for Poetry for *The Pisan Cantos, LXXIV–LXXXIV* (1948).

Often incorporating fragments of Chinese or Greek verse in his own poems, Pound was also an active translator. Trained in the Romance languages, he translated Latin, French, Italian, and Provençal poetry and, through his own teaching, translated other poetry – Anglo-Saxon, Chinese, Greek, Hindi, Japanese – and Greek and Japanese Noh drama. Pound was a self-taught economist and historian too, publishing idiosyncratic works such as *Jefferson and/ or Mussolini* (1935) and *ABC of Economics* (1933). Yet assigning particular genres to Pound's writing is often arbitrary, since many of his literary forms overlap. His poetry contains literary and political criticism, his economic and historical treatises analyze poetry and art, and his literary criticism theorizes about art, economics, politics, and history.

POETRY

*A lume spento*, 1908
*A Quinzaine for This Yule*, 1908
*Exultations*, 1909
*Personae*, 1909
*Provença*, 1910
*Canzoni*, 1911
*Ripostes*, 1912
*Lustra*, 1916
*Pavannes and Divisions*, 1918
*Quia Pauper Amavi*, 1919
*Hugh Selwyn Mauberley*, 1920
*Umbra*, 1920
*Poems 1918–1921*, 1921
*Indiscretions*, 1923
*A Draft of XVI Cantos*, 1925
*Personae: The Collected Poems of Ezra Pound*, 1926
*A Draft of the Cantos 17–27*, 1928
*Selected Poems*, 1928
*A Draft of XXX Cantos*, 1930
*Eleven New Cantos, XXXI–XLI*, 1934
*The Fifth Decad of Cantos, XLII–LI*, 1937
*Cantos LII–LXXI*, 1940
*A Selection of Poems*, 1940
*The Cantos of Ezra Pound*, 1948
*The Pisan Cantos, LXXIV–LXXXIV*, 1948
*Selected Poems*, 1949
*Section: Rock-Drill 85–95 de los cantares*, 1955
*Thrones: 96–109 de los cantares*, 1959
*Drafts and Fragments of Cantos CX–CXVII*, 1969
*Canto CXX*, 1969
*The Cantos of Ezra Pound, I–CXVII*, 1970
*Selected Poems: 1908–1959*, 1975
*Collected Early Poems*, 1976

NONFICTION

*The Chinese Written Character as a Medium for Poetry*, 1920 (editor)
*Imaginary Letters*, 1930
*ABC of Economics*, 1933
*Alfred Venison's Poems: Social Credit Themes*, 1935
*Social Credit: An Impact*, 1935
*Jefferson and/or Mussolini*, 1935
*Orientamenti*, 1938
*What Is Money For?*, 1939
*Carta da Visita*, 1942 (*A Visiting Card*, 1952)
*Introduzione alla natura economica degli S.U.A.*, 1944 (*An Introduction to the Economic Nature of the United States*, 1950)
*L'America, Roosevelt, e le cause della guerra presente*, 1944 (*America, Roosevelt, and the Causes of the Present War*, 1951)
*Oro e lavoro*, 1944 (*Gold and Work*, 1952)
*"If This Be Treason . . .,"* 1948
*The Letters of Ezra Pound, 1907–1941*, 1950
*Lavoro ed usura*, 1954
*Nuova economia editoriale*, 1962
*Pound/Joyce: The Letters of Ezra Pound to James Joyce*, 1967
*Selected Prose 1909–1965*, 1973
*"Ezra Pound Speaking": Radio Speeches of World War II*, 1978
*Letters to Ibbotson, 1935–1952*, 1979

*From Syria: The Worksheets, Proofs, and Text*, 1981
*Pound/Ford: The Story of a Literary Friendship*, 1982
*Ezra Pound and Dorothy Shakespear: Their Letters, 1909–1914*, 1984
*The Letters of Ezra Pound and Wyndham Lewis*, 1985

TRANSLATIONS

*The Sonnets and Ballate of Guido Cavalcanti*, 1912
*Cathay: Translations by Ezra Pound for the Most Part from the Chinese of Rihaku, from the Notes of the Late Ernest Fenollosa and the Decipherings of the Professors Mori and Ariga*, 1915
*'Noh' or Accomplishment*, 1916 (with Ernest Fenollosa)
*The Natural Philosophy of Love*, 1922 (of Remy de Gourmont's work)
*The Testament of François Villon*, 1926 (translation into opera)
*Rime*, 1932 (of Guido Cavalcanti's poetry)
*Homage to Sextus Propertius*, 1934
*Digest of the Analects*, 1937 (of Confucius' work)
*Italy's Policy of Social Economics, 1930–1940*, 1941 (of Odon Por's work)
*Confucius: The Unwobbling Pivot and the Great Digest*, 1947
*The Translations of Ezra Pound*, 1953
*The Classic Anthology Defined by Confucius*, 1954
*Women of Trachis*, 1956 (of Sophocles' play)
*Love Poems of Ancient Egypt*, 1964

ANTHOLOGIES

*Des Imagistes: An Anthology*, 1914
*Catholic Anthology 1914–1915*, 1915
*Active Anthology*, 1933
*Confucius to Cummings: An Anthology of Poetry*, 1964 (with Marcella Spann)

## Further reading

Beach, Christopher. *ABC of Influence: Ezra Pound and the Remaking of American Poetic Tradition*, 1992.
Bell, Ian. *Critic as Scientist: The Modernist Poetics of Ezra Pound*, 1981.
Dasenbrock, Reed Way. *The Literary Vorticism of Ezra Pound and Wyndham Lewis: Toward the Condition of Painting*, 1985.
Davie, Donald. *Ezra Pound*, 1975.
——. *Studying Ezra Pound*, 1991.
De Nagy, N. Christoph. *Ezra Pound's Poetics and Literary Tradition: The Critical Decade*, 1966.
Gallup, Donald. *A Bibliography of Ezra Pound*, 1983.
Goodwin, K. L. *The Influence of Ezra Pound*, 1966.
Grover, Philip, ed. *Ezra Pound: The London Years, 1908–1920*, 1978.
Homberger, Eric, ed. *Ezra Pound: The Critical Heritage*, 1972.
Kenner, Hugh. *The Pound Era*, 1971.
Materer, Timothy. *Vortex: Pound, Eliot, and Lewis*, 1979.
Olson, Charles. *Charles Olson and Ezra Pound at St. Elizabeths*, 1975.
Ruthven, K. K. *Ezra Pound as Literary Critic*, 1990.
Simpson, Louis. *Three on the Tower: The Lives and Works of Ezra Pound, T. S. Eliot, and William Carlos Williams*, 1975.
Stock, Noel, ed. *Ezra Pound Perspectives*, 1965.
Wilhelm, James. *The American Roots of Ezra Pound*, 1985.
Williams, William Carlos. "Ezra Pound," in *The Autobiography of William Carlos Williams*, 1951.
Wilson, Peter. *A Preface to Ezra Pound*, 1997.

STEVEN P. SCHULTZ

*See also* Eliot; Hulme; Marinetti

# The Prague School

The Prague School, the popular designation for the group of scholars associated with the Prague Linguistic Circle, came into existence during the mid-1920s and was an active movement until after World War II. For many years it was, as the official name implies, better known for the work done by its members in the field of linguistics, but since the 1960s it has become at least equally renowned for its contributions to literary theory and aesthetics. In talking of the Prague School it is misleading to insist on a strict separation of the two fields; the linguists were involved in the study of literature, particularly the nature of verse, and the most prominent of the literary theorists, Jan Mukařovský, started with the study of poetic language and was familiar with the work not only of the linguists in the Prague School, but also that of Ferdinand de Saussure, whose ideas were of importance in Mukařovský's work on semiotics. Besides applying sign theory to the study of the aesthetic object, the members of the Prague School formulated a modern theory of structuralism, in which the component elements of a literary work were seen to be in a dynamic, dialectical relationship; they also produced important work on reception theory and on the nature of literary history. Not only did their ideas, through the mediation of several of the school's members and students, go on to influence developments in Western literary scholarship and in Russia, but many of their writings have retained their vitality to the present day.

Although the focus here is on the school's literary significance, it is necessary to say a word about the role played by the Prague School in linguistic theory. Its international reputation grew primarily out of its work in phonology and the related areas of morphophonology and morphology. Thus Roman Jakobson, who came to Prague from Moscow in 1920, produced some of his most significant phonological studies during the nearly two decades that he spent in Czechoslovakia; while Nikolai Trubetzkoy, who also was of Russian origin, wrote a series of groundbreaking works on both general and Russian phonology and morphophonology. Among the Czech members, Bohumil Trnka studied aspects of Czech phonology, while Vilém Mathesius, regarded as the founder of the Prague School, wrote on English phonology as well as the structure of modern English. The concentration on phonology was ultimately crucial for the direction taken by the Prague Linguistic Circle in its study of literature as well, for by examining this "lower" level of language Prague School members were able to define the contours of a system and then to see language in general as a system of interrelated systems; in a similar way, they were then to see the literary work as also comprising a set of interlocking systems.

## History

The beginning of the Prague Linguistic Circle can be precisely dated: on October 6, 1926, a half dozen people met in the Charles University office of Vilém Mathesius, whose specialty was English philology: besides Mathesius, the gathering included three other Czech linguists; a visiting German scholar (Henrik Becker), whose paper was the subject of discussion, and Roman Jakobson, who, though living in Prague, was still a leading member of the Russian Formalist movement. Over the next few years some several dozen scholars became associated with the group, which had a decidedly international air: besides Trubetzkoy and Jakobson, the members who were of Russian origin included the folklorist Pyotr Bogatyryov and the linguist Sergei Kartsevsky; scholars from many European countries gave lectures before the Circle. During the early 1930s several younger Czech scholars joined the group, including René Wellek and Felix Vodička. The chief outlet for papers from the Circle significantly had a French title (*Travaux du Cercle Linguistique de Prague*); over a period of ten years, 1929 to 1939, some eight volumes appeared, with articles in French, German, and English. A Czech journal *Slovo a slovesnost* (the word and verbal art) began to appear only in 1935.

A major turning point for the Prague School in terms of literary and aesthetic theory occurred in 1934; during this year Mukařovský published several crucial papers that clarified the distinction between the Prague School and the Russian Formalists, helped define the structuralist orientation of the movement, and laid the groundwork for subsequent contributions to sign theory and reception theory. Over the next few years Mukařovský and others established the specific focus of Czech structuralism, working out principles of literary development, expanding their concern from just the literary work to all the arts, and, eventually, broadening their concern from the work itself to issues of its creation and perception. With the approach and then the outbreak of World War II, the Prague School began to suffer significant losses. Jakobson and Wellek emigrated to the West, while Bogatyryov returned to the Soviet Union. Trubetzkoy died in 1939, and several Czech scholars did not survive the war. Yet the movement was only slowed, not stopped. Meetings of the Circle continued through the war years, and important publications continued to appear, until the imposition of Communist rule in 1948 put an end to the structuralist approach in the field of literary scholarship; most notably, Mukařovský renounced his pre-1948 writings and became a supporter of the Marxist regime. Still, many of the leading figures remained active as scholars, and some of the linguists remained faithful to the movement's structuralist thrust.

## Key concepts

Although the Prague School shared not just some of its members with Russian Formalism, but also some of its theoretical underpinnings, it is too simple a matter to say that the Czech movement simply grew out of the Russian school. Granted, Jakobson himself brought to Prague some of the approaches to poetics developed by the Formalists, and other Russians associated either with the Petrograd or Moscow branches of Formalism – Iurii Tynianov, Boris Tomashevskii, and Grigory Vinokur – lectured to the Prague Linguistic Circle during its early years. The Czech members of the Prague School were also influenced, however, both by earlier schools of aesthetic theory within Czechoslovakia itself and also by their greater contact with currents in Western thought, including Edmund Husserl's phenomenology and Ernst Cassirer's *Philosophy of Symbolic Forms* (published in German 1923–1929 and in English 1953–1957). Formalism too was an evolving movement, which, during its declining years of the late 1920s, had moved well beyond its early programmatic statements; hence the 1928 article by Tynianov and Jakobson, "Problems in the Study of Literature and Language," published in Russia, is simultaneously a statement of early structuralist as well as late Formalist principles. From its start the Prague School had moved past the early and radical Formalist position, in which the work of art is seen primarily as a sum of devices, whose goal is to make perception more conscious and less automatic; nonetheless, Mukařovský, in his 1934 review of Viktor Shklovskii's *Theory of Prose* (which had appeared in Russian in 1925), expresses empathy for the achievements of Formalism and attempts to "rescue" Shklovskii from his own extreme statements, finding in his references to composition and literary schools an effort to characterize the literary work as a semantic whole. To Mukařovský, the Formalist effort to analyze the structural components of the literary work itself and to define their internal dynamics, rather than to look primarily at external elements, was a necessary step on the road to structuralist poetics.

In addition, the Prague School took from the Formalists, and particularly from Jakobson, the notion that linguistics itself offers a precise method for the study of literature. One of Jakobson's first major works after coming to Prague, *On Czech Verse: Particularly as Compared to Russian* (1923), demonstrated how careful analysis of a language's dominant prosodic features can lead to an understanding of developments in the poetic tradition. Mukařovský went on to apply linguistic principles to the study of poetry in, for instance, his 1928 examination of Karel Mácha's long poem *Máj* (May) and his 1933 discussion of the role played by intonation in structuring the verse line ("Intonation as the Basic Factor of Poetic Rhythm"). Poetry, with its inherent emphasis on the word and on literary devices, provides ready material for those looking to formulate principles of literary structure that are based on the qualities of language itself; thus it is not surprising that some of the earliest key structuralist works focus on the poetic tradition. Another lesson gleaned from Jakobson and Formalist tradition is the need to pay attention not just to linguistic devices and literary devices, but to elucidate their function(s) in the literary work. The notion, again, is to see the

various aspects of the literary work as creating a system, which becomes the basic principle behind the structuralist approach to verbal art. Another Formalist influence was the notion that literary development had special laws of its own, and that to understand those laws it is necessary to look at the evolution of the total literary environment within a given tradition, not just at a handful of leading works. Significantly, when Tynianov lectured to the Prague Linguistic Circle in 1928, his topic was "On Literary Evolution."

These last two ideas – the sense of the literary (and later any aesthetic) work as a system, and the conviction that literary history operates according to special principles that can be gleaned only by seeing works in a broad context – were to become greatly elaborated by Mukařovský and his colleagues. Indeed, the two principles eventually became intertwined, as in Mukařovský's 1946 lecture "On Structuralism." He notes that all the components in a work of art – down to individual sounds and grammatical forms in a poem, or lines and colors in paintings – convey meaning and thus take part in the semanticization of the work. The interrelations of these elements (such as euphonic links between words in a text, which can then evoke semantic connections even among etymologically unrelated words) also create meanings, as do the links between the work itself and the world outside it. Hence every feature, from the smallest constituent to the entire work of art itself, enters into a complex correlation; the overall meaning depends both on the system made up of individual elements and on the system (the sociocultural environment) of which the work is a part. That environment, in turn, evolves with time: the body of other works will change, as will artistic conventions, specific genres, and the broad social setting within which a work is perceived.

In "Art as a Semiotic Fact" (1934) Mukařovský had already made explicit the implication that the work of art, since it exists as part of a large and ever-evolving context, cannot be identified solely with the consciousness of its creator or with that of its perceiving subjects; rather, it is best seen as an autonomous "sign." His basic point is that the work of art does not refer to "reality" as such, but to the totality of social phenomena within a given milieu. The physical work functions as a sensory symbol, while the "aesthetic object" is something immaterial, lodged in the "social consciousness." Those works of arts with a subject are said to exhibit a second, communicative function, but this is seen as separate from the autonomous quality that defines the work as an instance of art. Not yet fully defined in this formulation is the manner in which the literary work is either produced or perceived; Mukařovský and also Vodička turned their attention to these issues as well. In "Intentionality and Unintentionality in Art" (1943) Mukařovský examines the qualities specific to artistic (as opposed to other kinds of) creation. Intentionality serves to give the individual aspects of a work the unity that imparts meaning. He points out that paradoxically the perceiver (even more than the creator) plays an active role in establishing that intentionality, for it is the "audience" that must make the effort to comprehend the relationships among the parts of the work that give rise to semantic unity. Unintentionality may enter into perception either through certain uncontrolled factors in the creator or in the creation (accidents of performance or imperfections in the physical object comprising the work). Vodička concentrates more specifically on the reception of the literary work rather than aesthetic creations in general; in "The Concretization of the Literary Work" (1941) he combines Roman Ingarden's use of "concretization" with Mukařovský's ideas regarding the evolution of the literary work. His reception history becomes a history of "concretizations"; not just of the work, but of the author and the context in which the work is perceived. The focus, as in Mukařovský, becomes not so much the work itself or its creator, as the specific literary and social consciousness within which they are perceived.

Finally, it is important to note that the structural approach of the Prague School was broadly applied to other fields of artistic endeavor, such as folklore (for example, Jakobson and Bogatyryov on the qualities distinguishing folk as opposed to literary creation), theater, and film. As with the studies on literature, particular attention is devoted to the component aspects of the specific art form, to issues of perception, and to the notion of the artistic work as a system.

## Aftermath and assessment

The immediate influence of the literary studies emanating from the Prague School on the broader scholarly community was slight; most were written in Czech and many ostensibly dealt with Czech works or authors not well known outside their homeland. However, with Jakobson and Wellek becoming prominent figures in the United States, and Bogatyryov, despite the difficulties he faced in Soviet Russia, affecting a generation of Russian folklorists, many key notions of the Prague School gained a wider audience. Both French structuralism (indirectly through the influence of Jakobson) and the Moscow-Tartu school (more directly through Bogatyryov and others) reveal the influences of Prague structuralism. Thanks to the numerous translations of literary studies by members of the Prague School since the 1960s, as well as the appearance of articles and books on its work, the role of Czech structuralism in twentieth-century critical studies has received ever increasing attention.

The achievement of the Prague School was to bring together various strands in the thought of its day to create a more comprehensive understanding of the artistic work. Its members established the notion that the work of art is a structure made up of interrelated elements forming a complex system, while the work as a whole is itself a part of another system, comprised of the aesthetic codes and norms within the general sociocultural context. This understanding in turn led to an expanded conception of literary evolution; it is not just the aesthetic value of the component elements in literary works that change, but so do the norms of the society and the context within which a given work is perceived. The Czech theorists were also apparently the first to describe a theory of reception based on the notion that aesthetic objects form a semiotic system. The Prague School was not without its limitations – Mukařovský, for instance, did surprisingly little to expand his analyses beyond Czech literature, and at times the emphasis on context seems to treat the aesthetic work more as a theoretical than an actual entity – but perhaps no other movement did so much both to anticipate and to affect trends in literary criticism since the middle of the twentieth century.

## Further reading

Doležel, Lubomír. "Structuralism of the Prague School," in *The Cambridge History of Literary Criticism*. Vol. 8, *From Formalism to Poststructuralism*, 1995.

Galan, F. W. *Historic Structures: The Prague School Project, 1928–1946*, 1985.

Garvin, Paul. *A Prague School Reader on Esthetics, Literary Structure, and Style*, 1964.

Luelsdorff, Philip A., ed. *The Prague School of Structural and Functional Linguistics: A Short Introduction*, 1994.

Matejka, Ladislav, ed. *Sound, Sign and Meaning: Quinquagenary of the Prague Linguistic Circle*, 1976.

Mukařovský, Jan. *The Word and Verbal Art*, 1977.

———. *Structure, Sign and Function*, 1978.

Pike, Christopher, ed. *The Futurists, the Formalists, and the Marxist Critique*, 1979.

Steiner, Peter, ed. *The Prague School: Selected Writings, 1929–1946*, 1982.

Striedter, Jurij. *Literary Structure, Evolution, and Value: Russian Formalism and Czech Structuralism Reconsidered*, 1989.

Tobin, Yishai, ed. *The Prague School and Its Legacy in Linguistics, Literature, Semiotics, Folklore, and the Arts*, 1988.

Toman, Jindřich. *The Magic of a Common Language: Jakobson, Mathesius, Trubetzkoy, and the Prague Linguistic Circle*, 1995.

Vachek, Josef. *The Linguistic School of Prague: An Introduction to Its Theory and Practice*, 1966.

———, comp. *A Prague School Reader in Linguistics*, 1964.

Wellek, René. *A History of Modern Criticism: 1750–1950*. Vol. 7, *German, Russian, and East European Criticism, 1900–1950*, 1991. (See also his similar account published as *The Literary Theory and Aesthetics of the Prague School*, 1969).

BARRY P. SCHERR

*See also* Jakobson; Russian Formalism; Structuralism

# Mario Praz

Italian writer on literature and art

**Born:** Rome, Italy; September 6, 1896
**Died:** Rome, Italy; March 23, 1982

## Biography

Mario Praz was born on September 6, 1896, in Rome, to Luciano Praz (a bank clerk) and Giulia di Marsciano. The family moved to Switzerland, where his father died when Mario was four. When his mother returned to her home in Florence, he attended school there. He first studied law but gave that up in favor of an interest in art and in literature, specifically English studies. He earned his Ph.D. in 1923 and immediately applied for a scholarship to England. He worked at the British Museum for a year, was senior lecturer of Italian at Liverpool University from 1924 to 1932, and professor of Italian studies at Manchester University from 1932 to 1934. Praz was professor of English at the University of Rome from 1934 until 1966. In March, 1934 he married an Englishwoman, Vivyan Eyles, with whom he had one daughter. He traveled in many countries, including the United States, doing research or on teaching assignments. His honorary degrees included those from the universities of Cambridge, Paris, Uppsala, and Aix-Marseilles. He died in Rome at the age of eighty-five.

## Influence

Mario Praz is considered the foremost Italian critic of English literature and one of the most important writers of his age. Although he championed T. S. Eliot and introduced Ernest Hemingway to his native people, his work is better known in England than in his native Italy. His style of criticism is unique, easily crossing borders between different art forms, time frames, and national literatures. He is the preeminent interpreter of the macabre in painting and in literature; the acceptance as literature of the writings of the Marquis de Sade is largely attributable to Praz.

In his studies of de Sade, Charles Baudelaire, Gabriele D'Annunzio, Lord Byron, Charles Dickens, and Charles Lamb, among many others, he combined his vast knowledge of literature and the plastic arts in a manner unlike that of any critic before him. Because of his vast command of periods, genres, and the arts, Praz introduced new readings of great bodies of literature and uncovered significant amounts of forgotten or obscure material.

## Analysis

"Literary criticism assumes the existence of a history of culture" in which "tendencies, themes, and mannerisms current in a writer's own day provide an indispensable aid to the interpretation of his work." Praz wrote these words in the introduction to his most important work, *The Romantic Agony*, at a time when the New Criticism was in its formative stage. While the New Criticism, in its concentration on the internal dynamics of literary works, did not explicitly deny the relevance of historical and biographical details, it was not attuned to the lonesome voice of this relatively unknown theoretician from the heart of Italy.

When *The Romantic Agony* first appeared, it provoked harsh criticism – it was dismissed as a book of "disjointed gimcrack" and a "gigantic pile of satanic bric-à-brac" – yet Praz's study has since been recognized as one of the most influential works written on the Romantic movement. One must focus on *The Romantic Agony* because it contains three principles central to Praz's critical approach. First, historical criticism is a legitimate, even preferred, approach to literary study. Second, the trait variously referred to as the macabre, the sadistic, the horrible, the morbid, or the grotesque is a major and unique aspect of the Romantic movement. Finally, the milieu of great works of art (including furniture, architecture, and music to a lesser degree) should be incorporated into any critical discussion of a body of literature.

In arguing for the historical approach, Praz does not deny a place for other approaches, such as the formalistic or aesthetic. He simply assumes that literary criticism presupposes the existence of a history of culture, whether one is dealing with a particular environment or a particular individual. In a work of increasing critical importance, *Mnemosyne*, he warns his readers that if they are interested in conclusions and deductive reasoning rather than sources and references, then the subject of his book will appear "academic" and "futile." In *The Hero in Eclipse in Victorian Fiction*, literary terms such as Baroque, Romantic, and neoclassical are defined as "approximations" of historical concepts, which "are intended merely to indicate where the accent falls, and acquire their meaning only within the compass of specified historical periods." Such names came to be assigned to specific moods or times and thus are contextual frames for literary history but are not exclusive to one period. Thus, though the grotesque and the horrific do stem from the Romantic period, and therefore must be studied within the context of the writers and events of that time, these terms can be identified in human nature outside a particular time frame.

*The Romantic Agony* is a seminal study of the decadent and the perverse in literature. It traces the development of a literary tradition in the nineteenth century which emphasized erotic cruelty, Byronic rakes, satanic heroes, and femmes fatales who lured men with their promise of the mysterious and the bizarre. Praz's extensive writings on the subjects of the erotic, the grotesque, and the mysterious are intended to show that prolonged involvement in the sensual and the sadistic culminates in nihilistic and suicidal impulses. While it is true that Praz produced some critical works that deviate from his inquiry into this subject, it is also true that many of his later studies (including *Bellezza e bizzarria* and *Perseo e la Medusa*) stem from or allude to this preoccupation.

Praz insisted on presenting a whole backdrop of cultural material as evidence for any thesis he was formulating. He was a ravenous collector, a meticulous assimilator, and a master weaver of quotes, facts, and images. Such collections did not apply to literary subjects alone. One saw it abundantly in his life, whether in his home, in his taste for Empire and Regency furniture, in his taste in the arts, or (if reviewer Aubrey Menen is to be believed) in his taste for women. Praz wrote a number of books on furniture, on architecture, on art, and on philosophical systems of various periods, such as *Machiavelli and the Elizabethans* and *Studies in Seventeenth Century Imagery*.

In practice as well as in theory, then, Praz compared, juxtaposed, entangled, and otherwise interrelated the plastic and verbal arts. His avowed aim was the discovery of the secrets of artistic inspiration. He hypothesized that the so-called sister arts had been so deeply rooted in the human mind since prehistory that there must be something in them organic and resistant to dismissal. Praz believed that by comparative probing into those mysterious relationships of artistic modes and themes he could uncover the textured layers hiding creative inspiration. The result is a critical theory which is as encompassing and as diverse as all the nations, periods, and movements of Europe.

Given the need to trace the genealogy of all the arts and to expose artistic techniques, how does Praz propose to proceed? Frequently he begins his discussion with a principle in dispute or a revelation hitherto unfocused. For example, he begins *On Neoclassicism* by claiming that "the Aristotelian unities were a creation of Italian critics; but it was reserved for the French tragedians to adhere strictly to them." In *The Romantic Agony*, he offers this stark summary: "The very objects which should induce a shudder – the livid face of the severed head, the squirming mass of vipers, the rigidity of death, . . . all these give rise to a new sense of beauty, a beauty imperilled and contaminated, a new thrill." Upon making these dramatic observations, he proceeds to build mountains of evidence in support of his thesis.

Praz quickly despaired of establishing a series of artistic correspondences on a scientific, logical basis. Praz's method, as presented in *On Neoclassicism*, is to "collect aspects, motifs, and personalities" of a period "in such a way as to give of the age a complex picture in which learning might go hand in hand with imagination." Indeed, Praz warns his readers not to judge any age prematurely, before they have a feeling for it.

Praz argues, further, that it is possible to identify the distinctive style of expression of a particular artist – a style manifested in all of his or her works, even those in different art forms. Thus, William Blake's paintings are not only compatible with, but also can be identified as coming from, the same hand that produced his writings. In his ongoing argument

with Benedetto Croce, Praz notes that he and Croce part ways at this point. Croce could never agree to a parallel between the various arts, since he finds that even translations from another tongue are new expressions. The location of that commonality in all the arts is precisely Praz's mission.

In *Mnemosyne*, Praz postulates his conclusions:

It can be maintained that there is a general likeness among all the works of art of a period . . . that there is either a latent or a manifest unity in the productions of the same artist in whatever field he tries his hand; and that traditions exert a differentiating influence not only between one art and another, but also within the same art.

To see Praz's method in action, one need only note his clustering of the antiart of Dadaism, the antiarchitecture of Le Corbusier, or the antinovel of Alain Robbe-Grillet and the French *nouvelle vague*. To take a more challenging method of unification, Praz shows how the "interpenetration of planes" in Impressionist paintings, sculpture, and architecture can be found in the "interpenetration of words" and rhythm in works such as James Joyce's *Ulysses* (1922), Lawrence Durrell's "stereoscopic" technique of running a common catalyst through a collection of stories, and Pablo Picasso's creation of a new language in art "through the fusion of unreconcilable manners." So it is that Virginia Woolf can successfully apply musical technique to literature in *To the Lighthouse* (1927), Marcel Proust's novel *Du côté de chez Swann* (1913; *Swann's Way*, 1922) can recall Claude Monet's art, or Charles Dickens can rival William Hogarth's mixture of the grotesque and tragic in his portraits.

As a critic, Praz is not easy to emulate. His ability to move at will in and out of Greek, Latin, German, French, English, Italian, Spanish, and Russian without translating makes him inaccessible to many readers, and the vast range of quotations and references which he routinely assembles can be intimidating. He clearly represents a break from the Italian tradition of writing long treatises on literary matters from a philosophical base. His long debate with Croce, who charged Praz with having neither a philosophical foundation nor an ability to synthesize his massive evidence, accents this break.

In one work, Praz compares two modes of writing; in another, he juxtaposes art against literature; elsewhere, he traces the roots of a quirk in the civilization process. In all instances, he relates voluminous data to a single phenomenon. He has profoundly influenced the course of criticism toward a fuller appreciation of literature's cultural and historical context.

## Principal criticism

*La fortuna di Byron in Inghilterra*, 1925
*Secentismo e marinismo in Inghilterra: John Donne – Richard Crashaw*, 1925

*Machiavelli and the Elizabethans*, 1928
*The Italian Element in English*, 1929
*La carne, la morte, e il diavolo nella letteratura romantica*, 1930 (*The Romantic Agony*, 1933)
*Studi sul concettismo*, 1934 (*Studies in Seventeenth-Century Imagery*, 1939–1947; 2 volumes)
*Storia della letteratura inglese*, 1937
*Studi e svanghi inglese*, 1937
*Gusto neoclassico*, 1940 (*On Neoclassicism*, 1969)
*Machiavelli in Inghilterra*, 1942
*Outline of English Literature*, 1943
*Ricerce anglo-italiane*, 1944
*Richard Crashaw*, 1945
*Motivi e figure*, 1945
*La poesia metafisica inglese del seicento: John Donne*, 1945
*Il dramma Elisabettiano: Webster, Ford*, 1946
*Geoffrey Chaucer e i racconti de Canterbury*, 1947
*La poesia di Pope e le sue origini*, 1948
*Cronache letterarie anglosassoni*, 1951–1966 (4 volumes)
*La casa della fama: Saggi di letteratura e d'arte*, 1952
*La crisi dell'eroe nel romazo vittoriano*, 1952 (*The Hero in Eclipse in Victorian Fiction*, 1956)
*The Flaming Heart: Essays on Crashaw, Machiavelli, and Other Studies in the Relation Between Italian and English Literature from Chaucer to T. S. Eliot*, 1958
*Belleza e bizzarria*, 1960
*Il libro della poesia inglese*, 1967
*Caleidoscopio Shakespeariano*, 1969
*Mnemosyne: The Parallel Between Literature and the Visual Arts*, 1970
*Il patto col serpente*, 1972
*Il giardino dei sensi: Studi sul manierismo e il barocco*, 1975
*Perseo e la Medusa: Dal romanticismo all'avanguardia*, 1979
*Voce dietro la scene, un'antologia personale*, 1980

## Other major works and literary forms

Mario Praz was not only a student of literature but also a recognized art critic, historian, translator, and scholar of languages. He has a respected following for his books on furniture, paintings, and objects of art, and his travels in Greece, England, France, and Spain produced popular literary diaries. In particular, *Penisola pentagonale* (1928; *Unromantic Spain*, 1929) is highly regarded. He wrote literally thousands of essays and reviews on various subjects, including some for the *Encyclopedia italiana*. He was coeditor of *La cultura*, editor of *The English Miscellany*, and considered the leading authority on Shakespeare editions in Italy. Praz translated hundreds of plays, poems, short stories, and essays, including works by William Shakespeare, Jane Austen, and Charles Lamb. His interest in artifacts led him to publish the first comprehensive bibliography of emblem books.

### NONFICTION
*Penisola pentagonale*, 1928 (*Unromantic Spain*, 1929)
*Viaggio in Grecia*, 1943
*La filosofia dell'arredamento*, 1945 (*An Illustrated History of Interior Decoration from Pompeii to Art Nouveau*, 1964)
*Lettrice notturna*, 1952
*Viaggi in Occidente*, 1955
*La casa della vitta*, 1958 (*The House of Life*, 1964)
*Scene di conversazione*, 1970 (*Conversation Pieces: A Survey of the Informal Group Portrait in Europe and America*, 1971)

### TRANSLATIONS
*I saggi di Elia*, 1924 (of Charles Lamb's collection *Essays of Elia*)
*Poetic inglesi dell'ottocento*, 1925
*Misura per misura*, 1939 (of William Shakespeare's play *Measure for Measure*)
*Troilo e Cressida*, 1939 (of Shakespeare's play *Troilus and Cressida*)
*Volpone*, 1943 (of Ben Jonson's play *Volpone: Or, The Fox*)
*Emma*, 1951 (of Jane Austen's novel)

## Further reading

Brendon, Piers. "Mario Praz," in *Books and Bookmen*. XVI (February/March, 1971), pp. 40, 51.
Gabrieli, Vittorio, ed. *Friendship's Garland: Essays Presented to Mario Praz on His Seventieth Birthday*, 1966.
Kermode, Frank. "Palace of Art," in *New Statesman*. LXVIII (September 25, 1964), pp. 446–447.
Menen, Aubrey. "On Exhibition," in *The New York Times Book Review*. LXIX (November 8, 1964), pp. 7, 26.
Wilson, Edmund. *The Bit Between My Teeth*, 1965.
——. "The Genie of the Via Giulia," in *The New Yorker*. XLI (February 20, 1965), pp. 152–162.

ERNEST R. PINSON

*See also* Anceschi; Croce; Erotic; Grotesque

# Vladimir Propp

## Russian folklorist and critical theorist

**Born:** St. Petersburg, Russia; April 17 (29), 1895
**Died:** Leningrad, Russia; August 22, 1970

## Biography

Vladimir Propp was born on April 17 (29), in St. Petersburg to a family of German descent. He studied Russian and German at the University of St. Petersburg where he graduated in 1918. His career started with teaching these languages at secondary school and soon he became a college instructor of German. His first publications concern textbooks for Russian students of German. In 1932 he was called to Leningrad University and he worked there until his death.

There is early evidence of Propp's interest in folklore. He began researching the "wondertale" as a genre in the 1920s and in 1928 published his first book, *Morfologija skazki* (*Morphology of the Folktale*), the work that would eventually make him famous. In 1938 he gave up language teaching and linguistics altogether and chaired the Department of Folklore until it was incorporated into the Department of Russian Literature. All Propp's subsequent writings testify to his continued preoccupation with the formation, structure, and historical typology of folk narrative. Yet despite all his research work, the list of his publications is not long. Apart from a limited number of books, he composed some long articles and many reviews and, together with M. J(u). Mel'c, compiled annual bibliographies of Russian folklore.

Throughout most of his writing career Propp was plagued by the political situation in Russia. The early 1930s saw a fierce fight by socialist realism against anything that was formalistic, including Propp's "morphology." During the war he was harassed because he was German. The publication of his second major book, *Istoričeskie korni volšebnoj skazki* (historical roots of the wondertale), ready in 1939, was delayed until 1946. The subsequent period of extreme Soviet nationalism produced virulent attacks against "unpatriotic" scholars including Propp who was humiliated into publicly recanting his admiration for the great Russian scholar Aleksandr Veselovskii and to criticizing his own works. As a result, his interest veered toward different forms of narrative, in the event Russian epic poetry. Moreover, his research now excluded any reference to Western critics. The breaking of the political frost coincided with the publication of the English translation *Morphology of the Folktale* (1958). It brought belated international fame and transformed his status. In 1965, on the occasion of his seventieth birthday, Leningrad University fêted Propp with laudatory speeches by distinguished scholars. A second edition of *Morfologija skazki* appeared in 1969 with an introductory essay by the leading Russian folklorist Eleazar Meletinsky.

## Influence

Propp's most influential work was his *Morphology of the Folktale* which, when it was first published in Russia in 1928, did not produce many reviews, either in Russia or abroad. Only very few articles, notably by Volodimir Peretz and Dimitrii Konstantinovich Zelenin, showed positive appreciation. The book's true importance was not recognized until it appeared in English some thirty years later. It is precisely this 1958 translation of Propp's work that produced spectacular resonance in academic circles on both sides of the Atlantic.

There were two ways in which the influence of Propp's morphological study manifested itself: to some the new method proved a stimulating example for practical application; to others it gave rise to critical discussion of its epistemological foundations. One of the first to realize the significance of *Morphology* and apply its principles to other texts was Alan Dundes (for example, *The Morphology of North American Indian Folktales,* 1964) and it was he who made Propp famous in the United States. In his introduction to the second edition of *Morphology of the Folktale* (1968), he stresses the growing number of structural analyses of folk-tale genres and the great impact the book was having on folklorists and literary critics.

In France, on the other hand, recent development of structural linguistics and semiotics made Propp's scientific discoveries highly attractive to structuralist thinkers. This led to the well-known controversy between the Russian

scholar and the anthropologist Claude Lévi-Strauss. In his lengthy review (1960), the latter expressed his great admiration for Propp and his method but also disagreed with some of the procedures and conclusions. Basically, Lévi-Strauss saw Propp as a formalist and identified himself as a structuralist. Propp felt misunderstood and offended. He published a reply to Lévi-Strauss in a postscript to the Italian edition of his work.

Other eminent French structuralists (Roland Barthes, A. J. Greimas, Claude Bremond, Tzvetan Todorov) followed Lévi-Strauss' example. Looking for universal structures, they adapted Propp's findings and incorporated them into semiotic models applicable to all narrative. German scholars, on the other hand, Karl Eimermacher (1972) among them, saw in Propp's typology potential progress for a general theory of genre definition of all literary works.

Despite justified criticism, there is no doubt that Propp's work was a theoretical breakthrough and that it has made an overwhelming impact on the study of folklore. Nonetheless, it is also important to note that its influence would seem to be restricted to *Morphology of the Folktale* which was translated into several European languages. Propp's other works are hardly ever quoted. In many cases they do not even exist in English translation.

## Analysis

As Meletinsky points out, contrary to popular assumption Propp was not a member of the Russian Formalist circle. He was undoubtedly familiar with their work and influenced by the ideas of prominent Formalists, Viktor Shklovskii and Iurii Tynianov, for example. Propp's interests, however, went in a slightly different direction. The novelty of his particular approach consisted both in his theory of genre definition and its methodological application. It is astonishing that the originality of his ideas did not emerge until a generation later, translated into a foreign language and discussed in different cultural contexts. Moreover, apart from Propp's response to Lévi-Strauss' review, there is little evidence of direct discussion or fruitful exchanges between their author and European or American scholars.

When Propp set out to write his morphology, he did not see his method of analysis as an end in itself. His overall intention was to compose a work about the history and genesis of Russian folklore. To do a diachronic study, however, he believed he needed first to examine the narrative invariants or constant elements synchronically in order to determine the specificity of the genre. Historical research would then provide an explanation for its uniform character. One hundred Russian fairy tales or "wondertales" taken from the Afanas'ev collection served as a corpus for analysis. He rejected the "motif" as basis for classification despite his reverence for Veselovskii, considering it too restrictive a narrative unit. Instead he divided the text into segments according to the most important actions that make up the story. Each segment was condensed into a short sentence, such as "An interdiction is addressed to the hero," "The interdiction is violated," or "The villain is punished." These narrative units, or types of actions, Propp called functions to denote their significance for the progress of the narrative. He discovered thirty-one such functions which together describe the structure of the Russian wondertale. No tale included all of them but those he found would always follow one another syntagmatically in strict logical order. Propp also found that the functions were distributed among a fixed set of seven character roles, those of villain, donor (provider), helper, princess (sought-after-person) and her father, dispatcher, hero (seeker or victim), and false hero. These he named spheres of action. By establishing in this way an abstract predicate/action and subject structure to the folk tale, Propp had set up what he called the grammar of the folk tale, albeit relevant only to the subgenre he had analyzed.

The specific purpose which Propp's morphological study served had placed restrictions on his findings in terms of their wider application. It fell to French structuralist thinkers to be stimulated and seduced by their scientific and epistemological potential. By reworking them, criticizing, and adapting them to their particular aims, however, these scholars also tended to modify and reduce their original importance. Claude Lévi-Strauss in his 1960 review reproached Propp with having analyzed only the form of the tale and not what he called its "raw content." Having in his own study defined myth in bundles of relationships, he found fault with the exclusively linear arrangement of Propp's narrative functions and tried to translate the compositional invariants of the folk tale into achronic signifying elements. Basically, Lévi-Strauss was looking for universally applicable paradigmatic models while Propp had been concerned with the syntagmatic pattern of a particular genre.

The semiotician A. J. Greimas also attempted to extract universally valid models by streamlining Propp's theory. In his book *Sémantique structurale* (1966; *Structural Semantics*, 1976) he presents a general narrative grammar largely elaborated from Propp's theoretical principles. He simplified the seven spheres of action to produce his own actantial narrative schema based on three sets of binary oppositions: subject/object, sender/receiver, helper/opponent. Presenting six key narrative functions (actantial roles) they account together for all possible relationships within a story. His canonical narrative schema, based on Propp's thirty-one functions, complements this actantial model by describing the logical stages of action in narrative. This schema comprises three tests (acquiring competence, the decisive contest, and the final stage of reward or punishment) preceded by a contract.

Claude Bremond was another theorist who, inspired by Propp's example, tried to reach beyond the wondertale to formulate a universal logic of narrative. He adapted Propp's schema to introduce notions of functional grouping, those of "pivot functions" (offering a choice of consequences), of freedom of order of the functions, and finally of "improvement" or "deterioration." The resulting schema is supposed to represent a model for all narrative. Other French thinkers, Todorov and Barthes among them, also experimented with adapting Propp's schema so that it could be applied in a more general fashion. Thus while its influence was by all accounts tremendous, *Morphology of the Folktale* itself was only the starting point, a first step in the direction of the elaboration of general laws of structure, a long way removed from the initial study of the folklorist. Propp was not interested in abstract reasoning. In his reply to Lévi-Strauss he referred to himself as an incorruptible empiricist. He studied his material, collected his data, and proceeded from there to his conclusions.

Propp's genius lies in recognizing the importance of invariant structure for the definition of genre and in devising a method of analyzing just one such structure. His limitations arise precisely from tailoring his method to the needs of only one subgenre and from examining it in isolation, that is, excluding social context or cultural conditions. But then, that was not his primary concern. Propp was a folklorist with a lifelong interest in history and typology. His subsequent works also testify to this fact. *Istoričeskie korni volšebnoj skazki* (1946) searches for affinities between the structure of the wondertale and primitive initiation and funeral rites. *Russkie agrarnye prazdniki* (1963; Russian agrarian festivals) investigates links between the traditional Russian calendar and socioeconomic factors in the life of the peasants. Even in his work on epic poetry (1955), Propp bases his theory of archaic epos on his studies of the wondertale. His final, posthumous book, on laughter and the comic (1976), once again concentrates on typology. Different aspects of the comic and types of laughter are meticulously classified and evaluated.

Thus Propp's early preoccupation with pedagogy and linguistics together with his pervading interest in folk narrative would seem to account for his critical theories. His method of analysis reflects the analogy with language investigation and his studies in Russian folklore established him as one of the most distinguished researchers in his field in the world.

## Principal criticism

"Transformacii volšebnyx skazok," 1928 ("Fairy Tale Transformations," in *Readings in Russian Poetics: Formalist and Structuralist Views*, 1971)
*Morfologija skazki*, 1928, second edition 1969 (*Morphology of the Folktale*, 1958 and 1968)
"Ritual'nyj smex v fol'klore," 1939 (ritual laughter in folklore)
*Istoričeskie korni volšebnoj skazki*, 1946 (historical roots of the wondertale)
"Specifika fol'klora," 1946 (the nature of folklore)
*Russkij geroičeskij èpos*, 1955 (Russian heroic epic poetry)
*Russkie agrarnye prazdniki*, 1963 (Russian agrarian festivals)
"Fol'klor i dejstvitel'nost'," 1963 (folklore and reality)

"Principy klassifikacii fol'klornyx žanrov," 1964 (the principles of classifying folklore genres)

"Generic Structures in Russian Folklore," ("Žanrovi sostav russkogo folklora"), in *Genre*, 3, 1971

"The Russian Folk Lyric" ("O russkoj narodnoj liričeskoj pesne"), introductory essay in *Down Along the Mother Volga. An Anthology of Russian Folk Lyrics*, 1975. Translated by Roberta Reeder.

*Fol'klor i dejstvitel'nost'. Izbrannye stat'i*, 1976 (Folklore and reality. Selected papers)

*Problemy komizma i smexa*, 1976 (problems of laughter and the comic)

"Study of the Folktale: Structure and History" (translation of Propp's reply to Claude Lévi-Strauss' review), in *Dispositio*, 1, 1976

*Theory and History of Folklore*, 1984, containing seven articles, two chapters from *Istoričeskie korni volšebnj skazki* (historical roots of the wondertale) and the introduction to *Russkij geroičeskij èpos* (Russian heroic epic poetry)

## Further reading

Eimermacher, Karl. "Nachwort des Herausgebers" ("Postscript by the Editor") in *Morphologie des Märchens*, 1972 (German translation of *Morphology of the Folktale*).

Greimas, A. J. *Sémantique structurale*, 1966 (*Structural Semantics*, 1976).

Lévi-Strauss, Claude. "La Structure et la forme. Réflexions sur un ouvrage de Vladimir Propp" ("Structure and Form: Reflections on a Work by Vladimir Propp"), in *Cahiers de l'Institut de Science Économique Appliquée*, 1960.

Liberman, Anatoly. "Introduction: Vladimir Jakovlevic Propp," in *Theory and History of Folklore*, 1984.

Maranda, Pierre, ed. *Soviet Structural Folkloristics*, 1974.

Meletinsky, Eleazar. "Strukturno-tipologicheskoe izuchenie skazki" ("Structural and typological study of the folk tale"), introductory essay to *Morfologija skazki*, 1969 (second edition).

Shishkoff, Serge. "The Structure of Fairy Tales: Propp vs Lévi-Strauss," in *Dispositio*, 1, 1976.

Shukman Ann. "The Legacy of Propp," in *Essays in Poetics*, 1, 1976.

FELIZITAS RINGHAM

*See also* Genette; Greimas; Narratology; Russian Formalism; Semiotics

# Marcel Proust

## French novelist and critic

**Born:** Auteuil, France; July 10, 1871
**Died:** Paris, France; November 18, 1922

## Biography

Marcel Proust was born on July 10, 1871, in Auteuil, a suburb of Paris, at the turbulent close of the Franco-Prussian War. He came from a well-to-do, highly cultured, quintessentially French family: he was of Jewish extraction on his mother's side but was reared a Roman Catholic, and his father was an eminent medical doctor. Proust was educated and lived most of his days in the heart of Paris. He spent childhood summers at Auteuil and the more rural Illiers, until he had a severe attack of asthma around the age of nine. He was educated at the Lycée Cordorcet. Despite his asthma, he completed a year of military service immediately after he graduated at the age of eighteen. A bachelor and homosexual, Proust remained extremely close to his parents until their deaths. After a bright, social beginning, he spent his later years as a virtual recluse with a strictly nocturnal social life.

His first published work, *Les Plaisirs et les jours* (1896; *Pleasures and Regrets*, 1948), a book of short stories and poems, was interpreted by his contemporaries in the light of the waning Decadent movement. One review was so insulting that Proust challenged the reviewer to a duel, which ended without injuries but strained his precarious health. Despite Proust's undisputed personal honor, the Decadent label stuck to him, and his personal eccentricities did not help to dispel it.

Proust participated in the journalism of his day, publishing brief, witty articles on literary and occasionally more general topics. Other, substantial works remained unpublished during his lifetime. In failing health, he undertook and lived to see part of the publication of his ambitious masterpiece *À la recherche du temps perdu* (1913-1927; *Remembrance of Things Past*, 1922-1931, 1981), a seven-part novel in fifteen volumes, presenting an ever-fresh and ever-deepening, uniquely created world. He died in Paris on November 18, 1922.

## Influence

Proust looms large on the French literary scene, but he stands apart. His most famous peer and contemporary, André Gide, was a rather hostile rival who grabbed the lion's share of prestige and made it clear that he owed Proust nothing. Proust had a marginal influence on the existentialists, who were interested chiefly in what they interpreted to be his atheism. Modern French critics, from Jean-Paul Sartre to Julia Kristeva, pay homage to his achievement. Nevertheless, Proust's dedication to a privileged aesthetic truth, amounting to what is often called a "religion of art," contradicts the mainstream of twentieth-century criticism, particularly in France. Proust drew on many more sources than merely the influences of his era; besides an encyclopedic knowledge of French literature, his range included Plato, Arthur Schopenhauer, Immanuel Kant, Buddhism, and the writers of the American nineteenth century, including the Transcendentalists. As his age fades from living memory, Proust himself is gradually being taken more seriously as the original thinker that he was.

## Analysis

Proust is more articulate than most other novelists about the secrets of how a novel is written. His critical and fictional writings form a whole, reflecting a subtle but cohesive aesthetic theory of all the arts in their relationship to reality.

Proust's first, unfinished novel, *Jean Santeuil* (1952; English translation, 1955), written between 1895 and 1899, already attempts to explain how a writer is formed. Proust's sense of the importance of the writer's cultural role did not diminish as he matured. A few years after *Jean Santeuil*, in a piece entitled "Poet and Novelist," he wrote: "We all come to the novelist as slaves stand before an emperor. He can free us with a word."

During the critical period of 1902–1905 (bounded by the breakdown of his health and the deaths of his father and of his mother), Proust began the soul-searching that led to *Remembrance of Things Past*, a monumental novel sometimes compared to a cathedral. The roots of this complex work are clearly seen in Proust's ambitious critical study, *Contre Sainte-Beuve* (1954; *By Way of Sainte-Beuve*, 1958), which was written in 1908 and 1909 but published posthumously. This book-length essay explores all the factors that were soon to make Proust's best writing possible: unusual states of consciousness that lead to creativity, Proust's innermost feelings and childhood development, the role of his aristocratic neighbors (with their palpable historic aura) in liberating Proust's imagination, the works of Honoré de Balzac and Gérard de Nerval, and the concept of the literary critic's moral obligation toward the writer whom he interprets for the public. A precipitating motive for the essay was Proust's indignation at the pusillanimous way in which the influential critic, Charles-Augustin Sainte-Beuve, despite his keen critical appreciation and personal friendship, had failed Charles Baudelaire when the great poet was socially pilloried.

According to Proust, the literary critic is an extremely important figure because literature itself is so important. He differs from Sainte-Beuve, and many modern critics as well, in regarding the arts and literature as a unique path to privileged truth, rather than as one of many interchangeable means of self-expression. While in Proust's opinion the writer ought indeed to retain his persona as an Everyman, Proust emphasizes that this weak, foolish, Everyman voice is not the "I" that writes the novels. From the confusing of the author's writing and nonwriting selves stems both the fallacy of the Sainte-Beuve method (which seeks to explain everything in a writer's work through reference to biographical details – a method by no means dead) and Sainte-Beuve's failure to respect and defend the dignity of Baudelaire when his human weaknesses brought him opprobrium.

Proust shows himself a perspicacious critic in *By Way of Sainte-Beuve* with his own analyses of Balzac, Baudelaire, and other masters of French literature. His insights have the shorthand quality of shoptalk as he looks into other writers' workshops with a refreshing lack of reverence and the brotherly love of a sibling rival. He effortlessly keeps his footing through the maze of novels that make up

Balzac's world, enjoying their ebullient and sometimes vulgar abundance and urging more timorous readers to do the same: "Because of this half-baked realism, too fabulous for life, too prosaic for literature, we often get very much the same kind of pleasure from Balzac's books that we get from life." Though the vulgarian and the aesthete would seem to be at opposite poles of sensibility, Proust shared and endorsed the goal of producing books that gave, not an artificial pleasure, but the enjoyment that can sometimes be had from life itself (at its better moments).

The critic's private lyrical digressions, in which intensely personal feelings are shared with the reader, lead into critical analysis, just as occurs in the art criticism of John Ruskin (so greatly admired by Proust that he translated two of his works into French). Thus, Proust begins *By Way of Sainte-Beuve* with the first known version of the experience that later became the famous "madeleine" scene in *Remembrance of Things Past*. The act of munching a bit of dry bread dipped in tea (a combination not tried since childhood) sets free a chain of memories that causes time to stand still for Proust, here the thoughtful critic still coming to terms with the role of literature: "Suddenly the shaken partitions in my memory gave way, and into my conscious mind there rushed the summers I had spent." Proust offers his own finest moments of experiencing life – in a timeless, perfect, involuntarily re-created form – as the standard by which to evaluate literature.

Proust's standard of realism rejects superficial naturalism and boldly aims at the essential experience of life. Thus a practitioner of "half-baked realism," such as Balzac, or a writer of deep dreams, such as Nerval, can be a far more successful realist, for Proust, than could a so-called materialistic novelist such as Romain Rolland. Even more than the best-selling, facile materialists, however, Proust scorns the precious, self-styled Decadent writers of his day who claimed to write for "the few," meaning that their work was too refined and too profound for a wide readership. "There is only one way of writing for the many," Proust reminds them, "and that is to write . . . for the sake of what is deep and essential in oneself." Repeatedly, in *By Way of Sainte-Beuve* and in his numerous occasional pieces of literary criticism, Proust excoriates superficiality, insincerity, and materialism, three traits that add up to worldliness. Though popularly regarded as the ultimate worldling, Proust as a critic, speaking from the heart, is unworldly, spontaneous, and direct. He has a Kantian emotionality about his reactions to art and beauty. Unlike Kant, however, Proust finds no contradiction between art and thought. He emphasizes the inwardness of the creative process: "Books are the work of solitude and the *children of silence*." They are not written for the sake of prattle, of having "something to say," but reflect a thought process deeper than words. When the well-achieved literary work finally emerges from the depths of subverbal thought, it "is written in a sort of foreign tongue. To each sentence we each attach a meaning ... which is often a mistranslation. But in great literature all our mistranslations result in beauty." In addition to the inward, psychological truth of the sheer quality of human consciousness, the great novelists, such as Lev Tolstoi and Balzac, convey the sense of a law at work behind the seeming accidents of their plots, lending to humdrum, everyday occurrences "a sort of literary quality" that had not been perceptible before.

Proust's group of five articles on painters is very consistent with his concepts of realism in literature and lends additional illumination to that theme. The greatest virtue of any painter, in his opinion, is in compelling the viewer to see reality more deeply, and this deeper vision, if it is true, must inevitably result in a perception of beauty. In painting, too, Proust rejects materialism, stating bluntly: "Picture galleries are dwellings that house only thoughts." He is especially eloquent on Jean-Baptiste-Siméon Chardin and Rembrandt and is a most suitable critic to belie the complaint of artists that the visual arts cannot be encompassed by words:

On the threshold of Rembrandt, let us pause. Chardin has taught us that a pear is as living as a woman, a kitchen crock more beautiful than an emerald. He has proclaimed the divine quality of all things under the light which beautifies them and to the mind which reflects on them. By opening the world to us, he has made us leave behind a false idealism in order to explore an ample reality where on all sides we have rediscovered beauty, no longer the dwindled prisoner of convention or false good taste, but free, strong, universal; and it is into the open sea of beauty that he launches us.

The same could be said of Proust's own work, both as novelist and as critic.

## Principal criticism
*Contre Sainte-Beuve, suivi de nouveaux mélanges*, written 1908–1909, published 1954 (*By Way of Sainte-Beuve*, 1958)

## Other major works and literary forms
Marcel Proust, a highly conscious literary artist, is best known for *À la recherche du temps perdu* (1913–1927; *Remembrance of Things Past*, 1922–1931, 1981), an integrated series of elegant, aesthetically fresh, psychologically adventurous novels about French society of the *belle époque* at the turn of the century. In the best-known work of the series, *Du côté de chez Swann* (1913; *Swann's Way*, 1922), the protagonist, Charles Swann, toys with the idea of becoming an artist. He is talented at both music and writing. Nevertheless, although life grants him a sudden privileged insight into the deeper, richer possibilities of life – which for Proust demand to be expressed in art – Swann turns aside and is thus a failure. Many of Proust's other characters participate in art or aesthetics, if only passively. The least fortunate are those who give way to emotional obsessions, particularly jealousy.

NOVELS
*À la recherche du temps perdu*, 1913–1927 (*Remembrance of Things Past*, 1922–1931, 1981), includes *Du côté de chez Swann* (*Swann's Way*), *À l'ombre des jeunes filles en fleurs* (*Within a Budding Grove*), *Le Côté de Guermantes* (*The Guermantes Way*), *Sodome et Gomorrhe* (*Cities of the Plain*), *La Prisonnière* (*The Captive*), *Albertine disparue* (*The Sweet Cheat Gone*), and *Le Temps retrouvé* (*Time Regained*)
*Jean Santeuil*, 1952 (written 1895–1899 English translation, 1955)

NONFICTION
*Pastiches et mélanges*, 1919
*Chroniques*, 1927

TRANSLATIONS
*Le Bible d'Amiens*, 1904 (of John Ruskin's *The Bible of Amiens*)
*Sésame et les lys*, 1906 (of John Ruskin's *Sesame and Lilies*)

MISCELLANEOUS
*Les Plaisirs et les jours*, 1896 (*Pleasures and Regrets*, 1948)

## Further reading
Brée, Germaine. *The World of Marcel Proust*, 1966.
Bucknall, Barbara J. *The Religion of Art in Proust*, 1969.
Carter, William C. *The Artist and the Aviator*, 1992.
Girard, René, ed. *Proust: A Collection of Critical Essays*, 1962.
Hayman, R. *Proust: A Biography*, 1990.
Kasell, Walter. *Marcel Proust and the Strategy of Reading*, 1980.
Kristeva, Julia. *Time and Sense: Proust and the Experience of Literature*, 1996.
Moss, Howard. *The Magic Lantern of Marcel Proust*, 1962.
Painter, George D. *Marcel Proust*, 1955–65 (2 volumes).
Stambolian, George. *Marcel Proust and the Creative Encounter*, 1972.
Strauss, Walter. *Proust and Literature: The Novelist as Critic*, 1957.
Warner, Sylvia Townsend. Introduction to *By Way of Sainte-Beuve*, 1958.

DIANA GOSSELIN NAKEEB

*See also* Bergson; French Literary Theory: Twentieth Century; Gourmont

# Psychoanalytic Criticism

If we date the emergence of psychoanalysis from the publication of Sigmund Freud's *The Interpretation of Dreams* (1900), then we can with equal certainty identify the beginnings of psychoanalytic criticism. In this work we find the first example of *applied psychoanalysis* with Freud's interpretation of William Shakespeare's play *Hamlet*. For Freud, *Hamlet* derives from the same psychic origins as Sophocles' *Oedipus Rex*, that is, repressed infantile sexual desires. We can account for the differing treatment within each play of essentially the same raw material through the "secular advance of repression in the emotional life of mankind." Freud goes on to say that in *Oedipus Rex*, "the child's wishful phantasy that underlies it is brought into the open and realized as it would be in a dream. In *Hamlet* it remains repressed; and – just as in the case of neurosis – we only learn of its existence from its inhibiting consequences." Hamlet, in other words, is the first modern psychopathological character on the English stage; he is a character who is able to perform any act "except take vengeance on the man who did away with his father and took his father's place with his mother, the man who shows him the repressed wishes of his own childhood realized." *Hamlet*, in short, reveals to us our deeply repressed Oedipal desire. Freud's brief interpretation of *Hamlet* has been vigorously criticized by Shakespearean scholars but at the same time it has remained a peculiarly enduring reading of the play, an ambivalence which has always been the hallmark of the relationship between psychoanalysis and literary criticism.

## Applied psychoanalysis

Applied psychoanalysis broadly designates two related forms of criticism: first, literature as *illustrative* of psychoanalytic concepts and, second, the *psycho-biography*. Ernest Jones' *Hamlet and Oedipus* (1949) exemplifies the former through its assertion of the universality of the Oedipus complex. In an extended defensive of Freud's initial interpretation, Jones sought to prove how the appeal of Shakespeare's play could be accounted for through Hamlet's Oedipal conflict, which he saw as a direct expression of Shakespeare's own unresolved Oedipal complex. These unconscious Oedipal desires then in turn resonate with the unconscious desires of the audience, which, he argues, accounts for the play's universal appeal and timelessness. Jones' interpretation was ingenious but it rested upon a number of fallacies and a large degree of speculation about Shakespeare's life. In order to assert that Hamlet has an unresolved Oedipal conflict we must first assume that he is a "real" person rather than a character on the stage. Jones, therefore, must insist on the *verisimilitude* of Shakespeare's text and ignore its literary and dramatic quality. Second, the critic must accept that the text is merely a *symptom* of the author's particular neurosis.

The text as a symptom of the author's unconscious is central to the notion of psycho-biography. In *The Life and Work of Edgar Alan Poe: A Psychoanalytic Interpretation* (1949), Marie Bonaparte argued that the literary work is analogous to a dream or a symptom and thus can be seen to reveal the author's psychopathology. Bonaparte identifies two incidents that irrevocably marked Poe's life: first, the sight of his dead mother and his subsequent infatuation with her; second, a night he spent in the same room as a consumptive niece and the desire this aroused in him. These two instances can be seen to recur in Poe's fiction,

albeit in disguised forms, thus the key to understanding Poe's work is his deeply repressed sadonecrophilia. As with Jones, Bonaparte uncovers some interesting insights into Poe's life and work but she also shares the problem of directly equating the fictional text with the biography of the author. This problem is further compounded by the analogy between the literary text and the dream.

In "Creative Writers and Day-dreaming" Freud had shown how the dreams of adolescents and adults were related to the play activities of children and how both represented fictive wish-fulfillment. Freud further suggested that a parallel between the process of daydreaming and creative writing existed. Creative writing gratifies the author's unconscious, infantile, wishes by allowing the author to express these fantasies in an imaginary and more or less disguised form. In other words, the author imaginatively represents his or her most secret and hidden desires and thus makes them both acceptable and accessible to a wider audience. Now, on the one hand, if the literary text is like a dream then psychoanalysis can provide an interpretive model through the notion of dream-work – condensation, displacement, secondary revision – for the analysis of texts (see Trilling, 1950). If, on the other hand, literary works are seen as merely another route to the author's unconscious then once the critic has identified the underlying pathology or neurosis of an author he or she simply has to search the text for the appropriate symbols or representations to confirm the analysis. The critic will inevitably find confirmation of his or her reading as all symbols will be suitably disguised and displaced forms of repressed wishful fantasies; the interpretation in other words, is circular and self-fulfilling.

Freud, Jones, and Bonaparte were first and foremost psychoanalysts and their sole interest in literature was what it could reveal about an individual author's psychology or how it could validate psychoanalytic concepts. What is missing from these writers is any appreciation of the *literariness* of literature. Their respective interpretations reduce the meaning of the text to the singular expression of an author's unconscious symptoms. Applied psychoanalysis was not restricted to psychoanalysts, however, and many eminent literary critics, such as Edmund Wilson and D. H. Lawrence, used psychoanalysis in a similar way.

## Archetypal criticism

Psychoanalysis is not restricted to the work of Freud; each major school of psychoanalysis can be seen to have developed its own distinctive form of criticism. The Swiss psychoanalyst Carl Jung, as well as being one of Freud's most important early collaborators, and dissenters, has had an extraordinary influence on both literature and literary criticism. Analytical psychology, as Jung distinguished his practice from Freudianism proper, has developed what is known as *archetypal criticism*. An archetype is a primordial image that does not exist in individual psyches as such but in what Jung called the "collective unconscious," which is transcultural and trans-historical. These archetypes or privileged symbols, such as anima and animus (feminine and masculine), puer and senex (age and youth), and the trickster, could be seen to recur not only in the unconscious of individuals but also in our myths and fictional representations.

The most influential work of archetypal criticism, and arguably one of the single most important works of Anglo-American criticism of the last forty years, is Northrop Frye's *Anatomy of Criticism* (1957). Frye used the notion of the archetype to develop his own system of classification of literary genres and modes. According to Frye, literature is structured around four "pregeneric" archetypes or narrative categories: the romantic (summer), the tragic (autumn), the ironic (winter), and the comic (spring). Frye saw each of these *mythoi* as governed by a particular narrative structure and ultimately representing the fulfillment of an unconscious desire. More recent Jungian-inspired criticism has included the poet Ted Hughes' *Shakespeare and the Goddess of Complete Being* (1992).

## Ego psychology
The main development of psychoanalysis in North America has been through ego psychology. Ego psychologists abandoned Freud's emphasis on unconscious processes, concentrating their work on strengthening the ego. Whereas Freud located the meaning of literary texts in the unconscious fantasy of the author, the ego psychologists see meaning as deriving from what is publicly shareable and socially encoded. In other words, meaning does not rest in the psyche of the author but in the conventions between reader and text; this kind of criticism is closely aligned with *reader-response theory*. In *The Dynamics of Literary Response* (1968) Norman N. Holland initially argued that the literary text was a kind of fundamental fantasy shared by both author and reader but in subsequent revisions of his work, *Poems in Person* and *Five Readers Reading* (both 1975), he placed the emphasis for meaning firmly on the side of the reader. In line with ego psychology, Holland has been concerned with the way in which readers adapt their identity in the process of interpretation and thereby confirm a sense of self and autonomy.

## Object relations theory
Within the United Kingdom the principal development of psychoanalysis has been through the work of Melanie Klein and object relations theory. This particular body of psychoanalytic theory has had little impact upon literary criticism although some notable work has recently been produced using D. W. Winnicott's notion of "transitional objects" and "potential space" (see Rudnytsky, 1993). By far the most significant influence on psychoanalytic criticism within Britain and the United States over the last three decades has been the work of the French psychoanalyst Jacques Lacan. By the mid-1960s applied psychoanalysis was a spent critical force, it was perceived to be inherently reductionist and to amount to little more than phallic symbol spotting. Lacan's work on desire and language was to fundamentally transform the nature of psychoanalytic criticism and to produce some of the most important literary theory of the 1970s and 1980s. Despite his notoriously difficult and esoteric style, Lacanianism in one form or another permeates current literary theory.

## Lacanian criticism
Like Freud, Lacan has written on a number of literary texts, including *Antigone*, *Hamlet*, and courtly love poetry, as well as the works of Edgar Alan Poe and James Joyce. Lacan's most influential piece of literary criticism is his seminar on Poe's *The Purloined Letter*. In this seminar Lacan sought to demonstrate how the human subject is constituted through language and within a symbolic order. His interpretation of Poe's tale focused upon two main themes: first, the anomalous nature of the letter itself, the contents of which are never revealed to the reader; second, the way in which possession of the letter by individual characters immediately sets them within a triangular relationship with the other main characters. Lacan also highlights the way in which Poe's tale repeats itself, reworking the same triangular scenario but in a slightly different form. According to Lacan, the contents of the letter remain a secret because it is a pure signifier (representation) without a signified (meaning) and it is the signifier that captivates the individual characters and positions them as subjects in the chain of signification. This, for Lacan, is the meaning of Poe's tale, the insistence of the signifying chain and the determination of the subject by the signifier.

Lacan's reading of *The Purloined Letter* has raised a great deal of debate and we can see within it the traditional methods of applied psychoanalysis, whereby literature is simply used to illustrate psychoanalytic concepts and the literariness of the text itself is ignored. It is not to Lacan himself, therefore, that we should turn for insights into literature. His significance for literary studies rests upon his transposition of the Freudian notion of the unconscious and repressed desire from the individual to the realm of language and a transindividual symbolic order. Lacan famously said that the unconscious is structured *like* a language, in other words, the unconscious functions according to rules of language, primarily metaphor and metonymy. This insight marked an important shift in psychoanalytic criticism away from its previous focus on the unconscious fantasies of the author or characters to the way in which desire works through language and the text. Indeed, Peter Brooks has gone so far as to suggest that literature and the psyche share the same structure and, therefore, psychoanalytic theory is directly superimposable upon narrative theory.

For Brooks, psychoanalysis is primarily a narrative art which offers us a systematic and dynamic account of a psychic process that directly corresponds to narrative or textual strategies. Against what he sees as the scientism of much semiotic and narrative theory, Brooks proposes a psychodynamic model of the text as a system of internal energies and tensions, compulsions, and resistances, above all driven by desire. Desire operates at a number of different levels in the text, initially as the desire to narrate itself, secondly, as the intrinsic textual desire of, or between, characters within the narrative. But more importantly there is the desire of the reader, the desire to continue and finish the narrative. Brooks' conception of a system of multilayered narrative desire is useful in understanding how readers invest narrative with their own desire and fantasy. The key to understanding how this process works is the psychoanalytic concept of *transference*.

## Transference and the text

Transference is essentially the process whereby, within analysis, the analysand *transfers* onto his or her relationship with the analyst infantile sexual fantasies or previous sexual experiences. Within the transference something of the past is reconstructed, or reenacted, in the present. According to Brooks, transference creates an intermediate region that is neither past nor present, it is neither inside nor outside, neither fiction nor reality. Transference is a *symbolic* reconstruction of past experiences, it is textual through and through just as much as the text is fundamentally transferential. Readers are involved in a dialogue with the text and, according to Brooks, the reader must grasp not only what is said but also what is left unsaid within the narrative, what is absent from the discourse but must be reconstructed if the reader is to understand how a text is working upon him or herself.

Shoshana Felman's analysis of Henry James' short story *The Turn of the Screw* is an extraordinary example of this kind of criticism. Felman is concerned to resist the reductionism of previous forms of psychoanalytic literary criticism that inevitably identifies the meaning of any text as an Oedipal drama. For Felman, Lacan's insight that desire motivates the signifying chain of language means precisely that meaning can never be fixed and determined. She therefore investigates the way in which readers and critics of James' short story are caught up in a complex transferential relationship with the text. In the act of interpreting the text, critics inevitably repeat the same gesture of identifying the meaning of the text which they initially set out to challenge. For Felman, this is not coincidental, as what psychoanalysis teaches us is precisely that we are all doomed to repeat what has gone before, but psychoanalysis also teaches us another lesson, that is the impossibility of ever completely determining this process or fixing meaning. She therefore highlights the ambiguity of James' text and the way in which unconscious desires refuse to allow any singular meaning to be fixed to the text. Psychoanalysis allows us to keep open the text in a constantly proliferating series of readings.

Psychoanalytic criticism has thus come full circle, from initially providing the hermeneutic key that reveals the true meaning of literature, as Freud said of *Hamlet*, to providing a dynamic model of how unconscious fantasy and desire works within language and texts to resist any fixed or determinate meaning.

## Further reading

Brooks, Peter. *Reading for the Plot: Design and Intention in Narrative*, 1984.
Ellmann, Maud, ed. *Psychoanalytic Literary Criticism*, 1994.
Felman, Shoshana, ed. *Literature and Psychoanalysis, The Question of Reading: Otherwise*, 1982.
Kofman, Sarah. *Freud and Fiction*, 1991.
Muller, John P., and William J. Richardson, eds. *The Purloined Poe: Lacan, Derrida and Psychoanalytic Reading*, 1988.
Rudnytsky, Peter·L., ed. *Transitional Objects and Potential Spaces*, 1993.
Trilling, Lionel. "Freud and Literature," in *The Liberal Imagination*, 1950.
Vice, Sue, ed. *Psychoanalytic Criticism: A Reader*, 1996.
Wright, Elizabeth. *Psychoanalytic Criticism: A Reappraisal*, 1998.

SEAN HOMER

*See also* Archetypal Criticism; Edel; Hartman; Holland; Irigaray; Kristeva; Lacan

# Aleksandr Pushkin

## Russian poet and writer

**Born:** Moscow, Russia; June 6, 1799
**Died:** St. Petersburg, Russia; February 10, 1837

## Biography

Aleksandr Pushkin was born in Moscow on June 6, 1799; he was the second child in the family of Nadezhda Osipovna and Sergei Pushkin. Many of his ancestors had been prominent in government and literature; indeed, it was claimed that for six centuries scions of the house of Pushkin had played leading roles in the nation's history. During his early years Pushkin displayed an intense interest in published works of every sort; he spent entire nights reading French books in his father's library. In 1811 he was one of the thirty students who were chosen for the first entering class at the imperial lycée near St. Petersburg.

Although he was only an adequate student, Pushkin's literary gifts were evident even during this early stage; his first published poems appeared when he was fifteen, and increasingly he became preoccupied with such efforts. In 1817 Pushkin accepted a position as junior secretary in the Ministry of Foreign Affairs. Much of his time, however, was spent reveling and composing lyrical poems. Some of his compositions had political overtones which brought him under suspicion at the imperial court. In 1820 Pushkin was exiled to southern Russia; the cities where he lived during the ensuing period provided him with settings and local color for his major writings.

Because of his personal associations, Pushkin was implicated in the Decembrist Uprising of 1825, yet he was allowed to reside in the capital when Emperor Nicholas I decided to supervise him and became his personal censor. For a time Pushkin was allowed access to historical archives, and in 1829 he joined the army for a brief period of active duty during one of Russia's wars with the Ottoman Empire. In the meantime he had become engaged to Natal'ia Goncharova, from a noted family in Moscow; in 1830 her parents presented Pushkin with an estate in Boldino, in central Russia. He married early the following year. During this time, however, a journal with which Pushkin had been associated was closed down, partly for political reasons. Subsequently, although Pushkin managed to compose many of his outstanding poems and narrative works, he also indulged his propensity for gambling and carousing.

Pushkin continued to be concerned with salient literary questions, and indeed in 1836 he helped establish the journal *Sovremennik* in order to promote public interest in such developments, but he was recurrently distracted by intrigues and rumors involving his wife. Although four children were born to them, theirs was not a happy union. He challenged one of her admirers, an adopted son of the Dutch ambassador, Georges d'Anthès, to a duel. When they fought, on February 8, 1837, Pushkin was shot in the abdomen while inflicting only a superficial wound on his opponent. Two days later, after painful struggles, he died at his house in St. Petersburg.

## Influence

Pushkin's literary legacy is almost unparalleled in the development of Russian culture, and his significance has been acknowledged by a number of important figures. While Nikolai Gogol' was one of the first major writers to see Pushkin's efforts as extraordinary, judgments of this sort were seconded by Ivan Turgenev and Fedor Dostoevskii. Indeed, while generations of authors have found different facets of Pushkin's work to emphasize, his place in Russian letters has seldom been challenged. For that matter, critics of widely disparate political leanings have cited his writings as essential. Official Soviet works have stressed his place in literary history, while poets such as Anna Akhmatova and Boris Pasternak, who fell out of favor with the government, attested the inspiration and insights provided by Pushkin's verse. Particularly during the twentieth century, Pushkin's stature has been recognized in many other countries as well.

## Analysis

While his critical works were not produced according to any systematic schedule or order, Pushkin's writings on literature were significant both in suggesting internal concerns which were important in the composition of his fictional works and in reflecting the problems and prospects of Russian culture during an important formative phase. Some of his critical studies dealt with the influences, Russian and foreign, that had affected his own efforts; on occasion he discussed writers and works generally well known at the time. Most of Pushkin's literary judgments were delivered when he had both the opportunity and the inclination to do so; his ideas were not openly identified with any specific school or group but represented an outlook which arose in the course of his own creative development. The elements of style that distinguished Pushkin's narrative prose were also featured in his essays on literature. Some of his criticism was couched in the form of aphorisms; other articles and studies were composed in spare, precise language that achieved its ends directly.

Although he was rarely inclined to do so, Pushkin occasionally responded to reviews of his works. For example, in discussing critical reactions to *Kavkazskii plennik* (1822; *The Prisoner of the Caucasus*, 1936), Pushkin acknowledged with gratitude the constructive point of view expressed by certain people who had written about his work. In the draft preface to *Boris Godunov* (1831; English translation, 1918), he defended his choice of poetic meter and contended that, when possible, he had attempted to achieve historical verisimilitude; indeed, in preparing that work he had consulted materials pertaining to the political activities of one of his ancestors. Other drafts and letters which appear in Pushkin's collected works reveal his scrupulous candor in assaying his own efforts. While in some instances he believed that the public estimate of his writings fell below their actual worth, he also suggested that, in relation to the rest, certain compositions of his were weaker than had generally been supposed. Pushkin sometimes reproached his critics for their obtuseness in objecting to metaphors and stylistic techniques he had used in his poetry; he also chided some of them for an excessive delicacy in protesting against some of the more plainly erotic passages in his works. On the whole, however, Pushkin did not devote much time to defending his own writings or expounding the principles upon which they had been composed. His other comments on Russian literature were about evenly divided between those dealing with specific authors and remarks of a more general nature.

An arresting observation which runs through much of Pushkin's critical writing is the contention that until that time Russia had had no real criticism. In his article "O zhurnalnoi kritike" (1830; "On Journal Criticism," 1969), he maintained that, apart from bibliographical notices, some rather uneven efforts at satire, and reviews of a rather pedestrian stamp, Russian writers had accomplished little in this area. Occasionally Pushkin found some glimmers of hope among various surveys of Russian literature. In "Dennitsa" (1830; "Morning Star," 1969), he discerned some positive qualities in a study of active writers composed by Ivan Kireevskii; while it was not clear that his expectations were vindicated when Kireevskii eventually became a prominent Slavophile publicist, Pushkin also, toward the end of his career, became interested in early critical writings of Vissarion Belinskii. He maintained that with more scholarship and experience major accomplishments could be expected from Belinskii, as already he had talent which would justify great hopes. In other notes on the practice of criticism, Pushkin maintained that it was a science which depended upon the exacting description and analysis of its subject matter; sound knowledge of the principles affecting an artist's or a writer's creations was a prerequisite. Critical undertakings could hardly be dispassionate, because realization of their tasks required profound and abiding love for literature and art. Pushkin often contrasted ideals of this sort to the rather squalid controversies that broke out from time to time in literary circles.

Where praise was due, Pushkin was more than willing to extend it. In discussing the lyric poetry of Evgenii Baratynskii, he acclaimed the grace and maturity of his elegies. He also found much that was meritorious in the poetry of his friend Anton Del'vig, the editor of journals to which Pushkin sometimes contributed. He maintained that Del'vig's idylls showed powers of imagination that were unusual for verses taken from classical models. In writings that employed historical themes, Pushkin had consulted Nikolai Karamzin's massive study of ancient Russia; he recommended this work for its use of original chronicles and for its great erudition. Indeed, his contention that Karamzin had discovered the nation's past as Christopher Columbus had discovered America was widely cited.

Pushkin's astuteness in recognizing literary talent perhaps was demonstrated most clearly in his reviews of early works by Gogol'. While he was most immediately impressed with Gogol''s fresh and lively humor, Pushkin also took note of the sly hints of social commentary, as well as the author's underlying sincerity. Indeed, he maintained that Gogol' would move on to yet greater achievements. In reviews of efforts by other authors, Pushkin intimated that he valued originality and genuine inspiration more than broad public appeal; in many respects, he remained suspicious of works that succeeded by attracting an extensive popular following over a relatively brief period. One of the most withering literary attacks Pushkin ever mounted was on Faddei Bulgarin, a notorious police spy who was also the author of some rather moralistic novels and the editor of an influential journal. Under the pseudonym Feofilakt Kosichkin, Pushkin published a searing examination of literary cronyism, in which he pointed out that other mediocre writers came to Bulgarin's support with favorable judgments of his rather ponderous works. Pushkin's essay suggested that Bulgarin and his allies were in no position to criticize the more compact and closely organized efforts of other authors.

Although Pushkin believed that native literary traditions were generally lacking in Russia, he did not advocate the craven imitation of foreign models; rather, he suggested that on many counts Russian resources could be used to advantage. For example, he contended that writers did not need to affect a tone of high-flown discourse; the everyday speech of common people was pure and correct and thus could serve as a model for authors seeking to portray real life. While Pushkin was well-read in European literature (he even composed a number of letters and other drafts in French), he opposed the wholesale borrowing of foreign words and phrases where Russian equivalents existed. Even where he had deplored the weakness of Russian critical theory, he did not propose that teachings propounded elsewhere should be adopted uniformly. Moreover, while Pushkin's critical prose showed a familiarity with the arbiters of European taste, from Nicolas Boileau-Despréaux and Jean-François de La Harpe to his contemporary Charles-Augustin Sainte-Beuve, references of this sort were made for the sake of illustration, to show that critical ideas had flourished where other forms of literature had taken root. Much of Pushkin's interest in foreign writing was centered on authors whose creative works were relevant to his own efforts.

Pushkin readily conceded that French literature had exercised a preeminent influence on Russian culture; yet, although its effects were pervasive, the results were not always felicitous. While Pushkin's judgments were sometimes inexact, particularly for early French authors, he showed a keen appreciation for some classical thinkers, and he openly acknowledged his indebtedness to writers of a romantic persuasion whose outlook and ideas in some ways ran parallel to his own. For example, François Auguste René Chateaubriand was mentioned in many of Pushkin's writings; although he took note of Chateaubriand's careless handling of factual matters, and he did not share the French writer's concern with religious quests, Pushkin found his works inspiring where contrasting images of settled ways and natural sensibilities arose. Pushkin also took interest in the efforts of Benjamin Constant and was especially fond of his novel *Adolphe* (1816; English translation, 1816). Some emotional and psychological insights certainly came from this source, and it has been maintained that Constant's romantic hero in some ways served as a model for the protagonist of Pushkin's *Evgenii Onegin* (1825–1832, 1833; *Eugene Onegin*, 1881). Other assessments of French literature were frequently discerning but sometimes idiosyncratic: Pushkin paid tribute to the poetry of André-Marie Chénier and found the works of Alfred de Musset extraordinarily vivid, but he had a low estimate of Victor Hugo's verse.

English and American literature also affected the development of Pushkin's views on art and criticism. He had a particularly high regard for the drama of William Shakespeare and considered his plays more clearly and incisively composed than classical French works, such as those of Jean Racine. Pushkin pondered Shakespeare's characterization of Henry IV during the composition of his own *Boris Godunov*. His attitude, however, never approached veneration; he maintained that his *Graf Nulin* (1827; *Count Nulin*, 1967), a pastiche, was better than Shakespeare's poem *The Rape of Lucrece* (1594). Pushkin also stated his interest in the works of John Milton, and he went to some lengths in considering both the achievements and the shortcomings of Lord Byron. During the early stages of his career Pushkin had been measurably affected by the atmosphere of exoticism, adventure, and Romantic melancholy that was associated with the English poet's work. In some senses, Pushkin regarded Byron as exhibiting both depth and variety, but on other points he found fault with Byron's inattention to problems of character and plot. Pushkin also came upon some passages in Byron's writings which dealt with Russia, and he commented caustically on inaccurate or implausible claims.

Pushkin also took interest in the stories of Washington Irving and indeed used material from one of Irving's stories as the point of departure for his *Skazka o zolotom petushke* (1834; *The Tale of the Golden Cockerel*, 1918). Moreover, a lengthy review of a work whose authorship is disputed but which appeared as *A Narrative of the Captivity and Adventures of John Tanner During Thirty Years Residence Among the Indians* (1830), available to Pushkin in a French translation, provided the opportunity for some commentary on American manners and mores. He seemed skeptical and somewhat fearful about democratic institutions, which he believed might yield to tyranny in a new guise; he apparently also regarded the United States as dominated by mercantile values. Perhaps the most interesting portion of this review, however, dealt with matters of authenticity and verisimilitude, for Pushkin contrasted the situation of the Native American as reported by an actual observer with the more idealized versions of life in the wild which fiction writers, including Chateaubriand and James Fenimore Cooper, had presented.

The scope of Pushkin's interests, although not all-embracing, certainly warranted the designation that has sometimes been made, that he was Russia's first professional man of letters. While critical musings about literature were secondary to his major creative efforts, Pushkin did much to promote serious theoretical consideration of literary problems. Such writings, when taken together with his poetry, his narrative fiction, and his dramatic works, reveal an intellect and a temperament that recorded major advances on several cultural fronts.

## Principal criticism

Articles appearing in *Moskovskii telegraf* (1825), *Severnye tsvety* (1828), *Literaturnaia gazeta* (1830–1831), *Russkii invalid* (1833), and *Sovremennik* (1836–1837)
*Pushkin-kritik*, 1934, 1950
*A. S. Pushkin o literature*, 1962
*The Critical Prose of Alexander Pushkin*, 1969
*Pushkin on Literature*, 1971, 1986

## Other major works and literary forms

Aleksandr Pushkin contributed much to Russian poetry during the early phase of its development; his poems achieved a sonorous grace which has never been equaled by later writers. His command of rhythm and diction was matched by a seemingly effortless mastery of narrative techniques, which were displayed in works such as *Kavkazskii plennik* (1822; *The Prisoner of the Caucasus*, 1936), *Tsygany* (1827; *The Gypsies*, 1957), and *Mednyi vsadnik* (1841; *The Bronze Horseman*, 1936). Pushkin's *Evgenii Onegin* (1825–1832, 1833; *Eugene Onegin*, 1881), which was composed as a novel in verse, evokes the enduring pathos of unrequited love, jealousy, and bitter conflict leading to a duel to the death. Other poetic works stand as sparkling examples of Pushkin's use of imagery and details in settings drawn from Russian history and folklore.

Pushkin's plays were written along classical European lines, but with some individual features added to reflect his own thematic concerns. His most notable work in this genre, *Boris Godunov* (1831; English translation, 1918), tells of political intrigue and social upheaval during the troubled period that preceded the rise of the Romanov dynasty. The play *Motsart i Sal'eri* (1832; *Mozart and Salieri*, 1920) depicts the resentment mediocrity held toward genius. Other dramatic works involve the retelling of time-honored tales and legends in a crisp and elegant fashion.

Many of Pushkin's prose works are distinguished by their charm and simplicity; the stories presented as a group in *Povesti Belkina* (1831; *Russian Romance*, 1875, better known as *The Tales of Belkin*, 1947) are studies in Russian life and mores which fascinated many readers by their meticulously crafted plots. *Pikovaia dama* (1834; *The Queen of Spades*, 1858) developed overtones of the fantastic in a haunting narrative of a young man's downfall in the wake of his efforts to master the secrets of gambling. Pushkin's longer fiction often features events from Russian history, providing panoramic studies of the violence and turmoil that surrounded crucial events. The novella *Kapitanskaia dochka* (1836; *The Captain's Daughter*, 1858), set during the period of the Pugachev Rebellion, is possibly the most renowned among his longer works of fiction; *Egipetskie nochi* (1841; *Egyptian Nights*, 1896) is an unusual foray into an exotic classical setting, with explicitly erotic overtones that aroused consternation in some quarters. Pushkin also wrote formal historical works based upon his own research. For example, *Puteshestvie v Arzrum* (1836; *A Journey to Arzrum*, 1974) presents his recollections of incidents along the Ottoman-Russian frontier during a period of war.

NOVELS
*Evgenii Onegin*, 1825–1832, 1833 (*Eugene Onegin*, 1881)
*Arap Petra velikogo*, 1828–1841 (*Peter the Great's Negro*, 1896)
*Kirdzhali*, 1834 (English translation, 1896)
*Kapitanskaia dochka*, 1836 (*The Captain's Daughter*, 1858)
*Dubrovskii*, 1841 (English translation, 1892)

*Egipetskie nochi*, 1841 (*Egyptian Nights*, 1896)
*Istoriia sela Goriukhina*, 1857 (*History of the Village of Goryukhino*, 1966)

SHORT FICTION
*Povesti Belkina*, 1831 (*Russian Romance*, 1875, better known as *The Tales of Belkin*, 1947)
*Pikovaia dama*, 1834 (*The Queen of Spades*, 1858)

PLAYS
*Boris Godunov*, 1831 (English translation, 1918)
*Motsart i Sal'eri*, 1832 (*Mozart and Salieri*, 1920)
*Pir vo vremia chumy*, 1833 (*Feast in Time of the Plague*, 1925)
*Skupoi rytsar'*, 1836 (*The Covetous Knight*, 1925)
*Rusalka*, 1837 (*The Water Nymph*, 1924)
*Kamennyi gost*, 1839 (*The Stone Guest*, 1936)

POETRY
*Ruslan i Liudmila*, 1820 (English translation, 1974)
*Gavriiliada*, 1822 (*Gabriel: A Poem*, 1926)
*Kavkazskii plennik*, 1822 (*The Prisoner of the Caucasus*, 1936)
*Brat'ia razboiniki*, 1824
*Bakhchisaraiskii fontan*, 1827 (*The Fountain of Bakhchisarai*, 1849)
*Graf Nulin*, 1827 (*Count Nulin*, 1967)
*Tsygany*, 1827 (*The Gypsies*, 1957)
*Poltava*, 1829 (English translation, 1936)
*Domik v Kolomne*, 1833 (*The Little House at Kolomna*, 1977)
*Skazka o mertvoi tsarevne*, 1833 (*The Tale of the Dead Princess*, 1924)
*Skazka o rybake i rybke*, 1833 (*The Tale of the Fisherman and the Fish*, 1926)
*Skazka o tsare Saltane*, 1833 (*The Tale of Tsar Saltan*, 1950)
*Skazka o zolotom petushke*, 1834 (*The Tale of the Golden Cockerel*, 1918)
*Mednyi vsadnik*, 1841 (*The Bronze Horseman*, 1936)
*Pushkin Threefold*, 1972
*Collected Narrative and Lyrical Poetry*, 1984
*Epigrams and Satirical Verse*, 1984

NONFICTION
*Istoriia Pugacheva*, 1834 (*The Pugachev Rebellion*, 1966)
*Puteshestvie v Arzrum*, 1836 (*A Journey to Arzrum*, 1974)
*Dnevnik (1833–1835)*, 1923
*Pis'ma*, 1926–1935 (3 volumes)
*The Letters of Alexander Pushkin*, 1963 (3 volumes)
*Pis'ma poslednikh let 1834–1837*, 1969

MISCELLANEOUS
*The Poems, Prose, and Plays of Pushkin*, 1936
*A. S. Pushkin bez tsenzury*, 1972
*Polnoe sobranie sochinenii*, 1977–1979 (10 volumes)
*Alexander Pushkin: Complete Prose Fiction*, 1983

## Further reading

Akhmatova, Anna Andreyevna. "Benjamin Constant's *Adolphe* in the Work of Pushkin," in *Russian Literature Triquarterly*. X (1974), pp. 157–179.
Bethea, David M. *Pushkin Today*, 1993.
Blagoy, Dmitry Dmitriyevich. *The Sacred Lyre: Essays on the Life and Work of Alexander Pushkin*, 1982.
Bloom, Harold, ed. *Alexander Pushkin*, 1987.
Briggs, A. D. P. *Alexander Pushkin: A Critical Study*, 1983.
Debreczeny, Paul. *Social Functions of Literature: Alexander Pushkin and Russian Culture*, 1997.
Gutsche, George J. "Puškin and Belinskij: The Role of the 'Offended Provincial,'" in *New Perspectives on Nineteenth-Century Russian Prose*, 1982. Edited by George J. Gutsche and Lauren G. Leighton.
Karlinsky, Simon. "Two Pushkin Studies," in *California Slavic Studies*. II (1963), pp. 96–120.
Lotman, Iurii. *Pushkin*, 1995.
Lunacharsky, Anatoly Vasilyevich. "Pushkin as Critic," in *Pushkin: Homage by Marxist Critics*, 1937. Edited by Irving D. W. Talmadge.
Maguire, Robert A. "A. S. Pushkin: Notes on French Literature," in *American Slavic and East European Review*. XVII, no. 1 (1958), pp. 101–109.
Mersereau, John, Jr. "Pushkin's Concept of Romanticism," in *Studies in Romanticism*. III, no. 1 (1963), pp. 24–41.
Todd, William Mills, III. *The Familiar Letters as a Literary Genre in the Age of Pushkin*, 1976.
Vickery, Walter. *Alexander Pushkin*, 1971 (revised 1992).

J. R. BROADUS

*See also* Belinskii; Romanticism; Zhukovskii

# George Puttenham

## English critic

**Born:** England; c. 1530
**Died:** England; 1590

## Biography

Most scholars agree that George Puttenham was born about 1530 and died in 1590. The grandson of Sir George Puttenham, who owned property at Sherfield and the manors of Puttenham and Long Marston on the borders of Hertfordshire and Buckinghamshire, Puttenham was an English gentleman who received a good liberal education and was well-read in English as well as classical literature. He was the second son of Robert Puttenham and Margery, daughter of Sir Richard Elyot and sister of Sir Thomas Elyot, the famous English Humanist who wrote scholarly works such as *The Boke Named the Governour* (1531). George had an older brother, Richard, born about 1520, and a sister, Margery. Where in England Puttenham was born, what schools he attended, what his occupation was, and how extensively he traveled are all matters of conjecture. Baxter Hathaway remarks that Puttenham "was educated at Oxford" and "may never have left England." Hyder E. Rollins and Herschel Baker believe that Puttenham attended Cambridge University, and D. C. Browning notes that Puttenham "travelled extensively on the Continent in his youth." Clearly, not much is certain about Puttenham's life.

George Puttenham married Elizabeth, daughter of Peter Coudray of Herriard. He was her third husband, and evidence exists to indicate that his relationship with both Elizabeth and her family was a stormy one. In December,

1578 he was apprehended by the sheriffs of London and imprisoned. By the summer of 1579, however, he was released. He continued to petition the queen for justice in his case, and in 1585 he was granted a large sum of money for his unjust suffering. Puttenham's dedication of *The Arte of English Poesie* to Queen Elizabeth was perhaps his way of repaying her.

## Influence

Coming as it does among the first few works of criticism in the English language, Puttenham's *The Arte of English Poesie* helped to establish the style and form of poetry in England during the Renaissance. His condemnation of "inkhorne terms," the introduction of foreign words and phrases into English poetry, set down in writing a dictum that was followed in poetry generally throughout the seventeenth century. Sir Philip Sidney and Puttenham represent the headwaters of a mainstream of critical theory that leads through Sir John Herrington to Roger Bacon and George Chapman. Both Herrington, in the preface to his 1591 translation of Ludovico Ariosto's *Orlando furioso* (1516–1532), and Francis Meres, in his *Palladis Tamia, Wits Treasury* (1598), refer to Puttenham's book in most admiring terms. The Renaissance dramatist and critic Ben Jonson owned a copy of *The Arte of English Poesie* (now in the British Library), and several seventeenth-century writers mention the book as an authority on English poetics. William Camden refers to the work familiarly in *Remaines of a Greater Work Concerning Britaine* (1605), and both William Vaughan, in *The Golden Grove* (1600, revised 1608), and Henry Peacham, in *The Compleat Gentleman* (1622), refer to the work as the authority for their comments on English poetry.

## Analysis

The most systematic and thorough book of literary criticism in early England is *The Arte of English Poesie*. William Caxton's observations of books and authors found in his prologues and epilogues show that critical opinions had become important enough to be printed and, one might presume, to be read. The Cambridge scholars Roger Ascham, Sir John Cheke, and Thomas Wilson had written in favor of a "pure" English in literature and against the use of over-elaboration and the use of "inkhorne" terms. It is in *The Arte of English Poesie*, however, that the first attempt at a discussion of English poetics can be found.

Scholars generally agree that *The Arte of English Poesie* was written by a Puttenham, and perhaps most agree that it was George, rather than his brother Richard, who was the author. The evidence is slight in either case, but what little exists weighs in favor of George.

The book reveals an author who had read widely in classical and English literature and had an intense and analytical interest in poetry. Because the book was probably written before the Puritan attack upon poetry, its purpose is not so much a "defense" of poetry, as are the works by Sidney and Thomas Lodge, as it is an analysis of poetry. Puttenham argues above all else for regularity in poetry, but in so arguing he does not require that poetry follow a classical mold or pattern. "A poet," Puttenham begins his work by saying, "is as much to say as a maker," using the Latin meaning of the term. A poet is like a god, having either divine inspiration or superior perception – or, more likely, both. Puttenham, therefore, can argue "that there may be an art of our English Poesie, aswell as there is of the Latine and Greeke," thus displaying English common sense and a refusal to limit English poetry to classical models. Poets, to Puttenham, were the first priests, prophets, legislators, philosophers, and politicians in the world.

*The Arte of English Poesie* is in three books. Beginning with a general account of poetry in book 1, Puttenham discusses the various kinds of poetry – such as tragedy, comedy, epic, pastoral – and the three major purposes of poetry: to praise God, to praise virtue and reprove vice, and to offer solace to humankind in this transitory life. Yet even with these lofty goals for poetry, Puttenham does not condemn poetry written for the sake of delight alone, as the Puritans were later to do.

Book 2 reviews the metrical forms used by English poets in the mid-sixteenth century. Using analogies with mathematics and theology, Puttenham asserts that poetry must "stand by proportion, and that without it nothing could stand to be good or beautiful." Differing with those who argued that rhyme should be eschewed in poetry because Greek and Latin poetry had none, Puttenham insists that rhyme is good, so long as the "good maker will not wrench his word to helpe his rime." He furthermore argues that "figures," by which he means the use of geometrical shapes in poetry, are good in that they yield "an ocular representation" to the reader. He offers examples of the rhombus, spindle, triangle, square, cylinder, spire, sphere, oval, and other shapes.

Book 3 deals with poetic devices, the ornamentation of poetry. The purpose of ornament is to allure, to delight the reader so that the general purposes discussed in book 1 can be achieved. The book takes up the matter of ornamentation by breaking it down it into three parts: language, style, and figure. The language to be used in poetry should, according to Puttenham, be "naturall, pure, and the most usuall of all his countrey," not jargon or "inkhorne terms." Concerning style, Puttenham argues for decorum: if the subject is high and lofty, so should be the style; if humble and base, the style should follow. The use of figures is a "lively or good grace set upon wordes, speaches, and sentences to some purpose." Again, the purpose is so to ornament the language that the style is delightful, causing the reader to learn.

Puttenham's idea throughout *The Arte of English Poesie* is that poetry generally, and English poetry specifically, should both reflect and glorify the ordered cosmos. The unchanging realities of good and evil are the subject matter of the poet/priest, and *The Arte of English Poesie* is the guidebook for the revelation of those realities. Chapter 24 of book 3, entitled "Of Decencie in Behaviour," shows the author to be a man of philosophical, gentlemanly interests, one who sees the poet's duty to be to rise to a perception of cosmic reality and to be craftsman enough to communicate his insight. Puttenham's purpose in this book is to show the way.

## Principal criticism
*The Arte of English Poesie, Contrived into Three Bookes: The First of Poets and Poesie, the Second of Proportion, the Third of Ornament,* 1589

## Other major works and literary forms
George Puttenham's critical work, *The Arte of English Poesie*, is clearly his magnum opus – and very nearly his only extant opus. If Puttenham is in fact the author of the critical work, then numerous other works – drama, poems, and prose – may also be attributed to him, for the author has supplied references to many such works throughout his book. The following works are mentioned in the book: *The Eclogue of Elpine, Partheniates, Ierotekni, A Ditty of Great Britaine,* a comedy entitled *Ginecocratia, Of the Originals and Pedigree of the English Tong,* two interludes, "Lustie London" and "The Woer," *A Hymn to the Queen Minerva, Triumphals, Philocalia, De Decoro,* and others. Among these works only *Partheniates,* an interesting collection of seventeen poems, is extant. Also remaining in the British Library is a copy of an autographed manuscript, written shortly before Puttenham's death, of a prose "Apologie or True Defens of Her Majesties Honorable and Good Renowne," a defense of Queen Elizabeth's treatment of Mary, Queen of Scots. Because no other significant work by Puttenham exists, were it not for his critical work, Puttenham would receive no attention from modern literary scholars.

PLAYS
*Ginecocratia*
"Lustie London"
"The Woer"

POETRY
*A Ditty of Great Britaine*
*The Eclogue of Elpine*
*A Hymn to the Queen Minerva*
*Partheniates*
*Triumphals*

NONFICTION
*De Decoro*
*Ierotekni*
*Of the Originals and Pedigree of the English Tong*
*Philocalia*

## Further reading
Hardison, O. B. *English Literary Criticism: The Renaissance,* 1963.
Hathaway, Baxter. *Marvels and Commonplaces: Renaissance Literary Criticism,* 1968.
Lewis, C. S. *English Literature in the Sixteenth Century,* 1954.
Rollins, Hyder E., and Herschel Baker. "George Puttenham," in *The Renaissance in England,* 1954.
Smith, Gregory. *Elizabethan Critical Essays.* Vol. 2, 1959.
Stephen, Leslie, and Sidney Lee. *The Dictionary of National Biography.* Vol. 16, 1967–1968.

EUGENE P. WRIGHT

*See also* Gascoigne; Gosson; Renaissance and Restoration Literary Theory; Sidney

# Q

## Qudāma Ibn Ja'far

Arabic theorist and philologist

**Died:** Baghdad (Iraq); c. 948

### Biography

Abū l-Faraj Qudāma Ibn Ja'far's place and year of birth is unknown. During the reign of the Abbasid caliph al-Muktafi (902–908) he converted from Christianity to Islam. He was employed as a *kātib* (scribe, secretary, or chancery official) in Baghdad, in mostly unimportant positions. Few facts about his life are reported, and of these many are uncertain and disputed, such as the year of his death, which occurred either in 948 or, according to others, during the reign of al-Muqtadir, which ended in 932. He was certainly present at the famous debate between the grammarian as-Sīrāfī and logician Mattā Ibn Yūnus that took place in 932.

### Influence

In the introduction to his highly ornate *al-Maqāmāt* (the assemblies), one of the most-studied literary texts in Arabic, al-Harīrī (died 1122) mentions Qudāma as if he were proverbial for his eloquence ("If I possessed Qudāma's eloquence . . ."). This encomium seems slightly misdirected, for if Qudāma became famous, it was not so much for his eloquence as for his scholarly treatment of it in several books, notably in his book on poetics. In it he was the first to subject poetry to a systematic treatment. Many of his ideas, formulations, and terms were adopted by later theorists and critics and became part of traditional Arabic poetics and stylistics, yet his approach was, apparently, considered too rigid and too "scientific," and was generally not taken over. Yāqūt (died 1229), in his biographical dictionary, calls Qudāma not only "eloquent" but "a good philosopher, someone outstanding in the science of logic." Some refutations of his poetics were written, but did not survive.

Medieval biblio-biographical compilations ascribe some fifteen titles to Qudāma. Most of these works are lost, including a few that, judging by their titles, may have been of an ethical or edifying nature, such as *Sābūn al-hamm*

(the soap of sorrow), or *Diryāq al-fikr* (the theriac of thought). Lost, too, are a work on dialectics (*al-Jadal*) and a partial commentary on Aristotle's *Physics*. Three works have survived, two of which are closely connected with his employment as an administrative civil servant. *Al-Kharāj wa-sinā'at al-kitāba* (land taxation and the art of the scribe) is a handbook on technical matters relevant for administrators and chancery officials, with a section that belongs to the genre of "mirrors for princes." The book included a section, unfortunately lost, on *balāgha* ("eloquence"). *Jawāhir al-alfāz* (the jewels among words) is a lexicographical work on words and idioms, thematically arranged in the form of a thesaurus, with a short introduction on figures of speech, of which he lists fourteen. It is on his poetics, however, that his fame must rest.

### Analysis

The nature and aim of his *Naqd ash-shi'r* (the criticism of poetry) are made clear in the opening paragraph:

> The knowledge of poetry is of several parts, one part relating to the knowledge of its prosody and meter, another to that of its rhymes and line-endings, another to that of its recondite vocabulary and its lexicon, another to that of its themes and purpose; and a part relating to the knowledge of good and bad poetry.

His aim is to develop a method for distinguishing good poetry from bad. The term *naqd*, which became the normal word for "criticism," literary or otherwise, is derived from the assaying of coins (*naqd* still means "cash"). Composing poetry is seen as an art, in the original sense of *technē*, or craft; in Qudāma's poetics, and in traditional Arabic literary criticism in general, there is little space for theories of inspiration by either Muses, demons, or God. Qudāma's definition of poetry, widely accepted by later theorists, as "metered and rhymed utterance indicating a meaning," containing the four elements of poetry (meter, rhyme, wording, and meaning), yields the framework of the book, in which the good and bad qualities of each element and their possible interactions are discussed in separate chapters. At the outset he points out that a poet is free to express any theme, from the lofty to the lowly and obscene. It is wrong, for instance, to condemn the pre-Islamic Imra' al-Qays for his description of extramarital sexual adventures ("Many a pregnant woman have I visited, or one suckling a child, distracting her from her amulet-bearing babe . . ."). Nor should a poet be condemned for contradicting himself in two different poems, as when he praises something and then blames it – on the contrary, this only serves to demonstrate his poetic abilities.

Strikingly, the great majority of Qudāma's examples are taken from pre-Islamic and early Islamic poetry; there are only a few lines by the "modern poets" (muhdathūn). Qudāma, no poet himself, writes as if he addresses would-be critics rather than would-be poets. His contemporary Ibn Tabātabā was indeed a poet and speaks at some length of the poetic process in his work on poetics, yet, like Qudāma, he quotes predominantly early poets. Most later works on poetics, however, freely quote "modern" poetry and seem to instruct their readers in the art of writing poetry, an art that in pre-modern Arab society was expected from any literate individual.

In the chapter on the wording or expression (Arabic lafz), its desired qualities are given in rather vague terms and shown mainly through examples. The section on its negative counterpart, bad expression, is more enlightening. Obviously, bad grammar, syntactical convolution, and the use of abstruse vocabulary are condemned. The chapters on meter and rhyme are closely connected with matters of wording. It ought to be pointed out here that classical Arabic poetry has a set of quantitative meters not unlike those of classical Latin and Greek. All lines of a particular poem have basically the same meter and are of equal length; all lines, moreover, must have the same rhyme. In the course of the centuries some new, strophic forms were developed, but the monorhyme in one of the accepted meters remained standard until well into the twentieth century and is still the norm in some conservative circles. The sciences of meter (ʿarūd) and rhyme (qāfiya), codified by al-Khalīl Ibn Ahmad in the late eighth century, remained substantially unchanged. Qudāma takes them for granted and only discusses some general qualities and technical defects.

The main part of the book deals with "meaning," Arabic maʿnā, a term that may also be rendered as "motif," "thought," or "theme." Since the number of "meanings" or literary motifs is infinite, as Qudāma says, he will only discuss the major and most frequent "purposes" (aghrād, singular gharad) of the poets, namely panegyric, invective, elegy, comparison, description, and love poetry. Compared with later lists of aghrād, the "purposes," modes, or themes of poetry, it is striking that some of the "modern" ones are lacking, such as the hunting poem, bacchic and gnomic verse, or the theme called mujūn (licentious, bawdy, or obscene verse). Theorists in general ignore genres such as narrative, didactic, religious, philosophical, or mystical poetry, partly because they do not belong to the traditional

pre- and early Islamic set of themes and modes. The mode that is prevalent in much of Arabic verse, especially that of the first few centuries, fakhr or vaunting poetry, is also absent from Qudāma's book, presumably because it is a subcategory of panegyric (madīh).

Striking, too, in Qudāma's list is the occurrence of "comparison" (tashbīh) and "description" (wasf) as independent modes, rather than as techniques to be employed in any mode. This is to some extent due to the "molecularistic" outlook of the theorists. Ideally, each line of verse or short passage could be said to have its own "purpose." Normally, the term gharad applies to somewhat larger sections, so that an average qasīda or ode consists of some two or three "purposes," such as love poetry, description (for example, of a camel), and praise (of a patron, one's tribe, or oneself). Qudāma is not interested in the structure of such polythematic poems.

Although, as pointed out above, he will not condemn a poet for writing "unethical" poetry, Qudāma bases his theory of poetic praise and blame firmly on an ethical framework of four cardinal virtues (intelligence, courage, justice, and continence) and their possible combinations; thus intelligence combined with courage results in "endurance" and "loyalty," for instance. In his discussion "justice" is replaced by "generosity," which more befits the Bedouin ethos expressed in early poetry and which always remained thought of as an "Arab" virtue par excellence. It is in this ethical theory, together with his formal definition of poetry in the manner of the philosophers, that Qudāma most clearly shows influence from Greek thought (he mentions Galen's work on ethics by name); there are no indications that Aristotle's Poetics or Rhetoric were among his sources.

In praise and blame, poets ought to select the proper virtues and vices, in accordance not only with the character but also the status of the addressee; an encomium on a ruler should differ from one written for a vizier or a craftsman. One should not attack someone for his or her physical defects or for being poor. Qudāma's poetics is here unambiguously prescriptive and running counter to what has always been customary in classical Arabic poetry, where people are often praised, and even more often vilified, for their physical, nonmoral qualities. Generally speaking, Arabic literary theory shows a mixture of prescription and description. It happens often that a poet-critic advocates ideas on poetry that he himself flatly contradicts in his poetical practice; as far as is known, Qudāma did not write poetry, however. Elegy, as Qudāma says, is a variant of panegyric, and he takes rather more pains to show the parallels between them than the differences, which are not as slight as he suggests.

The term Qudāma uses for "love poetry" is nasīb, thereby showing his conservative approach, for usually this term is restricted to the elegiac amatory introductory section of the traditional polythematic ode, in which a male poet speaks about his yearning for a female beloved who has departed. The independent love lyric which became popular especially in urban milieus is known as *ghazal*, a term at least mentioned by Qudāma, who fails to discuss the prevalence of homoerotic love in this genre since the eighth century.

One of the merits of *Naqd ash-shi'r* is the incorporation of a number of rhetorical figures and tropes as well as poetic defects into the framework described. For example, among the defects resulting from a poor cooperation of "wording" and "meter" he mentions "padding" and its opposite, "curtailing" (for example, shortening the name 'Isrā'īl' to 'Isrāl'). Later writers on tropes and figures (often called '*ilm al-badī*) directly or indirectly adopted his ideas, without the theoretical framework. Among the tropes discussed by Qudāma is hyperbole, in which he advocates a middle position between the opposing views epitomized in the sayings "the best poetry is the most truthful" and "the best poetry is that which lies most," the latter said to be the view of the Greek philosophers. The line by Abū Nuwās (died c. 813, one of the few "modern" poets quoted), "You [the caliph Hārūn ar-Rashīd] have frightened the unbelievers so that even the yet uncreated drops [of sperm] fear you" was condemned by some for being literally impossible. Yet it may be defended, according to Qudāma, because it conveys an effective image of extreme fear, and the implied meaning of the verse is that the uncreated creatures would *almost* fear the caliph.

A work entitled *Naqd an-nathr* (criticism of prose) used to be ascribed to Qudāma until, in 1949, a more complete manuscript was discovered which proves that its author was a certain Is'hāq Ibn Ibrāhīm Ibn Wahb and its true title *al-Burhān fī wujūh al-bayān* (the proof: on the ways of exposition), written after 946. The author belonged to a well-known family that yielded many "secretaries" or civil servants. The book is intended primarily as a handbook for these *kātibs*, although it does not wholly neglect poetry. It discusses practical matters of administration as well as more theoretical aspects of stylistics and rhetoric, with some Aristotelian influences being visible.

## Principal criticism
*Naqd ash-shi'r* (the criticism of poetry), 1956 (with English introduction and summary; S. A. Bonebakker, editor. Partial translation in Vicente Cantarino's *Arabic Poetics in the Golden Age*, 1975, pp. 118–124)

Pseudo-Qudāma:
*Naqd an-nathr* (criticism of prose), 1941
Is'hāq Ibn Ibrāhīm Ibn Wahb, *al-Burhān fī wujūh al-bayān* (the proof: on the ways of exposition), 1967

## Other major works and literary forms

MISCELLANEOUS
*Jawāhir al-alfāz* (the jewels among words), 1932
*al-Kharāj wa-sinā'at al-kitāba* (land taxation and the art of the scribe), 1981; facsimile edition 1986

## Further reading
S. A. Bonebakker. "Ḳudāma b. Dja'far,'" in *The Encyclopaedia of Islam*. Vol. 5, 1986 (new edition), pp. 318–322.

GEERT JAN VAN GELDER

*See also* 'Abd al-Qāhir al Jurjānī; Arabic Literary Theory; Hāzim al-Qartājānnī


# Quintilian
(Marcus Fabius Quintilianus)

Roman rhetorician and teacher

**Born:** Calagurris, Spain; c. A.D. 35
**Died:** Rome; c. A.D. 96

## Biography
Quintilian was born Marcus Fabius Quintilianus in about A.D. 35 in Calagurris (modern Calahorra), Spain, to a well-educated, although not aristocratic, family. It is believed that by the year 57 he was studying rhetoric in Rome, since he refers with familiarity to the trial of Capito which took place there at that time. His praise for the orator Domitius Afer suggests that the latter served as his individual mentor: certainly Afer's austere, classical, yet witty Ciceronian style was a strong influence on his young student.

Quintilian first became well known as an orator in the law courts, probably beginning his career with a ten-year legal practice in his hometown in Spain. The reason he went back to Spain is unknown, but by 88 he had returned to Rome and had become highly successful as the director of the first publicly funded school of rhetoric, where he presented lectures and declamations and evaluated the speeches of his adolescent and adult students. Aside from his work at the school, Quintilian continued to serve as an orator, or advocate, for clients in courts of law, where he gained a great reputation. Information concerning his family is brief, the most specific being in his preface to book 6 of the *Institutio oratoria*, where he writes poignantly about the successive deaths of his wife and the two older of his three sons.

After twenty years of teaching and advocacy, Quintilian retired at the consular rank, accorded him by Domitian. Perhaps he wanted to begin life as a wealthy gentleman, the only teacher ever to have become so (according to Juvenal); perhaps he wanted to retire while his "services were still desired"; or perhaps he wanted to escape service to Domitian, who, increasingly concerned about sedition, had executed several public figures.

It was during his retirement, probably in the years 94 and 95, that Quintilian wrote his only major work, the *Institutio oratoria*, at the request of his friends. He dedicated the work to Marcellus Vitorius, a Roman statesman and patron of the arts. The work was further intended for the education of Domitian's designated heirs, the two young sons of Flavius Clemens whom Quintilian tutored. Quintilian probably died in the year 96, although there is no extant record of his death. Later references suggest that he was dead by the beginning of the next century.

## Influence

Quintilian was a Roman rhetorician and teacher whose views on oratory and education are among the most comprehensive in all antiquity – views which had a profound impact not only during his own age but also during the Middle Ages and the Renaissance. His practical, humanistic, and yet idealistic description in the *Institutio oratoria* of the education of the orator from infancy through retirement is based on the premise that an orator is the most important individual in society since only he, with his great virtue, wisdom, and rhetorical skill, can became a worthy leader, a *vir bonus* (good man). Quintilian showed how the education of such a man must be very skillfully tended. To enhance and guide this education, Quintilian also created an extensive, annotated reading list of classical authors in book 10 of the *Institutio oratoria*. While literary criticism was not yet an established concept, his selections and judgments demonstrated considerable knowledge, sensitivity, and sophistication in literary judgment.

## Analysis

Ancient Romans believed that the development of an orator was one of the central goals of education. In fact, the entire classical world presumed that a man could be particularly effective and successful in only two careers: the military and oratory. Only through speech could beneficial change in society be effected. The speech of man was thought to separate him from the beast, and since speech is so intrinsic to humanness, the best speaker or orator was thought to be the best man. In order to become a fine orator, a boy needed three things: nature, art, and practice. The first required fortunate birth; the second required an education of lectures, reading, and world experience; and the last required self-consciousness and expert criticism. Such excellence in oratory meant excellence in government, law, and other areas of leadership. An education in rhetoric was vital for a successful Roman man.

The tradition for such an education began in the third century B.C., when Romans were introduced to the Greek rhetorical education in the Greek-speaking areas of southern Italy and Sicily, through Greek ambassadors to Rome, and later by Greek rhetoricians and grammarians working in Rome. By the first century B.C. rhetoric was taught in all the private Roman schools, and Rome abounded in great orators, such as Cato the Elder, Marcus Tullius Cicero, Caesar Augustus, Pompey, Mark Antony, and Gaius. Because Rome became an empire rather than a republic, the practical benefits of rhetoric in government

debate faded, yet rhetorical study grew to be even more central to education. The use of artifice became more popular, and exercises in the devices of rhetoric were practiced by both students and patrons.

This world of education which Quintilian entered in the first century was carefully structured to create orators. First, it provided a study of grammar to young boys and girls in about twenty schools throughout Rome. After that, a thorough study of rhetoric began, for upper-class boys, at approximately the age of fourteen in schools that offered several years of study in literature, business, and perhaps law or philosophy. Quintilian spent twenty years administering and teaching in the most successful school of that kind in first-century Rome.

It was to this world, which so highly valued the practical application of language, that Quintilian presented his single great work on the education of the orator, *Institutio oratoria*. The work now serves as the clearest extant presentation of the practice of education in Hellenistic and Roman schools, all of which focused on the teaching and practice of rhetoric, the art of persuasion.

Quintilian divided his work into twelve books, each of which is divided into an introduction and chapters, probably by a later scribe. Much of what Quintilian wrote is summary, criticism, and judgment on earlier conflicting opinions of rhetoric. For example, Quintilian chose to define rhetoric according to the traditional Stoic philosophers, especially Cleanthes and Chrysippus, as the "science of speaking well." Science here means knowledge, and speaking well means speaking with art and judgment, which are rooted in an orator's honor and virtue. An orator makes wise and moral judgments and creates oratory that is all the more effective because of its beauty.

In addition to such traditional material, Quintilian presented a method by which a man might be trained in oratory from infancy through adulthood. He believed, like Cicero, that nature intended both eloquence and wisdom to be joined within individuals, and the study of one without the other, beginning to predominate in his world, was leading orators to amoral materialism and philosophers to self-righteous arrogance and carping cynicism.

His *Institutio oratoria* is divided into 12 books arranged so as to provide a complete course of study: book 1 describes pre-rhetorical studies, speech, reading, writing, and grammar; book 2 outlines the nature of rhetoric; books 3 through 7 concern the rhetorical topics of invention and arrangement; books 8 through 11 describe *elocutio*, or style, memory, and delivery; and, finally, book 12 presents the sort of life the orator should live.

Some of Quintilian's most consistently influential ideas address early education. He blamed parents and teachers for uninterested young students and believed that play should be used to make palatable both moral and intellectual instruction. It is interesting that he argued against corporal punishment and for the child's attendance at a grammar school rather than a private education. Since an orator must function in the world among all sorts of people, a sheltered life would not help him. Quintilian claimed that an ideal student is good at imitation, excited by praise and success, and greatly saddened by failure. While he noted that the seven liberal arts of late antiquity, known as *enkyklias paideia* – grammar, logic, rhetoric, arithmetic, geometry, music, and astronomy – should be taught, he believed that grammar and rhetoric are the essence of education while the others serve only to enhance these two major arts.

In his discussion of the schools of rhetoric, Quintilian continued to emphasize the responsibility of the instructor, saying that the instructor should take over the responsibilities of the parent and should respond calmly, constructively, and moderately to his students' work, all the while showing only the highest morality himself. The primary function of this school is instruction in declamation, or the creation of an argument, and while many of the topics for argumentation proposed by Quintilian seem exotic or artificial – such as stepmothers, soothsayers, potions, or pirates – they were intended to excite student interest.

The lengthy section of more than nine books dealing with rhetoric in the *Institutio oratoria* covers many of the traditional topics of rhetoric discussed since the fifth century B.C. in Greece. Quintilian argued that the principles of rhetoric should not be ignored in favor of bombastic or highly ornamented oratory. He continued with the classification of oratory into the classical Greek categories laudative, deliberative, and judicial, the latter receiving the greatest emphasis, which was typical among ancient rhetorical treatises. He examined types and presentations of proofs; the overall arrangement of material; the use of *ethos*, which involves arguments based on the moral character of the speaker, and *pathos*, which involves arguments based on an appeal to the listeners' feelings.

Quintilian's discussion of style, or eloquence, follows. The goals of good style should be conformity to nature, directness, and charm, all of which may be achieved with correctness, clarity, ornamentation, and aptness, ideas Quintilian adopted from Cicero and Celsus. He stressed the problems of obscurity created by overextended sentences, exaggeration, parenthesis, grammatical ambiguity, redundance, and excessive brevity. Ornamentation, a virtue in oration, addressed at length, is classified into amplification, figures, rhythmical composition, and tropes, or nonliteral language.

While Quintilian's discussion of memory is short and seemingly obvious (he maintained that memory is a gift from nature, improved through practice), his discussion of delivery is the fullest of any classical writer, including Aristotle, Aristotle's student Theophrastus, and Cicero. He divided delivery into voice and gesture and wrote extensively on the subdivisions of each.

Most famous of the books of the *Institutio oratoria* is book 10, which enters into the realm of literary criticism, a genre which did not exist in Rome at the time. Quintilian needed to list works he believed a good orator should read. First, he begins with poetry, since it is pleasant, relaxing, and shows inspired, sublime, and emotional treatment of a subject. He prefers the conservative, even nationalistic Gaius Valerius Flaccus to Ovid, whom he thinks undisciplined, or Lucan, whom he finds too harsh and oratorical; he praises Virgil most highly of all. He claims that history is closest to poetry, but he names no specific historians. Similarly, he does not find philosophers inherently useful, because they often seem divorced from the practical world.

His discussion of classical authors is unique. It is not like those of Cicero, in which the latter created a literary history; rather it is an overview which ignores historical periods and classifies authors by genre instead. It is similar in organization only to *On Imitation* (c. 20 B.C.) by Dionysius of Halicarnassus and in purpose to a reading list of Dio Chrysostom. Many of Quintilian's comments on such authors as Quintus Ennius, Albius Tibullus, Virgil, and especially Cicero, the writer whom Quintilian considered closest to perfect, are considered insightful even by modern scholars of the classical period.

Quintilian's reputation and influence has fluctuated over the centuries. His insistence on morality as the most important prerequisite for the orator remained consistent with Roman and later Christian ideals for hundreds of years. His emphasis on the practical benefits of the oratorical ideal, however, was more appropriate for his own age. The political-philosophical climate of Quintilian's time, during Domitian's rule, provided little opportunity for orators to debate or even function as wise advisers to the emperor. Therefore, Quintilian wrote for the education of the rulers themselves, namely Domitian's two heirs.

Quintilian's goal of the ideal orator who speaks with eloquence and simplicity was shared by other men both during and after his time, including the Greek Second Sophists, a group which reached its peak of influence in the second century. Its most famous member was Dio Chrysostom, the philosopher who gave up all of his worldly possessions for a life devoted to preaching Stoic philosophy.

Roman concepts of oratory were less far-reaching and abstract than those of the Greeks. Yet even though the Romans were devoted to more practical goals of law and government, their oratory is no less to be valued. Quintilian's most immediate Roman follower was his student Pliny the Younger, who addressed a panegyric to the emperor Trajan in the year 100. In it, he used oratory for political reasons, to praise Trajan as a model emperor, a model for all future emperors. Marcus Cornelius Fronto, too, was influenced by Quintilian, serving as a mentor for both Marcus Aurelius Antoninus and Lucius Verus. Finally, Cornelius Tacitus wrote in his *Dialogue of the Orators* some scathing comments on society, saying that the rhetoric in common use was no longer eloquent and that no education, no school, including that of Quintilian, could improve it. Since the current empire under Nerva and Trajan was operating so successfully, however, not only the opportunity but also the need for political oratory had ceased to exist. Yet both Tacitus and Quintilian recognized that great orators were alive, although they differed on who these men were. Tacitus, for example, often praised informers, but Quintilian refused to approve of them, idealistically considering them of a morality too low for an orator.

Succeeding generations have varied in their appreciation of Quintilian. In the generation which followed him, he was praised as a moral and uniquely prosperous teacher by Pliny, Suetonius Tranquillus, and Juvenal, who may have been his student. In the late third century, after a period of being held in low esteem, Quintilian was rediscovered, along with other classical writers, because the concept of the statesman-orator again became popular. Still, his abstract ideas about the ideal orator were ignored in favor of his practical advice on oratory and his views on education. Jerome used Quintilian's educational theories in his description of a proper education for a girl; and the rhetoricians Julius Victor in the fourth century, Cassiodorus in the sixth century, and Isidore of Seville in the seventh century immortalized Quintilian's name for later medieval readers. After the ninth century, direct knowledge of his works was meager, since only one text was available and it lacked books 6 and 7 and large sections of books 1, 8, 9, 10, 11, and 12 – much of what was most interesting in the work.

Not until the Italian Renaissance of the fourteenth century did Quintilian regain popularity. Petrarch addressed one of his letters to the dead Quintilian, praising his understanding of the education of an orator, but not his own oratory. When an entire version of the *Institutio oratoria* was discovered in a dungeon in 1416 by the Italian humanist Gian Francesco Bracciolini Poggio, a new wave of Quintilian's influence was set off and inspired a humanistic philosophy of education. Through the sixteenth century, he was ranked with Cicero and Virgil as one of the great Roman writers. Pope Pius II, Maffeo Vegio, Luigi Palmieri, and Lorenzo Valla hailed his educational ideas and eventually northern European writers such as Roelof Huysman, Desiderius Erasmus, and Martin Luther praised his eloquence in the teaching of eloquence.

After this period, Quintilian's reputation waned. Although he was mentioned favorably by Michel Eyquem de Montaigne and by Alexander Pope and John Stuart Mill, Quintilian had no noticeable intellectual influence by the nineteenth century. Since he was never as popular in Britain as he was in continental Europe, there are only four complete or partially complete English translations of his work written between 1754 and 1921.

In the twentieth century Quintilian was respected as an educator who stressed the need for early, child-centered, play-oriented learning and as a rhetorician whose presentation of language is unusually thorough and rich. Quintilian remains an example of the Roman scholar whose concern for the link between oratory and both personal morality and civic good represents the height of Roman culture.

## Principal criticism

*Institutio oratoria*, c. A.D. 95 (*On the Education of an Orator*, 1856; better known as *Institutio oratoria*)

## Other major works and literary forms

Quintilian is known primarily for the *Institutio oratoria*. Although two sets of declamations – their dates unknown and extant only in manuscript form – have been attributed to Quintilian, they are not considered major contributions to his thought. Indeed, the first, *Declamationes maiores*, a set of nineteen full-scale declamations, does not seem to be a correct attribution, because the themes and style are not consistent with those in his other work. The second set, *Declamationes minores*, contains one hundred and forty-five of an original three hundred and eighty-eight shorter declamations which, based on their practical themes and somewhat restrained style, are more likely to be the work of Quintilian.

In addition, Quintilian was the author of a lost treatise, *De Causis corruptae eloquentiae* (89; on the causes of corrupted eloquence). In it, he probably discussed the styles of writing of which he disapproved. Since many of the ideas in this work are specifically referred to in the *Institutio oratoria*, its loss is not considered serious by scholars.

## Further reading

Curtius, Ernst Robert. *European Literature and the Latin Middle Ages*, 1953.

Kennedy, George. *Quintilian*, 1969.

Little, Charles E. Introduction to *The "Institutio Oratoria" of Marcus Fabius Quintilianus*, 1951 (2 volumes).

Newlands, Carole. Introduction to *Arguments in Rhetoric Against Quintilian: Translation and Text of Peter Rasmus' "Rhetoricae distinctiones in Quintilianum,"* 1986.

Peterson, W. Introduction to *M. Fabi Quintiliani Institutionis Oratoriae Liber Decimus*, 1967.

Watson, John Selby. Introduction to *Quintilian's Institutes of Oratory: Or, Education of an Orator*, 1910 (2 volumes).

VICKI K. ROBINSON

*See also* Cicero; Classical Greek and Roman Literary Theory; Longinus

# R

## Jean Racine

French playwright and writer

**Born:** La Ferté-Milon, France; December 22, 1639 (baptized)
**Died:** Paris, France; April 21, 1699

### Biography

Jean Baptiste Racine was born around December 22, 1639, the date of his baptism, in a small town about fifty miles from Paris, La Ferté-Milon. He was reared by his paternal grandmother, Marie Desmoulins Racine, who moved to Port-Royal, the center of Jansenist thought in France, after the death of her husband in 1647. The Jansenists accepted the precepts of predestination as elucidated by John Calvin and others, and they were extremely ascetic. At Port-Royal, Racine received a superb education, especially in Greek, a language less favored than Latin in most colleges. His marginal annotations of Greek tragedies and of Aristotle have survived.

Racine's second play, *Alexander the Great*, was produced in 1665 and became a contemporary success, but it led to a breach between him and Molière and to estrangement from Pierre Corneille. Racine promised the play to Molière at the Palais-Royal but then withdrew it. Apparently without informing Molière, he gave the play to the company at the Hôtel de Bourgogne. Racine's doubts about the ability of the Palais-Royal to handle tragedy appear to have prompted this action. He also seems to have preferred the more realistic style of recitation of the Hôtel de Bourgogne. Prior to production, Racine showed the manuscript of *Alexander the Great* to Pierre Corneille, asking for his comments. Corneille praised his versification but recommended that he stay away from the theater because he lacked a talent for drama.

During the next eight years, Racine composed masterpieces which also earned public acclaim. In 1673 he was admitted to membership in the prestigious French Academy. His last and favorite secular drama, *Phaedra*, was composed in 1676 and performed on New Year's Day the next year. A seven-year-long affair with the actress Marie Desmares Champmeslé had become increasingly unpleasant. At first he shared her favors with her husband, an actor in the company, but then he was replaced by younger, aristocratic rivals.

Racine's personal unhappiness was compounded by the actions of the Duchess of Bouillon, the Duke of Nevers, and the poet Antoinette Ligier de la Garde Deshoulières. They arranged for the playwright Pradon to write a play based on Euripides' *Hippolytos* (428 B.C.; *Hippolytus*) and then bought seats for *Phaedra* at the Hôtel de Bourgogne which they left vacant. They filled the hall at the rival performance by Pradon. Racine was threatened with beating when he responded with a scurrilous protest.

At thirty-seven Racine renounced the theater, destroyed his fragment based on Euripides' *Alkēstis* (438 B.C.; *Alcestis*), and married Catherine de Romanet, twenty-five, pious, and so uninterested in his literary achievements that she never read his plays. His youngest son, Louis, claimed that his father had renounced the theater because of his sinful past. The pull of his early Jansenist training at Port-Royal and the engineered "failure" of *Phaedra* may also have influenced his decision.

The only extant plays that Racine wrote after he renounced the theater have religious subjects, *Esther* (1689; English translation, 1715) and *Athalie* (1691; *Athaliah*, 1722); they were written for Saint-Cyr, the religious school established by Madame de Maintenon for the daughters of impoverished nobility. Racine died in Versailles on April 21, 1699. In his will he asked to be buried in Port-Royal at the foot of the grave of Monsieur Hamon, his teacher in the classics.

### Influence

Racine is one of the foremost poetic dramatists. He departed from the theoretical tenets established by his influential predecessor, Corneille, by simplifying the dramatic action and enhancing the psychological complexity of his characters. Racinian drama depicts characters during periods of intense self-recognition. His characters, particularly his women, experience passionate, often violent emotions and communicate great dramatic power. Racinian theater was copied by his contemporaries and by later writers as well, to the extent that Racine surpassed Corneille, in both popularity and critical acclaim.

Racine's influence on the eighteenth century was assured when Nicolas Boileau-Despréaux illustrated his discussion of tragedy in his *L'Art poétique* (1674; *The Art of Poetry*, 1683) with examples from Racine. Boileau lauded Racine's plays as the principal achievement in dramatic literature of seventeenth-century France, ensuring that Racinian drama would become the accepted model for neoclassical tragedy, which followed the rules by preserving the dramatic unities.

Because Racine was a classical scholar as well as a practicing dramatist, he was also a major exponent of classicism in the drama. Most of his secular plays are based on classical sources, and his style is frequently described as having recaptured the spirit of Greek tragedy.

Twentieth-century criticism, represented most notably by Roland Barthes in *Sur Racine* (1960; *On Racine*, 1964), has paid less attention to Racine's neoclassicism and concentrated on using the psychological patterns in his plays as a means of analyzing his aesthetic intentions.

## Analysis

Corneille, known as the founder of French classical tragedy, was the most important predecessor of Racine. *Le Cid* (1637; *The Cid*, 1637), his masterpiece, is an exciting story of love and honor. Although Corneille is credited with introducing the classical principles of dramatic construction, his plays have complicated plots in which the hero faces extraordinary obstacles. Racine's initial break with Corneille stemmed from the latter's critical appraisal that Racine was a gifted poet who lacked the ability to create drama, but this breach was intensified by their very different views concerning dramatic plots and style.

Corneille's heroic drama was considered the model for tragedy when Racine began his own career, and comparisons of the two playwrights have continued to occupy a central position in French criticism. Corneille's predilection for eventful drama and complex plots, however, was at odds with Racine's preference for simplicity. In the first preface to *Britannicus*, a play which was first produced in 1669, without mentioning Corneille, Racine attacks complex plots, claiming that they violate verisimilitude and take drama into the realm of the "extraordinary." In contrast to Racine, Corneille believed that in tragic drama the playwright should exaggerate his subject in order to gain the admiration of the audience. For Corneille, drama required an elaboration of events; his heroes encounter an astonishing number of obstacles. Racine consciously rebelled against the complexity of the action in Corneille's plays.

Like Corneille, Racine inherited the elaborate system of rules that derived from Aristotle and his Italian and French commentators, but he interpreted with particular rigor those principles which seemed to him essential if drama were to achieve verisimilitude. Even though his plays were less influenced by Neo-Aristotelian canons of taste than were those of his later imitators, Racine became established in literary theory as the forerunner for eighteenth-century neoclassicism.

Among the critical precepts associated with neoclassicism to which Racine paid particular attention were the dramatic unities. The dramatic unities included time (the duration of the action was to be no more than a twenty-four-hour period), place (the scene of action was to be within one town or city), and action (the fable, or plot, was to be arranged so that no part could be taken away or transposed). Racine followed the unities rigorously and used them to heighten dramatic effect. In spite of the ostensibly exotic settings of his plays in Rome or Constantinople, the scenes are staged inside palaces where stage settings are austere rather than elaborate. As was conventional in Greek drama, most of his catastrophes take place offstage and are reported by witnesses.

Racine did not leave an organized statement of his literary theories. The prefaces to his plays are principally responses to the critical appraisals of his contemporaries, but he makes general observations concerning drama from which his dramatic theories can be reconstructed. Frequently, the prefaces seem to function as defenses written for the printed editions in response to criticism leveled at the performance.

Three kinds of criticism were leveled at Racine in his own day: that he had departed factually from his classical sources by introducing an invented character or by altering some traditional aspect of the action or characterization, that his characters were either too immoral or, conversely, too moral, and that by departing from the complex plots typical of Corneille he had made his plots simple and barren. Corneille's dramatic theory was so well established that Racinian drama was frequently criticized for its lack of events. A frequent charge leveled against Racine was that he had violated the rules which governed the drama by excluding the "extraordinary."

In the second preface to *Andromache*, a play first produced in 1667, Racine acknowledges that he has been censured for altering his sources by keeping Astyanax alive longer than he is supposed to have lived. Underlying this criticism is the assumption that the author has no discretion concerning adapting plots or characters drawn from classical sources. Racine observes that in Euripides' tragedy of *Helenē* (412 B.C.; *Helen*) Euripides pretended that Helen never went to Troy with Paris and that only on the authority of Herodotus, Euripides has Menelaus find Helen in Egypt. Racine, however, does not rest his argument on the authority of Euripides. He points out that there is a great difference between destroying the foundation of a legend and altering a few incidents, particularly if several possible alterations have occurred. In conclusion, Racine quotes a commentator on Sophocles:

One must not delight in criticizing poets for the few changes that they may have made in legends; but rather strive to consider the excellent use they have made of these changes, and the ingenious way in which they have modified the legend to suit their theme.

Complaints concerning the moral and psychological blemishes in his characters seem to have plagued Racine. In the first preface to the 1667 play *Andromache*, Racine writes that he sympathizes with those who would like to reform all the heroes of antiquity to make them conform to standards of polite conduct; still, he ironically observes, it is not for him to change the "rules" of the drama. After a glance at Horace, he paraphrases Aristotle's comments on tragic characters to the effect that the punishment of an entirely good man will make the audience outraged. He adds that the hero should not be entirely wicked, because the audience will not pity the punishment of a wicked man. He concludes that the characters must be moderately good, that is to say, good with some defect, and should fall into misfortune through some fault which arouses pity rather than contempt or loathing.

The simplicity of Racine's action also elicited criticism from his contemporaries, who were accustomed to the variety of incidents in Corneille's plays. Racine's willingness to accept the constraints imposed by the unities, especially of time, led him to keep his action as simple as he could. In the interest of verisimilitude, or dramatic plausibility, most of his plays begin after a crisis has occurred and move inexorably to the final denouement. In the first preface to *Britannicus* Racine observes that to make his action more complex he would have to deviate from nature and common sense and plunge into the realm of the improbable. The time sequence of the play would have to extend to at least a month.

It should be noted that Racine's conscientiousness in observing the unity of time became a means of focusing his dramatic art. As he acknowledges in the first preface to *Britannicus* and reiterates in the preface to *Bérénice*, a play produced in 1670, he has deliberately striven for simplicity. He sacrifices preliminaries by beginning with a moment of crisis. His plots progress step-by-step to the end; they are sustained only by the interests, sentiments, and passions of the characters. It is true that character is fate in Racine's tragedies until *Phaedra*, a play in which the gods seem to have more influence on the action than in Racine's earlier dramas. The succeeding pattern of events rises out of the passions of his characters. Focus on these passions to the exclusion of all else assists him in achieving the verisimilitude and simplicity which he valued.

In a well-known passage in the preface to *Bérénice*, Racine states what he holds to be the fundamental principles of tragic poetry:

It is enough that the action should be great, that the actors should be heroic, that the passions of the audience should be aroused, and that everything should be imbued with that majestic sadness wherein lies the whole pleasure of tragedy.

His characters are kings, queens, and figures of nobility with remoteness from the everyday. In his preface to *Bajazet*, a play produced in 1672, Racine observes that in the interest of achieving the proper perspective, the action in a tragedy should take place at a distance from ordinary life.

Paradoxically, however, in the above passage from the preface to *Bérénice*, Racine emphasizes the "affective" nature of tragedy – its "majestic sadness." The resolution of the paradox is supplied in his comments in the second preface to *Britannicus*. In response to critical comments that the play should have ended at the narration of the death of Britannicus, he cites a number of examples from Greek tragedy in which scenes continue after the denouement. For Racine, what is "necessary" is not determined by the action or plot but by the affective power of the tragedy. Racine's annotations of Aristotle's *Poetics*, *Fragments du premier livre de la "Poétique" d'Aristotle* (written in 1662 and published 1865–1873), indicate that he was intrigued by the idea of catharsis and that he interpreted catharsis differently from many other critics.

Instead of believing that the tragic purgation should eliminate feelings of pity and terror from the audience, he believed that catharsis should rid the audience of excessive pity and terror. The equilibrium achieved by means of catharsis should contain pity and terror within reasonable bounds. This concept of purgation helps to explain Racine's theoretical impatience with the idea that the plot or action should determine what is necessary in a tragedy.

## Principal criticism

In 1676 Jean Racine published a collection of his plays. For that edition he rewrote many of the prefaces to his works. Of all the prefaces, the most important are:
First and second prefaces to *Alexandre le Grand*, 1666, 1676 (*Alexander the Great*, 1714)
First and second prefaces to *Andromaque*, 1668, 1676 (*Andromache*, 1674)
First and second prefaces to *Britannicus*, 1670, 1676 (English translation, 1714)
Preface to *Bérénice*, 1671 (English translation, 1676)
First and second prefaces to *Bajazet*, 1672, 1676 (English translation, 1717)
Preface to *La Thébaïde: Ou, Les Frères ennemis*, 1676 (*The Theban Brothers*, 1723)
Preface to *Phèdre*, 1677 (*Phaedra*, 1701)

## Other major works and literary forms

The complete works of Racine include lyrics, translations, epigrams, prefaces, and orations delivered before the French Academy. Racine wrote various odes to King Louis the XIV and his queen, including *La Nymphe de la Seine* (1660; nymph of the Seine), on the occasion of their marriage.

PLAYS

*La Thébaïde: Ou, Les Frères ennemis*, 1664 (*The Theban Brothers*, 1723)
*Alexandre le Grand*, 1665 (*Alexander the Great*, 1714)
*Andromaque*, 1667 (*Andromache*, 1674)
*Les Plaideurs*, 1668 (*The Litigans*, 1715)
*Britannicus*, 1669 (English translation, 1714)
*Bérénice*, 1670 (English translation, 1676)
*Bajazet*, 1672 (English translation, 1717)
*Mithridate*, 1673 (*Mithridates*, 1926)
*Iphigénie*, 1674 (*Iphigenia in Aulis*, 1700)
*Phèdre*, 1677 (*Phaedra*, 1701)
*Idylle sur la paix*, 1685 (libretto, with Jean-Baptiste Lully)
*Esther*, 1689 (English translation, 1715)
*Athalie*, 1691 (*Athaliah*, 1722)
*The Dramatic Works of Jean Racine*, 1889
*The Best Plays of Racine*, 1936
*Five Plays*, 1960
*The Complete Plays*, 1967 (Samuel Solomon, translator, with an introduction by Katharine Wheatley)

POETRY

*La Nymphe de la Seine*, 1660
*Ode sur la convalescence du roi*, 1663
*Idylle sur la paix*, 1685
*Cantiques spirituels*, 1694
*Mémoire pour les Religieuses de Port-Royal des Champs*, 1697

NONFICTION

*Fragments du premier livre de la "Poétique" d'Aristotle*, written 1662, published 1865–1873
*Abrégé de l'histoire de Port-Royal*, 1742 (first part), 1767 (full text)

## Further reading

Abraham, Claude. *Jean Racine*, 1977.
Barnwell, H. T. *The Tragic Drama of Corneille and Racine: An Old Parallel Revisited*, 1982.
Barthes, Roland. *On Racine*, 1964.
Brereton, Geoffrey. *Jean Racine*, 1951.
Butler, Philip. *A Student's Guide to Racine*, 1974.
Giraudoux, Jean. *Racine par Jean Giraudoux*, 1930.
Hawcroft, Michael. *Word as Action: Racine, Rhetoric and Theatrical Language*, 1992.
Koster, Serge. *Racine: une passion française*, 1998.
Maskell, David. *Racine: A Theatrical Reading*, 1991.
Pommier, René. *Le "Sur Racine" de Roland Barthes*, 1988.
Racine, Louis. *Mémoires sur la vie de Jean Racine*, 1747.
Vinaver, Eugene. *Racine and Poetic Tragedy*, 1957.
Weinberg, Bernard. *The Art of Jean Racine*, 1963.

JEAN R. BRINK
TINA M. RHEIN

*See also* Boileau-Despréaux; Corneille; La Bruyère; La Fontaine; Neoclassical Literary Theory

# John Crowe Ransom

American critic and poet

**Born:** Pulaski, Tennessee; April 30, 1888
**Died:** Gambier, Ohio; July 3, 1974

## Biography

One of four children, John Crowe Ransom was the son of John James and Ella Crowe Ransom. He was born in Pulaski, Tennessee, on April 30, 1888, and, being the son of a Methodist minister who was regularly transferred to new churches, had lived in Spring Hill, Franklin, Springfield, and Nashville, Tennessee, by the age of twelve. Because of this constant moving, the boy did not attend school until he was ten, although his father and mother (who had been a teacher of music and French) tutored him.

At the age of eleven Ransom entered the Bowen School in Nashville and was its best student. Shortly after his fifteenth birthday, he took the entrance examinations for admission to Vanderbilt University and received the highest score in each of the five subjects in which he was tested. He entered Vanderbilt in September, 1903. After two years away to earn tuition money by teaching, he graduated first in Vanderbilt's class of 1909. Following another year of teaching, he attended Oxford University as a Rhodes scholar. After service abroad in World War I, Ransom attended the University of Grenoble briefly before returning to Vanderbilt to teach. In 1920 he married Robb Reavil. The couple had three children.

Ransom taught at Vanderbilt University from 1914 until 1937, attaining the rank of professor. In 1937 he became Carnegie Professor of English at Kenyon College, a post from which he retired in 1958. He founded the *Kenyon Review* in 1939 and was its editor until 1959. He died in Gambier, Ohio, on July 3, 1974.

## Influence

Ransom played a significant role in two important literary movements: the New Criticism and the Agrarian movement. As one of the founders of *The Fugitive*, a literary journal that published verse and brief criticism, and later as editor for twenty years of *Kenyon Review*, Ransom assumed an active role in disseminating the philosophies of the two literary movements with which he was directly involved.

Through his participation in the informal literary group in Nashville that launched *The Fugitive* in 1922, Ransom interacted with a small group of his contemporaries who eventually became leaders in the New Criticism: Donald Davidson, Walter Clyde Curry, Stanley Johnson, and Alec B. Stevenson. His ideas affected their thinking and their ideas affected his.

An impressive roster of New Critics and literary figures studied with Ransom, and it is perhaps through them and through his own writing that his influence has been most broadly spread both nationally and internationally. Among his students were Cleanth Brooks, Peter Taylor, Robert Lowell, Robie Macauley, Allen Tate, Randall Jarrell, Ted Borgardus, James Wright, Eric Bentley, and Robert Penn Warren. As a visiting professor and guest lecturer, Ransom carried his critical theories to students in numerous colleges and universities. Ransom is probably the best known of the Vanderbilt group of New Critics.

## Analysis

Fundamental to the New Criticism is close reading, the deep and perceptive reading of any piece of literature so that it is experienced on as many levels as possible and so that it communicates to readers as much as it can of the total experience that inheres within it. The reader may, indeed, find more in the work being scrutinized than the writer of that work realized it contained. If such is the case, however, the reading can still be quite legitimate because the reader may be attuned to subconscious nuances that the writer was not. New Critics pay little attention to authors' lives and times, concentrating rather on the literary work.

One of Ransom's earlier essays, "Shakespeare at Sonnets," published in *The World's Body* (1938), illustrates well his critical stance. Refusing to join the throng that had for years worshipped at William Shakespeare's feet, Ransom examined specific Shakespeare sonnets and found them badly wanting in poetic quality as he defined it. Indeed, in this piece that raised the hackles of readers more, possibly, than anything Ransom ever wrote, Ransom demonstrates how, according to his own poetic standards, the sonnets under discussion were badly defective. He proceeds to call them "Romantic," alleging that they are little more than a diffuse, self-indulgent outpouring of emotion. Having sullied Shakespeare's poetic reputation on those grounds, he then attacks Shakespeare as a metaphysical poet, demonstrating his inferiority to John Donne.

Ransom, during more than a decade of reflection, found two major problems in the New Criticism as it had developed. In the preface to *The New Criticism* (1941), certainly his most important critical book, he objects to the psychological affective vocabulary that I. A. Richards used in making literary judgments about the feelings, emotions, and attitudes of poems at the expense of considering them in terms of their objects. He also strikes out against the moralism in some of the so-called New Criticism because he regards this moralism as a vestige of the old criticism.

Ransom demands intense consideration of the structural properties of poems and of their textures. Ransom views a poem's structure as its logic, its thesis, its argument. To structure Ransom adds "local texture" as a central element in any poem. In his view, local texture distinguishes a poem from a piece of prose. It is because of this quality that poetry offers a unique knowledge of the world, one that science cannot offer, because, in Ransom's view, science can provide only structure, as he defines the term. In the texture of a poem is found the very essence of its subject.

Perhaps the most surprising element in Ransom's contentions occurs in his statement that the texture of the poem is irrelevant to the structure. The two do not coexist harmoniously, each contributing directly to the other, as earlier critics had suggested and as one might expect. Indeed, according to Ransom, the texture of a poem affects its shape by impeding the argument. In so doing, it complicates the poem's argument (structure), diverts the reader, threatens the success of the poem's fundamental logic. Yet if the poem succeeds, its logic survives despite its texture, whose function it is to present those elements of the work that defy logic. It is in the tension that the interplay of structure and texture creates that effective poems succeed.

Ransom considered himself a reactionary in poetic technique. Using this word outside its conventional political context, Ransom implied by it that he believed that the highest order of poetry must concern itself with form and technique. It will not preach, nor will it reveal much about its author's personality. The author is an instrumentality and assumes a mask of anonymity. In order that poets achieve a proper aesthetic distance from their poems, Ransom would have them write from behind the mask that assuming a persona provides for them, as it did for John Milton in "Lycidas" (1637). He would have them objectify their poems as totally as they can.

Ransom shunned the poetry of ideas, which he called "Platonic poetry," in favor of a poetry that concerns itself with objects. He considered many poems of the Platonic type nothing but pseudosermons. With the exception of his first book of poems, *Poems About God* (1919), his own work is a poetry of objects, not a poetry of ideas. Ransom's first poem written in almost total conformity to his new poetic posture was "Necrological" (1921), in which he established the poetic style that characterized his writing for the next decade.

For Ransom, good poetry is the poetry that exists in the tension created by the interplay of structure and texture. He considers the poet's problem one of relating these two opposing forces in such a way that each retains its identity. He demands of critics that they approach poetry with a full appreciation of a poem's logic, of its structures, upon which the aesthetic judgment will partly be based, but that they not exclude a thoughtful consideration of the local textural elements, which will significantly color their judgments.

Ransom devised an ontological structure of the poem which is based upon five considerations: all poems have a content that can be paraphrased, and this content is the argument of the poem; the most significant matters for the critic are found not in the paraphrase (content), but in the texture of the poem; the texture consists of devices that present the poem's meaning in concrete terms – such devices as image, tone, irony, ambiguity, metaphor, paradox, and symbol; close analysis of formal devices is necessary because it is these devices that transform literary works into unique kinds of knowledge not yielded by prose or science; and, finally, close analysis demands that one can re-create the work of art, that one have the humility to allow the work of art to speak for itself through its form, and that one realize that the fundamental task of critics is discovery.

Ransom regards poems as logical structures with logical textures; the critic's task, then, is to move toward an understanding of these two inherent logics as a means of experiencing poems with all the impact they contain, despite the seeming contradictions that exist for Ransom in the tension between the two opposing logics. He considers heterogeneity rather than homogeneity to be the characteristic mode of poetry. A good poem, Ransom suggests, is not a steady, overall concentration but is rather a sequence of small concentrations evoked by each symbol, each image, each metaphor. Every poetic device evokes for Ransom a poem in miniature.

Ransom came of age in a period that was bristling with artistic redefinition. During 1922, the year in which he helped to launch *The Fugitive*, T. S. Eliot published *The Waste Land* and James Joyce published *Ulysses*. At that time, Ransom found himself surrounded in Vanderbilt University's department of English by a group of vigorous critics who were actively seeking new ways to assess literature, and significant guidelines were soon provided by critics such as I. A. Richards, whose *Principles of Literary Criticism* (1924) and *Practical Criticism: A Study of Literary Judgment* (1929) invented whole new contexts for literary criticism. T. S. Eliot's collection of critical essays, *For Launcelot Andrewes* (1928), and Yvor Winters' various essays which were collected in *Primitivism and Decadence* (1937) and *Maule's Curse* (1938) were also instrumental in shaping Ransom's critical views at that formative time in his life and of bringing him to his own critical maturity. Three of the four chapters in *The New Criticism* are devoted to extended assessments of the critical theories of Richards, Eliot, and Winters.

Ransom's views of poetic meter ran completely counter to those of many critics of his day, including most notably Richards'. For Ransom, meter is part of the structural element in a poem, and, as such, Ransom denies that it plays a part in expressing the poem's meaning or in evoking the feeling of a poem. Ransom views meter as something that goes on independently within the poem for the sole purpose of providing independent phonetic enhancement. He suggests that the independent activity of enjoying a poem's meter necessarily interferes with the reader's perception of a poem's meaning. Both the meter and the meaning (texture) set up their own irrelevancies, thereby creating a desirable tension.

Ransom posits that meter and meaning go their separate ways in a poem, the irrelevancies of one interfering with the impact of the other. This interference, however, is not destructive to the poem. Indeed, it is constructive because readers take pleasure in metrical irregularities per se. It is the irregularities and irrelevancies in the two basic components of any successful poem that cause readers to refocus, to reconsider, and to penetrate the intricacies of the communication as they read, with the result that poems yield experiences of which prose and science are incapable.

In arriving at his critical posture, Ransom immersed himself in the aesthetics of Plato, of G. W. F. Hegel, and of Immanuel Kant. For poetry, he rejected Platonic Idealism, acknowledging that a poem may focus essentially on two things, ideas or objects, the latter being mere imitations of Platonic ideas. He objected to the physical poetry of the Imagists because he considered its ideological base to be concealed. He objected with even greater vehemence to Platonic poetry because its images have no independent existence, but serve merely to illustrate Platonic ideas. For Ransom then, Platonic poetry and physical (Imagist) poetry are the thesis and antithesis of the Hegelian triad, whose synthesis is metaphysical poetry in which image and idea become one.

The early agrarianism of the Fugitives remained fundamental to Ransom's outlook throughout his life. He was instrumental in composing the credo of the Fugitive movement in 1922, and its conviction was that the arts, particularly poetry, flourish best in an agrarian culture dominated by small, subsistence-level farms. The Fugitives thought that industrial society, by separating people from nature, diminishes their artistic impulses. Ransom remained an Agrarian until his death.

## Principal criticism

*God Without Thunder: An Unorthodox Defense of Orthodoxy*, 1930
*I'll Take My Stand: The South and the Agrarian Tradition*, 1930 (with others)
*The World's Body*, 1938
*The New Criticism*, 1941
*Studies in Modern Criticism from the "Kenyon Review,"* 1951 (editor)
*American Poetry at Mid-century*, 1958 (with Delmore Schwartz and John Hall Wheelock)
*Symposium on Formalist Criticism*, 1967 (with others)
*The Kenyon Critics*, 1967 (editor)
*Beating the Bushes: Selected Essays, 1941–1970*, 1972

## Other major works and literary forms

Many literary pundits think that John Crowe Ransom will be remembered longer as poet than as literary critic, even though his poetic career lasted just over a decade, during which he published four slim volumes of verse. Subsequent collections of his poetry were published, but these consisted of previously published poems, some extensively revised. Ransom produced only one completely new poem after 1939. Although his lifetime production of poetry could be printed in fewer than one hundred pages, his poems endure as superior examples of poetic structure, and Ransom is numbered among the finest stylists in American poetry.

Except for the selections in his first volume, *Poems About God* (1919), Ransom's poetry provides valuable insights into his critical theories about poetry, the genre upon which his critical pronouncements concentrated. The poems in his first volume are atypical and were written before he had developed the critical posture for which he is best known. The poems in *Chills and Fever* (1924), *Grace After Meat* (1924), and *Two Gentlemen in Bonds* (1927) increasingly reflect his adoption of an authorial persona and of a poetry objectified to the point that structure and texture dominate.

Ransom produced two textbooks designed for use in freshman writing courses. One of these books suggests topics for freshman writing and gives students advice about how to select and limit topics. The other is essentially a handbook for freshman composition. Ransom also edited a collection of Thomas Hardy's poems.

POETRY
*Poems About God*, 1919
*Armageddon*, 1923
*Chills and Fever*, 1924
*Grace After Meat*, 1924
*Two Gentlemen in Bonds*, 1927
*Selected Poems*, 1945, 1963, 1969
*Poems and Essays*, 1955

NONFICTION
*Topics for Freshman Writing*, 1935
*A College Primer of Writing*, 1943
*Selected Letters of John Crowe Ransom*, 1985 (Thomas Daniel Young and George Core, editors)

ANTHOLOGY
*Selected Poems of Thomas Hardy*, 1969

### Further reading

Abbott, Craig, S., ed. *John Crowe Ransom: A Descriptive Bibliography*, 1998.
Buffington, Robert. *Equilibrist: A Study of John Crowe Ransom's Poems, 1916–1963*, 1967.
Jancovich, Mark. *The Cultural Politics of the New Criticism*, 1993.
Knight, Karl F. *The Poetry of John Crowe Ransom*, 1965.
Parsons, Thornton H. *John Crowe Ransom*, 1969.
Quinlan, Karen. *John Crowe Ransom's Secular Faith*, 1989.
Stewart, John L. *John Crowe Ransom*, 1962.
——. *Burden of Time: The Fugitives and Agrarians*, 1965.
Williams, Miller. *The Poetry of John Crowe Ransom*, 1972.
Young, Thomas Daniel, ed. *John Crowe Ransom: Critical Essays and a Bibliography*, 1968.
——. *Gentleman in a Dustcoat: A Biography of John Crowe Ransom*, 1976.
——, ed. *John Crowe Ransom: An Annotated Bibliography*, 1982.
——, ed. *Selected Letters of John Crowe Ransom*, 1985.

R. BAIRD SHUMAN

*See also* American Literary Theory: Twentieth Century; Brooks, C.; New Criticism

# Sir Herbert Read

English writer, poet, and critic

**Born:** Kirbymoorside, Yorkshire, England; December 4, 1893
**Died:** Malton, Yorkshire, England; June 12, 1968

## Biography

Herbert Edward Read was the son of a farmer, Herbert Read, and his wife, Eliza (Strickland) Read. He lived on his father's farm, Muscoates Grange, until his tenth year, when his father died, whereupon he went to a boarding school in Halifax. When he left school he worked as a bank clerk. In 1911 he matriculated at the University of Leeds, but World War I interrupted his education. In 1915 he joined the Yorkshire Regiment, in which he served as an infantry officer until the war ended in 1918. He served in combat in France and emerged from the war a staunch pacifist, whose pacifism grew into an intelligent and well-considered anarchism during the next two decades.

His first, immature, book of poetry, *Songs of Chaos* (1915), appeared in the year he entered military service and was followed in 1919 by two volumes of more seasoned verse, *Eclogues: A Book of Poems* and *Naked Warriors*. Although he is not essentially a war poet, his early books of verse reflect not only his war experience but also his adherence to the tenets of the Imagist school of poetry. From 1915 his verse appeared frequently in the pages of the avant-garde little magazine *The Egoist*, which also published the early work of T. S. Eliot, James Joyce, and Ezra Pound.

After the war Read was first employed by the Treasury. In 1922 he became an assistant curator at the Victoria and Albert Museum, a post he held until 1931. He also assisted Eliot on *The Criterion*, which Eliot founded in 1922. The first volume of Read's *Collected Poems 1913–1925*, published in 1926, was favorably received by Eliot, Pound, and William Butler Yeats.

After he left the Victoria and Albert Museum, Read devoted himself to writing and lecturing, although he held brief academic appointments in both art and literature at the University of Edinburgh (1931–1933), the University of Liverpool (1935–1936), the University of London (1940–1942), Harvard University (1953–1954), and the University of Cordoba (Argentina, 1962). He was knighted in 1953. In 1956 he shared the Erasmus Prize with René Huyghe. He was made a trustee of the Tate Gallery in 1965.

Read was married to Evelyn Roff in 1919, and one son was born of that union. His second marriage, to Margaret Ludwig, produced one daughter and three sons, one of whom is the novelist Piers Paul Read.

Herbert Read died in Yorkshire, near where he was born. He was convinced until the end that his aesthetic philosophy, which was for him a substitute religion, would survive and, if humankind did not destroy the world first, prevail.

## Influence

Herbert Read is not identified with any single school of literary criticism as are critics such as the Agrarians or the Marxist critics. He was, nevertheless, such an imposing figure in the intellectual and literary life of Great Britain for more than four decades that his frequently controversial critical postures evoked response from literary figures such as T. S. Eliot, particularly in *After Strange Gods* (1934), James Dickey in *Babel to Byzantium* (1968), George Woodcock in *Herbert Read: The Stream and the Source* (1972), and Graham Greene in *The Lost Childhood and Other Essays* (1951).

Read's pioneering efforts to relate literary assessment to the intellectual currents of his times, especially his interpreting literature first in terms of Freudian psychology and later in terms of Jungian psychology, led the way for much modern psychoanalytical literary criticism. His interest in Marxism also led him to make literary judgments in terms of this political philosophy, and as one of the earliest Marxist critics, he again led the way for many others.

Although Read did not earn his living primarily as a teacher, he frequently held university appointments and presented important lectures to audiences that certainly were affected by his critical thinking. Among his more significant lectures were his *Wordsworth* (1930), upon which he based his Clark Lectures; *Art and Society* (1937), delivered at the University of Liverpool, where he was Sydney Jones Lecturer in Art, in 1935-1936; *The Grass Roots of Art: Four Lectures on Social Aspects of Art in an Industrial Age* (1947), delivered as the Woodward and Trowbridge Memorial Lectures at Yale University in 1946; his controversial *Coleridge as Critic* (1949, 1964), delivered at The Johns Hopkins University in 1948; *Culture and Education in World Order* (1948), delivered at the Sixth Annual Conference of the Committee on Art Education in 1948; *Icon and Idea* (1955), delivered when he was Charles Eliot Norton Professor at Harvard University in 1953-1954; and *The Flower of Peace* (1958), delivered at the Eranos Conference in 1958. The Sir Herbert Read Collection in the McPherson Library of the University of Victoria (Canada) contains the manuscripts of scores of lectures that Read presented through the years. His ideas reached hundreds of thousands of people through these lectures and through his voluminous publications.

## Analysis

Herbert Read came of age in a world that, on the one hand, was reacting to the intellectual cross-currents attributable to the seminal writings of such giants as Charles Darwin, Karl Marx, Sigmund Freud, and Carl Jung, and that, on the other hand, was poised to engage in a war purported to be the one that would end all wars. A university student

when the war erupted, Read soon joined the armed forces, and during combat service in France, much that he had learned up to that point was put to the test. His philosophy was forged in the frightening crucible of combat. He emerged from service much decorated, quite disenchanted.

As a student of Marxism, Read was intimately familiar with the dialectic of the German philosopher, G. W. F. Hegel, upon which the Marxist dialectic is based. Hegel's concept of thesis, antithesis, and synthesis has provided the structure for much modern thought. Read adapted Hegel's dialectic to his own critical thinking and concluded that art, including literature, is born from a dynamic state of tension. Art is the synthesis that emerges from two opposing extremes, from pairs of opposites.

Read mused over past history and saw that Immanuel Kant's thinking had initiated a philosophical flow that extended to Hegel, as well as to Samuel Taylor Coleridge, William Wordsworth, Friedrich Schelling, Søren Kierkegaard, Friedrich Nietzsche, Martin Heidegger, and Edmund Husserl. John Locke's conception of the *tabula rasa* loosed a counterflow that extended to such thinkers as David Hartley, Jeremy Bentham, Karl Marx, Vladimir Ilich Lenin, Jean-Jacques Rousseau, and Étienne Condillac.

Read began to investigate contrarieties, and his thinking along these lines led him to make comparisons between Romanticism and classicism, an investigation perhaps sparked by Thomas Carlyle's early observation that classical and romantic are historically the systole and diastole of the human heart. Read concluded that Romanticism was older than classicism, and he traced its origins to Euripides' *Ion* (c. 411 B.C.).

Read thought that Surrealism, which, for his purposes, he renamed "superrealism," was in general a reaffirmation of the romantic principle in art. He takes Sir Herbert Grierson to task for identifying Romanticism with revolt and establishes his own dichotomy, in which he identifies Romanticism with the artist and classicism with society, thereby making classicism a political concept of art to which artists are expected to conform. Surrealist artists break from this expectation, as Read sees it, because it is an absolute impossibility for artists to produce work by the conscious exercise of their talents.

Read's thinking and writing about Surrealism led him inevitably to view artists in Hegelian terms. Classical and Romantic were his extremes in art, and superrealism became his mean. This line of thinking ultimately led him to consider artists and their work in psychoanalytical terms.

Insisting that one cannot be a competent artist without also being a good critic, Read reminds his readers of Alfred Adler's contention that what makes a work of art successful is its achieving a synthesis between opposing factions. Adler further contends that analysis of a work of art destroys this synthesis. Read, however, was constantly seeking more objective, scientific means of artistic evaluation, and analysis was essential to his scheme.

Read contended that the purpose of art is to impose an order on the chaos of life. Having considered ways to apply the methodology of physics to making valid, objective artistic and literary judgments, he dismissed the possibility, replacing physics with a science more applicable to critical method: psychology. Pressing on, he concluded that artists tend toward neuroticism, saved only by the art that diverts them from it.

In Freudian terms, Read contends that because we live in an age of savagery as manifested in occurrences such as World War I, one might expect artists to revert to a savage type of art. Still, even though a bit of the savage lurks in everyone, humankind's savage tendencies are sublimated in art, which becomes a safety valve for society. Art provides for those who practice it a pathway back to reality. Because psychology can view art as a system of symbols that mask an obscured reality, it can also analyze art in terms of how genuine its symbols are in achieving its purpose.

Read was for a time sympathetic to Freud's contention that the value and enjoyment of any work of art are in direct proportion to the psychic tensions it relieves in those upon whom it acts. Just as creating the work has permitted the artist to relieve psychic tensions, so does the product permit the viewer or reader to relieve such tensions. As Read's thinking moved away from Freud, he came for a time to embrace the physiological theories of some of the behaviorists, seeking correlations between glandular secretions and artistic responses.

As psychology came to be a more developed field of inquiry, however, Read moved from Freud and from the behaviorists, attracted now by Jungian psychology, whose concept of archetypes and of the collective unconscious lent themselves more easily to art criticism than the earlier psychological theories that Read had tried to superimpose upon his aesthetic. As he was working through these theories, Read wrote some of the earliest psychoanalytical criticism, first his *Wordsworth*, then *In Defence of Shelley and Other Essays* in 1936, in which, through a close and exemplary application of Freudian analysis to Shelley's work and life, Read reached the conclusion that Shelley was a repressed homosexual, a view that later criticism has not supported.

During his infatuation with the Freudian and behaviorist psychologies, Read glorified the irrational, contending that the worth of Coleridge's work is in inverse proportion to its logical sense, and pointing to "Kubla Khan" as the poem in which Coleridge reached the acme of his potential. He departed from such contentions as he moved toward Jung's theories, as he began to believe that works of art that survive and have lasting impact, while they are irrational and dreamlike, are in one way or another derived from the legendary myths and archetypes that Jung has identified.

As Read became increasingly engrossed in and concerned with Surrealism, he realized that it was more a leftist political movement in the service of eventual revolution than it was a sound and objective school. This realization led him to favor the Jungian outlook over the Freudian, the Surrealist, and the behaviorist approaches.

Read, who admired the formal precepts of Imagism and who, to his death, was stylistically influenced by it in the spare clarity of both his poetry and prose, had many quarrels with tradition, and in that stand was thoroughly modern. He believed that the only taste is a contemporary taste. He did not turn his back on the artistic monuments of the past, but he denied that they can be interpreted in terms of their own time. They communicate to contemporary human beings in contemporary ways or fail to communicate at all.

## Principal criticism

*Reason and Romanticism: Essays in Literary Criticism*, 1926
*English Prose Style*, 1928, 1983
*Phases of English Poetry*, 1928
*The Sense of Glory: Essays in Criticism*, 1929
*Wordsworth: The Clark Lectures*, 1930
*Form in Modern Poetry*, 1932
*The Innocent Eye*, 1933
*In Defence of Shelley and Other Essays*, 1936
*Collected Essays in Literary Criticism*, 1938
*Poetry and Anarchism*, 1938
*Coleridge as Critic*, 1949, 1964
*Byron*, 1951
*The True Voice of Feeling: Studies in English Romantic Poetry*, 1953
*Icon and Idea: The Function of Art in the Development of Human Consciousness*, 1955
*The Tenth Muse: Essays in Criticism*, 1957
*The Forms of Things Unknown: Essays Towards an Aesthetic Philosophy*, 1960
*Truth Is More Sacred*, 1961 (with Edward Dahlberg)
*The Contrary Experience: Autobiographies*, 1963
*Selected Writings: Poetry and Criticism*, 1963
*The Origins of Form in Art*, 1965
*Poetry and Experience*, 1967
*The Cult of Sincerity*, 1968

## Other major works and literary forms

Herbert Read is perhaps as well known a poet as he is a literary critic, although the total corpus of his poetry is relatively slim, totaling about 250 pages. Read also wrote one play, one novel, two collections of short stories, numerous books about art, several about politics, several more broadly about art and culture, two specifically about sculpture, and four about education and the role of art in education.

It is sometimes difficult to classify Read's books. He was passionately concerned with ideas and with the major intellectual currents of his day. His books, regardless of their major classifications, are usually far-ranging and might legitimately be reclassified in categories other than those that come most immediately to mind. When Read talks about art, for example, even though his initial focus might be on graphic art or on sculpture, he usually expands his consideration to include the other art forms with which he was also intimately concerned, particularly writing.

Read's political books, particularly such volumes as *The Philosophy of Anarchism* (1940), his collection *Anarchy and Order: Essays in Politics* (1954), and *To Hell with Culture, and Other Essays in Art and Society* (1963), confront and discuss as many problems in art and literature as they do in politics, which is their ostensible focus.

NOVEL
*The Green Child: A Romance*, 1935

SHORT FICTION
*In Retreat*, 1925
*Ambush*, 1932

PLAYS
*Lord Byron at the Opera*, 1953 (radio play)
*The Parliament of Women*, 1960

POETRY
*Songs of Chaos*, 1915
*Eclogues: A Book of Poems*, 1919
*Naked Warriors*, 1919
*Mutations of the Phoenix*, 1923
*Collected Poems, 1913–1925*, 1926
*Poems, 1914–1934*, 1935
*Thirty-five Poems*, 1940
*A World Within a War: Poems*, 1944
*Collected Poems*, 1946
*Moon's Farm, and Poems Mostly Elegiac*, 1955
*Selected Poetry*, 1994

NONFICTION
*English Stained Glass*, 1926
*Staffordshire Pottery Figures*, 1929
*The Meaning of Art*, 1931, 1977
*Art Now: An Introduction to the Theory of Modern Painting and Sculpture*, 1933
*Art and Industry: The Principles of Industrial Design*, 1934
*Essential Communism*, 1935
*Art and Society*, 1937, revised edition, 1966
*The Philosophy of Anarchism*, 1940
*Education Through Art*, 1943, 1974
*The Politics of the Unpolitical*, 1943
*The Education of Free Men*, 1944
*The Grass Roots of Art: Four Lectures on Social Aspects of Art in an Industrial Age*, 1947
*Culture and Education in World Order*, 1948
*Education for Peace*, 1949
*Existentialism, Marxism, and Anarchism: Chains of Freedom*, 1949
*Contemporary British Art*, 1951
*Art and the Evolution of Modern Man*, 1951
*The Philosophy of Modern Art: Collected Essays*, 1952
*Anarchy and Order: Essays in Politics*, 1954
*The Art of Sculpture*, 1956
*The Flower of Peace*, 1958
*A Concise History of Modern Painting*, 1959
*A Letter to a Young Painter*, 1962
*To Hell with Culture, and Other Essays in Art and Society*, 1963
*A Concise History of Modern Sculpture*, 1964
*Henry Moore: A Study of His Life and Work*, 1965
*Gothic Flame: Being a History of the Gothic Novel in England*, 1966
*Art and Alienation: The Role of the Artist in Society*, 1967

*The Coat of Many Colours*, 1973
*The Contrary Experience: The Autobiography of Herbert Read*, 1974
*A Concise History of Modern Art*, 1974

## Further reading

Berry, Francis. *Herbert Read*, 1961 (revised edition).
Dickey, James. *Babel to Byzantium*, 1968.
Eliot, T. S. *After Strange Gods*, 1934.
Fussell, Paul. *The Great War and Modern Memory*, 1975.
Greene, Graham. *The Lost Childhood and Other Essays*, 1951.
King, James. *The Last Modern: A Life of Herbert Read*, 1990.
Robertson, Seonaid M. *Rosegarden and Labyrinth: Studies in Art Education*, 1963.
Skelton, Robin, ed. *Herbert Read: A Memorial Symposium*, 1970.
Thistlewood, David. *Herbert Read, Formlessness and Form: An Introduction to His Aesthetics*, 1984.
Treece, Henry, ed. *Herbert Read*, 1944.
Woodcock, George. *Herbert Read: The Stream and the Source*, 1972.
Zekowski, Arlene. *Seasons of the Mind*, 1969.

R. BAIRD SHUMAN

*See also* British Literary Theory: Twentieth Century; Hulme

# Reader-Response Criticism

The term reader-response criticism refers not to a single theory or method but to a range of approaches in which the focus of critical attention is on how readers respond to a text. Its development was a reaction against New Criticism and other varieties of formalism, in which there is an emphasis on the *text*; and also against various biographical approaches to interpretation, in which the *author* is seen as the ultimate source of meaning (reader-response criticism developed mainly during the 1970s and 1980s, when the concept "death of the author," announced by Roland Barthes, was making an impact on critical theory). In their analysis of how a reader responds to a text, reader-response critics have drawn upon a number of theories and interpretative models, notably psychoanalysis, structuralism, and phenomenology.

To take a simple example, we can look at the opening of Charles Dickens' novel *Bleak House* (1852): "London. Michaelmas term lately over. Implacable November weather." How, as readers, do we respond to even such a fragment of text, let alone to a complete work? In the first instance, we must know that London is an English city, but the attitudes to it could be very different, from a Cockney (familiar), an American tourist (glamour, Buckingham Palace, the Changing of the Guard), a drug dealer (money), and so on. The next four words are much more specific: in England these can refer only to the Oxbridge universities or the law courts – and the next reference confirms that the latter is the right interpretation. The word "implacable" is much less easy to define, but probably anchors us in a Victorian London characterized by smog and mud, while denying any specificity as to kind or degree.

Clearly no two readers will respond in identical ways to a text or even a word. As William Wimsatt points out in a highly influential essay, "The Affective Fallacy" (in *The Verbal Icon*, 1954), there can be a confusion between the objective data of a text and the results – what the text does to the reader. Wimsatt's main aim is to show that random, affective responses are indeed fallacious and he does this by concentrating on language. For example, the word "rose" in a dictionary will have a purely denotative, botanical meaning; but used in a poem or a love letter can evoke a whole range of emotive connotations, and these will probably be different for every reader. So if no two readers will respond in identical ways to a text, is it at all possible to construct a grid of responses ranging from the absurd to the probable? Such a theory has been elaborated by the German scholar Wolfgang Iser. The main features of Iser's approach hinge round the basic distinction between what the text provides irrefutably ("schematised aspects") and how the reader, to use Iser's terms "actualises" or "realises" it in his or her mind. Hence, "London" is a *donnée* – you cannot substitute Paris, but the weather is up to the reader to imagine. Most texts hover between given facts and spaces which the reader can fill in in any way that seems appropriate. It is rather like the children's game of "join the dots": if the text simply says "two men were sitting in a room," it is up to the reader to actualize what they were wearing, how tall they were, the colour of the wallpaper . . . . I am already concretizing this snippet in my own way: perhaps there was no wallpaper. But I cannot refute the men or the room.

This is the most important element in reader-response theory and is variously described as *actualization, realization*, or *concretization*: they all refer to the process whereby the signifiers of the text are brought together in the reader's mental act of cognition to create the "world" of the text. The next crucial dimension lies in the distinction between *schematized aspects* and *virtuality*; the first refers to irrefutable aspects of the text which guide the reader to the perception of predetermined structural patterns, elements of plot, of character or location (though, of course, the author can cheat; in Agatha Christie's detective novel *The Murder of Roger Ackroyd* (1926) what should be a major foregrounded clue is quietly tucked away in a few words so that it is not until the end of the narrative that the reader realizes that the narrator of the story is himself the murderer!).

*Virtuality*, on the other hand, refers to the indeterminate dimension that results from the convergence of the *données* of the text with the individual subjectivity of the reader. Again, if the text simply says, "The door opened suddenly and a peculiar-looking stranger went up to Tom as he sat in his insalubrious room and said, 'Your time has come,'" we cannot deny the door, the seated Tom, or the words of the stranger; but it is entirely up to the reader to virtualize the appearance of the stranger and the degree of insalubrity of the room.

Iser also introduces the term *pre-intention*: this refers to the set of expectations aroused by the components of a text (which can be either fulfilled, unfulfilled, or modified). But these are in turn controlled by what Iser terms a *horizon*. We may be led at first to believe that the butler did it, only to find that the horizon of expectation precluded that possibility. It is here that, on the macroscopic level, we engage in what Iser terms *consistency-building*. In other words, we seek consistency within a text by taming alien allusions, domesticating apparent ornaments, and reducing the range of possible meanings until a coherent interpretation is arrived at, and all the components of the text (however seemingly diverse) are united in one all-embracing *gestalt*. It is no accident that reader-response theorists have borrowed this term from psychology, since clearly the "rage to order" disparate elements into a meaningful picture is an essentially human characteristic.

But free-ranging subjectivity must be restrained and limited, and what controls this kind of affectivism is described by reader-response theorists as the *repertoire*. This is the body of knowledge – linguistic, historical, cultural, generic – that the reader brings to the text to enable *actualization*. Crucially, it produces a horizon of extratextual material that limits unbounded subjectivity. Clearly John Milton's *Paradise Lost* (1667–1674) will indeed be lost on the reader with no knowledge of Christianity, and the satire of Jonathan Swift's *Gulliver's Travels* (1726) will lose its bite if the reader does not know that Flimnap is a caricature of Sir Robert Walpole. But, by the same token, it is often difficult to determine how *extensive* the repertoire must be. While the Flimnap–Walpole equation is clearly central, is it really necessary to know that the obscure allusion to "one of the King's cushions" refers to the Duchess of Kendal, one of King George's mistresses? This question of the extent of the repertoire is raised when editors ponder what and what not to gloss in, say, the footnotes to an edition of William Shakespeare's plays.

Reader-response criticism is generally regarded as a contemporary movement, reacting against the formalist doctrine of the text as an inviolably autonomous object, but in fact one of the first to have espoused this way of looking at texts was the Polish critic Roman Ingarden. In *The Literary Work of Art* (1931) he makes a crucial distinction between the ontological nature of a text (it simply "is") and the epistemological activity required by the reader to concretize or make that text cognitively come to life. Ingarden points out that the layers of sound, syntax, semantics, characters, and setting are nothing until *concretized* in the act of reading: they exist "ontically" as things, but must be actualized subjectively.

This is the basis for Wolfgang Iser's much more scientific study *The Act of Reading* (1978), in which he makes a central distinction between the "artistic" and the "aesthetic" poles of the literary work. The former relates to the objective and verifiable *données* of the text provided by the author; the latter to the subjective realization of these in the mind of the individual reader. As we have seen, there can be little control over the latter in terms of response, even within the restraining factors of the repertoire: two people have just watched the same film and one says, "I really love the cowboy" and the other replies, "Oh no, he was a vicious, cruel, obnoxious character." Obviously there was a cowboy, but nobody can adjudicate on the individual response of the viewer.

Iser has been criticized by Stanley Fish, a major American reader-response theorist, for being simplistic. Even the *données* of the text, he claims, do not exist until actualized: so what is the difference between schematized aspects and gaps? To Fish, *everything* is subject to an individual act of interpretation. In a seminal study, *Is There a Text in This Class?* (1980), Fish charts a course between the remains of intentionalism and the possible violation by the reader of the author's overt intention: in other words there is actually no "pre-existing text," in fact everything is determined by the consciousness of the reader. Fish can thus eliminate both the intentional and the affectivist fallacies and rather disarmingly he claims that readers' experiences are simply "different perspectives on the same interpretive act" and he goes on to ask, "What is that act an interpretation *of*?" To further problematize the issue, Fish claims, in his essay "Interpreting the *Variorum*" (1978), "I cannot answer that question, but neither, I would claim, can anyone else."

Finally, we must mention David Bleich's timely reminder that, however subjective a response may be, we all share one indisputable element – a common language. Words, quite simply, mean – and, as a result, we have intersubjective "communities" of readers who may argue about the *interpretations* of a text, but at least they are objectifying their subjectivity by "naming" their experience of the work under discussion. This idea of language as a lynchpin of objectivity, while allowing individual readers to let their imaginations wander, however subjectively, erratically, or idiosyncratically, has found favor with a new generation of reader-response critics and seems to provide a sound basis for the way that we (readers) actually read the text. As a good example of how a completely unrestrained subjectivity can actually distort the actuality of the external world, consider Vladimir Nabokov's comic novel *Pale Fire* (1962) in which the protagonist, who regards himself as the exiled king of Zembla, interprets an innocuous poem in the style of Alexander Pope by one of his colleagues at an American university as a disguised allegory of his (the ex-king's) own life. This is a delightful parody of *misreading* – the gaps between background (reality) and foreground ("subjective

misreading") are so immense that the reader can only come to the conclusion that the narrator is not only unreliable but actually mad. In this case, the reader feels a strange mixture of confusion, alienation, and yet fascination as the traditional solidarity of narrated text with implied reader is anarchically fragmented.

An extreme example perhaps, but since no-one can ever tell exactly what goes on in someone else's mind during the reading process, let alone his or her own, it is clear that the problematics raised by reader-response theory will be with us for some time to come.

## Further reading

Bennett, Andrew, ed. *Readers and Reading*, 1995.
Bleich, David. *Subjective Criticism*, 1978.
Eco, Umberto. *The Role of the Reader: Explorations in the Semiotics of Texts*, 1979.
Fish, Stanley. *Is There a Text in This Class? The Authority of Interpretive Communities*, 1980.
——. "Interpreting the *Variorum*," in *Is There a Text in This Class?*, pp. 147–173.
Freund, Elizabeth. *The Return of the Reader: Reader-Response Criticism*, 1987.
Holland, Norman N. *The Dynamics of Literary Response*, 1968.
——. *Five Readers Reading*, 1975.
Ingarden, Roman. *The Literary Work of Art*, 1931.
Iser, Wolfgang. *The Act of Reading: A Theory of Aesthetic Response*, 1978.
Riffaterre, Michael. *The Semiotics of Poetry*, 1978.
Slatoff, Walter J. *With Respect to Readers*, 1970.
Suleiman, Susan R., and Inge Crosman, eds. *The Reader in the Text: Essays on Audience and Interpretation*, 1980.
Tompkins, Jane P. *Reader-Response Criticism: From Formalism to Post-Structuralism*, 1980.
Wimsatt, William K. *The Verbal Icon*, 1954.

A. W. LYLE

*See also* Culler; Fish; Holland; Iser; Reception Theory

# Realism

Realism refers to the attempt to reproduce reality (both natural and social) in a truthful or verisimilar manner as it would appear to the normal consciousness of the individual. It is often associated with the ancient Greek term "mimesis," or the imitation of nature, and is usually spoken of in terms of late-nineteenth- and early-twentieth-century Western literature and painting/sculpture. Originally the term realism itself came from thirteenth-century scholastics who used it to mean the reality of ideas or concepts. As a literary term it came to mean quite the opposite – the reality of the physical world – during the eighteenth and nineteenth centuries, especially in connection with French literature. Realist style is characterized by precise description of prosaic details from the daily life of common people (often by the metaphoric mode of metonymy), descriptions of local nature and scenery, and the patterns of everyday speech (as opposed to the elevated discourse of "literary" language).

Stendahl and Honoré de Balzac were considered to be precursors to French realism. Stendahl once proclaimed that the ideal novel was akin to "a mirror that is walked along a road," merely reflecting everything as it "truly" appears without any distortion. Gustave Flaubert as well as Edmond and Jules de Goncourt and the younger Alexandre Dumas were regarded as its major exponents, although Flaubert (correctly in part due to the distinctly modernist elements in his writing) disputed the designation. In England the term was associated with George Moore and George Gissing during the 1880s. Henry James and W. Dean Howells were linked to the term in the United States during the same time period. French realists were the major influence on writers in other countries with the exception of mid-nineteenth-century German literature where the term "poetic realism" is sometimes (arguably) used in conjunction with writers such as Theodor Storm, Gottfried Keller, and Jeremias Gotthelf in whose texts there is a greater degree of the idyllic and/or didactic in the formulation of characters and events than can be commonly found in French authors. Russian writers such as Fedor Dostoevskii and Lev Tolstoi heatedly disagreed with any use of the term to describe their writings (the former, in particular, regarded his work as "psychological").

Realism is often mentioned in conjunction with and clearly distinguished from the term "naturalism." Again French writers – especially Émile Zola – were pivotal in establishing its meaning in narrative fiction. A naturalist was taken to mean a student of (social) nature akin to a biologist, a "scientific" writer for whom (romantic) ideals and visions are unimportant and for whom only the hard, cold, indeed even brutal, facts of social reality – a deterministic, almost Darwinian, materialism – should play a role in the creation of literature. Naturalism thus came to be associated with elements of social criticism. This is realism's focus on the everyday reality of common people brought to its logical (and political) conclusion; it does, however, run the risk at this point of becoming a mere tendentious pamphleteering rather than literary text. Realism and naturalism's focus on depicting the real also brought about its own transcendence when pursued consistently in the context of the individual's psychology. The attempt to reproduce a person's consciousness as it really is led to the psychological and modernist "stream of consciousness" narrative technique as in the later writers James Joyce, Virginia Woolf, and William Faulkner. At this point, psychological realism came to be both existential in its emphasis on individual reality and even surrealistic in its focus on the minute, fragmented, and at times hallucinatory, nature of the conscious and (in the post-Freudian era) unconscious mind. Contemporary postmodernist (that is, poststructuralist and deconstructionist) discussions of literary realism focus on issues such as the "truth" status

of its language and the complex fictional and linguistic strategies employed to generate such claims to truth.

Because of its focus on everyday/historical and material reality, realism has been held in high regard as the sole valid mode of artistic creation within traditional Marxist aesthetics. The Hungarian Marxist critic Georg Lukács is generally considered to be the premier socialist theoretician of the realist novel. He argued that realist writing should not depict merely the surface details of reality but rather the ideal "types" that exist behind appearance. The socially "progressive" novel should present the reader with recognizable characters and situations – it should be representative – through which he or she can identify the dialectical turns of the historical process as it is understood in Marxist philosophy. Lukács skillfully combines a notion of realism as being ideally mimetic with a clear-cut political ideology. In the post-World War II era, Soviet countries adopted an aesthetic of "socialist realism" which was really a tendentious (and didactic) art in the hands of its average practitioners and a sincere attempt to explore the dimensions of true social commitment by its more talented representatives (the former East German writer Christa Wolf, for example). Socialist realism was called for at the 1952 Communist Party Congress by Georgii Malenkov and demanded that the artist depict ideal socialist "types" or role models with whom the worker could identify and therefore strive to ever greater devotion to the socialist state.

## Further reading

Auerbach, Erich. *Mimesis*, 1953.
Devitt, Michael. *Realism and Truth*, 1984.
Furst, Lilian R., ed. *Realism*, 1992.
——. *Through the Lens of the Reader. Explorations of European Narratives*, 1992.
——. *All is True. The Claims and Strategies of Realist Fiction*, 1995.
Grant, D. *Realism*, 1970.
Hemmings, F. W. J., ed. *The Age of Realism*, 1974.
Nochlin, Linda. *Realism*, 1971.
Stern, J. P. *On Realism*, 1971.
Walder, Dennis. *The Realist Novel*, 1995.

THOMAS F. BARRY

*See also* Lukács; Mimesis

# Reception Theory

Reception theory, *Rezeptionsästhetik* or the aesthetics of reception, also known as the Constance School of reception aesthetics, was introduced by its main proponents, Hans Robert Jauss and Wolfgang Iser, at the University of Constance in Baden-Württemberg, Germany (formerly West Germany), shortly after this newly established center of educational reform was founded in 1967. Both Jauss and Iser attempted in different ways to shift critics' focus from the traditionally defined object of literary study, namely, from the author and his or her text, to studies of readers, readership, and the reading process. Like the practitioners of the broader school of reader-response theory, reception theorists are committed to reinstating the reader into the interpretive process by investigating the manner in which texts, readers, and society interact, and by analyzing the specific ways in which literary works are "received" both individually and collectively by their "consumers." This interpretive gesture constitutes a marked shift in German literary theory, away from critics' earlier fascination with individuals, mentalities, and formalistic concerns toward an appreciation of the constitutive role readers play in the creation of textual meaning.

## Political and cultural context

One of the most significant, innovative, and widely applied theoretical approaches of German literary criticism of the last few decades, reception theory evolved to a large extent in response to (1) the pressing sociopolitical and anti-authoritarian political climate in Germany in the late 1960s, (2) the expanding popularity of Marxist thought at that time, (3) demands for greater social relevance of humanities disciplines at German universities, and (4) the philosophical rift within phenomenology accompanied by a general skepticism of the knowability of objects. Taking the then current leftist political climate into consideration, it is not surprising that reception theorists applauded the focus on the historicity of literature, while denouncing the ahistorical aestheticism of these earlier critical approaches as elitist and reactionary. Accordingly, studies of biography, literary periods (*Geistesgeschichte*), and the work-centered (*werkimmanent*) analyses of New Criticism, yielded to a new fascination with the sociology of literary texts. It is within these larger sociopolitical and aesthetic contexts that the entire field of German *Rezeptionkritik* evolved, which, in addition to Jauss and Iser, also includes such West German critics as Hans Norbert Fügen, Hans Ulrich Gumbrecht, Karlheinz Stierle, Rainer Warning, and Harald Weinrich, several of whom were Jauss' students in Constance. Manfred Naumann, Rita Schober, and Robert Weimann certainly rank among the most notable reception critics of the former German Democratic Republic, although some were displeased with what they viewed as an overemphasis on consumption and outright disregard for the entire dimension of production.

## Philosophical sources

Reception theory reaches beyond the ancient notion of evaluating texts according to their effects on readers, as practiced much earlier by Aristotle and Plato, and incorporates premises from a variety of fields of inquiry, including aesthetics, semiotics, psychology, and philosophy. Its most salient arguments remain, however, firmly rooted in both phenomenology and hermeneutics, in inquiries into the complex relationship between text and historical context, and in discussions of the feasibility of writing objective literary history. In particular, reception theory evolved in reaction to the work of Hans-Georg Gadamer, whose *Wahrheit und Methode* (1960; *Truth and Method*, 1975) was published a few years earlier. A student of Martin Heidegger, Gadamer proposed that any attempt at historical objectivity could only end in illusion, given that all conclusions are inherently limited by the restricted perception (or *horizon*) of given and ever-changing moments in history. Gadamer terms this attempt to deduce or affix a meaning from the ongoing dialogue between our limited and mutable view of the past, our historical horizon, and the text present before us, *hermeneutics*, an interpretive act similar to what the reception theorists might term *reading*. For reception theorists, the reader's role in *Rezeption* or the activity of reading, includes not only the reader's response to the text, but also his or her contribution to the active construction of the text's meaning.

## Theory in practice

Jauss and Iser developed two different yet complementary branches of this theory and its application. In 1967 Jauss gave a lecture at the University of Constance entitled, "Was heisst und zu welchem Ende studiert man Literaturgeschichte?" (What is and for what purpose does one study literary history?), which he hoped would resonate with Friedrich Schiller's similarly titled 1789 essay, "Was heisst und zu welchem Ende studiert man Universalgeschichte?" (What is and for what purpose does one study universal history?), in which Schiller urges the reading public of his day to revitalize the present by imbuing it with a study of the past. Jauss' "provocation," published three years later in *Literaturgeschichte als Provokation* under the revised title "Literaturgeschichte als Provokation der Literaturwissenschaft" (1970; "Literary History as a Challenge to Literary Theory," 1982), was to become the foundation on which the new, socially conscious literary history was to be built, a history that would result from analyzing the changing reception of literary texts over time. Jauss, who was familiar with Roman Jakobson, hoped to move beyond both Russian Formalism and what he believed to be the Marxists' overemphasis on the materialistic and mimetic functions of literature by linking the reading of texts closely to the evolutionary nature of all systems. For Jauss, to write literary history is to document the experience of the reader. This experience which every reader brings to the text is proscribed by and defined according to the reader's *Erwartungshorizont*, or horizon of expectations. And it is these expectations which the reader ultimately relies on in order to make sense of the text. Among the aspects contributing to readers' expectations for a text are the reader's knowledge of and prior experience with literature in general, with the inherent workings of the genre, with other familiar works of the literary/historical context, and with his or her life experience. Texts reside suspended in all of these implicit relationships to the reader, resonating, shaping, and reshaping the historical consciousness of their readers. Because that consciousness or horizon is based in a stream of changing moments in history, the literary work offers different "views" at different times. Text and reader exist in a dialectical relationship. It is in this regard that literature forms society, but insofar as each work challenges the literary tradition stretching out behind it, it also challenges and constitutes that literary tradition.

Three years after Jauss' inaugural lecture in Constance, Iser further investigated the dialectical nature of reading as an interaction between reader and text in his *Die Appellstruktur der Texte: Unbestimmtheit als Wirkungsbedingung literarischer Prosa* (1970; *Indeterminacy and the Reader's Response in Prose Fiction*, 1971). Iser, who was influenced by Roman Ingarden, is more interested in defining the phenomenology of the process of reading and the construction of meaning than with establishing the task of literary history. Iser argues that every literary text contains gaps, or *Leerstellen*, which the reader has to "fill in" as an integral part of formulating an aesthetic response to the text. The meaning a reader takes from a text is derived from certain cues or readable qualities as well as limitations or hindrances to reading presented in the text itself. From this perspective, the text exists in a state of potentiality, presenting its readers with a kind of system of devices, which the reader then "deciphers" by filling in the missing pieces or gaps, by engaging both the expectations he or she brings to the text as well as expectations raised by the text itself. This "deciphering" or reading process reveals the manner in which individual readers fill in those ambiguous "gaps," as dependent on their horizon, which is in turn constituted by past experience. While the indeterminacies of the text are filled in by the reader, the "filling in" process is also carefully guided by the author, since, as Iser argues, every author writes with an "implied" reader in mind. Iser further broadens our understanding of the dialectical nature of reading by suggesting that readers are not only constituted by the texts they read, but that texts are also constituted by their readers.

## Current responses and applications

Reception theory, which dominated literary theory in Germany throughout the 1970s, only became known to most English-speaking scholars once the seminal theoretical texts were translated in the early 1980s. In more recent years it has been criticized for being reductionist, for giving priority to the consumption of the text at the expense of its production, and for being overly subjective and individualistic, insofar as it assigns the consciousness of individual readers the function of determining history. Other responses claim that the approach also focuses little attention on the variety of readers' economic, educational, and cultural backgrounds, and fails to indicate exactly how critics are to determine which of the multitude of potential readers is in fact "implied" in the text. Reception theorists have also come under attack for neglecting to provide clear criteria for evaluating either the text or the response.

Despite these criticisms, important echoes of reception theory can be found in contemporary theory, particularly in New Historicist and feminist approaches. Indeed, some of the basic tenets of reception theory, namely, that meaning is entirely context-dependent, that there is no pre-existing literary meaning residing in the text, but rather that it must be negotiated, are at the heart of most recent approaches to literary criticism. Critics from other countries, such as the feminist historian Jane P. Tompkins, push Jauss' idea further (as does Stanley Fish) by claiming that the reader's historical situation does not simply affect his or her view of the individual work, but actually produces whatever it is that can be defined as the text in the first place. Judith Fetterley elaborates on Jauss' and Iser's theses in *The Resisting Reader: A Feminist Approach to American Fiction* (1978), which maps the various effects that reading particular texts can have on women. Patrocinio Schweickart, a leader in feminist reader-response criticism, recommends in her essay "Reading Ourselves: Toward a Feminist Theory of Reading" (1986) that gender be taken into account when positing readers, noting that women have been taught to read like men. She theorizes that if it is possible to locate "difference" in women's writing, then it should also be possible to locate it in women's reading. Other contemporary critics, such as Michael Riffaterre, Gerald Prince, Jonathan Culler, Stanley Fish, Norman Holland, and David Bleich, have undoubtedly been influenced by reception theory as well, although due to the variety of their perspectives on readership, they are usually more commonly associated with reader response in general.

## Significance

Reception theory, as developed and practiced to large extent by German theorists, has had a variety of applications in different schools of criticism and a wide international appeal particularly outside of the United States, where literary theory is taught primarily in English departments within an American literary tradition. Reception theory is still most commonly represented in the United States through the work of Wolfgang Iser and often in the context of his affinities to narratology, completely ignoring reception theory's revolutionary beginnings and its indebtedness to phenomenology. Nonetheless, the theory has served not only to incite dramatically unique readings of literary texts, but also to expand the traditional limits placed on the literary canon to include new objects of literary study and alternative ways of viewing and defining literature. It has also helped to complicate our understanding of traditional literary genres and broaden literary tastes to include an appreciation of both high and low literature

(*Trivialliteratur*). One of the first critical theories to encourage an interdisciplinary approach to reading, it provided all literary theorists with a more thorough grasp of the complexity of the role of readers implicit in literary texts, while sparking new investigations into the social conditions of literary reception and the sociology of reception. German criticism has always assigned a pivotal role to historical context in its endeavor to outline a *Geistesgeschichte*; reception theorists took that interest in creating a mythologized past and provided it with a social present.

## Further reading

Bleich, David. *Readings and Feelings: An Introduction to Subjective Criticism*, 1975.

Culler, Jonathan. *Structuralist Poetics: Structuralism, Linguistics, and the Study of Literature*, 1975.

de Man, Paul. Introduction to Jauss, Hans Robert. *Toward an Aesthetic of Reception*, 1982.

Eco, Umberto. *The Role of the Reader: Explorations in the Semiotics of Texts*, 1979.

Fetterly, Judith. *The Resisting Reader: A Feminist Approach to American Fiction*, 1978.

Fish, Stanley. *Is There a Text in This Class? The Authority of Interpretive Communities*, 1980.

Freund, Elizabeth. *The Return of the Reader: Reader-Response Criticism*, 1987.

Holland, Norman. *Five Readers Reading*, 1975.

Holub, Robert. *Reception Theory: A Critical Introduction*, 1984.

———. *Crossing Borders: Reception Theory, Poststructuralism, Deconstruction*, 1992.

Iser, Wolfgang. *The Implied Reader: Patterns of Communication in Prose Fiction from Bunyan to Beckett*, 1974.

———. *The Act of Reading: A Theory of Aesthetic Response*, 1978.

Jauss, Hans Robert. *Literaturgeschichte als Provokation*, 1970.

———. *Toward an Aesthetic of Reception*, 1982.

McGregor, Graham, and R. S. White, eds. *Reception and Response: Hearer Creativity and the Analysis of Spoken and Written Texts*, 1990.

Prince, Gerald. "Introduction to the Study of the Narratee," in *Reader-Response Criticism: From Formalism to Post-Structuralism*, 1980. Edited by Jane P. Tompkins.

Riffaterre, Michael. *The Semiotics of Poetry*, 1978.

Schweickart, Patrocinio, and Elizabeth A. Flynn. *Gender and Reading*, 1986.

Stierle, Karlheinz. "The Reading of Fictional Texts," in *The Reader in the Text: Essays on Audience and Interpretation*, 1980. Edited by Susan R. Suleiman and Inge Crosman.

Suleiman, Susan R., and Inge Crosman, eds. *The Reader in the Text: Essays on Audience and Interpretation*, 1980.

Tompkins, Jane P., ed. *Reader-Response Criticism: From Formalism to Post-Structuralism*, 1980.

JENNIFER HAM

*See also* Gadamer; Heidegger; Iser; Jauss; Phenomenological Criticism; Reader-Response Criticism

# Renaissance and Restoration Literary Theory

Almost any definition of the Renaissance raises some problems, but the period indisputably brought a rebirth of literature, the arts, and the scientific spirit at the close of the Middle Ages. This revival, sparked by the study of ancient Greek and Roman classics, began in Italy in the fourteenth century and later spread to Germany, France, England, and other parts of Europe. The ancient Greek and Latin classics, as interpreted and elaborated first by Italian scholars of the fourteenth, fifteenth, and sixteenth centuries, provided the basis for Renaissance literary theory. The Humanists in Italy and, later, in other countries revived the knowledge of ancient Greek in the West, unearthed and disseminated many Greek manuscripts, and acquainted literate people with many more Roman authors than had been known in the Middle Ages. This rediscovery of the classics enlarged the pool of ideas, styles, genres, and subjects available to writers in the Renaissance – a trend accelerated by the invention of the movable-type printing press. The Humanist movement also fostered a new concept of human beings: that they possess an innate divinity and dignity; therefore, what is most worthy of study is humanity itself, and indeed wisdom begins with the study of humankind. For the Renaissance, the purpose of learning was to guide action and map out the discoveries of experience, and literature in all of its forms was the principal vehicle for ethical learning.

The rediscovery of the classics and the new Humanist approach to life encouraged a revolt against medieval scholastic and ecclesiastical authority in favor of the empirical approach that still dominates modern society. This revolt was reinforced by the fact that, whereas the Middle Ages had tended to look upon the past as all of a piece, the Renaissance made a distinction between the classical period and the nonclassical (or "barbarous" or "gothic") period, regarding the latter with disdain or condescension. At the same time, revived Greek texts allowed firsthand examination of basic treatises in philosophy and science that medieval thinkers often knew only from citation. Thus, in the Renaissance, the ancient authorities became far less awesome to those who could study them in the original, yet they provided an inspiring example.

In the scientific spirit, Renaissance authors formulated "new" psychologies of human behavior (heavily influenced by the ancients, especially Aristotle) to counter what they regarded as nebulous superstitions inherited from the Middle Ages. Literature portrayed experiments in life, reflecting both the intense scientific curiosity and the Humanism of the period. One outcome, which has been passed on to the present day, was the psychological drama. For example, in several plays William Shakespeare established conventional genre situations but created characters who did not react in the conventional way: *Hamlet* (c. 1600–1601), a generic revenge play modeled on Seneca, posits one conventional situation (the murder of Hamlet's father), in which Hamlet's course of action (to avenge his father's death) should be clear but is not, as Hamlet wavers between action and inaction and the audience watches the "real" story played out on the stage of Hamlet's mind.

In other ways besides the psychological drama, the influence of Renaissance literary theory extended well beyond its immediate period. Indeed, the Renaissance was the first age to witness literary criticism as an independent form of literature. The literary precepts originated, or adopted from the ancients, by the Renaissance were formalized during the neoclassical period, beginning in the second half of the seventeenth century. Renaissance Neo-Platonism would also provide inspiration to the Romantics of the nineteenth century: certain aspects of William Wordsworth's philosophy, for example, can be traced directly to Marsilio Ficino's fifteenth-century translations of several Neo-Platonic authors. Finally, with their successful defense of the literary art against charges of immorality or lack of social value, Renaissance critics helped to establish the virtually complete freedom of subject matter and interpretation that writers enjoy today.

## The influence of Petrarch

Petrarch (Francesco Petrarca, 1304–1374) can be seen as the epitome of the Renaissance literary theorist and practitioner. Actually, he established the model for the Renaissance literary life. Known as the literary arbiter of his own day, he defined several issues that remained current throughout the entire period of the Renaissance. During various stages of his own career, for example, he took both sides of the vernacular-classical language question. He wrote most of his earliest works in Latin, expecting them to make his literary fortune; in fact, two of these early works – *Africa* (1396; English translation, 1977) and *De viris illustribus* (1351–1353; of illustrious men) – earned for him a poet laureate's crown from the Roman senate (an honor he chose over a similar offer from the University of Paris). In addition to these writings, Petrarch's neo-Latin works, all begun around 1337, included the *Secretum meum* (1353–1358; *My Secret*, 1911), a deeply introspective work modeled on the *Confessiones* (397–400; *Confessions*) of Saint Augustine but written as a dialogue between Petrarch and Augustine.

Between 1342 and 1343, however, Petrarch began to compose in Italian, and two didactic vernacular-language poems in terza rima, *The Triumph of Love* and *The Triumph of Chastity* (two of his *Trionfi*, 1470), are noteworthy for their treatment of the courtly love theme that became obligatory for Renaissance writers. These *Trionfi* celebrate his unrequited love for Laura, a woman whose identity has never been conclusively established. Laura is also at the heart of Petrarch's most polished, enduring

Italian verse: the many poems, in various forms and on many subjects, that constitute the *Rerum vulgarium fragmenta* (1470; also known as the *Canzoniere*).

As a classical scholar, Petrarch was deeply involved in a campaign to rediscover ancient Greek and Latin works and, above all, to reestablish the values of their authors. He therefore has been called Europe's first true Humanist (although Desiderius Erasmus is hailed as the greatest Humanist). In his letters and verses, Petrarch continually praised classical literature, denounced medieval scholasticism, and discussed his unflagging efforts to recover classical manuscripts that were lost or corrupted in his time. Thanks in large part to Petrarch's influence, several academies had been established for this purpose throughout Europe by the end of the fifteenth century. At the same time, he was among the very first to attempt the classical Latin style in original works of literature. His letters (*epistolae*), addressed to the leading scholars and princes of his time, exhibit a Ciceronian fluency and perfection of style. His *De viris illustribus* resembles Plutarch's *Lives* (c. 105–115) in recounting the characters and destinies of great figures of antiquity.

Petrarch strove not only to emulate the style of the ancients but also to attain their philosophical discipline. The Petrarchan ideal represented a search for moral regeneration – a departure from what he and many contemporaries saw as medieval corruption – and it was to that end that he enlisted the aid of the classical authors. Petrarch's Christian works, including *De contemptu mundi* (of contempt for the world) and *De vita solitaria* (1346; *The Life of Solitude*, 1924), show a strong influence from the pagan Stoics. It was an influence he passed on to many generations after him.

It was Petrarch's sonnets in the vernacular-language *Canzoniere* that constituted his most pervasive and lasting influence on the Renaissance. Sir Thomas Wyatt and Henry Howard, Earl of Surrey, both of whom traveled extensively in Italy, introduced the sonnet form in England. Wyatt translated many Petrarchan sonnets into English, and more than thirty sonnets of his own survive. The popularity of the form is indicated by the list of great English authors – including Sir Philip Sidney, Edmund Spenser, John Milton, and William Shakespeare (who lent his name to the other dominant type) – who left behind collections of sonnets. All are indebted to Petrarch not only for the formal scheme but also for the contemplative tone, the identification of the beloved with a figure from classical mythology, and the religious-amatory tension of their sonnet sequences. Thus, Petrarch's influence extended well beyond the sonnet form. Indeed, he created a convention in love poetry and contributed heavily to the style, imagery, and sensibility of all Renaissance lyricism.

In the *Canzoniere*, Petrarch contemplates his passion for the unyielding Laura in terms of the myth of Daphne, who metamorphosed into a laurel tree to escape Apollo's overtures. Petrarch's tendency to use wordplay, especially on the name of Laura, was adopted with varying success by his many imitators throughout the Renaissance. He strongly influenced posterity, too, through his particular use of myth to express the paradox of fleeting human existence versus timeless poetic beauty – a commonplace theme that Shakespeare, for one, exploited to great advantage.

The Petrarchan sonnet became one of the two characteristic sonnet types, the other being the English, or Shakespearean. The Petrarchan sonnet is divided into an octave (eight lines), with the rhyme scheme *abba abba*, and a sestet (six lines), rhyming *cdecde*. This form allows the writer to set forth a question, philosophical reflection, or problem in the octave, then resolve or answer it in the sestet. Some critics have held that – because of the exacting requirements of the Petrarchan sonnet, or of sonnets in general – a bad example of the form is still better than a bad example of another poetic form.

Other Petrarchan writings that helped set the trend for later Renaissance literary endeavors were the prose treatises *The Life of Solitude* and *De otio religioso* (1376), both written about 1347, in which the author describes the benefits of solitude and leisure for the life of the mind. Indeed, although he developed his philosophy and literary work along secular lines, Petrarch remained close to the Church's ideal of the contemplative life and intellectual discipline in the service of religious self-development. (He supported himself in part through several canonries which he received from Pope Clement VI, though he turned down a bishopric and an apostolic secretaryship.) The celebration of his love for the mysterious Laura helped establish the courtly tradition, in which secular affections were expressed in terms hitherto reserved for religious mysticism.

Yet, like many Renaissance men and women of letters who followed him, Petrarch was also a man of action, carrying out many assignments for the papal court and for secular rulers such as King Robert of Naples. He was briefly an energetic supporter of Niccolà Cola di Rienzo's unsuccessful revolution in Rome, though he suffered no reprisals because, disenchanted with Cola's growing penchant for tyranny, he abandoned the cause before Cola's downfall.

Petrarch's ideal Humanist, as portrayed in his letters and elsewhere, is one who emulates the great personalities of antiquity. Implicit in this ideal is the pursuit of excellence in many varied endeavors; thus, the typical Renaissance individual aspired to be soldier, diplomat, courtier, philosopher, poet, mystic, and more. Petrarch himself had special admiration for Cicero, who excelled in law, government, oratory, and literature. This Petrarchan ideal influenced such later authors as Baldassare Castiglione (1478–1529), who codified it in *Il cortegiano* (1528; *The Courtier*, 1561).

## Literary theories of the Renaissance

What became the major issues of Renaissance literary theory were first explored in Italy, or, more specifically, in

the republic of Florence. The debate between the classical-language and vernacular partisans began with Dante Alighieri's *De vulgari eloquentia* (c. 1306; English translation, 1890), before the Middle Ages can be said to have ended. The fourteenth century also saw attacks on and defenses of poetry on moral and social grounds; Giovanni Boccaccio, for example, sought to defuse moralistic detraction of literature by asserting that poetry and religion are not in conflict. Neo-Platonic concepts of literature, another major Renaissance trend, first emerged in Florence at the end of the fifteenth century. Finally, the revival and interpretation of Aristotle's *De poetica* (c. 334–323 B.C.; *Poetics*), and the establishment of neoclassical rules, took place in Italy well before any other country.

The growth of vernacular literature – a trend dating from medieval times – came into conflict with the classical revival, even while the classics stimulated this growth. The impure Latin of the Middle Ages had provided no standard (nor was one wanted) by which to judge the vernacular. Spurred by the rediscovery of ancient Greek and Latin classics, some authors strove to develop their vernacular literatures so as to surpass those models. Florence, home of such vernacular masters as Dante, took the lead in the debate. Dante himself made the first plea for the vernacular (though he wrote it in Latin) in *De vulgari eloquentia*, which attempted to establish the appropriate dialect and forms for serious poetry in Italian. An additional goal was to surpass the ancients in specific genres, especially the epic. Petrarch wrote the Latin epic *Africa*, the first in a line that also included the vernacular work of Torquato Tasso and Edmund Spenser and culminated in John Milton's *Paradise Lost* (1667, 1674).

In the Italian-language *Governo della famiglia* (written 1433–1441; *The Family in Renaissance Florence*, 1969), Leon Battista Alberti argued that the vulgar tongue would become as polished as classical Latin if patriotic writers gave it their attention. Whoever championed literature in the vernacular had first to defend the choice of a particular dialect. In *Prose della volgar lingua* (1525), Pietro Bembo claimed not merely that the Florentine dialect was the equal of classical Latin, but that it excelled that language as a vehicle for modern subjects. The Florentine dialect, with its already strong literary tradition, became the language of choice for most Italians writing in the vernacular. Some, however, notably Castiglione, called for a national language which they dubbed "Italian." (These proponents borrowed most of their arguments from Dante's *De vulgari eloquentia*.) Ultimately, thanks to the poets, the Florentine dialect itself became the standard language for all Italy.

A later advocate of vernacular literature was Sperone Speroni, whose *Dialogo della lingue* (1542) influenced like-minded scholars in other countries as well as in Italy. Following Speroni's lead, for example, Joachim du Bellay, in *La Deffence et illustration de la langue françoyse* (1549;

*The Defence and Illustration of the French Language*, 1939), argues that the French are as good as the Romans and that there is no reason that their language should not be as good.

On the other side, many Renaissance authors preferred to demonstrate their proficiency in both classical languages, especially Latin. Indeed, the Humanist restoration of "good" Latin was an important part of the anti-medieval literary revolution. Moreover, Latin was the international diplomatic, scholarly, and ecclesiastical language (the Holy Roman Empire still incorporated much of Europe), and the Humanist outlook that actuated much Renaissance literary thought was marked by a profoundly internationalist spirit. Desiderius Erasmus of Rotterdam (1466?–1536), for example, could be called a Hollander only in a limited sense. Thus, to compose in one's own spoken language was not always easy. Roger Ascham confessed in *Toxophilus* (1545) that "to have written this book either in Latin or Greek . . . had been more easier."

These factors combined to produce a vogue for original writing in Latin that deeply influenced vernacular writing and, in itself, may have provided a sort of bridge from classical to modern literature. As this vogue gathered momentum between the fourteenth and sixteenth centuries, works in almost every genre were written. Petrarch's *Africa* was the first neo-Latin epic. Important neo-Latin comedies included Jacob Wimpheling's *Stylpho* (1470) and Johannes Reuchlin's *Henno* (1497). The first neo-Latin tragedy was Alberto Mussato's *Ecerinis* (1315; *The Tragedy of Ecerinis*, 1972). Later times produced several rather topical contemporary history plays, such as Roulerius of Lille's *Stuarta tragoedia* (1593), the first dramatic treatment of the death of Mary Stuart. More common, however, were tragedies on classical themes, such as *Julius Caesar tragoedia* (1544), by the French playwright Marc-Antoine Muret. Of all generic works in Latin, however, lyric poetry was most widespread, both numerically and geographically.

Some vernacular works, such as Boccaccio's *Decameron* (1349–1351; *The Decameron*, 1620) and Ludovico Ariosto's *Orlando furioso* (1516, 1521, 1532), attained international recognition primarily because they were translated into Latin (though the latter work gained additional fame when Sir John Harington translated it into English in 1591). A few authors initially staked their reputations on neo-Latin works. Petrarch himself expected his entire fame to rest on his Latin epic *Africa*, written early in his career.

Eventually, however, a growing national patriotism and distrust of foreign influences – especially in England and France, which had long since established national monarchies – led to the triumph of vernacular literature. Thus in England, Richard Mulcaster called his native language "the joyful title of our liberty and freedom, the Latin tongue remembering us of our thraldom and bondage." Nevertheless, while it lasted the cult of neo-Latin literature firmly established a major tenet of Renaissance literary

theory to which vernacular writers later adhered: the ideal of stylistic and generic perfection and elegant polish.

An important sidelight to the classical-vernacular issue was the debate over quantitative versus accentual meter. Even after vernacular became acceptable, literary thinkers – still reacting against the medieval hodgepodge – rejected the use not only of rhyme (somewhat contradictorily called a "papist" invention of Goths and Huns) but also of native stress-based (accentual) poetic meters. Only through ancient metrics, based on vowel length rather than syllabic stress, could modern poetry and drama hope to rival the classics.

Again, the Italians took the lead. Claudio Tolomei, in *Versi et regole della nuova poesia toscana* (1539), argued that Italian poetry written in quantitative meter could be made to sound like Latin verse. His followers – including Jacques de la Taille in France and Roger Ascham, Thomas Drant, Gabriel Harvey, and Thomas Campion in England – showed the ambition of the dedicated classicists to equal or surpass Homer and Virgil. Ascham, for one, was also convinced that any metrical scheme other than the quantitative was "unnatural." In *The Scholemaster* (1570), he wrote:

> as a foote of wood is a plaine shew of a manifest maime, euen so feete in our English versifying without quantitie . . . be sure signes that the verse is either borne deformed, vnnaturall, and lame, and so verie vnseemlie to looke vpon, except to men that be gogle eyed them selues.

Thomas Campion (1567–1620) described quantitative meter in musical terms:

> when we speake of a Poeme written in number, we consider not only the distinct number of the sillables, but also their value, which is contained in the length or shortnes of their sound. As in Musick . . . so in a verse the numeration of the sillables is not so much to be obserued as their waite [weight] and due proportion.

Edmund Spenser himself belonged, briefly, to the quantitative-meter party, so widespread was its appeal in England. In practice, however, attempts at quantitative English verse were largely failures, as illustrated by the following lines addressed from Spenser to Drant:

> See yee the blindfoulded pretie god, that feathered Archer,
> Of Lovers Miseries which maketh his bloodie Game?
> Wote ye why his Moother with a Veale hath coovered his Face?
> Trust me, least he my loove happely chaunce to beholde.

In time, even ardent classicists such as George Gascoigne (c. 1525–1577) came to accept the accentual prosody of their native languages. The most sophisticated and decisive argument on the accentual side came in Samuel Daniel's *A Defence of Ryme* (1603). Using Campion's own musical analogy against him, Daniel declares that quantity does *not* after all naturally fit the English language: "For as Greeke and Latine verse consists of the number and quantitie of sillables, so doth the English verse of measure and accent ... so that the English verse then hath number, measure and harmonie in the best proportion of Musicke." Nevertheless, the quantitative-meter movement did encourage experimentation – in keeping with the Renaissance scientific spirit – and probably helped lead to improved standards for dramatic blank verse.

Parallel to the debates over language, meter, and rhyme was the campaign to reestablish the classical literary genres, again in opposition to what the Renaissance considered the formlessness of medieval literature. It was the commentators on Horace and Aristotle who first worked out the classical genres and learned to distinguish among them. In 1548 Aristotle's *Poetics* became much more widely accessible with the publication of Francesco Robortello's *De arte poetica explicationes*, which included the Greek text, a Latin translation, and Robortello's commentary. This work opened up a whole new field of study in poetics, such as verisimilitude, poetic unity, the nature of imitation, plot structure, catharsis, and dramatic conventions. It was the beginning of the movement to formulate rules for each genre of poetry. Yet all but the most fanatic Renaissance neoclassicists understood that Horace and Aristotle had regarded themselves as observers of what actually was rather than as rule makers. To the Renaissance, the classics were an imitation of life (*mimesis*), a mirror held up to Nature.

The most influential figure in this movement was the French writer J. C. Scaliger, who in 1561 published *Poetices libri septem* (partial translation, *Select Translations from Scaliger's Poetics*, 1905). Other critics, such as Antonio Minturno in Italy and Sir Philip Sidney in England, codified these generic standards and produced their own treatises on poetics. The next step was to classify literary genres according to the type of life mirrored. The field of drama serves to illustrate this process.

Among dramatic types, tragedy was ranked highest because its characters are kings and princes (and because this genre receives the most thorough treatment from Aristotle in the *Poetics*). Thus, Scaliger in *Poetices libri septem* identifies the affairs of royalty – in court, fortress, and military camp – as the basis for the tragic plot. According to Giambattista Giraldi Cinthio, the actions of tragedy are "illustrious," not because they exemplify virtue, but because the characters who commit them are of society's most notable rank. All agreed that the language and style of composition must be worthy of kings and princes.

Comedy, in contrast, portrays middle-class people. Lodovico Castelvetro, in *Poetica d'Aristotele vulgarizzata et sposta* (1570; partial translation in *Castelvetro on the Art of Poetry*, 1984), maintains that while nobility is a law unto itself, the poor-spirited middle-class characters of comedy obey externally imposed laws and tend to run to magistrates with their squabbles. Thus, a Senecan revenge plot (in which the hero takes the law into his own hands) would be entirely unsuitable to middle-class comedy. The language of comedy must be drawn from everyday life. Farce, meanwhile, is reserved for the lowest classes, with appropriately low language and actions. Farces tended to be very short and limited to a single "trick," such as someone cheated out of his pot of gold.

Thus, the Renaissance approached ancient drama with a view to purification of its own dramatic forms. Critics of the period were reacting against medieval dramatic forms such as the May games, farces, and miracle, mystery, and morality plays. Renaissance playwrights, for the most part, adhered to the standard of generic distinction and purity, which they believed to be even more important than the unities of time, place, and action. Castelvetro had outlined these unities in his commentary on Aristotle in 1570, but they did not become dogma until the seventeenth century. Ben Jonson admitted having departed from the unity of time in *Sejanus His Fall* (1603), but he offered the following justification for his play:

First, if it be objected, that what I publish is no true poem, in the strict law of time, I confess it. . . . In the meantime, if in truth of argument, dignity of person, gravity and height of elocution, fullness and frequency of sentence, I have discharged the other offices of a tragic writer, let not the absence of these forms be imputed to me.

Renaissance neoclassicists agreed widely on this ranking and these generic definitions, and generally the playwrights adhered to the distinctions of rank, action, and language. Any mixture of ranks, actions, or language appropriate to different genres would be unacceptable to the theorist, because a play written in a specific genre was supposed to contain a set of moral lessons and elicit predictable audience responses peculiar to its type. The moralistic standard is implicit in Sidney's complaint against writers of tragicomedy in *An Apology for Poetry* (1595):

All their plays be neither right tragedies nor right comedies; mingling kings and clowns, not because the matter so carrieth it, but thrust in the clowns by head and shoulders to play a part in majestical matters, with neither decency nor discretion. So as neither the admiration and commiseration [an expected response of tragic audiences] nor the right sportfulness, is by their mongrel tragi-comedy obtained.

Aristotle had said that tragedy, having experienced many changes before his time, stopped developing when it found its proper nature. The Renaissance inferred that Aristotle saw tragedy was an organic genre. Sidney's criticism implies that tragicomedy is an artificial and "unnatural" genre. Other, more conservative, theorists went further in this direction, maintaining that if a work could not provide moral instruction – half of the Horatian equation – it did not deserve to exist. Horace, in *Ars poetica* (c. 17 B.C.; *The Art of Poetry*), held that literature exists to provide moral instruction as well as to delight audiences. Giasone De Nores, in his *Apologia* (1590), held that comedy instructs the average citizen on how to act, but a mixed genre, which cannot provide this instruction, serves no useful end. He added that, whatever the choice of settings, language, or rank, a mixed genre would always be inappropriate for one set of characters, one set of moral values. A tragi-comedian such as Battista Guarini, author of the popular *Il pastor fido* (1590; *The Faithful Shepherd*, 1602), did not dare violate such a major tenet of Renaissance literary thought by answering (though he strongly hinted) that he wrote solely to entertain.

The Horatian formula was common to both the literature and the rhetorical philosophy of the period. Thomas Wilson, in *The Arte of Rhetorique* (1553, revised 1560), for example, declared, "Three things are required of an Orator. To teach. To delight. And to instruct." In fact, the lines between criticism and rhetoric were indistinct. Many of the classical sources of Renaissance criticism – Cicero's *De inventione* (86 B.C.) and *De oratore* (55 B.C.; *On Oratory*); the anonymous *Rhetorica ad Herennium*; Quintilian's *Institutio oratoria* (c. A.D. 95), Aristotle's *Rhetoric* (c. 335–323 B.C.) – would today be called rhetoric rather than criticism. As in ancient times, so again in the Renaissance, the discipline of rhetoric became a central element of formal education. Part of the impulse to persuade through rhetoric was the desire to persuade men and women to right living through reason. It was an ethical impulse that pervaded the Renaissance quite independently of the need to defend literature against those who, following Plato or the Puritans, attacked it on moral grounds.

The ancient works of rhetoric, with the Renaissance works modeled on them, constituted the standard authorities on such aspects of rhetoric as *doctrina*, verisimilitude, decorum, and style. In addition, Horace's *The Art of Poetry* (elaborated by many scholarly glosses) formed the basis of a *raison d'être* of literature in the Renaissance. The works of Aristotle and Horace also provided a framework for analyzing "literary" and rhetorical components of a work, such as plot, characterization, diction, style, the dramatic unities, and the moral lesson of the piece.

What theories of rhetoric and of literary genre had in common was the belief that the best oratory and the best literature served to demonstrate moral truths. When, as generic purists saw it, the mixture of dramatic genres raised an obstacle to such demonstration, they borrowed an ancient term, *contaminatio*, to describe the phenomenon. Plautus had used the term *contaminatio* to describe his own play *Amphitruo* (second century A.D.; *Amphytrion*), but in his hands it had meant nothing more than a mixture of plots, implying conformity to the generic rules of tragedy and the generic rules of comedy. Renaissance neoclassicists, however, gave the term an undertone of moral pollution. Nor was it an accident that a mixed type such as tragicomedy should be called a "monstrous" or "bastard" genre.

Conflict was, however, inevitable: in addition to the newly revived classical literary forms, Renaissance audiences also had available to them a rich medieval heritage, including a well-developed narrative tradition, which they did not wish to abandon but which would not fit into classical definitions of genre. Moreover, at least in the field of drama, critical theory lagged somewhat behind actual practice – that is, critics were dealing with modern literary phenomena for which their ancient theoretical models were not always adequate guides. By the middle of the sixteenth century, many playwrights and audiences alike had developed a taste for blended dramatic forms in individual works. Ariosto, for example, abandoned the standards of generic purity that his own early comedies had helped to establish. In Giraldi Cinthio's tragicomedies, or "tragedies with happy endings," the characters are of noble rank, there are no slaves or bourgeois comic figures, but adverse circumstances always work out for the playwright's good characters in the end. In short, despite the tragic elements, these plays preserve an external moral basis in common with middle-class comedy; the good are rewarded while the bad are punished. Though there is nothing in these plays that is particularly comic in the modern sense of humorous or amusing, they all end happily.

Critics and authors may have argued among themselves over the "naturalness" of a given literary form, but clearly they shared the conviction that literature as a whole deserved to exist. Thus, when faced with a common enemy – those who questioned that right – their similarities tended to be more important than their differences. There was a puritanical, literal-minded, and anti-intellectual strain in many attacks on literature. If the moralistic conception of literature has not survived the Renaissance, perhaps the reason is that its proponents at the time successfully defended literature against those who attacked it from outside as immoral and socially useless.

Paradoxically, literature's enthusiasts and its detractors alike drew support from many of the same ancient classical sources, especially Plato. In book 10 of the *Republic* (between 388 and 368 B.C.), Plato attacked literature as a pale imitation of ideal reality. He asserted that only God creates an ideal – for example, the "ideal" of an actual object such as a bed or table – and that a craftsman creates an imitation of that ideal, such as a bed or table that can be seen or used. A poet or painter is even further removed from the ideal in that he creates an imitation of the craftsman's work. Thus, the artist creates only a useless imitation of an imitation. Further, said Plato, while those who are wise will bear losses and misfortune calmly, tragedy celebrates heroes who weep and lament their misfortunes, creating an evil influence on the dramatic audience. Again, literature has nothing to offer for the wise governance of the state – Plato's primary concern. He has Socrates imagine a conversation with Greece's most celebrated poet: "Friend Homer, . . . if you are able to discern what pursuits make men better or worse in private or public life, tell us what State was ever better governed by your help?"

Finally, in *Ion* (between 399 and 390 B.C.), Plato purported to explain poetic inspiration – predictably, to its detriment: "For the poet is a light and winged and holy thing, and there is no invention in him until he has been inspired and is out of his senses, and the mind is no longer in him: when he has not attained to this state, he is powerless and is unable to utter his oracles." Renaissance detractors of literature rightly took this passage as a criticism by the rationalist Plato, although one of literature's earliest Renaissance champions, Marsilio Ficino, missed the irony of this dialogue and celebrated the *furor poeticus* (poetic frenzy) as a divine sort of inspiration that recommended poetry and other genres. Ficino's many imitators cited the *furor poeticus* as one of poetry's virtues.

The doctrine of *furor poeticus* was combined with rhetorical considerations to encourage idealism and an allegorical treatment of literary subjects – the use of characters and objects to represent abstract philosophical or religious ideas. Inspired partly by the ancient Greek philosopher Theophrastus, those who made it their business to study and observe character approached it literally in terms of "emblems" – external signs of inner truth – and of human personality types based on the four humors.

It profoundly disturbed many antiliterary moralists, however, that literature had been invented by pagans. "Tragedies and comedies," said "I. G.," an English Puritan clergyman (in "A Refutation of the Apologie for Actors," 1615), "had their beginning *a Rebus Divinis*, from divine sacrifices . . . they were first instituted of devils and for devils, and therefore as things first consecrated to devils, ought to be abandoned." I. G. also complained that "a comedy is not like unto truth, because it is wholly composed of fables and vanities; and fables and vanities are lies and deceits; and lies and deceits are clean contrary to truth, and altogether unlike it, even as virtue is unlike to vice." Drawing on the works of the ancient Athenus, I. G. also charges that plays teach "how in our lives and manners we may follow all kind of vice with art. For they are full of filthy words and gestures . . . which infect the spirit, and replenish it with unchaste, whorish, cozening, deceitful, wanton and mischievous passions. . . ." He even cites Cicero's condemnation, in *Tusculanae disputationes* (44 B.C.; *Tusculan Disputations*,

1561), of drama as a corrupter of audiences. Finally, against those who assert that plays "instruct men what vices to avoid," I. G. claims that "God only gave authority of public instruction and correction but to two sorts of men: to his ecclesiastical ministers and temporal magistrates." The poets' use of Neo-Platonist doctrine – asserting that poetry imitated the ideal world or even created its own, like the God of Genesis, out of nothing – earned the displeasure of Girolamo Savonarola, a leader of the Inquisition, who charged Humanists with blasphemy for attributing to secular poetry an inspiration and depth of meaning found only in the Bible.

It was Giovanni Boccaccio (1313–1375) who created the model defense of literature in books 14 and 15 of *Genealogia deorum gentilium* (c. 1350–1375), by asserting, in opposition to moralistic detractors, that poetry and religion are not in conflict. Boccaccio found a moral-allegorical interpretation, sometimes rather convoluted, in everything: "When the ancient poets feigned that Saturn had many children and devoured all but four of them, they wished to have understood from their picture nothing else than that Saturn is time, in which everything is produced, and as everything is produced in time, it is likewise the destroyer of all and reduces all to nothing." Using Boccaccio's approach, the story of Leda and the swan could be interpreted as foreshadowing the Virgin Mary and the Dove. With this line of reasoning, one could rationalize virtually anything. Boccaccio and his followers helped to establish the virtually complete freedom of subject matter and interpretation that writers enjoy today.

Boccaccio also mirrored the values of the Renaissance by justifying poetry through its association with kings and other notables. Not only, he said, has poetry always been admired among all peoples, but also its patrons – and even, sometimes, its practitioners – have been kings, princes, and noble lords. Moreover, the poet has always been worthy of patronage, for he carries on the most godlike of functions: creation.

Boccaccio's arguments were echoed throughout the Renaissance, in the various "apologies for poetry" published in Italy, France, and England. Against contemporary charges that the poet's fictions are lies, defenders of literature, especially in Italy and England, claimed that poets teach by example and hence shape reality, which is amoral, to fit a moral ideal. By far the best example of its type, both as literature and as a piece of reasoning, is Sir Philip Sidney's *An Apology for Poetry*. It was directly influenced by Italian and French writings, which in turn were influenced by Boccaccio: Antonio Minturno's *De poeta* (1559) and *Arte poetica* (1563), Angelo Poliziano's *Nutricia* (1491), the work of Scaliger, and others. Typical of their approach was *Nutricia*, a verse essay on the early history of literature in which poetry is celebrated as the nurse of humankind, the font of religion, law, and science, and a divinely inspired prophetic vision.

Sidney answered conclusively several of the principal moralistic arguments against literature. To the charge that it is "the mother of lies," Sidney responded:

Now for the Poet, he nothing affirmes, and therefore neuer lyeth. . . . The Poet neuer maketh any circles about your imagination, to coniure you to beleeue for true what he writes.

And truely even Plato, whosoever well considereth, shall find, that in the body of his work, though the inside and strength were Philosophy, the skinne as it were and beautie, depended most of Poetrie: for all standeth upon Dialogues, wherein he feigneth many honest Burgesses of Athens to speake of such matters, that if they had been sette upon the racke, they would never have confessed them.

Answering the frequent charge that literature is "the mother of abuse, infecting us with many pestilent desires," he admitted that some poets do set a bad moral example, "but what, shall the abuse of a thing make the right vse odious?"

The recurring image of a "mother" suggests (against critics who contended that it was a bad imitation of life) that literature is the original source of religious and philosophical thought. Sidney expands on this metaphor:

And first, truly to al them that professing learning inveigh against Poetry, may justly be objected, that they goe very neer to ungratefulnes, to seek to deface that which, in the noblest nations and languages that are knowne, hath been the first light-giver to ignorance, and first Nurse, whose milk by little and little enabled them to feed afterwards of tougher knowledges: and will they now play the Hedghog that, being received into the den, drave out his host? . . . Let learned Greece in any of her manifold sciences be able to shew me one booke, before Musaeus, Homer, and Hesiodus, all three nothing els but Poets.

Critics and authors of the Renaissance were most uneasy with Plato's seeming exclusion of poets from his *Republic*. Detractors of literature such as Stephen Gosson and I. G. had been quick to capitalize on this point. Sidney grappled with the issue in *An Apology for Poetry*:

And lastly, and chiefely, they [moralists] cry out with an open mouth, as if they out shot *Robin Hood*, that *Plato* banished them out of hys Common-wealth. . . . *S. Paule* himselfe, who (yet for the credit of Poets) alledgeth twise two Poets . . . setteth a watchword vpon Philosophy, indeede vpon the abuse. So dooth *Plato* vpon the abuse, not vpon Poetrie. *Plato* found fault that the Poets of his time filled the worlde with wrong opinions of the Gods . . . the Poets did not

induce such opinions, but dyd imitate those opinions already induced. . . . *Plato* therefore (whose authoritie I had much rather iustly conster than uniustly resist) meant not in general of Poets, in those words of which *Iulius Scaliger* saith, *Qua authoritate barbari quidam atque hispidi abuti velint ad Poetas e republica exigendos* [which Sidney translates, "This authority (Plato's) certain barbaric and crude people wish to use to expell poets from the state"]; but only meant to driue out those wrong opinions of the Deitie.

Sidney turned the tables on those who asserted that other disciplines, such as history or philosophy, were better suited than poetry to provide effective moral lessons. Essentially, his argument was that poetry is better suited to provide vivid moral lessons:

Anger, the *Stoicks* say, was a short madnes: let but *Sophocles* bring you *Aiax* on a stage, killing and whipping Sheepe and Oxen, thinking them the Army of the Greeks, . . . and tell mee if you haue not a more familiar insight into anger than finding in the Schoolemen his *Genus* and difference. . . . I say the Philosopher teacheth, but he teacheth obscurely. . . .

. . . the Historian, being captived to the truth of a foolish world, is many times a terror from well dooing, and an incouragement to unbridled wickedness.

Onelie thus much now is to be said, that the Comedy is an imitation of the common errors of our life, which he representeth in the most ridiculous and scornefull sort that may be; so as it is impossible that any beholder can be content to be such a one.

Finally, unlike philosophy, poetry leads to action – another major tenet of the Renaissance ideal.

In another counterattack on "the morall Philosophers," Sidney, who wrote *An Apology for Poetry* as a refutation of Gosson's *The Schoole of Abuse* (1579), pointed to the many contradictions in their approach to the debate:

if wee can shewe the Poets noblenes, by setting him before his other Competitors, among whom as principall challengers step forth the morall Philosophers, whom me thinketh, I see comming towards me with a sullen gravity, as though they could not abide vice by day light . . . with bookes in their hands agaynst glory, whereto they sette theyr names, sophistically speaking against subtility, and angry with any man in whom they see the foule fault of anger. . . .

It is true that, as literature was attacked on moral grounds, so it had to be defended on those grounds. In view of the moral standards set by the critics themselves, however, it would clearly be a mistake to think that the moral concerns of Renaissance literary thinkers were merely a reaction against Puritans and those who interpreted the *Republic* as a slight on poetry. In fact, the Humanist movement carried with it a strong ethical impulse, because the ancients were interested in the right way to live.

The term "Humanism" could be construed narrowly to mean the scholarly movement that revived and reevaluated the writings of antiquity. In a larger sense, Humanism sees human beings as innately divine and worthy of study; indeed, wisdom begins with the study of humankind. For the Renaissance, learning was for living, to guide action and map out the discoveries of experience; and literature in all its forms was the principal vehicle for ethical learning. The ancient Roman or Greek was a fellow human being facing the same eternal moral and philosophical dilemmas as modern humanity. Thus, the past was a vital part of the present. There was value in knowing how the ancients had handled their problems. Literary imitation was not confined to form, but also encompassed content.

Moreover, ancient philosophical schools such as Stoicism provided a readily acceptable example for the Renaissance, easily reconciled to Christianity. Socrates and Plato, the same philosophers who had seemed to denounce literature, also provided inspiration to those who examined the right way to live. The Humanistic philosophy opened the way to intellectual pursuit, including a deep study of the ancient classics.

## Renaissance literary theory in practice

It is instructive to examine how Renaissance literary theory actually was applied by practicing authors. William Shakespeare has always been considered a Renaissance anomaly, yet in a surprising number of ways he is one of the period's best representatives. His employment of blank verse may be regarded as a positive outcome of the quantitative-meter resolution. He went beyond the vernacular-language advocates (the neo-Latin cult having nearly expired), excelling not merely in one but in many dialects. Witness, for example, the language of Fluellen in *Henry V* (c. 1598–1599). Shakespeare drew on the best classical models, both for material (Plutarch) and for form (Plautus, Terence, Seneca).

Shakespeare excelled, too, in the genre play – the courtly comedy of *Love's Labour's Lost* (1594–1595), the revenge tragedy of *Hamlet* (c. 1600–1601). Yet few of his plays fit exactly into any single genre. It was axiomatic in Renaissance genre theory that each literary form contributed to its audience's ideas about ethical behavior; that is, a work of literature could be judged for its ethical effect upon the reader or spectator. Implicitly, Shakespeare's development of generic *contaminatio* into a high art would pose a tremendous challenge to audiences concerned with the moral lessons of stock plots. Therefore, it is a valuable exercise to study Shakespeare's unique blendings of dramatic genres and the effects on his spectators.

Although *The Tempest* (1611) does not fit neatly into any generic category, its action upon an audience is typical of Shakespeare's plays. The protagonist is Prospero, the exiled Duke of Milan, whose brother, Antonio, has usurped his position. Antonio, with several companions, including King Alonso of Naples, is shipwrecked on Prospero's island, where they fall under the latter's magical power. Alonso, an ally of the usurping Antonio, begs Prospero's forgiveness; Antonio does not follow suit, but both are forgiven by the rightful Duke of Milan. The formulaic ending for a play such as *The Tempest* would be: *if* the villain repents and abjects himself, he is forgiven. If instead he is stiff-necked and unrepentant, he receives poetic justice. Such generic resolutions clearly require rhetorical management of action and dialogue: the dramatist attempts to secure the agreement of a reasonable-minded audience that the outcomes for certain characters are appropriate. Shakespeare, however, regularly manages action and dialogue in such a way that sincerely charitable audiences cannot approve instances of their highest ideals being put into action. He challenges the charitable Christian motives of spectators when Antonio in *The Tempest* (and this is only one example in one play) is forgiven but unrepentant.

The same action upon the audience is evident in *All's Well That Ends Well* (c. 1602–1603), in which not one but possibly three sets of conflicting generic values operate. There is the "secular saint" plot, with Helena as the tested figure, like the patient Griselda in Geoffrey Chaucer's "The Clerk's Tale." There is the "loathly lady" plot (like Chaucer's "The Wife of Bath's Tale"), in which Bertram must learn that his wife, the virtuous Helena, is not so "loathly" after all. There are also elements of the *senex* plot (as in Terence's *Andria*, 166 B.C.), in which an older person – usually a father, but in this case Bertram's mother – commands a young man to marry a woman but the young man wants another woman instead; the play ends with the young man married to the woman of his choice and the older authority content although foiled. Each plot has its own set of values, and each set of values conflicts with, but does not cancel out, the others. The title of the play implies that it has a happy resolution, yet an audience cannot forget that this resolution comes about as a result of two injustices: Bertram's casual seduction of a seemingly incidental virgin (who proves be his wife in disguise) and Helena's ruse to get him into bed. It is the presence of all three generic value-systems that so disturbs an audience of *All's Well That Ends Well*. If Helena were the sole focus, no one would be bothered by the bed trick through which she triumphs, for Bertram would be merely an impersonal catalyst in the test of the heroine. If Bertram were the sole focus, his seeming unfaithfulness to Helena would be similarly inoffensive, merely an error that he commits before learning wisdom and right values. As the play stands, however, the values operating in one type of plot loom up, intact, in the other.

Thus, the audience response evoked by a character, an action, or a spoken line in a Shakespearean dramatic situation is different from that predictably evoked by any given rhetorical or generic situation. This fact, however, does not make Shakespeare atypical of the Renaissance. In transcending the boundaries set up by generic values, he brings the dramatic situation closer to reality – a major Renaissance preoccupation that figured prominently in the antimedieval rebellion. Shakespeare's audience is carried beyond the predictable logic (in the Aristotelian sense) of the dramatic situation. The result is a crisis of understanding for the audience, which is challenged to affirm the principle of Christian mercy when it conflicts with that of Christian justice.

## The transition to neoclassicism

Near the end of the sixteenth century, clearly defined and somewhat conflicting schools of criticism emerged to quarrel over such issues as the ancients versus the moderns, the relative worth of Homer's and Virgil's poetry, and the legitimacy of romance and tragicomedy as literary forms. This division portended the later, more rigid neoclassicism of France and England in the eighteenth century. Meanwhile, in sixteenth-century Italy, a campaign was started to purify the language and crystallize the definitions of words – an anticipation of similar efforts later in France and England. Another school arose which considered metaphor, conceit, and wit the essential components of poetry. In Italy the vogue was known as *concettismo*; in Spain, Gongorism; in France, mannerism; and in England, the "Metaphysical style" of John Donne and the style known as Euphuism, after John Lyly's novel *Euphues, the Anatomy of Wit* (1579).

Although early Humanism was in part a rebellion against the literary and intellectual chaos of medieval times, it was clear by the seventeenth century that often the contemporary political milieu also bordered on chaos. For this reason, a movement from antiquity such as Stoicism – with its perception of disorder in the human world despite the ordered peace, beauty, and security always available to mortals – exerted a tremendous influence on the Renaissance and, later, the neoclassical mind. Literary thinkers of the period maintained their fellow-feeling for the ancients, whom they recognized as facing the same life issues as themselves, and thanks to this recognition, the past kept its vitality for Humanists and their successors, the neoclassicists.

As the seventeenth century wore on, however, the Humanist movement underwent a subtle change. The enthusiastic discussions of Sidney and other defenders of literature had not saved it from being under siege. In 1642, in England, with the overthrow of Charles I and the formation of a Puritan government, the theaters closed their doors

and a law was passed against playacting that remained in force for eighteen years. The political and religious upheavals of the seventeenth century called forth a variety of literary responses, chief among which was an intensification of neoclassical standards. Exactly how to define neoclassicism is a very difficult question. In England, the differences between creative literary works such as John Milton's *Paradise Lost* (1667, 1674) and Alexander Pope's *Essay on Man* (1733–1734), or Milton's *Samson Agonistes* (1671) and John Dryden's *All for Love* (1677), serve to illustrate the wide gulf separating Humanism from neoclassical ideas of literature.

In the realm of critical theory, the neoclassicists seemingly upheld the same principles as had the Humanists before them: that poetry is both morally useful and entertaining in the Horatian sense; that it is related to the "real world" and is not simply a third-hand copy of the Platonic ideal; that art is distinct from nature and imitates reality, though it cannot transcend nature's bounds. The profound difference that set the Age of Enlightenment apart from the age of Humanism is primarily one of emphasis. Whereas Renaissance Humanists had fervently believed that linguistic and stylistic purity was a sign of moral purity, critics and authors in the later seventeenth century believed in literary rules as proof against "enthusiasm." The ideal man possessed by *furor poeticus* was gradually replaced by the ideal man of letters. Verisimilitude, decorum, and wit gained credence, while the allegory and symbolism of a Spenser or a Milton fell out of favor. The earlier delight in ornament, digression, and fantasy, illustrated by Spenser's *The Faerie Queene* (1590, 1596), gave way to the ideal of precision and restraint, illustrated by Ben Jonson's *Epigrams* (1616) and *The Forest* (1616). The couplet became the major verse form. French critics first supplemented, then replaced, the Italians as the pacesetters of European critical theory.

Another difference between Humanism and neoclassicism lay in the two schools' respective attitudes toward scientific rationalism. The Humanists had an inspired faith that both their literary endeavors and the "new" science inspired by the rediscovery of ancient manuscripts fitted into a program of both religious and moral regeneration. In the English neoclassical period of literature, which was called the Age of Reason, the view was rather that religion could be contained by science and philosophy. Francis Bacon (1561–1626), a champion of scientific experimentation, contributed much to the critical tone of the period. Although accepting of literary fantasy and the concept of classical mythology as philosophical allegory, Bacon suggested in *The Advancement of Learning* (1605) that allegory was pure poetic creation, not necessarily corresponding to anything in the real world. To Bacon, poetry was a product of imagination, and imagination was, in turn, a fantasy-producing organ unless rigidly controlled by reason. In part because of Bacon's doctrines, the genres of epic and tragedy became all but extinct, while such "reasonable" poetic forms as verse essay, satire, and comedy flourished.

The older Renaissance literary tradition still had its defenders. Henry Reynold's *Mythomystes* (1632), an attack on the rationalistic side of Baconian doctrine, was heavily indebted to Marsilio Ficino, Giovanni Pico della Mirandola, and Angelo Poliziano. The seventeenth-century Spenserians and the Cambridge Neo-Platonists attempted in various ways to carry on the sixteenth-century tradition. The greatest champion of Humanistic values was John Milton (1608–1674), whose work in a sense culminated the entire movement. Milton's literary allegiance was to the Italy of Petrarch, Minturno, and Tasso and to the England of Spenser.

So long as neoclassical critics required a split between reason and imagination, they ran the risk of not contributing anything of significance or originality to literary theory. This view was implicit in the lines written by Thomas Carew (1594/1595–1640) in "An Elegie upon the Death of the Deane of Pauls, Dr. John Donne":

... So the fire,
That fills with spirit and heat the Delphique quire,
Which, kindled first by thy Promethean breath,
Glowed here a while, lies quench'd now in thy
    death;
The Muses garden with Pedantique weedes
O'rspred, was purg'd by thee; The lazie seeds
Of servile imitation throwne away,
And fresh invention planted; Thou didst pay
The debts of our penurious bankrupt age;
Licentious thefts that make poetique rage
A Mimique fury, when our soiles must bee
Possest, or with Anacreons Extasie,
Or Pindars, not their owne ...

Not that the classical rules lacked vigorous proponents. The early seventeenth century's most energetic example was Ben Jonson (1573?–1640). "Laws" and "principles which could not err" first entered English criticism through his agency. Although Sidney, in the *An Apology for Poetry*, had espoused the "three unities," Jonson successfully transmitted the message of literary order to the public, while exemplifying it in his own practice through his plays, prefaces, prologues, epilogues, and poems.

Like William Wordsworth nearly two centuries later, Jonson wanted normal facts stated in normal speech. In the prologue to *Every Man in His Humour* (1598, revised 1605), he says:

But deeds and language, such as men doe use;
And persons, such as comedy would chuse,
When she would shew an image of the times,
And sport with humane follies, not with crimes.

Jonson was a Humanist in the sense that he wished to employ the ideals and forms of classical literature to discipline the artlessness of his time and the "enthusiasm" that seemed to menace the ideal of aesthetic reason. He also wanted these ideals and forms to be accessible to every one of his fellow citizens. Unlike the Humanists of earlier times, he had a strong sense of literature as a closed nationalist system. Moreover, he chose the classical moralists and satirists as his literary models, and for reasons quite different from those for which they are admired today. Modern admirers of Pindar, for example, often stress his splendid style; for Jonson, Pindar was the quintessential author of moral odes.

But Jonson had another side as well. Although he adhered to the classical Greek and Roman standards of aesthetic expression, he drew on medieval English lyric forms for his hymns – partly, no doubt, as an expression of literary nationalism. He had a Spenserian sense of mutability, as expressed in the procession of images called forth by Phantasy in his masque *The Vision of Delight* (1617). In this masque, Phantasy yields place to Change – the Hour leading in the Spring (with Wonder following) – which is interpreted for the audience by Peace: King James had chosen "peace and plenty" as symbols of the Stuart reign.

In *Timber: Or, Discoveries Made upon Men and Matter* (1641), Jonson set forth in a highly selective manner what he believed to be important to the needs of England and English literature. In comparing literature and painting (following Plutarch), Jonson says, "They are both borne *Artificers*, not made. Nature is more powerful in them than study." The paradox is that, while progressing toward stricter interpretation of classical literary standards, Jonson and other neoclassicists began to admit some concepts (though these, too, had been anticipated in the early Renaissance) that could not be subsumed under classical doctrine. These concepts generally had to do with what is called "ineffable" in art: the phenomena that were not or could not be captured through traditional critical analysis. Thus, Bacon, despite his rationalism, first defined many aspects of literature that have since become associated with Romanticism. He was among the first to perceive literature as a part of something he called a "Time Spirit." He worked to define the relation of poetry to the imagination, although later eras have questioned his doctrine of rational control. His statement that art becomes more delightful when "strangeness is added to beauty" foreshadows the eighteenth-century definition of the sublime and the nineteenth-century definition of Romanticism. His assertion that art works by "felicity not by rule" places him in opposition to the whole tendency of criticism in the eighteenth century.

By the end of the seventeenth century, the notion of taste (*gusto* in Italy and Spain, *goût* in France) had became one possible, and frequently used, explanation for the puzzling differences of opinion among literary and dramatic audiences and for the unsupported judgments of some critics. Thomas Hobbes (1588–1679) had analyzed the process by which imagination transforms the materials of life into art. Hobbes' psychology became the groundwork of Restoration criticism. "Time and education," he says in his *Answer of Mr. Hobbes to Sir Will. D'Avenant's Preface Before Gondibert* (1650), "begets experience: Experience begets Memory; Memory begets Judgement and Fancy; Judgement begets the strength and structure, and Fancy begets the ornaments of a Poem." His distinction between judgment and fancy became a commonplace of criticism in the period of neoclassicism. Fancy, or wit, sees resemblance between disparate objects; judgment, or reason, finds differences in objects apparently similar; and so wit and judgment were placed in a sort of conventional opposition and became critical catchwords. Along with the French *je ne sais quoi* (or the Latin *nescio quid*) and Alexander Pope's later phrase "the grace beyond the reach of art," these concepts – which practically became technical terms in their own right – are also implicit admissions that the critical net of neoclassicism could not catch every aspect of the literary response. The stage was set for later studies of the sublime and the revival of interest in Longinus (whom the earlier Renaissance neglected in favor of Aristotle and Horace) and eventually for the total reassessments of fancy and imagination by William Wordsworth, Samuel Taylor Coleridge, and other Romantics.

## Further reading

Atkins, J. W. H. *English Literary Criticism: The Renaissance*, 1947.
Baldwin, Charles Sears. *Renaissance Literary Theory and Practice*, 1939.
Bush, Douglas. *English Literature in the Earlier Seventeenth Century, 1600–1660*, 1962.
Elledge, Scott, and Donald Schier. *The Continental Model*, 1960.
Hall, Vernon, Jr. *Renaissance Literary Criticism: A Study of Its Social Context*, 1945.
Hamilton, K. G. *The Two Harmonies*, 1963.
Hardison, O. B. *The Enduring Monument: A Study of the Idea of Praise in Renaissance Literary Theory and Practice*, 1962.
——. *English Literary Criticism: The Renaissance*, 1963.
Hathaway, Baxter. *The Age of Criticism: The Late Renaissance in Italy*, 1962.
Herrick, Marvin T. *The Fusion of Horatian and Aristotelian Literary Criticism, 1531–1555*, 1946.
Kinley, A. F. *Continental Humanist Poetics*, 1989.
Smith, G. Gregory. *Elizabethan Critical Essays*, 1904.
Spingarn, J. E. *Introduction to Critical Essays of the Seventeenth Century*, 1908–1909.
Wallerstein, Ruth. *Studies in Seventeenth-Century Poetic*, 1950.
Weinberg, Bernard. *A History of Literary Criticism in the Italian Renaissance*, 1961.

THOMAS RANKIN

**Britain** *See also* Bacon; Gascoigne; Gosson; Jonson; Puttenham; Sidney

**France** *See also* Du Bellay; Malherbe

**Italy** *See also* Bembo; Boccaccio; Castelvetro; Dante; Erasmus; Giraldi Cinthio; Humanism, Renaissance; Minturno; Petrarch; Scalinger; Trissino

# Rhetoric

Rhetorical criticism was the original form of verbal analysis in Western culture. The term *rhetor* in Greek means "speaker." Rhetoric was developed by the Greeks and Romans as a method for preparing orators for legal and/or political careers and by medieval Europeans for training religious clerics and priests. Throughout the Middle Ages, rhetoric was considered the skill of *dicandi et scribendi*, of both speaking and writing, and as such it underscored essential similarities and distinctions between oral and written discourse. Aristotle defined rhetoric as "the faculty of observing in any given case the available means of persuasion" – political, philosophic, religious, but also poetic persuasion, for he extended his study of rhetoric to poetry in the *Poetics* (c. 334–323 B.C.). An incredibly complicated system of rhetorical education developed over a period of nearly three thousand years to assist orators and priests in preparing persuasive speeches and sermons and ultimately to train writers to compose poems, begin, continue, and conclude narratives, and to embellish literary products with appropriate stylistic ornaments. Rhetoric, along with logic and grammar, was the mainstay of the *trivium* – the medieval curriculum for the study of the verbal arts. By the late medieval period *grammatica* developed into the science of the proper reading and interpretation of great literary works such as *The Iliad*, *The Odyssey*, and *The Aeneid*, and *rhetorica* became the discipline devoted to training in "speech" and written "composition."

Plato and Aristotle differed on the importance and function of rhetoric. Socrates argued against the sophists, the ancestors of modern lawyers, who felt that the truth could never be discovered in rhetorical discourse which was at best an argument engaged to be won regardless of the truth of the matter. The function of rhetoric, Socrates declared, was "making great matters small and small things great." Aristotle, on the other hand, provided the art with a thoroughgoing rationale and justification. His *Rhetoric* (348–336 B.C.) remains the major treatise on the art to this day. It lists three major categories of the discipline which, over the ensuing millennium, came to be applied to literature. "Of the modes of persuasion furnished by the spoken word there are three kinds. The first kind depends on the personal character of the speaker; the second on putting the audience into a certain frame of mind; the third on the proof, or apparent proof, provided by the words of the speech itself." Applied to literary discourse, the first category – *ethos* – pertains to the voice or persona constructed for the narrator of the work; the second – *pathos* – refers to the mood or tone generated by variables such as the genre or diction of the literary work, whether tragic, comic, romantic, and to the rhetorical devices utilized to evoke such emotional effects; and the third – *logos* – pertains to the plot or argument devised to convey the theme of the speech, poem, or novel.

In Cicero's *De oratore* (55 B.C.) and the pseudo-Ciceronian *Rhetorica ad herennium* (86–82 B.C.), the most influential treatises in the late classical and medieval periods, rhetoric is divided into five major processes any speaker or writer must consider in composing a speech or literary work: invention, disposition, style, memory, and delivery, categories that have remained remarkably constant over the last two thousand years. Invention involved the discovery of persuasive material or logical evidence, which was not composed *ex nihilo* – from inspiration or the divine madness that Plato suspiciously supposed motivated the poets – but from some prior oral or written source. Disposition pertained to the arrangement of the discourse – where to begin, how to continue, when to conclude – which provided an outline for the speaker or writer. Style involved the ornamentation of the discourse with appropriate figures or "colors," providing a literary work with its "clothing" or "dress" as a common metaphor for this process suggested. Rhetorical devices are divided into "tropes" such as metaphor, allegory, irony, and metonymy which suggest new directions in the discourse and "figures" that simply introduce special verbal effects such as antithesis, apostrophe, repetition, rhetorical question, personification, and oxymoron. Memory and delivery have to do with the mastery and presentation of a speech, of course, but are often applied to the notion of "voice" in literary analysis.

As literature developed into its own special discipline in the Early Modern period, "rhetorical" became a pejorative term used to describe passages that were considered superfluous, hyperbolic, self-evident, or downright untrue. By the nineteenth century poets like William Wordsworth, Samuel Taylor Coleridge, and Walt Whitman were in open rebellion against the prescriptive approach to discourse characterized by classical rhetoric which had enjoyed one last flowering in the ornate and highly artificial poetry of the neoclassical period in European letters. Romantic poets felt that the highly schematic nature of rhetorical analysis compromised the spontaneity and originality of the poet who worked more from inspiration and intuition than formal linguistic and grammatical training. However, by the twentieth century, with the rise of New Criticism and postmodernism, the notions of the primacy of the literary work as linguistic product and the death of the author as prime mover of literary discourse provoked a revival in rhetorical criticism. New Criticism, an Anglo-American branch of literary formalism, drew heavily on the constructive principles and figurative devices of rhetorical analysis in its analysis of poems and novels as ironic, allegorical, or hortatory statements. Kenneth Burke brought the old prescriptive categories and practices of traditional rhetoric up to date in developing a new system he dubbed "dramatism" which emphasized the theatrical nature of literature as a rhetorical construct. In *The Rhetoric of Fiction* (1961), Wayne Booth investigated "the art of communicating with readers" by examining "the rhetorical resources available to the writer of epic, novel, or short story." Postmodernism, in its declaration of the arbitrary nature of linguistic signs, re-creates the role of the writer as sophistic rhetor.

The study of rhetoric is bound to be with us for at least another millennium or two. It remains the backbone of the verbal arts in higher education as every student of freshman composition or the introductory speech course comes to discover the first day in class, often to his or her dismay. Literary analysis, especially on the elementary level, almost always pursues a rhetorical tack and every lawyer, whether he or she knows it or not, is a sophist skilled, as Stanley Fish has remarked, in "the art of constructing the verbal ground upon which (he or she) then confidently walks."

### Further reading

Atkins, J. W. H. *Literary Criticism in Antiquity: A Sketch of Its Development.* Vol. 1, *Greek*; Vol. 2, *Graeco-Roman*, 1961.

Black, Edwin B. *Rhetorical Criticism: A Study in Method*, 1978.

Booth, Wayne C. *The Rhetoric of Fiction*, 1961.

Bryant, Donald C., ed. *Rhetorical Dimensions in Criticism*, 1973.

Burke, Kenneth. *A Grammar of Motives*, 1947.

——. *A Rhetoric of Motives*, 1950.

——. *Dramatism and Development*, 1972.

Fish, Stanley. *There's No Such Thing as Free Speech*, 1994.

Murphy, James J. *Rhetoric in the Middle Ages: A History of Rhetorical Theory from Saint Augustine to the Renaissance*, 1974.

Nilsen, Thomas R., ed. *Essays on Rhetorical Criticism*, 1972.

Schleifer, Ronald. *Rhetoric and Death: The Language of Modernism and Postmodern Discourse Theory*, 1990.

Scott, Robert L., and Bernard L. Brock, eds. *Methods of Rhetorical Criticism*, 1972.

JAMES R. ANDREAS, SR.

*See also* Booth; Burke, K.; Classical Greek and Roman Literary Theory

# I. A. Richards

English critic, writer, and linguist

**Born:** Sandbach, England; February 26, 1893
**Died:** Cambridge, England; September 7, 1979

## Biography

Born in Sandbach, England, on February 26, 1893, Ivor Armstrong Richards was the son of a chemical engineer from Wales, William Armstrong Richards, and his wife, Mary Anne Haig. Richards had survived three extended bouts of tuberculosis by the age of twenty-three. To build up his strength and recover from his illnesses, Richards engaged in mountain climbing, an activity that provided the subject matter for many of his later poems. Through mountain climbing, Richards also met Dorothy Eleanor

Pilley, a journalist and proficient mountain climber whom he married in 1926.

Richards attended Clifton College in Bristol, then entered Magdalene College, Cambridge, where he studied the moral sciences. In 1915 he graduated in the moral sciences tripos. He pursued premedical studies from 1917 to 1918, when he began lecturing on literature in English at Cambridge. There he found his vocation. From 1922 to 1929 he was a lecturer in English and moral science at Cambridge, after which he was a visiting professor at Tsing Hua University in Peking (now Beijing).

In 1931 Richards was a visiting lecturer at Harvard University, to which he returned in 1939 on a five-year Rockefeller research grant. In 1944 he was appointed professor of English at Harvard, from which he retired in 1963. He spent much of his retirement writing poetry and verse plays. In the last year of his life, Richards returned to China to resume work on a language series he had begun there four decades earlier. He returned to England and died in Cambridge on September 7, 1979.

## Influence

All modern critics have been affected by the work of Richards, universally designated the father of modern critical theory. By focusing on authors' works detached from biographical considerations, Richards pointed the way for the so-called New Criticism, introduced at Vanderbilt University.

The New Criticism was early exported to schools of critical controversy such as Kenyon College and Yale University. Critics such as Donald Davidson, John Crowe Ransom, Cleanth Brooks, Allen Tate, Robert Penn Warren, and René Wellek, many of them products of Vanderbilt University, owe direct debts to Richards. Through their writing and graduate students, these "new critics" helped to disseminate new critical techniques throughout the United States and abroad, changing drastically the way that scholars assess literature.

Richards had an acknowledged influence upon William Empson, whose *Seven Types of Ambiguity* (1930) responds directly to Richards' early writing, particularly *The Meaning of Meaning*. The same may be said of Kenneth Burke's *Permanence and Change: An Anatomy of Purpose* (1935) and *The Philosophy of Literary Form* (1941), in which the debt to Richards is acknowledged. The first chapter of Empson's *The Structure of Complex Words* (1951) is largely a refutation of Richards' premise that the emotions of words in poetry are not dependent on the senses, and the entire book focuses considerably upon Richards' theories.

Richards' writing has sparked dialogue with the major critics of five decades: T. S. Eliot, Max Eastman, Irving Babbitt, David Daiches, R. P. Blackmur, F. R. Leavis, Stanley Edgar Hyman, Murray Krieger, and others who responded directly to Richards' work.

## Analysis

Richards matured in a time of considerable intellectual ferment. In the years following World War I, American and British expatriates were flocking to Paris, where art, both graphic and literary, was being redefined. British mathematician and philosopher Alfred North Whitehead was philosophizing about science in such works as *An Enquiry Concerning the Principles of Natural Knowledge* (1919), *The Concept of Nature* (1920), and *Science and the Modern World* (1925). James Joyce was applying highly psychological principles to the use of language in *Ulysses* (1922), and T. S. Eliot was creating a new poetry in *The Waste Land* (1922) and in "The Hollow Men" (1925). Such was the context in which Richards pursued his serious explorations into semantics, psychology, and literary assessment.

Richards' early collaborations, *The Foundations of Aesthetics* and *The Meaning of Meaning*, were directly concerned with defining human experience as it is transmuted by art and language. These two books led directly to Richards' two most significant works of critical theory, *Principles of Literary Criticism* and *Practical Criticism*.

Richards, who always considered himself fundamentally a poet, was well schooled in the sciences and particularly in modern psychology. He thought that the aesthetic school of literary criticism was untenable because it was deeply subjective and woefully unscientific. Just as Germany's universities had attempted to make humanistic studies more scientific a generation earlier, Richards now set out to develop a new, scientific way of assessing poetry.

*Principles of Literary Criticism* exploded like a bomb in intellectual and literary circles. The book was filled with new ideas but was so incredibly condensed that even the most resolute and perspicacious readers found its ninety-six pages frustratingly lacking in examples and development of ideas. In the book, Richards abjures interpretations of poetry based upon concepts of beauty and aesthetic contemplation and insists that poems be judged by the mental experience they offer readers and the success with which that experience is communicated.

Richards considers any works of art to be good, defective, or bad. A good one successfully communicates a valuable experience. A defective one is only partially successful in communicating an experience that is, nevertheless, valuable. A bad work of art is one which, no matter how successful its communication, communicates a worthless experience. The problem with Richards' pronouncements is that they are based upon terms such as "good" and "bad" that have no more universal meaning than do "truth" and "beauty," terms with which classical aesthetics was vitally concerned but which were never adequately defined. In his attempt to bring greater objectivity to critical analysis, Richards succeeds only in presenting his own absolutes, subjectively defined and superimposed upon those who would read critically.

Richards equates refined critical sensibilities, behavioristically, with a well-ordered nervous system and implies that people who lack such sensibilities lack them because of a neurological disorder, a specious argument that few neurologists would accept. Richards can be commended for wanting to free aesthetic judgments from emotional considerations. The absolutism of his method, however, puts him in control of deciding what is good, bad, or defective in a work of art.

*Principles of Literary Criticism* aroused considerable comment and forced critics to reassess their own ways of dealing with literature. The work was obviously the product of a fruitful and brilliant mind, and it set in motion patterns of critical thought that before had been only vaguely considered. Richards was constantly growing, ever reassessing his own pronouncements and revising them as his own thinking developed.

In *Practical Criticism*, he set out to explore how someone can teach another person to appreciate poetry and to judge it in ways Richards deemed correct. He began by giving his students poems of various quality and asking them to respond to these poems. None of the poems' authors was identified, so that students could not base their judgments on who had written the poems, on who they had been brought up to believe were the better poets. Richards analyzed the responses of a significant number of students and identified some of the problems inherent in their readings of poems.

He specified ten basic impediments to receiving from poetry all that it has to offer the reader in terms of the poetic experience: not understanding the plain sense of the poet's subject; not understanding the sensuous qualities of a poem, its rhythm and sound; perceiving the poet's imagery inaccurately; allowing mnemonic irrelevancies, purely personal associations, to intrude upon the poem's meaning; allowing stock responses to intrude upon one's interpretation; allowing sentimentality or emotions to dictate response; being inhibited or closed-minded about a poem; rejecting a poem because it challenges a reader's beliefs; expecting a poet to be technically consistent; and bringing preconceptions about poetry as a form to the reading of a poem.

Attempting to categorize and define the poetic experience, Richards identifies four ways in which language is normally used: to make sense, which Richards considers the scientific way; to bring about an attitude or emotion toward an object, which he identifies as the poetic way; to express an emotion toward a listener; or to carry out some ulterior intention. Without defining the ambiguous term "normal," Richards defines metaphor as a use of words that departs from the normal, distinguishing the "sense metaphor," found in prose and technical writing, from the "emotive metaphor," which is poetic.

*Practical Criticism* continually uses "normal" as one fundamental to defining the poetic experience, but Richards' failure to define the term makes much that he says in this work difficult to accept, despite the compelling ideas his theories raise and despite the significant barriers to understanding poetry his arguments identify. Richards was ever moving forward, however, expanding his critical horizons as he also moved into such other areas of interest as language-learning and reading; indeed, because of their ultimate concern with effective communication, both of these interests came to impinge substantially upon his critical views.

So widely was Richards discussed in his lifetime that he continually moved from a given critical posture to another, more refined one as the result of what other critics, most of whom had the utmost respect for Richards as a critic, questioned in his work. Whereas Louise Rosenblatt in *Literature as Exploration* (1938) centers the reading experience within the reader and implies that all individuals necessarily will create their own responses to literature, Richards throughout his career sought to find ways in which poems can mean essentially the same thing to every perceptive reader and can order all readers' experiences in essentially the same way. His search, while exciting and intensely interesting, was authoritarian and suffered from the obvious limitations inherent in trying to establish any absolute standards by which people can make judgments about anything as elusive of definition as beauty or goodness.

The vocabulary Richards devised for discussing literature has been of great value to subsequent critics, who still use many of Richards' coinages as a fundamental part of their own critical apparatus in writing and discussion. In a real sense, Richards' coinages have helped to define modern criticism and are fundamental to the modern discussion of literature. Among the specialized terms that come directly from his work and remain current in critical discourse are "pseudostatement," "stock response," "close reading," "vehicle of metaphor," "tenor of metaphor," "context," "appetency," "tension," "equilibrium of opposed attitudes," "tone," and "referential language."

*Coleridge on Imagination*, in which Richards demonstrates Samuel Taylor Coleridge's uncanny prescience about modern psychology, is the key book in modern Coleridge scholarship. Richards' system of reading literature is articulated well in it and in three books that followed his Coleridge volume. *The Philosophy of Rhetoric* is a thorough exploration of how metaphor is used in literature and of how it can be interpreted. *Interpretation in Teaching* suggests how to read a prose text and uses many of the methods suggested earlier in *Practical Criticism*. *How to Read a Page* is more pedagogical than critical, but it advances and elucidates some of the means by which people can read perceptively. Each of these books has an undercurrent of sentiment that favors uniformity of response.

Because of the discussion that Richards' ideas generated, he was clearly the most influential critic of his age. He made such brilliant critics as T. S. Eliot and John Crowe Ransom explore new, important critical horizons. That Richards sometimes erred in his own judgments and in his methodology does not diminish the fact that he planted the seeds of modern critical theory and succeeded in bringing a scientific methodology to the assessment of literature.

Before Richards, literary criticism was purely aesthetic, often more biographical than critical. The literary canon was self-perpetuating. The writers included in it were considered the great writers, and they were considered great because they had become a part of the traditional literary canon, a clearly circular arrangement. Their greatness was passed on unquestioningly from generation to generation as an inviolable legacy. Richards sought to change this situation, and in large measure he succeeded. He brought his keen intellect to bear upon critical literary assessment. He spurred the critics of his day and all subsequent literary critics into assessing literature from an analytical point of view strongly based in both semantics and behavioral psychology.

## Principal criticism

*The Foundations of Aesthetics,* 1922 (with C. K. Ogden and James Wood)
*The Meaning of Meaning: A Study of the Influence of Language upon Thought and of the Science of Symbolism,* 1923 (with Ogden)
*Principles of Literary Criticism,* 1924
*Science and Poetry,* 1926, revised 1935
*Practical Criticism: A Study of Literary Judgment,* 1929
*Mencius on the Mind: Experiments in Multiple Definition,* 1932
*Basic Rules of Reason,* 1933
*Coleridge on Imagination,* 1934
*The Philosophy of Rhetoric,* 1936
*Interpretation in Teaching,* 1938
*How to Read a Page: A Course in Effective Reading, with an Introduction to a Hundred Great Words,* 1942
*Speculative Instruments,* 1955

## Other major works and literary forms

Besides his extensive contributions to literary criticism, I. A. Richards produced verse plays and poems, many of which were anthologized. He was an active writer of textbooks, including picture books designed to teach several foreign languages, such as French, German, Italian, Spanish, and Hebrew.

Throughout his career, Richards was intensely interested in language, which accounts for his being involved in textbook projects in foreign languages produced under the auspices of a nonprofit institute, Language Research, which he codirected with Christine Gibson and which developed the extensive Language Through Pictures series. In part, his interest in semantics and his conviction, fueled by his early association with C. K. Ogden, that English could be a world language as Latin once had been, caused him to delve into studying language as it is used by poets and to approach literary criticism from a solid linguistic and semantic base.

So convinced was Richards that the world would be moved closer to peace if it had a universal, easily communicated language that he wrote numerous papers on the subject and developed a form of English that consisted of eight hundred and fifty words and a few important grammatical patterns through which everyone could learn enough of the language to use it for basic communication. These papers are gathered in *So Much Nearer: Essays Toward a World English* (1968) and *Design for Escape: World Education Through Modern Media* (1968).

PLAY
*Tomorrow Morning, Faustus! An Infernal Comedy,* 1962

POETRY
*A Leak in the Universe,* 1956
*Goodbye Earth and Other Poems,* 1958
*The Screens and Other Poems,* 1960
*Why So, Socrates? A Dramatic Version of Plato's "Dialogues": "Euthypro," "Apology," "Crito," "Phaedo,"* 1964
*Beyond,* 1974

NONFICTION
*Design for Escape: World Education Through Modern Media,* 1968
*So Much Nearer: Essays Toward a World English,* 1968
*Complementarities: Uncollected Essays,* 1976

MISCELLANEOUS
*Internal Colloquies: Poems and Plays,* 1972

## Further reading

Brower, Reuben, Helen Vendler, and John Hollander, eds. *I. A. Richards: Essays in His Honor,* 1973.
Constable, John, ed. *Selected Letters of I. A. Richards,* 1990.
Hotopf, W. H. N. *Language, Thought, and Comprehension: A Case Study of the Writings of I. A. Richards,* 1965.
Karani, Chetam. *A Study of the Writings of I. A. Richards,* 1989.
——. *I. A. Richards: A Critical Assessment,* 1989.
Needham, John. *The Completest Mode: I. A. Richards and the Continuity of English Literary Criticism,* 1982.
Russo, John P. *I. A. Richards: His Life and Works,* 1989.
Schiller, Jerome P. *I. A. Richards' Theory of Literature,* 1969.
Wellek, René. *A History of Modern Criticism: 1750–1950,* 1955.
Wimsatt, William K., Jr., and Cleanth Brooks. "I. A. Richards: A Poetics of Tension," in *Literary Criticism: A Short History,* 1959.
——. "The Semantic Principle," in *Literary Criticism: A Short History,* 1959.

R. BAIRD SHUMAN

*See also* British Literary Theory: Twentieth Century; Empson; New Criticism

# Christopher Ricks

English teacher, critic, and editor

**Born:** Beckenham, England; September 18, 1933

## Biography

Christopher Bruce Ricks was born on September 18, 1933, in Beckenham, Kent (now part of Greater London). He was educated at King Alfred's School, Wantage, and at Balliol College, Oxford. He was a Junior Research Fellow at Balliol while completing his B.Litt., and became a Fellow of Worcester College in 1958, a position he held until becoming professor of English at the University of Bristol in 1968. From 1975 to 1986 he was a Fellow of Christ's College, Cambridge, during which time he was appointed initially to a professorship in English and then to Cambridge's most prestigious chair in the subject, the King Edward VII Professorship in English Literature.

From 1965 to 1984 Ricks was a visiting professor at various universities in the United States: Berkeley and Stanford (1965), Smith College (1967), Harvard (1971), Wesleyan (1974), and Brandeis (1977, 1981, and 1984). Since 1975 he has been a Fellow of the British Academy, and since 1991 a Fellow of the American Academy of Arts and Sciences. A founding member of the Association of Literary Scholars and Critics, he has been professor of English at Boston University since 1986.

## Influence

Although Ricks studied at Oxford and taught at the universities of Oxford and Bristol during the formative years of his academic career, he has become associated with the Cambridge tradition of evaluative criticism centered on the close reading of literary texts. Apart from his Cambridge predecessors F. R. Leavis and William Empson, he is the only British critic whose influence is such that one can speak of there being "Ricksite" critics just as there are Leavisites or Empsonians. Yet Ricks prefers to think of himself as influenced rather than influencing, and he takes no interest in academic cliques or intellectual generalizations. Unlike Leavis, he has never professed a redemptive cultural program. Nor does he claim to have founded any school of criticism or to have established a theory of literature. Indeed, he regards such institutions as a failure of "vigilance" on the part of the critic. He has a list of significant writers, including John Milton, John Keats, Alfred, Lord Tennyson, T. S. Eliot, Samuel Beckett, Stevie Smith, and Bob Dylan, to whom he returns again and again. But there is no Great Tradition here, for although Ricks upholds the Enlightenment values of harmony, unity, and logical coherence, he also delights in diversity, heterogeneity, paradox, and the unexpected. Therefore he views canon-formations, like theories, as academic or "professionalized" abstractions which serve only to preserve literature from the larger world in which it participates. Moreover, for the most part he leaves grand statements to those critics he most admires, Eliot and Empson in particular: "I repeatedly find my beliefs best expressed by others."

Ricks' critical power derives from his appeal to both traditionalism and iconoclasm. Traditionalism in that his literary evaluation continues to defer to great poet-critics such as Samuel Johnson, Samuel Taylor Coleridge, Gerard Manley Hopkins, and Eliot, whose judgments are shown to be timelessly valid. In a 1990 lecture, "Literature and the Matter of Fact," Ricks declares that "in an age where literary critics have been getting above themselves (and above the artists upon whom they live), it is gratifying, and may be salutary, to find that the artist knew not only better but best," so it is hardly surprising that he looks to artists who are also critics (and in Empson's case a critic who is also an artist) for illumination. Iconoclasm in that his reverence for the artist is a matter of principle and not an article of faith. The critic may be something of a parasite whose primary function is to enable understanding of literary form and language; nevertheless, the ethical stance here involves distinguishing between good and bad argument, irrespective of whether one is responding to Spinoza or the man on the Clapham omnibus. Eliot, for example, can exhibit "shameful" prejudices even as he brings home "not only how inescapably available are the incitements to and of prejudice, but also how precarious they are; he understands how little information controls so much behaviour; and, how this fact of life must itself therefore be controlled." Lest this should be seen as an exercise in political correctness, Ricks quickly follows up by noting "the way in which people who would blench or blanch at anything resembling an ethnic slur" nevertheless reserve "the word 'ethnic' for certain privileged (dis-privileged) ethnicities or even restaurants," and are quite happy to use ethnically divisive terms (such as White Anglo-Saxon Protestant) to attack the powerful. Elsewhere, he finds that the ironic power of self-contradiction he values in Samuel Beckett's writing is reprehensible in Rudyard Kipling, the sarcastic reflex-action of colonial domination. Kipling wrote:

Once upon a time, on an uninhabited island on the shores of the Red Sea, there lived a Parsee from whose hat the rays of the sun were reflected in more-than-oriental splendour.

For Ricks, imperialist condescension in this passage is secured less by "more-than-oriental splendour" than by the assumption that an island containing no-one except a Parsee can be called "uninhabited." A Parsee, of course, being no-one. Central to Ricks' belief in vigilance is the ability to see that prejudice inhabits the zone of the taken-as-read, and to be able to identify it. The task of the critic is not to accept whatever orthodoxies are in place within a community (academic or otherwise), nor is it to maintain a lofty skepticism where ideology is concerned, but to combine political commitment with an ethical awareness of the bogus, muddled, and dishonest in any discourse, including one's own. In this respect, as in many others, Empson remains for Ricks the exemplary critic: eclectic, anti-authoritarian, witty, atheistic, attentive to the private and public subtleties of language, and able to write "some of the best Marxist and some of the best Freudian criticism of the century" without adhering slavishly to any one system of interpretation.

## Analysis

In his first book, *Milton's Grand Style* (1963), Ricks set out to rescue Milton from the charge brought by T. S. Eliot and F. R. Leavis that the magniloquent style of *Paradise Lost* sacrifices sense to musical value, being pompous, flabby, and abstract. At the time Ricks was writing, Milton's reputation had suffered so greatly from the "dissociation of sensibility" argument that it was thought not to respond to New Critical close reading. But, Ricks argues, considering that such doyens of New Criticism as Empson and Cleanth Brooks rank Milton highly, this can hardly be the case. What follows is a remarkable defense of the Grand Style which demonstrates its precision in using syntax, etymology, and word-play to create subtle effects of meaning. Ricks does encounter bad writing in Milton, but he finds it mainly in *Samson Agonistes*, and some of his most incisive points are made when contrasting *Samson* with *Paradise Lost*. For example, *Samson* is pedestrian in its frequent recourse to dead metaphors. One such is the word "flower." "We ought," says Ricks, "to resist the imaginative withering which results if we entirely cut off the literal meaning of the word from its application as 'the best, the élite.'" *Paradise Lost* re-energizes this common figure in the beautiful passage:

Proserpin gathring flours
Her self a fairer flour by gloomie Dis
Was gatherd . . .,

or in describing Eve, "Her self, though fairest unsupported Flour." In *Samson*, however, inappropriate and redundant usage of the metaphor ensures that it remains dead. When Samson brings down the temple

Upon the heads of all who sate beneath,
Lords, Ladies, Captains, Counsellers, or Priests,
Thir choice nobility and flower, not only
Of this but each Philistian City round
Met from all parts to solemnize this Feast,

"flower" has as little pressure in this context as the word "cream."

Ricks finds himself vindicating many of Milton's eighteenth-century editors, who in turn voice the essence of Ricks' critical method; as Jonathan Richardson advised Milton's readers, "they must Attend diligently, or Something Material will pass away." From the beginning, Ricks claims to be following in Empson's footsteps. But he thinks that Empson sometimes fails to substantiate his readings and sentimentalizes what he takes to be the author's intentions. Ricks requires a "balance of evidence" in order to substantiate a critical insight, and this involves respect for an author's statements of intention and for the contemporary reception of the text. One of the principles of New Criticism is to regard these factors as immaterial to

interpretation. Ricks is enough of an empiricist to want to re-establish the text's status as fact over and above the proliferation of interpretations. This is why his next two books, *Tennyson* (1972) and *Keats and Embarrassment* (1974), fly in the face of New Critical orthodoxy by exploring critical biography. Thus, he can attest to "the delicacy, humour, and humanity of Keats's feelings" as if there were no possible disparity between the subject of the poet's writings and the man himself. Yet at the same time Ricks is too strongly indebted to New Critical practice to allow contextual evidence to determine meaning. The final arbiter of truth is always the literary work's potential for revitalizing language as a civic medium. When Milton lets the flower metaphor wither, he fails poetically and pastorally; when he clarifies and intensifies it, he enriches the range of human expression. And this has nothing to do with the poet's intentions or the original context of the poem.

Colin MacCabe has accused Ricks specifically of lacking contextual understanding in the Milton debate. According to MacCabe, not only does Ricks conflate Eliot's argument against Milton with Leavis' argument, he ignores Eliot's Anglo-Catholic, monarchist opposition to a poet who was a Republican and (in Christopher Hill's words) a radical Protestant heretic. Ricks says nothing about the Civil War (the English Revolution); his notion of history is confined to a narrow literary context, and his "grammatical" defense of Milton submerges the political debate.

Since MacCabe and Ricks fought on opposing sides during Cambridge University's uncivil war over theory in the 1980s, it is hardly surprising that MacCabe allegorizes what he sees as the political difference between Ricks' humanist approach to literature and his own blend of Marxist and poststructuralist theory. However, if Ricks is a long way from professing revolutionary criticism, he is not politically conservative and has in fact attempted to relate literary form to political context. As in so many recent battles over the status of the literary text, the ideological issue here is centered on a fundamental disagreement about the nature of form. MacCabe reviews in a positive light Eliot's description of *Paradise Lost* as having "no poetic diction in the derogatory sense but a perpetual sequence of original acts of lawlessness." Milton's discordant images and fractured syntax mediate his heretically independent approach to scripture and anti-authoritarian politics. The lack of unity held against Milton by his critics becomes here a radical poetic force. Ricks, on the other hand, takes the principle of aesthetic unity as a necessary response to the poet's experience of political unrest. In a 1978 essay, he focuses on the similarities between Andrew Marvell and Seamus Heaney, both of whom "write out of an imagination of civil war and whose work is characterized by the use of reflexive images. These self-infolded and self-divided images (e.g., Marvell's dewdrop which 'shines with a mournful light;/ Like its own tear'; Heaney's waterfall which 'drowns steadily in its own downpour') simultaneously recognize and resist the 'perverse infoldings and divisions' which occur when a nation is at war with itself. They are an attempt to reconcile opposing forces by 'surmounting them with resilient paradox.' To bring contraries into a state of composition or composure is an act of '[r]eunion, unity, and identity: these may embody, as they do in the work of Marvell and Heaney, not only philosophical and psychological hopes, but also civil and political ones."

For Ricks, then, the word "civil" is a touchstone for the desire to restore social harmony: civic virtue, civility, civilization. Political analysis gets no further than noticing a shared response to figurative language in Republican poetry of the seventeenth and twentieth centuries. Ricks is really interested in the possibility of an ethics of speech which will overcome the "perversity" of division. Reconciliation can be achieved only by accepting the fact of difference. Ricks entertains versions of this rational humanist argument throughout his writing, redeeming the disturbing aspects of the work of great poets where other critics have failed. When Keats' poetry and letters refuse to shy away from embarrassing subjects, including himself, they allow threatening experiences to be refined, with the result that "art, in its unique combination of the private and the public, offers us a unique kind of human relationship freed from the possibility, which is incident to other human relationships, of an embarrassment that clogs, paralyses, or coarsens." Tennyson's *Maud* portrays a hero divided against himself; the poet's "sense of the relationship between madness and monodrama enabled him to create a living representation of the way in which a morbid self-consciousness precludes the consciousness of others' selves." Again, the recognition of division opens the way to an imaginative reconciliation. Unlike philosophers and theorists, the artist accepts division as a principle of existence and puts it to "good human purposes." Echoing Empson, Ricks believes that life involves maintaining oneself between contradictions which cannot be solved by analysis: "It is in philosophy that something is *stigmatized* as paradox."

The critic's job, then, is not to resolve or dismiss paradox and other linguistic complexities, but to point out their aesthetic and even moral significance. This is why Ricks delights in the rhetorical effects of double syntax and has a strong weakness for oxymorons, etymologies, and puns; why he is fascinated by misquotations, inconsistencies of translation, and the afterlife of clichés; and why he endorses Sigmund Freud's account of antithetical words. The latter is most apparent in *Beckett's Dying Words* (1993). Samuel Beckett's early work treats the word "death" as pejorative and "life" as meliorative, but his mature writing short-circuits any easy distinction between the two. Freud argued that the organism strives both for release from the pain of living (Keats' "easeful death") and to protect itself from mortal dangers which would prevent it from reaching its goal. The paradox is lived out in Beckett's mordant yet

comical prose, where words such as "quick," "still," and "last" yield poignant antitheses. Beckett makes bitter play with the phrase "the quick and the dead" when he writes of "a quick death/ that an outcast might not die quickly." "Still" is an insistent feature of the late prose, most notably in the title of *Stirrings Still*, where it connotes both immobility and continuance. And "last" oscillates between finality and endurance: *Krapp's Last Tape* is not necessarily his final recording. Beckett maintains his desire to end by forestalling the end, "to end yet again" and to "fail better next time." The ultimate paradox is writing itself. To bother to write is to envisage the work living on after oneself, even when all one writes of is the futility of living. Ricks draws a moral from this (though he would be the first to admit that it could hardly be the "last word" on the subject): "Art is as mortal as men, but it is a stay, though not triumphantly against immortality, yet enduringly against confusion or consternation about mortality."

Ricks rarely takes the text as a "whole," preferring to concentrate on localized effects of literary language and connect them with general questions of usage. The approach can appear fragmentary, and long digressions on matters obliquely related to the literary works under discussion are common. But these are only tangential if one fails to see that Ricks treats art as a special area of knowledge which prompts active engagement with reality. His belief that the literary should never be divorced from fact is directly opposed to what he calls the "living death which constitutes one of the present fashions in academic literary studies: the flaccid assurance that everything is fictive and verbal." Beckett criticism is littered with such complacent misapplications of structuralist theory. Ricks dispatches the lot with the observation that, if everything is fiction, the fictive has nothing against which to define itself. Confounding the idealist escape into pure fiction, the power of Beckett's art is to incarnate in language the irreducible human reality of "piteous bodily weakness," and to have "the strength to contemplate it."

At this point, Ricks' position begins to shift from ethics to moralism. The appeal to the weakness of the flesh is a familiar humanist argument which, like a cautionary tale, insists that while "we" may imagine ourselves to be free from what the German philosopher Friedrich Nietzsche calls the myth of the real, we will inevitably be corrected by life's disappointments, including the decay of the body. Great art is "moving" when it allows us to empathize with this general condition without arousing revulsion or self-pity. But already the question of "reality" has been transferred from the condition itself to the correct moral response to it. Ricks' 1982 essay on Philip Larkin argues that when the poet observes of young mothers "Their beauty has thickened./ Something is pushing them/ To the side of their own lives," his "responsible control of tone" allows the reader to experience a universal sense of pity. Whereas some might argue that these lines evince a pitilessly judgmental attitude toward their object, for Ricks the poem is "simply a flat fidelity" to the experiences of childbirth and growing old which holds not only for young mothers but for "all of us." Larkin's "art is varying and almost invariably lovely," and it reminds us of Samuel Johnson's remark: "The only end of writing is to enable the readers better to enjoy life or better to endure it." Ultimately, Ricks' criticism works to confirm this maxim, but its emphasis on the vitality of language gives precedence to enjoying over merely enduring.

## Principal criticism

*Milton's Grand Style*, 1963
*Tennyson*, 1972, revised 1989
*Keats and Embarrassment*, 1974
*The Force of Poetry*, 1984
*T S Eliot and Prejudice*, 1988
*Beckett's Dying Words*, 1993
*Essays in Appreciation*, 1996

## Other major works and literary forms

Christopher Ricks is first and foremost a teacher and communicator. Many of his principal books and essays began life as lectures. He is a lively and expressive speaker, and this is reflected in the conversational, digressive style of his criticism. Ricks is also a renowned editor. His major work in this field is the comprehensive annotated edition of *The Poems of Tennyson* (1969). This has been complemented by a thirty-one-volume collection of Tennyson's manuscripts in facsimile, *The Tennyson Archive* (with Aidan Day; 1987–1993). Most recently, *T S Eliot: Inventions of the March Hare* (1998) brings together Eliot's previously unpublished early poems, which Ricks has annotated in great detail. He is the editor (with Leonard Michaels) of the influential *The State of the Language* (1980 and 1990), *The New Oxford Book of Victorian Verse* (1987), *The Faber Book of America* (with William Vance; 1992), and he is set to follow Sir Arthur Quiller-Couch and Dame Helen Gardner as the editor of *The Oxford Book of English Verse*.

## Further reading

Barnes, Julian. *Flaubert's Parrot*, 1985.
Karlin, Daniel, and John Woolford. "Conversation with Christopher Ricks," in *Browning Society Notes*. Vol. 10, nos. 2 and 3 (1980).
Lennard, John. *But I Digress: The Exploitation of Parentheses in English Printed Verse*, 1991.
MacCabe, Colin. "'So truth be in the field': Milton's Use of Language," in *Teaching the Text*, 1983. Edited by Susanne Kappeler and Norman Bryson.

ANTHONY MELLORS

*See also* Bradbury; British Literary Theory: Twentieth Century; Heath; Lodge

# Paul Ricœur

## French critic

**Born:** Valence, France; February 27, 1913

## Biography

Paul Ricœur was born in Valence, France, on February 27, 1913. Both his father and his mother died before he reached the age of three, thus necessitating that Paul and his sister Alice be reared by an aunt in Rennes. His professional career began in 1933 after he received the *Licencié ès Lettres* from the University of Rennes. After teaching philosophy for two years, he entered the competition for the *agrégation de philosophie* administered by the University of Paris. Upon successfully completing the examination, he was granted a permanent teaching position.

Ricœur married Simone Lejas on August 14, 1935, and eventually became the father of five children. Only two, however, were born prior to his capture by the Germans in the spring of 1940. Ricœur's subsequent five-year internment kept him from his family. Nevertheless, he managed to keep himself active professionally, as many of the prisoners joined together in establishing a prison camp university, in which Ricœur taught philosophy. It was during these years that Ricœur became attached to the ideas and the method of Edmund Husserl's phenomenology and began his writing career. While still a prisoner, he translated Husserl's *Ideen zu einer reinen Phänomenologie und phänomenologischen Philosophie* (1913) to French (*Idées directrices pour une phénoménologie*, 1950).

At the end of World War II, Ricœur taught for three years at Collège Cevenol. He was appointed professor of the history of philosophy to the University of Strasbourg – a position which he held from 1948 to 1956. From 1956 to 1965 he held the prestigious position of professor of philosophy at the Sorbonne. In 1967 he left the Sorbonne and accepted a position at a branch of the University of Paris in Nanterre. From 1970 until his retirement in 1983, Ricœur divided his time between Paris and the University of Chicago, where he had been named to the John Nuveen Chair of Philosophy and Theology. Having earned his doctorate in 1950, he was awarded honorary degrees by several universities, including the University of Chicago, Université de Montréal, Ohio State University, and De Paul University.

## Influence

Ricœur has worked consistently on the fronts of both philosophy and the Christian religion. Having worked carefully through the phenomenology of Husserl, his interests carried him into analyses of Martin Heidegger, Karl Jaspers, and Gabriel Marcel, accompanying his repudiation of the Sartrean view of absolute freedom. In the place of Sartre's approach, Ricœur posited a dialectical relationship between freedom of action and the involuntary aspects of experience, somewhat reminiscent of the Heideggerian notions of facticity and possibility. His work in these areas has been of such a nature that in the August 9, 1967, issue of *Christian Century*, Sam Keen considered him "of the magnitude of the old men of existentialism – Marcel, Heidegger, Jaspers and Sartre."

In his sojourn into philosophical hermeneutics, Ricœur entered into the debate between Hans-Georg Gadamer and Jürgen Habermas. According to Gadamer, all understanding comes as a result of an immersion in the historical process. Ricœur takes the opposite view as he notes the difference between speaking and writing. According to Ricœur, the text decontextualizes itself from both the psychological conditions of the author's mind and the sociological and cultural conditions related to the text's production. The semantic autonomy thus produced allows for the necessary "distanciation" of the text for methodological inquiry, for example, structuralist explanations.

With his publication of *The Symbolism of Evil*, Ricœur established himself as a major figure in the theory of religious interpretation. In this book he offered a hermeneutic interpretation of various symbolic terms such as guilt, sin, defilement, stain, terror, and dread. From this point on, Ricœur seemed to shift his emphasis from the phenomenological concerns of the past toward his growing interest in hermeneutics.

## Analysis

In working carefully through a phenomenology of interpretation, Paul Ricœur has come to believe that the boundaries of a text must be defined. He thus begins his inquiry with a question, "What is a text?" This question in itself includes several questions. Should discourse be viewed in the same sense as a text, and how is each to be viewed in its relationship to a sender and receiver? For his purposes Ricœur distinguishes "discourse" from the meaning which a linguist might attach to it, that is, language. His particular usage has to do with messages which open up a world. Hence, he sees a triangular relationship between a speaker, a receiver/responder, and the world of things about which individuals talk. This primary level of approaching a text purports that discourse has the responsibility to show the quality of the world being revealed through communication.

When writing enters into this triangular relationship, a new dimension is added. No longer is the discourse intimately tied to the speaker, since, through this medium of writing, discourse can be preserved long after the disappearance of the speaker. Thus the text develops an autonomy, freeing itself from the history of its production and surviving the occurrence of speech. The audience of a written text becomes unlimited, as the text is open to whomever is able to read.

Another important category for Ricœur is that of "the work." The work of art is something beyond mere discourse

or the written symbolization of said discourse; it has its own form, adheres to its own genre, and functions within its own self-contained world. Therefore, in doing the work of literary criticism, the enterprise of formal analysis occupies a place of primary importance, as the critic seeks to reestablish the horizons of the world of the work. The act of reading takes place on varying levels. It involves a simple interpretation of sentences on a syntactic and semantic level; it also seeks to comprehend the work of an author in its totality. Semantics is bound to sentence-level interpretation; nevertheless, as Ricœur himself acknowledges, "hermeneutics begins with the work taken as a signifying totality, which is not simply a sum of sentences." The purpose of the reading is something other than listening to spoken discourse. As a result of the text being mute, and since it does not give feedback on a respondent's claims about it, it must be given life: this is the task of hermeneutics.

Building upon the linguistic distinctions laid down by Ferdinand de Saussure, Ricœur develops, through his typically dialectic approach, a dialectic of event and meaning. In the first lecture of a series given at Texas Christian University, which was later expanded and published in book form as *Interpretation Theory*, Ricœur emphasizes that "the notion of speech as an event provides the key to the transition from a linguistics of the code to a linguistics of the message." The system, or to use Saussure's term – the *langue* – has only a virtual existence; it is the message, *parole*, that gives actuality to language. It is not languages that speak, but people. When the speech occurrence takes place, the event side of the dialectic is inaugurated, which relates back to the reference of the speaker's discourse or the utterer's meaning. It is seen in the inner structure of the sentence, in which personal pronouns, adverbs of time and space, demonstratives, and verb tenses refer to the "now" of the speech event and of the speaker. In other words, discourse exhibits many means for displaying itself as event, through self-referentially pointing back to the speaker.

Ricœur also develops the subjective side of meaning, that is, the utterer's meaning, along the lines of the illocutionary dimension of the speech act, and the intention of recognition by the hearer. Although communication has the power to say things, it also has the ability to do things. In conjunction with the insights of J. L. Austin and speech act theory, Ricœur acknowledges the performative force of discourse through illocutionary and perlocutionary acts.

He says that to mean is what the speaker does; he also shows, however, that the sentence means. Inasmuch as he identifies the "utterer's meaning," he also seeks to capture the essence of the "utterance meaning." While the utterer means in a subjective sense, the utterance is the objective side of meaning. Just as there were several ways of viewing the subjective side of meaning, he develops two ways of approaching the utterance meaning. Following Gottlob Frege, Ricœur distinguishes between "sense" and "reference." Ricœur simplifies the terminology somewhat by showing that the sense is the "what" of discourse; whereas, its reference is the "about what." The "sense" is what displays the internal relationships within the sentence, while the "reference" shows the external relationships to the world.

As Ricœur progressively unfolds his dialectics of interpretation, he eventually gets to the dialectic of explanation and understanding. Having established the relationship of speech to writing, as well as the relationship of event to meaning, his journey does not allow him to stop until the process is complete. Whereas discourse is produced as an event, it is understood as meaning. When mutual understanding is achieved, this achievement is effected through the shared context of the sender and the receiver. Further, the process of understanding is circular by its very nature. He describes this circular process of interpretation (commonly known as the hermeneutical circle à la Gadamer, Heidegger, and others) as a move from understanding to explanation and then to comprehension.

Ricœur is convinced that the understanding of a text begins with a guess. Since the text is mute, an asymmetric relationship exists between the text and the reader, in which the reader must speak for both of them. The interpreter must guess at the meaning of the text because the author's intention is beyond his or her grasp. In conjunction with E. D. Hirsch, Jr., he believes that though there may be no rules for making good guesses, there are good methods for validating the conjectures which are made. Those which are projected in the interpretive process must be tested. What is sought by this testing is not any sort of positivistic empirical verification. Validation, not verification, provides the key to moving from the initial understanding stage (the guess), through the explanation process, and toward a viable comprehension of the text. Certainty is not what is provided, but rather probability. Textual interpretation is thus argumentative by nature – validating itself through the establishment of its relative probability – not unlike juridical procedures. Hence guess and validation function in a subjectively objective process which moves the interpreter toward comprehension.

The hermeneutic procedure involved in moving from guess through explanation (Gadamer calls it the art of projecting and revising) toward comprehension is what is known as establishing horizons. This is where Ricœur's phenomenological and hermeneutical methods intersect. Phenomenology seeks to recognize how meaning comes to the reader. Thus, the reader makes himself cognizant of the horizon of the genre of which the work is a part. In conjunction with this he takes note of formal considerations. Merely to recognize that a work is poetry is not nearly as beneficial as recognizing that it belongs to the category of the L-A-N-G-U-A-G-E poets as opposed to being an Elizabethan sonnet or a haiku. Moreover, some understanding of the conventions used helps the interpreter to establish the horizons of possible meaning in which an interpretation can be adjudged either valid or invalid. For example, it would be inappropriate to impose the Aristotelian unities of time, place, and action upon an interpretation of an absurdist drama, for Aristotle's unities are not a part of the conventions characteristically used in the Theater of the Absurd. Had the interpreter chosen instead to interpret the drama in terms of conventions such as tragicomedy, meaningless banter, repetition, and existentialist themes, then one could feel comfortable that he was viewing the drama in terms of conventions common to the genre. In this way horizons of meaning can be established in which valid interpretations can be achieved.

Although it is true that there is always more than one way of constructing a text, all constructions or interpretations are not equally valid. There are certain boundaries that are required by the text. The establishment of meaningful horizons tends to set the parameters within which interpretations might operate. The better these parameters are set, the better one is able to make judgments regarding validity. Whereas meaning can never be thought to be established in an absolute and determinant sense, the establishment of meaningful horizons will serve to invalidate many spurious attempts at interpretation. This criterion of adjudication functions similarly to the criteria of falsifiability proposed by Karl Popper.

Ricœur has been a prolific essayist, having written hundreds of articles. Although many of these pieces have been anthologized, many more remain in their original form. His interests have moved progressively from phenomenology to structuralism to hermeneutics, and some of his writings have been viewed as seminal pieces with respect to the interpretation of meaning and social involvement.

## Principal criticism

*Karl Jaspers et la philosophie de l'existence*, 1947 (with Mikel Dufrenne)
*Gabriel Marcel et Karl Jaspers: Philosophie du mystère et philosophie du paradoxe*, 1948
*Le Volontaire et l'involontaire*, 1949 (*Freedom and Nature: The Voluntary and Involuntary*, 1966)
*Philosophie de la volonté*, 1950, 1960 (2 volumes)
*Histoire et vérité*, 1955 (*History and Truth*, 1965)
*L'Homme faillible*, 1960 (*Fallible Man*, 1965)
*La Symbolique du mal*, 1960 (*The Symbolism of Evil*, 1967)
*De l'interprétation: Essai sur Freud*, 1965 (*Freud and Philosophy: An Essay on Interpretation*, 1970)
*Le Conflit des interprétations: Essais d'herméneutique*, 1969 (*The Conflict of Interpretations: Essays in Hermeneutics*, 1974)
*Political and Social Essays*, 1974
*La Métaphore vive*, 1975 (*The Rule of Metaphor*, 1977)
*Interpretation Theory: Discourse and the Surplus of Meaning*, 1976
*The Philosophy of Paul Ricœur*, 1978
*Essays on Biblical Interpretation*, 1980
*Hermeneutics and the Human Sciences: Essays on Language, Action, and Interpretation*, 1981
*Temps et récit*, 1983 (*Time and Narrative*, 1984, 1986, 1988)
*The Reality of the Historical Past*, 1984

*À l'école de la phénoménologie*, 1986
*Lectures on Ideology and Utopia*, 1986
*Du texte a l'action (From Text to Action: Essays in
    Hermeneutics*, 1991)

## Other major works and literary forms

Paul Ricœur is known primarily for his criticism.

TRANSLATION

Introduction to *Idées directrices pour une phénomenologie*,
    1950 (translator)

MISCELLANEOUS

*Le Critique et la Conviction*, 1998 (*Critique and Conviction:
    Conversations with François Azouvi and Marc de Launay*,
    1998)

## Further reading

Clark, Steven H. *Paul Ricœur*, 1990.
Gerhart, Mary. *The Question of Belief in Literary Criticism:
    An Introduction to the Hermeneutical Theory of Paul
    Ricœur*, 1979.
Klenm, David E. *The Hermeneutical Theory of Paul Ricœur:
    A Contructivist Analysis*, 1983.
Reagan, Charles E., ed. *Studies in the Philosophy of Paul
    Ricœur*, 1979.
——. *Paul Ricœur: His Life and His Work*, 1996
Sweeney, Robert. "A Survey of Recent Ricœur Literature by and
    About 1974–1984," in *Philosophy Today*. XXIX (Spring,
    1985), pp. 38–58.
Thompson, John B. *Critical Hermeneutics: A Study in the
    Thought of Paul Ricœur and Jürgen Habermas*, 1961.
Vanhoozer, Kevin J. *Biblical Narrative in the Philosophy of Paul
    Ricœur*, 1990.
Wood, David, ed. *On Paul Ricœur: Narrative and
    Interpretation*, 1991.

STEPHEN M. ASHBY

*See also* French Literary Theory: Twentieth Century;
Gadamer; Heidegger; Phenomenological Criticism

# Alain Robbe-Grillet

French novelist, writer, and theorist

**Born:** Brest, France; August 18, 1922

## Biography

Alain Robbe-Grillet was born in Brest, France, on August
18, 1922, but spent most of his youth in Paris. For a time
during World War II, he served as a virtual slave laborer
in German factories. Afterward, he was trained as an agronomist; although he lived mostly in France, his job as an
agronomist specializing in exotic fruits took him occasionally to Guinea, Morocco, Guadeloupe, and Martinique; he
also served as *chargé de mission* at the Institut National
des Statistiques. For many years, beginning in the 1950s,

he was literary adviser to the publisher Éditions de Minuet
in Paris. He married Catherine Rstakian in 1957. Since
gaining international fame in literature, Robbe-Grillet has
been a visiting writer at a number of universities, including
some in the United States, his longest tenure being at
Washington University in St. Louis.

## Influence

Robbe-Grillet is the leading figure behind the New Novel,
a radically innovative fiction that appeared in France as
early as the late 1930s and rose to its greatest influence in
the 1960s. Not only a skillful fiction writer, Robbe-Grillet
is also the New Novel's most widely published and
discussed theorist. In essays and reviews later collected in
*For a New Novel*, Robbe-Grillet analyzes and generally
dismisses what seem to him the outmoded conventions
employed by great novelists from the past, while praising
the innovations of lesser-known writers such as Jöe
Bousquet and Raymond Roussel. As outrageous as his theories sometimes seem to readers with more traditional tastes,
in essence what Robbe-Grillet calls for is no more than a
vital fiction that creates its own reality.

## Analysis

Alain Robbe-Grillet is among those writers whose works
generate not only discussion or even mere debate but anger.
Indeed, in some circles, he is less famous than infamous.
This outrage cannot be attributed to the experimental
nature of his fiction alone, for, innovative though he is, any
number of modern writers are equally so. Rather, the storm
centers on Robbe-Grillet because he articulates an adamant
– and one might say brusque and supercilious – theoretical
position in his essays and reviews, a position that by its
very nature is bound to seem threatening to conservative
writers and theorists.

Robbe-Grillet's theory of fiction may be likened to the
theories of the political anarchists of an earlier age, who
believed that the old order must be uprooted and destroyed
before a benevolent new order can arise. Robbe-Grillet, in
other words, insists that the emergence of the New Novel
depends on the recognition and rejection of outmoded
forms. His theory, then, extends in two directions, as a
critique of established conventions and an argument for
newer forms, and the one cannot be fully understood
without the other.

It must be noted at the outset, however, that Robbe-
Grillet's writings on fiction do not constitute a unified body
of critical theory, partly because no single work serves as
the bible of his theory. His one major critical document,
*For a New Novel*, is a collection of essays and reviews
published individually over several years. In successive
essays, Robbe-Grillet often responds to criticism of his
earlier fiction and literary theory, and in doing so, he sometimes alters his position. Some inconsistency results – but
interesting inconsistency.

If, in defending himself from critics, Robbe-Grillet's focus wavers over the years, it never wanders far from his program for the New Novel. The first part of the program is a rejection of the old. "Old" being defined as any fiction produced by writers preceding Robbe-Grillet – including innovative modern masters such as Marcel Proust, William Faulkner, and even Albert Camus and Jean-Paul Sartre – what does Robbe-Grillet wish to see rejected? Virtually everything. Among the most important, because most cherished by conservative writers, are character, story, "commitment" (serious intent), and form and content (when seen as distinguishable).

Although Robbe-Grillet discusses each of these conventions at some length in his criticism, in general he finds two faults with all of them. First, he believes that by isolating conventions, one distorts what fiction really is: an act of writing, or, as his contemporary Raymond Queneau might say, an exercise in style. To isolate the "story" convention, for example, is to reduce a piece of fiction to its anecdote, thereby reducing the writer to little more than a reporter. It is not that Robbe-Grillet believes the story to be no more important than style; rather, he believes it to be inseparable from style. The same complaint would hold for the conventions of character, setting, and so forth. Actually, most of these conventions could be subsumed under the general critical fallacy, in Robbe-Grillet's estimation, of form and content. Form and content, as discrete aspects of fiction, do not exist. Form is content, content form.

In a sense, this contention is at least as old as Samuel Taylor Coleridge and his argument for an "organic" style. The difference between, on the one hand, Coleridge and many subsequent critics who argue for a wedding of form and content and, on the other, Robbe-Grillet, is significant and leads to Robbe-Grillet's second general complaint about conventions. Coleridge and most critics contend, or at least imply, that they are describing the verities of literature, essentially changeless and eternal. Robbe-Grillet, however, abhors specific conventions less than the very concept of conventions. If Charles Dickens and Gustave Flaubert found the conventions of Henry Fielding and Laurence Sterne no longer useful, and if Marcel Proust and James Joyce rejected as outmoded the novels of Dickens and Flaubert, then perhaps, Robbe-Grillet would argue, it is the very idea of conventions that is suspect. Indeed, he would go beyond this. It is not enough to say that each new age must create its own conventions; rather, each book constitutes its own set of laws, applicable only to itself, answerable to its own inner logic. Robbe-Grillet demands of writers ever new fictions, trampling on the bones of the obsolete – little wonder that more conservative writers and critics find him so ominous.

The "destructive" half of Robbe-Grillet's theory of fiction, then, calls for the perpetual rejection of anything threatening to become a convention. Yet what of the "constructive" portion? Does Robbe-Grillet demand anything demonstrable from himself and fellow writers? He does; he demands the New Novel. It is necessary when discussing the New Novel, however, to distinguish between a general new novel, one which may be pursued by all writers present and future, and a more specific New Novel of the variety written by Robbe-Grillet and his avant-garde, largely French contemporaries such as Nathalie Sarraute, Michel Butor, and Claude Simon.

What Robbe-Grillet insists upon for all novels might come as a surprise to some who find him forbiddingly avant-garde. He insists upon realism. Indeed, conventions are sterile and to be avoided not because they have been used too frequently, but, more important, because they do not reflect the world as it is. Nevertheless, the New Novelists do more than merely reflect reality; they create reality, fostering a new and more intimate relationship between art and life:

> [The New Novel] is merely a convenient label applicable to all those seeking new forms for the novel, forms capable of expressing (or of creating) new relations between man and the world, to all those who have determined to invent the novel, in other words, to invent man. Such writers know that the systematic repetition of the forms of the past is not only absurd and futile, but that it can even become harmful: by blinding us to our real situation in the world today, it keeps us, ultimately, from constructing the world and man of tomorrow.

This "constructing the world and man of tomorrow" may seem on the verge of introducing a political impulse in Robbe-Grillet's theory, but such is not the case. Political intent – or any other intent or theme – would be just one other artificial impulse from beyond the work of fiction, hence a distortion and distraction. The novel never looks outward, only inward: "The book makes its own rules for itself, and for itself alone."

How a fiction can look only inward and still be said to reflect reality may seem an unresolvable paradox. Robbe-Grillet resolves, or at least eloquently addresses, the problem in his discussion of the writer Joë Bousquet, who becomes for Robbe-Grillet very nearly a personification of the creative process. Paralyzed by a war wound, Bousquet cannot go out into the world, and, more important, the world – in the form of a theme, a philosophy, a political goal, a conventional way of seeing – increasingly loses its power to intrude upon Bousquet's fiction. The more the outside world becomes a memory, the more it becomes Bousquet's "property." It is this inner reality that each artist must strive to re-create. Rather than being a step away from actuality, this "reinvented" world comprises "real things, clear, hard, and brilliant, of the real world. They refer to no other world. . . . And the only contact man can make with them is to imagine them."

Were Robbe-Grillet content with this general view of the goal and purpose of fiction, quite likely few critics would take very much exception to his views. It is the New Novel as actually practiced and Robbe-Grillet's descriptions of how it operates that strike some as puzzling or even absurd. He has not always been helped by his well-intentioned defenders, such as Roland Barthes, who sometimes distort his theory and practice. Many critics would have the reader believe that what Robbe-Grillet calls for and practices in the novel is a fiction made up of static descriptions of objects and meaningless gestures, totally objective, devoid of humanity. Robbe-Grillet himself has abetted this misinterpretation by vehemently denying any psychological impulse in the New Novel. By psychological, however, Robbe-Grillet refers to any specific theory of psychology to which all the elements of the fiction seem to be in service. This, for Robbe-Grillet, would simply be one more way for the novel to lose its own reality, to obey a "cause" outside itself.

If his fictions are not psychological, however, neither are they "objective" in the normal sense of the term. Instead, Robbe-Grillet notes that his fictive reality is always a highly subjective one; as for the New Novel's infamous objects, they

> never have a presence outside human perception, real or imaginary; they are objects comparable to those in our daily lives, as they occupy our minds at every moment.
>
> And, if the object is taken in its general sense (object, according to the dictionary: whatever affects the senses), it is natural that there should be only objects in my books.

Carefully considered, Robbe-Grillet's subjective reality allows for more "play" in the novel than his detractors admit. Still, the New Novel as practiced by Robbe-Grillet and his colleagues was idiosyncratic enough that its influence did not extend much beyond France, and by the late 1960s it had come to seem relatively feeble in contrast to newer forms appearing in Latin America and Central and Eastern Europe.

Much the same must be said for Robbe-Grillet's theoretical pronouncements. Although several of his colleagues and a number of scholars joined him in championing the cause of the New Novel, even at their height they could not be said to constitute a movement of much influence in the critical community. This result may be explained partly by the fact that criticism itself was not – at least in Robbe-Grillet's case – their major concern; writing fiction was. The criticism never seems to match, or even very accurately describe, the vigor and integrity of the fiction. Finally, the core idea of Robbe-Grillet's critical theory – that fiction obeys its own laws and has no necessary connection to the "actual" world – soon found more commanding and vigorous voice in the work of a far more influential critical movement, deconstruction.

Robbe-Grillet, then, is in a curious position. An internationally famous novelist, he is also the author of one of the most widely discussed works of critical theory concerning fiction since World War II. Yet his influence is, and probably always was, far less than is his fame. What this means for the lasting value of his critical theory, only time will determine.

## Principal criticism

*Pour un nouveau roman*, 1963 (*For a New Novel: Essays on Fiction*, 1965)

## Other major works and literary forms

Alain Robbe-Grillet's theory of fiction, which can be credited with creating a subgenre, the New Novel (*nouveau roman*), is put into practice in nearly a dozen novels, beginning with *Les Gommes* (1953; *The Erasers*, 1964), an experimental collection of short fiction, *Instantanés* (1962; *Snapshots*, 1965), and photo-essays. He also has written several screenplays; one, *L'Année dernière à Marienbad* (1961; *Last Year at Marienbad*, 1962), received the Academy Award for Best Foreign Film in 1961.

NOVELS
*Un régicide*, 1949 (*A Regicide*, 1978)
*Les Gommes*, 1953 (*The Erasers*, 1964)
*Le Voyeur*, 1955 (*The Voyeur*, 1958)
*La Jalousie*, 1957 (*Jealousy*, 1959)
*Dans le labyrinthe*, 1959 (*In the Labyrinthe*, 1960)
*La Maison de rendez-vous*, 1965 (English translation, 1966)
*Projet pour une révolution à New York*, 1970 (*Project for a Revolution in New York*, 1972)
*Topologie d'une cité fantôme*, 1976 (*Topology of a Phantom City*, 1977)
*La Belle Captive*, 1976 (illustrated by René Magritte)
*Souvenirs du triangle d'or*, 1978 (*Recollections of the Golden Triangle*, 1984)
*Djinn*, 1981 (English translation, 1982)
*Miroir qui revient*, 1985 (*Ghosts in the Mirror*, 1991)
*Angélique ou l'enchantement*, 1987
*Les derniers jours de corinthe*, 1994

SHORT FICTION
*Instantanés*, 1962 (*Snapshots*, 1965)

SCREENPLAYS
*L'Année dernière à Marienbad*, 1961 (*Last Year at Marienbad*, 1962)
*L'Immortelle*, 1963 (*The Immortal One*, 1971)
*Trans-Europ Express*, 1967
*L'Homme qui ment*, 1968
*L'Éden et après*, 1970
*Glissements progressifs du plaisir*, 1974

NONFICTION
*Rêves de jeunes filles*, 1971 (photographs by David Hamilton; *Dreams of a Young Girl*, 1971)
*Les Demoiselles d'Hamilton*, 1972 (photographs by Hamilton; *Sisters*, 1973)
*Le Rendez-vous*, 1981

## Further reading

Faris, Wendy B. *Labyrinths of Language*, 1988
Fletcher, John. *Alain Robbe-Grillet*, 1983.
Heath, Stephen. *The Nouveau Roman: A Study in the Practice of Writing*, 1972.
Jefferson, Ann. *The Nouveau Roman and the Poetics of Fiction*, 1980.
Morrissette, Bruce. *The Novels of Robbe-Grillet*, 1975.
Stoltzfus, Ben. *Alain Robbe-Grillet*, 1985.
Sturrock, John. *The French New Novel*, 1969.

DENNIS VANNATTA

*See also* Butor; French Literary Theory: Twentieth Century

# Romanticism

In the autumn, 1941, issue of *The Kenyon Review*, Edwin Berry Burgum warned, "He who seeks to define Romanticism is entering a hazardous occupation which has claimed many victims." Just as modern critics find the term elusive, so their late-eighteenth- and early-nineteenth-century counterparts seemed uncertain about the nature of the literature of this period. Heinrich Heine described Romanticism as "the re-awakening of the life and thought of the Middle Ages." F. W. J. Schelling, on the other hand, declared that "the classic temper studies the past, the romantic neglects it." Jean-Jacques Rousseau declared that Romanticism meant a return to nature, while Victor Hugo maintained that Romanticism offers "the complete truth of life." Yet William Blake's works are visionary rather than realistic, and he criticized William Wordsworth's poetry for stressing observation ahead of sensibility.

One finds similar disagreements over literary merit. In *The Four Ages of Poetry* (1820), Thomas Love Peacock condemned the English Lake Poets, among them Wordsworth and Samuel Taylor Coleridge; Coleridge, in his *Biographia Literaria* (1817) objected to Wordsworth's theory of poetic diction. Madame de Staël, who was immersed in the Romantic theories of the Germans and whose *De l'Allemagne* (1813; *Germany*, 1813) did so much to spread those ideas to England and France, disagreed with the brothers, Friedrich and August Wilhelm Schlegel, over the relative merits of the Greeks and Romans, preferring the latter. Schelling regarded Christian mythology as inferior to that of the Greeks, whereas Friedrich Schlegel, at least after his conversion to Catholicism in 1808, considered Christian literature better.

Amid such a welter of disagreement among critics of diverse nationalities writing during a period of more than five decades, can one discover anything resembling a Romantic school? Are there underlying tenets that link Peacock and Wordsworth, Schelling and Schlegel, Hugo and Heine?

The answer is a qualified yes. No movement is monolithic, and the Romantic movement, with its emphasis on individualism and its aversion to rules and imitation, can appear especially fragmented. Even individual critics changed their minds over time – Friedrich Schlegel before and after his conversion, for example. Yet the criticism that emerges from France, Italy, Germany, and England between 1770 and 1830 reveals an underlying similarity of outlook and judgment. Consistently it rejects neoclassicism and emphasizes the imagination, emotion, spontaneity, originality, and the exalted role of the writer. The unity in multeity that Romantics saw as characterizing the natural world thus exists in their own works as well.

## The sense of the past

In his *Racine et Shakespeare* (1823, 1825; *Racine and Shakespeare*, 1962), Stendhal claimed that great writers of all ages were Romantics because Romanticism is the art of creating literary works that please people at the moment, whereas classicism is the art that pleases their great-grandparents. In a similar vein, Charles Baudelaire in the "Salon de 1846" (1846; "Salon of 1846," 1964) equated Romanticism with modernism. Already quoted is Schelling's view that Romanticism dismisses the past in favor of the present.

The past that these writers dismiss, though, is in fact limited to the recent literary tradition. In his introduction to *Specimens of the Later English Poets* (1807), Robert Southey declared that "the time which elapsed from the days of Dryden to those of Pope is the dark age of English poetry." In his "Sketches of the Progress of English Poetry from Chaucer to Cowper" (1836), Southey added that "Pope closed the door against poetry" and called the age of Pope "the pinchbeck age of poetry." Francis, Lord Jeffrey, often regarded as an enemy of Romanticism because of his attacks on Wordsworth and Southey in the *Edinburgh Review*, agreed that the period between 1714 and 1760 was an "interregnum of native genius" and attacked Alexander Pope and his followers as "cold, timid, superficial." In the same essay in which Peacock satirized the Lake Poets, he wrote of neoclassical verse, "Its range is limited, and when exhausted, nothing remains but the *crambe repetita* of common-place, which at length becomes thoroughly wearisome, even to the most indefatigable readers of the newest new nothings." In continental Europe, Hugo rebelled against the tyranny of Jean Racine and Pierre Corneille, while Stendhal proclaimed himself the supporter of William Shakespeare against Racine, and of Lord Byron against Nicolas Boileau-Despréaux, whose *L'Art poétique* (1674; *The Art of Poetry*, 1683) had codified the tenets of neoclassicism. Gotthold Ephraim Lessing, Johann Gottfried Herder, Immanuel Kant, Novalis, and the Schlegels rejected the Enlightenment and mechanistic views of rationalists such as Johann Christoph Gottsched, who reduced literature and nature to formulas.

Turning away from the immediate past and its Roman sources of inspiration – one thinks of the numerous imitations of Horace, Juvenal, and Virgil in the neoclassical period – Romantic critics nevertheless did not reject history altogether. Indeed, they did much to stimulate interest in the achievements of classical Greece and the medieval period. Friedrich Schlegel was an early admirer of Aristophanes, praising the Greek comedian for his Dionysian freedom. In his long essay "Über das Studium der griechischen Poesie" (on the study of Greek poetry), written in 1794–1795 and published in 1797, he praised Greek literature as natural, spontaneous, original, and free of outside influences, all of which elements he saw lacking in the succeeding works of Rome. August Wilhelm Schlegel, Friedrich's brother, shared this view of the relative merits of Greek and Roman writing. August Wilhelm wrote his dissertation on Homeric geography and later published much about his views on classical civilization. He attacked Virgil, Ovid, Plautus, Terence, and Horace, considering them derivative, and preferred the plays of Aristophanes, Aeschylus, and Euripides. Jean Paul was another German to declare his affection for the ancient Greeks, whom he called "this beauty-intoxicated people with their serene religion in eye and heart." In works such as *Hyperion: Oder, Der Eremit in Griechenland* (1797, 1799; *Hyperion: Or, The Hermit in Greece*, 1965), Friedrich Hölderlin imagined himself a worshipper of the Greek gods and inspired by them. Johann Wolfgang von Goethe planned to write an epic about Achilles, and in his old age Heine undertook a pilgrimage to worship the Venus de Milo.

Such appreciation for classical Greece extended to France and England. Charles-Augustin Sainte-Beuve called François Auguste René Chateaubriand "Greek and pagan in spite of himself." The "in spite of himself" is superfluous, for when Chateaubriand left France for the United States in 1791, he took with him a copy of Homer. Chateaubriand's *Le Génie du Christianisme* (1799, 1800, 1802; *The Genius of Christianity*, 1802) also reveals a strong Hellenic bias, and in the preface to *Atala* (1801; English translation, 1802), Chateaubriand said that he sought "to restore in literature this love of antiquity which has been lost in our time." In 1844 two friends of Hugo, Paul Meurice and Auguste Vacquerie, presented an adaptation of Sophocles' *Antigonē* (441 B.C.; *Antigone*). In their preface they declared that Greek theater is Romantic because it is not bound by rigid rules of decorum. Sophocles mixes comedy and tragedy and is not squeamish about killing his characters. Edgar Quinet, Gérard de Nerval, and Byron traveled to Greece; John Keats added Psyche to the pantheon of Greek gods and built "a fane/ In some untrodden region of his mind" to the deity; Wordsworth wrote poems on Greek themes, such as "Laodamia" (1815) and "Ode to Lycoris" (1820). According to Peacock, the first golden age of literature was the time of Homer, Aeschylus, and Pindar. The Augustan period of Rome marked a falling off to silver, and by the latter days of the empire, poetry had degenerated to the age of brass.

Peacock maintained that this cycle of literary growth and decline repeated itself in more recent centuries: the modern golden age was the Elizabethan and Jacobean period. While the Romantics did not invent the cult of Shakespeare – that had started slightly earlier – they did much to support it and to increase public awareness of his contemporaries and predecessors. Charles Lamb's *Specimens of English Dramatic Poets Who Lived About the Time of Shakespeare* (1808) showed an early enthusiasm for the Jacobean playwright John Webster, and Lamb was among the first to appreciate the poetical qualities of non-Shakespearean drama of the sixteenth and early seventeenth centuries. Robert Southey edited the fourteenth-century *Morte d'Arthur* and wrote poems about ancient Wales. Wordsworth admired Thomas Percy's *Reliques of Ancient English Poetry* (1765), that collection of traditional ballads and folksongs dating back to the Middle Ages. No longer did the medieval period seem "dark"; "Gothic" ceased to be a term of opprobrium. Dante's *La divina commedia* (c. 1320; *The Divine Comedy*) appeared in partial English translation for the first time, reflecting this new attitude toward medieval art and literature.

France and Germany witnessed a similar Gothic revival. In the former, the writers of the age of Louis XII (1462–1515) were praised for their portrayal of the chivalric tradition, a key element of Romanticism according to Madame de Staël. August Wilhelm Schlegel argued that Gothic architecture and medieval literature were at least the equals of the works of the classical period, and this view found an echo in Wilhelm Heinrich Wackenroder's statement that "to God a Gothic temple is as pleasing as a temple of the Greeks; the crude war music of savages is to Him just as charming a sound as artful choruses and church songs." Like his brother, Friedrich Schlegel defended the age of chivalry and planned an edition of medieval Provençal poetry, a project he never completed. August Wilhelm Schlegel shared this interest in early French verse, publishing essays on the origins of chivalric romances, the Provençal literature and language, and the German *Nibelungenlied*. Herder and Friedrich Gottlieb Klopstock urged their compatriots to turn away from the Romans and instead find their inspiration in Teutonic myth. Johann Joseph Görres went so far as to describe the medieval period as "the garden of poetry, the Eden of romanticism" (*Die teutschen Volksbücher*, 1807). Yet another reflection of this newfound appreciation for the Middle Ages is Ludwig Tieck's modernized version of various *Minnelieder*, which he published in 1803. Just as Thomas Percy had collected old ballads in England and Allan Ramsay had sought out ancient Scottish poetry, so the Brothers Grimm, Görres, Clemens Brentano, and Achim von Arnim in Germany stimulated interest in the previously neglected works of their medieval compatriots.

In contrast to classical Greece and the Middle Ages, the present impressed many Romantics as artificial and prosaic. In *Northanger Abbey* (1818), Jane Austen satirized the Gothic novels of her day and the visions that they fostered. The heroine, Catherine Morland, influenced by Gothic novels such as those of Ann Radcliffe, has been imagining that bizarre and illicit activities are occurring within the Tilney household. Henry Tilney awakens her to reality when he reminds her that she is living in nineteenth-century England, not fourteenth-century Italy. In Catherine's world, "every man is surrounded by a neighbourhood of voluntary spies; and . . . roads and newspapers lay everything open."

That openness was precisely the problem for many Romantics, who saw in the Middle Ages and ancient Greece a more poetic time, when "holy were the haunted forest boughs,/ Holy the air, the water, and the fire," as Keats wrote in his "Ode to Psyche" before science had clipped the angels' wings and placed the "awful rainbow . . . in the dull catalogue of common things." Romantic critics therefore sought, and found, new historical sources for literary inspiration, themes, settings, and images, offering to writers avenues of escape from the dull world of reality.

## Imagination

Just as Romantic critics substituted for the neoclassical admiration of Rome an appreciation of ancient Greece and medievalism, so too they dethroned the neoclassical god of reason and deified the imagination in its stead. Moreover, the imagination offered another alternative to the common-sense world of the commonplace. This celebration of the imagination, like the new historical perspective, crosses national boundaries and constitutes one of the fundamentals of Romantic doctrine, even if disagreements arose over the definition of this faculty. Blake declared, "One Power alone makes a Poet; Imagination, the Divine Vision." In a letter to Walter Savage Landor dated January 21, 1824, Wordsworth says the same thing: "In poetry it is the imaginative only, i.e., that which is conversant or turns upon Infinity, that powerfully affects me."

While Blake and Wordsworth thus seem to echo each other's sentiments, in fact they do not. Wordsworth believed that the imagination permits the writer to see reality more clearly, to penetrate to what he calls in "Tintern Abbey" (1798) "the life of things." Blake, along with the majority of his contemporaries, regarded the imagination as more powerful, more creative. In his *A Vision of the Last Judgment* (1925), written about 1810, he states, "'What,' it will be Question'd, 'When the sun rises, do you not see a round Disc of fire somewhat like a Guinea?' O no no, I see an Innumerable company of the Heavenly host crying, 'Holy, Holy, Holy is the Lord God Almighty.'"

The Romantic imagination therefore frees the writer from the toils of the senses. As Blake observes in *There Is No Natural Religion* (1788), "Man's perceptions are not bounded by organs of perception; he perceives more than sense (tho' ever so acute) can discover." There is no natural religion because the senses alone never could discover the Infinite, which is accessible only through the inward eye. Such a view directly contradicts the neoclassical doctrine expressed by John Locke and Edmund Burke. In *An Essay Concerning Human Understanding* (1690), Locke stated, "It is not in the Power of the most exalted Wit, or enlarged Understanding, by any quickness or variety of Thought, to invent or frame one new single Idea in the mind." Almost seventy years later, Burke repeats this position in *A Philosophical Enquiry into the Origin of Our Ideas of the Sublime and Beautiful* (1757) when he maintains, "This power of the imagination is incapable of producing any thing absolutely new; it can only vary the disposition of those ideas which it has received from the senses."

In his famous definition of the Imagination in the thirteenth chapter of his *Biographia Literaria*, Coleridge shows how far Romantic literary theory had moved from these earlier views. Coleridge says that Burke and Locke are actually describing not Imagination but Fancy. Fancy, a lesser faculty than Imagination, merely recombines what the senses perceive. Imagination, though, is "a repetition in the finite mind of the eternal act of creation in the infinite I AM." This is the power that the true poet possesses, for, as Coleridge states in "Dejection, an Ode" (1802),

> And would we aught behold, of higher worth,
> Than that inanimate cold world allowed
> To the poor loveless ever-anxious crowd,
>     Ah! from the soul itself must issue forth
> A light, a glory, a fair luminous cloud
>     Enveloping the Earth –
> And from the soul itself there must be sent
>     A sweet and potent voice, of its own birth,
> Of all sweet sounds the life and element!

William Hazlitt agreed that "poetry is the language of the imagination and the passions" rather than an accurate rendition of reality: "Neither a mere description of natural objects, nor a mere delineation of natural feelings, however distinct or forcible, constitutes the ultimate end and aim of poetry, without the heightenings of the imagination." Consequently, he ranked poetry above painting, since the artist relies on and depicts reality, whereas poetry has the power to "represent objects, not as they are in themselves, but as they are moulded by other thoughts and feelings, into an infinite variety of shapes and combinations."

In his letter dated September 27, 1819, to his brother George, John Keats draws a similar distinction between his works and Byron's: "He describes what he sees – I describe what I imagine. Mine is the hardest task. You see the immense difference." Keats chose this more difficult path because he believed that it alone led to truth. As he writes to Benjamin Bailey (November 22, 1817), "What the imagination seizes as Beauty must be truth," and he makes an analogy to book 8 of John Milton's *Paradise Lost* (1667, 1674), in which Adam dreams of Eve, then awakes to find the vision true. In "The Eve of St. Agnes" (1820), Keats himself creates a similar illustration of the power of the imagination. Here Madeline awakens to discover the husband about whom she has just been dreaming.

Novalis is an important German spokesman for the imagination. His novel *Heinrich von Ofterdingen* (1802; *Henry of Ofterdingen*, 1842) presents the poet moving from the world of reality to that of illusion, the artist's proper realm. Another of Novalis' works, *Hymnen an die Nacht* (1800; *Hymns to the Night*, 1897, 1948), praises the night because it offers dreams and visions. By blocking one's perception of the outside world, it allows inner, truer reality to express itself. Since the fairy tale is the form of literature least tied to reality, Novalis deemed it the most poetic and advocated it as a model for prose fiction.

Along with so many of his fellow Romantics, Schelling endowed the imagination with the power to create its own worlds, and he praised most highly those writers, such as Miguel de Cervantes, Shakespeare, Goethe, and Dante, who used the imagination in that way. Wilhelm Heinrich Wackenroder claimed that in painting his celebrated Madonna, Raphael did not rely on an actual model but instead copied a dream vision, for to create such a masterpiece Raphael could only have relied on his imagination. This view suggests Jean Paul's belief that "poetry is kindred to dreaming and dreaming is involuntary poetry." It also reminds one of the supposed origins of works such as Coleridge's "Kubla Khan" (1816), subtitled "A Vision in a Dream," and Keats' *The Fall of Hyperion: A Dream* (1856).

Friedrich Schlegel, in *Geschichte der alten und neuen Literatur* (1815; *Lectures on the History of Literature, Ancient and Modern*, 1818), spoke of imagination as "raising the veil of mortality" to reveal "the secret of the unseen world." Similarly, Friedrich Schleiermacher's *Über die Religion* (1799; *On Religion*, 1892) saw the poet as presenting "the heavenly and eternal as an object of pleasure and unity," and Karl Wilhelm Ferdinand Solger glorified the artist's imagination as divine and its creative powers as godlike.

Elsewhere in Europe, Romantic critics made similar statements. Giacomo Leopardi rejected Locke and Burke as firmly as did Coleridge or Novalis when he maintained that "the imagination sees the world not as it is; it fabricates, invents." Alfred de Vigny again treats imagination as creative, and, in the "Salon of 1846," Baudelaire describes the North as Romantic, the South as classical because "the North is all for colour; dreams and fairy-tale are born of the mist." He saw the south of Europe as too concerned with depicting reality to qualify as Romantic.

Plato's concept of the Ideal is evident here; the artist's task is to pierce the mask that the senses impose, to move beyond the realm of shadows in order to bring to others true vision and understanding. Yet the Romantic Imagination can do still more. Not only can it perceive the ideal shrouded by the real, but also it can create a "Beauty .../ Surpassing the most ideal Forms/ Which craft of delicate Spirits hath composed/ From earth's materials," as even Wordsworth claimed in the prospectus to *The Excursion* (1814).

## Spontaneity and emotion

Together with the celebration of the imagination came a worship of spontaneity and the passions. Literature came to be perceived, at least in its higher forms, as the result not of labor and craft but rather of inspiration and emotion. As Wordsworth wrote in his preface to *Lyrical Ballads with Other Poems* (1800 edition), "Poetry is the spontaneous overflow of powerful feelings." He condemned the "meddling intellect" that would interfere with these feelings, and in "Essay upon Epitaphs" (1810, 1876), he claimed that such inscriptions were best when "instinctively ejaculated."

On this point all Romantic critics agree. Keats, writing to John Taylor on February 27, 1818, claims to have "a few Axioms," one of which is "that if Poetry comes not as naturally as the Leaves to a tree it had better not come at all." Later that same year, on October 18, he returns to this idea: "[The] genius of poetry must work out its own salvation in a man; it cannot be matured by law and precept, but by sensation and watchfulness in itself. That which is creative must create itself." Although Byron was among the few Romantics who admired Pope, he, too, claimed that "Poetry is the expression of excited passion" and "the lava of the imagination." Coleridge went so far as to assert that "passion was the true parent of every word in existence in every language" and lamented that he himself thought too much to be a poet. This belief in the emotional, spontaneous origins of poetry led Coleridge to condemn metaphysical poets such as John Donne because they abandoned "the passion and passionate flow of poetry, to the subtleties of intellect, and to the starts of wit."

In "A Defence of Poetry" (1840, written 1821), Percy Bysshe Shelley, too, argues that the writer cannot approach his art as a mechanic or a carpenter would his craft. "A man cannot say, 'I will compose poetry,'" Shelley states;

> The greatest poet even cannot say it: for the mind in creation is as a fading coal, which some invisible influence, like an inconstant wind, awakens to transitory brightness: this power arises from within, like the color of a flower which fades and changes as it is developed, and the conscious portions of our natures are unprophetic either of its approach or its departure.

As an example, Shelley cites *Paradise Lost*, which he considered a dictated poem, dictated to Milton before it could be dictated by him, because, for Shelley, the ideal poet resembles the skylark, which sings "In profuse strains of unpremeditated art," the penultimate word here being the key to the bird's excellence.

Alexander Smith likened true poetic expression to the groans of a suffering person, involuntary utterances that reveal his mental state. John Keble, professor of poetry at Oxford University from 1832 to 1842, regarded poetry as an outlet "which minds moved by strong excitement, and aspiring by a kind of blind impulse to high ideals, have sometimes found for themselves." Thomas Carlyle argued that spontaneity and unconsciousness were characteristic of good poetry, and John Stuart Mill objected to any art that is conscious of an audience. He considered historical painting and epic poetry – regarded by the eighteenth century as the epitomes of their respective art forms – inferior because they were clearly intended for others and were not even ostensibly a spontaneous overflow of feeling. For the same reason, he preferred Wolfgang Amadeus Mozart to Gioacchino Rossini, Raphael to Peter Paul Rubens. Mozart's music, Mill says, resembles a soliloquy; Rossini's is like a dialogue. Rubens' paintings rely too heavily on narrative, and narrative always implies an audience, hence a conscious rather than spontaneous presentation. So, too, he ranked Shelley above Wordsworth, claiming that despite the latter's definition of poetry, his verse "has little even of the appearance of spontaneousness: the well is never so full that it overflows."

These views are echoed in continental Europe. Madame de Staël in *Germany* claims that literature should be "improvised rather than composed." Hugo agreed, declaring in *Notre-Dame de Paris* (1831; *The Hunchback of Notre Dame*, 1833) that a work should "gush forth in a single surge" and never be revised. The advertisement to Alphonse de Lamartine's *Harmonies poétiques et religieuses* (1830) states that such is the case with the material to follow: "Here are four books of poetry written as they were felt, without connection, without order, without apparent transition." Leopardi maintained that his poetry began with sudden flashes of inspiration; without these, he said he could not write. Since he regarded all poetry as the product of spontaneous impulses, he shared Mill's opinion of the epic. Such an extended piece "demands a plan conceived and arranged in completely cold blood," so it cannot be true poetry. Leopardi managed to rescue *The Divine Comedy* from this category by classifying it as a "long lyric where the poet and his feelings are always in evidence."

This desire for spontaneity led in Germany to the elevation of the *Volksleid* over the *Kunstleid*, the folk song over the studied composition. Hence, poets such as Edward Friedrich Möricke, Joseph von Eichendorff, Ludwig Uhland, and Heinrich Heine sought to duplicate the feelings of the former even though they were composing the latter. The Brothers Grimm believed that poetry degenerates as it moves away from the natural toward the artificial; they therefore admired folktales and folk songs. Heinrich von Kleist asserted that reflection and gracefulness cannot coexist. Drawing an analogy to literary composition, he tells of a young man who inadvertently struck a pose identical to that depicted in an exquisite ancient bronze. When the youth attempted to reproduce that posture, though, he could not, for "all movement, everything involuntary is beautiful; but crooked and distorted is everything as soon as it understands itself. Oh the understanding! The unhappy understanding!" Arthur Schopenhauer considered *The Divine Comedy* great because it is a vision, and he justified the Romantic view of youth as the time of poetry because one is then most a dreamer. Friedrich Schlegel shares this preference for vision over reality and so condemned Henry Fielding's novels while praising those of Laurence Sterne, Denis Diderot, and Jean Paul, whose works are odd and fantastic. In his review of *Des Knaben Wunderhorn* (1806, 1808), Görres spoke for the entire Romantic movement when he wrote,

> We believe frankly in the existence of a special natural poetry which to those who practice it comes as if in a dream, which is not learned and not acquired in school, but which is like the first love that even the most ignorant knows in a flash and without effort practices best when he has least studied it, and likewise worst, the more he has examined it.

Poetry not only begins with emotion but also is synonymous with it. Again one finds widespread agreement on this point. Hugo observes, "Poetry is almost nothing but feeling"; Mill eliminates the "almost" in declaring, "Poetry is feeling, confessing itself to itself in moments of solitude." Alfred de Musset agrees, calling all art nothing but feeling. In poetry, passion is "the all in all" according to Lamb, and Keats writes to his brothers on December 22, 1817, "the excellence of every Art is its intensity."

Intensity, gusto, power – these are the critical terms that Keats, Hazlitt, and Thomas De Quincey use in describing the poetic ideal. To George and Georgiana Keats the poet writes, "Though a quarrel in the streets is a thing to be hated, the energies displayed in it are fine." How much better, then, must a work of art be when it exemplifies emotion. Hazlitt, claiming that "the greatest strength of genius is shown in describing the strongest passion," considered *King Lear* (1605–1606) to be Shakespeare's greatest play because it presents the most powerful emotions. In his essay "On Gusto" (1816), Hazlitt uses this quality as the touchstone of merit in art and literature, praising painters such as Titian, Michelangelo, and Rembrandt because they have gusto, condemning Claude Gellée and Antonio Correggio because they lack it.

So too De Quincey ranks the literature of power above literature of knowledge. In making this distinction between the two types of writing, he explains why *Paradise Lost* ranks above a cookbook even though the former teaches nothing and the latter reveals some new fact in every paragraph. Milton's poem, unlike the cookbook, moves the reader. As De Quincey writes, "Tragedy, romance, fairytale, or epopee, all alike restore to man's mind the ideals of justice, of hope, of truth, of mercy, of retribution." Underlying De Quincey's criticism here is again the Romantic preference for emotion over reason.

The greatest literature not only springs from the emotions and expresses strong feeling but also stimulates an emotional response in the reader. Coleridge and Wordsworth agree that "the poet must always aim at pleasure as his specific means." Hazlitt objected to the poetry of George Crabbe because it fails to arouse any feelings; Hazlitt preferred the universal tragedies of Shakespeare to the domestic dramas of George Lillo and Edward Moore for the same reason: Shakespeare, unlike the others, "rouses the whole man within us." Any work that can so move the reader merits the label of poetry for Hazlitt, who was willing to include John Bunyan's *The Pilgrim's Progress* (1678–1684), Daniel Defoe's *Robinson Crusoe* (1719), and Giovanni Boccaccio's *Decameron* (c. 1349–1351; *The Decameron*, 1620) in that category, since each of these "lifts the spirit above the earth [and] draws the soul out of itself, with indescribable longings." Alexander Smith also rejected an absolute distinction between poetry and prose, concurring with Hazlitt that any work capable of exciting an audience qualifies as poetry.

Madame de Staël and Stendhal use this same criterion to evaluate literature. The former considered *Die Leiden des jungen Werther* (1774; *The Sorrows of Young Werther*, 1779) Goethe's greatest book because it is his most moving, whereas *Faust* (1808, 1833; English translation, 1838) and *Wilhelm Meisters Lehrjahre* (1795–1796; *Wilhelm Meister's Apprenticeship*, 1824) lack passionate intensity. Ossian, Rousseau, Edward Young, and Thomas Gray she ranked as the greatest poets because they inspire tears. She also approved of the ghosts and witches in Shakespeare because they create a sense of terror. Stendhal criticized Sir Walter Scott's novels for their lack of such passion. Leopardi used this emotional yardstick in his criticism as well, praising Dante and Petrarch for revealing their feelings and so moving others, calling the works of Giuseppe Parini and Vittorio Alfieri philosophy rather than poetry because they convey no strong sentiments.

Romantic critics believed that studies of literature should also reflect an emotional bias and, ideally, move the reader as much as the literature being investigated. Wackenroder denied that reason could offer any useful insights:

Whoever with the divining rod of searching understanding wants to discover what can be felt only from inside, will always discover only thoughts about feeling and never the feeling itself. An eternal hostile gulf is fixed between the feeling heart and the investigations of research. Feeling can only be grasped and understood by feeling.

Achim von Arnim, reviewing a play by Adam Gottlob Oehlenschläger, argued that a critic could say little to affect anyone's appreciation of the piece, since "whoever has no sense of it, won't learn it by the most extensive explanations and who has, won't need them." Novalis agrees: "Who does not immediately know and feel what poetry is cannot be taught any idea of it." Hazlitt defended his subjective approach to criticism when he maintained, "I say what I think: I think what I feel. I cannot help receiving certain impressions from things; and I have sufficient courage to declare (somewhat abruptly) what they are."

Such views explain why so much of Romantic literary criticism is impressionistic; the critic reveals his feelings and hopes to reproduce that emotion in the audience. Hugo's *William Shakespeare* (1864; English translation, 1864) offers an excellent – or egregious – example of this approach. René Wellek describes the book as "an extremely exasperating series of incoherent, flamboyant meditations full of incredible verbiage and ecstatic rhetoric," and he cites statements such as "Macbeth *is* hunger" and "Othello *is* Night" as examples of Hugo's impressionistic approach to literary criticism.

Charles Lamb discusses Cyril Tourneur's *The Revenger's Tragedy* (1606–1607) in terms of its effect on him: "I have never read it but my ears tingle, and I feel a hot blush overspread my cheeks." His annotations in *Specimens of English Dramatic Poets* (1808) consist largely of remarks on the beauties of particular passages rather than analysis, and his observations on Izaac Walton's *The Compleat Angler* (1653) are similarly subjective: "Don't you already feel your spirit filled with the scenes? – the banks of rivers – the cowslip beds – the pastoral scenes – the neat alehouses – and hostesses and milkmaids." Wordsworth urges readers to judge his poetry by their feelings, not by what they think poetry should be or rules it should obey.

## Originality

Indeed, rules are the aversion of Romantic criticism, because they chain the imagination and seek to control the passions. Hugo's *La Préface de Cromwell* (1827; English translation, 1896) rejects the dramatic unities of time and place and then goes even further. "Let us take the hammer to theories and poetic systems" of all kinds, it urges. To those who demanded that writers look to good models, that is, the classical writers of Augustan Rome and their neoclassical worshippers, and imitate these, Hugo retorts, "Is the reflection equal to the light? Is the satellite which travels unceasingly in the same circle equal to the central creative planet? With all his poetry Virgil is no more than the moon of Homer." The Académie Française kept Hugo's play

Cromwell from the stage because it violated decorum, but the organization's members were fighting a losing battle against Romanticism. Three years earlier, *Le Globe*, the leading journal of French Romanticism, had begun publishing under the banner of freedom and originality, and in 1828 the Deschamps brothers declared in their preface to *Études françaises et étrangères* that writers could no longer imitate; they must either create new works or frankly translate old ones.

By the 1820s such views were commonplace elsewhere in Europe. As early as 1759 Gotthold Ephraim Lessing had attacked imitation and praised Shakespeare as a genius who created his own models and rules instead of relying on those of others. In that same year Edward Young's *Conjectures on Original Composition in a Letter to the Author of Sir Charles Grandison* had distinguished between imitation and originality and maintained that rules are necessary only for lesser artists. Young's work quickly appeared in German translation (1760) and thus influenced critics both in England and in continental Europe.

August Wilhelm Schlegel's *Vorlesungen über dramatische Kunst und Literatur* (1809–1811; *A Course of Lectures on Dramatic Art and Literature*, 1815) argues that great artists such as Dante, Ludovico Ariosto, Michelangelo, and Raphael do not follow prescriptions. He says further that the enduring reputation of Torquato Tasso and Luís de Camões derives not from their similarities to the classical epics of Virgil and Homer but rather from their differences, for "mere imitation is always fruitless." His brother Friedrich similarly argued that the novel is superior to the epic because prose fiction is not limited by conventions. Friedrich Schlegel's desire for originality reveals itself in another way as well; he replaced the conventional review with a mixture of aphorisms and the *Charakteristik*, a form he invented by combining philosophical observations, lyric, and impressions. *Gespräch über die Poesie* (1800; *Dialogue on Poetry*, 1968) provides another example of this refusal to adhere to conventional formats, for here he mingles lecture and Platonic dialogue as he offers his comments in a seemingly random fashion.

On this subject of originality Lord Jeffrey again shows himself to be a Romantic, despite his reservations about Wordsworth's poetry. In the *Edinburgh Review* for 1802, Jeffrey criticizes the Lake Poets on precisely this issue, accusing them of borrowing ideas from Rousseau and the Germans instead of developing their own. Hazlitt refutes the notion that "genius and taste are strictly reducible to rules." Instead he equates genius with originality, the ability to bring "out some new and striking quality in nature," for which no rules or models can therefore exist. Wordsworth believed that much of the merit of *Lyrical Ballads* lay in their pioneering a new species of poetry, and despite Coleridge's reservations about his former coauthor, the *Biographia Literaria* still praises the volume for breaking new ground.

## The artist

For rules and models, Romantic literary theory substituted the artist, who assumes godlike proportions. Wordsworth's preface to *Lyrical Ballads* in many ways reflects the democratic impulses of the age, stressing as it does humble life as the proper subject of poetry and claiming that a poet "is a man speaking to men." Wordsworth sent a copy of his book to the Whig leader Charles James Fox because he believed that poems such as "Michael" and "The Brothers" supported the agrarian democracy for which Fox was fighting. When Wordsworth turns to an extended definition of the poet, however, the egalitarian impulse vanishes, for Wordsworth sees his ideal artist as

> a man . . . endued with more lively sensibility, more enthusiasm and tenderness, who has a greater knowledge of human nature, and a more comprehensive soul, than are supposed to be common among mankind; a man . . . who rejoices more than other men in the spirit of life that is in him. . . . To these qualities he has added a disposition to be affected more than other men by absent things as if they were present; . . . and from practice, he has acquired a greater readiness and power in expressing what he thinks and feels.

Finally the poet becomes the "rock of defence of human nature [binding] together by passion and knowledge the vast empire of human society."

In *Anima Poetae* (1895), Coleridge called poets "the true protoplasts who tame the chaos," and John Keble saw them as priests and doctors who provide "healing relief to secret mental emotion." Hugo believed that the artist is the civilizer, the one who transforms "iniquity to justice, the crowd to a people, the mob to nation, the nations to humanity, war to love." Novalis declared the writer's mission to be no less than that of reshaping the world; the artist could accomplish this goal only by taking "possession of one's transcendental self, to be, as it were, the quintessential ego of one's ego." Johann Gottlieb Fichte preached this same cult of the self: "Heed only yourself: turn your gaze away from everything around you and look inward on yourself. . . . Nothing outside you matters, only you yourself." In his "A Defence of Poetry" Shelley quotes Tasso's statement that only the poet and God deserve the name of creator, and in a highly charged definition of the poet he ascribes to poets the origins of every aspect of civilization:

> Poets . . . are not only the authors of language and music, of the dance and architecture, and statuary, and painting; they are the institutors of laws, and the founders of civil society, and the inventors of the arts of life, and the teachers, who draw into a certain propinquity with the beautiful and the true, that partial apprehension of the agencies of the invisible

world which is called religion. . . . Poets are the hierophants of an unapprehended imagination; the mirrors of the gigantic shadows which futurity casts upon the present. . . . Poets are the unacknowledged legislators of the world.

This emphasis on poets' own sensibilities, their reaction to reality rather than on reality itself, gave impetus to the lyric, since this genre embraces the inward and abstract. Though treating the everyday life of the lower and middle classes, Wordsworth claims that the interest of his poetry derives from the underlying feelings he expresses, not the subjects themselves.

The cult of the individual also prompted an outpouring of autobiographies; the word "autobiography" itself first appears in print in English in 1809. Among the best known of these works are Rousseau's *Les Confessions de J.-J. Rousseau* (1782, 1789; *The Confessions of J.-J. Rousseau*, 1783–1790), De Quincey's *Confessions of an English Opium Eater* (1821), Byron's *Childe Harold's Pilgrimage* (1812–1818, 1819), and Alfred de Musset's *Confession d'un enfant du siècle* (1836; *The Confession of a Child of the Century*, 1892). In *The Prelude: Or, The Growth of a Poet's Mind* (1850), Wordsworth exemplifies the egotistical sublime by writing an epic about himself. He can regard himself as worthy of the same treatment as Achilles or Aeneas because he is a poet. Werther's claim that when he looked into himself he found an entire world expresses the Romantic view of the poet, one who contains within himself all that he needs to write and whose work becomes better as it more fully reveals that internal universe.

## Conclusion

Literary movements never die; they just fade away. About 1830, though, many important Romantic theorists did die – Blake and Ugo Foscolo in 1827, Friedrich Schlegel in 1829, Hazlitt in 1830, Hegel in 1831, Goethe in 1832, Coleridge and Charles Lamb in 1834, and Leopardi two years later. In this same period a number of satires on Romanticism appeared: Peacock's *Crotchet Castle* (1831), Heine's *Die Romantische Schule* (1836; *The Romantic School*, 1876), Karl Leberecht Immermann's *Die Epigonen* (1836). The victory of Hugo's *Hernani* (English translation, 1830) in 1830 marked the triumph of Romanticism over the forces of neoclassicism in France, but even here new forces were at work to drive literature toward realism and social responsibility.

Nevertheless, what Baudelaire said in his "Salon of 1846" remains essentially true; he who says "Romanticism" is still speaking of modern literature. The Romantic impulse remains powerful. Gustave Flaubert, who was ten years old when *Hernani* was produced, repeatedly called himself a Romantic. Émile Zola, who thought he was rejecting Romanticism, reveals its pervasive influence in statements such as "poetry is everywhere, in everything," stressing the

observer's sense of reality instead of reality itself. Marcel Proust reflects the literary revolution Romanticism wrought when he makes the artist his hero and focuses on the psychological, subjective responses of the writer and his characters. André Breton, founder of the Surrealist movement, emphasized the creative forces within humankind available by tapping the dream and unconscious state. He also rejected the word "because" as a symbol of the rationality humankind must transcend if happiness is to be found. Writing in *The Nation* in 1942, Randall Jarrell grouped Ezra Pound, Hart Crane, e. e. cummings, and Wallace Stevens as Romantics also. James Joyce's stream of consciousness and interior monologues, Franz Kafka's concentration on psychological states, Kurt Vonnegut's experiments with time and space all demonstrate the survival of the Romantic aesthetic. The genie loosed by the Schlegels, Wordsworth, Hugo, and Leopardi has not yet been put back into the lamp.

## Further reading

Abrams, M. H. *The Mirror and the Lamp: Romantic Theory and the Critical Tradition*, 1953.

Allen, Guy Wilson, and Harry Hayden Clark. *Literary Criticism: Pope to Croce*, 1941.

Furst, Lilian R. *Romanticism in Perspective*, 1970.

——. *Romanticism*, 1976.

McGann, Jerome J. *The Romantic Ideology: A Critical Investigation*, 1983.

Parrinder, Patrick. *Authors and Authority: A Study of English Literary Criticism and Its Relation to Culture, 1750–1900*, 1977.

Peyre, Henri. *What Is Romanticism?*, 1977.

Prickett, Stephen, ed. *The Romantics*, 1981.

Rajan, Tilottama. *Dark Interpreter: The Discourse of Romanticism*, 1980.

Wellek, René. *A History of Modern Criticism: 1750–1950.* Vol. 2, *The Romantic Age*, 1955.

JOSEPH ROSENBLUM

**America**  *See also* Emerson; Poe

**Britain**  *See also* Byron; Coleridge; Hazlitt; Keats; Shelley; Wordsworth

**France**  *See also* Baudelaire; Gautier; Hugo; Rousseau; Sainte-Beuve; Madame de Staël; Stendhal

**Germany**  *See also* Eichendorff; Goethe; Grillparzer; Hegel; Heine; Herder; Kant; Kleist; Lessing; Schelling; Schlegel, A. W.; Schlegel, F.; Schopenhauer; Solger

**Italy**  *See also* Mazzini

**Russia**  *See also* Belinksii; Pushkin; Zhukovskii

# Jean-Jacques Rousseau

Swiss-born French writer, critic, and social theorist

**Born:** Geneva, Switzerland; June 28, 1712
**Died:** Ermenonville, France; July 2, 1778

## Biography

Jean-Jacques Rousseau was born on June 28, 1712, in Geneva, Switzerland, and his mother died nine days later. Until his tenth year, he lived in Geneva with his father and brother. In 1722, when his father fled the city to escape imprisonment for dueling, the boy was sent to live in the home of a Protestant minister in the small village of Bossey. He stayed there two years, then was apprenticed to an engraver, a martinet who frequently enforced his narrow discipline with corporal punishment. Rousseau left his apprenticeship after three years and, abandoning Geneva, headed to the nearby Savoyard city of Annecy, where he was given protection by Madame de Warens, whose name had been given to him by a priest looking for converts. Indeed, less than a month after entering that household, he was on his way to Turin to take instruction at the hospice of the Holy Spirit.

From 1728 until 1749 Rousseau held a variety of menial positions in noble households – lackey, interpreter, tutor, secretary – but still managed to educate himself, improving his French and studying mathematics, science, history, and literature. He also acquired a knowledge of music sufficient to develop a theory of composition and write an operetta entitled *Le Devin du village* (1752; *The Cunning-Man*, 1766).

Rousseau's fame began with an essay attacking the proposition that a renaissance in the arts and sciences contributed to the purification of morals. His article won first prize in a literary competition sponsored by the Academy of Dijon in 1750 and the following year was published in the prestigious *Mercure de France*. This triumph gave him the confidence to become a writer, and the next fifteen years were his most productive. He produced a novel, articles on music and economics for Denis Diderot's *Encyclopédie* (1751–1772; *Encyclopedia*, 1965), a major work of political philosophy, and a treatise on education. He also reconverted to Protestantism.

Despite his acquaintance with the leading philosophes of the period, including Diderot, Jean d'Alembert, David Hume, and Voltaire, Rousseau was essentially a loner who had difficulty forming close relationships with others – with the possible exception of his lifelong companion Thérèse Levasseur, an illiterate serving girl who bore him five children, all of whom he abandoned to a Paris foundling home. He died in his sixty-sixth year, just five weeks after the death of his great adversary, Voltaire. Buried on the Island of Poplars on the estate of Ermenonville, his remains were transferred to the Pantheon in Paris in 1794, during the French Revolution.

## Influence

Rousseau was not a literary critic as such; his influence on criticism comes more from the example he set in his own writings on politics and society than from any attempt to analyze the works of others. He believed that true creativity lay in a refusal to imitate, in a willingness to encourage a spontaneous play of impulse and temperament. His stress on the imagination, plus his sentimentality and love of nature, helped to break down the conventional formalism of the age. Rousseau's passionate advocacy of popular sovereignty and social justice affected literary creativity by undermining academic models and encouraging a spirit of revolt, an essential component of the Romantic spirit.

## Analysis

Rousseau was an eternal pilgrim, forever longing for an impossible utopia. An egomaniac, he rarely bothered to analyze the works of other writers or deal objectively with the merits of their arguments. He felt himself to be a victim of injustice and blamed his inner turmoil on the prevailing oligarchical and autocratic system which, he believed, both caused and prolonged society's discontents and miseries. In his *Social Contract* (1762), Rousseau denounced the current establishment for corrupting natural human goodness, and he demanded its replacement with a new order founded on social equality and popular sovereignty. Naturally, those in power did not find such revolutionary ideas particularly attractive. The Councillors of the Geneva Republic branded him a dangerous agnostic, an offense and threat to public morality, political order, and Christianity. They ordered the city's executioner to burn a copy of the *Social Contract* and the educational treatise, *Émile* (1762), in the square before the City Hall. They tried Rousseau *in absentia* and sentenced him to exile.

Nevertheless Rousseau's determined individualism and open defiance of prevailing authority earned him a durable reputation not only as a political revolutionary but as a literary critic, although his reputation in the latter area rested primarily on *Discours sur les sciences et les arts* (1750; *A Discourse on the Arts and Sciences*, 1750), the published version of the essay that had won the Dijon competition. In this work Rousseau had already shown a special concern for social and political questions, setting forth the beliefs with which he would be popularly associated, although, true to form, would change as he got older.

*A Discourse on the Arts and Sciences* appeared at a crucial time, both politically and artistically. Monarchy by divine right was under increasing assault from those who believed in the legitimacy of natural law. Rousseau confirmed these attacks and directed them into the field of literary criticism. In the process, he gave the reform movement additional authority, dramatizing it, infusing it with his revolutionary credo of the General Will. The Dijon polemic also occupied an important place in an ongoing dispute over the nature of cultural authority, a controversy, known as the "Quarrel of the Ancients and the Moderns", which had begun two centuries before with the appearance of Joachim du Bellay's *La Deffence et illustration de la langue françoyse* (1549; *The Defence and Illustration of the French Language*, 1939). Du Bellay's work launched classicism as a leading force in French letters by advocating a return to the purity of Greco-Roman antiquity, in place of the corrupting influences of medievalism. Rousseau put himself on the side of the moderns, however, castigating those who had an overzealous reverence for past literary forms, and he turned the debate into a consideration of the basic nature of progress, in which science and literature are united. Thus, he linked the abolition of literary rules and models to the more precarious intent of reforming society. He put literature on trial, arguing that progress in the arts had not led to the betterment of society but to its increased immorality because it made people more willing to accept despotism. Sciences, literature, and the arts "spread garlands of flowers over the iron chains with which [people] are laden, throttle in them the sentiment of that original freedom for which they seemed born, make them love their slavery, and fashion them into what is called civilized Peoples."

Rousseau believed that art (used in a generic sense to denote culture) was responsible for humanity's artificiality and discouraged naturalness, choking it in an atmosphere of uniformity and deceit. The purity of taste was further injured by too much luxury. In short, progress in the arts and sciences had added nothing to human happiness. Men of letters and courtiers were often indistinguishable in their obsequiousness. "The only praise worthy of a King," he later wrote, "is that heard, not from the mercenary mouth of an Orator, but from the voice of a free People."

According to Rousseau, true literature was possible only in a free society. Yet nothing could be judged on literary merit alone; a critic must also consider a work's political intent. The worst evil was an abuse of state power: "As long as power remains by itself on one side, [and] enlightenment and wisdom by themselves on the other, the learned will rarely think great things. . . . Peoples will continue to be base, corrupt, and wretched." Rousseau denounced those who would shackle literature with forms and systems and restraints, substituting instead reliance on imagination, sentiment, and emotion – all essential elements of the Romantic movement which would dominate European thought for the next three generations.

In committing himself to the expansion of creativity and the emancipation of humankind, however, Rousseau established a new form of authority, one which proved to be as tyrannical as the old. He was the quintessential individualist, detesting all forms of coercion and championing the rights of those victimized by authority, but he was also an apologist for a collectivism in which few activities would be immune from state interference. Humanity could indeed be forced to be free. The logical extreme of this contention would appear in a long, rambling, open letter, written in 1758, protesting the installation of a theater in Geneva (advocated by Jean d'Alembert). *Lettre à d'Alembert sur les spectacles* (1758; *A Letter to M. d'Alembert Concerning the Effects of Theatrical Entertainments*, 1759), although primarily political, contained Rousseau's only formal attempt at literary criticism and marked his break with the mainstream of the Enlightenment.

Rousseau now advocated censorship. He opposed the establishment of a theater because it would not make people virtuous. Plays, he claimed, purged passions that audiences did not have and fostered those they did, therefore doing little to develop that pride and patriotism necessary for moral order. Rousseau was especially troubled by the destructive effects of comedy: "It is all bad and pernicious. . . . And since the very pleasure of the comic is founded on a vice of the human heart, it is a consequence of this principle that the more comedy is amusing and perfect, the more its effect is disastrous for morals."

He illustrated his point with Molière's *Le Misanthrope* (1666; *The Misanthrope*, 1709). Alceste, the title character, he found much maligned and hardly a fit subject for ridicule. Alceste was "a righteous man, sincere, worthy, truly a good man." Rousseau considered Molière's derogatory treatment of such a virtuous character "inexcusable" and a "perversion of nature." Taking the argument further, he remarked that plays such as those of Molière were even more sinister because they promoted the ascendancy of women over men.

Rousseau broadened his beliefs into a discussion of the shortcomings of the theater as a whole. In his didactic universe, no room remained for independent artistic expression. Everything would be judged by a standard of what was necessary for the proper development of society. Instead of theatrical entertainment, Rousseau believed that people should be treated to appropriate civic celebrations, official sporting events, and patriotic spectacles. He expressed special admiration for the kind of public spirit manifested in one of the most reactionary and totalitarian of ancient Greek societies: Sparta. In Sparta, the laws and morals were "intimately united in the hearts of the citizens" and "made, as it were, only one single body."

Voltaire was so incensed with Rousseau's admiration for authoritarianism and his betrayal of tolerance and freedom that he asked "Has [Rousseau] become one of the church fathers?"; and, when one of Geneva's few theaters, Théâtre Rosimond, caught fire, he insinuated that Rousseau had arranged to burn it down. Rousseau's contemporaries, however, notwithstanding Voltaire, considered him more a radical than an ultra-conservative. In their minds, his devotion to social equality and artistic freedom supported the need for reform and change. Posterity's verdict is more paradoxical. In politics Rousseau worked both sides of the street: he is the ideological father both of modern democracy and of modern totalitarianism.

In literature he exerted a strong hold on those who would be the founders of the Romantic movement. Madame de Staël believed Rousseau to be the most eloquent of French writers, and in her work *De la littérature considérée dans ses rapports avec les institutions sociales* (1800; *A Treatise on Ancient and Modern Literature*, 1803, also as *The Influence of Literature upon Society*, 1813) attempted to explain how the spirit of literature changed in accordance with moral and political causes. Nevertheless, her admiration for Rousseau never led her to forsake political liberalism and feminism. François Auguste René Chateaubriand, a staunch Royalist, writing in the wake of Rousseau's powerful influence, was primarily captivated by Rousseau's linguistic color and praise of natural beauty. Though Rousseau's reputation as a literary critic came almost by default – he left no clearly enunciated theory – the strength of his personality and his social values established the primacy of personal vision and relativism. After him, it became increasingly difficult to examine works of literature without considering them in the context of their political culture.

## Principal criticism

*Discours sur les sciences et les arts*, 1750 (*The Discourse Which Carried the Praemium at the Academy of Dijon*, 1751, better known as *A Discourse on the Arts and Sciences*, 1913)
*Discours sur l'inégalité*, 1754 (*A Discourse on Inequality*, 1756)
*Lettre à d'Alembert sur les spectacles*, 1758 (*A Letter to M. d'Alembert Concerning the Effects of Theatrical Entertainments*, 1759)
*Essai sur l'origine des langues*, 1781 (*On the Origin of Languages*, 1967)

## Other major works and literary forms

Jean-Jacques Rousseau's primary importance comes from such essays as *Discours sur l'inégalité* (1754; *A Discourse on Inequality*) and *Le Sentiment des citoyens* (1764; the opinion of the citizens). He created the prototypical Romantic novel with *Julie: Ou, La Nouvelle Héloïse* (1761; *Eloise: Or, A Series of Original Letters*, 1761; also as *Julie: Or, The New Eloise*, 1968; better known as *The New Héloïse*), became a major political philosopher with *Du contrat social: Ou, Principes du droit politique* (1762; *A Treatise on the Social Contract: Or, The Principles of Political Law*, 1764), proclaimed his pedagogical expertise with *Émile: Ou, De l'éducation* (1762; *Emilius and Sophia: Or, A New System of Education*, 1762–1763), and set the style of the modern autobiography with *Les Confessions de J.-J. Rousseau* (1782, 1789; *The Confessions of J.-J. Rousseau*, 1783–1790).

### NOVEL

*Julie: Ou, La Nouvelle Héloïse*, 1761 (*Eloise: Or, A Series of Original Letters*, 1761; also as *Julie: Or, The New Eloise*, 1968; better known as *The New Héloïse*)

### PLAYS

*Le Devin du village*, 1752 (*The Cunning-Man*, 1766)
*Narcise: Ou, L'Amant de lui-même*, 1752

### NONFICTION

*Dissertation sur la musique moderne*, 1743
*Du contrat social: Ou, Principes du droit politique*, 1762 (*A Treatise on the Social Contract: Or, The Principles of Political Law*, 1764)
*Émile: Ou, De l'éducation*, 1762 (*Emilius and Sophia: Or, A New System of Education*, 1762–1763)
*Le Sentiment des citoyens*, 1764
*Quatre Lettres à M. le président de Malesherbes contenant le vrai tableau de mon caractère et les vrais motifs de toute ma conduite*, 1779
*Les Dialogues: Ou, Rousseau juge de Jean-Jacques*, 1780, 1782
*Essai sur l'origine des langues*, 1781 (*On the Origin of Languages*, 1967)
*Les Rêveries du promeneur solitaire*, 1782 (*The Reveries of the Solitary Walker*, 1783)
*Les Confessions de J.-J. Rousseau*, 1782, 1789 (*The Confessions of J.-J. Rousseau*, 1783–1790)
*Political Writings*, 1915, 1954
*Religious Writings*, 1970

### MISCELLANEOUS

*The Works*, 1763–1773 (10 volumes)
*The Miscellaneous Works*, 1767 (5 volumes)
*Œuvres complètes*, 1780–1789 (33 volumes)
*Œuvres complètes de Jean-Jacques Rousseau*, 1959–1969 (4 volumes)

## Further reading

Besse, Guy. *Jean-Jacques Rousseau, l'apprentissage de l'humanité*, 1988.
Bonhôte, Nicolas. *Jean-Jacques Rousseau, vision de l'histoire et autobiographie: étude de sociologie de la littérature*, 1992.
Cassirer, Ernst. *The Question of Jean-Jacques Rousseau*, 1954. Translated by Peter Gay.
Chapman, John W. *Rousseau: Totalitarian or Liberal?*, 1956.
Crocker, Lester. *Jean-Jacques Rousseau*, 1968, 1973 (2 volumes).
Green, Fredrick. *Jean-Jacques Rousseau: A Critical Study of His Life and Writings*, 1955.
Grimsley, Ronald. *Jean-Jacques Rousseau: A Study in Self-Awareness*, 1961.
Hamilton, James F. *Rousseau's Theory of Literature: The Poetics of Art and Nature*, 1979.
Hartle, Ann. *The Modern Self in Rousseau's Confessions: A Reply to St. Augustine*, 1983.
Harvey, Simon, Marian Hobson, David Kelley, and Samuel Taylor, eds. *Reappraisals of Rousseau*, 1980.
Havens, George R. *Jean-Jacques Rousseau*, 1978.
Hendel, Charles. *Jean-Jacques Rousseau, Moralist*, 1934 (2 volumes).
Kavanagh, Thomas M. *Writing the Truth: Authority and Desire in Rousseau*, 1987.
Simon, Julia. *Mass Enlightenment: Critical Studies in Rousseau and Diderot*, 1995.
Starobinski, Jean, et al. *Jean-Jacques Rousseau: quatres études*, 1978.
Wokler, Robert. *Rousseau*, 1995.
Wright, Ernest. *The Meaning of Rousseau*, 1929.

WM. LAIRD KLEINE-AHLBRANDT

*See also* Diderot; Romanticism; Voltaire

# John Ruskin

English social and cultural critic

**Born:** London, England; February 8, 1819
**Died:** Coniston, Lake District, England; January 20, 1900

## Biography

John Ruskin was born on February 8, 1819, to John James Ruskin, a London wine merchant, and his cousin Margaret Cox Ruskin, a Scotswoman four years her husband's senior. After a childhood best described as oppressive, Ruskin attended Oxford University, where he concentrated on writing poetry, winning the Newdigate Prize in 1839 for his poem "Salsette and Elephanta." His studies were interrupted by illness in 1840, but he completed his degree in 1841.

His early public life was marked by his championing of J. M. W. Turner's painting, an interest which engendered *Modern Painters* and led him to become a highly influential art critic. He married Effie Gray, his cousin, in 1848, but the marriage was annulled six years later, still unconsummated. In the meantime, Ruskin continued to travel and to collect art, along with sketches and other materials for his later works on art, architecture, and society. During this middle period of his life, Ruskin brought serious attention to the works of the Pre-Raphaelites, especially those of William Holman Hunt, and he established himself as a social critic.

Ruskin's later years were marked by recognition and by trouble. In 1870 Oxford honored him by naming him Slade Professor, and his Oxford lectures on art gave him the chance to solidify his ideas and extend his influence. An intolerant, disparaging remark about James McNeill Whistler's painting *Nocturne in Black and Gold*, however, led to Whistler's successful libel suit and Ruskin's resignation from Oxford – for all practical purposes, his retreat from public life. Ruskin retired to his estate, Brantwood, in the English Lake District, where he was overtaken by his family's tendency toward insanity, suffering breakdowns in the years between 1878 and 1885 and again from 1889 to 1900, when he died. In the interval of lucidity between 1885 and 1889, Ruskin worked on his remarkable autobiography, *Praeterita*, which remained unfinished at his death.

## Influence

In *The Last Romantics* (1949), Graham Hough, exploring the origins of William Butler Yeats' poetry, found that Yeats owed much to the Pre-Raphaelites. The Pre-Raphaelites, in turn, found the wellspring of their ideas in John Ruskin. According to Hough, "The new ideas about the arts and their relations to religion and the social order all seemed to originate somewhere in the dense jungle of Ruskin's works." Ruskin brought criticism in general and art criticism in particular out of triviality and into the center of

intellectual life, tying art to morality, religion, and the social order. His seminal writings led to Matthew Arnold's position that poetry was a kind of religion, to Walter Pater's statement that success consisted of being able "to burn always with this hard, gemlike flame," to William Holman Hunt's remaking of English painting, and to William Morris' interrelating of art and politics. Ruskin's political writings are largely credited with inspiring the Labour movement, and Mahatma Gandhi, who as a young man translated *Unto This Last* into Hindi and reported that he found some of his deepest convictions in Ruskin's writings. Ruskin's influence has persisted, affecting the approaches of such critics as Harold Bloom and Northrop Frye and laying the groundwork for archetypal criticism in general.

## Analysis

John James Ruskin, the wine merchant, perhaps feeling too keenly the fact that his money could not win for him social acceptance, attempted roughly the same trick that Charles Dickens would later chronicle in *Great Expectations* (1860–1861): the creation of a gentleman. The elder Ruskin, acting the part of Magwitch to his son's Pip, provided young John with all the accoutrements of gentility: travel in Europe, the finest tutors, an Oxford education, and, especially, an acquaintance with art. This last element in Ruskin's up-bringing was the most crucial, since at that time in England art was the province of the very few, a closed group to which entry meant status. Ironically, the son turned the father's intentions upside down, for when the younger Ruskin gained access, his primary act as a power in the world of art was to widen art's province, to popularize art for the masses, and to assert that since all great art is essentially theophany (a manifestation of God's spirit to humankind), great art belongs to all people, not solely to the privileged few.

This democratization of art is the source from which flow not only Ruskin's ideas on art, but his basic tenets in social criticism as well. As interpreter, Ruskin was at great pains to train his audience's eyes to see again – to see nature as it really is, and to see art with something of the consciousness and sensibilities of the artist. That most people were incapable of seeing in these ways was, in Ruskin's view, not their fault, but the fault of a system which forced on them an unnatural disjunction. The manufacturing process, for example, divorced the workman from the product of his labor, reducing the human being to a pair of hands and eliminating all but monetary value from his labor. No wonder, then, that the worker took no pride in the product, and that the quality of the product declined. As people succumbed more and more to these alienating influences, they become equally alienated from art and from all that Ruskin saw as civilized. Thus, the same impulse that led him to write *Modern Painters* as a guidebook to the ideas of power, imitation, truth, beauty, and relation in painting also demanded, ultimately, that he attack the very social and economic evils which he believed had destroyed the ability of people to form wholesome relationships with one another. As a result, any treatment of Ruskin's critical theories necessarily begins with his aesthetic criticism and thence must lead into his views about civilization itself.

In *Modern Painters*, Ruskin urges his readers repeatedly to look, to see, to observe. Since nature is theophany, nature is an expression of the divine, and so to be an artist – or to appreciate art – one must first appreciate the natural world. Art, for Ruskin, merely fixes and interprets nature according to the artist's special vision, and Ruskin the critic stood in the place of priest, the mediator between the divine and the people. By heightening the public's appreciation of art, he also accomplished the improvement of his readers, by training them to share in his vision.

Foremost in the perceptions this vision produced was beauty, which for Ruskin was central to nature's theophanic message. Great art depends upon vision and imitation, and so close observation is its foundation. Although Ruskin did not simply advocate realism, a slavish faithfulness to the literal image, his views expressly run counter to the notions of the proponents of the grand style, who sought to improve upon nature. Ruskin demanded that beauty be combined with truth, which means that the artist combines the natural beauty of God's creation with the artist's own prophetic consciousness. Artists, to paraphrase William Wordsworth, half create what they perceive. As a result of this stance, Ruskin deplored such highly regarded figures as Canaletto and the Dutch realists as slavish copiers, while he hailed Turner's later works, such as *Steamer in a Snowstorm* and *Slave Ship*, as truer to nature, despite Turner's venturing beyond literal representation of the actual scenes.

These basic tenets became the foundation of Ruskin's architectural writings too, and these, *The Seven Lamps of Architecture* and *The Stones of Venice*, marked the beginning of his shift away from pure art criticism and toward the more overtly political writings of his later life. Ruskin anticipated the coming revolution in architecture, and he condemned laissez-faire capitalism, foreseeing that it would produce only a purely mechanical architecture, devoid of any recognizable human presence. Ruskin's answer to this new architecture was a return to Gothic. He perceived the Gothic city – Venice, for example – as equivalent to the heavenly city, contrasting that vision of loveliness with the modern manufacturing centers belching smoke and noise. The course of architecture was set in a direction away from the beauty and truth of nature and therefore that course was destructive to humanity. In what is almost certainly a conscious adaptation of Thomas Carlyle's philosophy of clothes from *Sartor Resartus* (1833–1834), Ruskin asserted that a return to the Gothic style would save humanity, placing it in a purer, more beautiful environment that more closely resembled nature, and therefore God. Without such a revival, Ruskin was convinced that humanity was bound toward ugliness, which he equated with death. Ruskin's vision of humankind as headed down the road to self-destruction is found at its fullest in his masterpiece of social criticism, *Unto This Last*, a stinging indictment of the evils of laissez-faire capitalism.

Ruskin's precise influence on the literature of his time, though certainly profound, is somewhat more difficult to trace than his influence on art and social criticism. Ruskin was the generative force in a new kind of art and a new kind of social criticism, but his contributions to literature took place within the context of a strong and vital tradition. Thus, in some ways Ruskin simply participated in the ongoing reformations of a period that would certainly have been significant without his influence. Yet in other ways his influence, as it did in art, paved the way for developments that would not have occurred so easily without his contribution.

The basic thrust of Ruskin's work, like that of Alfred, Lord Tennyson, Thomas Carlyle, Robert Browning, and so many other Victorians, is Romantic. The emphasis Ruskin places on individual perception – that is, the importance of vision – is also found in the works of Romantic poets such as William Blake and William Wordsworth, as well as in such poems as Tennyson's "The Lady of Shalott" and "The Holy Grail" and Browning's "Childe Roland" and *The Ring and the Book* (1868–1869). In addition, Ruskin helped return to literature the methods of biblical typology: the telescoping of historical events by using one event to refer to an entire sequence. In an age dominated by religious doubt, Ruskin removed typology from strictly biblical applications and made it a powerful literary device. In the famous opening to *The Stones of Venice*, for example, Ruskin uses typological references in order to conflate the distant past with the present, allowing the history of the powerful Renaissance city-state of Venice to stand as a warning to modern Britain, which Ruskin thinks is headed down essentially the same path toward destruction.

In addition to participating in ongoing literary movements, Ruskin's work also engendered important developments. His emphasis on the personal nature of vision and on the role of art as a force which leads the audience to share in the act of vision can be seen in Browning's concept of the artist as "Maker-see," for example. Ruskin's major influence, however, comes through the Pre-Raphaelites, whom Ruskin granted legitimacy. Ruskin's writings validating Turner's art led inevitably to applying the same tenets to literature, thus freeing the artist from many of the constraints laid on by centuries of British literary tradition. Thus, the Pre-Raphaelites, led by Ruskin's disciple Walter Pater, evolved into the aesthetic movement, where art became important, not for its social utility but for its own sake. The thrust of this movement also paved the way for modernism, which freed the novel to deal with more subjective kinds of reality, and for such modern and post-modern schools of criticism as archetypal criticism reader-response theory.

## Principal criticism

*Modern Painters*, 1843–1860
*The Seven Lamps of Architecture*, 1849
*The Stones of Venice*, 1851–1853
*Unto This Last*, 1860
*Sesame and Lilies*, 1865
*The Crown of Wild Olives*, 1866
*Lectures on Art*, 1870
*Fors Clavigera*, 1871–1884
*The Eagle's Nest*, 1872
*Deucalion*, 1875–1883
*The Storm Cloud of the Nineteenth Century*, 1884

## Other major works and literary forms

The bulk of John Ruskin's works, and certainly his most important, consists of nonfictional prose, from multivolume works to hundreds of journal essays. Besides these productions, his incomplete autobiography, *Praeterita* (1885–1889), is most important and most affecting. It has both biographical and psychological interest, since it was written during Ruskin's last long period of lucidity before he died. Ruskin also wrote minor poems, one of which won the Newdigate Prize at Oxford University, and for Euphemia Gray, whom he later married, he penned a children's tale entitled *The King of the Golden River: Or, The Black Brothers, a Legend of Syria* (1851).

CHILDREN'S LITERATURE
*The King of the Golden River: Or, The Black Brothers, a Legend of Syria*, 1851

NONFICTION
*Praeterita*, 1885–1889
*The Diaries of John Ruskin*, 1956–1959 (3 volumes; Joan Evans and John Howard Whitehouse, editors)
*The Brantwood Diary of John Ruskin*, 1971 (Helen Viljoen, editor)
*The Ruskin Family Letters: The Correspondence of John James Ruskin, His Wife, and Their Son*, 1801–1843, 1973 (2 volumes; Van Akin Burd, editor)

MISCELLANEOUS
*The Works of John Ruskin*, 1902–1912 (39 volumes; E. T. Cook and Alexander Wedderburn, editors)

## Further reading

Abse, Joan. *John Ruskin the Passionate Moralist*, 1982.
Ball, Patricia M. *The Science of Aspect: The Changing Role of Fact in the Works of Coleridge, Ruskin, and Hopkins*, 1971.
Birch, Dinah. *Ruskin's Myths*, 1988.
Evans, Joan. *John Ruskin*, 1954.
Fitch, Raymond E. *The Poison Sky: Myth and Apocalypse in Ruskin*, 1982.
Helsinger, Elizabeth K. *Ruskin and the Art of the Beholder*, 1982.
Hough, Graham. "Ruskin," in *The Last Romantics*, 1949.
Landow, George P. *The Aesthetic and Critical Theories of John Ruskin*, 1971.
Leon, Derrick. *Ruskin the Great Victorian*, 1949.
Miller, J. Hillis. "Myth as 'Hieroglyph' in Ruskin," in *Studies in Literary Imagination*, 8 (1975).
Rosenberg, John D. *The Darkening Glass: A Portrait of Ruskin's Genius*, 1961.
Sawyer, Paul. *Ruskin's Poetic Argument: The Design of His Major Works*, 1985.
Stein, Richard L. *The Ritual of Interpretation: The Fine Arts as Literature in Ruskin, Rossetti, and Pater*, 1975.

WILLIAM CONDON

*See also* Arnold; Literary Theory in the Age of Victoria; Pater; Swinburne

# Russian Formalism

The critical movement known as Russian Formalism attempted to focus attention on the literary work itself – on its linguistic and structural properties – and not on the author or on the sociohistorical conditions under which it was produced. For all its renown, Russian Formalism lasted only a short while as even a loose alliance of literary critics and theorists, arising in the mid-1910s and largely coming to an end as a recognizable movement by around 1930, due to the increasingly hostile opposition of the Soviet regime. Nonetheless, the movement's influence on subsequent developments in literary criticism has been substantial – some of its members went on to become part of the Prague School of structuralism, which was the direct successor of Russian Formalism, while in more modern times American New Criticism, both French and Russian structuralism, as well as other recent trends in critical thought can be seen as owing much to certain notions that derive ultimately from the Formalists.

Although reacting sharply against the predominant tendency in Russian criticism to interpret literature in terms of political ideas and the social message of the text, the Formalists were not without their predecessors in Russia. Aleksandr Potebnya's nineteenth-century lectures on poetic language, while at times disparaged by the Formalists, nonetheless recognized the uniqueness of poetic discourse as well as an awareness that the study of literature must be accompanied by a close study of language itself. The comparative literary historian Aleksandr Veselovskii carefully examined the nature of the literary work, arriving at the notion of the "motif" as the basic narrative unit and seeing the plot not so much in terms of story line as in the artistic arrangement of such units. The Russian Symbolist movement in poetry, which arose at the turn of the twentieth century, created a new interest in the poetic craft, resulting in a greater attention to the poetic word, to sound, to the relationship between the signifier (representation) and the signified (meaning). In terms of approach, two Symbolist poets, Valerii Briusov and especially Andrei Belyi, undertook notable studies of Russian versification; Belyi's detailed analyses of verse forms helped lay the groundwork for a statistical approach toward the analysis of meter and rhythm.

## History

Russian Formalism, though, was too fluid and too variegated a movement to be defined solely in terms of its antecedents. If in its initial period the emphasis was on a rather static and simplified definition of the literary work as the sum of its poetic devices, then by its later stages it viewed the individual text as a more elaborate system, in which the internal elements affect each other in complex ways and must also be viewed within the context created by other works. Formalism was constantly evolving as new hypotheses were put forth, tested, modified, and superseded. And as well, individual Formalists differed greatly in their backgrounds and their interests. One center, the Moscow Linguistic Circle, was, as the name implies, strongly oriented toward the role of language in the literary work; the other, in St. Petersburg, was the more heterogeneous *Opoyaz* (an acronym for the Russian phrase meaning Society for the Study of Poetic Language). The members of the former included Roman Jakobson and Petr Bogatyriov (both of whom were later associated with Czech structuralism as well), and Grigorii Vinokur. Leading figures in the St. Petersburg group during in its first years were Viktor Shklovskii, Boris Eikhenbaum, and Lev Yakubinskii. In 1920 the Division of Literary History at the Petrograd State Institute of Art History became a major focal point for Russian Formalism; Shklovskii and Eikhenbaum were participants in the research center, as were Iurii Tynianov and Boris Tomashevskii, two important figures in the movement during the 1920s, and several future eminent scholars who remained on the periphery of the movement, such as Viktor Vinogradov. The chair was Viktor Zhirmunskii, who had his differences with *Opoyaz* and the other Formalists, but whose own writings in many cases are in keeping with the broad program of Formalism. Others were more or less closely associated with Formalism at various times, including the folklorist Vladimir Propp and the theorist Osip Brik.

Along with Jakobson and Shklovskii, Brik was one of those who helped strengthen a natural link between the Formalists and the poetic movement known as Russian Futurism. The Futurists, in their attempts to do away with conventional language and to revolutionize both the syntax and vocabulary of poetry, were, already before the rise of Formalism, paying attention to language in a manner that had much in common with Formalist concerns. Of particular importance in this regard was the effort to create a "trans-sense language" (*zaumnyi iazyk*). The Futurist poet Vladimir Maiakovskii was personally close to several of the Formalists, but more important from a theoretical standpoint were the writings and poetry of Velimir Khlebnikov, who, *inter alia*, tried to find inherent meanings in various sounds and, even more radically than Maiakovskii, experimented with poetic neologisms.

During the 1920s Futurists and Formalists came together on the journal *Lef* (an acronym for Left Front of Art), and,

after that journal was closed, *Novyi lef* (the new Lef). However, both the journal and the critical movement came under increasingly fierce attack by Marxist critics; in response, Formalist critics moved from the "pure" Formalism of the school's early years to a greater concern with placing literature in a sociological context, while continuing to examine closely the purely literary features of the artistic work. The attempt at a reconciliation of Marxism and Formalism failed, however, and while the individual critics were, in many cases, to remain active and productive for several more decades, Formalism as a movement and as a theory was largely abandoned within the Soviet Union from about or soon after 1930.

## Key concepts

The Russian Formalists began with the notions that literature has specific features that differentiate it from other forms of human endeavor, and that the object of literary scholarship is to define these distinguishing qualities and focus narrowly on the actual text. In the oft-quoted words of Roman Jakobson, "the subject of literary scholarship is not literature as a whole, but literariness, or that which causes a given work to be a work of literature." The task, then, was to define literariness. Viktor Shklovskii, in some ways the liveliest and most programmatic of the Formalists, rejected the widely held idea that imagery is the distinguishing feature of literature; he pointed out that not all imagery is found in literature, nor are all literary texts necessarily based on imagery. Rather, as he noted in his early essay "Art as Device" (1916), the function of art is to renew the very art of perceiving, to deautomatize the manner in which objects are experienced. Therefore the primary device of literature, is "defamiliarization," which Shklovskii illustrates by citing Lev Tolstoi's story "Kholstomer," in which the human world is described through the eyes of a horse, and, in *War and Peace*, his literal description of an opera as though by a person totally unfamiliar with theatrical convention. Such descriptions undermine "automatic" social and linguistic conventions, slowing the act of perception, and ultimately calling attention to the device, to the formal qualities of the art. The very qualities that make the work artistic, therefore, become the chief object of aesthetic perception.

In studying prose fiction, the Formalists largely eschewed issues of psychological motivation or social theme, concentrating instead on structural elements and narrative technique. Thus Propp, in what has become the highly influential *Morphology of the Folktale* (published 1928; English translation, 1958), saw all Russian fairy tales, despite their ostensible variety in terms of theme and story, as exhibiting the same basic narrative structure and containing functionally similar characters. In examining texts belonging to the literary rather than the folk tradition, Formalists were particularly drawn to works in which the aesthetic qualities came to the fore: Shklovskii talks of the "laying bare of the device." He wrote an admiring essay (1921) on Laurence Sterne's *Tristram Shandy*, with its playful mockery of novelistic convention, its virtuosic parody, and its self-awareness of literary form; Shklovskii concludes by polemically calling *Tristram Shandy* "the most typical novel in world literature." Eikhenbaum's essay on "How Gogol''s 'Overcoat' Was Made" (1919) is equally polemical, undercutting the heretofore predominant readings of the story. According to Eikhenbaum, the work is not "about" the poor clerk who dies after his newly acquired overcoat is stolen; rather, he argues, the focus is on the telling itself, on a form called *skaz* (a concept elaborated elsewhere by Eikhenbaum and several other theorists associated with Formalism), in which the narrator takes on a distinctive voice. Here the *skaz* results in a grotesque effect through the accumulation of extraneous detail and abrupt shifts from the comic to the pathetic.

Implied in Eikhenbaum, and stated outright in Shklovskii, is the parodic intent of the author. If the Formalists studied literature as a more or less closed system, they nonetheless saw it as a system that was constantly evolving and shifting. Parody of form or genre is intrinsic to creative renewal; hence *Tristram Shandy* becomes the most typical of novels precisely because it serves as a parody of the form, thereby opening it up to new directions. In "Dostoevskii and Gogol': Toward a Theory of Parody" (1921) Tynianov shows how Fedor Dostoevskii's early imitation of Nikolai Gogol' was replaced by parody, which allowed Dostoevskii not just to appropriate Gogolian devices, but to refashion them into a system of his own.

This article was one of the first to present a Formalist view of literary history, and Tynianov went on to elaborate his views, most notably in "On Literary Evolution" (1927), where he argues that an emphasis on evaluative issues causes literary history to become a history of "generals." Instead, he sees literary change as involving an evolution of the total literary system; the "dominant" (roughly speaking, the defining characteristic of a mode or genre) shifts over time, as does the "attitude" of a given school, which, for instance, may come to employ forms that once were regarded as nonliterary. Tynianov, along with in particular Shklovskii and Eikhenbaum, developed a complex view of literary development; they saw it not as a straightforward process, but as an ongoing battle between tradition and innovation, as the constant interaction of complex forces. In reacting against recent trends an author may in fact go back to the more distant past, motifs and devices once belonging to subliterary genres may become "canonized" as literary, and the great writer is often influenced as much by second-rate literature as by other "generals." Literary influence is not so much direct, father to son, as oblique, uncle to nephew or perhaps grandfather to grandson. This approach to literary development led in turn to a revisionist view of (especially) Russian literature, with the significance of specific writers and works reevaluated.

## Verse theory

In no other realm did the Formalists have so lasting an impact as in the study of verse form. Eikhenbaum's *The Melodics of Russian Lyric Verse* (1923) explored the nature of poetic intonation as it arises through the interaction between rhythm and syntax, and Tynianov, in *The Problem of Verse Language* (1924), distinguished the language of verse from that of prose and argued for the importance of rhythm as the most prominent feature of verse. Roman Jakobson laid the groundwork for the linguistically based approach to verse that has retained its influence among students of Russian versification to the present day; of particular significance in this regard is his *On Czech Verse, Particularly as Compared to Russian* (1923), where he contrasted Russian and Czech verse in terms of their dominant prosodic feature (fixed versus free stress position) and pointed out that rhythmical patterns, rather than metrical scheme, determine the nature of verse. A trilogy of monographs written by Viktor Zhirmunskii during the 1920s (*The Composition of Lyric Poems*, 1921; *Rhyme: Its History and Theory*, 1923; *Introduction to Metrics: The Theory of Verse*, 1925) are still of value for their systematic analyses of verse form. The most important single contributor to the subsequent study of Russian versification, however, was Boris Tomashevskii, whose *Russian Versification: Metrics* (1923) and *On Verse* (1929) laid out the methodology and the principles for the statistical study of verse features that have governed much of the most important work by Russian meterists.

## Aftermath and assessment

Despite the demise of Russian Formalism as a unified movement, virtually all those associated with it went on to have distinguished and often varied careers. Jakobson became not only the leading Slavic linguist of his era, but an important contributor to fields ranging from versification to folklore to medieval studies. Tynianov's interests perhaps ranged the furthest afield; while continuing his literary studies, he went on to write film scripts (he and several other Formalists also wrote important theoretical articles on film) and gained renown for several historical novels on literary themes. Others pursued more conventional scholarly careers: Zhirmunskii, who published numerous studies on both Russian and comparative topics; Tomashevskii, who helped edit scholarly editions of the works by many nineteenth-century writers at the same time that he made further contributions to the study of verse; and Eikhenbaum, whose work on Tolstoi, begun during his Formalist years, continued right up to his death several decades later.

Nearly all the leading figures in Russian Formalism were born in the 1890s, and thus they were only in their twenties and thirties during its heyday. And perhaps for that very reason their early writings often exhibited an impetuousness and extremism. Eikhenbaum's insistence that the sympathy expressed toward the hero of Gogol''s "The

Overcoat" functions only as a stylistic device in the story seems surely an overstatement. More generally, "defamiliarization," while a striking literary technique, hardly seems as prominent as Shklovskii claims, and the exclusive focus on the literary text in early Formalist writings, while correcting the then prevalent tilt toward sociological and biographical interpretations, nonetheless seems excessively narrow. Still, their achievements are considerable. Even (or particularly) the most extreme of their pronouncements can to this day excite with their freshness and originality. The Formalists were among the first to place the actual literary text at the center of scholarly inquiry, and they emphasized the greater sensitivity to language that distinguishes the literary text. Their discussions of parody and of literary evolution created a more sophisticated and nuanced understanding of literary history. They created a heightened awareness of distinctive narrative voices (through the study of *skaz*), and in paying attention to the constituent elements of the literary work they were able to draw a distinction between the literal story (*fabula*) and the artistic arrangement of plot elements to realize the story within a literary work (*syuzhet*). Modern verse studies in particular owe their very essence to the Formalists, who called attention to the interaction of meter and rhythm, the significance of sound patterns, and the compositional role of rhyme and stanzaic forms. Thus the Russian Formalists contributed immensely to the development of modern literary theory, both in their own works, as well as through the direct and indirect influence they were to have on subsequent generations of critics who went on to revise and develop their insights.

## Further reading

Any, Carol. *Boris Eikhenbaum: Voices of a Russian Formalist*, 1994.

Bann, Stephen, and John E. Bowlt, eds. *Russian Formalism: A Collection of Articles and Texts in Translation*, 1973.

Erlich, Victor. *Russian Formalism: History–Doctrine*, 1969 (third edition).

Hansen-Löve, Aage A. *Der russische Formalismus: methodologische Rekonstruktion seiner Entwicklung aus dem Prinzip der Verfremdung*, 1978.

Jackson, Robert Louis, and Stephen Rudy, eds. *Russian Formalism: A Retrospective Glance: A Festschrift in Honor of Victor Erlich*, 1985.

Jameson, Fredric. *The Prison-House of Language: A Critical Account of Structuralism and Russian Formalism*, 1972.

Lemon, Lee T., and Marion J. Reis, eds. *Russian Formalist Criticism: Four Essays*, 1965.

Matejka, Ladislav, and Krystyna Pomorska, eds. *Readings in Russian Poetics: Formalist and Structuralist Views*, 1971.

Pike, Christopher, ed. *The Futurists, the Formalists, and the Marxist Critique*, 1979.

Pomorska, Krystyna. *Russian Formalist Theory and its Poetic Ambiance*, 1968.

Steiner, Peter. *Russian Formalism: A Metapoetics*, 1984.

Striedter, Jurij. *Literary Structure, Evolution, and Value: Russian Formalism and Czech Structuralism Reconsidered*, 1989.

Thompson, Ewa M. *Russian Formalism and Anglo-American New Criticism: A Comparative Study*, 1971.

Wellek, René. *A History of Modern Criticism: 1750–1950*. Vol. 7, *German, Russian, and East European Criticism, 1900–1950*, 1991.

BARRY P. SCHERR

*See also* Bakhtin; Eikhenbaum; Jakobson; Lotman; Prague School; Propp; Shklovskii; Todorov; Tynianov

# Thomas Rymer

English critic, translator, and editor

**Born:** Yafforth Hall (near Northallerton), Yorkshire, England; c. 1643
**Died:** London, England; December 13, 1713

## Biography

Although Thomas Rymer's birth date is uncertain, it is believed that he was born at Yafforth Hall, near Northallerton, Yorkshire, around 1643. His father, Ralph Rymer, a Puritan landholder in Yorkshire, was hanged for his part in the Presbyterian plot against Charles II in 1663. Rymer attended grammar school in Northallerton and was admitted to Sidney-Sussex College, Cambridge University, in 1659. He left Cambridge before taking a degree and later entered one of the London law schools, Grays Inn, where he remained from 1666 until 1673, when he was called to the bar.

It appears that he never practiced law but instead lived quietly in London as a man of letters, supported by a modest annuity left from his family estate. In 1674 he published his first significant work, a translation of René Rapin's *Reflections on Aristotle's Treatise of Poesie*, accompanied by a critical preface surveying English heroic poetry. Thereafter he produced additional translations and wrote original literary criticism, one tragedy, and a few lyric and occasional poems. Although his early works contain flattering references to Charles II, it is clear that Rymer's sympathies lay with the Whigs.

Following the death of Thomas Shadwell in 1692, Rymer was appointed Historiographer Royal to the government of William and Mary. In the following year he began work on his *Foedera*. For twenty years Rymer worked on this project, often having the transcribing and editing done at his own expense. Before his death he had completed fifteen volumes and had seen most of them through the press. Eventually, five additional volumes were completed under the editorship of Robert Sanderson. Rymer died on December 13, 1713, and was buried in the London Church of St. Clement Danes in the Strand.

## Influence

Rymer's rigid application of neoclassical principles and his emphasis upon ethical values influenced Jeremy Collier's

*A Short View of the Immorality and Profaneness of the English Stage* (1698). As Rymer had attacked tragedies of an earlier age for failure to teach a clear moral lesson, Collier attacked comedies of his own time for their immorality. Together, their critical assaults on English drama contributed to the public's favorable reception of sentimental comedies and domestic tragedies in the early eighteenth century. Yet most critics of his time, even John Dryden, John Dennis, and Charles Gildon, who generally accepted the neoclassical view of literature, found Rymer's approach too narrow and doctrinaire. As literary tastes gradually turned away from neoclassicism, Rymer's reputation suffered a decline. Comparing Rymer's criticism with Dryden's, Samuel Johnson observed that Rymer "has the ferocity of a tyrant," and Thomas Macaulay called Rymer "the worst critic that ever lived." Subsequent critics have been less harsh, yet even sympathetic scholars such as Curt Zimansky have found little to admire in Rymer's work.

## Analysis

Rymer's approach to literary criticism, both theoretical and applied, derives from assumptions about literature that were widely accepted during the neoclassical era, beginning in the mid-seventeenth century. Among these are assumptions about literary history and the development of national literatures. In his preface to Rapin's work on Aristotle, Rymer observed that unlike France, where Cardinal Richelieu encouraged literary criticism by founding the Académie Française, England enjoyed no continuing critical tradition. In his view, the absence of a body of literary theory adversely affected the development of the national literature, for critics, with their knowledge of theory, influence authors to write well. The critic identifies the principles and rules and exposes authors' faults and weaknesses, with a view toward improving the national literature.

Rymer genuinely believed that England could develop a great national literature, because he considered its language to be more refined than German but not refined to the point of weakness like Italian and French. Oddly enough, Rymer concluded that despite its strong tradition of literary criticism, France had not produced a great literature. Consistent with neoclassical values, Rymer concentrated on its two most respected genres, epic and tragedy. His treatment of epic is brief, limited largely to his preface to Rapin's work, in which he makes no distinction between epic and romance. His promised critical analysis of John Milton's *Paradise Lost* (1667, 1674) was not completed.

His two major critical essays, both devoted to tragedy, are closely related. *The Tragedies of the Last Age*, though it proposes to concern itself with tragedies by Francis Beaumont and John Fletcher, William Shakespeare, and Ben Jonson, actually takes up only Beaumont and Fletcher. *A Short View of Tragedy*, continuing where the earlier essay ended, examines Shakespeare's *Othello, the Moor of Venice* (1604) and *Macbeth* (1606) and Jonson's *Catiline* (1611). Although there are differences of emphasis and approach, the fundamental values and assumptions are similar in the two essays.

To further his objective of improving English tragedy, Rymer advocated two basic guides. First, dramatists should study Aristotle's *De poetica* (334–323 B.C.; *Poetics*) and Horace's *Ars poetica* (c. 17 B.C.; *The Art of Poetry*), since these two classical texts either state or imply all the important principles applicable to tragedy. Following these critical texts would enable playwrights to produce dramas superior to anything yet achieved by their English forerunners. Second, contemporary tragedians, ignoring all recent precedent, should model their dramas on the tragedies of Aeschylus and Sophocles, whose tragedies are based upon sound dramatic principles.

Thus, Rymer adhered to general attitudes of neoclassicism. He assumed that the role of modern authors was to re-create the genres of the classics. Models of ancient authors, supplemented by a study of the principles of classical critics, would serve as the best guides to this important end. By relying on a dramatic tradition that developed during the Middle Ages, contemporary tragedians had taken the wrong course and had veered sharply from the genre's proper development. Rymer's major contribution to literature, as he envisaged it at the outset, was to discredit major Elizabethan and Jacobean tragedies – plays that were still being performed on the Restoration stage and still exerting influence on practicing dramatists.

Rymer's view of tragedy places it above nature, as an improvement of reality. For the dramatist to reproduce reality, or nature unadorned, does not suffice. Pointing out that tragedy originated with religious ceremonies and that Athenians derived some of their laws from tragedy, he stressed the instructive role of the genre. While he acknowledged that all literature is written primarily to please, he believed that the nature of tragedy is such that it pleases only if it also instructs. Thus the fable or plot must be more instructive than history, and characters should represent idealized human types so that they become models for human behavior. The plot must have a clear and significant moral as its basis. This requirement, according to Rymer, is not met by the plays of Beaumont and Fletcher, or by Shakespeare's *Othello*, which, Rymer concludes, is a "Bloody Farce, without salt or savour." As a suitable plot he proposes a stark and simplified account of the English defeat of the Spanish Armada. To further indicate the need for acceptable plots, he compares the works of Greek tragedians such as Aeschylus and Euripides to modern plots.

It is in regard to character, however, that Rymer offered his most severe judgments. Like the French formalist critics, he strongly emphasized decorum, meaning propriety of action and speech. Decorum has to do with a character's class, sex, and rank. Rymer assumed that if the dramatist ignored decorum, the characters would not be credible to an audience and their moral impact would be thereby diminished.

Adhering to decorum means that a dramatist was to follow numerous specific rules and requirements. For example, a woman in tragedy must always be modest. Kings, having been accorded the highest rewards by society, must reflect the highest virtue. A woman cannot kill a man unless she is shown to be his superior, and no man can draw his sword against a woman. Characters are not allowed to engage in mortal combat unless they might legitimately challenge each other to a duel. A villain, having no wholesome moral influence, has no place in tragedy. To Rymer, Shakespeare's Iago, an arch villain, violates the type he is supposed to represent – the plain, honest soldier. Characters are also subject to the rule of poetic justice, which requires that no one may commit a crime for which his or her suffering cannot atone. Otherwise, the ethical expectations of an audience will not be satisfied.

In addition to plot and character, Rymer's method, derived from French critics such as Pierre Corneille, includes considerations of thought and expression. He devoted less attention to these two elements, perhaps because they become much more detailed. Rymer noted at one point that there was no need to dwell on specifics when so many of the essentials were defective. In examining thought and expression, he often used a commonsense approach, seeking to discover flaws and to reduce the passages to absurdities. Thus he noted that Desdemona, a senator's daughter, has no better manners and expression than an English chambermaid. He taxed Shakespeare for giving Brutus expression beneath the dignity of his character as history represents it.

In *A Short View of Tragedy*, he devotes brief attention to the dramatic unities of time, place, and action – subjects of endless refinement among the French neoclassicists. Rymer proposes that a chorus be restored to the English stage, so that the presence of the same group of personae at all times during the performance will limit the time of the plot and the locale. At the same time, he attacks Jonson for inept use of the chorus in *Catiline*.

To compare *The Tragedies of the Last Age* with *A Short View of Tragedy* is to discover that Rymer's judgments are inconsistent and that his views became increasingly narrow and rigid and his tone more acerbic. In *The Tragedies of the Last Age*, he makes no objection to romantic love as a theme, perhaps because it is an important theme of his tragedy, *Edgar*. In *A Short View of Tragedy*, he rejects it because it is absent from the best classical tragedies. In the first essay he praises Euripides; in the second, he concludes that Aeschylus and Sophocles are the best models, *Oidipous Tyrannos* (c. 429 B.C.; *Oedipus Tyrannus*) representing the only perfect model. In the first essay he largely ignores the works of his contemporaries; by the time of *A Short View of Tragedy*, he includes numerous allusions and quotations from George Villiers' *The Rehearsal* (1671) as an oblique satire of Dryden and other Restoration dramatists.

Among Rymer's achievements were the introduction of the term "poetical justice" into English criticism and the early use of quoted passages to assess writers' strengths as well as their weaknesses. In his preface to Rapin's study of Aristotle, for example, Rymer quotes a passage from Dryden to analyze its tone and style. Previous critics had used quotations to assail the grammar and logic of poets but not to call attention to their merit. In his preface to John Wilmot, Earl of Rochester's *Poems on Several Occasions*, Rymer demonstrates similar perception when he quotes a passage by Rochester and explains its superiority over comparable passages by two other poets. Rymer was also among the first critics to give the history of national literature an important place in his work. In *A Short View of Tragedy* he traces the development of English drama to the religious drama and strolling players of the Middle Ages. He also discerns the origin of modern poetry in the Provençal poetry of the twelfth century. One should note, however, that he cited historical evidence not as an objective scholar, but rather as a critic arguing the thesis that modern literature has murky and unworthy origins.

While he possessed an ability to recognize poetic merit, Rymer unfortunately concentrated his efforts on faultfinding. The tone of his criticism is frequently harsh; even in a time when neoclassic formalism was widely accepted, he was considered an extremist. Had the neoclassical movement continued and produced a rich flowering of literary works, he might well have been accorded a place as a pioneer champion of its principles. With the decline of the neoclassical movement and the beginning of Romanticism, however, Rymer's reputation suffered an eclipse. His assumption that neoclassical theory was sufficiently coherent and complete to serve as an adequate model for reforming national literatures proved historically unsound and intellectually flawed. His attempt to delineate the ethical purpose of literature rested upon interpretations of Aristotle that do not withstand scrutiny.

## Principal criticism

Preface to *Reflections on Aristotle's Treatise of Poesie*, by René Rapin, 1674
*The Tragedies of the Last Age*, 1678
Preface to *Poems on Several Occasions*, by John Wilmot, Earl of Rochester, 1691
*A Short View of Tragedy*, 1693

## Other major works and literary forms

Apart from his literary criticism, Thomas Rymer's contributions to literature are extremely obscure, though he produced a variety of works. His tragedy, *Edgar: Or, The English Monarch* (1678), written in heroic couplets, was never performed. The play reveals that in actual practice he did not follow the critical principles he recommended. Most of his occasional and lyric poetry remained in manuscript until after his death, and their posthumous publication brought him no distinction.

As a translator, Rymer contributed both verse and prose to published editions of his time, notably "Trista" in Ovid's *Epistles* (1680) and "Life of Nicias" in Plutarch's *Lives* (1683–1686), both edited by John Dryden. In the chapters concerning literary history in his *A Short View of Tragedy*, Rymer incorporates some of his own translations of poems and documents. His most significant achievement, however, was the historical work *Foedera, Conventiones, et cujuscunque generis Acta Publica* (1704–1735, best known as *Foedera*), a compilation of all treaties between Great Britain and foreign powers from the year 1101. To this project he devoted the final twenty years of his life, completing fifteen of its twenty volumes before his death.

PLAY
*Edgar: Or, The English Monarch*, 1678

NONFICTION
*Foedera, Conventiones, et cujuscunque generis Acta Publica*, 1704–1735 (20 volumes)

## Further reading

Grace, Joan C. *Tragic Theory in the Critical Works of Thomas Rymer, John Dennis, and John Dryden*, 1975.
Hume, Robert D. *Dryden's Criticism*, 1970.
Spingarn, Joel E., ed. *Critical Essays of the Seventeenth Century*, 1957 (3 volumes).
Zimansky, Curt A., ed. *The Critical Works of Thomas Rymer*, 1956.

STANLEY ARCHER

*See also* Dryden; Neoclassical Literary Theory

# S

## Edward Said

Palestinian-American cultural critic

**Born:** Jerusalem, Palestine; November 1, 1935

### Biography

Edward Said, born in Jerusalem, Palestine, on November 1, 1935, was educated in Western-style schools in Palestine and Cairo, Egypt. In 1948 he moved to the United States where he studied at Princeton University (B.A. 1957) and Harvard University (M.A. and Ph.D. 1960 and 1964). He was appointed to the Comparative Literature faculty of Columbia University in 1963, and has been a visiting professor at Yale, Stanford, Harvard, and Johns Hopkins universities. His distinguished academic career includes a Guggenheim fellowship (1972). A fellowship at the Center for Advanced Study in Behavioral Sciences at Stanford University (1975–1976) resulted in his influential book *Orientalism* (1978), which was nominated for the National Book Critics Circle Award. He was elected president of the Modern Language Association in 1999.

With a background in comparative literature and broad research interests, Said is one of the most erudite critics, commanding an encyclopedic knowledge of culture, both Eastern and Western. He has written about classical music (*Musical Elaborations*, 1991) and is music critic for *The Nation*. However, his importance to contemporary cultural and literary criticism develops from his own situation as an Arab with a Western education. As both dislocated Palestinian Arab and Western intellectual, he feels he belongs "to both worlds, without being completely of either one or the other." Rather than regarding his "exile" status as "something sad or deprived," Said believes it has been essential in helping him to understand "both sides" of the imperial and cultural divide which is the focus of his critical work. Despite his claim of seeing "both sides" and his self-image as mediator, Said has been perceived by some as fundamentally anti-Western, particularly in his major works, *Orientalism* and *Culture and Imperialism* (1993).

Said has clearly established himself as spokesperson and activist for the Palestinian cause, a position which has exposed him to particularly rancorous attack. A number of his books are frankly partisan: *The Question of Palestine* (1979), *Covering Islam* (1981), *After the Last Sky: Palestinian Lives* (1986), *The Politics of Dispossession: The Struggle for Palestinian Self-Determination 1969–1994* (1994), *Blaming the Victims* (1988). In 1993 he resigned his place in the Palestinian parliament-in-exile to protest Yasir Arafat's peace accord with Israel. Beyond Israeli-Palestinian politics, however, Said is a controversial figure because his analysis of Western culture and imperialism is unsettling.

### Influence

Said's style of broad cultural criticism is a reaction against formalist, New Critical tendencies to treat literary texts as privileged, self-sufficient verbal constructs, unconnected to social, political, historical, or biographical realities. Said also rejects postmodern criticism which in a different way severs literature from life, and tends to reduce literary criticism to games and "tiresome playfulness." In Said's view, "Too often literature and culture are presumed to be politically, even historically innocent; it has regularly seemed otherwise to me." Like the New Historicists, he is no respecter of traditional discipline borders, but ranges across them into anthropology, sociology, political science, history, or wherever a "full" reading of a text may take him.

His book *Orientalism* is a foundational text for many fields of study. His other landmark book, *Culture and Imperialism*, continued and extended his inquiry into the relationships between culture and power in a postcolonial world. Both books have profoundly influenced education in the humanities, in helping to move the debate over the Western literary canon from what should be read, to questions of how we read. His critiques of imperialism and Eurocentrism (and all other "isms") have helped fuel a demand for crosscultural studies and interdisciplinary education, now increasingly regarded not as exotic or esoteric, but as essential in a destabilizing but interdependent world.

Some important contemporary theorists who have influenced Said's thinking (Raymond Williams, Michel Foucault,

Frantz Fanon, Antonio Gramsci, to name a few) have gained increased exposure because of Said's judicious synthesis and application of their ideas. Not the least of Said's talents is the ability to convey complex ideas with clarity and precision to a large reading audience.

## Analysis

Beginning with his Ph.D. dissertation on Joseph Conrad (*Joseph Conrad and the Fiction of Autobiography*, 1966), Said has been concerned with the relationship between literature and politics, because he believes that texts have "materiality," they "are always enmeshed in circumstance, time, place, and society – in short, they are in the world, and hence worldly." The task of the critic is to read literature in the largest possible contextual framework, including history, politics, economics, institutions, language, learning, communications, and popular culture. His interpretative method is to examine closely a text's language, and to interrogate it: to question both what it states and what it omits. In this way he expands a reading of a Jane Austen novel, for example, by noting the imbalance in *Mansfield Park* (1814) between the "provocatively rich" evocation of English life, and the reticence about the West Indian slave-run sugar plantation on which this privileged lifestyle depends. To fill in what is missing, Said advocates reading the work of a Caribbean historian such as Eric Williams' *Capitalism and Slavery* (1961) alongside *Mansfield Park*.

Said calls this method of reading "contrapuntal" analysis: "extending our reading of texts to include what was once forcibly excluded – in *L'Étranger* [*The Stranger* by Albert Camus], for example, the whole previous history of France's colonialism and its destruction of the Algerian state, and the later emergence of an independent Algeria (which Camus opposed)" Said believes is relevant to a full reading of the novel. He sees such readings as "completing or complementing others, not discounting or displacing them." His purpose is not to deny that novels such as those by Austen or Camus are great works of literature, or to deny readers the pleasures of these texts: European literature is "no less complex, rich, or interesting for having supported most aspects of the imperial experience." Rather, a "contrapuntal" reading draws "connections that enrich and sharpen our reading."

In *Orientalism*, Said's concern is the way in which the West has "Orientalized" the Orient. By the Orient, he means specifically the Muslim Orient (the Near East); by "Orientalism" he means the collection of stereotypes, distortions, myths, and fantasies which the Occident (the West) has imposed in its drive to dominate it. Using Michel Foucault's concept of discourse, Said's purpose is to examine Orientalism, and to demonstrate "how the will to exercise dominant control . . . has . . . discovered a way to clothe, disguise, rarefy, and wrap itself systematically in the language of truth, discipline, rationality,

utilitarian value and knowledge." Such language is all the more effective because of its "naturalness, authority, professionalism, assertiveness, and anti-theoretical directness."

In examining language, whether of Western Orientalist "experts" or the "language" of popular culture, he finds a view basically unchanged from "the anti-Islamic polemics of the Middle Ages and the Renaissance." The Orient is aberrant, exotic, backward, passive, inferior (while the West is "rational, developed, humane, superior"). Images of Arabs in Western popular culture include slave trader, camel driver, money changer, treacherous oil sheik, colorful scoundrel, "oversexed degenerate." The Western view is that the Orient is "something either to be feared (the Yellow Peril, the Mongol hordes, the brown dominions) or to be controlled (by pacification, research and development, outright occupation whenever possible.)" He is particularly critical of the new "experts" on the Orient, the area-study specialists and social scientists who are largely ignorant of the language and literature of those they study, but prefer to rely on "facts" which reinforce their preconceptions.

Said, however, denies "that there is such a thing as a real or true Orient," one that an insider could conceivably give us. Rather, he notes that the "Orient" (like the "Occident") is a human construct, an invented essence which has gathered "a tradition of thought, imagery, and vocabulary" which makes it seem real. Here, as elsewhere, Said draws attention to the artificiality and inadequacy of categorizing. As he points out in *Culture and Imperialism*, "No one today is purely *one* thing. Labels like Indian, or woman, or Muslim, or American are not more than starting-points, which if followed into actual experience for only a moment are quickly left behind." One of the harmful legacies of Western imperialism is that it has so firmly fixed the belief "that everyone is principally and irreducibly a member of some race or category, and that race or category cannot ever be assimilated to or accepted by others – except as itself." One consequence of this view is identity politics, a kind of tribalism in which each separate group demands that its own needs be met. The ultimate expression of this philosophy is nationalism.

Said notes that the triumph of Orientalism seems complete when its ideas have been internalized in "the Orient" itself. Observing that there is no Arab equivalent of an Oxford or a Harvard for the study of the Arab world, he finds it alarming that Arab students and their professors turn to American Orientalists, and learn to teach their local audiences the clichés of "Orientalism."

Because *Culture and Imperialism* is a collection of revised lectures (originally delivered between 1985 and 1988 in Britain and North America on varied topics) it seems less satisfying than *Orientalism* to read, appearing disjointed and, at times, repetitious. However, beneath its diversity of topics (Italian opera, Irish poetry, nineteenth- and twentieth-century novels) it does have a unifying theme, pointed by its title: the relationship of culture (broadly defined) and power, in this case the imperial powers of Britain, France, and the United States over the last two hundred years.

Despite the vast scope of this book, some critics have faulted it because it fails to encompass all imperial history, beginning with the Egyptians, Persians, and Romans. Anticipating this complaint, Said stated he chose these three powers because they have "a unique coherence," "cultural centrality," a "systematic" style of spreading their culture not evident in other empires, and finally, that these are the three countries he knows best. Possibly the scope of the book is not the real problem; the abundant examples of Western complacency and arrogance may be.

*Culture and Imperialism* moves beyond instances of imperial cultural domination in the first half of the book, to a discussion of resistance to empire, decolonization, independence, and finally, liberation. Drawing extensively on Frantz Fanon's theories in *The Wretched of the Earth* (1961), Said charts the stages through which this process must move. Again, he assumes culture leads the way. Just as Western culture preceded the actual possession of territories, so the reclamation of cultural territories must precede the reclaiming of geographical territories. Poets of resistance and decolonization are needed for the struggle, followed finally by a genuinely revolutionary literature of new forms and consciousness.

The rejection of the colonizer's traditions leads to a desire to celebrate and return to a pre-imperial, unsullied past, a past naively and nostalgically conceived. This stage is what Said terms "nativism," an inevitable development in recovery from the oppression and humiliation of colonialism, but also a stumbling block for the achievement of true liberation. To remain at a stage of nativism is "to accept the consequences of imperialism, the racial, religious, and political divisions imposed by imperialism itself." To revaluate the hierarchy is no escape from hierarchical and "us versus them" thinking. Just as Said points out that Occidentalism is not the answer to Orientalism, so he believes that Arabism (or Islamism, or Afrocentrism) is not the answer to Eurocentrism. To achieve true human liberation is to move beyond imperialism's destructive dualisms of master/slave, white/colored, colonizer/colonized, civilized/uncivilized, superior/inferior. This is the legacy of "difference" that must be overcome.

A final chapter, "Freedom From Domination in the Future," discusses the United States, the newest and perhaps the last superpower. Will America's massive military, economic, and cultural power be used for world domination in the old imperial style, or will it become a force for human liberation? Said wisely leaves the question open, but his observations of American attitudes particularly after the 1991 Gulf War ("triumphalism") put him in mind of the British Raj in imperial India. Despite Said's belief that there has been in the twentieth century an increase in political and historical awareness, it may not be enough: "systems

of thought . . . discourses of power, ideological fictions – mind-forg'd manacles – are all too easily made, applied, and guarded."

Edward Said, one of the most provocative contemporary intellectuals, is truly a global critic who (in Salman Rushdie's words) "reads the world as closely as he reads books," and challenges his readers to do the same. *Orientalism* and *Culture and Imperialism*, vast works of analysis and synthesis, are of permanent importance: they stand as models of the kind of imaginative, integrative, and humane thinking a destabilizing world now requires.

## Principal criticism
*Joseph Conrad and the Fiction of Autobiography*, 1966
*Beginnings: Intention and Method*, 1975
*Orientalism*, 1978
*The Question of Palestine*, 1979
*Covering Islam*, 1981
*The World, the Text, and the Critic*, 1983
*After the Last Sky: Palestinian Lives*, 1986
*Culture and Imperialism*, 1993
*The Politics of Dispossession: The Struggle for Palestinian Self-Determination, 1969–1994*, 1994
*Representations of the Intellectual*, 1994
*Peace and Its Discontents*, 1996

## Other major works and literary forms
Edward Said has written many essays on classical music. Some of them are collected in *Musical Elaborations* (1991).

EDITED TEXTS
*Literature and Society*, 1980
*Blaming the Victims*, 1988 (with Christopher Hitchens)

## Further reading
Bove, Paul A. "Edward W. Said: A Special Issue," in *Boundary 2*. September, 1998.
Fraiman, Susan. "Jane Austen and Edward Said: Gender, Culture, and Imperialism," in *Critical Inquiry*. 21 (Summer 1995).
Gare, A. E. "Understanding Oriental Cultures," in *Philosophy East and West*. 45 (July 1995).
Groden, Michael, and Martin Kreiswirth, eds. *The Johns Hopkins Guide to Literary Theory and Criticism*, 1994.
Makiya, Kanan. *Cruelty and Silence*, 1993.
Parry, Benita, Keith Ansell-Pearson, and Judith Squires, eds. *Cultural Readings of Imperialism: Edward Said and the Gravity of History*, 1997.
Prakash, Gyan. "Orientalism Now," in *History Today*. 34, no. 3 (1995).
Salusinszky, Imre. *Criticism in Society: Interviews with Jacques Derrida, Northrup Frye, Harold Bloom, Geoffrey Hartman, Frank Kermode, Edward Said, Barbara Johnson, Frank Lentricchia, and J. Hillis Miller*, 1987.
Sprinker, Michael. *Edward Said: A Critical Reader*, 1993.
Veeser, Harold. *Edward Said*, 1998.
Xu, Ben. *Situational Tensions of Critic-Intellectuals: Thinking Through Literary Politics With Edward W. Said and Frank Lentricchia*, 1992.

KAREN A. KILDAHL

*See also* Foucault; Postcolonial Literature and Theory; Spivak

# Charles-Augustin Sainte-Beuve

French critic and writer

**Born:** Boulogne-sur-Mer, France; December 23, 1804
**Died:** Paris, France; October 13, 1869

## Biography

A posthumous child reared by his mother and a paternal aunt, Charles-Augustin Sainte-Beuve received an excellent grounding in Latin literature at the local pension. In 1818 he moved to Paris and there studied literature at the Lycée Charlemagne and later philosophy at the College Bourbon, where he won first prize for Latin verse. Choosing a career in medicine, he was enrolled at the École de Médecine from 1823 to 1827 but never practiced.

Sainte-Beuve's true calling was decided when his former rhetoric teacher, Paul Dubois, asked him to contribute to the new liberal journal, *Le Globe*, which he had helped to found in 1827. An event crucial for Sainte-Beuve's career and for the course of French Romanticism was his *Le Globe* review of Victor Hugo's *Odes et ballades* (1826) in that same year. Thereafter, through the 1840s, he wrote regularly for the *Revue de Paris*, the *Revue des deux mondes*, and the *National*. From their pages he later collected the essays in his volumes of literary *Portraits*. During 1837–1838 he delivered at the University of Lausanne, Switzerland, the lectures which over some twenty years he expanded into *Port-Royal*. In 1844 he was elected to membership in the French Academy. In 1848, glad to escape the revolutionary turmoil in Paris, he accepted an invitation from the University of Liège, Belgium, where he gave the course of lectures that later yielded *Chateaubriand et son groupe littéraire sous l'empire*.

Back home in 1849 he was engaged by Louis Véron to supply him with a critical article, every Monday, for his newspaper *Le Constitutionel*. Thus began the two-decade series of *Causeries du lundi* (Monday chats) which after a few years were continued in two rival papers. During this time Sainte-Beuve added to his academic activity by lecturing on Latin poetry in 1854 at the Collège de France. His failure there – he was driven from the podium by students protesting his political views – did not prevent his subsequent tenure of the chair in French letters at the École Normale Supérieure (1857–1861). In 1865 he became a member of Napoleon III's senate, where he won acclaim for his courageous advocacy of liberal ideas.

## Influence

At least by his late maturity and for some sixty years after his death, Sainte-Beuve's influence was immense. "He became *the* critic," René Wellek declared in *A History of Modern Criticism: 1750–1950* (1955–1992), "the master not only in France but all over Europe and the Americas." This influence had its initial stirring among French literati

of the historical-naturalist school such as Hippolyte Taine, Sainte-Beuve's most famous disciple. In England Matthew Arnold hailed him as the literary critic par excellence, whose work best embodied the quality of disinterestedness in which Arnold thought contemporary British criticism was woefully deficient. In the United States Sainte-Beuve's major impact was on academic literary study, whose most eminent representatives widely adopted as a norm of scholarly criticism his biographical method. Irving Babbitt of Harvard called him the greatest modern French critic. "To read Sainte-Beuve," he wrote in 1912, "is to enlarge one's knowledge, not merely of literature but of life." A few years earlier Paul Elmer More, Babbitt's fellow neo-humanist at Princeton, had confessed himself "almost overwhelmed" by the sheer magnitude of Sainte-Beuve's accomplishment in his "incomparable *Lundis*." A decade later the chief theorist and historian of literary criticism at Columbia, Joel E. Spingarn, took Sainte-Beuve as a model of the nondogmatic impressionism he was then propounding.

With the revolt during the 1930s against "extrinsic" approaches to literature, however, and especially to the biographical form of it, Sainte-Beuve's prestige suffered a decline from which it has since only partly recovered.

## Analysis

Both Sainte-Beuve's explicit comments on criticism and his critical practice constitute a complex and sometimes contradictory mixture of theories and methods. There is the subjective, "confessional" Sainte-Beuve, who maintained that in discussing what others had written he was really indulging in self-revelation. In diametric opposition stands the impressionist Sainte-Beuve, who in 1835 argued that critics should be openly receptive to the differing intellectual fare in the books they examine, ever ready to adopt all sides of a question and even if need be to contradict themselves for the sake of total empathy with the author under scrutiny at the moment. Then there is the scientific Sainte-Beuve, the detached analyst who told a correspondent that he had taken as his motto the English word "Truth." This last includes the scholarly Sainte-Beuve, who in his concern for minute accuracy often dispatched his manservant to the public library, during the composition of a *Lundi*, to verify a date or the precise ancestry of an obscure personage to whom he was making passing reference.

Most often though, and at his most readable best, the dispassionate cultural historian and literary biographer coexist in Sainte-Beuve with the erst-while poet, who insisted that his criticism was really a form of creative writing, more an art than a science. This role is brilliantly sustained in his masterpiece *Port-Royal*. There, in meticulous detail, he constructs the intellectual and social history of the Jansenist religious order from its founding in the early 1600s to its dissolution a century later by papal and royal decrees. What he produced is more than an energetic exercise in historiography. At intervals the unhurried progress of the narrative is suspended for critiques of eminent literary figures of the period, Pierre Corneille, Blaise Pascal, Nicolas Boileau-Despréaux, Jean Racine and others. As he declares in the "Preliminary Discourse," Sainte-Beuve conceived his subject poetically, and in dramatic terms, expressive of his affective involvement in what was a labor of love. It is "That Port-Royal so beloved of its own" ("Ce Port-Royal tant aimé des siens"), whose poignant fate is envisaged in Sainte-Beuve's ardent pages as a Greek tragedy, complete with the required unity of plot and lamenting chorus. This conception accords well with the goal he professed in 1844 of combining in criticism elements of both charm and reality, "poetry" and "physiology."

At the same time, Sainte-Beuve was far from immune to the all-embracing scientific naturalism of his day, by which every phenomenon – social and artistic as well as physical – was to be explained as an effect of causes discoverable by disciplined observation and induction. In this faith his younger admirer Taine wrote a literary history of England showing how the peculiar qualities of its literature from Anglo-Saxon times to the then-present had been shaped by the three fundamental determinants of race, moment, and milieu.

The Sainte-Beuve whom Taine emulated was the Sainte-Beuve who in mid-career recorded in a much-quoted *Pensée* his desire to establish a "literary natural history." What he meant he finally spelled out many years later. Having in the meantime often openly avowed his protean critical stance and at times even gloried in a perpetual metamorphosis of principle, he took the occasion of a two-part *Lundi* on François Auguste René Chateaubriand in 1862 to refute complaints by other writers that he had no consistent theory. He did so by embracing the biographical method for which he has ever since been chiefly celebrated and which, he maintained, his *Portraits* and *Lundis* had all along exemplified. For him, Sainte-Beuve explained, a literary work was inseparable from the person who created it. Though he could enjoy a work in and for itself, he felt unable to interpret or judge it except in reference to the author's character and total life experience. In conformity to the reigning scientific determinism, he was "quite willing to say, 'As the tree is, so is its fruit.' Quite naturally, therefore, literary study leads me to moral study." He then proceeded to outline a critical method structured on that of botany, with a classification of human psychological types paralleling the taxonomy of plants. For the final perfection of this method he looked to a future time when the further progress of science would make it possible. Sainte-Beuve was nevertheless confident that he had taken some preliminary steps toward that goal. He had discerned as the most inclusive genus of classification what he called "families of minds," which determined the quality of the writings their members produced. These grand types transcended historical periods. Virgil and Racine, for example,

as exemplars of classical restraint and conscious artistry, belonged to the same family even though they were separated by some sixteen hundred years.

By moral study Sainte-Beuve meant not a judgmental process based on a code of ethics but a thoroughgoing anatomy of the human psyche, individually and collectively, carrying forward a literary tradition of great moralists that starts in antiquity with Theophrastus' *Characters* and is enriched in modern times by two of Sainte-Beuve's own favorites, Jean de La Bruyère and Samuel Johnson. In the finest of his literary *Portraits* and *Lundis*, and in such critiques as those on Molière and Pascal in *Port-Royal*, Sainte-Beuve proved himself their worthy successor.

Sainte-Beuve was not the founder of biographical criticism, nor did he claim to be so. He freely acknowledged that pioneer work in that category had preceded his own, most notably Johnson's *Lives of the English Poets* (1779–1781). He became, however – as he still remains – its ablest representative by refining it to a degree of psychological and aesthetic subtlety probably never equalled and certainly never exceeded by anyone since.

Going beyond the assimilation of the critic to the botanist in his reply to the charge of having no theory, Sainte-Beuve described how his moral focus could be systematized into a quasi-scientific mode of inquiry. He argued that the proper appreciation of any book other than a treatise on geometry required the critic to find out the author's religious convictions, his attitude toward women and money, whether he was poor or rich, his daily routine, and his particular vice or weakness. These data were to be further supplemented by particulars of the author's ancestry because "the man of genius is inevitably found reflected in his relatives . . . especially in his mother." Fortunately, Sainte-Beuve's own better instincts kept him from making more than a very few abortive attempts to carry this heavy-handed investigative procedure into practice. Two years after making it public, he himself stated the reason which would alone suffice for not doing so. Conceding that criticism had profited and would continue to profit from advances in scientific and historical investigation, he nevertheless concluded that it could not itself "become a science. It will remain an art, and, in the hands of those who have the skill to apply it, a very delicate art."

For all his attraction to the deterministic historiography of his time, as represented most influentially in the work of Jules Michelet and Ernest Renan, Sainte-Beuve refused to reduce literature to a mere product of blind social forces to which writers are willy-nilly obedient, as his disciple Taine tried to demonstrate in his *History of English Literature* (1864). Reviewing that work, Sainte-Beuve argued that after all due allowance has been made for the parts played in literary creation by Taine's historical forces, there remains, as chief determinant, the writer himself. And he is himself no mere resultant, no passive focusing lens. He possesses a mirror of his own, which Sainte-Beuve called "his individual unique monad." The bulk of his critical legacy may be regarded as a sustained effort of some forty years' duration, as journalist and lecturer, to penetrate to that monad as he found it embodied in the hundreds of men and women whose minds and art he explored. Few if any of those who have emulated him in that enterprise have equaled him in the psychological sensitivity and analytical tact it demands.

The insatiable moral curiosity that motivated his successes also accounts in large measure for the three faults that have been imputed to Sainte-Beuve as critic. The one most often deplored and most pervasive is that he devoted too many of his essays to the minor works of major writers, to the neglect of their masterpieces; or to second- and third-rate writers; or – worst fault of all – to writings of no particular artistic value, such as the memoirs, diaries, or letters of some obscure general, statesman, or titled lady. Ironically enough, though of little intrinsic merit in themselves, such things may often be as fruitful to the moralist as a first-rate novel or book of verse. The second fault is that even when he deals with an imaginative work worth critical attention, his focus is too much on the author, too little on what he or she wrote.

Closely related to the second, the third fault, though perhaps less disturbing to the general reader, is the gravest of the three on theoretical grounds. Sainte-Beuve's biographism, both in the way in which he formulated it and in much of his practice, is an example of what during the last half-century or so has been authoritatively condemned as the "personal heresy" or, alternatively, the "biographical fallacy." This error consists in the assumption that in their fictional compositions writers invariably express their actual opinions and feelings; and on this assumption the interpreter turns to the author's life for evidence (in the form of letters, notebooks, records of conversation and the like) to guide his or her interpretation. Literary biographers, or the critics themselves for that matter, are guilty of the same flawed technique when they reverse the process and probe an author's fictive work to discover what that author did, suffered, or thought; loved, hated, or feared. In either direction the reasoning is fallacious because it overlooks the mass of evidence in literary history to show that writers imagine experiences they have never undergone, give fictive expression to opinions they have never held, and verbalize emotions they have never felt.

There is no question that Sainte-Beuve was often guilty of basing his critical judgments on a too direct, unmediated relationship between product and producer. The many instances of this in his essays seem only underscored by some of his more or less offhand remarks, such as his confident assertion that by simply knowing the state of a poet's health he could infer the quality of his or her poetry. There is also little question that the abrupt decline of Sainte-Beuve's reputation after World War I owes much to the

impact on modern critical opinion of T. S. Eliot's essay "Tradition and the Individual Talent" (1919), with its memorable pronouncement that "the more perfect the artist, the more completely separate in him will be the man who suffers and the mind which creates." By essentially the same argument the novelist Marcel Proust, in his posthumous *Contre Sainte-Beuve* (1954; *By Way of Sainte-Beuve*, 1958), severely berated his countryman for failing to understand that literary artists, by the very nature of their creative activity, really comprise two selves. One is the ordinary self of their quotidian existence; the other, distinct and in important respects frequently the contrary of the first, is alone the self which fashions the works associated with their names as authors.

There are certainly passages in Sainte-Beuve which lend color to Proust's indictment. In *Portraits of Celebrated Women*, for example, on highly select evidence he finds the personality and experiences of Madame de La Fayette to be perfectly mirrored in her novel *La Princesse de Clèves* (1678; *The Princess of Clèves*, 1769): "telle est la vie de Mme de La Fayette et le rapport exact de sa personne à son roman." Yet, inconsistent in this as in so much else, he sometimes stressed the distinction not only between poet and poem but also between the poet and his or her ordinary self, on which Proust based his objection. In a youthful essay on Corneille, Sainte-Beuve actually took to task literary biographers who supposed that authors' characters can be drawn exclusively from their writings. Moreover, the effort to reveal the individual behind the author, virtually Sainte-Beuve's trademark, would be meaningless if that elusive being were not taken to be disparate from the being visible in his or her works. It should also be noted that on some occasions his failure to maintain the separation involves some consciously expressive lyric poet in whom the duality is so tenuous as hardly to distort the interpretations of a critic who disregarded it. Of Alfred de Musset, for one, Sainte-Beuve observed that, as he put it, his lyre and his soul were one.

In any case there is general agreement that Sainte-Beuve's limitations do not seriously disfigure his best work. True, at rare moments his critical vision seems strangely in abeyance, as in his notorious blindness to the merits of great contemporaries like Honoré de Balzac, Stendhal, and Charles Baudelaire. At times too he seemed to forget that life and art are not the same. In an otherwise perceptive review of Gustave Flaubert's *Madame Bovary* (1857; English translation, 1886), he complained that the novelist had painted his characters and setting in too unrelievedly somber tones, since after all even in the French provinces where the story is set there are some admirable people.

Yet Sainte-Beuve was well aware that fictional probability typically deviates from literal truth. His alertness to the difference is perhaps nowhere more evident than in the brilliant pages on Molière in *Port-Royal*. What sets Molière above every other French dramatist, he notes, is his sure intuition of theatrical truth, something more profound than a slavish copy of normal human action. He points to a telling instance from the scene in *Tartuffe* (1664; English translation, 1732) in which the puritannical hypocrite tosses the pretty Dorine a handkerchief to cover her naked throat. "What truth!" Sainte-Beuve exclaims, "and what improbability!"

As the titles of his early volumes suggest, Sainte-Beuve strove to convey his moral insights in imaginative form, as verbal portraits. Whenever he succeeded the result was a composition graced with a literary attractiveness of its own quite apart from its instructive or explicative value. He was a master of verbal depiction, and few of his pieces lack passages of sheer visual appeal. Embarking on his massive study of Port-Royal, he thought of it, as noted above, in poetic terms. Nearing its completion years later, he reiterated the point with a shift of metaphor to the graphic art. "I am not writing the history of Port-Royal," he observed. "I am painting its portrait, and trying to capture its spirit."

For Sainte-Beuve's most memorable essays on individual writers, Proust's censure does not hold. Because in them the humanist in the critic's intellectual makeup prevailed over the naturalist, there is no attempt to force an author's literary progeny into a pat conformity with his biography. His manner instead is so to characterize the poem and the "man behind the poet" that the two are made to stand in a reciprocal explicative relationship. The "portrait" that emerges is neither of the creation in unreal isolation from its creator, nor of the latter seen through the necessarily distorting lens of his own art. The Beuvian portrait is rather a deft amalgam of the two. A spirited instance is a late pair of *Lundis* on the great seventeenth-century pulpit orator Bishop Jacques-Bénigne Bossuet. Sainte-Beuve states his intention to capture the unique intellectual constitution of the famous prelate: "bien saisir la forme particulière à son esprit." He does so by a display of critical empathy that reaches its climax in several paragraphs of eloquent prose admirably suited to his theme. Like the even more moving accounts of Pascal and his *Pensées* (1670) in the third volume of *Port-Royal*, the "Bossuet" and many *Portraits* and *Lundis* of comparable appeal have a double value. They are rewarding reading in themselves, and they whet the reader's appetite for the monuments of literary art which they limn. Taken together, they constitute the side of Sainte-Beuve's complex and uneven achievement that prompted T. S. Eliot, despite his own very different theoretical persuasion, to call him a critic of genius.

## Principal criticism

*Critiques et portraits littéraires*, 1832, revised 1836–1839
*Port-Royal*, 1840–1859 (5 volumes)
*Portraits littéraires*, 1844 (2 volumes; revised 1862–1864, 3 volumes)
*Portraits de femmes*, 1844 (*Portraits of Celebrated Women*, 1868)

*Portraits contemporains*, 1846 (3 volumes; enlarged 1869–1871, 5 volumes)
*Causeries du lundi*, 1851–1862 (15 volumes; partial English translation, 1909–1911)
*Derniers portraits littéraires*, 1852
*Étude sur Virgile*, 1857
*Chateaubriand et son groupe littéraire sous l'empire*, 1861 (2 volumes)
*Nouveaux lundis*, 1863–1870 (13 volumes)
*Premiers lundis*, 1874–1875 (3 volumes)
*Portraits of the Seventeenth Century, Historic and Literary*, 1904
*Portraits of the Eighteenth Century, Historic and Literary*, 1905
*Literary Criticism of Sainte-Beuve*, 1971 (Emerson Marks, editor and translator)

## Other major works and literary forms

Charles-Augustin Sainte-Beuve's earliest literary aspiration was creative, not critical. Between 1830 and 1840 he published three volumes of verse, not counting the poems included in his *Vie, poésies et pensées de Joseph Delorme* (1829), and the quasi-autobiographical novel *Volupté* (1834). Like the hero of *Volupté*, Delorme is a projection of Sainte-Beuve himself, in the image of the romantic, hypersensitive poet which in his mature criticism he subjected to destructive analysis. The consensus during his lifetime and ever since is that Sainte-Beuve's talents as novelist and poet were distinctly below those of his contemporaries. Nevertheless, his creative efforts retain interest as evidence of the youthful "romantic" phase of his literary outlook that found further expression in his earliest critical essays.

NOVEL
*Volupté*, 1834

POETRY
*Les Consolations*, 1830
*Pensées d'août*, 1837
*Le Livre d'amour*, 1843

MISCELLANEOUS
*Vie, poésies et pensées de Joseph Delorme*, 1829
*Sainte-Beuve, Selected Essays*, 1963 (Francis Steegmuller and Norbert Guterman, editors)

## Further reading

Arnold, Matthew. "Sainte-Beuve," in *Essays in Criticism*, 1888.
Babbitt, Irving. "Sainte-Beuve," in *Masters of Modern French Criticism*, 1912.
Chadbourne, Richard M. *Charles-Augustin Sainte-Beuve*, 1977.
Lehmann, A. G. *Sainte-Beuve: A Portrait of the Critic, 1804–1842*, 1962.
MacClintock, Lander. *Sainte-Beuve's Critical Theory and Practice After 1849*, 1920.
Wellek, René. "Sainte-Beuve," in *A History of Modern Criticism: 1750–1950*. Vol. 3, *The Age of Transition*, 1965.

EMERSON R. MARKS

*See also* Baudelaire; Continental Theory; Gautier; Hugo; Taine

# George Saintsbury

English critic, historian, and biographer

**Born:** Southampton, England; October 23, 1845
**Died:** Bath, England; January 28, 1933

## Biography

George Edward Bateman Saintsbury was born in the port of Southampton, on the south coast of England, on October 23, 1845. His father, superintendent of docks owned by a railroad company, died when George was fourteen. He lived with his mother and two elder sisters in the Notting Hill area of London. After attending a dame school and a prep school, Saintsbury entered King's College School in London when he was thirteen. In 1863 he was awarded a postmastership at Merton College, Oxford.

Saintsbury's years at Oxford gave him the chance to read widely and to develop his love of wine, as well as serving to strengthen his Tory and High Church views. His time at university ended in disappointment, however, when he failed to achieve the expected first-class degree, and was awarded only a second in Greats. In January of 1868 he began teaching at Manchester Grammar School; he stayed only six months before taking up a post at Elizabeth College in Guernsey. In the same year he married Emily Fern King, a Southampton friend of his sisters. In 1874 he was appointed headmaster of a new establishment, the Elgin Educational Institute in Scotland. He resigned after only two years, however, returned to London, and made a career as a literary journalist for the next eighteen years. He contributed extensively to many journals including the *St. James Gazette, Macmillan's Magazine*, the *Saturday Review, Blackwood's Magazine, Cornhill Magazine*, and, toward the end of the period, the *Manchester Guardian*. During these years he also contributed numerous essays to important works of reference, such as the *Encyclopædia Britannica*, and published many volumes of literary history, criticism, and biography.

After several unsuccessful attempts to obtain university posts, he was appointed, in 1895, Regius Professor of Rhetoric and English Literature at the University of Edinburgh. He became a popular and respected figure in the university until his retirement in 1915. He continued to publish prolifically, despite the considerable demands of his work in Edinburgh. Some of his major works, including his *History of English Prosody*, were written during these years. Upon his retirement he spent one year back in Southampton, before moving to 1a, Royal Crescent, Bath, where he lived until his death. His retirement from teaching and administration certainly did not prompt a similar retirement from writing and publishing, and work continued – albeit at a slightly slower rate – to pour from the press. He died quietly in Bath and was buried in Southampton.

His last will and testament stipulated that no biography should be written and that none of his letters should be published.

## Influence

To some of his contemporaries, George Saintsbury was "the official English critic" (Irving Babbitt) or the "King of Critics" (Christopher Morley). René Wellek describes him as "by far the most influential academic literary historian and critic of the early twentieth century." Prodigiously widely read, and immensely prolific, the informed enthusiasm of much of Saintsbury's writing made him an effective advocate for what he characterized as the "friendship of reading . . . not the least delightful and much the safest kind of friendship."

Saintsbury had a deep suspicion of any and all attempts to make criticism either a science or a philosophy, and certainly his own work as a critic is of continuing interest and value not for its systems or its theories but for its appreciation of individual authors and texts and for the fertility and richness of the comparisons and links which the range of Saintsbury's reading – and the retentiveness of his memory – made possible. He largely sees literature in isolation from the history of ideas or larger questions of cultural history; in the preface to the third volume of his *History of Criticism* he writes that "a friend who is at once friendly, most competent, and of a different complexion in critical thought, objected to me that I 'treat literature as something by itself.' I hastened to admit the impeachment, and to declare that this is the very postulate of my book." In striving, as far as possible, to see works of literature disentangled from the social and intellectual contexts of their production, it might be said that he overdid what many of his successors have failed to do at all – to see literary history as having its own distinctive patterns and structures.

Given such predispositions, it is not surprising that Saintsbury's critical and historical writings should predominantly concentrate on matters of form and style, especially where poetry is concerned. In his early book on John Dryden he declared that "so long as any one holds a definition of poetry which regards it wholly or chiefly from the point of view of its subject-matter, wide differences are unavoidable. But if we hold what I venture to think the only Catholic faith with regard to it, that it consists not in a selection of subjects, but in a method of treatment, then it seems to me that all difficulty vanishes. . . . What constitutes a great poet is supremacy in his own line of poetic expression." His position had not essentially changed when in one of his last major works, *A History of English Prosody*, he affirmed that "the formal part of English poetry . . . is to me the life of poetry." He was, however, willing to grant (*Miscellaneous Essays*) that "the novel is while the poem is not, mainly and firstly a criticism of life."

## Analysis

The reader of virtually any part of Saintsbury's voluminous output of literary criticism and literary history is likely to be impressed by the sheer intensity of the author's pleasure in what he is discussing. He writes with enormous gusto of all the many authors and texts which gave him pleasure; a kind of literary hedonism is often the most obvious hallmark of his writing. As Herbert Grierson has very well said of Saintsbury (in his Introduction to a 1946 reprint of *The Peace of the Augustans*), "he judged it [literature] simply and frankly by the pleasure which it gave him, as he judged of wine and food." In *A Cellar Book* Saintsbury frequently compares drinks to favorite authors; in doing so he was inverting a process of comparison he had often employed in his works of literary criticism. For Saintsbury the word "taste" used in a literary context was almost more than a metaphor. So, in *The Peace of the Augustans*, he distinguishes between "the novel gormandiser who spends whole days on his gormandising" and "the intelligent voluptuary who regards novels as things to be digested at leisure after his or her day's work." Some of the minor works of Jonathan Swift are recommended to "those whose taste can relish literary amontillado, olives, caviare, etc." The note of connoisseurship is, perhaps, never very far away. But the reader generally feels that this is a connoisseur of great and informed experience, of sharp discrimination, who has an articulate eagerness to share his pleasures.

For Saintsbury the critic's job (like the connoisseur's) essentially involved the making of comparisons. In "The Kinds of Criticism" (which serves as a Preface to the first volume of his *Essays in English Literature*) Saintsbury enumerates what he takes to be unsatisfactory ways of proceeding as a critic. These include the critic who is merely a "sayer of fine things" and "the scientific critic" (a phrase which Saintsbury dismisses as "a contradiction in terms"), who is constricted by his theories and helpless in the face of what Saintsbury calls "the splendid mystery of the idiosyncrasy of the artist," as well as the critic who replies purely on his or her impressions (though Saintsbury finds this preferable to the other two kinds of error). The work of the impressionistic critic, pure and simple, is inadequate because it fails to "render the whole virtue" of its subjects, something only possible to a critic who can "compare them with similar and dissimilar ones in the same and other languages, analyze the literary causes and effects, then place and value the work." All such activity "must be supported by wide knowledge of all literature, so that the critic may make the many comparisons central to the process." He put the case more forcefully still in "A Note on Criticism" (in *A Last Vintage*), asserting that "the comparison which takes This and That, puts them together, notes what This has and That lacks, observes how This excels That in one way, and That excels This in the other, appears to me to be [...] the one method by which you can get really luminous results." Luminous comparisons abound in the pages

of Saintsbury's writing. So, for example, the observation that "there are passages in Montaigne which might almost be the work of a French Bacon, and in Bacon passages which might easily be the work of an English Montaigne" (in *A History of Elizabethan Literature*) opens up possibilities which, characteristically, Saintsbury does not elaborate; similarly fascinating vistas are opened up when he compares (in his *Short History of French Literature*) Jean de La Fontaine with, by turns, Luigi Pulci, Ludovico Ariosto, and Giovanni Boccaccio. So central is this to his whole way of thinking and writing that it alone goes some way toward justifying Dorothy Richardson Jones' claim that he made a major contribution toward the development of the very idea of comparative literature in England (a claim also readily supportable by, for example, his editorship of a series such as *Periods of European Literature*).

Saintsbury was a pioneer critic and historian of French literature in English – there were few substantial works before his own. He was among the first to write at all intelligently of Charles Baudelaire. *A Short History of French Literature* long remained in print; it is characteristically wide-ranging and though, equally characteristically, it avoids discussion of most of the larger historical questions, and inevitably has areas of weakness (on the naturalists, for example) it continues to offer brilliant brief characterizations of authors both major and minor. His various histories of English literature are, unsurprisingly, variable in quality – but none are without local insights of enduring value and a continuing capacity to provoke thoughtful reflection. Few critics have ever equaled Saintsbury's capacity to identify, and communicate briefly, the distinguishing qualities of even a minor writer. Few before Saintsbury, in his introduction to the 1896 Muses Library edition of John Donne's poems, had perceived quite how Donne's work was characterized by its "union of the sensual, intellectual, poetical and religious temperaments." There is, too, a weight of reading and good sense behind such seemingly simple assertions as that (in his *History of Elizabethan Literature*) which observes that "about Dekker, hack and penny-a-liner as he undoubtedly was, there was a simplicity, a truth to nature, and at the same time, a faculty of dramatic presentation in which Greene, Lodge and Nash were wholly wanting; and his prose pamphlets smack of these good gifts in their measure as much as *The Honest Whore*."

Saintsbury's substantial late works, most notably his *History of Criticism* and *History of English Prosody*, are remarkable works of erudition written with their author's usual élan and frankness. The *History of Criticism* remains lively and readable over its considerable bulk. He often shows limited understanding when he deals with critics whose chief concern is with questions of morality, and little patience with the more philosophical kinds of criticism. His enthusiasm is most apparent when he deals with a critic such as Longinus who, according to Saintsbury, locates literary greatness in a work's capacity to compel "the 'transport,' the absorption of the reader." But for all its areas of relative weakness, and for all that has been sneeringly said of it by lesser minds than Saintsbury's, an open-minded reader of the *History* is likely to find grounds for endorsing T. S. Eliot's judgment (in *The Use of Poetry and the Use of Criticism*) that it is "always delightful, generally useful and most often right." The *History of English Prosody* is perhaps best read and enjoyed as a connoisseur's anthology of rhythmic effect. The work's terminology is often confused and contradictory, its judgments often idiosyncratic and inadequately explained. But there is hardly a page that does not have something stimulating to say to those who share Saintsbury's devotion to what he called "the Goddess Prosodia."

There are, to later eyes – as there were to those of some of his contemporaries (most notably represented in the violent attacks of John Churton Collins) – readily apparent weaknesses in Saintsbury's huge output. Herbert Read finds in his work "a certain treatment of literature as a refuge from life" and suggests that "there is one characteristic common to all the authors he preferred and recommended – they are all men without general ideas. He instinctively avoided those writers who probe deeply into the problems of human life." Given the extent and quality of Saintsbury's writings on, say, Swift and Honoré de Balzac, this is not a charge that can easily be sustained, though certainly it is true that Saintsbury was prone, particularly toward the end of his life, to approach literature too simply as "a place of Rest and Refreshment" (subtitle of *The Peace of the Augustans*). John Gross' rather condescending account of Saintsbury complains that "his catholicity, admirable up to a point, works against him in the end. His criticism is full of forthright judgments and downright opinions, yet ultimately shapeless, a wilderness of signposts" and characterizes his work as given to "rambling" down "side-paths of learned gossip." More judicious, and better-informed, is René Wellek's account, which balances the view that "Saintsbury's enormous reading, the almost universal scope of his subject matter, the zest and zeal of his exposition, the audacity with which he handles the most ambitious and unattempted arguments should be recognized as a great achievement" with an awareness that "the main objection to Saintsbury's work is not his neglect of philosophy or abstract theory or even the extreme individualism of his taste, but the poverty and haziness of his concepts and criteria of genres, devices, style, composition." Certainly many of Saintsbury's key terms remained resolutely undefined over his long career, their sense(s) often shifting and overlapping in ways that sometimes facilitate adroit rhetorical maneuvering but more often simply confuse. Other weaknesses are clear too. His writing on drama is often perfunctory and, in general terms, is at its best whenever he can treat dramatic texts as poems, rather than as texts for performance. He responds very poorly to the whole theatrical dimension of the history of drama. Though his implied definition of "literature" is fairly wide, he can seem very superficial when discussing discursive prose of various kinds, given his reluctance to engage with political or social ideas.

For all the obvious datedness of many of his assumptions – and of his often convoluted style – Saintsbury remains well worth the reading. Reading Saintsbury on a period is still a good way of discovering where to start in reading that period oneself; ideas of the canon, naturally, have changed since the period of Saintsbury's dominance but in the very difference lies a good reason for reading him. Reading a major critic from the beginning of the twentieth century is a very good way of coming to some recognition of just how partial our own view of things at the end of that century and the start of the next is. We may, in the mirror that Saintsbury provides, also find means to discern the strengths and weaknesses of our own increased specialization and our own far greater emphasis upon questions of theory.

## Principal criticism

*A Primer of French Literature*, 1880
*A Short History of Life and Writings of Le Sage*, 1881
*A Short History of French Literature*, 1882
*A History of Elizabethan Literature*, 1887
*Essays in English Literature: 1780–1860, First Series*, 1890
*Essays on French Novelists*, 1891
*Miscellaneous Essays*, 1892
*Corrected Impressions*, 1895
*Essays in English Literature: 1780–1860, Second Series*, 1895
*A History of Nineteenth Century Literature: 1780–1895*, 1896
*The Flourishing of Romance and the Rise of Allegory*, 1897
*A Short History of English Literature*, 1898
*A History of Criticism and Literary Taste in Europe from the Earliest Texts to the Present Day*, 1900–1904 (3 volumes)
*The Earlier Renaissance*, 1901
*A History of English Prosody from the Twelfth Century to the Present Day*, 1906–1910 (3 volumes)
*The Later Nineteenth Century*, 1907
*Historical Manual of English Prosody*, 1910
*A History of English Criticism*, 1911
*The Historical Character of English Lyric* (Warton Lecture on English Poetry), 1912
*A History of English Prose Rhythm*, 1912
*The English Novel*, 1913
*A First Book of English Literature*, 1914
*The Peace of the Augustans: A Survey of Eighteenth Century Literature as a Place of Rest and Refreshment*, 1916
*A History of the French Novel to the Close of the Nineteenth Century*, 1917–1919 (2 volumes)
*The Collected Essays and Papers 1875–1923*, 1923–1924 (4 volumes)
*A Consideration of Thackeray*, 1931
*Prefaces and Essays*, 1933
*Shakespeare*, 1934
*George Saintsbury: The Memorial Volume: A New Collection of His Essays and Papers*, 1945 (Augustus Muir, John W. Oliver, and Arthur M. Clark, editors)
*French Literature and Its Masters*, 1946
*A Last Vintage: Essays and Papers*, 1950

## Other major works and literary forms

George Saintsbury translated several French novels, including Balzac's *The Chouans* (1890), Prosper Mérimée's *Chronicles of the Reign of Charles IX* (1890), and Jean François Marmontel's *Moral Tales* (1895). He contributed prefaces to a huge number and range of editions and series (including, for example, forty volumes of Balzac's *Comédie humaine*, 1895–1898, and twelve volumes of the *Works of Smollett*, 1895–1900). His three-volume edition of *Minor Poets of the Caroline Period* (1905–1921) was an important and pioneering piece of work. He wrote biographies of *Dryden* (1881), *Marlborough* (1885), *The Earl of Derby* (1892), *Sir Walter Scott* (1897), and *Matthew Arnold* (1899). His *Notes on A Cellar Book* (1920) is a classic of wine-writing, and the series of his "Scrap Books" (*A Scrap Book*, 1922, *A Second Scrap Book*, 1923, *A Last Scrap Book*, 1924) mixes autobiographical memories with characteristically various reading (and characteristically forceful opinions).

## Further reading

Collins, John Churton. "Our Literary Guides. I. A Short History of English Literature," in *Ephemera Critica or Plain Truths about Current Literature*, 1902.
Elton, Oliver. "George Edward Bateman Saintsbury: 1845–1933," in *Proceedings of the British Academy*. 19 (1933), pp. 325–344.
Gross, John. *The Rise and Fall of the Man of Letters*, 1969.
Jones, Dorothy Richardson. *"King of Critics": George Saintsbury 1845–1933*, 1992.
Leuba, Walter. *George Saintsbury*, 1967.
Orel, Harold. *Victorian Literary Critics*, 1984.
Read, Herbert. "George Saintsbury," in *A Coat of Many Colours*, 1945.
Wellek, René. *A History of Modern Criticism: 1750–1950.* Vol. 4, *The Later Nineteenth Century*, 1965.
Wilson, Edmund. "George Saintsbury's Centenary" and "George Saintsbury: Gourmet and Glutton," in *Classics and Commercials*, 1950.

GLYN PURSGLOVE

# Jean-Paul Sartre

French philosopher and writer

**Born:** Paris, France; June 21, 1905
**Died:** Paris, France; April 15, 1980

## Biography

Jean-Paul Sartre was born on June 21, 1905, in Paris. His father died a year after his son's birth; his mother, a member of the famous Schweitzer family, took her child to live with her father, who was a professor of German in Meudon. They moved back to Paris in 1911, and his mother remarried in 1916. Sartre had enjoyed the company of his grandfather, who encouraged him to read; he felt a sense of estrangement, however, from his stepfather and became lonely and withdrawn.

Sartre attended the Lycée Henri IV and began to publish at the age of fifteen. He later entered the École Normale Supérieure to pursue a degree in philosophy. Strongly influenced by Cartesian rationalism, he explored the nature of consciousness in studies which prefigure his later philosophical works. In 1929 he met Simone de Beauvoir, with whom he formed an intellectual and emotional alliance which lasted until his death.

After teaching in Le Havre, he accepted a fellowship to study in Berlin in 1933; there he encountered works by Martin Heidegger and Edmund Husserl which provoked a crucial change in his intellectual development. German phenomenology came to dominate his thought for the next three decades. Mobilized in 1938, he was taken prisoner of war soon after. When released, he worked in the Resistance movement and returned to teaching and writing. A visit to the Soviet Union in 1954 led to his disillusionment with Soviet Communism, and he began to develop a personal theory of Marxist politics. He declined the Nobel Prize for Literature in 1964. Because of poor health and near blindness, he wrote little during the last decade of his life, but he continued to give strong support to a variety of left-wing causes. He died in Paris on April 15, 1980.

## Influence

In the 1950s and 1960s Sartre was the center of what almost amounted to a cult: people who never considered reading *L'Être et le néant* (1943; *Being and Nothingness*, 1956) were absorbing ideas from his plays, novels, articles, and interviews. It is difficult to make a specific assessment of the influence of a figure as prominent as he: it would be hard to imagine, for example, the existence of the Civil Rights movement, women's liberation, or gay activism without the all-pervasive undercurrent of Sartrian existentialism. His affirmation of people's freedom to choose for themselves and determine their own destiny heightened social consciousness in the young and inspired members of minority groups to work for changes in their own condition.

Sartre's blend of ideas from such thinkers as G. W. F. Hegel, Karl Marx, and Sigmund Freud quickly led to a popular philosophical attitude with important literary and psychological implications which continue to reverberate through Europe and America. These ideas filtered down from universities to the popular realm: revolutions ensued, techniques of psychotherapy were modified, and literature entered a different era as new ground was broken.

The full impact on the practice of literary criticism of the methods Sartre employed in his studies of Charles Baudelaire, Jean Genet, and Gustave Flaubert is yet to be determined. Sartre attempted to explore existential techniques of analysis to sketch a new approach which future critics could distill in order to produce studies of exceptional depth.

## Analysis

The totality of Sartre's literary criticism can best be understood by arranging his works into three categories: the early essays, which develop in general terms his Marxist view of the social purpose of all writing; his occasional short pieces on particular authors and artists, which clarify individual works and his judgment of their importance; and the extended aesthetic and biographical studies of Baudelaire, Genet, and Flaubert, which suggest new directions for the development of literary exploration and discovery.

Sartre's philosophical writings lay an important metaphysical foundation for his opinions on art and clarify the bases of his thought. His theory and practice of criticism, however, most often express either the position of an intellectual leftist or the subjective views of an individual with no apparent political bias, interested simply in exploring the imaginative world of a creator such as William Faulkner or Albert Camus. Seen in this perspective, Sartre's critical essays assume a significance, a shape and form, which they lack when surveyed chronologically.

*Qu'est-ce que la littérature?* (1947; *What Is Literature?*, 1949) explores the nationalization of literature, what it means to write and why one writes, the nature of the reader, and the situation of the French writer as Sartre saw it at that time. These essays express his concern for the writer's involvement in the life of his or her time, the social and political conditions which were determining the everyday reality of people of all classes, especially the proletariat. They are pervaded by Marxist views as Sartre develops his concept of *la littérature engagée*, the literature of commitment. He opposes the social and psychological determinism frequently encountered among writers at that time, wishing instead to stress human freedom and the duty writers have to awaken in their fellows an awareness of their liberty and the need to struggle heroically to further it.

Sartre distinguishes between works of music, painting, sculpture, and poetry, which exist as pure objects conveying different sensations to each person, and prose, which primarily conveys meanings simply and directly. It is significant that Sartre never wrote any poetry. His prose fulfills the ideals he promoted: it communicates clearly, and sometimes bluntly, his perception of the human condition. These perceptions, frequently shocking and offensive to the bourgeois public, which preferred what he called "literature of consumption," were intended to aid the lower classes in striving to fulfill their freedom. A prose writer who was an artist could no longer write books about boring puppets; "art for art's sake," at least in prose, could no longer be tolerated, given the conflicts of the contemporary world. He concludes that good writing must reveal the human condition to the reader, while suggesting the means for political and social change. For Sartre, the essence of literature is its content; style, by no means to be despised, should clearly be considered a secondary element in artistic expression.

Sartre's comments on François Mauriac are, then, predictably negative: his article "M. François Mauriac et la liberté" (1939; "François Mauriac and Freedom," 1957) attacks the suggestions of predestination which hover over this Catholic writer's work. Sartre is just as troubled, however, by the shifting perspectives of narrative technique and the stilted and artificial dialogue. Characters are presented sometimes from the outside, sometimes from within, changing the reader's perspective from their subjectivity to their objectivity, often in the same sentence. Sartre finds that Mauriac's books deal more with enslavement than with freedom. His review (1943) of Albert Camus' *L'Étranger* (1942; *The Stranger*, 1946) predicted that French literature, renewed with American vitality, would move in new directions. Sartre subtly analyzes the absurd condition of Camus' character Meursault and the ways it is revealed through detached, Hemingway-like sentences, equal to one another, which float like islands in a void. Camus' artistic vision provides bewildering glimpses into an absurd universe, a vision that would shortly be clarified in *Le Mythe de Sisyphe* (1942; *The Myth of Sisyphus*, 1955). It is not surprising that for a time Sartre and Camus enjoyed a close friendship.

Sartre's articles on American writers drew attention to such figures as William Faulkner and John Dos Passos. His essay "À propos de *Le Bruit et la fureur*: La Temporalité chez Faulkner" (1939; "On *The Sound and the Fury*: Time in the Work of Faulkner," 1957) discusses Faulkner's innovations in the presentation of time and chronology: the incoherent thoughts of the idiot Benjy establish a backward narrative motion, which creates a clockless time representing temporality rather than chronology. This technique of disorder, reflecting the monotony of everyday life, reveals Faulkner's metaphysics of irrational time: the present being essentially catastrophic, only the past, shattering the possibility of any future, can describe suffocation in a world dying of old age. In a 1938 essay on Dos Passos, Sartre continues to examine narrative techniques which, through jerky and uneven progressions, destroy the order of causality, creating characters who are "interior-exterior" beings described in a journalistic style. Sartre was later to use these techniques himself in parts of *Les Chemins de la liberté* (1945-1949; *The Roads to Freedom*, 1947-1950).

The influence of Freud became apparent in Sartre's monograph on Baudelaire, which sketched the outline for a new approach to the study of art and artists: a comprehensive understanding of an author was to be sought through a kind of existential psychoanalysis of his or her work. This analytic study, relatively short and easy to read, explores the mind and spirit of Baudelaire through his poems, diaries, and letters, examining them as if they were the utterances of a client on a couch. Neither ponderous nor superficial, Sartre probes the works and the intimate personal writings to discover both the man Baudelaire and his artistic essence. Marx and Freud combine to provide a framework within which Sartre could elaborate his commentary: this short book suggested new psychological and social directions which literary criticism could eventually take.

Sartre's analysis of Genet elaborates this preliminary technique into a systematic method: the work is an encyclopedia of existential explanation of the life and writing of the man. Taking an event from Genet's life, Sartre pauses to explore its multiple possible significances and lingers, sometimes excessively, upon the development of his explanations. He provides, in essence, a phenomenology of a living person. He proceeds in a similar fashion with the writings, elucidating small details from *Journal du voleur* (1948, 1949; *The Thief's Journal*, 1954) and *Notre-Dame des fleurs* (1944, 1951; *Our Lady of the Flowers*, 1949, 1963), exploring the significance of the details of his subject's experience and its expression in literature. Philosophy, psychology, and politics merge in this extraordinary analytical study. No comparable work of literary criticism had ever before been produced; one more was to follow.

Sartre spent his last years as a writer, handicapped by nearly total blindness, composing an extended analysis of the life and work of Flaubert which penetrates even more deeply into the psyche of a creative personality than his two earlier efforts. Left incomplete, Sartre's study, nearly three thousand pages long, explores the totality of Flaubert as man and artist.

Hazel Barnes, the translator of *Being and Nothingness*, wrote a condensation, with commentary, of the entire work as published. She believes that it will take many years for critics to digest this enormous work and discover how to apply its innovations in literary criticism. Few people have the time or patience to delve as deeply into the nature and character of an author as Sartre has done, but his method may eventually prove fruitful when condensed to reasonable dimensions. Sartre himself admitted in an interview that this huge work is an unedited rough draft: he was unable to see well enough to revise it, and, moreover, he believed that one should not attempt to write extremely well when dealing with a supreme master of style such as Flaubert. Perhaps, years from now, a new method of criticism will emerge from this experiment.

Offering a well blended synthesis of ideas drawn from the thinking of three giants of modern times – Hegel, Marx, and Freud – Sartre retained flexibility and versatility in his critical approaches. He supported the emerging black writers of the *négritude* movement and encouraged the controversial innovations of the New Novelists, such as Nathalie Sarraute and Michel Butor. He turned his attention to the visual arts in his existential investigations of the mobiles of Alexander Calder and the paintings of Tintoretto and Alberto Giacometti. Near the end of his life, Sartre expressed an interest in the work of the semiologist and structuralist Roland Barthes; he planned, in fact, to employ Barthes' technique of analysis in the fourth volume of his study of Flaubert, which unfortunately was never completed.

In both critical theory and practice, Sartre attempted to devise a totalizing critique, to propose a method on which another method could be constructed, to reveal the realities of literature and those who produced it in their condition of alienated freedom. He was convinced that empathy offered the key to the understanding of an artist, and that a "completed totality," to use his phrase, could emerge from a disciplined and detailed examination of a writer's work.

## Principal criticism

*L'Imagination*, 1936 (*Imagination: A Psychological Critique*, 1962)
*L'Imaginaire: Psychologie phénoménologique de l'imagination*, 1940 (*The Psychology of Imagination*, 1948)
*Qu'est-ce que la littérature?*, 1947 (*What Is Literature?*, 1949)
*Baudelaire*, 1947 (English translation, 1950)
*Situations I–X*, 1947–1975 (10 volumes)
*Saint-Genet: Comédien et martyr*, 1952 (*Saint Genet: Actor and Martyr*, 1963)
*Les Mots*, 1964 (*The Words*, 1964)
*L'Idiot de la famille: Gustave Flaubert, 1821–1857*, 1971–1972 (3 volumes; partial translation as *The Family Idiot: Gustave Flaubert, 1821–1857*, 1981)
*Un Théâtre de situations*, 1973 (*Sartre on Theater*, 1976)

## Other major works and literary forms

Seldom has a writer extended his attention over such a wide range of disciplines as did Jean-Paul Sartre. Known as an existentialist philosopher, novelist, playwright, literary critic, political and social theorist, and psychologist, Sartre exerted a major influence on the development of French – and international – thought in the twentieth century. His works were translated into many languages and have been widely studied throughout the world.

The first piece of fiction by this prolific writer was a novel, *La Nausée* (1938; *Nausea*, 1949), followed in short order by a collection of short stories, *Le Mur* (1939; *The Wall and Other Stories*, 1948). Sartre's early plays include *Les Mouches* (1943; *The Flies*, 1946) and *Huis-clos* (1944; *No Exit*, 1946). As he continued to write dramatic works, he produced a three-part novel, *Les Chemins de la liberté* (1945–1949; *The Roads to Freedom*, 1947–1950). The plays that followed, from *Morts sans sépulture* (1946; *The Victors*, 1948) to *Les Troyennes* (1965; *The Trojan Women*, 1967), served as effective vehicles for the dissemination of Sartre's existentialist ideas. He also wrote numerous essays on literature and its purposes for various journals, including *Les Temps modernes*, which Sartre founded in 1946 and continued to direct until his death.

NOVELS
*La Nausée*, 1938 (*Nausea*, 1949)
*Les Chemins de la liberté*, 1945–1949 (*The Roads to Freedom*, 1947–1950), includes *L'Âge de raison* (*The Age of Reason*), *Le Sursis* (*The Reprieve*), and *La Mort dans l'âme* (*Troubled Sleep*)

SHORT FICTION
*Le Mur*, 1939 (*The Wall and Other Stories*, 1948)

PLAYS
*Les Mouches*, 1943 (*The Flies*, 1946)
*Huis-clos*, 1944 (*No Exit*, 1946)
*Morts sans sépulture*, 1946 (*The Victors*, 1948)
*La Putain respectueuse*, 1946 (*The Respectful Prostitute*, 1947)
*Les Mains sales*, 1948 (*Dirty Hands*, 1948)
*Le Diable et le bon Dieu*, 1951 (*The Devil and the Good Lord*, 1953)
*Kean: Ou, Désordre et génie*, 1952 (adaptation of Alexandre Dumas, *père*'s play; *Kean: Or, Disorder and Genius*, 1954)
*Nekrassov*, 1955 (English translation, 1956)
*Les Séquestrés d'Altona*, 1959 (*The Condemned of Altona*, 1960)
*Les Troyennes*, 1965 (adaptation of Euripides' play; *The Trojan Women*, 1967)

SCREENPLAY
*Les Jeux sont faits*, 1947 (*The Chips Are Down*, 1948)

NONFICTION
*Esquisse d'une théorie des émotions*, 1939 (*The Emotions: Outline of a Theory*, 1948)
*L'Être et le néant*, 1943 (*Being and Nothingness*, 1956)
*Réflexions sur la question juive*, 1946 (*Anti-Semite and Jew*, 1948)
*L'Existentialisme est un humanisme*, 1946 (*Existentialism*, 1947)
*Critique de la raison dialectique, précédée de question de méthode*, 1960 (*Search for a Method*, 1963)

## Further reading
Barnes, Hazel E. *Sartre and Flaubert*, 1981.
Bauer, George Howard. *Sartre and the Artist*, 1969.
Collins, Douglas. *Sartre as Biographer*, 1980.
Cranston, Maurice. *Jean-Paul Sartre*, 1962.
Danto, Arthur C. *Sartre*, 1975.
Goldthorpe, Rhiannon. *Sartre: Literature and Theory*, 1984.
Halpern, Joseph. *Critical Fictions: The Literary Criticism of Jean-Paul Sartre*, 1976.
Howells, Christine. *Sartre's Theory of Literature*, 1979.
Jameson, Fredric. *Sartre: The Origins of a Style*, 1961.
LaCapra, Dominick. *A Dangerous Crossing: French Literary Existentialism and the Modern American Novel*, 1973.
McMahon, Joseph H. *Humans Being: The World of Jean-Paul Sartre*, 1971.
Murdoch, Iris. *Sartre: Romantic Rationalist*, 1987.
Schilpp, P. A. *The Cambridge Companion to Sartre*, 1992.
Suhl, Benjamin. *Jean-Paul Sartre: The Philosopher as a Literary Critic*, 1970.
Thody, Philip. *Jean-Paul Sartre: A Literary and Political Study*, 1960.

RAYMOND M. ARCHER

*See also* Absurd; Existentialism; French Literary Theory: Twentieth Century

# Ferdinand de Saussure
## Swiss linguist

**Born:** Geneva, Switzerland; November 26, 1857
**Died:** Vufflens, near Geneva, Switzerland; February 22, 1913

## Biography
Ferdinand de Saussure was born on November 26, 1857. His father, Henri de Saussure, came from a distinguished Huguenot family that had emigrated from France in the sixteenth century; among his forebears were the physicist Horace-Benedict de Saussure and the botanist Nicolas de Saussure. His mother came from the socially prominent de Pourtalès family, whose aristocratic origins had necessitated their emigration from France at the time of the French Revolution.

Saussure exhibited an interest in language at a very early age, although because of family tradition he began by studying science at the University of Geneva. He went on to read philology at the Universities of Leipzig and Berlin, and at the age of twenty-one he impressed his academic colleagues with the excellence of his monograph *Mémoire sur le système primitif des voyelles dans les langues indo-européenes*. This led to a post at the École Pratique des Hautes Études in Paris, where he taught from 1881 to 1891.

He then returned to the University of Geneva, where he became a professor of Indo-European linguistics and Sanskrit in 1901 and a professor of general linguistics in 1907, and spent the remainder of his career in a congenial academic environment. He published very little and gave only the lectures later published as *Course in General Linguistics*, when he was suddenly called upon to substitute for another professor, who had become ill. Saussure died on February 22, 1913, with no idea that two of his students, Charles Bally and Albert Séchehaye, would assemble his lecture notes into a book destined to become the bible of modern linguistics.

## Influence
Saussure is considered the father of modern linguistics, and as a consequence his work has influenced almost every critic or theorist involved with the serious investigation of language. More specifically, his ideas provided the impetus for the formation of the structuralist movement, and were instrumental in the intellectual development of the anthropologist Claude Lévi-Strauss and the critic Roland Barthes.

Saussure's influence on literary theory has been considerable. His synchronic study of language – as a self-enclosed system rather than a historical phenomenon – and his emphasis on the arbitrary nature of the linguistic sign have been adapted to literary study by a variety of structuralist and poststructuralist critics, who minimize or deny altogether literature's capacity to represent extraliterary reality.

As Sigmund Freud is to psychology and Charles Darwin to biology, so is Saussure to the analytic study of language.

## Analysis

Ferdinand de Saussure was instrumental in making linguistics the study of living languages rather than dead words. Where his predecessors had for the most part treated language as a collection of grammatical rules and historical texts, Saussure argued that it was a vital, constantly changing and to some extent socially determined phenomenon comprising speech as well as writing. Like many other late-nineteenth-century intellectual pioneers – Karl Marx, Max Weber, and Émile Durkheim among them – he conceived of humanity as an essentially interactive species which developed its characteristics within a social context rather than inside the minds of isolated individuals.

There was still an important historical element in Saussure's thought, but it was balanced by a social component that he considered at least as important. He identified language's social aspect as the "synchronic" and its historical aspect as the "diachronic." The synchronic was the realm of language conceptualized as an organic whole, in terms of the actual conditions of its use at a particular moment in time; the diachronic was the chart of its development over time, viewed in terms of changes in usage as exemplified by a series of examples taken from successive historical periods. A thorough investigation of language would require that both methods be utilized, although it was his advocacy of the synchronic approach that made Saussure's theory so revolutionary.

The primary source of information about language's synchronic character was human speech, which points to a second major distinction crucial for the understanding of Saussure's theory of language. He conceived of speech as the synthesis of *langue* and *parole*, the French terms for the language system and the act of speaking itself, respectively, which are often used in untranslated form in contemporary literary criticism. *Langue* is the sum total of individual language uses at any given time, a theoretically knowable if in practice only generally approximated description of language as a social system; *parole* is the individual's manifestation of *langue*, those speech acts which constitute the demonstration of how it is used in day-to-day life.

The distinction between *langue* and *parole* has been used by Noam Chomsky as the basis for his dichotomy between "competence" and "performance," and as such has become part of general intellectual culture. Although *parole* usually interests linguists only as the raw material from which to work toward the definition of *langue*, in literary criticism it has assumed greater significance because of its obvious relevance to questions of character construction and narrative voice.

A third crucial aspect of Saussure's linguistic theory was his notion of language systems, which he defined as groups of mutually defining entities called linguistic signs. The latter were composed of signifiers, or words, and the signified, the meanings to which they pointed, and the most important thing about this relationship was that it was arbitrary: there was no necessary logical connection between signifier and signified, and thus the signs themselves could not be identified with objects in the external world. From this it followed that linguistic signs could be defined only by other linguistic signs, a conception of complete systemic interdependence which constitutes one of the essential elements of structuralist thought.

Linguistics thus becomes the study of how signs relate to one another within the language system. Saussure here emphasized what he called the syntagmatic and paradigmatic character of such relationships: the syntagmatic referred to the sequence of signs within a sentence, the paradigmatic to a sign's participation in a subset of interchangeable signs. In the sentence "I never drink wine," for example, the syntagmatic aspect of its linguistic signs is the ordering of pronoun, adverb, verb, and direct object, while their paradigmatic feature consists in the possibility of substituting "You" for "I" – to focus upon one of its signs – because both are part of that particular group of signs known as pronouns. Since every word in the sentence has both syntagmatic and paradigmatic functions, both must be studied if one wishes to understand the structure of a language.

The highly technical nature of these various distinctions should not be permitted to obscure the explosive force with which they burst upon linguistic and literary theorists alike. Where language had been assumed to be a system of nomenclature, a collection of words which each had one-to-one correspondences with easily identifiable objects, Saussure conceptualized it as a system of differentiations. It is here that Saussure departs most radically from commonsense notions of language (and it is here, as several critics have pointed out, that his theory of language is most vulnerable to attack). According to Saussure, Jonathan Culler notes, "a language is a system of elements which are wholly defined by their relations to one another within the system." In Saussure's own words, linguistic differences are "differences without positive terms," established through mutual opposition (as with the phonemes that distinguish "pen" from "den") rather than by extralinguistic reality.

If linguistic signs are in essence arbitrary, this does not mean that they are irrational or incomprehensible. On the contrary, Saussure argues, their arbitrary quality points to the social processes through which each language's particular character is generated. In fact, society and language must be imagined as coming into the world at the same time, since social life would be impossible without a mutually understood signifying system and such a system could develop only within a social context. Given the mutual interpenetration of language and society, the study of one is in an important sense the study of the other.

The study of linguistics, Saussure believed, would ultimately yield a general science of signs, or semiology (now called semiotics). Once it was understood that linguistic signs were arbitrary, it would be but a short step to the realization that other socially generated signs, such as rituals, customs, and gestures, must also be seen as deriving their meaning from a system of relationships rather than their intrinsic qualities. Thus, principally through the work of Claude Lévi-Strauss, Saussure's linguistic theories influenced the development of structuralist anthropology.

It is difficult to overestimate Saussure's influence on contemporary literary theory. Roland Barthes, in the 1950s, was the first to give Saussure's ideas general currency; thereafter, the growing interest in Saussure coincided with the unprecedented growth of literary theory as a discipline. Indeed, much of the terminology of literary structuralism and poststructuralism is derived from Saussure. All traditional theories of literature, whatever their distinctive emphases, ascribe to literary texts a mimetic function. In contrast, many contemporary theorists assert that literature's claims to represent reality are grossly exaggerated, if not (as some insist) absolutely without foundation. In part, this contention is based on Saussure's theories.

As great as Saussure's impact on literary theory has been, there are indications that it has peaked. The 1980s saw reaction against the notion that literature is essentially self-referential; at the same time, there is increasing skepticism concerning the claim (so widely made during the heyday of structuralism) that linguistics will transform literary study into a science – or that such a goal is even desirable. Whatever the future direction of literary theory, Saussure's ideas have proved to be an extraordinarily rich source of intellectual stimulation, and there is every reason to expect that he will continue to be regarded as one of the seminal thinkers of the modern era.

## Principal criticism
*Cours de linguistique générale*, 1916 (*Course in General Linguistics*, 1959)

## Other major works and literary forms
Other than the reconstruction of his lecture notes posthumously published as *Course in General Linguistics*, Ferdinand de Saussure's only other published work was his *Mémoire sur le système primitif des voyelles dans les langues indoeuropéenes* (1879), a work of comparative philology whose theories concerning vowel alteration were confirmed fifty years later by other researchers.

NONFICTION
*Mémoire sur le système primitif des voyelles dans les langues indo-européenes*, 1879

## Further reading
Barthes, Roland. *Elements of Semiology*, 1967.
Culler, Jonathan. *Saussure*, 1976.
Gadet, Françoise. *Saussure and Contemporary Culture*, 1989. Translated by Gregory Elliot.
Gordon, W. Terrence. *Saussure for Beginners*, 1996.
Harris, Roy. *Reading Saussure: A Critical Commentary on the "Cours de linguistique générale,"* 1987.
——. *Language, Saussure and Wittgenstein: How to Play Games With Words*, 1988.
Holdcroft, David. *Saussure: Signs, System, and Arbitrariness*, 1991.
Koerner, E. F. K. *Ferdinand de Saussure: The Origin and Development of His Linguistic Thought in Western Studies of Language*, 1973.
Spinks, C. W., and John Deely, eds. *Semiotics*, 1996.
Starobinski, Jean. *Words upon Words: The Anagrams of Ferdinand de Saussure*, 1979.
Thibault, Paul J. *Re-reading Saussure: The Dynamics of Signs in Social Life*, 1997.

PAUL STUEWE

*See also* Deconstruction; Linguistics and Literary Studies; Semiotics; Structuralism

# Julius Caesar Scaliger
Italian-French scholar and writer

**Born:** Riva, Italy; April 23, 1484
**Died:** Agen, France; October 21, 1558

## Biography
Julius Caesar Scaliger was born in Italy at the La Rocca Castle, at Riva, near Lake Garda on April 23, 1484. His family claimed to be descended from the Della Scalas of Verona, who traced their lineage back to the time of the early Gothic kings. The Della Scalas called themselves Lescale in French and Scaliger in Latin.

This claim to be descended from the princes of Verona was not questioned during Scaliger's lifetime, but in 1607 Gaspard Schoppe, known by his Latin name of Scioppius, attacked it. Scioppius contended that Scaliger's father was a painter named Benedetto Bordoni. He also claimed that the name Della Scala derived from the ladder which Bordoni used in his trade and that the ladder had also been used as an identifying mark on the sign in front of Bordoni's shop. Scaliger's son, Joseph Justus, answered this charge in 1608, but the controversy over the lineage of the Scaligers continued for several centuries.

The elder Scaliger spent his early years as a soldier in the service of the Emperor Maximilian I and Alfonso d'Este; he also attended the University of Bologna, one of the most distinguished centers of European learning at that time. He studied medicine by reading the works of Hippocrates and Galen and by practical observation.

On a trip to France with Anthony Rovere, Bishop of Agen, he met and fell in love with Andiette de La Roque Lobejac, a very young heiress. When they married on

April 3, 1529, Andiette was sixteen and Scaliger forty-five. In order to persuade Andiette's guardians that he was a suitable husband, he spent three years establishing a medical practice in Agen. In March of 1528, a year before his marriage, he became a naturalized citizen of France.

Scaliger spent the rest of his life in Agen, where he died on October 21, 1558. His gout seems to have prevented him from traveling and even to have made it difficult for him to write. Of his fifteen children, Joseph Justus Scaliger, who is frequently confused with his father, was most inclined to scholarship; he became the teacher of the influential Humanist, Daniel Heinsius. Joseph Justus' pedantic approach to literary theory and scholarship contrasts sharply with that of his father, who believed that "to cull from books what authors have reported is exceedingly dangerous; true knowledge of things is out of the things themselves."

## Influence

Scaliger's *Poetices libri septem* (poetics – seven books) derives from Aristotle's *De poetica* (334-323 B.C.; *Poetics*), and, although Renaissance scholars of the sixteenth and early seventeenth centuries cited Aristotle as the supreme authority on poetry and drama, they canonized him as Scaliger interpreted him. Scaliger, in spite of his theoretical and practical differences from Aristotle, became one of the authoritative interpreters of Aristotle's *Poetics*. He was frequently cited by his contemporaries as second in importance only to Aristotle himself.

## Analysis

Scaliger's theories of literature are largely set forth in his *Poetices libri septem*, a seven-book treatise which was published posthumously in 1561. He introduces his treatise as a work intended to continue the education of his oldest son, Sylvius, for whom he had earlier written *De causis linguae latinae* (the principles of the Latin language).

Even among Humanists devoted to classical learning, Scaliger's Greek scholarship was formidable. He was the first systematic commentator on Aristotle's *Poetics* and one of the most influential. Until the first Greek edition of Aristotle's *Poetics* was printed by Aldus Manutius in 1508, all that was available were two corrupt editions, a summary by Averroës in 1481 and an incomplete Latin translation by Giorgio Valla in 1498. In 1531 Desiderius Erasmus included the full Greek text of the *Poetics* in his complete edition of Aristotle.

Although much of Scaliger's influence derived from his position as an early interpreter of Aristotle, his *Poetices libri septem* is intended as a comprehensive treatise on the subject of poetry. He provides an exhaustive description of metrics and genres, while elaborating theories which differ in significant respects from those of Aristotle. Scaliger's *Poetices libri septem* is divided into *Historicus* (the history of poetry), *Hyle* (the matter of poetry), *Idea* (the ideas of poetry), *Parasceve* (the preparation or composing of poetry), *Criticus* (criticism), *Hypercriticus* (criticism continued), and *Epinomis* (appendix).

The first book, *Historicus*, supplies a history and etymology of poetry and of poetic genres, such as comedy, tragedy, and satire. Scaliger was responsible for an addition to the theory of comic structure. Traditionally, comedy was supposed to have a three-part structure: *protasis* (exposition of the circumstances), *epitasis* (complications develop), and *catastrophe* (conversion of the debated complications into unexpected tranquillity). To this paradigm, Scaliger added *catastasis* (the full vigor and climax of the play). This term was first used in 1616 in England, and its origin can be traced to Scaliger.

The second book, *Hyle*, analyzes the material of poetry from a metrical and rhythmic perspective. Scaliger ranges widely over the Greek works and fragments known in his day, supplying metrical analysis and examples for each meter. It is important to note that he does not offer these descriptions from a prescriptive point of view. Scaliger encourages poets not only to imitate the ancients but also to experiment with new forms. As an indication that the modern poet can and should compete with the Greeks and Romans, he offers his own poem in pyrrhics, a foot of two short and no long syllables. Scaliger pointedly observes that no classical poet had written an entire poem in pyrrhics.

The third book, *Idea*, comments upon the meaning and form of poetry, emphasizing the conventions governing structure and arrangement. The fourth book, *Parasceve*, discusses character, decorum, and rhetorical style. The fifth and sixth books, *Criticus* and *Hypercriticus*, engage in practical or applied criticism of selected poets from the perspective of Scaliger's theories. In this section he compares Homer and Virgil, to the disadvantage of Homer. Scaliger engages in a highly biased stylistic comparison of the two poets in which unlike passages are compared; Virgil is always preferred. Scaliger's elevation of Virgil over Homer was controversial even with his contemporaries. George Chapman, the English translator of Homer, vehemently attacked Scaliger for his criticism of Homer: "But thou soule-blind Scalliger, that never hadst anything but place, time, and termes to paint thy proficiencie in learning, nor ever writest any thing of thine owne impotent braine but thy onely impalsied diminuation of *Homer*."

Many scholars and critics who know nothing else about Scaliger's literary theories know that he considered Virgil superior to Homer. In part, Scaliger's judgment derives from his own insistence that poetry must teach people to lead better lives. Virgil's Aeneas is nobler than Homer's Achilles and so functions better as a model of virtuous conduct. Scaliger's preference, however, was also motivated by his attitudes toward the relationship between the ancients and the moderns. He contends that "the arguments of Homer which nature proposed to him were corrected by Vergil as a schoolboy's theme by his professor. Make no mistake, this is true of all the works of the Greeks. If they had not said these things, we would have. All we took from them was for the purpose of improving it."

Scaliger's attitude toward the classics contrasts favorably with the idealization of Homer and Virgil which dominated European criticism for more than two hundred years after his death. Using the classical epics and dramas as models, neoclassical critics attempted to establish rules governing poetry and proceeded to censure the works of their contemporaries for not observing the classical unities or other conventions deduced from the practice of classical poets.

Scaliger's method of criticism, particularly of contemporary poets, influenced the direction French criticism was to take. He engages in a line by line analysis of poems, either stating that what is said is good or providing an example of how it might be improved. When he objects to a line, it is usually for one of two reasons: the statement is not true or does not make sense or it is not metrically effective. After praising Girolamo Fracastoro's *Syphilis sive morbus Gallicus* (1530; *Syphilis: Or, A Poetical History of the French Disease*, 1686), he corrects Fracastoro's medical statements, observing that syphilis is not necessarily limited to human beings because he has diagnosed syphilis in a dog. He also freely revises lines to improve their meter.

The seventh book appears to be an appendix or conclusion written after the completion of *Poetices libri septum*. Since book 7 contains an important summary of the points of disagreement between Scaliger and Aristotle relative to imitation and to the importance of plot and character in tragedy, it may be that Scaliger realized the full extent of his theoretical disagreements with Aristotle only after completing the work.

Only fragmentary portions of Scaliger's *Poetices libri septum* have been translated into English. Frederick Morgan Padelford translated selections from it in 1905, but these fragments do not do justice to the clarity of Scaliger's theories. Ignoring the systematic coherence of the *Poetices libri septum*, Padelford entirely omits book 2 on the grounds that it is "altogether taken up with the technical treatment of classical meters." This particular book was extremely influential in its own day because it supplied practicing poets with a handbook on metrics. In the preface to his translations, Padelford describes book 7 as "a salve to the exacting conscience of Scaliger, [which] helped to keep up the pleasing delusion of his omniscience" and comments that it is interesting because it "betrays how completely [Scaliger] failed to understand Aristotle's discussion of character and action." Padelford's unsympathetic evaluation of Scaliger fails to take account of the ways in which Scaliger consciously disagreed with Aristotle's theories.

Scaliger analyzes the implications of Aristotle's statements that imitation is the purpose and basic element in poetry and that only people imitate. Scaliger believes that lyrics, epigrams, and many other kinds of songs and poems cannot be regarded as true poetry if imitation is considered the basis of poetry. In lyric poetry, imitation does not occur because the singer sings and explains the emotions of his or her own spirit, not those of a fictionalized character. Scaliger further comments that if imitation is the purpose or end of poetry, then only those who imitate should be regarded as poets. In the epic, for example, the epic poet will be a true poet when he or she speaks as a fictional character but will not be when he or she speaks in his or her own person.

In addition, Scaliger contends that all speech is imitation, that words are the images of things; consequently, poetry and nonpoetry will be identical since they both use words. He is also skeptical about defining fiction as the end of poetry because poetry about truth rather than fiction – for example, historical, scientific, and philosophical verse – will be omitted from the literary canon. Pointing out that epic poetry is a mixture of history and fiction and that the best historians insert fictional speeches into their narratives, Scaliger insists that meter and rhythm are the basis of poetry and that works in verse will always be poems. Echoing Horace's dictum that poetry should teach and delight, he concludes that the end of poetry is to teach with pleasure.

Scaliger's definition of poetry as verse characterized by meter and rhythm results in the exclusion of prose fiction from the poetic canon. On the other hand, Aristotle's insistence upon imitation (or fiction) as the basis of poetry excludes philosophical poems, such as Lucretius' *De rerum natura* (c. 60 B.C.; *On the Nature of Things*, 1910), historical poetry, such as Lucan's *Pharsalia* (c. A.D. 60; *On the Civil War*, 1713), and all scientific verse from the literary canon. In the *Poetics*, Aristotle identifies "plot" as the essential and unifying element to which all other elements are subordinate. Scaliger argues against this principle largely because of his assumption that the end of poetry is persuasive teaching. Poetic drama should improve the characters of members of the audience by persuading them to lead better lives. For this reason, Scaliger claims that the depiction of character offers the audience models of behavior and so is of the utmost importance. Action reinforces the lessons in the drama rather than giving it unity.

Scaliger's *Contra poetices calumniatores declamatio* (declamation against the slanderers of poetry; published posthumously in 1600) is a *declamatio*, a highly rhetorical speech on a hypothetical law case. Scaliger is defending poetry against those who claim that it undermines piety and encourages vice. After devoting serious efforts to showing that Plato, who had attacked poetry, was himself a poet, Scaliger turns to the Bible and argues that if poetry is to be eliminated, all biblical stories will have to be deleted.

Once the Romantics substituted the poem for what the poem taught and affirmed ("art for art's sake"), Scaliger began to seem out of date. For Scaliger, poetry existed in the broader realm of politics, and, as a part of politics, poetry supplemented legislation and oratory in contributing to the institutions of the state and the welfare of the citizenry. Beyond the requirement that it must be in verse, poetry had no principles of its own; whatever could be said about philosophy or natural science also held true· for poetry. Scaliger's insistence upon the didactic function of poetry enabled him to claim that it had practical and theoretical value in the political realm.

## Principal criticism
*De causis linguae latinae*, 1540
*Poetices libri septem*, 1561 (partial translation as *Select Translations from Scaliger's Poetics*, 1905)
*Contra poetices calumniatores declamatio*, 1600

## Other major works and literary forms
Julius Caesar Scaliger exhibited the enthusiasm for learning characteristic of Renaissance Humanists. In addition to distinguishing himself as a theoretical and practical critic, he composed poetry, botanical commentaries, and treatises on physics, medicine, and philosophy. His voluminous correspondence with his Humanist contemporaries represents a record of the intellectual history of his times.

POETRY
*Poemata in duas partes divisa*, 1574

NONFICTION
*Oratio pro M. Tullio Cicerone contra Desiderium Erasmum Roterodamum*, 1531
*Adversus Desiderium Erasmi Roterodamum dialogum Ciceronianum oratio secunda*, 1536
*Exotericarum exercitationum liber quintus decimus de subtilitate ad Hieronymum Cardanum*, 1557
*Epistolae et orationes*, 1600

TRANSLATIONS
*Hippocratis liber de Somniis cum J. C. Scaligeri Commentariis*, 1539 (of Hippocrates' *Liber de Somniis*)
*In libros duos, qui inscribuntur de Plantis, Aristotele autore, libri duo*, 1556
*Animadversiones in Historias Theophrasti*, 1584

## Further reading
Billanovich, M. "Benedetto Bordon e Giulio Cesare Scaligero," in *Italia Medioevale e Umanistica*. XI (1968), pp. 187–256.
Bradner, Leicester. *Musicae Anglicanae: A History of Anglo-Latin Poetry, 1500–1925*, 1941.
Brink, Jean R. "Philosophical Poetry: The Contrasting Poetics of Sidney and Scaliger," in *Explorations in Renaissance Culture*. VIII–IX (1982–1983), pp. 45–53.
Campbell, Lilly B. "A Note on Scaliger's *Poetices*," in *Modern Philology*. XX (1922–1923), pp. 375–378.
Grafton, Anthony. *Joseph Scaliger: A Study in the History of Classical Scholarship*, 1983, 1993 (2 volumes).
Hall, Vernon. "Scaliger's Defense of Poetry," in *PMLA*. LXIII (1948), pp. 1125–1130.
——. "Life of Julius Caesar Scaliger (1484–1558)," in *Transactions of the American Philosophical Society*. XL (October, 1950).
Herrick, Marvin T. *The Fusion of Horatian and Aristotelian Literary Criticism, 1531–1555*, 1946.
Lintilhac, Eugene. *De J. C. Scaligeri Poetice*, 1887.
Weinberg, Bernard. "Scaliger Versus Aristotle on Poetics," in *Modern Philology*. XXXIX (1942), pp. 337–360.

JEAN R. BRINK

*See also* Bembo; Giraldi Cinthio; Renaissance and Restoration Literary Theory; Trissino

# Friedrich Wilhelm Joseph Schelling
German philosopher, writer, and critic

**Born:** Leonberg, Württemberg, Germany; January 27, 1775
**Died:** Bad Ragaz, Switzerland; August 20, 1854

## Biography
Friedrich Wilhelm Joseph Schelling, whose father was a Lutheran pastor and whose mother was the daughter of a pastor, was born on January 27, 1775, at Leonberg in Württemberg. Schelling was a precocious child, mastering Latin and Greek by the age of eight. Destined by his family for the ministry, he received his elementary education at the theological seminary in Bebenhausen, where his father was professor of Oriental languages. The boy's rapid intellectual development led to his admission at the age of fifteen to the University of Tübingen, where he studied theology, philosophy, and philology, and where he became friends with the philosopher G. W. F. Hegel and Romantic poet Friedrich Hölderlin. Schelling and his friends embraced the ideals of the French Revolution, and they celebrated together when they received news of the fall of the Bastille. These radical ideas caused Schelling to lose the Duke of Württemberg's patronage.

After intensively studying the works of Immanuel Kant and Johann Gottlieb Fichte, Schelling received in 1791 a master's degree in philosophy and in 1795 a master's degree in theology. After finishing his studies, for two years he tutored the sons of a noble family in Leipzig, where he also attended lectures in physics, chemistry, and medicine. These scientific studies turned him away from Fichte, who, Schelling believed, had not paid adequate attention to nature in his Idealist system.

In 1798 Schelling became, at the age of twenty-three, a professor at the University of Jena, the academic center of Germany. There he became part of the Romantic circle that included August Wilhelm Schlegel, Friedrich Schlegel, and Novalis. Schelling was particularly friendly with Caroline Schlegel, the intellectually gifted and charming wife of August, eventually marrying her in 1803, after her divorce. In keeping with the Romantic creed of freedom and faithfulness to feeling, the three remained friends. The marriage was a happy one, helping Schelling to produce his most successful works, but his disagreements with Fichte led him to accept an appointment at the University of Würzburg, where he served from 1803 to 1806. This period was followed by a call to Munich to become the general secretary of the Bavarian Academy of Fine Arts. Three years after their arrival in Munich, Caroline died; Schelling was devastated. From then on he was unable to publish anything substantial. He continued to lecture, at Erlangen and at Munich, and remarried, in 1812, to Pauline Gotter, the daughter of a friend of his late wife; although the marriage was harmonious, producing three sons and three daughters, Schelling's great passion for Caroline was unrepeatable.

In 1841 King Friedrich Wilhelm IV of Prussia, seeking someone to counteract the antimonarchical ideas of left-wing Hegelians, offered Schelling a post in Berlin. Despite his advanced age, he accepted the offer, and though he taught only a few years, among his students were Friedrich Engels, Søren Kierkegaard, Jakob Burckhardt, and Mikhail Bakunin. In 1846 Schelling retired from teaching, withdrew from public life, and eventually returned to Munich, where he devoted himself to perfecting his philosophy. Nevertheless, he was never able to put his thoughts into a form coherent enough to publish. He died in 1854 at Bad Ragaz in Switzerland.

## Influence

Schelling, despite being primarily a philosopher, had little philosophical influence because the right-wing Hegelians, the talented disciples of his rival, Hegel, occupied most of the important academic positions. Science historians, however, have discovered some Schellingian influence on such nineteenth-century scientists as Karl Ernst von Baer and Lorenz Oken, and his view of nature as a unity of polar forces may have contributed to Hans Christian Ørsted's discovery of electromagnetism. Schelling's greatest influence, however, was on German Romantic artists and writers, and he became known as the philosopher of Romanticism.

Some critics mark the start of Romanticism in England by the publication in 1798 of William Wordsworth's and Samuel Taylor Coleridge's *Lyrical Ballads*, a few months after the appearance of Schelling's first works in "*Naturphilosophie*" (the philosophy of nature). This chronological closeness symbolizes the intimate relationship between Schelling and English Romanticism. He certainly influenced Coleridge's aesthetics, and Schelling's views on individuality, freedom, and creativity attracted other English poets and literary critics.

In the United States, Schelling's ideas were used by Ralph Waldo Emerson in some of his essays and by Edgar Allan Poe in *Eureka: A Prose Poem* (1848). In Russia, Schelling appealed to the pan-Slavist group, and his religious ideas inspired Vladimir Soloviev. More recently, critics have written about Schelling's impact on modern existentialist writers. His insight that human actions are determined not only by conscious reason but also by unconscious impulses

is now valued as leading to a deeper understanding of humanity than that attained by Hegel.

## Analysis

Schelling was the most romantic of the German Idealists, but, like those classical and medieval ruins so beloved to Romantics, his work remained incomplete and he left behind no finished system. His ideas evolved from the past, and he consciously used Neo-Platonic and medieval German traditions as well as such modern philosophers as Baruch Spinoza and Gottfried Wilhelm Leibniz. Curious, enthusiastic, and sensitive, Schelling was able to invent new ideas and give new meaning to old ideas. He told his students that the beginning and end of all philosophy is freedom, and this free spirit characterized his philosophizing.

Deeply desiring unity, Schelling was concerned about the rift between humanity and nature, the subjective and objective, the ideal and real, thought and being, the ego and nonego. A main thrust of his thinking is to break down these barriers and see these things as interdependent poles of a single cosmic reality. Human reflection caused these rifts, and therefore reflection can be a spiritual sickness, since it turns humanity in on itself and away from nature. If one views existence properly, by philosophical reflection, however, then one realizes the healthy and holy bond among natural things and between these things and the human spirit. In this light, nature becomes visible spirit and spirit, invisible nature, or, as Schelling put it, nature is slumbering spirit.

This doctrine has implications for poetry because the poem is, for Schelling, nature's knowledge of itself. Poetry is not a mere play of words and notions but the result of an energy partly conscious and partly unconscious. Poetic knowledge has two poles, subjective and objective, and during poetic creation, these poles are so intimately united that a kinship of love develops. Schelling was also convinced that poetic activity depends on a grasp of the intelligibility of nature. The poet presupposes an ideal structure of nature, and the culmination of the poetic process is the revelation that human knowledge of nature, gained poetically, is nature's knowledge of itself. From the transcendental point of view, then, no rift exists between nature and spirit; they are one. The external world has the same character as the internal world, and Schelling clearly proclaimed the *Ichheit (I-ness)* of all things.

Schelling also viewed the universe as a divine organism. In every organism, unity and individuality must rule; thus God, the divine life, must rule the universe as One in all. This unifying force can be grasped only by the intuitive power of imaginative genius. For example, nature responds to questioning by the poetic genius because the poet possesses an intuitive faculty attuned to the spiritual activity of the universe; just as nature is God's playground, so the poem is the poet's playground. The creative activity of both God and poet are forms of individual self-expression, the stamping of a unique personality on the matter of experience. The poem, then, is like an organism in that both can be properly understood only teleologically, that is, as entities in which the parts serve the whole and the whole itself is purposive. The main difference between the poem and life is that in living organisms the activity of the organizing intelligence is hidden or unconscious whereas in the poem this activity is both conscious and unconscious. The unconscious element in poetic creation means that the poet never fully understands his poem.

According to Schelling, the purpose of the poem is neither utility, nor pleasure, nor morality, nor knowledge, but beauty – the realization of the infinite in the finite. In his aesthetics, he thought of himself as a prophet whose religious message was the revelation of the divine in art. He spoke, as did Wordsworth, of the sympathetic attraction between the poet's spirit and nature, and both saw this cosmic sympathy as a correlate of cosmic life. Art, then, crowns the creativity of the cosmos. In Schelling's view, theoretical intelligence contemplates the world and practical intelligence orders it, but aesthetic intelligence creates it.

The artistic genius, free from external laws though not from its own internal laws, reveals the hidden beauty of things. Schelling, along with Kant, helped establish the aesthetic as an autonomous faculty in the life of the mind. This faculty comes into play at special moments in the artist's experience. Schelling described this faculty as the flower of eternity unfolding in the temporal. He recognized that this free and playful faculty offered a way to revolt against the rationalist tradition in art with its emphasis on balance, its insistence on rules, and its morality of calculation. He escaped from the confinement of this rationalist creed by proclaiming art as an intuition of the Absolute in nature. In the universe, the same divine energy that, when unconscious, manifests itself as nature, is, when conscious, art. The ideal work of art and the real world of things are products of the same aesthetic activity. In this way, Schelling divinized art. Before him, the value of artistic and literary works had been utilitarian, ornamental, or didactic; after him, these works had spiritual dignity and value. In the early nineteenth century, the phrase "art for art's sake" began to be used to refer to this aesthetic doctrine. The phrase came to mean artistic rebellion against conventional bourgeois morality, with its prudery and hypocrisy. Instead Schelling asked his followers to conceive both nature and art as revelations of the odyssey of the spirit.

The beautiful in art and literature is, for Schelling, a revelation of the Absolute in sensuous garb. His idea that the beautiful is a symbolic representation of the infinite aided the spread of symbolism in art and literature. For example, he realized that a new mythology was needed by modern poets and offered his Idealist philosophy as a source for a modern mythology; some Romantic artists accepted his offer. Indeed, he was prophetic of the type of mythology that later materialized in the work of Friedrich Nietzsche and Richard Wagner.

Creative power, for Schelling, characterizes everything in nature, and it finds its highest expression in the human being. The artist's power is an extension of the creative force pervading all nature. This means that poetic genius is not reducible to technical proficiency, something that can be taught; rather, the creative poet is the vehicle of a power that acts through him. One of the vital elements in these poets, and in all Romantic artists, is a consciously recognized principle of organic form. This principle rests on the distinction between nature as it appears, *natura naturata* (nature as a system of particular things), and ideal nature, *natura naturans* (nature in her universal patterns). The central question for Schelling is how the artist, a creation of *natura naturata*, becomes aware of the process of *natura naturans*, the realm of essence. This is done through art, the active bond between the soul and nature, the universal and particular, essence and existence. Art is not a mere imitation of phenomena; it is the holy and creative elemental power of the world.

Such creative power leads to practical activity. Schelling defined the faculty that conceives and forms artworks the imagination (*Einbildungskraft*), whereas fancy (*Phantasie*) perceives art in an external way. Imagination is controlled by something nonarbitrary, whereas fancy is purely arbitrary. Imagination is the faculty of ideas (theoretical reason), whereas fancy, isolated from reason, gives birth to chimeras, which represent a retreat into subjectivity. As is well known, Coleridge, building on Schelling, distinguished sharply between the use of "imagination" and "fancy" by the poet, fancy being a mode of memory able to copy and embellish past examples, and imagination, the synthetic faculty, possessing the power to see things whole and to bring new worlds to life by creation.

For Schelling, an individual's emotions and his or her unconscious instincts constitute the first stage of imagination. He calls this combination of instinct and feeling *Gemüt*, and works of art result when these emotions are recollected in tranquillity. In this second stage of imagination, the artist remembers the emotion, its cause, and the relationship of all of these to the life of things. This theme, common to Wordsworth and Schelling, shows that the lower levels of the mind are not canceled out in the higher but are retained and transcended in a new unity.

In his later works, Schelling tried to construct a positive philosophy based on the evolution of the divine principle in human history, especially in myths and religion. He believed that this positive philosophy completed his own earlier, negative, merely rational philosophy. For the later Schelling, God gradually reveals His nature in the history of the cosmos and in human history, but there is dark ground or negative principle in God. Since only the Absolute is fully real, finite things exist only in a removal or fall from reality. God creates His own counterpart, freedom, which is both the cause of the fall and the trace of divinity carried by things after the fall. In this wrestling with the problems of God, freedom, and evil, Schelling arrived at a new realism, in contrast to his earlier Romanticism, and this idea of struggling, suffering humanity became a basic theme of existentialism. In his torturous later years, Schelling tried to express the pathos of existence in words halfway between poetry and philosophy. The issues he posed eventually found followers among the philosophical and literary writers of the twentieth century.

Thus, Schelling's philosophical pilgrimage took him a great distance from his starting point. As a young man he shared many traits with the literary figures who had embraced Romanticism in their reaction against the rationalism of the Enlightenment. One can see in his enthusiastic early writings an emphasis on freedom, feeling, the irrational, creative genius, and intuition. Later, he believed that philosophy must deal not only with the "what" of the world, its essence, but also with the "that" of the world, its existence. God, whose essence is existence, unifies this apparent opposition. Schelling uses love as a symbol of this union. Love constitutes the eternal bond of God's self-revelation, by which the infinite is resolved into the finite and the finite into the infinite. Love's transformation is the symbol for all the transformations of the human imagination, both artistic and literary. Indeed, for Schelling, life, love, and art are really earthly expressions of God.

## Principal criticism
Über Mythen, historische Sagen und Philosopheme der ältesten Welt, 1793
Ideen zu einer Philosophie der Natur, 1797 (Ideas for a Philosophy of Nature: Introduction to the Study of This Science, the first complete English translation, 1988)
System des transzendentalen Idealismus, 1800 (Introduction to Idealism, 1871)
Philsophie der Kunst, 1802–3 (The Philosophy of Art, 1989)
Über das Verhältniss der bildenden Künste zu der Natur, 1807 (The Philosophy of Art: An Oration on the Relation Between the Plastic Arts and Nature, 1845)
Zur Geschichte der neueren Philosophie, 1826 (partial translation as Practical Effects of Modern Philosophy, 1873)

## Other major works and literary forms
Friedrich Wilhelm Joseph Schelling, best known for his philosophical studies, was also a literary artist, though not a very good one. As a member of the Romantic circle which included the Schlegel brothers, Ludwig Tieck, and Novalis, he contributed regularly to the literary journals Athenäum and Musenalmanach. Because of his use of Bonaventura as a pseudonym, he was long thought to be the author of the novel Die Nachtwachen des Bonaventura (1805; The Night Watches of Bonaventura, 1971), an ascription now known to be false. His most important literary works are Das Epikurische Glaubensbekenntnis Neinz Widerporstens (1799), a poetic discourse exploring his attitudes toward

nature, and the Romantic epic poem Die Letzten Worte des Pfarrers zu Drottning auf Seeland (1802).

### POETRY
Das Epikurische Glaubensbekenntnis Neinz Widerporstens, 1799
Die Letzten Worte des Pfarrers zu Drottning auf Seeland, 1802

### NONFICTION
Philosophische Untersuchungen über das Wesen der menschlichen Freiheit, 1809 (Of Human Freedom, 1936)
Über die Gottheiten von Samothrace, 1815
Die Weltalter, 1913 (written 1811–1813; The Ages of the World, 1942)

### MISCELLANEOUS
Sämtliche Werke, 1856–1861 (14 volumes)
Erste Abteilung, 1856–1861 (10 volumes)
Zweite Abteilung, 1856–1858 (4 volumes)
Werke, 1907 (3 volumes)
Schellings Werke, 1927–1928, 1948–1956 (8 volumes)

## Further reading
Bowie, Andrew. Schelling and Modern European Philosophy: An Introduction, 1993.
Copleston, Frederick C. History of Philosophy. Vol. 7, Fichte to Nietzsche, 1963.
Esposito, Joseph I. Schelling's Idealism and Philosophy of Nature, 1977.
Gray-Smith, R. God in the Philosophy of Schelling, 1933.
Heidegger, Martin. Schellings Abhandlung über das Wesen der menschlichen Freiheit, 1971 (Schelling's Treatise on the Essence of Human Freedom, 1985).
Hirsch, Eric D., Jr. Wordsworth and Schelling: A Typological Study of Romanticism, 1960.
Marx, Werner. The Philosophy of F. W. J. Schelling: History, System, Freedom, 1984.
O'Meara, T. F. Romantic Idealism and Roman Catholicism: Schelling and the Theologians, 1982.
Read, Herbert. The True Voice of Feeling, 1953.
Snow, D. E. Schelling and the End of Idealism, 1996.
Watson, J. Schelling's Transcendental Idealism, 1892.
White, Alan. Schelling: An Introduction to the System of Freedom, 1983.
Zizek, S. The Indivisible Remainder: An Essay on Schelling and Related Matters, 1996.

ROBERT J. PARADOWSKI

See also Hegel; Kant; Romanticism; Schlegel, A. W.; Schlegel, F.

# Friedrich Schiller
## German poet, playwright, and theorist

**Born:** Marbach, Württemberg, Germany; November 10, 1759
**Died:** Weimar, Germany; May 9, 1805

## Biography
Friedrich Schiller was born on November 10, 1759, in Marbach in the state of Württemberg, to a career military

man and the daughter of an innkeeper. A bright and sensitive child, Schiller wanted to be a pastor, but Karl Eugen, the rather tyrannical Duke of Württemberg, determined that his subject should become a lawyer in order that he might serve the duchy. Schiller was sent to a famous military institution, the Karlsschule (named after Eugen), where he was finally allowed to study medicine. Because his first play, *Die Raüber* (1781; *The Robbers*, 1792), angered the duke with its critical portrait of a ruler, Eugen forbade him to write, and Schiller secretly fled in 1782 to Mannheim. The years of struggle and poverty that Schiller endured seriously impaired his health. In 1783 he became the resident dramatist of the Mannheim Theater, and in 1787 he moved to Weimar, where other well-known writers – Johann Wolfgang von Goethe, Christoph Martin Wieland, and Johann Gottfried Herder – resided. Schiller married Charlotte von Lengefeld in 1790. In the early 1790s he studied Immanuel Kant's philosophy; the latter's thought helped shape Schiller's mature aesthetic writings. Schiller became friends with Goethe, and their mutually respectful discourse stimulated their work. Schiller continued his intense productivity until his frail health finally gave out; he died in 1805 at the age of forty-six.

## Influence

Schiller's theories on art and literature were highly influential (to a greater degree than those of his colleague, Goethe) in formulating the aesthetic of Germany's era of Weimar classicism, a period considered by most critics to be one of the high points of the nation's cultural history. As the leading theoretician of this pivotal epoch, Schiller shaped the aesthetic thought and practice of subsequent German writers such as Friedrich Hebbel, Adalbert Stifter, Friedrich Nietzsche, Richard Wagner, and Thomas Mann. His work anticipated and helped form the ideas of Karl Marx as well as those of the twentieth-century neo-Marxist philosopher Herbert Marcuse. The aesthetician Susan Langer was greatly influenced by Schiller. In general, the central position assumed by artistic creation in Schiller's writings influenced the development of a "religion of art" that characterizes much modernist and postmodernist aesthetic thinking.

## Analysis

Friedrich Schiller's aesthetic theories are based upon the traditional notion that art serves an essentially didactic purpose; that is, following the Roman poet Horace, he believed that art should instruct as well as delight. Works of art should morally uplift their audience, leading to a higher, more spiritual plane of existence. This association of aesthetics with ethics is characteristic of the German tradition, especially during the Enlightenment. The moral function of art is clear from the title of one of Schiller's early pieces, a lecture given in Mannheim entitled *Die Schaubühne als eine moralische Anstalt betrachtet* (1784;

*The Theater as a Moral Institution*, 1845). There Schiller explicitly linked theater with religion as a means of educating the public. The stage, however, provides striking dramatic illustrations of moral principles and is thus, he argues, more effective as a mode of education than the moral codes and strictures of religious institutions.

In 1790 Kant published his *Kritik der Urteilskraft (The Critique of Judgment*, 1892), which contains his theories concerning aesthetics. Schiller immediately read his works, and the influence of Kant's ethical and aesthetic ideas as well as his philosophical vocabulary is evident in Schiller's aesthetic writings. (It must be admitted that Schiller's use of such terminology is not completely rigorous.) Before turning to Schiller, then, it would be helpful to summarize briefly some of the Kantian notions which shaped his writings. For Kant, the domains of ethics and aesthetics revolve around the issues of freedom versus determinism and the performance of moral duty. The central concept of Kant's ethics is the "categorical imperative," which commands that each human being act in a manner such that his or her behavior can be held up as a maxim for all others. This is essentially a rational version of the traditional and universal "golden rule". The most morally advanced individual has internalized this precept and automatically acts in a moral manner. Such a person is not involved in any inner conflict over the performance of duty and is thus free from the constraints or determinism of the material world. Art and the Beautiful (aesthetic ideas as opposed to logical ideas), which depict the appearance of autonomy within nature, allow the individual to contemplate in a disinterested fashion the freedom of the moral plane. The realm of Kant's aesthetic ideas is one of imagination, of free "play," because it is independent of the demands of both material necessity and moral order.

During the last decade of the eighteenth century, Schiller produced a number of important aesthetic treatises. The first major treatise, entitled *Über Anmut und Würde* (1793; *On Grace and Dignity*, 1845), presents Kantian ideas as aesthetic categories. Grace is an attribute of the "Beautiful Soul," an idealized vision of the free human being in whom there is no inner conflict between universal moral duty and individual inclination or desire. Such a person possesses an inner harmony of being which manifests itself as fluid grace or beauty in motion. Dignity, on the other hand, is evidenced by the individual who is in conflict with his or her inner desires and who overcomes them through an act of rational will in order to behave in a moral manner. This kind of person also manifests a spiritual freedom over the determinism of the natural or material world. (The title character of Schiller's play *Maria Stuart* (1800; English translation, 1801) is such an exemplary individual.) Both of these types have educational value in that they demonstrate kinds of moral behavior.

*Briefe über die ästhetische Erziehung des Menschen in einer Reihe von Briefen* (1795; *On the Aesthetic Education* of Man, 1845), written in a series of letters to the Danish prince Friedrich Christian of Schleswig-Holstein, is one of Schiller's most important aesthetic treatises. Its argument involves the question of how the individual can achieve the ideal (rational) political state, of how the individual can evolve from a social state based on force and violence to one based on reason and morality. The letters were written during the bloody aftermath of the French Revolution, and they present an idealistic solution to the problems of social change. Schiller, who, following Kant, sees humankind as torn between the material/instinctual (inclination) and the rational/spiritual (moral duty), asserts that humankind must pass from a natural condition of determinism, through one of aesthetic education, to one of rational moral freedom. The dialectically opposed states of Nature (evidenced by the sensuous drive) and Reason (evidenced by the formal drive) must not dominate the personality and must be brought into synthesis. When the instincts direct the individual, the person behaves as a mere savage, and when the rational faculties rule behavior, the person is, for Schiller, nothing more than a barbarian. In either case, the individual's actions are not free.

This synthesis can be attained through the aesthetic domain (the drive to play), since art presents as well as demands in the viewer a harmonious union of matter and form, feeling and reason. This produces an experience of freedom in the disinterested act of aesthetic contemplation. The end result of aesthetic education is a rational citizen, a balanced individual, like the Beautiful Soul, in whom feeling and reason are in harmony and who freely acts in a moral manner. At points in the essay, Schiller alludes to a triadic historical scheme: the ancient Greeks as a culture at one with nature and themselves; the contemporary age as a period of conflict and self-alienation in which duty and inclination are opposed within the personality; and a future period in which the rational/moral individual will prevail. Here he shares in the dialectical approach that characterizes many of his contemporaries such as G. W. F. Hegel, Friedrich Hölderlin, and Novalis, as well as later thinkers, including the young Karl Marx.

Schiller wrote Über naïve und sentimentalische Dichtung (1795–1796; On Naïve and Sentimental Poetry, 1845) as an attempt to define ancient versus modern poetry, an issue current in eighteenth-century aesthetic debates. It was also written in part in order to distinguish his approach to artistic creation from that of his friend Goethe, with whom he felt a degree of rivalry. The naive poet (Goethe or the classical poets of ancient Greece) is essentially childlike and lives in an instinctive union with nature, reason and feeling complementing each other. This type spontaneously creates works of art which reflect a natural harmony between self and world, a sensuousness that depicts objects and people in concrete simplicity. Goethe's "poetry of experience" (Erlebnislyrik) is, for example, intensely personal and highly visual. Schiller cites Homer and William Shakespeare as

representative of the naive poet. The sentimental artist (Schiller or the Romantic poet), however, has lost this primal harmony with the universe and thus experiences nature in an analytical fashion, the world becoming a reflection of abstract ideas more than of concrete objects. This latter type must deliberate over the creative process and produces works of art which portray nature as a spiritual rather than a sensuous phenomenon. The sentimental poet tends to write works which are either satirical or elegiac and idyllic. Schiller's "philosophical poetry" (Gedankenlyrik) presents content as a vehicle for the reflection upon ideas and concepts.

Schiller's last major treatise, Über das Erhabene (1801; On the Sublime, 1845) elaborates ideas contained in his earlier aesthetic writings, especially On Grace and Dignity. He begins by discussing the human will or spirit in its confrontation with the forces of nature. We have responded to the power of the material world, which limits our freedom, with the phenomenon of culture. There is physical culture which confronts nature with the force of the will, attempting to make the world conform to the demands of the spirit. Technology is an example of this type of culture. Nature, however, can be dominated only to a certain extent; then moral culture becomes an important factor. Here we submit to the finite conditions of existence and thereby remain spiritually above it. Religion, or our submission to the divine order, is an example of moral culture. Our tendencies toward aesthetic experience also provide, Schiller suggests, a mode of recognizing our inner freedom.

In On the Sublime, Schiller again distinguishes between two types of aesthetic conditions which also present visions of moral autonomy: the beautiful and the sublime. In the beautiful, one experiences a sense of freedom from necessity because sensuous and instinctive drives stand in harmony with the rational dictates of the moral order. In the experience of the sublime, the rational spirit, through an act of will, overcomes the drives of the instincts and is thus also free from material determinism. The sublime allows the individual to perceive the infinity of the spiritual self as opposed to the limitations of the finite physical body. The sublime is characterized by feelings of awe and delight at the experience of the infinite.

Schiller's views on aesthetics, especially with regard to those that address the didactic function that art can assume for the individual as well as society, have had a profound impact on subsequent authors and thinkers. Writers of the nineteenth century such as the Austrian Stifter were greatly influenced by the idealism of Schiller's vision of human aesthetic education; Stifter's novels and Novelle present the theme of the morally didactic role of art. The primacy of art as a cultural institution within human civilization, a notion which is so prominent in Schiller's ideas, helped shape the thought of the important nineteenth-century German thinker Nietzsche, as well as the aesthetic views of the composer Wagner. The aestheticism of early twentieth-century writers such as Mann, Stefan George, and Rainer Maria Rilke also owes a debt to Schiller's views on art. Mann even wrote a short story, "Schwere Stunde" ("A Weary Hour"), based on Schiller's life. The romantic view of humanity's self-estrangement in the modern world – an important aspect of Schiller's view of aesthetic education – is echoed in the young Marx's later analyses of alienation within capitalist society. The twentieth-century neo-Marxist philosopher Marcuse, in his well-known work *Eros and Civilization* (1955), also discusses the importance of the (Schillerian) impulse to play being associated with labor within the liberated society. Schiller's aesthetic theories, enacted in his plays and poetry, have clearly made their mark on the thought of succeeding generations.

## Principal criticism
*Die Schaubühne als eine moralische Anstalt betrachtet*, 1784 (*The Theater as a Moral Institution*, 1845)
*Über den Grund des Vergnügens an tragischen Gegenständen*, 1792 (*On the Pleasure in Tragic Subjects*, 1845)
*Über das Pathetische*, 1793 (*On the Pathetic*, 1845)
*Über Anmut und Würde*, 1793 (*On Grace and Dignity*, 1845)
*Briefe über die ästhetische Erziehung des Menschen in einer Reihe von Briefen*, 1795 (*On the Aesthetic Education of Man*, 1845)
*Über naïve und sentimentalische Dichtung*, 1795–1796 (*On Naïve and Sentimental Poetry*, 1845)
*Über das Erhabene*, 1801 (*On the Sublime*, 1845)
*Aesthetical and Philosophical Essays*, 1845

## Other major works and literary forms
Friedrich Schiller is known primarily as one of Germany's foremost dramatists and poets. He also wrote a number of prose fiction pieces as well as several treatises on history. His early dramas, such as *Kabale und Liebe* (1784; *Cabal and Love*, 1795), were produced in the rebellious spirit of the German *Sturm und Drang* (Storm and Stress) era, and his mature plays, such as *Maria Stuart* (1800; English translation, 1801), reflect the influence of the neoclassical period as well as his long-term friendship with Johann Wolfgang von Goethe, with whom he edited a literary journal. Schiller's ballads and later philosophical poems are ranked among the best lyric poems of German literature.

PLAYS
*Die Räuber*, 1781 (*The Robbers*, 1792)
*Die Verschwörung des Fiesko zu Genua*, 1783 (*Fiesco: Or, the Genoese Conspiracy*, 1796)
*Kabale und Liebe*, 1784 (*Cabal and Love*, 1795)
*Don Carlos, Infant von Spanien*, 1787 (*Don Carlos, Infante of Spain*, 1798)
*Wallensteins Lager*, 1799 (*The Camp of Wallenstein*, 1846)
*Die Piccolomini*, 1799 (*The Piccolomini*, 1800)
*Wallensteins Tod*, 1799 (*The Death of Wallenstein*, 1800)
*Maria Stuart*, 1800 (English translation, 1801)
*Die Jungfrau von Orleans*, 1801 (*The Maid of Orleans*, 1835)
*Die Braut von Messina: Oder, Die feindlichen Brüder*, 1803 (*The Bride of Messina*, 1837)
*Wilhelm Tell*, 1804 (*William Tell*, 1841)

*Historical Dramas*, 1847
*Early Dramas and Romances*, 1849
*Dramatic Works*, 1851

POETRY
*Anthologie auf das Jahr 1782*, 1782
*Xenien*, 1796 (with Johann Wolfgang von Goethe)
*Gedichte*, 1800, 1803
*The Poems of Schiller*, 1851
*The Ballads and Shorter Poems of Fredrick v. Schiller*, 1901

NONFICTION
*Historischer Kalender für Damen*, 1790, 1791
*Geschichte des dreissigjährigen Kriegs*, 1791–1793 (3 volumes; *History of the Thirty Years War*, 1799)
*Briefwechsel zwischen Schiller und Goethe*, 1829 (*The Correspondence Between Schiller and Goethe*, 1845)
*Schillers Briefwechsel mit Körner von 1784 bis zum Tode Schillers*, 1847 (*Schiller's Correspondence with Körner*, 1849)

MISCELLANEOUS
*Sämmtliche Werke*, 1812–1815 (12 volumes; *Complete Works in English*, 1870)

## Further reading
Behler, Constantin. *Nostalgic Teleology: Friedrich Schiller and the Schemata of Aesthetic Humanism*, 1995.
Garland, Henry B. *Schiller*, 1949.
Graham, Ilse. *Schiller's Drama: Talent and Integrity*, 1974.
Grossmann, Walter. "The Idea of Cultural Revolution in Schiller's Aesthetic Education," in *Germanic Review*. XXXIV (1959), pp. 39–49.
Kaufmann, W. F. *Schiller: Poet of Philosophical Idealism*, 1942.
Kerry, S. S. *Schiller's Writings on Aesthetics*, 1961.
Martin, Nicholas. *Nietzsche and Schiller: Untimely Aesthetics*, 1996.
Martinson, Steven D. *Harmonious Tensions: The Writings of Friedrich Schiller*, 1996.
Miller, R. D. *Schiller and the Ideal of Freedom*, 1970.
Murray, Patrick T. *The Development of German Aesthetic Theory from Kant to Schiller: A Philosophical Commentary on Schiller's "The Aesthetic Education of Man" (1795)*, 1994.
Reed, Terence James. *Schiller*, 1991.
Sharpe, Lesley. *Friedrich Schiller: Drama, Thought, and Politics*, 1991.
Simons, John D. *Friedrich Schiller*, 1981.
Witte, William. *Schiller*, 1949.

THOMAS F. BARRY

*See also* Goethe; Kant; Kleist; Romanticism

# August Wilhelm Schlegel
German translator and critic

**Born:** Hannover, Germany; September 8, 1767
**Died:** Bonn, Prussia; May 12, 1845

## Biography
August Wilhelm Schlegel was born on September 8, 1767, into a distinguished literary family. His father, Johann Adolf

Schlegel, was a Lutheran minister who wrote essays, hymns, and fables. His uncle, Johann Elias Schlegel, was a noted critic and dramatist. Schlegel was educated at the Hannover Gymnasium and at the University of Göttingen, where he studied theology and philology and wrote a dissertation in Latin on geography in the works of Homer. At Göttingen, he was attracted to the poetry of Gottfried Bürger and the classical scholarship of Christian Heyne.

For three years Schlegel worked as a private tutor in Amsterdam before moving to Jena in 1795, where he established contact with Friedrich Schiller and other Romantic theorists. The following year he married Caroline Böhmer (née Michaelis), a young widow who shared his interest in translating William Shakespeare's plays. Schlegel was appointed professor of art and literature at the University of Jena in 1798. His lectures on the Romantic conception of literature added to his growing reputation as a perceptive critic.

Schlegel's marriage collapsed when Caroline met the philosopher F. W. J. Schelling, whom she married in 1804. Between 1801 and 1804 Schlegel regularly visited Berlin, where he delivered a series of lectures summarizing the doctrines of the Romantic movement. In 1805, upon the recommendation of Johann Wolfgang von Goethe, who admired his work, Schlegel became secretary to the French writer Madame de Staël. He traveled throughout Europe with her and in 1808 they went to Vienna, where he gave his famous lectures on dramatic art and literature.

After serving as secretary to the Prince of Sweden from 1813 to 1815, Schlegel stayed with Madame de Staël at Coppet in Switzerland until her death in 1817. The following year he accepted a chair of Oriental languages at the University of Bonn. He returned to Berlin in 1827 to present lectures on the history and criticism of the fine arts. In the last twenty years of his life, Schlegel devoted himself to Eastern languages and literatures as a translator and scholar. He died in Bonn in 1845.

## Influence

Schlegel's criticism offered a broad philosophical base for the establishment of Romanticism in Germany. His writings are permeated by a historical attitude that dominated German philology in the nineteenth century. This historical sense is imbued with the nationalistic fervor that accompanied the growth of the Romantic movement in Europe, stimulating at the same time an interest in cultural origins and folklore.

Schlegel regarded criticism as the link between theory and history, and he developed this idea in highly influential lectures given at Berlin and Vienna. Furthermore, he clarified key concepts in Romantic aesthetic theory; his study of the theological differences between ancient and modern cultures formed the basis for the division of art into classical and Romantic categories. In providing line-for-line verse translations, which closely approximated the meaning and rhythm of Shakespeare's dramatic language, Schlegel greatly improved the prose texts of previous translations. This effort virtually guaranteed the favorable reception of Shakespeare in Germany. The universality of Schlegel's criticism contributed to the formation of a cosmopolitan spirit in literature.

## Analysis

Schlegel's criticism does not represent a systematic account of nineteenth-century Romantic theory. His interest in the unexplored and unfamiliar was the product of a pluralist imagination. According to Schlegel, criticism is essentially a collective art or dialectic. By means of rigorous empirical analysis, he strove to ground his theoretical speculation in a comprehensive interpretation of reality.

A number of themes permeate Schlegel's critical works, giving coherence to his fluid, eclectic ideas. First, he continually emphasizes the relationship of literature to linguistics. He also relies heavily on the philosophy of Immanuel Kant, Johann Gottlieb Fichte, and Schelling. In addition, he regards poetry as the highest mode of written expression, with primitive or natural poetry serving as a model of inspiration. Finally, he insists on the referentiality of criticism and history.

These themes were adumbrated in the essays written between 1798 and 1800 for *Das Athenäum*. By the time of the Berlin lectures, Schlegel's definition of the word *romantisch* was more explicit. He persuasively argued that the distinction between classical and Romantic, or ancient and modern, was chronological, not philosophical. Rather than use terminology that was becoming increasingly inflated, Schlegel developed the classifications of *die schöne Poesie*, the beautiful poetry, and *die interessante Poesie*, the interesting poetry. The former represents objectivity, and the latter subjectivity; they function as governing principles in artistic creation. Schlegel maintained that the craving for "the interesting" is an aspect of modern taste that should not be wholeheartedly endorsed, because it depends too insistently on the artist's ego. He regarded Greek literature as the basis of tradition and admired the work of the ancients, who perceived the general, not the particular, as the object of true art.

In the Berlin lectures, Schlegel stated that poetry should restore the figurative meaning (*Bildlichkeit*) of language. He promoted Karl Philipp Moritz's concept of *Bildungskraft* as a faculty of aesthetic production: that is, all art should engender meaningful images so that beauty can ultimately express, in symbolic form, the mystery behind appearances. To this concept, Schlegel added his own theory of correspondences, by which he traced the evolution of the arts (music, dance, and poetry) from their primal unity to their latter-day status as interrelated yet distinct cultural activities.

Schlegel's Vienna lectures, which were disseminated throughout Europe in translation, represent an insightful and wide-ranging discussion regarding the privileged status of dramatic art. His principal objective was to account for the fastidiousness and purity of Greek drama, as compared to the recklessness and indulgence found in modern theater. He held that the Romantic spirit requires for its gratification the creation of works distinct in structure from those which established the classical style – an artistic revolution which Schlegel attributed to profound religious differences.

The ancient Greeks adored the powers of nature; their vision of ideal perfection was embodied in the idols of superstitious worship and mythology. This system of religious adoration was confined to the senses and to life on Earth. Christianity represents the opposite of paganism; it added to the material world a mysterious world of spirits and substituted the infinite for the finite. Classical drama, then, was concerned with fixed types and natural order, viewed in the light of rational ideas. In contrast, the Romantic attitude is directed toward the process of instability and change; through imaginative feelings that feed on contemplation, the Romantic artist attempted to derive creative energy from the conception of an afterlife.

Schlegel maintained that, in like manner, sculpture was the dominant art form of antiquity, whereas painting conveyed the modern sensibility. Plastic art was centered on a person or group removed from external accompaniments; the picturesque, on the other hand, exhibited the surrounding locality and was open to a boundless perspective. Greek tragedy was compatible with sculpture in that it annihilated the external conditions of space and time, while the Romantic drama endowed these abstractions with mystical power. The classical idea of any person or object remained essentially the same and yielded the same impressions. Yet it was the association of ideas indigenous to the Romantic imagination that made an object interesting.

Schlegel located Shakespeare at the core of the Romantic imagination, because Shakespearean drama retains the vitality of lyric poetry and the objectivity of the epic. Schlegel extolled the richness of Shakespeare's textures and the pervasive irony of his characterization. Shakespeare's supremacy as a dramatist is rooted in his understanding of human nature and in his ability to reveal the feelings of characters as they adapt to changing circumstances: "What a field for a poet who, like Shakespeare, could discern the poetical aspect of the great events of the world!"

Schlegel also studied the structure of Shakespeare's plays and analyzed the qualities of language and versification desirable in dramatic art. From this emerged the concept of organic unity – perhaps the most seminal idea in his criticism. Organic form is innate, because it unfolds from within; it is connected to the attributes of plot and the function of character. The language of the personages is not determined by their respective idiosyncrasies, but by the place they occupy in relation to the whole. Thus, organic unity becomes a logic of the imagination which, in the hands of a genius, unites creativity and restraint, according to the purposes of the "action." Hence, Schlegel dismissed

the unities of "place" and "time" as relevant only to mechanical, or disjunctive form; the proper metaphor for the work of art, he argued, is biological. At the same time, every work of art is ultimately detached, like fruit from a tree, from the historical conditions that surround it. The function of criticism is to isolate and refine this autonomy.

At Göttingen, under the direction of Bürger and Heyne, Schlegel manifested an intense preoccupation with poetic and metrical forms. Bürger was considered one of Germany's most accomplished lyric poets. Schlegel appropriated many of his stylistic effects and advocated strict rules for German verse, based on classical metrics. Schlegel acquired a reputation for precision in these matters, and even Goethe asked him to evaluate his hexameters. Schlegel's own poetry presents a curious mixture of Christian, pagan, and Oriental conceits. Every poetic form is represented: odes, sonnets, elegies, and ballads. Schlegel intended to demonstrate the poetic range of German and to remold the language as Goethe had suggested. Schlegel made excellent use of the verse schemes of the Italian *canzone* and the Spanish *romancero*, with which he was familiar from his translations of Dante and Pedro Calderón de la Barca, respectively.

Before Schlegel, no translator had ever attempted to follow Shakespeare line-for-line. In collaboration with Bürger, Schlegel began a verse translation of *A Midsummer Night's Dream* (c. 1595–1596). Many of Shakespeare's meters were rearranged, and Bürger's insistence on sonority and vigor was incompatible with the light and tender verses. This early effort was superseded by the more successful translations Schlegel wrote in Jena after he escaped Bürger's influence. Through his reading of Schiller and Goethe, Schlegel came to realize that technical perfection is not an external quality acquired by tireless revision; it has an inward origin and is closely connected to a translator's willingness to appreciate the subtle characteristics of a foreign language. Unity of style is ultimately the result of a translator's disposition.

In his subsequent translations of Shakespeare's plays, Schlegel had numerous technical difficulties to overcome. In general, English words of Latin origin are lighter in texture than the Germanic equivalents. Nevertheless, without duplicating Shakespeare's style, Schlegel managed to render each line by a single line in translation and still reproduce in broad outline the contrasts of tempo and verbal melody of Shakespeare's language. The rough drafts and manuscripts of these translations represent the intellectual history of Schlegel's generation. His stylistic and linguistic achievements exercised a deep and lasting influence on German poetry.

Through his critical writings, Schlegel was instrumental in promoting not only the value of Shakespeare but also the importance of literary works not yet part of traditional scholarship; he conducted research on the *Nibelungenlied*, the Arthurian legends, and the Provençal poets. In his view, the spirit of true criticism is associated with the capacity to cultivate values and to appreciate, by means of an exclusive mode of seeing and feeling, works that seem alien to one's own language, manners, and social relations. In his introduction to the Vienna lectures, he emphasized the significance of this "true genius of criticism":

> No man can be a true critic or connoisseur without universality of mind, without that flexibility which enables him, by renouncing all personal predilections and blind habits, to adapt himself to the peculiarities of other ages and nations – to feel them, as it were, from their proper central point.

This attitude informs the critical temper and enables the discerning critic to illuminate those historical conditions indispensable to the creation of a masterpiece. In this way, criticism acts as an intermediary between theory and history; without criticism, these independent disciplines would be defective or inadequate.

In his creative writing, Schlegel attempted to unite theory with practice. For example, *Ion* (1803), his only drama, is a careful replication of Euripides and an attempt to demonstrate the versatility of the German language. In a work written in French and published in 1807, Schlegel compared Euripides to Jean Racine in order to expose the incongruities that arise when modern style and sentiments are grafted onto mythological and classical subjects. This criticism seems unduly harsh, but in later writings Schlegel consistently praised the diction and tenderness of language in Racine's tragedies. He insisted that the works of Racine, like those of other French neoclassical dramatists, retain an intrinsic value as elegant paraphrases of Greek tragedy, despite their self-consciousness and overblown rhetoric.

Schlegel was equally as severe in the epigrams and sonnets directed against August von Kotzebue, a prolific playwright who, according to Schlegel, had introduced into the drama a vulgar mixture of frivolity, sentiment, and moral skepticism. Schlegel shared Madame de Staël's view that a constrained and affected manner had prevailed in Europe since the middle of the seventeenth century. Working from this premise, Schlegel was at times too sweeping in his criticism, and he was prone to making unfair comparisons. Hence, he reversed his original enthusiasm for Ludwig Tieck, Novalis, and Friedrich Schiller, and he became disaffected with other German Romantics. He considered Goethe too classical, and he disparaged Molière and John Milton, accusing the latter of trying to invent a mythology. He overlooked the accomplishments of Johann Gottfried Herder, Jean Paul, and Christoph Martin Wieland, and dismissed the insights of Alexander Pope, John Dryden, Denis Diderot, and Voltaire.

In part, Schlegel's didacticism stemmed from his tenacious belief that art requires a willful submission to aesthetic laws; in order to be beautiful, and by implication meaningful, art must be free from external goals, such as the cleverness or ambition of the artist. Schlegel's notion of *romantische Poesie* is concomitant with this philosophy. His critical outlook is Romantic in the sense that it relies for its articulation on certain key concepts that he codified and expressed, yet this approach draws its strength from a cogent analysis of classical values. Schlegel's criticism is compelling because it provides an aesthetic frame within which these values can be reconciled with the Romantic affirmation of faith in holistic process.

## Principal criticism

*Spanisches Theater*, 1803–1809
*Vorlesungen über dramatische Kunst und Literatur*, 1809–1811
    (*A Course of Lectures on Dramatic Art and Literature*,
    1815)
*Geschichte der deutschen Sprache und Poesie*, 1818
*Vorlesungen über philosophische Kunstlehre*, 1827
*Vorlesungen über die Theorie und Geschichte der bildenden
    Kunst*, 1827
*Vorlesungen über schöne Literatur und Kunst*, 1884

## Other major works and literary forms

August Wilhelm Schlegel contributed articles to numerous periodicals, notably Friedrich Schiller's *Die Horen* and *Das Athenäum*, which represented, for the most part, the essays of Schlegel, his younger brother Friedrich, and Ludwig Tieck. The views presented in *Das Athenäum* promoted the first Romantic school of thought in Berlin. Schlegel, assisted by his wife, translated seventeen of William Shakespeare's plays; this achievement secured a position of prominence for Shakespeare in Germany. Schlegel also wrote a neoclassical tragedy and produced a volume of poetry. He translated extensively from Italian, Spanish, and Portuguese poetry and prose and initiated the study of Sanskrit in German universities.

PLAY
*Ion*, 1803

POETRY
*Gedichte*, 1800
*Ehrenpforte und Triumphbogen für den Theater-Präsidenten von
    Kotzebue*, 1801
*Blumensträusse italiänischer, spanischer, und portugiesischer
    Poesie*, 1804

NONFICTION
*Comparaison entre la "Phèdre" de Racine et celle d'Euripide*,
    1807

TRANSLATION
*Shakespeares dramatische Werke*, 1797–1810

## Further reading

Atkinson, Margaret E. *August Wilhelm Schlegel as a Translator of Shakespeare* (Studies in Shakespeare, No. 24), 1977.
Ewton, Ralph W. *The Literary Theories of August Wilhelm Schlegel*, 1972.
Grosse-Brockhoff, Annelen. *Das Konzept des Klassischen bei Friedrich und August Wilhelm Schlegel*, 1981

Hepworth, Brian. *The Rise of Romanticism: Essential Texts*, 1968.

Hughes, Glyn Tegai. *Romantic German Literature*, 1979.

Lacoue-Labarthe, Philippe, and Jean-Luc Nancy. *The Literary Absolute: The Theory of Literature in German Romanticism*, 1988.

Lohner, Edgar. "August Wilhelm Schlegel," in *Deutsche Dichter der Romantik. Ihr Leben und Werke*, 1971.

Lovejoy, Arthur O. *Essays in the History of Ideas*, 1948.

Robertson, J. G. *A History of German Literature*, 1962.

Wellek, René. *A History of Modern Criticism: 1750–1950*. Vol. 2, *The Romantic Age*, 1955.

Werner, Richter. *August Wilhelm Schlegel: Wanderer zwischen Weltpoesie und Altdeutscher Dichtung*, 1954.

Willoughby, Leonard Ashley. *The Romantic Movement in Germany*, 1930.

ROBERT J. FRAIL

*See also* Goethe; Hegel; Kant; Romanticism; Schelling; Schlegel, F.; Madame de Staël

# Friedrich Schlegel

German critic and writer

**Born:** Hannover, Germany; March 10, 1772
**Died:** Dresden, Germany; January 12, 1829

## Biography

Friedrich Schlegel was born in Hannover, Germany, on March 10, 1772, into a family with an illustrious literary background. His uncle, Johann Elias Schlegel, had been a successful dramatist and literary theorist during the Enlightenment and is generally regarded as the most significant forerunner of Gotthold Ephraim Lessing. His father, Johann Adolf Schlegel, made a name for himself as a translator and as the cofounder of an important literary group, the Bremer Beiträger. His brother, August Wilhelm Schlegel, became a leading Romantic philologist, critic, and translator of William Shakespeare's works.

At the age of eighteen, Schlegel entered the University of Göttingen to study law. He soon became disenchanted with his studies, however, and transferred to the University of Leipzig, where he majored in classical philology, philosophy, and art history from 1791 to 1794. As a student and later also as a freelance writer and lecturer in literature, history, and philosophy, Friedrich traveled extensively within Germany, France, and the Netherlands, meeting such luminaries as Johann Wolfgang von Goethe, Friedrich Schiller, Ludwig Tieck, Novalis, F. W. J. Schelling, Rahel Levin, and, finally, Dorothea Veit, whom he married in 1804.

In 1799 Schlegel briefly settled in Jena, the center of the German Romantic movement. There, he edited the periodical *Das Athenäum* together with his brother August Wilhelm – a periodical which, until 1800, was the official voice of Romanticism in Germany. Despite the fact that his efforts as a writer, lecturer, and editor were widely acclaimed, Schlegel was never able to profit from them financially. Indeed, it was not until 1815 that he managed to secure a steady, well-paying position, when he was appointed by Prince von K. W. N. L. Metternich to the Austrian Legation at the Diet of Frankfurt. Even though this position proved strenuous and entailed much travel, Schlegel was able to pursue his scholarly interests, making valuable contributions in the areas of literature, linguistics, philosophy, and history up until his death on January 12, 1829, in Dresden.

## Influence

Schlegel provided the theoretical framework for the entire Romantic movement in Germany by postulating Romantic literature as universal in nature and as closely tied to the *Roman* (novel). He also laid the groundwork for modern hermeneutics through his new, phenomenologically oriented method of literary evaluation. This method rejected the utilization of external (that is, classical) ideals in judging literature and, instead, focused on identifying the "individual ideal" within a given work. A significant feature of Schlegel's method is the high level of interaction between criticism and history. This interaction had important implications, providing the impetus for literary history to become the primary medium of German criticism during the nineteenth century. Schlegel's influence extends even beyond this, however, for he was also the first to use the *Charakteristik* (pen portrait) and the *Fragment* (longer aphorism) as vehicles for literary criticism. In addition, he thrust irony into the forefront of literary discussion both in Germany and abroad.

## Analysis

Schlegel, an avowed disciple of the famed German classicist Johann Joachim Winckelmann, began his career in literary criticism by elevating the Greek literature of antiquity to the standard against which all literary works must necessarily be measured. In an early essay entitled "Über das Studium der griechischen Poesie" (on the study of Greek poetry), he asserted that Greek literature was the ideal product of a natural and uncorrupted civilization devoted entirely to the achievement of absolute perfection and beauty in all artistic endeavors. He contrasted this with the literature of French and German Enlightenment, which he saw as the outgrowth of a rationalistic and hence totally artificial culture in which art did not strive toward the fulfillment of aesthetic ideals but was subservient to such "prosaic" interests as philosophy, science, ethics, and didactics. To raise itself to the aesthetic heights of its Greek counterpart, modern literature must, according to Schlegel, focus all of its efforts on the imitation (*Nachahmung*) of ancient works, while paying particular attention to their inner harmony, their enduring beauty and validity, and their consistent purity in content and form. Schlegel even went so far as to suggest specific models for modern literature to follow. These included Sophocles' tragedies, Doric poetry, and Homer's timeless epics, the *Iliad* (c. 800 B.C.) and the *Odyssey* (c. 800 B.C.).

Schlegel soon came to realize, however, that modern literature, even with the most faithful adherence to ancient models, could never arrive at the Greek ideal, as it is not predicated upon the same, almost utopian living and working conditions enjoyed by the ancient Greeks – conditions which he ultimately believed to be unique in the history of humankind. He also recognized that he had, through his one-sided idolization of the Greeks and their literature, unjustly neglected the outstanding literary contributions of postclassical authors such as Dante, Miguel de Cervantes, Shakespeare, and Goethe, whose works he generally admired despite their obvious deviation from Greek models.

As a consequence of these realizations, Schlegel soon turned away from all external ideals in judging literary works of art and, in such writings as *Geschichte der Poesie der Griechen und Römer* (history of the poetry of the Greeks and Romans) and "Dialogue on Poetry" proposed that modern works be evaluated strictly on their own merits by carefully weighing their inherent positive and negative traits. That implied a detailed explication of individual works aimed especially at determining whether they are, from an aesthetic standpoint, "whole" and "complete," whether their content is varied and dynamic, and whether they transcend that which is merely mundane and superficial to attain a truly symbolic and enduring quality.

Schlegel pioneered this new, essentially phenomenological method of criticism in his *Charakteristiken und Kritiken* (characteristics and criticisms), a collection of pen portraits designed to identify the "individual ideal" within the works of such "modern" German authors as Lessing, Friedrich Heinrich Jacobi, and Johann Georg Forster. This ideal was usually based on the various aesthetic considerations (or criteria) mentioned above and on literary innovations as they manifest themselves in individual works. In his portrait of Forster, for example, Schlegel identifies "social consciousness" as the ideal within this author's numerous travelogues – a consciousness which allows these works to rise above mere landscape descriptions to become meaningful sociopolitical documents of the late eighteenth century.

Schlegel was very careful in specifying the prerequisites for properly evaluating literary works. True critics, he maintained, must – in addition to possessing an impeccable (that is, consistent and sophisticated) taste in literature – be extremely well versed in literary history. Only through their intimate knowledge of what exists in the world of literature can they determine what is aesthetically valuable, innovative, and thus worthy of being praised as the ideal within a given work. In many respects, then, true critics must enter into a heuristic circle, where the correct evaluation of individual works presupposes a knowledge of their function within the history of literature and, in turn, where the ability to survey literary history presupposes a knowledge of the individual works that are its parts. The fact that Schlegel saw a direct connection between history and criticism easily explains his concentration on both critical and historical issues in his essays and numerous literary histories.

In the course of developing his new method of literary analysis, Schlegel completely revised his opinions concerning modern literature and ultimately praised many literary practices – for example, combining various genres within a single work – that he had condemned earlier as being completely incompatible with the Greek ideal. In fact, instead of idealizing a literature characterized by clarity and simplicity in content and form, he now promoted literary complexity, or "universality" – the topic of his now-famous aphorism 116 in the "Athenäums-Fragmente." To Schlegel, universality implied a literature in which authors were no longer forced to adhere to conventional (Aristotelian) poetics but indeed were free to explore the limits of their imagination by mixing various genres to create dramatic fairy tales and other hybrid forms, by allowing literature to become the voice of such disciplines as philosophy and didactics, and by commenting on and even parodying their own works via the subtle use of irony. Universality also meant a thorough mixture of classical (Greek) and "modern" elements in literature, resulting in a unique combination of seriousness and bawdiness, objectivity and subjectivity, reality and fantasy. Finally, Schlegel conceived of universal literature as being equally at home in the present as it is in the past, the golden age of medieval and Renaissance Europe.

In his renowned aphorism 116, Schlegel unified all aspects of universality by collectively referring to them as Romantic, a term he associated not only with the various Romanic literatures which, through the works of such authors as Dante and Cervantes, exercised a profound influence on the postclassical literary world, but also with the *Roman*, which he, on account of its length and potential for digression, perceived as the ideal genre for putting Romantic universality into practice. It should be noted that Schlegel actually wrote what he considered to be a perfect universal novel, namely his *Lucinde*. This work contains ethical and philosophical discussions on topics ranging from physical love to the emancipation of women and incorporates such diverse literary forms as letters, dialogues, allegories, and prose idylls.

At one point, Schlegel attempted to summarize his ideas on Romantic literature in a formulaic, pseudoscientific manner and arrived at the following equation:

The poetic (or Romantic) ideal = $1/0\sqrt{FSM/0}$ ($1/0=$God).

Here, he indicates that Romantic literature is a harmonious mixture of fantasy (or imagination), sentimentality (or spiritual feeling), and mimesis (or reality) and that this mixture, in turn, symbolizes the language of God. This language transcends ordinary communication to give the individual a glimpse into the secrets of nature, into his or her own most primitive beginnings, and into the deeper reaches of his or her own psyche. This godlike language also gives Romantic literature the sense of being timeless and everlasting, or what Schlegel would identify as *unendlich*.

Friedrich Schlegel ranks among the most influential German literary critics and theorists. His theories of Romanticism, with their constant emphasis on universality, became the foundation for the entire German Romantic movement – a movement which attracted such luminaries as August Wilhelm Schlegel, Tieck, Wilhelm Heinrick Wackenroder, Novalis, Achim von Arnim, Clemens Brentano, Joseph von Eichendorff, and the brothers Grimm. Central to Schlegel's concept of Romanticism was the *Roman*, which he elevated to the ideal genre of the entire movement, thus inspiring a long line of Romantic novels beginning with his own *Lucinde* in 1799.

In terms of the general history of criticism, Schlegel's new, largely phenomenological method of literary evaluation, which rested on the assumption that each work's "individual ideal" can be identified by means of interpretation, provided the theoretical basis for hermeneutics and understanding as formulated in later years by Friedrich Schleiermacher and August Boeckh. Schlegel's insistence on a close relationship between criticism and history also had extremely far-reaching implications. It gave rise to the so-called historical method in Germany and ultimately helped the literary history (Schlegel himself wrote several) to become the most popular medium of German criticism during the nineteenth century. Seen in this light, the great masters of the *kritische Literaturgeschichte* (Georg Gottfried Gervinus, Hermann Hettner, Julian Schmidt, Ricarda Huch, and so on) are all greatly indebted to Schlegel's ideas and initiatives.

Finally, Schlegel can be credited with having discovered the *Charakteristik* and the *Fragment* as vehicles for literary criticism, as well as with having introduced irony into general literary discussion. On the basis of these contributions, he extended his influence well beyond the confines of Germany and became known as an important literary force throughout the entire Western world.

## Principal criticism
"Lyceums-Fragmente," 1797 (English translation, 1968)
"Über das Studium der griechischen Poesie," 1797
*Der Griechen und Römer*, 1797 (includes "Lyceums-Fragmente," and "Über das Studium der griechischen Poesie")
"Athenäums-Fragmente," 1798 (English translation, 1968)
*Geschichte der Poesie der Griechen und Römer*, 1798
*Gespräch über die Poesie*, 1800 ("Dialogue on Poetry," 1968)
*Ideen*, 1800 ("Ideas," 1968)
*Charakteristiken und Kritiken*, 1801

*Geschichte der alten und neuen Literatur*, 1815 (*Lectures in the History of Literature, Ancient and Modern*, 1818)
*Von der Schönheit in der Dichtkunst*, 1935
*Literary Notebooks, 1797–1801*, 1957 (Hans Eichner, editor)
"*Dialogue on Poetry*" *and Literary Aphorisms*, 1968

## Other major works and literary forms
In addition to the major critical and theoretical works listed above, as well as to the many reviews and short essays he wrote for a variety of literary periodicals including his own *Das Athenäum*, *Europa*, *Deutsches Museum*, and *Concordia*, Friedrich Schlegel was able to publish a number of important writings in such nonliterary fields as history, philosophy, and linguistics. Some noteworthy examples of these writings are *Über die Sprache und Weisheit der Indier* (1808; on the language and wisdom of the Indians), *Über die neuere Geschichte* (1811; *A Course of Lectures on Modern History*, 1849), *Philosophie der Geschichte* (1828; *The Philosophy of History*, 1835), and *Philosophie des Lebens* (1828) and *Philosophie der Sprache und des Wortes* (1830), which were translated together as *The Philosophy of Life and Philosophy of Language* (1847). *Über die Sprache und Weisheit der Indier* carries a special significance, serving as Germany's first systematic introduction to Sanskrit and to the thought and culture of India.

Schlegel tried his hand at all major literary genres but with a rather limited degree of success. He has to his credit a collection of poetry (*Gedichte*, 1809; poems), a play (*Alarcos*, 1802), and a novel (*Lucinde*, 1799). *Lucinde*, partially translated in 1913, is the most famous of Schlegel's fictional works, as it deals with topics that were largely taboo during the eighteenth century, namely physical love and the emancipation of women. On account of its risqué elements, this work was actually considered pornographic when it first appeared.

NOVEL
*Lucinde*, 1799 (partial English translation, 1913)

PLAY
*Alarcos*, 1802

POETRY
*Gedichte*, 1809

NONFICTION
*Über die Sprache und Weisheit der Indier*, 1808
*Über die neuere Geschichte*, 1811 (*A Course of Lectures on Modern History*, 1849)
*Philosophie der Geschichte*, 1828 (*The Philosophy of History*, 1835)
*Philosophie des Lebens*, 1828, and *Philosophie der Sprache und des Wortes*, 1830 (translated together as *The Philosophy of Life and Philosophy of Language*, 1847)

## Further reading
Behler, Ernst. *Friedrich Schlegel: In Selbstzeugnissen und Bilddokumenten*, 1966.
Eichner, Hans. *Friedrich Schlegel*, 1970.

Hecht, Wolfgang. "Einleitung," in *Friedrich Schlegel: Werke in zwei Bänden*, 1980.

Immerwahr, Raymond. "The Subjectivity or Objectivity of Friedrich Schlegel's Poetic Irony," in *The Germanic Review*. XXVI (1951), pp. 173–191.

Mettler, Dieter. "Friedrich Schlegel–Walter Benjamin–Roland Barthes: Philosophische Begründungsversuche der Literaturkritik," in *Wirkendes Wort*. 40 (1990), pp. 422–434.

Moser, Hugo, and Benno von Wiese, eds. *Friedrich Schlegel und die Romantik*, 1969.

Peter, Klaus. *Friedrich Schlegel*, 1978.

Schanze, Helmut, ed. *Friedrich Schlegel und die Kunsttheorie seiner Zeit*, 1985.

Verstraete, Ginette. "Friedrich Schlegel's Practice of Literary Theory," in *Germanic Review*. 69 (1994), pp. 28–35.

Wellek, René. "Friedrich Schlegel," in *A History of Modern Criticism: 1750–1950*. Vol. 2, *The Romantic Age*, 1955.

DWIGHT A. KLETT

*See also* Hegel; Kant; Romanticism; Schelling; Schlegel, A. W.; Winckelmann

# Arthur Schopenhauer

German philosopher

**Born:** Danzig, Prussia; February 22, 1788
**Died:** Frankfurt am Main, Germany; September 21, 1860

## Biography

Arthur Schopenhauer was born on February 22, 1788, in the free Prussian city of Danzig (Gdansk). His father, Heinrich Schopenhauer, was a successful businessman interested in the arts and culture but given to periods of melancholy and depression. He died presumably by accidental drowning in 1805. Arthur's mother, Johanna, a refined and elegant woman much younger than her husband, was a rather popular author of romantic novels. After the death of the father, mother and son moved to Weimar, then the leading cultural center of Germany. As Schopenhauer grew older, he and his mother became increasingly antagonistic toward each other. Their relationship ended in complete estrangement.

Although his father had wished that he undertake a career in business, Schopenhauer studied philosophy. He first went to the University of Göttingen, where he applied himself to the writings of Plato and Immanuel Kant. In 1811 he went to Berlin, where he attended lectures by Johann Gottlieb Fichte and Friedrich Schleiermacher. He also began studies of Asian religious philosophy, primarily Hinduism and Buddhism. Schopenhauer completed his doctoral dissertation in 1813 at the University of Jena.

In an age dominated by the progressive dialectics of G. W. F. Hegel, Schopenhauer's philosophy of pessimism drew little attention, and his lectures at the University of Berlin attracted few students. Bitter and disappointed, he withdrew from academic life and devoted himself to further writing. Lonely, suspicious, and egotistical, he became increasingly eccentric and wrote a number of morbid essays on women, sex, and marriage. With the second edition of *The World as Will and Idea* in 1844, Schopenhauer's work began to receive a measure of critical acclaim, and he finally felt some degree of personal and professional vindication. He died on September 21, 1860.

## Influence

Schopenhauer's ideas, especially those on aesthetics, were of tremendous influence on subsequent writers and thinkers, many of whom are among the greatest in nineteenth- and twentieth-century art, literature, and philosophy. The importance which art assumes within his thought helped to shape the so-called religion of art of twentieth-century modernism. A partial list of those whose work was shaped by Schopenhauer's philosophy include Wilhelm Raabe, Theodor Storm, Friedrich Nietzsche, Richard Wagner, Thomas Mann, Franz Kafka, Sigmund Freud, and Ludwig Wittgenstein, as well as Thomas Hardy, D. H. Lawrence, and Samuel Beckett.

## Analysis

Since Schopenhauer's aesthetic theories are an important aspect of his overall philosophy, it is important to consider first the general context of his ideas contained in his major work, *The World as Will and Idea*. Schopenhauer is a post-Kantian thinker, that is, he accepts the latter's distinction between the phenomenal (reality as it appears structured through the categories of human perception) and the noumenal (reality as it is unto itself). Whereas Kant regarded the noumenal, which he termed "the thing-in-itself," as unknowable, Schopenhauer considered the ultimate ground of reality to be the "Will," a mindless, irrational, and ever-changing life force, indifferent to all human values and concerns. The Will is a dynamic force prior to all matter and consciousness and manifests itself continuously through the creation of the cosmos and its beings.

The Will seeks only its own objectification or perpetuation through the generation of ever-new forms, which Schopenhauer termed "Ideas," in never-ending cosmic cycles of creation and destruction. These Ideas – from the Greek *eidos*, meaning images or pictures – are only eternal manifestations of the life force, expendable and themselves without absolute ontological substance. All perceived "reality" – Kant's phenomenal world – is shaped by the Idea, a picture generated by the Will. All humanity, its hopes and fears, triumphs and achievements, is merely its phenomenal expression. The Ideas are immutable patterns of being that underlie the myriad phenomena of life, and they can only be intuited through aesthetic vision. These objectifications, or Ideas, present a hierarchy of levels – from the lowest, matter, to the highest, the human race – to the degree that they reflect the Will. Having been greatly influenced by Hindu philosophy and religion, Schopenhauer often used the Sanskrit term *maya* (illusion) to designate the insubstantial nature of the Ideas.

Since the Will seeks only the perpetual creation of ever-greater objectified forms, or Ideas, the basic principle, or energy, of the universe seems to be desire. Human desire – the individual's will – is merely a reflection, on a minor scale, of this grand cosmic longing for Being. Desire, however, can never be truly satisfied because the Will is infinitely dynamic, never static or at rest. Desire unsatisfied always produces suffering, and for Schopenhauer, this was the essential condition of human life. That is the case because desire and consciousness are infinite, and the world is finite. To exist is to will or desire, and that means the experience of ongoing suffering. Again reflecting the influence of Hindu and Buddhist philosophies, Schopenhauer believed that quietism, or a stilling of individual volition (the monk's abnegation of the world), was the only adequate response to existence.

Art, however, also serves as an escape from the pain of life: it permits the transformation of the ceaseless desire of the Will into detached contemplation. Art affords humankind a momentary sense of transcendence from the suffering that is existence. Aesthetic vision allows the individual to perceive the eternal essence of the Will as objectified Idea in the form of Beauty. As such, art represents the highest degree of objectification as abstraction. The Beautiful is not an expression, however, of humanity's respect for the divine perfection of creation or of its love for life; instead, it is a vision of existence abstracted as essence, free from the bondage of desire and suffering that it entails. Thus, the state of aesthetic contemplation parallels for Schopenhauer the Buddhist notion of Nirvana, the freedom and peace of a consciousness that has attained true detachment from life. The only liability of the aesthetic state is that it remains a transitory experience and offers only a momentary reprieve from the pain of existence.

The genius of the artist resides in the capacity of his or her intuitive knowledge to perceive the essence of the Idea in all of its purity. Most of humankind is capable of this to a limited degree insofar as they can achieve the aesthetic detachment involved in the contemplation of art; they are, however, subject to the demands of the Will expressed as instincts. The artist, on the other hand, lives, so to speak, in a continual state of aesthetic disinterest. Because he lives in a world of essences, he is also divorced from the concrete reality of existence and is, to that degree, like a madman – just as the enlightened monk is "mad" in his detachment from the world.

The mad genius is incapable of participating in the institutions of everyday bourgeois life, such as marriage and family, and lives a life of isolation as a perpetual outsider. This view of the genius/artist in Schopenhauer's philosophy was of great influence on later German writers such as Mann, whose works revolve around the dichotomy of the "diseased" artist versus the "healthy" bourgeois, and Kafka, whose writings often treat the guilty conscience of the artist who rejects the demands of normal life such as marriage, children, and career.

Schopenhauer ranks the individual arts according to the degree to which they express the objectifications of the Will. Architecture, for example, is one of the lowest ranked forms of art, because it deals in the rigid and heavy forms of matter, such as stone and wood, and depicts as such the most basic and crude forms of the Will as objectified Idea. Painting and sculpture, insofar as they represent the human form, are, on the other hand, superior art forms because they manifest the highest objectification of the Will, that is, humanity.

Considering Schopenhauer's pessimism, it is logical that he would consider tragedy to be the highest of the poetic arts. Tragedy depicts the suffering of the individual and thus represents the eternal indifference of the Will in its ongoing cycles of creation and destruction. It manifests in aesthetic vision the horrible essence of existence. Here, his ideas would provide the starting point for Nietzsche's early work *Die Geburt der Tragödie aus dem Geiste der Musik* (1872; *The Birth of Tragedy out of the Spirit of Music*, 1909).

Schopenhauer conceives of music as the highest form of all the arts because it is essentially different from other modes of artistic creation. Other traditional art forms – such as sculpture, painting, poetry, or tragedy – are basically referential or mimetic, that is, they depict the phenomenal world of people, places, and things. In Schopenhauer's terms, they represent the Ideas, or objectifications, of the Will and not the Will itself. These aesthetic forms are thus twice removed from what the philosopher holds to be the absolute reality. This more immediate vision, however, is accomplished in music, a nonmimetic genre. Music is a direct and abstract expression of the ceaseless movement of the Will – the joy, sorrow, and desire that is existence – and it thus allows the individual to contemplate the absolute reality in a less veiled or less mediated manifestation. This high evaluation of the musical arts made Schopenhauer an important influence on Wagner. It also pointed the way to the essentially "musical" or nonrepresentational aesthetic forms in painting, sculpture, and literature that characterize modernist art. Later, art movements such as cubism and abstract expressionism would be examples of this kind of musical aesthetic.

Schopenhauer's aesthetics is closely associated with his view of ethics. The good individual shares with the artist a similar insight into the essential reality of the Will. Individuals who are morally good behave with an awareness of the illusory nature of all existence and realize their essential oneness with the Will. They love conscious of the suffering that is life and thus act in sympathy with their fellow human beings. The moral individual avoids the lures and traps of the world and lives in an ascetic manner, in a style of life akin to that of a saint.

Aesthetic contemplation is significant for moral behavior, because it prepares the way for the ethical life in that it affords the individual essential insight into the processes of the Will. The artist's disinterested vision therefore occupies a privileged position. The aesthetic experience becomes a kind of moral meditation and represents a mode of knowledge superior to that of science, which deals only in the logical concept and not abstract symbolic essence. Conversely, morally bad people fall victim to the illusory attractions of life; they love self-centered and pitted against their fellows. They are hopelessly caught in the endless cycles of desire and suffering, wholly determined by the instincts. These people are the bourgeois philistines who have no sense of an appreciation for artistic creation.

Schopenhauer's philosophy, especially his aesthetics, has had an important influence on some of the best-known writers and thinkers of the nineteenth and twentieth centuries. His impact on Nietzsche has already been mentioned; through Nietzsche's works, Schopenhauer's influence was transmitted to later writers such as Mann and Kafka. Freud's notion of the individual libido as the instinctual energy within the psyche and his views concerning art and sublimation owe much to Schopenhauer. The fatalist Thomas Hardy, whose often-tragic novels portray the individual as existing within an indifferent and remote cosmos, was acquainted with Schopenhauer's thought. The idea of sexuality as the unconscious workings of the Will – the individual as subject to his or her instincts – appealed to D. H. Lawrence, whose works revolve around the theme of the irresistible drive of the erotic. Finally, Schopenhauer's nihilism and the existential theme of art as a mode of transcendence deeply influenced Samuel Beckett, whose texts confront a similar bleak and pessimistic outlook on life, with the transformation offered by the act of writing.

## Principal criticism
*Die Welt als Wille und Vorstellung*, 1819, 1844 (3 volumes; *The World as Will and Idea*, 1883–1886)
*Parerga und Paralipomena*, 1851 (*Parerga and Paralipomena*, 1974)

## Other major works and literary forms
Arthur Schopenhauer's writings were all in the area of philosophy and its various subfields: epistemology, ontology, logic, and, above all, aesthetics. His style is considered by many to be a model of elegant German prose.

NONFICTION
*Über die vierfache Wurzel des Satzes vom zureichende Grunde*, 1813 (*On the Fourfold Root of the Principle of Sufficient Reason*, 1889)
*Über das Sehen und die Farben*, 1816
*Die beiden Grundprobleme der Ethik*, 1841 (*The Basis of Morality*, 1903)
*Selected Essays of Schopenhauer*, 1951

## Further reading
Atwell, John E. *Schopenhauer: The Human Character*, 1990.
——. *Schopenhauer on the Character of the World: The Metaphysics of the Will*, 1995.
Copleston, Frederick C. "Schopenhauer's Philosophy of Art," in *A History of Philosophy*. Vol. 7, 1965.
Gardiner, Patrick. *Schopenhauer*, 1963.
Hamlyn, D. W. *Schopenhauer*, 1980.
Hubscher, Arthur, et al. *The Philosophy of Schopenhauer in its Intellectual Context: Thinker Against the Tide*, 1989.
Knox, Israel. *The Aesthetic Theories of Kant, Hegel, and Schopenhauer*, 1936.
Krukowksi, Lucian. *Aesthetic Legacies*, 1992.
Magee, Bryan. *The Philosophy of Schopenhauer*, 1983.
Safranski, Rüdiger. *Schopenhauer and the Wild Years of Philosophy*, 1989. Translated by Ewald Osers.
Simmel, Georg. *Schopenhauer and Nietzsche*, 1986.
Sorg, Bernhard. *Zur literarischen Schopenhauer-Rezeption im 19. Jahrhundert*, 1975.
Wellek, René. "Schopenhauer's Aesthetics," in *A History of Modern Criticism: 1750–1955*. Vol. 2, *The Romantic Age*, 1955.

THOMAS F. BARRY

*See also* Kant; Nietzsche

# Semiotics

Semiotics is the study of meaning in all its forms. It takes as its fundamental premise that human society – the world we inhabit – is essentially meaningful and hence open to interpretation. Semiotic activity can be described, therefore, as an operation of decoding and of delving beneath physical surfaces (signifiers) to arrive at underlying meanings (signifieds). If, for example, we see someone crying (the signifier), we conclude it is because they are upset (the signified).

The impact of semiotics on literary criticism in the twentieth century has clearly been enormous. Reading a literary text is envisaged as a process of discovery whereby ever more layers of meaning are unraveled until we arrive at a central underlying system of meanings and values. This process of interpretation involves the active participation of the reader in an ongoing encounter with cultural and political context.

The semiotic approach differs from both previous and current approaches to literature in a number of ways. Firstly, it envisages the text as an internally coherent unit. Meaning is established through an intricate network of structures. The point of departure and central focus of any study of literature, therefore, should be a close analysis of the language and structures of the text in question. Impressionistic or purely subjective readings of literature are no longer considered valid, nor is it acceptable to base one's analysis on predominantly biographical data. Indeed, a fundamental premise of semiotics is that form and content, structure and meaning, are inseparable. Semiotics thus claims for itself the status of a science, one of its far-reaching effects being to bridge the traditional divide between the arts and science.

Secondly, unlike more traditional/stylistic approaches to literature, semiotics posits the necessity to delve beneath the linguistic textual surface to uncover more abstract structures of meaning. These abstract structures pre-exist the text and are universal, that is, they are prelinguistic and common to all humankind.

Thirdly, although semiotic analysis focuses primarily on a specific text, this text is never viewed in isolation from its context. Indeed, the unraveling of layers and structures of meaning represents essentially a process of decoding that goes well beyond the frontiers of any given work. This process will necessarily bring into play the cultural and political climate in which the text is produced as well as that in which it is being interpreted (if different). Literary texts can thus be viewed as living organisms capable, with the passage of time, of acquiring ever-wider and more pertinent layers of meaning.

Broadly speaking, there are two principal branches or schools of semiotics, the American, represented by C. S. Peirce, and the French, represented by A. J. Greimas and the Paris School. Here we will be principally concerned with the Paris School.

## AMERICAN SEMIOTICS: C. S. PEIRCE

Founded by the philosopher Charles Sanders Peirce (1839–1914), American semiotics is concerned principally with a theory of signs. Indeed, Peirce considered the sign to be the logical basis of all human thought.

In Peirce's system a sign is not only something that stands for something else (the object). To exist as a sign, it also needs to be interpreted and so have an *interpretant*. A sign, therefore, has three aspects: (1) *The actual sign*. For example, the word STOP on a red background at a traffic junction. (2) *The object or meaning*. The sign STOP *means* that one must come to a halt. (3) *The interpretant*. The interpretant is the idea joining the sign to a particular object, usually by a process of induction or deduction. In the example of the traffic light it is the *idea of stopping*. Different interpretants will clearly produce different objects. The sign – the red light – could also indicate, for example, the presence of a main road or of a heavily populated area. According to Peirce, a process of *unlimited semiosis* (production of meanings) could be set in action through the function of the interpretant.

Much of Peirce's work in this field is concerned with developing and redefining sign categories. He divides signs into three types: the *icon*, *index*, and *symbol*.

*The icon*. An icon is a sign which resembles the object signified. A portrait, for example, is an icon because it resembles the subject represented. A diagram of a house is an icon of the house.

*The index*. An index is a sign physically linked to its object. The relationship could be causal or sequential. Examples given by Peirce are a weathercock, a barometer, and a sundial. Other examples might include knocking at the door indicating someone is there, or pointing a finger at someone. Smoke is an index of fire and high temperature the index of illness.

*The symbol*. A symbol is a sign whose relationship to its object is entirely arbitrary. An example would be the word "bus" where there is no causal or physical link and no resemblance between the sign and its object.

## The influence of Peirce: Umberto Eco

The work of Peirce has exerted a very strong influence not only on the development of American semiotics but also on the thought of the Italian philosopher and semiotician Umberto Eco. In his book *A Theory of Semiotics* (1976) Eco presents a theory of codes and of sign production that is based on Peirce's notion of unlimited semiosis. Later, in his *Semiotics and the Philosophy of Language* (1984), Eco shows how language, as a network of meanings, has more in common with an encyclopedia than with a dictionary.

Eco's most celebrated and perhaps most accessible theoretical work is his book *The Role of the Reader: Explorations in the Semiotics of Texts* (1979). The chapter "Narrative Strategies in Fleming," which focuses on the use of opposition and on the notion of "the Villain," may be of particular interest to students of literature and of the media. In another chapter, "The Poetics of the Open Work," Eco also develops the notion of an open and closed text. An open text is one where the meanings remain complex and in which ambiguities cannot be resolved. A closed text, on the other hand, is less susceptible to a wide range of interpretations and its ending would be relatively free of ambiguity. Examples of open texts would be the works of Samuel Beckett, whereas the traditional children's fairy tale would be considered a closed text.

Although the thought of Peirce has undoubtedly influenced his European counterparts, the American approach to semiotics – and to a certain degree that of Eco himself – differs in important respects from that of the French, as represented by A. J. Greimas and the Paris School. Unlike Peirce, the primary concern of the Paris School is not with the individual sign or with its classification but rather with the relationships or structures that underlie a text, giving rise to its meanings. In contrast to Peirce, the Paris School also attaches central importance to the practical application of its theories and to the development of a methodology for textual analysis. Its impact, therefore, can be felt in a very wide range of disciplines.

## FRENCH SEMIOTICS: A. J. GREIMAS AND THE PARIS SCHOOL

French semiotics is represented primarily by what is known as the Paris School (École de Paris) founded by the linguist Algirdas Julien Greimas. The Paris School is the name given to a group of researchers that emerged in the mid-1960s in France and whose members continue to meet at regular intervals in Paris. The theories of this school are outlined in a dictionary produced by Greimas and his colleague Joseph Courtés (*Sémiotique, dictionnaire raisonné de la théorie du langage*, 1979, 1986, two volumes; *Semiotics and Language: An Analytical Dictionary*, 1982, first volume) and practical examples of semiotic analysis also appear in their numerous publications. Current participants include Michel Arrivé, Denis Bertrand, Joseph Courtés, Jacques Fontanille, Jacques Geninasca, Eric Landowski, and Herman Parret.

## The Paris School definition of semiotics

The Paris School defines semiotics as a *theory for the production of meaning*. It takes issue with the more popular definition – that coined by Peirce which describes semiotics as a *science of signs*. This latter definition relates more accurately to the discipline of *semiology* – the word employed in the 1960s – from which semiotics, whilst acknowledging its debt, takes its distance.

## The genesis of the Paris School

Firmly rooted in an intellectual tradition, semiotics is also a product of the cultural climate of the 1960s. Greimas himself collaborated with influential figures of the period such as Roland Barthes, Gérard Genette, Claude Lévi-Strauss, and Julia Kristeva. Members of the Paris School were also familiar with the works of fashionable writers such as Émile Durkheim, Edmund Husserl, Maurice Merleau-Ponty, Jean-Paul Sartre, and Ferdinand de Saussure. The principal influences on the growth of semiotics at that time were linguistics, cultural anthropology (including mythology), and phenomenology.

### Linguistics

The development of semiotics is heavily indebted to structuralism and in particular to the work of Saussure. Saussure's central conviction that meaning does not lie in individual words but in a complex system of relationships or differences lies at the very core of the semiotic enterprise. As Greimas says in the opening chapter of his seminal work *Structural Semantics* (1976):

> We perceive differences and thanks to that perception, the world "takes shape" in front of us and for our purposes.

Binary opposition thus comes to form the basis of all meaning.

Saussure's work on the sign has also played a key role in the growth of semiotics. For Saussure words are not symbols corresponding to things, but are made up of two components: a mark or *signifier* and a concept or *signified*. The word (linguistic sign) "tree," for example, is made up of a sound or written mark (signifier) and also of the idea

or concept of a tree (signified). Saussure describes the relationship of the signifier to the signified as that between the front and back of a piece of paper. In other words, form and content cannot be disassociated. This too was to become a fundamental premise of semiotics.

### Cultural anthropology

Semiotics has also been strongly influenced by the work of the French anthropologist Claude Lévi-Strauss. In his *Structural Anthropology* (1972) and *The Raw and the Cooked* (1970), Lévi-Strauss sets out to identify the constituent parts of cultural behavior he studies as if it were a language. In other words, like the semiotician, he is not so much interested in the intrinsic nature of phenomena but in the way elements combine to form contrastive relationships.

In this search for a system underlying all cultures, Lévi-Strauss attaches particular importance to myth. His analysis of myths from different cultures brought to light a number of recurrent elements or *mythemes* that operate like the components of universal signifying structures. This discovery inspired Greimas and his colleagues in their development of universal narrative models.

At the same time, semiotics is heavily indebted to the findings of the Russian Formalist Vladimir Propp. An examination of numerous folk tales led Propp to conclude that there exist thirty-one functions that form the basis of any story. These functions are distributed amongst seven "spheres of action" such as that of villain, hero, and donor. They were later simplified by Greimas to produce what was to become the basic narrative model and indispensable working tool of the Paris School.

### Phenomenology

Phenomenology has also been of prime importance in the growth of semiotics. Of particular significance here is Maurice Merleau-Ponty's *Phenomenology of Perception* (1962). Merleau-Ponty defines original differences as perceptual and hence prelinguistic. Both Merleau-Ponty and the Paris School, then, reject the traditional dualistic separation of mind and body, of intellect and lived reality. Semiotic theory attaches central importance to the role of the perceptions in the construction of meaning. Indeed, the focus of much recent semiotic research has been on the role of the observer in the creation of a sense of place.

## The fundamental principles of Paris School semiotics

The basic tenets of French semiotics can be summarized as follows.

Meaning is not inherent in objects but is *constructed* by a human observer. In analyzing a literary text, central importance is attached to the position of the subject/observer from whose point of view – physical and mental – the fictive universe is constructed.

There is no meaning without difference. Items do not signify in themselves but only in relationship to a structure. Literary criticism, therefore, should not concern itself solely with the examination of individual lexical items, images, or themes, but rather with the intricate network of meanings/oppositions established within the text.

There exist universal structures that underlie and give rise to meaning. These structures can be represented in the form of models which can be applied to any signifying object to decode and interpret its meanings. In other words, these models can be applied to all kinds of literary texts be they lyrical, descriptive, or narrative, and so on.

Narrativity is a central feature of all discourse and not simply of literature. For instance, story patterns underlie legal texts as well as media, political, and bureaucratic discourse. The semiotic approach thus represents a narrowing of the divide between the literary and the nonliterary and between text and context.

There are three fundamental levels of meaning. All texts, including literary texts, can, therefore, be approached from three angles. These levels are: (1) *The discursive level* including the figurative component. This is a surface, concrete level of meaning where the illusion of time, place, and character is constructed. (2) *The narrative level*. This is more abstract than the discursive level. It is the level at which underlying narrative models operate. (3) *The deep, abstract level*. This is the level of the abstract or conceptual. It is the level at which the fundamental values of the text are articulated.

## How to analyze a literary text

The semiotic method has been used for several years now in the teaching of literature both in schools and at universities. The approach has yielded outstanding results, proving itself to be particularly effective in the uncovering of the multiplicity of meanings within – and beyond – the text. The following pages present the basic outline of this method, taking as an example the fairy tale *Sleeping Beauty*.

To briefly summarize the story, a King and Queen are very unhappy because they have no children. Eventually, to their joy, the Queen gives birth to a beautiful daughter and they celebrate the christening at their castle. All the fairies are invited to the feast except one (she is too bad-tempered) and they bring gifts of Beauty, Happiness, Goodness, Health, Gracefulness, and Kindness for the Princess. Suddenly the uninvited fairy appears and, seeking revenge, she curses the Princess, saying that on her sixteenth birthday she will prick her finger on a spindle and die. Immediately, a good fairy comes forward and weakens the curse: instead of dying, the Princess will fall asleep for a hundred years to be awakened by a Prince. And so, on her sixteenth birthday, as predicted, the Princess pricks her finger on an old woman's (the wicked fairy's) spindle and falls asleep in a high tower. A hundred years later a handsome Prince, hearing of the story of *Sleeping Beauty* from an old man, arrives at the castle, hacks down the surrounding hedge of thorns, climbs the tower, and wakes her with his kiss. The two instantly fall in love, marry, and live happily ever after.

Based on the notion of levels of meaning, a semiotic analysis commences with an examination of surface textual phenomena. It then proceeds through a process of decoding to uncover deeper and more abstract levels of meaning until we arrive at the fundamental values underlying the text. Broadly speaking, therefore, an analysis can be divided into three sections reflecting this overall movement from surface to depth.

## The discursive level

The discursive level is a surface level of meaning or level of manifestation. Here we examine the specific words – or grammatical items/structures that are visible on the surface of the text. Key components of this level are (a) the figurative component, (b) the grammatical/syntactical component, and (c) the enunciative component.

### *The figurative component*

The term figurative describes all those elements (figures) in a text that refer to the external, concrete, physical world and that can be apprehended by the five senses. Examples are: house, cat, small, hot, wet, loud, and so on. These elements can be contrasted with the inner world of the conceptual and abstract. The figurative component is an important feature of every literary text, and is an essential ingredient in the construction of a "reality effect" (the referential illusion) – that is, in creating an impression of time, of place, and of character.

To explore the figurative component we start with examining the vocabulary and grouping together words that have a similar meaning or common denominator. These groupings are termed *isotopies* and their construction is essential to the coherence of a text. For example, one might begin by listing all references to place, objects, time, and people. The following analysis is in fact based on a specific version of *Sleeping Beauty*. This, however, is a typical version and most of the key elements discussed below will be found in traditional treatments of the story. The isotopy of place can be presented thus:

*place*
kingdom
land
cradle
castle (7)
door/doorway (3)
place to hide
inside (2)
top (2)
room (3)
spiral staircase (3)

floor
ceiling
down
high tower.

Depending on the nature of the text, other useful headings or isotopies might include sound, vision, temperature, parts of the body, weather, size, shape, verticality, movement, clothes, gesture, color, animals, plants, country, and city.

Having extracted and made lists of the principal isotopies, the next stage in our analysis is to look for oppositions: as Saussure says, there can be no meaning without difference. These oppositions are to be found either within the individual isotopies, or between one isotopy and another. Let us take the example of the isotopy of place in *Sleeping Beauty*, where the following oppositions can be discerned.

1.  *high*          versus     *low*
    high tower                  ground
    the top                     floor
    ceiling                     down
    up

2.  *wild/natural*  versus     *cultivated/artificial*
    briars                      castle
    hedge of thorns             door/doorway
    hacked                      room/tower
                                spiral staircase

3.  *outside*       versus     *inside*
    outside                     inside
    hedge of thorns             castle
                                door/doorway

These oppositions can then be correlated: the *wild/natural* can be correlated with *outside* space whereas the *cultivated/artificial* is associated with *inside* space. Within the modern and avant-garde text this process of correlation is naturally both more complex and more subtle than in the traditional fairy tale. It is certainly an important factor in explaining a text's specificity or originality.

The next stage in our analysis is to ask what does the choice of isotopies and of oppositions signify? Indeed, the figurative component, viewed in isolation, is meaningless; it acquires significance only in relationship to a subject – narrator – and to the feelings and judgments of this narrator. It is at this point, therefore, that we bring to bear the isotopy of the emotions expressed in the opposition *euphoria* versus *dysphoria* (pleasant versus unpleasant). An isotopy of evaluative terms (*positive* versus *negative*) is also brought into play. In *Sleeping Beauty* these oppositions are of particular significance in the construction of the actors (characters). As is customary in the fairy tale, divisions between pleasant and unpleasant, happy and sad, positive and negative, are very clear-cut and unambiguous. An

examination of the text could produce the following lists and conclusions.

1.  The isotopy of the emotions expressed in the opposition *euphoria* versus *dysphoria*:

    | *euphoria* | versus | *dysphoria* |
    |---|---|---|
    | joy | | unhappy |
    | happiness | | bad-tempered |
    | excited | | furious |
    | surprise | | spitefully |
    | amazed | | hissed |
    | fell in love | | with horror |
    | happy life | | |

Here positive emotions are associated with one group of actors – the King, Queen, Princess, Prince, and seven fairies – whereas the negative are linked (with one exception at the beginning) to the wicked fairy. A process of evaluation is clearly taking place, producing a second grouping.

2.  The isotopy of evaluative terms (physical and moral) with the opposition *positive* versus *negative*:

    | *positive* | versus | *negative* |
    |---|---|---|
    | *physical* | | |
    | beautiful | | |
    | beauty | | |
    | lovely | | |
    | wonderful | | |
    | magnificent | | |
    | graceful | | |
    | gentle | | |
    | handsome | | |
    | health | | |
    | | | |
    | *moral* | | |
    | goodness | | evil |
    | kindness | | wicked |
    | kindest | | curse |
    | good | | cunningly |

Positive physical terms are associated with the Princess: beauty, grace, health. These are coupled with the positive moral terms of goodness and kindness. The Prince is described as handsome but he is not invested explicitly with any moral attributes. Implicitly, however, he could be linked to curiosity and determination. The other actors in the story are devoid of any physical attributes. The fairies, for example, are evoked in exclusively moral terms: the seven good fairies and the one wicked one.

## The grammatical/syntactical component

The illusion of a real world (the figurative component) may be strengthened through the use of linguistic devices such as repetition, ellipsis, the active/passive, nominalization, coordination/subordination, and cohesive markers. Most versions of *Sleeping Beauty* are written for children and so the sentence structure is kept simple. What is striking is the frequent use of temporal connectors (link words and phrases) particularly at the beginning of sentences, for instance: "there once," "not long after," "after a magnificent feast," "on your sixteenth birthday," "at last," "immediately." The effect is to heighten the drama and pace of a narrative in which the passage of time is itself an important theme.

Another interesting device is the use of repetition, a characteristic feature of children's writing. Nouns are frequently employed to refer to people where it would be more customary to use a pronoun. For instance, the terms "the wicked fairy" and "the good fairy" are repeated in close proximity. The effect once more is to heighten the drama by foregrounding the opposition between good and evil. A sense of symmetry is conveyed and of a universe that is highly ordered. The almost incantatory repetition of these two sets of terms in the last paragraph has the effect of reassuring the child that the threat has been lifted and that good is restored.

## The enunciative component

The enunciative stagies in *Sleeping Beauty* are those of traditional storytelling. The narrator is third person and extradiagetic (not an actor in the story). This hidden narrator is also omniscient in that the reader has access to the thoughts and emotions of the actors. The story is told in the past and we are kept at a distance from the events recounted; indeed, storytelling itself becomes a narrative motif: it is the old man's account of what happened in the castle that prompts the Prince to embark on his quest.

Looking at the use of modality (the degree of the speaker's adherence to the statement), the utterances can be described as categorical. They express certainty on the part of the narrator, and there are no tentative statements suggesting probability or possibility. An impression of narratorial distance and of complete objectivity is thereby conveyed.

At the same time, however, the presence of a narrator – of a subjectivity – can be discerned indirectly in the abundant use of evaluative terms. The sharp divisions between positive and negative, good and evil, that we have already noted suggest a particular interpretation of reality or vision of the world.

The enunciative strategies employed in *Sleeping Beauty* thus contribute to a strong sense of reality and to a fictive world whose authenticity is never open to doubt or to questioning. The explicit and clearly delineated categorization, whether in terms of space, time, or the actors, serves to reassure the reader, and the child in particular, suggesting a world that is stable and inherently meaningful.

## The narrative level

The next stage in our analysis is an examination of what is known as the narrative level. More abstract than the discursive, this is the level of story structure, that is, the level at which underlying universal narrative models operate.

These models can be applied globally to a whole story and/or they can be applied to smaller units or episodes. In order to decide on the approach, it may be helpful to ask the question what is (are) the principal event(s)? In other words, what is (are) the principal *transformation(s)*? If we are having difficulty in selecting key transformations, it may be useful to summarize the plot in one or two sentences. It may also help to look at the end of the story – the final event – and compare it with the beginning.

In *Sleeping Beauty* two principal transformations are apparent: (1) the Princess pricks her finger and falls asleep for a hundred years; (2) after a hundred years a Prince arrives, wakes her (breaks the spell), and marries her. These transformations are also marked on the surface level by actorial and temporal disjunctions: after her birthday party, the Princess meets an apparently new actor (an old woman) who hands her the spindle with which she pricks her finger; a new actor, the Prince, arrives on the scene "one day, a hundred years later." The story thus falls neatly into two parts or two major episodes (narrative programs). Mirroring this pattern, the following divisions can be made: Part 1 from the beginning to "Nearly everyone forgot about the King and Queen and their beautiful daughter," and Part 2 from "But one day, a hundred years later" to the end.

Our first step will be to examine the distribution of narrative roles in each of the two parts of the text. If we apply Greimas' *actantial model* to Part 1 of *Sleeping Beauty*, the following pattern emerges:

*Subject.* The subject of the quest is a collective actor, the King and Queen.

*Object.* The objects of the King and Queen's quest are both concrete (or pragmatic) and abstract (or cognitive). The concrete goals are to preserve the life of their daughter and to prevent the wicked fairy's spell from coming true. The abstract objects are (a) the protection of their daughter from all evil; (b) the preservation of the gifts/values of Beauty, Happiness, Goodness, Health, Gracefulness, and Kindness that she embodies; and (c) the triumph of good over evil.

*Helper.* An implied helper is the collective actor, the subjects of the King and Queen, who try to burn all the spinning wheels in the land. The magnificent party on the Princess' sixteenth birthday also functions as a helper: "they thought that this would stop her finding a spindle on that day."

*Opponent.* The Princess' desire to play hide-and-seek as well as her curiosity concerning the spinning wheel function as opponents.

*Sender.* The sender of the parents' quest to preserve the life of their daughter is the wicked fairy's curse that the good fairy can only weaken.

*Anti-subject.* The principal anti-subject is the wicked fairy herself who, in the guise of an old woman, lures the Princess into touching the spinning wheel. The object of her quest is the destruction of the Princess' life, in other words, her goal is in opposition to that of the King and Queen. Her own sender is her desire for revenge.

The quest of the King and Queen fails: they do not succeed in protecting their daughter from evil. The quest of the wicked fairy succeeds (partially) in that the Princess pricks her finger and falls to the ground "as if she were dead." The quest of the good fairy also succeeds, however, in that the Princes sleeps rather than dies. To put it more abstractly, the values of Beauty, Happiness, Goodness, Health, Gracefulness, and Kindness lie dormant rather than being destroyed altogether.

Having examined the distribution of narrative roles in the first part of *Sleeping Beauty*, we go on to divide the quest into a number of logical stages in accordance with the *canonical narrative schema*. These stages are:

*The Contract.* The contract is enacted in two episodes in the text: (1) the wicked fairy's curse, and (2) the good fairy's desire to weaken the curse by changing death to sleep. By pronouncing the curse whose effect the good fairy can only mitigate, the wicked fairy incites in the King and Queen the desire and need to protect their daughter both from death and from falling asleep. Put more abstractly, the parents must now fight to preserve the gifts or values that their daughter represents. The King and Queen, now in possession of the modalities of *wanting-to-do* and of *having-to-do*, become virtual subjects of a global narrative program or quest.

*The Qualifying Test.* Hoping to acquire the ability to carry out his quest (a *being-able-to-do*), the King orders every spindle in the land to be burnt. However, his efforts meet with only partial success: we learn later that not all the spindles are destroyed. His competence is undermined by an anti-subject, the wicked fairy. Her intention is to harm the Princess and, as she is in possession of magic powers, she is stronger than the King.

*The Decisive Test.* The arrival and celebration of the Princess' sixteenth birthday is the principal event (transformation) toward which the whole story has been moving; it is also the moment of confrontation between two opposing parties or forces. In this confrontation it is the wicked fairy with her lure who prevails over the father's attempts to protect his daughter.

*The Glorifying Test.* It is at this stage that the reader learns of the outcome of the decisive test; whether, for example, it has failed or succeeded. In other words, it is at this point that the decisive action is being evaluated. The Princess falls asleep: it can be said, therefore, that the parents have failed in their quest to protect their

daughter from the effects of evil. The narrator interprets the action of falling asleep as follows: "At once she fell to ground as if she were dead. The wicked fairy's curse had come true," and the next paragraph adds "But the good fairy's spell came true, too, for the Princess was not dead, only sleeping."

This global narrative program of the quest in the first part of the story is preceded by two significant episodes or smaller narrative programs (a narrative program designates a narrative unit expressing a transformation in the relationship between a subject and an object).

At the very beginning of the story, the King and Queen are introduced as separated or *disjoined* from their objects of value: a child and happiness. At the end of the paragraph, they are described as in possession or *conjoined* with these objects: they now have a baby and are happy. This opening is followed by an episode conveying a similar narrative program: after the feast the subject, the seven fairies, gives to the Princess a number of gifts. It is these objects (Beauty, Health, and so on) that, as we have seen, are at stake when the wicked fairy triggers the quest.

Let us now look at the second half of *Sleeping Beauty*, which starts with the arrival of the Prince and continues to the end. In the distribution of narrative roles in this section, the following pattern emerges.

*Subject.* The Prince.

*Object(s) of the Quest.* He wishes to discover if the old man's story about the Princess is true. The Prince's aim, therefore, is to see the Princess and implicitly (that is, by reference to other familiar versions of the tale) to be the one who awakens her with a kiss. At the same time, he may be in pursuit of the abstract values of, for example, Beauty, Kindness, and Happiness represented by the Princess.

*Helper(s).* The Prince's own impatience and impetuosity, together with his sword, function as helpers.

*Opponent(s).* The thorns and briars surrounding the castle are initially his opponents, but they transform into helpers ("the thorns seemed to part in front of him").

*Sender.* With his story of the Princess, the old man implants in the Prince the desire to go on this quest.

*Anti-subject.* The Prince meets with no resistance. A potential anti-subject, the wicked fairy, does not appear on the scene.

Let us proceed to divide the Prince's quest into the logical stages of the *canonical narrative schema*:

*The Contract.* The old man arouses in the Prince the desire to go on a quest. The Prince accepts the contract and decides to act on his desire.

*The Qualifying Test.* The Prince chops down the briars and thorns: by overcoming this obstacle he acquires the ability (a *being-able-to-do*) to attain his goal. In other words, he possesses the necessary competence enabling him to reach the castle and the Princess.

*The Decisive Test.* The arrival in the small room of the high tower of the castle and kissing the Princess constitute the decisive test or performance.

*The Glorifying Test.* We learn that the decisive test has been successful: the Princess wakes up, the spell is broken, Prince and Princess fall in love. The marriage, a further episode in the glorifying test, can be considered a reward for the Prince and a confirmation of the triumph of good – of love and happiness – over evil. The wicked fairy's curse no longer has any power.

Finally, a global view of the whole story still defines the King and Queen as the subject of a quest to protect their daughter from evil and death. In this perspective, however, the Prince and his actions function as helper and the overall quest can be deemed successful.

## The deep, abstract level

After analyzing the discursive and narrative levels of meaning, we can now examine the deep level, known also as the thematic level. This is the level of the abstract or conceptual: it relates to the inner world of the mind as opposed to the outer physical world represented by the figurative component. Most importantly, it is the level at which the fundamental values of the text are articulated. But how do we arrive at these values?

Let us begin by looking at the fundamental opposition(s) or transformation(s) underlying the text. To facilitate this task, it may be helpful to ask the following questions:

- Can we reduce all the oppositions found on the discursive and narrative levels to one or two basic oppositions that can function as a common denominator for the text?
- What are the two most abstract poles of meaning between which the text moves?
- What fundamental transformation of values is at stake?

Here it might help to bear in mind the object of the quest(s).

In *Sleeping Beauty*, a key opposition is that between evil and good. This opposition can be seen as an umbrella term encompassing on the discursive level the passage from high to low, asleep to awake, individual isolation to community. It marks, therefore, the fundamental transformation of the text.

This movement between two abstract poles of meaning can be mapped out on what Greimas calls a *semiotic square*. The diagram illustrates relationships of contrariety (evil versus good) and of contradiction (evil versus non-evil):

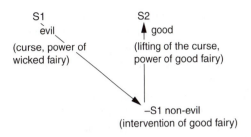

This transformation between evil and good parallels that between death and life:

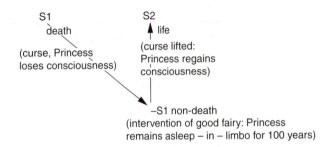

A third semiotic square could express these transformations in terms of the more specific values represented by the Princess:

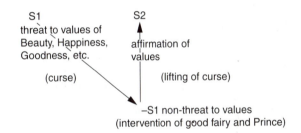

## Text and context

Having ascertained the universal values underlying the text, we then open up the analysis to broader considerations of sociopolitical and cultural context. What additional values can be brought to bear on the text by the contemporary reader? How relevant is *Sleeping Beauty* to us today? Does the story, like many fairy tales, lend itself to a multiplicity of levels of interpretation?

*Sleeping Beauty* has in fact been open to a wide variety of interpretations. It could be argued, for example, that the story is the embodiment of stereotypical images of friendships and relationships – that women are essentially passive and that once the Princess is rescued by the Prince they will both live "happily ever after." Furthermore, the story seems to give support to the view that it is those who are beautiful, handsome, and young who are good and who will be successful and happy.

However, it could also be argued that the story has more positive implications. One is that it presents in unambiguous terms the conflict between good and evil and the final triumph, through virtue or courage, of good. There are also mythical/religious interpretations; for instance, by representing a world in which the mundane and the magical coexist, a world shaped by unseen and irrational forces, *Sleeping Beauty*, it could be claimed, implicitly challenges the tyranny of "reason."

Semiotic analysis does not in itself support any specific interpretation, which depends on a wide range of social and cultural values. But semiotic analysis provides an invaluable tool for revealing the central deep structures upon which any convincing interpretation of such a narrative will depend.

## Recent developments

In the late 1960s and 1970s the focus was on the development of models on the narrative and deep levels. During the years that followed the publication of the semiotics dictionary (1979), attention was turned to the discursive level of meaning, to strategies of enunciation and to the spatial and temporal organization of texts. Interesting studies were carried out on the works of, in particular, Marcel Proust and Émile Zola.

The 1980s saw the emergence of a semiotics of passion as well as an interest in the notion of the aesthetic. Current research is directed toward the concept of figurativity and is concerned, in particular, with the development of a semiotics of the body.

## Further reading

Ali Bouchacha, A., and D. Bertrand. *Lectures de récits. Pour une approche sémio-linguistique des textes littéraires; parcours méthodologique de lecture de d'analyse*, 1981.

Courtés, Joseph. *Introduction à la sémiotique narrative et discursive*, 1976.

Eco, Umberto. *The Role of the Reader: Explorations in the Semiotics of Texts*, 1979.

Floch, Jean-Marie. *Une Lecture de Tintin au Tibet*, 1997.

Fontanille, Jacques. *Sémiotique et littérature*, 1999.

Greimas, A. J. *Structural Semantics*, 1976.

——. *On Meaning: Selected Writings in Semiotic Theory*, 1987.

——. *Maupassant, The Semiotics of Texts*, 1988.

——, and Joseph Courtés. *Semiotics and Language. An Analytical Dictionary*, 1982.

——, and Jacques Fontanille. *The Semiotics of Passion*, 1991.

——, et al. *Paris School Semiotics*, Vols 1 and 2, 1989.

Hawkes, Terence. *Structuralism and Semiotics*, 1977.

Hodge, Robert, and Gunther Kress. *Social Semiotics*, 1988.

Jackson, Bernard. *Semiotics and Legal Theory*, 1985.

Martin, Bronwen. *Semiotics and Storytelling: An Introduction to Semiotic Analysis*, 1997.

——. *The Search for Gold: Space and Meaning in J. M. G. Le Clézio*, 1998.

——, and Felizitas Ringham. *Cassell Dictionary of Semiotics*, 1999.

Peirce, C. S. *Peirce on Signs: Writings on Semiotics by Charles Sanders Peirce*, 1991. Edited by James Hope.

Savan, David. *An Introduction to C. S. Peirce's Semiotics*, 1988.

Schleifer, Ronald. *A. J. Greimas and the Nature of Meaning: Linguistic Semiotics and Discourse Theory*, 1987.

BRONWEN MARTIN

*See also* Barthes; Eco; Greimas; Kristeva; Lacan; Lévi-Strauss; Russian Formalism; Saussure; Structuralism

# Sensibility

The notion of sensibility comes to the fore in eighteenth-century aesthetic and moral discourse, although it has its roots in the terminology of medicine and philosophy. From about 1750 onward (and hence, significantly, coinciding with the emergence of aesthetics as an intellectual discipline), the term is practically interchangeable with the term "sentimentality," which acquired largely negative connotations in the nineteenth century that remain to the present day. But in *An Enquiry Concerning the Principles of Morals* (1751), David Hume was able to speak positively of "the blind, but sure testimony of taste and sentiment."

For purposes of clarity, it is helpful to compare the notion of sensibility with the German (and partly equivalent) term *Empfindsamkeit*. In fact, this term was directly derived, via Johann Jakob Bodmer and Gotthold Ephraim Lessing, from the English word "sentimental" as used in Laurence Sterne's novel *A Sentimental Journey through France and Italy* (1768). The German cult of *Empfindsamkeit* drew greatly on the works of such English writers as James Thomson's *The Seasons* (1726–1730), Edward Young's *The Complaint, or Night Thoughts on Life, Death and Immortality* (1742–1745), and the work of other members of the so-called "Graveyard poets" including, most famously, Thomas Gray, author of "Elegy Written in a Country Churchyard" (1751):

> The curfew tolls the knell of parting day,
> The lowing herd winds slowly o'er the lea,
> The ploughman homeward plods his weary way,
> And leaves the world to darkness and to me.

The cult of sensibility or sentimentality fed *Empfindsamkeit* in Germany, chiefly associated with such German writers as Friedrich Gottlob Klopstock, Christian Fürchtegott Gellert, and the members of the group known as the *Göttinger Hain*. In the context of Germany, *Empfindsamkeit* underpinned the thrust of the period known as *Sturm und Drang* ("Storm and Stress"), and the capacity for deep delicacy of emotions, whether positive or negative, characterizes the cult of sensibility in both cultures, too. But "greatness" (sublimity) of emotion is characteristic of *Sturm und Drang* (and, later, Romanticism), by contrast with the "delicacy" of *Empfindsamkeit*. Not for nothing, then, do the French refer to the *Sturm und Drang* as "*le préromantisme*" – a necessary anticipation of the full-blown sublimity of feeling to come.

The direct link between British and German literature is well demonstrated by the translated quotations from the work of Ossian, a fictitious Gaelic bard invented by the Scottish writer James Macpherson, in that prototypically Romantic novel by Johann Wolfgang von Goethe, *Die Leiden des jungen Werther* (1774, revised 1787; *The Sorrows of Young Werther*, 1779). In his drama *Der Triumph der*

*Empfindsamkeit* (performed 1778, published 1787; *The Triumph of Sensibility*), Goethe satirized the cult of sensibility as found not only his own early novel but also, more widely and even more influentially, in Jean-Jacques Rousseau's *La Nouvelle Héloïse* (1761). Whereas Henry Mackenzie's novel *The Man of Feeling* (1771) is arguably the most important example in English literature of the "novel of sensibility," Jane Austen's *Sense and Sensibility* (1811), among other works, represents the most famous reaction against its exaggerated, one-sided cultivation.

In the twentieth century, however, the word took on a rather different meaning in critical discourse. In his essay "The Metaphysical Poets" (1921), T. S. Eliot discerned, in English literature at any rate, a crisis in the seventeenth century which he referred to as a "dissociation of sensibility." Between the time of such so-called "Metaphysical poets" as John Donne and Henry Marvell and the age of Alfred, Lord Tennyson, and Robert Browning, Eliot perceived the existence of a caesura that he described as follows:

> The poets of the seventeenth century, the successors of the dramatists of the sixteenth, possessed a mechanism of sensibility which could devour any kind of experience.... A thought to Donne was an experience; it modified his sensibility. When a poet's mind is perfectly equipped for its work, it is constantly amalgamating disparate experience; the ordinary man's experience is chaotic, irregular, fragmentary. The latter falls in love, or reads Spinoza, and these two experiences have nothing to do with each other, or with the noise of the typewriter or the smell of cooking; in the mind of the poet these experiences are always forming new wholes.

Where do writers of sensibility, in the earlier sense, fit into this pattern? For Eliot, they rated very low: "The feeling, the sensibility, expressed in the *Country Churchyard* (to say nothing of Tennyson and Browning) is cruder than in [Marvell's poem] [*To his*] *Coy Mistress*."

From this remark and the quotations above, however, the modern sense of sensibility is also clear: it has the sense of a special poetic or, more generally, an aesthetic faculty. Thus, for example, T. E. Hulme wrote in his "Notes on Language and Style" (1925/1929): "The two tarts walking along Piccadilly on tiptoe, going home, with hat on back of head. Worry until could find exact model analogy that will reproduce the extraordinary effect they produce." The ability that is here ascribed to the "plastic imagination" is, perhaps, related to what Eliot, in "Hamlet and His Problems" (1919), termed the "objective correlative": "a set of objects, a situation, a chain of events which shall be the formula of that particular emotion."

Common to both senses of the word, then, is the notion that, as Goethe put it in "Fragment eines Romans in Briefen" (written c. 1770–1771; "Fragment of a Novel

in Letters"), "it is better to be bad out of emotion [*Empfindung*] than good out of understanding [*Verstand*]." And common to its high evaluation in both, too, is the belief that it is even better to express that emotion in the form of some kind of art.

## Further reading

Bredvold, Louis I. *The Natural History of Sensibility*, 1962.
Brown, Herbert Ross. *The Sentimental Novel in America, 1789–1860*, 1940.
Frye, Northrop. "Towards Defining an Age of Sensibility," in *ELH: A Journal of Literary History*. 23, no. 2 (June, 1956), pp. 144–152.
Hilles, Frederick W., and Harold Bloom, eds. *From Sensibility to Romanticism*, 1965.
Rawson, C. J. "Some Remarks on Eighteenth-Century 'Delicacy,' with a Note on Hugh Kelly's 'False Delicacy,'" in *Journal of English and Germanic Philology*. 61, no. 1 (1962), pp. 1–13.
Sherbo, Arthur. *English Sentimental Drama*, 1950.
Wright, Walter Francis. *Sensibility in English Prose Fiction, 1760–1814*, 1937.

PAUL BISHOP

# Third Earl of Shaftesbury

(Anthony Ashley Cooper)

English writer and critic

**Born:** London, England; February 26, 1671
**Died:** Naples, Italy; February 15, 1713

## Biography

Anthony Ashley Cooper was born in London on February 26, 1671, and almost immediately came under the tutelage of his grandfather, the first Earl of Shaftesbury and famous Whig statesman, satirized by John Dryden in *Absalom and Achitophel* (1681–1682). The philosopher John Locke, a close friend of the family, prescribed the principles and discipline for his education, and they were carried out by a gifted governess, Elizabeth Birch. By the age of eleven, when he was sent to a private school, he was fluent in both Latin and Greek. A year later he was enrolled at Winchester College, which he later condemned for its permissive attitude toward the vice of drinking among both students and faculty.

In July 1687 he set out on a grand tour of continental Europe, accompanied by his tutor and a younger friend, Sir John Cropley. He remained abroad for three years, acquiring an almost-native command of French and a sound knowledge of Italian fine arts. In 1694 he declined the governorship of Carolina and in the following year was elected to Parliament for the district of Poole. After the dissolving of that body in 1698, he decided not to run for reelection. Instead, he visited the Netherlands for a philosophical retreat, where he associated with Pierre Bayle and

Jean Le Clerc. He returned to England in the following year, shortly before his father's death, when he became Earl of Shaftesbury and entered the House of Lords. In 1699 his Deistic *An Inquiry Concerning Virtue in Two Discourses* appeared in print, arguing for the existence of a benevolent deity and a moral sense in human behavior. From 1708 to 1711 he completed the writings which would be published as *Characteristicks*. In August, 1709, he married, and two years later he set out for Naples for health reasons and to continue his artistic activities. He died there on February 15, 1713.

## Influence

So important is Shaftesbury's *Characteristicks of Men, Manners, Opinions, Times* as the first thorough treatment of aesthetics in English that Irving Babbitt gave him credit for making aesthetics a separate subject and then railed at him for doing so. Shaftesbury appealed to Gottfried Wilhelm von Leibniz, Denis Diderot, Voltaire, Johann Wolfgang von Goethe, and Friedrich Schiller during the Enlightenment and to Benedetto Croce and Ernst Cassirer in modern times. Paradoxically, he has been more widely praised in Europe than in the English-speaking world. Throughout the Enlightenment, Shaftesbury was celebrated for his doctrine of moral sense, which harmonized with neoclassical notions of harmony and order. By providing a philosophical basis for the joining of morality and aesthetics, he revitalized Platonic thought and created an intellectual bridge between the Renaissance and the Romantic period. In his philosophical system, universal order as a reflection of the Divine Being is necessary to beauty, and beauty is inherent in the Divine Being. Recent commentators have seen in Shaftesbury a revolt against empiricism, and, instead of portraying his thought as an orderly system, have emphasized individual concepts from his work, such as a cult of artistic genius, creative imagination, and the power of instinct.

## Analysis

Shaftesbury affirmed as the principal aim of the *Characteristicks* "to assert the reality of a beauty and charm in moral as well as natural subjects, and to demonstrate the reasonableness of a proportionate taste and determinate choice in life and manners." This concept fully conforms to the prevailing neoclassicism of his age. He believed that skill in writing is founded in the rules of art as well as in the knowledge of the world and humankind, and he reasserted the authority of Aristotle in requiring unity of plot and greatness with order as well as in making imitation the nature of poetry. He also quoted Aristotle to support the opinion that particulars should be sacrificed for the general design, an attitude that is almost the antithesis of Romanticism. He further venerated the ancients over the moderns and described William Shakespeare's *Hamlet* (1603) as one continued moral.

At the same time, Shaftesbury repeated the Platonic doctrine that truth, good, and beauty are essentially the same and discoverable by an inherent and universal moral sense. The latter provides only an initial impulse, however, which must be strengthened by means of a carefully cultivated taste. Because of the foundation of beauty in the absolute, taste is based on a universal standard, not upon individual whim or caprice. According to some metaphysical and formalistic critics, Shaftesbury believes that beauty as pure form is not perceived by the senses, but is the subject of contemplation alone. The perception of beauty is, therefore, a process transcending the created world or actual world of objective reality and making possible the penetration of the forces of creation as far as Divine Being itself. A contrary interpretation, more in line with Shaftesbury's milieu and the majority of his critical pronouncements, however, sees his system as a variant of the Stoic ideal, in which the individual conforms to the design and order of the universe. One is drawn to both good and beauty by means of a moral sense which must be cultivated and perfected. By rejecting opinion and developing reason, the individual acquires a right taste that allows for the perception of both good and beauty and the recognition of the harmony of the whole.

Shaftesbury could have derived from either Plato or the Stoics his view that beauty and good are one and the same, or, in his words, that "what is beautiful is harmonious and proportionable; what is harmonious and proportionable is true; and what is at once both beautiful and true, is, of consequence, agreeable and good." Although the term "taste" has the connotation of personal liking or preference, there existed for Shaftesbury a universal and absolute standard. He was, however, aware of the major objection to theories of absolutes, that no general agreement has ever been reached concerning the nature of the beautiful or the good. He had two answers to this objection: first, that the basic standard of beauty is universal, and that persons differ only in its application, and second, that the forces of custom and education may override natural impulses. Shaftesbury's portrayal of the standard of taste as a composite of the views of people of culture and refinement in all periods is practically identical with the neoclassical notion of the *consensus gentium*.

Even if it were granted that taste is not innate or a result of simple intuitive perception, there are three competing theories in the *Characteristicks* to explain its development. That most compatible with Shaftesbury's fundamental Stoic background bases moral and aesthetic perception exclusively upon reason; the contrary doctrine in *An Inquiry Concerning Virtue in Two Discourses* affirms the salutary influence of the passions or feelings. The only possible means of reconciling these contrary doctrines is to assume, as Shaftesbury does, that an innate proclivity toward the good and the beautiful is developed through experience and education. Shaftesbury does not treat the sublime as such, but he repeatedly admires the natural aspects of the cosmos. Indeed, he is extraordinarily ambivalent: in one passage he equates the sublime with beauty, but elsewhere identifies it with the pompous and the miraculous. Some critics have seen in Shaftesbury's theories of taste a precursor of Immanuel Kant's attempt to reconcile the sensuous world and the ideal world, or the relative appeals of pleasure and reason. He clearly indicates, however, that true taste is not innate, but the result of rigorous intellectual training.

Shaftesbury does not present a developed theory of creative imagination, but hints at it by his notions of innate ideas and of God as a creative artist. A true poet, he maintains, must recognize the elements comprising the harmony of a mind before he can presume to depict humanity and manners. Only then does the poet become a second maker or Prometheus in regard to Jove. The poet or moral artist is a creator in the way that God is, forming a unified whole, coherent and proportioned, and giving form to the inward structure (passions and sentiments) of others based upon a prior self-knowledge. Whether in painting, the epic, or the drama, the artist must portray moral truth in a work that is a whole by itself, independent, and as great and comprehensive as possible. Moral truth supersedes empirical reality. The painter is unnatural when following nature too closely and strictly copying life.

The main function of the poet is not to express his or her own feelings, personality, or attitudes, but to represent the beauties of a human soul or moral truth. In sum, the poet must describe both humanity and behavior in a coherent whole with due subordination of the constituent parts. Shaftesbury believed that his own function as a critic was that of improving the taste and manners of his contemporaries. In carrying out this objective, he formulated a number of critical principles and opinions. The classical rules he compared to philosophical sea charts or master drawings or anatomies for artists. Yet he realized that great art is not based on reality and these mechanical aids alone, but on mental graces and talents. The original critics, he affirmed, were equal in genius with those who practiced the persuasive arts, but were less eager for attention. They served to remind the poets that they were writing for ordinary human beings and must for this reason observe the mechanical rules of composition. Shaftesbury does not advocate pedantic adherence to any set of rules or principles, however, but merely the free exercise of rational examination and analysis. Indeed, the avoidance of pedantry ranks along with the attaining of unity and moral truth as the third of his critical principles. Shaftesbury states that the critic need not be a creative artist, but that a great writer is usually a good critic. The best modern criticism, he affirms, is comic or satirical since methodical analysis is not entertaining. Shaftesbury himself excels in raillery, pleasantry, and mirth. He has no brief for professional Grub Street critics, but is a great admirer of the art of criticism, that is, rigid and severe examination.

In his practical criticism as well as in theory, Shaftesbury asserts a universal standard. The sense of beauty is innate, he says, but recognizing it in concrete form may be difficult and a matter of debate. Critical ability based upon true taste requires labor, dedication, and time for the cultivation of natural genius. Individual taste is formed by both fancy and reason. When reason guides, taste coincides with the universal standard, but when whim or fancy are in control, critical opinions are likely to be erroneous. In some passages, Shaftesbury affirms that the critic should subordinate fancy to reason; in others he suggests that taste has an almost independent function. There are some elements in an artistic work that cannot be isolated through analysis, and for these he falls back upon the notion, already expressed in French criticism, of the *je ne sais quoi*, or the charm and enchantment that even the artist cannot explain.

Shaftesbury has much to say about the resemblances between poetry and painting, and many of his theoretical pronouncements apply equally to both, but he does not accept the traditional platitude that they are completely parallel. Before Gotthold Ephraim Lessing's *Laocöon* (1766), he recognized that the plastic arts cannot portray continued action, and he analyzed the importance of what he called the vital moment in the depicting of a historical or dramatic situation. In keeping with neoclassical theory, Shaftesbury believed in a hierarchy of genres. Indeed he considered many of the elements of which his own *Characteristicks* is composed – the miscellany, the pastiche, the satire, and all occasional writings – as works suitable enough to portray nature or physical reality, but not adequate to capture moral truth or the ideal. Among all the literary genres practiced in his day, he considered the romance the lowest for being gothic, effeminate, and false. He highly favored the dialogue, which he successfully practiced in his own work, as one of the most philosophical and beneficial of all forms.

A major element of Shaftesbury's critical thought, one which has been almost totally neglected by scholars, is the doctrine of the necessary connection of political liberty and culture or the inseparability of liberty and letters. The doctrine derives from his Whig background, the political experience of his grandfather, his own Parliamentary career, and to some degree the writings of John Locke and the Greek and Latin classics. The deistical message of the *Characteristicks* is also interwoven with the concept of political liberty. Although Shaftesbury accorded warm praise to French drama, he affirmed that the high spirit of tragedy cannot subsist without the spirit of liberty.

More generally recognized by scholars than Shaftesbury's political overtones is his notion, later associated with Baron de Montesquieu, of the influence of climate and national cultures upon literature. Among many other references, he traces the mutabilities in English writers to the variableness and inconstancy of the English climate.

Incorporating most of the critical preconceptions of his age, Shaftesbury's criticism represented a liberalizing force. He associated literature with philosophy, political liberty, and the plastic arts. Highly eclectic, he fluctuated between imagination and reason, between individual taste and tradition, as well as between innate ideas and empirical knowledge. He succeeded in reconciling Epicurean and Stoic strains and neoclassical rigor with individual taste.

## Principal criticism
*A Letter Concerning Enthusiasm*, 1708
*Sensus Communis: An Essay on the Freedom of Wit and Humour*, 1709
*The Moralists: A Philosophical Rhapsody*, 1709
*Soliloquy: Or, Advice to an Author*, 1710
*Characteristicks of Men, Manners, Opinions, Times*, 1711 (3 volumes; includes *A Letter Concerning Enthusiasm*, *Sensus Communis*, *The Moralists*, and *Soliloquy*)
*A Notion of the Historical Draught or Tablature of the Judgment of Hercules*, 1713
*A Letter Concerning the Art or Science of Design*, 1714

## Other major works and literary forms
The third Earl of Shaftesbury left in manuscript form other critical statements that have been published as *The Life, Unpublished Letters, and Philosophical Regimen of Anthony, Earl of Shaftesbury* (1900) and *Second Characters: Or, The Language of Forms* (1914). A religious satire, "The Adept Ladys," and three scatological poems were published in 1981 in volume 1 of the standard edition of Shaftesbury's complete works.

NONFICTION
*An Inquiry Concerning Virtue in Two Discourses*, 1699
*Paradoxes of State, Relating to the Present Juncture of Affairs in England and the Rest of Europe*, 1702
*Several Letters Written by a Noble Lord to a Young Man at the University*, 1716
*The Life, Unpublished Letters, and Philosophical Regimen of Anthony, Earl of Shaftesbury*, 1900
*Second Characters: Or, The Language of Forms*, 1914

MISCELLANEOUS
*Complete Works, Selected Letters, and Posthumous Writings*, 1981-1998 (6 volumes)

## Further reading
Aldridge, A. Owen. "Lord Shaftesbury's Literary Theories," in *Philological Quarterly*. XXIV (January, 1945), pp. 46-64.
——. "Shaftesbury and the Deist Manifesto," in *Transactions of the American Philosophical Society*. XLI (1951), pp. 297-385.
Brett, R. L. "The Third Earl of Shaftesbury as a Literary Critic," in *Modern Language Review*. XXXVII (April, 1942), pp. 131-146.
Brugère, Fabienne. "Esthétique et resemblance chez Shaftesbury," in *Revue de Métaphysique et de Morale*. C (1995), pp. 517-531.
Klein, Lawrence. "The Third Earl of Shaftesbury and the Progress of Politeness," in *Eighteenth-Century Studies*. XVIII (Winter, 1984 / 1985), pp. 186-214.
Townsend, Dabney. "From Shaftesbury to Kant: The Development of the Concept of Aesthetic Experience," in *Journal of the History of Ideas*. XLVIII (April / June, 1987), pp. 287-305.
Voitle, Robert. *The Third Earl of Shaftesbury, 1671-1713*, 1984.
——. "Lord Shaftesbury and Sentimental Morality," in *Studies on Voltaire and the Eighteenth Century*. CCLXIII (1989), pp. 489-491.
Weinsheimer, Joel. "Shaftesbury in Our Time: The Politics of Wit and Humor," in *The Eighteenth Century: Theory and Interpretation*. XXXVI (1995), pp. 178-188.

A. OWEN ALDRIDGE

*See also* Addison; Dryden; Pope

# George Bernard Shaw
## Irish dramatist and critic

**Born:** Dublin, Ireland; July 26, 1856
**Died:** Ayot St. Lawrence, England; November 2, 1950

## Biography
George Bernard Shaw was born in Dublin on July 26, 1856, the youngest child and only son of a declining Anglo-Irish family. His father was a failure in trade, and there is evidence that he was an alcoholic. His mother, however, was a positive influence. Her move to London in 1872 provided her son with an alternative to life in Dublin, and he joined her there in 1876.

In London, Shaw decided to be a writer. His early attempts in that profession were unsuccessful. A turning point in his career occurred in 1884, when he joined the Fabian Society. This attachment helped Shaw develop and exploit his gift for public speaking and his equal talent for public controversy. He held local public office in the London borough of St. Pancras between 1897 and 1903, by which time he was already well known as a literary figure.

Shaw had found work as a book reviewer and art critic in 1885. In 1888, under the pseudonym Corno di Bassetto, he began to distinguish himself as a music critic. He also worked as a drama critic during these years. It was not until 1892, however, under the stimulus of his literary mentor, William Archer, also a drama critic, that Shaw had his first play, *Widowers' Houses*, produced. This play, published the following year, like its immediate successors – *The Philanderer* and the banned *Mrs. Warren's Profession* (both written in 1893 and published in 1898) and *Arms and the Man* (1894) – had no commercial success. Shaw's first success was an American production of *The Devil's Disciple*, in 1897. The following year Shaw married Charlotte Payne-Townshend, who had nursed him through a general breakdown in health brought on by overwork.

Shaw's breakthrough in the theater occurred in 1904, when a number of his plays were featured in the repertory of London's Royal Court Theatre. His artistic reputation in the ascendant, Shaw pursued his career as a public polemicist, most notably in his trenchant published critique of World War I, which generated widespread public rage. A modification of this critique forms the basis of *Heartbreak House* (1919), produced in 1920, which Shaw considered his best play. (In terms of popularity, however, *Saint Joan*, produced in 1923, is his greatest stage success – though many may consider *Pygmalion*, 1913, to be more successful, as it provided the basis for the 1956 musical *My Fair Lady*.) The last twenty years of Shaw's long life were comparatively unproductive. He died at his English country home on November 2, 1950.

## Influence

Shaw's influence as a critic has not been great. His championing of Richard Wagner's music and of the drama of Henrik Ibsen did not distinguish him among his contemporaries; many of them already held these men in great esteem. Moreover, in the area where Shaw was at his most original and persuasive – reviewing for the daily and weekly press – his insistence on high artistic standards and his intellectual vigor have not found an obvious successor. Partly, that is a result of the public's long wait until Shaw's criticism became available in full. In addition, there is the problem of Shaw's range as a critic: it is inconceivable that a modern critic would cover the art world, in addition to London musical and theatrical life, as Shaw did. Indeed, Shaw's lack of impact as a critic is an excellent example of the degree to which the critical enterprise has, particularly after the time of Shaw, become institutionalized.

## Analysis

The whole of Shaw's literary and cultural career was a sustained act of criticism, exemplified by a consistency of polemical, adversarial tone through such ostensibly diverse forms as the prefaces to his plays, pamphlets for the Fabian Society, and sundry controversial contributions to the press. Shaw's formal critical writings on the arts are not necessarily the playwright's last word on any given subject.

Shaw's verve and pungency as a writer were developed in response to the extraordinarily difficult conditions in which he began his public literary life. Shaw, however, did more than meet his deadlines – a challenge itself, for he was reviewing books, plays, concerts, and art exhibits – he insisted on being analytical and demanding in his work, thereby not only effecting a revolution in reviewing but also establishing aesthetic and moral standards upon which his own creative work was to draw, as the prefaces to the plays reveal.

In addition, his work for *Saturday Review* and musical performances for *The Star* and *The World* led directly to two of Shaw's three major critical meditations,

*The Quintessence of Ibsenism* (1891) and *The Perfect Wagnerite: A Commentary on "The Ring of the Niblungs,"* (1898). (The third is *The Sanity of Art*, 1895.) His association with the Fabian Society made the main current of sociological analysis available to Shaw. The three critical essays represent a similar contemporaneity in his cultural analysis; in addition, they show the origins of Shaw's analytical technique in the Socialist orientation of his education as a Fabian: indeed, his Fabian proselytizing was the immediate occasion for *The Quintessence of Ibsenism* coming into being.

At the same time, however, it is important to note that these three exercises in criticism have ultimately more bearing on the development of Shaw's cultural doctrines than on the growth of Fabian social policy. This emphasis is seen in *The Quintessence of Ibsenism*, where the great Norwegian playwright's works are taken less for their significance in their own right than as a pretext for Shaw's own theorizing. While *The Quintessence of Ibsenism* contains numerous trenchant insights into Ibsen the playwright, Shaw's interest is in the social meaning of the plays. (This interest establishes Shaw as an early, original exponent of the "social text" approach to literature, though his originality has not found a place in the history of modern criticism.) *The Quintessence of Ibsenism* is a definitive account of Shaw's view of the artist and his role in society, the rhetorical emphasis being more on the latter component of his thought than on the artist as such. Shaw, a lifelong satirist and critic of romanticizing in all of its forms, had no time for ivory towers or their inhabitants, insisting rather on the essential reality of the artist's role.

Society, Shaw argues, consists of three ranks – those who are controlled, those who do the controlling, and the exceptional creatures who make themselves known by virtue of their relentlessly critical attitude of the two other groups (the former whom they wish to instruct and redeem socially, the latter whom they wish to expose as unhealthy influences). Such a diagnostic scenario is not entirely a travesty of a tendency in Ibsen's work. Yet Shaw's insistence on the significance of the superior being – the moral and cultural conscience of contemporary social arrangements, mocker of their hypocrisies and castigator of their injustices – owes more to the Victorian social critic Thomas Carlyle's sense of the hero, as well as to Friedrich Nietzsche, than it does to the European drama of the day.

With a playwright's thought for his focus, Shaw has found a typically apt and witty means of underlining the significance of ideas in action. Shaw's analysis is not merely literary or philosophical in the abstract, disinterested sense of the words. Rather, it is marked by a strong pragmatic streak. Hence, the essay concludes with remarks in support of an Ibsen theater, not as a cultural ideal but as a practical proposition, requiring funding and public support, complete with a sketch of a possible repertoire of plays to be produced. As Shaw's preface to the 1913 edition of

*The Quintessence of Ibsenism* implies, however, the essay's appeal for practical cultural rehabilitation by means of an outspoken, socially critical theater was not a success, and its failure is further underlined by the rather demoralized tone of the uncharacteristically brief introduction to the 1922 edition – though both prefaces hold unapologetically to the essay's original views.

It is possible to argue that Shaw himself saw certain limitations in *The Quintessence of Ibsenism* by, in effect, readdressing its issues in *The Perfect Wagnerite*. Like the plays of Ibsen, the musical dramas of Richard Wagner were changing the face of European theater, particularly that of the opera house, during Shaw's intellectually formative years. (Again, Nietzsche is a fascinating point of contact between author and subject. Indeed, Eric Bentley suggests that Shaw, in writing about Ibsen and Wagner, was using those well-known names as a means of gaining attention for his own analyses – just as Nietzsche was, Bentley claims, in his writings on Wagner and Arthur Schopenhauer.)

In *The Perfect Wagnerite*, Shaw modifies his schematic view of society, asserting the existence of four instead of three representative social types, the fourth being a subdivision of the "undermen." Such a modification does not affect the thrust of Shaw's argument. Yet, in his analysis of Siegfried, the protagonist of Wagner's *Der Ring des Nibelungen* (1876; *The Ring of the Nibelung*, 1901), Shaw has found a heroic presence which enables him to crystallize much of his thinking about the superior being and his destiny as a cultural exemplar, as the following extract shows:

> The philosophically fertile element in the original project of "Siegfried's Death" was the conception of Siegfried himself as a type of the healthy man raised to perfect confidence in his own impulses by an intense and joyous vitality which is above fear, sickliness of conscience, malice, and the makeshifts and moral crutches of law and order which accompany them. Such a character appears extraordinarily fascinating and exhilarating to our guilty and conscience-ridden generations. . . .

In addition to philosophical fertility, however, it should be noted that a conception of energy plays an important role in the above passage. It is in this idea, rather than in philosophical niceties, that glimpses of one of Shaw's most central articles of cultural hygiene may be had, most vividly characterized as the "Life Force" in Shaw's play *Man and Superman* (1903). Possession of this force constitutes the ultimate embodiment of cultural pragmatism, a synchronism of self and world which contemporary social shibboleths, whether in the realm of political administration or that of interpersonal behavior, inhibit.

It is a defense of the viability of such creative energy, and of the reality of art as its medium, that *The Sanity of Art* articulates. Unlike the other two essays, between whose dates of publication it appeared, *The Sanity of Art* was a commissioned piece. Shaw was asked, by an American editor, to repudiate the characterization of all contemporary art as degenerate by a German cultural analyst, Max Nordeau. Shaw responded with gusto, and the essay originally appeared with the title "A Degenerate's View of Nordeau." Ibsen and Wagner are given pride of place in a rebuttal which is so devastatingly comprehensive that when Shaw finds something to like in his opponent – "the freedom and boldness with which he expresses himself" – it is impossible not to suspect that even here Shaw is emphasizing the strength of his own case. The brief autobiographical overtures to some sections of the essay seem to bear out such a suspicion.

According to Shaw, the sanity of art consists in art's balance of freedom and restraint. Art's freedom derives from the necessity that the artist speak as fully and truthfully as possible. Restraint comes from the requirement that such speech accede to the discipline of objectively discernible form, in order that both the speaker and his or her audience be saved from mere self-indulgence. Shaw's love of music and his musicological expertise can perhaps be seen as a powerful influence on such a conception of art. Once again, however, in Shaw's view the sanity of art is crucially related to the social value of art. This value, as the essay (like all Shaw's criticism) makes clear, may be readily assessed by evaluating a given work's reformative, redemptive, and progressive tendencies. Art is sane, just as Ibsen and Wagner are important, because it delimits a zone of human energy, because it preaches the unimpeachable human delight which identification with that energy enjoins.

## Principal criticism

*The Quintessence of Ibsenism*, 1891
*The Sanity of Art*, 1895
*The Perfect Wagnerite: A Commentary on "The Ring of the Niblungs,"* 1898
*Our Theatres in the Nineties*, 1931 (3 volumes)
*London Music in 1888–1889 as Heard by Corno di Bassetto*, 1937

## Other major works and literary forms

George Bernard Shaw is frequently referred to as the best-known English dramatist after William Shakespeare, and it is as a playwright that his name has been remembered. In addition to his many plays, Shaw is celebrated for his prefaces to them. These often lengthy pieces, apart from the light that they throw on the prefaced works, provide an excellent introduction to Shaw's preoccupations, his powers of criticism, and his vivid, paradoxical style.

Shaw began his literary career as a novelist and wrote five works in this form: *Cashel Byron's Profession* (1886), *An Unsocial Socialist* (1887), *Love Among the Artists* (1900), *The Irrational Knot* (1905), and *Immaturity* (1930). His other important work of fiction is a collection of short stories, *The Adventures of the Black Girl in Her Search for God* (1932). Next to his work for the theater, however, Shaw is known for his voluminous polemical pamphleteering on behalf of the Fabian Society, the Socialist think tank which predated and subsequently provided ideological sustenance to the English Labour Party. The playwright's work in this vein culminated in his *The Intelligent Woman's Guide to Socialism and Capitalism* (1928).

Shaw also wrote extensively on controversial social issues of the day – for example, *Common Sense About the War* (1914), expanded in 1930 to be *What I Really Wrote About the War*. Finally, no sense of Shaw's range as a writer is complete without acknowledgment of his genius as a correspondent; his letters are available in a variety of compilations.

NOVELS
*Cashel Byron's Profession*, 1886
*An Unsocial Socialist*, 1887
*Love Among the Artists*, 1900
*The Irrational Knot*, 1905
*Immaturity*, 1930

SHORT FICTION
*The Adventures of the Black Girl in Her Search for God*, 1932.

PLAYS
*Widowers' Houses*, written 1885–1892, published 1893
*Mrs. Warren's Profession*, written 1893, published 1898
*The Philanderer*, written 1893, published 1898
*Arms and the Man*, 1894
*Candida: A Mystery*, 1897
*The Devil's Disciple*, 1897
*The Man of Destiny*, 1897
*You Never Can Tell*, 1898
*Captain Brassbound's Conversion*, 1900
*Caesar and Cleopatra*, 1901
*The Admirable Blashville*, 1903 (based on his novel *Cashel Byron's Profession*)
*Man and Superman*, 1903
*How He Lied to Her Husband*, 1904
*John Bull's Other Island*, 1904
*Major Barbara*, 1905
*Passion, Poison, and Petrifaction*, 1905
*The Doctor's Dilemma*, 1906
*The Interlude at the Playhouse*, 1907 (playlet)
*Getting Married*, 1908
*Press Cuttings*, 1909
*The Shewing Up of Blanco Posnet*, 1909
*The Fascinating Foundling*, written 1909, published 1926
*The Glimpse of Reality*, written 1909, published 1926
*The Dark Lady of the Sonnets*, 1910
*Misalliance*, 1910
*Fanny's First Play*, 1911
*Androcles and the Lion*, 1912
*Overruled*, 1912
*Pygmalion*, 1913
*Beauty's Duty*, written 1913, published 1932 (playlet)
*Great Catherine*, 1913
*Heartbreak House*, written 1913–1919, published 1919
*The Music Cure*, 1914
*The Inca of Perusalem*, 1916
*O'Flaherty, V. C.*, 1917

*Augustus Does His Bit*, 1917
*Annajanska, the Bolshevik Empress*, 1918
*Back to Methuselah*, 1921
*Jitta's Atonement*, 1923
*Saint Joan*, 1923
*The Apple Cart*, 1929
*Too True to Be Good*, 1932
*How These Doctors Love One Another!*, 1932 (playlet)
*On the Rocks*, 1933
*Village Wooing*, 1934
*The Six Men of Calais*, 1934
*The Simpleton of the Unexpected Isles*, 1935
*Arthur and Acetone*, 1936
*The Millionairess*, 1936
*Cymbeline Refinished*, 1937 (adaptation of William Shakespeare's *Cymbeline*, act 5)
*Geneva*, 1938
*In Good King Charles's Golden Days*, 1939
*Buoyant Billions*, 1947
*Shakes Versus Shaw*, 1949
*Far-fetched Fables*, 1950

NONFICTION
*The Fabian Society: Its Early History*, 1899
*The Common Sense of Municipal Trading*, 1904
*Dramatic Opinions and Essays*, 1907
*Common Sense About the War*, 1914 (expanded as *What I Really Wrote About the War*, 1930)
*Letters to Miss Alma Murray*, 1927
*The Intelligent Woman's Guide to Socialism and Capitalism*, 1928
*Ellen Terry and Shaw*, 1931
*Everybody's Political What's What*, 1944
*Sixteen Self Sketches*, 1949
*Correspondence Between George Bernard Shaw and Mrs. Patrick Campbell*, 1952
*Platform and Pulpit*, 1961
*The Matter with Ireland*, 1961
*Collected Letters, 1874–1897*, 1965
*An Autobiography: 1856–1898*, 1969
*An Autobiography: 1898–1950*, 1970
*The Nondramatic Literary Criticism of Bernard Shaw*, 1972
*Collected Letters, 1898–1910*, 1972
*Collected Letters, 1911–1925*, 1985

EDITED TEXT
*Fabian Essays in Socialism*, 1889

MISCELLANEOUS
*Works, 1930–1938* (33 volumes)
*Short Stories, Scraps, and Shavings*, 1932
*Works, 1947–1952* (36 volumes)
*The Bodley Head Bernard Shaw: Collected Plays with Their Prefaces*, 1970–1974 (7 volumes)

## Further reading

Adams, Elsie E. *Bernard Shaw and the Aesthetes*, 1971.
Bentley, Eric. *Bernard Shaw*, 1957.
Dukore, Bernard F. *Bernard Shaw, playwright: Aspects of Shavian Drama*, 1973.
Gerould, Daniel C. "George Bernard Shaw's Criticism of Ibsen," in *Comparative Literature*. XV (Spring, 1963), pp. 130–145.
Gibbs, A. M. *The Art and Mind of Shaw*, 1983.
Henderson, Archibald. *George Bernard Shaw: His Life and Works*, 1911.

——. *George Bernard Shaw: Man of the Century*, 1956.

Holroyd, Michael. *Bernard Shaw*, 1988–1992 (4 volumes).

Kauffman, R. J., ed. *Shaw: A Collection of Critical Essays*, 1965.

Kaye, Julian B. *Bernard Shaw and the Nineteenth-Century Tradition*, 1958.

Meisel, Martin. *Shaw and the Nineteenth-Century Theater*, 1984.

Ohmann, Richard M. *Shaw: The Style and the Man*, 1962.

Peters, Sally. *Bernard Shaw: The Ascent of the Superman*, 1996.

GEORGE O'BRIEN

*See also* Bentley; Brecht; Drama: Literary Theory and Criticism

# Percy Bysshe Shelley

## English poet

**Born:** Field Place, Sussex, England; August 4, 1792
**Died:** At sea off Viareggio, Italy; July 8, 1822

## Biography

Percy Bysshe Shelley was born on August 4, 1792, at Field Place, near Horsham, Sussex, the son of Timothy Shelley, a wealthy landowner and Whig Member of Parliament. Shelley attended Syon House Academy and Eton College; in 1810 he went into residence at University College, Oxford University. The following year he was expelled for writing a pamphlet entitled *The Necessity of Atheism* with his friend Thomas Jefferson Hogg. Later in the same year Shelley eloped with Harriet Westbrook and married her in Edinburgh, Scotland. In 1812 he visited Dublin and was active in radical political circles there. The following year he had his first major work, *Queen Mab: A Philosophical Poem*, privately printed.

In July 1814 Shelley abandoned Harriet and eloped with Mary Godwin, the daughter of William Godwin. They married in 1816, after Harriet Shelley committed suicide. In 1818 the Shelleys made their home in Italy, never to return to England. After a period of restless moving from place to place, they finally settled in Pisa in 1820, where they gathered around them the "Pisan circle," a group of friends which included Lord Byron. In Italy Shelley wrote many of his major works, such as *Prometheus Unbound*, *The Cenci*, "A Defence of Poetry," *Epipsychidion*, and *Adonais*. On July 8, 1822, Shelley was drowned after a sudden storm capsized the open boat in which he was sailing.

## Influence

Shelley's main work was as a poet rather than a theorist, and it is therefore difficult to isolate any specific influence he may have had as a literary critic from the general critical response to his poetry. The Victorians admired Shelley's "A Defence of Poetry" as a classic of literary criticism, but the New Critics of the twentieth century could find little good to say about it. They regarded Romanticism in general, and Shelley's poetry in particular, as an escape from reality, and Shelley's literary theory was dismissed as mystical and imprecise. Subsequent critics have seen more value in Shelley's poetry and have in consequence shown more appreciation of "A Defence of Poetry." As an attempt to make what Shelley calls "the unchangeable forms of human nature" the basis of critical understanding, "A Defence of Poetry" has been seen to have something in common with modern archetypal criticism, which attempts to identify recurring patterns in literature and the human mind.

## Analysis

Percy Bysshe Shelley's contribution to literary theory lies almost exclusively in his essay "A Defence of Poetry." It was written as a reply to an ironical essay by his friend Thomas Love Peacock entitled *The Four Ages of Poetry* (1820), in which Peacock suggested that poetry had become an anachronism in a materialistic age.

Shelley planned his essay in three parts, but the second two were never written. As it stands, "A Defence of Poetry" is not a systematic treatise, and critics have complained of its inconsistencies and contradictions (between expressive and mimetic theories, for example) and its apparent defense of automatic writing. It also offers little that would aid in the practical criticism of poems. To focus on such defects, however, is perhaps to miss its value. In its finest passages, "A Defence of Poetry" is an inspired and eloquent statement which affirms the universal value of the imaginative arts.

Beginning with a definition of the difference between reason (the "principle of analysis") and the imagination (the "principle of synthesis"), Shelley goes on to define poetry and the poet. The poet is the one who apprehends the beautiful, the true, and the good, and thereby participates in "the eternal, the infinite, and the one." In this broad definition, heavily influenced by Shelley's Platonic metaphysics, enlightened painters, musicians, philosophers, historians, and legislators are all understood to be poets. It is they who intuit the universal laws which underlie all creative activity.

Shelley's Platonic framework can also be seen in his definition of poetry, "the very image of life expressed in its eternal truth." He contrasts a poem with a story: "The story of particular facts is as a mirror which obscures and distorts that which should be beautiful: poetry is a mirror which makes beautiful that which is distorted." Renaissance Platonists frequently used the image of a mirror to convey the relationship between the transcendent world of ideas, which exist in the One, and the transient forms of the material world, which are only imperfect copies of eternity. As Shelley states later in his essay, poetry "strips the veil of familiarity from the world, and lays bare the naked and sleeping beauty which is the spirit of its forms." Shelley's is, however, a modified Platonism. The universal values which poetry reveals do not belong only to a transcendent Platonic One; they are "the unchangeable forms of human nature, as existing in the mind of the creator, which is itself the image of all other minds." The creator in this context is the human mind, which in Shelley's view is the container of all possibilities and the shaper of all worlds, because "all things exist as they are perceived."

This modified Platonism is further revealed in Shelley's discussion of the creative act itself. Like the poet described in Plato's *Ion*, (c. 399–390 B.C.) which Shelley had been reading about the time he was writing "A Defence of Poetry," Shelley's poet is an inspired being, but his inspiration comes not, as in the *Ion*, because he is possessed by a god or moved by divine impulse; it comes from within the depths of his own mind. It also comes unsought; it cannot be summoned by an act of the will because it acts "beyond and above consciousness." When composition begins, inspiration is already on the wane, so that the finished product can never be more than a shadow of the original, intuitive perception. Shelley also believed that the act of composition should be spontaneous and effortless; it is, he says, an "error to assert that the finest passages of poetry are produced by labour and study" (a view which he modified in the preface to *The Revolt of Islam*: "I have exercised a watchful and earnest criticism on my work as it grew under my hands"). Moreover, in one of numerous echoes of William Wordsworth's preface to *Lyrical Ballads* (1798), Shelley links the act of creation with pleasure: "The joy of the . . . creation of poetry is often wholly unalloyed," and he calls great poetry the record of the happiest and best minds in their happiest and best moments.

In this essay, Shelley characteristically exalts the power, beauty, and capabilities of the human mind and the sovereign authority of the poet's own experience. Poetic inspiration is self-validating. ("Let us believe," he writes elsewhere, "in a kind of optimism in which we are our own gods.") Nevertheless, for Shelley this celebration of individual power does not make for a rampant individualism. The poetic imagination may be autonomous, but in moments of inspiration the poet paradoxically becomes aware of the smallness of his individuality; the "self appears as what it is, an atom to a Universe." The emphasis here, however, is not on separation but on relationship and union. The inspired mind is no longer small because it has expanded to partake of all other human minds, as Shelley envisions it in act 4 of *Prometheus Unbound*: "Man, one harmonious soul of many a soul,/ Whose nature is its own divine control,/ Where all things flow to all, as rivers to the sea."

For Shelley, it is the poet who orchestrates this enlightened flowing of soul into soul; the poet touches "the enchanted chord" and reawakens others to their noblest emotions and ideals. Thus, for Shelley, "poetry is indeed something divine." Not only does it have the power to reconcile a wide range of seemingly opposite values, but, by making "familiar objects be as if they were not familiar," it also offers release from the binding and dulling effect of everyday, habitual perceptions. It re-creates the world anew. Shelley here echoes Samuel Taylor Coleridge in his comment on Wordsworth, that the poet of genius is the one who can give "freshness of sensation" to the most familiar scene.

Shelley then launches into a series of magnificent passages about the transforming spirit of poetry. The flavor of them can only be conveyed by a sample quotation:

> Poetry thus makes immortal all that is best and most beautiful in the world; it arrests the vanishing apparitions which haunt the interlunations of life, and veiling them or in language or in form sends them forth among mankind, bearing sweet news of kindred joy to those with whom their sisters abide – abide, because there is no portal of expression from the caverns of the spirit which they inhabit into the universe of things. Poetry redeems from decay the visitations of the divinity in man.

Many other passages could be quoted; they reveal Shelley at his lyrical best, inspired and lifted up by his transcendent vision.

Shelley goes on to tackle Peacock's argument, and that of the utilitarian philosophers of the time, that the imaginative arts are no longer necessary in a materialistic and scientific age. He argues to the contrary that the creative faculty is the foundation of all knowledge and that true utility lies in the production, not of goods, but of pleasure, understood in the highest sense of the word. It is only through the work of the great poets, who have effected an inestimable moral improvement in society, that the human mind has been freed to make world-changing scientific inventions and rational speculations about politics, economics, history, and morals (Shelley has in mind the works of such thinkers as John Locke, David Hume, Edward Gibbon, Voltaire, and Jean-Jacques Rousseau). Yet in the midst of technological and philosophical advances, the creative faculty itself has been allowed to wither. The result is that, although man has enlarged his dominion over the external world, his internal world, his capacity to enjoy and to be free, has been circumscribed: "Our calculations have outrun conception; we have eaten more than we can digest."

Anticipating the thrust of Matthew Arnold's essay "Literature and Science" several generations later, Shelley argues that humankind have to learn to assimilate the results of material progress to the internal laws of their nature, which can be understood as their need to arrange their knowledge and power within to conform to the beautiful and the good. Failing this integration, "man, having enslaved the elements, remains himself a slave."

Always the political radical, Shelley goes on to assess how poetry can transform society. First, he argues that the morally elevating effect of poetry is not produced by inculcating moral precepts or sentiments. To do so is to accept an "inferior office"; the power of poetry diminishes in direct proportion to its moralistic purpose (a view Shelley echoes in his preface to *Prometheus Unbound*, in which he declares his abhorrence of didactic poetry). Conversely, poetry expands the mind itself "by rendering it the receptacle of a thousand unapprehended combinations of thought"; it is itself a source of new knowledge. In the preface to *The Revolt of Islam*, Shelley puts the emphasis on feeling – poetry awakens the feelings of the reader in such a way as to inspire in him or her an enthusiasm for virtue, justice, and liberty and to stimulate his or her own search for truth. "A Defence of Poetry" puts forward a more sophisticated argument, as Shelley draws on the eighteenth-century philosophical concept of the sympathetic imagination. Because poetry awakens the imaginative faculty, and since the imagination is the faculty by which one can sympathetically identify with all things outside oneself, poetry promotes the kind of selfless love which strengthens the moral condition of society. It nourishes the higher aspects of the individual's nature. Poetry and the social good are therefore inextricably linked; the quality of a society's poetry is the measure of its civilization. It is because poetry can act as a catalyst for social change that Shelley regards poets as the "unacknowledged legislators of the World" and the transmission of poetry from one generation to the next as a "sacred chain." (The latter phrase is another echo of Plato's *Ion*.)

Shelley's poetic theories are embodied in many of his poems. One stanza from "To a Skylark," for example, actualizes his theory of the poet who transcends individual self and becomes the inspired seer, spontaneously uttering the holy words of poetry until by some kind of imaginative and spiritual osmosis the world is changed:

> Like a Poet hidden
>   In the light of thought,
> Singing hymns unbidden,
>   Till the world is wrought
> To sympathy with hopes and fears it heeded not.

The concluding stanzas of the "Ode to the West Wind," with their splendid driving energy, convey a vision of the poet as prophet, as an enlightened chanter of magical sounds which can stimulate a new awakening in humankind:

> Drive my dead thoughts over the universe
> Like withered leaves to quicken a new birth!
> And, by the incantation of this verse,
>
> Scatter, as from an unextinguished hearth
> Ashes and sparks, my words among mankind!
> Be through my lips to unawakened earth

> The trumpet of a prophecy! O, Wind,
> If Winter comes, can Spring be far behind?

One might also refer to "Ode to Naples," "Mont Blanc," and the first stanza of "Ode to Liberty."

"A Defence of Poetry" was not published until nearly twenty years after Shelley's death. Readers of the Victorian Age in which it first appeared thought highly of it because it accorded well with their belief in the moral influence of art, although they sometimes interpreted this influence in a narrower sense than Shelley had intended. Yet because "A Defence of Poetry" is not a systematic treatise, but more the work of a poet intoxicated by his own idealistic vision, its direct influence has been limited. It certainly represents a landmark in the Platonic and Neo-Platonic influence in English literary theory, but this tradition has had few twentieth-century adherents. The rise of the New Criticism and the general reaction against Romanticism in the 1920s and 1930s, in which Shelley fared very badly, resulted in a devaluing of "A Defence of Poetry" because it contains nothing of value to the close reading of literary texts. F. R. Leavis poured scorn on Shelley's idea of poetic inspiration, calling it nothing more than "surrendering to a hypnotic rote of favorite images, associations, and words." A later critic, Kathleen Raine, has defended Shelley, however, in an outstanding essay in which she describes "A Defence of Poetry" as "a recall to order, to the Platonic tradition, an eloquent descant upon those first principles also set forth by Coleridge in his *Biographia Literaria*."

## Principal criticism

Preface to *The Revolt of Islam*, 1818
Passages in *Prometheus Unbound*, 1820
"A Defence of Poetry," 1840

## Other major works and literary forms

Percy Bysshe Shelley is known primarily as one of the foremost poets of the Romantic age. His principal poems include *Alastor: Or, The Spirit of Solitude, and Other Poems* (1816), *The Revolt of Islam* (1818), *Adonais: An Elegy on the Death of John Keats* (1821), *Epipsychidion* (1821), the unfinished *The Triumph of Life* (1824), and lyric poems such as "Ode to the West Wind" (1820). He also wrote a tragedy, *The Cenci* (1819), and the lyrical dramas *Hellas* (1822) and *Prometheus Unbound* (1820), his masterpiece. He translated Plato's *Ion* (c. 399–390 B.C.), *Symposium* (c. 388–366 B.C.), and part of *Phaedo* (c. 388–366 B.C.) and wrote essays on metaphysical, religious, and political topics, such as "On the Science of Mind" (1815), "On Life" (1815), "On Love" (1815), "A Philosophical View of Reform" (1920), and "Essay on Christianity" (1819).

NOVELS
*Zastrozzi: A Romance*, 1810
*St. Irvyne: Or, The Rosicrucian*, 1810.

PLAY

*The Cenci*, 1819

POETRY

*Original Poetry by Victor and Cazire*, 1810 (with Elizabeth
   Shelley)
*Posthumous Fragments of Margaret Nicholson*, 1810
*Queen Mab: A Philosophical Poem*, 1813 (revised as *The
   Daemon of the World*, 1816)
*Alastor: Or, The Spirit of Solitude, and Other Poems*, 1816
*Rosalind and Helen: A Modern Eclogue, with Other Poems*, 1819
*Oedipus Tyrannus: Or, Swellfoot the Tyrant*, 1820
*Epipsychidion*, 1821
*Adonais: An Elegy on the Death of John Keats*, 1821
*Hellas: A Lyrical Drama*, 1822
*Posthumous Poems of Percy Bysshe Shelley*, 1824 (includes *Prince
   Athanase, Julian and Maddalo: A Conversation, The Witch of
   Atlas, The Triumph of Life, The Cyclops, Charles the First*)
*The Masque of Anarchy*, 1832
*Peter Bell the Third*, 1839
*The Poetical Works of Percy Bysshe Shelley*, 1839
*The Wandering Jew*, 1887
*The Complete Poetical Works of Shelley*, 1904 (Thomas
   Hutchinson, editor)
*The Esdaile Notebook: A Volume of Early Poems*, 1964

NONFICTION

*The Necessity of Atheism*, 1811 (with Thomas Jefferson Hogg)
*An Address to the Irish People*, 1812
*Declaration of Rights*, 1812
*A Letter to Lord Ellenborough*, 1812
*Proposals for an Association of . . . Philanthropists*, 1812
*A Refutation of Deism, in a Dialogue*, 1814
*History of a Six Weeks' Tour Through a Part of France,
   Switzerland, Germany, and Holland*, 1817 (with Mary
   Shelley)
*A Proposal for Putting Reform to the Vote Throughout the
   Kingdom*, 1817
*An Address to the People on the Death of the Princess
   Charlotte*, 1817?
*Essays, Letters from Abroad, Translations, and Fragments*, 1840
*Shelley Memorials*, 1859
*Shelley's Prose in the Bodleian Manuscripts*, 1910
*Note Books of Shelley*, 1911
*A Philosophical View of Reform*, 1920
*The Letters of Percy Bysshe Shelley*, 1964 (2 volumes; Frederick
   L. Jones, editor)

TRANSLATIONS

*The Cyclops*, 1824 (of Euripides' play)
*Ion*, 1840 (of Plato's dialogue)
"The Banquet Translated from Plato," 1931 (of Plato's dialogue
   *Symposium*)

MISCELLANEOUS

*The Complete Works of Percy Bysshe Shelley*, 1926–1930 (10
   volumes; Roger Ingpen and Walter E. Peck, editors)
*Shelley's Poetry and Prose: Authoritative Texts and Criticism*,
   1977 (Donald H. Reiman and Sharon B. Powers, editors)

## Further reading

Abrams, M. H. *The Mirror and the Lamp*, 1953.
Bunn, James. "The 'True Utility' of Shelley's Method in
   *A Defence of Poetry*," in *English Romanticism; Preludes and
   Postludes*, 1993. Edited by Donald Schoonmaker and John
   A. Alford.
Cronin, Richard. *Shelley's Poetic Thoughts*, 1981.
Delisle, Fannie. *A Study of Shelley's Defence of Poetry:
   A Textual and Critical Evaluation*, 1974 (2 volumes).
Keetch, William. *Shelley's Style*, 1984.
Roberts, Hugh. "Chaos and Evolution: A Quantum Leap in
   Shelley's Process," in *Keats–Shelley Journal*. 45 (1996),
   pp. 156–94.
Schulze, Earl J. *Shelley's Theory of Poetry: A Reappraisal*, 1966.
Solve, Melvin. *Shelley, His Theory of Poetry*, 1927.
Wasserman, Earl. *Shelley: A Critical Reading*, 1971.
Weisman, Karen A. *Imageless Truths: Shelley's Poetic Fictions*,
   1994.

BRYAN AUBREY

*See also* Byron; Coleridge; Hazlitt; Keats; Romanticism;
Shelley

# Viktor Shklovskii

Russian critic

**Born:** St. Petersburg, Russia; January 25, 1893
**Died:** Moscow, U.S.S.R.; December 5, 1984

## Biography

Viktor Shklovskii was born in 1893 to Boris Shklovskii, a
mathematics teacher, and his second wife, Varvara Bundel.
His father was Jewish, his mother of Latvian origin. He
had a half brother, Evgenii, from his father's first marriage
and a sister, Varvara. He was not a diligent student, being
far more interested in the shenanigans of the Futurists, but
he did succeed in matriculating at the University of
Petersburg in the fall of 1913. Early in 1914 he published
a booklet called *Resurrection of the Word*, which stated in
embryonic form his views on art. He took a copy of the
booklet to his professor, the renowned linguist Baudouin
de Courtenay, who introduced Shklovskii to his most gifted
students. Under Shklovskii's leadership, those students
joined forces with the local Futurists to form a group called
Opoiaz, the Society for the Study of Poetic Language.

When World War I began in 1914, Shklovskii enlisted.
He served with the czarist army in Galicia and the Ukraine
until 1916, when he was reassigned to Petrograd (the
former St. Petersburg) as an instructor in a school for
armored-car personnel. Once again, he began meeting with
the members of Opoiaz. When the February Revolution
broke out, he joined the insurgents. He served as a member
of the Petrograd Soviet and as a commissar on the Austrian
front. Disillusioned by the course of events, he requested
transfer to Persia, where he was serving when the October
Revolution broke out. When he returned to Petrograd, he
joined an underground organization plotting to restore the
Constituent Assembly. Threatened with arrest, he fled to
Kiev. After being exonerated of his crimes, he returned to
Petrograd. He married Vasilisa Kordi, with whom he eventually had two children: Nikita and Varvara. From early

1919 until the end of 1921 he played a major role in the literary activities of the beleaguered city. He participated in the activities of Opoiaz; he published his theoretical articles; he served as mentor to the talented young writers known as the Serapion brothers; he joined Lef, the new coalition of Futurists organized by Vladimir Maiakovskii in 1923.

In March, 1923, faced once again with arrest because of his ties to the Socialist Revolutionary Party, Shklovskii fled to Finland. Then he joined the growing Russian colony in Berlin. While there, he continued actively writing and publishing his books, but he hated the life of an émigré. When an amnesty was granted in the fall of 1923, he returned to the Soviet Union, settling in Moscow, where he lived until his death in 1984.

Shklovskii's life in the Soviet Union after his return in 1923 was not easy. He resumed his ties with the Serapion brothers, with Lef, and with Opoiaz, which were viewed as hostile to the tenets of Marxism. Throughout the 1920s and 1930s Shklovskii was under constant attack. The pressures on him, as on other writers, eased during World War II, in which Shklovskii served as a war correspondent. In the very last days of the war, his only son, Nikita, was killed. After the war he divorced his wife to marry Serafima Narbut.

The severe period of Stalinist repression that began after the war posed particular dangers to the Jews and to those associated with Western culture. Shklovskii, vulnerable on both counts, came under attack once again. Though he escaped imprisonment, he published very little. With the death of Joseph Stalin in 1953, he gradually regained his position as one of his country's foremost literary critics, publishing a series of new books that have been admired not only in the Soviet Union but in the West as well.

## Influence

Shklovskii viewed Russian society as stagnant and he found the art of that time either conventional (realism) or bloodless (Symbolism). He eagerly joined forces with the Russian Futurists in arguing for new forms and new language. Rejecting conventional criticism, which studied literature primarily for information about writers and/or their society, Shklovskii argued that a work of art does not exceed the sum of its stylistic devices. He coined the term "estrangement" to stress the major task of the writer: to select and arrange his or her material so that it will lose the familiarity acquired with long usage and gain the reader's attention. Shklovskii's controversial formulations attracted a wide following and provided the foundation for the school of criticism eventually known as Russian Formalism.

## Analysis

Shklovskii began his career as a Futurist. Strongly attracted by the poetry of Maiakovskii and Velimir Khlebnikov, he stated in theoretical terms the assumptions that underlay their poetry. That statement, *Resurrection of the Word*, caught the attention of the linguists Lev Iakubinskii and Evgenii Polivanov, who saw the language of Futurist poetry as a promising vehicle for linguistic analysis. Drawn together by their common interest, these individuals formed the group known as Opoiaz, the Society for the Study of Poetic Language.

What enabled Shklovskii to isolate the theoretical assumptions underlying Futurist poetry was, in the main, his adaptation of the hypotheses advanced by Aleksandr Veselovskii. In his numerous studies, Veselovskii had demonstrated that a work of literature can be effectively studied as a discrete formal entity, but he inevitably located the source of those forms in social conditions. Shklovskii divested Veselovskii's hypotheses of their genetic fallacy and converted his terms – image, motif, plot – into purely formal categories. Veselovskii had suggested that literary language differs from standard language primarily in its heightened perceptibility. Shklovskii elevated those few hints into a cardinal principle, identifying heightened perceptibility as the hallmark of Futurist poetry and of art in general. To describe the process of restoring words and objects to perceptibility, he coined the terms *ostranenie* (estrangement) and *zatrudnennaia forma* (obstructed form).

Shklovskii reacted against the traditional quest of Russian criticism for ideas in art; he reacted against the Symbolists' view of art as music and mystery. Instead, he advocated studying art as device – as a discrete verbal form, assembled by an author/technician. Since he promoted perceptibility of form, his studies of literature stressed the new ways in which writers used the limited number of forms available to them. These ideas provided the foundation for a new school of criticism: Russian Formalism, of which Shklovskii is usually regarded as the founder.

After delineating verse language as the initial concern of Opoiaz, Shklovskii demonstrated the efficacy of his system in the areas of prose structure and literary history. He argued that literary change occurs when once-dominant devices, plots, and/or genres cease to elicit perception and are replaced by new forms. He described the legacy as transmitted not from father to son but from uncle to nephew; that is, a newly dominant writer derives not from his or her dominant predecessor, but from the stockpile of peripheral writers and genres. Shklovskii's provocative insights opened new vistas and inspired major studies. In particular, he influenced the work of Boris Eikhenbaum and Iurii Tynianov.

Shklovskii developed his theoretical system in a series of articles that he published between 1916 and 1921. At the same time, he applied those theories in the numerous critiques of books, plays, and paintings that he wrote before his emigration in 1922. His criticism reflected the dominant concerns of his theoretical concepts: concentration on form and techniques, contemptuous dismissal of art seen as didactic and old-fashioned, appreciation of striking formal effects. His style displayed the same predilection for such effects that the Futurists had exhibited in their poetry.

During this period Shklovskii applied his critical tools to the works of Vasilii Rozanov, Laurence Sterne, and Andrei Belyi, writers united by their interest in experimental form and style. Those writers not only provided ideal subjects for Shklovskii's theories but also exerted a lasting influence on his own techniques of style and composition, which he now put to use in the three hybrid novels that he wrote during the 1920s: *A Sentimental Journey*, *Zoo*, and *Third Factory*. He cultivated stylistic and compositional nonchalance. He learned how to violate systematically the reader's expectations – with chronological displacement, digressions, and overt devices, all designed to expose the conventional nature of literature and to create an ironic tone. He mixed literary language with slang and conversational idioms. He discarded the conventional paragraph, resorting instead to the one-sentence paragraph, which became his trademark, or assembling incongruous ideas in the same paragraph. Such techniques created an impression of stylistic and compositional anarchy, but he offset his disruptive devices with an intricate system of leitmotifs, coterminous conceits, and interlocking cross-references.

Shklovskii's stimulating lectures at Opoiaz, at the Translators' Studio, at the House of Arts, and at the Institute of Art History amplified the effect produced by his articles and books. The literary theories that he so brilliantly formulated and demonstrated exerted an enormous influence on writers and critics of the time and left a permanent mark on twentieth-century Russian prose.

As the 1920s unfolded, a confluence of film work, changes in Russian reading tastes, and opposition from Marxist critics led Shklovskii to modify his earlier views. As a member of Lef, he abandoned his earlier insistence on intricate forms and irony. Invoking his theory of perception, he asserted that the new Russian reader had ceased to respond to those forms and now preferred unadorned factual material. Accordingly, he turned his attention to short, simple forms that would permit maximum orientation to the message. He led the exploration and refinement of such genres as the newspaper article, the *feuilleton*, and the sketch – those forms that dominated the Russian literary scene during the 1930s. After the death of Stalin in 1953, he emerged with a series of new books which represent at least a partial return to his earlier views.

## Principal criticism

*Voskreshenie slova*, 1914 (*Resurrection of the Word*, 1972)
"Iskusstvo kak priem," 1917 ("Art as Device," 1965)
"Sviaz priemov siuzhetoslozheniia s obshchimi priemami stilia," 1919 ("The Connection Between Plot Devices and General Stylistic Devices," 1972)
*Rozanov*, 1921 (English translation, 1982)
"Razvertyvanie siuzheta," 1921
"*Tristram Shendi* Sterna i teoriia romana," 1921 ("Sterne's *Tristram Shandy* and a Theory of the Novel," 1965)

*Khod konia*, 1923
*Literatura i kinematograf*, 1923
"*Evgenii Onegin* (Pushkin i Stern)," 1923 ("*Eugene Onegin* (Pushkin and Sterne)," 1975)
"Andrei Belyi," 1924 ("Ornamental Prose: Andrei Bely," 1982)
"Isaak Babel (kriticheskii romans)," 1924 ("Isaac Babel," 1973)
"Tekhnika romana tain," 1924 ("The Technique of the Mystery Novel," 1971)
*O teorii prozy*, 1925 (*Theory of Prose*, 1990)
*Udachi i porazheniia Maksima Gor'kogo*, 1926
*Piat chelovek znakomykh*, 1927
*Ikh nastoiashchee*, 1927
*Material i stil v romane L'va Tolstogo "Voina i mir,"* 1928
*Gamburgskii schet*, 1928
*Podenshchina*, 1930
*Zametki o proze Pushkina*, 1937
*Zametki o proze russkikh klassikov*, 1953
*Za i protiv: Zametki o Dostoevskom*, 1957
*Khudozhestvennaia proza: Razmyshleniia i razbory*, 1959
*Za sorok let: Stati o kino*, 1965
*Staroe i novoe: Kniga statei o detskoi literature*, 1966
*Povesti o proze: Razmyshleniia i razbory*, 1966
*Tetiva: O neskhodstve skhodnogo*, 1970
*Energiia zabliuzhdeniia: Kniga o siuzhete*, 1981
*Za shestdesiat let*, 1985
*Gamburgskii schet*, 1990

## Other major works and literary forms

In addition to the aforementioned books, Viktor Shklovskii has published hundreds of articles and reviews. His theoretical work and applied criticism involve not only literature but also film. Between 1926 and 1961 he wrote more than two dozen screenplays. Shklovskii's work also includes a series of books on neglected historical figures and three widely translated biographies of Vladimir Maiakovskii, Lev Tolstoi, and Sergei Eisenstein. His memoirs, highly experimental in style and structure, are concentrated in four books: *Sentimentalnoe puteshestvie* (1923; *A Sentimental Journey: Memoirs, 1917–1922*, 1970), *Zoo: Ili, Pisma ne o liubvi* (1923; *Zoo: Or, Letters Not About Love*, 1971), *Tretia fabrika* (1926; *Third Factory*, 1977), and *Zhili-byli* (1964; once upon a time). He has also written books for children and studies of children's literature.

### NOVELS

*Sentimentalnoe puteshestvie*, 1923 (*A Sentimental Journey: Memoirs, 1917–1922*, 1970)
*Zoo: Ili Pisma ne o liubvi*, 1923 (*Zoo: Or Letters Not About Love*, 1971)
*Tret'ia fabrika*, 1926 (*Third Factory*, 1977)

### SHORT FICTION

*Matvei Komarov, zhitel goroda Moskvy*, 1929
*Kratkaia no dostovernaia povest o dvorianine Bolotove*, 1930
*Zhitie arkhiereiskogo sluzhi*, 1931
*Chulkov i Levshin*, 1933
*Kapitan Fedotov*, 1936
*Marko Polo*, 1936
*Minin i Pozharskii*, 1940
*O masterakh starinnykh*, 1951
*Povest' o khudozhnike Fedotove*, 1955
*Istoricheskie povesti i rasskazy*, 1958

SCREENPLAYS
*Bukhta smerti*, 1926
*Krylia kholopa*, 1926
*Po zakonu*, 1926
*Predatel'*, 1926 (with Lev Nikulin)
*Prostitutka*, 1927
*Schastlivye cherepki*, 1927 (libretto)
*Tret'ia meshchanskaia*, 1927 (with A. Room)
*Dva bronevika*, 1928
*Dom na trubnoi*, 1928 (with others)
*Ivan da Maria*, 1928 (with B. Altshuler and V. Sirokov)
*Kazaki*, 1928 (with V. Barskii)
*Kapitanskaia dochka*, 1928
*Ledianoi dom*, 1928 (with G. Grebner and O. Leonidov)
*Ovod*, 1928 (with K. Marzhanov)
*Ukhaby*, 1928
*Poslednii attraktsion*, 1929
*Turksib*, 1929 (with E. Aron, A. Macherat, and V. Turin)
*Ochen' prosto*, 1931
*Mertvyi dom*, 1932
*Gorizont*, 1933
*Zhit'*, 1933
*Zolotye ruki*, 1933
*Minin i Pozharskii*, 1939
*Alisher Navoi*, 1948
*Dalekaia nevesta*, 1948 (with E. Pomeshchikov and Nikolai Rozhkov)
*Chuk i Gek*, 1953
*Dokhunda*, 1957
*Kazaki*, 1961

NONFICTION
*Room, zhizn' i rabota*, 1929
*O Maiakovskom*, 1940 (*Mayakovsky and His Circle*, 1972)
*Lev Tolstoi*, 1963 (English translation, 1978)
*Eizenshtein*, 1973

CHILDREN'S LITERATURE
*Puteshestvie v stranu kino*, 1926
*Nandu II*, 1928
*Turksib*, 1930
*Marko Polo, razvedchik*, 1931
*Skazka o teniakh*, 1931
*Zhizn' khudozhnika Fedotova*, 1936
*Rasskaz o Pushkine*, 1937

MISCELLANEOUS
*Svintsovyi zhrebii*, 1914
*Tekhnika pisatel'skogo remesla*, 1927
*Motalka, knizhka ne dlia kinematografov*, 1927
*Gornaia Gruziia: Pshaviia, Khevsuretiia, Mukheviia*, 1930
*Poiski optimizma*, 1930
*Kak pisat' stsenarii*, 1931
*Dnevnik*, 1939
*Vstrechi*, 1944
*Zhili-byli*, 1964
*Sobranie sochinenii v trekh tomakh*, 1973–1974
*Izbrannoe v dvukh tomakh*, 1983

## Further reading

Avins, Carol. "Emigration and Metaphor: Viktor Shklovsky's *Zoo: Or Letters Not About Love*," in *Border Crossings: The West and Russian Identity in Soviet Literature, 1917–1934*, 1983.
Bristol, Evelyn. "Shklovskii as Memoirist," in *And Meaning for a Life Entire: Festschrift for Charles A. Moser on the Occasion of his Sixtieth Birthday*, 1997. Edited by Peter Rollberg.
Erlich, Victor. *Russian Formalism: History, Doctrine*, 1955.
Flaker, "Shklovsky and the History of Literature: A Footnote to Erlich's *Russian Formalism*," in *Russian Formalism: A Retrospective Glance, A Festschrift in Honor of Victor Erlich*, 1985. Edited by Robert Louis Jackson and Stephen Rudy.
Galushkin, A. Iu. "Novye materialy k bibliografii V. B. Shklovskogo," in *de Visu*. No. 1 (1993).
Gifford, Henry. "Viktor Shklovsky," in *Grand Street*, 1988.
Grits, T. *The Work of Viktor Shklovsky*, in *Third Factory*, 1977.
Haber, Edythe. "Bulgakov and Shklovsky: Notes on a Literary Antagonism", in *New Studies in Russian Language and Literature*, 1987.
Holub, Robert C. "Russian Formalism," in *Reception Theory: A Critical Introduction*, 1984, pp. 15–22.
Laferriere, Daniel. "Potebnja, Shklovskii, and the Familiarity / Strangeness Paradox," in *Russian Literature*. IV, no. 2 (1976), pp. 175–198.
Lary, N. M. "Afternoon in Peredelkino," in *Sight and Sound*, 1984, pp. 217–220.
——. "Shklovsky and Dostoevsky as Demons of Darkness," in *Dostoevsky and Soviet Film: Visions of Demonic Realism*, 1986.
Loveridge, Mark. "Sterne and the Russian Novel," in *Laurence Sterne and the Argument about Design*, 1982, pp. 18–24.
Nicholas, Mary A. "Formalist Theory Revisited: On Shklovskii 'On Pilnyak,' " in *Slavic and East European Journal*. 36. no. 1(1992), pp. 68–83.
Sheldon, Richard. "Shklovsky, Gorky, and the Serapion Brothers," in *The Slavic and East European Journal*. XII (1968), pp. 1–13.
——. "The Formalist Poetics of Viktor Shklovsky," in *Russian Literature Tri-Quarterly*. II (1972), pp. 351–371.
——. "Viktor Shklovskii and the Device of Ostensible Surrender," in *Slavic Review*. 34, no. 1 (1975), pp. 86–108.
——. *Viktor Shklovsky: An International Bibliography of Works by and about Him*, 1977.
Sherwood, Richard. "Viktor Shklovsky and the Development of Early Formalist Theory on Prose Literature," in *Russian Formalism*, 1973.
Smart, Robert A. "Viktor Shklovskii and Sentimental Journey," in *The Nonfiction Novel*, 1985.
Stacy, R. H. "The Formalists," in *Russian Literary Criticism*, 1974, pp. 163–174.
Steiner, Peter. "The Praxis of Irony: Viktor Shklovsky's Zoo," in *Russian Formalism: A Festschrift in Honor of Victor Erlich*, 1985. Edited by Robert J. Jackson and Stephen Rudy.
Thompson, Ewa M. "V. B. Shklovskii and the Russian Intellectual Tradition," in *Aspects of Modern Russian and Czech Literature*, 1989, pp. 11–21.

RICHARD SHELDON

*See also* Belyi; Lunacharskii; Russian Formalism

# Sir Philip Sidney

## English poet and critic

**Born:** Penshurst, England; November 30, 1554
**Died:** Arnhem, the Netherlands; October 17, 1586

## Biography

Philip Sidney was born on November 30, 1554, at Penshurst, Kent, to Sir Henry Sidney, a future colonial administrator under Queen Elizabeth I, and Lady Mary Sidney, daughter to John Dudley, Duke of Northumberland, and sister to the queen's great early favorite, Robert Dudley, Earl of Leicester. With this pedigree and remarkable native ability, the boy was destined for greatness. An education begun at Shrewsbury School and Christ Church, Oxford, was capped by three years of travel in continental Europe. When he returned to England in 1575, he spent a few months at court and then saw military service in Ireland. Thereafter he undertook diplomatic missions for the queen. *An Apology for Poetry* followed sometime after Stephen Gosson's *Schoole of Abuse* (1579), at which time Sidney was probably working on the old *Arcadia*, which he appears to have finished the next year while visiting his sister and her husband at Wilton, their country estate.

In 1581 Sidney was elected to Parliament, most likely completed *An Apology for Poetry*, and began *Astrophel and Stella*, an extraordinarily influential sonnet cycle when published. His new *Arcadia* probably dates from 1582. In the following year he was knighted and married Frances Walsingham, a daughter of Queen Elizabeth's principal secretary. Sidney numbered among his interests American exploration and in 1584 planned to accompany a proposed expedition under Sir Francis Drake but instead accepted the post of Governor of Flushing in the Netherlands, where England had long been opposing Spanish influence. In 1586, after the death of both parents, he was mortally wounded while leading troops at Zutphen. He lingered a month, then died on October 17. The nation mourned the loss of this brilliant young man. Amid lavish ceremonies and tributes from all over Europe, he was buried in St. Paul's Cathedral in London on February 16, 1587, the works for which he is now best known yet unpublished.

## Influence

*An Apology for Poetry* is the first major critical treatise in English and is all the more remarkable as the work of a man known in his short lifetime as a courtier, soldier, and diplomat rather than as a writer. Sidney wrote this work in response to a puritanical attack on poetry by Gosson, who, without permission, dedicated *The Schoole of Abuse* to him. Sidney shared the aversion of English aristocrats of his time to print publication, but *An Apology for Poetry*, constructed in the form of a classical oration, certainly circulated in manuscript before his death. Since its initial publication under two titles by two different publishers in 1595, the treatise has attained the stature of the major statement in any language of the literary critical views that animated the Renaissance.

*An Apology for Poetry* is a compilation and attempted harmonization of critical thought by Plato, Aristotle, Horace, and others up to Sidney's own time, but it is more than that. It is the witty and graceful work of an early prose master. It is an eloquent argument for the moral value of great literature. It is a plea to his countrymen to acknowledge the value of their literary tradition, in the process incorporating the first history of English literature. Sidney set English neoclassicism on a course that eschewed slavish devotion to classical models but proved a liberating and creative force in English letters from the time of Ben Jonson, in the early seventeenth century, to that of Samuel Johnson, a century and a half later.

## Analysis

Sidney was the first of a long line of important poet-critics writing in English. Earlier discussions of poetic theory had concentrated on the analysis and classification of meters and figures of speech. Sidney's work is an "apology" or defense in the largest sense: a justification of poetry in an era of growing Puritan suspicion of any art which did not patently subserve the interests of piety and Christian morality.

In responding to Gosson's *Schoole of Abuse*, aimed particularly at the emerging English theater, Sidney wisely chose to enlarge the topic and place it in historical context. His review of poetry's longstanding reputation as "first light-giver to ignorance" implicitly condemns the historical ignorance of poetry's puritanical opponents. The great achievements of Greece and Rome, he pointed out, coincided with, and were promoted by, superior poetry, while even in places devoid of other achievements poetry is honored. He makes an etymological excursus to demonstrate poetry's reputation. The Romans called the poet a *vates*, or prophet, and the Roman word for songs, *carmina*, is the basis of "charms," artifacts by which spirits are commanded. The word "poet" itself comes from the Greek and signifies "maker."

In exploring the nature of poetry, Sidney draws upon the greatest of Greek philosophers. Plato acknowledged the power of poetry but argued that it is only an imitation of the concrete world, which itself is only a pale shadow of ultimate reality. Aristotle granted that poetry was an imitation, but he saw nature, which it imitated, as a process of development whereby reality is manifested in the concrete and takes on meaning. Art also is a process by which form and meaning emerge from sensory images of things and actions. Sidney's strategy was to combine and retain the most attractive aspects of both approaches. He honors nature but sees poetry as capable of transcending it. The poet "doth grow in effect another nature" and produces something different from anything in nature and superior to it. Aristotle would have thought such a notion presumptuous, but Aristotle did not understand that humankind was made in God's likeness and hence superior to all other worldly creations. Thus Plato, Aristotle, and Christianity contribute to Sidney's conception of poetry.

After defending poetry's reputation and providing a Christian's philosophical account of its nature, Sidney adapts a tripartite classification made earlier in the century by J. C. Scaliger, whom he follows in categorizing religious poets, such as David, Solomon, and Moses (not neglecting to remind Puritan fundamentalists that the Bible contains divine poems), and philosophical ones, such as Lucretius and Virgil (in his *Georgics*, 36–29 B.C.). Scaliger's miscellaneous third category becomes Sidney's "indeed right poets," who fulfill Horace's popular requirement that poetry instruct and delight its audience. In this respect poetry exceeds both history, which is tied to a factual account of the past, and philosophy, which is abstract and difficult. The "right poets" achieve this end because they imitate not merely "what is, has been, or shall be; but range, only reined with learned discretion, into the divine consideration of what may be, and should be." Thus poetry is much closer to what later critics would call "creation" than to the classical notion of imitation.

Sidney's concept of the right poet furnishes a strategy for answering moralistic critics of poetry. Sidney accounts the greatest poets great moralists also, for they are free to inspire their audience with "notable images" of a "golden world." Here he is planting the seed that would grow into Romantic theories of the creative imagination, but his intention is to explain poetry's motivational superiority to both history and philosophy. The poet "doth not only show the way, but giveth so sweet a prospect into the way, as will entice any man to enter into it." Sidney is aligning himself with Renaissance Neo-Platonists such as Marsilio Ficino and Giovanni Pico della Mirandola, who combined Plato's view of the soul as capable of ascending a ladder of perfection through higher and higher degrees of love, beauty, knowledge, and goodness with ideals of Christian perfection. As a good Protestant Christian, Sidney understood the implications of Original Sin, which he saw as affecting human will more profoundly than reason. Humankind sees the way but has difficulty "reaching unto it." Enter the great motivational force of poetry, however, and even the fallen can aspire to Plato's ladder. Sidney acknowledges the possibility that such a force might also lead one astray, but the fault is not in poetry, only in its misuse.

Yet Sidney does not see poetry flourishing in England, which has become a "stepmother to poets." Although modern students see Sidney himself as one of the inaugurators of a great literary period in England, Sidney shared his nation's sense of inferiority to France and Italy, where the Renaissance blossomed earlier. Sidney reminds his countrymen, nevertheless, of what the English poets have already accomplished. His assessment is rudimentary – the only medieval work he mentions is Geoffrey Chaucer's *Troilus and Criseyde* (1382) – but it is important as the first such effort. Here, as in his introduction, he puts to work a developing Renaissance historical sense. Largely conceived as a dichotomy between "ancients" and "moderns" – a contrast which itself later exercised John Dryden, Jonathan Swift, and Alexander Pope at greater length – Sidney's embryonic literary history foreshadowed a now-familiar form of study.

His insistence on poetry's capacity for "moving" its audience had a more immediate impact. The Renaissance faith in the efficacy of education to promote human improvement produced manuals, usually called courtesy books, designed to guide the prince, courtier, governor, magistrate, and schoolmaster in his occupation. "The ending end of all earthly learning being virtuous action," the most important courtesy book of all would be one calculated to produce the virtuous person. Given this confidence in the practical value of moral as well as vocational education, and given Sidney's stature and verbal felicity, it would have been strange if his contemporaries had not responded to *An Apology for Poetry*. While Edmund Spenser would not necessarily have had to read Sidney before declaring his purpose in *The Faerie Queene* (1590–1596) – "to fashion a gentleman or noble person in virtuous and gentle discipline" (a doubtless deliberately ambiguous statement suggesting the "fashioning" not only of his hero but also of his reader) – he does pay explicit tribute to Sidney's influence in a dedicatory sonnet to Sidney's sister, the Countess of Pembroke, and elsewhere in his writings.

The Sidneyan moral emphasis continues strongly into the generation of John Milton, who in *Of Education* (1644) patently echoes the very language of *An Apology for Poetry*:

> I will point you out the right path of a virtuous and noble education; laborious indeed at the first ascent, but also so smooth, so green, so full of goodly prospect and melodious sounds on every side that the harp of Orpheus was not more charming.

Milton's *Paradise Lost* (1667, 1674) is the last great poem reflecting the Renaissance confidence in "notable images" to perform such an exalted task as justifying the ways of God to humankind. By the time Pope attempts a similar theme in *An Essay on Man* (1733–1734), he does not even try to "show the way" but conducts a rational argument in verse.

A more representative seventeenth-century poet, such as Abraham Cowley, much more celebrated in his time than today, illustrates both the continuing development of Sidney's theory and the decline of the transcendental ambitions that fired it. In his ode "The Muse," he elaborates Sidney's "second nature" into a "new world" populated by creatures of poetic invention such as centaurs, satyrs, and fairies. Although Spenser's *The Faerie Queene* abounds in such creatures, in Cowley's world they have lost their connection with lofty doctrine and moral purpose.

The idea of another and superior nature of the poet's fashioning continued to attract poets and critics. In 1674 Dryden echoes it in a preface to an edition of William Shakespeare's *Troilus and Cressida* (1609). By the time of Joseph Addison's *The Spectator* essays (1711–1712), poetry is routinely touted as a new creation revealing new worlds. This aspect of *An Apology for Poetry* thus becomes a significant element in the theory of poetic imagination developing in the eighteenth century and cresting with the great Romantics. Percy Bysshe Shelley's *A Defence of Poetry* (written in 1821, published in 1840) owes much more than its title to Sidney. Like his predecessor, Shelley was sensitive to charges that poetry promoted immorality and eager to defend it in large and positive terms. He constructed his argument along lines similar to Sidney's and employed an enthusiastic rhetoric unapproached in English criticism since *An Apology for Poetry*.

Matthew Arnold is often cited as retaining the idea of the golden world of poetry in the Victorian period, but perhaps the most important legacy from Sidney persisting in his criticism can be seen in his essay "Literature and Science" (1882), from which affirmations of the ethical value of literature passed into twentieth-century defenses of its vitality in the curricula of schools and colleges. If modern skepticism forbids the specifically Christian and Platonic enthusiasm of Sidney the Renaissance man, advocates continue to defend literature on the grounds of its capacity to enlarge and refine the moral imagination. In such terms Joseph Brodsky, the 1987 Nobel Prize winner, praised poetry more than four centuries after Sidney's death.

Sidney's continuing influence over the centuries testifies to the generosity of his mind and to his capacity for selecting, codifying, and expressing the best in previous European poetic theory. He is susceptible to charges that he distorted the thought of some of his sources in his eagerness to harmonize competing and sometimes antagonistic philosophical stances, but the ingenuity of his effort still gratifies his readers. *An Apology for Poetry* remains the single most eloquent and useful primary source for the study of Renaissance poetics.

Sidney clearly established a valuable precedent for English literary criticism. As the author of two important creative works, *Astrophel and Stella* and *Arcadia*, he undoubtedly emboldened subsequent poets to follow his lead by defending or exploring their craft. The roster of great poet-critics in English, which includes Ben Jonson, John Dryden, Alexander Pope, Samuel Johnson, William Wordsworth, Samuel Taylor Coleridge, Percy Bysshe Shelley, Matthew Arnold, and T. S. Eliot, has no equal in any other European language. Although many of these men have written much more extensively on their craft than did Sidney, they have for the most part followed him in subordinating the discussion of technical matters and the assessment of individual writers to the investigation of large philosophical questions. Thus Sidney may be said to have begun a critical tradition which has encouraged poets to formulate the principles by which they work and to produce a body of theory much less intimidating to the general reader than much of the work produced by professional critics in other languages. His spirit breathes through his work and continues to stimulate his readers.

## Principal criticism
*Defence of Poesy*, 1595 (also as *An Apology for Poetry*)

## Other major works and literary forms
Sir Philip Sidney composed two other major literary works, *The Countesse of Pembroke's Arcadia* (1590, 1593, 1598; best known as *Arcadia*), a prose romance with many interpolated poems, and *Astrophel and Stella* (1591), a sequence of 108 sonnets and eleven songs. Both contain literary critical ideas, but these are incidental to the main purpose in each case. All Sidney's works were published posthumously, some in forms of which he certainly would not have approved. He wrote one version of the *Arcadia*, usually called the "old" *Arcadia*, and later began a substantially different and more ambitious revision, with the result that editors have difficulty in deciding whether to print the old *Arcadia*, the new *Arcadia*, a composite of the two, or both separately.

His other works include an early pastoral entertainment, *The Lady of May* (1578); a collection titled *Certaine Sonnets* (1598); other uncollected poems, some of which later editors inserted into *Arcadia*; and, with Mary Sidney Herbert, Countess of Pembroke, *The Psalmes of David, Translated into Divers and Sundry Kindes of Verse* (1823). These works, too, have complicated publishing histories.

FICTION
*The Countesse of Pembroke's Arcadia*, 1590, (revised 1593, third edition 1598; best known as *Arcadia*)

PLAYS
*The Lady of May*, 1578
"Fortress of Perfect Beauty," 1581 (with Fulke Greville, Lord Brooke; Phillip Howard, Earl of Arundel; and Baron Windsor of Stanwell)

POETRY
*Astrophel and Stella*, 1591
*Certaine Sonnets*, 1598
*The Complete Poems of Sir Philip Sidney*, 1873 (2 volumes)

TRANSLATION
*The Psalmes of David, Translated into Divers and Sundry Kindes of Verse*, 1823 (with Mary Sidney Herbert, Countess of Pembroke)

MISCELLANEOUS
*Miscellaneous Prose of Sir Philip Sidney*, 1973

## Further reading
Buxton, John. *Sir Philip Sidney and the English Renaissance*, 1954.
Hager, Dennis. *Dazzling Images: The Masks of Philip Sidney*, 1991.
Hamilton, A. C. *Sir Philip Sidney: A Study of His Life and Works*, 1977.
Kay, Dennis, ed. *Sir Philip Sidney: An Anthology of Modern Criticism*, 1987.
Kinney, Arthur F., ed. *Sidney in Retrospect: Selections from English Literary Renaissance*, 1988.
Kimbrough, Robert. *Sir Philip Sidney*, 1971.

Myrick, Kenneth O. *Sir Philip Sidney as a Literary Craftsman*, 1965 (second edition).
Robinson, Forest G. *The Shape of Things Known: Sidney's "Apology" in Its Philosophical Tradition*, 1972.
Weiner, Andrew. *Sir Philip Sidney and the Poetics of Protestantism*, 1978.

ROBERT P. ELLIS

*See also* Bacon; Gascoigne; Gosson; Puttenham; Renaissance and Restoration Literary Theory; Sidney

# Sincerity

The use of the term "sincerity" mirrors closely the changing conception of literature. One of the oldest literary forms, classical epic, is characterized by its use of stock formulas, such as the so-called "Homeric epithet," and is thus essentially derivative rather than sincere. This is also true of such later forms as medieval epic. Drawing on classical sources, writers in the Middle Ages used the motif of "sincerity" as a *topos* (basic theme), particularly in medieval (or "courtly") love poetry, which is anchored neither in the poet's biography nor the audience's reality but occupies a space created and defined by the act of performance. So, from today's perspective, it is largely in the Romantic period that the notion of "sincerity" becomes all-important, denoting that the poet has personally experienced what he or she describes in his or her work. William Wordsworth's definition of poetry as "emotion recollected in tranquillity" (Preface to the *Lyrical Ballads*, 1800), Thomas Carlyle's encomium of sincerity in *On Heroes* (1840), and Matthew Arnold's praise of "the high seriousness which comes from poetry" ("The Study of Poetry," 1880) illustrate not only the importance they attached to sincerity but also its apparently ethical implications.

In theories of aesthetics, the notion of sincerity is an ancient one. In Plato's *Republic* (388–368 B.C.), Socrates attacks poets (such as Homer) because of their technique of *mimesis* (imitation), thus practicing deception and conniving at *eikasia* (the crudest level of understanding) (Books II, X). Hence the very nature of poetry, Socrates argues, demands its exclusion from the state. On this account, poetry can never be "sincere," yet in Latin classical criticism, poetic form in general and rhetoric in particular are seen as a means, not an obstacle, to "sincere" expression. In his *Art of Poetry* (c. 17 B.C.), Horace advised: "If you want to move me to tears, you must first feel grief yourself," thus stating in the first century B.C. that very principle to which the Romantics were so attached. In his turn, Lev Tolstoi claimed in *What is Art?* (1898) that "art is not a handicraft, it is a transmission of feeling the artist has experienced."

From the Renaissance onward, however, a more precise conception of the aesthetic renders void the need to praise (or condemn) a work because of (its lack of) sincerity. In *An Apology for Poetry* (1595), for example, Sir Philip Sidney wrote that the poet "nothing affirmeth, and therefore never lieth." By the time of the Enlightenment, the focus in aesthetic thinking shifts even further away from the disposition of the author and toward his or her exploitation of language. *Über die neuere deutsche Literatur* (1767; on recent German literature) by Johann Gottfried Herder includes a passage that both constitutes a response to Horace and acts as a programmatic statement for "sincerity" in terms of Weimar classicism: "Poor poet! You have to paint your feelings onto a page, make them flow through a channel of black juice, you have to write so that it can be felt, and yet you have to renounce the real means of feeling: you're not supposed to soak your paper with tears so that the ink runs, you're supposed to paint your entire living soul in dead letters, and merely talk, instead of expressing." For Herder, the poet's task was to "present in an artificial way the natural expression of feeling," and to communicate tone and gesture in written language: the poet must make "everything cleave to expression," exploiting the formal and physical, as well as conceptual, aspects of language. Or as Johann Wolfgang von Goethe put it, "the work born of a true marriage between mind and medium may well surpass either parent." In *On the Aesthetic Education of Man* (1795), Friedrich Schiller made a distinction between logical semblance (which provides false information in order to deceive) and aesthetic semblance (Letter 26). Thus art is, so to speak, a lie which tells the truth. More forcefully, at the end of the nineteenth century, Oscar Wilde expressed the view in his essay "The Decay of Lying" (1891) that "art never expresses anything except itself," concluding with a rebuttal of Plato: "The final revelation is that Lying, the telling of beautiful untrue things, is the proper aim of Art." The debate over sincerity also lies behind T. E. Hulme's discussion in "Romanticism and Classicism" (1911–1912) of "freshness," which he briskly dismisses – "works of art aren't eggs" – only to reinstate: "Freshness convinces you, you feel at once that the artist was in an actual physical state." And in 1921 (in his essay "The Metaphysical Poets"), T. S. Eliot implicitly reinvoked the notion of sincerity by arguing that its opposite, a "dissociation of sensibility" (a separation of thought and feeling), had taken place in the period between the seventeenth and nineteenth centuries.

The persistence of the notion of sincerity may be gauged by Roland Barthes' allusion in *Writing Degree Zero* (1953) to René Descartes' motto *Larvatus prodeo* (I advance, pointing to my mask). In the context of discussing the novel, Barthes claims that "sincerity here needs evidently false signs to last and to be consumed." One might even see the survival of the notion of sincerity in the celebration of its absence by postmodernism. Faced with the avowed abandonment of such related notions as authenticity, to say nothing of most logico-rational categories, sincerity is replaced by the "simulacrum," and art by the advertisement, leaving Coke as indeed the only "real thing." Nevertheless, such American critics as Lionel Trilling and E. D. Hirsch have carried forward the notion of sincerity in the form of "authenticity" and "validity."

Hence the notion of sincerity, despite its long history, has come to be tainted with the suspicion of lack of theoretical sophistication. In *Theory of Literature* (1949), René Wellek and Austin Warren wrote: "As for 'sincerity' in a poem: the term seems almost meaningless." More recently, in *The Western Canon* (1994), the critic Harold Bloom has quoted with approval Wilde's (and Heinrich Heine's) view that "all bad poetry is sincere" and added: "Had I the power to do so, I would command that these words be engraved upon every gate at every university, so that each student might ponder the splendor of the insight." In conclusion, one might say that it is essential to distinguish between the sincerity of the artist, which is a moral judgment, and the sincerity of the work itself, which is an aesthetic judgment; between *being* sincere (or "authentic"), and *seeming* sincere.

## Further reading

Ball, Patricia M. "Sincerity: The Rise and Fall of a Critical Term," in *Modern Language Review*. 59 (1964).

Burris, Sidney. "Sincerity," in *The New Princeton Encyclopedia of Poetry and Poetics*, 1993.

Hirsch, E. D. *Validity in Interpretation*, 1967.

Spacks, P. M. "In Search of Sincerity," in *College English*. 29 (1968).

Trilling, Lionel. *Sincerity and Authenticity*, 1972.

Wellek, René, and Austin Warren. *Theory of Literature*, 1949.

PAUL BISHOP

# Andrei Siniavskii

("Abram Tertz")

## Russian writer and critic

**Born:** Moscow, U.S.S.R.; October 8, 1925
**Died:** Fontenay-aux-Roses, France; February 25, 1997

## Biography

Andrei Siniavskii was born in Moscow on October 8, 1925. His father had been active in the Revolution and was then high in Party favor. The young man joined the Komsomol, the Communist youth organization which provided Party leaders, but he did not fulfill the pattern, usual for advancement, of joining the Communist Party. In spite of this omission, he made a position for himself in Soviet academic life.

He served briefly in World War II, but at nineteen he began his studies in philology at Moscow University, obtaining the candidate degree (roughly a Western Ph.D.) in 1952 with a dissertation on Maksim Gor'kii. He embarked at once on an academic career, becoming a lecturer on Russian literature at the university and a senior staff member at the Gor'kii Institute of World Literature. He was a popular teacher and an active scholar, collaborating on anthologies and histories of Soviet literature. He also wrote articles and reviews for the liberal journal *Novyi mir*, defining himself as a sensitive and liberal critic.

In 1951, in one of the last of Joseph Stalin's purges, Siniavskii's father was arrested, a blow to the young writer's hopes for his own society. The death of Stalin and the revelations by Nikita Khrushchev destroying the dictator's image further challenged Siniavskii's commitment to the Revolution and the Communist dream. Boris Pasternak's image of independence toward the regime, both before and after his forced rejection of the Nobel Prize for *Doctor Zhivago*, the novel published abroad, evidently attracted Siniavskii, who had the courage to be a pallbearer at the funeral of the officially ostracized Pasternak.

In 1959 Siniavskii sent his essay *On Socialist Realism* to Paris by way of a former school friend. Thus began some seven years of a double life as the experimental satirical novelist and theorist Abram Tertz abroad and the conventional academic Siniavskii at home. The double identity was discovered and the critic, along with Iulii Daniel', brought to trial in 1966 on the grounds that three of his works aimed at "subverting or weakening the Soviet regime," a crime punishable by imprisonment and exile under article 70 of the Soviet Criminal Code. It was the first time writers were put on trial for what they had written, and the affair received international attention. Siniavskii was convicted and sentenced to seven years of hard labor and exile from intellectual centers. Nevertheless, it was during this period that Siniavskii wrote *A Voice from the Chorus* and his studies of Aleksandr Pushkin and Nikolai Gogol'. He was released after completing most of his sentence, after which he, among other dissident writers, emigrated. He settled in Paris in 1973, began teaching at the Sorbonne, and continued to write fiction, criticism, and polemical essays until his death in 1997. He founded and contributed to the literary journal *Sintaksis*. His Russian citizenship was restored in 1990.

## Influence

Siniavskii's decision to publish the essay *On Socialist Realism* abroad followed Boris Pasternak's lead in publishing *Doctor Zhivago* (1957) in Europe. Unlike Pasternak, however, Siniavskii offered the book to Western publishers under a pseudonym and never tried to publish it in the Soviet Union at all. Following the essay with the novel *The Trial Begins*, Siniavskii helped to establish the flow to the West of manuscripts unpublishable in the Soviet Union in the 1960s, making the West aware, after the long Stalinist winter, of the dissident movement and its method of secret publication inside the U.S.S.R. This system, called tamizdat, led by the 1970s to a large emigration of Soviet dissident writers and the establishment of active centers of Russian writing and criticism in Paris and other Western cities.

More important in influence was the critical theory itself. *On Socialist Realism* was the first post-Stalin public challenge of the officially imposed theory of Socialist Realism, a literary policy in place since the early 1930s. Siniavskii's attack on the resulting Soviet literature and his proposal of a "phantasmagoric" art both freed writers from the straitjacket of Socialist Realism and made possible a return to literary experiments. The two effects made accessible the exciting literature of Soviet writers heretofore written "for the drawer" and made it possible to assess much of the officially sanctioned literature as the stultifying mediocrity that it was.

Siniavskii's theoretical development since his trial and opportunities in emigration moved him to a position of influence as a sophisticated Western critic in émigré circles, while Western literary critics have yet to come to appreciate fully his penetrating work. His latest work on the cultural and intellectual history of the Soviet Union and post-Soviet experience may yet influence understanding in the West.

## Analysis

Siniavskii, in defending his publication abroad under a pseudonym, said at his trial, "Literary criticism for me was not a mask, it was my life's work, and there was always a close relationship between my work as a critic and my work as a writer." Richard Lourie, in *Letters to the Future: An Approach to Sinyavsky-Tertz* (1975), points out that Siniavskii's critical works differ in nature, however, on the basis of their circumstances of publication, ranging from scholarly editions for the Soviet Institute of World Literature and reviews and critical pieces for *Novyi mir* to the work of the pseudonymous Abram Tertz, and from highly individual publications such as *A Voice from the Chorus* to postemigration criticism for *Sintaksis* and other publications. Several of Siniavskii's shorter critical works have become available in English in the collection *For Freedom of Imagination*, but much remains available only in Russian.

Three of the academic projects especially contribute to the content of Siniavskii's critical positions. In a collaboration with A. Menshutin, he studied carefully the earliest poetry of the post revolutionary period, *Poeziia pervykh let revoliutsii, 1917–1920*. This intense work on the innovative poetry of this silver age of Soviet verse gave the critic a close knowledge of modern Russian poetry against which to measure later work. Further, his collaboration with I. Golomshtok on a study of Pablo Picasso (1960) gave him his detailed acquaintance with modernist European painting as a way into contemporary Western thought. The grotesque elements in the works of Picasso especially interested him. Beyond these two works, Siniavskii's

introductions to two selections of Pasternak's poetry present that poet's links with nature, compatible with the critic's later views, and develop a theory of metaphor growing out of a world-view similar to the poet's.

Works of the second group, those of *Novyi mir* at the time of its liberal policy during the post-Stalin thaw, allowed the development of Siniavskii's own critical position on Socialist Realism in reviews and articles attacking inferior works and appreciating the work of poets such as Anna Akhmatova and Pasternak.

Siniavskii's first great contribution, however, came with *On Socialist Realism*. The timing and political content of the work allowed its extraordinary impact, but the critical stance led to new experimentation in fictional forms. Its ironic tone was a relief in the context of a managed literature. His challenge was that the concept of Socialist Realism, made official policy in 1934 as a uniform guide for creative work in support of socialist society, had proved impossible to achieve. Siniavskii at this point ostensibly accepted the view that art should support the great Purpose emerging from the Revolution, and he said that he thought a Socialist Realist art was theoretically possible. Still, he rejected the practice of the theory as it had emerged over thirty years in the Soviet Union. The problem arose from incompatible aims in the official definition: Socialist Realism was to be "the truthful, historically correct representation of reality in its revolutionary development." This formulation meant, according to Siniavskii, that Soviet writers must combine the complex psychological realism of their beloved nineteenth-century fiction writers with descriptions of not the real, but the ideal – the society as it should be. Siniavskii linked the faith in the great Purpose of a Communist utopia to religious faith; he noted, however, that the art of religious cultures chose convention, fantasy, and imagination to express ideals. It was impossible, he said, to produce the necessary "positive hero" by the use of a psychological realism developed to depict the contradictory and purposeless "superfluous man" of the nineteenth-century Russian novel. The classicism of the eighteenth century, with its didacticism, pathos, elevated style, allegory, and decorum, Siniavskii somewhat deviously suggested, was more suited to the teleological demand. In fact, some of these classical elements appeared in Socialist Realist works; they were precisely the elements that he had attacked as absurd in reviews of mediocre Soviet works. Siniavskii proposed instead, in what he then called his artistic credo, "a phantasmagoric art, with hypotheses instead of a Purpose, an art in which the grotesque will replace realistic descriptions of ordinary life." He thought the "fantastic imagery" of E. T. A. Hoffmann and Fedor Dostoevskii, of Francisco de Goya, Marc Chagall, and Vladimir Maiakovskii could teach them "how to be truthful with the aid of the absurd and fantastic." His fiction, in the form of science fiction, fantasy, the grotesque and absurd, and ironic satire, does in fact explore this alternative to Socialist Realism.

The experience of imprisonment and exile, however, allowed developments and shifts in Siniavskii's views of literary art. *Unguarded Thoughts*, a collection of brief reflections and aphorisms somewhat like the work of Vasilii Rozanov, traces Siniavskii's facing the fact of death and his shift from a political to a religious consciousness, linked to an understanding of nature that he sees as the artist's role to penetrate. In *A Voice from the Chorus*, drawn from letters he wrote to his wife while he was in the labor camps, Siniavskii moved to a view of art harmonious with those of some advanced Western critics, though without the same critical vocabulary.

First, he saw art as self-consciously thinking about itself, "preening before a mirror," a view that suggests the preoccupation of Western art with art itself. He explored a parallel between "realistic" painting, pantomime, and narrative theory. He saw decoration and illustration of ancient texts in such a way as to emphasize the text as artifice and as object. In links with Russian Formalists, he showed how Jonathan Swift and Daniel Defoe "estrange" reality so as to let the readers see it anew, and he suggested in another passage a "verbal texture so dense that it fairly dances before the reader's eyes" in what sounds like the "impeded" style of Viktor Shklovskii and others.

In a variety of ways, he emphasized the "imprecision" and "reversibility" of texts, to demonstrate that a literary text is not static. Of Nikolai Leskov's "chaotic" style he said Leskov runs up "by accident against something which will spring to life and soar up – under the impact of so much incoherence – in 'dense and headlong disharmony.'" In reflecting on fairy tales, he showed the connection of the grotesque and the beautiful. In a contemplation about character, he questioned the nature of realism in terms suggesting "codes." (In his novels he used a very complex narrator, and applied the Russian technique of *skaz* as revealing character codes.) In discussing metaphor as arising "in response to the need for impelling it towards . . . a transfiguring . . . direction," he explained that readers notice an image only insofar as it "displaces what it is supposed to depict." He even spoke of distrust of the written word as against the spoken, but also discussed possibilities for punctuation as textual elements. Siniavskii's literary reflections in *A Voice from the Chorus* are rich indeed.

Art became for Siniavskii an integral part of all life: "It could be that particles of art are strewn like grains of salt throughout our existence and that the artist's job is to discover them, refine them, and gather them together in their pure state." Openness to these particles gets rid of the artist's self-consciousness and puts him or her in touch with the absolute; so Siniavskii sees Pushkin's genius, in the unconventional critical study *Strolls with Pushkin*. Art conquers death: "Anything that singles out the species or the individual in defiance of the levelling action of death belongs to the realm of art." In representing the transformation of his understanding of art, he said, "A man enters into art in rather the same way as he comes into the world at his birth. Thereafter everything is art for him."

With such views, Siniavskii's remarks made at a 1981 conference on Russian literature in emigration are understandable: "Politics, ethics, philosophy, even religion, and even truth or the whole fullness of truth – all this, in my subjective view, still does not save a writer. And especially politics. The very best politics is still not the criterion of artistry."

Siniavskii's bold and accurate assessment of the long rule of Socialist Realism as dominant critical theory in the Soviet Union was a breakthrough allowing imaginative innovations to emerge in his own work and that of others. His political alienation and punishment shifted his perspective and his emigration changed his context, moving his influence on Russian literature from Moscow to Paris. Still writing in Russian, Siniavskii must look to translation to carry his influence to Western criticism. His orientation was liberal and pluralistic, appealing to Western critics, and translations since the end of Soviet power have enhanced his long-term reputation. After the fall of the Soviet Union, his focus shifted to analyzing Soviet culture and the role of the intelligentsia.

## Principal criticism

*Istoriia russkoi sovetskoi literatury*, 1958, 1961
*Chto takoe sotsialisticheskii realizm*, 1959 (as Abram Tertz; *On Socialist Realism*, 1961)
*Poeziia pervykh let revoliutsii, 1917–1920*, 1964 (with A. Menshutin)
*Mysli vrasplokh*, 1966 (as Abram Tertz; *Unguarded Thoughts*, 1972)
*For Freedom of Imagination*, 1971
*Golos iz khora*, 1973 (*A Voice from the Chorus*, 1976)
"Literaturnii protsess v Rossii," 1974 ("The Literary Process in Russia," 1976)
*V teni Gogolia*, 1975 (*In the Shadow of Gogol*)
*Progulki s Pushkinym*, 1975 (*Strolls with Pushkin*, 1993)
"Opavshie listia" V. V. Rozanova, 1982

## Other major works and literary forms

Andrei Siniavskii was a multifaceted writer. He is best known in the West for his innovative novels and stories, published under the pseudonym Abram Tertz. In addition, he has published art criticism and polemical essays addressed to the Russian émigré community. After his emigration to Paris in the early 1970s, he edited the journal *Sintaksis*.

NOVELS
*Sud idet*, 1960 (as Abram Tertz; *The Trial Begins*, 1960)
*Liubimov*, 1964 (as Abram Tertz; *The Makepeace Experiment*, 1965)
"Pkhentz," 1966
*Spokoinoi nochi*, 1984 (*Goodnight*, 1989)

SHORT FICTION
*Fantasticheski povesti*, 1961 (as Abram Tertz; *Fantastic Stories*, 1963)

NONFICTION
*Pikasso*, 1960 (with I. Golomshtok)
*The Russian Intelligentsia*, 1997 (Lynn Visson, translator)
*Soviet Civilization: A Cultural History*, 1990 (Joanne Turnbull and N. Formozov, translators)

MISCELLANEOUS
*Kroshka tsores*, 1980 (as Abram Tertz; *Little Jinx*, 1992, Larry P. Joseph and Rachel May, translators, foreword Edward J. Brown)

## Further reading

Aucouturier, Michel. "Writer and Text in the Works of Abram Terc," in *Fiction and Drama in Eastern and Southeastern Europe: Evolution and Experiment in the Postwar Period*, 1980. Edited by Henrik Birnbaum and Thomas Eekman.

Dalton, Margaret. *Andrei Sinyavsky and Iiuli Daniel': Two Soviet Heretical Writers*, 1973.

Field, Andrew. "Abram Tertz's Ordeal by Mirror," in *Mysli vrasplokh*, 1966.

Glad, John. *Coversations in Exile: Russian Writers Abroad*, 1993. Interviews by Richard and Joanna Robin.

Labedz, Leopold, and Max Hayward, eds. *On Trial: The Case of Sinyavsky (Tertz) and Daniel (Arzhak)*, 1967.

Lourie, Richard. *Letters to the Future: An Approach to Sinyavsky-Tertz*, 1975.

Mihajlov, Mihajlo. "Flight from the Test Tube," in *Russian Themes*, 1968.

Nussbaum, Andrew J. "Literary Selves: The Tertz–Sinyavsky Dialogue," in *Autobiographical Statements in Twentieth-Century Russian Literature*, 1990. Edited by Jane Gary Harris.

MARTHA MANHEIM

# Karl Wilhelm Ferdinand Solger

German philosopher and critic

**Born:** Schwedt, Brandenburg, Germany; November 28, 1780
**Died:** Berlin, Prussia; October 25, 1819

## Biography

Karl Wilhelm Ferdinand Solger was born on November 28, 1780, in the town of Schwedt in northern Brandenburg. He received his preparatory education in Berlin beginning in 1795, and in 1799 he took up the study of jurisprudence at the University of Halle. Classical philology and philosophy captured his interest, however, and he transferred to the University of Jena in 1801 to study under F. W. J. Schelling (at which time he also came into contact with Johann Wolfgang von Goethe and Friedrich Schiller). In 1804 he attended Johann Gottlieb Fichte's lectures at Berlin. In that year he also completed his translation of Sophocles' *Oedipus*. Solger then fought in the struggle against Napoleon Bonaparte, resuming his literary and philosophical studies in 1806. He received his doctoral degree in 1809 and joined the faculty of the University of Frankfurt,

returning to Berlin as full professor in 1811. He married Henriette von Groeber in 1813 and was made rector of the university the next year.

Most of Solger's professional life was spent as a professor in Berlin. There, he lectured in aesthetics and speculative philosophy. He was determined to revitalize the genre of the dialogue as a vehicle of philosophical inquiry, an intention which led to the publication of *Erwin: Vier Gespräche über das Schöne und die Kunst* (Erwin: four conversations on beauty and art) in 1815. In Berlin, Solger enjoyed the society of Ludwig Tieck, Friedrich Schleiermacher, and the philologist Freidrich von der Hagen. He developed poor health early, however, and died on October 25, 1819, not yet forty years old.

## Influence

Solger's philosophy, which unites transcendence and immanence in a universal continuum, is often considered the link between the nature philosophy of his teacher Schelling, the teaching of Johann Gottlieb Fichte, and the world system of G. W. F. Hegel. In the field of literary theory, however, his influence is felt most directly, not in sustained critical attention to his own writings beyond the nineteenth century but in the works of his friend, the dramatist and prose writer Ludwig Tieck, who was sympathetic to Solger's concept of irony, as were other Romantics. Solger is the only serious philosopher to follow Friedrich Schlegel as a systematizer of the new Romantic poetics. His highly sophisticated arguments suggest that irony allows the artist through fantasy to recognize and resolve the dichotomy between the "real" world of ideas beyond the individual ego and the imperfect manifestations of ideas in art. Irony is for Solger the transcendent, unifying principle in all art, even tragedy, and it was this idea of "tragic irony" that influenced German dramatists such as Friedrich Hebbel, the most notable early proponent of poetic realism.

## Analysis

Solger's aesthetic theory represents an attempt to resolve dualities and reconcile contradictions in a unified vision of art, religion, and philosophy. In his emphasis on subjective experience and revelation one notes the influence of the German mystics, while the writings of Benedictus de Spinoza furnished inspiration for Solger's conception of Being as an orderly continuum virtually identical with God.

Solger proceeds from a basically Platonic assumption: that there are two distinct realms of knowledge – the realm of mere appearance and the realm of higher spiritual or divine truth. Yet these two realms are ultimately only relations of one and the same reality, or ground of being, for appearance itself is revelation and points to the divine. Revelation, or manifestation, which includes the phenomenal world and thus by necessity the creations of art, is an aspect of what has been called the "dialectical unity" of the universal and the particular in Solger's thinking. The divine takes physical form in the revealed world, and in a similar way the higher Idea, which is antithetical to forms of common perception and cognition, becomes manifest when individual consciousness reveals it through creative activity. This process of creation is thus a unifying process, resolving the opposition of perfect Idea (the sphere of the divine) and imperfect cognition (the empirical).

The activity of consciousness unifies the particular and the universal, the phenomenal and the absolute. Artistic creation makes the realm of ideas, or spirit, manifest and perceivable in the world of appearances, and the result, manifest beauty, shares both in immanence and transcendence, as do expressions of truth and the good.

For the antithetical transcendent and immanent realms Solger sought a synthesis, whereas Hegel located the absolute within the phenomenal world and made the spiritual purely immanent. Solger's synthesis is reflected in the symbol, which is the physical manifestation of the Idea. In the symbol the physical and spiritual cannot be demarcated or separated; the symbol actually is what it signifies. As in the case of visual or literary allegory, all art is symbolic.

Concerning this level of synthesis and its relation to subjective experience, Solger makes his original and most interesting contributions to aesthetic theory. Solger's style is, however, not only demanding but also unappealingly static, and it has inhibited the general diffusion of his ideas. His best-known work, *Erwin*, is an ambitious attempt to revive dialogue as a genre of philosophical prose, but it suffers from obvious artificiality and is occasionally so hypotactic that it rivals the difficulty of both Hegel and Immanuel Kant. In addition, most scholars point out the necessity of studying Solger's more philosophical writings, *Philosophische Gespräche* (1817) and the posthumously published lectures on aesthetics, *Vorlesungen über Ästhetik* (1829), for example, in order to comprehend fully the issues discussed in *Erwin*, a book in which three of the four characters speak with the voices of Fichte, Schelling, and Solger, as they engage in a lengthy and arcane discussion of the aesthetic concerns specific to the period.

In his day Solger was known for distinguishing between two aspects of imagination, as Schelling had. Solger wrote about two categories, *Phantasie* and *Einbildungskraft*, or fantasy and imagination. *Phantasie* is a faculty that might be best described as "ideational imagination," the spontaneous and active realm of ideas, whereas *Einbildungskraft* refers to the manipulative or directive power that endows the conception with form or representation and thus leads to physical manifestation in art. An additional distinction in Solger's view of the subjective process of artistic creation should be noted: Solger separated *Verstand*, understanding, or reasoned thought, and *Witz*, which corresponds approximately to the English "wit." *Verstand* is the analytic power of consciousness, the antithesis of the spontaneous ideational activity of *Phantasie*, and necessary for art – free imagination alone cannot create works of consequence. As

the Idea becomes part of empirical reality through artistic activity, contemplation is also at work. In Solger's controversial formulation, the activity of *Witz* is an essentially negative process, dissolving the antitheses of universal and particular, of Idea and manifestation, to a point where neither antithesis exists. The essence of art is found in this moment of dissolution, when the Idea by becoming reality also ceases to exist as Idea, destroying itself – which is, in turn, the point at which "artistic irony" arises. Thus, irony is not merely rhetorical detachment but a part of the process of art.

In one of his last writings, a review of August Wilhelm Schlegel's *Vorlesungen über dramatische Kunst und Literatur* (1809–1811; *A Course of Lectures on Dramatic Art and Literature*, 1815) in 1819, Solger attacked Schlegel and his brother Friedrich for their inability to recognize this concept of irony as the dissolution of the contradiction between imperfect reality and perfect Idea and, moreover, to appreciate the evidence for irony in tragedy as well as comedy. Clearly irony is present in the relationship of the audience to the players in a comedy – it is essential that the audience knows or thinks it knows more about the actions and entanglements of the players than the players themselves know. Yet this light irony of "mood" is not what Solger intends. Solger's irony exists on an ontological level beyond the mere techniques of dramatic humor or even, as with Tieck and the Romantics, the destruction of the illusion of art through the interruption of action on the stage (authorial commentary and so on), although these surely grow out of the ironic character of artistic creation.

By suggesting that irony permeates tragedy, Solger endowed unenvisaged irony with a profundity previously unknown. Accordingly, the genre of tragedy, in resolving the conflicts to which the individual is prone, requires the death and transfiguration of the individual in much the same way that the process of aesthetic creation itself requires the dissolution of the spiritual and perfect in the empirical and thus the imperfect.

Solger's concept of irony received considerable attention in the nineteenth century. Hegel acknowledges his debt to Solger but objects that the idea of dialectic dissolution in irony represents a kind of "absolute negation" of the infinite in the material. Søren Kierkegaard, on the other hand, would later argue in his *Am begrebet ironi med stadigt hensyn til Socrates* (1841; concept of irony with respect to Socrates) that Solger's idea ultimately reduces all creative acts, even divine creation, to an ironic diversion or pastime.

In his reply to August Wilhelm Schlegel's arguments on dramatic art and literature, however, Solger emphasized the affirmative power of irony, particularly in the aesthetic experience of tragedy, where the mood created by the action onstage reveals in the vanity and limitations of human life not senselessness but the very presence of the divine or transcendent. Nor is this mood necessarily absent in comedy; it is to be found in the work of Aristophanes as well as

William Shakespeare. Schlegel's belief that the ancients celebrated the senses more openly and were less "melancholy," less conscious of human inadequacy and sinfulness, than modern writers was for Solger a false distinction. Just as Solger identified a mood of irony in comedy and in tragedy, he also found "a certain sadness" as well as cheerfulness (*Heiterkeit*) in all forms of art. Drama, in particular, exhibits art's capacity for allowing one to experience the pain and sadness of mortal existence. Yet in drama one could also experience the destruction of earthly contradictions and the ironic transcendence of the immediate world.

Heinrich Heine, in *Die romantische Schule* (1836; *The Romantic School*, 1876), praised Solger as superior to Schlegel in critical acumen. Solger's relatively early death, however, confined his literary production to two books. Tieck, with whom Solger had planned to collaborate on a new literary journal, went to great lengths, along with Friedrich von Raumer, to collect and publish correspondence and other writings so as to preserve the memory of Solger, and Solger's student K. W. L Heyse contributed to this cause by reconstructing the Berlin lectures on aesthetics, published as *Vorlesungen über Ästhetik*, which contain the essential positions of Solger's literary theory.

## Principal criticism
*Erwin: Vier Gespräche über das Schöne und die Kunst*, 1815, 1971
*Nachgelassene Schriften und Briefwechsel*, 1826 (2 volumes)
*Vorlesungen über Ästhetik*, 1829

## Other major works and literary forms
Karl Wilhelm Ferdinand Solger is known primarily for his contributions to philosophy and aesthetic theory. As a young man, however, he tried his hand at translation from the Greek and published an edition of Sophocles' *Oedipus* in 1804. He also wrote reviews of works by Friedrich Schiller, Johann Wolfgang von Goethe, Zacharias Werner, and August Wilhelm Schlegel.

NONFICTION
*Philosophische Gespräche*, 1817
*Tieck and Solger: The Complete Correspondence*, 1933

TRANSLATION
*Oedipus*, 1804 (of Sophocles' play)

## Further reading
Decher, Friedhelm. *Die Ästhetik K. W. F. Solgers*, 1994.
Hegel, G. W. F. "Über Solger nachgelassene Schriften und Briefwechsel," in *Jahrbücher für wissenschaftliche Kritik*, 1828.
Heller, J. E. *Solgers Philosophies der ironischen Dialektik*, 1928.
Henckmann, Wolfhart. Introduction to *Erwin: Vier Gespräche über das Schöne und die Kunst*, 1971.
Wellek, René. "Solger," in *A History of Modern Criticism: 1750–1950*. Vol. 2, *The Romantic Age*, 1955.

MARK R. McCULLOH

*See also* Hegel; Heine; Kant; Romanticism; Schelling; Schlegel, F.

# Susan Sontag
American essayist, critic, and novelist

**Born:** New York, New York; January 16, 1933

## Biography
Born on January 16, 1933, in New York City, Susan Sontag grew up in Tucson, Arizona, and Los Angeles, California. Always precocious – she began her writing career at about the age of eight – she entered the University of California at Berkeley when she was only fifteen. A year later, she transferred to the University of Chicago, where she took a B.A. in philosophy in 1951, after marrying social psychologist Philip Rieff, with whom she had a son, born in 1952. Sontag went on to Harvard University, where she took an M.A. in philosophy in 1957, and where she was a Ph.D. candidate from 1955 to 1957. She also studied at St. Anne's College, Oxford, and at the University of Paris. She and Rieff were divorced in 1959.

Sontag has held a number of academic positions, serving as lecturer in philosophy at City College of New York and at Sarah Lawrence, as instructor in religion at Columbia University, and as writer-in-residence at Rutgers University. The recipient of numerous prestigious fellowships, among them the Guggenheim and the Rockefeller, she has also received awards for individual works, including the National Book Critics Circle Award for *On Photography* in 1977. In 1959 Sontag served briefly as an editor at *Commentary*, and she has continued her association as consultant and contributor with a number of periodicals, most notably *The New York Review of Books* and *Partisan Review*.

## Influence
The emphasis of Sontag's critical endeavors has been on modern culture, which she has attempted to analyze through a multitude of approaches, first aesthetic – through literature, art, film, and photography – then, in a sense, philosophical and moral – through politics and through culture as a social phenomenon. She gained her reputation initially as an essayist with a penchant for overstatement and an inclination toward provoking controversy, and these same characteristics are apparent in her explorations of other modes of expression, for example, in her equation of Communism and Fascism during a 1982 rally for the Polish trade union movement, Solidarity. Such commentaries have garnered for Sontag a large measure of harsh criticism, but even her detractors have been forced to acknowledge the originality, seriousness, and high intelligence of her work.

## Analysis
Although it was not her first published work, the appearance of *Against Interpretation and Other Essays* in 1966 occasioned Susan Sontag's debut on the American cultural

scene, in which she immediately became an influential presence. The book is a coherent collection of meditations on a wide variety of subjects, ranging from anthropology to film, but the two most frequently cited selections are the eponymous essay and her "Notes on 'Camp.'"

Although seemingly different in their concerns, "Against Interpretation" and "Notes on 'Camp,'" taken together, helped to define the territory Sontag made peculiarly her own in subsequent years. Citing examples from among her favorite practitioners of contemporary art – Alain Resnais, Alain Robbe-Grillet, and Ingmar Bergman – she declares her credo: interpretation, with its concentration on meaning and its dissection of form and content, violates art. "Against Interpretation" then ends with a characteristically provocative statement couched, also characteristically, in loaded language: "In place of a hermeneutics we need an erotics of art."

What follows helps to elaborate Sontag's meaning, but nowhere else in the volume is her theory so memorably and entertainingly explored as in "Notes on 'Camp,'" which helped to define both a term and a branch of aesthetics:

Camp is the consistently aesthetic experience of the world. It incarnates a victory of "style" over "content," "aesthetics" over "morality," of irony over tragedy.

The experiences of Camp are based on the great discovery that the sensibility of high culture has no monopoly upon refinement. Camp asserts that good taste is not simply good taste; that there exists, indeed, a good taste of bad taste.

Camp taste is, above all, a mode of enjoyment, of appreciation – not judgment.

With pronouncements such as those quoted above, Sontag ran the risk of becoming high priestess of the avant-garde. A collection of criticism that soon followed, however, *Styles of Radical Will* (1969), signaled Sontag's shift in interest from literature to film, a shift certainly anticipated in "Notes on 'Camp'": "And movie criticism . . . is probably the greatest popularizer of Camp taste today, because most people still go to the movies in a high-spirited and unpretentious way."

Sontag's long-standing belief that film is the most alive, most interesting form of contemporary artistic expression led her to write and direct three screenplays, *Duet for Cannibals* (1969), *Brother Carl* (1972), *Unguided Tour* (1983), and the documentary *Promised Lands* (1974). Throughout her career as a filmmaker, she protested that her interest lay not in writing the screenplays, but in directing and editing the films, which allowed her a structural, rather than critical, method of expression. She has made the same observation about her fiction, but as

numerous commentators have remarked, her intellectual rigor is better suited to the essay form than to film or fiction. Sontag's forays into the novel, *The Benefactor* (1963) and *Death Kit* (1967), have both been exercises in the experimental New Novel mode, where emphasis on elaborate, apparently gratuitous, structures and details replaces character delineation and plot development. Sontag's novels are extensions of her critical theory, stressing the inseparability of form and content, but neither they nor her 1978 collection of short fiction, *I, etcetera*, has been as well received as her nonfiction writing. But *The Volcano Lover* (1992) constituted both a popular and critical success, winning her a new audience for her fiction.

In 1977 Sontag translated her interest in film into an interest in what William Gass has called "the act of photography," publishing *On Photography*, a collection of essays on photographers such as Alfred Stieglitz and Diane Arbus. Despite its title, *On Photography* is notable for its lack of illustration and for the infrequency with which it treats individual images. Indeed, photographers who reviewed her book complained of her lack of interest in interpreting photographs. They took her to task for pursuing what was basically an intellectual approach to the phenomenon of photography. This was exactly Sontag's point: "I came to realize that I wasn't writing about photography so much as I was writing about modernity, about the way we are now. The subject of photography is a form of access to contemporary ways of thinking and feeling. And writing about photography is like writing about the world."

It is not surprising, then, that the greatest influence on her view of photography is that of Walter Benjamin, who is celebrated for his ground-breaking essay, "Das Kunstwerk in Zeitalter seiner Reproduzierbarkeit" (1936; "The Work of Art in the Age of Mechanical Reproduction," 1968). In that essay, Benjamin argues that the way works of art have come to be replicated in photography and film had a fundamental impact on the very definition of art in the twentieth century. Like Benjamin, Sontag discusses technical devices, such as the close-up, to suggest that the human personality has been explored with an intimacy and psychological complexity unavailable to artists in previous centuries. At the same time, the mechanical quality of the reproduction has raised disturbing questions about the uniqueness of the work of art and about the way in which human identity has been transformed by the very instruments that were intended simply to convey it.

*On Photography* is characteristic of Sontag's method in that she convincingly summons up one's sense of the power photographs have over ways of seeing, yet photographs per se, as physical objects, scarcely have a place in her criticism. As Cary Nelson has noted:

When we pair that decision not to quote and explicate with her commitment to evoke her own experience of her subjects, we reach the curious conclusion that the things she describes constitute in each case an informing absence at the core of her essays. To be convinced by her analysis of a work is to be led to yearn for what is not "there" in her prose.

Surely this proposition goes to the heart of Sontag's success as an essayist and comparative failure as a fictionist. By refraining from subsuming the work at issue in her essays in her own pronounced style, she allows the work to continue its own existence, to retain a sense of immediacy. Paradoxically, however, in refusing to supply what T. S. Eliot called an adequate "objective correlative" (adequate motivation) in her fiction – despite a surfeit of detail – Sontag leaves her reader only with a sense of emptiness, an intuition of fairly meaningless form without substance.

Sontag's next major book was an extended essay, *Illness as Metaphor* (1978), which was based in part on her own experience with cancer. Reviewer Peter Brooks found it to be marked by a "sense of incompletion" that is the "price of its polemical vigor" and also Sontag's primary virtue as a writer: "Sontag has always carried out with a rare penetration, a capacity to turn one metaphor against another with the polemic thrust that lays bare the unrecognized cultural assumption." If Brooks is accurate in his assessment, Sontag has achieved in her own writing what her essays prescribe, and *Illness as Metaphor* may be the best illustration of her art. *Illness as Metaphor* takes as its subject the contemporary scourge of cancer and its predecessor, tuberculosis, and shows how pernicious can be the results of reading too much into a phenomenon. Sontag's message in this book is in essence the same one as that in *Against Interpretation and Other Essays*: links between consciousness and the phenomenal world are illusory; to search for higher meaning can be to engage in a deadly game that murders art and life. *AIDS and its Metaphors* (1989) was less well received – in part because it added little to Sontag's earlier book on disease, and in part because it failed to address the concerns of gay readers.

Alfred Kazin has accused Sontag of being a "café intellectual" inhabiting a rarefied atmosphere, but this characterization seems wide of the mark. There can be no question about Sontag's intellectualization of culture and society, but she thereby arrives at some stunningly original truths that help to clarify the modern condition. *Illness as Metaphor*, for example, does not toy with the idea of cancer, but suggests that civilization as a whole does so. While her observations may not help find a clinical cure for the disease, they might help remove some psychological obstacles to doing so, or at least to coping with the implications of the disease.

Sontag is frequently criticized for employing inflammatory language to approach controversial subjects, but her methods seem to grow out of a passionate involvement with her subjects and a desire to engender a similar concern in

her readers. If she often dwells on reflections of society rather than on its conspicuous ills (the opening chapter of *Illness as Metaphor* is titled "In Plato's Cave"), her observations nevertheless carry a great weight of immediacy for most contemporary thinkers. Sontag is clearly heir to an honored tradition of cultural essay writing and successor to such figures as Ralph Waldo Emerson and Matthew Arnold.

## Principal criticism

*Against Interpretation and Other Essays*, 1966
*Styles of Radical Will*, 1969
*On Photography*, 1977
*Illness as Metaphor*, 1978
*Under the Sign of Saturn*, 1980
*AIDS and its Metaphors*, 1989

## Other major works and literary forms

The collections of essays and extended essays on social and cultural subjects cited above constitute Susan Sontag's primary contribution to the critical debate. Sontag has, however, made an effort to change the focus of public attention to her work in other genres. In addition to her critical output as an essayist, she has published dozens of pieces of short fiction and prose nonfiction in periodicals. She has published three works of fiction, *The Benefactor* (1963), *Death Kit* (1967), and *The Volcano Lover* (1992), and a collection of short fiction, *I, etcetera* (1978). One of her ongoing interests has been film; she has directed, from her own screenplays, the films *Duet for Cannibals* (1969), *Brother Carl* (1972), *Promised Lands* (1974), and *Unguided Tour* (1983). She has also directed plays by Luigi Pirandello and Milan Kundera, and she has published one play, *Alice in Bed* (1993).

NOVELS
*The Benefactor*, 1963
*Death Kit*, 1967
*The Volcano Lover*, 1992

SHORT FICTION
*I, etcetera*, 1978

SCREENPLAYS
*Duet for Cannibals*, 1969
*Brother Carl*, 1972
*Promised Lands*, 1974
*Unguided Tour*, 1983

PLAYS
*Alice in Bed*, 1993

NONFICTION
*Trip to Hanoi*, 1968

EDITED TEXTS
*Selected Writings*, by Antonin Artaud, 1976
*A Barthes Reader*, 1982

MISCELLANEOUS
*A Susan Sontag Reader*, 1982

## Further reading

Bruss, Elizabeth. *Beautiful Theories: The Spectacle of Discourse in Contemporary Criticism*, 1982.

Gass, William H. "A Different Kind of Art," in *The New York Times Book Review*. LXXXII (December 18, 1977), pp. 7, 30–31.

Gilman, Richard. *The Confusion of Realms*, 1970.

Hickman, Larry. "Experiencing Photographs: Sontag, Barthes, and Beyond," in *Journal of American Culture*. VII (Winter, 1984), pp. 69–73.

Kennedy, Liam. *Susan Sontag: Mind as Passion*, 1995.

Nelson, Cary. "Soliciting Self-Knowledge: The Rhetoric of Susan Sontag's Criticism," in *Critical Inquiry*. VI (Summer, 1980), pp. 707–726.

Paglia, Camille. *Vamps and Tramps*, 1994.

Poague, Leland. *Conversations with Susan Sontag*, 1995.

Sayres, Sohnya. *Susan Sontag: Elegiac Modernist*, 1990.

Smith, Sharon. *Women Who Make Movies*, 1975.

Solotaroff, Theodore. *The Red Hot Vacuum*, 1970.

CARL ROLLYSON
LISA PADDOCK

*See also* American Literary Theory: Twentieth Century

# Wole Soyinka

## Nigerian playwright, poet, and novelist

**Born:** Abeokuta, Nigeria; July 13, 1934

## Biography

Akinwande Oluwole Soyinka was born on July 13, 1934, at Abeokuta, in Western Nigeria. The son of Ijegba parents who were both Christian, Soyinka sustained Christian influences throughout his early life and through his education in the British school system. He began his undergraduate study at University College, Ibadan (where he studied from 1952 to 1954), completed it at the University of Leeds with honors in English in 1957, and did some work toward an M.A. before devoting his time to drama. What affected him more than Christianity or Western culture, however, was his Yoruba heritage with its indigenous rituals and practices. He studied Yoruba mythology as a scholar, developed a theory of tragedy from it, and has used it as the basis and inspiration of his fiction, poetry, and drama. It has also motivated him as a critic to defend the "repleteness" of African world-views.

After Nigeria's independence in 1960, Soyinka returned home to take up his career as dramatist, director, and professor of literature, but he continued to make frequent trips abroad as a visiting lecturer and playwright. At home, he became engaged in political controversy and skirmishes with government figures, resulting in his arrest and trial for a pirate radio broadcast (he was acquitted), his detention in prison from August, 1967, to October, 1970 (for his position on the Biafran War), and his self-imposed exile

(from 1971 to 1975) because of political disagreement with Nigeria's head of state. While Soyinka was often critical of regimes in power, his bitterness became intense during and after his detention, darkening his poetry, his plays, and his novel *Season of Anomy*. Soyinka has received several significant awards, most notably the Nobel Prize for Literature in 1986.

## Influence

Soyinka is one of several prominent contemporary African writers – including Chinua Achebe and Ngugi wa Thiong'o – who have devoted some of their energies to literary criticism. It is a natural complement considering their sociopolitical situation. Their literary works themselves are attempts at "racial self-retrieval," as Soyinka calls it. Their criticism combines an evaluation of other African writing, a defense of their own, and a raising of their evaluations to theoretical and philosophical levels. The criticism is not purely "literary"; it proposes to clarify what Africa is and what it needs. Of all the well-known African critics, Soyinka is the most academic and philosophical. If anything, his intellectualism has, in many instances, alienated his peers and the younger generation rather than influenced them, but in the long run his eclectic, comprehensive, independent (rather than ideological) approach to African culture and art will have its effect. Soyinka himself would wish the effect to be genuine self-critical debate among critics, less literary criticism and more unrestricted creative expression.

## Analysis

Soyinka has called literary criticism, as it is often practiced, both "an incestuous activity" and a "whoring profession." He speaks from the point of view of a creative writer, an African writer, who has frequently been the object of criticism for a supposed failure to understand adequately his responsibility as an African spokesman. Soyinka has responded not only by continuing to write according to his own creative insights but also by becoming a literary critic himself. His criticism is both theoretical and practical. It ranges from stylistic and linguistic analysis to myth theory, ritual, and generic distinctions. It covers, and emphasizes at different times, the four critical approaches that M. H. Abrams outlined in *The Mirror and the Lamp: Romantic Theory and the Critical Tradition* (1953) – mimetic, affective, expressive, and objective – although Soyinka is reluctant to accept art as having an objective existence independent of the people, the culture, and the language that create it.

While it would be difficult, and unfair, to pigeonhole Soyinka's criticism, certain guiding principles do underlie it. *Myth, Literature, and the African World* is his only book-length critical work, but during his career he has made numerous statements in published articles and speeches. His views have developed and the emphases have shifted, but what he regards as the purpose of both literature and criticism has not changed. They are, at their best, in the service of one's culture and of humanity. The writer is a laborer and, like other laborers, offers a product. Soyinka would like to convince the public and governments that the product has value essential to society. If Soyinka has a complaint against most critics and some writers it is that they do not treat literature as a "cultural" necessity; they misunderstand the nature of artistic creation, of audience response, and of literature's contribution to society's health.

Those critics who complain about Soyinka as a writer do so on the grounds of "social conditioning": his Western education has corrupted him, tempted him to join the ranks of experimental aesthetes who are more concerned with form than with substance, who champion complexity over direct communication. Soyinka's rebuttal has turned that issue into a frontal assault against his critics. It is they who do not understand traditional African literature or African culture. African art, often described as "holistic, animist, protean, totalist," is, according to Soyinka, "governed by a creative contextualism – that which, while proceeding from its context, enlarges and extends it even as it faithfully explores its initial bearings." This "creative contextualism" requires immersion in one's own culture. Soyinka's critics have only a superficial notion of the creative process; they do not understand what it is to be an African writer, or even a writer. Ironically, they themselves judge the African writer by Western standards. Soyinka applies the criterion of "social conditioning" to the critics, an application that needs, according to Soyinka, to be made more often. The critic should not escape criticism.

Under the heading "aesthetic illusions," Soyinka identifies certain groups of literary critics of African literature who pretend to defend authentic African values but who in fact represent Western orientations. Soyinka is best known for his attacks on "negritude," a theoretical position taken by writers, critics, and cultural theorists to define the African character. Soyinka contends that negritude may have made its contributions to the development of modern Africa but that it is essentially a reaction to European conceptions, a positing of the African as mainly emotional and intuitive in contrast to the European's technical and abstract thought rather than a true definition. Soyinka points to the fact that foreigners and Africans exiled on foreign soil conceived the theory. As an artificial construct, it cannot help identify African literature or generate new literature.

In defense, Soyinka coined the term "neo-Tarzanism" to describe some African critics. Again, while pretending to describe characteristics of authentic African poetry, critics of African literature further a composite of an "American hard sell" reductionist mentality – a "poetics of limited sensibilities" which favors extreme positions for short-term effect – and a contemporary version of the old "noble savage" idea, which Soyinka calls "beatific pristinism." It sees Africa through the naive haze of a Tarzan film. Finally, Soyinka attacks the functionalists who have condemned him for his concern with aesthetic values. While they appear to be leftist, even Marxist, in their insistence on literature as a social instrument, they are actually motivated by the "Euramerican puritanic ethic"; they are "missionary salvationists" who have taken their missionaries seriously and have accepted the verdict of evangelical Christianity that "aesthetic functionalism is sinful."

In all these attacks, Soyinka has turned the theory of social conditioning back on his accusers. These critics have not been self-critical; they do not know their own minds. They do not realize that their own training has carried them away from an authentic African spirit. In an essay written in 1981, "The Critic and Society: Barthes, Leftocracy, and Other Mythologies," Soyinka gives this approach a linguistic twist, as he uses Roland Barthes and Ferdinand de Saussure to dissect the language of these Western-oriented critics in order to determine what their remarks really signify. By using the language of their own class, these critics exploit a piece of literature "for the edification of a microsociety," in order to develop their own reputation among their academic peers. These petit bourgeois "leftocrats" take "a work of art . . . a value of labor . . . without any self-criticism" and "appropriate [it] to ends other than the ends for which the work is produced and marketed."

Lest this attack on would-be revolutionary critics seems to resemble too closely, even in language, that of a Marxist, Soyinka clearly differentiates himself from Barthes' ideology. He does pay respect to Barthes' own honesty: Barthes knows that he is, paradoxically, a "leftist scholar, a would-be academic popularizer who, however, does not employ a 'popular' *langue*." Unlike the others, he is self-critical. Still, Soyinka takes issue with Barthes' argument that language is totally historical and therefore not only helpless but also obtrusive in the search for "essence." Barthes' purpose is to explode the bourgeois assumption that its language communicates essences rather than perceptions. Soyinka applauds Barthes' effort but would argue that there is real "experiencing": even if a mountain is not always what European literature and travel posters would have it be, real human beings living on the mountain know from experience what it is. It is those experienced truths to which literature must return. Sadism, "that predilection of certain human beings to inflict horrid pains – mental, physical, economic, or psychological – on others," is a fact of experience, whatever word signifies the fact. Certain ideas, such as power and love, exist, and music reminds humans that "subterranean structures of feelings" exist. It is "a language of man's aesthetic strivings, but one which reinforces, yet resists, the language of other forms of artistic production, it leads remorselessly to a value which 'radical' theories of art attempt to deny and even deride." It "does not pretend to express *everything*, but insists that there is everything to be expressed, comprehended, embraced, and ravaged."

This objection to Barthes' bias points to a tenet crucial to Soyinka's own creative practices and to what he regards as essential to the future of art in Africa. It underlies his objections to the various ideologies that other critics bring to African literature. Ideology itself is the danger:

> The correlation of artistic forms and idioms with ideological precepts of any one persuasion is full of pitfalls which leave the agent or arbitrator dangerously exposed – and, ironically, the greater the agent's intellective faith, the worse his exposure. Despite all evasions and rationalizations, those penalties of willed adherence to compact systems of ideas, the language of art and creativity continues to pose problems beyond the merely linguistic or semiological.

The history of art is a history of "*langues* of individual art forms" that have attempted "to make *meaning*." The key word for Soyinka is "change." Art does not live by ideological preconceptions. It looks at reality honestly; it records human beings responding to their experiences. Bad criticism tries to dictate to the artist what he or she must do. Bad art follows such dictates. When asked to define what an African writer is, Soyinka responds with the question "What is a writer?" A writer must be allowed the freedom to respond to his or her own cultural context as it is honestly perceived. The test of success will be the depth of the writer's vision. The answer is not to abandon the search for meaning. Writes Soyinka, "The solution is to begin by creating a new language."

Soyinka's own social conditioning within the African setting has affected significantly his critical theory. Not only was his early childhood spent largely within a traditional, non-Western framework but he also lived at a time when Africa was under great pressures from the West to alter its traditional beliefs. His parents were Christian, as was his education under the British system. He turned to biblical sources for some of his imagery and myth, if not his beliefs, and to Western authors from Greek to modern European and American for stylistic techniques and mythical and philosophical constructs. Friedrich Nietzsche's interpretation of Greek culture obviously impressed him, as did Romantic revolutionary angst and ritual theory. He was attracted by stylistic complexities in writers from Gerard Manley Hopkins to James Joyce and William Faulkner. These influences had a tremendous effect on his creative writing, but in his critical statements he makes clear that what he draws from these sources, especially those that he finds compatible with his own cultural temperament, is not imitation. He finds them useful because they resemble essential elements in his own Yoruba mythology and artistic tradition.

As much as Soyinka is a student of the Western tradition, he is even more a devotee of his own. His criticism, like his literature, draws in particular from the story of Ogun within that mythology. It gives him a base from which to describe and evaluate foreign cultural conceptions. It is the paradigm that enables him confidently to reject Marxist ideological criticism as not truly revolutionary and hence not truly beneficial to society. If Soyinka goes to other cultures for his sources it is not because he needs to fill a gap in his own. He insists that complexity is traditionally a part of African art, including oral poetry and drama; it is not the naive, primitive expression that westernized observers, the neo-Tarzanists and negritudinists, conceive it to be. African art has traditionally been eclectic and assimilative; it has thrived on dialectic and synthesis. The Ogun myth is essentially one of challenge and change, not of stasis. Soyinka's criticism advocates a literature that is revolutionary.

Ogun, the central figure in the revolutionary concept, is the Yoruba god who first dared to enter the abyss that separated human beings from their gods, the dead, and the unborn. Ogun shaped a bridge from the chaotic elements to span the abyss. This act of courage for the benefit of gods and human beings alike risked extinction, disintegration of the personality; an act of will reasserted identity, and Ogun, the god of the forge, henceforth became the symbol of active creativity, the warrior god of poetry. He then became the symbol of the destructive principle as well, when he, in a drunken stupor, killed in battle both friend and foe. The central action, with the reminder of an underlying chaotic potential, became the basis of Soyinka's thinking about art, in its psychological (personal) and ritual (communal) aspects.

The poet-artist, as a "true devotee" of Ogun, faces the abyss, "knows, understands and penetrates the god's anguish." His "inner being encounters the precipice" and, as he feels his identity disintegrating, he saves himself by "channelling the dark torrent into the plastic light of poetry and dance." In addition to this definition of the poetic act, Soyinka also defines literary forms in terms of ritual action, specifically as reenactment of Ogun's quest. Poetry constitutes "the celebrative aspects of [Ogun's] resolved crisis." The profundity of the poem depends on the degree of the poet's awareness of the abyss – the danger of disintegration and the need of will to achieve wholeness. Ritual drama is a transcription of the Ogun experience: it is "an integral part of man's constant efforts to master the immensity of the cosmos with his minuscule self." The protagonist in any drama that draws from ritual experience (Soyinka thinks that the distinction between ritual and drama is "largely artificial") enters the abyss, the inner world of "primal reality," and brings back its essence which he or she communicates to "the choric participants of the rites – the community." The "mythic inner world" is real; it is "the cumulative history and empirical observations of the community." The stage is literally the cosmic setting for the confrontation. "All profound drama," Soyinka argues, transpires in "a complete, hermetic universe of forces . . .

or being." The distinction that Soyinka makes between epic and tragedy lies in the treatment of Ogun's journey. The epic "celebrates the victory of the human spirit over forces inimical to self-extension." Tragedy, on the other hand, is more realistic: the unknown realm of essences is a real threat, the challenge of confrontation an ultimate test. The ritual protagonist is to the "transitional gulf" as the tragic hero is to "his contemporary reality." Comedy and the grotesque Soyinka defines as the evasion of cosmic horror.

These definitions, resonating with Nietzschean tones, are clearly speculative, highly individualistic, and imprecise. Yet the imprecision about forms should not be surprising, since Soyinka always addresses spiritual dimensions and actual effects on an audience more than "speculative projections of the nature of literature," "the ontology of the idiom" being "subservient to the burden of its concerns." He prefers to define literature in terms of its "social vision," which he specifies as a "genre." The great danger in society is "the entrenchment of the habitual." Literature of social vision allows for "extension," in that literature should be not only "the reflection of experience" but also the extension of experience. Ogun's confrontation with the gulf in his struggle for harmony provides the rationale for the genre:

A creative concern which conceptualizes or extends actuality beyond the purely narrative, making it reveal realities beyond the immediately attainable, a concern which upsets orthodox acceptances in an effort to free society of historical or other superstitions, these are qualities possessed by literature of social vision.

Such a theory of art seems especially appropriate for a continent in a stage of rapid transition, with ancient traditions and new ideologies vying for power.

Even though the myth on which Soyinka's thinking is based is African, he finds parallels in other mythologies, of which his reading of Nietzsche's Apollonian-Dionysian balancing act is the prime example. Perhaps it is the presence of such divine/human confrontations with chaos outside Africa that gives Soyinka confidence when he goes outside African literature to apply his theory. In any case, he does make such applications. In a speech delivered at the University of Washington, "Drama and the Revolutionary Ideal," Soyinka focuses on leftist doctrinaire literature in support of the proletarian revolution. His main complaint against the authors is that they are bourgeois intellectuals who do not understand the actual cultural situation of their audience. They impose on their plots false resolutions based on closet bourgeois values. Ironically, a play that Soyinka saw produced in Cuba, Edward Albee's *Who's Afraid of Virginia Woolf?* (1962), a product of a bourgeois society for a bourgeois society, turns out to be more revolutionary than any of the conscious attempts at conversion and social purgation. It is revolutionary because

it is ritual drama: its plot is the confrontation of four characters with their inner reality. In purging themselves of their past lives they are achieving "self-liberation." Purgation is a basic ritual experience. Because this play "does not condescend, [it] is ultimately more enriching, more liberating than" proletarian art.

According to Soyinka, it is crucial that any writer adopt "what has become integrated within the cultural matrix of a society – whatever and wherever it is – into the idiom of the ritual for making new social and, we hope, revolutionary statements." Further, it is important that the writer be a part of, and be perceived as a part of, the community he or she serves. Soyinka is fighting against the mental attitude which has militated against the artist and the intelligentsia in society, against their unreserved acceptance by the community with which they are involved in the process of change. The dramatist, the actors, the audience, all are involved together in the ritual enactment that takes place on the cosmic stage.

For Soyinka, art should serve all these functions: it must use language that "addresses the proletariat directly," a "*l'engage*" that engages "the differential to deliver a socially active meaning." It must face the problem of power in society, by confronting its abuse as Ogun confronted the abyss. It must perform the act of "desuetude" to destroy old social forms that are no longer functional. It must force the audience to join the protagonist in confronting inner reality and purging itself of its shameful past. It must, in this way, lead the audience to change intellectually and emotionally and to become, like Ogun, creative. All these functions Soyinka reaffirmed, directly or indirectly, in his Nobel lecture, "This Past Must Address Its Present."

Even though Soyinka is a liberal critic and argues for complete artistic freedom, he does have his preferences. After the Nobel lecture, in an interview, he divided literature into two classes: the "shotgun" variety that tries to effect immediate social change and the more complex, aesthetic, profound literature that he finds enriching and continually compelling. This latter kind offers the potential for spiritual change and is truly revolutionary. Such an assessment is not merely a self-defense against attacks. It is his prescription for the future of African and other "third-world" literatures.

It would be impossible to determine Soyinka's influence as a dramatist, poet, or novelist on his fellow African writers. His career is far from over, and his highly individual style and extraordinary talent have elicited as much blame as praise and will probably continue to do so in spite of his being awarded the Nobel Prize. It certainly would be impossible to assess his impact as a literary critic, since that is not his major endeavor. Still, the Nobel honor should call even more attention to him. The depth of his scholarship in critical theory and practice, his ability to assimilate non-African sources into his essentially African theoretical base, his insistence on the cultural and long-term value of literature, his experience as a writer himself (which lends credibility to his judgments about how the artist must function), and finally his obviously genuine commitment to human freedom – both political and cultural – will no doubt result in a future recognition of his importance to the cultural retrieval in which Africa is currently engaged. Soyinka's emphasis on myth and ritual as fundamental to revolutionary change in Africa may encourage future African critics and writers to avoid clichéd constructs and face the realities of the contemporary scene.

## Principal criticism

"From a Common Back Cloth: A Reassessment of the African Literary Image," 1963
"The Writer in a Modern African State," 1967
"The Choice and Use of Language," 1971
"Drama and the Revolutionary Ideal," 1973
"African Writers: A New Union," 1975
"Neo-Tarzanism: The Poetics of Pseudo-Tradition," 1975
"Aesthetic Illusion: Prescriptions for the Suicide of Poetry," 1975
*Myth, Literature, and the African World*, 1976
"The Critic and Society: Barthes, Leftocracy, and Other Mythologies," 1981
"This Past Must Address Its Present," 1986

## Other major works and literary forms

Wole Soyinka's principal literary form is drama. Generally regarded as the best dramatist to have emerged during the African literary resurgence since the 1950s, Soyinka has published and produced at least a dozen plays of exceptional quality, including comedies such as *The Lion and the Jewel* (1959), undefinable plays such as *The Road* (1965), and bitter satires such as *Madmen and Specialists* (1970, 1971). Soyinka is also the author of two novels, *The Interpreters* (1965) and *Season of Anomy* (1973), some books of poetry, two autobiographical memoirs, and a translation of a Yoruba novel. All these works reveal the philosophical and mythological concerns about African culture that underlie Soyinka's critical theory.

NOVELS
*The Interpreters*, 1965
*Season of Anomy*, 1973

PLAYS
*The Swamp Dwellers*, 1958
*The Lion and the Jewel*, 1959
*The Invention*, 1959 (one act)
*The Trials of Brother Jero*, 1960
*A Dance of the Forests*, 1960
*Camwood on the Leaves*, 1960 (radio play)
*The Strong Breed*, 1963
*Three Plays*, 1963
*Five Plays*, 1964
*Kongi's Harvest*, 1964
*The Road*, 1965
*Madmen and Specialists*, 1970, 1971
*Jero's Metamorphosis*, 1973
*The Bacchae*, 1973 (adaptation of Euripides' play)
*Collected Plays*, 1973, 1974 (2 volumes)
*Death and the King's Horseman*, 1975

*Opera Wonyosi*, 1977 (adaptation of Bertolt Brecht's play *The Threepenny Opera*)

POETRY
*Idanre and Other Poems*, 1967
*Poems from Prison*, 1969
*A Shuttle in the Crypt*, 1972
*Ogun Abibiman*, 1976

AUTOBIOGRAPHY
*The Man Died: Prison Notes of Wole Soyinka*, 1972 (autobiography)
*Aké: The Years of Childhood*, 1981 (autobiography)
*Ibadan: The Penkelemes Years. A Memoir: 1946–1965*, 1994

TRANSLATION
*Forest of a Thousand Daemons: A Hunter's Saga*, 1968 (of D. O. Fagunwa's novel *Ogboju Ode Ninu Igbo Irunmale*)

## Further reading

Chinweiza, Onuchekwa Jemie, and Ihechukwu Madubrike. *Toward the Decolonization of African Literature*, 1982.
Gibbs, James, ed. *Critical Perspectives on Wole Soyinka*, 1980.
Irele, Abiola. *The African Experience in Literature and Ideology*, 1981.
Last, Brian W. "Ngugi and Soyinka: An Ideological Contrast," in *World Literature Written in English*. XXI, no. 3 (1982), pp. 510–521.
Maduakor, Obiajuru. "Soyinka as Literary Critic," in *Research in African Literatures*. XVII (Spring, 1986), pp. 1–38.
Maja-Pearce, Adewale, ed. *Wole Soyinka: An Appraisal*, 1994.
Nkosi, Lewis. *Tasks and Masks: Themes and Styles of African Literature*, 1981.
Olaniyan, Tejumola. *Scars of Conquest/Marks of Resistance: The Invention of Cultural Identities in African, African-American, and Caribbean Drama*, 1995.

THOMAS BANKS

*See also* Black Literary Theory and Criticism; Mphahlele; Ngugi wa Thiong'o; Postcolonial Literary Theory

# Gayatri Chakravorty Spivak

Indian cultural critic

**Born:** Calcutta, India; February 24, 1942

## Biography

Gayatri Chakravorty was born into a middle-class family in Calcutta in 1942. In 1957 she went to Presidency College at the University of Calcutta, graduating in 1959 with first class honors in English. She followed the "brain drain" from India to America in 1961; her postgraduate work was carried out in the Department of Comparative Literature at Cornell University, this being the only department to offer her funding. She completed an M.A. in English in 1962 and received her Ph.D. (on William Butler Yeats, supervised by Paul de Man) in 1967. During this period she also met, married, and divorced an American, Talbot Spivak.

In the course of her career Spivak has taught widely in America, Britain, and India. In 1987 she was made Andrew W. Mellon Professor of English at Pittsburgh University and in 1991 she took up the post of Avalon Foundation Professor in the Humanities at Columbia University (a position she continues to hold). She has been a Fellow of the National Humanities Institute, the Center for the Humanities at Wesleyan, the Humanities Research Center at the Australian National University, the Center for the Study of the Social Sciences at the University of Calcutta, the Davis Center for Historical Studies at Princeton University, and the Rockefeller Foundation. She has also been a Guggenheim Fellow and holds the Tagore Fellowship at the Maharaja Sayajirao University of Baroda in India. Spivak is on the editorial boards of a number of journals, including *Cultural Critique, boundary 2, new formations, Diaspora, ARIEL, Re-thinking Marxism, Public Culture, Parallax, Interventions,* and *The Year's Work in Critical and Cultural Theory.* She is also involved with rural literacy teacher training in India and Bangladesh.

In terms of her intellectual interests, Spivak states that she came to feminism through Jacques Derrida's critique of phallogocentrism and through Luce Irigaray's work on Sigmund Freud. Often her own experiences and her own cross-cultural background form the backdrop to many of Spivak's comments on more general dimensions of culture, identity, and marginality.

## Influence

Spivak first came to the attention of literary and critical theory through her translation of and substantial introduction to Derrida's *De la grammatologie* (1967; *Of Grammatology,* 1976). Since the late 1970s and early 1980s, however, her work has been associated with the emergence of postcolonial theory and, in particular, she is frequently considered to be one of the most influential figures who draw upon poststructuralism to approach questions about colonialism and identity. Spivak combines her interest in poststructuralist thinkers (such as Derrida, Gilles Deleuze, and Michel Foucault) with arguments associated with Marxism and feminism in order to consider the complex formation of subjectivity and cultural identity. Her work is often concerned with the construction of margins and centers and it focuses on the status of women, those in the so-called "Third World" compared to those in the "First World," as well as the particular status of Third World women. Frequently, as Spivak herself readily admits, these positions reveal shortcomings in theoretical models and much of her work is concerned not only with the productive elements in poststructuralist, feminist, and Marxist theory but also with the problems and weaknesses of such approaches. One consequence of this complex theorization is that Spivak's work can seem dense, oblique, and difficult to grasp; as Robert Young observes,

Spivak's work offers no position that can be quickly summarized: in the most sustained deconstructive mode, she resists critical taxonomies, avoids assuming master discourses. To read her work is not so much to confront a system as to encounter a series of events.

Spivak therefore refuses to attempt a single or coherent explanation of complex cultural formations, preferring instead to draw upon different theoretical models to explore the various "subject-positions" that emerge out of colonialism. Literary and critical theories for Spivak provide not only a number of approaches for describing imperialism and colonialism, they also provide the basis for intervening in the different manifestations of neocolonialism.

In disciplinary terms, Spivak's interests are widespread and her work falls into several categories. She is interested in cultural studies in general, her writings focus on literary texts, cinema, philosophy, institutions, economic structures, and history and historiography, and, as Spivak herself states, she explores, "the margins at which disciplinary discourses break down and enter the world of political agency."

## Analysis

Like many other recent commentators on colonialism and imperialism, Spivak is concerned with the discursive and epistemological dimensions of Europe's intrusions into other cultures. Edward Said in *Orientalism* (1978) charts the ways that the "Orient" was invented and reinvented not only through economic forces and through institutional regulation but also through the governance of "truth" by language, literature, and ideology. Spivak similarly focuses on the relationship between textuality and cultural subjugation and although she certainly explores both the implementation of physical force under colonialism and the economic dispossession of colonized nations by the West, her overriding concern is with the way that these processes are constantly mediated by representational structures.

One of Spivak's most significant arguments develops out of Derrida's critique of what he calls "the metaphysics of presence" in Western thought and culture. For Derrida, the West is regulated by a conventional series of oppositions (such as inside/outside or self/other) which privileges concepts relating to proximity, immediacy, and identity while at the same time subordinating concepts relating to absence, distance, and difference. Within this metaphysical tradition, Derrida maintains, "being" has been construed in terms of essence, substance, consciousness, and foundation. Spivak extends Derrida's model by claiming that this tradition of giving primacy to presence can be found both in colonialist identifications of non-Western cultures and in the resistance to such identifications that emerged in anti- and postcolonial intellectual activity. Spivak argues that Western colonial nations have racialized cultural classifications in terms of innate, essential, and natural characteristics and the traces of these classifications can be detected in countercolonial work. Consequently, for Spivak, greater theoretical vigilance is needed since the conceptual structures of the West (that is, structures associated with metropolitan or "mother" countries – France, Britain, Spain, or Portugal – which figure identity in terms of presence and absence, same and other, and in terms of original and immutable properties) continue to organize so-called "peripheral" or nonmetropolitan cultures even after decolonization.

A number of Spivak's essays are concerned with essences, origins, and their mediation by representational forms. Her argument is that the reclamation of "subaltern" (subjugated and silenced) consciousness often takes place through a nonsubaltern narrative of origins and nationality. In "Can the Subaltern Speak?" (1988), for example, she maintains that the search for an authentic subalternity is a doubly misguided enterprise. Not only is this essay "committed to the notion that . . . a nostalgia for lost origins can be detrimental to the exploration of social realities within the critique of imperialism," but it also observes that a diversity of subject-positions under colonialism needs to be recognized: "One must . . . insist that the colonized subaltern *subject* is irretrievably heterogeneous." "Can the Subaltern Speak?" traces this heterogeneous construction through the practice of widow self-sacrifice (or *Sati*), in which women immolated themselves on their dead husband's funeral pyre in Hindu cultures. For Spivak, this tradition illustrates what she calls the "double displacement" of women in India, since *Sati* has been regulated both by patriarchal customs in India and by British colonial law. On the one hand, there is what Spivak terms "the Indian nativist argument," which sets out to establish the intentions of those women who performed *Sati* and concludes that these women were active agents who wanted to die. On the other hand, British legislators in 1929 implemented laws which were grounded in notions of human nature and universal civilization and which saw itself, as Spivak summarizes it, as "White men saving brown women from brown men." With both practices, however, the voices of women disappeared and the history of *Sati* must therefore be understood as a history of a double repression: instead of recovering the essential truths of those women who committed *Sati*, history must instead be interpreted as a narrative which selectively documents Hindu customs and which needs to be read in terms of its exclusions.

In the work of the Subaltern Studies Group, made up of Indian historians who research the effects of colonialism and who challenge the inaccuracies of colonialist history, further examples of colonial essentialisms can be found. For Spivak, however, this group's work needs to be read in terms of both its problematic adoption of "elite" theory and its resistant critique of colonialist history. In "Subaltern Studies: Deconstructing Historiography" (published in *In Other Worlds: Essays in Cultural Politics*, 1987) she states

that problems exist in the attempts of this group to re-present subordinated identities and in their professed aims of recovering a lost consciousness: for Spivak, "To investigate, discover, and establish a subaltern or peasant consciousness seems at first to be a positivistic project which assumes that, if properly prosecuted, it will lead to firm ground, to some *thing* that can be disclosed." What Spivak is most concerned with here is that a number of underlying tensions can be identified in the work of the Subaltern Studies Group. Certainly, there are methodological contradictions with the group's search for lost origins and their seemingly irreconcilable claim that, as Spivak puts it, "consciousness is *the* ground that makes all disclosures possible." In other words, while attempting to recover subaltern or peasant consciousness, the Subaltern Studies Group also declares that any disclosure must be mediated by forms of consciousness (such as history or representation); as Spivak observes, the group constantly suggests that "subaltern consciousness is never fully recoverable, that it is always askew from its received signifiers, indeed that it is effaced even as it is disclosed, that it is irreducibly discursive."

More importantly, for Spivak, these methodological and metaphysical problems are evidence of a persistent colonialism since the historiography of the Subaltern Studies Group is derived from a recognizably Eurocentric post-Enlightenment tradition of thought. In "Subaltern Studies," Spivak argues that the reclamation of "peasant" or "subaltern" consciousness takes place through a nonsubaltern narrative of origins and nationality: not only does the Subaltern Studies Group problematically attempt to disclose a presence which must ultimately remain irrecuperable, it does so by adopting the conceptual structures of elite – Western – thought. It is because of these problems, Spivak claims, that the conclusions of the Subaltern Studies Group must be thought of as "theoretical fictions." In spite of this, however, "Subaltern Studies" crucially argues that these fictions can be rethought as part of a tactical resistance to the authority of Western conceptual structures. Since European colonial practices included the dissemination of values, ideologies, and beliefs in colonized cultures and, consequently, since this process included the transmission of "First World" essentialisms, it would be naive to think that essentialisms could be avoided in resistance thought. While arguing that the notions of origin and essence at the core of colonial, neocolonial, and postcolonial conceptuality are based upon a series of misunderstandings about the relationship between identity, consciousness, and culture, Spivak also recognizes that it would be a mistake to believe that essentialisms can be avoided and that resistance theory can exist outside of colonial structures of thought. In other words, Spivak argues that the work of the Subaltern Studies Group should be interpreted as an insurgent foundationalism or strategic essentialism, countering colonial authority not by challenging the notion of innate, original, or essential truth, but by providing differently essentializing accounts of Indian consciousness and subjectivity which dismantle the "truths" established by European representations.

Unsurprisingly, given that Spivak's essays on history and culture are preoccupied with the overriding significance of narrative, her writings on literary and fictional texts are concerned with essentializing accounts of knowledge, identity, and nationhood. The first section of *In Other Worlds* draws upon developments in late-twentieth-century literary and critical theory to reread canonical writing; Marxism, feminism, psychoanalysis, and deconstruction all provide Spivak with models for reading Dante, William Butler Yeats, Virginia Woolf, and William Wordsworth. The final section, entitled "Entering the Third World," also explores narrative interpretation, though in this section Spivak is more concerned with texts that have been excluded from European canons. As a result, she includes two short stories by the Bengali writer Mahasweta Devi and one of these stories ("Stanadayini") forms the focus for the last essay in *In Other Worlds*, "A Literary Representation of the Subaltern: A Woman's Text From the Third World." In this essay Spivak contrasts several interpretational approaches – Marxist feminism, liberal feminism, and Lacanian psychoanalysis – when discussing Devi's story about Jashoda, a wet nurse. This story, Spivak argues, highlights the dilemma facing resistance narratives since Jashoda is usually read as a parable for decolonized India: India, like Jashoda is a "mother-by-hire," abused and exploited by those who worship her and who will collapse unless something is given back to her. However, such parabolic or allegorical reading requires an exclusion of the subaltern subject – to disclose the parable and to read Jashoda as India ultimately requires the eradication of Jashoda from Devi's narrative; for Spivak, such exclusions necessarily occur when nationhood is the sole focus for criticism and when other textual elements are ignored. "If the story of the rise of nationalist resistance to imperialism is to be disclosed coherently," Spivak observes, "it is the role of the indigenous subaltern that must be strategically excluded."

Spivak's reading of "Stanadayini" is, of course, preoccupied with the figuring of national identity in Devi's text, though she also considers other aspects of this narrative. She claims that Devi's text unsettles the assumptions of both the dominant Anglo-American "radical" reader (who "reactively homogenizes the Third World and sees it only in the context of nationalism and ethnicity") and the humanistic "Indian reader" (who embraces the preoccupations of the orthodox Anglo-American reader by seeking the natural and commonsense meaning of texts). This unsettling occurs partly because "Stanadayini" is concerned with political economy (class, commodification, surplus value, and so on) and with the status of women, but also because Devi's story disrupts the stability of knowledge. Devi's story conspicuously resists the expectations of liberal (and liberal feminist) criticism since Jashoda does not possess an affirmed and fully developed identity at the end of the tale. Instead, Spivak argues, "Stanadayini" shows how knowledge and consciousness are made and unmade through the body: at the end of the story Jashoda develops breast cancer and dies, and while this can be read as an allegory for decolonization, for Spivak the fact that Jashoda cannot name her disease suggests that subjectivity cannot be reduced to rational consciousness. For Young, this interpretation of Devi's tale illustrates Spivak's claim that Third World texts can intervene in and disturb Western assumptions about knowledge and identity:

> A narrative such as Devi's does not simply provide a haven of realism for the nostalgic critic at a time when First World literature has graduated into language-games; rather it can deconstruct First World discourse by inverting it and displacing it, thus initiating the process of the First World's own necessary decolonization.

Spivak's work has attracted a number of criticisms, some of which question specific features of her methodology while others challenge more substantial aspects of her theoretical arguments and affiliations. Young, for example, points out that Spivak constantly seeks a vigilance toward the heterogeneity of subject-positions assigned to women in the Third World; however, Spivak often refers to her own experiences as an Asian woman who teaches in the Western academy and in doing so, Young observes, "she runs the inevitable risk of presenting herself as the representative of that very 'Third World Woman.'" Peter Childs and Patrick Williams point out that Spivak has attempted to rethink the political consequences of poststructuralist theory in terms of imperialism, colonialism, and neocolonialism and in so doing she broadly retains much of poststructuralism's preoccupation with representations of identity. What this of course suggests is that Spivak prioritizes the discursive over the historical and material, and that she fails fully to explore the ways that insurgent practices challenge European colonialism. In an influential essay entitled "Problems in Current Theories of Colonial Discourse" (1987), Benita Parry also argues that Spivak places too great an emphasis on the constitutive status of discourse, and according to Parry there are further problems with the way that Spivak treats hegemonic discourse as entirely constitutive. Parry argues that:

> while protesting at the obliteration of the native's subject position in the text of imperialism, Spivak gives no speaking part to the colonized, effectively writing out the evidence of native agency recorded in India's 200 year struggle against British conquest and the Raj – discourses to which she scathingly refers as hegemonic nativist or reverse ethnocentric narrativization.

## Principal criticism

"Love Me, Love My Ombre, Elle," in *Diacritics*, 1984
"Three Women's Texts and a Critique of Imperialism," in
    *Critical Inquiry*. 12, no. 1 (1985), pp. 243–261
*In Other Worlds: Essays in Cultural Politics*, 1987
*Selected Subaltern Studies*, 1988 (editor, with Ranajit Guha)
"Can the Subaltern Speak?," 1988. Republished in *Colonial
    Discourse and Post-Colonial Theory: A Reader*, 1993
    (Patrick Williams and Laura Chrisman, editors)
*The Post-Colonial Critic: Interviews, Strategies, Dialogues*, 1990
*Outside in the Teaching Machine*, 1993
*The Spivak Reader*, 1996 (Donna Landry and Gerald MacLean,
    editors)

## Other major works and literary forms

Before translating Jacques Derrida's *De la grammatologie*
(*Of Grammatology*), Gayatri Chakravorty Spivak worked
mainly on English and French poetry and published extensively on William Butler Yeats' poetry. She has subsequently
continued to write about European poetry and fiction,
though most of her work is predominantly concerned with
theoretical issues in Marxism, feminism, and poststructuralism. In 1995 Spivak added to her critical readings of
Mahasweta Devi's fiction by collecting and translating
*Imaginary Maps: Three Stories by Mahasweta Devi*.

## Further reading

Childs, Peter, and Patrick Williams. *An Introduction to Post-
    Colonial Theory*, 1997.
Parry, Benita. "Problems in Current Theories of Colonial
    Discourse," in *Oxford Literary Review*. 9, nos. 1–2 (1987),
    pp. 27–58.
Young, Robert. *White Mythologies: Writing History and the
    West*, 1990.

PHILIP LEONARD

*See also* Feminist Criticism; Postcolonial Literature and
Theory; Said


# Madame de Staël

(Anne Louise Germaine, Baroness of
Staël-Holstein)

French critic and writer

**Born:** Paris, France; April 22, 1766
**Died:** Paris, France; July 14, 1817

## Biography

Anne Louise Germaine Necker was born in Paris on April
22, 1766, the only child of Jacques Necker and the former
Suzanne Cuchod from Geneva. A wealthy Swiss banker who
became the minister of finance to Louis XVI, Necker was
idolized by his daughter. Ostensibly because the king had
dismissed Necker from his ministry, the French people
stormed the Bastille in 1789, carrying its seven prisoners
away in triumph; as a result, the king was forced to ask
Necker to return. Necker returned but was ineffective and
resigned in September of 1790; he retired to Coppet, leaving
two million francs of his own in the state treasury. One
trait that Germaine shared with her indulgent father was
her ability to preserve the Necker fortune and to pass it
on, undiminished, to her children.

She received an Enlightenment education. Taught by
her Calvinist mother until the age of thirteen, she was
subjected to a rigorous course of study which included Latin
and English. The writings of the Baron de Montesquieu,
the Marquis de Condorcet, Voltaire, and Jean-Jacques
Rousseau were major and early influences on her. More
important, before she could walk, she became part of her
mother's salon, which was frequented by the *philosophes*,
including Denis Diderot, Jean Le Rond d'Alembert, and the
Comte de Buffon. It was clear to the young girl that public
attention from men for brilliant conversation was not only
to be expected but was her birthright as well.

Her arranged marriage to Eric Magnus, Baron de Staël-
Holstein, was bereft of emotional and intellectual ties.
Nevertheless, his position as the Swedish ambassador to the
French court led to an increased sphere of political influence for his wife. Her passionate need for intellectual
dialogue and her own temperament, which readily
subscribed to Rousseau's damnation of human institutions
such as marriage, led her into a number of intense love
affairs, the most celebrated being with the writer and politician Benjamin Constant, who described their relationship
in his novel *Adolphe* (1816). While her biographers often
discuss her faults, no one questions her courage and
generosity. Her loyalty to friends and ex-lovers was
unfailing, and even her enemies received her support. She
lacked any sense of vindictiveness: when she learned of a
plot to assassinate Napoleon after his exile to Elba, she was
ready to go herself to warn him.

Although her Parisian salon was extremely important to
her (Napoleon knew that exile from Paris was the worst
torture he could inflict on her), Madame de Staël had less
need for a home than for dialogue. Truly cosmopolitan
at a time when nationalism was becoming increasingly fanatical, she traveled throughout Europe, from England to Italy,
Scandinavia, Germany, and Russia, and planned to go to
the United States as well. She was accustomed to dealing
with royalty and heads of state. No beauty by contemporary standards, she was criticized not only for her liaisons
and devouring intellect but also for her outlandish costumes.
She nevertheless fascinated men with her candor, her guile-
less curiosity, and her brilliant gift for conversation.

After her years of exile, she returned to Paris in 1814
and reopened her salon, gathering about her the leading
young republicans of France, who were to overthrow the
Bourbon dynasty in 1830. Even after her death on July 14,
1817, her ideas lived on, reflected in the members of her
last and greatest salon.

## Influence

The influence of Madame de Staël on her contemporaries and successors is incalculable and much greater than can be ascertained from her writings alone. Her ideas were developed in her conversations with the great leaders and writers of the time. The force of her personality and intellect, regardless of whether others agreed with her opinions, is indisputable. The salon was her world: she gathered about her, wherever she was, the great minds of her era. Those who were not in attendance, such as Johann Wolfgang von Goethe and Friedrich Schiller, she visited. She regularly corresponded with European heads of state and with Americans, such as Thomas Jefferson, Governeur Morris, Albert Gallatin, and John Quincy Adams. She has been described by scholar Morroe Berger as "often linked with England and Russia as one of the three great 'powers' of Europe in the nineteenth century."

Such prominence, combined with her vocal opposition to despotic rule, led inevitably to a long and losing battle with Napoleon Bonaparte. Her salon, a refuge for disaffected royalists and republicans alike, was more than the emperor could tolerate, and he exiled her from Paris. When *Germany*, the last of her works to be published while she was alive, was being printed in France in 1810, he had thousands of copies, the plates and, he hoped, the manuscripts destroyed. He succeeded in keeping her out of Paris for ten years, but he scarcely diminished her impact on Western intellectual history.

## Analysis

While she introduced German Idealism and Romanticism to the French, Madame de Staël formulated no systematic literary theory. In the rigorous dialectic of the salon, her ideas were examined and refined over a period of thirty years of violent political change. The ideas she set forth in *Essay on Fiction* and *A Treatise on the Influence of the Passions upon the Happiness of Individuals and Nations* are essentially the same ones that she developed in her later and most significant works, *The Influence of Literature upon Society*, *Germany*, and *Considerations on the Principal Events of the French Revolution*. Consistent throughout her writings is the assertion that literature must encompass all facets of human life and that, therefore, the study of art is inextricably linked to the study of the political, legal, religious, and social issues of her day.

Her interest in government began in her mother's salon and with her father's attempts to make the French government solvent. Necker had hoped that France might follow the British into a constitutional monarchy. Like her father, Madame de Staël had argued for a constitutional monarchy, but in accordance with her belief in the necessity of constitutional government, she sought to support the new government of France. When the National Convention voted to guillotine Marie-Antoinette, Madame de Staël wrote vehemently in the queen's defense. Earlier, she had, in fact,

provided a means of getting the king and his family out of France.

Brought up in the tradition of the *philosophes* and believing that all individuals ought to be guaranteed political liberty, she tried to extend these rights even to the king and queen. She had witnessed the hungry mobs and the bloodletting of the Reign of Terror and had saved as many individuals as she could, including Louis Narbonne. Throughout her life, she acted upon her belief that humankind could and would develop an international community based on reason and moderation, on the rule of law. She looked to the United States as the land free to develop the best society without the evils of the old – if slavery were abolished.

Never, she argued, could one accept bloodshed and tyranny. No end justified violent means, and tyranny could not be defended by pretending that its imposed order was necessary: "When one does not know how to convince, one oppresses; in all power relations among governors and governed, as ability declines, usurpation increases." Civil liberty supports enlightened rule and protects individuals from themselves.

Napoleon ranked her as a danger to his empire on the basis of her political views. Her Protestant thinking threatened the Catholicism he wanted to see reestablished in France, and he damned her as anti-French because of her admiration for British government and literature and German Romanticism. Specific in her criticism as well as in her praise, she admired Great Britain for approximating her ideal: "Happy the land where the writers are sad, the merchants satisfied, the rich melancholic, and the populace content." Such concerns were alien to Napoleon.

Yet Madame de Staël was no believer in utopias. She saw human history as a struggle toward improvement and away from violence; only by engaging in that struggle could humanity perfect its temporal existence. While she conceived of happiness as a series of contradictions – love without jealousy, belief without fanaticism, religion without superstition – she knew that such a perfect state was impossible. The degree of happiness attainable by individuals is dependent upon the nature of their government, and the quality of that government depends entirely upon the enlightenment of the rulers. As a humanist, Madame de Staël argued that education is the only effective means of combating superstition, prejudice, and authoritarianism in government and religion. Because of her belief in the improvement of the human condition, in spite of the senseless violence of recent history, she argued for the development of the sciences and emphasized that scientific progress must be accompanied by moral progress.

She paid tribute to Rousseau as her literary forebear and agreed with his emphasis on the emotions. For Rousseau, emotion is the only means by which human beings can go back to their paradisiacal perfection, and art is the undisciplined expression of feeling. In accord with Rousseau,

Madame de Staël believed that enthusiasm or divine inspiration (the passion that propels people toward their ideals) is the source of human nobility. Unlike Rousseau, however, she saw the past as preparation for the future.

Knowing that uncontrolled emotion was harmful and recognizing the deleterious effects of the passions which subvert both individual and social happiness, she sought to offset potential harm by insisting on reason. Yet while the emotions either control or are controlled by the individual, they are nevertheless essential to human progress. Reason alone is not sufficient, but the emotions must be confirmed by reason. For Madame de Staël, the human condition requires a constant struggle to balance emotion with reason.

She also rejected Rousseau's theories of education, advocating an early, rigorously disciplined education – including the study of foreign languages – which would provide the necessary foundation for enlightened thinking. Language must be the basis of education as it has been for the best minds in the past: "Grammar connects ideas as calculation links numbers." She also equated sloppy expression with sloppy thinking: "When one deals with thoughts that are boundless, obscurity of style is sometimes an indication of the very reach of the mind, but obscurity in the analysis of the affairs of life only shows that one does not understand them." Written or spoken, the power of language was beyond question.

She made a distinction between the imaginative arts and the intellectual arts. The imaginative arts include poetry, art, and music. Among the intellectual arts, she included philosophy, both moral and political, and modern fiction. The imaginative arts are the product of the emotions, which do not change; therefore, the poetry of the Greeks, for example, can never be surpassed. The intellectual arts, however, are the product of exploration of the emotions by reason. Because intellectual art will lead humanity to an ever increased understanding of itself and the world, it is, in her view, the literary form of the future. In her *Essay on Fiction*, she argued for the novel's capacity to depict the full range of human emotion; ambition, pride, vanity, avarice, and the desire for glory, and not merely the portrayal of love. Opposed to allegorical and historical fiction, she argued for the novel as an imitation of the lives of its readers, as it provides the insight that history does not offer. Indeed, the novel should explore the complexity of emotions and character in depth.

Whether she was examining political, social, or ethical issues, Madame de Staël invariably returned to her considerations of national character. She asked: what is the relationship between the writer and his or her audience? How exactly is the artist a product of his or her society? When does literature reflect the social life of a time and place? What social change can literature effect? She believed that such literary forms as the novel and the essay can re-create as well as reflect a particular society.

Her focus on the novel led her into further exploration of Germanic literature. She discovered in Goethe a quality which she identified with a melancholy, Romantic tradition of the north. Moreover, British and German literature favors freedom from restrictive forms and commitment to action; it was the literature of the north which spoke directly to her. She perceived in the form-conscious, classical tradition of the south, with its emphasis on order, pleasure, and beauty, little relevance in an age that had seen the chaos of revolution followed by the absolutism of tyranny. She saw the southern classical literature as imitative, not innovative. In France, this classical tradition had led to stagnation and even fostered the oppression that led to the Revolution. Yet Madame de Staël did not believe that the classical tradition should be rejected: she argued instead that a reconciliation or harmonious synthesis of the two traditions was necessary.

She sought in *Germany* to introduce German Idealism and Romanticism to the French rather than to explicate German thought (scholarly accuracy and detail was never her concern), and she led French writers, such as Charles-Augustin Sainte-Beuve, Alphonse de Lamartine, Alfred de Vigny, and Victor Hugo, to confront and assimilate the ideas of Romanticism. If this work was directed to the French, it was nevertheless widely and carefully read, by Lord Byron, for example. According to Byron, who recorded his tribute to her, as Corinna, in a note to canto 4 of *Childe Harold's Pilgrimage* (1812–1818, 1819), she "is sometimes right, and often wrong, about Italy and England; but almost always true in delineating the heart, which is of but one nation, and of no country, – or, rather of all."

*Considerations on the Principal Events of the French Revolution* provides without doubt valuable insights into the Revolution, its aftermath, and Napoleon, but most significantly, it enabled the French to come to terms with the immediate horrors of the past and to look to the future with hope. Madame de Staël convinced her readers that the best of the French tradition had not been destroyed.

It is impossible to imagine a more representative individual of any era than Madame de Staël. Her literary stand was both revolutionary and an integral part of her political, moral, and social ideas. The effect of her words, even when unacknowledged, as in Hugo's *La Préface de Cromwell* (1827; English translation, 1896), on her contemporaries and successors, is staggering. Her ideas remain significant in that, as Morroe Berger points out,

The eighteenth century's ethics and rationalism have not yet been superseded as ideals; its distillation of the accumulated knowledge about social life remains largely valid. Madame de Staël spoke for rationality and also for feeling. She saw European civilization as a whole, not in order to oppose it to other civilizations but to give it its place among them. She did not believe that Europe's energy, integrity, and greatness depended upon injustices like slavery and imperialism, or that to end these injustices would reduce Europe's cultural potentialities .... She saw the defeat of reason many times but never doubted it as an ideal.

While her approach to literature would now be classified as sociological, her thought is not so easily classified. She focused both on the ideas presented and on the power of those ideas to change society for the better. She certainly promoted the study of comparative literature, of foreign languages, and of politics as a science. She believed in the supremacy of language: "I still believe that if speech uttered before a large number of people and books judged by the entire public have no effect whatever, then it is the orators and the writers who are to blame."

## Principal criticism
*Essai sur les fictions*, 1795 (*Essay on Fiction*, 1795)
*De l'influence des passions sur le bonheur des individus et des nations*, 1796 (*A Treatise on the Influence of the Passions upon the Happiness of Individuals and Nations*, 1798)
*De la littérature considérée dans ses rapports avec les institutions sociales*, 1800 (*A Treatise on Ancient and Modern Literature*, 1803; also as *The Influence of Literature upon Society*, 1813)
*De l'Allemagne*, 1813 (*Germany*, 1813)
*Considérations sur les principaux événemens de la Révolution française*, 1818 (*Considerations on the Principal Events of the French Revolution*, 1818)

## Other major works and literary forms
Madame de Staël wrote voluminously throughout her life, producing essays on innumerable subjects as well as fiction and plays. Her tribute to Jean-Jacques Rousseau was written when she was only twenty-two. Aside from her critical works, which gained wide and immediate renown, she was famous for her two novels, which present heroines of intelligence and sensibility who suffer much. Her volume of memoirs, *Dix années d'exil* (1821; *Ten Years' Exile*, 1821), includes an account of her travels in Russia in 1812.

NOVELS
*Delphine*, 1802 (English translation, 1803)
*Corinne: Ou, L'Italie*, 1807 (*Corinne: Or, Italy*, 1807)

NONFICTION
*Dix années d'exil*, 1821 (*Ten Years' Exile*, 1821)

## Further reading
Behler, Ernst. "Cross-Roads in Literary Theory and Criticism: Madame de Staël and August Wilhelm Schlegel," in *Carrefour de Cultures*, 1993, pp. 129–141. Edited by Regis Antoine.
Berger, Morroe. *Madame de Staël on Politics, Literature, and National Character*, 1964.
Forsberg, Roberta J., and H. C. Nixon. *Madame de Staël and Freedom Today*, 1963.
Goldberger, Avriel H., ed., and Germaine Bree (introd.). *Woman as Mediatrix: Essays on Nineteenth-Century Women Writers*, 1987.

Gutwirth, Madelyn. *Madame de Staël, Novelist: The Emergence of the Artist as Woman*, 1978.
Herold, J. Christopher. *Mistress to an Age: A Life of Madame de Staël*, 1958.
Larg, David Glass. *Madame de Staël: Her Life as Revealed in Her Work, 1766–1800*, 1926.
Posgate, Helen B. *Madame de Staël*, 1968.

CAROL BISHOP

*See also* Romanticism; Rousseau

# George Steiner
French-born American critic and writer

Born: Paris, France; April 23, 1929

## Biography
George Steiner was born on April 23, 1929, in Paris, France, the son of Frederick George and Elsie (née Franzos) Steiner. His first language was German; during his early education in Paris he mastered French, and he learned English as another language spoken at home. Thus Steiner was trilingual from his earliest years. In 1940 his parents emigrated to the United States, where he became a naturalized citizen in 1944. Steiner received a B.A. from the University of Chicago in 1948, an M.A. from Harvard University in 1950, and a D.Phil. in 1955 from Oxford University, where he was a Rhodes Scholar. From 1952 to 1956 he served on the editorial staff of *The Economist* in London. Between 1956 and 1958 he was a member of the Institute for Advanced Study in Princeton, and in 1959–1960 he was Gauss Lecturer at Princeton University. In 1961 he returned to England, where he became a Fellow of Churchill College, Cambridge University. He has been Albert Schweitzer Visiting Professor in the Humanities at New York University and has taught at Stanford University, Princeton University, Harvard, and Yale University. In 1974 he became professor of English and comparative literature at the University of Geneva. Most recently he has been teaching at Cambridge University and has been a visiting professor at Oxford. Among his many honors are an O. Henry Short Story Award, Fulbright and Guggenheim fellowships, and the Morton Zabel Prize awarded by the National Institute of Arts and Letters. He is married to Zara Alice Shakow; they have two children.

## Influence
Steiner's extraordinarily wide knowledge of languages and literatures places him in that small group of critics who may truly be called "international." He is a philosophical critic and historian of ideas who believes that criticism is or ought to be "an act of pivotal social intelligence." He believes critics should "work outward from the particular

literary instance to the far reaches of moral and political argument." His acute awareness of the world outside literature, the world of politics and science, enables him to make of literary criticism what he believes it should be: a critique of society. He has been most influenced by critics of high moral and social seriousness: Georg Lukács, Walter Benjamin, Edmund Wilson, and F. R. Leavis. Steiner believes, however, that their criticism has begun to seem dated because the humanist assumptions on which their work is based have been called into doubt by recent world history, particularly by the Holocaust. Steiner is a critic unafraid of major questions and provocative themes, even though he is well aware that "to ask the larger questions is to risk getting things wrong." Not to ask them, however, is to acquiesce in the intellectual sterility and moral frivolity of our age. Measured against much late-twentieth-century literary criticism (which has been trivialized into a kind of "initiate sport"), the work of Steiner looks unfashionably, refreshingly large.

## Analysis

Steiner acknowledges that "much of my work has concerned itself, directly or indirectly, with trying to understand, to articulate, causal and teleological aspects of the holocaust." Some of Steiner's readers may find an obsessive concern with the Holocaust to be understandable in a Jewish writer who escaped the fate of millions of Jews only by chance – his family's 1940 emigration to the United States. Steiner is, then, "a kind of survivor," as he explains in his essay of that title, but he is no longer intact, nor does he believe that anyone else is either. He believes that human beings everywhere have been diminished and maimed by the knowledge that genocidal atrocity was possible in the midst of civilized Europe. As Elie Wiesel stated, "at Auschwitz, not only man died but also the idea of man." Steiner returns again and again to the idea that the death camps incinerated (along with some six million human beings) a civilization, a world. For Steiner, the Holocaust is nothing less than "a second Fall . . . a voluntary exit from the Garden." Humankind now lives among the ashes of the Judaic-Hellenic tradition. "Our time is not ordinary," he reminds his readers. "There is nothing *natural* about our present condition," for "we come *after*."

Steiner rejects the relatively comfortable explanation of the Holocaust as "a purely German phenomenon or some calamitous mishap rooted in the persona of one or another totalitarian ruler." For him, it signifies the failure of humanistic culture itself and the collapse of the language on which such culture has traditionally been based. He argues that one cannot continue one's teaching and reading of literature or one's assumptions about education "as if nothing very important had happened." High culture and barbaric action coexist; Steiner's need to know why, to understand how such a phenomenon is possible, pervades his writing, even to the title of one of his early books, *Language and Silence*.

Many questions about the relationships between language and politics, language and cultural decay, "language and other codes of meaning (music, translation, mathematics)," language and silence, are raised in his writings. A dominant interest, however, is in "aspects of linguistic devaluation and dehumanization" brought about not only by the corruption of language under totalitarian regimes such as Adolf Hitler's, but also by "the great load of vulgarity, imprecision, and greed it is charged with in a mass-consumer democracy." Education, rather than being something to shore against the ruin of humankind, is participating in the general cultural collapse, in the "retreat from the primacy of the word" on which Western civilization has been based. Universal education has at best produced a kind of semiliteracy or subliteracy, generations of readers who are unable to read the great works of Western civilization because they are written in an alphabet that has been lost – that is, they require more knowledge of classical myth, Scripture, Christian symbolism, and previous literatures than footnotes can provide. He identifies, in addition, a widespread "natural illiteracy," an ignorance of the names and shapes of the natural world (flowers, trees, stars) which "served Ovid and Shakespeare, Spenser and Goethe, as a current alphabet." Steiner concedes that other, primarily nonverbal and now-dominant language-worlds (mathematics and natural sciences) have just claims upon the person who wishes to be considered educated. He believes, however, that these fields are "only rarely of ultimate interest" because "they have added little to our knowledge or governance of human possibility." Despite the humanities' at times "arrogant . . . assertions of centrality," it remains true that there is more insight into human beings in Homer or William Shakespeare or Fyodor Dostoevski "than in the entirety of neurology or statistics." In Steiner's view, the greatest achievement of the sciences, their moral neutrality or objectivity, also bars them from "final relevance."

For Steiner, the current state of "humane literacy" as reflected in literary criticism is particularly disheartening: the servant of literature is now being taken as its master. Honest acknowledgment that criticism is of secondary importance is necessary. A critic "writes *about*"; thus, "criticism exists by the grace of other men's genius," a truth that is being forgotten. Modern people often read reviews and criticism instead of the literary work and thus miss the essential personal encounter with the literature and evade the valuable "effort of personal judgment." This loss is the greater because, even though modern culture is a "post-culture" (after the radical human defeat represented by the Holocaust), Steiner continues to believe that some of the most crucial knowledge obtainable about the human condition comes through literature. Literature, however, has become the province of "specialists," and literary criticism is increasingly marked by jargon, triviality, and megalomania. "The proliferation of verbiage in humanistic scholarship, the trivia decked out as erudition or critical re-assessment, threatens to obliterate the work of art itself."

In such a world, the threefold functions of literary criticism are more important than ever. First, criticism can help readers choose from the plethora and confusion those works which speak "to the present with particular directness or exaction." Second, criticism must help readers make connections among languages, literatures, and cultures. Steiner believes that comparative study is essential if literature is to avoid the "chauvinism [which] has cried havoc in politics." Third, and most important, is the evaluation and understanding of contemporary literature. A critic has "special responsibilities toward the art of his own age," not merely in evaluating technique, style, and originality, but also in asking what a work "contributes to or detracts from the dwindled reserves of moral intelligence." Critics need to be aware, however, that their judgments are not necessarily of lasting validity, because "the work of art stands in a complex, provisional relation to time." Nevertheless, Steiner believes that a critic's concern is with masterpieces. A reviewer or literary historian can distinguish between the good and the bad; a critic's job is to distinguish "between the good and the best." Social conditions of the twentieth century have made the task of literary criticism in helping people to "read as total human beings, by example of precision, fear, and delight" more crucial than ever. Thus, though criticism is secondary to creation "it has never counted more. Without it, creation itself may fall upon silence."

Steiner's meditations on silence are at times paradoxical. There is the crime of silence during the Holocaust, when vast numbers of Europeans seemed indifferent to what was happening. Afterward, the unspeakable nature of the atrocity makes silence the only appropriate response, or so Wiesel and numerous witnesses at the Eichmann trial came to believe. Steiner agrees that language is inadequate to such realities, that silence is the best response, but it is obvious that he has opted for "the next best" response, which is "to try and understand, to keep faith with what may well be the utopian commitment to reason and historical analysis." Steiner is certain that the garrulous, glib modern society talks too much, but he also wonders whether writers are writing too much, "whether the deluge of print . . . is not itself a subversion of meaning." Particularly in a time when language itself has become debased, "silence *is* an alternative. When the words in the city are full of savagery and lies, nothing speaks louder than the unwritten poem." Steiner's detractors have not been slow to observe that his own prodigality contradicts this counsel of silence, that his attitude toward the silence which he at times extols is ambiguous at best. Nor have they failed to criticize his tendency toward overstatement, or to wonder at his failure to reflect that a poet who does not write ceases to be a poet.

Steiner's fascination with language is evident in his interest in linguistics. In an essay entitled "Whorf,

Chomsky, and the Student of Literature," he analyzes the controversy between the relativists (Benjamin Whorf) and the universalists (Noam Chomsky) and finds that, at bottom, the controversy is over whether language is an ill-defined or a well-defined system. Steiner believes that students of literature are necessarily relativists because of the complex relationship between reader and text and the inexhaustibility of meaning in a great literary work. Students and critics can learn from linguistics (particularly from linguistic anthropology, sociolinguistics, and psycholinguistics), yet "the order of complexity, the order of relation between analysis and object as they occur in the study of literature are generically beyond anything that can be dealt with in linguistics." Linguistics will be a part of any future for literary studies, yet the study of literature itself necessarily involves numerous "messy" contingencies. It will always resist the effort to contain it within formal linguistic systems.

Frank Kermode describes Steiner as a "moral terrorist," Kant's term for "his contemporaries whose view of history was colored by the belief that they lived i. a period when the world was so far gone in decadence that universal catastrophe was at hand." Steiner's obsession with the Holocaust, his apocalyptic pronouncements on the state of Western culture, his "love of the abyss" (as one commentator expressed it), have irritated some of his readers, and his rhetorical style has been variously described by his detractors as melodramatic, grandiose, feverish, theatrical, repetitious, sensationalist, and arthritic. Some of Steiner's contemporaries complain that he has made a vocation of his Jewishness, others that he exploits the atrocities he condemns, and still others appear exasperated that one scholar should have the vast erudition that Steiner appears to have. Considering the fact that he is openly contemptuous of the narrowness and megalomania which he finds all too frequently in the literary criticism establishment, it is not surprising that he has aroused some hostility. Yet Kermode concludes that, regardless of whether one likes Steiner's "moral terrorism," his ideas, or his style, one is compelled to respect the evident sincerity of his motives and the "power of intellect" which combine to make him one of the most challenging and least provincial of contemporary critics.

## Principal criticism

*Tolstoy or Dostoevsky*, 1959
*The Death of Tragedy*, 1961
*Language and Silence: Essays on Language, Literature, and the Inhuman*, 1967
*Extraterritorial: Papers on Literature and the Language Revolution*, 1971
*In Blue-beard's Castle: Some Notes Toward the Redefinition of Culture*, 1971
*Nostalgia for the Absolute*, 1974
*After Babel: Aspects of Language and Translation*, 1975, revised 1992
*On Difficulty and Other Essays*, 1978

*Heidegger*, 1978 (also as *Martin Heidegger*, 1978)
*Antigones*, 1979
*Real Presences*, 1986
*No Passion Spent: Essays 1978–1995*, 1996

## Other major works and literary forms

George Steiner is a prolific writer. He has been principal literary critic for *The New Yorker* and is a regular contributor to numerous periodicals and journals including *Commentary, Harper's Magazine, The Nation,* and *The Times Literary Supplement.* In addition to reviews and essays, Steiner has written novellas, *Anno Domini* (1964) and *Proofs and Three Parables* (1993), as well as a controversial political novel, *The Portage to San Cristóbal of A. H.* (1979). Steiner has edited *The Penguin Book of Modern Verse Translation* (1966) and (with Robert Fagles) *Homer: A Collection of Critical Essays* (1962). His interest in chess produced *Fields of Force: Fischer and Spassky at Reykjavik* (1974), his impressions of the 1972 Bobby Fischer-Boris Spassky chess tournament.

NOVEL
*The Portage to San Cristóbal of A. H.,* 1979

AUTOBIOGRAPHY
*Errata: An Examined Life,* 1998

SHORT FICTION
*Anno Domini: Three Stories,* 1964
*Proofs and Three Parables,* 1993

NONFICTION
*Fields of Force: Fischer and Spassky at Reykjavik,* 1974

EDITED TEXTS
*Homer: A Collection of Critical Essays,* 1962 (with Robert Fagles)
*The Penguin Book of Modern Verse Translation,* 1966

## Further reading

Abel, Lionel. "So Who Is to Have the Last Word? (On Some of the Positions Taken by George Steiner)," in *Partisan Review.* LIII, no. 3 (1986), pp. 358–371.
Boyers, Robert. "George Steiner's Holocaust: Politics and Theology," in *Atrocity and Amnesia,* 1985.
Hassan, Ihab. "The Whole Mystery of Babel: On George Steiner," in *Salmagundi.* 70–71 (Spring–Summer, 1986), p. 331.
Kermode, Frank. "The Uses of Catastrophe," in *Book Week.* (March 26, 1967), p. 3.
Scott, Nathan, and Ronald Sharp, eds. *Reading George Steiner,* 1994.
Simon, John. "The Theatre Critic and His Double," in *Acid Test,* 1963.
Solotaroff, Theodore. "A Kind of Survival," in *The New Republic.* CLVI (May 13, 1967), pp. 21–24.

KAREN A. KILDAHL

*See also* Leavis; Trilling; Wilson

# Stendhal

(Marie-Henri Beyle)

French novelist

**Born:** Grenoble, France; January 23, 1783
**Died:** Paris, France; March 23, 1842

## Biography

Marie-Henri Beyle, whose pseudonym was inspired by the small East German town of Stendal, was born on January 23, 1783, in Grenoble, a provincial city in southeastern France. He hated his father, Chérubin Beyle, an unsuccessful lawyer and land speculator, but adored his mother, who died when Henri was seven. Privately educated by the "tyrant" Abbé Raillane, Stendhal later studied mathematics at Grenoble's École Centrale preparatory to admission to the prestigious École Polytechnique in Paris. In addition, he read Jean-Jacques Rousseau, Molière, William Shakespeare, Miguel de Cervantes, and the French philosophes and ideologues, whose works he found in his beloved Grandfather Gagnon's library.

Stendhal never did take the École Polytechnique entrance examinations. Instead, helped by his influential cousin Pierre Daru, he joined Napoleon Bonaparte in Milan as a sublieutenant in the Sixth Dragoons: thus began Stendhal's lifelong love affair with Italy. Bored with army life, he soon resigned his commission, returned to France, and planned to "write comedies like Molière." Several years of financial difficulties forced Stendhal to reenter Imperial service, from 1806 to 1814, in various high-level war administration posts in Germany and Austria and during the Russian campaign. Following Napoleon's fall, he was placed on half pay and lived in Milan from 1814 to 1821 before moving back to Paris.

After the July Revolution in 1830, Stendhal was appointed consul at Civitavecchia, near Rome, a post he filled from 1831 to 1842. This responsibility did not prevent him from writing or taking extended leaves to France. It was during one such leave that, on March 23, 1842, Stendhal died in Paris from an apoplectic stroke.

## Influence

As a literary theorist and critic, principally of the theater, Stendhal did not have an immediate impact on his contemporaries, except on Prosper Mérimée and, to a lesser extent, Alexandre Dumas *père.* Only later, when dramatists rejected verse form, long monologues, and complicated plots, were his ideas recognized and accepted. Moreover, because his novels refused to follow the pattern Sir Walter Scott had so successfully developed, the majority of contemporary critics found little merit in them (Honoré de Balzac was a lone admirer in France). Not until the publication of Hippolyte Taine's *Nouveaux Essais de critique et d'histoire* (1865; new essays on criticism and history) and Paul

Bourget's *Essais de psychologie contemporaine* (1883; essays on contemporary psychology) did Stendhal the writer, the stylist, and above all the theorist of love and the human heart, finally receive praise and recognition. His nonfiction, too, has influenced later generations: authors as diverse as Marcel Proust, James Joyce, and André Gide discovered in such works as *Souvenirs d'égotisme* (1892; *Memoirs of an Egotist*, 1949) a model for their own works.

## Analysis

Having decided to embark on a literary career, Stendhal focused his efforts on writing for the theater. He read, analyzed, and even dissected the plays of the French repertoire, especially the comedies of Molière, going so far as to keep a record of those passages that elicited any laughter from the audience. Further, at his grandfather's urging, he studied the works of the eighteenth-century sensationalists, behaviorists, and psychophysiologists, all of whom saw human beings not as essentially rational but rather as dominated by passions and desires. The influence of these works helped to determine his critical outlook concerning behavior and ethics.

In addition to absorbing the materialistic ideas of this group, Stendhal followed with great enthusiasm writers of his generation such as Lady Morgan, August Wilhelm Schlegel, and Madame de Staël. The theoretical writings of these authors questioned the validity of such sacrosanct principles of French classicism (as codified by Nicolas Boileau-Despréaux in the seventeenth century) as plot lines taken from Greek or Roman antiquity and the unities of time and place. Quickly, therefore, Stendhal began to side, in this new quarrel between the ancients and the moderns, with his rebellious contemporaries against the right-thinking members of the Academy: to their exaggerated – and highly biased – praise of Pierre Corneille and Jean Racine he proposed William Shakespeare, "the truest painter I know."

In the summer of 1822, when an English company was scheduled to perform Shakespeare on the French stage, much to the chauvinistic consternation of the Paris literary establishment, Stendhal felt compelled to respond with two articles published in the English-language *Paris Monthly Review*. Later these two articles were reprinted in the first part of *Racine and Shakespeare*. Although he readily admitted to the genius and beauty of Racine's plays, he contended in the preface "that henceforth tragedies should be written for us, the young people of the year of grace 1823, who are argumentative, serious, and a bit envious."

Rather than slavish imitation of their elders, who had written for their own public, Stendhal argued that dramatists must now mine French history for their subject matter. Following Shakespeare's brilliant accomplishments (particularly in *Othello*, 1604, and *Macbeth*, 1606), they must reject the outdated restrictions regarding time and place as both unrealistic and false. In an additional attack on the old order, Stendhal advocated the use of prose over verse,

because kings and queens do not speak in verse, and, furthermore, "in our day, the alexandrine line is often nothing more than a means of concealing stupidity."

Tragedy is not, however, the only genre that he handled roughly; classical comedy, too, whether written by old-fashioned, contemporary playwrights or by Molière himself, was considered by Stendhal to be irrelevant and shallow. It did not depict France in the 1820s and, again, it sought to hide its shortcomings behind pretentious language and situations. Summarizing his ideas, Stendhal defined Romanticism as

> the art of presenting to different peoples those literary works which, in the existing state of their habits and beliefs, are capable of giving them the greatest possible pleasure. *Classicism*, on the contrary, presents to them that literature which gave the greatest possible pleasure to their great-grandfathers.

From John Locke, Étienne de Condillac, and Claude-Adrien Helvétius, Stendhal understood the importance of sound intelligence and the need for observation and analysis, along with the concept that the formation of ideas is purely materialistic, since it derives from sensations. From Pierre-Jean-Georges Cabanis he learned that judgmental values cannot be given to sensations and that the moral phenomenon is thus the reverse of the physical: "Since we see the world and men only as our sensations record them in our minds, we must know this mind . . . must know the mind and the passions," Stendhal wrote in 1804 in his *Pensées, filosofia nova* (thoughts, new philosophy).

At the same time, Rousseau's works had taught him to favor personal emotions, with the result that Stendhal's critical theories were on the one hand based on psychophysiology and, on the other, on the critiqued writers' own lives. Thus he sometimes changed his opinion of an author's literary merits after he had uncovered either a flaw in that author's character (for example, Schlegel's "arrogance") or a lack of firsthand experience, as in the case of Scott. The English novelist, Stendhal told his friend Adolphe de Mareste, did not analyze love in his novels, for "to know how to depict it, one must have felt it." Conversely, he admired the writings of those who had themselves experienced their protagonists' emotions and upheavals (Abbé Prévost, Lord Byron, Madame de La Fayette).

Faced with this conflict between the outer and the inner worlds, therefore, Stendhal turned to prose fiction, because "I look at the novel as the comedy of the nineteenth century." Here also he wanted to imitate life, but without the trappings and weaknesses of much historical literature; he refused outright to create local color by the abuse of quaintness, and he rejected long, unnecessary descriptions: "Should one describe the clothes worn by the characters, the landscape around them, and their facial features? Or is it preferable to depict the passions and other feelings that stir their souls?"

In order to attain his dual goal of realism and sensitivity, Stendhal had developed, first in his art histories and criticism, then in *Racine and Shakespeare* and in his fiction, the now-famous notion that painting in general and the novel in particular form "a mirror one moves along the highway." In *Mimesis* (1946), Erich Auerbach recognizes in this metaphor a very modern novelistic practice: "Contemporary political and social conditions are woven into the action in a manner more detailed and more real than had been exhibited in any earlier novel, and indeed in any works of literary art."

To complement the mirror's reflection of the world, Stendhal advocated the use of "small true facts" that would unobtrusively reinforce the mimetic qualities of literature, combined with an understated, elliptical style, akin, he often declared, to that of the Civil Code. Just as, in an attempt to preserve sincerity, he avoided correcting or revising his works, Stendhal achieved psychological truth through indirection rather than straightforwardness. Relying as much on commonly shared emotions as on the readers' own creative faculties, he expected their active participation and hoped for their understanding as well.

That his works, critical and literary alike, did not meet with instant success on their publication is a result of their daring ideas and avant-garde originality as well as of his refusal to pander to the masses. One typical contemporary reviewer called *Maxims of Love* "that bizarre treatise" and later argued that *Racine and Shakespeare*, by calling for a literary revolution, went completely against the French temperament and French mores. Indeed, according to this same critic, if Shakespeare were alive in the 1820s he would want to imitate Racine.

Victor Hugo saw Stendhal as the enemy of poetry, and, in any case, Hugo's side won the Romantic battle with the tumultuous performance of his *Hernani* (1830). Balzac, however, raved about *The Charterhouse of Parma* as "a novel of ideas" which Machiavelli himself "would have written if he were living banished from Italy in the nineteenth century." English critics were on the whole more admiring than their French counterparts. For one thing, Shakespeare was their bard; for another, they had long been won over to Romanticism. It is no wonder, then, that so many of Stendhal's books were dedicated "to the happy few", or, in the case of *Racine and Shakespeare*, to "*intelligenti pauca*" (the few intelligent ones).

Stendhal's short-term influence was quite minimal, except on Mérimée, whose *Le Théâtre de Clara Gazul* (1825; *The Plays of Clara Gazul*, 1825), a series of Romantic plays, incorporated most of the principles elaborated in *Racine and Shakespeare*. Mérimée's novels and short stories also fulfilled the master's demanding standards of style and narrative, objective skepticism, and psychological veracity.

Most of Stendhal's ideas of the theater have by now become so well assimilated as to be taken for granted; only his fiction and his autobiographical works continue to offer succeeding generations new ways of looking at and thinking of the world. As Stendhal himself anticipated, he was not to be understood and appreciated until around 1880, although he did have some admirers before then. Taine had already studied Julien Sorel, the hero of *The Red and the Black*, whom he considered the perfect example of social and scientific determinism, while Émile Zola viewed the novelist as a precursor of naturalism and Friedrich Nietzsche described him as "the last great psychologist of France." The battle scenes in *The Charterhouse of Parma* inspired those of Leo Tolstoy (*War and Peace*, 1865–1869) and of Ernest Hemingway (*For Whom the Bell Tolls*, 1940).

Finally, thanks to Stendhal's obsession to see himself both as subject and object, analysts of egotism, from Maurice Barrès to André Gide and from Marcel Proust to James Joyce, have found in *The Life of Henri Brulard* and *Memoirs of Egotism* the necessary justifications for their own "cult of the self." Paul Valéry best summed up the legacy of this unique writer-critic when he wrote: "We should never have done with Stendhal. I can think of no higher praise."

## Principal criticism
*De l'amour*, 1822 (*Maxims of Love*, 1906)
*Racine et Shakespeare*, part 1, 1823, part 2, 1825 (*Racine and Shakespeare*, 1962)
*Pensées, filosofia nova*, 1931

## Other major works and literary forms
Stendhal was very much interested in all areas of human activity, whether politics or music, fine arts or tourism. He wrote numerous articles and reviews for several cosmopolitan publications (for example, the *Edinburgh Quarterly Review*, the *Paris Monthly Review*, and the *New Monthly Magazine*); some of these pieces later appeared in book form.

Stendhal's most important and lasting contribution, however, remains his fiction, especially his two novels, *Le Rouge et le noir* (1830; *The Red and the Black*, 1898) and *La Chartreuse de Parme* (1839; *The Charterhouse of Parma*, 1895), as well as his collection of short stories. His correspondence and autobiographical writings (published posthumously) have further contributed to understanding both the writer and the man.

NOVELS
*Armance*, 1827 (English translation, 1928)
*Le Rouge et le noir*, 1830 (*The Red and the Black*, 1898)
*La Chartreuse de Parme*, 1839 (*The Charterhouse of Parma*, 1895)
*Lucien Leuwen*, 1855, 1894, 1926–1927 (English translation, 1950)
*Lamiel*, 1889, 1971 (English translation, 1950)

SHORT FICTION
*Chroniques italiennes*, 1839, 1855 (*The Abbess of Castro and Other Tales*, 1926)

NONFICTION

*Vies de Haydn, de Mozart et de Métastase*, 1815 (*The Lives of Haydn and Mozart, with Observations on Métastase*, 1817)

*Histoire de la peinture en Italie*, 1817

*Rome, Naples et Florence en 1817*, 1817, 1826 (*Rome, Naples, and Florence in 1817*, 1818)

*Vie de Rossini*, 1823 (*Memoirs of Rossini*, 1824, also as *Life of Rossini*, 1956)

*Notes d'un dilettante*, 1824–1827

*D'un nouveau complot contre les industriels*, 1825

*Promenades dans Rome*, 1829 (*A Roman Journal*, 1957)

*Mémoires d'un touriste*, 1838 (partially translated in *Memoirs of a Tourist*, 1962)

*Voyage dans le midi de la France*, 1838 (*Travels in the South of France*, 1971)

*Correspondance inédite*, 1855, 1968 (partially translated in "*To the Happy Few*," 1952)

*Vie de Napoléon*, 1876 (*A Life of Napoleon*, 1956)

*Journal*, 1888, 1937 (partially translated in *The Private Diaries*, 1954)

*Vie de Henri Brulard*, 1890, 1949 (*The Life of Henri Brulard*, 1925)

*Souvenirs d'égotisme*, 1892, 1950 (*Memoirs of Egotism*, 1949)

*Correspondance*, 1933–1934

*Courrier anglais*, 1935–1936

*Journal littéraire*, 1970

MISCELLANEOUS

*The Works*, 1925–1928 (6 volumes)

## Further reading

Auerbach, Erich. *Mimesis*, 1946.

Barzun, Jacques. *Classic, Romantic, and Modern*, 1961.

Bloom, Harold, ed. *Stendhal*, 1989.

Booth, Wayne C. *The Rhetoric of Fiction*, 1961.

Brombert, Victor. "Stendhal, Analyst or Amorist?," in *Yale French Studies*. XI (Summer, 1953), pp. 39–48.

Caraccio, Armand. *Stendhal*, 1965.

Cremin, Joan. *Selfhood, Fiction, and Desire in Stendhal's "Vie de Henry Brulard" and "Armance*," 1998.

Day, James T. *Stendhal's Paper Mirror*, 1987.

Del Litto, V. *La Vie intellectuelle de Stendhal: Genèse et Evolution de ses idées*, 1962.

Jefferson, Ann. *Reading Realism in Stendhal*, 1988.

Pearson, Roger. *Stendhal's Violin: A Novelist and His Reader*, 1988.

Peyre, Henri. *What Is Romanticism?*, 1976.

Talbot, Emile J. *Stendhal and Romantic Esthetics*, 1985.

———. *Stendhal Revisited*, 1993.

PIERRE L. HORN

*See also* Madame de Staël; Romanticism

# Structuralism

In Western scholarship, structuralism most often refers to an analytical method that came to the fore in France during the 1950s, reached its peak during the following decade when it came to exert a strong influence on Anglo-American thinkers as well, and continued as an important force through the 1970s. However, the use of the term "structuralism" to define an approach to literary analysis first appears in a 1928 paper by Roman Jakobson (who was then living in Czechoslovakia) and Iurii Tynianov; the Prague School, which flourished from 1926 until 1948, went on to refine literary structuralism in ways that anticipate many positions of the French structuralists. More recently, and largely independently of developments in France and the United States, structuralism has served as the predominant method of the so-called "Moscow-Tartu School" in Russia.

Structuralism has its roots in the linguistics of Ferdinand de Saussure, who called for replacing the prevalent historical and comparative study of language with a more analytical approach, which would examine language synchronically (at any given moment rather than historically). At least three of the basic notions that he developed in course lectures from 1907 to 1911 were to be adapted by the structuralists: (1) the importance of considering language as a system (which Saussure called *langue*, as opposed to the individual speech act, or *parole*); (2) the recognition that language can be seen as a system of signs in which the relationship between the signifier (the sound-image) and the signified (the concept or thing) is essentially arbitrary; and (3) the need to define linguistic entities relationally, that is, in terms of the ways in which they combine with or are opposed to each other. Saussure himself felt that his conclusions about signs, while based on specifically linguistic investigations, could be applied more broadly to other social and cultural phenomena; what he called "semiology" has more popularly come to be known as semiotics. The effort to apply both the terminology and the techniques of linguistic scholarship to literary and other entities has remained an essential feature of structuralism.

## Czech and Russian structuralism

While the focus here will be largely on French and Anglo-American structuralism, it is necessary to say a word as well about the two other major schools. The Prague School consisted largely of linguists, several of whom shared Saussure's interests in phonology, which, in dealing with the most elemental building blocks of language, served as the most suitable area in which to work out a structural methodology. At the same time, the school's contributions to literary studies were not inconsiderable. Roman Jakobson, while a member of the Prague School, created several of his most important statements on the relationship of linguistics to literary study. Jan Mukařovský, the leading literary theorist in the school, by the mid-1930s was applying sign theory to the study of the aesthetic object in a remarkably sophisticated manner; unfortunately, his major works were translated from Czech too late to influence most French and American structuralists during the formative period of their writing.

In Russia, the Moscow-Tartu School arose around 1960, attracting an outstanding group of linguists and literary critics. Despite the suspicion of official Marxist circles toward a methodology that was essentially non-ideological in its orientation, the school flourished for more than two decades, until emigration, political upheaval, and new directions taken by some of its leading members diminished its force by the late 1980s. While not dissimilar to French and Anglo-American structuralism in its basic approach to literature, the influence of its Slavic antecedents (Russian Formalism and the Prague School) has understandably been more direct. The Moscow-Tartu School has also been less affected than Western structuralism by developments in philosophy and, especially, psychoanalysis (Sigmund Freud, after all, was a "non-person" in the Soviet Union), though it too has applied structuralist and semiotic analyses not just to language and literature but also to a wide variety of other cultural and social phenomena (to such systems as folklore, film, and icon painting, as well as to activities like card playing). One emphasis of the Moscow-Tartu School, seen most fully in Iurii Lotman's *The Structure of the Artistic Text* (1977), combines the Prague School notion of the poetic text as a dynamic system of interrelated systems, along with certain elements of both information theory (via Jakobson) and Russian Formalism. Lotman notes that the literary text has a higher density of information than other forms of communication, in part because it contains an entire hierarchy of codes, in which every element is meaningful (and thus appreciation of the text requires a careful and knowledgeable reading). Structuralism, understood abstractly, can be seen as studying only the inner system or *langue* of the objects it investigates; the Moscow-Tartu School, however, has more and more emphasized the flexible boundaries of the literary work, whose system intersects with other cultural structures, all of which themselves are constantly evolving. The other distinctive feature of the Russian school has been its attention to the study of verse, employing statistical and linguistically based analyses to establish important findings about the nature and variety of metrical and rhythmic forms in the Russian tradition as well as to offer innovative approaches to studying the relationship between verse forms and their (acquired) semantic associations.

## French and Anglo-American structuralism

The figure linking all twentieth-century structuralisms is Roman Jakobson. A key member in one of the two centers of Russian Formalism during the late 1910s, he was a founding member of the Prague School, and several decades later his writings exerted a powerful influence on the Moscow-Tartu School. French structuralism was inspired in a variety of ways by its Russian and Czech predecessors (it is noteworthy, for instance, that both Tzvetan Todorov and Julia Kristeva, the latter from the start more a critic than an adherent of structuralism, are from Bulgaria, where they were introduced early on to the basic teachings of the Russian scholars), but Jakobson's own ideas were to prove formative. In 1942, due to the exigencies of World War II, both Jakobson and Claude Lévi-Strauss were teaching at a school founded by French exiles in New York. Lévi-Strauss attended Jakobson's lectures on linguistics in order to gain some knowledge that would help with his efforts to record native languages of Brazil. Instead, Lévi-Strauss was introduced to Saussurian concepts and to Jakobson's further work in phonology, especially the notion of phonemic distinctive features that stand in opposition to each other. Lévi-Strauss quickly saw the broad applicability of linguistic concepts to create a more formal approach to anthropology, whether for elaborating the system that lies behind kinship relations or determining the underlying structural similarities that link the different versions of a myth.

While Lévi-Strauss was creating a school of structural anthropology, Roland Barthes, who also adopted linguistic notions from Saussure and was familiar with the writings of Jakobson as well as other linguists, developed an extensive treatment of literature in terms of language, endeavoring, for instance, to define the essentials of narrative in terms of its constituent units. His structuralist approach, informed by sign theory, was applied to other cultural phenomena as well; for example, in *The Fashion System* (1983) he almost playfully shows that the captions in fashion magazines can be read as a semiotic system. Following Lévi-Strauss and Barthes, structuralist notions can be discerned in the writings of scholars seeking to understand a broad range of human endeavors, ranging from psychoanalysis to political philosophy. Structuralism soon had a major impact on critical thought in the United States, as summarized in Jonathan Culler's *Structuralist Poetics* (1975). However, already in 1966, during a conference at the Johns Hopkins University, Jacques Derrida gave a paper which seriously questioned the entire structuralist endeavor; he pointed out that in order to analyze a structure one has to be able to view it from without, but it is impossible to stand outside the broad systems that create meaning for various human endeavors. Derrida's ideas were developed in subsequent publications and gave the impetus to what has become known as poststructuralism, which over the next decade or so supplanted structuralism as the dominant movement in critical thought.

## Key concepts

The crucial insight guiding structuralist approaches is the notion that the codes governing other systems can be studied with the same scientific precision, and by using many of the same concepts, as language. The Moscow-Tartu School in fact has referred to the products of human endeavors which are definable by signs as "secondary modeling systems" (with language understood as comprising the primary modeling system). The various kinds of systems – whether literature, kinship relationships, clothing, or traffic signals – are said to operate according to a set of rules or a code equivalent to the *langue* distinguished by

Saussure. This code, like the grammatical rules governing language, is not "visible"; it is precisely the task of the linguist or literary critic or anthropologist to discover and elucidate the inner workings of the system.

In other words, the structuralist approach goes beneath the surface to examine the dynamic and complex relationships among the various structural entities; at the same time, by describing the internal construction in all its richness, this method is ultimately interested in understanding the totality. The relationships are most often described in terms of binary oppositions, which, like much of structuralism, can be traced back to the influence of structural linguistics and specifically to investigations into the nature of phonological correlations. In order to discover all the sets of oppositions operating within the work actual structuralist analyses tend to be quite detailed. Often cited as the archetypal instance of such criticism is the article by Lévi-Strauss and Jakobson on Charles Baudelaire's sonnet "Les Chats," in which the two scholars devote approximately twenty pages of printed text to analyzing the syntactic, rhythmic, and phonological qualities of this fourteen-line poem. They note how symmetries, parallelisms, and contrasts among the constituent elements both underlie and create various structures within the work, and, what is more, that these phenomena have "a semantic foundation" – in other words, the inner form of the work both accentuates and creates meaning.

The painstaking search for such structures is justified by the consideration that they are what make a text literary. In "Linguistics and Poetics" (1960), Roman Jakobson elaborates a communicative model, which consists of six elements. On one side stands the addresser, on the other the addressee, in the middle is the message; the message in turn is conveyed through a "contact" (the means of communication, be it speech, a written text, or whatever), is composed in a mutually intelligible "code," and refers to a "context." Jakobson goes on to note that any one of these six elements may be the focus of a given communication; for instance, if the communication is oriented toward the context, then it is basically "referential" (informative). In a poetic text the orientation is toward the message itself: that is, repetitions, parallels, sound echoes, and so on highlight the constituent elements of the text and call attention to it. Jakobson specifically uses the word "poetic," since the effects in poetry are both more concentrated and more integral to the very genre, but the basic principles are at work in prose as well.

However, some of the most significant work by structuralists has resulted from an effort to go beyond the level of phonemes, words, and grammatical parallels in order to examine the nature of narrative structure. "Narratology," as this field is known, owes much to certain concepts originally elaborated by the Russian Formalists. Most important in this regard is Vladimir Propp's *Morphology of the Folktale* (originally published in 1928). Propp reduced the fairy-tale story units to thirty-one functions (actions defined in terms of their role within the plot) – for instance, interdiction, violation of an interdiction, struggle (of hero and villain), and so on. Not all functions will necessarily appear in every tale, but those that do appear always appear in the same order. And Propp found that the characters in these tales fulfill just seven basic roles. His basic insight into the nature of narrative structure, while deriving solely from his work with folk literature, was adapted by Lévi-Strauss in his work on myths and then by A. J. Greimas, who, in his *Structural Semantics* (1983) and other works, attempted to generalize and simplify the categories of Propp's functions and character types. Other scholars have drawn on the Russian Formalist distinction between *fabula*, the "actual" order of the events described in the text, and *siuzhet*, the plot as it is unfolded within the literary work. Thus Gérard Genette, whose focus is on the work as discourse, has considered this demarcation as part of his effort to categorize the different manners in which the narrator relates to events. That is, if Propp examines the narrative, the story that has been told, then Genette offers a structuralist approach to narration, the act of telling the tale.

## Aftermath and assessment

Already by 1970 Barthes, in *S/Z*, an analysis of Honoré de Balzac's story "Sarrasine," was taking a poststructuralist rather than a structuralist approach to the literary work: the story was no longer seen as a fixed structure subject to analysis, but as something analyzable in infinite ways, with ultimately indeterminate meaning. Others created conceptual frameworks that challenged structuralism even earlier. For instance, Jacques Lacan's psychoanalytic theory, with its central notion that the unconscious is structured like a language, draws heavily from the structuralist concepts of Saussure and Jakobson (and Lacan's own analyses of such works as *Hamlet* have helped make his approach of particular interest to literary scholars). Even early on, though, Lacan emphasizes divisions and conflict in his descriptions of the self, thereby undercutting the sense of a coherent structuralist system in his view of the unconscious. Ultimately, then, many French thinkers whose thought was regarded as structuralist in the 1950s and 1960s were seen as poststructuralists by the 1970s, while among literary theorists in the United States, deconstruction, essentially a poststructuralist enterprise, soon become the predominant trend.

Literary structuralism, as embodied in its purest form, has been criticized on a number of counts. Its focus on the inner workings of the text and on describing literature as an independent system can result in a lack of attention to the author and to the context in which the work is created. If literary evolution is to be regarded as operating according to its own laws, then it seems to be isolated from human history, and from social and political developments.

The exhaustive analysis of inner structure also tends to leave aside questions of evaluation; it is possible to carry out impressive and convincing structural studies of political slogans or nursery rhymes, and structuralism itself does not seem to offer an answer as to why a Shakespearean sonnet is to be valued more highly than an advertising jingle. Indeed, the very fact that structuralism can serve as an analytic tool for many fields in the social sciences as well as the humanities calls into question its ability to place adequate emphasis on the particular emotional and aesthetic qualities of literature. Attacked from the other side, structuralism has been accused of being less scientific than it claims to be; just as Derrida and others have denied the possibility of objectively studying a system from within, others have questioned whether the specific parallelisms and structures that structuralism privileges are necessarily either the most important aspect of a work or even perceptible to the "normal" reader.

And yet structuralism has left (and continues to create) a significant and enduring legacy. At the most basic level, it has established tools for analyzing the literary work with greater care and insight; merely subjective statements about the power or beauty of a work seem inadequate in light of structuralism's ability to discover the qualities that may in fact account for that power or beauty. The more sophisticated adherents of structuralism, beginning already with the Prague School, attempted to find ways to study not just the literary work, but to see it as part of a set of systems that included an author's other writings, the artistic norms of a given period, the works within a given genre, and so on – in other words, broader structural analysis can in fact not only account for the author and the context of the work, but also take into consideration artistic quality. Even poststructuralist analyses, in their very attack on the structuralist assumptions, make use of concepts and an understanding of language that would not have been possible without the original work of the structuralists. Thus the legacy of structuralism, which survived the opposition of Marxist governments to remain a vital tradition in the Slavic countries, remains an integral part of the Western critical tradition as well.

## Further reading

Baran, Henryk, ed. *Semiotics and Structuralism: Readings from the Soviet Union*, 1976.

Barthes, Roland. *Essais critiques*, 1964 (*Critical Essays*, 1972).

——. *Éléments de sémiologie*, 1964 (*Elements of Semiology*, 1967).

——. *Système de la mode*, 1967 (*The Fashion System*, 1983).

Berman, Art. *From the New Criticism to Deconstruction: The Reception of Structuralism and Post-Structuralism*, 1988.

Culler, Jonathan. *Structuralist Poetics: Structuralism, Linguistics, and the Study of Literature*, 1975.

Eagleton, Terry. *Literary Theory: An Introduction*, 1983.

Eco, Umberto. *A Theory of Semiotics*, 1976.

Ehrmann, Jacques, ed. *Structuralism*, 1970.

Galan, F. W. *Historic Structures: The Prague School Project, 1928–1946*, 1985.

Genette, Gérard. *Figures*, 1966–1972 (selections translated as *Figures of Literary Discourse*, 1982).

Greimas, A. J. *Sémantiqe structurale: Recherche de méthode*, 1966 (*Structural Semantics: An Attempt at Method*, 1983).

Hawkes, Terence. *Structuralism and Semiotics*, 1977.

Jakobson, Roman. *Selected Writings*, 1962–1987 (8 volumes; see especially vols. 2–3, 7–8).

Jameson, Frederic. *The Prison-House of Language: A Critical Account of Structuralism and Russian Formalism*, 1972.

Lane, Michael, ed. *Introduction to Structuralism*, 1970.

Lévi-Strauss, Claude. *Anthropologie structurale*, 1958 (*Structural Anthropology*, 1963).

Lotman, Iurii. *The Structure of the Artistic Text*, 1977 (Russian original, 1970).

Prince, Gerald. *Narratology: The Form and Functioning of Narrative*, 1982.

Riffaterre, Michael. *Semiotics of Poetry*, 1978.

Saussure, Ferdinand de. *Cours de linguistique générale*, 1916 (*Course in General Linguistics*, 1959).

Scholes, Robert. *Structuralism in Literature: An Introduction*, 1974.

Selden, Raman, ed. *The Cambridge History of Literary Criticism*. Vol. 8, *From Formalism to Poststructuralism*, 1995.

Todorov, Tzvetan. *Introduction à la littérature fantastique*, 1970 (*The Fantastic: A Structural Approach to a Literary Genre*, 1973).

BARRY P. SCHERR

*See also* Barthes; Culler; Deconstruction; Lévi-Strauss; Linguistics and Literary Studies; Russian Formalism; Saussure; Semiotics

# Style

Style has been traditionally defined in one of two ways. According to the first approach, style is a property of the form of a discourse, in contrast to the content it communicates: *how* a thing is said as opposed to *what* is said. The second approach defines style as the expressive function of language as opposed to its referential function: *connotation* versus *denotation*.

Aristotle, whose brief discussion in his *Poetics* (c. 334–323 B.C.) and much longer treatment in his *Rhetoric* (348–336 B.C.) constitute the foundation of most stylistic criticism, emphasizes the former approach, and casts the subject/style distinction as one between Thought and Diction. Style, or Diction, is assumed to be a matter of fitting the appropriate words, metaphors, and ornaments to previously established ideas. In proper written or verbal expression, form corresponds to this prior content. Considerations of genre are also determinants of style. Strange words or metaphors, for example, should be used more sparingly in prose than in poetry, an observation that seems to imply that a given text might have more or less style. Drawing what will become a commonplace analogy between style in language and style in clothing, Aristotle observes that a red cloak will suit a young man (poetry) better than it will an old man (prose). The underlying assumption is that the man (the content) is inherently either old or young, and that his clothes (the style), whether appropriate or not, can only make him look distinguished or silly, not change his age.

If the appropriate analogy for the formal model of style is that of clothing, the analogy for the expressive model of style is the fingerprint. Whereas the former approach sees style as a wardrobe of clothing options that any given writer might select for outfitting a particular content or idea, the latter approach sees style as the set of unique fingerprints that every writer leaves behind as he or she creates a given work. This position implicitly posits a sort of objective, descriptive writing that can be seen as stylistically neutral. Style in literature is restricted to only the expression of emotions and feelings, language that exploits the connotations and not just the denotations of words and examples. In this view, style expresses not just the ideas but the idiosyncratic character and personality of the individual writer. In the famous phrase attributed to the French critic Georges de Buffon (1707–1788), "The style is the man himself." By extension, some critics have argued for period or national styles, which express the distinctive characteristics of a time or culture.

Both the formal and expressive premises pose difficulties. The formal assumption that the subject of a discourse is a fixed given ignores the point that style can affect content; contrary to the Aristotelian implication, clothes can to some extent make the man. Style and subject seem to mutually influence one another in greater and lesser ways, and *what* is said would seem in most cases to depend to some degree on *how* it is said. The logical conclusion that form and content are inseparable becomes one of the central dogmas of most twentieth-century criticism. In Gérard Genette's formulation, "Style is the perceptible surface of discourse, the surface that by definition accompanies it at every point without interruption or fluctuation." Paradoxically, this valorization of style in effect empties the concept of meaning, since *every* feature of the text can count as stylistic. The subject/style distinction has been further undercut by consideration of fields such as architecture and music that have no obvious subject, yet can be discussed in terms of their style independently of any form/content distinction. Related arguments have been invoked against the expressive model; language and ideas are not infinitely malleable, and what an author says, as well as the language and culture within which he or she says it, are materials that set parameters as to how it can be said. To adapt the analogy proposed by the nineteenth-century critic Walter Pater, the linguistic and cultural materials writers work in and upon are no more their own creations than the sculptor's marble. The twentieth-century French theorist Michael Riffaterre has argued for the collapse of both the form/content and expressive/objective dichotomies; in a pointed reformulation of Buffon's famous dictum, Riffaterre has declared that "style is the text itself."

The American philosopher Nelson Goodman has proposed the use of the idea of "exemplification" in the discussion of style, a suggestion that many critics see as a path around these traditional oppositions. Some qualities, he argues, are not merely referred to or expressed in a text, but exemplified by it, just as color and weave are exemplified by the swatch of cloth used by a tailor or upholsterer as a sample. The word "short" not only refers to or expresses brevity, but also exemplifies brevity by being a short word, whereas "long" does not exemplify length. The principle is of course not restricted to single words: sonnets by different authors on different subjects expressing different emotions may still exemplify the same form and therefore some of the same qualities. While style can refer to what is said, what is expressed, or what is exemplified, not every such feature counts as stylistic. The swatch of fabric exemplifies the color, weave, and thickness of the fabric, but not its size and shape: no one orders a thousand tiny rectangles of cloth to cover a couch. Similarly, only certain aspects of the subject, form, and feeling of a work are relevant to the analysis of its style, while others, like the size and shape of the swatch, are not stylistically functional. Obviously, determining which aspects of the swatch of fabric are significant is a simple matter compared to the complex task of specifying which features are crucial to the functioning of a work of art. Goodman argues that a property counts as stylistic only when it associates a work with other works of one rather than another artist, period, region, school, and so on, but it remains to be seen to what extent his ideas will bear critical fruit.

## Further reading

Aristotle. *Rhetoric* and *Poetics*.
Auerbach, Erich. *Mimesis: The Representation of Reality in Western Literature*, 1953.
Genette, Gérard. "Style and Signification," in *Fiction and Diction*, 1993, pp. 85–141.
Goodman, Nelson. "The Status of Style," in *Ways of Worldmaking*, 1978, pp. 23–40.
Hough, Graham. *Style and Stylistics*, 1969.
Riffaterre, Michael. *Text Production*, 1983.
Ullmann, Stephen. *Style in the French Novel*, 1957.

WILLIAM NELLES

# Sublime

Sublime is a term that is associated with a feeling, experience, or process that is overpowering, awe-inspiring, and excessive. Sublime differs from many other literary terms in that it appears explicitly within literature, can be used to define traditions of literature, and is a metacritical term employed in discussions of aesthetics and society. In some cases it is used as an adjective to describe objects in nature, works of art, artists, as well as poetic language, imagery in texts, and characters in novels. In other cases, it designates challenges to perception and judgment. More often, it names a combination of the two, as in Edmund Burke's *Philosophical Enquiry into the Origin of our Ideas of the Sublime and Beautiful* (1757). Burke provides a catalogue of the objects in nature and art that elicit a sense of the sublime, which he defines as "the strongest emotion which the mind is capable of feeling." Storms, mountains, and elevated passages of poetry, such as John Milton's description of Satan, evoke fear or apprehension through their "obscurity" and "darkness." The fear, however, is distanced and speculative rather than physical, affecting comprehension rather than actual life. In this way, the sublime is also delightful, because the perceiving subject is able to experience the danger and at the same time celebrate being alive.

The sublime first gained prominence through Nicolas Boileau-Despréaux's influential 1674 translation of *Peri Hypsous* (*On the Sublime*), attributed to Longinus. Longinus' detailed analyses of passages of classical poetry with an eye to the workings of genius influenced late-seventeenth- and early-eighteenth-century aesthetic theory by demonstrating how great poetry overpowers the reader and the conventions of literature itself. Longinus writes that "genius does not merely persuade an audience but lifts it to ecstasy," and it is by feeling this power that a reader can recognize greatness. Genius also demands awe, even if the works have flaws, because such writers have "more than human capacity" and are akin to gods. Longinus had an interesting place in the long-standing debate of the time over what criteria determined a great work of art. French neoclassical critics such as Boileau and René Rapin enlisted Longinus into the battle which emphasized regularity and conformity in literature. However, Longinus' text obviously makes arguments equally valid for the critics who valued challenges to classical form and expression. Joseph Addison represents Longinus in a position that transcends the division between ancients and moderns, writing that while poetry should respect the Aristotelian unities, "there is still something more essential to the art, something that elevates and astonishes the fancy, and gives a greatness of mind to the reader, which few of the critics besides Longinus have considered."

Samuel Monk's study of the sublime describes the way the emphasis on the feelings evoked in the reader develop throughout the eighteenth century in works by Addison, David Hume, and Edmund Burke. What begins as a means of judging great poetry becomes, in Immanuel Kant's *Critique of Judgment* (1790), a means of discussing the mind that judges. Like Burke, Kant describes the sublime as a combination of pleasure and pain. He emphasizes more so than Burke, however, that the sublime is a judgment and "cannot be contained in any sensuous form." The sublime arises first as a failure of the mind to give form to what is "absolutely great" or "great beyond all comparison." In the attempt, however, the mind is freed to reflect on the power of reason and its independence from nature. In other words, the thought process that attempts to comprehend the infinite is sublime, not the mountain or ocean that began the train of thought. The subjectivism evident in Kant's theory of the sublime extends into Romantic poetry, although the relationship between the mind and nature alters. As Thomas Weiskel explains, the sublime becomes a system of meaning within a poem and a strategy of authorship that allows the poet to transcend fragmentary experience and speak as an "I." The Romantic persona hopes to find a greater bond to nature in the dominance over nature. In Percy Bysshe Shelley's "Mont Blanc," for instance, the result of "a trance sublime and strange" inspired by the mountain frees the speaker's mind to hold "unremitting interchange/ with the clear universe of things around."

Sublime dropped out of the literary and critical vocabulary as the nineteenth century progressed, but has returned to critical discourse, at least, with a vengeance. The same issues of transcendence and boundaries that interested eighteenth-century aesthetic theory are being re-examined by contemporary poststructuralist theory. Some critics have interrogated the configurations of gender and power in literary and philosophical discussions of the sublime, while others delve into the economic and political contexts of the sublime. Contemporary work on the sublime not only looks backward to critique earlier versions of the sublime, it often takes the self-reflective aspect of the sublime into account and questions its own project. Jean-François Lyotard's work returns to Kant's "Analytic of the Sublime," reading it as both an example and discussion of the way critical frameworks of thought reach their own limits and find themselves ungrounded, provisional, and conditional. The "Analytic of the Sublime," according to Lyotard, "exposes the 'state' of critical thought when it reaches its extreme limit – a spasmodic state." The dizzying variety of sublimes in contemporary critical theory, including the Longinian sublime, Kantian sublime, Gothic sublime, negative sublime, feminine sublime, and postmodern sublime, certainly seem to attest to the dynamic Peter de Bolla describes whereby the sublime "becomes part of the text which locates, analyses and describes the experience."

## Further reading

Burke, Edmund. *A Philosophical Enquiry into the Origin of our Ideas of the Sublime and Beautiful*, 1757; edited by James T. Boulton, 1958.

De Bolla, Peter. *The Discourse of the Sublime: History, Aesthetics and the Subject*, 1989.

Kant, Immanuel. *Kritik der Urteilskraft*, 1790 (*Critique of Judgment*, 1951).

Longinus. *On the Sublime*, 1927. Translated by W. Hamilton Fyfe.

Lyotard, Jean-François. *Leçons sur l'analytique du sublime*, 1991 (*Lessons on the Analytic of the Sublime*, 1994).

Monk, Samuel H. *The Sublime: A Study of Critical Theories in XVIIIth-Century England*, 1935.

Weiskel, Thomas. *The Romantic Sublime: Studies in the Structure and Psychology of Transcendence*, 1976.

DONYA SAMARA

*See also* Burke, E.; Longinus

# Surrealism

The term "surrealism" is used to characterize both an early twentieth-century modernist movement and a philosophical concept in the history of art and literature. The prefix "sur-" means "about" or "concerning," and also "above" or "transcending," and its appearance in the word suggests that surrealism represents both a concern with given reality and also its transcendence, perhaps to achieve another level of reality. This relation is fundamental to both the historical movement known as "Surrealism" and present-day philosophical developments which it has influenced.

## The Surrealist movement

The Surrealist movement is generally regarded as originating in Dada, a loosely-knit collective of European artists which germinated during the years between 1916 and 1924, and whose ideas spread to North America during World War I. Dada artists reacted against all that they saw as boring, conventional, traditional, or bourgeois in art and society, and their art varied from performances of nonsense poems, songs, and plays to displays of "ready-mades" – junk and everyday objects such as ironing-boards and urinals, or a reproduction of Leonardo da Vinci's *Mona Lisa* with a mustache scribbled on it – in art exhibitions. The eclecticism of Dada, however, is illustrated by the appearance in its exhibitions and publications, *Dada* and *Cabaret Voltaire*, of works not only by key Dadaists such as Hugo Ball, Marcel Duchamp, Marcel Janco, and Richard Huelsenbeck, but also cubist pieces by Pablo Picasso, expressionist paintings by Vasilii Kandinskii, articles by the futurist Filippo Marinetti, and poetic texts by Guillaume Apollinaire, Jean Arp, and André Breton, who were later associated with Surrealism.

The transition from the anarchistic philosophy of Dada, which on principle had to reject its own institutionalization as a convention of art, to the positive idealism and ethics of Surrealism took place during the years 1921 to 1924, when a group of (mostly French) artists, playwrights, and poets were brought together under the leadership and doctrines of André Breton. These included the poets Paul Éluard, Robert Desnos, and Guillaume Apollinaire (who coined the term "surrealism"); the artists Max Ernst, Jean Arp, Joan Miró, André Masson, Yves Tanguy, René Magritte, and Salvador Dali; the novelists Louis Aragon and Georges Bataille; playwrights Alfred Jarry, Jean Cocteau, and Antonin Artaud; and filmmakers Luis Buñuel and Man Ray.

The movement crystallized in 1924, when the Bureau of Surrealist Research was established, the publication *La Révolution surréaliste* appeared, and Breton published his first *Surrealist Manifesto*. A second *Manifesto* followed in 1929, and during the 1930s Surrealism was a powerful influence in almost every area of literature and art in Europe. With the outbreak of World War II in 1939, most of the Surrealists left Europe for New York, and the group gradually dissipated; their ideas, however, continue to influence contemporary art.

## Philosophy and concerns

While the Surrealists continued the criticism of society that Dada had initiated, rejecting social institutions and systems viewed as oppressive, their voluminous writings and works of art reflect a more positive concern with transcending given social realities to reveal what they hide or repress, in order to build a better society. Thus Breton's *Manifesto* defines surrealism as "thought dictated in the absence of all control exerted by reason, and outside any aesthetic or moral preoccupation," and as a philosophy based on "belief in the superior reality of certain forms of association neglected until now, in the omnipotence of the dream, and in the disinterested play of thought." Rejecting conventional notions of artistic style and technique, and in particular the idea that a work of art is mimetic, or imitative of a perceived reality, the Surrealists advocated a spontaneous creative act, which would reveal not perceived "reality," tamed by reason and logic, but what this given reality concealed: the strange aphasiac logic of unconscious reality. Surrealist images are thus characterized by surprising juxtapositions and visual and verbal puns; and the shock they give to the viewer's perceptual logic and rationality is often caused by a disjunction between verbal and visual language.

Breton's main sources for these ideas were Leon Trotskii's social critiques and studies of the human condition, Hippolyte Taine's questioning of the human senses as valid means of experiencing reality, and Sigmund Freud's work on the unconscious as it is revealed in dreams. The interrogation of given social reality led to the development of various methods of creation by which unconscious forces and images could be revealed free of all conscious control: Max Ernst's *frottage*, the creation of an image by placing a piece of paper over an object and making a charcoal rubbing, and *grattage*, the scratching and scraping of surfaces coated in thick layers of paint to produce changes in the layers and effects of light and shade; Breton's automatic writing, where the writer simply recorded whatever spontaneous thoughts and images appeared in his or her mind (with results similar to the literary technique of "stream of consciousness"); and the children's game *cadavre exquis*, where each player draws a body part without seeing the others, and the results are combined to produce a grotesque image of a person.

In seeking to express the unconscious forces of human nature, the Surrealists produced diverse works of literature and art, but works described as surrealistic are generally characterized by a dreamlike quality, which may range from the grotesque and monstrous (Odilon Redon, Buñuel) to the witty and childlike (Miró, Paul Klee) and the mystical (Paul Éluard, Edmond Jabès). A hallucinatory style is particularly apparent in Surrealist novels such as Breton's *Nadja* (1928; English translation, 1960) and Aragon's *Le Paysan de Paris* (1926; *Paris Peasant*, 1995), where dream characters drift through streets and parks, jostled randomly by passers-by and unexpected occurrences. The forces of the Freudian unconscious also include repressed desires such as violence, sexuality, incest, and murder-dominant themes in Bataille's novels and Artaud's treatises on the "theater of cruelty."

## Sources and influences

The various artists associated with Surrealism claimed different antecedents and precursors, most famously Isidor Ducasse (Comte de Lautréamont), whose novel *Les Chants de Maldoror* (1868; *The Songs of Maldoror*, 1978) both stylistically and thematically contains all the elements of Surrealist writing; Charles Baudelaire and Edgar Allan Poe, for their concern with the problems of evil and death; and the French Symbolists Stéphane Mallarmé and Arthur Rimbaud, whose experiments with poetic language anticipated the Surrealists' concern with language as both a constraining and liberating medium.

In retrospect, however, the concepts involved in the Surrealist movement have implications far beyond its historical moment. The project of Surrealism may be seen as simply one moment in a long historical tradition of anti-aesthetic and counter-philosophical questioning which runs parallel to (and often intervenes in) the history of rational philosophy. This tradition of "irrationalism" or unreason may be considered a movement of self-questioning within systems of thought based on reason: its faces and figures are found in the grotesques and gargoyles on Gothic churches, in the visual images of Hieronymus Bosch, Francisco Goya, Henri Rousseau, and Giorgio de Chirico, and in the writings of the Marquis de Sade and Friedrich Nietzsche. In twentieth-century literature, surrealist elements are ubiquitous and international, and appear in works by authors as diverse as Franz Kafka, Italo Calvino, Ralph Ellison, Will Self, Angela Carter, Chinua Achebe, Gabriel García Márquez, and Carlos Fuentes. In the world of music, the work of John Cage and Pierre Boulez; in modern dance, the performances of Merce Cunningham; in film, productions ranging from Buñuel's *An Andalusian Dog* to Peter Greenaway's *The Cook, the Thief, his Wife and her Lover*; and in video, the remarkable special effects and computer-aided designs of MTV – all these developments are built on the foundations laid by the Surrealists.

The influences of Surrealism on literary criticism and theory have also been remarkable, although very little work has been done in this area: philosophers and theorists ranging from Walter Benjamin and Theodor Adorno to Jacques Lacan and Gilles Deleuze have written on the Surrealists. Deleuze and Félix Guattari's influential two-volume work *Capitalism and Schizophrenia* (1985) makes frequent references to Surrealist aesthetics; Roland Barthes, Susan Sontag, and others have written on Bataille; Julia Kristeva and Jacques Derrida have addressed the implications of Surrealism in general and Artaud's theater of cruelty; and Michel Foucault, in addition to books on Magritte and the Surrealist novelist Raymond Roussel, has provided a theoretical framework for analyzing Surrealism in his seminal work *Madness and Civilization: A History of Insanity in the Age of Reason* (1965). It is an indication of the extraordinary achievement and continuing legacy of Surrealism that its questioning of the given social reality has developed into the critique of canons, systems, and institutions which characterizes the dominant modes of literary theory and criticism at the start of the twenty-first century.

## Further reading

Ades, Dawn. *Mirror Images: Women, Surrealism and Self-Representation*, 1998.
Balakian, Anna. *Surrealism: The Road to the Absolute*, 1986.
Burke, Kenneth. *Surrealism Pro and Con*, 1973.
Chenieux-Gendron, Jacqueline. *Surrealism*, 1994.
Conley, Katharine. *Automatic Woman: The Representation of Woman in Surrealism*, 1997.
Foucault, Michel. *Death and the Labyrinth: The World of Raymond Roussel*, 1986.
Higgins, Ian. *Surrealism and Language: Seven Essays*, 1987.
Nadeau, Maurice. *The History of Surrealism*, 1965.
Rose, Alan. *Surrealism and Communism: The Early Years*, 1991.
Sawin, Martica. *Surrealism in Exile and the Beginning of the New York School*, 1995.

JOHANN PILLAI

*See also* Absurd; Breton

# Algernon Charles Swinburne

English poet and critic

**Born:** London, England; April 5, 1837
**Died:** London, England; April 10, 1909

## Biography

In terms of setting, Algernon Charles Swinburne's country childhood might seem idyllic. Yet his was not to be a happy life. Like his poetic "father," Percy Bysshe Shelley, Swinburne was an anomaly of an aristocrat: born to an admiral and an earl's daughter, he was almost from the first a misplaced rebel, never at home among middle-class people, never shedding his patrician tastes and habits, yet prophesying at every opportunity against institutional Christianity and mad with fervor for Giuseppe Mazzini, Italian liberation, and political revolution. His later ill health and perhaps his well publicized sexual aberrations were dictated by the peculiarities of his physique – a sensitive, puny body topped by a large head and flaming red hair.

Probably the crucial event of his adolescence was an intense attachment to his cousin, Mary Gordon. Though ultimately frustrated (they were considered too closely related to marry), the relationship fed his literary ambitions, as did his voracious reading – experiences more important to his intellectual development than his years at Eton College and Oxford University, which he left without taking his degree. At Oxford, however, he was introduced to the Pre-Raphaelites; from 1862 until 1864 he and Dante Gabriel Rossetti shared a London home. The relationship triggered Swinburne's most productive decade as both poet and critic.

By the late 1870s Swinburne's heyday was over. He had long been a semi-alcoholic, and in August of 1879 his health collapsed. In September began what some have regarded as his imprisonment and vegetation in suburban Putney. Here, until his death from pneumonia, he was devotedly cared for by Walter Watts-Dunton, a lawyer with literary leanings.

## Influence

Without Swinburne there might have been no Walter Pater, no Arthur Symons, no Oscar Wilde – in short, no basis upon which these later (and, in Pater's case only, greater) critics could build a tradition of impressionistic aesthetic criticism. More generally, Swinburne's sensitive and serious, even severe, sense of critical duty had a profound influence upon the young men of the 1860s. In method, tenor, and theory, if not in style, he is a strikingly "modern" critic. Also ahead of their time were his reassessments of the Elizabethan and Jacobean dramatists; still more bold, and fruitful for subsequent criticism, was his pioneering work on William Blake and his championing of such unorthodox and unpopular figures as Walt Whitman, Charlotte Brontë, James McNeill Whistler, and his idols Victor Hugo and Charles Baudelaire.

## Analysis

The story of Swinburne's criticism is bound up with that of his poetry: the two flowered side by side, each pollinating the other. The 1860s were years when, as Edmund Gosse put it, "the advent of the *Fortnightly Review* with a critical article by Swinburne in it was looked forward to as a great event," and when Swinburne as poet was able to hold his own against a barrage of largely hostile (and sometimes morally outraged) criticism. Much of his importance as a critic and theorist, too, rests in the corrective as well as the inspiring force he exerted on his immediate contemporaries: he is a critic who must be seen in context.

A picture of that context can be built up through consideration of the contemporary critical tendencies which Swinburne viewed as faults and tried to correct, thus laying foundations for modern critical practice as well as theory. His own more scholarly work on the Elizabethan and Jacobean dramatists, particularly on William Shakespeare, aimed to understand and assess artistic development, spirit, and achievements through the internal evidence of changing style. This emphasis of itself set him at loggerheads with contemporary textual criticism, which was preoccupied with the letter rather than the spirit and the wholeness of a work. Swinburne not entirely unfairly characterized the well-meaning pedants of the New Shakespere Society and others as the "Polyseudocriticopantodapomorosophistico-metricoglossematographicomaniacal Company for the Confusion of Shakespeare and Diffusion of Verbiage (Unlimited)."

Most offensive, given Swinburne's protomodernist belief in the integrity of the literary text, were such current editorial practices as "regularizing" punctuation, enforcing anachronistic grammatical rules (for example, William Michael Rossetti's substituting "you" for "thee" and "thou" in his 1870 edition of Shelley), removing and adding lines (notoriously from *Macbeth*, 1606) on the basis of ultimately unprovable theories about their authorship, and bowdlerizing books and plays in the dubious cause of morality and "purity." Swinburne hated such critical arrogance. Also anathema to him was the still current practice of anonymous or pseudonymous reviewing. The critic, Swinburne wrote, must have the courage of his critical convictions. Too many critics wailed about the degeneracy of their own day and failed to detect and foster greatness in contemporary writers. Swinburne set out to correct this latter fault by his championship of such writers and artists as Brontë, Whistler, and Whitman. The ideal Swinburnian critic must also avoid the biographical fallacy, what he called the "Johnny Keats stage of criticism."

In advocating the primacy of the text over the life, Swinburne sounds one of his most modern notes. Each text must be judged on its merits and on its own terms. In the same way that destructive negative criticism is of little value, so it is ridiculous to indulge in false comparisons, becoming "surprised and indignant" not to "find grapes on a fig-tree or figs on a vine." Pointed characterization and comparison of like with like is another matter. In Swinburne's own criticism, for example, the Jacobean dramatist James Shirley may remind the reader of Ben Jonson " – with all the sap squeezed out of him, or of [John] Fletcher – with all his grace evaporated." With regard to the frequent pairing of Shelley with Lord Byron, he writes, with sure discrimination:

I can no more accept [Byron] as a poet equal or even akin to Shelley ... than I could imagine Shelley endowed with the various, fearless, keen-eyed, and triumphant energy which makes the greatest of

Byron's works so great. With all his glory of ardour and vigour and humour, Byron was a singer who could not sing; Shelley outsang all poets on record but some two or three throughout all time.

Finally, the ideal critic must eschew the pervasive critical habit, common to both his contemporaries and such Romantic critics as Charles Lamb, of isolating the "gems" and "beauties" of a writer's work and then judging him or her upon them, not upon his or her work as a whole, failures and all. In all, Swinburne's strictures and dictums (unlike some of his poetry) breathe luminous common sense.

What he sought to correct was what he called a wrong "system of criticism." The phrase is revealing. Like his call for a new critical vocabulary able to engage more fully with the lyric form, it demonstrates Swinburne's sense of criticism as a discipline, backboned by theory. For although some of his individual works lack shape and construction, and despite his renunciation, late in life, of his earlier heroes Baudelaire, Whitman, and Whistler, Swinburne's criticism adds up to a coherent œuvre, as Robert Peters has demonstrated. What unifies his criticism is partly what also ties his criticism to his poetry, for as consistently and as courageously as in his poetry, in his critical prose Swinburne grappled with the crucial Victorian issue of Art versus Morals, of "art for art's sake." His supremely intelligent exposition of this central doctrine of the aesthetic movement positions him midway in critical history (a history of which he himself was well aware) between the doctrinaire Matthew Arnold, with whose sociomoral emphasis he quarreled but whose work he often admired, and the aesthetic criticism of Pater and Wilde:

No work of art has any worth or life in it that is not done on the absolute terms of art.... On the other hand we refuse to admit that art of the highest kind may not ally itself with moral or religious passion, with the ethics or the politics of a nation or an age. ... In a word, the doctrine of art for art is true in the positive sense, false in the negative; sound as an affirmative, unsound as a prohibition.

Another unifying force in his criticism is his impressionistic style, expressly designed simultaneously to comment on the work and to express it, to stand both outside and inside the work. (Not surprisingly, he was also an accomplished writer of parody and burlesque.) Thus, his style and stance reflect the doubleness of vision evident in the quotation above. Also, they distinguish his work from Romantic criticism, which was often much more concerned with the critic's subjective response to the text, as well as more coy about making judgments and analyzing the how and why of a work's success. Certainly, they reflect his belief that poets make the best critics, that creative genius demands a comparable critical genius to complete it or to meet it. This belief, coupled with his achievements, very nearly earns for him a place in the alternative tradition of the great poet-critics – Ben Jonson, John Dryden, Samuel Johnson, William Wordsworth, Samuel Taylor Coleridge, Matthew Arnold, William Butler Yeats, T. S. Eliot, and the great Frenchman whose impressionistic critical essays were perhaps the strongest influence on Swinburne as critic, Baudelaire. His early critical masterwork, the study of Blake, is a case in point. Here, he shifts between blunt criticism and expressive sympathy within a single paragraph. Of Los, Enitharmon, Theotormon, Oothoon, Blake's gods and heroes, he writes:

This monstrous nomenclature, this jargon of miscreated things in chaos, rose as by nature to his lips, flowed from them as by instinct. Time, an incarnate spirit clothed with fire [Los], stands before him in the sun's likeness.

The flip side of the flexibility and fluency of his prose and of the desire to express his subject, however, is a tendency to overindulge in words and to overpraise. Sometimes, as Harold Nicolson puts it (writing at the height of the early modernists' reaction against all things Victorian, but still with justice), "having already expended all his superlatives in the rambling course of his argument, he often reaches the portals of his main thesis with not a 'divine,' not even a 'magnificent,' or a 'superb,' left in his pocket." To such frequent excesses can be added Swinburne's other faults as critic: on the one hand, his half-blind hero-worship, and on the other hand, his violent prejudices (against William Hazlitt, for example, surely an impressionist Romantic ancestor, but a critic whose very name was taboo in Putney). These dislikes issue forth in spluttering, even childish, alliterative invective. Similarly, the breadth of reading that allows Swinburne to place an author judiciously in the context of all Western literature has as an unfortunate corollary a ludicrous assumption, particularly evident in his later scholarly work on the dramatists, that the general reader will recognize his flurries of allusions.

Much of this later work was privately published and reached only a small audience. Yet this half of Swinburne's influence – his impact on textual scholarship, editing, and commentary, what one might call his "academic" side – has proved long-lasting indeed. The twentieth century saw a drift away from the pedantic and philological excesses he attacked and toward the text-centered, text-respectful approach that he advocated and pioneered. The other half of his influence – what one might call his "critical" side – was more widespread and more immediate, springing from accessible articles published preeminently in *The Fortnightly Review*, but also in *The Spectator*, *The Nineteenth Century*, and *The Quarterly Review*; it has proved no less long-lasting. In these pieces he forged some of the critical tools and language that would be employed by the aesthetic critics and, indeed, all later critics (Pater was particularly affected by the imaginative critical prose of *Essays and Studies*). Here, too, appeared his very early, provocative, and clear-sighted statements of the doctrine of "art for art's sake," a contribution that was both theoretical and methodological. Further, his total detachment from the bourgeois world and its tastes, his openness to originality and innovation, and his critical vision command respect. It was these attributes, coupled with sheer industry, that enabled him, in defiance of current critical opinion, to carve a path through the difficulties and obscurities of Blake's prophetic books, to challenge Shakespeare scholars at their own game, and to build powerful cases for disparaged and unfashionable contemporaries and predecessors. These qualities were recognized even by the early modern critics, perhaps because of an underlying sense of indebtedness. "He put new life," wrote J. W. Mackail, "into poetical criticism, gave it a new range and scope and brilliance, in something of the same way as he discovered or revealed new potentialities in poetry itself."

## Principal criticism
Preface to *A Selection from the Works of Lord Byron*, 1866
*William Blake: A Critical Essay*, 1868
*Under the Microscope*, 1872
*Essays and Studies*, 1875
*George Chapman*, 1875
*A Note on Charlotte Brontë*, 1877
*A Study of Shakespeare*, 1880
*A Study of Victor Hugo*, 1886
*Miscellanies*, 1886
*A Study of Ben Jonson*, 1889
*Studies in Prose and Poetry*, 1894
*The Age of Shakespeare*, 1908
*Shakespeare*, 1909
*Charles Dickens*, 1913
*Contemporaries of Shakespeare*, 1919

## Other major works and literary forms
Although he was often neglected and maligned in the twentieth century, Algernon Charles Swinburne must be regarded as one of the dominant poetic voices of the Victorian era, an original lyric poet of remarkable technical skill and fluency. He is also memorable for his verse dramas – classical pieces intended for private reading – particularly *Atalanta in Calydon: A Tragedy* (1865) and *Erechtheus: A Tragedy* (1876). Notwithstanding his Shelleyan Romanticism, his intellectual depth and instinct for irony and parody are apparent in his epistolary novel, *Love's Cross-Currents: A Year's Letters* (1905) and the unfinished *Lesbia Brandon* (1952).

NOVELS
*Love's Cross-Currents: A Year's Letters*, 1905 (serialized as *A Year's Letters*, 1877)
*Lesbia Brandon*, 1952

PLAYS
*The Queen-Mother, Rosamond: Two Plays*, 1860
*Atalanta in Calydon: A Tragedy*, 1865
*Chastelard*, 1865
*Bothwell*, 1874
*Erechtheus: A Tragedy*, 1876
*Mary Stuart*, 1881
*Marino Faliero*, 1885
*Locrine*, 1887
*The Sisters*, 1892
*Rosamund, Queen of the Lombards*, 1899
*The Duke of Gandia*, 1908

POETRY
*Poems and Ballads*, 1866
*A Song of Italy*, 1867
*Ode on the Proclamation of the French Republic*, 1870
*Songs Before Sunrise*, 1871
*Songs of Two Nations*, 1875
*Poems and Ballads: Second Series*, 1878
*Songs of the Springtides*, 1880
*The Heptalogia*, 1880
*Tristram of Lyonesse and Other Poems*, 1882
*A Century of Roundels*, 1883
*A Midsummer Holiday and Other Poems*, 1884
*Gathered Songs*, 1887
*Poems and Ballads: Third Series*, 1889
*Astrophel and Other Poems*, 1894
*The Tale of Balen*, 1896
*A Channel Passage and Other Poems*, 1904
*Posthumous Poems*, 1917
*Rondeaux Parisiens*, 1917
*Ballads of the English Border*, 1925

NONFICTION
*Byron*, 1866
*Notes on Poems and Reviews*, 1866
*Three Plays of Shakespeare*, 1909

MISCELLANEOUS
*The Complete Works of Algernon Charles Swinburne*, 1925–1927

## Further reading
Bloom, Harold, ed. *Pre-Raphaelite Poets*, 1986.
Binyon, Laurence, ed. *The Works of Algernon Charles Swinburne*, 1995.
Cheney, Liana De Girolami, ed. *Pre-Raphaelitism and Medievalism in the Arts*, 1992.
Connolly, Thomas E. *Swinburne's Theory of Poetry*, 1964.
Eliot, T. S. "Swinburne as Critic," in *The Sacred Wood*, 1920.
Louis, Margot K. *Swinburne and His Gods: The Roots and Growth of an Agnostic Poetry*, 1990.
McGann, Jerome J. "Conversation on Aesthetics; on Impressionistic Prose; Lastly, on Swinburne's Prose Criticism in Particular," in *Swinburne: An Experiment in Criticism*, 1972.
Peters, Robert L. *The Crowns of Apollo: Swinburne's Principles of Literature and Art*, 1965.
Raymond, Meredith B. *Swinburne's Poetics: Theory and Practice*, 1971.
Robbins, Ruth. "'But One Thing Knows the Flower': Whistler, Swinburne, Derrida," in *Applying: To Derrida*, 1996. Edited by John Brannigan, Ruth Robbins, and Julian Wolfreys.

Rooksby, Rikky. *A. C. Swinburne: A Poet's Life*, 1997.
——, and Nicholas Shrimpton, eds. *The Whole Music of Passion: New Essays on Swinburne*, 1993.

JOSS MARSH

*See also* Aestheticism; Literary Theory in the Age of Victoria; Pater; Wilde

# Symbolism

In addition to its meaning as the use of any kind of symbol, the term Symbolism also refers to works produced, predominantly but not exclusively in France, during the period from the 1880s to, at the latest, 1914. As such, it overlaps to a large extent with such other critical terms as aestheticism, *art nouveau*, decadence, *fin-de-siècle*, and *Jugendstil*, in the discussion of music and painting, as well as literature.

The term "*symbolisme*" was first applied to a group of French poets by the poet and critic Jean Moréas (Yánnis Papadiamantópoulos). In 1885 he proposed to replace the term "decadent," which had been applied to himself and the French poet Stéphane Mallarmé, by "symbolist": "The so-called decadents seek the pure concept and the eternal symbol in their art, before everything else." In his *Manifeste littéraire*, published in *Le Figaro* on September 18, 1886, Moréas wrote: "Symbolist poetry tries to cover the idea in a sensible form, which is not an end in itself, but which, while serving to express the idea, remains the subject of it." On October 1, 1886, the first issue of *Le Symboliste*, cofounded by Mauréas, appeared, but only four editions were published and on September 14, 1891, Moréas announced in *Le Figaro* that Symbolism was dead. Yet the term continued to be used by such other critics as Gustave Kahn, one of Moréas' collaborators, together with Jacques Plowert (Paul Adam), who published a *Petit Glossaire* of the bizarre neologisms and archaic expressions used by many Symbolist writers. More important, those writers continued to produce literature, even if, like Mallarmé, they never used the term "symbolist" or, like Paul Verlaine, they rejected it (Verlaine spoke parodically of "Cymbalisme").

The sources of Symbolism include Edgar Allan Poe, whose short stories were translated by Charles Baudelaire and whose poems were translated by Mallarmé. Baudelaire also translated Poe's essay "The Philosophy of Composition," an account of writing the poem "The Raven," and took it seriously, although the essay was, as Mallarmé realized, probably not meant to be. Poe's debt to Samuel Taylor Coleridge and, in turn, F. W. J. Schelling, says much about Symbolism's ultimate relationship to Romanticism (another major influence on Baudelaire was E. T. A. Hoffmann). Although Baudelaire's output predates the coining of the term Symbolism, his poem "Correspondences," which alludes not just to the mystic writer Emanuel Swedenborg but to an ancient topos (basic theme) of the world as the "signature of God," was highly influential: "Nature is a temple where living pillars/ Sometimes allow confused words to escape;/ Man traverses it through forests of symbols,/ That watch him with a familiar gaze." And in another poem, "The Swan," Baudelaire wrote: "everything for me becomes an allegory." Harking back to antiquity's identification of the bird with the poet (*cycni poetae*), homophonic in French with the word for "sign" (*le cygne/le signe*), and rich in erotic associations (for example the myth of Leda and Zeus), the swan was also the subject of a famous sonnet by Mallarmé ("The virginal, living, and beautiful day"). Two statements by Mallarmé help explain his aesthetics, and also illuminate the essence of Symbolism. First, in his letter to Henri Cazalis of 1864, he wrote: "I am inventing a language which must necessarily spring from a very new type of poetics that I could define in two words: paint, not the thing, but the effect it produces"; and second, from the essay "Crisis in Verse": "I say: a flower! and, out of the forgetfulness where my voice banishes any contour, inasmuch as it is something other than known calyxes, musically arises, an idea itself and fragrant, the one absent from all bouquets." Hence Symbolism preserves and intensifies two central aspects of Baudelairean Romanticism: the sense of the *au-delà*, the beyond; and the desire to *faire rêver*, to make us dream. Furthermore, Mallarmé's connection between literature and music was explicitly stated by Verlaine in his poem "Art poétique": "Music above everything else," and, for many, embodied in the music-dramas of Richard Wagner.

In critical terms, possibly the most insightful contemporary discussion of Symbolism was offered by Des Esseintes, the main character of Joris-Karl Huysmans' ultra-decadent novel *À rebours* (1884). The French critic Charles Morice and the Polish-born critic Téodor de Wyzéwa consolidated "symbolism" as a term of critical discourse, while Arthur Symons' *The Symbolist Movement in Literature* (1899) mediated the notion to England. As well as Maurice Bowra's *The Heritage of Symbolism* (1943), another notable discussion of Symbolism was Edmund Wilson's still useful *Axel's Castle* (1931), whose title alluded to a play by Auguste, Comte de Villiers de l'Isle Adam, that contained the celebrated phrase "Live? Our servants will do that for us." The works of the Irish writers Oscar Wilde and William Butler Yeats show the influence of Symbolist doctrines. Although the aestheticist doctrine of "*l'art pour l'art*" ("art for art's sake") is often attributed to the French *Parnassien* poet Théophile Gautier, the late German Romantic poet Heinrich Heine used the phrase "art is the purpose of art" in a letter to Karl Gutzkow of August 23, 1838. Possibly its earliest occurrence, albeit with different implications, is in the essay collection *Kritische Wälder* (1769; critical forests) by the German Enlightenment thinker Johann Gottfried Herder: "A work of art is there for the sake of art." Thus it is no surprise that Symbolism, being closely allied to aestheticism, also had its German exponents. Stefan George attended the celebrated *mardis* (Tuesday evening meetings) in Mallarmé's house in Paris, and he subsequently translated poems by Baudelaire and Mallarmé (as did Rainer Maria Rilke). In Austria, Hugo von Hofmannsthal emphasized the importance of the symbol in his essay "Conversation about Poetry" (1903). In Russia, Symbolism is seen as forming two groups, one centered around the stylistic concerns of Valerii Briusov, and another more "metaphysical" school of V. A. Ivanov, Aleksandr Blok, and Andrei Belyi. Many Symbolists, however, came from Belgium (Maurice Maeterlinck, Albert Mockel, Georges Rodenbach, and Émile Verhaeren), as well as France (René Ghil [Guilbert], Félix Fénéon, Rémy de Gourmont, Jules Laforgue, Arthur Rimbaud, and Paul Valéry). So when, in his *Cahiers*, Valéry wrote that "symbolism is the group of people who believed that the word symbol had a meaning," he is referring to the difficulty of defining the term, not denying the significance of the writers and artists associated with it.

## Further reading

Balakian, Anna. *The Symbolist Movement: A Critical Appraisal*, 1967.
——. "Symbolism," in *The New Princeton Encyclopedia of Poetry and Poetics*, 1993.
Cassou, Jean. *Encyclopédie du symbolisme: peinture, gravure et sculpture, littérature, musique*, 1979 (*The Concise Encyclopedia of Symbolism*, 1979).
Chadwick, Charles. *Symbolism*, 1971.
Cornell, Kenneth. *The Symbolist Movement*, 1951.
——. *The Post-Symbolist Period*, 1958.
Donchin, G. *The Influence of French Symbolism on Russian Poetry*, 1958.
Lehmann, A. G. *The Symbolist Aesthetic in France 1885–1895*, 1950, 1968.
Michaud, Guy. *Message poétique du symbolisme*, 1947.
Peyre, Henri. *Qu'est-ce que le symbolisme?*, 1974 (*What is Symbolism?*, 1980).
Plowert, Jacques (Adam, Paul). *Petit Glossaire*, 1888; new edition 1998.
Wilson, Edmund. *Axel's Castle: A Study of the Imaginative Literature of 1870–1930*, 1931.

PAUL BISHOP

*See also* Aestheticism; Baudelaire; Continental Theory; George; Gourmont; Mallarmé; Symons; Valéry; Yeats

# John Addington Symonds

English critic

**Born:** Bristol, England; October 5, 1840
**Died:** Rome, Italy; April 19, 1893

## Biography

John Addington Symonds' father, whose literary remains his son edited and published in 1871, was a physician with literary tastes that foreshadowed those of his scholar son;

in his lifetime were published lectures on knowledge, dreams, and the "Principles of Beauty." Symonds' mother died of tuberculosis when he was four years old – another and more sinister foreshadowing.

Symonds was a shy and sickly boy at Harrow, starting to blossom only at Balliol College, Oxford University, under the wing of the great Benjamin Jowett. He was to take a brilliant double first honors in classics and to proceed smoothly to an open fellowship at Magdalen College in 1862. Meanwhile, in 1860 and again in 1863, his life was given a decisive direction when he won first the Newdigate Prize for his poem "The Escorial" and then the Chancellor's Prize for an essay on the Renaissance. The toil that these achievements entailed was too much. His health broke down altogether.

After a long convalescence, marriage to Janet Catherine North, and a move to London to study law, which proved uncongenial, Symonds moved to Clifton, near Bristol, in 1868 and embarked on a literary life. His lectures there led to his first important critical publications, *An Introduction to the Study of Dante* and *Studies of the Greek Poets*; a visit in 1873 to Sicily and Greece both inspired him to begin his eleven years' work on *The Renaissance in Italy* and granted him the respite from ill health he needed to do so. Ten years later, however, precarious health obliged him to begin a lifelong exile in the Alpine village of Davos Platz, Switzerland. His remarkable output, large even by Victorian standards, continued virtually until the day of his untimely death from pneumonia.

## Influence

Symonds' influence on literary criticism has been limited in terms of general theory; it is more important but still diffuse in terms of particular works and of the understanding of literary and cultural history. Most important for subsequent scholars has been his work on Italian literature and the Renaissance. His more speculative and theoretical criticism died (perhaps unfairly) with its century, although it pointed the way to more systematic theoretical analysis of such subjects as literary form. The differing tastes and scholarship of the twentieth century made his work on ancient Greek literature outdated.

## Analysis

It may not be an overstatement to say that Symonds' homosexuality to some degree determined both his primary choices of subject – the Italian Renaissance and ancient Greece – and the way in which he treated them. "Ancient Greece," as Richard Jenkyns remarks in his excellent study *The Victorians and Ancient Greece* (1980), "had produced the literary treatments of homosexuality and Italy was where it was practised at the present day." Symonds was not the only wealthy later-Victorian homosexual man of letters who sought the Mediterranean world both literally and figuratively. Indeed, his experience at the age of seventeen reading Plato's fourth-century B.C. work *Phaedrus* (in 1858 the only intelligent discussion of homosexual love available), his sense of spellbound recognition, self-dedication, and gratitude almost exactly prefigures the reactions of E. M. Forster's Clive Durham in *Maurice* (1971). Plato's dialogue, indeed Greek literature as a whole, seemed devoid of the sense of sin that marred even the Renaissance. Plato's Socrates was a virile hero-philosopher, a pure ideal – Symonds himself referred to Socrates as the Christ of Greece. Symonds came to Greek literature with an immense sense of liberation and identification but also with what Jenkyns pithily terms the literary voyeurism so distinctive of late-Victorian attitudes about Greece: Symonds' Greece was too much a fantasy land of wrestling athletes, public baths, and frank and merry boys who would have been more at home on British public school playing fields. Nevertheless, he was by no means merely the "Platonic amorist of blue-breeched gondoliers" whose "renascent blossoms" earned the sneers of Algernon Charles Swinburne in a famous diatribe of 1893.

Symonds' work on Greek literature is quintessentially Victorian, valuable to later generations only for its occasional felicities of judgment and phrase, or, perhaps more important, for the illuminating light it throws on the critical preoccupations of the Victorian era. The pervasive sense of the sinlessness of Greek sensuality, for example, lent a particular edge to Symonds' articulation, in his critical works and also in his well received travel writings, of the established contrast between the Scandinavian north and the Mediterranean south. At one pole, the north represented not only the present life of the world but also Romantic anguish, darkness, pollution, and guilt-ridden, repressive puritanism; at the other, the south represented not only the ancient past and a living communion with that past but brightness, purity, and uninhibited paganism. Despite this difference, for Symonds, as for Percy Bysshe Shelley, Swinburne, Charles Kingsley, and John Ruskin, all civilized nations are colonies of ancient Greece.

Symonds was also very much at the center of the Victorian critical tradition in emphasizing, following August Wilhelm Schlegel, the statuesque perfection, serene grandeur, and simplicity of classical Greek drama. To his credit, however, Symonds did not avoid Aeschylus, who did not fit into this peculiar but dominant view; instead, dubbing the great tragedian "rough-hewed like a Cyclops," he mustered his bloodiest epithets to do justice to the tide of gore that he saw sweeping through the *Agamemnon* (458 B.C.; *Agamemnon*). Like Matthew Arnold, he emphasized the fresh youthfulness of the Greek ethos. Like another contemporary, Walter Pater, he wrote of the soothing transparency and austerity of the Greek spirit and even of the Greek landscape. Like all earnest Victorians, he also attempted to redeem the pagan Greeks for a culture that was, if no longer wholeheartedly Christian, at least Christian in its ethical and moral tradition. "Ethical

philosophy," he wrote at an unguarded, over-earnest moment, "is more than ever substantive in verse."

His agnosticism is again evident in *Studies of the Greek Poets* and is characteristically Victorian, reminiscent of the Arnold of *Empedocles on Etna* (1852). The urge to establish links and to find support for agnostic views pushes him into a most unhistorical view of the Greeks as a nation of Wordsworthian pantheists, for whom Apollo was not a pagan god but "the magic of the sun whose soul is light" and for whom Pan was nothing more specific than "the mystery of nature." His adherence to the then dominant rise-and-fall theory of history and literature also led him into some foolish ideas. Like Arnold viewing the fifth century B.C. as the culminating epoch of Greek history, the less circumspect Symonds based some of his judgments about Greek sculpture upon evidence that simply did not exist. In addition, like nearly all Victorian classicists, Symonds in his Greek criticism fell into the temptation of evaluation and of establishing rules: because the serene and happy Greeks wrote this way, so should everyone. That type of thinking created the dead technical perfection of Swinburne's classical dramas after *Atalanta in Calydon* (1865) and Symonds' own forgotten volumes of verse. By way of complement was Symonds' verdict against the novel, the most vital and characteristic literary form of his era, but one which, like many Victorians, he shortsightedly dismissed as a trivial art form with a suspect lineage. In his opinion, novel-reading is a form of enjoyment and self-indulgence; life-like characters cannot uplift readers as can the ideal heroes of the great classical plays.

Symonds' work on the Italian Renaissance and its literature, however, belongs to another and higher class. Not original in terms of ideas (like most subsequent work, it owes obvious debts to the seminal studies of the German scholar Basel Burckhardt), it is to some degree original in its method. *The Renaissance in Italy* was the first full-scale work on the subject to appear in English, opening up new fields of study and doing so with scrupulous attention to detail, a breadth of view, and a refusal to distort the picture by concentrating exclusively on a few well-known names. This objectivity was quite new in British literary criticism and was conspicuously absent in his more famous fellow Renaissance scholar Pater. For his efforts, Symonds earned both the criticism of his contemporaries and the praise of later scholars, for whom his text might still serve as a model for exhaustive scholarship. Another aspect of his running against the Victorian grain in this more mature work is his tendency to describe rather than to feel, in addition to the overwhelming fact that, according to his contemporary Frederic Harrison, "the general reader" so beloved of Victorian critics "may complain that [the volumes of *The Renaissance in Italy*] stoop to register [too] many conceits and ... filth" in Symonds' efforts to track literary forms thoroughly. "A history of literature, no doubt," Harrison adds, "must take note of all popular books, however pedantic or obscene. But we are constantly reminded how very much Symonds is absorbed in purely literary interests rather than in social and truly historical interests. . . . This exhaustive treatment brings its own Nemesis." For the Victorians, bred on Thomas Carlyle, Ruskin, and Arnold, the fact that Symonds was not what might be called a "mixed" critic but a literary specialist was an anomaly and even a drawback. To modern readers, it marks him as a precursor. Symonds himself seemed to be aware of his position; his eulogy of Renaissance scholarship was an interesting mix of agnostic fervor and special pleading:

It was scholarship, first and last, which revealed to men the wealth of their own minds, the dignity of human thought, the value of human speculation, the importance of human life regarded as a thing apart from religious rules and dogmas.

Some of the criticism of his contemporaries Symonds does deserve. As in his classical criticism, he tended to overemphasize personalities and to view each subject as an occasion for another exquisite and picturesque sketch. There was also some lack of unity in the work as a whole. Finally and most damagingly, science was completely omitted – Galileo Galilei and Christopher Columbus scarcely figured in the picture. Usually stylish, Symonds sometimes succumbed to a "fatal proneness to Ruskinese" and became "luscious"; according to Harrison, as in earlier work "we feel sometimes . . . as if we were lost in a plantation of sugar-cane." To others, it often seemed that spontaneity had been sacrificed for overstudied effect ("No phrase is fresh," complained the poet Francis Thompson, "Mr. Symonds has deflowered his words"). Nevertheless, there are ample compensations.

One result of Symonds' detachment was that, unlike Ruskin, he did not feel the moralist's urge to "stigmatise the Renaissance as a monstrous growth of pride and infidelity." Since this attitude led Ruskin to dismiss the Renaissance entirely, it was a not inconsiderable compensation for Symonds' lack of Ruskin's intensity and rigor. Then again, Symonds struck a more modern note. His view of Renaissance Italy was less earnest and distorted than his view of ancient Greece. His stress on Renaissance individualism and enjoyment of life was a healthy corrective to the fallaciously sensationalist Romantic view, propagated even by the young Ruskin, of Italy as "a land of tombs [where] the air is full of death" and to the exclusive classicism of Edward Gibbon and other eighteenth-century humanists for whom modern Italians were dirty foreigners. Symonds filled out the insights of his elder, the poet Robert Browning. Poems such as "My Last Duchess" and "The Bishop Orders His Tomb at Saint Praxed's Church" evidenced the same interest in types of humanity and the same sensuous appreciation of Renaissance Italy as a new flowering of the pagan spirit of ancient times.

Nevertheless, it is also true to say that objective detachment is only half the picture. Symonds' Italy was also visibly the pagan heaven (an alternative to stuffy Victorian society) of decadent critics such as Swinburne and Pater, one that was most humanly valuable not for its achievements but precisely for its paganism, vitality, color, beauty, and amorality. Yet Symonds, though now less remembered, avoided the narrowness of the aesthetic and elitist Pater ("His view of life gives me the creeps," Symonds commented on the publication of Pater's *Studies in the History of the Renaissance* in 1873; "I am sure it is a ghastly sham"). Occasionally, too, he was as brilliant. His attempt to identify and evoke the life spirit of Renaissance Italy was part of a desire to reconnect his own age to the creative impulse that had made past ages great (and from which it had been severed by the political traumas and the Romantic explosion at the end of the previous century). This effort resulted in such wonderfully thoughtful passages as that on one phrase that reappeared time and again in the pages of Tasso, "un non so che." Its vagueness, Symonds wrote, suggests what cannot be put into words, much as does modern music, born in the Renaissance. Symonds' desire, however, was also intertwined with a somewhat too literal belief in the *genius loci*. His belief that contact with the Mediterranean and the life-enhancing richness it represented could do sophisticated Northern people only good, a belief swallowed whole by many contemporaries, was utterly without the complexity and awareness of danger of Henry James' *Daisy Miller* (1879) or E. M. Forster's *Where Angels Fear to Tread* (1905).

*The Renaissance in Italy*, reissued in 1897–1898, was the standard work on the subject for a generation. Popularized by the publication of an authorized abridged edition in 1893, it remained in print until well into the 1920s. Two of its volumes, collectively titled *Italian Literature*, are still considered a full and insightful introductory survey. The whole, scholar Kenneth Churchill succinctly comments, "demands respect for having brought a broad picture of that age before a wide audience," and can still "stimulate serious thought."

It is curious therefore that immediately after his death, in direct opposition to current views, Symonds was celebrated above all for what were believed to be his crucial contributions to literary theory and cultural criticism, born of his attempt to bring to these nascent disciplines some of the rigor of scientific thought and to apply to them evolutionary principles. *Essays Speculative and Suggestive* has long since been dismissed as outdated. This opinion, however, may be unfair. After all, in the 1980s the same ideas brought critical acclaim to the film scholar Thomas Schatz. Symonds' proto-Marxist emphasis on period and form over individual author, his sense of form as embodying national spirit and a particular mythos, and his persuasive development of the well-worn organic metaphor of growth and decay and application of it to the test cases of

Elizabethan and Attic drama, Greek sculpture, Gothic architecture, and Italian painting are lucidly presented.

## Principal criticism

*An Introduction to the Study of Dante*, 1872
*Studies of the Greek Poets*, 1873, 1876
*The Renaissance in Italy*, 1875–1886 (7 volumes)
*Essays Speculative and Suggestive*, 1890
*In the Key of Blue, and Other Prose Essays*, 1893

## Other major works and literary forms

John Addington Symonds' excursions into biography bore mixed fruit. His lives of Percy Bysshe Shelley and Sir Philip Sidney were undistinguished. *The Life of Michelangelo Buonarroti* (1893), however, was remarkable for its exhaustive scholarship and its treatment of its subject's homosexuality; the former may well have contributed to Symonds' early death, while the latter was a courageous attempt to treat a subject at that time ignored but nevertheless essential to an understanding of the biographer as well as of his subject.

Symonds also published six volumes of elegant and forgettable lyrical poems. Far more worthy of attention is his work as a translator; here, his lack of poetic originality was no handicap, while his considerable technical skill and extensive vocabulary were immense benefits. Particularly striking are his verse translations of the crabbed and difficult sonnets of Michelangelo and Tommaso Campanella, the translations of the Latin songs of medieval students that appeared under the title *Wine, Women, and Song: Medieval Latin Students' Songs* (1884), and his masterful, racy prose translation of *The Life of Benvenuto Cellini* (1888), the work on which, together with his seven volumes on the Italian Renaissance, his reputation in his lifetime and immediately after his death largely rested.

POETRY
*Many Moods*, 1878
*New and Old*, 1880

NONFICTION
*Sketches in Italy and Greece*, 1874
*Shelley*, 1878
*Sketches and Studies in Italy*, 1879
*Italian Byways*, 1883
*Life of Ben Jonson*, 1886
*Sir Philip Sidney*, 1886
*The Life of Michelangelo Buonarroti*, 1893
*Walt Whitman: A Study*, 1893

TRANSLATIONS
*The Sonnets of Michelangelo Buonarroti and Tommaso Campanella*, 1878
*Wine, Women, and Song: Medieval Latin Students' Songs*, 1884
*The Life of Benvenuto Cellini*, 1888
*The Memoirs of Count Carlo Gozzi*, 1890

MISCELLANEOUS
*The Memoirs of John Addington Symonds*, 1984 (Phyllis Grosskurth, editor)

## Further reading

Churchill, Kenneth. "The Victorians and the Renaissance," in *Italy and English Literature, 1764–1930*, 1980.
Grosskurth, Phyllis. *John Addington Symonds: A Biography*, 1964.
Harrison, Frederic. "John Addington Symonds," in *Tennyson, Ruskin, Mill, and Other Literary Estimates*, 1900.
Jenkyns, Richard. *The Victorians and Ancient Greece*, 1980.
Wellek, René. *A History of Modern Criticism: 1750–1950*. Vol. 4, *The Later Nineteenth Century*, 1965.

JOSS MARSH

*See also* Aestheticism; Literary Theory in the Age of Victoria; Pater; Wilde

# Arthur Symons

English writer and critic

**Born:** Milford Haven, Wales; February 21, 1865
**Died:** Wittersham, Kent, England; January 22, 1945

## Biography

Arthur William Symons was born on February 21, 1865, at Milford Haven, Wales, the only son and second child of the Reverend Mark Symons and Lydia (née Pascoe) Symons, both originally from Cornwall, England. In the first twenty years of Symons' life, his father, a Wesleyan Methodist minister, had charge of nine different circuits; the transient nature of his early home life gave Symons a sense of vagabondage that he would turn to his own account during the 1890s. Educated at various Devonshire schools, Symons dedicated himself to literature from an early age, and by the age of twenty-one had published an essay on the French poet Frédéric Mistral, an introduction to William Shakespeare's *Venus and Adonis* (1593) in F. J. Furnivall's Shakespeare Quarto reprint series, and *An Introduction to the Study of Browning* (1886). His first volume of poetry, *Days and Nights*, appeared in 1889 and was dedicated to Walter Pater, who had helped him with the publisher, George Macmillan, and also with the page proofs. Symons lived the life of a man of letters to the full in the 1890s: he joined the Rhymers' Club, contributed to *The Yellow Book*, edited *The Savoy*, and wrote his most important work, *The Symbolist Movement in Literature* (1899). Married to Rhoda Bowser in 1901, he continued a productive literary career until he suffered a mental breakdown in Italy in 1908. He recovered somewhat two years later and, between 1919 and 1930, regained some of his workmanlike strength as a writer but not his full acuity. He died at Islanda Cottage, Wittersham, Kent, on January 22, 1945.

## Influence

Symons' greatest impact on the history of literary theory and practice was the introduction of French Symbolist theory and poetry to the English-speaking world. A disciple of Pater, he shared Pater's enthusiasm for French literature and began, in the 1880s, modeling his poetry on French writings, discovering his contemporaries in Paris, translating their works, and promoting them in England among his Rhymers' Club colleagues, notably William Butler Yeats. His most important volume, *The Symbolist Movement in Literature*, dedicated to Yeats, had a profound effect on Ezra Pound, T. S. Eliot, Wyndham Lewis, and James Joyce.

## Analysis

A self-conscious champion of modernity, Arthur Symons strove to explore and explain the era in which he lived; he achieved prominence as the principal interpreter of contemporary and near-contemporary French writers. It can be argued that his critical perspective, first formed under the influence of Pater's writings, began with aestheticism and Impressionism (until about 1893), evolved into Symbolism (ending about 1900), and further evolved into expressionism until his breakdown in 1908. Although he resumed his writing career nearly a decade after his mental collapse, his work did not focus on contemporary culture, but looked back to the Yellow Decade. He became the spokesman for art and life in the 1890s, frequently reprinting material written during that period and writing reminiscences about those with whom he had associated at the height of his career.

Aestheticism, as Pater defined it and as Symons and others practiced it, depends upon knowing one's impression of a work of art, discriminating the virtue that is the source of one's impression, and elucidating that virtue for oneself and for others. For Symons in his early phase of criticism, this activity consisted principally in identifying how essentially different one writer or artist is from any other. Symons' aestheticism led him to imitate Pater's language and style in his early phase; the influence lingered into his Symbolist period, so that the conclusion to *The Symbolist Movement in Literature* closely resembles Pater's conclusion to *Studies in the History of the Renaissance* (1873; better known as *The Renaissance*). Symons adopted the role Pater had set for himself and refined the art of "appreciation" in a dazzling series of essays, reviews, introductions, and commentaries in the late 1880s and early 1890s. Also following Pater's lead, Symons turned much of his literary attention to France, finding there not only the source of Pater's aesthetic criticism and of his own adopted aestheticism but also the source of the Symbolist theories he would espouse. In his highly important essay, "The Decadent Movement in Literature," published in 1893 as a rejoinder to Richard Le Gallienne's acerbic criticism of Decadence as insane thinking, he sought to champion the new movement in France but conflated Decadence, Impressionism, and Symbolism under the single heading of Decadence and further attempted to exemplify the Decadent as a linguistic phenomenon as well as a cultural phenomenon peculiar to France. Given the context of the essay, it would have been better titled "The Impressionist Movement in Literature." This essay, reminiscent of Pater's work in "Style" and borrowing from his *A Prince of Court Painters: An Imaginary Portrait* (1885), opened to Englishmen a new world of poetic and literary theory and practice.

Having announced his plan to publish "The Decadent Movement in Literature," Symons deepened his own study of recent French literature and its antecedents at the same time that he sought a unitary explanation of all the arts and, indeed, of life itself. What he fixed upon was at the heart of Decadence and Impressionism and emerged in his most famous and far-reaching work, *The Symbolist Movement in Literature*. For Symons, as for his friend Yeats, Symbolism was more than a literary technique: it was an occult, mystical means of explaining humanity's place in the universe as an interpreter of that universe. Rooted in William Blake's poetry, Yeats brought to Symons a perspective that helped him to reassess his literary and spiritual position and to see the writers whom he had characterized as expressing perfect Decadence as artists in search of transcendence. Thus *The Symbolist Movement in Literature* fixed upon the transcendent elements in literature that tend to spiritualize it and make it into a kind of religion; its conclusion sets forth Symons' profession of faith in Symbolism.

In elaborating the Symbolist creed, Symons both explicates the French and adumbrates the modernists among British, American, and Irish writers of the early twentieth century. Working toward a definition of Symbolism, Symons cites Albert Joseph Goblet d'Alviella's dictum that a symbol is a representation that does not aim at being a reproduction and, pursuing the definition further, identifies it as every conventional representation of idea by form, of the unseen by the visible. Taking up Thomas Carlyle's terminology, Symons avers that in a symbol there is concealment yet revelation and that the symbol constitutes an embodiment or revelation of the infinite, so that the infinite is made to blend with the finite and to stand visible and attainable there. This unity of finite and infinite is at the heart of all symbolism; the distinguishing feature of modern symbolism, according to Symons, is that it is self-conscious. The literature of which he writes, then, is one in which the visible world is no longer a reality and the unseen world no longer a dream. This state of transcendence is precisely the artistic nexus Symons himself sought and the mystical philosophy to which he surrendered himself during this period.

The work's doctrinaire elements apart, it was an epoch-making volume in that it introduced together such important French writers as Honoré de Balzac, Gérard de Nerval, Charles Baudelaire, Edmond and Jules de Goncourt, Stéphane Mallarmé, Paul Verlaine, Joris-Karl Huysmans, Arthur Rimbaud, Jules Laforgue, and Maurice Maeterlinck. It was also useful in providing bibliographies, notes, and translations from Mallarmé and Verlaine to Englishmen previously unaware of the great wealth of literature in this later flowering of French Romanticism. The work is also important for understanding Symons' critical perspective in this phase of his development as well as in his later, expressionist phase, a phase that was at the end of a developmental continuum and may be characterized as an aggressive stage of Symbolism incorporating a vitalistic mysticism. Although in Symons' last true critical lustrum, between 1900 and 1908, he rejected nearly all of those he had praised in *The Symbolist Movement in Literature*, his earlier discovery of the Symbolists left a lasting mark on his contemporaries and his successors.

The extent to which Symons influenced Yeats and Yeats influenced Symons remains open to investigation, but clearly some cross-fertilization existed through the 1890s, particularly when they were next-door neighbors and traveled together through Ireland. Symons' Symbolist and mystical leanings found sympathetic resonances in Yeats, who would later incorporate both into his highly complex mythology in *A Vision* (1925, 1937) and in poems in *The Tower* (1928), *The Winding Stair* (1929), and *Words for Music Perhaps and Other Poems* (1932), especially the Byzantium poems.

Joyce and Pound also owe a debt to Symons, principally for his introduction of the French Symbolists. Joyce's many-layered prose, his highly allusive narrative, and his early poetry appealed to Symons, who was quick to recognize the affinity between Joyce and Verlaine, an affinity Symons himself may have fostered, not only through his own work but also through his early meeting with Joyce in 1902 and his subsequent service as literary agent in persuading Grant Richards to publish *Chamber Music* (1907). Symons also recognized Joyce's more pronounced affinity with Mallarmé in his linguistic quest. Pound quite openly admitted that the French influence on his work came through Symons; he listed Symons, with Plato, Dante, Benedict de Spinoza, Longinus, and Pater, among his household gods.

Laboring under what Harold Bloom would call the anxiety of influence, Eliot both acknowledged his early debt to Symons and sought to trivialize it by attacking Symons' criticism. While he stated in "The Perfect Critic" that Symons' *The Symbolist Movement in Literature* was for him an introduction to wholly new feelings, a revelation, he also noted that his own readings of Verlaine, Laforgue, and Rimbaud differed from Symons' readings. Although the book, he concluded, had a less than permanent value for him, it led to results of permanent importance to him. Symons, indeed, was the object of Eliot's severe dismissal as "the aesthetic critic" in much the same way that Pater became such an object in Eliot's "Arnold and Pater." It is nevertheless telling that the epigraphs for both parts of "The Perfect Critic" are drawn from the French Symbolist critic Remy de Gourmont, whose works Eliot might not have known without Symons' introduction.

While Eliot's criticism was derived in part from Symbolist thought, his poetic practice was more clearly influenced by the Symbolists, particularly Laforgue, to whom Symons introduced him – a point he would reiterate in *For Lancelot Andrewes* (1928).

A combination of factors conspired to put Symons out of favor and fashion for most of the twentieth century. Eliot's criticism was surely a primary factor in the decline of Symons' popularity; so, too, was Symons' own longevity, the loss of his critical powers after 1908, and his later work as a raconteur of a time that became increasingly quaint after World War I. Thus Richard Jennings in *New Statesman* (February 17, 1945) marked Symons' death with the observation that he had died mentally in 1908 and that all work published after that date should be received with caution. Just after mid-century, however, Symons began to receive deserved critical attention from Ruth Z. Temple, Frank Kermode, and Richard Ellmann in a rebirth of interest in the roots of modernism and in the Symbolist legacy to the twentieth century. Since that time, Symons has been the object of two reliable biographies and numerous studies, many of which deal with his crucial role in bridging the gap between the Victorian era and the modern world in what has been called the transitional age.

## Principal criticism
*An Introduction to the Study of Browning*, 1886
"The Decadent Movement in Literature," 1893
*Studies in Two Literatures*, 1897
*The Symbolist Movement in Literature*, 1899
*Studies in the Seven Arts*, 1906
*William Blake*, 1907
*The Romantic Movement in English Poetry*, 1909
*Charles Baudelaire: A Study*, 1920
*A Study of Oscar Wilde*, 1930
*A Study of Thomas Hardy*, 1930
*A Study of Walter Pater*, 1932

## Other major works and literary forms
The volumes listed above represent only a fraction of Arthur Symons' literary work. He published more than fifty books and edited, translated, or introduced another fifty on such varied topics as music, literature, painting, sculpture, the theater, and travel. He also published several volumes of poetry, some remarkable for their decadence, others for their application of French Symbolist theory to English verse. Symons was a prolific essayist and reviewer; in much of his early writing, especially in the 1890s, he was clearly on the frontier of modernism in prose and in poetry. His work after 1908, the year of his mental collapse in Italy, was rarely up to his earlier standard.

POETRY
*Days and Nights*, 1889
*Silhouettes*, 1892
*London Nights*, 1895
*Amoris Victima*, 1897
*Poems*, 1902 (2 volumes)

NONFICTION
*Dramatis Personae*, 1923
*Confessions: A Study in Pathology*, 1930
*From Toulouse-Lautrec to Rodin: With Some Personal Impressions*, 1930
*Selected Letters*, 1989 (Karl Beckson and John M. Munro, editors)

EDITED TEXTS
Introduction to *The Poems and Prose of Ernest Dowson*, 1919

## Further reading

Beckson, Karl. *The Memoirs of Arthur Symons*, 1977.
———. *Arthur Symons: A Life*, 1987.
Clements, Patricia. "Symons," in *Baudelaire and the English Tradition: Canonization of the Subversive*, 1985.
Ellmann, Richard, ed. *The Symbolist Movement in Literature*, 1958.
Gibbons, Tom. *Rooms in the Darwin Hotel*, 1973.
Kermode, Frank. "Arthur Symons," in *The Romantic Image*, 1957.
Lhombreaud, Roger. *Arthur Symons: A Critical Biography*, 1963.
Munro, John M. *Arthur Symons*, 1969.
Stern, Carol S. "Arthur Symons: An Annotated Bibliography of Writings About Him," in *English Literature in Transition*. XVII, no. 2 (1974), pp. 77–133.
Temple, Ruth Z. "Arthur Symons," in *The Critic's Alchemy: A Study of the Introduction of French Symbolism into England*, 1953.

JOHN J. CONLON

*See also* Aestheticism; Pater; Symbolism; Wilde; Yeats

# T

## Hippolyte-Adolphe Taine

French critic and writer

**Born:** Vouziers, France; April 21, 1828
**Died:** Paris, France; March 5, 1893

### Biography

Hippolyte-Adolphe Taine was born on April 21, 1828, in Vouziers, France. He was the son of Jean-Baptiste-Antoine Taine, a country lawyer, and the former Marie-Virginie Bezanson. After his father's death in 1840, the young Taine was sent to Paris, where, in 1848, he was admitted to the École Normale Supérieure at the top of his class. In 1853 Taine earned his doctorate in letters, presenting two theses, one on Plato and the other on Jean de La Fontaine. The latter was published that same year as the *Essai sur les fables de La Fontaine* (essay on the fables of La Fontaine).

Taine's career as a literary critic formally began in 1855 with articles in respected publications, such as *La Revue des deux mondes*, *La Revue de l'instruction publique*, and *Le Journal des débats*; in 1855 also his *Essai sur Tite-Live* (1856; essay on Livy) won a prize from the French Academy. After the appearance of several books of literary criticism had securely established his reputation as a critic and literary historian, Taine became a professor of aesthetics and art history at the École des Beaux-Arts in Paris, assuming that position in 1864. He would subsequently publish books of art criticism comprising his lectures, which also contained some of his theories relative to literary criticism.

Taine's celebrity in the 1860s was such that he could frequent the salon of Princess Mathilde and dine at Magny's in the company of Gustave Flaubert, Théophile Gautier, and the Goncourt brothers, among others. In 1871 Taine accepted an invitation to lecture at Oxford University, where he was granted an honorary degree. Election to the French Academy, coming in 1878 on the third try, officially confirmed Taine's lofty standing in the French intellectual community. He died in Paris on March 5, 1893.

### Influence

The prestige that Taine enjoyed in France as an intellectual mentor during the second half of the nineteenth century was matched only, perhaps, by that of Ernest Renan and, at a later date, by that of Ferdinand Brunetière. Like the latter, Taine was a highly influential exponent of the scientific method as applied to the analysis of literature, although Brunetière – who denounced the naturalists for maintaining that the art of literary creation could be scientific – disagreed with Taine as to precisely how the techniques of science should relate to literary criticism. Yet Brunetière, although with reservations, endorsed and was influenced by Taine's scientific frame of reference, as were, more willingly and more particularly, foreign admirers, among whom was the American literary historian Vernon L. Parrington.

With the reaction against scientism at the end of the nineteenth century, Taine's prestige suffered appreciably. Marxist criticism, structuralism, and psychoanalytic methodologies all drew from his work, however, indicating that his attempt to render literary criticism objective, while obviously flawed in some respects, continued still to constitute an instructive and stimulating example of how scientific principles could be profitably applied to the study of literature.

### Analysis

Hippolyte-Adolphe Taine's critical writings reflected his age's immense faith in science and its effort to apply the scientific method to the analysis and appreciation of literature. In the latter regard, Auguste Comte's positivism had already shown the way, and Ernest Renan's work, *L'Avenir de la science* (1890; *The Future of Science*, 1890) had affirmed the almost boundless optimism of a generation convinced that science would provide the answers to most, if not all, humankind's problems.

Early in his career, Taine sought to introduce the scientific spirit into literary criticism, as is demonstrated by the theoretical aspects of the *Essai sur Tite-Live* and of *Les Philosophes français du XIXᵉ siècle* (1857), whose definitive title became, for the third edition in 1868, *Les Philosophes classiques du XIXᵉ siècle en France*. It was only in the 1858 and 1866 prefaces to his *Essais de critique et d'histoire*, and in his *Histoire de la littérature anglaise* (1863–1864; *History of English Literature*, 1871), however, that Taine gave shape and coherence to his theories. In these writings, he put forth the notion that a literary work could be meaningfully studied only in its historical setting, and in specific relation to the factors of race, milieu, and moment which had conditioned its production. Beyond the influence of Spinozistic and Hegelian propositions about the geometrically rational and systematically deterministic organization of the universe, implicit in Taine's reasoning was the principle of analogy as adapted to the study of literary phenomena. According to this principle, originally applied to biological phenomena by Étienne Geoffroy Saint-Hilaire, constant characteristics could be observed in a nation or race whatever the modifications occurring as a result of external pressures. According to Taine, this principle meant that a basic determinism underlay the production of a literary work. The latter was necessarily shaped – whatever the individual caprices of its author – not only by the moment (seen as a kind of cultural momentum as well as a historical epoch) and the milieu (viewed as political and social institutions in addition to geography) but also by the writer's racial stock, which for Taine involved the elementary idea of "blood," or hereditary traits.

Nevertheless, Taine was not content to examine authors and their works against the background of these overmastering and irresistible forces, nor was the critic satisfied merely to progress to the next step of analyzing an individual work in its relation to an author's output within the context of the literary movement to which he or she belonged. Inspired by Thomas Carlyle's approach in *Oliver Cromwell's Letters and Speeches with Elucidations* (1845), and by the critical technique of Charles-Augustin Sainte-Beuve, Taine firmly held that the critic's obligation was, ultimately, to gain access to the inner man. The author of a literary work having been inevitably conditioned by powerful determinants external to his or her will, it remained for the critic, having surveyed those determinants, to probe inside and to discover how the mechanism of the individual mind responded to this conditioning process – vice and virtue themselves being merely, according to the introduction to the *History of English Literature*, products like vitriol and sugar. What the critic strove to discern, in the inner man, was the *faculté maîtresse*, or dominant trait, which caused him or her to mirror his or her race, milieu, and moment in a distinctive way.

In seeking to ascertain inductively the literary consequences which flowed from the influence of external forces on an artistic temperament, Taine was pursuing a grandiose yet understandable goal: the establishment of laws basic to a deductive procedure for explaining literary history. Beyond this aim, however, he curiously endeavored to graft a set of aesthetic values on his deterministic methodology. When combined with such aesthetic values, Taine's deterministic logic seemed to lead to the conclusion that the greatest writers were by definition those who best represented their nation and their time, those in whom the dominant individual trait was best equipped to reflect the dominant racial trait of their people.

At first glance, Jean Racine, the finest exponent of French classical tragedy in the seventeenth century, appeared to incarnate this dual excellence. In the *Nouveaux Essais de critique et d'histoire* (1865; new critical and historical essays), Taine observed that, no less than Sophocles and William Shakespeare, Racine was a national poet, his theater being as French as one could desire, his personal genius being the very image of the French national genius, his works portraying the very heart of the French race. Taine contended that what enabled Racine to be so incomparably French was the dominant trait within him, the superior endowments of the court poet which allowed him to give unique expression to *la raison oratoire* (oratorical reason), the latter being the dominant trait of the French people at that time. Racine's accent on psychological verisimilitude in the broad universal sense, his cultivation of the rational and harmonious expression of human emotion, his abhorrence of excess, and his banishment of violence from the French stage were all marvelously consistent, in Taine's view, with the essence of the French spirit and character in the seventeenth century.

Yet despite Racine's superb encapsulation of this essence, Taine could not be unequivocal in his praise of the seventeenth-century dramatist. At odds with the conclusions of his "objective" assessment of Racine's greatness were Taine's personal biases as a nineteenth-century critic prone to deplore in Racine's theater the abstract portrayal of life and the refusal to imitate it in a realistic, concrete way. In Taine's final estimation paradoxically it was the fabulist La Fontaine, and not Racine, who turned out to be the chief poet of seventeenth-century France. In the third edition of his *Essai sur les fables de La Fontaine*, revised and bearing the definitive title of *La Fontaine et ses fables* (1861), Taine had rationalized his preference by claiming that La Fontaine, in contradistinction to a Racine confined within the rules of classicism, embodied the Gallic spirit of all ages of French history. Nevertheless, Taine was then hard put to explain why, if this Gallic spirit was so fundamental, it was not prominent also in the French theater of the classical period, instead of being restricted to the relatively minor genre of the fable that La Fontaine represented.

Nor were Taine's analyses any more consistent when he turned to other writers and other historical periods. A nineteenth-century novelist who both attracted the critic's attention and provoked his considerable admiration was Stendhal, at a time – and this is much to Taine's credit – when the novelist was either ignored or unfavorably treated by French critics in general. What fascinated the psychologist in Taine was, predictably, the singular psychological insight that Stendhal brought to the portrayal of his characters, his relentless scrutiny of the inner man. Having already called Stendhal, in *Les Philosophes classiques du XIXᵉ siècle en France*, the greatest psychologist of the century, Taine added to his enthusiastic commendation in the 1866 edition of the *Essais de critique et d'histoire*. In this work – and his commendatory article would appear also in editions of the *Nouveaux Essais de critique et d'histoire* – Taine identified Stendhal's dominant trait as being a superior mind. It was this superior mind that enabled the novelist to penetrate to the very soul of his protagonist, dispensing with the massive description of external reality so cultivated by lesser novelists.

The further he advanced in his analysis of Stendhal's literary genius, however, the more Taine became caught up in the contradictions of his method. Nor was it simply that he appeared to be extolling, in Stendhal's unremitting pursuit of the inner man, the very preoccupation with psychology to the detriment of the realistic material detail that the critic had found objectionable in the classical theater of Racine. Rather, it was that Taine seemed to suspend, inexplicably, his insistence on the primordial determinative factors of race, milieu, and moment: if anything was profoundly characteristic of Stendhal, it was that his literary genius asserted itself not as the splendid embodiment of the major currents or values of his environment and time but as the defiant rejection of those currents and values.

When Taine attempted to extend his aesthetic judgment to the internal analysis of individual literary works and to apply moral criteria to them, his method betrayed further inconsistencies. In *De l'idéal dans l'art* (1867; *The Ideal in Art*, 1868), Taine not only sought – amid considerations relative to style and convergence of artistic effects – to evaluate characters as to whether they were important (that is, fully representative of the historical period); he also sought to evaluate characters as to whether they were beneficent (that is, noble and heroic, ideally balanced in their physical and spiritual qualities). These criteria complicated even more Taine's attempt to apply his deterministic principles in a detached manner. While some of his observations regarding Honoré de Balzac in the *Nouveaux Essais de critique et d'histoire* were remarkably insightful, for example, Taine was unable to appreciate fully the novelist's extraordinary art: given the critic's moral standards, Balzac's seeming obsession with monomaniacal characters constituted an inexcusable flaw. Because of still more serious violations of Taine's aesthetic and moral codes, Émile Zola was not even considered worthy of extended critical commentary; and, in the light of the fact that some of the naturalist's novels appeared tailor-made for the effective illustration of the critic's deterministic theories, the absence of such a commentary would be generally viewed as one of the most incongruent and glaring omissions in Taine's survey of nineteenth-century French literature.

Despite the many contradictions in Taine's method, the impact of his critical doctrine was, nearly from the very beginning of his career, quite considerable. Ironically, his ideas shaped some of Zola's works, and Maurice Barrès paid homage to him in a novel, *Les Déracinés* (1897). With specific reference to literary criticism, Taine's scientific approach was adopted – but not without qualification – by another nineteenth-century French critic later to be most influential, Ferdinand Brunetière; though an adversary of naturalist scientism, Brunetière elaborated a theory of the evolution of literary genres. Other European critics, such as Georg Brandes, accepted Taine's ideas more readily. In the English-speaking world, the work of the American literary historian Vernon L. Parrington would be only one example of the extent of Taine's influence, reflected in Parrington's *Main Currents in American Thought* (1927–1930).

Even during his lifetime, however, Taine's views on criticism provoked vigorous opposition in certain quarters. It was noted that Barrès paid tribute to Taine in a novel; in another, *Le Disciple* (1889; *The Disciple*, 1898), Paul Bourget created a character, Adrien Sixte, who was clearly modeled on Taine and whose scientific theories led to disaster. Around the same time, Anatole France stated his objection to literary criticism which was inspired by an illusion of objectivity and defended his own impressionistic technique in *La Vie littéraire* (1887–1893; *On Life and Letters*, 1910–1924).

The rebellion against scientism in the arts that partially characterized the 1890s would later culminate in Dadaism, Surrealism, and Henri Bergson's intuitionism, further undercutting Taine's prestige. The critic Albert Thibaudet would subsequently treat Taine severely in his *Réflexions sur la littérature* (1938–1941; reflections on literature), finding Taine's formidable constructions void of meaning, since they were strapped to laws of causality and took no notice of other sources of human creation.

Such assaults on Taine's ideas, however, would not succeed in disqualifying entirely his contribution to literary criticism. What remained worthy in his method was the attempt to limit the subjective aspect of criticism by creating a scientific basis for critical commentary: the systematic consideration of external factors as they conditioned the author's mental mechanism. Taine may have been either too rigid, on the one hand, or too inconsistent, on the other, in his application of this method, but his approach had the salutary effect of causing him to eschew the vague impressionism of nineteenth-century critics such as Jules Lemaître, even as he, Taine, significantly advanced a tendency already present, though not fully developed, in Sainte-Beuve, who had tried to study an author within the latter's sociopolitical context and with reference to psychological factors bearing on his or her work. Interestingly enough, Taine's emphasis on environmental forces was not appreciated by Marxist critics because of his bourgeois values and his failure to interpret those forces in strict terms of class struggle. Yet the Marxist methodology was indebted to him, notwithstanding the fact that the degree of indebtedness – evident, for example, in Lucien Goldmann's *Le Dieu caché* (1955; *The Hidden God*, 1964) – was rarely, if ever, acknowledged.

Through his conception of literature as the result and illustration of relationships within a structural system, the modification of one of whose elements necessarily brought about the modification of all the others, Taine was also indirectly a forerunner of the structuralist thinkers, such as Claude Lévi-Strauss. Finally, while Taine's psychology was to appear primitive in the wake of Sigmund Freud and Carl Jung, his demonstration of the importance of the psychological dimension in literary creation would not be lost on those inclined to practice a psychoanalytic approach to literary criticism, or on those who, like Roland Barthes and Charles Mauron, endeavored to incorporate aspects of the psychoanalytic approach into their own particular methodologies.

In spite of its frequent rigidity and partial obsolescence, Taine's critical method therefore continued to influence constructively the conduct of literary criticism well beyond the era of scientific positivism that, in so many respects, he epitomized. Critics who followed him, however averse they were to certain features of his inflexibly deterministic outlook, often shared Taine's ambitious and supremely challenging goal: to devise a means of introducing into the practice of literary criticism the comprehensiveness, precision, and objectivity associated with science.

## Principal criticism
*Essai sur les fables de La Fontaine*, 1853 (revised as *La Fontaine et ses fables*, 1861)
*Essai sur Tite-Live*, 1856
*Les Philosophes français du XIXᵉ siècle*, 1857 (revised as *Les Philosophes classiques du XIXᵉ siècle en France*, 1868)
*Essais de critique et d'histoire*, 1858
*Histoire de la littérature anglaise*, 1863–1864 (4 volumes; *History of English Literature*, 1871)
*L'Idéalisme anglais: Étude sur Carlyle*, 1864
*Le Positivisme anglais: Étude sur Stuart Mill*, 1864 (*English Positivism: A Study on John Stuart Mill*, 1870)
*Nouveaux Essais de critique et d'histoire*, 1865
*De l'idéal dans l'art: Leçons professées à l'École des Beaux-Arts*, 1867 (*The Ideal in Art*, 1868)
*Derniers Essais de critique et d'histoire*, 1894

## Other major works and literary forms
Hippolyte-Adolphe Taine's publications were not limited to the field of literary criticism. He also wrote works on philosophy and psychology, books of art criticism, travel narratives, and a multivolume history of France entitled *Les Origines de la France contemporaine* (1876–1894; *The Origins of Contemporary France*, 1876–1894). Taine even tried his hand at fiction, leaving the fragment of an unfinished autobiographical novel, *Étienne Mayran: Fragment de roman inachevé* (1910).

NOVEL
*Étienne Mayran: Fragment de roman inachevé*, 1910

NONFICTION
*Voyages aux eaux des Pyrénées*, 1855 (*A Tour Through the Pyrenees*, 1874)
*Philosophie de l'art: Leçons professées à l'École des Beaux-Arts*, 1865 (*Philosophy of Art*, 1865)
*Philosophie de l'art en Italie*, 1866 (*The Philosophy of Art in Italy*, 1875)
*Voyage en Italie*, 1866 (translated as *Italy: Naples and Rome*, 1867, and *Italy: Florence and Venice*, 1869)
*Notes sur Paris: Vie et opinions de M. Frédéric-Thomas Graindorge*, 1867 (*Notes on Paris*, 1875)
*Philosophie de l'art en Grèce*, 1869 (*The Philosophy of Art in Greece*, 1871)
*Philosophie de l'art dans les Pays-Bas*, 1869 (*The Philosophy of Art in the Netherlands*, 1871)
*De l'intelligence*, 1870 (2 volumes; *On Intelligence*, 1871)
*Notes sur l'Angleterre*, 1872 (*Notes on England*, 1872)
*Les Origines de la France contemporaine*, 1876–1894 (6 volumes; *The Origins of Contemporary France*, 1876–1894)
*Carnets de voyage: Notes sur la province, 1863–1865*, 1897 (*Journeys Through France: Being Impressions of Provinces*, 1897)
*H. Taine: Sa Vie et sa correspondance*, 1902–1907 (4 volumes; *Life and Letters of H. Taine*, 1902–1908, 3 volumes)
*Voyage en Allemagne*, 1920

## Further reading
Babbitt, Irving. *The Masters of Modern French Criticism*, 1912.
Charlton, D. G. *Positivist Thought in France During the Second Empire, 1852–1870*, 1959.
Eustis, Alvin Allen. *Hippolyte Taine and the Classical Genius*, 1951.
Evans, Colin. "Taine and His Fate," in *Nineteenth-Century French Studies*. 6, nos. 1–2 (1977–1978) pp. 118–28.
Gates, Lewis E. "Taine's Influence as a Critic," in *Studies and Appreciations*, 1900.
Gullace, Giovanni. *Taine and Brunetière on Criticism*, 1982.
Kahn, Sholom J. *Science and Aesthetic Judgment: A Study in Taine's Critical Method*, 1953.
Michaud, Stéphane, and Michèle Le Pavec, eds. *Taine au carrefour des cultures du XIXᵉ siècle: colloque organisé par la Bibliothèque Nationale et la Société des Études Romantiques et Dix-neuviémistes, 3 décembre 1993*, 1996.
Nordmann, Jean Thomas. *Taine et la critique scientifique*, 1992.
Weinstein, Leo. *Hippolyte Taine*, 1972.

NORMAN ARAUJO

*See also* Bourget; Brunetière; Continental Theory; Zola

# Allen Tate
## American writer and critic

**Born:** Winchester, Kentucky; November 19, 1899
**Died:** Nashville, Tennessee; February 9, 1979

## Biography
John Orley Allen Tate was born in Winchester, Kentucky, near Lexington, on November 19, 1899, the son of John Orley and Eleanor (Varnell) Tate. His father, an orphan

since the age of eleven, but with a financial legacy from his grandfather, engaged in various ill-fated business ventures while Tate was growing up. After scattered schooling in Louisville and Ashland, Kentucky, as well as Cincinnati, Ohio, Tate entered Vanderbilt University in Tennessee in September, 1918, where he enrolled in classes under the young instructor John Crowe Ransom and was invited to join a discussion group led by Ransom which included Donald Davidson and others. Until his graduation from Vanderbilt in 1922, Tate participated in the creation and contributed to the development of *The Fugitive*, an influential journal published by the group which, along with Ransom, Tate, and Davidson, included Cleanth Brooks and Robert Penn Warren and which formed the seminal origins of the New Criticism.

Tate married the novelist Caroline Gordon in 1924, and they moved to New York, where he began his literary career, publishing a prodigious number of poems, papers, and reviews, as well as the biography of Stonewall Jackson. During the 1930s and 1940s Tate participated in the Agrarian movement, published his one novel, *The Fathers* (1938), continued to write poetry and critical essays, and took on various teaching and editing jobs, including the editing of the prestigious *The Sewanee Review*. In 1951 he was appointed professor of English at the University of Minnesota, a position he held until his retirement in 1968. Tate received numerous awards, including being elected to both the American Academy of Arts and Letters and the American Academy of Arts and Sciences. He would be married two more times: to Isabella Gardner in 1959 and Helen Heinz in 1966. Tate died on February 9, 1979, in Nashville, Tennessee.

## Influence

As one of the original members of the self-styled Fugitive group from Vanderbilt University in the 1920s and thus, along with Ransom, Davidson, Brooks, and Warren, one of the members of the New Critics, Allen Tate has shared in the influence of that group on the way literature was taught and written about by American academics from the 1930s until the 1960s. Although his works have not been as central as the theoretical studies of other members of the group, such as Ransom and William K. Wimsatt, and although his pedagogical studies have not been so pervasive in the classroom as Brooks and Warren's *Understanding Fiction* (1943, 1959) and *Understanding Poetry* (1938, 1950), nevertheless, such essays by Tate as "Tension in Poetry" (1938), "Three Types of Poetry" (1936), and his studies of Emily Dickinson and Edgar Allan Poe affected the way literature in general and the works of these authors in particular were taught and thought about in the twentieth century.

## Analysis

Tate's criticism cannot be considered apart from his role in the most influential critical and pedagogical movement in literary studies in the twentieth century, the New Criticism – a formalist approach to the study of literature which was established in the 1920s by such critics as I. A. Richards, T. S. Eliot, and Ransom, and propagated by Ransom's pupils Tate, Brooks, and Warren.

The New Criticism began as an attempt by both British and American critics to establish the value of literature on literary grounds. It arose in rebellion against the prevailing pedagogical practice of teaching the study of literature as simply historical scholarship as well as the prevailing artistic assumption in the 1930s of writing literature to serve the purposes of propaganda. Although the Anglo-American formalists share many of the same assumptions about the nature of literature as the group of 1920s theorists known as the Russian Formalists, they clearly developed independently of each other. In fact, one of the earliest mentions of the Russian Formalists in American criticism appears only in 1949 with the publication of *Theory of Literature* by René Wellek and Austin Warren.

Tate's primary critical assumptions are much the same as those of his mentor Ransom and his colleagues Brooks and Warren – that is, that literature, in its style and structure, is a symbolic form of the human experience which uses language in a radically different way from the way language is used in logical or discursive prose. Whereas logical prose, the tool of science, aims toward abstraction and generality, the language of literature, as most essentially seen in lyric poetry, aims toward concretion or the unique particular. Whereas the language of science makes use primarily of the concept, the language of poetry primarily makes use of the image or the iconic sign – what Eliot called an "objective correlative" – a language complex which somehow embodies and communicates the concrete complexity of human life emotionally and cognitively.

Although the New Critics differed in the particular ways in which they taught or wrote about this approach to literature and thus never developed what could be called a unified theory of literature, they all agreed that the literary work was not simply a means of communicating pre-existing knowledge. It was not merely a medium for the simple communication of ideas, but rather the literary work was, in itself, a means of knowing, of discovering knowledge in its own unique symbolic, iconic, and organic way.

In his first book of criticism, *Reactionary Essays on Poetry and Ideas* (1936), Tate insisted on the literary nature of literature, as opposed to those positivist thinkers who believed that literature was only a branch of politics. Furthermore, Tate rebelled against those professors in English departments across the country who believed that the serious study of literature could only be the scholarly pursuit of knowledge about the historical context of literary works, and who scorned criticism as being a subjective pursuit which required no schooling, in which anybody could engage. The function of criticism for Tate is to demonstrate and communicate that unique knowledge which the great forms of literature create. Tate argues strongly against historical and sociological scholarly pursuits, which he says are dominated by the "doctrine of relevance," that is, that the subject matter of the literary works must be tested against the external world they represent. For Tate, the only touch stone for the validity of the work is the integrity of the work itself, not how well it imitates the world it takes for its subject matter.

Tate's one constant antagonist in his criticism is the scientific spirit – a point of view which he argues is characterized by "positive Platonism," that is, the scientist's confidence that humans have unlimited power to impose practical abstractions on experience. By the same token, urges Tate, any literary form, such as allegory, which attempts to communicate these predetermined abstractions oversimplifies human experience and is therefore inferior to genuine art works. Poetry is not history, emotion, propaganda, or religion, as the scientific positivists claim; the value of poetry is intrinsically cognitive, for it provides knowledge that did not exist before its creation.

"Tension in Poetry" is one of Tate's most important essays. In it he directly attacks what he calls the fallacy of communication in poetry and the kind of poetry which is most guilty of the fallacy – those poems which communicate an affective state by the irresponsible denotation of words. Such poetry is most often characterized as romantic or symbolist, what Tate calls the poetry of "intension." At the other extreme is rationalistic poetry, the poetry of "extension." Each of these types is the ultimate end of a continuum; Tate, however, proposes a poetry of the middle of the scale, which he calls a poetry of "tension," in which there is a unification of the two. Tate gets the word "tension," an important concept in all New Criticism, from chopping off the prefixes of the logical terms extension and intension. Tension, or the meaning of poetry, results from the organization of all the extension and intension that one can find in the poem.

It is this notion, inspired by Eliot, of a poetic unification of emotion and thought in a concrete way which made the New Critics, including Tate, rebel against both the discursive poetry of the eighteenth century and the emotional poetry of the nineteenth century and instead turn back to the Metaphysical poets, such as John Donne, George Herbert, and Andrew Marvell, of the sixteenth and seventeenth centuries. Tate says that modern poetry, such as the poetry of Eliot, Ezra Pound, and Hart Crane, is difficult for the same reason that sixteenth-century poetry was difficult: it requires the direct and active participation of the reader in the texture, style, and form of the work itself.

Readers cannot understand the foundations of poetry, says Tate, unless they eliminate from their thinking the demands of the will with its instrument, the practical intellect. The problem with positivism, he argues, is that it offers a single field of discourse which may be called "physicalism" and then pretends that it is the sole field of discourse. Those teachers who suggest that historical scholarship is the only way to study literature are thus guilty of pernicious positivism. Tate notes that he is not trying to dispense with historical scholarship or the study of the external elements of literature; in fact, he finds it helpful at times, especially in understanding the historical context of words in poetry. The historical study of literature as the positivists see it, however, makes the student of literature into an amateur sociologist or psychologist and puts literature itself into the subordinate position of being an empty container for ideas. Furthermore, the so-called historical method, at least as it was practiced before the New Critics, says Tate, is unhistorical, for it is removed from living history and insists on the necessity of documents for the study of literature; it ignores the unique characteristics of literature as literature.

In a 1950 essay entitled "Is Literary Criticism Possible?" Tate notes that the humanities have no rationale such as that of the sciences or even the social sciences. The study of literature particularly can have no rationale or justification of its own as long as literature is seen to be a secondary delivery system for preestablished ideas. Literary criticism, says Tate, cannot be practiced apart from what it confronts, and what it confronts is the literary work itself.

The focus of Tate and the other New Critics on the individual work, particularly the style, technique, and form of the work, transformed college literature classes all over the US into sessions focusing on explication of the individual text. Given the critical preference of the group, the most prized texts were the lyric poems of the seventeenth-century Metaphysical poets and their twentieth-century heirs. Tate's choices of artists to write about in his collected essays are reflective of this predisposition: Donne, Eliot, William Butler Yeats, Crane, and the most metaphysical of the English and American Romantic poets – Dickinson and John Keats.

The best-known exceptions to this predilection toward Metaphysical writers are the two essays on Poe which Tate published in *The Forlorn Demon: Didactic and Critical Essays* in 1953. In "Our Cousin, Mr. Poe," Tate begins by recounting his adolescent fascination with Poe and proceeds to discuss what he considers to be the serious religious and therefore symbolic basis of Poe's work. In "The Angelic Imagination," he begins by refuting Eliot's criticism of Poe's adolescent immaturity and then explores more fully his conviction about Poe's essentially religious nature by examining several of his most mystical and metaphysical works, including *Eureka: A Prose Poem* (1848). The two essays seem radical departures in approach for Tate, and just as he says he is somewhat embarrassed to be playing amateur theologian in them, other critics were somewhat embarrassed at the time for his spending such an inordinate amount of work on a writer who many considered to be definitely inferior. The seriousness with which Tate treats Poe has since been validated by subsequent studies, and the essays have become central not only in the study of Poe but also for the study of the dilemma of the modern artist.

Like the others of the American formalist movement, Tate places central emphasis on the form and technique of poetry, for within technique lies the means of poetic discovery. Thus his analyses of individual authors and works continually emphasize the means by which art creates and communicates by the tension of its literary elements. For Tate, the form of a work takes on an objectivity which he claims the subject matter of the work, abstracted from the form, totally lacks. It is a mode of criticism that has become so pervasive since Tate and the other New Critics that it sometimes seems the only approach possible.

## Principal criticism
*Reactionary Essays on Poetry and Ideas*, 1936
*Reason in Madness, Critical Essays*, 1941
*On the Limits of Poetry: Selected Essays, 1928–1948*, 1948
*The Hovering Fly and Other Essays*, 1949
*The Forlorn Demon: Didactic and Critical Essays*, 1953
*The Man of Letters in the Modern World: Selected Essays, 1928–1955*, 1955
*Collected Essays*, 1959
*Essays of Four Decades*, 1968

## Other major works and literary forms
Allen Tate is one of the few American writers in the twentieth century who deserves the honorable and all-encompassing title "man of letters." Although Tate has gained considerable respect as a literary critic because of his association with and contribution to the influential 1930s literary movement known as the New Criticism, he began his career as a poet and a biographer, publishing two volumes of poetry as well as biographies of Stonewall Jackson and Jefferson Davis by the time he reached the age of thirty. In 1932 his *Poems: 1928–1931* was published, and by 1937 his poetry was prominent and important enough to deserve a volume entitled *Selected Poems*. His most famous poem, "Ode to the Confederate Dead" (1928), has been reprinted numerous times in anthologies and textbooks.

Tate also has received belated critical praise for his only novel, *The Fathers* (1938), a first-person historical account set in the South in the late nineteenth century. In addition to his critical studies of literature, Tate is well known for his polemical essays on politics and his espousal of the sectionalist social view known as Agrarianism, especially in a 1930 volume he edited entitled *I'll Take My Stand: The South and the Agrarian Tradition*. Finally, Tate is also the editor of numerous important textbooks including *The House of Fiction: An Anthology of the Short Story* (1950), which he edited with his first wife, writer Caroline Gordon, and *Modern Verse in English, 1900–1950* (1958), which he edited with British critic David Cecil.

NOVEL
*The Fathers*, 1938

POETRY
*The Golden Mean and Other Poems*, 1923 (with Ridley Wills)
*Mr. Pope and Other Poems*, 1928
*Poems: 1928–1931*, 1932
*The Mediterranean and Other Poems*, 1936
*Selected Poems*, 1937
*Poems: 1920–1945*, 1947
*Poems: 1922–1947*, 1948
*Poems*, 1960
*The Swimmers and Other Selected Poems*, 1971
*Collected Poems: 1919–1976*, 1977

NONFICTION
*Stonewall Jackson: The Good Soldier*, 1928
*Jefferson Davis: His Rise and Fall*, 1929

ANTHOLOGIES
*I'll Take My Stand: The South and the Agrarian Tradition*, 1930
*Who Owns America? A Declaration of Independence*, 1936 (with Herbert Agar)
*American Harvest: Twenty Years of Creative Writing in the United States*, 1942 (with John Peale Bishop)
*The Language of Poetry*, 1942
*A Southern Vanguard*, 1947
*The Collected Poems of John Peale Bishop, 1892–1944*, 1948
*The House of Fiction: An Anthology of the Short Story*, 1950 (with Caroline Gordon)
*Modern Verse in English, 1900–1950*, 1958 (with David Cecil)

## Further reading
Arnold, Willard B. *The Social Ideas of Allen Tate*, 1955.
Bishop, Ferman. *Allen Tate*, 1967.
Bradford, M. E. *Rumors of Mortality: An Introduction to Allen Tate*, 1969.
Cowan, Louise. *The Fugitive Group: A Literary History*, 1959.
Hemphill, George. *Allen Tate*, 1964.
Meiners, R. K. *The Last Alternatives: A Study of the Works of Allen Tate*, 1963.
Squires, Radcliffe. *Allen Tate: A Literary Biography*, 1971.
——, ed. *Allen Tate and His Work: Critical Evaluations*, 1972.
Stewart, John L. *The Burden of Time: The Fugitives and Agrarians*, 1965.

CHARLES E. MAY

*See also* American Literary Theory: Twentieth Century; New Criticism

# Tzvetan Todorov
## Bulgarian-born French theorist

**Born:** Sofia, Bulgaria; March 1, 1939

## Biography
Tzvetan Todorov was born on March 1, 1939, in Sofia, Bulgaria, to Todor Borov Todorova (a university professor) and the former Haritina Todorova (a librarian). After taking his M.A. in philology at the University of Sofia in 1963, he emigrated to France and enrolled at the University of Paris. Roland Barthes directed his doctoral thesis, which

was published in 1967 as *Littérature et signification.* Todorov took his *doctorat de troisième cycle* (equivalent to the Ph.D.) in 1966, and his *doctorat ès lettres* in 1970. He was appointed to his post as a director of research at the French Centre Nationale de la Recherche Scientifique in 1968. In 1970 he helped to found the journal *Poétique*, of which he remained one of the managing editors until 1979. With Gérard Genette, he edited the *Collection Poétique*, the series of books on literary theory published by Éditions de Seuil, until 1987.

## Influence

Todorov has been one of the most systematic and versatile of the French structuralist literary theorists and semioticians. Although his most important work has been in the study of narrative and, in particular, of narrative "syntax" – the study of the "horizontal" structure of narrative, the structure of fictional events – he has also done important work in the theory of genre and in the theory of verbal "symbolism" and interpretation. Perhaps equally influential has been his work as a translator and editor of the Russian Formalists and Mikhail Bakhtin, as well as his work as coeditor of the journal *Poétique: Revue de théorie et d'analyse littéraires.*

## Analysis

Although his work has remained clear, systematic, and analytically rigorous, over the years Todorov's theoretical stance has shifted radically, from that of a "scientist" to that of a "humanist" and "moralist," as the context in which he has considered literature has expanded from what he once saw as the closed system of literature itself out into the world of social reality, and as he has become interested in discourses other than literary discourse. His early work, from *Littérature et signification*, the published version of his 1967 doctoral thesis, to the late 1970s, most clearly aspires to being scientific. During that period Todorov, in the range of topics he wrote about and in the consistency with which he applied characteristically "structuralist" methods and insights to literature, was the most representative of the French structuralist literary theoreticians.

Todorov has frequently discussed the opposition between "poetics," the study of the general laws of literature, and what he has variously called "description," "interpretation," "commentary" "criticism," and "exegesis" – the study, from various perspectives, of the individual literary work. None of these activities occurs in complete isolation from the others; they are equally important and mutually illuminating, since, as he observes in the preface to the English-language edition of *Poétique* (1973; *An Introduction to Poetics*, 1981), "the theoretician criticizes the exegete's discourse, and the exegete in his turn shows the inadequacies of theory in relation to the object studied, the works." Nevertheless, Todorov, like most of the French structuralists, is primarily a poetician rather than

an exegete. Even when he does focus on individual literary works, it is usually with ulterior theoretical motives. To those who object to the poetician's approach on the grounds that it neglects what is "specific" and "unique" about an individual work, Todorov replies that one cannot talk about literature without generalizing, since language is "essentialist and generic by nature: as soon as I speak, I enter into the universe of abstraction, of generality, of the concept, and no longer of things."

Todorov observes that one sense of "structuralism" is "the study of abstract structure." Poetics (and, by implication, his own work) is by definition "structuralist" in this broad sense, since the object of poetics is an abstract structure, the general laws of literature. Yet his work is also "structuralist" in a narrower sense. In *Critique de la critique* (1984; *Literature and Its Theorists*, 1987), he says that Northrop Frye's *Anatomy of Criticism* (1957) is structuralist in that it combines two traits: an "internal approach to literature" and a "systematic attitude"; it shares both traits with French structuralist poetics, including Todorov's work. In *Introduction à la littérature fantastique* (*The Fantastic*, 1970), however, he judges Frye's theory to be insufficiently "internal" and "systematic": the categories that make up Frye's classificatory scheme are all "borrowed . . . from philosophy, psychology, or a social ethic." Since Frye does not indicate that he uses these categories in special literary senses, "they lead us outside of literature." Thus, to take an "internal" approach to literature in Todorov's sense is to try to understand literature as constituted by its own categories and the relations between those categories.

Todorov's work (and French structuralist poetics in general) is "structuralist" in a still narrower sense: what most clearly distinguishes it from other internal, systematic theories of literature is its heavy reliance on structural linguistics and on semiotics (the more general science of sign-systems that has developed from and now includes structural linguistics) as sources for the basic categories in terms of which it describes the systems of literature. Although French structuralist poeticians generally agree that their adoption of linguistic categories is authorized to some extent by the fact that language and literature are both sign-systems, and by the further circumstance that literature is a "secondary" sign-system whose material of expression is the "primary" sign-system of language, they disagree among themselves about just how intimate the relationship between language and literature is. Some (such as Gérard Genette) see the relationship as little more than one of suggestive analogy. Todorov, on the other hand, hypothesizes rigorous homologies between language and literature; in *Poétique de la prose* (1971; *The Poetics of Prose*, he quotes with provisional approval Paul Valéry's dictum: "Literature is, and can be nothing other than, a sort of extension and application of certain properties of language." In *Grammaire du Décaméron* (1969), he adopts the "methodological hypothesis" of a kind of deep-structural identity between language and literature: underlying all sign-systems is a "universal grammar," which is also universal in the sense that "it coincides with the structure of the universe itself." He remarks that whereas in the past most of those who believed in a universal grammar thought that its structure reflected the structure of the universe, many now think that what one perceives as the structure of the universe is a projection of the structure of the universal grammar; he does not hazard an opinion himself.

One of Todorov's explicit borrowings from linguistics is his division of the literary work into "semantic" and "syntactic" aspects, along with a "verbal" aspect that does not have a parallel in language. Todorov applies this division in most of his writings about literature. The semantic aspect, which he also calls the "paradigmatic" aspect (a term borrowed from Ferdinand de Saussure), refers to "relations between elements present and absent," which are "relations of meaning and symbolization." For example, relations between a text and the other texts which it evokes, or between a text and its genre(s), or between a text and its themes – all of these are semantic relations. The syntactic aspect, which he also calls the "syntagmatic" aspect (again borrowing from Saussure), refers to "relations between copresent elements," which are "relations of configuration, of construction." Examples of syntactic relations include causal and temporal relations, relations of similarity and contrast among the fictional events evoked by a given text, and relations (more important in poetry than in fiction) of similarity and contrast among verbal structures in a given text. The verbal aspect of literature includes questions of "point of view" and of the relationship between the order in which fictional events are narrated and the order in which they occur in story time.

*Grammaire du Décaméron*, Todorov's most detailed elaboration of the homology between language and literature, is also typical of his work in that it is about narrative, the subject of much of his most influential work, and in that it exhibits particularly clearly his will to a "scientific" degree of abstraction and methodological rigor. For the most part setting aside consideration of the semantic and verbal aspects of Giovanni Boccaccio's *Decameron*, he outlines a grammar of its "narrative syntax," of the relations among the elements – the characters and events – of the fictions evoked by the tales. Todorov calls the most general actions in a narrative "propositions." The narrative proposition, which is the fundamental unit of narrative syntax, is homologous to the linguistic sentence, although it need not be (and usually is not) narrated in a single sentence. The fictional event evoked by the sentence "The king kills his grandson" is a narrative proposition that occurs in the *Decameron*, although that precise sentence does not.

Each proposition is made up of one or two "agents," which are homologous to the linguistic subject and object, and a "predicate." The agent is the syntactic category that corresponds on the semantic level to one or more characters (several characters can act as a single agent, just as several nouns can act as a single subject), which are like proper names in that they have no semantic content but "personhood" unless other qualities are predicated of them. Predicates can be either "verbs" or "attributes" (respectively homologous to linguistic verbs and adjectives); the three basic categories of narrative verbs are "situation-modifying actions," "transgressions," and "punishments," and the three basic categories of attributes are "states," "properties," and "statuses." Narrative propositions, like sentences, are sometimes in "modes" other than the indicative (Todorov's narrative "mode" is the attitude of the agent, the "subject" of the proposition, toward the proposed state of affairs, rather than the attitude of the speaker of the proposition, the narrator, as in the case of linguistic mode). Propositions may also be "negated," or transformed into their opposites, or appear in "comparative" forms, and can be the objects of false "visions" – that is, can be misperceived by agents.

Groups of propositions, among which there may be various sorts of "temporal" and "causal" relations, combine into "sequences," which are characterized by the reader's sense that they are "complete," able "to constitute an independent story." Formally, a typical well-formed sequence ends with the same proposition with which it begins, usually modified somehow (often by negation or opposition). Todorov represents the syntactic structure of a simple "attributive" sequence (one which involves a change in, or an attempt to change, some attribute) as follows:

$$X - A + (XA)_{\text{opt } \alpha} \rightarrow Ya \rightarrow XA$$

That is, agent X does not possess attribute A(X – A) then (+) agent Y desires that agent X possess attribute A: $(XA)_{\text{opt } Y}$ ("opt" indicates that this proposition is in the "optative" mode, the mode of desire); as a result ($\rightarrow$), Y performs situation-modifying action a (Ya), which results ($\rightarrow$) in X's possession of attribute A(XA).

Many of the tales of the *Decameron* consist of more than one sequence. Sequences can be combined in three different ways: by means of "linking" (*enchaînement*), the simple succession of sequences; by means of "embedding" (*enchâssement*), the inclusion of one sequence within another, often as a proposition of the inclusive sequence (the familiar story-within-a-story situation); and by means of "alternation" (*alternance*) between the propositions of two or more sequences. Todorov admits that his narrative grammar of the *Decameron* may not be generalizable to all narrative, and that there may even be a more economical way of formulating the grammar of the *Decameron*, but he concludes that the notion of a comprehensive grammar of narrative syntax is itself valid.

Todorov has devoted almost as much attention to the theory of genre as to the theory of narrative. His brief consideration, in *Littérature et signification*, of the genre of the epistolary novel, as exemplified by Pierre Choderlos de Laclos' *Les Liaisons dangereuses* (1782; *Dangerous Connections*, 1784, also as *Dangerous Liaisons*, 1962), already follows a major guiding principle of his later genre theory: the assumption that the various features of a given genre are intimately interrelated. He continues to follow the guiding principle of considering a given genre as a system of interrelated features in *The Fantastic*, his most extended discussion of genre. According to Todorov, texts belonging to the historical genre of the "fantastic" have three basic features. The first is verbal: the "implicit reader," whose perception, unlike that of the actual reader, "is inscribed in the text with the same precision as the movements of the characters," must hesitate between the natural and supernatural explanations of a narrated event. The second feature is both syntactic and, since it results in the thematization of the fantastic hesitation, semantic: a central character may also (although he need not necessarily) experience the fantastic hesitation, thus helping to promote the first feature by providing a model within the story for the implicit reader's hesitation. The third feature "transcends" the three aspects of literature, being a requirement for a particular "mode" of reading: the fantastic text must "refuse an allegorical or 'poetic' interpretation," since both of these modes of reading interfere with the evocation of the fiction, and the first, defining feature of the fantastic is precisely the implicit reader's attitude toward the fiction.

Todorov has come to generalize the notion of genre to include all forms of discourse established by social convention. "Scientific discourse," for example, displays certain relatively constant "generic" traits, including the exclusion of "reference to the first and second persons of the verb, as well as the use of other tenses than the present." This development is in part a consequence of Todorov's having come to question the possibility of distinguishing between "literature" and "nonliterature" on the basis of purely structural, internal features. In *Littérature et signification*, he followed a traditional line on the "literary," identifying it with fictionality: the most "outstanding" characteristic of "literary language" is that in it "words do not have a referent (denotatum), but only an imaginary reference." By 1973, however (the year in which he published *An Introduction to Poetics*), he had decided that there probably is no structural trait or group of traits that is possessed by every instance of what is called literature, and that is not possessed by any instance of "nonliterature." What counts as literature changes over time; in fact, European languages had no word for the category "literature" until the eighteenth century. If there is some greatest common denominator of what is called "literature," it is not structural but "functional"; that is, "literature" may perhaps be distinguishable from other discourses, not by what it is, but by what it does. The role of "poetics" has been primarily

"transitional": because it has focused on the most "opaque" discourses, it has sharpened its audience's awareness of discourse as such; all the "genres of discourse" should now be given the careful attention that has hitherto been accorded to literature.

Although there is nothing particularly poststructuralist or deconstructive about the way Todorov comes to reject the idea of an essential opposition between literature and nonliterature, his rejection of the opposition does seem to align him with poststructuralism. Yet Todorov has never denied the value of structuralism; he has only come to deny that by itself it can account for every important dimension of literature. Moreover, his ideas about the way language works and about the proper role of the critic put him into clear opposition to what Robert Scholes, in *Textual Power: Literary Theory and the Teaching of English* (1985), calls "hermetic interpretation," the current of poststructuralism, exemplified by the work of Jacques Derrida and Paul de Man, that "sees texts as radically self-reflective and non-referential." For example, the grounding premise of Todorov's analysis of indirect verbal signification, *Symbolisme et interprétation* (1978; English translation, 1982) – that there is an essential difference between the way one arrives at the "direct," or "literal," sense of a given utterance and the way one arrives at its "indirect," or "symbolic," sense – is directly contrary to deconstructive thought about language, as Todorov recognizes. He is referring to deconstruction when he refers to "a Nietzsche or his modern descendants" who (expressing an opinion that probably derives ultimately "from the Romantic refusal of hierarchies, even in the heart of language") "will say that there is no proper sense, that all is metaphor." Todorov's response to this deconstructive dogma is a commonsense appeal to his own "intuition as a subject engaged in the verbal exchange": "To be able to recognize that difference seems to me an inherent trait of the human being."

In *Symbolism and Interpretation*, Todorov analyzes two different interpretive strategies in detail: "biblical exegesis," which is a form of what he calls "finalist" interpretation, interpretation that takes the content of the text to be interpreted as a given (the given content of biblical exegesis was Christian dogma) and that sees its primary task as showing how one may get from text to the given truth; and "philological exegesis," which is a form of what he calls "operational" interpretation, interpretation that takes the ways of getting from a text to its meaning as a given and that sees its task as restricted to determining that meaning, without asking whether it is "true." What most strikingly distinguishes Todorov's recent work, both from poststructuralism and from his own earlier structuralism, is his rejection of a purely "operational" interpretive strategy, one that renounces any consideration of questions of "truth." He asserts in *Literature and Its Theorists* that "literature has to do with human existence; it is a discourse, too bad for those who are afraid of big words, oriented towards truth and morality," and criticism should admit that it too is a "search for truth and values."

Todorov sees that in rejecting operational "relativism," one risks lapsing into a finalist dogmatism; in *Literature and Its Theorists*, he explores the thought of twentieth-century literary critics in an attempt to find a way to "transcend" this "dichotomy." The form that Todorov finally suggests the critical "search for truth and values" should take is partly inspired by ideas advanced by Mikhail Bakhtin. Todorov calls for a "dialogic criticism" – one that does not try to deny, either by rendering the critic's "voice as inaudible as possible" or by assuming a position of mastery with regard to the literary text – that partakes of what Bakhtin saw as the essential "dialogism" of all discourse, its orientation toward the discourse of other subjects. Taking truth as "an ultimate horizon and a regulating idea" rather than as "given in advance," the critic should attempt to engage in a dialogue with the author of the text he or she is studying, granting him or her as far as possible full status as a speaking subject and equal partner in the exchange.

It is difficult as yet to measure the influence of Todorov's notion of "dialogic criticism," although it has already provoked discussion in major literary-critical forums. So far it is his structuralist theory that has had the greatest influence. His importance has partly been that of a synthesizer and organizer: he helped to define the program of structuralist poetics by providing it with its most coherent and comprehensive manifesto in his *An Introduction to Poetics* (first published in 1967 in the anthology *Qu'est-ce que le structuralisme?*), and he helped to give structuralist poetics its most important forum, as a cofounder and coeditor of the journal *Poétique*. His example brought greater methodological rigor and clarity of expression to structuralism (perhaps in part because French, the language in which he writes, is not his native language, he is the most lucid and approachable of the eminent French literary theorists). His most influential work has been in the theory of narrative. He was not the first to attempt to formulate a grammar of narrative syntax; in *Grammaire du Décaméron*, he acknowledges the Russian Formalists, Vladimir Propp, Étienne Souriau, Claude Bremond, and A.-J. Greimas as predecessors and influences. Todorov, however, developed the structural parallel between narrative and the sentence in greater detail and with greater rigor than anyone before him, and his attempt helped to prompt a number of similar, though often more elaborate, formulations (see Gerald Prince's *A Grammar of Stories*, 1973, for an example of a narrative grammar constructed along the lines of Noam Chomsky's transformational-generative sentence grammar). Gérard Genette's application, in *Narrative Discourse* (1979) – another major document of narrative poetics – of the categories "voice," "mood," and "tense" to the verbal aspect of narrative is inspired by Todorov's work. It is fitting that Todorov, who has done so much to shape modern narrative poetics, was the one who, in *Grammaire du Décaméron*, gave it the name by which it is generally known today: narratology.

## Principal criticism

*Littérature et signification*, 1967
*Grammaire du Décaméron*, 1969
*Introduction á la littérature fantastique*, 1970 (*The Fantastic: A Structural Approach to a Literary Genre*, 1973)
*Poétique de la prose*, 1971 (*The Poetics of Prose*, 1977)
*Poétique*, 1973 (*An Introduction to Poetics*, 1981)
*Théories du symbole*, 1977 (*Theories of the Symbol*, 1984)
*Symbolisme et interprétation*, 1978 (English translation, 1982)
*Les Genres du discours*, 1978
*Mikhaïl Bakhtine: Le Principe dialogique*, 1981 (*Mikhail Bakhtin: The Dialogical Principle*, 1984)
*Critique de la critique: Un Roman d'apprentissage*, 1984 (*Literature and Its Theorists: A Personal View of Twentieth-Century Criticism*, 1987)
*Frêle bonheur: Essai sur Rousseau*, 1985
*La Notion de littérature et autres essais*, 1987 (slightly revised versions of eight essays from *Les Genres du discours* and two essays from *Poétique de la prose*)

## Other major works and literary forms

Besides the books listed above, Tzvetan Todorov has published dozens of articles on the theory of literature and related topics, particularly semiotics and linguistics. With Oswald Ducrot, he has written *Dictionnaire encyclopédique des sciences du langage* (1972; *Encyclopedic Dictionary of the Sciences of Language*, 1979). He has helped to make the thought of major Russian literary theorists (most notably, the Russian Formalists and Mikhail Bakhtin) more available to the West through his translations, editions, and summaries of their works. Several tendencies of his recent thought – his growing interest in questions of practical morality, in discourses other than literature, in the relationship between discourse and its social context, in the relationship between the self and the "Other" – come together in *La Conquête de l'Amérique: La Question de l'autre* (1982; *The Conquest of America: The Question of the Other*, 1984), in which Todorov examines the connections between the sixteenth-century conquest of America by Spain and the two civilizations' differing ways of using language and perceiving the Other.

NONFICTION
*Dictionnaire encyclopédique des sciences du langage*, 1972 (with Oswald Ducrot; *Encyclopedic Dictionary of the Sciences of Language*, 1979)
*La Conquête de l'Amérique: La Question de l'autre*, 1982 (*The Conquest of America: The Question of the Other*, 1984)

TRANSLATIONS
*Théorie de la littérature: Textes des formalistes russes*, 1965
*Mikhaïl Bakhtine: Le Principe dialogique, suivi de Écrits du cercle de Bakhtine*, 1981

EDITED TEXTS
*Recherches sémantiques*, 1966
*Huit questions de poétique*, by Roman Jakobson 1977
*French Literary Theory Today: A Reader*, 1982

## Further reading

Bialostosky, Don H. "Dialogics as an Art of Discourse in Literary Criticism," in *PMLA*. CI (October, 1986), pp. 788–797.

Culler, Jonathan. *Structuralist Poetics*, 1973.

Jefferson, Ann. "Structuralism and Post-Structuralism," in *Modern Literary Theory: A Comparative Introduction*, 1986 (second edition). Edited by Ann Jefferson and David Robey.

Scholes, Robert. *Structuralism in Literature: An Introduction*, 1974.

SCOTT VASZILY

*See also* Bakhtin; Genette; Greimas; Narratology; Russian Formalism; Structuralism; Tynianov

# J. R. R. Tolkien

## South African-born English novelist and scholar

**Born:** Bloemfontein, South Africa; January 3, 1892
**Died:** Bournemouth, England; September 2, 1973

## Biography

John Ronald Reuel Tolkien was born on January 3, 1892, in Bloemfontein, South Africa, the first son of British bank manager Arthur Reuel Tolkien and his wife, Mabel (née Suffield) Tolkien. Dislocations and bereavements marked his childhood and left him with a lifelong reverence for the past. At the age of four, Tolkien was sent to England with his mother, and his father died in Africa soon after. Living in a hamlet outside Birmingham, young Tolkien learned to love rural England and dislike urban life. Mabel Tolkien taught her son Latin and drawing at home before he entered school. In his view, her family's hostility to her Roman Catholic conversion precipitated her death when he was twelve.

Under the guardianship of the family priest, Tolkien began precocious study of historic languages while inventing imaginary languages, histories, and mythologies. He entered Oxford University in 1911, first in classics, later in English language and literature, and in 1915 married Edith Bratt. After experiencing trench warfare in France as a second lieutenant, Tolkien tutored at Oxford and was a researcher for the *Oxford English Dictionary* until his appointment in 1920 to Leeds University, where he built a reputation as a lexicographer, bibliographer, and editor. In 1925 he was elected Rawlinson and Bosworth Professor of Anglo-Saxon at Oxford, where he led reforms in the English program, and in 1945 became Merton Professor of English Language and Literature. Tolkien's scholarly and critical publications were influential but few, the bulk of his time devoted to scrupulous lecture preparation and to his imaginary languages and mythic stories. Shortly before his retirement from Oxford in 1959, the success of *The Lord of the Rings* brought him fame and wealth.

## Influence

Tolkien is important, first, for reading medieval poetry, particularly *Beowulf* (c. eighth century B.C.), as poetry, not merely as historical document. He bridged the rift between the language and literature sections of English departments in the early decades of the twentieth century, using his fluency in languages to interpret medieval poetry thematically and structurally as well as historically, a critical stance which helped to revitalize medieval studies.

Second, he argued learnedly against the privileging of realism in modern fiction and in defense of "escapist" genres, particularly fairy stories. Writing what may be read as an apologia for his own eccentric stories, he provided guidelines for interpreting seriously not only his own work but also other modern fantasy and science fiction.

## Analysis

Tolkien's contributions to the twentieth century sprang from his conservative distaste for modern literature and culture. He not only understood but also had experienced traumatically the squalor of urbanization, the horrors of mechanized war, and the eclipse of traditional religion. Convinced that he lived, like his hobbits, in a dark age, Tolkien sought within it a medieval salvation. He wished to recover the spirit of the old lost order of which the modern world was a ruin. This worldview gave religious urgency to his study of historical language and literature and led him to revive and defend antique literary forms in defiance of contemporary taste. Ironically, the resulting fiction and criticism spoke directly to the students of the 1960s and to others whose values appeared radically different from Tolkien's own.

Nearly all Tolkien's critical influence derives from two frequently reprinted lectures. The first, "Beowulf," begins by insisting that the Old English poem be interpreted as an authoritative literary text within the ethos of its own time. In a respectful examination of recent critical judgments, Tolkien exposes the contradictions of using a legendary work as a historical document and of condemning a powerful medieval work for violating classical canons of taste. *Beowulf* evidently appeals to readers in ways which classical theories of narrative cannot explain. Tolkien's own explanation affirms the mythic core of the poem and sees in the monsters killed by the doomed hero a profound and direct expression of the human condition – a myth of mortality that is at once universal and characteristically Northern. The strongest hero eventually falls, glorified by his futile resistance to mundane evil. Previously incongruous elements in the poem make sense when Tolkien places *Beowulf* before a Christian audience that remembers and venerates the Norse heroic ethos in its overlap with Christian values.

The rising-falling pattern of the story, Tolkien suggests, parallels the Old English verse line, and the talk of *Beowulf*'s flawed plot derives from a critical error of false expectations. Like Leonard Bloomfield and other descriptive grammarians who during the 1930s were reinventing English grammar outside the assumptions of Latin, Tolkien trusted the text to define its own narrative grammar. For all of his conservatism, his critical style was quite contemporary – in part, no doubt, because of the methodological similarities between 1930s New Criticism and medieval biblical exegesis. His intimate knowledge of medieval language and culture helped him to reconstruct a living theme and expressive structure in a poem that had seemed incoherent to previous students.

When he wrote his second important lecture, "On Fairy-Stories," Tolkien had begun writing his three-volume fantasy masterpiece, *The Lord of the Rings*, and clearly felt a need to justify investing so much time in a genre which many of his contemporaries considered juvenile and escapist. Tolkien's defense of fairy stories assumed the universality and reality of mythic patterns, a Platonic assumption similar to Carl Jung's theory of archetypes and William Wordsworth's belief in "the permanent forms of nature." Given the universality of myth and rightness of what satisfies "primordial human desires," ordinary reality may be more ephemeral than fantasy. Fantasies express natural patterns and remind readers of the kind of lives they ought to be leading, in contrast to the manufactured patterns of what Tolkien calls the "Robot Age." Horses, elm trees, and lightning are more elemental than automobiles, factories, and electric lights. Thus, while acknowledging fantasy literature to be escapist, Tolkien distinguishes the "Flight of the Deserter" from the "Escape of the Prisoner." Readers do well to escape imprisonment in their modern lives.

Tolkien inverts Samuel Taylor Coleridge's concepts of Fancy and Imagination. Choosing to take Imagination in its simple sense as image-making, Tolkien declares Fantasy (the uncontracted form of Fancy) to be the higher mode of creation. Distinguished from the incoherence of delirium and the woodenness of allegory, literary Fantasy is subcreation, the making of a Secondary World which has "the inner consistency of reality" and thereby creates in a reader Secondary Belief. Tolkien's Secondary Belief is not willing suspension of disbelief; in fact, it is not suspension of ordinary disbelief at all. Readers absorbed in a fantasy about dragons continue to disbelieve in dragons in the Primary World. Rather, Secondary Belief is a different kind of belief maintained by what Tolkien calls Enchantment. The storymaker enchants by creating a coherent Secondary World which satisfies profound human desires. In effect, Tolkien accepts Coleridge's distinction between symbol and allegory and affirms as symbol the unified experience of a story as told, not its plot or abstracted motifs.

When Tolkien wrote, myth had already been studied by comparative mythologists such as Sir James Frazer and exploited with irony by authors such as James Joyce and T. S. Eliot – authors whom Tolkien joined his friend C. S. Lewis in disliking – but to Tolkien it seemed that his contemporaries misunderstood the need for myth in the modern world. They either analyzed myths or adapted them ironically. For Tolkien only the story itself holds in solution both the world of ordinary experience and the world of Faërie beyond. Any failure to accept the Secondary World seriously on its own terms – even if it is a comic world – destroys the Secondary Belief by which myth addresses spiritual and moral issues. Condemning his own equivalent of the New Critical "heresy of the paraphrase," Tolkien argues that a well-told story is richer and more profound than any interpretations of it; his own literary criticism, as opposed to his philology, is metaphorical and allusive, avoiding the orderly proofs so often found in interpretations of historic texts.

There is nothing childish, Tolkien insists, about Secondary Belief. Indeed, its effect is heightened by a strong reason and a strong sense of reality: the Frog Prince would not be so appealing to readers who genuinely believed that frogs talked. The writer of Fantasy is engaged in a sober adult activity: becoming creator-god of a Secondary World closer to human and divine nature than is the fallen Primary World. This is an old critical concept which Randel Helms traces to Cristoforo Landino, a fifteenth-century commentator on Dante, though a likely English source is Sir Philip Sidney's *Defence of Poesie* (1595), which asserts that "Nature never set forth the earth in so rich tapistry, as divers Poets have done . . . . Her world is brasen, the Poets only deliver a golden."

The benefits of fairy stories, and by extension of mythic fantasy in general, Tolkien lists as Recovery, Escape, and Consolation. Recovery, a romantic concept suggestive of William Wordsworth, involves regaining a clear mental view, so that readers learn to see afresh the particularity and strangeness of the Primary World. Tolkien calls the recovered state Mooreeffoc, a reference to the sign seen in reverse from behind a "coffeeroom" window. The second benefit, Escape, may not only be from a prison of a particular place and time – a mere trick of historical setting – but more elemental escape from human limitations: from the inability to fly and speak with animals; from hunger, pain, and injustice; or from death. Finally, fairy stories offer the Consolation of the Happy Ending, for which Tolkien invents the word *Eucatastrophe*. This "sudden joyous 'turn'" gives a fleeting glimpse, he says, of Joy beyond the limits of the world, which leads him to describe the Christian gospel as a fairy story that happened.

The influence of Tolkien on *Beowulf* criticism is unquestionable. His "*Beowulf*" has been required reading in college courses for fifty years, and discussions of the poem's theme or structure usually cite Tolkien's groundbreaking interpretation. He was a scholar of demonstrated authority in the close work of editing and textual analysis, extraordinary in his grasp of Old and Middle English history and dialectology. These precritical skills he demonstrated for years in editions and philological articles. Then, when Tolkien stepped back from his workbench in middle age and offered a critical interpretation of *Beowulf* at the broadest philosophical and structural levels, he stimulated rereadings of other Germanic poems which had previously seemed of only antiquarian interest.

"On Fairy-Stories" had less immediate impact. It was not widely read until after the success of *The Lord of the Rings*, when it was reissued as the first half of *Tree and Leaf* (1964) and later reprinted in *A Tolkien Reader* (1966), a mass-circulation paperback. Suddenly available to his millions of admirers, this essay provided a theoretical basis for reading Tolkien's stories seriously and provided arguments against those who doubted the legitimacy of modern fantasy. At the time the works of classic fantasy writers such as William Morris, George Macdonald, Edgar Rice Burroughs, and Lord Dunsany were being reissued to a new generation of readers initiated by Tolkien's hobbit books, and many young writers began to work seriously with heroic fantasy. The part Tolkien's criticism, as opposed to his best-selling fiction, may have played in this trend is difficult to assess, but his overall influence has been enormous. In his lecture on fairy stories he presented so many new ideas – new to his century – in so few pages that he seemed to be issuing a rallying cry as much as a systematic theory. Nevertheless, as fantasy and science fiction have emerged as academic fields since 1960, Tolkien's own defense of Faërie has been part of the theoretical background of critics working in the area.

## Principal criticism
"*Beowulf*: The Monsters and the Critics," 1936
"On Fairy-Stories," 1938

## Other major works and literary forms
J. R. R. Tolkien is best known as the author of *The Hobbit: Or, There and Back Again* (1937) and *The Lord of the Rings* (1954-1955), heroic fantasies set in a fairy-tale world of his own creation. These "hobbit" books, published during his lifetime, drew from an unpublished personal mythology in prose and verse which he began during World War I and revised and expanded for more than half a century. Much of the mythology has been collected by his son Christopher and issued posthumously as *The Silmarillion* (1977), *The Book of Lost Tales* (1983-1984), and *The Lays of Beleriand* (1985). Tolkien also published shorter children's books and translated medieval English poetry into modern verse. Before the late 1950s, however, his reputation rested chiefly on a Middle English glossary (1922) and an edition of *Sir Gawain and the Green Knight* (1925; with E. V. Gordon) – and on his brilliance as a lecturer about medieval literature.

### NOVELS
*The Hobbit: Or, There and Back Again*, 1937
*The Lord of the Rings*, 1954-1955 (includes *The Fellowship of the Ring*, *The Two Towers*, and *The Return of the King*)
*The Silmarillion*, 1977

### SHORT FICTION
*Farmer Giles of Ham*, 1949
*Tree and Leaf*, 1964
*Smith of Wootton Major*, 1967
*The Father Christmas Letters*, 1976
*Unfinished Tales of Numenor and Middle-earth*, 1980 (Christopher Tolkien, editor)
*The Book of Lost Tales*, 1983-1984

### PLAY
*The Homecoming of Beorhtnoth Beorhthelm's Son*, 1953

### POETRY
*Songs for the Philologists*, 1936 (with others)
*The Adventures of Tom Bombadil and Other Verses from the Red Book*, 1962
*The Road Goes Ever On: A Song Cycle*, 1967
*The Lays of Beleriand*, 1985

### NONFICTION
*A Middle English Vocabulary*, 1922
*The Letters of J. R. R. Tolkien*, 1981

### TRANSLATIONS
*Sir Gawain and the Green Knight, Pearl, and Sir Orfeo*, 1975
*The Old English Exodus*, 1982

### EDITED TEXTS
*Sir Gawain and the Green Knight*, 1925 (with E. V. Gordon)
*Ancrene Wisse: The English Text of the Ancrene Riwle*, 1962

### MISCELLANEOUS
*The Tolkien Reader*, 1966
*Pictures by J. R. R. Tolkien*, 1979
*Finn and Hengest: The Fragment and the Episode*, 1983

## Further reading
Carpenter, Humphrey. *Tolkien: A Biography*, 1977.
——. *The Inklings: C. S. Lewis, J. R. R. Tolkien, Charles Williams, and Their Friends*, 1979.
Flieger, V. *Splintered Light: Logos and Language in Tolkien's World*, 1983.
Helms, Randel. *Tolkien's World*, 1974.
Hillegas, Mark R., ed. *Shadows of Imagination: The Fantasies of C. S. Lewis, J. R. R. Tolkien, and Charles Williams*, 1969.
Isaacs, N. D., and Rose A. Zimbardo, eds. *Tolkien: New Critical Perspectives*, 1981.
Purtill, Richard L. *J. R. R. Tolkien: Myth, Morality, and Religion*, 1984.
Rosebury, Brian. *Tolkien: A Critical Assessment*, 1992.

WILLIAM H. GREEN

*See also* British Literary Theory: Twentieth Century; Lewis

# Lev Tolstoi

Russian novelist and writer

**Born:** Iasnaia Poliana, Russia; September 9, 1828
**Died:** Astapovo, Russia; November 20, 1910

## Biography

Count Lev Tolstoi was born on September 9, 1828, on his mother's ancestral estate, Iasnaia Poliana, near Tula, the fourth of five children. The family was of the landed gentry, not wealthy but comfortable. Since his mother died before he was two and his father when he was nine, Tolstoi was reared mainly by various collateral relatives and tutors. He entered Kazan University in 1844, but in 1847 he withdrew without completing the course. In 1851 he joined his eldest brother, an army officer, in the Caucasus, entering the army himself the following year. He served until 1856 and saw considerable action, first against rebellious mountain peoples and later in the Crimean War.

Tolstoi had begun writing for publication in 1852, and his early works were highly successful. By about 1860, however, his reputation appeared to be fading. In 1862 Tolstoi married Sof'ia Behrs, the daughter of a Moscow doctor. They had thirteen children. The next two decades were the period of Tolstoi's greatest artistic achievements. *Voina i mir* (1865–1869; *War and Peace*, 1886) was completed in 1869 and *Anna Karenina* (1875–1878; English translation, 1886) in 1878.

In the late 1870s Tolstoi underwent an existential crisis, after which he vowed to devote himself to religion. He now undertook to cleanse Christianity of all the accumulated impurities of the ages, an enterprise that occupied the rest of his life. His unorthodox religious beliefs evoked considerable controversy within his family, especially with his wife. His disciples were harassed by the government, though the authorities dared not touch Tolstoi himself. He was, however, officially excommunicated by the Orthodox church in 1901. During his later years Tolstoi did return from time to time to the writing of fiction, some of it left unpublished at his death. In 1910, seeking respite from the constant turmoil in his household, Tolstoi stole away from Iasnaia Poliana. He was taken ill on the train, however, and on November 20 died at a wayside station, Astapovo, now renamed for him.

## Influence

Tolstoi's direct influence as a literary theorist, strictly speaking, is rather small. Early in the twentieth century his major treatise on aesthetics, *Chto takoe iskusstvo?* (1898; *What Is Art?*, 1898), was excitedly discussed all over the world, but more because of the author's towering reputation as a novelist than because of its intrinsic theoretical merits. The same is even more true of the celebrated iconoclastic essay, "O Shekspire io drame" (1906; "Shakespeare and the Drama," 1907). Tolstoi's views have generally been written off as eccentric and extreme; it is, however, recognized that as a theorist Tolstoi argues with eloquence and conviction in support of his belief that art should be judged mainly for its moral impact and its "truth." It is rather Tolstoi's example as a practitioner of literary art that has had an immense influence, both in Russia and elsewhere, and several important works of criticism have been devoted to the analysis of his writings.

## Analysis

Lev Tolstoi's appearance on the literary scene in Russia coincided with the flourishing of the "natural school" – a movement, inspired especially by the critic Vissarion Belinskii, away from the Romantic preoccupations of the previous era in the direction of social concerns and "truth." Though Tolstoi's favorite models, Jean-Jacques Rousseau and Laurence Sterne, came from an earlier era, his insistence on uncompromising psychological observation and his intense social and moral concerns made him a pioneer in the development of Russian realism. Though in the late 1850s he briefly adhered to the "art for art's sake" camp and opposed the utilitarian views of such plebeian radicals as Nikolai Chernyshevskii and Nikolai Dobroliubov, Tolstoi always conceived of literature as having a purpose outside itself, whether cognitive or didactic.

Most of his major critical statements were written in the latter part of his life, when he was attempting to subordinate his art to the religious principles he now espoused. First, he insisted that art should strive for simplicity and maximal accessibility. Far too much of the world's heritage of art, he believed, could be appreciated only by a parasitic educated elite. Tolstoi's "ideal reader" now became the archetypal Russian muzhik – an intelligent, sensible, down-to-earth, literate peasant aged about fifty. Anything such a reader would not understand or appreciate was obviously not needed by the world. Tolstoi would not admit that a better solution might be to provide his peasant with enough education so that he could comprehend more complex art; he claimed that unlike science, any true art can be freely assimilated without preparatory training, for it "infects any man whatever his plane of development." Tolstoi's argument for accessibility was partly economic: vast resources were being expended to provide elaborate entertainments such as Richard Wagner's operas for a class of idle exploiters. Nevertheless, Tolstoi's principles had a strong moral aspect as well. Literature should be a guide to life; though it need not be explicitly didactic, it should clearly show the distinction between good and evil.

The insistence on truth remained a cornerstone of Tolstoi's philosophy of art. The truth of art was not to be obtained, however, simply by literal or photographic copying of reality. True artistic talent enables its possessor to perceive deeper layers of reality than appear to the layman's eye. In *Anna Karenina*, the artist Mikhailov in his paintings "removes the veils" of conventionality that prevent an object from being fully seen. His portrait of Anna reveals her soul as well as her features. In a similar vein, Tolstoi wrote that Guy de Maupassant possessed "that particular gift called talent, ... this gift of seeing what others have not seen." In "Posleslovie k rasskazu Chekhova 'Dushechka,'" (1905; "An Afterword by Tolstoy to Chekhov's story 'Darling,'" 1929) Tolstoi claimed that Chekhov's talent, his innate gift for seeing the truth, forced him, despite feminist beliefs that impelled him to condemn her, to reveal the spiritual beauty of the central character, a woman who completely changes the focus of her life to match those of a series of male companions.

Another important imperative which Tolstoi laid upon the artist was sincerity. Artists not only think, they feel; the communication of these feelings is the very essence of art. Following Eugène Veron, Tolstoi used the word "infection" to describe this process. Artists infect the reader (or viewer or listener) with their own emotions, and the honesty with which they impart these feelings is one of the bases for judging their art.

Tolstoi found little to admire in the accumulated philosophical writings on aesthetics. First in the writings of Plato and Aristotle and then in modern times in those of writers from Alexander Baumgarten to Herbert Spencer, he found the same dilemma: their definitions of art and its relation to "beauty" and "goodness" mingled in a cacophony of contradictions. Yet definitions of art that avoided the beauty-goodness trap proved equally unsatisfactory, notably those that defined art in terms of the pleasure which it affords, for pleasure is clearly derived from many experiences that are not art. Tolstoi found a way out of this dilemma by defining art as a form of communication, specifically the communication of emotions. "Art is a human activity consisting in this, that one man consciously, by means of certain external signs, hands on to others feelings he has lived through, and that others are infected by these feelings and also experience them."

This definition, however, provided Tolstoi with no basis for judging the quality of art. For that he was forced to rely exclusively on ethical criteria: "good" art is art that infects one with "good" feelings. The trouble with this principle is that it provides no basis for qualitatively distinguishing a rightminded but dull sermon from a great poem. Tolstoi never confronted this issue squarely; in a late essay on Nikolai Gogol', "O Gogole" (1909), he said that the "terrible, repulsive nonsense" of Gogol''s last writings resulted from his setting for art goals not suited to it and preaching the official version of Christianity. In any case, the goodness of feelings can be determined only by criteria specified by (true) religion, and all religions, especially Christianity, according to Tolstoi, have been corrupted by their priests. Nevertheless, at the root of all religions lies the innate knowledge of good and evil, and on this basis simple people have always instinctively known that art was "good only when it served goodness (as they understood goodness), and bad when it was in opposition to that goodness." He believed that notions of goodness have, however, progressed with time. The ancient Greeks "were so little developed morally that goodness and beauty seemed to them to coincide." This mistaken identification became the basis for the so-called science of aesthetics. Because of Baumgarten and his successors, Tolstoi argued, the world labored under the extraordinary delusion that the art of the ancient Greeks, "a small, semi-savage, slave-holding people," represented some sort of pinnacle that has never been surpassed. Only Homer was exempted from this wholesale disparagement of the Greeks.

Despite the ethical progress represented by Christianity, Tolstoi believed that almost all that passed for art was even more grounded in error and delusion, for it had abandoned its religious foundation. Lacking any ethical norms, art could not distinguish between good and evil feelings, and it further alienated itself from ordinary people by becoming so complex and obscure that special education was required to comprehend it. Furthermore, despite its formal complexity, the feelings it could transmit were limited to three: pride, sexual desire, and world-weariness. Examples of this overrefined, degenerate art abounded in all European countries. Tolstoi singled out for especial condemnation the poets Charles Baudelaire, Paul Verlaine, Stéphane Mallarmé, and Maurice Maeterlinck; the artists Camille Pissarro, Édouard Manet, Claude Monet, Pierre-Auguste Renoir, and Alfred Sisley; the dramatists Henrik Ibsen and Gerhart Hauptmann; the composers Franz Liszt, Hector Berlioz, Johannes Brahms, and Richard Strauss; and novelists Joris-Karl Huysmans, Rudyard Kipling, Émile Zola, and August de Villiers de L'Isle-Adam. Nevertheless, the figure that best epitomized all that was wrong with art was Wagner, that "limited, self-opinionated German of bad taste and bad style, who has a most false conception of poetry."

Tolstoi's repudiations by no means stopped with art. Throughout the ages much that has passed for art is not simply bad art, it is "counterfeit art." Into this trash-can category he ruthlessly cast countless works that have been celebrated as supreme examples of human achievement by critics; critics, almost by definition, lack the capacity to be infected by art. The list of rejects is long and includes the work of Sophocles, Euripides, Aeschylus, Aristophanes, Dante, Torquato Tasso, John Milton, William Shakespeare, Raphael, Michelangelo, "including his absurd 'Last Judgment,'" Johann Sebastian Bach, and Ludwig van Beethoven. Sometimes it appears that in Tolstoi's parlance counterfeit art is simply a rhetorically heightened substitute for "bad art," but Tolstoi claimed a distinction: bad art infects with bad feelings, while counterfeit art does not infect at all.

Art which Tolstoi acknowledged to be good may be divided into two classes: first, religious art, "transmitting both positive feelings of love of God and one's neighbour, and negative feelings of indignation and horror at the violation of love"; second, "universal art, transmitting feelings accessible to all." Tolstoi's examples of the first class from the literature of his day included Friedrich Schiller's *Die Räuber* (1781; *The Robbers*, 1792), Victor Hugo's *Les Misérables* (1862; English translation, 1862), Charles Dickens' *A Tale of Two Cities* (1859), Harriet Beecher Stowe's *Uncle Tom's Cabin: Or, Life Among the Lowly* (1852), George Eliot's *Adam Bede* (1859), and Fedor Dostoevskii's *Zapiski iz mertvogo doma* (1860–1861; *The House of the Dead*, 1915). Contemporary examples of the second class were hard to find, but Tolstoi allowed this designation to *Don Quixote de la Mancha* (1605, 1615; English translation, 1612–1620), Molière's comedies, Dickens' *David Copperfield* (1849–1850) and the *Pickwick Papers* (1836–1837), Gogol''s and Aleksandr Pushkin's tales, and some pieces by Guy de Maupassant. Archetypal examples of universal art were the Joseph story in Genesis and Homer's *Iliad* (c. 800 B.C.) and the *Odyssey* (c. 800 B.C.). In his own work, Tolstoi exempted from the category of "bad art" only two short stories: "God Sees the Truth but Waits," which qualifies as religious art, and "A Prisoner of the Caucasus," which is acceptable as universal art.

The art of the future, being universal and accessible to all, will be unspecialized, unprofessionalized, and unpaid. It will promote the peaceful cooperation of men, making the "feeling of brotherhood and the love of one's neighbour . . . the customary feeling and the instinct of all men."

Tolstoi's most extravagant feat of debunking was his famous attack on Shakespeare, written in 1903 and published in 1906. Urged on by aesthetically minded friends such as Ivan Turgenev, Tolstoi claimed to have read through all of Shakespeare three times – in Russian, German, and English. Each time he had been unable to find any of the greatness touted by others but had doubted his own judgment. Now, in his old age, he resolved to speak out. The world's idolatry of Shakespeare, he proclaimed, was a form of mass hypnotism. Over the centuries people had been duped into idolizing a man who was at best "a clever actor and a good stage-manager" and "managed verse well enough." It was time to reveal the emperor's nakedness, for the idolatry of Shakespeare was "a great evil, as every falsehood is."

Tolstoi attacked Shakespeare on many grounds: Shakespeare is indifferent to religion, and his morality is loose. He stands for "action at all costs, the absence of all ideals, moderation in everything, the maintenance of established forms of life, and the maxim that 'the end justifies the means.'" He is an English chauvinist. He glorifies the powerful and despises the common folk. These accusations are bad enough, but his plays are failures on aesthetic grounds as well. All of his characters speak the same unnatural, inflated, undifferentiated language. His plots are illogical and absurd and his characters inconsistent and unconvincing; it is clear that the dramatist is not sincere,

but only playing for cheap effects. To illustrate his points, Tolstoi provided an extended analysis of the absurdities of *King Lear* (c. 1605–1606), concluding that its model and source, the chronicle play *King Leir* (1594), was a better work of art than Shakespeare's adaptation. (Essentially, as G. Wilson Knight and George Orwell have shown, Tolstoi faulted Shakespeare for writing Elizabethan verse plays rather than realistic novels.) The drama of the future, Tolstoi concluded, liberated from the pernicious Shakespearean influence, "will serve for the elucidation and confirmation in men of the highest degree of religious consciousness."

## Principal criticism

"Komu u kogo uchit'sia pisat', krestianskim rebiatam u nas: Ili, nam u krestianskikh rebiat?," 1862 ("Are the Peasant Children to Learn to Write from Us?," 1904)
"Neskol'ko slov po povodu knigi *Voina i mir*," 1868 ("A Few Words Concerning the Book *War and Peace*," 1905)
"Predislovie k sochineniiam Gyui de Mopassana," 1894 ("Guy de Maupassant," 1898)
"Predislovie k *Krestianskim rasskazam* S. T. Semenova," 1894 ("S. T. Semenov's Peasant Stories," 1905)
*Chto takoe iskusstvo?*, 1898 (*What Is Art?*, 1898)
"Predislovie k romanu V. fon Polenca *Krestianin*," 1902 ("Introduction to W. von Polenz's *Der Büttnerbauer*," 1905)
*Tak chto zhe nam delat'?*, 1902 (written 1886; *What to Do?*, 1887)
"Posleslovie k rasskazu Chekhova 'Dushechka,'" 1905 ("An Afterword by Tolstoy to Chekhov's Story 'Darling,'" 1929)
"O Shekspire i o drame," 1906 ("Shakespeare and the Drama," 1907)
"Predislovie k romanu A. I. Ertelia *Gardeniny, ikh dvornia, priverzhentsy i vragi*," 1909
"O Gogole," 1909
*"What Is Art?" and Essays on Art*, 1929
*L. N. Tolstoi o literature: Stat'i, pis'ma, dnevniki*, 1955
*Lev Tolstoi ob iskusstve i literature*, 1958

## Other major works and literary forms

Literary criticism forms a small and relatively insignificant part of Lev Tolstoi's enormous output, which extends to ninety volumes in *Polnoe sobranie sochinenii* (1928–1958), the Russian jubilee edition. He is known primarily as a writer of novels and short stories; these have been translated into hundreds of languages and have earned a place among the world's greatest classics. He also wrote plays, the number and quality of which are at least sufficient to give him a leading place in the history of the Russian drama. In the latter part of his life, Tolstoi's major efforts were philosophical treatises and religious tracts. These are less read than they once were, but they too have had a substantial impact, via such disciples as Mohandas Gandhi, as powerful statements of the principle of nonviolent resistance to evil.

NOVELS
*Detstvo*, 1852 (*Childhood*, 1862)
*Otrochestvo*, 1854 (*Boyhood*, 1886)
*Iunost'*, 1857 (*Youth*, 1886)

*Semeinoe schast'e*, 1859 (*Family Happiness*, 1888)
*Kazaki*, 1863 (*The Cossacks*, 1872)
*Voina i mir*, 1865–1869 (*War and Peace*, 1886)
*Anna Karenina*, 1875–1878 (English translation, 1886)
*Smert' Ivana Il'icha*, 1886 (*The Death of Ivan Ilyich*, 1887)
*Kreitserova sonata*, 1891 (*The Kreutzer Sonata*, 1890)
*Voskresenie*, 1899 (*Resurrection*, 1899)
*Khadzhi-Murat*, 1911 (written 1904; *Hadji Murad*, 1911)

SHORT FICTION
*Sevastopol'skiye rasskazy*, 1855–1856 (*Sebastopol*, 1887)
*The Kreutzer Sonata, The Devil, and Other Tales*, 1940
*Notes of a Madman and Other Stories*, 1943
*Tolstoy Tales*, 1947

PLAYS
*Vlast' t'my, ili korotok uviaz, vsei ptichke propast'*, 1887
    (*The Power of Darkness*, 1888)
*Plody prosveshcheniia*, 1889 (*The Fruits of Enlightenment*,
    1891)
*Zhivoi trup*, 1911 (*The Live Corpse*, 1919)
*I svet vo t'me svetit*, 1911 (*The Light Shines in Darkness*, 1923)
*The Dramatic Works*, 1923

CHILDREN'S LITERATURE
*Azbuka*, 1872
*Novaia azbuka*, 1875
*Russkie knigi dlia chteniia*, 1875

NONFICTION
*Ispoved'*, 1884 (*A Confession*, 1885)
*V chom moia vera*, 1884 (*What I Believe*, 1885)
*O zhizni*, 1888 (*Life*, 1888)
*Kritika dogmaticheskogo bogosloviia*, 1891 (*A Critique of
    Dogmatic Theology*, 1904)
*Soedinenie i perevod chetyrekh evangelii*, 1892–1894 (*The Four
    Gospels Harmonized and Translated*, 1895–1896)
*Tsarstvo Bozhie vnutri vas*, 1894 (*The Kingdom of God Is
    Within You*, 1894)
*The Diaries of Leo Tolstoy, 1847–1852*, 1917
*The Journal of Leo Tolstoy, 1895–1899*, 1917
*Tolstoi's Love Letters*, 1923
*The Private Diary of Leo Tolstoy, 1853–1857*, 1927
*Leo Tolstoy: Last Diaries*, 1960

MISCELLANEOUS
*The Complete Works of Count Tolstoy*, 1904–1905
    (24 volumes)
*Tolstoy Centenary Edition*, 1928–1937 (21 volumes)
*Polnoe sobranie sochinenii*, 1928–1958 (90 volumes)

## Further reading

Christian, R. F. *Tolstoy: A Critical Introduction*, 1969.
Galagan, Galina. *L. N. Tolstoi: Khudozhestvenno-eticheskie
    iskaniia*, 1981.
Gibian, George. *Tolstoi and Shakespeare*, 1957.
Knight, George Wilson. *Shakespeare and Tolstoy*, 1934.
Levin, Yu. D. "Tolstoy, Shakespeare, and Russian Writers of the
    1860s," in *Oxford Slavonic Papers*. N.s. I (1968),
    pp. 85–104.
Orwell, George. "Lear, Tolstoy, and the Fool," in *Shooting an
    Elephant and Other Essays*, 1950.
Šilbajoris, Rimvydas. "Tolstoy's Aesthetics in Soviet
    Perspective," in *Bucknell Review*. XVIII (Winter, 1970),
    pp. 103–116.
——. "Lev Tolstoj: Esthetics and Art," in *Russian Literature
    Triquarterly*. I (1971), pp. 58–72.
——. *Tolstoy's Aesthetics and His Art*, 1990.
Steiner, George. *Tolstoy or Dostoevsky: An Essay in Old
    Criticism*, 1980.
Wasiolek, Edward. "A Paradox in Tolstoi's *What Is Art?*," in
    *Canadian American Slavic Studies*. XII (1978), pp. 583–591.
Wellek, René. *A History of Modern Criticism: 1750–1950*. Vol.
    4, *The Later Nineteenth Century*, 1965.
Wimsatt, William K., Jr., and Cleanth Brooks. *Literary
    Criticism: A Short History*, 1969.

HUGH MCLEAN

*See also* Chernyshevskii; Dobroliubov; Dostoevskii

# Jane P. Tompkins

American critic and educator

**Born:** New York, New York; January 18, 1940

## Biography

Jane P(arry) Tompkins was born on January 18, 1940, in
New York, New York, the only child of Henry Thomas and
Lucille Reilly Parry. She received her elementary and high-
school education in the public schools of New York City
and suburbs, completing her final year of high school in
Ardmore, Pennsylvania. She attended Bryn Mawr College
in Bryn Mawr, Pennsylvania, graduating *magna cum laude*
in 1961 with a bachelor of arts degree in literature. She
attended Yale University on a Woodrow Wilson Fellowship,
and received her M.A. degree in 1962 and Ph.D. in 1966.
She married Daniel P. Tompkins, a fellow graduate student
at Yale, in September, 1963 (from whom she was divorced
seven years later). Short-term teaching appointments at
Connecticut College and Greater Hartford Community
College were followed by a long association with Temple
University, which began in 1970 (she served as visiting assistant professor from 1970 to 1976, associate professor from
1976 to 1982, and professor of English from 1982 to 1983).
She married E. Daniel Larkin in 1975. She later left this mar-
riage for a relationship with Stanley Fish, then a member of
the English faculty at The Johns Hopkins University in
Baltimore, Maryland, whom she married in August, 1982.
Tompkins served as visiting professor at Columbia
University, New York, during the 1983–1984 academic
year, and the following year at the Graduate School and
University Center of the City University of New York. She
joined the faculty of the Duke University Department of
English in Durham, North Carolina, as a professor in 1985,
where she remained until 1999, when she left Duke
University for an appointment in the College of Education
at the University of Illinois at Chicago, in conjunction with
her husband's appointment as the dean of the College of
Liberal Arts and Sciences at the same institution.

## Influence

Tompkins' earliest critical work was deeply influenced by New Criticism, as practiced and taught at Yale University by Cleanth Brooks and others, emphasizing formalist analysis of literary texts as autonomous, free-standing works of art divorced from questions of intention and effect. However, the critical revolutions sparked by reader-response theory, poststructuralism, and feminism in the 1960s, 1970s, and 1980s offered critical perspectives which gave Tompkins opportunities to make significant contributions to new developments in American literary history and feminist criticism. The essays comprising the book *Sensational Designs: The Cultural Work of American Fiction, 1790–1860* (1985) are particularly noteworthy since they fired some of the most important salvos in the "canon wars" in the American literary establishment during the 1980s and 1990s: the popular and critical success of this volume encouraged major changes in university teaching about nineteenth-century American literature. Tompkins' latest work combines her interests in the ways readers interact with literature with a growing concern for the emotional and spiritual aspects of higher education.

## Analysis

Tompkins' critical writings, though diverse, have followed a general direction that may be traced through the essays that comprise her four major works: by locating texts in time, place, effect, and use, she consistently argues for the power of literature, for good or ill, to influence emotions, lives, and society.

The two essays that Tompkins contributed to an anthology she edited (published in 1980 as *Reader-Response Criticism: From Formalism to Post-Structuralism*), "An Introduction to Reader-Response Criticism" and "The Reader in History: The Changing Shape of Literary Response," provide a valuable summative purpose by placing the development of reader-response theory – a critical tradition that moves the focus of critical attention away from the autonomous text toward the reader who engages the text and the ways that meaning is produced through this engagement – in the context of ideas about the power of literature to inspire and influence readers. She argues that reader-response theories that attempt to objectify the experience of reading, by emphasizing literature as signification and discounting literature as experience, fail to account for the most fundamentally important aspect of literature, and are, as a result, as inadequate to the task of providing a full explanation of "language as a form of power" as the schools of formalist criticism which they sought to dis/replace.

In the essays that comprise *Sensational Designs: The Cultural Work of American Fiction, 1790–1860*, Tompkins advocates "a redefinition of literature and literary study" because she believes that the works she discusses, including novels by Susan Warner, Charles Brockden Brown, James Fenimore Cooper, and Harriet Beecher Stowe which were included grudgingly, if at all, in university literature classes at the time of this volume's first publication, "should be studied not because they manage to escape the limitations of their particular time and place, but because they offer powerful examples of the way a culture thinks about itself."

Tompkins' revisionist attack on the formalist canon of American literature emerges from a critique based in post-structuralist theory: according the status of "masterwork" only to those texts that have "stood the test of time" hides the elitist, exclusionary, political character of the academic, social, and gender hierarchies of privilege that profit from such a restricted, restrictive canon. Her subtitle indicates, as well, her disagreement with the formalist critical conviction that texts can attain, in the words of reviewer Ann-Janine Morey, "a disinterested aesthetic or a disinterested universality of literary worth." Tompkins' view is ultimately a functional one: hierarchies of valuation are always embedded in "interested" contexts, so the question that literary scholars should really be asking is not "Is it art?" but "What work is this text performing, and how well?"

The examples Tompkins uses in her extended argument are drawn from the ranks of American writers active during the first half of the nineteenth century, including Nathaniel Hawthorne (Tompkins argues that his inclusion in the canon of American literature can be understood not by appeals to "essential greatness" as defined by their complexity, subtlety, and psychological realism but "as a function of the circumstances in which [they] were read" and his relative status in hierarchies of gender, region, religion, social status, and other nonliterary value systems); Charles Brockden Brown (she approaches his novels *Wieland* and *Arthur Mervyn* as texts that successfully depict Brown's concerns about the political problems of the early Republic rather than as unsuccessful artistic efforts), the Leatherstocking novels of James Fenimore Cooper (Tompkins reads these texts not as sensational melodramas but as deliberately constructed "social criticism written in an allegorical mode"), Harriet Beecher Stowe (she argues that *Uncle Tom's Cabin* should not be dismissed as a "mere" sentimental novel, but studied as a "world-shaking" example of "[t]he enterprise of sentimental fiction" which was, in Tompkins' view, "a monumental effort to reorganize culture from a woman's point of view"), and Susan Warner (whose novel *The Wide, Wide World* Tompkins reads from the perspective of nineteenth-century revivalism, the American Home Missionary Society, and what Tompkins identifies as "claims that sentimental fiction made for the importance of the spiritual life and for women's crucial role in the salvation of the race," reversing the modernist notion that sentimental fiction was primarily a consolatory and apologist medium in acting to persuade women to remain complicit in their social and political disenfranchisement).

Tompkins' arguments, which are punctuated by moments of autobiographical reflection (a technique that becomes a characteristic rhetorical device in subsequent essays), conclude with a plea for the incorporation of the texts she discusses into academic curricula. She also offers an answer to the question "but are these works really any *good?*" which reconfigures the debate in functional and political terms:

> I see them doing a certain kind of cultural work within a specific historical situation, and value them for that reason . . . . It is the notion of literary texts as doing work, expressing and shaping the social context that produced them, that I wish to substitute finally for the critical perspective that sees them as attempts to achieve a timeless, universal ideal of truth and formal coherence . . . . The struggle now being waged in the professoriate over which writers deserve canonical status is not just a struggle over the relative merits of literary geniuses; it is a struggle among contending factions for the right to be represented in the picture America draws of itself.

The accessible language of *Sensational Designs* contributed to the volume's popular success; it also earned considerable praise in the critical community, and even those who dispute Tompkins' terms and conclusions acknowledge the persuasive power of her writing.

Tompkins moved from her reevaluation of Stowe, Warner, Cooper, Brown, and Hawthorne to the American historical-adventure genre known as the Western. In *West of Everything: The Inner Life of Westerns* (1992) Tompkins discusses Westerns, in a compositional style that combines autobiography with critique, as a narrative field that needs to be understood as a coherent system of meaning and fictive experience, rather that divided into discrete analytical categories based upon the medium of production or publication: "What matters is not the medium but the identity of the imaginative world."

Tompkins divides her argument into two parts. The first deals with "some of the genre's main features – death, women, language, landscape, horses, cattle," and in her discussion, draws on films and fiction; the second part presents case studies concerned with novels by Owen Wister, Zane Grey, and Louis L'Amour, the Buffalo Bill Museum in Cody, Wyoming, and readers of Westerns (including her father-in-law, Max Fish). She concludes that the Western is a genre she loves, but which "exists in order to provide a justification for violence." She sees the Western performing this cultural work through its devaluation of women, language, and emotion and its valorization of silence, suffering, and death, creating a fictional world in which power resides not with women but with men. *West of Everything* has thus been accurately described by John Seelye as "an annex or sequel to *Sensational Designs*, in

that it explicates the Western as a male-designed and -determined effort to disempower the sentimental novel."

*West of Everything* has been criticized by scholars of the Western for its reliance upon a very limited number of Westerns and related critical works; historians of the West express concern about the limited attention she gives to the specific historical circumstances of the regions that make up the West and to the particular circumstances of the creation and reception of many of the Westerns she analyzes; and historians of art and film chide her for her willingness to elide (or ignore) the particularities of film, art, and literature as essentially different modes of representation. Nevertheless, *West of Everything* was nominated for a Pulitzer Prize for nonfiction in 1992, and received widespread attention in the academic and popular press, winning high praise for its accessibility and its serious attention to a persistently popular twentieth-century genre.

In *A Life in School: What the Teacher Learned* (1996) and ancillary essays including "Pedagogy of the Distressed" (1990), Tompkins argues that the American educational system, from elementary school to colleges and universities, fails to help students develop an authentic sense of self, because the educational system "does not focus on the inner lives of students or help them to acquire the self-understanding that is the basis for a satisfying life. Nor, by and large, does it provide the safe and nurturing environment that people need in order to grow." Writing in a way that combines autobiography with analysis, Tompkins describes her own journey toward enlightenment: it was not until she learned to approach teaching as an opportunity to provide students with an emotional education and for professors to abandon the pose of mere "performer" that she understood how to transform education from "training for a career" into "the introduction to a life." She goes on to urge a transformation of education that emphasizes emotional experience connected to students' and teachers' lives, seeking to integrate life and learning.

Thus we see that Tompkins' criticism, from reader-response theory to expressive pedagogy, has followed a path that has been poststructuralist in orientation, feminist in intention, autobiographical in mode, expressive in voice, and accessible to the general reader. Her work represents a populist impulse in academic criticism: she writes for the common reader (even when she is concerned with professional pedagogical matters). How we respond to texts, and what they mean to us, as historians, as critics, as educators, as students, as cultural agents, and as readers, are the critical questions for her, which make literary criticism and teaching a matter of critical importance to culture.

## Principal criticism

"Studies in Melville's Prose Style," 1967
"'The Beast in the Jungle': An Analysis of James's Late Style," 1970
*Twentieth Century Interpretations of "The Turn of the Screw" and Other Tales: A Collection of Critical Essays,* 1970 (editor)

"The Redemption of Time in *Notes of a Son and Brother*," 1973
"Criticism and Feeling," 1977
" 'Sartre Resartus' A Reading of *Les Mots*," 1980
*Reader-Response Criticism: From Formalism to Post-Structuralism*, 1980 (editor), incorporating:
   "An Introduction to Reader-Response Criticism," 1980
   "The Reader in History: The Changing Shape of Literary Response," 1980
"Graff Against Himself," 1981
*Sensational Designs: The Cultural Work of American Fiction, 1790–1860*, 1985, incorporating:
   "No Apologies for the Iroquois: A New Way to Read the Leatherstocking Novels," 1981
   "Sentimental Power: *Uncle Tom's Cabin* and the Politics of Literary History," 1981
   " 'Pray, therefore, without ceasing': From Tracts to Texts," 1983
   "Masterpiece Theater: The Politics of Hawthorne's Literary Reputation," 1984
   "The Other American Renaissance," 1985
Afterword to *The Wide, Wide World* by Susan Warner, 1987 (editor)
"Me and My Shadow," 1987
"A Short Course in Post-Structuralism," 1988
"All Alone, Little Lady?" 1990
*West of Everything: The Inner Life of Westerns*, 1992, incorporating:
   " 'Indians': Textualism, Morality, and the Problem of History," 1986
   "West of Everything," 1987
   "A Visit to the Museum," 1989
   "At the Buffalo Bill Museum – June 1988," 1990
   "Language and Landscape: An Ontology for the Western," 1990
   Introduction to *Riders of the Purple Sage* by Zane Gray, 1990 (editor)
"Susanna Rowson, Father of the American Novel," 1993
"Saving Our Lives: *Dances with Wolves*, *Iron John*, and the Search for a New Masculinity," 1994
*A Life in School: What the Teacher Learned*, 1996, incorporating:
   "Fighting Words: Unlearning to Write the Critical Essay," 1988
   "Pedagogy of the Distressed," 1990
   "Scenes from a Conference: Discovering the True Nature of Liberal Conversation," 1991
   "Teaching Like It Matters: A Modest Proposal for Revolutionizing the Classroom," 1991
   "The Way We Live Now," 1992
   "Postcards from the Edge," 1993

## Further reading

Carroll, Michael. "A Comment on 'Pedagogy of the Distressed,'" in *College English*. 53, no. 5 (September, 1991).
Clubbe, John. "Review Essay, *West of Everything: The Inner Life of Westerns*," in *ANQ*. 7, no. 1, new series (January, 1994).
Flynn, Elizabeth A. "Women as Reader-Response Critics," in *New Orleans Review*. 10, no. 2/3 (Summer/Fall, 1983).
Kerrigan, William. "The Western Hero and the Christian Woman," in *Raritan*. 12, no. 4 (Spring, 1993).
Margolis, Anne T. "Designing Readers," in *American Quarterly*. 38, no. 2 (Summer, 1986).
Messer-Davidow, Ellen. "The Philosophical Bases of Feminist Literary Criticisms," in *New Literary History*. 19, no. 1 (Autumn, 1987).
Olson, Gary A. "Jane Tompkins and the Politics of Writing, Scholarship, and Pedagogy," in *Philosophy, Rhetoric, Literary Criticism: (Inter)views*, 1994.
Perez, Gilberto. "Review: West of Everything," in *The Nation*, September 14, 1992.
Schneider, Alison. "Jane Tompkins's Message to Academe," in *Chronicle of Higher Education*, July 10, 1998.

ALISON M. SCOTT

# Translation

One of the central questions concerning the translation of literature within the field of literary criticism is whether (or to what degree) it is an "art" (a creative act involving the translator's interpretation of the source text and its aesthetic re-creation in the target language) or a "science" (an exercise in technical expertise involving the translator's linguistic knowledge of the source and the target languages). The answer is, of course, that a successful translation is a creative act of mediation between languages and cultures; it involves both dimensions of creativity and technique and is dependent on a variety of factors such as how wide or disparate are the linguistic, social, and cultural gaps between the source and target languages, for example. A translator's general guideline is to render the original source text as *closely* as is possible in the target language but as *freely* as is necessary to make it comprehensible and viable *as a literary text* within the target language and culture.

The translation of literary texts involves a complex field of problems and difficulties ranging from the purely linguistic to the constantly shifting hermeneutic questions of interpretation. An example of a simple linguistic problem can be found even in closely related languages such as in the translation from German into English. German has the capacity to build large composite nouns in a manner not found in English. Hermann Hesse's novel *Demian* (1919) contains the following acceptable, albeit unusual, noun formation as only one element of a larger sentence – *das Nichtmehrkindseindürfen* – which literally means "the state or condition of no longer being permitted to be a child." As a noun within a single sentence, the nuances of this unique German formulation are difficult to convey in English translation. Simple noun translations such as "puberty" or "adolescence" are not quite adequate. Differences between the source and target language societies and cultures pose even greater difficulties, as in the following example between Japan and America. In Japanese there is the noun *amae* (usually simply translated as "dependence") from the verb *amaeru* (translated as "to count/depend upon the indulgence/consideration/goodwill of others"). The concept is etymologically related to the adjective *amai* meaning "sweet" and contains nuances of a childlike indulgence upon the good graces – the "sweetness" – of others including parents, spouse, teachers, and work colleagues. In Japanese culture, where individual identification with the group is more or less the norm, the notion of dependence is socially acceptable and even encouraged (within carefully proscribed limits, of course). In Occidental cultures, especially American, where individual freedom is highly valued, any suggestion of dependence upon others is a rather negative concept with nuances of helplessness, powerlessness, and even psychological addiction. Within the context of a Japanese literary text in which the idea of *amae* is central, the novels of Natsume Sōseki (1868–1916) for example, its translation into a Western language and cultural setting is fraught with difficulties and virtually impossible without extensive background "cultural notes" by the translator.

Aesthetic language, as opposed to everyday language and the logical discourses of the sciences, poses a special difficulty for translation as in the use of the common rhetorical literary figure of metaphor, for example. The easiest to translate are universal metaphors (and proverbs) such as "the *river* or *road* of life," which usually have an equivalent in the target language. Stock or common metaphors are sometimes very culturally specific, such as the Japanese expression *daikon ashi* meaning a person with legs like thick *daikon* radishes, that is, short and stubby, and are more difficult to render literally in the target language. Creative metaphors unique to the author of the source language text are most difficult to render successfully and here the translator's own creative talent and his or her personal interpretation of the author's meaning and artistic intentions are called into play. Sometimes they may be simply rendered literally but when this produces an incomprehensible construction a figurative rendition becomes necessary. Here too comes the problematic side of translation as a creative mediation since the translator's interpretation is by necessity only one of several possible ways of reading the source text. An interpretive choice must often be made by the translator and this invariably limits the target language reader's view of the source text.

The difficulty of translating literary texts is also marked by the aesthetic nature of the different literary genres. Poetry as the linguistically and artistically most compacted form of text remains the most challenging to the skill of the translator. Short fiction and short prose texts such as aphorisms are probably in second place, since textual interpretation may hinge on the translation of a single word or sentence. This is also the case with dramatic dialogue in plays. Longer fiction pieces such as novellas and novels allow the translator the most freedom since sheer size allows for varied multiple renderings of crucial textual elements. A motif or metaphoric construction used repeatedly by the source language author may be rendered in different ways so that the target language reader may have more interpretive choices when decoding the text.

Translation has traditionally been regarded as having a somewhat denigrated status with respect to "real" literature. Literary criticism, even in the field of comparative literature in which translation is essential, has always placed a high value on the "original sanctity of the source" of the author and the text – with all the hierarchical social privileging this implies – and thus translation, however skillful, remained a second-class entity, an inferior reproduction, a mere "handmaiden" to the source text; it has been forever maintained – at times with all the proper smugness of the elitist sensibility – that one should always read a work "in the original." This normative estimation changed somewhat during the 1980s and 1990s as a result of critical inquiry (stimulated in part by feminist literary criticism) into the nature of literature and the literary canon and their place within society. Translation as a creative activity of mediation assumes here the more egalitarian status of a genre or subgenre, much like dialect or minority literature, for example, within the overall canon of texts within a culture.

## Further reading

Bassnett, Susan, and André Lefevere. *Constructing Cultures. Essays on Literary Translation*, 1998.
Classe, Olive, ed. *Encyclopedia of Literary Translation*, 1998.
Hermans, Theo, ed. *The Manipulation of Literature. Studies in Literary Translation*, 1985.
Johnston, David, ed. *Stages of Translation*, 1996.
Newmark, Peter. *Approaches to Translation*, 1988.
——. *A Textbook of Translation*, 1988.
——. *About Translation*, 1991.
——. *More Paragraphs on Translation*, 1998.
Raffel, Burton. *The Art of Translating Prose*, 1994.

THOMAS F. BARRY

# Lionel Trilling

American critic and writer

**Born:** New York, New York; July 4, 1905
**Died:** New York, New York; November 5, 1975

## Biography

Lionel Trilling was born on July 4, 1905, in New York City to David and Fannie (Cohen) Trilling. Trilling grew up in the city in a Jewish environment, although his family was not particularly religious, and Trilling himself did not dwell on his Jewish identity. He graduated from DeWitt Clinton High School in 1921, and two years later began contributing stories and reviews to *The Menorah Journal* under the editorship of Elliot Cohen. This period – 1923 to 1931 – represents the only time he became involved in specifically Jewish activities. While not denying his Jewish heritage, he was one of a generation of Jewish intellectuals who exhibited little interest in their religious and ethnic background and who preferred to seek what they regarded as the larger frame of reference: American and European literature and politics.

After taking his bachelor's and master's degrees at Columbia University in 1925 and 1926, Trilling taught briefly at the University of Wisconsin and at Hunter College. He joined the faculty of Columbia in 1931 and completed his Ph.D. there in 1938. He remained at Columbia for the rest of his life, although he accepted prestigious visiting professorships at Oxford (1965, 1972–1973) and Harvard (1969–1970).

Trilling was the recipient of numerous honorary degrees, from schools such as Harvard University, the University of Leicester, Brandeis University, and Yale University. He received his second Guggenheim Fellowship in 1975. His national reputation is reflected in his election to the National Institute of Arts and Letters and his membership in the American Academy of Arts and Sciences. He married Diana Rubin in 1929; they had one son, James. After her husband's death in 1975, Diana Trilling organized an archive of his papers and edited the uniform edition of his works.

## Influence

Trilling is one of the two or three most important American literary critics of the twentieth century. Highly influential during his lifetime, his work has continued to be debated and discussed among literary critics and cultural historians, who often include him in studies of the "New York intellectuals" who framed much of the political and literary discussion of the 1930s, 1940s, and 1950s. He has been the subject of several monographs – which is rather unusual for a literary critic – and a twelve-volume uniform edition of his works was published between 1977 and 1980. In 1975 the reprinting of his only novel, *The Middle of the Journey*, occasioned considerable controversy because it was accompanied by an introduction in which Trilling expressed considerable sympathy for Whittaker Chambers, a former Communist Party secret operative who vehemently attacked the Party and testified against Alger Hiss, who was convicted of spying for the Soviet Union. The novel served to underscore the broad cultural and political implications of Trilling's criticism, in which he became absolutely committed to the primacy of the self over all ideological and aesthetic considerations.

## Analysis

*The Liberal Imagination* is the book that made Lionel Trilling's reputation. A collection of essays on individual American authors and on broader subjects (such as "Reality in America"), the book presented a subtle and elegant critique of literature and society. To gauge the book's impact, it is necessary to describe the cultural climate in which it appeared. Trilling was the inheritor of the 1930s emphasis on "the social responsibility of the writer." This was true of what he calls "liberal criticism" and of Stalinist criticism – the latter taking its cue from Joseph Stalin's formulation of Socialist Realism, in which it was incumbent upon the artist to reflect accurately the feelings and the material conditions of the people. In Trilling's view, so much concern and sympathy was given to socially responsible writers that the quality of their work and the consequences of their ideas were never adequately assessed. Opposed to Stalinism in all its forms, Trilling set out to define the liberal imagination in such a way as to make it more sophisticated and more attuned to what he terms in the preface to his book, "the sense of variousness and possibility." His method in *The Liberal Imagination* is to concentrate on how the self is shaped in modern society and on how the individual writer responds or fails to respond to the novel's peculiar ability to mirror and to criticize society.

In "Reality in America" – perhaps the most influential essay in *The Liberal Imagination* – Trilling attacks Vernon L. Parrington's standard text, *Main Currents in American Thought* (1927–1930; three volumes), because it takes a passive attitude toward reality. In Parrington's work, American writers are praised or condemned depending on how well they fit the critic's sense of a stable, uniform reality. As a result, Edgar Allan Poe – who fits none of Parrington's formulas – is dismissed as a freak. This conclusion is surely wrong, Trilling argues. American writers have responded to, defined, and transformed reality; they have not simply been the purveyors of some agreed-upon version of the cultural heritage.

This issue was extremely important to Trilling in 1950 because of the Stalinist tendency to presume that reality was a given that the writer should copy. Parrington was no Stalinist, but he was a liberal with an unimaginative sense of reality that dangerously played into Stalinist dogma. As Trilling bluntly puts it at the end of "Reality in America," once the writer's sense of social responsibility is approved of in the Parrington school of criticism, then the writer "is not really responsible for anything, not even for his ideas."

A case in point was the different reputations of Henry James and Theodore Dreiser among American critics. For a generation James had been attacked by liberal critics because of his turning away from American reality, his removal to Europe, and his convoluted style. Dreiser, on the other hand, was lauded for his attention to the urban poor, to economic inequality, and to the struggles of American workers. In reversing the critical tide, Trilling may overstate his point in "Reality in America," but there is no question that he is right in showing that James, not Dreiser, is most acute on the subject of the American sensibility. James has the supple style that reveals and assesses reality in new and exciting ways. Dreiser, for all of his social commitment, writes in an inflated, literary style full of contradictory notions. Trilling proves his point in the essay by deftly exposing embarrassing passages from Dreiser and by himself exhibiting a subtlety of argument absent in

Parrington and other earlier American critics. In effect, Trilling's own example in *The Liberal Imagination* testifies to the force of a unique sensibility that does not take reality for granted but shows that it must be sought for and argued into existence.

In *Beyond Culture*, Trilling extends his point that the great modern writers do much more than reflect their culture; they judge, sometimes condemn, and "perhaps revise" the culture that has produced them. While this body of modernist literature is extraordinarily valuable for the insight it provides on culture, it is also quite dangerous. Unlike many critics who give their total devotion to literature, Trilling contends that there are moral values that supersede the work of the art, values that may call literature into question: "art does not always tell the truth or the best kind of truth and does not always point out the right way, . . . it can even generate falsehood and habituate us to it." In his preface to *Beyond Culture*, Trilling admits that he is surprised to take this view and knows that many readers will consider it disastrous. By 1965, it must be pointed out, he was writing in a very different cultural climate. Stalinism was long out of favor, and liberal critics had adopted the subtle ways of reading literature which Trilling had advocated in 1950. Now the opposite danger seemed likely: the work of art was to be valued in and for itself, as an autonomous authority in its own right and not subject to any sort of "reality principle" outside itself. Perhaps that is why Trilling suggests that "on frequent occasions" art "might well be subject, in the interests of autonomy, to the scrutiny of the rational intellect." In other words, if reality is not something artists simply copy, it is also not merely something artists create. There must be a fruitful tension between art and society.

*Beyond Culture* also demonstrates that Trilling is a thoughtful critic of American education. In "On the Teaching of Modern Literature," he expresses reservations about "the educational propriety of its being studied in college." The very institutionalization of a literature that is highly personal seems a contradiction in terms to Trilling. How, in a classroom setting, can the teacher articulate his or her personal feelings, convince students of literature's individual power, and then assign standardized test questions that take the vital life right out of the literature that students should find deeply moving and challenging? Such a dilemma makes Trilling uncomfortable because the very power of literature is sapped in the college classroom: "Time has the effect of seeming to quiet the work of art, domesticating it and making it into a classic, which is often another way of saying that it is an object of merely habitual regard."

Such concerns serve to emphasize the fact that Trilling never considered himself merely an academic critic writing for his peers. He wrote with the largest literate audience in mind, an audience that would be concerned not only with literature but also with the current state of the culture.

Trilling therefore presented himself as a very active figure – not a scholar codifying and canonizing works of literature, but a contemporary figure writing even as the culture changed. In *A Gathering of Fugitives* this led him to a dynamic view of "culture being not a free creation but a continuous bargaining with life, an exchange in which one may yield less or more, but never nothing."

In "Some Notes for an Autobiographical Lecture," Trilling explains how he first became engaged with Matthew Arnold and how the example of Arnold turned Trilling toward the writing of an intellectual biography that was to have a profound impact on all his criticism. In the beginning, Arnold represented "the melancholy poet, the passive sufferer from the stresses and tendencies of his culture." By the time Trilling finished his book on Arnold, the poet had become "the man who had pitted himself against the culture, who had tried to understand the culture for the purpose of shaping it." That is also the critic Trilling became: never sure that literature, the teaching of literature, or the writing of literary criticism were self-justifying activities, he actively took on the point of view of society and argued for and against it. In his autobiographical lecture, Trilling calls his stance "novelistic," by which he seems to mean that all his assumptions have to be tested against experience and that ideas are not sacrosanct – they have no permanent truth – but must be constantly reevaluated in a changing environment. While many critics might echo Trilling's sentiments, very few have embedded this "novelistic" imagination in their prose. Trilling's work, read in its entirety, confirms that his views of literature and society continued to develop in response to the changing times.

In *Art, Politics, and Will: Essays in Honor of Lionel Trilling* (1977), Steven Marcus points out that alongside Arnold, "the figure of Freud was for [Trilling] something very close to a moral ideal," especially "Freud's fierceness, boldness, honesty, and independence, his sense of tragedy and stoical resistance." Trilling was hardly an orthodox Freudian, but Sigmund Freud's emphasis on the self as the locus of meaning was a cardinal principle for the critic. If Trilling's thought is neither as bold nor as disturbing as Freud's, it is distinctive, in Mark Krupnick's words, for its relentless probing of "the relation of culture and personality," and for its orientation toward "styles of self-definition."

## Principal criticism
*Matthew Arnold*, 1939
*E. M. Forster*, 1943
*The Liberal Imagination: Essays on Literature and Society*, 1950
*The Opposing Self*, 1955
*A Gathering of Fugitives*, 1956
*Beyond Culture: Essays on Learning and Literature*, 1965
*Sincerity and Authenticity*, 1972
*Speaking of Literature and Society*, 1980 (Diana Trilling, editor)

## Other major works and literary forms

Lionel Trilling is the author of one novel, *The Middle of the Journey* (1947), and several highly regarded short stories. In "Some Notes for an Autobiographical Lecture" (in *The Last Decade: Essays and Reviews, 1965–1975*, 1979, edited by Diana Trilling), Trilling remarks that he always had it in mind to be a novelist. This fact is important in assessing the consistent concentration in all of his work on the self, on the way the personality shapes and is shaped by its culture. Trilling tried to be as concrete as possible about literature and criticism, since he saw both as directly connected to the experience of life and not above or beyond the way people actually lived. For him, literary matters were matters of morality; how the self chose to define itself was of utmost importance – more important, in fact, than literature in and for itself. His novel, not surprisingly, is about moral choice, and it is set in the post-World War II years during a time of political and spiritual crisis that has commonly come to be known as the Cold War. The main characters of the novel, liberals and radicals, struggle to define the nature of the good society. In many ways, Trilling's novel defines the agenda of the distinguished criticism he went on to write in the 1950s.

NOVEL
*The Middle of the Journey*, 1947

SHORT FICTION
*Of This Time, of That Place, and Other Stories*, 1979

NONFICTION
*Freud and the Crisis of Our Culture*, 1955
*Mind in the Modern World*, 1973
*Prefaces to "The Experience of Literature,"* 1979 (Diana Trilling, editor)
*The Last Decade: Essays and Reviews, 1965–1975*, 1979 (Diana Trilling, editor)

EDITED TEXTS
*The Portable Matthew Arnold*, 1949
*The Selected Letters of John Keats*, 1951
*The Experience of Literature: A Reader with Commentaries*, 1967
*Literary Criticism: An Introductory Reader*, 1970
*The Oxford Anthology of English Literature*, 1973 (with others)

## Further reading

Anderson, Quentin, Stephen Donadio, and Steven Marcus, eds. *Art, Politics, and Will: Essays in Honor of Lionel Trilling*, 1977.
Boyers, Robert. *Lionel Trilling: Negative Capability and the Wisdom of Avoidance*, 1977.
Chace, William M. *Lionel Trilling: Criticism and Politics*, 1980.
Krupnick, Mark. *Lionel Trilling and Cultural Criticism in America*, 1985.
Leitch, Thomas, M. *Lionel Trilling: An Annotated Bibliography*, 1993.
O'Hara, Daniel T. *Lionel Trilling: The Work of Liberation*, 1988.
Shoben, J. Edward, Jr. *Lionel Trilling: Mind and Character*, 1981.
Tanner, Stephen. *Lionel Trilling*, 1988.
Trilling, Diana. *The Beginning of the Journey: The Marriage of Diana and Lionel Trilling*, 1993.

CARL ROLLYSON

*See also* American Literary Theory: Twentieth Century

# Giangiorgio Trissino

Italian poet and scholar

**Born:** Vicenza, Italy; July 8, 1478
**Died:** Rome, Italy; December 8, 1550

## Biography

Giangiorgio Trissino was born into an extremely wealthy aristocratic family of the Venetian city of Vicenza. Orphaned at the age of nine, married at sixteen to a daughter of another branch of the family, Trissino undertook his studies relatively late, only after the death of his first wife (with whom he had five children, two of whom survived). In 1506 he went to Milan to study Greek under Demetrio Calcondila. Trissino was in Vicenza to take part in the celebrations there when Emperor Maximilian I took possession of the city in 1509. He was exiled as a member of the imperial party when the League of Cambrai restored Vicenza to Venice. The banishment would be revoked in 1516; in the meantime, after a period of exile in Germany, Trissino frequented the highest levels of contemporary Italian society. After a time in Milan, he was welcomed in 1512 into the circle of Lucrezia Borgia at Ferrara. He visited Florence following the return of the Medici in 1512 and participated in the discussions of the famous Orti Oricellari, assuming an attitude that Benedetto Varchi characterized as "more like a master or superior than as a companion and equal."

After 1514 Trissino was drawn to the papal court of Leo X, where he fraternized with scholars and poets such as Bernardo Dovizi, Pietro Bembo, and John Lascaris. It was during this period that he composed *La Sofonisba* (1524). In Venice in 1523 he presented a vernacular oration which celebrated the installment of the doge Andrea Gritti. That same year he married Bianca Trissino, the widow of another member of the family. Eventually, two children were born to them. Trissino celebrated Bianca's beauty in his *I ritratti* (portraits), published in 1524. Attached to the court of Pope Clement VII, to whom he dedicated his letter proposing the orthographic reform of the Italian language, Trissino took his place among the assembled dignitaries at the coronation of Charles V in Bologna in 1530.

Separated from his wife, Bianca, in 1535, Trissino spent the rest of his life traveling between Rome and various Venetian cities, including Vicenza, Venice, Padua, Cornedo, and Cricoli, where he had a magnificent villa. The last years of his life were embittered by a violent dispute over the family patrimony with Giulio Trissino, a son from his first marriage who was supported in his claims by some members of the Trissino clan. At Rome in the mid-1540s Trissino became a patron of Andrea di Pietro, to whom he gave the name Palladio. In 1547 the first nine books of Trissino's *La Italia liberata dai Goti* (Italy liberated from the Goths) appeared, and he would publish the remaining eighteen books the following year. Following a last trip to Germany in search of imperial patronage (he had dedicated the epic to Charles V), he returned to Rome, where he died at the age of seventy-two on December 8, 1550.

## Influence

Generally considered failures by posterity as well as by his contemporaries, Trissino's ambitious and idiosyncratic critical and poetic efforts nevertheless represent cumulatively one of the most important literary-critical programs of the first decades of the sixteenth century. In his adoption of Aristotelian principles in both theory and practice, Trissino was an important precursor of the theoreticians who dominated the field by the middle of the century. His proposals for orthographic reform, his rediscovery and translation of Dante's *De vulgari eloquentia* (c. 1306; English translation, 1890), and his dialogue *Il castellano* (the chatelain) characterize and form the vernacular *questione della lingua* as that discussion evolved during the 1520s and 1530s. Scholars generally view Trissino as the principal representative (along with Baldassare Castiglione) of the courtly position on the language question, in opposition to the vernacular Humanism championed by Pietro Bembo in his *Prose della volgar lingua* (1525; writings in the vernacular language) and to those who argued for the primacy of contemporary Florentine language – for example, Niccolò Machiavelli in his *Discorso o dialogo intorno a la nostra lingua* (1525; discourse or dialogue on our language). Though many of Trissino's positions, proposed innovations, and poetic works were not well received, his highly original contributions are nevertheless central to an understanding of the cultural debate taking place in Italy during a formative period in the development of the Italian language and its literature.

## Analysis

The high point of Trissino's achievement as a literary theorist came in 1529 with the simultaneous publication of the first part of *La poetica*, the *Dubbi grammaticali*, the translation of Dante's *De vulgari eloquentia*, *Il castellano*, and *La grammatichetta*, as well as the republication of *Epistola del Trissino de le lettere nuovamente aggiunte ne la lingua italiana*, *La Sofonisba*, and *Le rime* (poems). This massive critical and poetic offensive reflects the programmatic and polemical character of Trissino's contribution to the linguistic and literary debate which was taking place in Italy during the early decades of the sixteenth century. It also

reflects his remarkable conscious recognition of the crucial nature of the historical moment from a linguistic and literary perspective. Indeed, it was in the years following 1525 (the date of the publication of Pietro Bembo's *Prose della volgar lingua*) that the Italian language and Italian literature began to emerge as modern cultural institutions. Trissino's was certainly one of the principal voices in the complex, conflict-ridden process that resulted in the emergence of modern Italian literature. In this light, Trissino's opposition to Bembo's Tuscanizing vernacular Humanism served to some extent a complementary function insofar as Trissino expanded the terms of the discussion; he addressed questions having to do with areas of the vernacular tradition such as the epic and the tragedy, as well as metrical issues excluded by Bembo's primarily Petrarchistic lyric program. Neither the isolated and autodidactic nature of Trissino's culture nor what has been described as the rhetorically feudal or reactionary mode of its presentation should obscure the fact that he clearly recognized the epoch-making proportions of the process which was taking place.

Trissino's most important theoretical work is *La poetica*, a treatise ordered in six divisions, which are in turn divided into two parts corresponding to two dates of publication. The first part (divisions 1–4) was published in that busy editorial year, 1529, while the second (5–6) was only published posthumously, in 1562. The first part of the work is largely concerned with grammatical and metrical problems, following a tradition of vernacular linguistic and rhetorical treatises including Antonio da Tempo's *Summa artis rithmici vulgaris dictaminis* (1332), Dante's *De vulgari eloquentia*, and Pietro Bembo's *Prose della volgar lingua*. The second part of the work addresses tragedy, the epic poem, and comedy; it provides Aristotelian definitions of unity, mimesis, and catharsis, concepts which Trissino presented as applicable to the nascent national literature. Of particular importance is Trissino's promotion of *verso sciolto* – that is, of blank verse hendecasyllables – as the appropriate meter for epic and tragedy, in opposition to the vernacular tradition of rhymed verse. This innovation derived from his admiration for the Greek poets, for, although they invented rhyme, "it was not often adopted by them, perhaps because of its defects." Rhymed verse is relegated by Trissino to the periphery: the chorus of tragedy and the comic register. Trissino's position on blank verse represents from his perspective a surpassing of his contemporaries, including "noble and elegant talents like Sannazzaro and Bembo, and a few others, who composing in rhyme did not dare to depart from the simple imitation of Petrarch." Though Trissino's contribution to the discussion of Aristotelian poetics was marginal compared to those of subsequent writers such as Francesco Robortello (whose commentary was published in 1548) and Giambattista Giraldi Cinthio, it was Trissino who as early as the dedication to his tragedy *La Sofonisba* marked the Renaissance revival of Aristotelian influence in vernacular letters.

Certainly, Trissino distinguishes himself in his emphasis on the importance of Aristotelian rules, which he programmatically promoted and followed in his own works.

Trissino was also one of the principal figures in the controversy that arose over the Italian language question, beginning in the second decade of the century with *Epistola del Trissino de le lettere nuovamente aggiunte ne la lingua italiana* (addressed to Pope Clement VII; Trissino's epistle on the letters recently added to the Italian language), a work which stimulated a series of violently polemical responses from certain Tuscan writers, who attacked Trissino for what they considered to be the misappropriation of their language by a foreigner. Trissino proposed to rationalize Italian orthography by introducing letters from the Greek alphabet in order to make clear the distinctions between open and closed vowels *e* and *a* and between voiced and unvoiced *z*. He even went so far as to introduce these reforms in the printed editions of his poetic and critical works. His initiative led to the polemical interventions of Angelo Firenzuola with his *Discacciamento delle nuove lettere inutilmente aggiunte nella lingua toscana* (1524; the ousting of the new letters uselessly added to the Tuscan language), Lodovico Martelli with his *Risposta alla epistola del Trissino delli lettere nuovamente aggionte alla lingua volgar fiorentina* (1525; response to Trissino's letter); Claudio Tolomei with his *Il polito* (1531), and even Niccolò Machiavelli. More offensive to the Tuscans than the proposed modifications of the alphabet (through which they discerned imperfections in Trissino's pronunciation of their language) was Trissino's designation of their language as Italian rather than Tuscan. Trissino's answer came in the barrage of 1529, which included – besides *Dubbi grammaticali* (questions of grammar) in which he further elaborated and somewhat modified his proposals for orthographic reform – a translation of Dante's *De vulgari eloquentia*, which had been rediscovered by him after nearly two hundred years of neglect, as well as the dialogue *Il castellano* (both published under the pseudonym Arrigo Doria).

The principal interlocutors in the dialogue include Giovanni Ruccellai, the Florentine "castellano" of Castel Sant' Angelo who is the spokesman for Trissino's point of view. Another Florentine, Filippo Strozzi (who cites verbatim lengthy passages from Martelli's *Risposta alla lettere del Trissino*), represents the position of Trissino's Tuscan detractors. In Trissino's view, the Italian language spoken by the elite in the courts of Italy represents an autonomous linguistic model to be distinguished from and preferred to the language of either the city of Florence or the region of Tuscany. Trissino's account of the origins of the vernacular lyric in Italy emphasizes the role of the Sicilian poets (by virtue of their not being Tuscan) against the account of the Tuscanizing Bembo, who had asserted that the vernacular lyric had passed directly from Provence to Tuscany. Trissino further observes that Petrarch himself had avoided municipal Florentine vocabulary.

Most important, however, is Trissino's appeal to the authority of Dante's *De vulgari eloquentia*. Trissino's reading of that treatise interprets Dante's poetic ideal of *volgare illustre* (illustrious vernacular) to correspond to the Italian language as it was spoken in the courts of Italy, not to any of the local languages of Italy. One of the crucial characterizing adjectives of Dante's linguistic ideal – that is, the illustrious vernacular's *curialitas* – offers convenient support for Trissino's promotion of the language of the court as a national linguistic model: "What does curial mean? It means a language spoken by the men at the court of the pope and the duke, who, on account of their being literary men, speak better than the way one speaks in the particular regions of Italy."

Trissino proposes, then, the language of the courtly elite, not the language spoken by contemporary Florentines nor that found in the classical vernacular authors of the trecento. Within the context of the *questione della lingua*, Trissino placed himself in opposition to both the vernacular Humanism championed by Bembo and the proponents of the contemporary Florentine language. In opposition to Bembo, Trissino proposes the courtly position on the language, analogous to that of Baldassare Castiglione in *Il libro del cortegiano* (1528; *The Book of the Courtier*, 1561). According to the courtly thesis, the ideal Italian language, similar to the classical Attic literary language of the Greek-speaking world, would be a distillation of the finest elements of the various courts of Italy.

Bembo had already revealed the theoretical weaknesses of this position in the first book of *Prose della volgar lingua*: the language of the Italian courts was excessively heterogeneous and offered no textual models for an Italian language and literature. What actually sealed the fate of the courtly position, however, was unavoidable historical and political realities. Indeed, the cultural mirage of a courtly Italian *koine* could not survive the political crises which had engulfed the courts of Italy, crises which culminated in the Sack of Rome in 1527. The political reality of Italy would continue for centuries to be one of disunity and foreign domination, beginning during Trissino's own time with the domination of imperial Spain. The Italian language and literature as cultural institutions were forced, in the absence of political unity, to fall back upon the vernacular Humanistic solution elaborated by Bembo. The linguistic and literary model of the vernacular classics, especially Petrarch and Giovanni Boccaccio, would function as models for the new Italian literature.

Nevertheless, the discussion which Trissino stimulated during the 1520s and 1530s about whether to call the language Italian, Tuscan, or Florentine, despite its academic character and apparent superficiality, was symptomatic of the nature of the process which was taking place at the time. In his *Discorso o dialogo intorno a la nostra lingua*, Machiavelli chastised those who would take away the language from the Florentines. As a target of Machiavelli's *vis polemica*, Trissino can be said to have been in good company, if one considers that another target was the non-Tuscan Ludovico Ariosto, author of what is generally recognized to be the literary masterpiece of the Italian Renaissance. While Trissino's proposal of an illusory courtly linguistic ideal was misguided, the response of a younger generation of Florentines, such as Ruccellai (who wrote a tragedy in imitation of *La Sofonisba*) or Francesco Guicciardini (who carefully annotated and considered Bembo's recommendations in the *Prose della volgar lingua* while revising his own *Ricordi*, 1513–1530), represents evidence in support of Trissino's position. The Florentine or Tuscan language had indeed ceased to be the exclusive property of the Tuscans and Florentines: it had become Italian and national in character.

## Principal criticism

*La grammatichetta*, 1524
*Espistola del Trissino de le lettere nuovamente aggiunte ne la lingua italiana*, 1524
*Il castellano*, 1529
*Dubbi grammaticali*, 1529
*La poetica*, 1529–1562 (partial translation in *Literary Criticism: Plato to Dryden*, 1962)

## Other major works and literary forms

Giangiorgio Trissino's theoretical positions regarding poetics and the question of vernacular language found their practical expression and exemplification in a series of ambitious literary works. The most successful and influential of these was Trissino's *La Sofonisba* (1524; written 1515). Written in Italian blank verse (*endecasillabi sciolti*), the work derives directly from the author's study of Greek tragedy and Aristotle and has traditionally been considered the first modern tragedy to observe classical rules. Trissino's other major opus was *La Italia liberata dai Goti* (1547–1548; Italy liberated from the Goths); here, Aristotle and Homer serve as theoretical guide and poetic model respectively. This epic poem in twenty-seven plodding books of blank verse was twenty years in the making and is widely considered one of the most notorious poetic failures in the Italian tradition. A comedy, *I simillimi* (1548; the twins), represents Trissino's attempt to reconcile Plautine situations with Hellenic technique – for example, in the suppression of the prologue and the introduction of a chorus. He was the author of a relatively small *canzoniere* (*Le rime* – poems – of 1529) consisting of seventy-seven compositions including *canzoni*, sonnets, ballads, *sirventes*, and madrigals. These are distinguished by metrical experimentation which reflects Trissino's desire to look beyond Petrarch and the Roman classics for his vernacular models, seeking them instead in the lyric of ancient Greece. Other minor works include the courtly dialogue *I ritratti* (1524; portraits), the *Espistola de la vita, che dee tenere una donna vedova* (1524; letter concerning the manner of life a widow ought to follow), an oration for the Venetian doge Andrea

Gritti, an encomium for Emperor Maximilian I, and a Latin grammar, *Grammatices introductionis liber primus* (first introductory book of grammar).

PLAYS
*La Sofonisba*, written 1515, published 1524
*I simillimi*, 1548 (based on Plautus' *Menaechmi*)

POETRY
*Le rime*, 1529
*La Italia liberata dai Goti*, 1547–1548

NONFICTION
*I ritratti*, 1524
*Epistola de la vita, che dee tenere una donna vedova*, 1524
*Grammatices introductionis liber primus*

TRANSLATION
*De la volgare eloquenzia*, 1529 (of Dante's *De vulgari eloquentia*)

MISCELLANEOUS
*Tutte le opere di Giovan Giorgio Trissino, gentiluomo vicentino*, 1729 (2 volumes)
*Giangiorgio Trissino: Scritti scelti*, 1950

## Further reading

Castelvecchi, Alberto, ed. *Scritti linguistici: Giovan Giorgio Trissino*, 1986.
Herrick, M. T. "Trissino's *Art of Poetry*," in *Essay on Shakespeare and Elizabethan Drama in Honor of Hardin Craig*, 1962.
Pozza, Neri, ed. *Convegno di studi su Giangiorgio Trissino: Vicenza 31 marzo–1 aprile 1979*, Oseo del Teatro Olimpico, 1980.
Roditi, E. "The Genesis of Neo-Classical Tragedy," in *The South Atlantic Quarterly*. XLVI (1947), pp. 93–108.
Steadman, John M. "Verse Without Rhyme: Sixteenth Century Italian Defences of *Versi Sciolti*," in *Italica*. XLI (December, 1964), pp. 384–402.
Weinberg, Bernard. *A History of Literary Criticism in the Italian Renaissance*, 1961.
Williams, R. C. "Epic Unity as Discussed by Sixteenth Century Critics in Italy," in *Modern Philology: A Journal Devoted to Research in Medieval and Modern Literature*. XVIII (November, 1920), pp. 383–400.
——. "Metrical Form in the Epic as Discussed by Sixteenth Century Critics," in *Modern Language Notes*. XXXVI (December, 1921), pp. 449–457.
——. "Tasso's Annotations to Trissino's Poetics," in *Modern Language Notes*. LXIII (1943), pp. 153–158.

THEODORE J. CACHEY, JR.

*See also* Bembo; Giraldi Cinthio; Renaissance and Restoration Literary Theory; Scaliger

# Ts'ao P'i

Chinese poet

**Born:** Ch'iao, Pei, China; A.D. 187
**Died:** China; A.D. 226

## Biography

Ts'ao P'i was born in A.D. 187 in Ch'iao, Pei (Anhui Province), China. His father, Ts'ao Ts'ao, was not only a powerful political figure but also a renowned poet of his time. At the age of five Ts'ao P'i began to learn archery and horseback riding from his father. In addition to military training he received an education in the classics and began his creative career at the age of eight. Ts'ao P'i frequently went on expeditions with his father, helping him to expand his military power. Because of Ts'ao Ts'ao, who served as premier in 211, Emperor Hsien appointed Ts'ao P'i, then twenty-four years old, vice premier.

Shortly after his father became the King of Wei in 216, a struggle for political power broke out between Ts'ao P'i and his younger brother, whose literary talent was greatly appreciated by his father. In the winter of 217 Ts'ao P'i emerged from the struggle as the crown prince. Upon his father's death in 220, he succeeded his father as the King of Wei and as premier. By this time Ts'ao P'i had virtually become the political and literary leader of northern China, which was, as opposed to the south, under the direct control of the central government of the Han Dynasty. Less than a year after he became premier he pressured Emperor Hsien to yield the throne, founded the Wei Dynasty, and took the title Emperor Wei Wen. He died at the age of thirty-nine in 226.

## Influence

Ts'ao P'i's concept of literature not only guided the development of the empire he established but also set the stage for a coming civilization renowned most for its creations of literature. His contributions, though clearly wrought through the generating force of political domination, brought about a new understanding of literature. The pursuit of literature as an end in itself, as opposed to a function of social etiquette, was a new dimension in the history of Chinese literature, attributable to Ts'ao P'i.

## Analysis

Most of the literary works written by Ts'ao P'i were lost by the time of the Sung Dynasty (A.D. 960–1270). His literary theory can be seen in his extant works: "Yü Wang Lang shu," "Yü Wu Chi shu," and "Tien lun lun wên." The first work of literary criticism in Chinese history, "Tien lun lun wên," though brief in length, has had a tremendous influence on the development of Chinese literature. The essay appeared at a time when literature was flourishing in China. Under the patronage of his father, Ts'ao

P'i and other great writers engaged themselves seriously in the creation of literary works. Before Ts'ao P'i literature had been placed in a subordinate position in Chinese cultural tradition. In Confucianism, literature, though useful, is less important than pragmatic achievements, such as political feats and virtuous deeds; in Taoism, literature is a distraction from the sage's ideal to be one with nature. Taking exception to these traditional views of literature, Ts'ao P'i attached unprecedented importance to literary creativity. Literature, he says, is equivalent to the ruling of a kingdom or the great achievement of immortality. Glory, happiness, and life will end, he argues, but literature is infinite. Ts'ao P'i therefore encouraged everyone, whether rich or poor, prominent or obscure, to pursue immortal fame through literary achievement.

Ts'ao P'i also disagreed with the traditional Confucianist view of literary history. According to Confucianism, ancient literature is always superior to contemporary writings, and the older the literary work is, the more value it has. To rectify this retrogressive concept, Ts'ao P'i proposed to view literary figures of every age in the light of their individual accomplishments rather than simply the time period in which they lived. Acknowledging the achievements of the ancient writers, he equally appreciates the merits of contemporary writers. His critical study of seven contemporary figures, in "Yü Wu Chi shu" and "Tien lun lun wên," further demonstrates his interest in the literature of his time. The opposition to the retrogressive view actually complements Ts'ao P'i's promotion of literature in that it fostered contemporary writers' confidence in their ability to compose works of enduring value. Together, these ideas initiated a new phase of literary creativity.

It is commonly acknowledged that Ts'ao P'i was the first literary critic who systematically applied the term *Ch'i* to literary writing. By *Ch'i* (which literally means "air" or "breath"), he indicates in "Tien lun lun wên," he means both a writer's creative spirit and the reflection of that spirit in a work, namely, style. Earlier, Mencius (c. 371–289 B.C.), a great Confucianist, had used the term to refer to the powerful universal spirit springing up from one's moral good, which one needs to cultivate. When introducing the term into literary criticism, Ts'ao P'i makes *Ch'i* a unique and inherent quality, which varies from writer to writer and which cannot be acquired through learning. Because of these inherent differences in the creative spirit, there exists a great variety of styles among writers' works. In this light, literary criticism, as Ts'ao P'i conceives it, is the analysis of the unique spirit of the writer as well as the work.

Focusing on the style of a writer, this critical theory is different from the traditional didactic theory which had been prevalent before Ts'ao P'i. According to Confucius (551–479 B.C.), literature should be judged by a standard of moral canons, which are extrinsic to the work, rather than by its intrinsic merits. Since the elevation of

Confucianism to a state of supremacy by Emperor Wu (140–87 B.C.) in the Han Dynasty (206 B.C.–A.D. 220), this view had been the guiding principle for all writers. Although Taoist scholars did not endorse the didactic concept of Confucianism, they essentially held an unfavorable view of literature. Confucianism gradually lost its power as a result of the decline of the Han empire. When Ts'ao Ts'ao rose to power, he made individual talent rather than morality the criteria for the evaluation of his officials – a policy which was opposed to moralistic Confucian doctrine. Freed from the limitations of Confucian tradition, Ts'ao P'i applied his father's criteria for evaluation to the writer. In his analysis of the strengths and weaknesses of contemporary writers, Ts'ao P'i focused on the distinctive features of their literary styles rather than on the moralistic nature of their works. This approach to literature amounted to the first appearance of literary criticism in the history of Chinese literature.

In his concentration on the distinctive features of various literary works, Ts'ao P'i discovered different genres in Chinese literature. For the first time in the history of Chinese literary criticism, literature was classified into four genres: report, treatise, epitaph, and poetry. In the classical Chinese literary tradition, the first two genres belong to prose, while the last two belong to verse. Earlier in the Han Dynasty, though writers had defined these terms linguistically, they had not undertaken a systematic study of the nature of these genres. Ts'ao P'i not only systematically discussed different kinds of literary forms but also explored their distinctive characteristics. Each genre, according to Ts'ao P'i, has its own special feature: a report should be elegant, a treatise should be rational, an epitaph, genuine, and a poem, beautiful. As each writer has his or her own unique talent, Ts'ao P'i notes, few writers can become adept at every genre. Consequently, Ts'ao P'i, a versatile writer himself, maintained that writers of varying talents should not belittle one another and that literary genres should not be placed in a hierarchical order.

Simple yet original, the literary theory of Ts'ao P'i had a tremendous influence on Chinese literature. Because of his position as emperor, his words had the effect of an edict in the empire that he had founded. During his lifetime Ts'ao P'i often summoned various scholars to his court in order to examine and discuss his own works. In 230, several years after his death, his son, who succeeded him on the throne, commanded that the writings of Ts'ao P'i be inscribed on stone tablets and placed at the entrance of the temple of the royal family. By virtue of political power, the literary theory of Ts'ao P'i therefore spread throughout China. His glorification of literature not only justified a writer's occupation but also created an atmosphere conducive to literary creativity.

Originally, when Ts'ao P'i equated literature with the ruling of a kingdom, he intended implicitly to divert his officials' attention from his usurpation of the throne. In addition to having a genuine love for literature, he needed to secure his own power by making literature an appealing substitute for the throne. He thus promoted literature with the ulterior motive of making politically minded officials think more of the value of literature than of the advantages of political power. In having this alternative outlet, these officials, Ts'ao P'i hoped, would not aspire to usurp the throne as he once had.

Regardless of his political motives, Ts'ao P'i's promotion of literature gave rise to a new era when literature flourished and also began to be appreciated more for its intrinsic worth than for its social function. Owing to his effort, the two centuries after his death witnessed the appearance of spectacular cultural development, created by the next five dynasties. The influence of Ts'ao P'i reached another climax in the tenth century. The founding emperor of the Sung Dynasty, T'ai Tzu (A.D. 960–976), followed the example of Ts'ao P'i in overtaking the throne as well as in issuing a policy which emphasized the importance of literature. This literature-oriented policy guided the development of the civilization of the Sung empire for more than three centuries.

With his literary criticism, Ts'ao P'i laid the foundation for later Chinese critics. His classification of literary genres has become the basic framework for further studies of the forms of classical Chinese literature. Moreover, his application of the term *Ch'i* to both the writer and the work has been so widely accepted that the term has become an essential concept in the criticism of literature and art in general. Most important, his "Tien lun lun wên" gave immediate birth to a long tradition of Chinese literary criticism.

## Principal criticism
"Yü Wang Lang shu," 217
"Yü Wu Chi shu," 217
"Tien lun lun wên," 220

## Other literary forms
In addition to gaining fame for his literary criticism and reigning as emperor, Ts'ao P'i is known as one of China's most renowned poets. His poetry, which is generally concerned with the sorrows and transience of life, is admired for its simple yet elegant style. Ts'ao P'i invented the poetic form that consists of seven characters in each line. Previously, Chinese poets had normally used four- or five-character lines. The new poetic form became popular among writers after Ts'ao P'i's reign as a result of the increasingly advanced cultural development in China. Allowing for a more sophisticated expression of thought for each line written, the form widened the range of possibilities for poetic expression. In addition to his poetic creations, Ts'ao P'i was well known for his songs, elegies, epitaphs, epistles, treatises, and edicts. Most of his works have been lost; what remains can be found in *Han wei*

liu-ch'ao pai-san ming-chia chi (c. 1630–1640; Chang P'u, editor).

## Further reading

Ch'en, Shou-yi. *Chinese Literature*, 1961.
Giles, Herbert A. *A History of Chinese Literature*, 1958.
Liu, James J. Y. *Chinese Theories of Literature*, 1975.
Liu, Wu-chi. *An Introduction to Chinese Literature*, 1966.
Rickett, Adele Austin. *Chinese Approaches to Literature from Confucius to Liang Ch'i-ch'ao*, 1978.

VINCENT YANG

*See also* Chinese Literary Theory; Liu Hsieh; Lu Chi

# Ki no Tsurayuki

Japanese critic and editor

**Born:** Kyoto?, Japan; c. 884
**Died:** Kyoto, Japan; c. 945

## Biography

Little is known about the family of Ki no Tsurayuki, and the years of his birth and death are uncertain. Though the Ki family was among the most distinguished of the Nara period (646–794), by the mid-ninth century, with the movement of the capital to Kyoto, the family's fortunes were eclipsed by the rise of the Fujiwara regents, forcing the Ki sons to seek advancement through scholarship and artistic accomplishment. As a young man, Tsurayuki devoted himself to the study of Chinese poetry, but he gained a reputation by excelling in Japanese poetry contests and was eventually appointed head of the imperial palace library. At the turn of the tenth century, along with Ki no Tomonori, Oshikochi no Mitsune, and Mibu no Tadamine, Tsurayuki was ordered by the emperor to compile the first official anthology of Japanese poetry, to which he added a preface written in the Japanese syllabary. In 930 he was appointed governor of the province of Tosa on the island of Shikoku, and on his return around 935 he wrote the *Tosa Diary*, describing the return passage to Kyoto. None of the official posts Tsurayuki held in his life was particularly distinguished, but the achievement of the *Kokinshū* gave him unrivaled authority in the composition of Japanese verse. Tsurayuki is believed to have died around 945.

## Influence

Along with Sugawara no Michizane, preeminent in Chinese poetry, Tsurayuki was the chief literary authority of the early Heian period (794–1185). He is credited with four original achievements of the first magnitude: his preface to the *Kokinshū* marks the birth of literary criticism in the Japanese language; the *Kokinshū* itself, of which he was the chief editor and principal poet, is the first imperial anthology of Japanese verse; his *Tosa Diary* represents the beginning of the poetic diary in Japanese; and his works in prose, chiefly the preface to the *Kokinshū* and the *Tosa Diary*, inaugurate *wabun*, prose in *hiragana* (the Japanese cursive syllabary), which was to be the medium of prose during the rest of Heian and flowed directly into the mainstream of prose thereafter. The expressive poetics he developed in the preface to the *Kokinshū*, occurring so early in the classical period, relieved subsequent writers and critics of the need to justify the expressive nature of literature.

## Analysis

Tsurayuki's contributions to Japanese literary criticism and his influence on the literary practice of subsequent centuries can be conveniently grouped around three "firsts": in the preface to the *Kokinshū*, (1) he wrote the first Japanese treatise on poetics and (2) provided the basis for subsequent expressive theories of literature, setting an enduring standard of literary taste; and in the *Tosa Diary*, (3) he initiated the genre of the poetic diary. To understand the significance of these contributions, something must be known about the early Heian era or classical period and its literary traditions.

In his three-volume *A History of Japan* (1958–1963), Bailey Sansom names the central quality of the Heian period as "the rule of taste," a shorthand notation for the striking aestheticism of the ruling aristocracy. During the rule of the Fujiwara regents the court nobility pursued the ideal of courtly elegance summed up in the word *miyabi*, the kind of aesthetic pleasures portrayed in Lady Murasaki's *Genji monogatari* (c. 1004; *The Tale of Genji*, 1925–1933, 1935, 1960, 1976): music, dance, painting, calligraphy, flower and moon watching, the blending of incense, but chiefly poetry.

The major poetic monument before the complete adaptation of the Chinese writing system to Japanese was the *Manyōshū* (c. 759; the *Manyōshū*, 1929–1969). It was written in a cumbersome mix of phonetic and semantic characters; the sheer difficulty of reading it prevented it from commanding an influence comparable to its position. The century and a half between the *Manyōshū* and the *Kokinshū* was marked in its early phase by a decline of the status of Japanese verse and an elevation of Chinese, with three imperial anthologies of Chinese verse appearing between 800 and 850. In the remainder of the century, however, as poets assimilated the techniques learned from Chinese poets of the Six Dynasties, the status of Japanese poetry rose. The compilation of the *Kokinshū* commemorates its resurgence and returns it officially to the public arena. Tsurayuki's preface expresses a critical consciousness of this resurgence, defining a theory and practice for Japanese poetry and legitimizing the theory by basing it on Chinese sources.

The preface offers the kind of poetics which M. H. Abrams in *The Mirror and the Lamp* (1953) labeled "expressive," centering on the poet. The key passage, which inscribed itself on the memory of posterity, is the opening paragraph:

> The seeds of Japanese poetry lie in the human heart and grow into leaves of ten thousand words. Many things happen to the people of this world, and all that they think and feel is given expression in description of things they see and hear. When we hear the warbling of the mountain thrush in the blossoms or the voice of the frog in the water, we know every living being has its song.

The heart as the fertile ground of poetry recalls William Wordsworth's expressive theory of spontaneous overflow in the 1800 preface to the *Lyrical Ballads* (1789, 1800). Yet Tsurayuki's evocation of the thrush and the frog do not fall into John Keats' "egotistic sublime," because these creatures do not become the poet. Rather, they possess a capacity for song which, putting them on a level with the poet, suggests an underlying equality of life forms, a notion characteristic of Japanese Buddhism and Shinto. Tsurayuki's expressive theory is powerfully restated in the *Tosa Diary*, a work to which the writing of poetry is central and which argues the centrality of art to life. Its narrator, contemplating the splendor of nature, finds it impossible not to compose a poem, explaining, "I do not set down these words, nor did I compose the poem, out of mere love of writing. Surely both in China and in Japan art is that which is created when we are unable to suppress our feelings."

The preface to the *Kokinshū* also argues that poetry has a "pragmatic" function, one that centers on the audience: "It is poetry which, without effort, moves heaven and earth, stirs the feelings of the invisible gods and spirits, smooths the relations of men and women, and calms the hearts of fierce warriors." The harmonizing of husband and wife is a didactic function (a subcategory of Abrams' "pragmatic"), whose origins can be traced to the *Lun-yü* (c. 551–479; *Analects of Confucius*, 1938). Poetry's ability to move the gods shows an even greater power to affect the audience. It should be emphasized that it is not the gods that speak through the poet, as in the Western tradition of inspiration; rather, the poet moves the gods through his or her own unaided talent. Just as the song of the frog is akin to human song, so the power of the poet shares in the divine: gods, humans, and frogs inhabit one world.

An additional contribution of Tsurayuki's preface is its introduction of three technical terms: *kotoba* ("diction"), *kokoro* ("feeling"), and *sama* ("style"). These emerge as part of Tsurayuki's poetic standard, an ideal reflected in the poems gathered in the *Kokinshū* and one accepted and elaborated by succeeding anthologies. A good poem was characterized by diction and feeling in proper balance: the words used should be only those Japanese (not Chinese) words accepted by tradition, but the feelings should be the

poet's own and arise from his or her unique situation or original perception. In his comments on the poet Ariwara no Narihira and five other contemporary poets, Tsurayuki uses the term *sama*, which refers in particular to the techniques learned from the Chinese poets of the Six Dynasties and assimilated to Japanese practice in the *Kokinshū*.

Style in the *Kokinshū* means the style of the *waka*, the classic thirty-one syllables patterned 5–7–5–7–7 (the precise term for the form is *tanka*, "short poem"). The emergence of the *waka* as a serious art form on a par with Chinese verse was tied to the question of style – the demonstration of the *waka*'s ability to absorb the wit and the techniques of Chinese poetry (including the *kakekotoba*, the "pivot word" or complex pun, and *engo*, word associations that create supplementary patterns of imagery), the whole sensibility summed up in the word *miyabi*, "courtly elegance."

The *Tosa Diary* is the first extant example of what was to become a characteristic genre of Japanese literature, the poetic diary, a form freely mixing poetry with prose narrative; it is arguably the first extant work of fiction in Japanese; together with the Japanese preface to the *Kokinshū* it is the first example of *wabun* Japanese prose written in *hiragana*, the medium of Japanese prose for the remainder of the Heian period. The *Tosa Diary*'s claim to be fiction opens a complex subject, and here it must suffice to note that its use of a first-person female narrator is a striking breakthrough in point of view.

The *Tosa Diary* looks toward the future with two faces: one turned toward the poetic diary written by the great women writers of the later Heian period, which developed into the travel diary, culminating in the masterpieces of Matsuo Bashō, and the other turned toward the novel, first in the *monogatari* tradition given classic form by the author of *The Tale of Genji*, then in modern times in the *watakushi shōsetsu* (the "I novel"), with its autobiographical basis.

Yet Tsurayuki's chief influence and legacy to literary posterity derives from the expressive theory of his preface to the *Kokinshū* and the rules of taste, the aesthetic of *miyabi*, to which its poems became a permanent monument. The expressive theory may be traced through two key points on its way to assimilation within the general culture. The first is the famous passage in *The Tale of Genji*, where Genji discusses the art of the novel:

> I have a theory of my own about what this art of the novel is, and how it came into being . . . it happens because the storyteller's own experience of men and things, whether for good or ill – not only what he has passed through himself, but even events which he has only witnessed or been told of – has moved him to an emotion so passionate that he can no longer keep it shut up in his heart.

Given the importance of poetry to the *monogatari*, it should not be surprising that Tsurayuki's expressive poetics thus passes into the theory of the Japanese novel, helping to account for that lyric strain which is one of its chief characteristics. A second key instance, this one specific to poetic theory, is the preface to the *Kindai Shūka* (c. 1209; superior poems of our times) by Fujiwara no Teika (1162–1241), joint compiler of the second great imperial anthology of classical verse, the *Shin kokinshū* (c. 1205; the new collection of ancient and modern poems). Teika writes, "In the expression of the emotions originality merits the first consideration. That is, one should look for sentiments unsung by others and sing them. The words used, however, should be old ones." The authority of Teika has probably been the greatest of any Japanese literary critic, and his echo of Tsurayuki's expressive theory signals its lasting influence.

The influence of the style embodied in the poems of Tsurayuki and other *Kokinshū* poets was decisive for the twenty imperial anthologies which followed (the last in 1433). Teika makes the diction of the *Kokinshū* the classic standard when he restricts diction to the old words, meaning the words of the *Kokinshū*; it is noteworthy in this regard that the foremost technique which the *Shin kokinshū* adds to the repertoire of the *Kokinshū* is the *honkadori*, the technique of allusive variation, for the allusions of the *Shin kokinshū* are to the poems of the *Kokinshū*. Teika not only lent his authority to the view of the *Kokinshū* as the source book for *waka*, but also in compiling the *Haykunin isshu* (c. 1235; one hundred poets, one poem each) he transmitted its aesthetic and twenty-four of its poems, including one by Tsurayuki, to popular culture. The *Hyakunin isshu* became a traditional card game which remains popular today, with the result that a large part of the population knows its poems by heart.

The poetic mainstream inaugurated by the *Kokinshū* and defined by its Japanese preface flows uninterrupted until the late nineteenth century when poets such as Yosano Tekkan (1873–1935) and Masaoka Shiki (1867–1902) called for a return to the *masuraoburi* ("masculinity" or "martial spirit") of the *Manyōshū* and for a modern poetics free of the rhetorical devices of the *Kokinshū*. In *Utayomi ni atauru sho* (1898; letters to the Tanka poets) Shiki writes: "Tsurayuki is a bad poet and the *Kokinshū* is a stupid collection." In particular he rebelled against the limited diction of the *Kokinshū* tradition, declaring, "Any word used literarily is a part of the Japanese poetic vocabulary." Yet the aesthetic of *miyabi* defined by Tsurayuki has outlasted its critics, for the imagery of nature defined by the *Kokinshū* – the transience of the cherry blossoms, the colors of the autumn leaves, the places made famous by poetic association – has become part of the consciousness of the ordinary Japanese. Here again it was Teika who guaranteed Tsurayuki's permanence: in 1970 Teika's *Hyakunin isshu*, that popular monument to the tradition inaugurated by the *Kokinshū*, was sealed in a time capsule (now at Osaka Castle); with other artifacts of twentieth-century culture, it is scheduled to be opened in the year 6970, after the passage of 5,000 years.

## Principal criticism
Preface to the *Kokinshū*, c. 905 ("Kanajo: The Japanese Preface," in *Kokinshū: A Collection of Poems Ancient and Modern*, 1984)
Preface to the *Oigawa gyōkōwaka*, c. 907
Preface to the *Shinsen Wakashū*, c. 934

## Other major works and literary forms
Ki no Tsurayuki was the chief editor and principal poet of the *Kokinshū*, also editing the two lesser collections referred to above. Apart from the famous preface to the *Kokinshū*, his principal prose work is the *Tosa Diary*, an example of the poetic diary combining narrative and poetry. Its discussions of poetry extend the expressive theory of the preface to the *Kokinshu*, and later generations viewed it as a handbook for writing poetry. Tsurayuki contributed one hundred and two poems to the famous collection, more than any other poet, and later imperial anthologies preserve about three hundred and fifty more of his poems, with another fifty contained in privately compiled anthologies.

MISCELLANEOUS
*Tosa Nikki*, c. 935 (*Tosa Diary*, 1969)

## Further reading
Brower, Robert H., and Earl Miner. *Japanese Court Poetry*, 1961.
Kato, Shūichi. *A History of Japanese Literature*. Vol. 1, *The First Thousand Years*, 1979.
McCullough, Helen Craig. *Brocade by Night: Kokin Wakashū and the Court Style in Japanese Classical Poetry*, 1985.
——. *Kokin Wakashū: The First Imperial Anthology of Japanese Poetry, with "Tosa Nikki" and "Shinsen Waka,"* 1985.
Miner, Earl, ed. and tr. *Japanese Poetic Diaries*, 1969.
Rodd, Laurel Rasplica, and Mary Catherine Henkenius, eds. and trs. *Kokinshū: A Collection of Poems Ancient and Modern*, 1984.

WAYNE POUNDS

*See also* Japanese Literary Criticism; Yoshimoto

# Iurii Tynianov
## Russian theorist

**Born:** Rezhitsa (modern Rezekne), Latvia, Russia; October 6, 1894
**Died:** Moscow, U.S.S.R.; December 20, 1943

## Biography
Iurii Tynianov was born into a doctor's family; he lived in Vitebsk Province and studied from 1912 to 1918 in a Pskov secondary school. He undertook a program of study in Slavic languages at Petrograd University and graduated

from the departments of history and philology in 1918. His seminars at the university included such fellow students as Boris Eikhenbaum and Boris Tomashevskii, who were early exponents of Viktor Shklovskii's Russian Formalist theory. Yet he was also urged to retain a historical focus in his studies by a traditional instructor, S. A. Vengerov. After leaving the university, Tynianov joined Opoiaz, the Society for the Study of Poetic Language, and embarked on the most important phase of his career.

Tynianov's first published work, *Dostoevskii i Gogol'* *(k teorii parodii)* (Dostoevskii and Gogol' (toward a theory of parody)), established his interest in the intertextual literary system by treating the relation of two key prose writers. While a member of the faculty at the Institute for the History of Arts from 1921 to 1930, Tynianov continued to pursue the historic aspect of literary texts and systems, producing the book that was to cement his reputation, *Problema stikhotvornogo iazyka* (1924; *The Problem of Verse Language*, 1981), as well as a series of extremely interesting essays on problems of general literary and film theory. The literary essays were collected in a volume entitled *Arkhaisty i novatory* (archaists and innovators), while the film essays appeared in such classic collections as *Poetika kino* (1927; *The Poetics of Cinema*, 1982), edited by Eikhenbaum.

By 1929 Tynianov was convinced that the mechanistic approach to formal analysis was dead, not only because it was officially under attack but also because it was lacking the promise of further development on account of its limited critical basis. He traveled first to Berlin, seeking treatment for the sclerosis that would later cause his death, and then to Prague, where he lectured for the Prague Linguistic Circle on literary evolution. In Prague he exchanged ideas with Jan Mukařovský and decided to coauthor with Roman Jakobson their later celebrated "Voprosy izucheniia literaturi iazyka" (1929; theses on the study of language and literature). Though these theses failed in their intended task of reviving Opoiaz, the work has since been translated into more than ten languages and is a fundamental text in the transition from Formalism to structuralism in literary studies.

Through the 1930s Tynianov worked successfully as both a creative writer and an author of film scripts, sometimes adapting his own novellas and other times concentrating on the historical experience of some major figure. Typical of the latter is his fascination with Aleksandr Pushkin. He began working on *Pushkin* in 1932, and by the time of his death he had proceeded, in the course of several hundred pages and three separate volumes, only to the great writer's "youth." In 1936 Tynianov again left the Soviet Union to seek medical help, traveling to Paris. In 1939 he was awarded the Order of the Red Banner of Labor for his achievements in historical fiction, having re-fashioned the genre to fit the ruling doctrine of Socialist Realism. He also translated Heinrich Heine for a poetry series.

In 1941, with the Nazi invasion in process, Tynianov was evacuated from Leningrad to Perm. He was living in Moscow in 1943, working on his Pushkin manuscript, when he died.

## Influence

Tynianov had considerable influence upon the dissemination of late Russian Formalist concepts. In particular, he played a vital role in the transmission of Formalism from Moscow to Prague, where it was taken up by the Prague School linguists and theorists such as Jan Mukařovský and Felix Vodička. Tynianov's reputation as a novelist permitted his critical work to be reexamined in the Soviet Union during the postwar era, when he became an important precursor for the Tartu School semiologists. Perhaps no less vital was Tynianov's part in the international rediscovery of Formalism, carried out by scholars such as the French structuralist Tzvetan Todorov and the German scholar Juri Striedter. Such remarks as Tynianov's suggestion that "literary history, the elucidation of the character of the literary work and its factors, is a kind of dynamic archeology" anticipate the later, much more acclaimed theoretical viewpoints of French scholars such as Michel Foucault.

## Analysis

Tynianov's principal contribution to Russian literary study was his response to the isolating tendency of early Formalism, which sought to establish the autonomy of literary works and of literary art. Tynianov's was always an informed, sympathetic reply to the careful reading that the Formalist method encouraged, but he consistently refused to abstract the work from its historical and especially its literary context. History was for Tynianov part and parcel of any contemporary moment, and he specialized in problems such as parody, problems which involve the relation of historical texts to new works.

Tynianov's first published work, on Fedor Dostoevskii and Nikolai Gogol', has been cited by Victor Erlich as an example of the way an individual question tended to mushroom into a general problem in the development of Formalist theory. Tynianov suggests in the essay that the bombastic utterances of Foma Opiskin, an important character in Dostoevskii's *Selo Stepanchikovo i ego obitateli* (1859; *The Friend of the Family*, 1887), parody critical sections of Gogol''s *Vybrannye mesta iz perepiski s druz'iami* (1847; *Selected Passages from Correspondence with Friends*, 1969). The notion of quotation, whether parodic or more allusive, forms the foundation for the development of Tynianov's theory of literature and the literary experience as an emergent system. He would return to the problem of parody in a later essay, not printed until 1977, and his whole process of historical writing in the 1930s involved the incorporation of historical quotation into novelistic material.

Tynianov's primary interest as a theorist, however, was not parody but the structure of the literary sequence. This received its most complete, most famous treatment in *The Problem of Verse Language*. Tynianov examines the material and the "constructive principle" of literary language in the book, emphasizing the time-related aspects of each. Rather than conceiving structure as a static, architectural aspect of the complete work, implicit in its very origins, Tynianov declared that

> the unity of the work is not a closed, symmetrical intactness, but an unfolding, dynamic integrity. Between its elements is not the static sign of equality and addition, but the dynamic sign of correlation and integration. The form of the literary work must be recognized as a dynamic phenomenon.

Tynianov's emphasis upon the work as an event in progress provided a healthy alternative to Shklovskii's insistence on the work as the "sum of its devices." Moreover, in his view of the various strands of a work entering into conflict and opposition, he anticipated the Prague School's focus on relational poetics. Formal disagreements, and conflict between sense and form, tend to energize a work rather than cause its disintegration. As Tynianov notes, "Dynamic form is not generated by means of combination or merger . . . but by means of interaction, and, consequently, the pushing forward of one group of factors at the expense of another." The idea of the dominant component, so important to early Formalist studies of devices such as *siuzhet*, or plot, is here placed in the context of the work itself, so that dominance is seen in relative terms rather than as a mechanical absolute.

Corollary to this concept is the principle of "deformation" that Tynianov introduces to account for the influence of the dominant component – the "constructive principle" – upon the remaining aspects of the literary work. Tynianov's explication of the dynamic of semantic deformation in verse is a fascinating example of his thesis:

> Verse is revealed as a system of *complex interaction, and not of combination*. Metaphorically speaking, verse is revealed as a struggle of factors, rather than a collaboration of factors. It becomes clear that the specific plus of poetry lies precisely in the area of this interaction, the foundation of which is the constructive significance of rhythm and its deforming role relative to factors of another order.

The relation of poetic meter to the sense of verse language becomes the primary subject of Tynianov's book *The Problem of Verse Language*, and this "antinomy of poetic creation" is established as the defining "dialectic of form" for the idea of verse. The continuity of flow implicit in the formal patterns of verse restructures the sense of the words used and disrupts the normal intonational patterns of other, more referential, kinds of language use. Rhythm versus sense is the "minimum of conditions" that creates the effect of verse. language, even in borderline forms such as free verse, the prose poem, and the verse novel, where the tensions are emphasized by their very denial. The accepted meanings of words are "deformed" by the verse sequence, the power of rhythm, which Tynianov isolates into four primary factors:

1. the unity of the verse series;
2. its compactness;
3. the dynamization of the vocal material; and
4. the successiveness of the vocal material in verse.

These four factors provided the formal basis for Tynianov's response to the Saussurean distinction between *langue* and *parole*, which is probably the most important contribution of Tynianov to Slavic poetics (and the reason its exponents remained considerably more sophisticated than their French counterparts in techniques of literary and cultural analysis).

Tynianov takes issue with the Saussurean idea of the isolated word, or *langue*, the objective sense of words. As Peter Steiner emphasized in his appraisal of Tynianov, Ferdinand de Saussure's static notion of the language system is methodological fiction, used to establish synchronic linguistics as an acceptable field of study. Tynianov denies the need for such a heuristic convenience, insisting that language has no existence outside usage, that "a word does not have one definite meaning. It is a chameleon, in which not only various shades, but even various colors arise with each usage." Taking as his case in point the various uses of the word "man," Tynianov opposes the static, lexicographical definition with the contemporary, deconstructive notion that "the word 'man' may be a *play* of meanings." In this regard, he also uses the example of the pun, which creates a tension between two meanings of the same word – the divergence and reconvergence of meanings that the contemporary critic Michael Riffaterre calls "syllepsis." Rather than a definitive meaning, the word enjoys a place in a flexible field of meaning within the text, within the literary tradition, and within language itself. Tynianov calls the nucleus of this meaning the principal expression of the work, a phrase which has unfortunately been translated as "principal sign" in the English version of the book. Consequently, the conclusion of Tynianov regarding the influence of meter upon sense reads:

> The rhythmical verse series presents an entire system of conditions which distinctively influence the principal and secondary signs of meanings and the appearance of oscillating signs.

The remainder of Tynianov's study then shows how various conventions of verse, such as rhymes, puns, names, and "equivalents" (nonverbal markers), deform the sense of the words in poetry.

Tynianov's other theoretical contributions come in the form of occasional essays, of which two are particularly important. The first of these is his essay "Literaturny fakt" (1924; literary fact). Here he suggests that the principle of "literariness," so essential to the Formalist argument for the autonomy of literature, had been misconceived. Rather than locate that idea of literariness in the thing itself, the literary artifact, Tynianov argues that literariness can only be realized in the process of perception, that is, during its social, relational life: "Literature is a speech construction perceived precisely qua construction, i.e., literature is a *dynamic speech construction*." In pointing out that construction itself is the constitutive factor of literature, Tynianov verges on the functional linguistic perspective that would be developed from Karl Bühler's organon model into Jakobson's acclaimed definition of poetic function as the focus within the message on the message itself.

In the second of these key essays, "O literaturnoi evoliutsii" (1927; "On Literary Evolution," 1971), Tynianov develops the idea that the historical system of literature provides a key context for the recognition of the literary work as such: "The literary epoch, the literary present, is not at all a static system opposed to the dynamic, evolving historical series. The same historical struggle of different layers and formations which exists in the diachronic historical series goes on in the present." Implicit in the evolution of the literary system and the literary work is the reader's knowledge of – memory of – its past and its literary relations. Tynianov states his assumption baldly, as the only premise from which the study of literature can proceed: "It must be agreed that a literary work is a system, as is literature itself." This system is not absolutely autonomous but relatively so: "Before us is the infinite variety of literary phenomena, a plurality of systems of interacting factors. However, in these systems are generalizing lines and divisions, embracing a great quantity of phenomena."

Implicit in Tynianov's theory is the whole notion of the intertext, the relational aspect of textuality that provides the linchpin of postmodernist poetics. There is no absolute closure but only a discrete series of conventional borders that allows the work to open endlessly outward or collapse inward to the least detail. All combinations are not exhausted by the contemporary moment's complexity; instead, the present state of the system provides a changing context within which the novelty of poetic effect can be continuously and effectively created: "Evaluation itself must be freed from its subjective coloring, and the 'value' of a given literary phenomenon must be considered as having an 'evolutionary significance and character.'" Tynianov's emphasis on historical problems encouraged him to emphasize novelty as the highest criterion of literary value, making his theory an extremely useful tool for the analysis of the avant-garde (despite his own fascination with nineteenth-century problems).

Tynianov's contribution to the theory of film also bears mention, since it is entirely consistent with his general critical theory and had an important role in the self-conscious development of cinematic technique in Russia. He wrote primarily about the black-and-white silent films of his era, and, like many other Formalist commentators on film, he tended to emphasize the creative challenge of its primitive form rather than lament its lack of representational "authenticity." As with his analysis of verse, Tynianov emphasized the energy of the formal conflicts within the art:

The poverty of cinema, its flatness and its colourlessness are in fact its constructive essentials: this poverty does not demand new devices to fill it out, but new devices are created by it, grow on its basis. The flatness of film (which still does not deprive it of perspective), this technical 'failing' is expressed in the art of cinema through the positive constructive principles of simultaneity of several sequences of visual images, on the basis of which a quite new interpretation of gesture and movement is achieved.

Maintaining his interest in the time sequence of art, Tynianov pays careful attention to the development of montage in relation to considerations of plot and style. He views the dramatic and technical aspects of film as existing in a kind of constructive antinomy, like the conflict between rhythm and sense that is the "dialectic of form" underlying verse. Tynianov chooses many examples from films that he wrote and emphasizes the point that "the lack of work on theory leads to even more critical errors in practice." If, as he maintains in *The Problem of Verse Language*, "the task of literary history is . . . the baring of form," then film in its stage of technical development needs to stress the immanent development of its own forms and devices. Tynianov's essay "Ob osnovakh kino" (1927; "The Fundamentals of Cinema") anticipates in range and interest the later, more mature semiotics of film written by Christian Metz and Iurii Lotman.

Tynianov's contributions to literary and film theory were first recognized in the West in the 1960s. In his concept of literary history and literary experience as evolving systems, he anticipated many of the primary issues of contemporary practice. His analysis of the relational effects of the different components of an art work, his idea of primary expression (so similar to the notion of "semantic gesture"), and his emphasis upon the disruption and renewal of habitual perceptions in art all confirm his place as a primary theorist of the early modern era – one who pointed the way toward the future of literary studies.

## Principal criticism

*Dostoevskii i Gogol' (k teorii parodii)*, 1921
*Problema stikhotvornogo iazyka*, 1924 (*The Problem of Verse Language*, 1981)

*Arkhaisty i novatory,* 1929
"Voprosy izucheniia literatury i iazyka," 1929 (with Roman
   Jakobson)
*Poetika, istoriia literatury, kino,* 1977

## Other major works and literary forms

During the 1920s, when changes in Soviet policy began
to exert ideological pressure upon Iurii Tynianov and his
Russian Formalist colleagues, he switched his emphasis
from critical to creative writing, producing three screenplays – *Shinel'* (1926; the overcoat), *S.V.D.* (1927; the club
of the big deed), and *Poruchik Kizhe* (1934; Lieutenant
Kije) – and a series of acclaimed historical novels. The
historical novels address either scholarly concerns or literary
values. *Kiukhlia* (1925), for example, focuses on the
Decembrist W. K. Küchelbecker. The most interesting from
the standpoint of literary criticism and theory are the three-
part, unfinished work *Pushkin* (1936–1943) and *Smert'
Vazir-Mukhtara* (1929), the latter being a treatment of the
life of the early Russian dramatist Aleksandr Griboedov
which was unfortunately abridged in its English translation,
*Death and Diplomacy in Persia* (1938), to eliminate much
of the literary commentary. Tynianov's works are considered standards of Russian historical prose, yet his sensitivity to historical processes is a direct result of the
theoretical experimentation that he undertook during his
Formalist period. He also translated a number of poems by
Heinrich Heine.

NOVELS
*Kiukhlia,* 1925
*Smert' Vazir-Mukhtara,* 1929 (*Death and Diplomacy in Persia,*
   1938)
*Pushkin,* 1936–1943 (3 volumes)

SHORT FICTION
"Podporuchik Kizhe," 1927 ("Second Lieutenant Likewise," 1953)
"Voskovaya persona," 1930
"Maloletnii Vitushishnikov," 1933

SCREENPLAYS
*Shinel',* 1926
*S.V.D.,* 1927
*Poruchik Kizhe,* 1934

## Further reading

Broekman, Jan M. *Structuralism: Moscow-Prague-Paris,* 1974.
Erlich, Victor. *Russian Formalism: History-Doctrine,* 1980.
Jameson, Fredric. *The Prison-House of Language: A Critical
   Account of Structuralism and Russian Formalism,* 1972.
Matejka, Ladislav, and Krystyna Pomorska. *Reading in Russian
   Poetics: Formalist and Structuralist Views,* 1978.
Steiner, Peter. *Russian Formalism: A Metapoetics,* 1984.
Striedter, Juri. "The Russian Formalist Theory of Literary
   Evolution," in *PTL: A Journal for Descriptive Poetics and
   Theory of Literature.* III (1978), pp. 1–24.
Todorov, Tzvetan. "Some Approaches to Russian Formalism," in
   *Russian Formalism,* 1973. Edited by Stephen Bann and John
   Bowlt.

MICHAEL L. QUINN

*See also* Prague School; Russian Formalism; Todorov

# U

## Miguel de Unamuno y Jugo

Spanish philosopher, writer, and critic

**Born:** Bilbao, Spain; September 29, 1864
**Died:** Salamanca, Spain; December 31, 1936

### Biography

Miguel de Unamuno y Jugo was born on September 29, 1864, in Bilbao, Spain, the third of six children. His father, Felix Unamuno, was a baker, and his mother, Salomé de Jugo, was Felix's niece. After completing his secondary education in Bilbao, Unamuno enrolled at the University of Madrid, where he completed his studies, writing a dissertation on the development of Basque language and culture and receiving his doctorate in 1884. For the next few years he supported himself as a tutor and newspaper writer and prepared himself to compete for a university position. After several attempts he won an appointment as professor of Greek at the University of Salamanca in 1891, and that same year he married Concepción Lizarranga, his childhood sweetheart. The couple had nine children, eight of whom survived childhood.

Concerned for the fate of his country – during Unamuno's young adulthood, Spanish society had been charged with political tensions – and seeking answers to questions regarding the interplay between religious faith and individual identity, Unamuno began to formulate some of the ideas for which he became famous. He published his first insights in such works as *En torno al casticismo* (1895, a series of essays urging the modernization of Spanish institutions, and *Amor y pedagogía* (1902; love and pedagogy), a novel that explores the conflict between reason and faith.

In 1900 he was appointed rector of the University of Salamanca, a post he held until 1914, when he was dismissed for political reasons. He was exiled to the Canary Islands in 1924, after expressing his opposition to King Alfonso XIII and the dictatorship of Primo de Rivera, established with royal approval in 1923. From 1925 until 1930 Unamuno lived in exile in France, returning to Spain to reclaim the rectorship of the University of Salamanca offered to him this second time by the government of the Spanish Republic. He was named rector for life in 1934, following his retirement from teaching. After the outbreak of the Spanish Civil War in 1936, Unamuno withdrew support and openly opposed the ideology and tactics of Francisco Franco and the Falangist Party, for which he was censured. He died on December 31, 1936, while under house arrest.

### Influence

Although Unamuno's theory was for the most part presented unsystematically, his ideas – emphasis on the individual, on humankind as an end in itself, the conflict between faith and reason and the need for a "leap of faith" to overcome skepticism, the need for the committed life in the face of the immanence of death – are powerful currents that have found their way into the thinking of later theorists.

An innovator and a dissenter, he was the most outstanding member of what came to be called the Generation of '98, which was marked by a determination to seek the regeneration of Spain through new principles. Unamuno's views on language – as a mode of being, an actual rather than symbolic embodiment of an idea – have influenced such later thinkers as Maurice Merleau-Ponty and Martin Heidegger.

### Analysis

Unamuno, a learned, successful, and respected writer, nevertheless scorned what he considered the "professionalization of writing," by which he meant the strict adherence of writers to a rigid system. He criticized the excessive dependence on aesthetic motifs, the frivolity, and the "sonorous vacuities" of modernists such as Rubén Darío. Unamuno emphasized the priority of content over form, the ideas expressed in a work rather than the perfection with which these ideas are expressed. Scorning labels, he claimed for himself the label of "ideoclast," claiming to break in ideas as though they were boots. In his own writing Unamuno displayed wide-ranging thematic interests and concerns and a willingness to express himself in a variety of forms. He wrote about politics, religion, philosophy, art, and literature; he was also an accomplished writer of fiction. He was an enthusiastic reader of the English poets

Samuel Taylor Coleridge, Alfred, Lord Tennyson, William Wordsworth, Robert Browning, and John Keats, and an ardent admirer of Walt Whitman's poetry. He showed keen interest in the novelists Benito Pérez Galdós, Honoré de Balzac, Gustave Flaubert, and Émile Zola, but found serious flaws in the content of their work. He was a faithful admirer of the theater of Henrik Ibsen and believed that Lope de Vega y Carpio was Spain's greatest playwright. He was also the first European author to recognize the merits of José Hernández's two-part poem on the gaucho, *El gaucho Martín Fierro* (1872) and *La vuelta de Martín Fierro* (1879), translated into English in 1935 as *Martín Fierro*.

Perhaps because of Unamuno's strong opposition to specialization, he did not develop a systematic theory of criticism, nor did he use any particular principles of analysis in his many essays and commentaries. Both in his philosophical writings and in his fiction, he was preoccupied with questions emerging out of his need to resolve certain personal and religious doubts and his longing for immortality. His sense of the conflict between the requirements of human existence and the requirements of reason produced in him a sense of perennial agony – at the uncertainty of existence and the tragic nature of life – a condition he considered universal. Unamuno's writing was the medium through which he could express his deeply felt concerns; his work was the public expression of his internal struggles.

Inevitably, then, a highly personal philosophy and literary criticism converge in Unamuno. An early example of this convergence is his *Vida de Don Quijote y Sancho* (1905; *The Life of Don Quixote and Sancho*, 1927). Ostensibly a critical analysis of Miguel de Cervantes' masterpiece, Unamuno's commentary is actually the deliberate appropriation of the life and character of Don Quixote as a metaphor for Spain, representing Unamuno's hope for the redemption and regeneration of a defeated and demoralized society.

Several of Unamuno's central themes can be detected in his study of Don Quixote: his sense of the priority of the individual, his emphasis on personal integrity, the conflict of reason and faith, the idea of commitment to an ideal which demands a blind leap of faith in order to achieve an authentic human existence. Added to his idea of life as a tenuous cluster of experiences bordered by the two mysteries of birth and death, these ideas exemplify Unamuno's existentialism, born out by his deep admiration for the existentialist thinker Søren Kierkegaard.

The relationship between an author and the characters he or she brings into existence, a theme that emerged in Unamuno's treatment of Don Quixote, received careful scrutiny in his 1914 novel *Niebla* (*Mist*, 1928). While this conceit would elicit much attention in European letters after the 1921 premier of Luigi Pirandello's *Sei personaggi in cerca d'autore* (*Six Characters in Search of an Author*, 1922), Unamuno preceded the Italian playwright by a number of years in exploring some of the implications of this complicated relationship. The plot of *Mist* centers on Augusto, an irresolute man, who at the prime of his life is disappointed and duped by a woman whom he thinks he loves and wants to marry. When he decides to end his life, he calls on Unamuno for advice. Unamuno rejects the plan, arguing that as a fictional character Augusto has no right to such autonomy. Augusto retorts by questioning Unamuno's own reality – suggesting the inevitable existence of an ultimate Creator – and the two argue the merits of their respective positions until the author decides that Augusto must indeed die, not as a suicide but from a heart attack, a solution Augusto finds terrifying; he is, however, powerless and must accept the death decreed for him by his creator.

Unamuno saw himself as being on the threshold of a new literary era. He wanted to create a kind of novel that would express his philosophy of existence. Art is the expression of the vital, and life itself is a form of fiction. Art and life reach their fullest expressions when both attain their authentic level of creativity. This creativity cannot be achieved if the novel is subject merely to the laws of reason, such as causality. He criticizes the realistic novel as merely showing events occurring that have been determined by previous events:

> The people of the realists are puppets dressed up in costumes and moving about as their strings are pulled, and with phonographs wound up somewhere in their insides to repeat remarks which their puppet-master has picked up on the sidewalks or in the cafés, and jotted down in a note-book.

Instead of springing full-fledged into the predetermined action of the novel, the characters must, in a sense, create their own reality, they must have their own independence: the novel takes shape as the characters create themselves. In inventing their characters, authors are revealing themselves to themselves, and in doing so are becoming themselves. This is also true of the readers of the novel: as they take part in the experience of self-creation undergone by the author, readers, too, undergo a change. Thus, author, character, and reader share the responsibility for the creation of art. According to Unamuno, "Every reader who in reading a novel worries about how the characters will finish, without worrying about how *he* will finish, does not deserve to have his curiosity satisfied."

In the creation of the novel, the guiding principle is that of spontaneous vitality, achieved by what Unamuno calls the "come what may" method. As a people create themselves through the workings of chance, so does a work of art. The *nivola* (the term was created by Unamuno to distinguish it from the realistic novel) is characterized by freedom of invention, which, guided by chance, leads to unexpected situations. Neither life nor art can be created through the use of reason. Art is a part of life and is created in the same way. Life and fiction are equally real and equally fictitious. The highest form of art is that which enables the person, both writer and reader, to achieve that which it was in him or her to become. This, too, is the aim of art.

Unamuno was an innovator in his writing, experimenting with several genres, refusing to be bound by rigid definitions. He created characters who, like Don Quixote, assume an existence independent of, and challenging to, their author/creator, foreshadowing the work of such twentieth-century writers as Pirandello and Jorge Luis Borges. Finally, Unamuno was among the first to recognize the importance of Kierkegaard and to adapt his ideas to his own theories. He was a pioneer of existentialism – opening the way to territories explored by only a few daring minds, making them accessible to those who would follow.

## Principal criticism
*En torno al casticismo*, 1895
*Vida de Don Quijote y Sancho, según Miguel de Cervantes Saavedra, explicada y comentada por Miguel de Unamuno*, 1905 (*The Life of Don Quixote and Sancho According to Miguel de Cervantes Saavedra Expounded with Comment by Miguel de Unamuno*, 1927)
*Soliloquios y conversaciones*, 1911
*Contra esto y aquello*, 1912
*La agonía del Cristianismo*, 1925 in French, 1931 in Spanish (*The Agony of Christianity*, 1928)
*Cómo se hace una novela*, 1927 (*How to Make a Novel*, 1976)
*Ensayos*, 1942 (2 volumes)

## Other major works and literary forms
Miguel de Unamuno y Jugo was an accomplished philosopher, essayist, journalist, poet, novelist, and dramatist. He published more than thirty separate book titles, evenly divided among all genres. Much of his international reputation rests on his philosophical ideas – expounded in such works as *Del sentimiento trágico de la vida en los hombres y en los pueblos* (1913; *The Tragic Sense of Life in Men and Peoples*, 1921) – and on a number of novels such as *Niebla* (1914; *Mist*, 1928), *Abel Sánchez: Una historia de pasión* (1917; *Abel Sánchez*, 1947), and *San Manuel Bueno, mártir* (1931; *Saint Manuel Bueno, Martyr*, 1956). Unamuno, however, considered himself a poet, arguing that there was little difference between philosophy and poetry. His substantial poetic output – there are seven separate collections of his verse – represents a deliberate reaction against the aesthetic code that placed artistic considerations and form before content, as pronounced by the Nicaraguan poet Rubén Darío, the apostle of *Modernismo*. Unamuno's works have been collected in sixteen volumes as *Obras completas* (1959–1964).

### NOVELS
*Paz en la guerra*, 1897 (*Peace in War*, 1983)
*Amor y pedagogía*, 1902
*Niebla*, 1914 (*Mist: A Tragicomic Novel*, 1928)
*Abel Sánchez: Una historia de pasión*, 1917 (*Abel Sanchez*, 1947)

*Tres novelas ejemplares y un prólogo*, 1920 (*Three Exemplary Novels and a Prologue*, 1930)
*La tía Tula*, 1921 (*Aunt Tula*, 1976)
*San Manuel Bueno, mártir*, 1931 (*Saint Manuel Bueno, Martyr*, 1956)
*Dos novelas cortas*, 1961 (James Russell Stamm and Herbert Eugene Isar, editors)

### SHORT FICTION
*El espejo de la muerte*, 1913
*Soledad y otros cuentos*, 1937

### PLAYS
*La esfinge*, written 1898, published 1909
*La venda*, written 1899, published 1913
*La difunta*, 1910
*El pasado que vuelve*, written 1910, published 1923
*Fedra*, written 1910, published 1918 (*Phaedra*, 1959)
*La princesa doña Lambra*, 1913
*Soledad*, written 1921, published 1953
*Raquel encadenada*, written 1921, published 1926
*El otro*, written 1926, published 1932 (*The Other*, 1947)
*Sombras de sueño: o, Tulio Montalbán y Julio Maceda*, 1927
*El hermano Juan: o, El mundo es teatro*, written 1927, published 1934
*Teatro completo*, 1959, 1973

### POETRY
*Poesías*, 1907
*Rosario de sonetos líricos*, 1911
*El Cristo de Velázquez*, 1920 (*The Christ of Velázquez*, 1951)
*Rimas de dentro*, 1923
*Teresa*, 1924
*Romancero del destierro*, 1928
*Poemas*, 1952
*Cancionero, Diario poético*, 1953

### NONFICTION
*De la enseñanza superior en España*, 1899
*Nicodemo el fariseo*, 1899
*Tres ensayos*, 1900
*Paisajes*, 1902
*De mi país*, 1903
*Recuerdos de niñez y de mocedad*, 1908
*Mi religión y otros ensayos breves*, 1910
*Por tierras de Portugal y de España*, 1911
*Del sentimiento trágico de la vida en los hombres y en los pueblos*, 1913 (*The Tragic Sense of Life in Men and Peoples*, 1921)
*La ciudad de Henoc*, 1941
*Cuenca ibérica*, 1943
*Paisajes del alma*, 1944
*La enormidad de España*, 1945
*Visiones y commentarios*, 1949

### MISCELLANEOUS
*Obras completas*, 1959–1964 (16 volumes)

## Further reading
Barcia, José Rubia, and M. A. Zeitlin, eds. *Unamuno: Creator and Creation*, 1967.
Durán, Gloria. "What Is to Be Done About History? A Comparative Study of the Insights of Tolstoy and Unamuno," in *Confluencia: Revista Hispánica de Cultura y Literatura*. II, no. 1 (1986), pp. 4–9.

Hynes, Laura. "La tia Tula: Forerunner of Radical Feminism," in *Hispanofila*. 117 (1996), pp. 45–54.

Ilie, Paul. *Unamuno: An Existential View of Self and Society*, 1967.

——. "Autophagous Spain and the European Other," in *Hispania*. LXVII, no. 1 (1984), pp. 28–35.

Kirkpatrick, Judith A. " 'La lengua pantalónica?': Unamuno and Women's Relationship to the Literary Text," in *Siglo XX–20th Century*. 15, nos. 1–2 (1997), pp. 95–108.

Labanyi, Jo. "Masculinity and the Family in Crisis: Reading Unamuno through Film Noir," in *Romance Studies*. 26 (1995), pp. 7–21.

Nozick, Martin. *Miguel de Unamuno*, 1971.

Perez, Janet. "Rereading *Amor y pedagogía*: Unamuno's as Baroque Stylist, Comic Satirist and Anti-Machista," in *Letras Peninsulares*. 9, no. 1 (1996), pp. 49–66.

Ribbans, Geoffrey. " 'Indigesto, Mezquino, Pedestre, Confuso': A Hostile Contemporary Critique of Unamuno's *Poesías* (1907)," in *Revista Canadiense de Estuidos Hispánicos*. 21, no. 1 (1996), pp. 203–216.

Rudd, Margaret Thomas. *The Lone Heretic: A Biography of Miguel de Unamuno y Jugo*, 1963.

Speck, Paula K. "The Making of a Novel in Unamuno," in *South Atlantic Review*. XLVII, no. 4 (1982), pp. 52–63.

Spires, Robert C. *Beyond the Metaphysical Mode: Directions in the Modern Spanish Novel*, 1984.

Turner, David G. *Unamuno's Webs of Fatality*, 1974.

CLARA ESTOW

*See also* Menéndez y Pelayo

# V

## Paul Valéry

French writer and poet

**Born:** Sète, France; October 30, 1871
**Died:** Paris, France; July 20, 1945

### Biography

Ambroise-Paul-Toussaint-Jules Valéry was born to parents of Italian and Corsican origin on October 30, 1871, in the Mediterranean port of Sète, which would later provide him with the starting point for his best-known poem, "Le Cimetière marin" (1920; "The Graveyard by the Sea"). He read for a law degree at the University of Montpellier, while pursuing, outside the classroom, the study of mathematics (Henri Poincaré was an important influence) and mysticism, together with the writing of Symbolist verse. Through Pierre Louÿs, he developed an important and lasting friendship with André Gide. In October 1891 he was introduced to Stéphane Mallarmé, whom he revered above all other poets and at whose legendary "Tuesday evenings" he would subsequently become a regular presence. In the course of a violent thunderstorm one night in Genoa in June 1892, he underwent a profound crisis (the so-called "Nuit de Gênes"), out of which was born a new self free of its former passions and now devoted to a single idol: the Intellect. Thus began a lifetime's devotion to the scientific study of the interrelation of language, thought, and consciousness, pursued independently of an adherence to any single philosophical approach or school. For the following two decades, he all but abandoned the writing of poetry.

His new concerns found their expression in *Introduction à la méthode de Léonard de Vinci* (1895), which Ralph Freedman has described as "an amazingly coherent yet abstract blueprint of the 'universal mind,'" and *La Soirée avec Monsieur Teste* (1896). (The cerebral Teste, the representative of pure thought, whose opening remark is "Stupidity is not my *forte*," has often, though erroneously, been seen as a self-portrait.) After a brief interlude in London, England, during which he was employed by Cecil Rhodes' British Standard South African Chartered Company to translate and adapt material aimed at influencing French public opinion, and commissioned by W. E. Henley's *New Review* to write an article (in French) entitled "The German Conquest" (1897), he was appointed to a position in the French War Ministry. In 1900 he married Jeannie Gobillard, a niece of the painter Berthe Morisot, and became secretary and superior factotum to Édouard Lebey, the infirm managing director of the Havas News Agency. This post he held until Lebey's death in 1922. His duties involved the discussion of literature, philosophy, and religion as much as his employer's business affairs. It was in this period that he began to fill the famous exercise books (*Cahiers*), some two hundred and fifty of them, with his reflections on the mental life. The twenty-nine volumes of the posthumous facsimile edition run to some 30,000 pages.

In 1913 Gide prevailed upon Valéry to collect the poems he had written in his youth. Finding them wanting, he embarked on their revision; the *Album de vers anciens* did not appear until 1920. A new poem, conceived as his farewell to poetry, finally saw the light of day in 1917: "La Jeune Parque" ("The Young Fate"), a five-hundred-line dramatic monologue in imitation of a Gluck recitative for contralto voice. Far from its signaling the end of Valéry's poetic activity, the next five years saw the composition of the poems which form his supreme poetic achievement and which were collected in *Charmes* (1922), a volume which did mark the end of his poetic career. His role as France's leading poet and theoretician of poetry was nonetheless assured. Valéry was elected to the French Academy in 1925. The many lectures and essays he delivered or wrote in the 1920s and 1930s were often in response to official commissions, but, as with his participation in the lucrative market for limited, luxury editions, they also provided him with an important source of income. In 1933 he was appointed administrator of the newly founded Centre Universitaire Méditerranéen in Nice. In 1937 he was elected to the chair of poetics at the Collège de France; regrettably, only the first of his lectures was worked up for publication. In 1939 he gave a remarkable Zaharoff lecture at the University of Oxford, England, under the title "Poésie et pensée abstraite" ("Poetry and Abstract Thought"). Paul Valéry died in Paris on July 20, 1945.

## Influence

"My work is undertaken on behalf of whoever might succeed me." (*Cahiers*)

It was Valéry's achievement to have established poetics as a fundamental subject for study in the post-Romantic age and to have presented it as being of yet more fundamental importance than the production, or critical appreciation, of individual literary works themselves, his own poetry included. Thus instead of poetics being a prescriptive or otherwise systematic doctrine placed in the service of literature, the latter was seen by Valéry as providing the empirical means by which access could be gained, through rigorous analysis, to an understanding of universals that lay beyond the individual text. Such a stance represented a significant overturning of existing hierarchies whereby, according to the Romantic credo, the actual poetic creation constituted the supreme achievement, being the product of the "divinely" inspired artist. This provocative reversal was destined to shape much twentieth-century French thinking about the status of the literary text, though in less subtle minds (and, it should be added, in less creative imaginations), it could lead to an artistic and intellectual impoverishment that Valéry would have been the first to abhor.

The question of Valéry's specific influence on the French New Criticism and on the poetics of the French New Novel has been much debated. There is no doubt that Valéry shares with Roland Barthes and other structuralists the starting point that a literary text is, by nature, a linguistic construct. It is from a volume by Valéry that the Tel Quel group would appear to have taken its name, while in "Poetry and Abstract Thought," Valéry, like Ferdinand de Saussure (the Swiss linguist whose theories provided the basis for structuralism), senses the need to start out, at least, from the basic observation that there is no natural or inevitable link between what Saussure called the "signifier" and the "signified." In common with the Marcel Proust of *Against Sainte-Beuve*, he was instrumental in bequeathing the notion of an essential difference between the writer's autobiographical and writing selves. His inability to contemplate writing a phrase of the type "The marchioness went out at five o' clock," or indeed even to imagine himself inventing fictional characters, forms part of a view of the novel which not only continues the Symbolist hierarchy of genres which informed his literary upbringing, but could be said to seek to undermine the (Balzacian) novel in advance of Alain Robbe-Grillet or Jean Ricardou, leading advocates of the French New Novel during the 1960s. Yet these were, very largely, positions or prejudices Valéry shared with his age, even if his was a voice of unusual authority. From such shared starting points, the subsequent practices would be many and diverse. In the final analysis, Valéry was a unique practitioner of his own "method," one whose subordination of poetics to a wider investigation into his intellectual and affective lives remains inimitable.

## Analysis

In his 1939 Oxford lecture, Valéry made the oft-quoted statement: "Every genuine poet is perforce a critic of the first order." Yet by his own terms, Valéry was not a literary critic, nor even a poet-critic in the manner of T. S. Eliot. For his peculiar intellectual project dictated that the study of literature was merely part of a wider exploration of the mind. In one of his *Cahier* jottings, he observed, "Literature is only of interest to me if it leads towards and contributes to the growth of the mind." With a rare obsession he reiterated that his motivation was never "literary," that he, in fact, detested literature, and that his basic literary principle was "anti-literary." It is, however, clear that such views related to the limitations inherent in literary creation, limitations which he nonetheless sought to transcend, while remaining conscious of the ultimate futility of his ambition. Judged by the yardstick of mathematics, literature, for Valéry, was an imperfect form of expression, firstly as a result of the fact that it was linguistic in nature ("Literature is, and can only ever be, a kind of extension and application of certain properties of language") and, secondly, because it could not exist independently of a (necessarily imperfect) reader. At the same time, he sought to define literary activity (and its shortcomings) in the physiological terms that were crucial to his attempts to characterize mental endeavor. In stating that the greatest poet was the nervous system, he might be regarded as both highlighting the inadequacy of poetry and setting it a goal to emulate.

Throughout Valéry's sustained reflection on the nature of writing, his concern was with the process of creation rather than with the object created. For what interested him ultimately was the state of self-reflexivity, the heightened self-awareness which becomes possible through a certain kind of writing that works against inherited conventions, precisely in order to provide the writing self with an image of its own consciousness. Thus writing is pursued, by Valéry the poet and Valéry the critic alike, in terms of a relentless denial of its representational function, so that the poet and reader might experience as pure a state of consciousness as possible, one that is consciousness of "something" beyond itself only to the most limited degree.

Yet if Valéry's persistent concern is with locating the specificity of writing, and his essential strategy that of definition, it is an activity that eschews all notion of "system." For it is a restless activity that never settles down, just as the creative process for Valéry is one in which movement is paramount. To respect this requires a resolve, on the reader's part, to resist the temptation to regard Valéry's aphoristic definitions as definitive. To a certain extent, an interpretative response is inevitable, but to see Valéry's critical writings as an accumulation of scientifically verified tenets is to fail to identify their provocative, strategic, and necessarily oversimplified, not to say self-contradictory, nature. Many scholars have pointed out that Valéry's thinking undergoes a process of evolution, but more importantly, his "method" is, in essence, experimental. A typical utterance by Valéry is both beguiling (through its paradoxical stance in relation to convention) and preposterous (by virtue of its exploitation of a rhetoric of overstatement, though at first this may not always be self-evident). Put more simply, the utterance will always be both true and false, and often in a number of different ways. This unresolved complexity must be extracted from the individual utterances before they are discarded. What Valéry is revealing, at least implicitly through his steadfast commitment to the fragment, is that his critical investigations, like poetry (especially his own), possess their significance at the level of process rather than product. The truth that he seeks will always defy expression in straightforward conceptual terms and must therefore seek alternative means of communication.

At the same time, there emerges undeniably from Valéry's critical writings a certain relocation of emphasis that permits us to situate him in literary-historical terms. The following declaration, while an example of the rhetorical activity previously described, is echoed throughout his writings: "Poetry has never been for me a goal but an instrument and an exercise, from whence derives its character: artifice, will." It was from Edgar Allan Poe's *Eureka* that he claimed to have derived the insight that poetry was construction, a mechanical activity, an act of will. (He attributed his own abandonment of poetry in 1892 to an inability to "construct.") His determination to demolish the Romantic attribution of poetry to a state of inspiration is clear and his compelling anti-Romantic poetics earns him a place as a leading theoretician of modernism, even if he was led subsequently to seek to redefine the (limited) role played by "inspiration" rather than continuing to deny it totally. Nevertheless, as he himself appears to have realized, his gigantic mental project represented a return to the most fundamental of Romantic ambitions. He was certainly drawn to at least the idea of a "Comedy of the Intellect" to stand beside Honoré de Balzac's *Human Comedy*. It was if he was seeking to become the reincarnation of Balzac's alter ego Louis Lambert, though without imitating the latter by falling prey to madness.

For all his dismissive comments about the writing of poetry, Valéry, who identified artistic perfection with Mallarmé and Richard Wagner, was ready not only to see poetry as the highest literary form, but to encourage precisely those attributes that distinguished it from prose. In "Homage to Marcel Proust" (1923) he wrote:

While a poem brings our physical organism directly into play and has as its final term song, which is an exercise in precise and continuous liaison between the sense of learning, the form of the voice, and articulate expression, the novel aims at awakening the general and intermittent sense of expectation which is the same as that aroused in us by real events . . .

And while the world of the poem is essentially closed and complete in itself, being a pure system composed of the ornaments and happy accidents of language, the world of the novel, even the fantastic novel, is bound to the real world in the same way that the *trompe-l'oeil* blends into the tangible objects among which the spectator moves.

"Poetry," he observed in *Tel Quel I*, "was simply literature reduced to its essential active principle." For it to realize its full potential required an adherence to an aesthetic of "pure poetry," in which the poetic utterance was characterized exclusively in terms of form. Not only did such a strategy relate poetry to the ideal of music, form provided the desired transition between poetry and the exemplary language of mathematics.

Valéry wrote a number of essays devoted to individual authors, but it was his wont to raise such discussions to the general plane of definition at the earliest opportunity. As Georges Poulet has observed, "his concern with others was a form of egotism." His natural affinity was with such "universal men" as Leonardo da Vinci and Johann Wolfgang von Goethe. Presentation of their work is a continuation of the self-exploration he engages in elsewhere. The resulting emphases can often be idiosyncratic, as when he seizes upon Goethe's desire for botanical concepts to be given the clarity of "algebraic formulas" as a welcome contradiction of his more characteristic "lack of mathematical sense." Stendhal, the subject of one of his most admired essays, is, on the other hand, praised for having "preserved a somewhat remarkable reverence for mathematics." But his essays on individual writers were also an occasion for him to reaffirm the primordial importance of language and form. Thus, while ready to accept that Jacques Bossuet's thought was unlikely to provide much intellectual stimulus in a later age, he observed that there is

none who is surer of his words, stronger in his verbs, more forcible and more subtle in all the procedures of discourse, bolder and more felicitous in his syntax, or, in a word, more a master of language – that is to say, of himself.

Of the "beeswax passage" in René Descartes' *Second Meditation*, he enthused:

These few lines are perfect. They are untroubled by any appeal extraneous to what they have to say; no desire to create an effect mars their purity of tone or the sober simplicity of their restrained movement. There is not a word which is inevitable and which does not appear at the same time to have been chosen with exquisite taste. I see in them a model of the way in which language is adapted to thought, blending the smooth and detached manner that belongs to the geometer who is propounding a problem, with a certain discreetly poetic grace, heightened by the rhythm, the harmony, and the careful construction of this tiny fragment.

As for the sixteenth-century poet Pontus de Tyard's alleged abuse of syntactical inversion, he defended the device, somewhat hyperbolically, as "a useful and significant liberty, for it inflicts a noble torture on the normal and humdrum course of expression."

Yet, here too, there is a danger in taking Valéry's remarks at face value. His strangely dismissive remarks on Gustave Flaubert are a case in point. Even so distinguished a Valéry scholar as Lloyd Austin falls into the trap of the very half-truth against which he issues so salutary a warning with regard to Valéry's "method," when he upbraids him for attributing to Flaubert a realist credo to which the latter did not subscribe. Such censure fails to take into account, *inter alia*, the fact that Valéry goes on to observe: "Realism ended curiously enough by giving an impression of deliberate artifice." Far from being blind to the way in which Flaubert's work was not the product of a naive commitment to realism, Valéry is engaged, in the essay in question, in an exemplary rhetorical (and ironic) reaffirmation of his own definition of literature as artifice. It would have been curious indeed if he had been blind to Flaubert's self-conscious artistry. If there is criticism of Flaubert, it is in the form of the implicit charge of having perversely pursued Art through the least amenable genre for such a purpose. The lesson, however, is clear: the reader charges Valéry with ignorance or imperfect understanding at his peril.

In short, careful consideration of Valéry's critical writings reveals a provocative tension between affirmation and denial, not to say a subtle art of contradiction necessitated by his scrupulous conviction that any formulation in words is irredeemably flawed. The paradox remains that his self-conscious exploitation of overstatement and understatement alike will often enhance our understanding of a given writer and his medium to a far greater extent than many forms of criticism which are concerned to advance a more measured set of conclusions.

## Principal criticism

"Poésie et pensée abstraite," 1939
*Tel Quel I–II*, 1941–43
*Variété I–V*, 1924–44

The contents of the above volumes, and many of Valéry's other lectures and essays on aesthetics, are contained (in French) in *Œuvres* (1957–1960, 2 volumes), edited by Jean Hytier, and (in English) in *The Collected Works of Paul Valéry* (1956–1975, 15 volumes), edited by Jackson Mathews. Both collections contain important notes and other valuable editorial matter. *The Art of Poetry*, Volume 7 of *The Collected Works of Paul Valéry*, has an

introduction by T. S. Eliot. Volume I of *Œuvres* includes a minutely detailed chronology of Valéry's life by his daughter, Agathe Rouart-Valéry.

## Other major works and literary forms
In addition to his poetry (in verse and prose), his essays on poetics and on individual writers, and the remarkable intellectual enterprise represented by the *Cahiers*, Valéry devoted a number of essays to art (see the 1938 collection entitled *Pièces sur l'art; Degas, Danse, Dessin et divers écrits sur la peinture*). Noteworthy among his political (or "quasi-political") essays is "The Crisis of the Mind," which first appeared, in John Middleton Murry's translation, in *The Athenaeum* in 1919, and which opens with the celebrated words: "We civilizations now know that we are mortal." His three major dialogues, *Eupalinos ou l'architecte* (1923), *L'Âme et la danse* (1923; *Dance and the Soul*), and *L'Idée fixe* (1932), are among his finest achievements; the clash of ideas (the first two are mock-Socratic) is presented with considerable verve and virtuosity.

## Further reading
Austin, Lloyd. *Poetic Principles and Practice. Occasional Papers on Baudelaire, Mallarmé and Valéry*, 1987.
Crow, Christine M. *Paul Valéry: Consciousness and Nature*, 1972.
——. *Paul Valéry and the Poetry of Voice*, 1982.
Eliot, T. S. *From Poe to Valéry*, 1948.
Freedman, Ralph. "Paul Valéry: Protean Critic," in *Modern French Criticism. From Proust and Valéry to Structuralism*, 1972. Edited by John K. Simon.
Gibson, Robert. *Modern French Poets on Poetry*, 1961.
Hytier, Jean. *The Poetics of Paul Valéry*, 1953 (English translation, 1966).
Ince, W. N. *The Poetic Theory of Paul Valéry. Inspiration and Technique*, 1970.
Mossop, D. J. *Pure Poetry. Studies in French Poetic Theory and Practice 1746–1945*, 1971.
Robinson, Judith. "The Place of Literary and Artistic Creation in Valéry's Thought," in *Modern Language Review*. 56 (1959), pp. 497–514.
Stimpson, Brian. *Paul Valéry and Music. A Study of the Techniques of Composition in Valéry's Poetry*, 1984.

MICHAEL TILBY

*See also* Continental Theory; Mallarmé; Symbolism

# Giovanni Verga

Italian writer and critic

**Born:** Catania, Sicily, Italy; September 2, 1840
**Died:** Catania, Sicily, Italy; January 27, 1922

## Biography
Giovanni Carmelo Verga was born in Catania, Sicily, on September 2, 1840, the eldest child of Giovanni Battista

Verga Catalano and Caterina di Mauro. The family, which could trace its name to noble ancestry, was well-to-do and locally prominent. In 1857, when only seventeen, Verga wrote his first work, a historical novel entitled *Amore e patria*, based on the American Revolution. The following year he entered the University of Catania as a law student. In 1861, however, he left the university to pursue a career as a writer. It was to aid this career that he went to Florence in 1865, where he entered literary circles and came into close contact with the leading intellectuals of his day.

Verga remained in Florence until 1872, at which time he went to Milan, where he would spend the next twenty-two years. In Milan his already successful career flourished: he frequented the *salotto* of the Contessa Maffei, where he met other writers, among them Giuseppe Giacosa, Arrigo Boito, and Gerolamo Rovetta.

In 1894 Verga, who throughout his years in northern Italy had never lost contact with his Sicilian origins, made a definitive return to Catania. In his native city the pace of his literary output became considerably slower than it had been during his years in Milan.

Despite the uneven response of literary critics to his works, on his eightieth birthday Verga received the nationwide recognition of a hero; it was in that same year, 1920, that he was made Senator of the Republic. He died in Catania two years later, on January 27, 1922.

## Influence

The name of Giovanni Verga has become closely identified with the Verism movement. Drawing from the French naturalism of Émile Zola, Verga formulated his own theories of realism. The impact of Verga's works may be identified primarily in two areas. The first is the author's attention to the oppressed working classes of Sicily, shifting the focus of mainstream literature from the concerns of bourgeois and aristocratic classes to the pressing problems of the underprivileged.

The other principal contribution to Italian literary history is Verga's work in establishing new guidelines and requirements for literary language, within the limits allowed by Verism. Although Verga's writing reflects his strong ties to the ancient ways and beliefs of Sicilian tradition, his modernity and his innovation are revealed in his use of discursive prose and in the intertwining of direct and indirect speech, a technique that foreshadows interior monologue.

## Analysis

The break between modern literature and the Romantic movement can clearly be witnessed in Verga's writings. His divergence from the Romantics was neither sudden nor easy. If during his lifetime his works often received a less than enthusiastic reception, it may also be said that Verga was ahead of his time in foreseeing, consciously or not, the literary changes demanded by the transition into modernity.

Verga's work follows a distinct evolution; the reader may without difficulty identify an initial developmental phase characterized by the presence of residual Romantic traits. In the early years of his career, Verga still shared the nineteenth-century taste for the exaggerated, the melodramatic, and the fantastic. Also in adherence to the Romantic literary tradition, the protagonists of Verga's early stories are often members of the bourgeois class. *Una peccatrice* (1866) and *Storia di una capinera* (1871) are exemplary of this period, in which he grappled with the task of bringing the solid backing of realism to a literature embedded in a tradition of melodrama and idealism. The narrative is pervaded by remnants of Romantic sentimentality, and the plots, predictably, center on ill-fated love.

*Vita dei campi* (1880; *Under the Shadow of Etna*, 1896) marks the beginning of Verga's movement toward establishing the parameters of a *verista* literature, a "human document" that would provide for the reader a deliberately unadorned representation of reality. Verga returned to that subject matter with which he was most comfortable and most familiar: life in Sicily. Leaving aside the bourgeois characters of his previous fiction, he turned to the Sicilian common people as they can be observed in everyday life. Verga's deep knowledge of his own Sicilian compatriots permitted him to write about them with almost scientific exactness.

Verga's choice of protagonists has a stylistic and ideological base, and thus it is pivotal in his literary theory. *Under the Shadow of Etna* is the proving ground for the author's theories regarding the search for truth and objectivity in literature. In a letter to Salvatore Farina, which serves as preface to one of the stories, "L'amante di Gramigna," Verga makes the following declaration: "The simple human fact will always provide food for thought; it will always have the effectiveness of *what has been*, of real tears, of fevers and sensations that have passed through the flesh." The most effective, and indeed the only possible, way of arriving at the unadorned, photographic representation of the human condition is to write about the places and people one knows best.

From an ideological point of view, Verga's return to his origins underscores his belief in the author's obligation to expose the realities of the human condition. In his view, modern society is structured principally on its economic system. Pecuniary gain is of primary importance, and survival is very much dependent on one's financial means. A reader of Charles Darwin, Verga placed evolutionary theories in an economic context. According to his perception, the individuals most fit for survival are those with the greatest wealth; those with the least means are clearly marked for extinction. The human struggle for survival and search for happiness, in Verga's analysis, amount to nothing more than the struggle for economic and social success.

This depiction of the human condition is one of the main characteristics of Verism; it seeks the "frank and self-evident manifestation and the conscious observation of art, in a word, its sincerity." The events of life are in the hands of chance, and the individual "who looks at this spectacle does not have the right to judge it."

Verga's approach to realism is similar to that of Zola in its impersonal observation of the world. Like the naturalism upheld by the French, Verga's realism assumes an unemotional and unobtrusive approach to the subject matter. Verga differs from Zola, however, on at least one major point. The Italian *veristi* reject the determinism advocated by the French. Determinism is based on the belief that to a great extent a person's situation and destiny are set by the laws of heredity. In Verga's work, it is not heredity but chance that decides a person's destiny.

In his novel *I Malavoglia* (1881; *The House by the Medlar Tree*, 1890, 1953, 1964), Verga applies the precepts of Verism, showing his protagonists to be completely at the mercy of outside forces. Members of the Malavoglia family, all fundamentally upright individuals, are ruined one by one, victims of circumstance, not (as Zola would have it) of their natural condition. Verga stressed the need to keep within the limits of fact and to maintain the author's impersonality in the narrative. To achieve the impression that the characters themselves, not the narrator, are the source of the facts being recounted, the author consciously employed a simple regional language: "I shall tell [the story] to you as I heard it on country lanes and in the fields, more or less with the same simple and picturesque words of popular storytelling." Thus Verga moved away from the traditional use of Florentine Italian in favor of a more realistic language.

Verga differed in his use of regional language from some of the northern Italian writers who composed in dialect. His fiction does not actually present dialect to his reader, but rather the idea of dialect. It was Verga's belief that, although to be most faithful to realistic representation the writer must reproduce the language that he hears, writing in the Sicilian dialect would make his narrative incomprehensible. He therefore resorted to techniques that would render the impression of the dialect without reducing the clarity of the speech.

Verga relied, particularly in direct discourse, on such devices as the repetition of words, the intentional adoption of a cadence, and expressions and aphorisms of local provenance. His aim was to create a language that would be easily understood by all of his readers, while still leaving the impression that the characters themselves were the sole protagonists, without the intrusion of a more literate narrator.

The particular attention that Verga gave to the use of language was certainly an integral part of his concern with realism, but was also in keeping with the ongoing *questione della lingua* in Italian literature. The most immediate example for Verga was probably that of Alessandro Manzoni, who, in writing the final version of *I promessi sposi* (1827, 1840–1842; *The Betrothed*, 1868, 1951), had chosen Florentine Italian over more regional language.

Choosing truth once more as his guideline, Verga says in the preface to *The House by the Medlar Tree*, "One must be truthful in order to show the truth, since form is as inherent in the subject as every part of the subject itself is necessary to the development of the general theme." Verga's manipulation of time in the narrative is yet another expression of his Verism. Rather than follow the traditional chronological arrangement, Verga often chose a more impressionistic, antichronological sequence. This device aids in the assimilation of the entire narrative into the protagonist's perspective, thereby excluding any extraneous narrative voice. It is a rather innovative approach which demonstrates the modernity of Verga's theories of literature, anticipating the rupture of traditional narrative techniques with the introduction of interior monologues, stream-of-consciousness writing, and psychological rather than chronological time.

Character, language, and landscape are all parts of the whole in the *verista* application. Each necessarily describes and participates in the existence of the others. Thus, the exotic wildness of the Sicilian landscape is a part of and a reflection of Verga's primitive, untamed characters. Like the characters who utter them, the words used are unadorned and essential. Realism, then, as intended by Verga, depends upon the successful integration of the character with his or her environment and upon a language that to all appearances is spontaneously generated by the character; the presence of the author must not be felt.

Because of its innovative aspects, Verga's work was not unanimously praised. Some of his major works – *The House by the Medlar Tree*, for example – were met by critics and readers with some ambivalence. Consequently, circumscribing his sphere of influence is an elusive task. That is not to say, however, that Verga did not have a direct influence on other artists. Indeed, his style and theories can be credited with playing a strong role in the writing of such figures as Gabriele D'Annunzio and Grazia Deledda (who won the Nobel Prize for Literature in 1926). In *Le novelle della Pescara* (1892, 1902; *Tales from My Native Town*, 1920), D'Annunzio assembled a collection of stories which, with Verghian simplicity, describe the primitive and difficult life of the poor people of Abruzzo, the author's native region. Deledda took up Verga's concern for the plight of the forgotten islander, writing about her native Sardinia. She adopted Verga's stark realism as a strong base for her more impressionistic writing. Ignazio Silone, as an exponent of the neorealist movement that began in the 1930s, also followed Verga's formula of Verism, but transformed it into a tool for social protest.

## Principal criticism

"Lettera a Salvatore Paola," 1878
Preface to "L'amante di Gramigna," 1880 (English translation, 1964)

Preface to *I Malavoglia*, 1881 (Preface to *The House by the Medlar Tree*, 1890)

## Other major works and literary forms

Although the literary theories upheld by Giovanni Verga have played a major role in Italian literary history, his ideas found their expression principally in practical application. Verga is known chiefly as a novelist and short-story writer. In addition, he experimented with the theater, often rewriting his stories for the stage. Perhaps the best known of these is "Cavalleria rusticana," made famous by Pietro Mascagni's opera of the same name; the story first appeared in 1880 and was rewritten as a one-act play in 1884.

NOVELS
*Amore e patria*, 1857
*I carbonari della montagna*, 1861–1862 (also as *I carbonari della montagna: Sulle lagune*; includes *Sulle lagune*, serialized 1863)
*Una peccatrice*, 1866
*Storia di una capinera*, 1871
*Eva*, 1873
*Eros*, 1874
*Tigre reale*, 1875
*I Malavoglia*, 1881 (*The House by the Medlar Tree*, partial translation, 1890, 1953; complete translation, 1964)
*Il marito di Elena*, 1882
*Mastro-don Gesualdo*, 1889 (English translation, 1893, 1923)
*Dal tuo al mio*, 1906

SHORT FICTION
*Primavera ed altri racconti*, 1876 (also as *Novelle*, 1880)
*Vita dei campi*, 1880 (*Under the Shadow of Etna*, 1896)
*Novelle rusticane*, 1883 (*Little Novels of Sicily*, 1925)
*Per le vie*, 1883
*Cavalleria rusticana ed altre novelle*, 1892 (*Cavalleria Rusticana and Other Stories*, 1928)
*The She-Wolf and Other Stories*, 1958

PLAYS
*Cavalleria rusticana*, 1884 (English translation, 1893)
*In portineria*, 1884
*La lupa*, 1896
*La caccia al lupo*, 1901 (*The Wolf Hunt*, 1921)
*La caccia alla volpe*, 1901
*Dal tuo al mio*, 1903
*Teatro di Giovanni Verga*, 1912
*Rose caduche*, 1928
*Teatro*, 1952

NONFICTION
*Lettere al suo traduttore*, 1954
*Lettere a Dina*, 1962, 1971
*Lettere a Luigi Capuana*, 1975

## Further reading

Bergin, Thomas Goddard. *Giovanni Verga*, 1969.
Cecchetti, Giovanni. Introduction to *The She-Wolf and Other Stories*, 1973.
——. *Giovanni Verga*, 1978.
Chandler, S. Bernard. "The Impossible Quest: From Verga's Early Novels to I Malavoglia," in *Perspectives on Nineteenth-Century Italian Novels*, 1989. Edited and introduced by Guido Pugliese.
Lawrence, D. H. "Essay on Verga," in *Cavalleria Rusticana and Other Stories*, 1928.
Lucente, Gregory L. *The Narrative of Realism and Myth: Verga, Lawrence, Faulkner, Pavese*, 1979.
O'Grady, Deirdre. "The Vicious Circle: Giovanni Verga as Storyteller," in *Italian Storytellers: Essays in Italian Narrative Literature*, 1989. Edited by Eric Haywood and Cormac O'Cuilleanain.
Ragusa, Olga. *Verga's Milanese Tales*, 1964.
Russo, Luigi. *Giovanni Verga*, 1966.
Smith, Jonathan. "Naturalism and Anti-Naturalism in Italy," in *Naturalism in the European Novel: New Critical Perspectives*, 1992. Edited by Brian Nelson.
Woolf, D. *The Art of Verga: A Study in Objectivity*, 1977.

SUSAN BRIZIARELLI

*See also* Continental Theory; Zola

# Aleksandr Veselovskii

Russian critic and translator

**Born:** Moscow, Russia; February 16, 1838
**Died:** St. Petersburg, Russia; October 23, 1906

## Biography

Aleksandr Veselovskii was born in Moscow in 1838 into an intellectual family of minor nobility. He was a schoolboy in the great years of Russian socioliterary theory, encountering the work of Vissarion Belinskii, Nikolai Dobroliubov, Nikolai Chernyshevskii, and others. In 1858 he graduated from Moscow University in philology, having studied classical and Slavic linguistic history. Professor Fedor Buslaev helped to shape his scholarly habits, but the telling impact on his work came from German and Italian academics when he did graduate work abroad.

The young man became a tutor in the family of the Russian ambassador to Spain, visiting Spain, Italy, France, and England, thereby beginning his mastery of the languages and literatures of Western Europe. In 1862 he received financial support for study abroad, and he first attended the University of Berlin in German and Romance philology, gaining an excellent knowledge of medieval German and Romance languages and of German epic and the Provençal lyric. Here, too, he found the ground for his historical approach to literary genre in lectures on folk psychology.

Veselovskii spent the next year in Prague, extending his knowledge of Slavistics. From 1864 to 1867 he was in Italy as an independent scholar. He became an expert in Renaissance literature and published his first book, in Italian, on a novel of the fifteenth century that he had discovered in manuscript.

Returning home, he defended his work for the master's and doctoral degrees and joined the faculty of the University of St. Petersburg, becoming a professor in 1872, first of general literature and later as a specialist in Western European literature and philology. He founded a new specialty – Western philology – and in 1885 organized a society for the study of Western European literature. Veselovskii became a member of the St. Petersburg Academy of Sciences in 1880 and served as president of the academy's section of Russian literature. He died in St. Petersburg in 1906. Veselovskii's younger brother Aleksei Veselovskii also became a literary historian, publishing in 1896 *Zapadnoe vlianie v novoi russkoi literature*, a book on Western influence in Russian literature.

## Influence

Though Veselovskii is little known by Western literary theorists and very little of his work has been translated, René Wellek, Victor Erlich, and others place him as perhaps the greatest comparatist in Russia in the nineteenth century. Through his university position and his voluminous writing he helped to establish a productive school of comparative literature in Russia and the Soviet Union. Much of the work of his students and successors, excellent though it is, also has small distribution in the West. The third edition of the *Great Soviet Encyclopedia* calls him, in the article on comparative literature, the "founder of Russian comparative literary studies," and in the article on U.S.S.R. literary theory, "a scholar of broad erudition" who developed the comparative-historical method, "the highest achievement of pre-Marxist literary scholarship, not only in Russia but in the West as well." His continuing effort was to make a science of literary criticism.

Most Western scholars who do know Veselovskii have encountered his work by way of his influence on two groups: the Formalists in literary theory and the folklorists in the collection and isolation of recurring motifs across national lines. The Formalists used his idea of separating form and content, and the folklorists developed structural analysis of tales. His work on borrowing is valued and sophisticated.

## Analysis

Veselovskii's contributions are impressive in three areas: comparative theory and practice, folklore theory and collection, and literary theory and criticism. His lifelong commitment to establishing the study of literature as a science, and his broadening of the conception of comparative historical study to include oral material linked the three areas. Over his lifetime, he moved from the study of the history of culture to the history of poetics.

As a young man, Veselovskii rejected both Jakob Grimm's approach to romantic nationalism (the narrowly specialized philological approach of German literature professors) and also the cultural-historical approach (the "great writer and his milieu") of French criticism in the 1860s. Though he believed that research by these groups

was useful to Russian philologists, he was stimulated (by lectures on *Volkpsychologie* and by the comparative approach of linguists in identifying the dispersion of Indo-European through Europe) to apply comparative techniques to the origin of genres and to persisting motifs and patterns in literary works.

His opening lecture as professor of general literature at the University of St. Petersburg set the terms of his whole scholarly career, suggesting even his latest interest in style as related to creativity. The necessity of the comparative approach to Russian literature is evident: for example, he says that "the German sagas and the French *chansons de geste* can illuminate for us many peculiarities of Russian folk poetry," and "Russian literature of the eighteenth century is incomprehensible without a solid acquaintance with contemporary intellectual movements in England and France." He objects to the focus on the great man in French criticism, even when some attention was paid to the "movement of the masses," on the grounds of the "rhetorical" effect. He questions the value of current generalizations about cultural milieu because they are based on too little scientifically gathered evidence. Further, he recommends the systematic collection of not only major historical phenomena but also everyday trivia which shape the larger events. Tracing cause and effect in a variety of cultural contexts, with ceaseless verification, allows finally a sounder and more comprehensive generalization. In a development of the historical method, he repeats studies on parallel lines in many national literatures. Some working hypothesis is essential, but collecting data to fit a preconception is not scientific, he says. He believes that his comparative and scientific method has replaced the aesthetic, philosophical, and less accurate historical methods of the past. The accumulation of specific and verifiable evidence also guides his views on folklore, thus avoiding the guessing of the mythological school.

Veselovskii argues in this first statement of his views that genres are "the natural expression of the mind." At one point he suggests something like Theodore Benfey's theory of diffusion from a common root. Yet his inductive approach makes him posit also the possibility of independent emergence of parallel items (polygenesis) when no evidence of borrowing can be found. He adds, like a good Darwinian, that "between these forms and the changing content of the world viewpoint are established relationships of natural selection, as it were, dictated by conditions of everyday life and the accidents of history."

The critic then reaches further, suggesting an interest he was to explore only in his latest work. Out of the comparative study of poetry must come altered conceptions of creativity, he thinks.

Is not poetic creativity limited to certain specific formulae, to constant motives which one generation has received from the preceding one, and that one from a third, the prototypes of which we will inevitably meet in epic antiquity and further, at the level of myth, in the concrete formulations of the primal word? Does not each new poetic epoch work upon images inherited from time immemorial, necessarily operating within their limits, allowing itself only new combinations of the old, and only filling them with that new understanding of life which in fact constitutes its progress over the past?

Veselovskii proposes the new task of the literary historian as the analysis of the progress of the collective mind as expressed in the series of unchanging formulas of ancient poetry, epic, and myth all the way through history to contemporary literature. The new work is to "trace in what modes the new content of life, this element of freedom which surges with each generation, penetrates the old in these forms of necessity into which preceding development has inevitably been cast." Veselovskii explored the ways in which borrowing did and did not take place, and he altered the romantic mythological approach by means of comparative ethnographic research.

In line with these views, the scholar's work during the 1870s and 1880s was the collection of data in Russian and Western European medieval literature and folk poetry. In such studies as those on the connection of Slavic tales with those about Merlin in the West, Russian spiritual verse, South Russian *byliny* (epic folk songs), and Christian legends, he amassed a broad base of specific knowledge and extended his ideas into the lively field of folkloristics. His lectures and published articles on the history of the epic, the characteristics of the novel, the short story, the tale, the drama, and the lyric grew out of these investigations. He also published further papers on stylistic devices such as epithets and refrains, developing his understanding of the evolution of style.

As a result of this broad, detailed research, more and more the interest of the critic turned to the development of a theory of historical poetics, and his work from the 1890s to the end of his life focused this shift. Lectures, then a preliminary *Tri glavy iz istoricheskoi poetiki* (1899; Three Chapters from a Historical Poetics), pointed toward a major study that he did not live to complete. A collection of his writing on the subject was, however, published as *Istoricheskaia poetika* (historical poetics) in 1940, with an introduction by Viktor Zhirmunskii, a member of the then highly developed school of comparatists which arose in the Soviet Union on the basis of the work of Veselovskii and others. This collection included the unfinished exploration "Poetika siuzheta" (Poetics of Plot). His most advanced speculation was on the nature of poetic creativity, made substantial by his extended knowledge of the poetic materials writers have as givens: language, stylistic devices, genres, and plot elements and patterns. While not "penetrating the curtain hiding the secrets of creation

itself," he could measure more accurately the nature of the individual's contribution with this kind of broad-gauge knowledge.

As a result of his extensive activity, Veselovskii's influence was felt in his country not only in comparative studies, which proliferated, but also in literary theory and its application to particular works, and in folklore. The critic's split of a work's form and content and his distinction between motif and plot were picked up by the Formalists, influencing significant figures in that movement such as Viktor Shklovskii and Boris Eikhenbaum, with their emphasis on literary device and structure. The distinction between motif and plot and Veselovskii's work on the way borrowed material adapts to the country of the borrower underlay Vladimir Propp's work on morphology of the folktale. A vigorous group of Russian comparatists wrote many interesting works about literary interplay of East and West between the time of the Revolution and World War II.

Unfortunately, after World War II a painful episode interrupted but did not destroy the long-term reputation and influence of Veselovskii in the Soviet Union. Professor Gleb Struve, in the 1955 and 1957 issues of the *Yearbook of Comparative and General Literature*, gives a circumstantial account of the affair. The problem arose in the Party control of literature after 1925, and especially in its definition of what Soviet literature should be, making Socialist Realism the only acceptable mode. The directives also implied a strictly nationalistic focus. With their emphasis on international literature and on the artistic work rather than on politics, comparatists and Formalists were politically vulnerable from the late 1920s through World War II, and many suffered exile and death.

After the war a resolution of the Central Committee of the Party set forth the necessity to root out "relics of bourgeois mentality" and "servility" to the capitalist West in Soviet literature. Andrei Zhdanov carried out the policy with a vengeance. The whole effort of showing parallels with Western literatures was looked upon as a crime against Soviet society. Aleksandr A. Fadeev, at the Union of Soviet Writers, gave Veselovskii a sort of backhand homage, charging (rather than crediting) the critic with being father of the comparative approach. Numerous articles appeared attacking "Veselovskyism" and all of its progeny. Both Shklovskii and the comparatist V. F. Shishmarev attempted Veselovskii's defense, but not until the death of Joseph Stalin in 1953 could Veselovskii be rehabilitated. The third edition of the *Great Soviet Encyclopedia* uses Veselovskii's idea of "crosscurrents" in borrowed literature to affirm the individuality of national adaptations, forgiving the scholar the limitations of his bourgeois and positivist approach. Comparatists renewed their activity in the 1960s, and the field continues to be vital. A recent volume in Russian explores Veselovskii's legacy, but his work continues untranslated in the West.

## Principal criticism

*"Il Paradiso o degli Alberti" e gli ultima trecentisti*, 1868
*"O metode i zadachakh istorii literatury kak nauka,"* 1870
    (*"On the Method and Aims of Literary History as a
    Science,"* 1967)
*Slavianskie skazaniia o Solomone i Kitovrase i zapadnye legendy
    o Morol'fe i Merline*, 1872
*Opyty po istorii razvitiia khristianskoi legendy*, 1875–1877
*Razyskanie v oblasti russkogo dukhovnogo stikha*, 1880–1891
*Yuzhnorusskie byliny*, 1881–1884
*Tri glavy iz istoricheskoi poetiki*, 1899
*V. A. Zhukovskii: Poeziia chuvstva i serdechnogo voobrozheniia*,
    1904
*Sobranie sochineniia*, 1908–1938 (16 volumes)
*Izbrannye stat'i*, 1939
*Istoricheskaia poetika*, 1940, 1970

## Other major works and literary forms

All Aleksandr Veselovskii's writings (some 280 articles and books) were in the field of comparative literature. He did one translation, of Giovanni Boccaccio's *Decameron*, in 1891–1892.

TRANSLATION
*Dekameron*, 1891–1892 (of Giovanni Boccaccio)

## Further reading

"A. N. Veselovskii i sravnitel'noe literaturovedenie," in
    *Sravitel'noe literaturovedenie*, 1979.
Erlich, Victor. "Alexander Veselovsky," in *Yearbook of
    Comparative and General Literature*. VIII (1959), pp. 33–36.
"On the Study of Comparative Literature," in *Oxford Slavonic
    Papers*. XIII (1967), pp. 1–13.
Struve, Gleb. "Comparative Literature in the Soviet Union,
    Today and Yesterday," in *Yearbook of Comparative and
    General Literature*. IV (1955), pp. 1–20.
——. "Comparative Literature of the Soviet Union: Two
    Postscripts," in *Yearbook of Comparative and General
    Literature*. VI (1957), pp. 7–10.
Zaborov, P. R., ed. *Nasledie Aleksandra Veselovskogo:
    issledovaniia i materialy*, 1992.
Zhirmunsky, V. M. Introduction to Veselovskii's *Istoricheskaia
    poetika*, 1940.

MARTHA MANHEIM

*See also* Pisarev; Plekhanov; Russian Formalism

# Giambattista Vico

Italian philosopher

**Born:** Naples, Italy; June 23, 1668
**Died:** Naples, Italy; January 23, 1744

## Biography

From his earliest childhood, Giambattista Vico regarded himself as an autodidact, having received only a limited and discontinuous education from tutors and institutions. In his youth he studied law and philosophy and cultivated poetry,

but his real education began in 1686, when, having been appointed tutor to the children of the marquess Domenico Rocca, he had the opportunity to pursue his studies in his employer's library in Vatolla, where he spent several months each year with the Rocca family until 1695.

In the meantime, when in Naples Vico frequented circles that were at the forefront of intellectual life. He had extensive contacts with a group of Lucretian atomists who, under the influence of Pierre Gassendi, were promoting materialistic conceptions of life; these views were regarded as dangerous enough for the group to be tried by the Inquisition. Vico's earliest published work, the canzone *Affetti di un disperato* (1692; English translation, 1935), was written under their influence.

In 1699 Vico obtained the post of professor of rhetoric at the University of Naples, which he held throughout all of his professional life. In 1723 he competed for the much more prestigious chair of Roman law, which had been recently vacated, but the post was offered to an under-qualified contender. This was a severe blow for Vico, but he was able to overcome his bitterness by rationalizing his loss as a sign that God did not want him to waste away his life writing Latin footnotes to the law, as was expected of a professor of law. Instead, he would devote himself to the development of an entirely original and much-needed science of humanity, to be written in Italian so that it might be read outside academia. This he did uninterruptedly for the rest of his life, and it filled him with a heroic spirit that enabled him to face all manner of adversity. When he died in 1744 the final version of the work for which he is now celebrated, *The New Science*, was in press.

## Influence

Although Vico was much more widely known in the eighteenth century than is generally assumed, one can speak of his influence on mainstream thought – in increasing magnitude – only in connection with the following two centuries. The fields in which his influence has been greatest are aesthetics, the philosophy of history, literary criticism, the philosophy of language, and ontology. In the literary criticism of the 1970s and 1980s, different principles from these and other fields are frequently brought together in the attempt to establish better categories for the understanding of literary works, and Vico, either directly or indirectly, serves as a plexus for many of them.

## Analysis

The science of humanity pursued by Vico in *The New Science* is at once theoretical and empirical, since it seeks to uncover universal principles as well as to explain specific facts. Vico called the two aspects of his science philosophy and philology, insisting that, like the two sides of a coin, they are inseparable components of a conceptual and methodological unity indispensable in the study of all fields, including poetry. His criticism may therefore be regarded as a study of the interrelations between general principles and individual works: individual works validate general principles and are illumined by them. His major theoretical concerns have to do with the conceptual and temporal link of poetry to history; the chief authors on whom he rehearses his criticism are Homer and Dante, though he makes brief references to myriad other poets, from the most ancient to the most recent.

At the heart of Vico's criticism are the notions that poetry and metaphysics tend toward mutual exclusion and that history is the development of humanity from a naturally poetic state to a naturally metaphysical one. Humanity's barbarian progenitors, who imaginatively projected sense on reality – like children still unable to infer the causes of phenomena – created the myths, that is to say the first poems, which form the semantic basis and historical beginnings of Western civilization. They were poets and founders of nations. Their descendants retain that poetic capacity in inverse proportion to their ability to think rationally. When humanity's rational vigor reaches the crest of the cycle of existence, its poetic faculty sinks to the trough.

The principal implications of this critical theory are, first, that poetry is prior to rational discourse and, second, that history hierarchizes poets in descending order. With respect to the first of these, it is clear that poetry is prior to metaphysics not only in a temporal sense, but also in that it is primordial and foundational, whereas rational discourse can only be evaluative and analytical, practicing its power on what has already been achieved prerationally. This is a position to which Vico adhered in all the philosophical works of his maturity; it represents his ontological valuation of the Humanist tradition, which he pitted against the Cartesian rationalism of his day. In the Humanist tradition he saw that the dignity of philosophy could not be denied to rhetoric, especially to that branch of it called "topics," which is the art of finding things to say. Topics leads quite naturally to inventive poetic thinking, in opposition to rational analysis, which is not in the least creative, since it can only judge the truth value of what has already been said. Through inventive poetic thinking, humanity's ancient forefathers brought forth their own historical being from the welter of their brute senses, creating the institutions, the arts, and the sciences which in time would refine and spiritualize their minds. Whereas most thinkers since Plato begin with metaphysics as the science from which all other sciences derive their methods and their thematic delimitations, Vico begins with poetry and goes on to show that it alone is primordial, nonderivative, and creative. By imagining things, primitive people brought them into being in the realm of figuration, and they did this in such a vivid manner that they believed in the phenomenal reality of their creations and let themselves be guided by them on the path to refinement. The dictum that poetry, like the music of Orpheus, is a civilizing force must be understood literally in the case of Vico.

It is clear from all of this that, at the ontological level, Vico did not see the need to distinguish between poetry and myth. The first and greatest poets were the ancient mythmakers, who gave what they regarded to be true accounts of reality; they created the greatest poem of all when they imagined that the thundering sky was Zeus. At the phenomenological level, however, where poetry figures as a special form of discourse, there can be no doubt that he separated it conceptually from myth, though he did not do so terminologically. In this sense, poetry did not begin when primitive humans anthropomorphized the thundering sky, but when language had developed to a degree sufficient for thought to be expressed figuratively but insufficient for it to be stated literally and exactly. Originally, tropes were not artificial embellishments of discourse but necessary circumlocutions to which the ancients had recourse to supplement the incomplete nomenclature at their disposal. Metaphors were used only because the proper names of their referents were not known. Poetic speech, in other words, was a direct consequence of the descriptive and expressive inadequacy of archaic language. If this philological fact is generalized and restated without reference to the historical beginnings of tropes, it yields the following principle: linguistic poverty is a necessary condition of great poetry.

The issue now naturally arises whether true poetry is at all possible in the age of reason, when an abundant nomenclature distinguishes every aspect of physical and spiritual reality from every other. Vico's answer is an unequivocal yes. With respect to poetic thinking, Vico observes in *The New Science* that poetic language, much like a mighty river surging into the sea and retaining the freshness of its water for a fair distance, retains some of its poetic character as it is engulfed by rational language. The question of poetry as a special form of discourse is most explicitly formulated and answered in the *De Constantia Jurisprudentis Liber Alter* (1721) and in Vico's letter to Gherardo degli Angioli of December 26, 1725. In these texts, Vico asserts that those who would write poetry in the age of reason must place themselves in the linguistic circumstances of the ancient poets, that is to say they must impose on themselves such lexical and prosodic restrictions as could reasonably simulate the linguistic indigence of the naturally poetic period of history. When it finds itself in such fetters, the mind necessarily thinks and expresses itself poetically. Because the naturally poetic age of Europe was the medieval period – when the nascent vernaculars were still underdeveloped with respect to Latin – Vico's observation implies that in the age of metaphysics poetry is possible only if poets undergo a linguistic self-medievalization that undermines their modern propensity toward rational discourse.

That poetry is possible in a period dominated by metaphysical speculation does not mean that it is also common; it is indeed very rare. In fact, from this perspective, the history of any culture may be described as the story of the progressive impoverishment of its initial capacity for poetry. This is the second major implication of Vico's literary theory: the natural hierarchization of poetry through the centuries. According to Vico, the history of each nation is patterned on a potentially recurrent tripartite structure in which the first two ages (the divine and the heroic) are propelled by poetic thinking, whereas the third (the human age) unfolds under the power of increasing ratiocination. In the first edition of *The New Science*, Vico looked at the chronology of Greece and discovered the advent of Homer toward the end of the heroic age. He then searched for analogues in the chronologies of other cultures, thereby giving shape to a Homeric typology, according to which a primitive and self-made epic poet appears during the waning of the heroic ages of universal history under different guises but with epic songs that have certain common features. As Homer remained unequaled in Greece, each of his types stands sovereign at the beginning of a national poetic line destined to become thinner and weaker with each generation. Homer became for Vico the ideal of excellence and a source of concepts and categories for the interpretation of other poets. In the first edition of *The New Science*, Quintus Ennius is the Homeric type of Rome, while Dante is the Homeric type of modern Europe. As for the relative excellence of Dante and Homer – the question is irrelevant in regard to Ennius, since only a few of his verses are extant – Vico claims that Dante is inferior to Homer because Dante's poetry was weakened by a substratum of Latin scholasticism, which interfered with his perceptual primitiveness and tainted his vernacular discourse.

This appraisal of Dante is *not* Vico's definitive view of the matter. It is mentioned in the present article in the attempt to correct a popular misconception, since many scholars and historians of criticism, under the influence of pseudo-Romantic theories of poetry, erroneously present it as definitive. In the last edition of *The New Science*, Vico states unequivocally that Dante is the Tuscan Homer *in spite of* his scholasticism, which proved to be no obstacle for the force of his poetic thinking. In this version of his work, Vico paid little heed to his original typology in his treatment of Dante, since by this time the linguistic, stylistic, and conceptual heterogeneity of the *Iliad* and the *Odyssey* (both c. 800 B.C.) – within themselves and with respect to each other – had brought him to doubt their author's historical existence and to interpret the name "Homer" as a metaphor for the whole of ancient Greece, collectively narrating and celebrating its own history through the voice of its many minstrels. In Latin culture, the analogue is no longer Ennius but the law of the twelve tables, the "severe epic poem" of Rome whose author could also be regarded as an entire people. Dante's historical existence, however, could not be dismissed, and *La divina commedia* (c. 1320; *The Divine Comedy*) could not be replaced with any other work of collective authorship. Dante therefore remains a conspicuous typological

anomaly, constantly threatening the logical status of Vico's original interpretive scheme.

These ideas on poetic thinking, on the relationship between poetry and history, and on Homer and Dante constitute Vico's principal legacy for modern literary criticism. Since the turn of the twentieth century several well-known scholars have acknowledged their debt to these and other aspects of Vico's philosophy, especially his epistemological principle that human beings can understand only what can be humanly made (that is, poetry but not nature) and their discovery that poetic thinking proceeds by means of imaginative or concrete universals. In the twentieth century his foremost philosophical heir, Benedetto Croce, considered Vico the founder of aesthetics and a precursor of his own neo-Idealistic philosophy. Croce's ideas largely determined the course of mainstream criticism and Vichian studies in Italy during the first half or so of the twentieth century. Other distinguished critics who have claimed the same lineage are Erich Auerbach (especially for the idea of philology) and Mario Fubini (for the concept of imaginative universals). Since the late 1960s Vico studies have flourished on both sides of the Atlantic, and many theorists (such as Edward Said, Hayden White, and Ernesto Grassi) have found far-reaching affinities between their ideas and Vico's. The name of Vico has thus come into frequent mention in literary discussions of diverse orientations from semiotics to hermeneutics. The task of recording these affinities as they arise has been undertaken by the Institute of Vico Studies in its annual publication, *New Vico Studies*. That there is a need for such a service is a further indication of the vitality and profundity of Vico's thought.

## Principal criticism
*De Nostri Temporis Studiorum Ratione*, 1709 (*On the Study Methods of Our Times*, 1965)
*De Antiquissima Italorum Sapientia*, 1710 (partial translation in *Selected Writings*, 1982)
*De Constantia Jurisprudentis Liber Alter*, 1721
*Vita di Giambattista Vico scritta da sé medesimo*, 1725 (*The Autobiography of Giambattista Vico*, 1944)
*Principi di scienza nuova intorno alla natura delle nazioni per la quale si ritruovano i principi di altro sistema del diritto naturale delle genti*, 1725 (partial translation in *Selected Writings*)
Letter to Gherardo degli Angioli dated December 26, 1725, 1783
*Discoverta del vero Dante*, written c. 1728, published 1818 (*Discovery of the True Dante*, 1961)
*Principi di scienza nuova d'intorno alla comune natura delle nazioni*, 1744 (*The New Science*, 1948)

## Other major works and literary forms
The fields other than philosophy which for various reasons attracted Giambattista Vico were poetry, rhetoric, and history. Vico's poetry is in general studied for the light that it can shed on his intellectual development as well as to document a lingering Baroque literary taste in late-seventeenth-century Naples. His rhetorical works were originally lecture notes for his course on rhetoric at the University of

Naples; until the 1980s, when attempts were first made to study them with the seriousness that they deserve, these writings were relegated to the outer margins of Vico scholarship. His two historical works were written on commission; his life of Antonio Caraffa, however, is especially relevant to the development of Vico's philosophy, since in the course of his research for it he first read Hugo Grotius and formulated some of his most important ideas on the nature of law.

## Further reading

Auerbach, Erich. "Vico's Contribution to Literary Criticism," in *Studia Philologica et Litteraria in Honorem L. Spitzer*, 1958. Edited by A. G. Hatcher and K. L. Selig.

Croce, Benedetto. *The Philosophy of Giambattista Vico*, 1913. Translated by R. G. Collingwood.

Fubini, Mario. "Quel che ho appreso dalla mia esperienza di critico," in *Rassegna della letteratura italiana*. LVIII (1954), pp. 525–533.

Goetsch, James Robert. *Vico's Axioms: the Geometry of the Human World*, 1995.

Grassi, Ernesto. *Rhetoric as Philosophy: The Humanist Tradition*, 1980.

Kunze, Donald. *Thought and Place: The Architecture of Eternal Place in the Philosophy of Giambattista Vico*, 1987.

Lilla, Mark. *Giambattista Vico: The Making of an Anti-Modern*, 1993.

Littleford, Michael S. *Giambattista Vico, Post-Mechanical Thought, and Contemporary Psychology*, 1988.

Mali, Joseph. *The Rehabilitation of Myth: Vico's New Science*, 1992.

Miller, Cecilia. *Giambattista Vico: Imagination and Historical Knowledge*, 1993.

Pietropaolo, Domenico. "Premesse e metodi degli studi vichiani in America," in *Belfagor*. XLI (1986), pp. 263–277.

——. "Vico and Literary History in the Early Joyce," in *Vico and Joyce*, 1987. Edited by D. P. Verene.

——. *Dante Studies in the Age of Vico*, 1988.

Pompa, Leon. *Human Nature and Historical Knowledge: Hume, Hegel and Vico*, 1990.

Tagliacozzo, Giorgio, and H. White, eds. *Giambattista Vico: An International Symposium*, 1969.

Verene, Donald Phillip. *The New Art of Autobiography: An Essay on the Life of Giambattista Vico Written By Himself*, 1991.

DOMENICO PIETROPAOLO

# Voltaire

(François-Marie Arouet)

## French writer and critic

**Born:** Paris, France; November 21, 1694
**Died:** Paris, France; November 30, 1778

## Biography

After a precocious youth in which he came into personal contact with the leading libertine poets of the age and dabbled in light verse under their tutelage, François-Marie Arouet succeeded in having his play *Œdipe* (1718; *Oedipus*, 1761), written under the pseudonym Voltaire, presented at the Comédie-Française. Encountering obstacles in his efforts to ascend into French nobility, he journeyed to England, where his epic poem *La Henriade* (1728; *Henriade*, 1732) was published under the patronage of George I. While there Voltaire made the acquaintance of the leading writers, attended the theater, studied Newtonian science, and, above all, observed and admired British liberty. On his return to France, he extended his scientific studies under the guidance of his mistress, a highly competent mathematician and scientist, Mme Émilie du Châtelet. Both submitted projects for a prize offered by the French Academy of Sciences and both had their papers published. After her death Voltaire sought solace at the court of Frederick the Great of Prussia, but his residence there degenerated into a prolonged dispute with Frederick based primarily on conflicting artistic sensibilities. Taking refuge in Switzerland, Voltaire continued writing for the stage and composed his prose masterpiece *Candide: Ou, l'Optimisme* (1759; *Candide: Or, All for the Best*, 1759). Although geographically removed from France, he became involved in a number of celebrated causes concerning religious freedom, using his pen and purse to protect innocent victims of persecution. In 1777, in his eighty-third year, he made a triumphal return to Paris for the production of his latest play, *Irène* (1778). He attended the sixth performance in March and died on November 30, 1778.

## Influence

Voltaire was by no means the originator of an eighteenth-century critical new wave or of any radical method of literary analysis. On purely aesthetic matters he did not depart substantially from the prevailing attitudes of his age; it was in extending the range of literature to social areas, especially history and religious controversy, that he was a great innovator. His philosophical cosmopolitanism moreover, paralleled his influence as a comparatist. In his essay on epic poetry (1727) he revealed the unified requirements in this literary genre while revealing the differences in various national treatments. In his English letters (1733) he introduced William Shakespeare to France and recognized the importance of Newtonian philosophy. He stressed the value of universal history, insisting that it should take account of Asia and the Near East. He became an outstanding Sinophile, basing one of his own dramas, *L'Orphelin de la Chine* (1755; *The Orphan of China*, 1756), on an actual Chinese play and arguing in his preface that it should be played as realistically as possible. Finally, in joining the concepts of liberty and letters, he made his greatest impact upon both contemporary life and posterity. As weapons in the crusade for freedom of expression in every area, his satires and tracts had a substantial effect in promoting religious toleration in France and elsewhere in the Western world.

## Analysis

If it is true, as is sometimes affirmed, that Voltaire was the greatest French critic of the eighteenth century, criticism as applied to Voltaire must not be confined to belles lettres but must extend to all aspects of human concern, comprising even his battle cry against religious intolerance, "*Écrasez l'infâme*" (stamp out infamy). Voltaire classed as genres of literature everything from mathematics to the epigram and defined literature as knowledge of the objects of belles lettres, a somewhat circular manner of referring to masterpieces. Yet he also termed it a perpetual battle between bees and hornets, a discrimination between creative writers and the critics who disparaged them. Rejecting systems of all kinds, literary as well as philosophical, his criticism is more empirical than theoretical, particular than general, but, nevertheless, not chaotic. Voltaire believed in universal standards even though most of his pronouncements were highly subjective. Pure literature, for Voltaire, consisted in what would be called today fugitive or occasional verse, that which diverts the serious thinker and maintains the French national character of wit and refinement. Important as it is, this pure literature Voltaire considered inferior to writing that carries a philosophical message. He esteemed poetry only as it functions as the ornament of reason. In an epistle to Mme du Châtelet, he declared that his century was a period when a poet had to be a philosopher and a bold woman was able to be a poet. Voltaire's other major category of literature consists of the drama, a genre that must stir human emotions and reflect life, not comment on it. Despite Voltaire's many pronouncements on the preeminence of philosophy over poetry, he remained somewhat ambivalent on the subject, expressing a number of stylistic principles that have nothing to do with philosophy. He also applied to several works the method of criticism known as beauties and faults, that is, citing outstanding examples of each characteristic in various works under scrutiny. Despite occasional inconsistencies and discrepancies in Voltaire's judgments, many of which were the result of experience and broadening vision over a lifetime of eight decades, he reveals on the whole a surprising uniformity.

Like nearly everyone else in the early eighteenth century, Voltaire accepted without question neoclassical standards as set forth by such established predecessors as Nicolas Boileau-Despréaux but did not cite them as infallible guides or follow them slavishly, relying more on individual taste and good sense than on absolute prescriptions. Indeed, he declared that to judge only by the rules is to judge badly. In satirizing Platonic notions of eternal beauty, Voltaire affirmed that a toad would locate beauty in the large eyes and small head of a female toad. As evidence of the diversity in human attitudes, he added that what is decent in Japan is indecent in Rome and what is in vogue in Paris is not so in Peking (Beijing). Nevertheless, in agreement with the notion of the unity of moral and plastic beauty, he

argued that some actions are universally regarded as beautiful – for example, dying for the benefit of one's friend or father. Material artifacts are relative; a Jesuit who had seen the magnificent palaces of China was disappointed by Versailles, whereas some visitors from Germany were ecstatic about it. Yet the great ethical maxims of Zoroaster and Confucius are universally accepted as beautiful. Voltaire's standard for literary judgment is highly personal: the only good books are those which the reader would like to read a second time; these are the ones that appeal to the imagination and please the ear by their harmony. In his own reading, he allowed himself to be led by his author, rejoicing in his pleasure and never quibbling.

Since Voltaire's epic *Henriade* did not conform fully to strict neoclassical prescriptions, Voltaire argued that the modern epic is different from that of the ancient and that the French is different from the Italian and English. His essay on the subject, presenting a brief history of the genre in seven literatures, is a pioneer contribution to comparative literature. There can be no doubt concerning Voltaire's cosmopolitanism. He maintained that a true man of letters must cultivate several genres, not confine himself to novels, plays, or sermons, and know other languages besides his own. Apart from the classical languages, he considered Italian and English most vital for his own compatriots. The literary individual need not possess a universal knowledge but should be able to traverse the various terrains even if unable to cultivate all of them. He called for French journals to compare new French works with those of other nations on the same subjects and to trace the treatment of themes in various literatures. Parallels of this kind, he suggested, are like comparative anatomy, giving insight into the workings of nature. He even hoped that journals would report on literary and other developments in China and the Near East. In his own dramas, moreover, he adapted themes from China, Egypt, Turkey, and South America. In regard to what was then called "universal history," he took the radical position that it should cover the origins of civilization in Africa and Asia instead of beginning with the Old Testament.

Voltaire drew a distinction between a critic, a man of letters, and a genius. Following classical precedent, he regarded critics as an ill-natured inferior race, labeling them the veterinarians of literature because they never find a healthy author. They make their living saying bad things about good works and good things about bad ones. If good critics existed, they would be artists possessing considerable knowledge and taste, but without prejudice or envy. Nevertheless, critical writing even at its best cannot be ranked with works containing beauty, those such as poetry and well-written history. Beauty is lacking even in such useful forms of criticism as interpretations of authors and chronological research. One never speaks of a beautiful commentary or a beautiful critique as one does of a beautiful passage by a great writer. A man of letters in the best sense is a journalist who describes the masterpieces of others, but the authors of these masterpieces, men such as Horace and Pierre Corneille, are men of genius.

For Voltaire, genius is the same thing as talent or a disposition to succeed in art, but he applies the term only to those writers whose gifts are extraordinary. He observed that genius guided by taste will never make mistakes, but that without taste, it will make enormous blunders and not even recognize them as such. Taste he defined as the recognition of beauties and faults in the arts. It is not entirely an intellectual quality but must please the senses as well. A person of literary taste recognizes the mixture of styles as a gourmet senses a blending of liquors. Nevertheless, reliance on taste does not mean capitulation to relativism. Good taste is based on reason and deviations from it may be corrected. The truism that one must not argue about taste is valid only in regard to food and does not apply to the arts. Although sense perception cannot be changed, a knowledge of the arts may be cultivated. One person who knows the ancient authors and who has compared their translations and commentaries on them is a better critic than another of greater taste who merely knows the good authors of his or her own country and is guided by a facile pleasure. Even in taste the *consensus gentium* reigns. Depraved taste is preferring that which disgusts others. The best taste in every literary genre imitates nature with the utmost grace and fidelity. Grace, as distinguished from wit, consists in giving life and sweetness to represented objects. Wit is a purely verbal adornment, inferior to simple and natural statement. Voltaire also maintained that those who have excelled in thought are those who have excelled in style. In keeping with his cosmopolitanism, Voltaire observed that as a single artist develops his or her taste, an entire nation may do so also. Aware of both national differences and universal qualities, he observed that some beauties prevail in all times and places, whereas others are mainly local. Although Voltaire lived for most of his life outside Paris, he believed that taste is present only in the capitals of great empires and even then is the property of a small community.

Voltaire regarded French letters, especially the French theater, as humanity's highest artistic achievement. About Shakespeare, he was ambivalent. He took credit for having introduced this "natural and sublime genius" to his compatriots and declared that Shakespeare's genius was his own, but that his faults were those of his century. In analyzing Shakespeare's plays, however, he considered these faults, such as vulgarity, bombast, and mixing the base with the sublime and buffoonery with terror, as personal characteristics of the author. Voltaire nevertheless wrote a play, *La Mort de César* (1733), based to some degree on Shakespeare's *Julius Caesar* (c. 1599–1600) and a preface comparing his work with Shakespeare's. He also translated the first three acts of *Julius Caesar* and compared them unfavorably with Corneille's *Cinna: Ou, La Clémence*

*d'Auguste* (1640; *Cinna*, 1713), remarking that Shakespeare was a genius in a period when taste had not yet been formed. Voltaire also took credit for introducing John Locke and Sir Isaac Newton to French thought and wrote extensively on both.

In the great battle between the partisans of the ancients and the moderns, Voltaire enlisted on the side of the moderns, although reluctantly at first. It was only logical that he should subsequently become a fervent believer in the doctrine of progress in all aspects of human life. He ridiculed the spirit of criticism that, tired of persecuting individuals, had taken to crying that the earth was degenerating and that the population was shrinking, stating that humanity's value and number were both increasing. From the perspective of artistic creation, he could conceive of nothing finer than the Golden Age of Louis XIV.

As one of his century's most fiery advocates of the union of liberty and letters, Voltaire argued for toleration in both religion and literature. He admitted that many books are boring, but he said that he knew of none that had done any real harm. Voltaire maintained that if people were allowed the freedom to read and dream, these two amusements would never bring evil into the world. In his personal struggle for intellectual liberty, Voltaire promoted Deism, religious toleration, international understanding, and freedom of the press.

Voltaire did not shine as a pure theorist, and he was no critical innovator, accepting and applying most of the neoclassical presuppositions of his age. He made an important independent contribution, however, in recognizing and tracing the historical development of literary genres and themes. He introduced Shakespeare to France and sought to maintain the prestige of the great French dramatists of the seventeenth century while expanding the stage to incorporate international themes. In practical criticism, he worked to substitute rational analysis for personal bias. He exalted taste and good sense over mechanical rules and conceived of literature in general as a powerful instrument in the struggle for human progress.

## Principal criticism

*An Essay upon the Civil Wars of France . . . and Also upon the Epick Poetry of the European Nations from Homer Down to Milton*, 1727
*Le Temple du goût*, 1733 (*The Temple of Taste*, 1734)
*Letters Concerning the English Nation*, 1733
Articles in *Dictionnaire philosophique portatif*, 1764 (*A Philosophical Dictionary for the Pocket*, 1765; also as *Philosophical Dictionary*, 1945)
*Commentaires sur le théâtre de Pierre Corneille*, 1764

## Other major works and literary forms

As one of the most prolific and versatile authors of his century, Voltaire contributed to almost every literary genre then practiced. Although today his philosophical fiction is most popular, he himself took greatest pride in his dramas and in his title as "the modern Sophocles." In addition to much occasional verse, he wrote *La Henriade* (1728; *Henriade*, 1732), the major European epic to appear between those of John Milton and Nikos Kazantzakis, and one of the wittiest parodies of that genre, *La Pucelle d'Orléans* (1755, 1762; *The Maid of Orleans*, 1758, also as *La Pucelle*). He contributed to social history with his *Histoire de Charles XII* (1731; *The History of Charles XII*, 1732), *Le Siècle de Louis XIV* (1751; *The Age of Louis XIV*, 1752), and *Essai sur les mœurs* (1756, 1763; *The General History and State of Europe*, 1754, 1759). In addition, Voltaire brought the genre of the philosophical tale to perfection with *Zadig: Ou, La Destinée, histoire orientale* (1748; *Zadig: Or, The Book of Fate*, 1749); *Le Micromégas* (1752; *Micromegas*, 1753); his masterpiece, *Candide: Ou, L'Optimisme* (1759; *Candide: Or, All for the Best*, 1759); and *L'Ingénu* (1767; *The Pupil of Nature*, 1771, also as *Ingenuous*). Outstanding among his works on Deism is a poem, *Épître à Uranie* (1732), and on social criticism a prose tract, *Traité sur la tolérance* (1763; *A Treatise on Religious Toleration*, 1764). Also recommended are the prefaces, introductions, and dedications to Voltaire's plays, especially those of *Oedipe* (1718; *Oedipus*, 1761), *Zaïre* (1732; English translation, 1761), *Sémiramis* (1748; *Semiramis*, 1760), *Oreste* (1750), *L'Orphelin de la Chine* (1755; *The Orphan of China*, 1756), *L'Écossaise* (1760; *The Highland Girl*, 1760), *Les Scythes* (1767), *Don Pèdre* (1775), and *Irène* (1778).

## NOVELS

*Zadig: Ou, La Destinée, histoire orientale*, 1748 (originally as *Memnon: Histoire orientale*, 1747; *Zadig: Or, The Book of Fate*, 1749)

*Le Micromégas*, 1752 (*Micromegas*, 1753)

*Histoire des voyages de Scarmentado*, 1756 (*The History of the Voyages of Scarmentedo*, 1757, also as *History of Scarmentado's Travels*, 1961)

*Candide: Ou, L'Optimisme*, 1759 (*Candide: Or, All for the Best*, 1759)

*L'Ingénu*, 1767 (*The Pupil of Nature*, 1771, also as *Ingenuous*, 1961)

*L'Homme aux quarante écus*, 1768 (*The Man of Forty Crowns*, 1768)

*La Princesse de Babylone*, 1768 (*The Princess of Babylon*, 1769)

## SHORT FICTION

*Le Monde comme il va*, 1746

*Memnon: Ou, La Sagesse humaine*, 1749 (*Memnon: Or, Human Wisdom*, 1961)

*La Lettre d'un Turc*, 1750

*Le Blanc et le noir*, 1764 (*The Two Genies*, 1895)

*Jeannot et Colin*, 1764

*L'Histoire de Jenni*, 1775

*Les Oreilles du comte de Chesterfield*, 1775 (*The Ears of Lord Chesterfield and Parson Goodman*, 1826)

## PLAYS

*Oedipe*, 1718 (*Oedipus*, 1761)

*Artémire*, 1720

*Mariamne*, 1724 (English translation, 1761)

*L'Indiscret*, 1725 (verse)

*Brutus*, 1730 (English translation, 1761)

*Ériphyle*, 1732

*Zaïre*, 1732 (English translation, 1736)

*La Mort de César*, 1733

*Adélaïde du Guesclin*, 1734

*L'Échange*, 1734

*Alzire*, 1736 (English translation, 1763)

*L'Enfant prodigue*, 1736 (verse; *The Prodigal*, 1750? Prose translation)

*La Prude: Ou, La Grandeuse de Cassette*, written 1740, published 1747 (verse, based on William Wycherley's play *The Plain-Dealer*)

*Zulime*, 1740

*Mahomet*, 1742 (*Mahomet the Prophet*, 1744)

*Mérope*, 1743 (English translation, 1744, 1749)

*La Princesse de Navarre*, 1745 (verse, music by Jean-Philippe Rameau)

*Sémiramis*, 1748 (*Semiramis*, 1760)

*Nanine*, 1749 (English translation, 1927)

*Oreste*, 1750

*Rome sauvée*, 1752

*L'Orphelin de la Chine*, 1755 (*The Orphan of China*, 1756)

*Socrate*, 1759 (*Socrates*, 1760)

*L'Écossaise*, 1760 (*The Highland Girl*, 1760)

*Tancrède*, 1760

*Don Pèdre*, written 1761, published 1775

*Olympie*, 1763

*Le Triumvirat*, 1764

*Les Scythes*, 1767

*Les Guèbres: Qu, La Tolérance*, 1769

*Sophonisbe*, 1770 (revision of Jean Mairet's play)

*Les Pélopides: Ou, Atrée et Thyeste*, 1772

*Les Lois de Minos*, 1773

*Irène*, 1778

*Agathocle*, 1779

## POETRY

*Poème sur la religion naturelle*, 1722

*La Ligue*, 1723

*La Henriade*, 1728 (revision of *La Ligue*; *Henriade*, 1732)

*Épître à Uranie*, 1732

*Le Mondain*, 1736 (*The Man of the World*, 1764)

*Discours en vers sur l'homme*, 1738–1752 (*Discourses in Verse on Man*, 1764)

*Poème de Fontenoy*, 1745

*Poème sur les événements de l'année 1744*, 1745

*Poème de la loi naturelle*, 1752 (*On Natural Law*, 1764)

*La Pucelle d'Orléans*, 1755, 1762 (*The Maid of Orleans*, 1758, also as *La Pucelle*, 1785–1786)

*Poème sur le désastre de Lisbonne*, 1756 (*Poem on the Lisbon Earthquake*, 1764)

*Poème sur la loi naturelle*, 1756

*Le Pauvre Diable*, 1758

*Épître à Horace*, 1772

## NONFICTION

*Histoire de Charles XII*, 1731 (*The History of Charles XII*, 1732)

*Discours de métaphysique*, 1736

*Éléments de la philosophie de Newton*, 1738 (*The Elements of Sir Isaac Newton's Philosophy*, 1738)

*Vie de Molière*, 1739

*Le Siècle de Louis XIV*, 1751 (*The Age of Louis XIV*, 1752)

*Essai sur les mœurs*, 1756, 1763 (*The General History and State of Europe*, 1754, 1759)

*Traité sur la tolérance*, 1763 (*A Treatise on Religious Toleration*, 1764)

*Dictionnaire philosophique portatif*, 1764 (*A Philosophical Dictionary for the Pocket*, 1765, also as *Philosophical Dictionary*, 1945)
*Avis au public sur les parricides imputés aux Calas et aux Sirven*, 1775
*Correspondence*, 1953–1965 (102 volumes)

MISCELLANEOUS
*The Works of M. de Voltaire*, 1761–1765 (35 volumes), 1761–1781 (38 volumes)
*The Complete Works of Voltaire*, 1968–1977 (135 volumes)

## Further reading

Aldridge, A. Owen. *Voltaire and the Century of Light*, 1975.
Besterman, Theodore. *Voltaire*, 1969, 1976.
Mason, Haydn. *Voltaire: A Biography*, 1981.
Navès, Raymond. *Le Goût de Voltaire*, 1938.
Pomeau, René, and others. *Voltaire en son temps*, 1995 (2 volumes).
Ridgway, R. S. *Voltaire and Sensibility*, 1973.
*Studies on Voltaire and the Eighteenth Century*, 1955– . Under the directorship of Theodore Besterman, 1955–1977, and Haydn Mason, 1977–
Truit, Marie-Paule. *La poétique de Voltaire d'après sa correspondance de 1704 à 1757*, 1984.
Wade, Ira Owen. *The Intellectual Development of Voltaire*, 1969.

A. Owen Aldridge

*See also* Diderot; Hume; Neoclassical Literary Theory; Rousseau

# Robert Penn Warren

American teacher, critic, poet, and novelist

**Born:** Guthrie, Kentucky; April 24, 1905
**Died:** Stratton, Vermont; September 15, 1989

## Biography

Robert Penn Warren was born on April 24, 1905, in Guthrie, Kentucky, to Robert Franklin and Anna Ruth Penn Warren. His father was a small-town banker. Warren often spent his summers on the farm of his grandfather, Gabriel Thomas Penn, who had been a cavalryman in the Confederate Army. The young Warren absorbed the folklore of both the local tobacco wars and the Civil War, as well as various frontier legends, elements of which appear in his poetry and fiction.

He enrolled in Vanderbilt University in 1921, where he became a member of the literary group known as the Fugitives, which published some of his first verse. John Crowe Ransom and Allen Tate were his special friends. After he graduated from Vanderbilt, he earned an M.A. from the University of California at Berkeley and did postgraduate work at Yale University.

Warren taught in the English department at Vanderbilt from 1934 to 1936, then joined the faculty of Louisiana State University. While there he absorbed the folklore of Huey Long, which was to result in *All the King's Men* ten years later. He also began his fruitful partnership with Cleanth Brooks, an association that began when the two coedited *The Southern Review* and resulted in their collaboration on numerous textbooks.

Warren was a professor of English at Yale University from 1961 to 1973. When he was seventy-three years old he won his second Pulitzer Prize for Poetry. In later years he revised *Brother to Dragons* and produced several more volumes of poetry. In 1986 he was named the first poet laureate of the United States.

## Influence

Warren is important not for originating the so-called New Criticism but, often in collaboration with Cleanth Brooks, for promulgating its methods of detailed explication of the texts of poetry and fiction. With their widely used texts, *An Approach to Literature: A Collection of Prose and Verse with Analysis and Discussions* (1936), *Understanding Poetry: An Anthology for College Students* (1938), and *Understanding Fiction* (1943), Brooks and Warren revolutionized methods of teaching literature in American colleges. Both teachers and students became more aware of the rhetorical principles that account for the emotional and intellectual impact of literature. This rhetorical analysis of literary texts was intended to compensate for the fact that teachers in graduate schools were generally trained to focus on biographical and social backgrounds of literature, while students were accustomed to direct, denotative prose and deaf to the niceties of metaphor, symbol, and irony. Thus, Warren and Brooks, though perfectly aware of the importance of social milieu and the personal background of the artist, provided what seemed to be most needed at that time – a better understanding of how literature works.

## Analysis

Warren's special contribution to the study of literature is a clear, forceful exposition of the reasons for reading literature, the rhetorical principles involved in poetry and fiction, and the nature of the process of writing poetry. He also produced perceptive critical essays on William Faulkner, Ernest Hemingway, Katherine Anne Porter, Joseph Conrad, and Samuel Taylor Coleridge.

At the 1979 College English Association meeting, Cleanth Brooks addressed the group on "Forty Years of Understanding Poetry," providing a short history of the most famous of the textbooks that he wrote with Warren and correcting some misconceptions about their intentions. Brooks pointed out that he and Warren were excited about new trends in literature, especially the critical essays and poetry of T. S. Eliot and the theory and practical criticism of I. A. Richards. Moreover, they were faced with students who approached a poem as they would an advertisement in a Sears, Roebuck catalog, expecting plain delivery of information. Apparently, no one had demonstrated the functions of metaphorical language, irony, symbol, imagery, or rhythm. Most anthologies provided meager footnotes that might provide the meaning of allusions or difficult words or helpful historical or biographical facts. The students needed more help.

Thus, the first "book" was born – a set of mimeographed class notes, much of it Warren's, to distribute to their classes. Their first real book, entitled *An Approach to Literature*, met with considerable distaste from colleagues at Louisiana State University and was often referred to as "the Reproach to Literature," a witticism that Warren and Brooks themselves adopted.

Opposition to the methods of Brooks and Warren focused mostly on what they had left out of the discussions – references to history, biography, and cultural background. It was not their intention, however, to slight such matters. It would be absurd to assume that Warren, to whom history and cultural milieu are so important, would be uninterested in such literary influences. Warren and Brooks were simply supplementing literary study where it seemed weakest. Since graduate schools that molded instructors of the 1930s stressed background, biography, and history, Warren and Brooks assumed that instructors would provide those elements for their students.

Some of Warren's comments appear in other college anthologies, such as *The Short Story: An Inductive Approach* (1967), which includes his "Why Do We Read Fiction?" Here Warren explores the function of role-taking, which is a part of the enjoyment of fiction. Only by role-playing can children come to know that other people really exist and have needs, hopes, fears, and even rights. Reading or listening to stories aids this process of acquiring empathy. It also contributes to an awareness and understanding of oneself.

Warren considers that an individual is not born with a self, but must create it, bit by bit, in a long process of trial and error. Even after the emergence of the official self, the ringmaster who claims to be in charge, the secret self is still rife with contradictions. As Warren expresses it, there is knife-fighting in the inner dark. Fiction in its more subtle forms may offer release from these hidden conflicts even when they are not consciously recognized as personal problems. Thus, successful fiction brings some sense of reconciliation with the world and with oneself. Warren compares the life process to a lover's quarrel, oscillating between conflict and reconciliation, a pattern enriched in fiction with many variations.

Warren's explanation of the psychological function of literature for the reader reflects what he expresses elsewhere when he discusses writing from the artist's standpoint of working through internal conflicts. Perhaps his best-known essay on this topic is "Pure and Impure Poetry," published in *Selected Essays* (1958). Actually, Warren had ironically put his concept of impurity in poetry into the mouth of Slim Sarrett, the sleazy intellectual in his novel *At Heaven's Gate* (1943). In his essay, he points out that "Poetry" wants to be pure, but poems do not. Therefore, poems may be marred with ugly words, jagged rhythms, argument, even clichés and seemingly inappropriate details, all of which call the reader back to prose and imperfection. The poem must earn its point of reconciliation by working through the ambiguities and ironies that impede the desired purity. Poetry which has no trace of internal ambiguity is often simply sentimental, an unhindered toboggan slide of the emotions.

He illustrates the principle of impurity by referring to the famous garden scene in William Shakespeare's play *Romeo and Juliet* (c. 1595). Surely here is an example of purity in poetry, the expression of young love as yet unsullied by exploitation or carnality. Yet its special poignancy is heightened by one's realization that on the other side of the garden wall Mercutio is making bawdy jokes. Moreover, the earthy nurse is close by, and even Juliet herself ("Swear not by the inconstant moon . . .") tempers the romanticism of Romeo. The effect is not to destroy the vision of romantic love, but to show how very fragile and therefore precious it is.

*Selected Essays* also contains articles on Ernest Hemingway, Robert Frost, William Faulkner, Katherine Anne Porter, Joseph Conrad, and Samuel Taylor Coleridge. Warren's reflections on the last two are especially illuminating, not only concerning the subject under discussion, but also regarding Warren's own attitudes toward humanity and nature and what is worthy of expression in fiction and poetry. "The Great Mirage: Conrad and *Nostromo*" is surely one of the most cogent pieces in Conrad criticism. Warren's explication of the enigmatic speech of Stein in *Lord Jim* (1900), beginning "A man that is born falls into a dream like a man who falls into the sea," is remarkably insightful. He interprets the dream as humanity's necessity to justify itself by the "idea," to idealize itself and its actions into moral significance. The difficulty lies in people's egotistical savage impulses, never completely adapted to the dream sea of ideas. Yet those who take a purely naturalistic view, denying the dream, refusing to create values that are "supernatural" (and therefore human), will drown. The person who learns to swim in the unnatural sea of ideas realizes that the values he or she creates are illusion, but that the illusion is necessary and the mark of his or her humanity. Anyone who has read Warren's novels *World Enough and Time* (1950), *Meet Me in the Green Glen* (1971), and *Wilderness: A Tale of the Civil War* (1961) must realize how vital to his own fiction is this dream sea of ideas, this illusion by which people justify themselves.

Warren classifies thematic elements in Conrad's stories as built around three kinds of persons: the person who lacks imagination but clings to fidelity and duty (exemplified by the old captain in *Youth*, 1902), the sinner against human solidarity and the human mission (such as Kurtz in *Heart of Darkness*, 1902, and Decoud in *Nostromo*, 1904), and the redeemed sinner (such as Lord Jim or Dr. Monygham in *Nostromo*). This classification happens to be useful in analyzing Warren's fictional characters as well, especially in *At Heaven's Gate*.

The longest and most complex study in *Selected Essays* is "A Poem of Pure Imagination: An Experiment in Reading," which deals with Coleridge's *The Rime of the Ancient Mariner* (1798). The essay includes a detailed consideration of most of the critical controversies that have surrounded Coleridge's poem, such as the complaint that the killing of the albatross is unmotivated or simply frivolous. Warren explains that its very lack of motivation helps to establish the killing as an especially perverse act – a crime against nature and therefore a crime against God. Further, the killing is a crime of the imagination. Warren suggests that the poem has a primary theme, which is the sacramental vision, or the theme of the "one life," culminating in the message explicitly stated ("He prayeth best, who loveth best/ All things both great and small"). No less important, however, is the secondary theme, which concerns the imagination.

Warren then sets the poem in the framework of a general effort among Romantic poets to combine moral and aesthetic principles in the same creative activity. Beauty is truth, truth beauty, as John Keats put it, and morality is part of the same process. Warren's argument is that *The Rime of the Ancient Mariner* was written both out of and about this general belief.

In 1974 the National Endowment for the Humanities chose Warren to deliver the third annual Jefferson Lecture in the Humanities, published as *Democracy and Poetry* (1975). Warren here uses the term "poetry" to represent art in general, reviewing American literature as a criticism of Americans' actual achievements in democracy.

Warren points out that in Jefferson's time, the term "democracy" was almost synonymous with "anarchy." Jefferson did envisage a society in which free men – of independent self – would exercise their franchise in the light of reason." Walt Whitman and Ralph Waldo Emerson express a more romantic and mystical view of democracy, while James Fenimore Cooper, who, unlike Jefferson, declared himself a democrat, deplores both the tyranny of majority rule and the corrupting influence of plutocracy, which uses the language of democracy for demagogic perversions. After the Civil War, even Whitman in *Democratic Vistas* (1871) sounds disillusioned with the masses he once extolled.

Warren passes from the acrid social criticism of Mark Twain to the amoral protagonists of Theodore Dreiser, who represent "a land of fictive values seized, or yearned after, by fictive selves." The "fictive selves" march on through F. Scott Fitzgerald's *The Great Gatsby* (1925), Faulkner's Popeye and Joe Christmas, and Hemingway's Frederick Henry, who resigns from society in *A Farewell to Arms* (1929). Warren maintains that the absolute individualism of the lonely hero can only result in another fictive self, since the valid self derives from a relationship between the individual and society.

In spite of this critical and subversive message, Warren demonstrates that "poetry . . . is a dynamic affirmation of, as well as the image of, the concept of the self" which is so crucial for a responsible expression of democracy.

## Principal criticism

*An Approach to Literature: A Collection of Prose and Verse with Analysis and Discussions*, 1936 (with Cleanth Brooks and John Thibaut Purser)
*Understanding Poetry: An Anthology for College Students*, 1938 (editor, with Brooks)
*Understanding Fiction*, 1943 (editor, with Brooks)
*Modern Rhetoric*, 1949 (editor, with Brooks; better known as *Fundamentals of Good Writing: A Handbook of Modern Rhetoric*, 1950)
*Selected Essays*, 1958
*Faulkner: A Collection of Critical Essays*, 1966 (editor)
*A Plea in Mitigation: Modern Poetry and the End of an Era*, 1966
*Randall Jarrell, 1914–1965*, 1967 (editor, with Robert Lowell and Peter Taylor)
*American Literature: The Makers and the Making*, 1974 (2 volumes, with R. W. B. Lewis)
*Democracy and Poetry*, 1975

## Other major works and literary forms

Robert Penn Warren published eighteen volumes of poetry, including two winners of Pulitzer Prizes, *Promises: Poems 1954–1956* (1957) and *Now and Then: Poems 1976–1978* (1978). Some of his notable long poems include a frontier legend, "The Ballad of Billie Potts," and biographical poems about John James Audubon and Chief Joseph of the Nez Percé. The unique book-length poetic drama *Brother to Dragons: A Tale in Verse and Voices* (1953) is a grisly tale combining philosophical speculations with a true story of the brutal murder of a young slave perpetrated by a nephew of Thomas Jefferson.

Warren's first significant publication in nonfiction was a biography, *John Brown: The Making of a Martyr* (1929). He published one volume of short stories, *The Circus in the Attic and Other Stories* (1947), which includes his well-known short story "Blackberry Winter."

He also published ten novels, including the Pulitzer Prize-winning *All the King's Men* (1946), based loosely on the legend of Huey Long, the Louisiana politician who led a populist revolt against a traditional governing elite. Other significant novels are *Night Rider* (1939), *World Enough and Time* (1950), and *The Cave* (1959), all of which have some reference to actual events in Southern experience. Both his poetry and his fiction explore the themes of identity and the tendency to live in socially dictated illusions.

NOVELS
*Night Rider*, 1939
*At Heaven's Gate*, 1943
*All the King's Men*, 1946
*World Enough and Time*, 1950
*Band of Angels*, 1955
*The Cave*, 1959

*Wilderness: A Tale of the Civil War*, 1961
*Flood: A Romance of Our Time*, 1964
*Meet Me in the Green Glen*, 1971
*A Place to Come To*, 1977

SHORT FICTION
*The Circus in the Attic and Other Stories*, 1947

PLAY
*All the King's Men*, 1960

POETRY
*Thirty-six Poems*, 1935
*Eleven Poems on the Same Theme*, 1942
*Selected Poems, 1923–1943*, 1944
*Brother to Dragons: A Tale in Verse and Voices*, 1953, 1979
*Promises: Poems 1954–1956*, 1957
*You, Emperors, and Others: Poems: 1957–1960*, 1960
*Selected Poems: New and Old, 1923–1966*, 1966
*Incarnations: Poems 1966–1968*, 1968
*Audubon: A Vision*, 1969
*Homage to Theodore Dreiser, August 27, 1871–December 28, 1945, on the Centennial of His Birth*, 1971
*Or Else – Poem / Poems 1968–1974*, 1974
*Selected Poems: 1923–1975*, 1976
*Now and Then: Poems 1976–1978*, 1978
*Being Here: Poetry 1977–1980*, 1980
*Ballad of a Deep Dream of Peace*, 1981
*Rumor Verified: Poems 1979–1980*, 1981
*Chief Joseph of the Nez Percé*, 1983
*New and Selected Poems, 1923–1985*, 1985
*The Collected Poems of Robert Penn Warren*, 1998

NONFICTION
*John Brown: The Making of a Martyr*, 1929
*Segregation: The Inner Conflict of the South*, 1956
*Who Speaks for the Negro?*, 1965
*Portrait of a Father*, 1988

## Further reading

Blotner, Joseph Leo. *Robert Penn Warren: A Biography*, 1997.
Bradbury, John M. *The Fugitives: A Critical Account*, 1958.
Burt, John. *Robert Penn Warren and American Idealism*, 1988.
Clark, William Bedford. *The American Vision of Robert Penn Warren*, 1991.
Cowan, Louise. *The Fugitive Group: A Literary History*, 1959.
Cowley, Malcolm, ed. *Writers at Work: The Paris Review Interviews*, 1958.
Grimshaw, James A., ed. *Cleanth Brooks and Robert Penn Warren: A Literary Correspondence*, 1998.
Guttenberg, Barnett. *Web of Being*, 1975.
Jancovich, Mark. *The Cultural Politics of the New Criticism*, 1993.
Justus, James H. *The Achievement of Robert Penn Warren*, 1981.
Koppelman, Robert S. *Robert Penn Warren's Modernist Spirituality*, 1995.
Snipes, Katherine. *Robert Penn Warren*, 1983.
Strandberg, Victor. *The Poetic Vision of Robert Penn Warren*, 1977.
Walker, Marshall. *Robert Penn Warren: A Vision Earned*, 1979.

KATHERINE SNIPES

*See also* American Literary Theory: Twentieth Century; Brooks, C.; New Criticism

# Joseph Warton and Thomas Warton

English critics and poets

### Joseph Warton
**Born:** Dunsfold, Surrey, England; April 22, 1722 (baptized)
**Died:** Wickham, Hampshire, England; February 23, 1800

### Thomas Warton
**Born:** Basingstoke, Hampshire, England; January 9, 1727
**Died:** Oxford, England; May 21, 1790

## Biography

Joseph Warton and Thomas Warton were born into a clerical and literary family. Their father, Thomas Warton, the elder, was a professor of poetry at Oxford between 1718 and 1723. In 1723 he became vicar at Basingstoke; he headed a small grammar school, where his sons received their early education. Joseph went on to Winchester College and then to New College, Oxford. He, too, became a cleric and joined his father in Basingstoke, serving as curate until his father's death in 1745. He held various church appointments during the next ten years. In 1755 he was asked to return to Winchester; he served as headmaster there from 1766 to 1793. His good nature, modest scholarship, and interest in letters led him into the literary circles of London, and for several years he was an intimate of Samuel Johnson. On leaving Winchester he settled in his church living in Wickham, continuing his literary writing. He died there on February 23, 1800, and was buried at Winchester Cathedral.

Thomas was kept at home and entirely educated by his father before going up to Trinity College, Oxford. He graduated in 1747 and took holy orders, but remained in Oxford as a college don throughout his life. Aside from his university work and his writing, he developed an enthusiasm for archaeological studies, and his journeys to old castles and churches were to feed his lifelong interest in the medieval arts.

Appointed professor of poetry in 1757, he held that post for ten years, going on to become Camden Professor of History (1785–1790). His most prestigious public recognition, however, was his appointment in 1785 as poet laureate. His work on the history of English poetry occupied much of his time from the 1770s onward; together with his final scholarly work, an edition of the minor poems of John Milton, it established his reputation as a man of letters. In 1790, suffering from gout, he was felled by a stroke while sitting in his college common room and died the following day (May 21). He was buried in his college chapel.

## Analysis

The Warton brothers, who wrote independently of each other, seem unlikely figures for the positions of importance and influence which their work finally attained, given the modesty of their talents and their rather benign, gentle-manly, and often-amateurish ways of scholarship. Indeed, their work on the major poets of England has not stood up well in the long run. Their importance results from the happy chance of their presence at a time when the ideas about poetry in Great Britain were in a state of flux. The Wartons championed new theories about how poetry should be judged and, quite as significantly, how it should be written.

Early in the course of his critical work, Joseph Warton realized that an understanding of any artist, particularly one of an earlier age, required an understanding of the kind of world in which the artist lived. Thus, the standards that were generally accepted in the early eighteenth century were not always appropriate for judging the work of poets of earlier times. That insight was coupled by both the Wartons with another proposition which was to be even more impor-tant: that the standards of the Restoration and the early eighteenth century might no longer be of use in the latter half of the century, and that the poetry of the Restoration and the early eighteenth century was, perhaps, not quite as good as it had seemed to be.

The general attitude toward politics, religion, society, the arts, and personal relationships which obtained in the period immediately after the restoration of the monarchy in 1660 was stunningly different from that which had existed when England was under the rigorously righteous hand of the Cromwellian Commonwealth. The transfer of political power had enormous cultural consequence: the arts leaped into lively and often riotously sophisticated cele-bration of life at its most pleasurable. What Charles II wanted in the arts (particularly in the theater) was wit, charm, sophistication, and smart sexual shenanigans. Members of the middle and upper classes wanted what the king wanted, not simply in order to flatter him but also in reaction to the dourness of the Puritan regime. The theater was the center of London frivolity. Though the tragedies of William Shakespeare were appreciated, and a handful of the best playwrights wrote moderately successful tragedies, the preferred drama was comic, with strong doses of social satire. To satisfy the public's cravings, new playwrights such as William Wycherley, Sir George Etherege, William Congreve, and Sir John Vanbrugh produced splendidly witty, often ribald plays. This flowering of the theater was paralleled in other literary fields. John Dryden, who was also a playwright, established a new style of satirical poetry during the period between Charles II's return and the turn of the century; he was followed by Jonathan Swift, who was probably better as a prose satirist than as a poet, but formidable in both genres, and Alexander Pope, who honed the heroic couplet to satirical perfection.

Expressions of serious feeling, however, were rare; there seemed to be a gentleman's agreement that shows of emotion in the arts were bad form and that sharp wit was to be prized above all other literary skills. As early as the first decade of the eighteenth century, however, there were signs that some critics were dissatisfied with the prevailing emphasis upon the intellect, not only as manifested in current works but also for the corresponding denigration of earlier literature, particularly that of the medieval period, because it was seen as being tastelessly inclined to the explo-ration of feeling and fancy. Joseph Addison, in his *The Tatler* and *The Spectator* essays, tentatively suggested that the old ballads had something to offer and that the imag-ination, as well as the intellect, had a role to play in liter-ature and life. Anthony Ashley Cooper, the third Earl of Shaftesbury, produced an eccentric, rambling set of essays, *Characteristicks of Men, Manners, Opinions, Times* (1711), attacking satire as a tool for mending the social structure and suggesting that a more sensitive approach might be more fruitful. Pope himself ventured to express his melan-choly streak in *Epistle from Eloisa to Abelard* (1717) and "Elegy to the Memory of an Unfortunate Lady" (1717). By mid-century, novelists such as Samuel Richardson, Henry Fielding, and Laurence Sterne were inclined to explore char-acters' emotions, and some poets sought to express feeling in their poetry and to elicit feeling in their readers.

If the sudden shift in the artistic sensibility in the late seventeenth century can be directly connected to the fall of the Puritan Commonwealth and the accession of the high-spirited Charles II, the slow subsequent movement toward expression of emotion in art can be seen as a natural reac-tion to the exaggerated elevation of intellect. The Wartons joined this movement, taking on the task of putting the poets of the past in the context of the new ideas about art. In his editions of Pope's works, Joseph Warton took the opportunity to express his views on poetry and on Pope's proper place in any hierarchy of greatness. Fully aware of Pope's importance as an intelligent, skeptical commentator on the human comedy, Warton radically denied Pope's standing as a great poet on the simple grounds that the highest poetry is that which explores sublime and pathetic experience. Warton thus put Longinus' emphasis on intense feeling into a hierarchical scheme, deeming poetry of the Sublime and the Pathetic the best, the Ethical and Panegyric of second importance; the Witty and the Tasteful fell to third place, with Pope's work as the finest example of that limited kind of poetry.

This radical (though respectful) demotion of the greatest poet of the century was not Joseph Warton's only challenge to conventional critical wisdom; he also took on the task of revaluing poets whom he believed had been given less than their due. From early in the century there had been an awareness that Shakespeare could not be evaluated by the rules of classical poetry, and Warton suggested that Shakespeare's case was not an isolated one. For example, Warton judged that John Milton's greatest achievement was to be found in the poetic passages that represent imag-inative flights of fancy. Warton named Thomas Gray the eighteenth century's greatest poet.

Joseph Warton advocated that writers of pastoral poetry avoid stock descriptive phrases, attempting instead to render a particular experience of nature. His emphasis upon the emotions as the basis for the best poetry and his undermining of classical rules cannot be said to represent original critical contributions, for he drew heavily from the ideas of other critics. Still, his work, together with that of his brother, became influential enough to give rise to a "school of the Wartons," not only in literary criticism but also in the practice of poetry. Joseph Warton's standards for poetry would find their fullest expression in the emotionalism of the Romantics.

Thomas Warton was in several ways a more substantial scholar than his older brother. If Joseph Warton broke new ground as a critic in assigning Pope a relatively low place in a hierarchical scheme of poetry, the younger Warton was determined to consider the entire range of English poetry in a systematic history. Like his brother, he espoused the idea that poets had to been seen first in the context of their own time. His work on Edmund Spenser led him to explain Spenser's use of the romance (a form that had fallen out of favor in the early eighteenth century) as a legitimate example of a major poet working within the popular traditions of his own time. His insistence upon Spenser's status as a major artist was consistent with his argument for reading artists in cultural context, an idea which Johnson praised and which came to be taken for granted in later literary criticism.

Although *The History of English Poetry* was never finished, Thomas Warton established a sense of continuity in English literature, tracing its development step-by-step from the medieval period forward and rescuing from patronizing disdain and indifference earlier authors who had seemed technically, thematically, and emotionally vulgar by neoclassical standards. The task that Addison had begun in his essays – that of broadening the taste of readers to extend to earlier English literature – had been carried on unsystematically through the eighteenth century. Thomas Warton was to show how all English poetry could be appreciated and understood by the use of a combination of the historical and comparative approaches, a method that he had used with great success in his earlier work, *Observations on "The Faerie Queene" of Spenser*.

In his studies of the classical pastoral tradition. Thomas Warton commended the naturalness of Theocritus' depictions of nature over what he saw as the dryness and spareness of Virgil's work in the genre. Like his brother, Thomas seized the moment of critical comment to make the case for realism, for vitality, for the "unevenness of actual life." As was the case with Joseph, he put his critical weight behind the ideas that the imagination and human feelings, even at their most eccentric, were the proper subjects of poetry, and that the peculiarity of the past was not to be ignored or rejected, but appreciated and absorbed. His writings on English Gothic architecture (a style which had been considered tasteless by neoclassical standards) were to contribute to the development of neo-Gothic themes in the art of the late eighteenth century, particularly in the Gothic novel, following the model of Horace Walpole's *The Castle of Otranto* (1764).

The Warton contribution is not so much a matter of originality as it is a matter of systematization. The ideas of Longinus, Nicolas Boileau-Despréaux, Addison, Shaftesbury, David Hume, Francis Hutcheson, Edmund Burke, and Johnson were readily at hand for them. What they did was to apply these ideas, not only challenging established neoclassical notions but also putting them into the historical context of English poetry. They insisted that poets had to be seen in the context of their own time and in the wider context of the whole history of English literature.

Joseph and Thomas Warton also insisted that the neoclassical strictures on poetry were too narrow – that they might support artists of the quality of Pope, but they could not produce artists such as Shakespeare or Spenser, who worked in a much wider world of imagination, fancy, and, above all, deep personal feeling. The late-eighteenth-century poets had been struggling to follow the path of feeling; what the Wartons gave them was the proof that feeling had always been there, and that the great poets of the past had been firmly committed to expressing it.

## Joseph Warton·

### Principal criticism
*The Works of Virgil in Latin and English*, 1753
*An Essay on the Writings and Genius of Pope*, 1756 (also as
    *An Essay on the Genius and Writings of Pope*, 1762)
Notes to *The Works of Alexander Pope*, 1797 (9 volumes)

## Thomas Warton

### Principal criticism
*Observations on "The Faerie Queene" of Spenser*, 1754, 1762
*Theocriti Syracusii Quae Supersunt, with Notes by T. Warton*,
    1770
*The History of English Poetry, from the Close of the Eleventh
    to the Commencement of the Eighteenth Century*,
    1774–1781 (3 volumes)

## Other major works and literary forms
Both Joseph Warton and Thomas Warton wrote poetry early in life. Joseph published one poem in *The Gentleman's Magazine* while he was still a schoolboy; his verses, though evidencing only modest poetic skill, were brought together in book form in *Odes on Various Subjects* (1746). His real talent lay in criticism. He became involved in Samuel Johnson's literary circle and wrote several essays on wide-ranging aesthetic topics for Johnson's periodical, *The Adventurer*. His edition of Virgil's works in both Latin and English included his versions of the *Eclogues* (43–37 B.C.) and the *Georgics* (c. 37–29 B.C.), but it is most notable for Warton's comments on Virgil and on various poetic forms.

Thomas Warton was also a precocious, if limited, poet; as early as 1745, he published a collection titled *Five Pastoral Eclogues*. His heroic poem *The Triumph of Isis* (1749) gained for him some renown, particularly in academic circles, for its praise of Oxford University, its scholars, and its Gothic architecture. In 1760 he satirized the conventional Oxford guidebook in *A Companion to the Guide, and a Guide to the Companion, Being a Complete Supplement to All the Accounts of Oxford Hitherto Published*. He produced biographies of two Oxford scholars, Ralph Bathurst and Sir Thomas Pope, but his serious scholarship is best seen in his 1770 edition of Theocritus, although its accuracy was questioned, and it was superseded by other editions in the early nineteenth century.

## Joseph Warton

POETRY
*The Enthusiast: Or, The Lover of Nature*, 1744
*Odes on Various Subjects*, 1746

## Thomas Warton

POETRY
*Five Pastoral Eclogues*, 1745
*Pleasures of Melancholy*, 1747
*The Triumph of Isis*, 1749
*The Poems on Various Subjects of Thomas Warton*, 1791

NONFICTION
*A Companion to the Guide, and a Guide to the Companion, Being a Complete Supplement to All the Accounts of Oxford Hitherto Published*, 1760
*The Life and Literary Remains of Ralph Bathurst*, 1761
*The Life of Sir Thomas Pope, Founder of Trinity College, Oxford*, 1772.

ANTHOLOGY
*Poems upon Several Occasions*, by John Milton, 1785

## Further reading

Bate, Walter J. *From Classic to Romantic*, 1949.
Hipple, Walter J. *The Beautiful, the Sublime, and the Picturesque in Eighteenth-century British Aesthetic Theory*, 1957.
MacDonald, W. L. *Pope and His Critics*, 1951.
MacLean, Kenneth. *John Locke and the English Literature of the Eighteenth Century*, 1936.
Pittock, J. *The Ascendancy of Taste: The Achievement of Joseph and Thomas Warton*, 1973.
Rinaker, C. *Thomas Warton*, 1916.
Vane, John, A. *Joseph and Thomas Warton*, 1983.

CHARLES PULLEN

*See also* Burke, E.; Hume; Johnson; Lord Kames

# Ian Watt

## English critic

**Born:** Windermere, England; March 9, 1917

## Biography

Ian Watt was educated at St. John's College, Cambridge. During World War II he served in the infantry, and in 1942 he was wounded while defending Singapore from the invading Japanese forces. He was reported as missing in action, presumed killed, but was captured by the Japanese and held as a prisoner of war. While in captivity he was among the British servicemen forced to participate in the construction of the famous bridge on the River Kwai.

After the war, Watt returned to St. John's College, Cambridge, where he taught from 1948 until 1952 when he became dean of the new School of English Studies at the University of California at Berkeley. He went to Stanford University in 1964, and was appointed the Jackson Eli Reynolds Professor of Humanities. At Stanford he served as chair of the English Department between 1968 and 1971, of the Program in Modern Thought and Literature from 1977 to 1980, and was director of the Stanford Humanities Center from 1980 to 1985. Since his retirement, Professor Watt has taught on a part-time basis in the English Department at Stanford. He is a member of the American Academy of Arts and Sciences.

## Influence

Watt's most important and influential work has been *The Rise of the Novel: Studies in Defoe, Richardson and Fielding* (1957), which was immensely successful and widely read in the years following its publication. For a time it was generally taken to be the single essential study of the origins of the novel as a literary genre in the eighteenth century, and continues to be a recommended text on many university literature courses. Watt's study owes its textual method to the tradition of Anglo-American New Criticism, but attempts to challenge the historical positivism of this school, and to provide an economic historicism as a theoretical backdrop to its discussion of the early development of the novel within British society. Watt's analysis unashamedly focuses on notions such as the individual genius and talent of fiction writers such as Daniel Defoe and Samuel Richardson, and in doing so it clearly predates the highly textualized and non-author-based approaches that were to develop in literary theory in the decades immediately following its publication.

Later academic objections to the argument and method of *The Rise of the Novel* are testament to its wide-reaching influence, and tend to center on Watt's selective choice of authors – all of whom are securely canonical – and his ambitious and occasionally sweeping approach to historical circumstance and its relation to the production of fiction.

Watt's achievement in the study is to have firmly based his criticism on a theoretically assured historical framework that assumes that the material situation of the production of the early novel should be vital to its aesthetic analysis. The most lucid objection to Watt's economic discussion is to be found in the work of the Daniel Defoe scholar Maximillian Novak. Watt's failure to survey the countless other exponents of the new narrative form, many of whom undoubtedly informed the writings of his chosen subjects, is a further unavoidable criticism, but it is also integral to his judgmental thesis: that the formal, aesthetic achievement of Daniel Defoe, Samuel Richardson, and Henry Fielding is inseparable from these writers' ability, as Watt determines it, to have surpassed the efforts of their precursors and contemporaries by delineating the unique complexities of their historical milieu within a new popular medium.

## Analysis

*The Rise of the Novel* was a substantial reworking and enlargement of Watt's fellowship dissertation for St. John's College, Cambridge, entitled "The Reading Public and the Rise of the Novel." Watt acknowledges that the subject of his discussion is potentially immense, and he signals early on in *The Rise of the Novel* that his treatment is to be "necessarily selective." Given that his chosen novelists of the eighteenth century – Defoe, Richardson, and Fielding – do not in any way constitute a school, he deduces that there must have been strong common sociological causes which enabled them to flourish at that time. He assumes that:

> the appearance of our first three novelists within a single generation was probably not sheer accident, and that their geniuses could not have created the new form unless the conditions of the time had also been favourable.

Watt avoids employing historical facts as merely incidental illustrations to the critical argument of *The Rise of the Novel*, and this argument is that the individual talents who created the best early examples of modern narrative were reliant on the amenability of their social environment to the subject and form of their imaginative work. The aim of Watt's thesis is "to discover what these favourable conditions in the literary and social situation were, and in what ways Defoe, Richardson and Fielding were its beneficiaries." Watt makes clear that precisely what is to constitute the definition of the novel is that which is already "commonly" held – long prose fiction beginning with the writings of Defoe, Richardson, and Fielding. In some sense his thesis is to be its own proof. Since the term "novel" did not enter into common usage until the end of the eighteenth century, Watt requires a definition that is "sufficiently narrow to exclude previous types of narrative and yet broad enough to apply to whatever is usually put in the novel category." His conclusion is that "realism" – itself

a problematical term – is what distinguishes the new form from the prose romances that had preceded it.

Watt sets out to analyze the epochal transitions that took place within Western civilization during the Renaissance, and the manner in which these fundamental shifts in thought and perception were to manifest themselves in the content, form, and style of European literature. Watt's focus is British fiction, but he necessarily includes a discussion of Continental writing, particularly Miguel de Cervantes and his *Don Quixote* (1605, 1615). He is keen to suggest that the uniqueness of fictional characters such as Don Quixote and Defoe's Robinson Crusoe lies in their ability to have transcended their narrative form and become individualist myths of modern Western culture. They were able to do so due to their appropriateness to the economic structure of modern society. Watt argues that the more scientific and empirical conceptions of time and place that developed in the early modern period across Europe were directly reflected in the form of the novel; the novel assumes pseudo-historical characteristics that emulate the historical importance of the precise time and location of events, and the new narratives emphatically involve "a developing but unplanned aggregate of particular individuals having particular experiences at particular times and at particular places."

Watt's historical definition of the uniqueness of the novel is that it discards the ahistorical characteristics of the literature which preceded it: the dislocated and universal poetics of William Shakespeare, whose work played upon a continually consistent "wheel of time" throughout the plays, representing little difference between the medieval English court and ancient Rome, for example; and the emblematic timelessness of the prose romance. These works made reference to particular historical milieus, of course, but Watt's argument is that the entirely specific referentiality of the novel, in terms of time and space, constitutes a "formal realism" that makes a distinct break with the literature of the immediate past. It is the novel's aspiration to accurate representation in terms of historical or empirical denotation, its provision of a false "air of total authenticity," that characterizes it. For Watt, it was Defoe who instigated the novel in England with *Robinson Crusoe* (1719) and *Moll Flanders* (1722); and typically Defoe's historical and fictional writings tend to exhibit a continuing embellishment of the one with the other. In the novel we are to find a widely referential use of language that relates directly to its surrounding culture, far more so than is usual in other literary forms. Essentially, Watt is putting forward an approach to the novel that simultaneously apprehends its formal and historical characteristics; his critical method is a synthesis of formal and historical criticism, which he deems fully appropriate to the inherent characteristics of the new genre in prose fiction; he aims to determine how it differs from its antecedents and what determining social factors led it to do so when it did.

The question of "realism" and its relation to the novel is particularly troublesome and Watt necessarily explores it at some length. The nineteenth-century French school of Realists, which provides the most common aesthetic association of the term, usually implies the portrayal of "low" or immoral aspects of life and is placed in opposition to "idealism." Watt avoids this definition of the term, and similarly discards its philosophical meaning from the Middle Ages which denotes the Platonic universals that constitute the abstract, ideal "reality." Watt identifies the realism of the novel form to be the philosophical realism which followed and reversed the classical and medieval conceptions of the term: the modern realism of René Descartes and John Locke, that concerns itself with the individual's apprehension of observable facts which delineate the external world. Watt recognizes in the content and form of the early novel an analogous relationship to the critical and questioning rigor of modern philosophical realism; it is inherent in the novel's concentration upon the specificity of characters, time, and location, and in the *post res* suggestion of emergent, general truths from the incidental particulars of the narrative. He argues that its formal realism makes implicit the notion that the novel, while fictional, is still "a full and authentic report of human experience," and as such the "air of total authenticity" that it assumes is its very premise. Watt emphasizes that he is not proposing that the formal realism exhibited by writers like Defoe and Richardson is their invention by any means, but that their application of its devices to the portrayal of individual characters is more consistent and conscious than any in earlier literature. While vivid characters and their environments have momentarily emerged from works by classical authors, and later, Geoffrey Chaucer, Watt sees a clear distinction:

> in Homer and in earlier prose fiction these passages are relatively rare, and tend to stand out from the surrounding narrative; the total literary structure was not consistently oriented in the direction of formal realism, and the plot especially, which was usually traditional and often highly improbable, was in direct conflict with its premises.

Watt goes on to survey in some statistical detail the evolution of the reading public in Britain in the eighteenth century. His assessment is that the rise of the novel as a popular form of literature corresponds directly to the increasing influence, affluence, and size of the middle class, for whom the printed novel was an affordable and desirable entertainment. Journalism had enabled secular literature to flourish, and periodicals such as the *Gentleman's Magazine*, founded in 1731, catered not simply to the educated middle classes as the *Spectator* had for some years, but to the less-educated yet entrepreneurial journalists and booksellers who were gaining power within the economic culture. Watt determines that Defoe and Richardson, themselves London tradesmen of the middle class, fully immersed in the growing business worlds of journalism and book selling, were circumstantially well placed to reflect the interests of their readership in the fictional medium.

In Watt's analysis, Defoe's *Robinson Crusoe*, and its eponymous shipwrecked character, represent the aspirations of the modern age in society: "the island offers the fullest opportunity for him to realise three associated tendencies of modern civilization – absolute economic, social and intellectual freedom for the individual." He regards Crusoe as a hero of the mercantile society, he is "an inspiration to economists and educators, and a symbol both for the displaced persons of urban capitalism . . . and for its practical heroes, the empire builders." All of Crusoe's ingenious success on the island is reliant upon his liberation of an enviable set of modern tools from the shipwreck; Watt considers this as symptomatic of the character's wholly economic nature. He is not a primitive hero, or a proletarian hero, but rather a fully-fledged capitalist:

> In the island he owns the freehold of a rich though unimproved estate. Its possession, combined with the stock from the ship, are the miracles which fortify the faith of the new economic creed. But only that of the true believers: to the sceptic the classic idyll of free enterprise does not in fact sustain the view that anyone has ever attained comfort and security only by his own efforts. Crusoe is in fact the lucky heir to the labours of countless other individuals; his solitude is the measure, and the price of his luck, since it involves the fortunate decease of all the other potential stockholders; and the shipwreck, far from being a tragic peripety, is the deus ex machina which makes it possible for Defoe to present solitary labour, not as an alternative to a death sentence, but as a solution to the perplexities of economic and social reality.

For Watt, *Robinson Crusoe* represents "the ultimate consequences of absolute individualism," one which was necessary before the development within fiction of a new representation and consideration of complex social interaction:

> it is appropriate that the tradition of the novel should begin with a work that annihilated the relationships of the traditional social order, and thus drew attention to the opportunity and the need of building up a network of personal relationships on a new and conscious pattern.

Watt argues that Samuel Richardson resolved some of the formal insufficiencies of Defoe's writing, when considered as part of the development of the modern novel; in particular, Richardson managed to avoid the episodic plot structure of Defoe's work by directing his fiction toward a single action – in *Pamela* (1740–1741), a courtship. He argues that due to his subtle and complex portrayal of personal relationships, it was Richardson who managed to produce "the first true novel," surpassing Defoe's isolated and unpsychologized characters. Henry Fielding's contribution to the novel form was to have produced the "comic epic in prose," and Watt sees his particular achievement as having provided in *Tom Jones* (1749) a wise assessment of human relationships that casts its view far wider across human affairs than Defoe or Richardson had done – he contrasts Richardson's "realism of presentation" (the detailed delineation of thought and action) to Fielding's "realism of assessment" (pragmatic moral adjudication upon the actions of the characters). Fielding's work establishes a panoramic vision of society that was to be instrumental to the development of the novel in the hands of Tobias Smollett, Charles Dickens, and William Thackeray in subsequent years.

*Myths of Modern Individualism: Faust, Don Quixote, Don Juan, Robinson Crusoe* (1996) is a historical analysis of the treatment of several post-Renaissance fictional characters. Watt had intended to write this comparative study – of the notion of individualism as an opposing force to society within early modern literature – decades before, and its themes and argument are implicit in *The Rise of the Novel*, but it was not until 1980 that he began what was to be the final version. Perhaps in the light of criticism of the broad sweep and omissions of *The Rise of the Novel*, Watt insists that his study is highly and subjectively selective, and that it is directed toward the general reader rather than the literary scholar. Watt develops arguments which are touched upon in the earlier work, of which it is very much a continuation, but its focus upon the fictional characters as types of modern Western culture. His approach is comparative – studying operas, plays, poems, and novels as parallel treatments of recurrent cultural myths. Watt is particularly interested in the continuing appeal of the figures to writers from various countries and eras, and their continual reinvention of the archetypes within their own social and historical context. The four mythical characters were to be recast by writers including Jean-Jacques Rousseau, Johann Wolfgang von Goethe, Lord Byron, and Fedor Dostoevskii (Watt refers to this particular process as the "Romantic apotheosis of Renaissance Myths") where, in the case of Faustus and Don Juan, hubristic tales of spiritual punishment and suffering were developed into secular myths. Watt identifies the individualism common to all the characters, and their representation of futile solitude in opposition to social integration; he traces their often reactionary transformations through various historical periods and artistic media. His survey regards these enduring fictional characters not as reinventions of classical types but as wholly "historically new; and in this they reflected their period's new emphasis on the social and political primacy of the individual." *Myths of Modern Individualism* confirms that Watt is a consistently historical and comparative critic,

with a broad grasp of the relationship between modern Western culture and its popular literature.

## Principal criticism
*The Rise of the Novel: Studies in Defoe, Richardson and Fielding*, 1957
*Conrad, The Secret Agent: A Casebook*, 1973
*Conrad in the Nineteenth Century*, 1980
*Joseph Conrad: Nostromo*, 1988
*Myths of Modern Individualism: Faust, Don Quixote, Don Juan, Robinson Crusoe*, 1996

## Other major works and literary forms
Ian Watt has written extensively on novels and prose fiction from the Elizabethan period up to the modern period, where his specialty has been the work of Joseph Conrad, an enthusiasm for which he developed in childhood. His uncollected critical essays serve as a supplement to his major critical publications and are available in various journals. Watt has also provided numerous introductions to classic works of fiction.

EDITED TEXTS
*Jane Austen: A Collection of Critical Essays*, 1963

MISCELLANEOUS
"Serious Reflections on *The Rise of the Novel*," in *Novel*. 1 (1968), pp. 205–218.

## Further reading
Dijkstra, Bram. *Defoe and Economics: The Fortunes of Roxana in the History of Interpretation*, 1987.
Hirsch, David H. "The Reality of Ian Watt," in *Critical Quarterly*. 11 (Summer, 1969), pp. 164–179.
Johnson, Bruce. "Conrad's Impressionism and Watt's 'Delayed Decoding,'" in *Conrad Revisited: Essays for the Eighties*, 1985. Edited by Ross C. Murfin.
McKeon, Michael. *The Origins of the English Novel, 1600–1740*, 1987.
Novak, Maximillian. *Realism, Myth, and History in Defoe's Fiction*, 1983.
Schwarz, Daniel R. "The Importance of Ian Watt's *The Rise of the Novel*," in *Journal of Narrative Technique*. 13, no. 2 (Spring, 1983), pp. 59–73.
Watts, Cedric. "'Solidarity' in The Nigger of the 'Narcissus': A Defence of Ian Watt," in *Conradiana: A Journal of Joseph Conrad Studies*. 20, no. 2 (Summer, 1988), pp. 165–166.
Wolfe, Charles. "Fictional Realism: Watt and Bazin on the Pleasures of Novels and Films," in *Literature and Film Quarterly*. 9, no. 1 (1981), pp. 40–50.

MICHAEL BRETT

*See also* British Literary Theory: Twentieth Century; Leavis; Lodge; Lukács; Novel: Theory and Criticism

# René Wellek

Austrian-born American theorist

**Born:** Vienna, Austria; August 22, 1903
**Died:** New Haven, Connecticut; November 10, 1995

## Biography

René Wellek's heritage and the intellectual milieu of his formative years explain in large measure his eminence as a critic and scholar. His father was a high government official of Czech ancestry in Vienna, and his mother was a cosmopolitan beauty fluent in several languages. At home, Wellek developed a knowledge of music and Czech literature; at school, he studied Latin, Greek, German, and English. After World War I he pursued Germanic philology at Charles University in Prague, also visiting England to prepare a thesis on Thomas Carlyle and Romanticism. In 1927 he was invited to Princeton as a fellow in English and subsequently taught German there. After returning to Prague, Wellek became a lecturer on Czech literature at the University of London.

At the outbreak of World War II he came to the United States, joining the faculty of the University of Iowa. His encounter there with Austin Warren led to their collaboration on the *Theory of Literature* (1949), a manifesto of their joint dissatisfaction with the contemporary state of literary scholarship. In 1955 he published the first two volumes of *A History of Modern Criticism*. His address at the 1958 meeting of the International Comparative Literature Association, "The Crisis in Comparative Literature," led to an academic debate over methodology that transfigured the study of comparative literature throughout the Western world.

Wellek began a long association with Yale University in 1946 as professor of Slavic and comparative literature, becoming chair of the Slavic department two years later and chair of comparative literature in 1960. That same year, he received honorary doctorates from Yale, Harvard, and Oxford universities, followed subsequently by many others. In 1962 he became president of the American Comparative Literature Association. A distinguished teacher as well as a scholar and a critic, Wellek directed more than fifty Ph.D. dissertations. His former students have been consistently loyal and appreciative, in large measure because of his practice of inculcating the highest standards of scholarship while encouraging each student to follow his or her own interest.

## Influence

Wellek did more than any other critic in the postwar period to turn the teaching of literature in the United States from a concentration on historical and biographical events and relationships to an emphasis on the text itself. At the same time, he raised the prestige of literary criticism to a peak it had never before reached. As the guide of the international comparative literature movement, he led the practitioners of the discipline away from what he considered to be the excesses of positivism – the accumulation of unrelated facts and the attempt to discover scientific causes in literature. His ideas were widespread during the 1950s and 1960s, and his distinctions among theory, criticism, and history prepared the way for later, extreme claims about the importance of theory and for radical changes in its nature. Methodologies of the 1970s and 1980s based on the notion of the autonomy of literary criticism, such as deconstruction, of which he did not approve, may nevertheless be considered developments of his principles.

## Analysis

The great paradox in Wellek's theoretical system is that he sought to be objective, almost scientific, without being a positivist – that is, without emphasizing facts and seeking to trace causes between one event and another. He proposed to attain this objectivity essentially by concentrating on individual literary texts and rejecting consideration of elements extrinsic to them. At the same time he believed in a type of evolution in literary history which could be perceived by classifying apparently meaningless series of events into essential and unessential elements. Yet very little evolution or change is to be found in his own ideas, which were formed in an early essay, "The Theory of Literary History" (1936), developed and crystallized in *Theory of Literature*, and applied in his series of books and articles on literary criticism. These works represent elements of Russian Formalism and American New Criticism vitalized by Wellek's personal ingenuity and buttressed by his enormous erudition.

In keeping with his basic principle of objectivity, Wellek distinguishes between literature as a simultaneous order and as a series of works arranged chronologically and considered as integral parts of the historical process. He tried to steer a middle course between the synchronic and the diachronic perceptions. His emphasis on the intrinsic aspects of the text suggests the synchronic in theory, but his practical contributions to literary history represent the diachronic. In his view, literature is both eternal and historical – an example of eclecticism rather than evidence of inconsistency. He admires the eclectic spirit as the tendency "to melt, to polish, and to blunt the edges of other ideas." The texts that he considers are also strictly limited. He rejects sermons, essays, travel accounts, philosophical discourses, and *Trivialliteratur*, a restriction based on subject matter. He consequently affirmed stylistic elements as crucial to defining literature, that is, the use of imagination and a language separated from that of the scientific and everyday. Considering the work of literary art a stratified structure of signs and meanings, he argues that the critic should not take into consideration the mental processes of the author or the possible influences that may have occupied his or her mind. At the same time Wellek insists that literature not be dehumanized, that it contains both meaning and value. Although accepting oral literature as a province of literary study, he failed to express an opinion about whether film will also qualify. He was also in the forefront of the movement to legitimatize the study of modern literature at a time when academic literary study ordinarily did not consider works published later than the nineteenth century.

The keynote of Wellek's system is the division of literary study into the triad of criticism, theory, and history. Literary theory he describes as the *organum* of methods for perceiving abstract relationships, methods such as categorizing, defining, and evaluating. Both criticism and history, on the other hand, deal with specific, concrete works. He nevertheless defines criticism as "simply a part of the history of aesthetic thought – at least if it is treated in itself, without reference to the creative work contemporary with it." He also asserts that the study of the history of criticism is equivalent to the study of criticism itself. Several writers have maintained that criticism cannot be separated from theory, and Wellek himself continually stated that pure literary history, criticism, or theory cannot exist without the other two elements. The critical process is dialectic: a mutual intercourse of theory and practice. It is obvious that even the scientific historian makes value judgments in deciding what material to emphasize and what to ignore. In this sense, criticism and history are alike. Mere description of the triad and its theoretical balance, however, does not indicate the division among practicing critics between aesthetic and historical criticism, a distinction of which Wellek was acutely aware. Supporting aesthetic criticism, he opposed the view that literary history should be based solely on the standards and attitudes of previous ages as well as the more simplistic opinion that it should limit itself to verifiable facts. He argues in essence that the theoretical part of literary history should reflect aesthetic standards rather than the times. Wellek reconciled theory and history, however, by affirming that aesthetic standards are the norms of history. The question remains, however, whether these are the norms of past history or of the present. A similar elusiveness remains about the interrelationships in his triad of theory, criticism, and history. In explications of his system, Wellek clearly advocated a synthesis of the three, but his continual repetitions of the categories imply a separation.

Wellek never declared that critics must themselves formulate new theories, but he believed that the ideal critic should resemble the creative artist in forming an organic whole based on the activity of the imagination. Contrary to the belief of some neoclassicists that art is immediately comprehensible to even the most primitive minds, Wellek believed that the critic must have an extensive training and knowledge as well as artistic genius and that he or she must be a scientific historian as well as a showman and authoritarian

judge. Not foreseeing the later excesses, in which criticism would come to be regarded as an autonomous discipline and the critic as an independent creative force equal to the author, Wellek concluded "The Crisis of Comparative Literature" by affirming that "literary scholarship becomes an act of the imagination, like art itself, and thus a preserver and creator of the highest values of mankind." In his writings, he did not address the issue of whether the moral content of literature is relevant to its values other than to point out the aesthetic limitations of simple didacticism. Because the purpose of literature is not to convey knowledge, he strongly suggested that moral considerations, if relevant at all, are greatly subsidiary to those of aesthetics. He found objectionable, for example, the use of a sublime style to express a trivial theme.

In some contexts, Wellek regards norms and values as equivalent, but in others, he makes a profound distinction between them. Most frequently, norms as elements of concordance or similarity in several works of art are significant enough to be considered as comprising a common structure. A genre is a simple illustration. More complicated is the theory in linguistics concerning the existence of a language independent of the use of that language by particular individuals. The language in the abstract would be the norm and the words used by individuals would be approaches to this norm. Wellek, therefore, conceives of a literary work of art as a stratified system of norms. In this sense, a norm has no connotation of value. In other contexts, however, Wellek believes that norms represent value based upon a historical consensus. His intellectual career can thus be regarded as an attempt to discover a series of norms by which to measure or analyze an entire literary work despite the constant, historical shifting of the theoretical basis. One of his major problems was the conflict between relative and absolute criteria – his theory verges toward the latter, but practical considerations made him compromise with the former.

Recognizing that both extreme absolutism and extreme relativism are unsound, he affirmed that literature has a meaning and that there are right and wrong readings; he made no attempt to account for contradictory interpretations, however, other than to indicate that all points of view are not equally right. His solution is a process of perceiving composed of structure, sign, and value, elements that – like those in his other triad – cannot be artificially separated from one another, while the element of value retains its elusive character. Although offering various standards such as inclusiveness, awareness of complexity, ironies, and tensions, Wellek at length falls back upon the *consensus gentium*: the great names in the canon are there because "the largest reputations survive generational tastes." They survive not because of fixed rank but because of the permanence of the aesthetic norm. Wellek rejected the theory that each individual as well as each generation reinterprets a work of art, in other words, that there are as many versions of Dante's fourteenth-century poem, *The Divine Comedy*, as there are readers. He admits in regard to Homer's *Iliad*, however, that one cannot assert an identity between the work as interpreted by its contemporary Greeks and that read by a modern university student.

Despite Wellek's opposition to historicism or judging works solely by the criteria of the age in which they were written, he made outstanding contributions to periodization or describing literary time-segments in connection with the then-prevailing norms. He revealed that the term "baroque" when applied to literature is arbitrary and fluctuating and that nineteenth-century realism, although sharply differentiated from Romanticism, has much in common with eighteenth-century classicism. His most famous writing on periodization is a polemic, "The Concept of Romanticism in Literary History" (1949), rejecting Arthur O. Lovejoy's thesis that there are several different Romanticisms rather than a single unified movement. Although he asserted in his essay on the subject that there does exist a unity based on imagination, symbol, myth, and organic nature, Wellek admitted elsewhere that Romanticism has no stylistic unity and that there are different Romanticisms in England, France, and Germany. He also did the definitive work on the meaning of such period designations as classicism and Romanticism and on the dates when these terms entered literary history. The only period on which he did not make important contributions is that of the Enlightenment, no doubt because of his belief that periods should be established upon purely literary criteria.

In a highly subjective article written late in his career, "Destroying Literary Studies" (1983), Wellek warns the literary world against the excesses of theory that are eroding literary studies from the inside and admits that he sometimes felt guilty for having propagated the theory of literature. The worst of the skeptical or nihilistic tendencies he decried are the denial of the aesthetic nature of literature, the view that language has no relation to reality, and the blurring of the distinction between criticism and fiction.

In short, Wellek more than any other critic shaped the nature of graduate instruction in American English departments in the 1950s and 1960s and changed the mainstream of American scholarship in the discipline of comparative literature during the same period. In the areas of both graduate education and scholarship, he successfully imposed his dogma that attention should be concentrated on the text itself, ignoring considerations extrinsic to it. His companion doctrines that literary history, criticism, and theory are separate concerns and that theory should be treated as an autonomous discipline were hailed less broadly, but with equal enthusiasm by their adherents. When later theoretical systems such as structuralism, deconstruction, and their offshoots gained instant popularity in the United States, Wellek deplored their excesses, particularly the ideas that criticism can be carried on without reference to specific literary texts and that meaning in literature can never be determined because of the inherent ambiguity of language.

## Principal criticism
*Theory of Literature*, 1949 (with Austin Warren)
*Concepts of Criticism*, 1963
*Essays on Czech Literature*, 1963
*Confrontations: Studies in the Intellectual and Literary Relations Between Germany, England, and the United States During the Nineteenth Century*, 1965
*The Literary Theory and Aesthetics of the Prague School*, 1969
*Discriminations: Further Concepts of Criticism*, 1970
*"The Attack on Literature" and Other Essays*, 1982

## Other major works and literary forms
From one perspective, everything that René Wellek wrote can be considered literary criticism or theory, but from another, that of his own distinctions among criticism, theory, and history, he wrote a considerable amount on literary theory, more on literary history, and less on practical criticism. In accordance with this distinction, his remaining books are most accurately described as literary history; they include *Immanuel Kant in England: 1793–1838* (1931); *The Rise of English Literary History* (1941); *A History of Modern Criticism: 1750–1950* (1955–1986), which includes *The Later Eighteenth Century, The Romantic Age, The Age of Transition, The Later Nineteenth Century, English Criticism: 1900–1950,* and *American Criticism: 1900–1950.* *Four Critics: Croce, Valéry, Lukács, Ingarden* appeared in 1981.

NONFICTION
*Immanuel Kant in England: 1793–1838*, 1931
*The Rise of English Literary History*, 1941
*A History of Modern Criticism: 1750–1950*, 1955–1986, includes *The Later Eighteenth Century, The Romantic Age, The Age of Transition, The Later Nineteenth Century, English Criticism: 1900–1950,* and *American Criticism: 1900–1950*
*Four Critics: Croce, Valéry, Lukács, Ingarden*, 1981

## Further reading
Bucco, Martin. "René Wellek: Profession of Criticism," in *Journal of Comparative Literature and Aesthetics*. I (Winter, 1978), pp. 13–24.
———. *René Wellek*, 1981.
Demetz, Peter. "Third Conversation with Rene Wellek," in *Cross-Currents: A Yearbook of Central European Culture.* XI (1992), pp. 79–92.
Lawall, Sarah. "Rene Wellek and Modern Literary Criticism," in *Comparative Literature.* XL (1988), pp. 3–28.
McGann, Jerome. "Reviews and Retrospects: Rethinking Romanticism," in *E.L.H.* LIX (1992), pp. 735–754.
Nichols, Stephen G., Jr. *Introduction to Concepts of Criticism,* 1963.
Parker, Mark. "The Lovejoy-Wellek Debate and Romantic Periodization," in *Theoretical Issues in Literary History,* 1991, pp. 227–247. Edited by David Perkins.
Sutton, Walter. "Histories, Theories, and Critiques of Criticism," in *Modern American Criticism,* 1963.

Uitti, Karl D. "The Study of Language and Literature," in *Linguistics and Literary Theory*, 1969.

Winner, Thomas G., and John P. Kasik. "René Wellek's Contribution to American Literary Scholarship," in *Forum*. II (1977), pp. 21–31.

A. OWEN ALDRIDGE

*See also* Ingarden; The Prague School

# Oscar Wilde

Irish writer, dramatist, and essayist

**Born:** Dublin, Ireland; October 16, 1854
**Died:** Paris, France; November 30, 1900

## Biography

Oscar Fingal O'Flahertie Wills Wilde was born on October 16, 1854, to Sir William Wilde and Jane Francesca Elgee Wilde. His father was an eye doctor famous for his development of cataract surgery, and his mother was a dedicated Irish Nationalist who wrote under the name "Speranza." Wilde's accomplishments at Portura Royal School in Enniskillen earned him a scholarship to Trinity College, Dublin, where he won the Berkeley Gold Medal for Greek and a scholarship to Magdalene College, Oxford. His career at Oxford was brilliant. He studied under Walter Pater, Cardinal Newman, and John Ruskin; began publishing poems in 1876; and received a double first in Classics as well as the Newdigate Prize for his poem "Ravenna."

By 1880 Wilde was a prominent figure in London literary circles, enough so that his preciosity had become a standard target for satire in *Punch*. After a greatly successful lecture tour across North America in 1882, Wilde lived briefly in Paris before marrying Constance Lloyd, daughter of an Irish barrister, in 1894 and settling down in London, where his two sons were born, Cyril in 1885 and Vyvyan in 1886.

In 1886 Wilde met the seventeen-year-old Robert Ross, who was to maintain that he then introduced Wilde to homosexual acts. The decade following their meeting was richly productive for Wilde, marked by two years as editor of *The Woman's World* and the publication of reviews, essays, his sole novel, and the plays that remain his greatest achievement.

Wilde began in 1891 the relationship with Lord Alfred Douglas that was, in one way or another, to dominate the remaining nine years of his life. At the peak of his career as a dramatist, Wilde in 1895 sued Lord Douglas' father, the Marquess of Queensbury, for criminal libel as the result of a sneering card the Marquess had left at Wilde's club in London. The suit was a crucial mistake for Wilde. The Marquess was quickly acquitted, but Wilde was soon charged with numerous sexual offenses and eventually sentenced to two years at hard labor. Out of this experience came a letter to Lord Douglas, later published as *De Profundis*, and "The Ballad of Reading Gaol," two of Wilde's most powerful works. Wilde saw his wife, Constance, for the last time in 1896 when she visited him at Wandsworth to tell him his mother had died.

The prison years broke Wilde's spirit and destroyed his health. Upon his release from Reading in 1897, Wilde moved to Berneval, France, where he assumed the name of Sebastian Melmoth. Constance Wilde died in 1898, and in the same year Wilde moved to Paris. Traveling in Italy with Lord Douglas in 1900, Wilde became severely ill. He had never fully recovered from an ear injury caused by a fall in prison, and he suffered excruciating pain in the head during his final sickness before dying on November 30, probably from cerebral meningitis. He was buried in Bagneux Cemetery, Paris, from where his body was moved to Père Lachaise Cemetery in the same city.

## Influence

Wilde inspired no school of criticism, but he was a significant figure in the art-for-art's-sake movement of the later nineteenth century, and it is also possible to read into "The Critic as Artist" and "The Decay of Lying" an anticipation of such later critics as Roland Barthes and the reader-response school of theorists. Wilde admired both Théophile Gautier and, especially, Charles Baudelaire for the satanism reflected in the title of his famous collection *Les Fleurs du mal* (1857; *Flowers of Evil*, 1909) and for his conviction that a beautiful work of art could never be immoral. Art had a transcendental magic for Baudelaire even when it was diabolical, a tenet that Wilde would quickly have agreed with.

The publication of Algernon Charles Swinburne's *Poems and Ballads* in 1866 established aestheticism in Britain, where it flourished till the century's end under the auspices of Walter Pater, James Whistler, and Wilde. In *De Profundis* Wilde proclaimed, "I treated art as the supreme reality and life as a mere mode of fiction," a philosophy from which a corollary emerged in Wilde's dandified attire and mannerisms. The importance of emotion for its own sake, asserted Wilde in "The Critic as Artist," explained why all art is "immoral." Aestheticism's whole bohemian revolt against Philistinism encouraged the bizarre and the gilded as subjects, as well as Wilde's exhortation in "The Critic" to "Start with the worship of form, and there is no secret in the world that will not be revealed to you." Wilde's collection of essays, *Intentions* (1891), was probably the most important statement of the principles of art for art's sake and makes him the movement's leading spokesman.

Of all modern critics, Roland Barthes shares the most critical dicta with Wilde. In *Le Degré zéro de l'écriture* (1953; *Writing Degree Zero*, 1967), Barthes' opposition to Jean-Paul Sartre's *Qu'est-ce que la littérature?* (1947; *What Is Literature?*, 1949) offers a close analogue to

Wilde's reaction to the moral criticism of Matthew Arnold. Both Wilde and Barthes reject any doctrine of mimesis in literature, Wilde describing art as lying and illusion and Barthes contending that literature is a self-reflexive activity that generates a "myth" of literature. Barthes' later turn to structural analyses dismissed the author as no more than an amanuensis. For the structuralist Barthes, the reader became the imaginative creator of meaning in a text. One can imagine that Oscar Wilde, always a keen student of French fashion, would have reveled in these Gallic lucubrations. The affinities between Wilde and Barthes, and the influence of Barthes in modern criticism, suggest that Wilde would have felt quite comfortable in postmodernist Yale and Paris.

## Analysis

Wilde's first major essay in criticism, "The Truth of Masks," responded to Lord Lytton's contention that, in Wilde's summary, "archaeology is entirely out of place in the presentation of any of Shakespeare's plays, and the attempt to introduce it one of the stupidest pedantries of an age of prigs." This is heresy to Wilde, for whom costume is "a means of producing certain dramatic effects," a position that he supports by numerous quotations from Shakespeare. Archaeology, or "the ornamentation and costume of the ancient world," was "a means by which they could touch the dry dust of antiquity into the very breath and beauty of life, and fill with the new wine of romanticism forms that else had been old and outworn."

Wilde agrees that Shakespeare's plays do not depend on facts, but on "Truth, and Truth is independent of facts always, inventing or selecting them at pleasure." As Shakespeare puts facts to the service of "the great art of illusion," he goes about creating for England "a national historical drama." Historical accuracy would have been "a most important adjunct to his illusionist method," for "unless a dress is archaeologically correct, and artistically appropriate, it always looks unreal, unnatural, and theatrical in the sense of artificial."

Wilde concludes by deconstructing his own essay, in which, he says, "there is much with which I entirely disagree. The essay simply represents an artistic standpoint, and in aesthetic criticism attitude is everything. For in art there is no such thing as a universal truth. A Truth in art is that whose contradictory is also true. And just as it is only in art-criticism, and through it, that we can apprehend the Platonic theory of ideas, so it is only in art-criticism, and through it, that we can realize Hegel's system of contraries. The truths of metaphysics are the truths of masks." Thus says Oscar Wilde, Hegelian dialectician.

"The Decay of Lying" is presented as a dialogue in which Vivian lectures his straight man, Cyril. Vivian's opening remarks suggest that Wilde had been reading Ralph Waldo Emerson, who had said in his essay "Nature" (1836) that in the outdoors "all mean egotism vanishes." Wilde does not mention Emerson but he agrees, tipping Emerson upside down, however, with his contempt for Nature: "Egotism itself, which is so necessary to a proper sense of human dignity, is entirely the result of indoor life." Emerson had confessed to being "glad to the brink of fear" when walking across a common amid snow puddles, but Vivian says, "Whenever I am walking in the park here, I always feel that I am no more to her [Nature] than the cattle that browse on the slope, or the burdock that blooms in the ditch." This connection to Emerson is not so fanciful as it might seem, since in the next paragraph Vivian alludes to Emerson, citing the injunction in "Self Reliance" to write "Whim" over one's lintel.

The essay is brilliant, witty, and salted with paradoxes. Nature in its common role as instinct rather than "self-conscious culture" always produces works that are "old-fashioned, antiquated, and out of date." And Nature considered as "phenomena external to man" presents only what the observer projects into it. "Wordsworth went to the lakes, but he was never a lake poet. He found in stones the sermons he had already hidden there."

Wilde's example of Life imitating Art is vivid: "the silly boys, after reading the adventures of Jack Sheppard or Dick Turpin, pillage the stalls of unfortunate apple-women, break into sweet-shops at night, and alarm old gentlemen who are returning home from the city by leaping out on them in suburban lanes, with black masks and loaded revolvers." As for Hamlet's pessimism, "The world has become sad because a puppet was once melancholy."

Not only does Life imitate Art but so does Nature. What we see in those Wordsworthian stones depends on the Arts that have influenced us, for Nature is no "great mother" but our own creation: "It is in our brain that she quickens into life." Wilde's social construction of the past extends to the Middle Ages, which appear to us now as "simply a definite form of style." Vivian chides Cyril for his fondness for Japanese things, declaring wittily but at least half-seriously that "In fact, the whole of Japan is a pure invention. There is no such country, there are no such people." Vivian praises the Church for "keep[ing] alive that mythopoeic faculty which is so essential for the imagination." Unfortunately, the Church is under siege by rationalists, and "The growth of common sense in the English Church is a thing very much to be regretted."

Speaking directly to the issue of lying, Vivian admits that "Lying for the sake of a monthly salary is, of course, well known in Fleet Street, and the profession of a leader writer is not without its advantages." But it all comes down to the fact that the only honorable lie is that done for its own sake, in the service of Art. Thus it is that "those who do not love Beauty more than Truth never know the inmost shrine of Art."

"Pen, Pencil and Poison" repeats many of the arguments of the two earlier essays, exploiting the strange life of Thomas Griffiths Wainewright for moralizing about masks and lying. Wainewright was not simply an aesthete and antiquarian, affectations dear to Wilde's heart, but also a forger and a poisoner who suited Wilde's need to separate art and morals. "There is no essential incongruity between crime and culture," Wilde concludes. "We cannot re-write the whole of history for the purpose of gratifying our moral sense of what should be."

"The Portrait of Mr. W. H." is another essay pretending to be a conversation in which the narrator relates to his friend Erskine the theory of another friend, Cyril Graham, regarding the identity of Mr. W. H., the dedicatee and "Onlie Begetter" of Shakespeare's sonnets. A beautiful boy-actor, Willie Hughes, is constructed from such passages in the sonnets as "A man in hew, all Hews in his controlling" and "Thou art as fair in knowledge as in hew." The extent to which Wilde works this all up in one of his longest essays, and the careful amassing of many effective quotations from the sonnets and the plays, are both remarkable. Wilde struggles to provide a Neo-Platonic philosophical rationale for the common love of men for boys that he seems to find implicit in Renaissance teachings about friendship:

> Friendship, indeed, could have desired no better warrant for its permanence or its ardours than the Platonic theory, or creed, as we might better call it, that the true world was the world of ideas, and that these ideas took visible form and became incarnate in man, and it is only when we realize the influence of neo-Platonism on the Renaissance that we can understand the true meaning of the amatory phrases and words with which friends were wont, at this time, to address each other. There was a kind of mystic transference of the expressions of the physical world to a sphere that was spiritual, that was removed from gross bodily appetite, and in which the soul was Lord. Love had, indeed, entered the olive garden of the new Academe, but he wore the same flame-coloured raiment, and had the same words of passion on his lips.

Friends tried to dissuade Wilde from publishing this speculation on Shakespeare's erotic urges, a venture into the school of criticism now called queer or homosexual theory.

"The Soul of Man under Socialism" makes two points, one extremely prescient considering its time, and the other embarrassingly naive. Altruism as a solution to poverty only complicates the problem, Wilde says, and hence "Charity creates a multitude of sins." The universal goal should be a Socialist state that frees the individual for self-fulfillment, but – and here's the prescience – an authoritarian Socialism would be an even worse evil. Under the system of his time, Wilde admitted that while "a great many people are enabled to develop a certain very limited amount of Individualism," even more were denied its benefits. But "under an industrial-barrack system, or a system of economic tyranny, nobody would be able to have any such freedom at all. It is to be regretted that a portion of our community should be practically in slavery, but to propose to solve the problem by enslaving the entire community is childish." What grim visions of Eastern Europe and the Soviet Union are implicit in this warning.

The naiveté of Wilde's dream of Socialist Individualism emerges in his depiction of a "new Hellenism" nurtured to maturity by the teachings of Christ. The Greek exhortation to "Know thyself" will be complemented by the commandment to "Be thyself," which is "the secret of Christ." One feature of the new Individualism will be the annihilation of family life consequent upon the eradication of private property (a view shared by Karl Marx and Friedrich Engels). Individualism "converts the abolition of legal restraint into a form of freedom that will help the full development of personality, and make the love of man and woman more wonderful, more beautiful, and more ennobling." One can agree with Wilde that "Unless there are slaves to do the ugly, horrible, uninteresting work, culture and contemplation become almost impossible" without seeing in his hopes for Socialist Individualism any realistic progress toward amelioration.

Wilde's masterpiece of criticism is "The Critic as Artist." In this dialogue, Gilbert instructs Ernest as they sit in their library smoking cigarettes and being witty ("Now, whatever music sounds like, I am glad to say that it does not sound in the smallest degree like German"). Gilbert's theme, the creative role of the critic as he wrestles with the raw material provided by the artist, is now a postmodernist commonplace, but Wilde generates considerable vitality in the observations that he strings out alongside this thesis. Robert Browning, for instance, has "moments when he wounds us with his monstrous music" and will be remembered as "the most supreme writer of fiction." Only George Meredith can compare with Browning, for "Meredith is a prose Browning, and so is Browning."

A serious note emerges in the observation that for the Greeks writing was simply "a method of chronicling," whereas "Their test was always the spoken word in its musical and metrical relations." We must return to the voice, Wilde says, and then he (Gilbert) modulates into facetious self-mockery: "Sometimes, when I have written a piece of prose that I have been modest enough to consider absolutely free from fault, a dreadful thought comes over me that I may have been guilty of the immoral effeminacy of using trochaic and tribrachic movements, a crime for which a learned critic of the Augustan age censures with most just severity the brilliant if somewhat paradoxical Hegesias."

The most serious parts of Gilbert's disquisition are finely stated. He judges the difference between the creative faculty and the critical as "entirely arbitrary," arguing that "Without the critical faculty, there is no artistic creation at all worthy of the name." Wilde repeats the claim of "The Decay of Lying" that Art is living, Nature is inert; the most apparently natural and artless work is the most self-conscious, and "self-consciousness and the critical spirit are one." Wilde sounds like Thomas Carlyle and Emerson when he asserts that "behind everything that is wonderful stands the individual, and it is not the moment that makes the man, but the man who creates the age." As he talks of "critical ages" and explains that it is to the "critical faculty in man" that each "new school" owes its origin, Wilde sounds like Matthew Arnold lecturing on alternating epochs of expansion and epochs of concentration.

"The Critic as Artist" is a rich and satisfying essay, a creative work in its own right that thereby proves its thesis. The incidental commentary on John Ruskin, Walter Pater, Walter Turner, and others enjoys not only the benefit of Wilde's sharp mind but also the "exuberance of diction" that Harold Bloom ascribes to great writing. And when Gilbert promises that "Criticism will annihilate race-prejudices, by insisting upon the unity of the human mind in the variety of its forms," he seems to have plunged head-first into the multiculturalism debates of the century that succeeded him. Wilde may have been born a hundred years too soon.

## Principal criticism
"The Portrait of Mr. W. H.," 1889
*Intentions*, 1891 (includes "The Truth of Masks" [1885], "The Decay of Lying" [1889], "Pen, Pencil and Poison" [1889], and "The Critic as Artist" [1890])
"The Soul of Man under Socialism," 1891
*Reviews*. Volume XIII of *Works of Oscar Wilde*, 1908
*The Artist as Critic: Critical Writings of Oscar Wilde*, 1968 (Richard Ellmann, editor)
*Literary Criticism of Oscar Wilde*, 1968 (Stanley Weintraub, editor)

## Other major works and literary forms
A century after his death Oscar Wilde is introduced to new audiences mainly through the witty comedies that he wrote for the stage, especially *Lady Windermere's Fan* (1892), *A Woman of No Importance* (1893), *An Ideal Husband* (1895), and what is probably his greatest play, *The Importance of Being Earnest* (1899). These works have long been honored in anthologies as well as on the stage. His play *Salomé*, scheduled to star Sarah Bernhardt in 1892 but banned by the Lord Chamberlain, was published in 1893 in French and remains among Wilde's important works. Wilde's only novel, *The Picture of Dorian Gray* (1891), enraged critics who were offended by its depiction of a beautiful young man who remained young while his portrait aged. His long poem "The Ballad of Reading Gaol" (completed in 1898) has always attracted readers, and his *De Profundis*, a letter to Lord Alfred Douglas first published in part in 1905, is a painful account of the two men's relationship. Wilde also published several volumes of stories and poems.

## Further reading
Adams, Elsie. *Bernard Shaw and the Aesthetes*, 1971.
Buckler, William E. "Building a Bulwark against Despair: 'The Critic as Artist,'" in *English Literature in Transition*. XXXII, no. 3 (1989), pp. 279–289.
Ellmann, Richard. "Introduction: The Critic as Artist as Wilde," in *The Artist as Critic. Critical Writings of Oscar Wilde*, 1968.
———. *Oscar Wilde*, 1984.
Gagnier, R., ed. *Critical Essays on Oscar Wilde*, 1991.
Mikolyzk, Thomas A. *Oscar Wilde: An Annotated Bibliography*, 1993.
Nassaar, Christopher S. *Into the Demon Universe: A Literary Exploration of Oscar Wilde*, 1974.
Small, Ian. *Oscar Wilde Revalued: An Essay on New Materials and Methods of Research*, 1993.

FRANK DAY

*See also* Aestheticism; Literary Theory in the Age of Victoria; Swinburne; Symbolism; Symons; Pater

# Raymond Williams

## Welsh critic and writer

**Born:** Llweyn Derw, Pandy, Abergavenny, Gwent, Wales; August 31, 1921
**Died:** London, England; January 28, 1988

## Biography
Raymond Williams was born in the Welsh farming village of Pandy. Both his mother and his father came from farming families. Pandy was a border village with two distinct social structures: localized farm workers and unionized wage earners on the railway. Thus, this little village, although a model of rural, residential life, hinted at a much wider social system beyond. A sense of class and place, which Williams experienced very young, affected him well into his writing career.

Williams earned a scholarship to the Abergavenny Grammar School in 1932. In 1938 he was awarded a state scholarship, and in 1939 he entered Trinity College, University of Cambridge. Much later in life Williams speculated that a university in Wales would have suited him better. At Cambridge he was acutely conscious of class distinctions; during his years there he met only one other person from a working-class family. Williams immediately joined the Socialist Club, which served to heighten his political awareness, and within a month of entering Cambridge he had joined the Communist Party. By 1941, however, he lapsed from Party work and finally left the Party altogether.

Between 1941 and 1945 Williams was a member of the Guards Armoured Division, serving as an officer in the war.

During his four years of military service Williams married Joyce Mary Daling, and they had a daughter, Merryn, born in July, 1944. When, in October, 1945, he was released from the army, he and his family returned to Cambridge; he graduated with his degree in English in 1945. With his second child, Ederyn, on the way, Williams turned down a senior research scholarship at Cambridge in lieu of an adult education job at the University of Oxford. He kept that job, teaching evening classes, until he was invited back to Cambridge as a lecturer in English and Fellow at Jesus College in 1961. His establishment of the journal *Politics and Letters*, together with Wolf Mankowitz and Clifford Collins, proved to be the tilling of fertile ground for his future writing endeavors, even though the journal itself lasted only two years.

In 1950 Williams' second son, Madawc, was born. This was also the year his first book, *Reading and Criticism*, was published – the first of many books of criticism and the beginning of an impressive career. Williams died in 1988, at the age of sixty-six.

## Influence

When Williams began to write in the late 1940s and early 1950s, the context for writing literary criticism within the framework of British Marxism had not been firmly established. Responding to the Stalinism which permeated Christopher Caudwell's writings and the tendency toward elitism found in the socialist magazine *Scrutiny*, Williams began to chart a new course with his criticism. He strongly emphasized the theme of "culture experienced," or "lived culture," in contrast to an artificial distinction between economic life and culture which he found in Karl Marx's writings. This focus, along with his collapsing of traditional Marxist categories of base and superstructure, has had a significant impact upon the way later Marxist critics such as Terry Eagleton have approached their work. In fact, Eagleton himself acknowledges Williams' considerable influence:

> Williams' achievement, then, has been to pursue the implications of felt personal experience to the point where they have organically emerged as methods, concepts, strategies. . . . What he did, then, he did almost single-handedly, working from his personal resources, without significant collaboration or institutional support. The product of that unflagging, unswerving labour was the most suggestive and intricate body of socialist criticism in English history, . . . which must be referred for comparative assessment to the aesthetic production of a Lukács, Benjamin or Goldmann.

## Analysis

Williams has been a very influential figure in the emergence of a "new" Marxism which has sought to revise many of the key concepts within classical Marxism. In his book *Marxism and Literature* (1977) Williams states:

> Any modern approach to a Marxist theory of culture must begin by considering the proposition of a determining base and a determined superstructure. From a strictly theoretical point of view this is not, in fact, where we might choose to begin. It would be in many ways preferable if we could begin from . . . the proposition that social being determines consciousness.

Although Williams starts with the traditional Marxist categories of base and superstructure, he quickly moves the emphasis out of the realm of hard determinism and toward the idea of a reciprocity of social influences. Hence, in his writings one can see the role of human subjectivity and human culture working reciprocally in the production of social relations.

This concept of reciprocity means that social relations are both received and made – indeed, even revalued and transformed. This remarkable shift of emphasis from the classically formulated notion that a mode of production strictly determines the categories within the superstructure – for example, the legal system, the educational system, the military apparatus, and, more broadly, culture and ideology – leads to a significant revaluation of the products of culture. They are no longer mere reflections of the determining forces within the base; rather, they may now be seen as viable and contributing forces in the production of society. For this reason, Williams succinctly states, "Real social relations are deeply embedded within the practice of writing itself, as well as in the relations within which writing is read. To write in different ways is to live in different ways."

It is important to recognize that Williams is not moving away from Marxism; instead, he is giving a new focus to his Marxism – a focus in which the products of culture play a much more significant role than before. He is thoroughly convinced that all writing carries references, meanings, and values. Yet he does not view language as being a conduit, or a "pure medium," through which experiences and reality can flow in an unadulterated fashion. The references and values carried by language result from its being a socially and reciprocally shared activity which is already based in active relationships. Thus, a primary goal for the critic would be to uncover the social significance that is embedded in what often looks like natural, neutral, or straightforward accounts. Particularly when studying works written in class-divided societies, an analysis may need to show exactly how themes of dominance and subservience make their way into pieces of writing through means that are generally thought to be neutral – genres, forms, conventions, and the like.

Genres, for example, are typically thought to be neutral means of organizing works of art. Works might be classified according to their literary form, their subject matter, or their intended readership. Some examples of these categorizations might be the novel, romance, short story, comedy, tragedy, melodrama, children's literature, and so on. In any Marxist account, however, social and historical explanations loom large. In fact, Williams held that certain social and historical relations exist between particular literary forms and the societies and periods in which they were originated or practiced. Indeed, though genre classification might be best left to merely academic pursuits or formalist criticism, Williams believed that "recognition and investigation of the complex relations between these different forms of the social material process . . . are necessarily part of any Marxist theory."

Williams views form in terms of what he would call a social theory of literature. Whereas literary forms have historically been recognized and described according to rules which set their limits, theorists typically fail to recognize that forms have been constructed; the rules have been devised through a process of active shaping. Readers collectively modify both traditional and emerging forms, by means of acceptance, rejection, or mere neglect of an individual artist's use of the form.

At this point Williams' use of the concept of "hegemony" (initially formulated by the Italian Marxist Antonio Gramsci) comes into play. Gramsci's notion of hegemony emphasizes the ideological and cultural authority of one social group over another. Williams notes that this cultural hegemony is so pervasive that it determines the limits of "common sense" for most people.

This hegemonic culture is made up of a central and dominating system of meanings and rules, wherein people are reared, socialized, educated, and employed for the purpose of continually reaffirming this dominant culture. The dominant culture reproduces itself through what Williams calls the "selective tradition." Through the process of "selection," those holding the power emphasize and privilege certain meanings and practices, while others are either marginalized or excluded altogether. Attempts to project alternative values and practices invariably invoke reactions by the dominant culture, which aims to maintain its privileged position. Because of the hegemonic forces at work, however, such reactions are not always necessary. Thus, alternative views are typically undervalued or sometimes even go unrecognized.

Williams makes clear the relationship of form to the idea of hegemony. Since no culture is able to incorporate or exhaust all human potential, there will always be both residual and emergent forms which do not comply with the dominant mode. As Williams states in his article "Base and Superstructure in Marxist Cultural Theory":

> No mode of production, and therefore no dominant society or order of society, and therefore no dominant culture, in reality exhausts human practice, human energy, human intention. . . . On the contrary,

it is a fact about the modes of domination that they select from and consequently exclude the full range of human practice.

Williams also insists upon seeing the functional value of literary conventions in terms of social theory. According to Williams, all established relationships operate in certain particular ways. Thus, conventions must be seen as the customs and practices whereby a particular community signifies meanings; conventions should not be thought to be self-evident or universal. For example, historically the tragic hero had to be a person of rank. In modern class societies the delegation of roles is invariably based upon class distinctions. The hierarchy need never be mentioned in such cases, because it is accepted without question. This is the power of the assumptions carried by conventions. The ways in which people are presented in literary works are never merely based upon "literary" or "aesthetic" decisions: people are social beings, and they are being presented in a social context.

Presentation of characters is often done in terms of their work or income as well; or, conversely, these factors are strategically left out of the presentation. It should not be assumed that these inclusions or omissions, or indeed the relative place of importance given to them, is simply accidental. Such conventional factors as position, work, income, place, action, and even speech patterns all carry within them implicit social messages. Williams puts all of this into context, stating:

> Significant facts of real relationships are thus included or excluded, assumed or described, analyzed or emphasized by variable conventions which can be identified by formal analysis but can be understood only by social analysis.

Williams set as his goal the fusing of social criticism with that of literary criticism. He believed that literary theory must not be separated from cultural theory – even though it is possible to distinguish between the two. He constantly sought to reject the abstractions of aesthetics, wishing rather to emphasize specific intentions and responses as seen within historical and social contexts. He worked for the dissolution of bourgeois aesthetic theory, that is, art as a categorically separate dimension. With his effective collapsing of the notions of base and superstructure, he dismissed the idea that art could be an extrasocial phenomenon. For Williams, creating literature was a material practice not unlike other material practices which function as means of production.

## Principal criticism
*Reading and Criticism*, 1950
*Drama from Ibsen to Eliot*, 1952, 1964 (revised as *Drama from Ibsen to Brecht*, 1968)
*Drama in Performance*, 1954

*Preface to Film*, 1954 (with Michael Orrom)
*Culture and Society, 1780–1950*, 1958
*The Long Revolution*, 1961
*Communications*, 1962
*Modern Tragedy*, 1966, 1979
*The English Novel from Dickens to Lawrence*, 1970
*George Orwell*, 1971
*The Country and the City*, 1973
*Television: Technology and Cultural Form*, 1974
*Keywords: A Vocabulary of Culture and Society*, 1976, 1983
*Marxism and Literature*, 1977
*Problems in Materialism and Culture: Selected Essays*, 1980
*Culture*, 1981 (U.S. edition, *The Sociology of Culture*, 1982)
*Towards 2000*, 1983 (U.S. edition, *The Year 2000*, 1984)
*Writing in Society*, 1983
*The Politics of Modernism: Against the New Conformists*, 1989
*Raymond Williams on Television: Selected Writings*, 1989
*The Writings of Carlos Fuentes*, 1996

## Other major works and literary forms

Raymond Williams is best known for his works of literary and social criticism, but he was also the author of five novels, four plays, and several short stories. Although he never considered his fiction writing to be a mere extension of his social criticism, he did believe that literary theory must not be separated from cultural theory, and he acknowledged that some of the themes of his novels overlapped with those of his social criticism. Still, Williams insisted that he would only write in novel form that which he was certain could not be written in essays and analysis. An excerpt from an interview with H. Gustav Klaus, found in *Contemporary Novelists* (1986), helps to sum up Williams' attitude toward his fiction writing. He states:

> I find novel-writing very important and rewarding, and I have given much more time to it than my list of publications might suggest. But I revise and rework a great deal, and shall be satisfied if by the time I have finished I have five or six novels which I can feel are really my own.

NOVELS
*Border Country*, 1960
*Second Generation*, 1964
*The Volunteers*, 1978
*The Flight for Manod*, 1979
*Loyalties*, 1985

SHORT FICTION
"Sack Labourer," 1941
"This Time," 1943
"A Fine Room to Be Ill In," 1947

PLAYS
*Koba*, 1966
*A Letter from the Country*, 1966
*Public Inquiry*, 1967
*The Country and the City*, 1979

## Further reading

Bennett, James R. "The Novel, Truth, and Community," in *D. H. Lawrence Review*, 1970–1971.
Eagleton, Terry, ed. *Raymond Williams: Critical Perspectives*, 1989.
Eldridge, John, and Lizzie Eldridge. *Raymond Williams: Making Connections*, 1994.
Goldstein, Leonard. "Aspects of Raymond Williams' *Second Generation*," in *Essays in Honour of William Gallacher*, 1966. Edited by P. M. Kemp-Ashraf and Jack Mitchell.
Hooker, Jeremy. "Idea of a People," in *Planet*, 1979.
Inglis, Fred. *Raymond Williams*, 1995.
O'Connor, Alan. *Raymond Williams: Writing, Culture, Politics*, 1989.
Ryan, Kiernan. "Socialist Fiction and the Education of Desire," in *The Socialist Novel in Britain: Towards the Recovery of a Tradition*, 1981. Edited by H. Gustav Klaus.
Wallace, Jeff, Rod Jones, and Sophie Nield, eds. *Raymond Williams Now: Knowledge, Limits, and the Future*, 1997.
Ward, J. P. *Raymond Williams*, 1981.

STEPHEN M. ASHBY

*See also* British Literary Theory: Twentieth Century; Cultural Criticism; Eagleton; Gramsci; Marxist Theory and Criticism; McLuhan

# Edmund Wilson

## American writer and critic

**Born:** Red Bank, New Jersey; May 8, 1895
**Died:** Talcottville, New York; June 12, 1972

## Biography

Edmund Wilson, Jr., was born on May 8, 1895, in Red Bank, New Jersey, the only child of Edmund Wilson, Sr., and the former Helen Mather Kimball. His father was attorney general of New Jersey until his legal career was ended by depression and hypochondria. The young Wilson was strongly influenced by two father figures: Alfred Rofle, a master of Greek at the Hill School in Pottstown, Pennsylvania, instilled in him a sense of the excitement of literature, and Christian Gauss, a professor of French at Princeton University, taught him about the interrelatedness of literature from different cultures and periods and encouraged him to learn French, Russian, Hungarian, and Hebrew. At Princeton, Wilson wrote for and edited the *Nassau Literary Magazine* and was close friends with classmates F. Scott Fitzgerald and John Peale Bishop.

After receiving his degree in 1916 Wilson became a reporter for the New York *Evening Sun* for a year before enlisting in the army. He served first as a wound dresser in a hospital unit before joining military intelligence just prior to Armistice Day. Like most of the artists and intellectuals of his generation, Wilson was horrified by World War I and pledged to devote himself to "Literature, History, the Creation of Beauty, the Discovery of Truth."

He began his career in literary journalism in the 1920s in New York as an editor for *Vanity Fair* and *The New*

*Republic* and was later a longtime contributor to *The New Yorker*. His work was interrupted briefly by a nervous breakdown in 1929. Wilson had four wives, the third being novelist Mary McCarthy, and three children. He was living in his mother's family home in upstate New York when he died on June 12, 1972.

## Influence

Wilson is widely considered to be America's preeminent man of letters and perhaps the last major critic to be a professional – as opposed to academic – writer. He showed that a critic need not be a scholarly dissector of a limited segment of the literary world but could be one who writes knowledgeably about numerous aspects of literary, social, and political endeavors while attempting to show how society's multifaceted affairs are interrelated. He made groundbreaking studies of the Symbolists and the literature of the Civil War, but he was important primarily as one of the major twentieth-century forces for keeping the significance of literature before the public. Wilson was a spokesman, says Warner Berthoff, "for nearly every important development in contemporary literature." According to Anthony Burgess, "no man has had a profounder influence on the capacity of a couple of generations . . . to form . . . judgments on a very large and important sector of European literature."

## Analysis

"There are few things I enjoy so much," wrote Wilson, "as talking to people about books which I have read but they haven't, and making them wish they had – preferably a book that is hard to get or in a language that they do not know." Wilson considered himself a journalist more than a critic. He rejected schools of critical thought, seeing his primary function as informative and his audience as the educated general reader. He prided himself on being a "practicing critic" with a public as opposed to the academics who, in his view, wanted to keep literature an arcane secret among themselves.

Wilson believed that the literary journalist

should be more or less familiar, or be ready to familiarize himself, with the past work of every important writer he deals with and be able to write about an author's new book in the light of his general development and intention. He should also be able to see the author in relation to the national literature as a whole and the national literature in relation to other literatures.

This latter point is the lesson he learned from Christian Gauss and is considered one of Wilson's greatest contributions to literary criticism. He displays it in his first major critical work, *Axel's Castle* (1931). This analysis of the works of William Butler Yeats, James Joyce, Marcel Proust,

Paul Valéry, T. S. Eliot, and Gertrude Stein shows how these moderns descended from the French Symbolists and is the first work to explain the central role of Symbolism in modern writing. Wilson was largely responsible, according to Robert M. Adams, "for the advent and widespread acceptance in America of what had been almost entirely a foreign or expatriate movement."

Despite Wilson's professed distrust of literary theory, certain tenets become clear in *Axel's Castle*, as he attacks writers who ignore everyday reality while preferring to "live only in the imagination." He thinks more highly of such a writer as Anatole France, who is of the world, as opposed to an elitist such as Valéry. Wilson disapproves of art grounded in the private and privileged world, emphasizing how it has a responsibility to the public and to the larger world of politics, objecting to the Symbolists' "lack of curiosity about life." Wilson contends that too many writers withdraw from the world, as Arthur Rimbaud did. He wants them to confront the evils of society in their art.

Wilson, however, does not ask that literature be dogmatic: in "Marxism and Literature" (1937), he takes Marxist critics to task for seeking simple social morals in literature instead of attempting to discover its complexities. Wilson tries to find in a work of literature some understanding of life; he looks for the expression of systems of value based upon human experience. His critics point out that what he means by value never becomes completely clear. They also observe that as Wilson aged he seemed to resemble more and more those he disparages in *Axel's Castle*, becoming aloof from humanity, perhaps even misanthropic.

Another of Wilson's important tenets is also stated in *Axel's Castle*:

The real elements . . . of any work of fiction, are the elements of the author's personality: his imagination embodies in the images of characters, situations and scenes the fundamental conflicts of his nature or the cycle of phases through which it habitually passes.

His main approach to literary analysis is biographical and psychological as he attempts to discover revelations about the writer in his or her works, an attitude directly opposite to that of the New Critics so influential for much of Wilson's career. This approach makes Wilson, in Berthoff's words, "a natural historian of the literary life." Wilson explains this biographical emphasis, "writing about literature for me, has always meant narrative and drama." In other words, he discusses writers almost as if they are fictional characters.

Wilson's penchant for psychoanalyzing his subjects can be seen when he finds in Eliot's *The Waste Land* (1922)

the peculiar conflicts of the Puritan turned artist: the horror of vulgarity and the shy sympathy with the common life, the ascetic shrinking from sexual experience and the distress at the drying up of the springs of sexual emotion, with the straining after a religious emotion which may be made to take its place.

In discussing Henry James, one of his favorite writers, Wilson is concerned less with the works than with discovering the "real" man behind them. He argues that in *The Sacred Fount* (1901) James is dramatizing the frustrations he felt with his life without admitting to himself that he is doing so. Wilson says James' characters cannot consummate love affairs because their creator was sexually unfulfilled himself. In *The Wound and the Bow* (1941), Wilson's thesis is that an artist's creativity compensates for some psychological wound: "Genius and disease, like strength and mutilation, may be inextricably bound up together." He thus looks into the fiction of Charles Dickens and Rudyard Kipling to find scars left by their childhood experiences. (Wilson and George Orwell were the first critics to pay serious attention to Dickens.) While this type of biographical/psychological analysis has been widely criticized, even ridiculed, critics such as Irving Howe and Alfred Kazin have compared Wilson to Plutarch for his skill at capturing the essence and paradoxes of a life.

In "We Don't Know Where We Are" (1959), Wilson admits he is as interested in history as in literature. This interest can be seen in his treatment of the relation of the lives of writers to their times and in his efforts to pinpoint how the concerns of literature are part of the social fabric. He explores the connections between literature and history most closely in *Patriotic Gore* (1962). Wilson examines fiction, poetry, letters, diaries, and memoirs to reveal how combatants on both sides regarded the war, how the war affected civilians, and how it shaped American society. This blend of literary analysis, biography, and social and political criticism is most typical of Wilson's writing, and he considered *Patriotic Gore* to be his best book.

*Patriotic Gore* has been criticized for barely mentioning the Civil War poetry of Herman Melville and Walt Whitman. In fact, perhaps precisely because Wilson is so widely known, he has constantly been attacked for such omissions and numerous other sins. His critics say he regards literary technique only as it serves meaning: thus he is interested in the social and moral content of Gustave Flaubert's fiction but not in his genius as a stylist. Wilson often confuses the narrative voice in a work for that of its author. He describes works more than he analyzes them. Despite his psychological emphasis, he has a limited understanding of the writings of Sigmund Freud and of psychoanalysis in general. Although he was such a dominant factor in the literary scene for half of the twentieth century, Wilson had virtually nothing to say about such significant writers of his time as William Faulkner, Albert Camus, Samuel Beckett, Günter Grass, and Saul Bellow. Berthoff, whose brief study is virtually a catalog of what he considers to be Wilson's deficiencies, attacks him for smugness, describing him as "conservatively radical, out of an unshakable assurance about his own privileged position." To Berthoff, Wilson's "is finally an arrogant and airless mind. It is acquainted with a great many ideas, but ideas become things to it, counters to score with."

While many critics concede Wilson's right to refuse to impose a theory upon literature, they also persist in their irritation at a lack of unity in his work. According to Robert M. Adams, "The most sympathetic and painstaking analyst could not tell what his philosophical position was, if he had one at all. He was interested in literature as a pageant, a parade of experience; but what it was all about he scarcely tried to say." "Like a pianist picking out an unfamiliar tune by ear," Adams continues, "Mr. Wilson often guesses, dodges, or skips where he should be forthright, and is satisfied with the ingenuities of verbal neatness, instead of solid intellectual consistency."

Although such weaknesses stand out when Wilson's literary criticism is regarded as a whole, even Berthoff acknowledges that the critic's "persistent element of serious, thoroughgoing, personal concern gives his reports a vividness and an urgency that fix them in the mind." Van Wyck Brooks called Wilson "one of the few critics who can also be called writers," and for Kazin, "there is no other critic who so evenly and so hauntingly writes criticism as a work of art." The bulk of his writing – unlike most criticism – is clear and frequently energetic. He knows much about literature, history, politics, and religion and has something interesting to say about an amazing variety of topics. Wilson chose to live his life through literature and saw such a life as fulfilling. He committed himself to spreading the word about the vitality, humanity, and importance of literature. As F. Scott Fitzgerald said of his feelings for his friend, Wilson tried to be the literary conscience of his generation.

## Principal criticism

*Axel's Castle: A Study in the Imaginative Literature of 1870–1930*, 1931
*The Triple Thinkers: Ten Essays on Literature*, 1938
*The Boys in the Back Room: Notes on California Novelists*, 1941
*The Wound and the Bow: Seven Studies in Literature*, 1941
*Classics and Commercials: A Literary Chronicle of the Forties*, 1950
*The Shores of Light: A Literary Chronicle of the Twenties and Thirties*, 1952
*Eight Essays*, 1954
*Patriotic Gore: Studies in the Literature of the American Civil War*, 1962
*The Bit Between My Teeth: A Literary Chronicle of 1950–1965*, 1965
*A Window on Russia: For the Use of Foreign Readers*, 1972
*The Devils and Canon Barham: Ten Essays on Poets, Novelists, and Monsters*, 1973
*The Edmund Wilson Reader*, 1997 (Lewis M. Dabney, editor)

## Other major works and literary forms

Edmund Wilson wrote poetry, plays, fiction, history, social and political commentary, travel books, and autobiography in addition to literary criticism. His major creative work, the 1929 novel *I Thought of Daisy*, paints a vivid picture of the artistic life of Greenwich Village in the 1920s. His many nonfiction subjects included the Depression, the Dead Sea Scrolls, the tribulations of the Iroquois, and the Modern Language Association. The most highly regarded of such works is *To the Finland Station: A Study in the Writing and Acting of History* (1940), an account of the causes of the Russian Revolution.

Since his death, selections from the extensive journals and diaries Wilson kept most of his adult life have been edited by his friend Leon Edel, offering an inside account of a considerable part of the American literary life of the twentieth century.

### NOVELS
*I Thought of Daisy*, 1929, 1957
*"Galahad" and "I Thought of Daisy,"* 1957

### SHORT FICTION
*Memoirs of Hecate County*, 1946

### PLAYS
*Discordant Encounters: Plays and Dialogues*, 1926
*The Room and This Gin and These Sandwiches*, 1937
*The Little Blue Light*, 1950
*Five Plays*, 1954
*The Duke of Palermo and Other Plays, with an Open Letter to Mike Nichols*, 1969

### POETRY
*The Undertaker's Garland*, 1922 (with John Peale Bishop)
*Poets, Farewell!*, 1929
*Note-Books of Night*, 1942
*Three Reliques of Ancient Western Poetry Collected by Edmund Wilson from the Ruins*, 1951
*Night Thoughts*, 1961

### NONFICTION
*The American Jitters: A Year of the Slump*, 1932
*Travels in Two Democracies*, 1936
*To the Finland Station: A Study in the Writing and Acting of History*, 1940
*Europe Without Baedeker: Sketches Among the Ruins of Italy, Greece, and England*, 1947
*The Scrolls from the Dead Sea*, 1955 (revised as *The Dead Sea Scrolls, 1947–1969*, 1969)
*Red, Black, Blond, and Olive: Studies in Four Civilizations: Zuni, Haiti, Soviet Russia, Israel*, 1956
*A Piece of My Mind: Reflections at Sixty*, 1956
*The American Earthquake: A Documentary of the Twenties and Thirties*, 1958
*Apologies to the Iroquois*, 1960
*The Cold War and the Income Tax: A Protest*, 1963
*O Canada: An American's Notes on Canadian Culture*, 1965
*A Prelude: Landscapes, Characters, and Conversations from the Earlier Years of My Life*, 1967
*The Fruits of the MLA*, 1968
*Upstate: Records and Recollections of Northern New York*, 1971

*The Twenties: From Notebooks and Diaries of the Period*, 1975
*Letters on Literature and Politics 1912–1972*, 1977
*The Nabokov-Wilson Letters 1940–1971*, 1979 (Simon Karlinsky, editor)
*The Thirties: From Notebooks and Diaries of the Period*, 1980 (Leon Edel, editor)
*The Forties: From Notebooks and Diaries of the Period*, 1983 (Edel, editor)
*The Fifties: From Notebooks and Diaries of the Period*, 1986 (Edel, editor)

### EDITED TEXTS
*The Last Tycoon: An Unfinished Novel by F. Scott Fitzgerald, Together with "The Great Gatsby" and Selected Stories*, 1941
*The Shock of Recognition: The Development of Literature in the United States Recorded by the Men Who Made It*, 1943
*The Crack-Up: With Other Uncollected Pieces, Note-Books, and Unpublished Letters*, by F. Scott Fitzgerald, 1945
*The Collected Essays of John Peale Bishop*, 1948
*Peasants and Other Stories*, by Anton Chekhov, 1956

## Further reading

Adams, Robert M. "Masks and Delays: Edmund Wilson as Critic," in *The Sewanee Review*. LVI (Spring, 1948), pp. 272–286.
Berthoff, Warner. *Edmund Wilson*, 1968.
Burgess, Anthony. "The Triple Thinker," in *Urgent Copy: Literary Studies*, 1968.
Castronovo, David. *Edmund Wilson*, 1984.
Douglas, George H. *Edmund Wilson's America*, 1983.
French, Philip, ed. *Three Honest Men: Edmund Wilson, F. R. Leavis, Lionel Trilling*, 1984.
Groth, Janet. *Edmund Wilson: A Critic of Our Time*, 1989.
Howe, Irving. "A Man of Letters," in *Celebrations and Attacks: Thirty Years of Literary and Cultural Commentary*, 1979.
Kazin, Alfred. "Edmund Wilson: The Critic and the Age," in *The Inmost Leaf: A Selection of Essays*, 1955.
Meyers, Jeffrey. *Edmund Wilson: A Biography*, 1995.
Paul, Sherman. *Edmund Wilson: A Study of Literary Vocation in Our Time*, 1965.
Ramsey, Richard David. *Edmund Wilson: A Bibliography*, 1971.
Wain, John, ed. *Edmund Wilson: The Man and His Work*, 1978.

MICHAEL ADAMS

*See also* Edel; Tate; Trilling

# William K. Wimsatt, Jr.

## American critic and editor

**Born:** Washington, D.C.; November 17, 1907
**Died:** New Haven, Connecticut; December 17, 1975

## Biography

William K. Wimsatt, Jr., was born on November 17, 1907, in Washington, D.C. His mother was the former Bertha McSherry. After attending local schools he received his bachelor's degree *summa cum laude* (1928) and master's degree (1929) from Georgetown University. He continued his graduate education at Yale University, where he was granted his doctorate in 1939. That same year he began teaching at Yale, where he spent the rest of his academic life. In 1944 he married Margaret E. Hecht, with whom he had two sons, William Alexander and James Christopher.

Wimsatt's Yale career – he was promoted to assistant professor in 1943, to associate professor in 1949, and to full professor in 1955 – was a distinguished one. The recipient of a Guggenheim Fellowship (1946–1947) and of a Ford Foundation Fellowship (1953–1954), he was named Frederick Clifford Ford Professor in English in 1965 and Sterling Professor of English in 1974. He served on the Yale Editorial Board in charge of the publication of Boswell's journals (he had coedited one of the volumes) and was appointed president of the Connecticut Academy of Arts and Sciences. Active on the national level, he chaired the influential and prestigious English Institute and served on the executive committee of the Modern Language Association. His accomplishments were recognized by Villanova University, the University of Notre Dame, and Le Moyne College, institutions that awarded him honorary doctoral degrees. He died of an embolism on December 17, 1975, in a New Haven hospital, where he was recovering from a hip operation.

## Influence

Though he specialized in eighteenth-century English literature, particularly the work of Samuel Johnson and Alexander Pope, Wimsatt was also a significant literary theorist who actively participated in the critical debates of his time. While he did not found any school of literary theory, he did summarize and restate the basic tenets of New Criticism, which his Yale University colleagues Cleanth Brooks and Robert Penn Warren had promulgated. He championed "objectivism," a literary theory that directed the reader's attention to the literary work itself. In two seminal papers written with Monroe C. Beardsley, he attacked two fallacies, the "intentional" and the "affective," which stressed, respectively, the author's intention and the audience's emotional/psychological response to the work of art. Wimsatt's *The Verbal Icon* (1954), in which the two essays appeared, established him as a formidable opponent of other types of criticism, especially the Chicago Neo-Aristotelians, who were then in vogue. In his insistence on the literary work as a union of style and content, sound and meaning (he was particularly interested in metrics), he posited the poem as an organic whole with interdependent parts. Because so much of his criticism was not only theoretical but polemical as well and because his two early fallacy essays were especially confrontational, he bore the brunt of the attacks against the New Criticism. His last book, *Day of the Leopards* (1976), which was published posthumously, was essentially a restatement and development of his early work, but by 1976 New Criticism had been superseded by Marxism, semiotics, structuralism, and other theories.

## Analysis

When, in collaboration with Beardsley, Wimsatt published "The Intentional Fallacy" and "The Affective Fallacy" in *The Sewanee Review* (1946 and 1949), he established himself as a major spokesman for New Criticism, the literary theory that had been founded by John Crowe Ransom, Brooks, Allen Tate, René Wellek, and Warren. Although he had in 1942 denied being an advocate of Ransom, who was a maverick within the loosely knit "school," Wimsatt nevertheless had much in common with the New Critics, some of whom were his Yale University colleagues. Influenced by T. E. Hulme's call for objectivity, Ezra Pound's theory of the impersonality of the artist, and T. S. Eliot's and I. A. Richards' close readings of poetry, the New Critics focused on the work of art itself, on its internal circumstances, rather than its external ones. When Wimsatt wrote that "the design or intention of the author is neither available nor desirable as a standard for judging the success of a work of literary art" (*The Verbal Icon*), he turned the reader's attention from the author, with biographical and historical "externals," to the literary work.

Wimsatt's objection to intention as a criterion for the explication and evaluation of literature (he appropriately titled a 1963 collection of essays *Explication as Criticism: Selected Papers from the English Institute, 1941–1952*) was initially limited to authorial intention; in *Day of the Leopards*, however, he extended his definition of "intention" to include ideas relating to "inspiration, expression, authenticity, sincerity, purpose and the like." As Wellek has observed, Wimsatt's extended definition implies a criticism of several contemporary critical theories, among them Freudianism and biographical and historical determinism, including Marxism. The literary work cannot be explicated or evaluated in terms of psychological or historical considerations.

Wimsatt's other influential essay with Beardsley addressed what he termed the "affective fallacy," the mistaken belief that a literary work may be interpreted in terms of its effect on the reader. Among Wimsatt's targets was Richards, ironically a peripheral New Critic whose close readings tended to rely on what Richards called the "emotive" power of words, the meanings suggested viscerally to the reader. Wimsatt was particularly concerned with critics, such as D. H. Lawrence, who relied on their feelings, since those feelings in turn led to impressionistic criticism, or criticism that varies with the critic. As Wimsatt noted, the critic's emotions do not lead to an interpretation of the poem; the poem, instead, contains the emotion, which must be read objectively by the critic.

Since he ruled out both the author's intention and the reader's affective response as appropriate focuses for interpretation, Wimsatt concentrated his attention on the literary work itself, that entity which is "hypostatized as an objective and metaphorically as a spatial object" (*Day of the Leopards*). It is a "verbal icon" not unlike the "well-wrought urn," a metaphor used as the title of the New Critical "bible" written by Brooks (*The Well Wrought Urn: Studies in the Structure of Poetry*, 1947). The verbal icon is itself a union of poetic "form" and poetic "substance" (*Day of the Leopards*); the poem exists as an organic unity that holds opposites in a state of tension. In this somewhat Coleridgean model, the parts of the poem are interdependent with one another and with the whole.

The poem, for Wimsatt, is rooted in words – their meaning and their arrangement in meter and rhyme, in effect, their form and content, their "sound and sense." In fact, much of his work was devoted to demonstrating, as in the case of Alexander Pope, how sound and meaning are interconnected. According to Wimsatt, critics of Pope's rhymes fail to do justice to him because they view rhyme as an isolated component of poetry, not as being tied to "reason," or meaning (*The Verbal Icon*). In his *The Prose Style of Samuel Johnson* (1941), Wimsatt observed that such a separation of style and content might be plausible if the writer had a bad style, but he concluded that even "bad style," because it must rely on words, ultimately has meaning that is inextricably related to the words themselves. The first chapter of the Johnson book, "Style as Meaning," reflects Wimsatt's view.

In his *Philosophic Words* (1948), a study of "style and meaning" in Johnson's essays in *The Rambler* (1750–1752) and in *A Dictionary of the English Language* (1755), Wimsatt explored the "public qualities of language" in terms of the "concord" between the "biographical and the linguistic and critical," but he was careful to state that there is not "a logical dependence of the two latter upon the former." That disclaimer was necessary to avoid the "intentional fallacy," but the linking of "linguistic" and "critical" does pose some potential problems because without the historical and "external" information about the words, the noncontemporaneous reader may encounter problems in "reading" the poem or "icon." As an eighteenth-century specialist, Wimsatt read Pope and Johnson as if he were their contemporary, but as an "ideal" reader, he is not the typical reader who needs notes and information extrinsic to the poem.

Although he stresses the words of a poem and their relationships, Wimsatt related those words to the world outside the poem: "Poetry . . . is a type of discourse where a certain kind of thing knowledge is intimately dependent on word knowledge and compressed into it" (*Hateful Contraries*, 1965). The word is a sign, a symbol, an "icon" which presents reality metaphorically and symbolically. The poem is not the slavish reproduction of reality but the creative interpretation of reality, which is rendered through metaphor, seen by Wimsatt as fulfilling almost the same role as Samuel Taylor Coleridge's "imagination." Metaphor, which holds opposites together, provides a fresh vision of the world through its use of wit, irony, and paradox, which Wellek identified as the "key-words of the New Criticism."

Rather than being a practicing New Critic providing his audience with "close readings" of literary works from different periods, Wimsatt was an explicator of primarily eighteenth-century texts; his practical, applied criticism was overshadowed by his theoretical literary criticism. He was, in effect, a critic of critics. His *Literary Criticism*, written with Brooks (though most of the book is Wimsatt's), provided him with the opportunity not only to review but also to assess the literary theories and literary critics of the past and even the present. In his literary history and his later *Day of the Leopards*, Wimsatt revealed his sympathies with those who see literature as tradition, as being a continuum dating back to antiquity; he maintained that past writers have as much relevance and value in the present as they did in their own time. In fact, there is much in Wimsatt that is reminiscent of Eliot, whose "Tradition and the Individual Talent" and discussion of the seventeenth-century "dissociation of sensibility" undoubtedly influenced him. In his own treatment of the dissociation, Wimsatt found that the split between "the feeling and responding side of human consciousness" and "the knowing and rational valuing" side led to concerns with the author's inspirations and the responses of his or her audience, or to the "intentional" and "affective" fallacies.

Instead of focusing on intent or affect, the literary critic, according to Wimsatt, should focus on the literary work; commenting on the text, explicating its meaning, and demonstrating its coherence and unity, the critic should then evaluate the work: "Our main critical problem is . . . how to make our understanding evaluative" (*The Verbal Icon*). As Wellek has indicated, valuation for Wimsatt was not purely subjective, because he believed in a hierarchy of universal moral values which transcend time and place. Criticism is "objective and absolute" (*The Verbal Icon*). While he acknowledged that such criticism had its limits, that the poem may contain that which cannot be paraphrased or "reduced by theory," Wimsatt was unwilling to engage in mysticism or to capture the mystery. Instead, he insisted that criticism be objective, theoretical, and rational; he even illustrated literary theories with diagrams and charts.

According to Wimsatt, the literary work is to be evaluated on its own terms, without regard to an end outside itself. Consequently, while admitting that literature presents moral and ethical guidelines, Wimsatt distinguished it from religion and philosophy. Not to make the distinction is to risk applying extraliterary standards to the literary work, thereby falling prey to the intentional or affective fallacies. Similarly, Wimsatt carefully drew the lines between literature and the other arts – painting, music, and sculpture. Unlike a poem, composed and made in the mind, the painting is made, though conceived in the mind, only on canvas: "Nevertheless, we would ordinarily think of a poem in the head, though not written down, as a bird in the hand; but of a painting in the head, though not painted, as a bird in the bush" (*Literary Criticism*).

Literary critics who have not observed these distinctions and who have slighted the text in favor of intention or affect have been the targets of Wimsatt's critical writings. Arnold L. Goldsmith called Wimsatt's essay "The Chicago Critics" the "most critical and incisive evaluation" of the Chicago School (*American Literary Criticism, 1905–1965*, 1979). Wimsatt faulted the Chicago School for their psychologism (the affective fallacy), their hypocrisy in attributing to others their own intolerance and dogmatism, their categorizing, their failure to acknowledge verbal analysis, and their preference for theoretical over practical criticism. Since Northrop Frye's myth criticism and E. D. Hirsch's genre criticism also rely on categorizing and applying outside criteria to the text, Wimsatt rejected their theories. In Hirsch's case, Wimsatt observed that genre criticism proceeds from the conventions to the poem rather than from the poem to the genre (*Day of the Leopards*). In a particularly vitriolic essay "Battering the Object" (*Day of the Leopards*), Wimsatt attacked the more current threat posed by structuralism, derided as "the contemporary Parisian vogue or energy." Because Marxists have made Formalism suspect, Wimsatt asserted that structuralism was created to be "reconciled with temporal experience and hence with the essentially romantic subjectivism of the human consciousness." Structuralists such as J. Hillis Miller are as guilty of the affective fallacy as was Richards.

In some ways *Day of the Leopards* reads like a jeremiad; Wimsatt appears as an articulate voice crying in a "wilderness" in which critical fads appeared to have captured the worship of literary scholars. Perhaps as a result of his somewhat reactionary opposition to change, he himself became a target of those he took to task. Eliseo Vivas, who wrote an early overview of Wimsatt's views, took exception to the narrowness of the New Critical focus. Vivas was particularly skeptical about Wimsatt's elimination of psychological factors: "To deny without qualification that there is a relationship between the psychological reactions by means of which the reader grasps the poem and the poem itself is to ask him to talk about a poem he has neither heard nor seen." In effect, Wimsatt seemed to overlook the fact that all readers bring different values, beliefs, and tools to their reading of a poem. Other critics have been less gentle than Vivas. Some have ignored Wimsatt's views as "totalitarian instructions to ignore certain realities" of a poem and have claimed that he desired to reduce poetry to a "science."

Regardless of whether the reader agrees with Wimsatt's literary views, he is a literary force critics cannot ignore. In 1975 David Newton-de Molina edited *On Literary Intention*, a collection of essays attempting to refute Wimsatt; in 1986 J. Timothy Bagwell began his book *American Formalism and the Problems of Interpretation* with an attack on Wimsatt's "intentional fallacy." Nevertheless, Wimsatt is a spokesman for those literary scholars who fear the political, obscurantist critics who see the literary text as a cultural artifact important only in terms of what it can reveal about its culture. Wimsatt, concerned about maintaining his "humanism" and identity as a critic of literature rather than of economics or politics (*Day of the Leopards*), was upset about current trends in literary criticism; events since 1976 have proved him to be a prophet.

## Principal criticism
*The Prose Style of Samuel Johnson*, 1941
*Philosophic Words: A Study of Style and Meaning in the "Rambler" and "Dictionary" of Samuel Johnson*, 1948
*The Verbal Icon: Studies in the Meaning of Poetry*, 1954 (with Monroe C. Beardsley)
*Literary Criticism: A Short History*, 1957 (with Cleanth Brooks; 2 volumes)
*Hateful Contraries: Studies in Literature and Criticism*, 1965 (with Beardsley)
*The Portraits of Alexander Pope*, 1965
*Day of the Leopards: Essays in Defense of Poems*, 1976

## Other major works and literary forms
In addition to the books listed above, William Wimsatt published numerous uncollected articles and notes, wrote many book reviews, and edited collections of literature and of criticism. While he is considered primarily an eighteenth-century literary scholar, Wimsatt wrote extensively on other literary critics, American literature, and meter. His only extraliterary publication was *How to Compose Chess Problems and Why*, which was privately printed in 1966.

NONFICTION
*CEA Chap Book: What to Say About a Poem*, 1963
*How to Compose Chess Problems and Why*, 1966

EDITED TEXTS
*Selected Poetry and Prose by Alexander Pope*, 1951
*English Stage Comedy: Six Essays*, 1955
*Parodies of Ballad Criticism, 1711–1787*, 1957
*Boswell for the Defense, 1769–1774*, 1959 (with F. A. Pottle)
*Samuel Johnson on Shakespeare*, 1960 (also known as *Dr. Johnson on Shakespeare*, 1969)
*Explication as Criticism: Selected Papers from the English Institute, 1941–1952*, 1963
*The Idea of Comedy: Essays in Prose and Verse, Ben Jonson to George Meredith*, 1969
*Versification: Major Language Types*, 1972
*Literary Criticism: Idea and Act: Selected Essays from the English Institute, 1939–1972*, 1974
*Samuel Johnson: Selected Poetry and Prose*, 1977 (with Frank Brady)

## Further reading
Bagwell, J. Timothy. "Wimsatt and Beardsley and the Problem of the Intentional Fallacy," in *American Formalism and the Problem of Interpretation*, 1986.
Brady, Frank, John Palmer, and Martin Price, eds. *Literary Theory and Structure: Essays in Honor of William K. Wimsatt*, 1973.
Goldsmith, Arnold L. "The Case Against the Chicago Critics," in *American Literary Criticism*. Vol. 3, *1905–1965*, 1979.
Lentricchia, Frank. *After the New Criticism*, 1980.

Lodge, David. "Review of *Hateful Contraries*," in *Modern Language Review*. 61.4 (October, 1966), pp. 647–648.

Vivas, Eliseo. "Mr. Wimsatt on the Theory of Literature," in *Comparative Literature*. VII (Fall, 1955), pp. 344–361.

Wellek, René. "The Literary Theory of William K. Wimsatt," in *Yale Review*. LXVI (Summer, 1976), pp. 178–192.

——. *A History of Modern Criticism: 1750–1950*. Vol. 6, *American Criticism, 1900–1950*, 1986.

THOMAS L. ERSKINE

*See also* American Literary Theory: Twentieth Century; Brooks, C.; New Criticism

# Johann Joachim Winckelmann

## German art historian and critic

**Born:** Stendal, Prussia; December 9, 1717
**Died:** Trieste, Italy; June 8, 1768

## Biography

Johann Joachim Winckelmann was born on December 9, 1717, the son of a cobbler in Stendal, Prussia. A curious child, he requested an education from his parents well above their means. Through the financial assistance of various benefactors, he made his way to the Köllnische Gymnasium in Berlin and then to the Altstäditsche Schule in Salzwedel. After his studies in theology at the University of Halle, Winckelmann became a tutor. He then took up studies in medicine at the University of Jena from 1741 to 1742. After his Jena years he accepted a position as tutor and then as schoolmaster.

During these years of unsatisfactory employment he continued his studies in Greek literature. His love for the Greek language and culture was quite unusual in eighteenth-century Germany, since most scholars favored the Roman language and culture over the Greek. When he finally achieved a more suitable position as a librarian with Count Bünau near Dresden, Winckelmann gained access to the elaborate art collections at the court in Dresden. It was here that he assisted the count in collecting the materials for a history of the German Empire, and it was through the Catholic court of August III that he met his future benefactor, Count Archinto, the Italian papal messenger. After some deliberation – Winckelmann had to convert to the Catholic faith – he decided to join Archinto in Rome as his librarian. His ample free time allowed for frequent archaeological excursions, and Winckelmann gained valuable insights into the nature of the visual arts. Travels to Naples and Florence in 1758 provided additional stimulation.

After the death of Count Archinto, Winckelmann joined the household of Cardinal Alessandro Albani in 1759. There he produced two of his most important works:

*Geschichte der kunst des Alterthums* (1764, 1776; *History of Ancient Art*, 1849–1873) and *Monumenti antichi inediti* (1767–1768). In 1763 he was appointed prefect of antiquities in Rome, where he often served as a guide to important visitors. His reputation earned for him an invitation to his native Germany, but when, after long deliberations, he decided to undertake the journey north in 1768, he soon regretted his decision and could hardly be persuaded to continue farther than the Tirolian mountains. His travel companion, an Italian painter, convinced him to travel to Vienna, where he was rewarded by Empress Maria Theresa with gold coins of considerable value. He could not be persuaded to continue his journey to Germany, and on May 28 he traveled back to Italy alone, where he arrived on June 1, 1768. A week later, while waiting for his boat to Venice, he was robbed and murdered in his hotel room in Trieste.

## Influence

Winckelmann's masterpiece, *History of Ancient Art*, laid the foundation for art history in the eighteenth century. His appreciation for the visual arts of the ancients, especially the Greeks, opened the world of ancient art to Germany. His description of the Laocoön statue had a profound influence on Gotthold Ephraim Lessing, the author of *Laokoon: Oder, Über die Grenzen der Mahlerei und Poesie* (1766; *Laocoön: An Essay on the Limits of Painting and Poetry*, 1836). His analysis of antiquity paved the way for German classicism, with its return to the simplicity of the ancients in art and literature. In his classical phase, Johann Wolfgang von Goethe utilized Winckelmann's thoughts and integrated them into his aesthetics of literature.

Winckelmann's aesthetic and autobiographical writings also allow glimpses at the often neglected homosocial and homoerotic contours of eighteenth-century German culture in the confluence of the enthusiasm for classical Greece and the celebration of male heroic friendship. Winckelmann was the architect of a powerful vision of Greece as the embodiment of aesthetic, moral, and sexual freedom in which male friendship – including the celebration of the male body – was incorporated into social and political institutions.

Winckelmann's work on imitation, *Gedanken über die Nachahmung der griechischen Werke in der Malerei und Bildhauerkunst* (1755; *Reflections on the Paintings and Sculpture of the Greeks*, 1765), became most influential during the period of German classicism. His characterization of Greek beauty as containing the qualities of serenity and simplicity ("*edle Einfalt, stille Groösse*") influenced classicist aesthetics until the end of the eighteenth century. His organic conception of culture as the birth, growth, and death of civilizations and their artistic representations was continued by Johann Gottfried Herder, especially in *Ideen zur Philosophie der Geschichte der Menschheit* (1784–1791; *Outlines of a Philosophy of the History of Man*, 1800).

## Analysis

Winckelmann's theory of aesthetics was contained in his first major publication, *Reflections on the Paintings and Sculpture of the Greeks*; he elaborated on the concepts contained in this work but never radically altered them. He soon followed his study with a supposedly anonymous critique, no longer extant, in which he anticipated the criticism of art historians and tried to deflect it.

Winckelmann's work on imitation had a great influence on his contemporaries. In an age when Baroque art was predominant in Germany, the turn toward Greek art was a radical departure from contemporary tastes. The Laocoön statue exemplified for him the perfect law of art. In his words, the "universal, dominant characteristic of Greek masterpieces is noble simplicity and serene greatness in pose as well as in expression." He recognized and explored the twofold aspect of beauty: the physical and the spiritual. According to Winckelmann, the ideal of inner beauty combined with outer beauty was realized in Greek statues, especially those of males.

Winckelmann also observed that historical conditions had a strong influence on art. He was convinced that the mild climate and the beautiful landscape, combined with a vigorous, free life-style, were responsible for the physical beauty of the Greeks. The cultural practices of the Greeks, such as nude or seminude sports activities and festivities, provided ample opportunity to observe the beautiful body in motion. The artist, therefore, had ideal conditions to view the body in its full range of movement. The observation of the body in motion enabled the artist to obtain a more precise look at human nature than is possible through observation of a studio model. In addition, the imitating artist was able to glimpse the underlying emotions informing the beautiful body while it engaged in various activities.

According to Winckelmann, this frequent exposure to physical beauty was also the reason Greek artists were able to formulate an abstract ideal of beauty by mentally combining features observed in sensual nature. Thus, Winckelmann's advice to his contemporaries who did not have the opportunity to observe such living beauty was to take Greek art as a model. He perceived this to be a more certain way to achieve true beauty than imitating nature.

Greek art became influential for literary theory and practice, especially during the period of German classicism, because it was perceived as the ideal expression of human nature and, therefore, as a moral model for classical Germany. In Greece, the arts were not merely a passion, as they were in Germany during the eighteenth century, but an integral and important part of mainstream culture, at least as Winckelmann perceived it. Thus, the admiration for Greek society and culture was also a critique of contemporary society, with its separation of art and life and its division of labor. Hellenistic life, in contrast, was seen as the epitome of human nature, produced by ideal social and climatic conditions which provided an opportunity to develop the rational as well as the sensual. Winckelmann was influential also through his love for Greek literature. In particular, his high regard for Homer directed the attention of German literary critics from Lessing to Goethe and back to ancient Greek literature.

The common element in his other works on the visual arts – which were less influential for literary criticism than the work on imitation – is the establishment of aesthetic criteria based on historical conditions. The historical dependency of art was an important concept which was taken up and expanded by Herder and the positivists of the nineteenth century.

Especially in his *History of Ancient Art*, Winckelmann developed a new concept of art history as an organically growing evolution from one style to another (a contradiction in the light of his propagation of the Hellenistic art as the ultimate achievement in aesthetics). The *History of Ancient Art* is divided into two parts; a philosophical investigation into the nature of art is followed by a historical section on Greek art. In the first part, Winckelmann discusses the origin of art, which he sees as having developed out of necessity, out of religious practice. Art arose spontaneously in many countries but not usually at the same time. He goes on to explain that the materials available had an important influence on the individual form the artifact eventually took. Winckelmann first discusses art among the Egyptians, Phoenicians, Persians, and Etruscans, and then moves to the most substantial part, art among the Greeks. He reiterates the absolute superiority of their concept of art. For the same reasons which he stated in his earlier work – the social, political, climatic, and cultural superiority of the Greek state which had led to the full integration of art into life – he once again assigns superiority to Greek art.

As in the earlier work, the concept of beauty remains nebulous and eludes a thorough analysis. Winckelmann attempts to illuminate it by two quasi opposite terms: *Unbezeichnung*, nonexpressiveness, and *Ausdruck*, expression. Beauty must have as little expression or emotion as possible, because strong emotions tend to distort the features and rob the body of the calm grandeur it was supposed to display. Ideally, the artifact should embody both nonexpressiveness, or calm grandeur, and expression. Therefore, Winckelmann considered beauty of form to be more important than the expression it is to convey. An affect which alters the facial features and the body's posture is seen to destroy true beauty. As an illustration for this somewhat vague concept of beauty he lists individual beautiful features based on their occurrences in the works of art he encountered. Unlike his contemporaries, who developed systematic definitions of beauty, Winckelmann concludes that beauty is one of the great secrets of nature which can be experienced but never fully explained.

Winckelmann's achievement in the *History of Ancient Art* lies in its organization and its broad scope. He was not the first to mention climatic factors for the cultural development of a people, and the organic concept of history had already been popularized. In addition, he was not the first to uphold the works of the ancients as ideal models for contemporary art. While all these ideas had already been discussed in one form or another, Winckelmann connected them into one unified history of art backed by a thorough sociohistorical analysis. He is, therefore, often referred to as the founder of two new disciplines: art history and archaeology. Winckelmann observed as precisely as possible and supplemented his findings with information from many different fields, such as philosophy, mathematics, and numismatics. Winckelmann followed the *History of Ancient Art* with a set of postscripts, *Anmerkungen über die "Geschichte der Kunst des Alterthums"* (1767). Here, he corrected some errors and attempted to expand his study in certain areas. He was working on more extensive revisions when he was murdered in Trieste. The revised edition was completed by others and was published in 1776.

Apart from Winckelmann's service to art history, his contribution to archaeology was also important. In his *Nachrichten von den neuesten herculanischen Entdeckungen* (1764; reports on the most recent discoveries made at Herculaneum), he criticized the blunders that were made by incompetent bureaucrats in the excavation of antique treasures in Portici and Naples and eventually effected changes in the procedures.

Winckelmann was a sensitive interpreter of the artifacts, because he was able to analyze the given object in its own right and, at the same time, assign it to its spatial and temporal field. He took the religious, political, and climatic aspects into consideration when interpreting a newly discovered object. This ability to integrate information of various disciplines into a unified picture of an artifact in its historical context was Winckelmann's greatest achievement.

## Principal criticism

*Gedanken über die Nachahmung der griechischen Werke in der Malerei und Bildhauerkunst*, 1755 (*Reflections on the Paintings and Sculpture of the Greeks*, 1765)
*Von der Grazie in den Werken der Kunst*, 1759
*Geschichte der Kunst des Alterthums*, 1764, 1776 (*History of Ancient Art*, 1849–1873)

## Other major works and literary forms

In addition to the books listed above, Johann Joachim Winckelmann produced several other studies on classical art and sculpture. His reviews on newly discovered works of classical sculpture were collected in *Monumenti antichi inediti* (1767–1768), written in Italian. Another of his important art-historical works is his description of the famous Apollo statue *Beschreibung des Torso im Belvedere zu Rom* (1759; *Description of Apollo Belvedere*, 1873)

NONFICTION
*Beschreibung der vorzüglichsten Gemälde der Dresdener Galerie*, 1752
*Gedanken vom mündlichen Vortrag der neueren allgemeinen Geschichte*, 1754
*Beschreibung des Torso im Belvedere zu Rom*, 1759 (*Description of Apollo Belvedere*, 1873)
*Nachrichten von den neuesten herculanischen Entdeckungen*, 1764
*Versuch einer Allegorie, besonders für die Kunst*, 1766
*Anmerkungen über die "Geschichte der Kunst des Alterthums,"* 1767
*Monumenti antichi inediti*, 1767–1768
*Sämtliche Werke*, 1825–1829 (12 volumes)

## Further reading

Butler, E. M. *The Tyranny of Greece over Germany*, 1935.
Flavell, Kay M. "Winckelmann and the German Enlightenment: On the Recovery and Uses of the Past," in *The Modern Language Review*. 1979, pp. 79–96.
Hatfield, Henry. *Aesthetic Paganism in German Literature, from Winckelmann to the Death of Goethe*, 1964.
——. *Winckelmann and His German Critics, 1755–1781*, 1943.
Leppmann, Wolfgang. *Winckelmann*, 1970.
Morrison, Jeffrey. *Winckelmann and the Notion of Aesthetic Education*, 1996.
Potts, Alex. *Flesh and the Ideal: Winckelmann and the Origin of History*, 1994.
Richter, Simon. "Winckelmann's Progeny: Homosocial Networking in the Eighteenth Century," in *Outing Goethe and His Age*, 1996, pp. 33–46. Edited by Alice Kuzniar.
Sweet, Denis M. "The Personal, the Political, and the Aesthetic: Johann Joachim Winckelmann's German Enlightenment Life," in *The Pursuit of Sodomy: Male Homosexuality in Renaissance and Enlightenment Europe*, 1989, pp. 147–162. Edited by Kent Gerard and Gert Hekma.

KARIN WURST

# Yvor Winters

## American critic and poet

**Born:** Chicago, Illinois; October 17, 1900
**Died:** Palo Alto, California; January 25, 1968

## Biography

Arthur Yvor Winters was born on October 17, 1900, in Chicago. His childhood years were divided between Chicago and Eagle Rock (an area of Los Angeles), California. He graduated from high school in Chicago and attended the University of Chicago in 1917–1918. In 1918 he was forced to move to Santa Fe, New Mexico, having contracted tuberculosis; he spent three years in a sanatorium there.

Winters later graduated from the University of Colorado, where he also received an M.A. In 1927, after two years of teaching French and Spanish, he entered Stanford University, an institution with which he was to be associated for the rest of his life. He received a Ph.D. from

Stanford in 1935 and was a professor of English there until his retirement in 1966.

In 1937 Winters published his first book of criticism, *Primitivism and Decadence*, and established himself as an important literary critic. In 1960 he won the Bollingen Award and in 1961 a Guggenheim Fellowship. Winters was married to the writer Janet Lewis, with whom he had two children. He died of cancer in Palo Alto, California, in 1968.

## Influence

Winters' criticism was not as influential as that of other poet-critics, such as T. S. Eliot, because he remained stubbornly independent of all critical trends and movements. His uncompromising insistence on a rational and a moral aesthetic were alien to a generation brought up on the doctrine of the "objective correlative" and the New Criticism's doctrine of irony. Nevertheless, Winters' passionate, and at times scornful, discussions and judgments did alter the critical consensus about the reputations of some writers and critics. For example, Winters had much to do with the deflating of the reputation of Hart Crane, and he helped raise the standing of the poetry of Edward Arlington Robinson. His attack on Robert Frost as a "Spiritual Drifter" and his campaign to promote Frederick Goddard Tuckerman's poem "The Cricket" were largely unsuccessful.

There were only a small number who followed the precepts that Winters outlined in his critical works, but those followers tended to be very committed and saw themselves as a minority fighting against carelessness and sloppy thinking. Chief among those followers are the former students of Winters, J. V. Cunningham and Edgar Bowers.

## Analysis

Winters has been called a humanist, a New Critic, and a moral critic. There are elements from all of these critical systems in Winters' developed theory, but the mixture is individual and unique. For example, he was drawn to the moral view of such humanist critics as Irving Babbitt and Paul Elmer More but was forced to reject their theories because of their demand for a didactic content for literature. He was attracted to the New Critics' method of analyzing a work of art but was put off by their lack of interest in historical traditions and their emphasis on irony and paradox as requisite to good poetry and fiction. He devised his own theory, which emphasized a full discussion of form to reveal the moral and intellectual order of the work. His critical principles are stated most clearly in a chapter of *The Function of Criticism*, entitled "Problems for the Modern Critic of Literature":

I believe that a poem (or other work of artistic literature) is a statement in words about a human experience. . . . In each work there is a content which is rationally apprehensible. . . . The work is thus a judgment, rational and emotional, of the experience – that is a complete moral judgment in so far as the work is successful.

These principles are already present in Winters' first book, *Primitivism and Decadence*. Winters attacks such "experimental" methods as "Repetition," "Pseudo-Reference," and "Qualitative Progression," while defending the "Logical Method." The chief culprit is Eliot, who uses both "Pseudo-Reference" and "Qualitative Progression," while such traditional poets as Andrew Marvell use the "Logical Method." Winters' methods of classification continue as he places D. H. Lawrence and Edgar Allan Poe into the "primitive" category because their style is undeveloped or inadequate. The "Decadents" are those poets, such as Crane and Ezra Pound, who have a finely developed sense of language but are "incomplete formally." One of the few poets of the twentieth century, according to Winters, who does not succumb to either the primitive or the decadent is T. Sturge Moore, and he praises highly Moore's poem "To Silence," since the "structure of the poem is logical."

Winters also insists on the necessity of a regular meter in poetry. He does acknowledge the success of the "sprung rhythm" of Gerard Manley Hopkins and he praises Robert Bridges' use of syllabic meter. He is suspicious, however, of such experiments as free verse and gave up writing free verse when he saw its limitations. His final judgment is that "experimental meter, like other aspects of experimental convention, is incomplete."

In *Maule's Curse*, Winters focuses on prose writers rather than poets, but the principles and standards of judgment remain the same. He praises Nathaniel Hawthorne's *The Scarlet Letter* (1850) very highly for using allegory against the Puritans, who had an allegorical view of the world. He states that Hawthorne has brought "his allegory to perfect literary form." In *The Blithedale Romance* (1852) and other works, however, he mixed allegory and the realism of the novel and marred the form; these novels are not fully realistic and the allegory cannot be discovered. For Winters, it is a failure to unify the form.

Winters condemns Hawthorne for murky symbolism but finds Herman Melville's symbolism to be not only appropriate but also effective. He goes so far as to call *Moby Dick: Or, The Whale* (1851) a "tragic drama" and a "great epic." One of the most important reasons for Melville's success, in Winters' view, is that he understands the Puritan mentality and portrays it in Ahab. Winters also praises *Billy Budd, Foretopman* (1924) as a "masterpiece" that deals with a moral problem, although the style is somewhat awkward.

Winters is most critical of Poe and declares that Poe is both a bad poet and a bad critic. He objects most strongly to Poe's condemnation of "didacticism" in a work of art;

Winters recognizes that some works are marred by "unsound" didacticism but refuses to dismiss all "didactic" works. He also finds Poe's focus on an abstract "Beauty" to be faulty, since it cannot be communicated to a reader, and his metrics to be "crude" and unsuccessful.

Predictably, Winters has little use for Ralph Waldo Emerson and calls him a "sentimentalist and a fraud." Winters believes that Emerson not only has an inadequate view of life but also that he influenced others, such as Walt Whitman, who revealed even more fully "the implications of such an attitude in life and in art." He does attempt to balance his total rejection of Emerson by promoting one of Emerson's contemporaries, Jones Very; Winters claims that Very has "been neglected" and wishes to establish him "permanently in his rightful place in the history of our literature." Winters' campaign for Very was only partially successful; he is still not considered to be a major American writer.

When Winters evaluates Emily Dickinson and Henry James, he relates both to their New England heritage. He believes that Dickinson was one of the very few writers of the period to find a way out of the Calvinist morality and "made her life a moral drama" while not succumbing to "moral confusion." Yet this same tradition robbed her poetry of "lightness and grace" and led her into poetic experiments and mannerisms which prevented her from fulfilling her potential. Winters also finds some defects and obscurities in James' fiction, but the defects fade in the face of James' creation of plots that deal with "ethical problems." Winters does connect the form and the moral content of the work in both these analyses but, at times, the demand for the representation of moral or ethical problems in literature seems to overwhelm the formal analysis.

In *The Anatomy of Nonsense*, Winters restates his critical principles in a series of propositions and "problems." Winters reasserts the possibility and necessity of making value judgments about a work of art and insists that the criteria for judgment are rational and traditional. When he applies these standards to such poets as Eliot and Wallace Stevens, the rational and philosophical content of the work can invalidate or corrupt such elements as style and form. For example, Winters calls Stevens a "hedonist," and even though he calls "Sunday Morning" one of the great poems of the century, he declares that Stevens is a "debased talent." In one of the better relationships of form and content, Winters suggests that Stevens' hedonistic philosophy is at odds with "the traditional seriousness of attitude and a traditional rhetoric"; the result is the gradual diminishment of a potentially great poet into triviality.

Winters is harsher on Eliot than Stevens, since Eliot was an influential critic as well as an important poet. He criticizes Eliot's theory of "autotelic," or self-referential, art as nonsense masquerading as profundity, while Eliot's famous "objective correlative" is, for Winters, self-contradictory and a "reversal of the normal processes of understanding human experiences." Winters also finds confusion and error in Eliot's view of the relationship between poetry and belief; he even suggests that Eliot wants to relate the two but is held back by the fashionable literary theories of the time. He also discovers significant problems in Eliot's poetry when he compares Eliot to Charles Baudelaire. Baudelaire, according to Winters, was able to "judge" the world he presented while Eliot "is merely exhibiting it." Such a failure to make moral judgments of experience is a central failing in Winters' critical system.

In *Forms of Discovery*, Winters returns to his central subject, the "short poem." He discusses and evaluates major and minor short poems from the Renaissance to the mid-twentieth century. He again finds very little to like and much to condemn. He first locates the main tradition in the plain style of George Gascoigne, Barnabe Googe, and George Turberville while diminishing the accomplishment of such poets as Sir Philip Sidney, Edmund Spenser, and John Donne. He specifically attacks Donne – who was a major figure to the New Critics – for being obscure or careless and using mere "decoration." John Milton is also criticized, since the "rational structure" of which Winters approves "began to break down toward the middle of the seventeenth century: the signs are most obvious in 'Lycidas.' "

Winters cannot find much to like in all of the eighteenth and nineteenth centuries. He admires certain poetic qualities in William Blake but cannot accept the religious or social ideas that dominated his poetry. William Wordsworth, Samuel Taylor Coleridge, Percy Bysshe Shelley, and John Keats are bad poets in an "unfortunate age." Winters is consistent in applying his doctrine of rational structure for the short poem in the face of the greatest reputations of the last four hundred years, but there is little left of those reputations in Winters' redrawing of the history of English and American poetry.

When Winters reaches the twentieth century, he also has some surprising judgments to make. He does not find much that is of value in the poetry of William Butler Yeats, and what is good is marred by Yeats' esoteric philosophy; Winters refuses to ignore the ideas in order to enjoy the "poetry." In contrast, he does praise highly Thomas Hardy's blend of clear metrics and "natural detail"; Hardy does have faults, as does Dickinson, to whom he is compared, but he remains an important poet for Winters. Another poet he praises is Frederick Goddard Tuckerman, and Winters asserts that his poem "The Cricket" is the finest poem of the nineteenth century. At this point, many readers might wonder if Winters' revision of the poetic tradition has become too individual and based on too narrow grounds. This concern is extended when Winters claims that "J. V. Cunningham seems to me the most consistently distinguished poet writing in English today." Winters does make the reader take another look at the poetic tradition, but he seems, at times, to wrench it out of its former shape and leave a handful of unknown or minor poets to represent the tradition.

Winters can be compared to the British critic F. R. Leavis. Both Winters and Leavis were irascible and opinionated critics who demanded moral vision from a literary work and were satisfied with nothing less than what they considered the best. Many have questioned their criteria or their particular selections of the best, but no one ever doubted their passion for their subject or the essential seriousness with which they went about informing and persuading others.

## Principal criticism

*Primitivism and Decadence: A Study of American Experimental Poetry*, 1937
*Maule's Curse: Seven Studies in the History of American Obscuranticism*, 1938
*The Anatomy of Nonsense*, 1943
*In Defense of Reason*, 1947
*The Function of Criticism: Problems and Exercises*, 1957
*On Modern Poets: Stevens, Eliot, Ransom, Crane, Hopkins, Frost*, 1959
*Forms of Discovery: Critical and Historical Essays on the Forms of the Short Poem in English*, 1967

## Other major works and literary forms

Yvor Winters was an important poet as well as a distinguished literary critic. He put into practice in his poetry many of the doctrines of his criticism. His 1960 revised edition of *Collected Poems*, first published in 1952, is filled with examples of the "short poem" with a rational and logical structure and a very identifiable meter. Many poems describe the California landscape, and several deal with social issues, such as "Ode on the Despoilers of Learning in an American University 1947." A few touch on personal life memorably, such as "The Terminal," on the departure of his daughter. Winters also did a number of translations from the French, which are included in the *Collected Poems*, published one work of short fiction, and edited four volumes of poetry.

SHORT FICTION
"The Brink of Darkness," 1932, revised 1947

POETRY
*The Immobile Wind*, 1921
*The Magpie's Shadow*, 1922
*The Bare Hills*, 1927
*The Proof*, 1930
*The Journey*, 1931
*Before Disaster*, 1934
*Poems*, 1940
*The Giant Weapon*, 1943
*To the Holy Spirit*, 1947
*Collected Poems*, 1952, revised 1960
*The Early Poems of Yvor Winters, 1920–1928*, 1966
*The Collected Poetry of Yvor Winters*, 1978 (Donald Davie, editor)

NONFICTION
*Edward Arlington Robinson*, 1946
*The Poetry of W. B. Yeats*, 1960
*The Poetry of J. V. Cunningham*, 1961

*The Uncollected Essays and Reviews of Yvor Winters*, 1973
*Hart Crane and Yvor Winters: Their Literary Correspondence*, 1978

EDITED TEXTS
*Twelve Poets of the Pacific*, 1937
*Selected Poems*, by Elizabeth Daryush, 1948
*Poets of the Pacific, Second Series*, 1949
*Quest for Reality: An Anthology of Short Poems in English*, 1969 (with Kenneth Fields)

## Further reading

Brown, Ashley. "The Critical Legacy of Yvor Winters," in *The Southern Review*. 17 (1981).
Davis, Dick. *Wisdom and Wilderness: The Achievement of Yvor Winters*, 1983.
Hyman, Stanley Edgar. *The Armed Vision: A Study in the Methods of Modern Literary Criticism*, 1955 (revised edition).
Issacs, Susan. *An Introduction to Yvor Winters*, 1981.
McKean, Keith F. *The Moral Measure of Literature*, 1961.
Ransom, John Crowe. *The New Criticism*, 1941.
Sexton, Richard J. *The Complex of Yvor Winters' Criticism*, 1973.

JAMES SULLIVAN

*See also* American Literary Theory: Twentieth Century; New Criticism; Leavis

# Virginia Woolf

### English novelist and critic

**Born:** London, England; January 25, 1882
**Died:** Sussex, England; March 28, 1941

## Biography

Virginia Woolf was born in 1882 into an upper-middle-class Victorian household. Her father, the noted literary critic Sir Leslie Stephen, educated his daughter at home, allowing her to read freely in his huge library. Her mother's death, when Virginia was thirteen, caused the first of many mental breakdowns she was to suffer throughout her life.

When Sir Leslie died in 1904, Virginia, her sister Vanessa, and her two brothers left their home in Hyde Park Gate and went to live in Bloomsbury, a slightly disreputable section of London. They leased a house which they later shared, to the horror of their conservative relatives, with several young men from Cambridge. This was the beginning of the literary group called "Bloomsbury." Vanessa and Virginia both chose husbands from the group, Virginia marrying the socialist writer Leonard Woolf, whom she described to a friend as a "penniless Jew."

Virginia's life with Leonard was outwardly uneventful. They divided their time between a country house in Sussex and a home in London, where the two began a publishing house, Hogarth Press. Virginia wrote voluminously: novels, diaries, criticism, letters, and stories. She also entertained friends, including the old Bloomsbury circle with fellow artists such as E. M. Forster. Her close friendships, including a romantic companionship with Vita Sackville-West, added impetus to her writing.

Throughout her life Virginia Woolf was plagued by mental illness. She frequently suffered attacks when she had just finished a book; sometimes a week of rest would suffice to cure her, while at other times several months would elapse before she recovered. Fear of these terrifying interludes of madness haunted her. During the height of World War II, depressed over Nazi advances, she felt this disease overtaking her again, and unable to face it, she drowned herself in the River Ouse in Sussex.

## Influence

Early in her career Virginia Woolf became a successful reviewer, writing for the most prestigious journals of the time. Her writings were well received: G. Lowes Dickinson said that she was quite simply the best critic writing. Woolf saw her influence waning in the 1930s as she and others were labeled as irrelevant or worse by younger, politically oriented writers. Woolf's novels and criticism were both castigated, her criticism scorned as insubstantial and apolitical. Later, her novels would be recognized as groundbreaking experiments in both form and content.

Ironically, Woolf has had a lasting influence in one very political area, feminist literary criticism. *A Room of One's Own* and other essays set out issues about women and writing upon which feminist writers have been building since. When feminist literary criticism became a major force in the early 1970s, Woolf was hailed as a progenitor of its thinking. Ellen Moers, in *Literary Women* (1977), called Woolf the finest of all critics of women's writing. *A Room of One's Own* proposed basic ideas about women as writers: women's particular style, the relationship between women's oppression and their creativity, and the subject matter most often chosen by women writers. All of these issues continue to frame discussion for feminist writers.

Many writers have played upon Woolf's famous and evocative title; Elaine Showalter's *A Literature of Their Own: British Women Novelists from Brontë to Lessing* (1976) is most notable. Such borrowing is a reminder of Woolf's role as a pioneer in the field. Contemporary feminist critics do not always see Woolf as a perfect model: some, such as Showalter herself, see Woolf as too passive, too concerned with showing how women's experiences have hurt them, rather than how such experiences have been strengthening. In spite of this and other divergences, Woolf remains the point of origin for feminist literary discussion.

## Analysis

All of her adult life, Woolf was a working critic. Her criticism was written in counterpoint to her novels, and only the two taken together can give the reader a full picture of her achievement and her genius. Criticism offered Woolf an escape from the intensity of her creative writing and a chance to look at literature from the other side. Also, the discipline and focus of assigned review articles pushed her into a direct style of discourse, a tightness, which she recognized as a useful opposition to the looseness she feared in her novels.

In a sense, Woolf was born into her vocation as a critic. Her father, Sir Leslie Stephen, was a noted critic and literary biographer. As a child, she kept notes on her readings and discussed her evolving tastes and literary values with her father. The breadth of her youthful reading and appreciation helped to shape her lifelong values as a critic: her criticism ranges more broadly than perhaps any other comparable writer's work. Because Woolf's literary education came solely from reading, not from schools, she liked to see herself as a "common reader," one who read for pleasure and with the hope of finding wholeness of vision. She looks at all genres, all eras, and most nations in her criticism, and she evaluates all that she finds with a few simple tests.

These tests were not learned only from her father. Woolf was aware that much of the literature she admired would have shocked or baffled her Victorian father. She was quite self-consciously a "modern," a product of the breakdown of Victorianism and the coming of Post-Impressionism. Late in her life, Woolf wrote, half-humorously, that human nature had changed in December, 1910. She was referring to the First Post-Impressionist Exhibition, which had for her generation expressed the sense of the new, the rebellion of young artists. With this event, Woolf believed, a new artistic era had genuinely begun. Those who ignored it would find themselves ignored in turn. Thus, in evaluating her contemporaries as writers, Woolf persistently used the word "original" as a criterion. To attempt something new was bold and brave, even if one failed. Woolf has kind words for Dorothy Richardson's stream-of-consciousness experiments, flawed though they were, and less generous evaluations of her friend Vita Sackville-West, whose stylistically traditional novels were written with a "pen of brass," according to Woolf.

To Virginia Woolf, to be truly modern in writing was not merely to be different, but to use that different mode to express reality. Perhaps every literary era sees itself as moving closer to an expression of life as it really is: such was Woolf's ambition for herself and her contemporaries. Her realism was a recognition that life is not truly perceived as a flat, factual narrative; rather, it has "moments of being," instances of full awareness which emerge from the blandness of day-to-day life. These impressions, which Woolf described as "an incessant shower of innumerable atoms," form the consciousness which ought to be the artist's true subject. For his faithfulness to such portrayal, Woolf praises James Joyce: "He is concerned at all costs to reveal the flickerings of that innermost flame which flashes its messages through the brain."

Yet experimentation, or even the successful portrayal of consciousness, does not for Woolf guarantee an entirely successful modern work. Joyce's *Ulysses* (1922), for example, may portray much of life fully through the "modern" method, yet Woolf finds that there is still too much of life left out. A vital criterion – indeed, Woolf's highest standard – is a novel's power to "enclose the human heart." In this judgment, Woolf was turning back to her Victorian heritage, to the lesson learned in her father's library that great literature had to speak powerfully to the human condition. This belief was strengthened in her by her friends, the other "Bloomsberries," as they were called. The men of the group had been heavily influenced by the Cambridge philosopher and ethicist G. E. Moore. Moore and his disciples believed that above all else stood the goodness possible in human relationships. Already attuned to such values, Woolf came to believe more deeply in them through her Bloomsbury connections. For her, literature, especially novels, had to show characters involved in human relationships. When the "damned egotistical self" was allowed to dominate, the literature suffered irreparably. This dominance, she believed, ruined *Ulysses*, and she feared its intrusion into her own work. This risk was inevitable for a writer whose style demanded concentration on the vagaries of human consciousness.

The contemporaries Woolf judged most harshly were those who rejected that risk altogether. H. G. Wells, John Galsworthy, and Arnold Bennett fall into the group Woolf labeled as "materialists." These writers are usually called "realists," but Woolf's more pejorative label emphasizes the fact that the reality they dealt with was rather superficial. To Woolf, these so-called modern writers missed the essentials. In her famous essay "Mr. Bennett and Mrs. Brown" (1924) she imaginatively constructs a situation in which a realist such as Bennett might try to represent the life of an elderly woman he meets on a train. Though the reader would be brought to see every bead on her shawl and every wrinkle in her dress, the essential Mrs. Brown would remain unknown. For Woolf, the successful writer must enter Mrs. Brown's mind. Although such a writer takes more risks, the potential reward is also greater: the author may genuinely approach the wholeness of human consciousness and experience.

Wholeness was Woolf's preoccupation with regard to subject matter as well as style. She believed that literature had for too long neglected the full representation of humanity by neglecting the full humanity of women: "There is the girl behind the counter . . . I would as soon have her true history as the hundred and fiftieth life of Napoleon." In *A Room of One's Own*, Woolf worked out her ideas about the role of women in society and the subsequent stunted development of female artists. Women, Woolf argues, will never come into their own as artists until they have adequate incomes and privacy, "a room of one's own." The few women who have managed to create have done

so against staggering odds, and their works have often suffered as a consequence. Furthermore, Woolf contends, all of literature has suffered because of this absence; women who have been denied a chance to write or to achieve their full stature as writers could have offered a unique presence to literary history.

Having passionately addressed this absence, Woolf also takes note of women who wrote but who have been mostly ignored. Nearly half of *The Common Reader* deals with women writers, some of whom are virtually unknown: Margaret Cavendish and Margaret Paston, for example. Louise Bernikow has written that literary figures become accepted into the canon largely because of who noticed them and who chose to record that notice. In this regard, Woolf seems intent upon opening the closed door of the canon, if only a crack, for the disenfranchised writers she champions.

Woolf's feminist concerns permeate her literary criticism. She is never hostile toward male writers, but her essays, letters, and diaries show an unfailing awareness of the favorable circumstances which have allowed and encouraged many men to become artists. She offers a complex response to such art: she takes pleasure in it, first, in its sureness and ample tradition, but she finds that it in fact often lacks the fullness of life. Woolf's discussion of John Milton's *Paradise Lost* (1667) provides a good example: "How smooth, strong, and elaborate it all is. . . . I can conceive that this is the essence, of which almost all other poetry is the dilution." Yet when she applies her most basic standard for literary value, she discovers that the epic is flawed by the "impersonality of the emotion."

For Woolf, all of literature would be enhanced by the greater and more varied presence of women: "Poetry ought to have a mother as well as a father." The great writer, whether male or female, will be able to "enclose the human heart" because of a power to see with an androgynous vision. In the future, Woolf believes, one's sex will enhance but not limit one's artistic vision, and literature will be the richer.

That large, forward view of literature characterizes Woolf's literary criticism overall. Her assessments are thoroughly generous. For example, while she disparages the "materialism" of Bennett, Galsworthy, and Wells, she compliments them, too, on what they have achieved, their skills, and their humanity. When Woolf must complain about a writer's performance, the negative comment is always couched in terms of genuine and gentle disappointment. Late in her life Woolf came to believe that she might have done better to write with a sharper pen, a less conciliatory note; perhaps she was influenced in this opinion by the decidedly unambiguous, hostile criticism which her own novels engendered in the 1930s.

The urbane and sensible tone of Woolf's criticism creates a convincing subtext which urges the reader to join her, to read what she has read. Her freedom from prejudice, her breadth of study, her generous yet keen opinions combine to make her a fine critic. She is also more. Woolf the novelist is not excluded from the writings of Woolf the critic. The splendid readability of many of the essays, and especially of *A Room of One's Own*, comes from a rather dramatic entrance of the novelist, who imposes texture on critical comments by gathering a fiction about them. In her essay on the Paston family letters, for example, Woolf imagines the circumstances under which the letters must have been written. In *A Room of One's Own*, she imagines the careers of several women; these embedded short stories help to make her critical point. Woolf was more than a "common reader," and she was an uncommonly good writer. These qualities combine to make her a critic of eternal value.

## Principal criticism

*The Common Reader*, 1925
*A Room of One's Own*, 1929
*The Common Reader: Second Series*, 1932 (published in the United States as *The Second Common Reader*, 1932)
*A Writer's Diary*, 1953
*Collected Essays*, 1966–1967 (4 volumes)

## Other major works and literary forms

Virginia Woolf is best known as a novelist. Her novels, published between 1915 and 1941, show a steady growth in her ability to leave behind the limits of the traditional novel and create experimental structures more adequate to the inner life of her characters. She also published short stories occasionally and authored one play, *Freshwater: A Comedy in Three Acts* (1976). At his family's request, she wrote a biography of her friend Roger Fry.

Always searching for the appropriate voice in her writing, Woolf saw her criticism as a focusing discipline and her novels as the durable product. Yet she excelled, too, in the personal voice, through letters and diaries. She was perhaps the most prodigious in these genres of any writer of her day: her published letters fill six large volumes, her diaries five. The quality of her writing in these forms is uniformly high, so that in her hands they may legitimately be considered as literary forms.

NOVELS
*The Voyage Out*, 1915
*Night and Day*, 1919
*Jacob's Room*, 1922
*Mrs. Dalloway*, 1925
*To the Lighthouse*, 1927
*Orlando: A Biography*, 1928
*The Waves*, 1931
*Flush: A Biography*, 1933
*The Years*, 1937
*Between the Acts*, 1941

SHORT FICTION
*The Mark on the Wall*, 1919
*Kew Gardens*, 1919
*Monday or Tuesday*, 1921
*A Haunted House and Other Short Stories*, 1943

*Mrs. Dalloway's Party*, 1973
*The Complete Shorter Fiction of Virginia Woolf*, 1985

PLAY
*Freshwater: A Comedy in Three Acts*, 1976

NONFICTION
*On Being Ill*, 1930
*Beau Brummell*, 1930
*A Letter to a Young Poet*, 1932
*Three Guineas*, 1938
*Roger Fry: A Biography*, 1940
*The Death of the Moth and Other Essays*, 1942
*The Moment and Other Essays*, 1947
*The Captain's Death Bed and Other Essays*, 1950
*Granite and Rainbow*, 1958
*Contemporary Writers*, 1965
*The London Scene*, 1975
*The Flight of the Mind: The Letters of Virginia Woolf, Vol. I, 1888–1912*, 1975 (published in the United States as *The Letters of Virginia Woolf, Vol. I: 1888–1912*, 1975)
*The Question of Things Happening: The Letters of Virginia Woolf, Vol. II, 1912–1922*, 1976 (published in the United States as *The Letters of Virginia Woolf, Vol. II: 1912–1922*, 1976)
*Moments of Being*, 1976
*The Diary of Virginia Woolf*, 1977–1984 (5 volumes)
*A Change of Perspective: The Letters of Virginia Woolf, Vol. III, 1923–1928*, 1977 (published in the United States as *The Letters of Virginia Woolf, Vol. III: 1923–1928*, 1978)
*A Reflection of the Other Person: The Letters of Virginia Woolf, Vol. IV, 1929–1931*, 1978 (published in the United States as *The Letters of Virginia Woolf, Vol. IV: 1929–1931*, 1979)
*The Sickle Side of the Moon: The Letters of Virginia Woolf, Vol. V, 1932–1935*, 1979 (published in the United States as *The Letters of Virginia Woolf, Vol. V: 1932–1935*, 1979)
*Leave the Letters Till We're Dead: The Letters of Virginia Woolf, Vol. VI, 1936–1941*, 1980

## Further reading

Bell, Quentin. *Virginia Woolf: A Biography*, 1972.
Bowlby, Rachel, ed. *Virginia Woolf*, 1992.
De Salvo, Louise. *Virginia Woolf: The Impact of Childhood Sexual Abuse on Her Life and Work*, 1989.
Good, Graham. "Virgina Woolf: Angles of Vision," in *The Observing Self: Rediscovering the Essay*, 1988.
Gorsky, Susan Rubinow. *Virginia Woolf*, 1978.
Hussey, Mark. *The Singing of the Real World: The Philosophy of Virginia Woolf's Fiction*, 1986.
Kronenberger, Louis. "Virginia Woolf as a Literary Critic," in *The Republic of Letters: Essays on Various Writers*, 1955.
Marcus, Jane, ed. *Virginia Woolf: A Feminist Slant*, 1983.
Rose, Phyllis. *Woman of Letters: A Life of Virginia Woolf*, 1978.
Rosenberg, Beth Carole. *Virgina Woolf and Samuel Johnson: Common Readers*, 1995.
Rosenthal, Michael. *Virginia Woolf*, 1979.
Sharma, Vijay L. *Virginia Woolf as Literary Critic: A Revaluation*, 1977.
Wellek, René. "Virgina Woolf as Critic," in *Southern Review*. 13 (1977), pp. 419–437.

DEBORAH CORE

*See also* British Literary Theory: Twentieth Century; Feminist Criticism; Forster

# William Wordsworth

English poet

**Born:** Cockermouth, Cumberland, England; April 7, 1770
**Died:** Rydal Mount, Westmorland, England; April 23, 1850

## Biography

William Wordsworth was born on April 7, 1770, in the village of Cockermouth, on the border of the Lake District in northwest England. After attending Hawkshead Grammar School, on the shores of Esthwaite Lake, he developed a love for the Lake District which was to endure for the rest of his life. He entered St. John's College, Cambridge University, in 1787 and graduated in 1791. In the same year he paid his second visit to France, where he enthusiastically embraced the revolutionary cause.

His first published poetry, *An Evening Walk* and *Descriptive Sketches*, appeared in 1793, and two years later he and his sister Dorothy moved to Racedown, in Dorset, where they met Samuel Taylor Coleridge. In 1798, with the publication of *Lyrical Ballads*, Wordsworth embarked on the most creative decade of his life. During this time he wrote most of his great poems, such as "Ode: Intimations of Immortality from Recollections of Early Childhood," an early version of *The Prelude*, "Michael," and a preface to the 1800 edition of *Lyrical Ballads*; he also planned a long poem entitled "The Recluse." In 1802 Wordsworth married Mary Hutchinson, by whom he had five children.

In midlife Wordsworth became a political and religious conservative, and in 1813 he accepted a government position as Distributor of Stamps for the county of Westmorland. The following year he published *The Excursion*, and in 1820 a series of sonnets, *The River Duddon*, appeared, to popular acclaim. Wordsworth became poet laureate in 1843; he died on April 23, 1850.

## Influence

In demolishing the polished artifices of neoclassical poetry, Wordsworth established new criteria for the writing and evaluation of poetry which had profound effects on later theory and practice. His rejection of traditional poetic diction in favor of simplicity and naturalness, along with his emphasis on feeling, emotion, spontaneity, and the creative imagination, made him the standard-bearer of an entire literary movement. His belief in the moral influence and responsibility of poetry took a deep hold in the nineteenth century, particularly in the work of Percy Bysshe Shelley and Matthew Arnold.

## Analysis

Wordsworth's literary theory is found chiefly in his preface to *Lyrical Ballads* (1800 edition), in which he defended his poetic practice against the widespread criticism which had been leveled against it. The preface marked a major new direction in English critical theory; it served almost as a manifesto of the emerging Romantic movement. Wordsworth's argument falls under three main headings: subject matter, poetic diction, and the status of poetry and the poet.

In *Lyrical Ballads*, Wordsworth was attempting to write in a new way, using unadorned style and language to reveal the workings of the human heart in its elemental simplicity. His purpose was to make the incidents of common life interesting "by tracing in them . . . the primary laws of our nature." Many of the poems center on emotional crises, what Wordsworth called "the fluxes and refluxes of the mind when agitated by the great and simple affections of our nature." In such intense situations, Wordsworth believed, the emotions would be expressed in a way which was free of artificiality and conventional restraints. The subject matter of the poems was drawn largely from "low and rustic life," because Wordsworth believed that there the "essential passions of the heart" found more sincere expression. Social outcasts, such as beggars, vagrants, convicts, an idiot boy, and a mad mother, all became subjects for poetry, although none of them would have been considered suitable by neoclassical standards of the eighteenth century. It was an attempt to create a poetry of the common man, and it is no coincidence that Wordsworth was writing at the threshold of the democratic age.

In Wordsworth's theory, the best guide to understanding the deep, permanent, and universal feelings to which mankind is subject is the highly developed feelings of the poet himself, for "all good poetry is the spontaneous overflow of powerful feelings." In this famous definition, Wordsworth outlines a radically new idea: that poetry is an expression of the contents of the poet's own mind and heart. The emphasis switches from the objective to the subjective realm; what becomes important is the inner life of feelings and thoughts, rather than objects or actions in the external world. Wordsworth makes this point in the poem "Simon Lee," from *Lyrical Ballads*, in which, after a detailed description of the old huntsman, he cautions the reader:

> . . . I'm afraid that you expect
> Some tale will be related.
>
> O reader! had you in your mind
> Such stores as silent thought can bring,
> O gentle reader! you would find
> A tale in every thing.

Small incidents can be infinitely revealing to the sensitive mind; the poet must possess stores of "silent thought" in abundance. Wordsworth is careful to point out that although the spontaneity of the creative act is paramount, the poet's feelings can only fruitfully express themselves when he has also "thought long and deeply." In *The Prelude*,

Wordsworth uses the phrase "feeling intellect" to express this harmonious combination of thought and feeling in the imaginative mind. Under these conditions, the poem which "overflows" is not wholly subject to conscious design; "spontaneous" is a key attribute (and one which virtually all other Romantics would seek). This was in sharp contrast to eighteenth-century theory, according to which poetry was an art which could be learned by following traditional rules and procedures.

Wordsworth did, however, have some eighteenth-century antecedents in the school of thought which M. H. Abrams has called "cultural primitivism." These theorists – Hugh Blair's *Lectures on Rhetoric and Belles Lettres* (1783) provides a good example – believed that poetry originated in the passionate, spontaneous speech of primitive peoples. Ideas about the "noble savage" were also popular, and there was a vogue for poets of humble origins, such as Stephen Duck the thresher and James Woodhouse the shoemaker.

Wordsworth's ideas about the kind of language which is appropriate for poetry were, like his choice of subject matter, radical departures from mainstream theory. Because the poet was "a man speaking to men," he must use the language "really spoken by men." Wordsworth therefore strove to avoid using standard poetic diction, which cut him off "from a large portion of phrases and figures of speech which from father to son have long been regarded as the common inheritance of poets." He also suggested that there was no "essential difference between the language of prose and metrical composition."

Efforts to determine Wordsworth's precise meaning here have engendered much discussion. Certainly, his views mark the beginning of the Romantic revolt against eighteenth-century poetic diction. In terms of the old antithesis of nature and art, the neoclassicists stood for art, but Wordsworth opted for nature. He preferred to use the everyday, conversational language of simple folk, because they "hourly communicate with the best objects from which the best part of language is originally derived." He elaborates on this in his second "Essay upon Epitaphs," which was prompted by a survey of epitaphs in a country churchyard. The most moving epitaphs are simple and sincere, without the affectation of supposedly "poetic" language. The latter are constructed "by the . . . *head* as opposed to *heart*" and are based on the common misconception that what is natural in prose would be out of place in verse. For this reason Wordsworth disliked the epitaphs of Alexander Pope; they are "almost wholly destitute of . . . universal feelings and simple movements of mind." Indeed, Pope has "corrupted the judgment of the Nation." Wordsworth's primary objection, however, was not to Pope but to the mediocre verse of many of his contemporaries, "the gaudiness and inane phraseology of many modern writers" as he puts it in the brief advertisement which appeared with the first edition of *Lyrical Ballads* in 1798. He would have disliked, for example, a line such as "First

the gay songsters of the feather'd train," which appeared in a poem in *The Monthly Magazine* in 1797. For Wordsworth, "The little birds began to stir," a line from his "The Idiot Boy" in *Lyrical Ballads*, was more effective, because it was more natural. His objection to contemporary poetic diction was that it falsified the object, whereas he always "endeavored to look steadily at [his] subject."

Wordsworth's advocacy of simple language does not mean that he was trying to write dialect poetry, and it has often been pointed out that the language of "Lines Composed a Few Miles Above Tintern Abbey" is not especially simple. Wordsworth would have argued, however, that it too arose out of genuine passion and feeling. Furthermore, in spite of arguing that the distinction between poetry and prose was unnecessary, he acknowledged that metrical language does have an effect on the reader. It appeals to "the perception of similitude in dissimilitude" which is fundamental to the human mind, and its pleasing regularity serves to keep the emotions, once aroused, from becoming too intense. Yet on the other hand (and Wordsworth seems oblivious to the apparent contradiction), if the poet's words cannot rouse readers "to a height of desirable excitement," the pleasurable associations evoked by the presence of meter will accomplish this for them.

Wordsworth then comments further on his own experience of the creative process. Poetry is indeed "the spontaneous overflow of powerful feelings; it takes its origin from emotion recollected in tranquillity." During this process of contemplation, the tranquillity gradually disappears, until the original emotion exists once more in the mind. Yet a catharsis has taken place; even if the original emotion was painful, the mind is now in a "state of enjoyment." It is in this method that composition takes place, and the purpose of the resulting poem is to communicate to the reader an "overbalance of pleasure." Wordsworth's famous poem "I Wandered Lonely as a Cloud" illustrates this process.

Wordsworth held an exalted concept of the status of poetry: "Poetry is the first and last of all knowledge – it is as immortal as the heart of man." Unlike his contemporaries William Blake and John Keats, Wordsworth did not view science as an enemy of poetry. The two could work hand in hand:

> If the time should ever come when what is now called science . . . shall be ready to put on, as it were, a form of flesh and blood, the poet will lend his divine spirit to aid the transfiguration, and will welcome the being thus produced, as a dear and genuine inmate of the household of man.

Wordsworth believed that all knowledge, whether that of the poet or the scientist, was rooted in pleasure, a pleasure which arises from an inner understanding of the beauty of the universe. When a man "has no pleasure he has no knowledge."

The poet himself was a man possessed of "more lively sensibility, more enthusiasm and tenderness . . . a greater knowledge of human nature, and a more comprehensive soul, than are supposed to be common among mankind." The poet can enlarge the human capacity to feel without recourse to "gross and violent stimulants." Wordsworth was particularly aware of the dehumanizing and isolating effect of large-scale industrialization and the consequent drift of the population to the cities. He believed, however, that the poet could counteract the harmful effects of this kind of social change because "he is the rock of defense of human nature; an upholder and preserver, carrying everywhere with him relationship and love. . . . The poet binds together by passion and knowledge the vast empire of human society, as it is spread over the whole earth, and over all time."

In the preface to *Lyrical Ballads* Wordsworth does not address the role of the imagination, but he turns to this question in his preface to his 1815 *Poems*. The imagination played a limited role in neoclassical theory. Poetry was thought to originate in the rational mind; the imagination merely supplied modifications and adornments to the central structure, and it was usually considered a lesser power than fancy. Wordsworth, however, turned these categories upside down. For him, the imagination is the true creative faculty; it is an "endowing" power, which "shapes and *creates*." It accomplishes creation through many processes, particularly that of "consolidating numbers into unity, and dissolving and separating unity into number." The imagination "recoils from every thing but the plastic, the pliant, the indefinite." It is "conscious of an indestructible dominion; – the Soul may fall away from it, not being able to sustain its grandeur; but, if once felt and acknowledged, by no act of any other faculty of the mind can it be relaxed, impaired, or diminished." The almost godlike power which Wordsworth attributes to the imagination can scarcely be exaggerated. It is the functioning of the mind in touch with its transcendent source. In book 6 of *The Prelude*, it is "that awful Power" which rises from "the mind's abyss" and gives the soul a glimpse of its true glory. In book 14, the imagination "Is but another name for absolute power/ And clearest insight, amplitude of mind/ And Reason in her most exalted mood."

Wordsworth's poetic theory was a guiding influence for the entire Romantic age, particularly in terms of the importance of feeling, spontaneity, and the imagination. Shelley's "A Defence of Poetry" (1840) is deeply imbued with Wordsworthian ideas, and when Keats declared his belief in "the holiness of the heart's affections," he was writing in a climate of opinion which Wordsworth had done more than anyone to create. Coleridge acknowledged that his own theory of the imagination had been originally inspired by Wordsworth, and John Stuart Mill's essays "What Is Poetry?" and "Two Kinds of Poetry" (both 1833) were partly based on the preface to *Lyrical Ballads*.

Wordsworth perhaps claimed too much for some of his ideas about poetic diction, and his belief that the language most suited to poetry was that of peasants and simple folk did not find general acceptance. Coleridge in particular would not accept that there was no difference between the language of poetry and that of prose; commenting on Wordsworth's poem "The Thorn," he said that it was not possible for a poet "to imitate truly a dull and garrulous discourser without repeating the effects of dulness and garrulity."

Leaving these objections aside, however, it can be said that Wordsworth profoundly extended the range of what poetry could attempt. He broke through the stuffy exclusivism of the age in which he was born and attempted to create an art which would express universal values. He affirmed the power of poetry to counteract the dehumanizing effects of the technology and urbanization which he saw at work in his own age – and which have increased in the years since.

## Principal criticism
Preface to *Lyrical Ballads, with Other Poems*, 1800
"Essay upon Epitaphs I," 1810; preface to *Poems*, 1815
"Essay, Supplementary to the Preface," in *Poems*, 1815
*A Letter to a Friend of Robert Burns*, 1816
"Essays on Epitaphs II, III," 1876

## Other major works and literary forms
William Wordsworth is known primarily as the greatest poet of the Romantic age. His first major work, written with Samuel Taylor Coleridge, was *Lyrical Ballads* (1798), which contained "Lines Composed a Few Miles Above Tintern Abbey." This work was followed by poems such as "Michael" (1800), "Ode: Intimations of Immortality from Recollections of Early Childhood" (1807), *The Excursion* (1814), and his greatest work, *The Prelude: Or, The Growth of a Poet's Mind* (1850).

POETRY
*An Evening Walk*, 1793
*Descriptive Sketches*, 1793
*Lyrical Ballads*, 1798 (with Samuel Taylor Coleridge)
*Lyrical Ballads, and Other Poems*, 1800 (with Coleridge)
*Poems in Two Volumes*, 1807
*The Excursion*, 1814
*Poems*, 1815
*The White Doe of Rylstone*, 1815
*Peter Bell*, 1819
*The Waggoner*, 1819
*The River Duddon*, 1820
*Ecclesiastical Sketches*, 1822
*Poems Chiefly of Early and Late Years*, 1842
*The Prelude: Or, The Growth of a Poet's Mind*, 1850
*Poetical Works*, 1940–1949 (5 volumes)

NONFICTION
*Letters of William and Dorothy Wordsworth*, 1935–1939 (6 volumes)

## Further reading

Abrams, M. H. *The Mirror and the Lamp*, 1953.

Altieri, Charles. "Wordsworth's 'Preface' as Literary Theory," in *Criticism*, 1976.

Barstow, Marjorie L. *Wordsworth's Theory of Poetic Diction*, 1917.

Coleridge, Samuel Taylor. *Biographia Literaria*, 1817 (2 volumes).

Leask, Nigel. "Pantisocracy and the Politics of the 'Preface to Lyrical Ballads,'" in *Reflections of Revolution: Images of Romanticism*, 1993. Edited by Alison Yarrington and Kelvin Everest.

Owen, W. J. B. Introduction and notes to *Wordsworth's Preface to "Lyrical Ballads,"* 1957.

——. *Wordsworth as Critic*, 1969.

Parrish, Stephen Maxfield. *The Art of the Lyrical Ballads*, 1973.

Pfau, Thomas. "'Elementary Feelings' and 'Distorted Language': The Pragmatics of Culture in Wordsworth's Preface to *Lyrical Ballads*," in *New Literary History: A Journal of Theory and Interpretation*. 24, no. 1 (Winter, 1993), pp. 125–146.

Winberg, Christine. "A Poet's Prose: The Preface to *Lyrical Ballads*," in *Unisa English Studies*. 29, no. 2 (September, 1991), pp. 18–28.

BRYAN AUBREY

# Y

## The Yale School

The Yale School is the general name given to a group of four literary critics – Paul de Man, J. Hillis Miller, Geoffrey Hartman, and Harold Bloom – who taught at Yale University in New Haven, Connecticut, and became highly influential during the 1970s and 1980s as a result of their innovative "deconstructive" approaches to analyzing texts.

### Controversies and misconceptions

The Yale critics have been criticized from various academic quarters; and while much of the criticism has been knowledgeable and productive, leading to new and important developments in literary theory and analysis, much has also taken the form of angry, indignant, or contemptuous denunciations in journals, newspapers, and popular media. In responding, proponents of deconstruction argue that these popular attacks are generally founded on superficial readings or oversimplifications of the theory; and that the misconceptions about "deconstruction" and various beliefs attributed to the Yale School are usually based on phrases or sentences taken out of context or mistranslated.

The most common popular misconceptions are: (1) that critics who subscribe to deconstructive theories believe that everything is constructed of language and that reality does not exist; (2) that Yale criticism is antihistorical, and rejects the traditional values of humanistic studies; and (3) that the deconstructive theories of the Yale School have proved ineffective and are passé, having been superseded by recent developments in literary theory. The Yale critics have also been criticized on nationalistic or xenophobic grounds in both Britain and the United States for "importing" continental European theories and philosophies rather than making use of home-grown ones; and on popular grounds for being elitist, by virtue of the complexity of their analyses, their use of technical jargon, and their association with the institutional power and authority of Yale University.

### Sources and origins

It is a practical impossibility to list all of the theories and philosophies which have influenced the Yale critics and their colleague, the Paris-based philosopher Jacques Derrida; a short list would include most of the major philosophers in the Western tradition, numerous European and American writers, the Anglo-American New Criticism, early Christian practices of textual interpretation, and the writings of Jewish mystics on the Kabbala. The writings of these critics, however, are always focused on the interpretation of specific texts, and their theories are derived from their readings. The texts under analysis can thus be considered both as sources of the theories and as a canon of major works generated by the theories.

Derrida's early philosophical works which influenced the Yale critics include *Dissemination* (1981), a study of G. W. F. Hegel, Plato, and Stéphane Mallarmé; *Of Grammatology* (1976), a study of language based on the theories of Ferdinand de Saussure and Jean-Jacques Rousseau; *Margins of Philosophy* (1982), a collection of essays on Edmund Husserl, Martin Heidegger, Hegel, Rousseau, and Saussure; and *Writing and Difference* (1978), essays on Emmanuel Levinas, Sigmund Freud, Antonin Artaud, Edmond Jabès, and Michel Foucault. The sources of Derrida's unique writing style include James Joyce's *Finnegans Wake* and certain moments in modernist art, in particular Dada and Surrealism, and the collage techniques introduced by the cubists.

The most influential literary criticism of Paul de Man, who taught in the humanities during the *floruit* of the Yale School, consisted of a collection of long, analytical essays: *Allegories of Reading* (1979), which studied the use of language in Rousseau, Friedrich Nietzsche, Rainer Maria Rilke, and Marcel Proust; a second collection, *The Rhetoric of Romanticism* (1984), containing essays on Mallarmé, Johann Hölderlin, William Wordsworth, Percy Bysshe Shelley, William Butler Yeats, and Heinrich von Kleist; and *Blindness and Insight* (1983), a book of highly theoretical essays analyzing the work of other theorists, such as Georg Lukács, Maurice Blanchot, Georges Poulet, Derrida, and Harold Bloom.

J. Hillis Miller's early work in English literature was associated with the Geneva School of phenomenological criticism, and includes three books on nineteenth- and twentieth-century poetry and fiction: *The Disappearance of God* (1963), *Poets of Reality* (1965), and *Thomas Hardy:*

*Distance and Desire* (1970). His later works, however, reflect the change in his theoretical position, by which he became one of the leading exponents of the literary criticism associated with the philosophy of Derrida: *Fiction and Repetition* (1982), intricate analyses of seven English novels; *Ariadne's Thread* (1985); and *The Linguistic Moment* (1987), a collection of essays on poets from Wordsworth to Wallace Stevens.

Geoffrey Hartman's prolific works in English and comparative literature, in addition to articles on Romanticism, particularly Wordsworth, include *Beyond Formalism* (1970), a collection of essays on such authors as Virginia Woolf, John Milton, Albert Camus, Maurice Blanchot, Andrew Marvell, Gerard Manley Hopkins, and William Blake; *Saving the Text* (1981), a commentary on Derrida's book *Glas*; and *Criticism in the Wilderness* (1980), a rich meditation on the past century and a half of literary criticism and theory, ranging from Thomas Carlyle through Freud to Derrida and de Man.

Harold Bloom, who teaches in the humanities at Yale, has developed a highly original and idiosyncratic approach to literature, which is argued theoretically in four influential books: *The Anxiety of Influence* (1973), *A Map of Misreading* (1975), *Kabbalah and Criticism* (1975), and *Poetry and Repression* (1976). Several of Bloom's books, such as *The Visionary Company* (1961) and *The Ringers in the Tower* (1971), focus on revising traditional views of Romantic poetry; his later works are intricate studies of the relations between such authors as William Shakespeare, John Milton, Ralph Waldo Emerson, Walt Whitman, and Wallace Stevens.

Bloom's relationship to the other Yale critics is complex: although he joined them in what has been considered a "manifesto" of the Yale School, the volume of essays entitled *Deconstruction and Criticism* (1979), he has at various times denied any theoretical affinity with deconstruction. Influences on Bloom's approach to literature include the writings of Freud, classical rhetorical theory, Jewish Gnosticism, and the Kabbala.

## Theory and method

Each of the Yale critics has an individual approach to literature and a particular style of criticism, and there are significant differences between them; it is therefore misleading to summarize their work as a whole – or even the œuvre of a particular critic – by reducing it to a formulaic "method" or "technique" of analyzing texts. Certain common interests and theoretical concerns, however, are found in all of their writings, and it is these concerns which bring them together as a revolutionary school of criticism.

A basic understanding of the Yale critics' interests requires some knowledge of key moments in the Western theoretical tradition in which they are engaged; and while to select particular examples is necessarily to greatly limit and vastly oversimplify, the moments of Plato, Nietzsche, Barthes, Saussure, and Derrida provide useful reference points.

The Western theoretical tradition, for practical purposes, begins with Plato's theory (in his *Republic*, 388–368 B.C.) that all objects in the world may be considered second- or third-order copies of perfect models, ideas, forms, or essences in the divine mind: since ultimate reality exists only in the divine realm of pure essence or "Being," the world perceived by human beings can only be an illusion, merely an imitation or mimesis of reality. A Platonic view of a work of literature would consider the text to be either a written representation of an idea or intention in the "divine" mind of the author; or a depiction, a reflection, of some external reality. Thus biographical or author-based criticism has traditionally sought the meaning or "reality" of a literary text not in its language, but in the state of mind and life of its creator or author; and, analogously, conventional historical scholarship has related the themes, characters, and ideas of literary works to the historical period in which they were produced, assuming that literary works mirror – are mimetic representations of – some empirical historical reality.

This Platonic world-view is thrown into question in the writings of the German philosopher Friedrich Nietzsche, one of the founding figures of existentialism. In his essay "On Truth and Lie in an Extra-Moral Sense," Nietzsche famously argues that Platonic ideas such as "God," "honesty," or "essence" are not universal or objective realities already existing "out there" somewhere, but notions that human beings have created and constructed by generalizing and abstracting their specific experiences, and then forgetting this process of abstracting: "truths are illusions about which one has forgotten that this is what they are."

Nietzsche's writings raise a number of interesting issues. From a Judeo-Christian theological perspective, the existence of God is what makes life and history meaningful; the absence of God means that any hope of redemption in an extraterrestrial afterlife disappears, and that the course of human events is determined not by predetermined fate or divine will, but by chance or the human will to power. In literary criticism, the absence of God is analogous to what Roland Barthes has termed the "death of the author," the implication of which is the recognition that each reader of a text, depending on his or her cultural and historical background and approach, understands and interprets it in a different way: "the birth of the reader must be at the cost of the death of the Author." These statements constitute a direct attack on traditional author-based literary criticism, since they imply that the meaning of a literary text is ultimately created by the reader's will to understand, and not controlled absolutely by the author's intention. They lead to very basic questions at the heart of the Yale criticism: if the meaning of a text is not intrinsic to the text, then what is a text? How does it work, and what is its relation to meaning?

One answer is that a text is a linguistic moment; and a preoccupation with language, in particular the theories of the Swiss linguist Ferdinand de Saussure, is characteristic of the Yale critics. Saussure, in lectures collected under the title *Course in General Linguistics*, identifies the basic unit of language as the sign, which is understood to be composed of two inseparable parts: a representation (signifer) and its meaning (signified). Thus, for example, the word "dog" is a signifier, representing the image, concept, or meaning (signified) of a four-legged animal which barks; and the signifier and signified together constitute a sign. Since different languages use different words to represent the same object (for example, a *dog* in English is *chien* in French), it is clear that the meaning of a word – or, in Saussure's terms, the signified of a signifier – in a particular language is determined by socially agreed conventions of usage, rather than by any intrinsic or direct relation between words and things; for if indeed words and things were directly connected, then a particular object would be designated by the same word in every language.

Saussure's statement of this obvious fact – that "the bond between the signifier and the signified is arbitrary," in other words determined by social convention – is the source of the first misconception regarding deconstruction: Saussure's phrase "the linguistic sign is arbitrary" has frequently been misunderstood, when taken out of context, to imply that language does not refer to reality. In fact, however, this theory of the sign (which, through the work of Barthes and others, has become a basic principle of semiotics and media analysis) has far more interesting consequences for the Yale critics. If the link between signs and reality is determined by social convention, then the relations between a text (a collection of signs) and what it refers to – for example, an author's intention, or a historical reality – may be considered as being fixed by conventions agreed upon among members of a community of critics. The way in which meaning is produced in texts, in other words, depends on the method used to read them: what we have traditionally understood as the "meaning" residing in or behind a text is in fact a meaning constructed by criticism, and thus the meaning or intent "found" in a text is actually planted there by the process of reading; it is, in de Man's phrase, an "allegory of reading." The proper study of texts must therefore begin with the study of methods and conventions of reading, and this is why much of the Yale critics' writing is about other critics and theorists: literary theory is the investigation of this "ungracious relationship between the criticized text and the indebted critic of that text," and its imperative is to question the most fundamental assumptions about truth, history, and reality which underlie literary studies.

In this theoretical endeavor the Yale critics take the deconstruction of Jacques Derrida as a paradigm. Although it is commonly understood to refer to the literary analysis of the Yale School, "deconstruction" is indefinable, because it functions in Derrida's writings not as a theory or method or approach, but as a monkey-wrench thrown into the works of philosophy, indicating cracks and fractures in the foundations and structures of systems of thought. Because it raises questions about how the limits of systems are demarcated, "deconstruction" cannot appear inside a system as part of it (in other words, to define it would be to assimilate it into one's system of thought and thereby miss the point); nor can it intervene within the system if it is outside it: deconstruction thus appears as a cat's paw on the threshold of thought, constantly chasing and unraveling the yarns of philosophy.

The stance maintained by deconstruction on the margins of systems, its resistance to being assimilated and reduced into a system by being summarized or defined, manifests itself in the Yale critics' works through a writing style characterized by endlessly proliferating ironies, puns, verbal plays, and allusions. This playfulness destabilizes the systemic logic of the text by refusing to allow its "meaning" to be controlled, unified, or fixed by conventional references to an author or a historical event; Derrida's phrase, "there is nothing outside of the text" is often misinterpreted to mean that "reality" does not exist – whereas in fact it simply indicates that linguistic communities decide on how to organize, structure, and hierarchize the ways in which language refers to reality.

Deconstruction exposes the assumptions and ideologies behind such decisions, and hence it can be argued – against traditional scholarship – that there is no such thing as an objective or universal "reading" of a text; there are only (individually, culturally, and ideologically determined) "misreadings." The question remains, however: what is a text? A work of literature does not exist in a vacuum: it is always embedded in an explicit or implicit tradition or canon; and a tradition represents a conventional, ideological linking together and systematization of literature. Thus Harold Bloom understands "tradition" or "influence" to mean that "there are no texts, but only relationships between texts. These relationships depend upon a critical act, a misreading. . . ." In other words, far from being anarchistic, ahistorical, or culturally relativistic – and in contrast to the "practical" approach of the Anglo-American practitioners of New Criticism – the Yale critics argue that their work is deeply engaged in problems of system, history, and culture; as Geoffrey Hartman comments, "the tradition of practical criticism, so narrow at present, has limited our awareness of the relation of literature to the practical life, which includes law, religion, economics, and the process of institutionalization itself." This engagement is illustrated by the recent work of Derrida on politics, Bloom on religion, Hillis Miller on ethics and education, and Hartman on Holocaust archives and testimony.

## Influences and implications

The moments of Plato, Nietzsche, Barthes, Saussure, and Derrida reveal a shift in the orientation of literary studies:

away from the study of past history and the life of the author as the controlling factors determining meaning in a text, to the study of the historical contexts of readers, who looking through the eyes of the present, construct images of past history, figures of authors, and meanings in texts. The playful subversion effected by deconstruction lays bare the tacit or hidden ideological factors in the present which control meaning, limit the freedom of interpretation, and shape our notions of what is meant by such things as "literature," "historical reality," and "truth."

In this relentless questioning and exposure of concealed institutional values, the Yale critics are heirs to the Renaissance and Enlightenment humanistic traditions of curiosity and inquiry (and perhaps also to the student protests of the 1960s); and from this perspective of – in Hillis Miller's phrase – an ethics of reading, it may be argued that deconstruction represents a democratization of literary studies, a revolution against the authoritarianism (and indeed, antihistorical stance) of traditional scholarship, which passes value judgments on literature, establishes canons of "great" writers, and decides on "what the author meant," without ever making explicit its assumptions about what constitutes literature; what ideologies are involved in the logic of canon formation; or how criticism, no less than literature, is embedded in history.

The scope of the Yale Criticism clearly extends well beyond the interpretation of literary texts to the critique of institutions (including universities such as Yale itself) which influence the present of interpretation, and in this regard relates in complex ways to other theoretical currents, including existentialist ethics, reader-response criticism, reception theory, various Marxisms and feminisms, and psychoanalysis. The election of J. Hillis Miller as president of the Modern Language Association of America in 1986, and the proliferation of courses and programs in literary theory both in Britain and in the United States, are indications of how profoundly the concerns of the Yale critics have affected literary studies. Their work has laid the foundations for theories of poststructuralism and postmodernism, and contributed to theoretical developments, revisions of literary canons, and the formation of programs of study in such areas as gender studies, African-American studies, and postcolonial theory. A direct consequence of the Yale critics' work has been the development of the area of law known as Critical Legal Studies; the contemporary American critical movements and schools referred to as "New Historicism" and "Cultural Studies" are also (although they are often mistakenly seen, even by their own advocates, as reactions to deconstruction) in fact built on the foundations laid by the Yale critics and Derrida. These contemporary developments (despite occasionally lacking its theoretical rigorousness) are natural extensions of the work of the Yale School; and while the terminology and specific examples may have changed over the last two decades, the directions taken by contemporary theories

testify to the vitality and continuing importance of the fundamental premises and concerns of the Yale critics.

## Further reading

Arac, Jonathan, et al. *The Yale Critics: Deconstruction in America*, 1983.
Bloom, Harold, et al. *Deconstruction and Criticism*, 1979.
de Man, Paul. *The Resistance to Theory*, 1986.
Derrida, Jacques. *Memoires for Paul de Man*, 1986.
Gasche, Rodolphe. *The Tain of the Mirror: Derrida and the Philosophy of Reflection*, 1986.
——. *The Wild Card of Reading: On Paul de Man*, 1998.
Gates, Henry Louis, ed. *"Race," Writing, and Difference*, 1986.
Handelman, Susan. *The Slayers of Moses: The Emergence of Rabbinic Interpretation in Modern Literary Theory*, 1982.
Harari, Josue V. *Textual Strategies: Perspectives in Post-Structuralist Criticism*, 1979.
Johnson, Barbara. *The Critical Difference: Essays in the Contemporary Rhetoric of Reading*, 1980.
Leitch, Vincent B. *Deconstructive Criticism: An Advanced Introduction*, 1983.
Lentricchia, Frank. *After the New Criticism*, 1980.
Spanos, William, ed. *The Question of Textuality: Strategies of Reading in Contemporary American Criticism*, 1982.
Taylor, Mark C. *Deconstruction in Context: Literature and Philosophy*, 1986.
Young, Robert. *Untying the Text: A Post-Structuralist Reader*, 1981.

JOHANN PILLAI

*See also* Bloom; Deconstruction; de Man; Derrida; Hartman; Miller

# William Butler Yeats

Irish poet, dramatist, and critic

**Born:** Sandymount, near Dublin, Ireland; June 13, 1865
**Died:** Cap Martin, France; January 28, 1939

## Biography

William Butler Yeats was born in 1865 in Sandymount, County Dublin, near the strand across which James Joyce's fictional Stephen Dedalus would walk into eternity thirty-nine years later. His father's family, originally English, had been in Ireland for over two hundred years, while the Pollexfens, his mother's family, also originally English, had settled in Sligo, a rural and windswept county on the west coast of Ireland. From these twin familial sources Yeats absorbed most of the dynamic conflict that informed his artistic life. From his father, John Butler Yeats, he acquired much of his rebel spirit and skeptical attitude to religion and science. Moreover, his father had abandoned a promising career in the law in order to devote his life to painting, or what Yeats senior called "poetic belief" which – in contrast to the tyranny of "religious belief" – could bring "absolute freedom" to the practicing artist. Yeats' struggle with the shadow of his father's radicalism informs much of his work and was particularly influential in his decision to champion John Millington Synge's dramatic tale of Oedipal struggle and self-definition, *The Playboy of The Western World* (1907), with which Yeats consolidated the reputation of the Abbey Theatre in Dublin. His role in establishing the National Theatre of Ireland in 1899 was yet another one of the enormous achievements that punctuate the life of this poet and critic who was awarded the Noble Prize for Literature in 1923.

Through his mother's rural background – and as a welcome respite against his patriarchal struggles – Yeats became steeped in the folklore of the west of Ireland. As a result of this grounding in an oral culture composed of ancient Celtic myths, fairy tales, and songs which document a particularly imaginative human relation to nature, he developed a keen and often encyclopedic appreciation of myth and the regenerative powers of mythology, an appreciation that furnished him with the raw materials upon which his work as a poet is based. His appreciation of poetry was consolidated by his exposure to the canonical traditions of English poetry during his schooling in London between 1874 and 1883, during which time he was drawn to William Blake and to the Romantic poets – particularly Percy Bysshe Shelley – as his inspiration. Upon leaving school, a brief dalliance with the Metropolitan Art College gave way to a decision to try poetry as a viable vocation, and in 1891 he was instrumental in forming the Rhymer's Club in London with such late-Victorian English luminaries as Lionel Johnson and Ernest Dowson.

However, it was Irish nationalism and the charismatic figure of John O'Leary, the eloquent and visionary patriot, that provided Yeats with a focus for the raw energies he had revealed in his earlier poetry, and also contributed to a simplification of style in order to make himself understood by the general Irish public. During the rapid and seismic changes that took place in Ireland between 1916 and 1922 – changes wrought in part by Yeats' nationalist poetry – he found his political vocation and spent the remainder of his life engaged in the daunting project of creating a viable and vibrant identity for his recently decolonized compatriots in the newly established Irish Free State. His success has shown how disparate influences such as patriarchal struggle, national mythology, foreign (English) literary models, and patriotic idealism can cohere in an art that fuses them together and yet results in a radical transformation of them. Appointed to political office as an Irish Senator in 1922, Yeats died in 1939 when what he referred to as "this filthy modern tide" consumed Europe in conflict. Buried in Drumcliff graveyard in Sligo, his epitaph reads

Cast a cold eye
on life, on death.
Horseman pass by!

yet it was the warmth and astonishing energy of Yeats' artistic vocation that made him, arguably, the single most important figure in the history of modern Ireland, and in the words of Richard Ellmann, "the dominant poet of our time."

## Influence

With T. S. Eliot and Ezra Pound, Yeats completes a triumvirate of the most influential twentieth-century poets and critics of poetry. Moreover, in his capacity as artistic director of the Abbey Theatre, Yeats reintroduced the mask and other classical elements into the explicitly naturalist drama of the very early twentieth century and also familiarized audiences with the more esoteric disciplines of Oriental drama such as the Noh and Kabuki traditions. In so doing he had no little influence in fostering the heterogeneous plurality that characterizes modern European theater. Additionally, and as a result of his project of national reconstruction through art, he paved the way for much of our current literary critical investigations into colonial and postcolonial forms of artistic representation. Finally, and perhaps most importantly, in 1937 his critical work *A Vision* went some way toward consolidating his father's belief in the religion of art by proposing a history of the world of artistic representation as an alternative belief system to that of deistic religion and/or science.

Although an avowed classicist, Yeats also straddles the early twentieth century's classical/modern artistic divide in work such as the *Crazy Jane* series of poems and in his constant desire to see less verbal, more gestural and innovative forms of theater. Such contradictions were deeply in keeping with a man who valued the creative flux that characterizes the artistic personality above any ideal or monologic truth. In this adherence to the contradictions, or what he called "antinomies" of the artistic spirit, Yeats had a profound influence on some of the major artists of the modernist movement. Both James Joyce and Samuel Beckett, his fellow countrymen, struggled – as Yeats had done with his own father – to find a voice that escaped Yeats' hermetically sealed vision of Irish identity; and both acknowledged the degree to which he was instrumental in establishing the parameters of the twentieth century's literary preoccupation with individual and national identity, and also with the division between classical and modern, elite and popular modes of artistic representation.

Precisely because Yeats prioritized the artistic imagination and so openly embraced its contradictions, it is next to impossible to make clear distinctions between his critical and artistic work; his imagination is so embedded in the fabric of both that it is difficult to identify anything that we might acknowledge as objective critical analysis. By definition, given that his art was his life, his artistic life incorporates its own contribution to literary criticism that cannot be finally separated from the life of the art. As Yeats himself wrote, "[t]he abstract is not life and everywhere draws out its contradictions. You can refute Hegel but not the Saint or the *Song of Sixpence*." However, Yeats' stock as the subject of appreciative contemporary criticism (from Paul de Man and Geoffrey Hartman's use of Yeats' poetry to deconstruct the distinction between criticism and literature to Edward Said and Chinua Achebe's admiration for his sensitivity to the role of art in the construction of decolonized identities) illustrates how the most resonant and powerful of art remains the principle stake of literary criticism.

## Analysis

It is a plain fact, as Declan Kiberd states in *Inventing Ireland: The Literature of the Modern Nation* (1996), that Yeats' "skill with words far outstripped his abilities as a thinker." Yeats frequently refers to this dilemma in his poetry; the opening line of "The Circus Animal's Desertion" ("I sought a theme and sought for it in vain"), for example, indicates the search for some contextual detail that will provoke another adventure in figurative language. It is also true that his most memorable poetry is memorable precisely because it is not lucid, or immediately accessible. In other words, it communicates its own importance as poetry long before its theme is fully absorbed by the reader. For this reason alone his critical writings are fascinating, for they provide us with a glimpse into his methodology as a poet; a glimpse which reveals his archly mystical approach to creative writing. This mysticism is facilitated by his use of symbolism, of which he is a practical and key critic. Influenced by the stories of his Sligo youth, by the French Symbolist poets, by William Blake's personal, symbolic universe, by Shelley's vibrant use of symbols, and by the Theosophical movement led by Madame Blavatsky and popular among artists in the late nineteenth century, Yeats absorbed and interrogated much symbolist practice.

"The Symbolism of Poetry," published in 1900, documents Yeats' opposition to poetic practice evolving out of faith in science. In the essay he argues that Alfred, Lord Tennyson's "brooding over scientific opinion" extinguishes "the central flame" in his poetry. As an alternative, Yeats suggests that if "people were to accept the theory that poetry moves us because of its symbolism" then it is less the immediate power of words but to what the words refer and the processes of cognition and emotional response involved in this recognition that produce powerful, or meaningful poetry. He writes that

> [a]ll sounds, all colours, all forms, either because of their preordained energies or because of long association, evoke indefinable and yet precise emotions, or as I prefer to think, call down among us certain disembodied powers, whose footsteps over our heart we call emotions.

So, although he would appear to believe that symbols are invested with meaning through usage – and in so doing

suggests that symbols work in the imagination with their own code and consequences which have been consolidated through history and cultural practice – he also believes that they call on emotions or some more profound form of recognition/response which is not so easily explained. Essentially, he is arguing that a symbol cannot be discursively explained without losing its vitality and significance as a symbol. In other words, it is both a figurative substitute for a more mechanistically determined or foreclosed "reality" and, simultaneously, an escape from such reality. Thus, when he defines a symbol as "the only possible expression of some invisible essence, a transparent lamp about a spiritual flame" he is defining a symbol through symbolism to escape from the rational, and therefore scientific, necessity of explaining what he believes to be essentially unexplainable within a scientific idiom.

Yet, one aspect of Yeats' faith in mystic symbolism appears, initially, to be critical, or intellectual. The best symbols evoke emotional and/or intellectual responses:

> If I say "white" or "purple" in an ordinary line of poetry, they evoke emotions so exclusively that I cannot say why they move me; but if I bring them into the same sentence with such obvious intellectual symbols as a cross or a crown of thorns, I think of purity or sovereignty.

Utilizing these distinctions, Yeats claims that William Shakespeare is the great emotional symbolist, while Dante Alighieri is the master of intellectual symbolism. And yet the distinction is only short-lived for he announces that intellectual symbolism is often "too subtle for the intellect" itself. Ultimately, for Yeats, symbolism would appear to be nothing short of a revelation through which we can glimpse "the hidden laws of the world." He argues that "unless [the poet's words] are as subtle, as complex, as full of mysterious life, as the body of a flower or of a woman" then poetry is simply "the invention of the will with its eyes always on something to be done or undone." In contrast, Yeats' great artistic will demands a "return to imagination" and, hence, a belief in the essentially mystical powers of poetry.

If the Symbolist tradition in poetry was a profound influence on Yeats, equally so were the English Romantic poets and their earnest belief in the importance of poetry and poetic practice. In "The Courage of the Artist," first published in its entirety in 1965, Yeats demands that a poet must be "by the very nature of things a man who lives with entire sincerity." He questions as to why we should "honour those that die upon the field of battle [when] a man may show as reckless a courage in entering into the abyss of himself." The emotional aspect of this proposition notwithstanding, those of a culturally secure national identity may scoff at the pompousness of such a belief. Yet for Yeats, as for the Irish people before the formulation of the Irish

Republic in 1916, identity was an unfathomable abyss born from the colonial confusion engendered both by the loss of a native language and by the close proximity and pervasive nature of English culture in an Irish context. Yeats became painfully aware of such oppositions at work in his own personality; the fact that as a Protestant he was neither wholly Irish nor English in the divided Irish psyche to which he adhered caused him great emotional difficulty. Working with an appreciation of Blake's subtle deconstruction of oppositions, Yeats' believed that "[e]verything calls up its contrary, unreality calls up reality" and given that "life [in Ireland] has been sufficiently perilous to make men think" he attempted to use poetry to resolve the opposites, or what he calls, "antinomies," at work in Irish culture and in himself. His belief in symbolism as a source of revelation and his conviction in the regenerative power of the mythological imagination instilled in him the belief that his poetry could actually formulate, or rephrase, the ingredients that he believed were essential to the success of Irish nationalism. Moreover, his immersion in folklore gave him the raw materials to be refigured in a modern Irish poetic impulse in which the Protestant ascendancy could take a part. He believed that "we might bring the halves together if we had a national literature that made Ireland beautiful in the memory, and yet had been freed from provincialism by an exacting criticism, an European pose." This he achieved in poetry that is at once sophisticated, accessible, erudite, and easy to read, while also being comprehensively engaged in stressing the essential artifice, the essential imaginative leap required to build the image of a new nation.

Yet if poetry was one prong in this attack, theater was another one. In Synge and O'Casey he found a Protestant flagship to lead the National Theatre Association into the twentieth century. Moreover, his passion for innovation and his friendship with Ezra Pound led him to Japanese Noh drama which helped to develop his own theories of "the Mask" and produce a symbolic drama in keeping with the symbolism of his poetry. Whereas Yeats had labored hard to produce a favorable postcolonial image for his nation, his awareness of its contrivance led him to believe "that all happiness depends on the energy to assume the mask of some other self; that all joyous or creative life is a re-birth as something not oneself, something which has no memory and is created in a moment and perpetually renewed." For Yeats, the mask is the social self; in the later words of T. S. Eliot, "a face to meet the faces that you meet." Ultimately, we are detached from the experiences we have while wearing the mask and so it functions like a social safety net.

In the context of theater practice, Yeats utilized the mask in conjunction with the stylized movement of the Noh and Kabuki traditions in order to create a Western drama that could be "a mysterious art ... doing its work by suggestion, not by direct statement, a complexity of rhythm, colour, gesture, not space-pervading like the intellect but a

memory and a prophecy; a mode of drama Shelley and Keats could have used without ceasing to be themselves." In this style, Yeats wrote the plays *At the Hawk's Well* (1916) and *The Cat and the Moon* (1917). With the actors wearing masks and employing stylized rhythmic language and dance, and by utilizing a chorus to reflect interior realities or imaginings, Yeats created a drama of symbolism.

Yeats' theories of the mask also function within his most complete and systematic critical appraisal of the history of art, *A Vision*, written between 1925 and 1937. *A Vision* proposes that artistic or abstract thought is an organic aspect of history, which is itself a drama that moves cyclically but which is never identically repetitive. Yeats uses the metaphor of a winding stair which moves spirally and on which you can find yourself in the same place although now temporally and spatially elevated. Individuals move within this differential history and compose its component parts. The soul – a word Yeats wants to avoid because it is theological – is both subjective and objective. He separates it into four faculties consisting of "the Will," which is the "first matter" of the personality. Then he envisages "the Mask," which is the Will's anti-self and "the image of what we wish to become" (here he echoes the function of the mask within his experimental theater, where he was striving not for "a theatre but the theatre's anti-self, an art that can appease all within us that becomes uneasy as the curtain falls and the house breaks into applause"). As the third faculty he substitutes the idea of intellect for what he calls "the Creative Mind," and as the fourth he posits a notion called "the Body of Fate" which is "any reality that exists outside of us."

To illustrate how history is cyclical and how the composition of the individual, artistic subject functions within this paradigm, Yeats became diagrammatic, designing a spiral symbol to represent these abstract concepts. Referring to it as a "gyre," Yeats proposes two interacting cones, one subjective and the other objective. These cones, as visualized antinomies, interpenetrate in a circular fashion rather like a turning wheel and represent both human history and the soul in its movement from subjectivity to objectivity and back again. In its wheel-like movement these cones move through phases delineated by Yeats from one to twenty-eight. The Will, as "first matter" of the personality, is instrumental in determining the individual's phase and in this regard perfect form or "Unity of Being" – the most complementary unity of the four faculties for each respective individual – is found close to phase 15. In phase 15 "all is beauty" which cannot be directly experienced by any individual, but, on the wider horizon of the development of a whole civilization, corresponds to identifiable historical periods in which collected individual's imaginative production reinvents the world. Thus within the three millennial periods to date, Yeats identifies Phidias (born c. 500 B.C.), Aeschylus (525–456 B.C.), and Sophocles (c. 496–405 B.C.) and the date 460 B.C. as the first artistic cultural zenith. In the second millennium he distinguishes phase 15 as corresponding to 560 A.D. and the age of Justinian in Byzantium, and for the third he identifies the period from 1450 to 1550, especially that of "the principal activity of the Academy of Florence" and the work of "Botticelli, Crivelli, Mantegna, Da Vinci." In other words, the historical repetition of phase 15 is recurrent around certain dates but always differential and resulting in a new explosion of artistic creativity. These periods are considered by Yeats to be the highest in artistic terms, cyclical recurrences which point to the constant regeneration of imagination.

There is no sense in which this is objective analytical or critical thinking in a scientific idiom; it is an area where criticism meets philosophy and prioritizes again the power and ceaseless energy of the imagination in forging its own reinvention. Ultimately, Yeats wished to "reveal the hidden laws" of an artistic world in which poets could live, breathe, and nurture their art as an organic part of classical tradition. If one agrees that Hegel can be refuted, but not "the *Song of Sixpence*," then Yeats formulates an artistic philosophy that is so imaginative it is also singularly irrefutable. It is this ceaseless exposition of imaginative prowess that transforms all of Yeats' work into a type of criticism; a criticism that advocates the necessity of imaginative invention as the potential, and, according to *A Vision*, inevitable regeneration of the world, a world made up from nothing, as Yeats himself was, in his own imagination.

## Principal criticism

*Ideas of Good and Evil*, 1903
*The Cutting of an Agate*, 1912
*Essays*, 1924
*A Vision*, 1925, 1937
*A Packet for Ezra Pound*, 1929
*Essays, 1931–1936*, 1937
*On the Boiler*, 1939 (poems and essays)
*If I Were Four and Twenty*, 1940
*Essays and Introductions*, 1961
*Explorations*, 1962
*Uncollected Prose*, 1970–1976 (2 volumes)

## Other major works and literary forms

SHORT FICTION
*John Sherman and Dhoya*, 1891, 1969
*The Celtic Twilight*, 1893
*The Secret Rose*, 1897
*The Tables of the Law, The Adoration of the Magi*, 1897
*Stories of Red Hanrahan*, 1904
*Mythologies*, 1959

PLAYS
*The Countess Cathleen*, 1892
*The Land of Heart's Desire*, 1894
*Cathleen ni Houlihan*, 1902 (with Lady Augusta Gregory)
*The Pot of Broth*, 1902 (with Lady Gregory)
*The Hour-Glass*, 1903

*The King's Threshold*, 1903 (with Lady Gregory)
*On Baile's Strand*, 1904
*Deirdre*, 1906 (with Lady Gregory)
*The Shadowy Waters*, 1906
*The Unicorn from the Stars*, 1907 (with Lady Gregory)
*The Golden Helmet*, 1908
*The Green Helmet*, 1910
*At the Hawk's Well*, 1916
*The Cat and the Moon*, 1917
*The Player Queen*, 1919
*The Only Jealousy of Emer*, 1919
*The Dreaming of the Bones*, 1919
*Calvary*, 1921
*Four Plays for Dancers*, 1921 (includes *Calvary, At the Hawk's Well, The Dreaming of the Bones, The Only Jealousy of Emer*)
*The Resurrection*, 1927
*The Words upon the Windowpane*, 1930
*The Collected Plays of W. B. Yeats*, 1934
*The King of the Great Clock Tower*, 1934
*A Full Moon in March*, 1934
*The Herne's Egg*, 1938
*Purgatory*, 1938
*The Death of Cuchulain*, 1939
*Variorum Edition of the Plays of W. B. Yeats*, 1966

POETRY
*Mosada: A Dramatic Poem*, 1886
*Crossways*, 1889
*The Wanderings of Oisin and Other Poems*, 1889
*The Rose*, 1893
*The Wind Among the Reeds*, 1899
*In the Seven Woods*, 1903
*The Green Helmet and Other Poems*, 1910
*Responsibilities*, 1914
*Responsibilities and Other Poems*, 1916
*The Wild Swans at Coole*, 1917, 1919
*Michael Robartes and the Dancer*, 1921
*The Tower*, 1928
*Words for Music Perhaps and Other Poems*, 1932
*The Winding Stair and Other Poems*, 1933
*The Collected Poems of W. B. Yeats*, 1933, 1950
*A Full Moon in March*, 1935
*Last Poems and Plays*, 1940
*The Variorum Edition of the Poems of W. B. Yeats*, 1957
*W. B. Yeats: The Poems*, 1983
*The Poems: A New Edition*, 1984

NONFICTION
*Autobiographies*, 1926, 1955
*The Letters of W. B. Yeats*, 1954
*The Senate Speeches of W. B. Yeats*, 1960
*Ah, Sweet Dancer: W. B. Yeats – Margaret Ruddock, A Correspondence*, 1970
*Memoirs*, 1972

## Further reading

Bloom, Harold. *Yeats*, 1970.
Brooks, Cleanth. "W. B. Yeats as a Literary Critic," in *A Shaping Joy: Studies in the Writer's Craft*, 1971.
Cross, K. G. W., and R. T. Dunlop. *A Bibliography of Yeats Criticism*, 1971.
de Man, Paul. *The Rhetoric of Romanticism*, 1984.
Donoghue, Denis. *William Butler Yeats*, 1971.
Ellmann, Richard. *The Identity of Yeats*, 1964.

___. *Eminent Domain: Yeats Among Wilde, Joyce, Pound, Eliot and Auden*, 1967.

Faulkner, Peter. "Yeats as Critic," in *Criticism: A Quarterly for Literature and the Arts*. IV (Fall, 1962), pp. 328–339.

Jeffares, A. Norman. *A New Commentary on the Poems of W. B. Yeats*, 1984.

Kermode, Frank. *Romantic Image*, 1964.

Said, Edward. "Yeats and Decolonisation," in *Nationalism, Colonialism and Literature*, 1990. Edited, with introduction, by Seamus Deane.

Sena, Vinod. *W. B. Yeats: The Poet as Critic*, 1980.

RODNEY SHARKEY

*See also* Aestheticism; British Literary Theory: Twentieth Century; Eliot; Symbolism; Symons; Pound

# Nijō Yoshimoto

Japanese poet

**Born:** Heian, Japan; 1320
**Died:** Heian, Japan; 1388

## Biography

Although Nijō Yoshimoto was born into one of the most prestigious families of his day, it was a time when prestige did not usually entail political power, a fact reflected in his appointment at the age of seven as a captain in the Left Palace Guard. His father had held the highest post in the imperial administration, that of Chancellor, and his mother was the daughter of a Minister of the Right (the third highest post). He himself became Minister of the Right in 1343 and was Chancellor from 1346 to 1358. Yoshimoto served the emperors of the northern court in the old capital (modern-day Kyoto), who were supported by the military might of the Ashikaga shoguns. This line was opposed by a rival imperial line known as the southern court, which was established in Yoshino by Emperor GoDaigo.

Yoshimoto, like all aristocrats, studied poetry, choosing to ally himself with the tradition of the Nijō family. One of his teachers was Ton'a, an important priest-poet of the age. Yoshimoto participated in poetry meetings attended by all the important poets of the day, including Yoshida Kenkō, the author of *Tsurezuregusa* (1340; *Essays in Idleness*, 1967). The Nijō school is known for its conservative attitudes and uninspiring poetry, and Yoshimoto was a typical adherent. He made his mark instead in the world of *renga* (linked verse). He studied under Kyūsei from the age of twenty. There is record of his study of the Japanese classics, the *Manyōshū* (c. 759; *The Manyōshū*, 1929–1969, 20 volumes) and *Genji monogatari* (1000–1010; *The Tale of Genji*, 1934), and of Chinese poetry in the 1360s.

Thanks to his intimate knowledge of court precedent and etiquette he served as adviser to three shoguns, Ashikaga Takauji (1305–1358), Ashikaga Yoshiakira (1330–1367), and Ashikaga Yoshimitsu (1358–1408).

## Influence

Before Yoshimoto, *renga* was more a parlor game than an art. *Renga* is the group composition of interconnecting verses so that the meaning of the poem changes continually. In early *renga* the major objective was to compose a verse which would be hard to follow or to meet such a challenge cleverly. Yoshimoto provided the crucial influence in establishing *renga* as a legitimate literary art. He lent his reputation as a poet of *waka* (the traditional Japanese poem of thirty-one syllables) and as an aristocrat of the highest rank to the practice of *renga* by compiling the anthology of *renga* verses called *Tsukubashū* (the Tsukuba collection), which was granted imperial recognition as second only to the imperially authorized anthologies of *waka*. Yoshimoto claimed for *renga* the weight and dignity of ancient tradition and spiritual value, as had been claimed for *waka* over the centuries. Yoshimoto's compilation of rules concerning associations between verses and repetition of words in various categories, *Renga shinshiki* (the new rule of *renga*), was received as the standard version of such rules for the rest of the medieval period.

## Analysis

The aim of Yoshimoto's several treatises on *renga* theory and criticism was to change the practice of *renga* from a group pastime into a literary art. The anthology he compiled, *Tsukubashū*, probably did the most to achieve that end. Until this anthology was completed, *renga* had been appreciated as participatory performance. Its most enjoyable feature was the display of quick wit as members of a group took turns composing connecting links. By compiling an anthology of especially good pairs of verses, Yoshimoto presented *renga* as poetry to be appreciated even after the event of its composition. He identified fifteen ways in which verses could be linked, so that depth and beauty became the virtues of *renga*, rather than mere wit. Wordplay was still an acceptable technique for linking verses, but so was the straight-forward development of a concept presented in a first verse. Moreover, literary values of the *waka* tradition, the elegance of *sabi* (quiet, thoughtful loneliness) and of *yūgen* (depth), are to be found in *renga*, he wrote, along with the trademark of *renga*, casual or commonplace vocabulary.

In promoting *renga* as an art, Yoshimoto was joining the two types of *renga* then being composed. *Jige renga* was linked verse composed by those of less than the highest aristocratic status, or, to put it broadly, by commoners, a group which included Yoshimoto's teacher, Kyūsei, a leading *renga* master. *Dōjō renga* was verse by aristocrats whose status gained for them access to the imperial palace, a group to which Yoshimoto belonged. Kyūsei's contribution to this alliance was originality and the expansion of the poetic vocabulary. Yoshimoto offered prestige.

Completed in 1356, *Tsukubashū* contains 2,190 verses, usually presented in pairs or as a sequence of three or four verses, not in one-hundred-verse units as *renga* was typically composed. Pairs were chosen in order to illustrate the chief objective of *renga*, skillful and interesting associations between links. By including examples of *renga* from the historical work, *Nihon shoki* (720; *Chronicles of Japan*, 1896), and from the first major collection of Japanese poetry, *The Manyōshū*, Yoshimoto claimed for *renga* the dignity of tradition. *Tsukubashū* was organized into categories of verses on spring (198 poems), summer (73), fall (190), winter (104), Shinto deities (59), Buddhist deities (74), love (337), miscellaneous (599), travel (185), celebration (64), miscellaneous forms (188), and *hokku* (opening verses, 119). This reflects the organizational principles of the prestigious Imperial Anthologies, such as the *Kokinshū* (c. 905; *Kokinshū: A Collection of Poems Ancient and Modern*, 1984), a conscious effort to secure the same respect for *renga* as was enjoyed by *waka*.

In *Tsukuba mondō* (1357–1372; The Tsukuba Dialogues), using the narrative setting of two poets discussing *renga*, Yoshimoto furthers his argument for the appreciation of *renga* as a venerable art. He traces the origins of *renga* as far back as a dialogue between the mythical deities Izanagi and Izanami, who created much of the world. He also claims benefits from *renga* for the government of the nation as well as progress toward the spiritual goal of enlightenment for the individual. Because the meaning of *renga* changes with the addition of each new link, it reflects the changeability of the mortal world. Thus *renga* teaches the Buddhist lesson of the transience of all things and of the fruitlessness of the desires which are the source of human suffering.

Yoshimoto did not intend, however, for the essential character of *renga* to be sacrificed for respectability. In *Renri hishō* (c. 1349; a secret treatise of *renga* principles), he addressed the question of how and where to conduct the group sessions at which *renga* were composed. Yoshimoto describes the ideal meeting place as an environment in which poetic feelings will naturally arise. The view, whether it is moonlight on snow or trees in blossom, a mountain or pond, should be one which will elicit the appropriate atmosphere. Guided by the *renga* masters, there should be harmony among the participants, who become so absorbed in their activity that they lose track of the time.

Until Yoshimoto's time there were several schools of *renga* composition, each with its own rules. With the emergence of Kyūsei and his adherents as the leading *renga* composers, their preferred list of rules, which had been compiled between 1275 and 1277, became the standard rule book. Yoshimoto had made previous efforts to supplement these old rules, but ultimately, with Kyūsei's help, he wrote *Renga shinshiki*, which is better known as *Ōan shinshiki* (1372; The New Rules of the Ōan Era, 1372). Although this was modified in subsequent years, it remained the basis for *renga* composition throughout the medieval period. Such rule books concerned themselves with the technical aspects of composing *renga*: avoid any repetition in three succeeding verses, avoid using the same associative technique more than once in a one-hundred-verse sequence. Some admonitions are very specific: subjects, such as fresh leaves, should not be mentioned more than once in one hundred verses; subjects, such as the spring moon, may be used twice per one hundred verses; certain subjects may be mentioned after skipping one, three, five or seven verses; the topics of spring, fall, and love may be sustained for five verses, but summer, winter, travel, and Shinto or Buddhist deities may be discussed in only three subsequent verses.

In *Kyūshū mondō* (1376; the Kyūshū dialogues), Yoshimoto answered larger questions about *renga* put to him by Imagawa Ryōshun, a shogunal official posted in Kyūshū. When considering a *renga* sequence (usually of one hundred, sometimes of one thousand links) as a whole, poets should employ a principle of composition called *umon-mumon* (brilliant and plain). The objective is to set an occasional magnificent verse against a ground of merely adequate verses so as to give the whole a variegated pattern. Moreover, there should be three stages of development through a complete sequence: *jo, ha, kyū* (slow, moderately paced, and quick), a concept borrowed from music. In the case of *renga*, the first quarter of the poem should be calm and tranquil, the second quarter should be variable, with highs and lows, and the third portion, the second half, should be smooth and light. To these ends, Yoshimoto suggests that a poet prepare by composing a number of verses in advance of a meeting. This proposal may seem contrary to the nature of *renga* composition as a spontaneous group project, but it served Yoshimoto's goal of making *renga* into a worthy literary art.

Yoshimoto's last important work was *Jūmon saihi shō* (1383; ten questions: a most secret selection), written for Ōuchi Yoshihiro, also a powerful military figure. Here Yoshimoto presents a refined version of his ideas. In particular, he discusses style, which refers inclusively to content, expression, and conception. Not only should a skillful poet develop a style independent of his teacher's, but also each age should display a distinctive style. Nevertheless, poets should always compose with an unchanging basic spirit of propriety, sincerity, and depth. While masterpieces may be found in a wide range of styles, the best *renga* are characterized by a vague, penetrating depth, by a bright beauty, and by elegance.

Except for his considerable accomplishment in establishing *renga* as a respectable art, Yoshimoto's influence was short-lived. Although his rule book remained a standard, his aesthetics did not. Before long even the *Tsukubashū* was rarely consulted. Yoshimoto had tried to apply the aesthetics of *waka* to linked verse by encouraging elegance, but the trend in *renga* was to be toward including the *zoku*, that is, the "vulgar" or commonplace and even humorous elements of life.

## Principal criticism
*Renri hishō*, c. 1349
*Tsukubashū*, 1356 (editor)
*Tsukuba mondō*, 1357–1372
*Renga shinshiki*, 1372 (better known as *Ōan shinshiki*)
*Kyūshū mondō*, 1376
*Renga jūyō*, 1379
*Jūmon saihi shō*, 1383

## Other major works and literary forms
While best known today for his work in *renga*, or linked verse, Nijō Yoshimoto was also a traditional *waka* poet of the Nijō (no relation) school. *Waka*, later known as *tanka*, uses a five-line, thirty-one-syllable form. Some three hundred of Yoshimoto's *waka* are extant in various collections, of which sixty can be found in the prestigious Imperial Anthologies: *Fūgashū* (1346; collection of elegance), *Shin senzaishū* (1359; new collection of a thousand years), *Shin shūishū* (1364; new collection of gleanings), *Shin goshūishū* (1384; new later collection of gleanings), and *Shinzoku kokinshū* (1439; new collection of ancient and modern poetry continued).

Of historical interest are his detailed descriptions of events and ceremonies at the imperial court. *Ojima no kuchizusami* (1353; murmurings at Ojima) is a record of the weeks that he spent in Ojima with Emperor GoKōgon, having fled the capital during a rebel attack. *Kinukazuki no nikki* (1363; diary behind veils) describes in great detail a *kemari* (kickball) match held in the summer of 1363. Borrowing the perspective of court women who observed from behind their veils, Yoshimoto notes costume and procedure, apparently with the intention of creating a guidebook for use by future generations.

An important source of information on Buddhist music is his *Kumoi no minori* (1380; rites for the lofty one), a record of the week-long memorial services held in 1380 to mark the seventh anniversary of the death of Emperor GoKōgon. Here his narrator is an elderly nun, who includes a description of Yoshimoto and his role as adviser in conducting the proper rituals. For the shogun Ashikaga Yoshimitsu, he wrote *Hyakuryō kunyōshō* (1368–1388; treatise explaining the essentials of the hundred offices), a text which explains official and unofficial posts in the imperial bureaucracy. By this time these were only honorary positions, but they were coveted by the military class as prestigious titles. Finally, Yoshimoto is considered to be the most likely candidate as author of *Masukagami* (1338–1376; the clear mirror), an anonymous history of court politics from 1180 to 1333.

### POETRY
*Bunna senku*, 1355
*Embun hyakushu*, 1357
*Nenjū gyōji utaawase*, 1366
*Ishiyama hyakuin*, 1385

### NONFICTION
*Masukagami*, 1338–1376 (probable author)
*Ojima no kuchizusami*, 1353

*Gumon kenshū*, 1363 (with Ton'a)
*Kinukazuki no nikki*, 1363
*Hyakuryō kunyōshō*, 1368–1388
*Kumoi no minori*, 1380
*Kinrai fūtaishō*, 1387

## Further reading
Carter, Steven D. *The Road to Komatsubara*, 1987.
——. *Waiting for the Wind*, 1989.
Keene, Donald. "The Comic Tradition in Renga," in *Japan in the Muromachi Age*, 1977. Edited by John Whitney Hall and Toyoda Takeshi.
——. *Seeds in the Heart*, 1993.
Kidō, Saizō. *Rengashi ronkō*, 1971–1973 (2 volumes).
Konishi, Jin'ichi. *Sōgi*, 1973.
Miner, Earl. *Japanese Linked Poetry*, 1979.
Shimazu, Tadao. *Renga no kenkyū*, 1972.

MARGARET H. CHILDS

*See also* Japanese Literary Criticism; Tsurayuki

# Edward Young

## English poet and critic

**Born:** Upham, Hampshire, England; July 3, 1683 (baptized)
**Died:** Welwyn, England; April 5, 1765

## Biography
Edward Young's baptism, on July 3, 1683, is the only recorded acknowledgment of his birth in the parish of Upham, where his father was the church rector. Young studied at Oxford University and became a Fellow at All Souls College, hoping for a political appointment. He was defeated as a candidate for Parliament in 1721 and later took holy orders, becoming a chaplain to George II in 1728. Upon his appointment as rector at Welwyn in 1730, he had already written religious and satirical poems, and two of his three blank-verse tragedies had had short runs in London. Although dedicatory letters, prefaces, and commemorative odes were common literary products in Young's day, biographers have always seen his work in these genres as part of the evidence of personal disappointment in his career goals. Letters and anecdotes reinforce this interpretation, even though he associated with the important literati of his day and gained entrance into Joseph Addison's cadre of coffee-house wits.

The popularity of *The Complaint: Or, Night Thoughts on Life, Death, and Immortality* (hereafter called *Night Thoughts*) dominated Young's public life, religious duties notwithstanding. These and his *Love of Fame, the Universal Passion*, an earlier serial publication, helped to make him Alexander Pope's "nearest rival" in the popular mind. The popularity of the poems also helped call attention to his prose, including his social commentary and the famous letter to Samuel Richardson containing his major theoretical statement, published as *Conjectures on Original Composition* about three years after Young first wrote it.

## Influence

The immediate and widespread contemporary popularity of Young's *Night Thoughts* often eclipses any modern notice of his other works. Nevertheless, while the poem survives usually as an example of the graveyard school, *Conjectures on Original Composition* continues to generate interest in its opposition to rationalism as the dominant force in neoclassical criticism. Young's theory illustrates eighteenth-century absorption with the Greek Longinus, whose rediscovered first-century treatise *Peri hypsous (On the Sublime)*, translated in France in 1674, offered an alternative to the standard criticism based on the three unities. The bold emphasis on originality in Young's treatise established it as a precursor of the Romantic period, and its commitment to the modern side in the "Quarrel of the Ancients and Moderns" gave the work an oracular function.

This manifesto was well received throughout Europe and developed an almost completely European influence at first. The essay became a stimulus toward individualism for younger writers in France and especially in Germany. Young's analogy between organic growth and artistic creation seemed new and appropriate to philosophers and poets alike; its focus on the mysteries of artistic genius helped to pinpoint an important area of study for the developing psychology of art.

## Analysis

In the prefaces to *Love of Fame, the Universal Passion* and *Imperium Pelagi: A Naval Lyrick* as well as in "A Discourse on Lyric Poetry," Young reveals some major theoretical interests of his era and suggests his emphasis in the forthcoming *Conjectures on Original Composition*. These early statements address "emulation" as opposed to imitation, which he defines as the copying of earlier works; intimidation by the reputations of the ancient writers; and the concept of the sublime stimulated by neoclassical interest in the Greek Longinus.

Young takes the standard moral approach to satire but concludes frankly that it "may not do much good." Many of his critical reasons in these early essays are based upon audience reaction. His rationale is thus founded on taste as opposed to "rules" or judgment. The essay on the lyric suggests an antidote to intimidation from the past by means of experimentation with the ode.

One common problem in these incipient critical documents develops from the inadequacy of vocabulary for critical discussions of the affective matters in which Young is interested. With hardly any psychological vocabulary at hand, his attempts to explain individuality in the creative process and to adjust it so that it fits the standard of truth to nature go off in whimsical and sometimes meaningless directions. These ventures, however, are also anticipations

of the truly important organic metaphor developed in *Conjectures on Original Composition*.

Circumstances surrounding the appearance of Young's major critical statement explain its full title, *Conjectures on Original Composition in a Letter to the Author of Sir Charles Grandison*. In 1756 Richardson had seen the manuscript and, judging from evidence in his correspondence, had begun to edit it. The sententious moralism of the essay probably can be attributed to Richardson's intrusion, as can the attention given to Addison at the expense of writers such as John Dryden. Samuel Johnson had heard the essay read aloud before its publication and is reported by James Boswell to have recognized as "commonplace maxims" that which Young considered "novelties" in the work.

Young's ideas are not usually seen as innovative and are examined in the context of antirationalist reactions to standard rationalist theory, primarily the English interest in the concept of the sublime as originating with Longinus. Nevertheless, Young exceeds Longinus in developing a manifesto for "original genius," a call for turning away from external models from the past toward the inner self. In short, Young calls for originality, and in doing so he begins to substitute individual perception and independent imaginative interpretation of experience for external standards for truth.

The urgent tone of *Conjectures on Original Composition* makes it a striking final salvo in the "Quarrel of the Ancients and Moderns" even while Young tries to accommodate both sides simultaneously. With examples drawn from the very classical models with which he wants his contemporaries to compete, he also creates a definition of originality which locates him as a Modern. Self-consciously he challenges the arts to progress as science and technology have done.

The inadequacy of critical vocabulary may be one reason that Young protects his theory with the label "conjectures" and encloses it in a letter to a friend, thereby establishing informality. The patterns of Aristotelian and neoclassical criticism may be another.

The variety of topics reveals many standard points in Longinian criticism and rudiments of eighteenth-century aesthetics: imitation, classical and native authors, inspiration, progress, the problem of belief, catharsis, use of rhyme, and critical comments on specific writers interspersed with anecdotes. The wit of Young the poet sometimes hurts the discussion, making it diffuse when consistency is needed.

The word "originality" did not actually appear in writing until later in the century, although "original" was already both a noun and an adjective. "Genius" was well known, but a new meaning, which Young's work may have helped to establish, was developing: "instinctive extraordinary capacity for imaginative creation." In *Conjectures on Original Composition*, original genius is defined by example, organic metaphor, moral analogy, and negation.

Young lists Francis Bacon, Robert Boyle, Sir Isaac Newton, William Shakespeare, and John Milton as "great *Originals*." His philosopher-scientists reinforce the competition established in an earlier passage between the "arts mechanic," which are progressive and the "liberal" arts, which are retrograde. He also sets up contrasts between genius and learning thus: "learning is borrowed knowledge; genius is knowledge innate." Even in the context of original composition as subject he asserts that many geniuses "probably . . . could neither write, nor read." This statement reinforces his argument that "genius, that supreme lustre of literature, is less rare than you conceive." He picks up this idea later in the context of the ancient-modern debate in referring to "an impartial Providence."

Early in the work, Young hints at the organic concept, and metaphors of the "*vegetable* nature" of original composition are scattered throughout his treatise. Nature, the object of imitation, becomes his foundation for the analogy, often seen more literally than the neoclassical concept of general nature, or natural laws, allows: "The mind of the man of genius is a fertile and pleasant field . . . it enjoys a perpetual spring." He also asserts, "An original genius rises spontaneously from the vital root of genius; it *grows*, it is not *made*." When he does talk about structures "made" by genius, he says that their form develops "by means invisible." Allusions to the oracular role of genius support his figurative language. The analogy operates further in Young's contrast between ancient and contemporary conditions for the growth of genius: "An evocation of vegetable fruits depends on rain, air, and sun . . . the fruits of genius no less depends upon externals."

This analogy leads to an essential part of Young's theory, serving as the introduction to his concept of the self. Beginning a passage that seems commonplace in borrowing "two golden rules from *ethics*," he begins by advising his reader to "know thyself," stating "an *Original* author is born of himself, is his own progenitor." Then, exhorting his reader not to be intimidated, he says something peculiar: "Thyself so reverence as to prefer the native growth of thy own mind to the richest import from abroad." According to Young, the process of knowing the self is confrontation with "the stranger within thee." He explains his shift into moral philosophy on the basis of "ignorance of the possible dimensions of the mind of man"; borrowing further from this source he calls genius "the god within," equating it with conscience.

On the negative side, Young's rejection of imitation offers "emulation" as a substitute: "Imitation is inferiority confessed; emulation is superiority contested, or denied." If his discussion seems to call merely for putting new subjects into old forms, his examples of genres may be at fault. He refers to the novel, for example, only by implication, in his title and in veiled addresses to Richardson. He seems to depend on the ode as his method for opening the door to creative initiation. His comments on Pope within the

discussions of emulation, imitation, and translation reinforce his attention to the ode, and the challenges to imitate the "spirit" and "taste" of ancient writers do not close the door to new forms.

References to Bacon are major parts of Young's strategy, especially in the psychological context. He credits the philosopher with initiating the study of "the human mind," and with revealing "blank spaces," some of which "have been enlightened since," while others remain "benighted." From this position, he moves to artistic creation as reflective of the divine process, resulting in "quite-original beauties we may call paradisaical, *Natos sine semine flores*" (flowers produced without seed).

Neoclassicals would charge arrogance here, especially regarding the references to enthusiasm seen in the essay; anticipating this reaction, Young often apologizes. Conversely, his criticism of Addison as a tragedian introduces an aesthetic counter to self-importance: "For the writer must be forgotten by his audience, during the representation, if for ages he would be remembered by posterity." Aesthetic disinterestedness is the obvious theoretical concept here.

Young depends primarily upon affective reasons for his theory, and his foundation is audience response. This position is the basis for his commentary on both Addison's and Dryden's failures in tragedy: "The tragedian's point is rather to *feel*." Couched in the neoclassical terms for catharsis and in Thomas Hobbes' psychology, Young's theory sounds familiar. Another contemporary debate, the choice between blank verse and rhyme, evolves out of his comparisons of Milton and Pope. Taking Pope to task for imitation, he calls the Homeric translations "childish shackles, and tinkling sounds." The novelty of Jonathan Swift's *Gulliver's Travels* (1726), however, does not please him; he falls back upon the neoclassical guide, judgment, to condemn what he considers Swift's excesses.

The account of Addison's death which ends the essay seems gratuitous, even with Young's careful preparation for it in the discussion of moral genius. Since Young states that telling the story is his reason for writing, the death scene must be taken into account. As noted above, evidence from Richardson suggests the novelist's influence here, while Young seems uncomfortable enough about including the anecdote to promise a sequel on Addison later.

Young's theory has been less influential than his poetry, and contemporaries talked about him more as a poet and a public figure than as a theoretician. Edmund Burke's *A Philosophical Enquiry into the Origin of Our Ideas of the Sublime and Beautiful* (1757), which takes pride of place on the subject of the sublime, was published during this same period and still dominates the discussion. Young's treatise was initially viewed in connection with the theory of the sublime, and it is still seen thus in English criticism. The parallel studies of the association of ideas, which started English aesthetics in the modern sense, have also taken attention away from Young's work. Study of Young has concentrated on tracing parallels and discovering possible studies instead of recognizing Young's contribution. Twentieth-century concepts, such as the affective and the genetic fallacies, have shown that *Conjectures on Original Composition* has the problem common to all works considered *sui generis* or perhaps ahead of their time: obscurity. From the viewpoint of Longinian tradition, however, Young's work does not seem original.

Yet in Europe, Young's theory received much attention, influencing not only younger French and German writers but also the interest in aesthetics. The abiding interest in *Night Thoughts* helped to call attention to *Conjectures on Original Composition*, so that the latter became, according to M. H. Abrams, "a primary document in the canon of the Storm and Stress" movement in Germany. Young's theory was known to Johann Gottfried von Sulzer, who studied the organic analogy, and subsequently to Gotthold Ephraim Lessing and Johann Wolfgang von Goethe. Denis Diderot and the leaders of the French Revolution were aware of Young's message through both his poetry and theory. One of the best biographies of Young was published in France in 1901. From these European bases, Young has often been placed in the pre-Romantic category, and his work is often anthologized as a transitional marker between English antirationalist critical methods and Romanticism. Young's concept of originality is an early development of the concept of critical relativism; as a source of the organic metaphor for the creative process, it is considered a contribution to later developments in aesthetics.

## Principal criticism

Preface to *Love of Fame, the Universal Passion*, 1725–1728
"A Discourse on Lyric Poetry," in *Odes Occasioned by His Majesty's Encouragement of the Sea-Service*, 1728
Preface to *Imperium Pelagi: A Naval Lyrick*, 1730
*Conjectures on Original Composition in a Letter to the Author of Sir Charles Grandison*, 1759 (best known as *Conjectures on Original Composition*)

## Other major works and literary forms

Edward Young was known in his day primarily as a poet, often judged second only to Alexander Pope. The two treated some of the same topics from contemporary life, using a similar type of end-stopped heroic couplet characterized by the witty epigram. Young's body of work is reflective of popular neoclassical themes and genres: satires on current behavior and attitudes, written in heroic couplets; epistles in this same verse form, on current writers; prose letters finding fault with fashionable life; panegyrics addressed to aristocratic patrons; occasional lyrics and odes adapted after the manner and style of Pindar; paraphrases of biblical sources; and tragedies in blank verse. Young not only defended blank verse in his criticism but also chose it

for his most popular work, a group of meditative poems eventually collected under the title *The Complaint: Or, Night Thoughts on Life, Death, and Immortality*, in 1797, with illustrations by William Blake following their initially anonymous serial publication from 1742 through 1746. Only a few sermons have regularly been included in collections of his works; his most interesting letters in the light of his literary career are those addressed to other well-known figures, such as the novelist Samuel Richardson.

PLAYS
*Busiris, King of Egypt*, 1719
*The Revenge*, 1721
*The Brothers*, 1753

POETRY
*A Paraphrase on Part of the Book of Job*, 1719
*Two Epistles to Mr. Pope, Concerning the Authors of the Age*, 1730
*The Complaint: Or, Night Thoughts on Life, Death, and Immortality*, 1742–1746, 1797
*The Works of the Author of the Night-Thoughts*, 1757
*Resignation*, 1761

NONFICTION
*A Letter to Mr. Tickell Occasioned by the Death of Joseph Addison*, 1719
*A Vindication of Providence: Or, A True Estimate of Human Life*, 1728
*An Apology for Princes: Or, The Reverence Due to Government*, 1729
*The Centaur Not Fabulous: In Six Letters to a Friend on the Life in Vogue*, 1755
*An Argument Drawn from the Circumstances of Christ's Death for the Truth of His Religion*, 1758
*The Correspondence of Edward Young, 1683–1765*, 1971

MISCELLANEOUS
*Complete Works*, 1854

## Further reading

Abrams, M. H. *The Mirror and the Lamp: Romantic Theory and the Critical Tradition*, 1953.
Bate, Walter Jackson. *The Burden of the Past and the English Poet*, 1970.
Bliss, Isabel St. John. *Edward Young*, 1969.
Cordasco, Francesco. *Edward Young: A Handlist*, 1950.
Kaufman, Paul. "Heralds of Original Genius," in *Essays in Memory of Barrett Wendell*, 1926.
Monk, Samuel Holt. *The Sublime: A Study of Critical Theories in Eighteenth-century England*, 1935.
Morley, Edith J., ed. *Edward Young's Conjectures on Original Composition*, 1918.
Pettit, Henry, ed. Introduction to *The Correspondence of Edward Young, 1683–1765*, 1971.
Shelley, Henry C. *The Life and Letters of Edward Young*, 1914.
Steinke, Martin W. *Edward Young's Conjectures on Original Composition in England and in Germany*, 1917.

EMMA COBURN NORRIS

*See also* Johnson; Pope; Warton and Warton

# Z

## Vasilii Zhukovskii

Russian poet, translator, and critic

**Born:** Mishenskoe, Russia; February 9, 1783
**Died:** Baden-Baden, Germany; April 19, 1852

### Biography

Vasilii Andreevich Zhukovskii was born on February 9, 1783, the illegitimate son of Afanasii Ivanovich Bunin and a Turkish woman, Salkha, who had become a house servant for the Bunins after being taken captive by Russian forces following a 1770 battle. He was named for his godfather, Andrei Zhukovskii, a poor nobleman who lived on the estate, but he was brought up within the Bunin household and educated as a member of the gentry, first at a school in nearby Tula and then in a boarding school for the nobility at Moscow University.

Zhukovskii's interest in literature appeared early; he began to write poetry while still a child, and his first work came out shortly after he arrived in Moscow in 1797, when he was only fourteen years old. His first major work, "Sel'skoe kladbishche," an adaptation of Thomas Gray's *Elegy Written in a Country Churchyard* (1751), appeared in an 1802 issue of *Vestnik evropy* (messenger of Europe), perhaps the most important literary journal of the day. The editor was Nikolai Karamzin, the prominent writer, historian, and publicist, whose views on both politics and poetry were to have a strong influence on Zhukovskii. From then on his career advanced rapidly; over the next few years his translations and original lyrics made him one of the leading poets in Russia. In 1808 and 1809 he edited *Vestnik evropy*; most of the critical essays that he published during his lifetime date from this period and the two years that immediately followed. In 1815, along with other followers of Karamzin, he formed the society known as Arzamas, in opposition to those who took a more conservative stance on the trends in literature and the literary language. That same year the first collection of his poetry began to appear, and he was invited to the court as a reader to the czarina.

The peak of his literary prominence came during the 1810s and early 1820s, when he created many of his ballads and much of his original poetry, culminating in the three-volume collection of his works that came out in 1824. From the middle of the decade on his influence waned. Part of the fault can be traced to his ever-closer court ties (he tutored the future Aleksandr II) and the growing conservatism of his views, which also took on a definite religious tinge late in life. Much of the explanation also lies simply in the appearance of a new generation of writers whose concerns differed from Zhukovskii's. His remaining in Europe after he married in 1841 further isolated him from literary currents in Russia. Still, his talents did not diminish; during the years abroad, he produced numerous essays and translations. He died on April 19, 1852, in Germany.

### Influence

Both as a poet and as a critic Zhukovskii played an enormously important role in the establishment of modern Russian literature. His efforts were crucial for introducing Romanticism and for making leading German and English poets of his day widely known in Russia. In Zhukovskii's search for new themes and new verse forms, in the importance that he gave to the imagination in the creative process, in his concern with beauty and the ideal, and through the mellifluousness that distinguished his own verse, he had a great effect on other poets of his generation, most notably the young Aleksandr Pushkin. Through his practice more than his theory, Zhukovskii also came to popularize certain genres. He was the leading practitioner of the literary ballad in Russia, while his 1817–1821 translation of Friedrich Schiller's *Die Jungfrau von Orleans* (1801; *The Maid of Orleans*, 1835) helped set the fashion for verse drama. Similarly, his 1822 rendering of Lord Byron's *The Prisoner of Chillon* served to create an interest in the Romantic narrative poem.

### Analysis

In his essays, poems, letters, and journalistic activity Zhukovskii arguably did more than any other single individual to introduce Romanticism to Russia. His critical writing, though important, comprised only a small portion of that contribution. Thus his contemporaries, while expressing high regard for Zhukovskii's intellect and analytical insights, voiced disappointment that he did not write more criticism. Only a handful of literary essays appeared during his lifetime, the great majority between 1808 and 1811, when he was closely associated with *Vestnik evropy*. Zhukovskii's contributions as a theorist depend equally on some of his poems (particularly several of his epistles, but also on "Lalla Rookh," 1821, inspired by Thomas Moore's poem of that title) and on passages that appear in letters to his contemporaries. Some of his critical writing remained in the form of unpublished notes and surveys; thus, his endeavors were in fact more extensive than was realized at the time. Surprisingly, despite his acknowledged importance, these writings have come out only piecemeal. By coincidence, the first two collections to be devoted solely to his criticism appeared almost simultaneously in 1985, one hundred and thirty-three years after his death.

Consideration of Zhukovskii's critical thought is further complicated by his attitude toward translation. As with his poetry, he regarded translated works as equal in importance to his original writing and did not always indicate whether a foreign source existed. Furthermore, since the translated essays were chosen in order to support his own views, neither his contemporaries nor recent compilers have drawn clear distinctions between the two: both of the 1985 collections contain translated items mixed in with his own articles. One piece, "O poezii drevnikh i novykh" (on the poetry of the ancients and the moderns), long thought to be by Zhukovskii, was shown only in 1985 to come from an unsigned article published in a series of volumes appended to Johann Georg Sulzer's *Allgemeine Theorie der schönen Künste* (1771–1774, 1792–1799; universal theory of the fine arts). Yet the new attribution does not alter the work's significance; it was influential at the time and clearly expresses certain aspects of Zhukovskii's own thought. The author examines the strengths and weaknesses of ancient as well as of modern art, implying that each needs to be appreciated on its own terms and that the new perhaps speaks best to its own age. The thrust, then, is to open the way to acceptance of the more recent art (Romanticism) without necessarily denying the merits of the classical practitioners. This acceptance is exactly what Zhukovskii himself was trying to accomplish in his *Vestnik evropy* articles.

Not surprisingly, Zhukovskii uses a translated article to lend support to his views of translation. "O perevodakh voobshche, i v osobennosti o perevodakh stikhov" (1810; on translations in general, with particular reference to translations of verse) comes from the last part of Jacques Delille's introduction to his French translation of Virgil's *Georgics* (c. 37–29 B.C.). Delille makes several points: poetry should always be translated by verse and not prose; a translation is not necessarily inferior to the original; and finally, the successful translator remains true to the spirit and achievements of the original even if that means sacrificing literalism. Not only could the article stand as a fine summary

of Zhukovskii's practice, but it also echoes comments he himself makes. In "O basne i basniakh Krylova" (1809; on the fable and on the fables of Krylov), he notes that Jean de La Fontaine borrowed the ideas for his fables, while Ivan Krylov in turn took both the ideas and the actual stories from La Fontaine. In Zhukovskii's opinion, both created original works. In order to reproduce a verse fable in another language, the translator must rely on imagination and on poetic talent no less than did the author being imitated. Zhukovskii particularly admires the effort required to create poetry; the prose translator, he claims, is a slave, while the verse translator is a rival.

Only one decade into the nineteenth century, when Russian literature was still struggling to find its own voice, translated works were especially prominent. Zhukovskii's views on translation could be seen as justifying his own practice, but he was also pointing Russian writers and readers to models that would inspire the development of a mature literature. Also programmatic were Zhukovskii's comments on the role of the critic and the writer. One of his earliest essays, "Pis'mo iz uezda k izdateliu" (1808; letter from a district to a publisher), apparently questions the need for critics, but only because Russia lacks a literature worthy of serious consideration. In "O kritike" (1809; on criticism"), he goes on to state that critics are indeed quite important. They bring to bear on works a "dispassionate" and "free" judgment that reflects an educated taste. By teaching readers how to appreciate what is good and beautiful in a work, the critic elevates the public's sensibility. The critic and writer are not opponents, but they possess different talents and play different roles. The poet creates intuitively, through inspiration. The passion and absorption that are necessary for creativity often make the poet appear aloof or alone, as Zhukovskii states in "Pisatel' v obshchestve" (1808; the writer in society) The critic, on the other hand, relies more on reason and informed judgment in an effort to explain and to enlighten.

Zhukovskii's chief influence on his contemporaries came through his championing of Romanticism. No single early essay contains a full statement of his ideas, but his comments about writers and critics hint at the essential points. Zhukovskii wants both writers and critics to rely on "taste" rather than to judge success according to an adherence to classical forms. The process of creation is intuitive; the special understanding that enables a poet to write great works is a gift that separates the writer from others. While the writer begins with observations and a knowledge of the world, creative work strives toward an ideal (of the good and the beautiful) that exists only in the imagination ("Rafaelova 'Madonna,'" Raphael's "Madonna," which became a key statement of Russian Romantic thought). Of particular importance to Zhukovskii are the concepts of passion and action. The creator becomes totally absorbed in art, while the most effective works are those that express strong feelings – a point that comes out in his poetry as much as in his critical writing. The references to action reflect a view of life as a process. Not only do people develop and change, but so does human thought as well. For art to express the nature of life and speak to a broad audience, it must capture this sense of movement.

Zhukovskii's concerns may explain his decision to write about the fable and about satire. Both "O basne i basniakh Krylova" and "O satire i satirakh Kantemira" (1810; on satire and on the satires of Kantemir) follow a similar plan: general remarks on the genre, some historical observations, and then analyses of works by the authors in question. In each case, he is attracted to the genre for nearly identical reasons. The fable is described as a "moral in action," in which general lessons about morality are extracted from a specific example. The fabulist acts on the reader's imagination, forcing him or her to compare the invented world with life as it is. The satirist, through use of ridicule and exaggeration, creates a disjunction between the familiar and what is depicted in the work, and the reader is again asked to compare the two. In both cases, the moral instils a deeper awareness of what is good.

In addition to defining and propagandizing Romanticism, Zhukovskii helped influence the subsequent history of Russian literary criticism. His interest in Western European critics and thinkers, evidenced throughout his career, was reflected in many of his successors, who relied heavily on an initial reading of foreign works before turning to practical criticism. Zhukovskii's early statements regarding the paucity of good literature in Russia would crop up again in the writings of critics from the next generations, many of whom were to assert that until at least the second or third decade of the nineteenth century Russian writers did not live up to their calling. Furthermore, Zhukovskii was one of the first in Russia to describe literature as passing through a series of stages, to see it in terms of a natural and logical development. Perhaps most important was his insistence that literature serve a purpose. His call for a moral in literature was to be echoed some years later by Lev Tolstoi, while the liberal and then the radical thinkers, to whom Zhukovskii's politics and religion were alien, remained no less insistent that literature had both the power and the responsibility to better humanity.

Zhukovskii's most lasting effects, though, came through his direct influence on his contemporaries. His significance for the poets who were to form the Pushkin Pleiad, including Pushkin himself, is indisputable. Through his essays and his poetry he helped assure the triumph of Romanticism in Russian literature and its turn away from many of the models that it had been following into the beginning of the nineteenth century. After the mid-1820s, when he was no longer so prominent a figure, his friendships with leading writers assured that his voice would still be heard by many of those who counted. Even in the late 1840s, when he was living abroad, he was to exert an influence on Nikolai Gogol'; thus, his essay "O poete i

sovremennom ego znachenii" (1848; on the poet and his contemporary significance) is in fact a letter to Gogol', in which Zhukovskii offers an excursus on the significance of the word in literature. Along the way, he summarizes many of his basic views on art, although with a more obvious religious overlay than earlier. Thus in many ways it was Zhukovskii the man, as much as Zhukovskii the critic or the poet, who has proved to be of greatest importance for Russian literature.

## Principal criticism

"O *Puteshestvii v Malorossiiu*," 1803
"Pis'mo iz uezda k izdateliu," 1808
"Pisatel' v obshchestve," 1808
"O basne i basniakh Krylova," 1809
"O kritike," 1809
"O satire i satirakh Kantemira," 1810
"O poezii drevnikh i novykh," 1811
"Rafaelova 'Madonna,'" 1824
"O poete i sovremennom ego znachenii," 1848
"O melankholii v zhizni i v poezii," 1856 (written 1846)
"Ob iziashchnom iskusstve," 1857 (written late 1840s)
"Konspekt po istorii russkoi literatury," 1948 (written 1826–1827)
"Obzor russkoi literatury za 1823 god," 1978 (written 1824)
"Konspekt po istorii literatury i kritiki," 1985 (written 1805–1811)

## Other major works and literary forms

Vasilii Zhukovskii's fame during his lifetime resulted primarily from his endeavors as a poet and translator. He saw no firm line between poetic translation and original verse; sometimes he would follow his source more closely, sometimes less so. Thus he originally "Russianized" Gottfried Bürger's "Lenore" (1773) as "Liudmila" (1808) and soon after wrote "Svetlana" (between 1808 and 1812), a treatment of the same theme but a quite different work. In 1831 Zhukovskii retranslated Bürger's work as "Lenora." Whatever the approach, he regarded all of his poetic translations as original creations and frequently did not indicate whether a given poem was his own or derived from a foreign source. For that matter, many of his translations are in fact superior to the originals as works of poetry and to this day are regarded as part of the Russian tradition. His thirty-nine ballads, for the most part based on German and English sources, may well be his greatest literary achievement. His poetic heritage, however, includes numerous elegies, epistles, and songs, many of them original works. His best lyrics have enjoyed enduring popularity – for example, "Vecher" (1806; evening), "Pevets vo stane russkikh voinov" (1812; "A Bard in the Camp of the Russian Warriors," 1823), the song beginning "Minuvshikh dnei ocharovane" (1818; "Enchantment of Bygone Days," 1962), and "More" (1822; "The Sea," 1916). Between 1831 and 1845 Zhukovskii also wrote several fairy tales in verse (three of them adaptations of foreign tales and three based on Russian sources). Except for an early Romantic tale,

"Mar'ina roshcha" (1809; Mariia's grove), Zhukovskii avoided literary prose; indeed, as in the case of Friedrich de La Motte-Fouqué's *Undine* (1811), which Zhukovskii translated in 1837, he would occasionally translate a prose work by means of verse. During the latter part of his career he turned his attention to epic poetry, retranslating portions of several Eastern epics from German and also, with the aid of a Russian crib, producing a fine translation of Homer's *Odyssey* (1842–1849).

POETRY
*Stikhotvoreniia*, 1815–1816, 1824

TRANSLATIONS
"Sel'skoe kladbishche," 1802 (of Thomas Gray's poem *Elegy Written in a Country Churchyard*)
*Orleanskaia deva*, 1817–1821 (of Friedrich Schiller's play *Die Jungfrau von Orleans*)
*Shil'onskii plennik*, 1822 (of Lord Byron's poem *The Prisoner of Chillon*)
*Undina*, 1837 (of Friedrich de La Motte-Fouqué's poem *Undine*)
*Odyssey*, 1842–1849 (of Homer's poem)

MISCELLANEOUS
*Polnoe sobranie sochinenii*, 1902 (12 volumes)
*Sobranie sochinenii v chetyrekh tomakh*, 1959–1960 (4 volumes)

## Further reading

Brown, William Edward. *A History of Russian Literature of the Romantic Period*. Vol. 1, 1986.
Katz, Michael R. *The Literary Ballad in Early Nineteenth-century Russian Literature*, 1976.
Leighton, Lauren G. *Russian Romanticism: Two Essays*, 1975.
Merserau, John, Jr. *Russian Romantic Fiction*, 1983.
Oblensky, Dmitri. *The Penguin Book of Russian Verse*, 1962.
Pein, Annette. *Schiller and Zhukovsky: Aesthetic Theory through Translation*, 1991.
Semenko, Irina M. *Vasily Zhukovsky*, 1976.
Zenkovsky, V. V. *A History of Russian Philosophy*. Vol. 1, 1953.

BARRY P. SCHERR

*See also* Pushkin; Romanticism

# Émile Zola

French novelist, writer, and critic

**Born:** Paris, France; April 2, 1840
**Died:** Paris, France; September 29, 1902

## Biography

Although Émile Zola was born in Paris, the first seventeen years of his life were spent in Provence, and his experiences there shaped much of his creed and literary philosophy. His father, a civil engineer of Greek and Italian ancestry, died suddenly when Zola was seven; increasing poverty became a fact of the life he shared with his mother and her aging parents, moving to progressively poorer lodgings as Mme Zola pursued an unsuccessful lawsuit to compensate for the death of her husband and the canal project he had planned. Undisciplined, Zola spent much of his time exploring the countryside around Aix-en-Provence with his close friend Paul Cézanne; his education was still incomplete when the family moved to Paris in 1858. In the two years that followed Zola was both homesick and ill with typhoid fever; twice he failed the *baccalauréat* examination that would qualify him for a professional career. He was innocent and hopeful but overwhelmed by doubt, because of incidents of his youth and the brutal reality of the life he faced. In 1862 Zola became a naturalized citizen and, with the help of a family friend, an apprentice to Hachette, the publishing house. His literary ambitions grew as he came to know publishers and authors; he had early stories published and turned to journalism to supplement his income. After four years Zola could outline the course of his life; by the end of the 1860s, with an engineer's precision, he had completed the blueprint for his life's work.

In 1870 Zola married Gabrielle-Eléonore-Alexandrine Meley, with whom he built a fortune and a brilliant home at Médan. In the spring of 1888 he began an affair with Jeanne-Sophie-Adèle Rozerot, with whom he had two children. If the fruitfulness of this relationship was not part of his plan, it certainly was in keeping with the creed he now advanced in his writing; so too, his involvement in the Dreyfus affair, which brought the indictment that compelled him to leave France and, later, the honor for which his remains were reinterred in the Panthéon.

## Influence

Although Zola won fame and made his fortune as a novelist, he was at heart a journalist – a commentator on his time. His primary contribution to literary theory can be seen from this perspective. As the creator and leading exponent of naturalism, Zola established a school of thought that synthesized much of the nineteenth century. Profoundly influenced by Honoré de Balzac, Gustave Flaubert, Hippolyte Taine, and the brothers Edmond and Jules de Goncourt, he in turn exerted extraordinary influence on those who followed him and formed his "school" – Guy de Maupassant, Joris-Karl Huysmans, Octave Mirbeau, Édouard Rod, and many others. American novelists Sinclair Lewis, Frank Norris, and Theodore Dreiser reflected Zola's influence, as did the Anglo-Irish writer George Moore. Ivan Turgenev, affected by both the theory and substance of Zola's work, introduced it to Russia. In Scandinavia, August Strindberg wrote for the theater from Zola's critical model; in France, André Antoine founded the Théâtre Libre; and in Germany, Otto Brahm helped to build the Freie Bühne from the clear vision of a new dramatic art Zola provided. The psychological novel and, in time, Symbolism were successors of Zola's naturalistic theories, as surely as Romanticism and realism were antecedents.

Inextricably tied to Zola's naturalism was his concept of the "experimental" novel. Here, too, his ideas were precise, borrowed liberally from Dr. Claude Bernard's 1865 study of experimental medicine and Dr. Prosper Lucas' 1850 treatise on natural heredity. These works provided a Darwinian backdrop for Zola's microscopic study of the human animal and ensured both the public outrage and popular success of his work and that which followed it.

## Analysis

"Nothing he ever wrote has damaged Zola's reputation more than the six volumes of critical theory and comment, published in a block between 1880 and 1882." F. W. J. Hemmings, preeminent Zola scholar and biographer, has cogent reason to lament the reprinting of criticism that underscored Zola's literary career, but this collection of articles – from four different periodicals, written over a period of seven years – has provided a useful academic tool. From these volumes comes the outline Zola drew for his work and, in his reactions to others of his time, a sense of the traditions that motivated it.

The point of Zola's journalistic fervor was not to be missed. His criticism was replete with repeated catchwords and slogans, the most popular of which was "naturalism" and, with it, the explanation that art is a part of nature seen through a temperament – terms he continued to use long after they served his primary purpose. As early as 1866, in a review of Taine's essays, Zola began to graft the idea of naturalism onto a literary context. He considered that his friends who were men of letters were also naturalists – Flaubert, Turgenev, Edmond de Goncourt, and Alphonse Daudet – as well as a number of younger disciples he labeled the "Médan group." Certainly with Goncourt and Daudet he shared that sturdy pessimism that came to be a hallmark of his theory.

Zola's early criticism reflected the growth of the French novel along increasingly "clinical" lines, in Balzac's *La Comédie humaine* (1829–1848; *The Comedy of Human Life*, 1885–1893, 1896, also as *The Human Comedy*) and Flaubert's *Madame Bovary* (1857; English translation, 1886), for example, and he determined to go further and take the "human animal" into the laboratory. Although his first three novels were marked with the Romanticism and idealism of his youth, the two that followed – *Thérèse Raquin* and *Madeleine Férat* – he considered to be "autopsies." Characters, he decided, should be conceived according to the laws of heredity and psychophysiology. Observed with scientific scrutiny, they could then be placed in environments that accurately reflect time and space. Their conduct would be a natural result.

Unfortunately, the temperament through which Zola made his microscopic examinations was darkened by the cruel facts of his youth. Naturalism came to be associated with a mechanistic and materialistic vision of brutalized humanity; carnal love, blind instinct, nightmares, hypocrisy,

corruption, and death – these were Zola's literary focus by the time his collected criticism was reprinted. The fatalism and bitterness that stalked his fiction began to be reflected in his theoretical work; he broke frequently with his literary forebears. Unlike Flaubert, Zola argued, the naturalistic writer should not be artistically selective; he must remove any subjective judgment from his creative product. Imposing his own shaded perspective on the contemporary environment, he advocated the "simple formula of naturalism," a perception of the "bourgeois of our time, a grotesque, unsightly man" with all of his "passions and feelings."

Zola's discussion of the experimental novel was similarly "scientific" in its approach. (It was saved from being a plagiarized version of Bernard's study of medicine only by the claims that it was intended to be just such an adaptation.) In it Zola viewed the novel like a test tube where chemical compounds were brought together to react. He saw the novelist's work as that of reporting "the facts just as he has observed them," and then instituting experiments "to show that the succession of facts" are those "required by the determinism of the thing studied." The naturalistic novelist, in other words, was the passive instrument of science, allowing truth to emerge from the confluence of heredity and environment. Zola used the term "experimental" much as he came to use "naturalistic" – to refer to literature that emerged from a "century of science." He pressed into service scientific treatises that explained his own earlier novels.

In *The Experimental Novel*, he offered a simple argument for a literary application of the scientific method: "Experimentation," as he defined it, was the process of drawing conclusions from observation. His critical concern was with the accuracy of the observation and the strict determinism of the outcome. For his own part, he filled thousands of pages with research for his novels; this first step of the process he called "the constitution of a portfolio." For each work he read volumes of background material and spent weeks visiting locales; he composed "sketches" of character description and conversation, exactly as he perceived them, and built general, then specific, "plans." For each of his voluminous novels, the mass of research data was from two to three times as long as the finished product. As his work on the Rougon-Macquart cycle progressed, his doctrine continued to adapt and reflect the technique he was developing.

Much of Zola's later criticism was preoccupied with a "formula." His passion for modernity continued to drive him to refine something new, "revolutionary," that would sweep away the traces of the past and ensure his own lasting fame. Scholars speculate on a number of causes – his childlessness, the deaths in 1880 of both his mother and Flaubert, a concern for his own mortality, perhaps all of these – but in any case, from that time, in his creative work he began to advance a creed that glorified productive labor and human fecundity. In his theoretical work he tried to define an aesthetic plan.

As Hemmings suggests, in Zola's critical volumes of the period from 1880 to 1882 "it is possible to disentangle a set of literary criteria," but many of these are "quite irreconcilable with those that guided" him in the years before. At twenty, unemployed and living in the filth and poverty of the Latin Quarter with the help of Cézanne, Zola reached the heights of Romantic inspiration. He remarked to his friend, "you are painting pictures that are denuded of poetry! I have never been able to make anything out of this realism." With hunger and squalor his Rousseauism waned. His passion for the sweeping panoramas of Balzac was replaced by respect for the craftsmanship and organization of Flaubert and the tormented style of the Goncourts. Within ten years he published five novels and sheaves of journalistic criticism, trying to evolve a "system," a "philosophy" that would represent his time. In the manuscript plans for *The Fortune of the Rougons*, he explained his dilemma: "There is no great novelist whose work does not contain a philosophy . . . I must search for the law to which all things must be submitted . . . [to] become the greatest novelist of my country and time," and then reasoned with himself for a solution: "I want a system that is entirely new . . . taken from the movement of ideas of my own time . . . . What is it? . . . We believe in Science." He turned to science "to explain life" and announced that he was now "a positivist, an evolutionist, a materialist; my system is heredity." Finally, he concluded, "I am going to picture the physiological man . . . . It will be a new art, . . . my own art. *I, I alone will be Naturalism.*"

Within another ten years Zola had completed the first half of the Rougon-Macquart novel cycle. In his criticism he left no doubt that realism was the superior literary system even as he sought to go beyond it. The fire of his journalistic rhetoric grew to the point that he equated the future of the French Republic with naturalism and its methods. His concern for "formula" came to mean something infinitely more precise than it had in the past. He broke entirely with the traditions of Balzac, Hugo, and Flaubert, completely removing imagination and the personality of a writer from his work. In this last stage of his critical development Zola went beyond literature in his flourish of "*méthodes scientifiques.*" Hemmings equates this "furious theorizing" with the same drive that compelled Zola to defend the Impressionist painters in 1866 and, later, to defend Alfred Dreyfus in 1898, as an "impulse to proclaim a 'truth' of which he was the sole repository." Whatever its cause, it assured that Zola was noticed, and if it cost him friendships, it ensured his enduring reputation.

In the collected criticism of *Naturalism in the Theater*, Zola provided a synthesis of much of his work and an important vehicle for assessing his continuing influence on literary theory. When he spoke of a need for "revolution," it was based on a clear assessment of the current situation.

The weaknesses of Romantic drama, he explained, made it no less a part of the "logical succession" of formulas that need to supplant one another: "Romantic drama was a first step in the direction of the naturalistic drama," with its "impulse towards real life." Although he found Romanticism to be an outdated formula, its back-to-nature movement made possible an association of the arts with the pulsing growth of interest in the natural sciences. Naturalism thus emerged "from the very entrails of humanity."

Zola repeated earlier discussions of writers and subjects, reasserting his interest in the "daily life" of the epoch, advocating the "substitution of physiological man for metaphysical man." The unique value of the work is clear at this point, as Zola transcended his earlier rhetoric with precise recommendations. He suggested details of costuming, stage design, and language and ushered in a new era of theater history, one that was free for a time from the conventions of artifice. In Russia – where his ideas had previously won favor as proletarian tract – his criticism affected the work of Konstantin Stanislavsky and the acting experiments of the Moscow Art Theater, and it was reflected in the plays of Anton Chekhov. In England and Germany as well as in France, Zola fueled a revolution in the theater. Although in time his dramatic theories, like his evolution of the experimental novel, came to be flattened by excesses, it was not before his impact had been felt in much of Western art.

Naturalist "theology" was also fulfilled in Zola's later years. In his novels, venal man, who had fallen from the provincial garden, was redeemed by the birth of a child and hope; here and in his criticism Zola preached a social gospel and a search for truth. His impassioned defense of Dreyfus – known to the world as "J'accuse," the title given it by Georges Clemenceau – attacked the military establishment and the President of France in the cause of common justice. As recorded in *La Vérité en marche* (the march of truth), this was no ordinary journalistic brawl. Zola violated his previous tenets with political protest, became the champion of Dreyfus, and ensured international recognition beyond any he had won with his writing.

Zola was at last a revolutionary hero. Public outrage was louder and more violent than it had been before; in time, the honor he earned was greater. His legacy was complete. The controversial and passionate man of thought had risked everything for his principles, and won.

Finally, Hemmings' lamentation of Zola's criticism is merely subjective musing. Over a century after the work was complete critics continue to find meaning in it, not only to support Zola's aesthetic contributions and reassert the significance of science and art, but to vindicate his political zeal. In a final assessment, Zola's maturing criticism can be seen as a manifesto to the twentieth century.

It was not naturalist vulgarity Zola advocated so much as truth. Ironically, vulgar images and prose were used to level accusations of indecency and immorality against him. The contradictions continued. For sixty years the best of critics viewed *Vérité* as a symptom of Zola's "faltering imaginative powers"; only recently have others begun to reassess its value, perceive the allegory and myth in its structure, and, more significantly, the point it attempted to make. An increase in attention to Zola's work, prompted perhaps by the centennial commemoration of the Dreyfus Affair, continues to open perspectives on his work. These will continue to be colored by new editions and Zola's "belief in the unstoppable power of truth," as it rages against xenophobia, miscarriages of justice, religious fundamentalism and self-serving lies.

## Principal criticism

*Mes haines*, 1866 (*My Hatreds*)
Preface to *Thérèse Raquin*, 1867 (English translation, 1881)
Preface to *La Fortune des Rougon*, 1871 (*The Rougon-Macquart Family*, 1879, also as *The Fortune of the Rougons*, 1879)
*Le Roman expérimental*, 1880 (*The Experimental Novel*, 1893)
*Les Romanciers naturalistes*, 1881
*Documents littéraires*, 1881
*Le Naturalisme au théâtre*, 1881 (*Naturalism on the Stage*, 1894, best known as *Naturalism in the Theater*, 1968)
*Nos auteurs dramatiques*, 1881
*Une Campagne*, 1882
*Nouvelle Campagne*, 1897
*La Vérité en marche*, 1901

## Other major works and literary forms

Émile Zola published significant work in every literary genre during his lifetime. He remains one of the most prolific and controversial French novelists of the nineteenth century, primarily on the merits of his twenty-volume fictional history of the Rougon-Macquart family, *Les Rougon-Macquart* (1871–1893; *The Rougon-Macquart Novels*, 1885–1907). Five earlier novels and six later ones substantiate scholar Henri Barbusse's claim that whatever else Zola may have been in his life, he was first a novelist.

His novels necessitated Zola's theories as well as demonstrated them; his short stories provided a testing ground for both. Like his novels, the short fiction works were initially published in periodicals and intended as a source of revenue, as well as being a means of exploring character, setting, and plot development. His works in the theater – including full-length plays, drafts of his novels in dramatic form, and at least six opera librettos – were "experiments" that had essentially the same value for him. Zola was also a lyric poet, essayist, art historian, and political advocate. Only a small portion of his journal articles have been published in collections, and these, as well as his letters, provide a significant body of work for further scholarship.

NOVELS
*La Confession de Claude*, 1865 (*Claude's Confession*, 1882)
*Le Vœu d'une morte*, 1866 (*A Dead Woman's Wish*, 1902)

*Les Mystères de Marseille*, 1867 (*The Flower Girls of Marseilles*, 1888, also as *The Mysteries of Marseilles*, 1895)
*Thérèse Raquin*, 1867 (English translation, 1881)
*Madeleine Férat*, 1868 (English translation, 1880)
*Les Rougon-Macquart*, 1871–1893 (*The Rougon-Macquart Novels*, 1885–1907), includes *La Fortune des Rougon* (*The Rougon-Macquart Family*, also as *The Fortune of the Rougons*), *La Curée* (*The Rush for the Spoil*, also as *The Kill*), *Le Ventre de Paris* (*The Markets of Paris*, also as *Savage Paris*), *La Conquête de Plassans* (*The Conquest of Plassans*, also as *A Priest in the House*), *La Faute de l'abbé Mouret* (*Albine: Or, The Abbé's Temptation*, also as *Abbé Mouret's Transgression*), *Son Excellence Eugène Rougon* (*Clorinda: Or, The Rise and Reign of His Excellency Eugène Rougon*, also as *His Excellency*), *L'Assommoir* (English translation, also as *The Dram-Shop*), *Une Page d'amour* (*Hélène: A Love Episode*, also as *A Love Affair*), *Nana* (English translation), *Pot-Bouille* (*Piping Hot*), *Au bonheur des dames* (*The Bonheur des Dames*, also as *The Ladies' Paradise*), *La Joie de vivre* (*Life's Joys*, also as *Zest for Life*), *Germinal* (English translation), *L'œuvre* (*His Masterpiece*, also as *The Masterpiece*), *La Terre* (*The Soil*, also as *Earth*), *Le Rêve* (*The Dream*), *La Bête humaine* (*Human Brutes*, also as *The Human Beast*), *L'Argent* (*Money*), *La Débâcle* (*The Downfall*), and *Le Docteur Pascal* (*Doctor Pascal*)
*Les Trois Villes*, 1894–1898 (*The Three Cities*, 1894–1898), includes *Lourdes* (English translation), *Rome* (English translation), and *Paris* (English translation)
*Les Quatre Évangiles*, 1899–1903 (English translation, 1900–1903), includes *Fécondité* (*Fruitfulness*), *Travail* (*Work*), and *Vérité* (*Truth*)

SHORT FICTION
*Contes à Ninon*, 1864 (*Stories for Ninon*, 1895)
*Esquisses parisiennes*, 1866
*Nouveaux Contes à Ninon*, 1874
*Le Capitaine Burle*, 1882 (*A Soldier's Honor and Other Stories*, 1888)
*Naïs Micoulin*, 1884
*Contes et nouvelles*, 1928
*Madame Sourdis*, 1929

PLAYS
*Thérèse Raquin*, 1873 (English translation, 1956)
*Les Héritiers Rabourdin*, 1874 (*The Heirs of Rabourdin*, 1893)
*Le Bouton de rose*, 1878

NONFICTION
"*The Experimental Novel*" *and Other Essays*, 1894 (includes *The Experimental Novel* and *Naturalism in the Theater*)

MISCELLANEOUS
*Œuvres complètes*, 1966–1968 (15 volumes)
*The Dreyfus Affair: "J'accuse" and Other Writings*, 1998 (Alain Pages, editor, and Eleanor Levieux, translator)

## Further reading

Baguley, David, ed. *Critical Essays on Émile Zola*, 1986.
——. *Zola et les genres*, 1993.
Barbusse, Henri. *Zola*, 1933.
Berg, William J. *The Visual Novel: Émile Zola and the Art of His Times*, 1992.
Brown, Frederick. *Zola: A Life*, 1995.

——. *Émile Zola: Critical Essays*, 1999.
Carter, Lawson A. *Zola and the Theater*, 1999.
Hemmings, F. W. J. *Émile Zola*, 1966.
Josephson, Matthew. *Zola and His Time*, 1928.
King, Graham. *Garden of Zola*, 1978.
Lethbridge, Robert, and Terry Keefe, eds. *Zola and the Craft of Fiction*, 1990.
Richardson, Joanna. *Zola*, 1978.

Schom, Alan. *A Biography of Émile Zola*, 1987.
Vizetelly, Ernest Alfred. *Émile Zola, Novelist and Reformer*, 1904.

JOAN COREY SEMONELLA

*See also* Baudelaire; Bourget; Brunetière; Continental Theory; Gautier; Taine

# TITLE INDEX

The titles listed are those which appear in the "Principal criticism" section of the essays on individuals and the name following is that of the critic whose work it is. For full details of the works mentioned refer to Principal criticism.

"À la grande nuit: Ou, Le Bluff surréaliste" ("In the Dark: Or, The Surrealist Bluff") (Artaud)

À l'école de la phénoménologie (Ricœur)

À Propos of Lady Chatterley's Lover (expansion of My Skirmish with Jolly Roger) (Lawrence)

A. S. Pushkin o literature (Pushkin)

ABC of Reading (Pound)

Abinger Harvest (Forster)

The Abolition of Man: Or, Reflections on Education with Special Reference to the Teaching of English to the Upper Forms of Schools (Lewis)

An Abyss Deep Enough: Letters of Heinrich von Kleist, with a Selection of Essays and Anecdotes (Kleist)

The Accursed Share see La Part maudite (Bataille)

The Achievement of T. S. Eliot: An Essay on the Nature of Poetry (Matthiessen)

The Act of Reading: A Theory of Aesthetic Response see Der Akt des Lesens: Theorie ästhetischer Wirkung

"L'Activité du Bureau de Recherches surréalistes" ("The Activity of the Surrealist Research Bureau") (Artaud)

Acts of Literature (Derek Attridge, editor) (Derrida)

Ad me ipsum (Hofmannsthal)

Additional Prose: A Bibliography on America, Proprioception, and Other Notes and Essays (Olson)

An Address Delivered Before the Senior Class in Divinity College, Cambridge (better known as Divinity School Address) (Emerson)

Addresses Delivered at the Library of Congress (Mann)

Adel des Geistes: Sechzehn Versuche zum Problem der Humanität (Essays of Three Decades) (Mann)

Adiciones a las obras del muy ilustre y reverendísimo padre maestro D. Fr. Benito Jerónimo Feijóo y Montenegro (Feijóo Y Montenegro)

"Adieu" in Philosophy Today (Derrida)

Adrastea (Herder)

The Advancement of Learning see The Two Bookes of Francis Bacon of the Proficience and Advancement of Learning, Divine and Humane (enlarged as De Augmentis Scientiarum)

The Aeneis (dedication) (Dryden)

Aesthetic as Science of Expression and General Linguistic see Estetica come scienza dell'espressione e linguistica generale

Aesthetic Experience and Literary Hermeneutics see Ästhetische Erfahrung und literarische Hermeneutik (Jauss)

"Aesthetic Illusion: Prescriptions for the Suicide of Poetry" (Soyinka)

"Aesthetic Relationshiop of Art to Reality" see Esteticheskie otnosheniia iskusstva k deistvitel'nosti

Aesthetic Theory see Ästhetisch Theorie

Aesthetical and Philosophical Essays (Schiller)

The Aesthetics of Thomas Aquinas see Il problema estetico in San Tommaso

Aetia (passages in) (Callimachus)

The African Image revised (Mphahlele)

"African Writers: A New Union" (Soyinka)

After Babel: Aspects of Language and Translation (Steiner)

After Bakhtin: Essays on Fiction and Criticism (Lodge)

After Strange Gods: A Primer of Modern Heresy (Eliot)

After the Fact: Two Countries, Four Decades, One Anthropologist (Geertz)

After the Last Sky: Palestinian Lives (Said)

"An Afterword by Tolstoy to Chekhov's Story "Darling'" see "Posleslovie k rasskazu Chekhova "Dushechka'"

Against Interpretation and Other Essays (Sontag)

Against the Academics see Contra academicos

Against the Grain: Essays (Eagleton)

The Age of Shakespeare (Swinburne)

The Age of Television (Esslin)

Agésilas (Préface) (Corneille)

Agon: Towards a Theory of Revisionism (Bloom)

La agonía del Cristianismo in French, in Spanish (The Agony of Christianity) (Unamuno y Jugo)

The Agony of Christianity see La agonía del Cristianismo

Agricultural Involution, the Processes of Ecological Change in Indonesia (Geertz)

"Ai Poeti Del Secolo XIX" ("Thoughts Addressed to the Poets of the Nineteenth Century") (Mazzini)

AIDS and its Metaphors (Sontag)

Der Akt des Lesens: Theorie ästhetischer Wirkung (The Act of Reading: A Theory of Aesthetic Response) (Iser)

Die Aktualität des Schönen (The Relevance of the Beautiful) (Gadamer)

Albion and Albanius (preface) (Dryden)

Alexander Pope: A Critical Anthology (Bateson)

Alexandre le Grand (Alexander the Great) prefaces (Racine)

"Alienation Effects in Chinese Acting" see "Verfremdungseffekte in der chinesis-chen Schauspielkunst"

"Alison's History of the French Revolution" (Mill)

"All Alone, Little Lady?" (Tompkins)

All for Love (preface) (Dryden)

Allegories of Reading (de Man)

The Allegory of Love: A Study in Medieval Tradition (Lewis)

# SUBJECT INDEX

A page number in **bold** indicates the main entry for an individual or a topic; the names of people who are the subject of individual essays are also in **bold**.

# NOTES ON CONTRIBUTORS

Every attempt was made to find original contributors and include change of address or affiliation. For those whom the publishers were not able to locate the last known affiliation is given.

**Adams, Michael.** Associate professor, City University of New York Graduate Center Library. Contributor of articles to reference works, including *Dictionary of Literary Biography* and *Masterplots II*, and journals. Assistant editor, *Henry James Review* (1982–1984); editor, *Urban Library Journal* (1998–2000); assistant editor, *Biblio–Notes* (1999–2000), editor from 2000. **Essays:** Lubbock; Wilson.

**Adcock, Patrick.** Professor of English, Henderson State University, Arkadelphia, Arkansas. Author of *Mugsbottom and Me: A Study in Anglo-Arkansas Relations* (1993) and of articles in *Evelyn Waugh Newsletter* and *PAPA*. Former associate editor and editor of *Academic Forum* (1987–1991) and editor and coeditor of *Proscenium* (1973–1998). **Essays:** Byron; Comedy; Hazlitt; Lewis; Plot.

**Adler, Jacob H.** Purdue University, West Lafayette, Indiana. Author of *The Reach of art: A Study in the Prosody of Pope* (1964). **Essay:** Pope.

**Aldridge, A. Owen.** Professor emeritus, University of Illinois at Urbana-Champaign. Author of *Man of Reason: The Life of Thomas Paine* (1959), *Benjamin Franklin: Philosopher and Man* (1965), *Thomas Paine's American Ideology* (1984), *The Reemergence of World Literature* (1986), *The Dragon and the Eagle: The Presence of China in the American Enlightenment* (1993). Founder and editor of *Comparative Literature Studies* (1963–1986), currently editor emeritus. Editorial board member, *Modern Age*, *Eighteenth Century Theory and Interpretation*. **Essays:** Shaftesbury; Voltaire; Wellek.

**Andreas, James R., Sr.** Professor of English and director, Clemson Shakespeare Festival, Clemson University, South Carolina. Editor, *The Upstart Crow: A Shakespeare Journal*; former member of University Board of Editors, University of Tennessee Press (1983–1985). Author of several articles on Chaucer, Shakespeare, and Voltaire. **Essays:** Biblical Criticism: Allegory and Typology; Classic; Dialogic Criticism; Geoffrey of Vinsauf; Rhetoric.

**Angyal, Andrew J.** Professor of English, Elon College, North Carolina. Author of *Loren Eiseley* (1983), *Lewis Thomas* (1989), *Wendell Berry* (1995), and articles in *The Robert Frost Review* and *The Literature of Science*. **Essay:** Cowley.

**Araujo, Norman.** Associate professor of French, Boston College, Massachusetts. Author of *In Search of Eden: Lamartine's Symbols of Despair and Deliverance* (1976) and articles in *French Review*, *Forum for Modern Language Studies*, and *Dictionary of Literary Biography* (1992). **Essays:** Brunetière; Gautier; Taine.

**Archer, Raymond M.** Indiana University at Kokomo. **Essays:** Butor; Sartre.

**Archer, Stanley.** Former professor of English, Texas A&M University, College Station, Texas. Author of *Richard Hooker* (1983) and *Somerset Maugham: A Study of the Short Fiction* (1993) and numerous articles, reviews, and essays on seventeenth-century British literature and the Renaissance. Former contributing editor, *Seventeenth Century News*. **Essays:** Dryden; Rymer.

**Ashby, Stephen M.** Assistant professor of philosophy and religious studies, Ball State University, Muncie, Illinois. Author of *Acts of the Apostles* (forthcoming) and articles on European and Russian literature and philosophy; coeditor (with Kent Johnson) of *Third Wave: The New Russian Poetry* (1992). **Essays:** Ricoeur; Williams.

**Ashley, Bob.** Principal lecturer, Nottingham Trent University, Nottingham, England. Editor of *The Study of Popular Fiction* (1989) and *Reading Popular Narrative* (1997). **Essays:** Popular Literature: Approaches to Genre; Popular Literature: Critical Reception.

**Aspinwall, Dorothy B.** Emeritus professor of European languages, University of Hawaii at Manoa. Author of *French Poems in English Verse, 1850–1970* (1973), *Modern Verse Translations from French* (1981), and *Choice Poems of Ilarie Voronca* (1988); translator of *The Riddle* (1963) by Albert Camus, *The Portico of the Mystery of the Second Virtue* (1970) by Charles Péguy, and *Récitatif* by Jacques Réda (*The Party is Over*, 1983). **Essay:** Breton.

**Aubrey, Bryan.** Independent scholar. Author of *Watchmen of Eternity: Blake's Debt to Jacob Boehme* (1986) and *English Romantic Poetry: An Annotated Bibliography* (1991). **Essays:** Arnold; Shelley; Wordsworth.

**Aubrey, James R.** Professor of English, Metropolitan State College of Denver, Colorado. Author of *John Fowles: A Reference Companion* (1991) and articles in *Studies in Eighteenth Century Culture* (1994) and other books, also in *Studies in Philology*, *CLIO*, and other journals. Founding editor of *War, Literature and the Arts* (1987–1989). **Essay:** Edmund Burke.

**Bahr, Ehrhard.** University of California at Los Angeles. **Essays:** Bodmer; Lukács.

**Baird, James.** Associate professor of English, University of North Texas, Denton. Author of articles in *Contemporary Philosophy*, *Mid-America Folklore*, and *Jeffers Studies*. Associate editor, *Popular Culture Review* (from 1989). **Essays:** Abrams; Matthiessen.

**Baker, Joseph O.** Brigham Young University, Provo, Utah. Author of *The Ethics of Life and Death with Heinrich von Kleist* (1992) and *Im Nonnengarten: An Anthology of German women's Writings 1850–1907*, edited with Michelle Scott (1997). **Essay:** Kleist.

**Baker, Simon C.** Lecturer in English, University of Wales, Swansea. Contributor to *Scottish Fiction 1945 to Present* (1997), *Appropriations and Impositions* (1997), and *Dylan Thomas: New Casebook* (1999); editor of *Rhys Davies: Print of a Hare's Foot* (1998) and *Ron Berry: Collected Short Stories* (1999). **Essay:** Novel: Theory and Criticism.

**Banks, Thomas.** Ohio Northern University, Ada. **Essay:** Soyinka.

**Barnard, Laura Stone.** University of Wisconsin-Milwaukee. **Essays:** Horace; Plato.

**Barry, Peter.** Senior lecturer in English, University of Wales, Aberystwyth. Author of *Beginning Theory: An Introduction to Literary and Cultural Theory* (1995). Editor of *Issues in Contemporary Critical Theory* (1987) and *New British Poetries* (1993, with Robert Hampson); joint editor of *English* (from 1988). **Essays:** Bateson; Criticism; Perloff.

**Barry, Thomas F.** Associate professor of English and comparative literature, Himeji Dokkyo University, Himeji City, Japan. Author of numerous articles and book reviews on modern literature. **Essays:** Aestheticism; Existentialism; Hegel; Metaphor; Metonymy; Modernism; Moi; Nietzsche; Realism; Schiller; Schopenhauer; Translation.

**Beebee, Thomas O.** Associate professor of comparative literature and German, Pennsylvania State University, University Park. Author of *Clarissa on the Continent* (1990), *The Ideology of Genre* (1994), *Epistolary Fiction in Europe* (1999), and articles in *Revue de littérature comparée*, *Prooftexts*, and

*The Comparatist*. Associate editor of *Comparative Literature Studies* (from 1993). **Essays:** Lacan; Lévi-Strauss.

**Benton, Richard P.** Professor emeritus, Trinity College, Hartford, Connecticut. Author of numerous articles and book reviews on Chinese, Japanese, and Western literature. Editor of *New Approaches to Poe: A Symposium* (1970) and *Poe as Literary Cosmologer – Studies on Eureka, A Symposium* (1975). Editorial board member, *Poe Studies* and *University of Mississippi Studies in English*. **Essays:** Bashō; Chinese Literary Theory; Japanese Literary Theory; Lu Chi.

**Bilhartz, Terry D.** Professor of history, Sam Houston State University, Huntsville, Texas. Author of *Francis Asbury's America: An Album of Early American Methodism* (1984), *Urban Religion and the Second Great Awakening: Church and Society in Early National Baltimore* (1986), and *Constructing the American Past: A Source Book of a People's History* (1991, with Randy Roberts and Elliot Gorn). Editor (with Paul Ruffin) of *Images of Texas in the Nation* (1991). **Essay:** American Literary Theory to 1900.

**Bily, Cynthia A.** Instructor of English and the Honors Program, Adrian College, Michigan. Author of articles on literary subjects for reference books and electronic media. **Essay:** Fulgentius.

**Bishop, Carol.** Indiana University Southeast. **Essays:** Pirandello; Staël.

**Bishop, Paul.** Senior lecturer, University of Glasgow, Scotland. Author of *The Dionysian Self: C. G. Jung's Reception of Friedrich Nietzsche* (1995), *The World of Stoical Discourse in Goethe's Novel "Die Wahlverwandtschaften"* (1999), and several articles on German literature and thought. Editor of *Jung in Contexts: A Reader* (1999). **Essays:** Erotic; Frankfurt School; Sensibility; Sincerity; Symbolism.

**Branam, Harold.** University of Pennsylvania. **Essay:** Gates.

**Brand, Gerhard.** Professor emeritus of comparative literature, California State University at Los Angeles. Author of articles in *Dictionary of Literary Themes and Motifs* (1988) and reviews and essays on literary texts and topics. **Essay:** Poulet.

**Brett, Michael.** Graduate student, University College London, England. Author of several articles on Anglo-American literature and film; contributor to first Sheffield International Conference (1999) on the films of David Lynch. **Essays:** Knights; McGann; Watt.

**Brink, Jean R.** Professor of English and comparative literature, Arizona State University, Tempe. Author of *Michael Drayton* (1990) and articles on sixteenth-century English literature. **Essays:** Racine; Scaliger.

**Briziarelli, Susan.** Associate professor of Italian, University of San Diego, California. Author of *Enrico Annibale Butti: The Case of the Minor Writer* (1994) and articles on Grazia Deledda, Leonardo Sciascia, and Elsa Morante. **Essay:** Verga.

**Broadus, J. R.** Independent scholar. **Essays:** Belinskii; Dostoevskii; Lunacharskii; Mann; Marinetti; Pushkin.

**Büsges, Michael J.** Assistant professor of German and comparative literature, The Catholic University of America, Washington, D.C. Author of several articles on German literature and book reviews. **Essays:** Gadamer; Herder.

**Buttigieg, Joseph A.** Professor of English, University of Notre Dame, Indiana. Author of *Antonio Gramsci's Triad* (1987), *Criticism Without Boundaries* (1987), currently editing and translating *The Prison Notebooks of Antonio Gramsci*. **Essay:** Gramsci.

**Cachey, Theodore J., Jr.** Associate professor of Romance languages and literatures and director of the Devers program in Dante studies, University of Notre Dame, Indiana. Author of *Le isole fortunate: appunti di storia letteraria italiana* (1995) and articles on Italian literary history and historiography of the Middle Ages and Renaissance; editor of *Dante Now: Current Trends in Dante Studies* (1995). Book review editor, *Speculum: A Journal of Medieval Studies* (1999–2002); editorial board member, *Italica* and *Italian Studies* (1997–2001). **Essays:** Bembo; Dante; De Sanctis; Trissino.

**Campion, Edmund J.** Professor of French, University of Tennessee, Knoxville. Author of *Montaigne, Rabelais, and Marot as Readers of Erasmus* (1995) and articles in *Cahiers du dix-septième* and *The European Legacy*. Editorial board member, *Classical and Modern Literature* (from 1994). **Essays:** Du Bellay; Erasmus; Humanism, Renaissance; La Bruyère; Malherbe; Mimesis.

**Carravetta, Peter.** Queens College, City University of New York. Author of *Prefaces to the Diaphora: Rhetorics, Allegory, and the Interpretation of Postmodernity* (1991) and *The Sun and Other Things* (1998). **Essay:** Anceschi.

**Childs, Margaret H.** Associate professor of Japanese, University of Kansas. Author of *Rethinking Sorrow: Revelatory Tales of Late Medieval Japan* (1991); literature editor for *The Journal of the Association of Teachers of Japanese* (from 1997). **Essay:** Yoshimoto.

**Chowenhill, Dennis C.** Instructor, Chabot College, Hayward, California. Author of several articles on modern international literature. **Essay:** Keats.

**Cofresi, Lina L.** North Carolina State University, Raleigh. **Essays:** Feijóo y Montenegro; Gilbert and Gubar.

**Condon, William.** University of Michigan, Ann Arbor. **Essay:** Ruskin.

**Conlon, John J.** Adjunct associate professor of English and lecturer in theater, University of Massachusetts at Boston. Author of *Walter Pater and the French Tradition* (1982) and several articles on nineteenth and twentieth-century literature. Editorial board member, *English Literature in Transition, 1880–1920*. **Essays:** Literary Theory in the Age of Victoria; Pater; Symons.

**Core, Deborah.** Professor of English, Eastern Kentucky University, Richmond. Author of several articles on twentieth-century literature. **Essay:** Woolf.

**Cory, Mark E.** Professor of German, University of Arkansas, Fayetteville. Author of *The Emergence of an Acoustical Art Form: An Analysis of the German Experimental Hörspiel of the 1960's* (1974) and several articles on German literature and radio drama; editor of *Politics in German Literature* (1998, with Beth Bjorklund). **Essay:** George.

**Davis, Liselotte M.** Senior lector German, Yale University, New Haven, Connecticut. Author of *Gelebte und geschriebene Geschichte* (1998) and articles on German literature. **Essay:** Eichendorff.

**Day, Frank.** Professor of English, Clemson University, South Carolina. Author of *Sir William Empson: An Annotated Bibliography* (1984) and *A Reader's Guide to Arthur Koestler* (1987). Editor, Twayne's United States Authors Series and *The South Carolina Review*. **Essays:** Callimachus; Empson; Hume; Wilde.

**Denton, Robert F.** Northern Illinois University. **Essay:** Hartman.

**Deredita, John F.** Independent scholar. **Essay:** Borges.

**Draper, R. P.** Emeritus professor of English, University of Aberdeen, Scotland. Author of publications on D. H. Lawrence, Thomas Hardy, and George Eliot; editor of *Tragedy: Developments in Criticism* (1980) and *The Epic: Developments in Criticism* (1990); contributor to several books and scholarly publications. **Essays:** Auden; Pastoral.

**Edwards, Bruce L.** Associate dean, College of Arts and Sciences, Bowling Green, Ohio. Author of *The Taste of the Pineapple: Essays on C. S. Lewis as reader, critic and imaginative writer* (1988). **Essay:** Booth.

**Ellis, Robert P.** Professor emeritus, Worcester State College. Author of articles in *America*, *New England Galaxy*, and *Commonwealth Review*. **Essays:** Montaigne; Sidney.

**Erskine, Thomas L.** Professor of English, Salisbury State University, Salisbury, Maryland. Coeditor (with Gerald Barrett) of *From Fiction to Film: Ambrose Bierce's "An Occurrence at Owl Creek Bridge"* (1973), *From Fiction to Film: D. H. Lawrence's "Rocking-Horse Winner"* (1974), and *From Fiction to Film: Conrad Aiken's "Silent Snow, Secret Snow"* (1975); coeditor (with Connie Richards) of *Charlotte Perkins Gilman's "The Yellow Wall-Paper"* (1993) and Rutgers University Press' American Women Short Story Writers series. Founding editor of *Literature/Film Quarterly* (1972); currently associate editor. **Essays:** Babbitt; Wimsatt.

**Estow, Clara.** Professor of Hispanic studies, University of Massachusetts at Boston. Author of *Pedro the Cruel of Castile, 1350–1369* (1995) and numerous articles and reviews on Spanish literature and history. **Essays:** Luzán y Claramunt; Menéndez y Pelayo; Unamuno y Jugo.

**Falk, Thomas H.** Associate professor emeritus, Michigan State University, East Lansing. Author of *Elias Canetti: A Critical Study* (1993) and articles on Austrian and German literature. Coeditor (with Julia S. Falk) of *Otto Jesperson: Critical Assessments* (forthcoming). **Essays:** Benjamin; Brecht.

**Forman, Robert J.** Professor of English, St. John's University, New York. Author of *Classical Greek and Roman Drama: An Introduction and Annotated Bibliography* (1989) and *Augustine and the Making of a Christian Literature* (1995). **Essays:** Saint Augustine; Classical Greek and Roman Literary Theory.

**Frail, Robert J.** Associate professor of English and French, Centenary College, Hackettstown, New Jersey. Author of several articles on European literature; contributor to *Great Lives from History* and *European Writers*. **Essays:** Gourmont; August Wilhelm Schlegel.

**Frank, Margot.** Randolph-Macon Woman's College. **Essay:** Eikhenbaum.

**Garnier, Camille.** Indiana University Southeast. Author of *Women Playwrights in England, Ireland and Scotland 1600–1823*, with David D. Mann and Susan Garland Mann (1996). **Essay:** La Harpe.

**Gosselin Nakeeb, Diana.** Adjunct associate professor of Russian, Pace University, New York City. Author of articles on Russian, American, French, and German literature and Baltic and Slavic linguistics. **Essays:** Kant; Kristeva; Proust.

**Green, William H.** Chattahouchee Valley State College. Author of *The Hobbit: A Journey into Maturity* (1995). **Essay:** Tolkien.

**Griffin, William.** Appalachian State University, Boone, North Carolina. **Essay:** Hugo.

**Gullace, Giovanni.** Formerly of the State University of New York at Binghamton. **Essay:** Croce.

**Habib, M. A. R.** Associate professor of English, Rutgers University, Camden, New Jersey. Author of *The Dissident Voice: Poems of N. M. Rashed: Translated from the Urdu* (1991), *The Early T. S. Eliot and Western Philosophy* (1999), and numerous articles in journals. **Essays:** American Literary Theory: Twentieth Century; British Literary Theory: Twentieth Century; Eagleton.

**Ham, Jennifer.** Associate professor of German, University of Wisconsin-Green Bay. Author of *Ideological Structures in Frank Wedekind's Dramatic Works* (forthcoming) and several articles and reviews on modern German culture and literature; editor (with Matthew Senior) of *Animal Acts: Configuring the Human in Western History* (1997). **Essays:** Jauss; Reception Theory.

**Haney, William S., II.** Professor, Eastern Mediterranean University, Gazimagusa, Turkey. Author of *Literary Theory and Sanskrit Poetics* (1993) and articles on Eastern philosophy and literature and deconstruction. **Essays:** Anandavardhana; Bharata; Bhartrhari; Derrida; Indian Literary Theory; Jameson; Phenomenological Criticism.

**Harvey, Stella.** Associate research fellow, Department of French, Birkbeck College, University of London, England. Author of *Myth and the Sacred in the Poetry of Guillevic* (1997) and articles on French literature. **Essay:** Bataille.

**Henderson, Greig E.** Associate professor, University of Toronto, Ontario, Canada. Author of *Kenneth Burke: Literature and Language as Symbolic Action* (1998) and articles on Burke, semiotics, and contemporary criticism; editor (with David Cratis Williams) of *Unending Conversations: Essays by and about Kenneth Burke* (forthcoming). **Essay:** Kenneth Burke.

**Homer, Sean.** Lecturer in psychoanalytic studies and tutor in English literature, University of Sheffield, England. Author of *Fredric Jameson: Marxism, Hermeneutics, Postmodernism* (1998) and articles on literature and psychoanalysis. Coeditor (with Douglas Kellner) of *Fredric Jameson: A Critical Reader* (forthcoming). Editorial board member, *PS: The Journal of the Universities Association for Psychoanalytic Studies* (from 1998). **Essays:** Althusser; Psychoanalytic Criticism.

**Horn, Pierre L.** Professor of French, Wright State University, Dayton, Ohio. Author of numerous books on nineteenth and twentieth-century French literature, including Marguerite Yourcenar, Honoré de Balzac, Stendhal, Gustave Flaubert, André Gide, and Elie Wiesel. Editor, *Handbook of French Popular Culture* (1991); series editor for *Greenwood's Guides to the World's Cinema*. **Essay:** Stendhal.

**Houlahan, Mark.** Lecturer in English, University of Waikato, Hamilton, New Zealand. Author of articles on Thomas Hobbes, John Milton, William Shakespeare, and early modern literature. **Essays:** Geertz; Grotesque; New Historicism.

**Hughes, Rowland.** Postgraduate researcher and teacher of English literature, University College London, England. Author of several articles on popular fiction and film; contributor to *The Devil Himself: Aspects of Villainy in Fiction and Film* (forthcoming). Regular contributor to conferences on crime fiction and American literature. **Essays:** Culler; Geneva School; Heath.

**Hussey, Barbara L.** Professor of English, Eastern Kentucky University, Richmond. Author of several articles on twentieth-century Latin American fiction and women's and African American autobiography. **Essay:** Barthes.

**Jayaswal, Shakuntala.** University of New Haven, West Haven, Connecticut. **Essay:** Girard.

**Kildahl, Karen A.** Professor of English, South Dakota State University, Brookings. Contributor of articles on modern literature to *Magill's Literary Annual* and other publications. **Essays:** Forster; Said; Steiner.

**Kleine-Ahlbrandt, Wm. Laird.** Associate professor, Purdue University, West Lafayette, Indiana. Author of *The Policy of Simmering: A Study of British Policy during the Spanish Civil War, 1936–1939* (1962), *La Tosca: The Drama Behind the Opera* (1990), *Europe Since 1945: From Conflict to Community* (1993), *Twentieth-Century Europe* (1993), and *The Burden of Victory: France, Britain and the Enforcement of the Versailles Peace, 1919–1925* (1995). **Essays:** Baudelaire; Rousseau.

**Klett, Dwight A.** Educator, Newark Public Schools, Newark, New Jersey. Author of *Tieck-Rezeption: Das Bild Ludwig Tiecks in den deutschen Literaturgeschichten des 19. Jahrhunderts* (1989), *Ludwig Tieck: An Annotated Guide to Research* (1993), and articles and book reviews on German literature. **Essays:** Holz; Friedrich Schlegel.

**Kopacz, Paula.** English Department, Eastern Kentucky University, Richmond. **Essays:** Fuller; Poe.

**Kraszewski, Charles S.** Assistant professor, King's College, Pennsylvania. Author of *The Romantic Hero and Contemporary Anti-hero in Polish and Czech Literature* (1997) and *Four Translation Strategies Determined by the Particular Needs of the Receptor* (1998). Translator of *Jan Kochanowski's Dismissal of the Grecian Envoys* (1994), *Hanging Bridges: Selected Poetry of Rio Preisner* (1996), and *The Gospel of Matthew, with Patristic Commentaries* (1999). **Essays:** Gombrowicz; Graves; Hopkins; Ingarden.

**Kuhlmann, Elizabeth.** Graduate student, Indiana University, Bloomington. Contributor to *Reader's Guide to Literature in English* (1996). Editorial assistant, *Genders* (1994–1995). **Essay:** Deconstruction.

**LaHay, William.** Independent scholar. **Essay:** Van Wyck Brooks.

**Landauer, Carl.** University of California at Berkeley. **Essay:** Auerbach.

**Leonard, Philip.** Lecturer in English, Nottingham Trent University, Nottingham, England. Author of articles on literary and critical theory, recently focusing on poststructuralist and postcolonial theory. Editor of *Trajectories of Mysticism in Theory and Literature* (1999). **Essays:** Irigaray; Spivak.

**Lewis, Leon.** Professor of English, Appalachian State University, Boone, North Carolina. Author of *Henry Miller: The Major Writings* (1986) and articles on twentieth-century British and American writers. **Essay:** Olson.

**Liladhar, Janine.** Associate lecturer, Open University, and researcher, Sheffield Hallam University, England. Author of articles on feminist and racial issues in literature. **Essay:** Feminist Criticism.

**Livingston, James.** Professor, English Department, Northern Michigan University, Marquette. Author of articles on American, British, and European literature. Assistant editor, *Paddler* (from 1997), *Ben Jonson Journal* (from 1995),

*Passages North* (1984–1988), and *South Shore* (1981–1984). **Essays:** Coleridge; Hulme.

**Luckett, Perry D.** United States Air Force Academy. **Essay:** Edmund Burke.

**Lutz, R. C.** Professor, University of the Pacific, California. Author of articles on European literature. **Essay:** Bacon.

**Lyle, A. W.** Freelance lecturer in English literature, University of Sheffield, England. Author of articles on Renaissance literature and modern critical theory, and an edition of the poems of Edmund Spenser in Japanese (1983). **Essays:** Narratology; Parody; Reader-Response Criticism.

**Lyons, John D.** Commonwealth professor of French, University of Virginia, Charlottesville. Author of *Exemplum* (1989) and *The Tragedy of Origins* (1996). Member of advisory board, *Philosophy and Literature* (from 1992); former editor of *Academe: Bulletin of the American Association of University Professors* (1994–1998). **Essay:** Fénelon.

**McCulloh, Mark R.** Professor of German, Davidson College, North Carolina. Author of articles in *Germano-Slavica*, *Modern Language Notes*, *Euphorion*, *Choice*, and other publications. **Essays:** Curtius; Heidegger; Hermeneutics; Postmodernism; Solger.

**McDonald, William.** Lecturer in English, Baylor University, Waco, Texas. **Essay:** J. Hillis Miller.

**McLean, Hugh.** Professor emeritus, Slavic Department, University of California at Berkeley. Author of *Nikolai Leskov: The Man and His Art* (1977) and articles on Lev Tolstoi and Simon Karlinsky; editor, *In the Shade of the Giant: Essays on Tolstoy* (1989). **Essays:** Jakobson; Tolstoi.

**McLeod, John.** Lecturer in English, University of Leeds, England. Author of *Beginning Postcolonialism* (forthcoming) and several articles and reviews on postcolonialism and postmodernism. **Essay:** Black Literary Theory and Criticism.

**MacPherson, Kerrie L.** University of Hong Kong. **Essay:** Hu Shih.

**Manheim, Martha.** Emeritus professor, Siena Heights College, Adrian, Michigan. Author of articles on Russian drama and literature; editor of *Soviet Theaters: 1917–1941* (as Martha Bradshaw, 1954). Press editor, *Slavic and East European Review* (1950–1953). **Essays:** Siniavskii; Veselovskii.

**Marks, Emerson R.** Professor emeritus, University of Massachusetts at Boston. Author of *Relativist and Absolutist* (1955), *Poetics of Reason* (1968), *Literary Criticism of Sainte-Beuve* (1971), *Coleridge on the Language of Verse* (1981), and *Taming the Chaos: English Poetic Diction Since the Renaissance* (1998). Editor, *Criticism: A Quarterly for Literature and the Arts* (1963–1968). **Essay:** Sainte-Beuve.

**Marks, John.** Reader in French studies, Nottingham Trent University, Nottingham, England. Author of *Gilles Deleuze: Vitalism and Multiplicity* (1998) and articles on contemporary French literature and culture. **Essay:** Deleuze.

**Marsh, Joss.** Associate professor of English and Victorian studies, Indiana University, Bloomington. Author of *Word Crimes: Blasphemy, Culture, and Literature in 19th-Century England* (1998) and articles on Charles Dickens, nineteenth-century literature and film, film design, F. Scott Fitzgerald and cinema, and nineteenth-century spectacle. **Essays:** Swinburne; Symonds.

**Martin, Bronwen.** Associate research fellow, Birkbeck College, London University, England. Coauthor (with M. Renouard and D. Ditner) of *Living English: Thinking, Speaking, Writing* (1993), coauthor (with Felizitas Ringham) of *Cassell Dictionary of Semiotics* (1999); author of *The Search for Gold: Space and Meaning in J. M. G. Le Clézio* (1995), *Semiotics and Storytelling* (1997). **Essays:** French Literary Theory: Twentieth Century; Greimas; Semiotics.

**Matson, JoAnne Liebman.** Associate vice chancellor of academic affairs, University of Arkansas at Little Rock. **Essays:** Fish; Iser.

**May, Charles E.** Professor of English, California State University, Long Beach. Author of *Short Story Theories* (1976), *Modern European Short Story* (1989), *Edgar Allan Poe: A Study of Short Fiction* (1991), *The Reality of Artifice: A Study of the Short Story* (1994), and *The New Short Story Theories* (1994). **Essays:** Holland; Modern Literary Theory; Tate.

**Mazzeno, Laurence W.** President, Alvernia College, Reading, Pennsylvania. Author of *The Victorian Novel* (1989), *Herman Wouk* (1994), *Victorian Poetry* (1995), *The British Novel* (1997), and *Matthew Arnold's Critics* (1999). Editor of *Nineteenth Century Prose* (1986–1989); consulting editor of *Masterplots: Revised Edition* (1996, twelve volumes). **Essay:** James.

**Mellors, Anthony.** Independent writer; former lecturer at Oxford, Durham, and Manchester universities, England. Author/editor of *Stephen Crane, The Red Badge of Courage and Other Stories* (1998), and author of articles on modern literature. General editor, *Fragmente: A Journal of Contemporary Poetics*; issue editor, *Angelaki: Journal of the Theoretical Humanities*. **Essay:** Ricks.

**Mills, Sara.** Professor, Sheffield Hallam University, Sheffield, England. Coauthor (with Pearce Spaull and Millard Routledge) of *Feminist Readings/Feminists Reading* (1989), author of *Discourses of Difference – Women's Travel Writing* (1991), *Feminist Stylistics* (1996), and *Discourse* (1997); editor of *Language and Gender* (1994) and *Gendering the Reader* (1994). **Essays:** Discourse; Linguistics and Literary Studies.

**Mittleman, Leslie B.** California State University, Long Beach. **Essay:** Lawrence.

**Morace, Robert A.** Professor of English, Daemen College, New York. Coauthor (with Kathryn Van Spanckeren) of *John Gardner: Critical Perspectives* (1982), author of *John Gardner: An Annotated Secondary Bibliography* (1984) and *The Dialogic Novels of Malcolm Bradbury and David Lodge* (1989). Consulting editor, *Critique: Studies in Contemporary Fiction* (from 1981). **Essays:** Bradbury; Eco; Gardner; Kermode; Lodge.

**Morris, Francis J.** Professor of English, St. Joseph's University, Philadelphia, Pennsylvania; former English department chair (1979–1991). Author of articles on Emily Dickinson, Geoffrey Chaucer, C. S. Lewis, Owen Barfield, and others. **Essay:** Barfield.

**Murray, Simone.** Tutor, University College London, England. Author of articles on feminist publishing. **Essays:** Intertextuality; Kolodny.

**Nelles, William.** Associate professor, University of Massachusetts at Dartmouth. Author of *Frameworks: Narrative Levels and Embedded Narrative* (1997) and articles on European literature and narrative fiction. Associate editor, *Style* (from 1991); editor of *Chaucerian Poetics* (special issue of *Style*, 1997). Editorial board member, *Interdisciplinary Literary Studies: A Journal of Criticism and Theory*. **Essays:** Genette; Lyric; Medieval Literary Theory; Style.

**Newton, K. M.** Professor of English, University of Dundee, Scotland. Author of *George Eliot: Romantic Humanist* (1981), *In Defence of Literary Interpretation: Theory and Practice* (1986), *Twentieth-Century Literary Theory: A Reader* (1988, 1997), *Interpreting the Text* (1990), and *Theory into Practice: A Reader in Modern Literary Criticism* (1992). Joint editor of *English* (from 1995). **Essays:** Marxist Theory and Criticism; New Criticism; New Pragmatism.

**Norris, Emma Coburn.** Former professor of English, university archivist, and director of university honors, Troy State University, Troy, Alabama. Author of articles on European and American literature for reference works. **Essay:** Young.

**Nosco, Peter.** Professor, University of Southern California, Los Angeles. Author of *Remembering Paradise: Nativism and Nostalgia in 18th-Century Japan* (1990); editor of *Confucianism and Tokugawa Culture* (1986). **Essays:** Kamo No Mabuchi; Motoori Norinaga.

**O'Brien, George.** Georgetown University. **Essay:** Shaw

**Otten, Robert M.** Dean, Center for Comprehensive Learning, Marymount University, Sterling, Virginia. Author of *Joseph Addison* (1982), *English Literature* (1997), and *English Composition* (1998). **Essays:** Johnson; Neoclassical Literary Theory.

**Paddock, Lisa.** Independent scholar and freelance writer. Author of *Facts About the Supreme Court* (1996) and contributor to *The Encyclopedia of American Biography* (1996) and *American National Biography* (1998). Editor of *Courtroom Drama* (1998). **Essay:** Sontag.

**Pagan, Nicholas O.** Associate professor and chair, Department of English Literature and Humanities, Eastern Mediterranean University, Gazimagusa, Turkey. Author of *Rethinking Literary Biography: A Postmodern Approach to Tennessee Williams* (1993) and articles on Roland Barthes and postmodernism. **Essay:** Film Criticism.

**Paradowski, Robert J.** Professor, Rochester Institute of Technology, New York. Author of numerous articles on literature, science, and history. **Essays:** Bergson; Saint Isidore of Seville; Ong; Plotinus; Schelling.

**Patterson, David.** Oklahoma State University. **Essay:** Bakhtin.

**Pemberton, William E.** Professor of history, University of Wisconsin-La Crosse. Author of *Bureaucratic Politics: Executive Reorganization during the Truman Administration* (1979), *Harry S. Truman: Fair Dealer and Cold Warrior* (1989), *George Bush* (1993), and *Exit with Honor: The Life and Presidency of Ronald Reagan* (1997). **Essay:** Blackmur.

**Peters, George F.** Professor and chair, Michigan State University, East Lansing. Author of articles on German literature. Translator of *Adelheit von Rastenberg* by E. Thon (1997). Editor, *Die Unterrichtspraxis/Using German* (1988–1994). **Essay:** Heine.

**Picard, Christopher L.** San Juan College, Farmington, New Mexico. **Essay:** De Man.

**Piepke, Susan L.** Professor of foreign languages, Bridgewater College, Virginia. Author of articles on Franz Grillparzer, Wilhelm Raabe, Friedrich Duerrenmatt, and Sor Juana Inés de la Cruz. Translator (with introduction) of *Women and Their Vocation: A 19th-Century View* (1999), by Luise Buechner. **Essay:** Grillparzer.

**Pietropaolo, Domenico.** Michaels College, University of Toronto, Canada. Author of *Dante Studies in the Age of Vico* (1989), *The Science of Buffoonery: Theory and History of the Commedia del'arte* (1989) and *Pirandello and the Modern Theatre* (1992). **Essay:** Vico.

**Pillai, Johann.** Eastern Mediterranean University, Gazimagusa, Turkey. **Essays:** Surrealism; Yale School.

**Pinnell, Lorraina.** Assistant professor, Eastern Mediterranean University, Gazimagusa, Turkey. Author of articles and reviews on modern and postcolonial literature. Assistant editor, *Hawaii Pacific Review* (1987–1989). **Essays:** Author; Postcolonial Literature and Theory.

**Pinson, Ernest R.** Former professor at William Carey College, Hattiesburg, Mississippi. **Essays:** Hofmannsthal; Praz.

**Pounds, Wayne.** California Polytechnic State University, San Luis Obispo. **Essay:** Tsurayuki.

**Powell, David.** Western New Mexico University. **Essay:** Chaucer.

**Prinsky, Norman.** Associate professor of English, Augusta State University, Georgia. Contributor of articles for reference works, notably *Masterplots II*, the American fiction, short stories, British and Commonwealth fiction, world fiction, and nonfiction series, and poetry supplement. **Essay:** Gascoigne.

**Pullen, Charles.** Professor emeritus, Queen's University, Kingston, Ontario, Canada. Author of *The Life and Times of Arthur Malone, The Last of the Tribunes* (1994) and numerous articles on Jonathan Swift, Lord Chesterfield, eighteenth-century aesthetics, modern British novels and drama, and Samuel Beckett. **Essays:** Addison; Joseph Warton and Thomas Warton.

**Pursglove, Glyn.** Senior lecturer in English, University of Wales, Swansea. Author of *Francis Warner's Poetry* (1988); editor of *Henry Reynolds: Tasso's "Aminta" and Other Poems* (1991), *I poeti ferraresi nel Rinascimento inglese* (1992), *The Poems of Henry Hughes* (1997), and *Peter Russell: From The Apocalypse of Quintilius* (1997). Reviews editor, *Acumen* (from 1989); editor, *Swansea Review* (from 1991). **Essays:** Archetypal Criticism; Bowers; Bradley; Davie; Saintsbury.

**Quinn, Michael L.** University of Iowa. **Essays:** Bentley; Krieger; Tynianov.

**Ramraj, Victor J.** Professor, University of Calgary, Alberta, Canada. Author of *Mordecai Richler* (1983), *A Concert of Voices: An Anthology of Word Writing in English* (1995), and numerous articles on postmodern and postcolonial literatures. Editor, *ARIEL: A Review of International English Literature* (from 1989). **Essays:** Leavis; Mphahlele.

**Rankin, Thomas.** Independent scholar. **Essay:** Renaissance and Restoration Literary Theory.

**Rhein, Tina M.** Arizona State University. **Essay:** Racine

**Ringham, Felizitas.** Associate research fellow, Birkbeck College, University of London, England. Coauthor (with Bronwen Martin) of *Cassell Dictionary of Semiotics* (1999) and articles in journals including *Lectures, Seventeenth Century French Studies, La Chouette,* and *French Studies.* **Essay:** Propp.

**Robinson, Vicki K.** State University of New York, A&T College at Farmingdale. **Essays:** Alan of Lille; Macrobius; Quintilian.

**Rollyson, Carl.** Professor of English, Baruch College, City University of New York. Author of *Marilyn Monroe: A Life of the Actress* (1986), *Lillian Hellman: Her Legend and Her Legacy* (1988), *Nothing Ever Happens to the Brave: The Story of Martha Gellhorn* (1990), *The Lives of Norman Mailer: A Biography* (1991), *Biography: An Annotated Bibliography* (1992), and *Rebecca West: A Life* (1996). **Essays:** Edel; Sontag; Trilling.

**Rosefeldt, Paul.** Professor of English, Delgado Community College, New Orleans, Los Angeles. Author of *The Absent Father in Modern Drama* (1995) and articles on George S. Kaufman, Caryl Churchill, and Wendy Wasserstein, among others. **Essays:** Artaud; Castelvetro.

**Rosenblum, Joseph.** Independent scholar. Author of *Shakespeare: An Annotated Bibliography* (1992) and *Thomas Holcroft* (1995); editor of *The Plays of Thomas Holcroft* (1980), *American Book Collectors and Bibliographers* (1994, 1997), *Shakespeare* (1998), and *Prince of Forgers* (1998). **Essay:** Romanticism.

**Samara, Donya.** Assistant professor of English, Denison University, Granville, Ohio. Author of articles on Gothic criticisms and the Sublime. **Essays:** Cultural Criticism; Sublime.

**Scerbo, Nancy.** Independent scholar. **Essay:** Baretti.

**Scherr, Barry P.** Professor of Russian, Dartmouth College, Hanover, New Hampshire. Author of *Russian Poetry: Meter, Rhythm, and Rhyme* (1986) and *Maxim Gorky* (1988); editor (with Dean S. Worth) of *Russian Verse Theory: Proceedings of the 1987 Conference at UCLA* (1989), (with Lev Loseff) *A Sense of Place: Tsarskoe Selo and Its Poets* (1993), and (with Simon Karlinsky and James L. Rice) *O RUS!: Studia litteraria slavica in honorem Hugh McLean* (1995); editor and translator (with Andrew Barratt) of *Maksim Gorky: Selected Letters* (1997). **Essays:** Chernyshevskii; Dobroliubov; Pisarev; Prague School; Russian Formalism; Structuralism; Zhukovskii.

**Schuler, Marilyn V.** Emeritus member, Department of Classical and Modern Languages, University of Louisville, Kentucky. **Essay:** Corneille.

**Schultz, Steven P.** Independent scholar. **Essay:** Pound.

**Scott, Alison M.** Head librarian, Popular Culture Library, Bowling Green State University, Ohio. Author of articles on popular culture and literature; contributor to *The Dictionary of Literary Biography* (1994, 1997). Editor (with Christopher D. Geist) of *The Writing on the Cloud: American Culture Confronts the Atomic Bomb* (1997). Librarian of the Year, Romance Writers of America (1999). **Essay:** Tompkins.

**Semonella, Joan Corey.** Professor, Riverside Community College, Riverside, California. **Essays:** Jarrell; Zola.

**Senior, Matt.** Associate professor of French, University of Minnesota at Morris. Author of *In the Grip of Minos: Confessional Discourse in Dante, Corneille, and Racine* (1994); contributor and editor of *Animal Acts: Configuring the Human in Western History* (1997). **Essay:** Baudrillard.

**Sharkey, Rodney.** Assistant professor, Eastern Mediterranean University, Gazimagusa, Turkey. Author of articles on Irish literature and film. Researcher and editor (with Anthony Cronin) of *Samuel Beckett: The Last Modernist* (1996). Editor, *EMU Prospectus.* **Essays:** Absurd; Gothic; Yeats.

**Sharma, Govind Narain.** Acadia University. Author of *Literature and Commitment* (1988). **Essay:** Ngugi wa Thiong'o.

**Sheldon, Richard.** Chair, Russian Department, Dartmouth College, Hanover, New Hampshire. Author of articles on Viktor Shklovskii; translator and editor of books by Shklovskii: *A Sentimental Journey* (1970), *Zoo, or Letters Not About Love* (1971), and *Third Factory* (1977); translator of articles by Shklovskii. Compiler of *Viktor Shklovsky: An International Bibliography of Works by and about Him* (1977). **Essay:** Shklovskii.

**Sherberg, Michael.** Associate professor of Italian, Washington University, St. Louis, Missouri. Author of critical edition of Torquato Tasso's *Rinaldo* (1990), *Rinaldo: Character and Intertext in Ariosto and Tasso* (1993), and articles on Italian literature. Editor, *Boccaccio Newsletter* (from 1987). **Essay:** Giraldi Cinthio.

**Sherwood, John C.** University of Oregon. Author of *R. S. Crane: An Annotated Bibliography* (1983). **Essays:** Crane; Jonson; Minturno.

**Short, Bryan C.** Professor of English, Northern Arizona University, Flagstaff. Author of *Cast by Means of Figures: Herman Melville's Rhetorical Development* (1992) and articles on Harold Bloom, Emily Dickinson, Herman Melville, American literature, and rhetoric. Editorial board member, *Leviathan.* **Essays:** Bloom; Kames.

**Shuman, R. Baird.** Professor emeritus of English, University of Illinois at Urbana-Champaign. Author of *Robert E. Sherwood* (1964), *William Inge* (1989, revised edition), *Classroom Encounters: Problems, Case Studies, Solutions* (1989), and *Georgia O'Keeffe* (1993). Editor of *Nine Black Poets* (1968), *A Galaxy of Black Writing* (1970), and *American Drama: 1918–1960* (1992). Executive editor, *The Clearing House* (from 1974). **Essays:** Continental Theory; Ransom; Read; Richards.

**Sienkewicz, Thomas J.** Minnie Billings Capron Professor of Classics, Monmouth College, Illinois. Author (with Vivien Edwards) of *Oral Cultures Past and Present: Rappin' and Homer* (1990), *The Classical Epic: An Annotated Bibliography* (1991), *World Mythology: An Annotated Guide to Collections and Anthologies* (1996), and *Theories of Myth: An Annotated Guide* (1997). Editor of *World Dictionary of Foreign Expressions* (1999), by Gabriel Adeleye and Kofi Acquah-Dadzie. **Essays:** Aristotle; Drama: Theory and Criticism; Epic.

**Singer, Armand E.** Professor emeritus of Romance languages, West Virginia University, Morgantown. Author of *Paul Bourget* (1976), *The Don Juan Theme: Annotated Bibliography of Versions, Uses, Analogues, and Adaptations* (1993), and numerous articles, reviews, and essays on literary, pedagogical, travel, and philatelic subjects; editor of *Essays on the Literature of Mountaineering* (1982). Editor-in-chief, *West Virginia University Philological Papers* (1948–1950 and from 1952). **Essays:** Boileau-Despréaux; Bourget; Diderot.

**Slomski, Genevieve.** Independent scholar. **Essays:** Adorno; Lotman.

**Smelstor, Marjorie.** Professor of English, University of Wisconsin-Eau Claire. Author (with Joyce Steward) of *Writing in the Social Sciences* (1984) and numerous articles on American and world literature. Coeditor, *English in Texas* (1981–1985). **Essay:** Emerson.

**Smith, David P.** Instructor, Naval War College, Newport, Rhode Island. Author of introduction to *Mister Roberts* (1992), articles on classical and modern literature, and reviews of military and political publications. **Essays:** Dionysius of Halicarnassus; Lucian.

**Smith, Gilbert.** Professor of Spanish, North Carolina State University, Raleigh. Author of *Juan Pablo Forner* (1976) and articles on nineteenth and twentieth-century Spanish literature. **Essay:** Alonso.

**Snipes, Katherine.** Professor emeritus, Eastern Washington University, Cheney, Washington. Author of *Robert Graves* (1979) and *Robert Penn Warren* (1983); contributor to *American Women Writers* (1979, 1980, 1981), *Critical Survey of Short Fiction* (1981), and *Critical Survey of Long Fiction* (1983). **Essay:** Warren.

**Stephens, Joanna.** Research associate, Harvard University, Cambridge, Massachusetts. Author of articles on Italo Calvino and European literature. **Essays:** Calvino; Esslin.

**Stevenson, David R.** Former associate professor of history, University of Nebraska at Kearney. Author of articles on David Hume and Giambattista Vico, and numerous other works on modern intellectual history. **Essays:** Gundolf; Maritain.

**Stuewe, Paul.** Independent scholar. **Essays:** Belyi; Foucault; Mallarmé; Saussure.

**Sullivan, James.** Professor of English, California State University at Los Angeles. **Essays:** Eliot; Frye; Winters.

**Sutherland, John.** Lord Northcliffe Professor of Modern English Literature at University College London. Author of *The Longman Companion to Victorian Fiction* (1988), *The Life of Walter Scott* (1995), *Is Heathcliff a Murderer? Great Puzzles in Nineteenth-Century Literature* (1996), and *Can Jane Eyre Be Happy? More Puzzles in Classic Fiction*, (1997). Professor Sutherland is Consultant to the *Encyclopedia*.

**Swanson, Roy Arthur.** Professor of classics and comparative literature, University of Wisconsin-Milwaukee. Author of *Odi et Amo: The Complete Poetry of Catullus* (1959), *Pindar's Odes* (1974), *The Love Songs of the Carmina Burana* (1987, with E. D. Blodgett), *Pär Lagerkvist: Five Early Works* (1989), and *Pär Lagerkvist: Literary Art and Pictorial Art* (1991, with Everett Ellestad). Editor, *The Minnesota Review* (1964–1967) and *The Classical Journal* (1968–1973). **Essay:** Longinus.

**Thompson, Spurgeon.** Ph.D. candidate, University of Notre Dame, Indiana. Author of articles on Irish literature and culture. Cultural studies advisory editor, *New Hibernia Review*; coeditor, "Irish Cultural Studies," *Cultural Studies*. **Essays:** Canon; Ellmann.

**Tilby, Michael.** Fellow of Selwyn College, Cambridge University, England. Author of *André Gide: "Les Faux-Monnayeurs"* (1981) and numerous articles and essays on nineteenth- and twentieth-century French literature. Editor of *Beyond the Nouveau Roman* (1990) and *Balzac* (1995). **Essay:** Valéry.

**Udris, Jan.** Lecturer in film studies, Middlesex University, London, England. **Essay:** Ideology.

**Udris, Raynalle.** Senior lecturer, Middlesex University, London, England. Author of *Welcome Unreason* (1993), coauthor (with Renée Birks and Charmian O'Neil) of *Français en Gros Plans* (1998); coeditor (with C. Rodgers) of *Duras lectures plurielles* (1998). Editor for bulletins of the Duras Society (UK) (from 1997); contributing editor for the UK for the American review *Women in French Studies* (from 1999). **Essay:** Cixous.

**Usilton, Larry W.** Former chair of department of history, University of North Carolina at Wilmington; secretary-treasurer for the Carolinas Symposium on British Studies from 1998. Author of *The Kings of Medieval England, c. 560–1485* (1996). **Essays:** Boccaccio; Cicero.

**Van Cleve, John.** Associate professor, Augsburg College, Minneapolis, Minnesota. Author of *Harlequin Besieged: The Reception of Comedy in Germany during the Early Enlightenment* (1980), *The Merchant in German Literature of the Enlightenment* (1986), *The Problem of Wealth in the Literature of Luther's Germany* (1991), *Sebastian Brant's "The Ship of Fools" in Critical Perspective* (1993), and *Remarks on the Needed Reform of German Studies in the United States* (1993, with A. Leslie Wilson). **Essay:** Goethe.

**Van Devender, George W.** Professor emeritus of English, Hardin-Simmons University, Abilene, Texas. Author of articles on William Faulkner, Aristotle, Alexandre Dumas, Mikhail Bakhtin, and others. Assistant bibliographer, *Christianity and Literature*. **Essay:** Cleanth Brooks.

**Van Gelder, Geert Jan.** Laudian Professor of Arabic, University of Oxford, England. Author of *Beyond the Line: Classical Arabic Literary Critics on the Coherence and Unity of the Poem* (1982), *The Bad and the Ugly: Attitudes Towards Invective Poetry (Hijā') in Classical Arabic Literature* (1988), and numerous articles on Middle Eastern and Arabic literature and culture; editor of *Two Arabic Treatises on Stylistics: al Marghīnānī's al-Maḥāsin fī 'l-naẓm wa-'l-nathr and Ibn Aflaḥ's Muqaddima, Formerly Ascribed to al-Marghīnānī* (1987). **Essays:** 'Abd al-Qāhir al-Jurjānī; Arabic Literary Theory; Hāzim al-Qartājannī; Qudāma Ibn Ja'far.

**Vannatta, Dennis.** Professor of English, University of Arkansas at Little Rock. Author of *Nathanael West: An Annotated Bibliography of the Scholarship and Works* (1976), *H. E. Bates* (1983), *Tennessee Williams: A Study of the Short Fiction* (1988), *This Time, This Place: Stories* (1991); editor of *The English Short Story, 1945–1980: A Critical History* (1985). Criticism editor, *Crazy Horse* (from 1980). **Essay:** Robbe-Grillet.

**Vaszily, Scott.** Northern Illinois University. **Essay:** Todorov.

**Vizzier, Anne R.** University of Arkansas, Fayetteville. **Essay:** Petrarch.

**Walker, William T.** Vice president for academic affairs and professor of history, Chestnut Hill College, Philadelphia. Author of *Europe, 1848–1914* (1991) and *Disraeli, An Annotated Bibliography* (1999). **Essays:** Mazzini; Mill.

**Wilson, John.** Independent scholar. Editor of *Best Christian Writing 2000* (forthcoming). Founding editor of *Books and Culture* (from 1995) and editor at large for *Christianity Today.* **Essay:** Kenner.

**Winchell, Mark Royden.** Professor of English, Clemson University, South Carolina. Author of *William F. Buckley* (1984), *Leslie Fiedler* (1985), *Talmadge* (1987, with Herman E. Talmadge), *Joan Didion* (1980, 1989), *Neoconservative Criticism* (1991), and *Cleanth Brooks and the Rise of Modern Criticism* (1996). Managing editor, *South Carolina Review* (1988–1994). **Essay:** Fiedler.

**Windhausen, John D.** Emeritus professor of history, Saint Anselm College, Manchester, New Hampshire. Author of articles on Russian history; editor and translator of Sergei Soloviev's *History of Russia: The Reign of Ivan the Great* (1978) and his *History of Russia: Russian Society in the Age of Ivan III* (1979); contributor (in Russian) to *Kontinent* special issue (January 1999). Editor, *Sports Encyclopedia North America* (1987–1993). **Essay:** Plekhanov.

**Wink, Johnny.** Professor of English, Ouachita Baptist University, Arkadelphia, Arkansas. Contributor to *Christianity and Literature* and *PAPA: Publications of the Arkansas Philological Association.* **Essay:** La Fontaine.

**Witkoski, Michael.** Vice president, Ferillo & Associates, Columbia, South Carolina. Contributor to *Public Relations Strategist* and *PR Tactics.* **Essays:** Gosson; McLuhan.

**Woods, Gregory.** Professor of gay and lesbian studies, Nottingham Trent University, Nottingham, England. Author of *Articulate Flesh: Male Homo-Eroticism and Modern Poetry* (1987), *We Have the Melon* (1992), *This is No Book: A Gay Reader* (1994), *May I Say Nothing* (1998), and *A History of Gay Literature: The Male Tradition* (1998). **Essay:** Gay Theory and Criticism.

**Wright, Eugene P.** Professor of English, University of North Texas, Denton. Author of *Joanna Southcott* (1969), *Thomas Deloney* (1981), and *The Structure of Shakespeare's Sonnets* (1993). **Essay:** Puttenham.

**Wurst, Karin.** Professor of German, Michigan State University, East Lansing. Author of *"Familiale Liebe is die wahre Gewalt." Zur Repräsentation der Familie in Lessings dramatischem Werk* (1988), *Unpopular Virtues: J. M. R. Lenz and the Critics. A Reception History* (1999, with Alan Leidner), and articles on German literature. Editor of *Frau und Drama im achtzehnten Jahrhundert* (1991), *J. M. R. Lenz als Alternative? Positionsanalysen zum 200. Todestag* (1992), and *Eleonore Thon's "Adelheit von Rastenberg"* (1996). **Essays:** Gottsched; Lessing; Winckelmann.

**Yang, Vincent.** Pennsylvania State University, University Park. **Essays:** Liu Hsieh; Ts'ao P'i.

**Yearley, Clifton K.** State University of New York at Buffalo. **Essay:** Hu Shih.